A Turbulent Voyage

Readings in African American Studies
Third Edition

Edited by

Floyd W. Hayes III

North Carolina State University

Collegiate Press

Collegiate Press
San Diego, California

Executive Editor: Christopher Stanford
Senior Editor: Steven Barta
Senior Developmental Editor: Jackie Estrada
Design and Typography: Christopher Davis
Cover art: Paul Slick

Library of Congress Card Number: 00-130334

ISBN: 0-939693-52-6

Printed in the United States of American

10 9 8 7 6 5 4 3 2 1

Photos courtesy of the Schomburg Center for Research in Black Culture,
Office of Special Collections, The New York Public Library.

to Alyssa Nicole St. Franc,
my granddaughter

Acknowledgments

During the 1960s and 1970s, my early thoughts about African American Studies and related issues were shaped by conversations, and sometimes fierce intellectual debates, with a number of individuals. Significantly, there is much difference of opinion, but I have learned a great deal from association with them. The list includes Molefi K. Asante, Thais Aubry, Ronald Bailey, Josef ben-Jochannan, Robert CheeMooke, John Henrik Clarke, Eugenia Collier, Daphne Duval Harrison, Samuel A. Hay, Mary Jane Hewitt, Caulbert A. Jones (deceased), Alfred and Bernice Ligon, Maulana Karenga, Mazi Elechukwu Njaka (deceased), Boniface I. Obichere, James Turner, Seneca Turner, Herbert West, C. S. Whitaker, and Arthur Williams.

From the 1980s to the present, I have benefitted enormously from intellectual exchanges about African American Studies and related issues with an equally important assortment of individuals. They include Margaret Adams-Dorsey, Lisa Anderson, JoAnne Cornwell, Harold Cruse, William A. Darity, Jr., Robert Fikes, Nancy Elizabeth Fitch, Lewis R. Gordon, H. Eugene Grigsby, Kwasi Harris, Rickey Hill, Njeri Jackson, Carolyn E. Johnson, Frances A. Kiene III, Theodore Kornweibel, Marilyn E. Lashley, Joy A. James, Charles E. Jones, Edward L. Jones, Mack Jones, Steve McCutcheon, James Mack, Eddie Meadows, Michael Mitchell, B. Lewis Ratcliffe, Clovis Semmes (Jabulani Makalani), T. Denean Sharpley-Whiting, Earl Smith, Carl Spight, Ronald W. Walters, Renee T. White, Sloan Williams II (deceased), Leonard Wash, Shirley Weber, Alex Willingham, and Betty and Antonio Zamora.

This third edition also benefits from the numerous individuals who took time to evaluate the previous edition. To those of you who are educators and students, I express my deep appreciation. I also want to thank those who read the second edition and then sent letters or telephoned me regarding aspects of the anthology. I hope that all of you will receive this third edition of *A Turbulent Voyage* with the same enthusiasm.

For over a decade, I have benefitted enormously from participating in the annual Black Studies conference at Olive-Harvey College in Chicago, Illinois. I want to thank Armstead Allen and his colleagues at that institution for providing a setting in which scholars, educators, students, activists, and local citizens challenge each other regarding the burning issues of the day. This conference at Olive-Harvey College is now the longest standing college-based conference in the field of African American Studies.

Since the publication of the second edition of this anthology, my granddaughter, Alyssa Nicole St. Franc, was born. I dedicate this anthology to her.

For their inspiration and support, I want to thank the members of the Challenge Karate Club of Purdue University and especially the chief instructor, Sensei Jackie Martinez. I also want to acknowledge Nancy Elizabeth Fitch, Judson L. Jeffries, Edward L. Jones, Mack H. Jones, and Antonio Zamora. I continue to be indebted to my family—Charlene Moore Hayes, my wife; Thelma Ruth Person Hayes, my mother; Kia-Lillian Nicole Hayes, my teenage daughter; and Ndidi Nkechinyere Hayes St. Franc, my adult daughter and Alyssa's mother.

Once again, I want to thank my weight-lifting partner, Doug Harney, for his coaching skill and encouragement, which helped me set a national record in the deadlift (525 pounds) at the USA Powerlifting Nationals in Bedford Heights, Ohio, on October 10, 1999. Finally, I wish to thank my new editor at Collegiate Press, Jackie Estrada, for her patience and attentiveness.

Contents

Preface to the Student

African American Studies, as an organized academic enterprise, grew out of the late 1960s struggle for black liberation. Before that, only historically black colleges in the South had paid attention to the scholarly examination of Africa and its American legacy, particularly in the discipline of history. The field of Black Studies (as it was originally called) developed simultaneously with the social movements that sought to transform both American society and its academy. By the mid-1960s, the Black Power movement was challenging the cultural and racial exclusivity of American society and its social institutions, including the academic institutions. Accusers of the academy said that the policies, practices, and curricula at historically white universities discriminated against African Americans. Consequently, the demand grew for more African American students and faculty and for Black Studies.

In the years since the beginning of African American Studies, indications are that American society seems to be headed toward increasing state violence, citizen rage, and social anarchy. In the 1960s, African Americans demanded attention to their charges of white supremacy and economic oppression, but the conventional channels of demand largely were blocked or ineffective for working-class and impoverished urban residents. The dispossessed urban African American scarcely experienced the tangible benefits of civil rights legislation and policies. As a result, a number of major American cities were engulfed in a rising tide of violent disturbances. The 1965 Watts rebellion signaled the watershed of urban black frustration and anger with anti-black racism, police brutality, and economic disenfranchisement. Almost thirty years later, the 1992 Los Angeles insurrection (triggered by the exoneration of white policemen whose vicious beating of a black man had been captured on videotape by a local citizen and later shown on television to the nation and to the world) reflected mounting discontent among impoverished Los Angelenos (African American, Latino, Asian American, and white), who destroyed property throughout much of the city. As in the 1960s, America's cities are becoming the visible terrain of frustration, rage, hopelessness, cynicism, and unrest brought on by decades of society's indifference to the growing pain and suffering associated with urban economic and political underdevelopment.

In contrast to the 1960s, it is apparent that as the twenty-first century begins, popular feelings of cynicism, resentment, and anger are expanding beyond impoverished African American communities to include Latino and dispossessed white Americans. Such recent incidents of political rage as expressed by the discourse of the Unabomber Manifesto, the 1995 bombing of an Oklahoma City federal building that killed 168 people, the growing presence of the militia movement, and the mass murders of teachers and fellow students by white secondary school students represent a veritable **culture of violence** in America. Moreover, today's increasing white racist hate crimes against, along with mounting police assaults on and murders of, black female and male citizens, from New York to California, represent continuing patterns of violence similar to the lynching, anti-black race riots, and segregation of the early twentieth century. Like the **culture of racism**, the culture of violence is deeply embedded in the origin and development of American civilization. What must no longer be ignored is the historical fact that America began as a nation when Western European immigrants conducted annihilating wars against Native Americans and brutally enslaved captured Africans. The process continued as Euro-Americans savagely confiscated Native American and Mexican territories, forcing the original inhabitants to become aliens in their own homelands. Therefore, deeply ingrained cultures of racism and violence characterize Americaís increasingly multicultural society. If these frightening trends and developments continue to worsen, chaos, anarchy, and disaster will characterize twenty-first-century America society.

Since the 1960s and the Great Society programs of the Johnson administration, there has been a progressive economic polarization between more affluent and less affluent Americans. The economic policies of the Reagan and Bush administrations speeded up this process. Moreover, the welfare reform policies of the Clinton administration threaten the very survival of economically impoverished Americans. The effects of this economic development are of particular significance to African Americans. Even though the 1960s breakthroughs resulted in a growing middle class of African American professionals and managers, many other African Americans slid further down the slope toward economic disaster. Trapped by poverty and powerlessness, black residents of the central city remain alienated from America's mainstream, while their institutions are under attack and their children are betrayed in public schools, where the fundamental tools of knowledge building have been discarded. Embittered, angry, and cynical, an expanding underclass struggles to survive in a nation where unemployment is rising steadily. Not surprisingly, crime and other social problems associated with persistent impoverishment increase. Therefore, whether we speak of the liberal Johnson administration's welfare capitalist state policies, the reactionary Reagan-Bush competitive capitalist state policies, or even the Clinton regime's neoliberal managerialism, the fundamental social conditions of the African American dispossessed seem to be worsening. The racial division of labor, the social problems of disenfranchisement, and the legacy of racial stereotyping—which have been inherited from the master-slave tradition and which have been employed by America's ruling elite to express effectively their determination to maintain the subordination of the African American masses—remain, and are indeed expanding as we begin the twenty-first century.

If American society continues on its present trajectory toward socio-economic polarization and cultural clash, this nation cannot hope to remain a great power in the emerging global economic order, which is organized increasingly on the production, distribution, and consumption of knowledge. The earlier social-scientific conception of American society as "melting pot" actually meant the engineering, as closely as possible, of a white Anglo-Saxon Protestant culture. However, it is not racial and cultural assimilation but racial and cultural domination of diverse groups that historically has characterized the American social order. The result has been the suppression of America's historic multicultural reality. Such practices must give way to practices that acknowledge, value, and encourage the multicultural character of American society.

To achieve this goal, quality education for all is critically important. Educational institutions at all levels must ensure that all students master the fundamental tools of knowledge (reading, writing, computational skills, and critical thinking); gain academic motivation; and receive positive character-building. In an increasingly knowledge-intensive age, advanced learning will constitute the essential ingredient of occupational advancement and robust citizenship. Additionally, the time is now for educational institutions to (re)develop curricula that recognize and respect the historical and contemporary contributions that people of color have made to America's multicultural society. This is the quest of African American Studies, for this field challenges America to refashion its self-understanding.

The white American cultural tradition has long ignored or excluded the contributions and experiences of others. African American Studies and the other "new studies"—American Indian, Latino, Asian American, and Women's Studies—challenge and correct the Euro-American interpretation of history and contemporary affairs, which is the source of much misunderstanding. African American Studies and the other "new studies" do not fragment America, as some writers have claimed; rather, they encourage the recognition and appreciation of the diverse cultures that make up the American experience. America's continued prominence in the coming global order will depend on its ability to provide to all of its people a quality education—from preschool to postgraduate—that encourages all Americans to value their multicultural society. African American Studies meets this challenge.

At the beginning of the twenty-first century, African American Studies has the potential for exploring aspects of America's transition toward a postindustrial-managerial society. In the new social order in which knowledge and managerial skill are rapidly becoming the essential societal resources, professional experts, as the manipulators of new knowledge, gain increasing power and influence in the governmental and policy-making process. Governmental and other policy makers more and more are influenced by policy *specialists*, who define complex social problems and provide alternative perspectives for solving them. These specialists, it is expected, will be able to avoid short-sighted solutions, such as continued insistence on school busing for racial balance or the banning of teenage mothers from high school. Courses in African American Studies can lay out numbers of social problems that policy makers and citizens will have to try to solve. Such courses can provide the knowledge and viewpoint that can allow policy makers and specialists to come up with creative solutions to pressing social problems. While a single course in African American Studies cannot, of course, give you as a student and as a citizen such knowledge, it can give you quick glimpses of various points of view as a foundation for further learning.

This anthology is designed to introduce the reader to the contours and content of African American Studies. The text and readings included here not only impart information but seek as their foremost goal to precipitate in the reader an awareness of the complex and changing character of the African American experience—its origins, developments, and future challenges. The book aims to engage readers in the critical analysis of a broad spectrum of subjects, themes, and issues: the importance of Africa, the transatlantic slave trade and chattel slavery, African American expressive culture, the psychology of oppression, family and educational policies, economic issues, and racism and resistance. Discussions of some of the fundamental problems and prospects related to the African American experience are presented in this anthology.

African American Studies is a broad field concerned with the examination of the black experience, both historically and presently. Hence, the subjects, themes, and issues included in this text transcend the narrow confines of traditional academic disciplinary boundaries. Reality, after all, is not disciplinary. In selecting materials for this text, I was guided by a historical approach in the general compilation of each section's readings. Each section generally contains historical materials, which provide a context for examining the remaining readings. In this way, I hope that the reader will be enabled to arrive at a critical understanding of the conditions and forces that have influenced the African American experience.

I need to say something about the scope and limitations of this anthology. I already have suggested that African American Studies includes the global African experience; this means Africa, the Caribbean, Latin America, African America, and any other areas inhabited by African-descended people. However, no single text or African American Studies enterprise can be this expansive. Although African American Studies programs in Africa, Asia, Europe, or the Caribbean might include different emphases, in the United States of America the field has focused largely on the life experiences of African-descended North Americans. This text focuses mainly on the interrelationship between Africa and African America as a basis for understanding developments in the United States of America.

In revising this anthology for the third time, again I have benefited from many people who have read, used, evaluated, and commented on it. I have made changes—deleting some readings and adding others—which I hope will make this anthology more "user-friendly."

Part I, "African American Studies: Trends, Developments, and Future Challenges," presents ideas that have influenced the genesis and current development of African American Studies. Considered the father of black history, Carter G. Woodson made a classic statement about the role of education that inspired many early formulators of African American Studies. Included here is an excerpt from his 1933 book, *The Mis-Education of the Negro*. Harold Cruse provides a vision of African American Studies as the field began in the late 1960s. Gloria T. Hull and Barbara Smith put forward the goals and objectives of Black Women's Studies. Manning Marable advocates radical democratic multiculturalism and argues for the central importance of African American Studies enterprises in higher education.

Part II is a discussion of "Africa and the Diaspora: Ties That Bind." Although African Americans are descendants largely of the West Africans brought to these shores in chains, their historic efforts to reclaim and reconstruct a positive cultural identity and sense of human worth have resulted in a desire to connect with Africa in all of its diversity. Boniface Obichere discusses the inadequate examination and false interpretation of African history by European and African historians. In a classic essay, C. L. R. James argues that the Atlantic slave trade and the enslavement of Africans in the Americas not only contributed much to the economic development of modern Western Europe but also influenced the elaboration of the American personality and political culture. Angela Davis challenges the false image of black women derived from a distorted history of the slave family in America. Vincent Harding uses David Walker, a free African American, and Nat Turner, a chattel slave, to examine the African American struggle against chattel slavery. Michael Mitchell examines the discovery of a black community that had preserved an original African language brought to Brazil by captives generations ago. Lydia Lindsey and Carlton Wilson explore the significance of the African Diaspora in Europe and its relationship to the philosophy of Afrocentricity.

Part III explores "African American Expressive Culture: Music and Literature." Although largely overlooked, the culture of African-descended Americans has directly influenced and enhanced the development of American culture. One could easily argue that without African American expressive culture there would be little American popular culture of significance. The complex character of African American cultural expressions also has served as a mechanism of survival and salvation for an oppressed yet strong-willed people. Portia Maultsby investigates the relationship between African and African American musical traditions. Daphne Duval Harrison describes the blues tradition in the 1920s, specifically focusing on the variety of themes expressed by urban black female singers. Nelson George dissects the complex interaction between the emergence of soul music and the political economy of the American music world in the 1950s and 1960s. Richard Wright reflects on how he developed the ideas about the tragic hero in one of his novels, Bigger Thomas. Larry Neal examines the interrelationship between the Black Power Movement and the Black Arts Movement of the 1960s and 1970s. Nobel Prize winner Toni Morrison investigates the impact of African American culture and literature on the study of white American literature.

Part IV is devoted to "Discovering the Meaning of Black Identity: Psychic Dimensions of Oppression." The roots of the problems between blacks and whites can be traced back to the modern encounter between Africans and Western Europeans and the collective psyches that emerged from this encounter, which began in the fifteenth century. Europe's violent enslavement of Africans constituted a human disaster of major proportions, which was driven by the West's desire for power, privilege, and pleasure. In this manner, black people became the victims of modern Western civilization. Dislocated from their African homeland, relocated to the Americas, and then isolated on plantations, African slaves and their American descendants were forced over the centuries to refashion their sense of identity and community; this process of self-refashioning continues. The violent legacy of the West and of the United States (by means of imperialism, colonialism, slavery, segregation, and racism) has been the systematic dehumanization, exploitation, degradation, and hatred of African-descended Americans. What resulted from this perverse relationship can be best described as the psychology of oppression, the violent psychic terrain that forces black people to search for their identity. Wade W. Nobles attempts to develop a black psychology based on an interpretation of West African philosophical and cultural traditions of spiritual and community life. Kenneth M. Stampp tells the story of slaveowners' use of psychological and physical violence in an effort to destroy the slaves' self-image. W. E. B. Du Bois writes about the black man's struggle to refashion a black identity in an anti-black American world.

Part V addresses "The Black Family: Historical and Policy Issues." The breakdown of the family is a major challenge facing American society today. The crisis of family instability is even greater in many African American communities, which are plagued with economic impoverishment and resulting hopelessness. How did matters reach this crisis point, and what are suggestions for improvement? From the dehumanizing chattel slave experience to the present, African American families have been characterized by cycles of instability and stability. Andrew Billingsley studies the patterns of traditional West African family life and the impact of chattel slavery on the development of the African American family. E. Franklin Frazier investigates the social and economic forces and conditions that shaped the structure and dynamics of African American families from slavery to freedom. The major objective of this section is to engage the reader in a critical dialogue about the growing and complex problem of African American family instability by including competing perspectives. Glenn Loury provides a conservative assessment of this dilemma. William Darity, Jr. and his colleagues examine the destabilization of the black family in the emerging managerial age.

Part VI focuses on "The African American Struggle for Literacy and Quality Education." It is concerned with major trends in the development of African American education and contradictions and dilemmas in the provision of quality equal educational opportunity to African Americans. Frederick Douglass, the slave who became a statesman, describes the challenges he faced as a child learning to read and write and developing an appreciation for knowledge. Jewell Mazique critically analyzes the subversion of urban public school systems during the 1960s. My contribution examines the politics of public school desegregation in Washington, D. C., during the late 1950s and 1960s. Joy James proposes a practice of teaching philosophy and theory that is rooted in black women's experiences and that is committed to social change and black liberation.

Part VII explores the "Political Economy of the African American Situation." This section examines the changing character of the American political economy and its constraints on the African American struggle for collective survival and economic well-being. Harold Baron investigates America's economic exploitation and racial oppression of African Americans from the Colonial Era to the mid-1960s. Daniel Fusfeld and Timothy Bates analyze the economic condition of African Americans from World War II to the 1980s, suggesting a growing polarization between an emerging middle class and a developing class of urban disinherited.

Part VIII examines "Racism, Resistance, and Radicalism." It is concerned with contemporary anti-black racism and the struggle against it. This section punctuates the continuing contradictions and dilemmas associated with the theory and practice of American democracy. Although articulating lofty democratic principles of liberty, justice, and equality for all of its citizens, the founders of the American system of government and politics denied the humanity of African slaves and their descendants (and of Native Americans) and excluded them from membership in the political community. This legacy of African American subordination and exclusion has become deeply embedded in the fabric of American political culture, continuing to shape individual and institutional attitudes, values, and practices. In the face of this brutal legacy, black people have waged an ongoing struggle for human dignity, social development, and self-determination. Lewis R. Gordon provides a theory of contemporary anti-black racism. Martin Luther King, Jr. advocates civil disobedient direct action as a strategy for resisting racial injustice and for securing civil rights. Malcolm X calls for black nationalism, self-defense, and human rights as the means to fight against American racism. Kathleen Cleaver reviews three stories of black women's leadership styles during the civil rights and black power movements. Hayes and Kiene investigate trends, developments, and contradictions related to the emergence and transformation of the Black Panther Party's ideology and social practice. Melvin L. Oliver and his colleagues analyze the causes of the Los Angeles uprising of 1992. Judson L. Jeffries examines the issue of local state violence against black citizens, particularly the 1999 San Diego police execution of former college and professional football player Demetrius DuBose. Maulana Karenga analyzes the factors that contribute to the contemporary crisis of black middle-class leadership.

The guiding spirit of this volume accepts as an initial educational premise that an introductory text in African American Studies should be broadly based. Hence, the readings that make up this volume cover a range of areas—from history to sociology, from economics to politics, from music to literature, and from education to ideology. Academically, African American Studies is located primarily in the human sciences. Practically, the field deals with social change. This anthology's driving theme centers on the historic black struggle against cultural domination and for human rights, socioeconomic advancement, and collective survival. As you explore the issues raised in this book, you should reflect on the following questions: What does this reality (for example, oppression and resistance or the struggle for identity and community) mean? How did it come into existence? What are its contradictions and dilemmas? How does this reality affect the quality of our lives? How can we change this existing reality? Why does it matter?

The broad purpose of this volume, then, is to pose questions, articulate differing responses, evaluate them, and set the stage for further questions. African American Studies faculty and students need to be engaged in an ongoing struggle for knowledge, the gaining of which will allow the development of wisdom, moral courage, and social responsibility.

Preface to the Instructor

African American Studies made its appearance with the promise of solving some of the educational problems of African Americans and of challenging the American academy's de facto racial exclusivity. Not only had individuals of African descent been excluded from university faculty and student bodies, but the curricula of many disciplines had ignored African and African American achievements and points of view.

The field emerged in the 1960s as part of a larger and turbulent social movement, which was itself a product of a transformation of American society. That transformation—and the field of African American Studies—is more than thirty years old. And now we are facing another transformation, a quiet, progressive one that has profound implications for all Americans: the shift from an industrial-manufacturing to a postindustrial-managerial society. This quiet, all-encompassing change requires us to reconsider the role and place of African American Studies not only within the academy but also in American society.

My intent in this introductory essay is to attempt such a reconsideration. To do this, I must examine the field's major intellectual tendencies—past and present, complementary and contradictory. My concern is to locate the logic and follow the trajectory of this evolving field. In the discussion that follows, I do not purport to provide an exhaustive genealogy of African American Studies; rather, my intention is to examine some of the representative intellectual trends and developments characterizing the field so far. After this examination, I will address the possible future challenges to African American Studies and black educational advancement posed by the current transformation of America from an industrial-manufacturing society to a postindustrial-managerial society. Although the intellectual roots of African American Studies can be traced back to a much earlier period (as shown in several of the readings included here), I will limit the scope of my analysis to the intellectual and social forces that have contributed to the field's development from the 1960s to the present. Having been involved in African American Studies for more than twenty years, I write this essay not as an outsider looking in, but as an insider looking around.

A note on naming: In the early years, African Americanists called the field Black Studies. Later, the terms Afro-American Studies, Pan African Studies, African American Studies, and Africana Studies also came to be used. Although there might exist some distinctions or variations among these names—particularly regarding the extent of an inclusion of African Studies and Caribbean Studies—for the purposes of this discussion, these titles are interchangeable.

THE TURBULENT EMERGENCE OF BLACK STUDIES

In the late 1950s and the 1960s, after the momentous *Brown v. Board of Education* ruling that, in effect, outlawed racial and ethnic segregation in schools, public school systems across the nation tried to find ways to evade the law and continue segregation. In response to such practices by local school boards, a powerful coalition of civil rights leaders, educational experts, and public policy makers was created, and the coalition determined to use all means available, and especially the courts, to make school systems comply with the desegregation orders. Many school systems, black as well as white, were caught in the middle of the war.

Scarce resources—intellectual as well as financial—were allocated to the policy battles and to moving children in buses instead of being allocated to education. Many black community leaders and organizations tried to point this out. They challenged the schools to implement policies and programs that would promote quality education, no matter what a school's racial makeup. But the movement for school integration had gathered such momentum that it could not be stopped by rational argument or even by evidence of blatant failure. As the coalition grew more and more powerful, imposing on urban communities racial integration at any cost, the quality of classroom teaching declined. Parents increasingly were intimidated by and excluded from an urban bureaucracy in which the policy-making process was dominated by a nonlocal elite with its own agenda—an agenda based solely on civil rights, ignoring students' rights to quality education.

As the civil rights movement began to wind down in the mid-1960s, many African American high school and college students looked for an alternative. They found it in the more militant social movements of the late 1960s, particularly the Black Power movement. These powerful, and in some way, anarchic, tendencies, along with resentment toward the educational establishment, served as the crucible for the turbulent appearance of African American Studies.

As an organized academic enterprise, African American Studies emerged at historically white universities and colleges during the late

1960s in the context of complex social changes that affected virtually every sector of American society. The African American Studies movement converged with mass movements of protest against the brutalizing effects of social injustice, socioeconomic inequality, racial antagonism, the Vietnam War, and university paternalism. Militant students challenged the hegemony of traditional modes of thinking and social practice, inaugurating an assault on what they perceived as the hypocrisy and immorality of many of the nation's social institutions. Institutions of higher education became primary targets of criticism as students challenged them to address the burning questions and urgent social problems of the day. Students attacked the university's conventional disregard of their everyday life experiences and demanded, increasingly, that the content of their university education be relevant to the solution of social problems.

While agreeing with the general student demand for a growing interaction between the academy and the world outside of its walls, African American students also audaciously called into question the American academy's dominant Eurocentric perspective—the unchallenged assumption that Western European culture is superior, neutral, and normative. Labeling this orientation ethnocentric, African American students charged that Western education, wittingly and otherwise, diminished, distorted, and, in many instances, obliterated the contributions of African peoples to world development generally and the contributions of African Americans to America's development specifically. Therefore, African American students demanded that the university establish courses of study that provided a systematic examination of African and African-descended peoples' experiences.

Responding to the powerful challenge of these student activists, many institutions of higher learning across the nation hurriedly implemented African American or Black Studies programs as appeasement measures. Under these circumstances, little long-range planning (academic or financial) took place, since many university officials considered the issue an aberration or fad and hoped that it would shortly disappear. Significantly, many universities decided to isolate Black Studies enterprises rather than to force traditional academic departments to transform their curricula to include the study of the black experience. In many instances, early African American Studies units drew on any African American faculty member already at the university—even if the person had no intellectual interest or academic preparation in the area—or any white faculty member who might be interested in race-related issues. More commonly, as African American students demanded that courses on the black experience be taught by black people, universities quickly sought to hire more black faculty members. In that highly charged period, some new faculty possessed Ph.D.'s in their fields, but many did not; some well-established black scholars decided not to affiliate with Black Studies; and some well-prepared black intellectuals were overlooked. Consequently, the view emerged in this early period that many African American Studies enterprises were designed to fail.

The eruption of what generally was called Black Studies in the late 1960s can best be understood as an institutional representation of the contemporary African American struggle for collective survival, socio-economic advancement, and human rights. After having seen the white South's terroristic reaction to civil rights activists' peaceful protests, African Americans found it difficult to believe that the American social order would soon end the oppression of African Americans.

Citing the limitations of the integrationist civil rights philosophy and social practice for bettering the circumstances of black Americans, the Nation of Islam and its chief spokesman, Malcolm X, urged urban African American masses across the nation to unite on the basis of black nationalist ideology and to expand their struggle beyond the narrow confines of the civil rights agenda to the global issue of human rights. Calling on African Americans to take their cause to the United Nations, Malcolm viewed human rights as an overall framework that included a struggle for the following: (1) personal worth and human dignity, (2) family stability and community solidarity, (3) literacy and quality education, (4) economic self-sufficiency and collective well-being, and (5) democratic political rights and self-determination. Malcolm X urged African Americans to take pride in themselves and their African heritage. He argued that black communities should control and support their own political and economic institutions. He admonished black Americans to respect their women and to clean up themselves and their communities by removing the socially destructive evils of family disintegration, alcoholism, drug abuse, and crime. In short, Malcolm challenged African Americans to improve the overall moral character and social stability of their communities.

The rhetoric of civil rights leaders and the decade of actual advances in legal rights had meanwhile fostered hopes in black communities for quick changes in economic and social conditions. Such changes, of course, were not forthcoming, and the dashed hopes for social and political self-determination produced violent revolts in Harlem, Watts, Detroit, Cleveland, Newark, and other cities outside of the American south. These powerful and defiant protests shook the nation and, in the summer of 1966, ushered in a new era, signaled by the discourse of "black power" (Forman, 1972; Stone, 1968).

On May 29, 1966, Congressman Adam Clayton Powell, Jr., chairman of the U.S. House of Representatives' Committee on Education and Labor and one of America's few progressive African American politicians, articulated the need for "black power" in his baccalaureate address at Howard University. He asserted: "Human rights are God-given. Civil rights are man-made. . . . Our life must be purposed to implement human rights. . . . To demand these God-given rights is to seek *black power*—the power to build black institutions of splendid achievement"

(Stone, 1968, p. 189). A week later, during the James Meredith protest march in Mississippi, Student Non-Violent Coordinating Committee activists Willie Ricks and Stokely Carmichael led the chant, "We want black power, we want black power" (Carson, 1981; Forman, 1972; Stone, 1968).

As with any political slogan, interpretations of black power differed. Although many civil rights leaders criticized the term, others appropriated it for their own agendas by articulating a variety of meanings, including group solidarity, cultural pride, political power, economic power, defensive violence, anti-integrationism, community control, black nationalism, and human rights. In 1967, Stokely Carmichael and Roosevelt University political scientist Charles Hamilton sought to define and clarify this new political vision when they wrote that black power

> is a call for black people in this country to unite, to recognize their heritage, to build a sense of community. It is a call for black people to begin to define their own goals, to lead their own organizations and to support those organizations. It is a call to reject the racist institutions and values of this society. (1967, p. 44)

This conception of black power set forth the vivid necessity for African-descended Americans to center their political outlook and social practice on their own collective concerns. The concentrated focus on black power—its accentuation of African American collective interests—characterized the ideological milieu within which African American Studies emerged.

The establishment of African American Studies was insurrectionary and emancipatory in at least two ways. First, as case studies of events at San Francisco State University (Chrisman, 1969; McEvoy and Miller, 1969), Merritt College (Walton, 1969), and Cornell University (Edwards, 1970, 1980) disclose, African American Studies erupted in the context of university protest. African American students and their supporters sought to challenge and transform the policies and practices of institutional racism. Second, African American Studies represented a bold movement that undertook to unmask the power/knowledge configuration of Eurocentrism and the white cultural domination characteristic of the American academy. The new field of study sought to resist the rigid barriers between traditional academic disciplines by emphasizing an innovative multidisciplinary approach to teaching and learning. Additionally, African American Studies challenged the ideological basis of the Eurocentric paradigm, which assumes that the Western European structure of knowledge is true, objective, and politically neutral, applicable equally to all peoples and circumstances. This organization of knowledge resulted in a representation of civilization that not only idealizes Western culture and thought but devalues all others. From the standpoint of the Eurocentric knowledge structure,

Western European views and values are and should be the human norm; hence, other cultures can be discounted insofar as theory deviate from the norm. In this regard, literary scholar Edward Said has observed:

> The entire history of nineteenth-century European thought is filled with such discriminations as these, made between what is fitting for us and what is fitting for them, the former designated as inside, in place, common, belonging, in a word above, the latter, who are designated as outside, excluded, aberrant, inferior, in a word *below*. . . . The large cultural-national designation of European culture as the privileged norm carried with it a formidable battery of other distinctions between ours and theirs, between proper and improper, European and non-European, higher and lower: they are to be found everywhere in such subjects and quasi-subjects as linguistics, history, race theory, philosophy, anthropology, and even biology. But my main reason for mentioning them here is to suggest how in the transmission and persistence of a culture there is a continual process of reinforcement, by which the hegemonic culture will add to itself the prerogatives given it by its sense of national identity, its power as an implement, ally, or branch of the state, its rightness, its exterior forms and assertions of itself—and most important, by its vindicated power as a victor over everything not itself (1983, pp. 13–14).

In similar fashion, Carolyn Gerald, arguing from the standpoint of the Black Aesthetic movement—a cultural and literary movement that paralleled the emergence of African American Studies in the late 1960s—assailed white American racial and cultural projections of its self-image and the historic practice of excluding a projection of the African American self-image. She stated:

> Concomitant with that projection for several hundred years—ever since the black man has come within the sphere of influence of the white—the moral and aesthetic associations of black and white have been mixed up with race. Thus, the negative reflection of ourselves is, in the white man's system, the reverse side of his positive projection of himself. The white man has developed a myth of superiority based on images which compare him symbolically with the black man. The very fact of this interconnection is at once a holdover from previous bondage and the most effective means of perpetuating that bondage. We realize now that we are involved in a black-white war over the control of image. For to manipulate an image is to control a peoplehood. Zero image has for a long time meant the repression of our peoplehood. (1972, pp. 352–353)

Since Eurocentrism lay at the base of most discourse within the American academy, many African American Studies theorists and practitioners saw their task as contesting and transforming the received ideas, entrenched institutions, and questionable values of the Eurocentric tradition. But there was no consensus on what Black Studies programs should attempt. There were differing intellectual and ideological tendencies corresponding largely to the ambiguous interpretations of black power. Therefore, during its first decade, Black Studies was character-ized by a variety of orientations even while improvising upon the academy's Eurocentric tradition.

The advocacy of a critical approach grounded in black cultural na-tionalism was a major intellectual tendency during the establishment of African American Studies enterprises. Harold Cruse, author of the widely read and debated book *The Crisis of the Negro Intellectual* (1967) was one of the strongest proponents of this view. At the 1968 Yale University symposium of Black Studies, Cruse attacked the integration-ist ethic of American scholarship, arguing that it had precluded the development of a viable black social theory on which to ground Black Studies. For him, any intellectually valid Black Studies curriculum had to rest on the ideology of black cultural nationalism and had to employ a critical historical approach. Cruse remarked:

> It is my belief that cultural nationalism as an ideology, nurturing the whole desire and thrust toward a Black Studies program, can only be understood if it is approached, first, historically, and then, by analyzing many of the deep problems which enmesh the Negro intelligentsia today. All over the country, in different aspects of the black movement we can see a general thrashing about, a frenetic search for method, and a search for both internal and external criticisms. (1968, p. 7)

Cruse suggested that Black Studies should focus its attention on black institutional development on all levels—cultural, political, eco-nomic, and social. While he called for a self-critical analysis—that is, investigation of the impact of the Protestant Ethic on African American social development; of W. E. B. Du Bois's talented tenth thesis and the historical origins of the black intellectual class; and of the clash be-tween radical-revolutionary and reformist-gradualist tendencies within the black movement—Cruse cautioned that Black Studies should not be too narrowly conceived. Rather, he argued for a critical investigation of the larger American cultural dynamic:

> Black cultural nationalism has to be seen as an attempt, a necessary historical attempt, to deal with another kind of cultural nationalism that is implied in our society, namely, the cultural nationalism of the dominant white group. You might call it a kind of cultural "particularism" which is found when you examine the cultural particularism of the Anglo-Saxon group or the WASP. . . . I think we find that an ideology exists which *has* to deny the validity of other kinds of cultural values that might compete with its own standards—whether in the social sciences, the arts, literature, or economic activity. We find this particularism of the Anglo-American implicit in all that is done in our society, whether it is done unconsciously or consciously. (1968, p. 9)

Cruse goes on:

> Black Studies must make the dominant particularism, the dominant racial creed, more capable of dealing with the internal crises facing us all.

... I think that those who would institute the black studies program must not only understand their own particular black history but must also grapple with, and understand, the dual tradition that has been nurtured in this society and that has given our society its unique character. I think the question of a Black Studies program—even if it expresses black particularism—is a kind of particularism which understands its own limits and its social function. Its social function is not to replace one particularism with another particularism but to counterbalance the historical effects and exaggeration of particularism toward a more raciallv balanced society, a society which would include expectations regarding the democratic creed. (1968, pp. 9–10)

For Cruse, then, Black Studies needed to employ a historical approach, grounded in black cultural nationalism, that critically examined both developments and contradictions within the African American population as well as the manifestations of the larger American cultural apparatus and its effects on black consciousness.

Another intellectual tendency during the formative stage of Black Studies was to define the new enterprise as almost solely an examination of the black experience because the white academy had omitted it. Although advocates of this program also sought to break the interpretive domination of the conventional Eurocentric paradigm, the effect ultimately would have been to replace white particularism with the black particularism against which Harold Cruse earlier had cautioned. In an article titled "Toward a Sociology of Black Studies," Maurice Jackson advocated this point of view when he defined the meaning and scope of Black Studies in the following manner:

> Black Studies, simply put, is the systematic study of black people. In this sense Black Studies differs from academic disciplines which stress white experiences by being based on black experiences. Black Studies is an examination of the deeper truths of black life. It treats the black experience both as it has unfolded over time and as it is currently manifested. These studies will examine the valid part that black people have played in man's development in society. In so doing, Black Studies will concentrate on both the distinctiveness of black people from, and their interdependence with, other people. To develop this kind of knowledge, Black Studies must extend beyond the limits prejudice has placed on knowledge of black people. (1970, p. 132)

By studying African American achievements, Jackson maintained, Black Studies could foster a sense of black pride among African Americans. In the examination of the African American experience, however, Jackson rejected the race-relations and ethnic minority approaches of conventional sociological analysis. Noting that these approaches assumed that black people could or should be studied only in relation to white people, Jackson argued that black people should be studied on their own terms. Because of different life experiences and values, white scholars lacked the necessary sensibility to gather and assess adequately information about the African American experience. Therefore, according to Jackson, black scholars were more appropriate for examining the African American experience, past and present. They would be the best interpreters of that experience.

This intellectual tendency within Black Studies also questions the notion of the political or value neutrality of received knowledge. Jackson pointed out that "cultural values play a dominant part in the selection of problems for study and the application of formulated knowledge" (1970, p. 134). A similar view is expressed by James Turner, of Cornell University's Africana Studies and Research Center, who criticized the idea that scholars have little control over the application of knowledge. Turner wrote:

> For many professional black educators any question of the relationship of ideology to what they teach makes them uneasy. They would most likely be inclined to consider the discussion of Black Studies . . . as a subjective approach to learning and a sort of sectarian encroachment that would demean the academic quality of their work. But, while it is true that facts must derive from objective discourse, we must not become confused by the facade that education is value-free and above the social system when in fact it is the axis for the development of the ideology of society. Education for blacks must consider the need to break down "false consciousness." It must seek to reveal to black people—by facts, by emotionally powerful experiences and by argument—the machinations of oppression. (quoted in Hare, 1974, pp. 256–257)

Although the focus on the "black experience" generally referred to the African American experience, another intellectual tendency defined African American Studies in more global terms. According to this view, the Eurocentric knowledge system is a particularism that is at best fragmented and partial knowledge; at worst, it is fictionalized data that is widely accepted. This more global intellectual perspective sees African American Studies as an expansion of the frontiers of knowledge beyond the singular and limited discourse of Eurocentrism. The original statement of objectives of the African American Studies Program at the University of Maryland, Baltimore County, exemplified this orientation:

> The broad goal of the UMBC African American Studies program is to provide a new horizon in liberal arts education that seeks a reunification of knowledge of the human experience. By broadening the basis of knowledge, it hopes to strike at the narrowness and ethnocentrism of the traditional disciplines which are at the root of much prejudice and racial misunderstanding. Western education developed alongside Western civilization and understandably to serve the needs of the West; consequently, it has been one-sided in approach, incomplete in content and culture bound in orientation. In the process, it wittingly and otherwise played down and in places distorted the contributions of other peoples to world development. The African American Studies program thus seeks to provide a center for the systematic study, research and dissemination of information about the contributions of Africans and peoples of the African Diaspora to the development of the world. (UMBC, 1973–1974, p. 78)

Finally, African American Studies, from its inception, sought to challenge and change the Eurocentric paradigm's rigid barriers between traditional academic disciplines by emphasizing multidisciplinary and interdisciplinary studies. Not only were African American Studies programs to incorporate courses from manv conventional disciplines (multidisciplinary), but faculty and courses would seek to trespass and criss-cross traditional academic disciplinary boundaries. Describing this more global approach, University of Pittsburgh administrator Donald Henderson pointed out:

> The primary goal of this department should be to provide the student with an encompassing knowledge of the history, culture, life-styles and futures of Africans and/or Afro-Americans. Such a department, unlike present substantive departments, would have to be truly interdisciplinary. Its membership would of necessity represent most of the established departments of the social sciences and the humanities. It is conceivable that geologists, biologists, geneticists and others from the natural sciences might be responsible for certain aspects of this department's program. The department would offer a broad concentration in African and Afro-American studies which would include, for example, surveys of art, literature, history, philosophy, religion, biology, economics, etc., as these areas contribute to an understanding of the world black experience. A student would be able to specialize, for example, in African Studies or Afro-American Studies with emphasis on the black experience in anglo-saxon cultures, or Afro-American Studies with emphasis on the black experience in latin cultures. . . . In short, the student would become reasonably knowledgeable about the experiences of black people in a certain large geographical area and their relations to all other blacks in the world. (1971, pp. 15–16)

Summing up this expansive approach to African American Studies, Henderson remarked:

> The Department of African and Afro-American Studies must be truly interdisciplinary and its members must be meta-disciplinarians. They must be academically and intellectually able to range across a variety of traditional areas with facility and sophistication. Obviously the selection of personnel will be a principal factor in the operation of such a department. The traditional and often arbitrary boundaries that divide sociology from history or philosophy from economics will not only be undesirable but dysfunctional in carrying out the mission of this department. (1971, pp. 16–17)

Clearly, a number of differing ideological positions found expression in the implementation of early Black Studies enterprises. In addition, depending on local institutional arrangements and circumstances, a variety of organizational designs (programs, centers, departments) characterized the emerging field's formation. The highly charged times of the late 1960s and early 1970s did not promote ideological and organizational uniformity. In light of Black Studies' turbulent implementation process—the often nonnegotiable demands of strident student advocates for Black Studies and the differing definitions of the field by its theorists and practitioners—it was largely inevitable that problems would emerge and that criticisms would arise. The next section addresses these matters.

BLACK STUDIES: CONTRADICTIONS AND DILEMMAS

By the late 1970s, Black Studies began to suffer growing pains resulting from the 1974–1975 economic recession and the repression of black student and other insurgent movements (see Donner, 1980, 1990; O'Reilly, 1989). Many Black Studies operations, implemented hastily and often without much thought and planning in the late 1960s and early 1970s, closed down. The financial crisis sweeping the nation caused many universities to experience severe financial setbacks. Many universities had to reduce the budget and resource allocations of academic programs. Perhaps hardest hit were disciplines within the humanities; students reflected the uncertainties of economic crisis by choosing courses of study more immediately job related. Because Black Studies units still were in their infancy, resource and budgetary reductions especially hurt them.

It also was during the mid-1970s and early 1980s that criticism of Black Studies gained increasing professional and public attention. Some critics charged that Black Studies was reverse racism. Others noted that many Black Studies programs suffered because of internal conflicts and poor leadership. Still others maintained that Black Studies was intellectually bankrupt. Additionally, there were critics who both pointed out some weaknesses of Black Studies program and blamed universities for not adequately supporting Black Studies enterprises (Allen, 1974; Colt, 1981; Malveaux, 1980; Poinsett, 1973: *U. S. News and World Report,* 1973). What follows is a brief attempt to capture some aspects of the critical environment surrounding Black Studies at its beginning and later during the 1980s.

At the 1968 Yale University symposium on Black Studies, Harvard political scientist Martin Kilson declared a profound skepticism regarding the establishment of Black Studies as an organized academic unit. Kilson, like many black scholars, chose not to affiliate with Black Studies but to remain in the traditional academic department. He was particularly concerned about what the impact of a "black racialist outlook" would be on the interpretation of the black experience. He argued that black nationalists would be selective in marshaling evidence and historical data in order to fashion an analysis of the black experience that would ipso facto castigate whites and thus endow black people with a special aura of righteousness. Pointing to the African entrepreneurial involvement in the Atlantic slave trade, Kilson contended that oppression has been practiced not only by whites but by human beings everywhere. Therefore, he maintained, "the black experience is little more than an offshoot of the human experience—no better and no worse" (1968, p. 15). Kilson then rejected "the viewpoint that the black man's experience with white oppression has endowed black men with a special insight into oppression and thus a special capacity to rid human affairs of oppression" (1968, pp. 15–16).

Five years later, in a *Journal of Black Studies* article, Kilson renewed his concern for the future development of Black Studies. He discussed four issues. First, he maintained that because of the interdisciplinary complexity of Black Studies, its faculty should originate from the traditional academic disciplines and that students should receive a sound background in a conventional discipline in addition to coursework in Black Studies. Kilson wrote:

> The significant issue is to guarantee that students—especially those marked for graduate school and professional schools—who pursue Black Studies are simultaneously grounded in an established academic and technical discipline. A Black Studies curriculum, like other interdisciplinary curricula (American Studies, Asian Studies) cannot stand alone: it must, so to speak, be clothed in the tested scholarly and technical garment of an established discipline. (1973, p. 307)

Second, in discussing who should major in Black Studies, Kilson soundly criticized the tendency among some militant black students to discourage white students from participating in Black Studies. He condemned this separatist tendency in Black Studies, arguing that in fact most black students should major in the scientific and technical fields. This is the kind of educational preparation required to transform the subordinate economic and political status of the black community. Kilson asserted:

> No amount of psychological, therapeutic, or symbolic dependence upon Black Studies should be permitted to prevent this development; if it does, the road to group suicide awaits us, for in the coming decades American society will be more, not less, dependent upon scientific and technological skills. (1973, p. 309)

In Kilson's view, majors in Black Studies should be "those special students, black or white, who have a serious appreciation of and good aptitude for the social sciences and the humanities" (1973, p. 310).

Finally, Kilson called for the depoliticization of Black Studies in order to ensure that the education of students in this field would rest on an academically and technically sound foundation. He charged that white university administrators and faculty members contributed to the academic weakness of Black Studies by yielding to militant student demands and by ignoring usual academic standards and procedures in the organization of Black Studies units and the appointment of black faculty. Concluding, Kilson issued a major challenge to Black Studies.

Unless this psychological immaturity, nearly endemic to the militants in the Black Studies movement, soon ceases, a large section of blacks who seek intellectual status will be relegated to the backwaters or the trash-heap of American academic and intellectual life. Perhaps, alas, this is the unconscious wish—a kind of death wish—of large segments of militant black students and intellectuals. Lacking the stamina and special stuff required of first-class students and scholars, these militant black students and teachers sport a fashionable and psychologically gratifying militant style in order to achieve a protected and segregated (but academically undemanding and inferior) educational niche called a Black Studies program. (1973, p. 313)

Kilson made his case in the early and heady days of Black Studies. As university campuses quieted down after the turbulent 1960s, a seeming (and probably inevitable) backlash occurred in the late 1970s and 1980s in the form of mounting complaints about the academic and intellectual integrity, viability, and adequacy of the Black Studies enterprise. The youthful field of inquiry was under attack.

Duke University English professor Kenny Williams is representative of this backlash. Writing in a 1981 issue of *Change* magazine, she leveled a harsh critique at the field. Williams contended that the image of Black Studies had come to be confused, wittingly or otherwise, with the relaxation of academic and professional standards. Echoing Kilson's previous concerns, Williams charged that students, faculty, and administrators perceived Black Studies as a collection of easy courses that was intellectually empty and simply gratified political and emotional demands. Examining trends in the development of Black Studies, Williams blamed many universities for yielding to strident black student demands and hastily installing Black Studies curricula taught by newly hired faculty who often lacked conventional academic credentials and preparation. Williams charged:

Unwittingly colleges and universities that prided themselves on their broadmindedness and their commitment to the "search for truth" supported the notion that Black Studies ought to be a program for black students. Even the academic purists, who insisted upon standards for everyone else, were frequently convinced that this was one area where relaxed standards were acceptable. They were aided in this misconception by students who often found some emotional security in minority-based social programs passed off as Black Studies. And to make these efforts the more fascinating and visible, many colleges and universities hired popular radicals and "media darlings" to augment the staff. In time few institutions were without their house radical who shouted at them and made them feel guilty, while they themselves dismissed as "inconsequential" such things as academic standards and honest research. (1981, p. 31)

According to Williams, many Black Studies enterprises remained unstable because institutions of higher learning employed a revolving door policy in regard to faculty hiring. This instability may have been inevitable, given the impact of the economic challenges and retrenchment of the times and the growth of the other "new studies": Women's Studies, Latino Studies, Asian American Studies, and Native American Studies. Nevertheless, because universities consistently applied the law of publish or perish, many Black Studies faculty were refused tenure and left the department. Black faculty members who could marshal enough protest support from black students and white sympathizers were able to win tenure by way of political bargaining. The outcome of all this was that many Black Studies programs were viewed as temporary while their faculty remained virtual outsiders or invisible within the university community.

Williams leveled a series of additional charges. She attacked university officials for employing budgetary management strategies to constrain Black Studies operations. She criticized black students' contradictory behavior and attitudes with respect to Black Studies. Some of these students, Williams observed, advocated Black Studies but refused to take these courses, not wanting Black Studies courses to appear on their transcripts. Some students enrolled in Black Studies courses seeking racial pride, while others expected African American professors to pass them automatically because of their common racial heritage. Finally, she criticized as racist the academy's rejection of Black Studies as an intellectually sound enterprise but its willing acceptance of the field as academically marginal. Speaking about the foreseeable future, Williams remarked cynically:

> There will, of course, remain for some time the brand of academic racism—both intentional and otherwise—that negates Black Studies as a scholarly discipline while accepting the Black Studies syndrome as a substitute. Our colleagues will remain for some time well-meaning and self-serving; continue to smile tolerantly when we speak of literary standards as applied to Afro-American literature; expect all of us to be authorities "on the race"; and in their discussions with us, unwittingly support Du Bois' 1903 declaration that the major problem of the twentieth century will be the color line. (1981, pp. 36–37)

With contradictions and dilemmas confronting Black Studies, an awareness emerged about the need to address critics'charges (see Davidson and Weaver, 1985; Farrell and Bridges, 1987). Leading Black Studies professionals and theorists put forward proposals to improve the status and image of the field. Perhaps the major strategies for renewal were efforts to stabilize, standardize, and (re)conceptualize the African American Studies' curriculum and philosophical foundation.

FROM BLACK STUDIES TO AFRICAN AMERICAN STUDIES: TOWARD INSTITUTIONALIZATION

Over the past decade, a major goal of African American Studies practitioners has been to institutionalize the field—to build a permanent foundation within the academy. Although some tensions remain between the university and African American Studies, there has been a gradual shift from the strictly reactive strategies by both parties that characterized the turbulent 1960s to forms of mutual adjustment. This and the desire for a more uniform name of the field might explain why many newer enterprises, developing in the late 1970s and after, called themselves African American Studies.

In its current and still evolving phase, a major strategy to institutionalize African American Studies has been the endeavor to standardize the curriculum. In 1980, the National Council for Black Studies, the field's professional organization, adopted a core curriculum for Black Studies (see Alkalimat and Associates, 1986; and Gordon, 1981). The purpose was to establish a model curriculum that would provide a coherent framework for standardizing African American Studies as a consistent field of study. The model core curriculum includes three broad course areas—social/behavioral studies, historical studies, and cultural studies—with four levels of courses. The first level is an introduction to the three broad course areas. The second level contains courses that review and survey basic literature on the black experience within the categories of social/behavioral studies, historical studies, and cultural studies. The third level includes advanced courses that explore current research methods and analysis on emerging issues within the three broad categories. The fourth level consists of senior seminars that integrate, synthesize, and apply knowledge acquired in previous courses with the goal of reconsidering and reassessing current issues in the field. At this level, students prepare for further research, graduate study, or the work world.

An ongoing issue in the attempts at institutionalization is the search for a philosophical or theoretical grounding for the field of African American Studies. There are a number of competing theoretical, philosophical, and ideological viewpoints in the evolving field. Maulana Karenga, chair of the Pan-African Studies Department at California State University at Long Beach, sets forth a conceptualization of the field in his textbook, *Introduction to Black Studies* (1982). Karenga's contribution is grounded in his long-standing black cultural nationalist theory of Kawaida, which seeks to encompass all aspects of the black experience. As he states:

> The scope of Black Studies as a discipline is the totality of historical and current Black thought and practice, but expresses itself most definitively in seven core subject areas: 1) Black History; 2) Black Religion; 3) Black Social Organization; 4) Black Politics; 5) Black Economics; 6) Black Creative Production (Black Art, Black Music and Black Literature); and 7) Black Psychology. As an interdisciplinary discipline concerned with the coherence and unity of its subject areas, Black Studies, of necessity, has core integrative principles and assumptions that serve as thematic glue which holds together these core subject areas.

Karenga continues by identifying four "integrative principles and assumptions":

> Each subject area of Black Studies is a vital aspect and area of the Black experience and, therefore, contributive to the understanding and appreciation of its wholeness. Secondly, the truth of the Black experience is whole and thus, any partial and compartmentalized approach to it can only yield a partial and incomplete image and understanding of it. Thirdly, effectively integrated into the pattern of the discipline as a whole, each subject area becomes a microcosm of the macrocosm, the Black experience, which not only enriches our knowledge of the Black experience, but also enhances the analytical process and products of the discipline itself. Finally, all the subject areas mesh and intersect not only at the point of their primary focus, i.e., Black people in the process of shaping reality in their own image and interest, but also in their self-conscious commitment and contribution to the definition and solution of the social and discipline problems which serve as the core challenges to Black Studies. (1982, pp. 37–38)

Molefi K. Asante, editor of the *Journal of Black Studies* and chair of the Department of African American Studies at Temple University, is another leading African American Studies theorist and well-known formulator of "Afrocentricity" or "Africalogy" (Asante, 1980, 1987, 1990; Asante and Asante, 1990). Afrocentricity is an interpretive strategy and theoretical framework that is directed at the examination of all human phenomena from an African-centered world view. This world view comes out of an exhaustive investigation of African and African American cultural history.

This African-centered standpoint can offer an alternative to the dominant Eurocentric paradigm and reveal its shortcomings by exposing its particularity, ethnocentrism, and subjectivity. While maintaining that the Eurocentric tradition is valid within its own context, Asante asserts that this tradition becomes imperialistic when it is presumed to be objective and equally applicable to all people and circumstances. Hence, Afrocentric criticism emphatically rejects Eurocentrism's representation of its view as universal and absolute. Asante does not arrogantly assert that Afrocentricity is the only interpretation of the world. Afrocentric critical practice is an interpretation of the world, according to Asante, from a particular philosophical and ideological standpoint. For example, Asante suggests that one of Afrocentricity's crucial elements is the notion of harmony and complementarity—the idea that entities can be different and yet complement each other. Asante remarks:

> In the Afrocentric conception of literature and orature, the critical method would be employed to determine to what degree the writer or speaker contributed to the unity of the symbols, the elimination of chaos, the making of peace among disparate views, and the creation of an opportunity for harmony and hence balance. . . . Harmony, in the sense that I am speaking of it, is an equilibrium among the various factors impinging upon communication. (1987, pp. 177–178)

Asante points out how much the Afrocentric concept of harmony differs from the conception of oppositional dichotomies so fundamental to Eurocentric consciousness. He notes that dichotomization pervades the Eurocentric structure of knowledge; people and things are generally grouped on the basis of their opposition to each other—for example, European/African, male/female, mind/body, reason/emotion, or science/nature. Moreover, the opposing categories are hierarchically related within the Eurocentric dualist conception of the world. That is, one of the dichotomous elements is superior to and therefore should dominate or negate the other: European over African, male over female, mind over body, reason over emotion, or science over nature. Parenthetically, this central dimension of the Eurocentric outlook might well be a driving force behind Western cultural aggression and exploitation based on class, race, and gender.

Asante suggests that Afrocentricity should become the theoretical and critical framework of African American Studies:

> As a relatively new field African-American Studies must take steps that might appear rather undramatic to most observers yet these steps are essential for a proper understanding of this novel coalescence within the academy. One of those steps involves the definition of the field in a way that distinguishes it from the study of black people in general by scholars, black and white, in other fields. In other words, the study of black people is not African/African-American Studies. If that were so we could argue that African-American Studies has existed for a hundred years. It is not the study of blacks that is the fundamental issue but the study of blacks and others from an afrocentric perspective; this is the locus of African-American Studies. . . . It is the congruence of object and subject. (1986, pp. 258–259)

Another effort to conceptualize and institutionalize African American Studies is found in sociologist Abdul Alkalimat and associates' textbook, *Introduction to Afro-American Studies* (1986). Although the underlying interpretive approach of the text is Marxist, the authors indicate that their aim is to provide a unifying theoretical framework that can incorporate competing ideological tendencies in African American Studies.

> Our text is based on a paradigm of unity for Black Studies, a framework in which all points of view can have the most useful coexistence. While maintaining a dynamic process of debate, everyone involved can remain united and committed to the field. This includes Marxists, nationalists, pan-Africanists, and old-fashioned civil rights integrationists as well. Further, our specific orientation is anti-racist, anti-sexist, and anti-capitalist. We are basing our analysis on most of our Black intellectual tradition and that leads us, as it did Langston Hughes, Paul Robeson, and W. E. B. Du Bois, to a progressive socialist position. This text, therefore, has a definite point of view, but it presents the basis for clarity, understanding, and dialogue between different schools of thought and different disciplines. (1986, pp. 21–22)

Besides the competing viewpoints just discussed, there are differences in programs, the organization and curricula of African American Studies, according to their institutional environments. So the outcome of current efforts to standardize the curriculum and to develop a critical theoretical practice of African American Studies is uncertain. Moreover, it is not clear that the National Council for Black Studies can ensure that African American Studies enterprises across the nation will conform to a model core curriculum. In fact, one must ask whether there should be conformity to a model curriculum and a single theoretical or ideological orientation in African American Studies. Most fields of study do not display this kind of uniformity. Perhaps an alternative is to allow a more flexible and innovative atmosphere in which African American Studies can continue to grow and develop.

Clearly, one future challenge for African American Studies is to move beyond its marginal image and status within the academy. An equally if not more important future challenge is to deal with the intellectual and social implications of the changing character of American society as the declining industrial-manufacturing order gives way to a rising postindustrial-managerial order.

CONCLUSION: AFRICAN AMERICAN STUDIES IN THE EMERGING POSTINDUSTRIAL-MANAGERIAL AGE

The postindustrial-managerial transformation of American society is characterized by the transition from a capital-intensive economy based on physical resources, which dominated the first half of this century, to a knowledge-intensive economy based on human resources, which characterizes the last half of this century. The principal resource in America's declining capital-intensive economy has been finance capital, invested in industrial plants, machinery, and technologies to increase the muscle power of human labor. In the emerging knowledge-intensive economy, the decisive resource is cultural capital: the nation's investment in and management of education, knowledge, computers, and other technologies that enhance the mental capacity of workers (Botkin, Dimancescu, and Stata, 1984; Drucker, 1969; Lyotard, 1984; Machlup, 1962, 1980, 1982, 1984; Reich, 1991; Toffler, 1990). Important now are specialized knowledge, communication skills, the capacity to process and utilize collections of information in strategic decision-making processes, and an increasingly professionalized/bureaucratic approach to managing people. With this expanding role for formal or specialized knowledge, professionals and experts—intellectuals and the technical intelligentsia—are becoming a "new class" in the public and private spheres, particularly with regard to policy making (see Bazelon, 1971; Derber, Schwartz, Magrass, 1990; Ehrenreich and Ehrenreich, 1979; Freidson, 1970; Galbraith, 1971; Nachmias and Rosenbloom, 1980; Perkin, 1989).

Mental capacity and managerial skills are supplanting money and manufacturing as the source of power. Learning, therefore, becomes an indispensable investment for social development, and educational credentials are more and more the key to a person's role in society (Collins, 1977). In view of these trends, many parents are becoming preoccupied with the educational advantages they can confer on their children, and many university students are realizing the importance of advanced education.

Society's new power wielders are located in government, elite universities, philanthropic foundations, the mass media, elite law firms, political action committees, and major policy research institutions (see Benveniste, 1972; Burnham, 1960; Fischer, 1990; Keane, 1984; Lebedoff, 1981; Smith, 1991). Their influence comes from the capacity to conceptualize the character of social issues and to design strategies for handling them; they also produce and manage ideas and images that direct the cultural, intellectual, and ideological development of society. For example, the current debate about the urban underclass and social welfare policy reform includes policy intellectuals of various ideological persuasions (see Auletta, 1982; Cottingham, 1982; Jencks and Peterson, 1991; Jones, 1992; Lawson, 1992; Mead, 1992; Murray, 1984; Wilson, 1987). Living by argumentation and persuasion, the new elite is not only a socioeconomic class, but it is also a cultural elite (see Darity, 1986; Fischer, 1990; Gouldner, 1979; Luke, 1989; Majone, 1989; Perkin, 1989).

This new elite does not rise to dominance by itself. To be effective, the new elite must be allied to a political, legal, or organizational base. Their power comes from their access to and their ability to influence policy makers in government and private organizations. They operate at many levels to influence the intellectual direction, content, and contours of public decision making. They may be policy specialists within the offices of political executives, intellectual activists who appear at local school board hearings, renowned university professors who consult with government officials on important policy matters, or social scientists whose research findings contribute to major court rulings.

What role will African American Studies intellectuals and scholars play in the evolving society? I think we need to respond with innovation and a critical consciousness in regard to curriculum development and strategies for social development. African American scholars will be required to pursue new knowledge that can prove useful for handling complex social problems—for example, the progressive impoverishment of urban black communities. Moreover, in the evolving global political economy that is anchored in knowledge production, distribution, and consumption (see Reich, 1991; Toffler, 1990), African American Studies will be compelled to strengthen its transdisciplinary and global thrusts by designing curricula that transgress upon the conventional academic disciplinary boundaries between the humanities and the social, behavioral, biological, and physical sciences. African American Studies needs to destroy old stereotypes, break new ground (conceptually and empirically), and broaden its intellectual scope and horizons to include attention to such areas of study as policy studies and advocacy, critical social theory, critical cultural studies, social and political ethics, futures research, organizational development, and leadership preparation.

In the process, African American Studies theorists, practitioners, and students need to remain skeptical of received knowledge and must continue to disturb the intellectual and ideological hegemony of Eurocentrism and white American chauvinism within the academy. I am not at all suggesting an end to the study of Western culture. However, because the Eurocentric perspective and white American chauvinism continue to set the terms of intellectual discourse and dictate the academy's accepted structure of knowledge, I advocate a more careful and critical investigation of Western European culture and its American legacy—but with a different and even irreverent interpretive lens refracted by African American Studies and the other "new studies" (see Hayes, 1989). Western civilization and its cultural heritage need to be seen and understood not as superior to others but as part of a democratic community of world civilizations and cultures. There is no normative civilization and culture.

Importantly, African American Studies scholars and intellectuals must be determined to grapple with the implications of the emerging postindustrial-managerial estate for African Americans and other historically oppressed peoples. How will this new social order affect such real human concerns as individual dignity and human worth; family stability and community solidarity; literacy and quality education; economic well-being and self-sufficiency; and democratic political rights and self-determination? African American Studies cannot ignore the examination of the consequences of a progressively changing world.

African American Studies, as a critically conscious intellectual endeavor, needs to hammer out a concept of social justice and morality that encompasses the growing multicultural and multiracial nature of America's evolving society. Cultural critic Jim Merod sets forth some guidelines for this project:

> The critic's task is not only to question truth in its present guises. It is to find ways of putting fragments of knowledge, partial views, and separate disciplines in contact with questions about the use of expert labor so that the world we live in can be seen for what it is. Thus the virtue of defining critical work in terms of opposition to the state rather than (or at least alongside) transgression of intellectual norms is that it offers the possibility of defining criticism as an ally of demoted people and of an intensified political process. Critical analysis cannot be relegated to text-bound labor unless critics insist upon fighting among themselves for purely professional authority. That, ironically, is what Foucault's transgressive strategy calls

for. The larger authority of the democratic enterprise—to put public needs and general human welfare into open conflict with the depoliticized mystique of Western institutions (the professionalization of expert knowledge in government, science, technology, law, and education)—can be fought for, nevertheless, by critics who work against the authorization of existing power by technical and professional elites. Such work requires not just negational suspicion, rampant skepticism, but proposals and concepts from which more just institutions may emerge. Justice requires that everyone have access to all information in a political system that develops the organized energy of once excluded interests and identities. This access is not wholly a matter of illuminating previously invisible discourse; *it depends on the emergence of previously invisible people and political positions* [emphasis added]. (1987, pp. 188–189)

Thus, intellectual work is not apolitical, and African American Studies theorists and practitioners need to consider themselves involved in a struggle for identity and community beyond the domination of manipulative images and exploitative policies. This battle resides in cultural, political, and economic systems and can only culminate in dynamic systems that are not more exclusive but more inclusive.

In the last analysis, African American Studies needs to decide whether it will continue to consume the dominant modes of thinking and knowledge of the academy's intellectual and managerial elites or whether it will engage in new thinking and design an independent critical social theory and practice that will promote the expansion of the frontiers of new knowledge (for example, see Wynter, 1984a, 1984b, 1984c, 1987). These critical and uncertain times demand, therefore, that African American Studies give leadership in the academic and nonacademic world by developing new strategies and tactics that could save humanity and thereby save the world African community. As we begin the twenty-first century, African American Studies will continue to develop to the extent that it remains innovative, critical, self-reflective, and emancipatory. The general purpose of this anthology is to contribute to that intellectual and practical project.

References Cited

Alkalimat, Abdul, and Associates, *Introduction to Afro-American Studies: A Peoples College Primer,* Chicago: Twenty-First Century Books & Publications, 1986.

Allen, Robert L., "Politics of the Attack on Black Studies," *The Black Scholar,* Vol. 6, No. 1 (September 1974), pp. 2–7.

Auletta, Ken, *The Underclass,* New York: Random House, Inc., 1982.

Asante, Molefi K., *Afrocentricity: The Theory of Social Change,* Buffalo: Amulefi Publishing Co., 1980.

___, "A Note on Nathan Huggins' Report to the Ford Foundation on African-American Studies," *Journal of Black Studies,* Vol. 17, No. 2 (December 1986), pp. 255–262.

___, *The Afrocentric Idea,* Philadelphia: Temple University Press, 1987.

___, *Kemet, Afrocentricity and Knowledge,* Trenton: Africa World Press, Inc., 1990.

___, and Kariamu W. Asante, eds., *African Culture: The Rhythms of Unity,* Trenton: Africa World Press, Inc., 1990.

Bazelon, David T., *Power in America: The Politics of the New Class,* New York: The New American Library, 1971.

"Black Studies Run into Trouble on U. S. College Campuses," *U. S. News and World Report,* Vol. 74, No. 5 (January 29, 1973), pp. 29–32.

Benveniste, Guy, *The Politics of Expertise,* Berkeley: The Glendessary Press, 1972.

Botkin, James, Dan Diamancescu, and Ray Stata, *The Innovators: Rediscovering America's Creative Energy,* New York: Harper & Row, Publishers, Inc., 1984.

Burnham, James, *The Managerial Revolution,* Bloomington: Indiana University Press, 1960.

Carmichael, Stokely, and Charles V. Hamilton, *Black Power: The Politics of Liberation in America,* New York: Random House, 1967.

Carson, Clayborne, *In Struggle: SNCC and the Black Awakening of the 1960s,* Cambridge: Harvard University Press, 1981.

Chrisman, Robert, "Observations on Race and Class at San Francisco State," in James McEvoy and Abraham Miller, eds., *Black Power and Student Rebellion,* Belmont: Wadsworth Publishing Company, Inc., pp. 222–232.

Collins, Randall, *The Credential Society: An Historical Sociology of Education and Stratification,* New York: Academic Press, Inc., 1979.

Colt, George H., "Will the Huggins Approach Save Afro-American Studies?" *Harvard Magazine,* September–October 1981, pp. 38–46, 62, 70.

Cottingham, Clement, ed., *Race, Poverty, and the Urban Underclass,* Lexington: Lexington Books/D. C. Heath and Company, 1982.

Cruse, Harold, *The Crisis of the Negro Intellectual,* New York: William Morrow and Company, Inc., 1967.

___, "The Integrationist Ethic as a Basis for Scholarly Endeavors," in Armstead L. Robinson, Craig C. Foster, and Donald H. Ogilvie, eds., *Black Studies in the University: A Symposium,* New Haven: Yale University Press, 1969, pp. 4–12.

Darity, William A., Jr., "The Managerial Class and Industrial Policy," *Industrial Relations,* Vol. 25 (Spring 1986), pp. 217–227.

Davidson, Douglas V., and Frederick S. Weaver, "Black Studies, White Studies, and Institutional Politics," *Journal of Black Studies,* Vol. 15, No. 3 (March 1985), pp. 339–347.

Derber, Charles, William A. Schwartz, and Yale Magrass, *Power in the Highest Degree: Professionals and the Rise of a New Mandarin Order,* New York: Oxford University Press, 1990.

Donner, Frank J., *The Age of Surveillance: The Aims and Methods of America's Political Intelligence System,* New York: Alfred A. Knopf, 1980.

___, *Protectors of Privilege: Red Squads and Police Repression in Urban America,* Berkeley: University of California Press, 1990.

Drucker, Peter F., *The Age of Discontinuity: Guidelines to Our Changing Society,* New York: Harper & Row, 1968.

Edwards, Harry, *Black Students,* New York: The Free Press, 1970.

___, *The Struggle That Must Be: An Autobiography,* New York: Macmillan Publishing Co., Inc., 1980.

Ehrenreich, Barbara, and John Ehrenreich, "The Professional-Managerial Class," in Pat Walker, ed., *Between Labor and Capital,* Boston: South End Press, 1979, pp, 5–45.

Farrell, Walter C., Jr., and Edgar F. Bridges, "Black Studies at the Crossroads," *Thought & Action: The NEA Higher Education Journal,* Vol. 3 (September 1987), pp. 103–112.

Fischer, Frank, *Technocracy and the Politics of Expertise,* Newbury Park: Sage Publications, 1990.

Forman, James, *The Making of Black Revolutionaries,* New York: The Macmillan Company, 1972.

Freidson, Eliot, *Professional Dominance: The Social Structure of Medical Care,* Chicago: Aldine Publishing Company, 1970.

Galbraith, John K., *The New Industrial State,* Boston: Houghton Mifflin Company, 1971.

Gerald, Carolyn F., "The Black Writer and His Role," in Addison Gayle, Jr., ed., *The Black Aesthetic,* Garden City: Doubleday & Company, Inc., 1971, pp. 349–356.

Gordon, Vivian V., "The Coming of Age of Black Studies," *The Western Journal of Black Studies,* Vol. 5, No. 3 (Fall 1981), pp. 231–236.

Gouldner, Alvin W., *The Future of Intellectuals and the Rise of the New Class,* New York: Seabury Press, 1979.

Hare, Nathan, "The Contribution of Black Sociologists to Black Studies," in James E. Blackwell and Morris Janowitz, eds., *Black Sociologists: Historical and Contemporary Perspectives,* Chicago: The University of Chicago Press, 1974, pp. 253–266.

Hayes, Floyd W. III, "Politics and Education in America's Multicultural Society: An African-American Studies' Response to Allan Bloom," *The Journal of Ethnic Studies,* Vol. 17, No. 2 (Summer 1989), pp. 71–88.

Henderson, Donald, "What Direction Black Studies?" in Henry J. Richards, ed., *Topics in Afro-American Studies,* Buffalo: Black Academy Press, Inc., 1971.

Jackson, Maurice, "Toward a Sociology of Black Studies," *Journal of Black Studies,* Vol. 1, No. 2 (December 1970), pp. 131–140.

Jencks, Christopher, and Paul E. Peterson, eds., *The Urban Underclass,* Washington, D.C.: The Brookings Institution, 1991.

Jones, Jacqueline, *The Dispossessed: America's Underclasses from the Civil War to the Present,* New York: Basic Books, 1992.

Karenga, Maulana, *Introduction to Black Studies,* Inglewood: Kawaida Publications, 1982.

Keane, John, *Public Life and Late Capitalism: Toward a Socialist Theory of Democracy,* New York: Cambridge University Press, 1984.

Kilson, Martin, Jr., "The Intellectual Validity of Studying the Black Experience," in Armstead L. Robinson, Craig C. Foster, and Donald H. Ogilvie, eds., *Black Studies in the Universiy: A Symposium,* New Haven: Yale University Press, 1969, pp. 13–16.

___, "Reflections on Structure and Content in Black Studies," *Journal of Black Studies,* Vol. 3, No. 3 (March 1973), pp. 297–313.

Lawson, Bill E., ed., *The Underclass Question,* Philadelphia: Temple University Press, 1992.

Lebedoff, David, *The New Elite: The Death of Democracy,* New York: Franklin Watts, 1981.

Luke, Timothy W., *Screens of Power: Ideology, Dominance, and Resistance in Informational Society,* Urbana: University of Illinois Press, 1989.

Lyotard, Jean-Francois, *The Postmodern Condition: A Report on Knowledge,* trans. Geoff Bennington and Brian Massumi, Minneapolis: University of Minnesota Press, 1984.

McEvoy, James, and Abraham Miller, "San Francisco State 'On Strike . . . Shut It Down'," in McEvoy and Miller, eds., *Black Power and Student Rebellion: Conflict on the American Campus,* Belmont: Wadsworth Publishing Company, Inc., 1969, pp. 12–31.

Maclup, Fritz, *The Production and Distribution of Knowledge in the United States,* Princeton: Princeton University Press, 1962.

___, *Knowledge and Knowledge Production,* Princeton: Princeton University Press, 1980.

___, *The Branches of Learning,* Princeton: Princeton University Press, 1982.

___, *The Economics of Information and Human Capital,* Princeton: Princeton University Press, 1984.

Majone, Giandomenico, *Evidence, Argument, and Persuasion in the Policy Process,* New Haven: Yale University Press, 1989.

Malveaux, Julianne, "Black Studies: An Assessment," *Essence,* August 1980, pp. 78–79, 95, 98, 103–104.

Mead, Lawrence M., *The New Politics of Poverty: The Nonworking Poor in America,* New York: Basic Books, 1992

Merod, Jim, *The Political Responsibility of the Critic,* Ithaca: Cornell University Press, 1987.

Murray, Charles, *Losing Ground: American Social Policy, 1950–1980,* New York: Basic Books, 1984.

Nachmias, David, and David H. Rosenbloom, *Bureaucratic Government, USA,* New York: St. Martin's Press, 1980.

Perkin, Harold, *The Rise of Professional Society: England Since 1880,* New York: Routledge, 1989.

Poinsett, Alex, "The Plight of Black Studies," *Ebony,* Vol. 29, No. 2 (December 1973), pp. 128–134.

Reich, Robert B., *The Work of Nations: Preparing Ourselves for 21st-Century Capitalism,* New York: Alfred A. Knopf, 1991.

Said, Edward W., *The World, the Text, and the Critic,* Cambridge: Harvard University Press, 1983.

Smith, James A., *The Idea Brokers: Think Tanks and the Rise of the New Policy Elite,* New York: The Free Press, 1991.

Stone, Chuck, *Black Power in America,* Indianapolis: The Bobbs-Merrill Company, 1968.

___, "The National Conference on Black Power," in Floyd B. Barbour, ed., *The Black Power Revolt: A Collection of Essays,* Boston: Extending Horizons Books, 1968, pp. 189–198.

Toffler, Alvin, *Powershift: Knowledge, Wealth, and Violence at the Edge of the 21st Century,* New York: Bantam Books, 1990.

UMBC Catalog 1973–1974, Baltimore: University of Maryland Baltimore County, 1973.

Walton, Sidney F., *The Black Curriculum: Developing a Program in Afro-American Studies,* East Palo Alto: Black Liberation Publishers, 1969.

Williams, Kenny J., "The Black Studies Syndrome: Down by One Is Still Losing," *Change* (October 1981), pp. 30–37.

Wilson, William J., *The Truly Disadvantaged: The Inner City, the Underclass, and Public Policy,* Chicago: The University of Chicago Press, 1987.

Wynter, Sylvia, "New Seville and the Conversion Experience of Bartolome de Las Casas," Part One, *Jamaica Journal,* Vol. 17, No. 2 (May 1984), pp. 25–32.

___, "New Seville and the Conversion Experience of Bartolome de Las Casas," Part Two, *Jamaica Journal,* Vol. 17, No. 3 (August 1984), pp. 46–55.

___, "The Ceremony Must Be Found: After Humanism," *Boundary 2,* Vol. XII, No. 1 (Spring/Fall 1984), pp. 19–70.

___, "On Disenchanting Discourse: 'Minority' Literary Criticism and Beyond," *Cultural Critique,* No. 7 (Fall 1987), pp. 207–244.

Advisory Board

I

African American Studies: Trends, Developments, and Future Challenges

Why African American Studies? Why do we study any human experience? We do so in order to learn about ourselves and others. We do so in order to understand the character of social development so that we can improve the human condition. African American Studies, as the study of Africa and its global legacy, developed as a consequence of the historical relationship between Africans and Western Europeans that resulted in the dynamics of slave trading and chattel slavery, imperialism and colonialism, annihilating wars and exploitation, and segregation and racism. The field of study draws its strength from the legacy of African peoples' historic struggle for liberation and self-determination, intellectual and cultural advancement, and socioeconomic and political development. By examining the experiences of African peoples, African American Studies can provide to black students a sense of individual identity and community and a sense of personal and collective dignity. For both black and nonblack students, African American Studies can be of help in understanding other cultures, an ability especially needed in the increasingly multicultural American society. By challenging and correcting the misrepresentations of Africa and Western Europe and their cultural legacies, African American Studies can give students the intellectual tools and the moral courage to improve the human condition.

The essays in this section explore aspects of the background and character of African American Studies—why the field developed, the concern to link scholarship and social practice, the inauguration of Black Women's Studies, and the relationship between African American Studies and multiculturalism.

In his essay "The Study of the Negro," written early in the twentieth century, Carter G. Woodson decries American history's treatment of Africans and African Americans and concludes that a study of such "history" can only have a negative psychological impact on African Americans. He puts forward views similar to those of the creators of African American Studies in the late 1960s. Woodson, who founded the Association for the Study of Negro Life and History in 1916 and who is often referred to as the father of African American history, argues that the strategy of omitting or misrepresenting the contributions that Africans have made to the development of human civilization encourages African-descended people to hate themselves and to worship Europeans. Woodson sees traditional American education as a form of intellectual control, which has behavioral consequences: "The education of the Negro then must be carefully directed lest the race may waste time trying to do the impossible. Lead the Negro to believe this and thus control his thinking. If you can thereby determine what he will think, you will not need to worry about what he will do. You will not have to tell him to go to the back door. He will go without being told; and if there is no back door he will have one cut for his special benefit." Unaware of their past, "mis-educated" African Americans become the tools of their oppressors and are of little use to the salvation and survival of African-descended people. The alternative to "mis-education," according to Woodson, is for African-descended people to think for themselves and to act in their own interests. This requires that they undertake their own systematic study and examination of the African and African American experience.

The essay by Harold Cruse, "The Integrationist Ethic as a Basis for Scholarly Endeavors," provides a vision of African American Studies propounded in the 1960s. At the 1968 Yale University symposium on Black Studies, Cruse attacked the liberal racial integrationist ethic of American scholarship, arguing that it had precluded the development of a viable black social theory on which to ground African American Studies. For him, any intellectually valid African American Studies curriculum had to rest on the ideology of black cultural nationalism and had to employ a critical historical approach.

Cruse suggested that African American Studies should focus its attention on black institutional development on all levels—cultural, political, economic, and social. While he called for a self-critical analysis—that is, investigation of the impact of the Protestant Ethic on African American social development; of W. E. B. Du Bois' talented tenth thesis and the historical origins of the black intellectual class; and of the clash between black radical-revolutionary and reformist-gradualist tendencies within the black movement—Cruse cautioned that African American Studies should not be too narrowly conceived. Rather, he argued for a critical investigation of the larger American cultural dynamic.

In many ways, the male voice dominated the character of the black liberation struggle and the early African American Studies movement of the late 1960s and 1970s. Moreover, the white woman's outlook shaped the content and contours of the women's liberation and the Women's Studies movements of the early 1970s. Emerging in the late 1970s as a result of an apparent marginalization by both of these social and intellectual movements, Black Women's Studies sought to fill the spaces left in the intersection of African American Studies and Women's Studies. Gloria T. Hull and Barbara Smith, in "The Politics of Black Women's Studies," establish a rationale for the development of Black Women's Studies. For Hull and Smith, the inauguration of Black Women's Studies expands the struggle for black liberation as it dignifies the everyday life-experiences of black women.

The authors are conscious of the political dynamics surrounding the advancement of Black Women's Studies. As guidelines for their project, Hull and Smith assert the significance of four themes. First, Black Women's Studies needs to be informed by the recognition that the history of black women has been one of extreme oppression and exploitation by a white male–dominated society. Hence, an objective of this emerging field is to transform society, empowering black women to live with freedom, dignity, and respect. Second, because black women are plagued by race, class, and sexual domination, only a black feminist perspective can adequately describe and analyze black women's experiences. Third, Black Women's Studies must incorporate a radical analysis of all black women's experiences regardless of sexual orientation. Finally, Hull and Smith call for an autonomous Black Women's Studies enterprise that builds alliances with African American Studies and Women's Studies programs.

The article by Manning Marable, "Black Studies, Multiculturalism and the Future of American Education," focuses on the meanings of multiculturalism in light of the increasing cultural diversity of American society. Marable asserts that the growing awareness of cultural difference within the United States makes African American Studies a primary participant in the discourse about multiculturalism. He then discusses four interpretations of multiculturalism: corporate multiculturalism, liberal multiculturalism, racial essentialism, and radical democratic multiculturalism. He notes the strengths and weaknesses of each perspective but advocates radical democratic multiculturalism because it emphasizes transforming the system of cultural and political power in America. Pointing out the difference of perspectives among radical democratic multiculturalists, Marable nonetheless asserts that the adherents of this view agree on the need to overturn the structure of racism that is based on elite white-skin privilege by employing "color-conscious" policy strategies.

In a critical analysis of American universities and their relations with historically excluded groups from the 1970s to the present, Marable argues that many of these institutions hired people of color as faculty and administrators and then placed them not in positions of power and importance but in less than significant positions without proper mentoring. Marable also maintains that many liberal and conservative university officials, who never valued the importance of teaching and researching the African American experience, employed the same strategy as they installed and then isolated African American Studies programs merely in order to pacify students who demanded them. Accordingly, some African American Studies enterprises became academic ghettos.

As a positive alternative and corrective to this academic corruption, Marable demands a principled criticism both of the ghettoization of some African American Studies programs and of conservative black intellectuals who deny the value of African American Studies in the academy. Looking to the future, he advocates high-caliber African American Studies programs and research institutes that affect the learning experiences of all university students regardless of cultural or ethnic background. Additionally, Marable recommends that all university students be required to take African American Studies as a general requirement for graduation. Finally, Marable contends that African American Studies should recapture the relationship between academic excellence and social responsibility by engaging in research that helps to improve the social conditions of impoverished black communities and that contributes to building a new class of African American leaders who value policy-relevant knowledge and who are committed to social change.

Taken together, the views put forward in these essays represent progressive expressions of the intellectual vocation and collective concern of African American Studies. Carter G. Woodson's criticism of traditional education's cultural and racial exclusivity and his call for the study of the black experience is at the heart of African American Studies. The conventional academic bias for Western European culture and civilization and against all others initially energized, and continues to inspire, the demand for African American Studies. Challenging the university's cultural parochialism and the integrationist approach of mainstream scholarship, Harold Cruse demands that African American Studies employ a critical and historical approach that is grounded in black cultural nationalism. Going beyond the often male-centered examination of the black experience in early African American Studies programs and the silencing of the black female voice in Women's Studies programs, Gloria Hull and Barbara Smith call for a radical black feminist interpretation as the foundation for Black Women's Studies. Finally, Manning Marable suggests a linkage between high-quality African American Studies programs and radical democratic multiculturalism, demanding a more rigorous project that is committed to improving the life-chances of impoverished black communities. Although this field is situated within the academy, teachers and researchers in African American Studies need to be aware of their responsibility to be actively engaged in changing society for the better.

The Study of the Negro

CARTER GODWIN WOODSON

The facts drawn from an experience of more than twenty years enable us to make certain deductions with respect to the study of the Negro. Only one Negro out of every ten thousand is interested in the effort to set forth what his race has thought and felt and attempted and accomplished that it may not become a negligible factor in the thought of the world. By traditions and education, however, the large majority of Negroes have become interested in the history and status of other races, and they spend millions annually to promote such knowledge. Along with this sum, of course, should be considered the large amount paid for devices in trying not to be Negroes.

The chief reason why so many give such a little attention to the background of the Negro is the belief that this study is unimportant. They consider as history only such deeds as those of Mussolini who after building up an efficient war machine with the aid of other Europeans would now use it to murder unarmed and defenseless Africans who have restricted themselves exclusively to attending to their own business. If Mussolini succeeds in crushing Abyssinia he will be recorded in "history" among the Caesars, and volumes written in praise of the conqueror will find their way to the homes and libraries of thousands of mis-educated Negroes. The oppressor has always indoctrinated the weak with this interpretation of the crimes of the strong.

The war lords have done good only accidentally or incidentally while seeking to do evil. The movements which have ameliorated the condition of humanity and stimulated progress have been inaugurated by men of thought in lifting their fellows out of drudgery unto ease and comfort, out of selfishness unto altruism. The Negro may well rejoice that his hands, unlike those of his oppressors, are not stained with so much blood extracted by brute force. Real history is not the record of the successes and disappointments, the vices, the follies, and the quarrels of those who engage in contention for power.

The Association for the Study of Negro Life and History is projected on the fact that there is nothing in the past of the Negro more shameful than what is found in the past of other races. The Negro is as human as the other members of the family of mankind. The Negro, like others, has been up at times; and at times he has been down. With the domestica-

From *The Mis-Education of the Negro,* edited by Charles H. Wesley and Thelma D. Perry. Africa World Press, Trenton, New Jersey.

Carter G. Woodson, founder of the Association for the Study of Negro Life and History in 1916.

tion of animals, the discovery of iron, the development of stringed instruments, an advancement in fine art, and the inauguration of trial by jury to his credit, the Negro stands just as high as others in contributing to the progress of the world.

The oppressor, however, raises his voice to the contrary. He teaches the Negro that he has no worthwhile past, that his race has done nothing significant since the beginning of time, and that there is no evidence that he will ever achieve anything great. The education of the Negro then must be carefully directed lest the race may waste time trying to do the impossible. Lead the Negro to believe this and thus control his thinking. If you can thereby deter-

mine what he will think, you will not need to worry about what he will do. You will not have to tell him to go to the back door. He will go without being told; and if there is no back door he will have one cut for his special benefit.

If you teach the Negro that he has accomplished as much good as any other race he will aspire to equality and justice without regard to race. Such an effort would upset the program of the oppressor in Africa and America. Play up before the Negro, then, his crimes and shortcomings. Let him learn to admire the Hebrew, the Greek, the Latin and the Teuton. Lead the Negro to detest the man of African blood—to hate himself. The oppressor then may conquer, exploit, oppress and even annihilate the Negro by segregation without fear or trembling. With the truth hidden there will be little expression of thought to the contrary.

The American Negro has taken over an abundance of information which others have made accessible to the oppressed, but he has not yet learned to think and plan for himself as others do for themselves. Well might this race be referred to as the most docile and tractable people on earth. This merely means that when the oppressors once start the large majority of the race in the direction of serving the purposes of their traducers, the task becomes so easy in the years following that they have little trouble with the masses thus controlled. It is a most satisfactory system, and it has become so popular that European nations of foresight are sending some of their brightest minds to the United States to observe the Negro in "inaction" in order to learn how to deal likewise with Negroes in their colonies. What the Negro in America has become satisfied with will be accepted as the measure of what should be allotted him elsewhere. Certain Europeans consider the "solution of the race problem in the United States" one of our great achievements.

The mis-educated Negro joins the opposition with the objection that the study of the Negro keeps alive questions which should be forgotten. The Negro should cease to remember that he was once held a slave, that he has been oppressed, and even that he is a Negro. The traducer, however, keeps before the public such aspects of this history as will justify the present oppression of the race. It would seem, then, that the Negro should emphasize at the same time the favorable aspects to justify action in his behalf. One cannot blame the Negro for not desiring to be reminded of being the sort of creature that the oppressor has represented the Negro to be; but this very attitude shows ignorance of the past and a slavish dependence upon the enemy to serve those whom he would destroy. The Negro can be made proud of his past only by approaching it

scientifically himself and giving his own story to the world. What others have written about the Negro during the last three centuries has been mainly for the purpose of bringing him where he is today and holding him there.

The method employed by the Association for the Study of Negro Life and History, however, is not spectacular propaganda or fire-eating agitation. Nothing can be accomplished in such fashion. "Whom the gods would destroy they first make mad." The Negro, whether in Africa or America, must be directed toward a serious examination of the fundamentals of education, religion, literature, and philosophy as they have been expounded to him. He must be sufficiently enlightened to determine for himself whether these forces have come into his life to bless him or to bless his oppressor. After learning the facts in the case the Negro must develop the power of execution to deal with these matters as do people of vision. Problems of great importance cannot be worked out in a day. Questions of great moment must be met with far-reaching plans.

The Association for the Study of Negro Life and History is teaching the Negro to exercise foresight rather than "hindsight." Liberia must not wait until she is offered to Germany before realizing that she has few friends in Europe. Abyssinia must not wait until she is invaded by Italy before she prepares for self-defense. A scientific study of the past of modern nations would show these selfish tendencies as inevitable results from their policies in dealing with those whom they have professed to elevate. For example, much of Africa has been conquered and subjugated to save souls. How expensive has been the Negro's salvation! One of the strong arguments for slavery was that it brought the Negro into the light of salvation. And yet the Negro today is all but lost.

The Association for the Study of Negro Life and History, however, has no special brand for the solution of the race problem except to learn to think. No general program of uplift for the Negroes in all parts of the world will be any

7

more successful than such a procedure would be in the case of members of other races under different circumstances. What will help a Negro in Alabama may prove harmful to one in Maine. The African Negro may find his progress retarded by applying "methods used for the elevation of the Negro in America." A thinking man, however, learns to deal wisely with conditions as he finds them rather than to take orders from someone who knows nothing about his status and cares less. At present the Negro, both in Africa and America, is being turned first here and there experimentally by so-called friends who in the final analysis assist the Negro merely in remaining in the dark.

In the furtherance of the program of taking up these matters dispassionately the Association had made available an outline for the systematic study of the Negro as he has touched the life of others and as others have functioned in their relation to him, *The African Background Outlined: A Handbook*. This book is written from the point of view of history, literature, art, education, religion and economic imperialism. In seventeen chapters as Part I of the work a brief summary of the past in Africa is presented; and courses on "The Negro in Africa," "The Negro in the European Mind," "The Negro in America," "The Negro in Litera-

ture," "The Negro in Art," "The Education of the Negro," "The Religious Development of the Negro," and "Economic Imperialism" follow as Part II with ample bibliographical comment for every heading and subhead of these outlines. This facilitates the task of clubs, young peoples' societies, and special classes organized where the oppressors of the race and the Negroes cooperating with them are determined that the history and status of the Negro shall not be made a part of the curricula.

In this outline there is no animus, nothing to engender race hate. The Association does not bring out such publications. The aim of this organization is to set forth facts in scientific form, for facts properly set forth will tell their own story. No advantage can be gained by merely inflaming the Negro's mind against his traducers. In a manner they deserve to be congratulated for taking care of their own interests so well. The Negro needs to become angry with himself because he has not handled his own affairs wisely. In other words, the Negro must learn from others how to take care of himself in this trying ordeal. He must not remain content with taking over what others set aside for him and then come in the guise of friends to subject even that limited information to further misinterpretation.

Essay/Discussion Questions

1. According to Carter G. Woodson, why should we study the experiences of African and African-descended people?

2. Woodson argues that their oppressors have indoctrinated black Americans. What is the effect of this practice?

3. What is the value of Woodson's essay to the development of African American Studies?

The Integrationist Ethic as a Basis for Scholarly Endeavors

HAROLD CRUSE

On behalf of the Black Student Alliance of Yale, I am pleased to be called before you to discuss this very unique and very important problem: the significance of the black experience to intellectual pursuits and scholarly studies. I have been asked to concentrate on one theme, namely the failure of the integrationist ethic as a basis for scholarly studies. And from that point of departure, I will attempt to deal with this problem in a way which will be in consonance with what you call the "framework," or method of attack on this problem.

It is my belief that the integrationist ethic has subverted and blocked America's underlying tendency toward what I would call a democratic ethnic pluralism in our society. This ethic has been a historical tendency stimulated both by Anglo-Saxon political ideology, rampant industrialism, racism, and an Americanism whose implied goal has been the nullification of all competing subcultures indigenous to North America. It is my belief that both black and white scholarly rationalizations have historically supported the integrationist ethic in pursuit of the ideal of the American creed. This approach was obviously predicated on an intellectual consensus which held that the political, economic, and cultural values of the Anglo-American tradition were sufficiently creative and viable enough to sustain the American progression to realization of its ultimate potential. But the present internal social and racial crisis we are experiencing proves beyond a doubt the failure of this integrationist ethic. As a result of this failure, at this present moment we have no viable black philosophy on which to base much-needed black studies programs.

Upon examining the black and white reactions to this failure, we find different reactions on both sides of the racial fence. You have separatist reactions coming from the black side of the equation, and you have white intellectual resistance toward acceptance and ratification of another ethic in scholarly endeavors. In response to pressures for black studies, whites often attempt to speed up piecemeal integrative processes in favor of black integrationists. Another response to demands for black

From *Black Studies in the University, A Symposium*, edited by Armstead L. Robinson, Craig C. Foster, Donald H. Ogilvie. Yale University Press, 1969.

studies involves questioning the validity of separatist doctrines; whites question the nihilist, irrational, or anarchistic tendencies they note in separatist doctrines and, by extension, question whether the whole approach, including a trend toward black studies, is valid. Thus, black intellectual critics of the integrationist ethic—students, writers, scholars, critics, historians and so on—must assume an obligation to establish black studies in the curricula whose subject matter, critical thrust, and social objectives fully answer those who would question curriculum reform in the direction of black studies.

Such black studies programs must achieve or establish certain critical and/or creative criteria which would make manifest their validity in the face of white intellectual criticisms. Needless to say, this is a big question and a complex one. I don't know how far we can go into the analysis of it today. However, from my own point of view, having thought about these perplexing questions for many years, having based my whole creative life on the examination of, and the response to, these pressures, I have something which I think is of value in lending understanding to the problem.

I believe that if it were left to the black students themselves, the black scholars, the undergraduate students, the graduate students, the writers and the critics, to create this black studies curriculum, they would employ a historical approach. I think one of the main points of departure in an approach to the content and the thrust of a black studies program can begin with an analysis of black middle-class formation from generation to generation, beginning possibly after the Civil War and proceeding down to our day; this would involve a minute analysis of the class ideology noted in middle-class formation from era to era. I think an investigation into plantation life should begin to verify whether there were sharp class divisions on slave plantations between field hands and so-called "house Negroes," and to see whether the social carry-over into Recon-

struction and twentieth-century developments really reflects a sharp class division, evolving out of plantation origins. All this I think could be verified as a historical basis for the beginning of a black studies curriculum.

I think an examination should be made of the extent to which the white Protestant ethic has achieved the American creed's stated aims of democratic inclusion of the Negro in American society. To what extent has the Protestant ethic aided, abetted, or checked what we would call normal middle-class development on the black side of the racial fence in American life? Was the intention of the Protestant ethic to aid and abet the development of a black middle class? Or was the racism inherent in the approach meant to deny the democratic inclusion of this black middle-class development into the American mainstream? Carrying this analysis further, how has the retardation of the black bourgeoisie historically affected the outlook of the "intellectual class" in black life? For example, how did this retardation of normal development affect W. E. B. DuBois' contention that the black race in America required the development of a kind of talented-tenth leadership stratum which would deliver the Negro mass from its degradation? I believe that a black studies curriculum should investigate DuBois' thesis of the talented-tenth and ascertain to what degree this expectation was rooted in our historical development. These questions are some important points of departure toward laying the basis of a black studies program.

I make these assertions mainly to answer certain questions about intellectual procedure in the approach to the establishment of a black studies program. From the standpoint of these historical considerations I think that by looking at the problem of developing intellectually valid black studies curricula, one can see a legitimate point of departure.

To get deeper into this problem, I think that the whole question of the demand for a black studies program falls under the heading of what we would call a movement, a tendency, an ideology of "black cultural nationalism." This phenomenon is emerging today among the young black intelligentsia, the young black students, and the young black activists. This tendency is emerging in response to the feeling that at present there is no viable intellectual approach to the problems facing both blacks and whites in American society. Though these activists have espoused cultural nationalism, it is understandable that at this moment the historical roots and implications of cultural nationalism in our society are quite unclear to some members of the younger generation.

It is my belief that cultural nationalism as an ideology, nurturing the whole desire and thrust toward a black studies program, can only be understood if it is approached, first, historically, and then, by analyzing many of the deep problems which enmesh the Negro intelligentsia today. All over the country, in different aspects of the black movement we can see a general thrashing about, a frenetic search for method, and a search for both internal and external criticisms. We see splits and factions; we see movements running into dead ends and, we see the assassination of Martin Luther King and the outpouring of people's anguish, both black and white. We see all this and we have to ask, as King asked before he was assassinated, "Where do we go from here?" And how?

I have cited several historical antecedents to make it easier to understand how to deal with the current manifestations of these historical problems in the black world. These problems must be confronted; the effort to resolve them should be reflected in affirmative actions in relation to the demand for black studies. Black studies must be geared to the question of black institutional development on all levels—political, economic, cultural, and social. I believe that the black studies program, using the thrust of cultural nationalism, might for example base one of its approaches upon the study of the development of the black church,

especially from the class aspect, from the Episcopal and other "higher" denominations down to the store-front church. It might deal with institutions such as the theater. It should deal with black business trends and it must investigate, on an economic level, how the black movement is going to adjust its aims within the context of American society.

How best to respond to demands for black studies is a very complicated problem because we have two distinct trends in the black movement, even though these trends are seldom verbalized. We have implied here what is often called a "radical" or "revolutionary" thrust, and we also have what can be described as a "slow reformist" thrust. Even though this conflict is not verbally expressed in all instances, we can see, if we look closely enough, a clash of aims and methods involved in these underlying trends. We can describe this problem in terms of a conflict between "radical-revolutionary" and "reform" or "gradualist" thrusts toward the achievement of stated goals.

This conflict presents a peculiar problem in America for the simple reason that at any moment it cannot be determined precisely whether American society, as now constituted, is conducive to a revolutionary rate of social change for any kind of adjustment, be it for the black man or for the white man or for any other kind of man or class. Moreover, the implied rate of social change, as it is effected in the reactions of certain strata in our society, may lead one to accept slow reformist methods for social change. This presents a very complicated problem for all concerned, particularly for the spokesmen, the activists, and the leaders of the black movement. It also presents a difficult problem for those who want to institute black studies programs, because in either case we have to deal with a method of study which is related to the realities of the society around us; this throws everyone into a quandary—"everyone," black and white—but particularly the blacks, because the young generation today is very impatient. They do not desire slow change; they demand rapid change.

Whether we are going to have rapid change or slow change is important. Aside from that, we must determine the quality, the thrust, and the approach of any black studies program. Will its content accept—or be based on—slow gradualism? Or will the studies thrust the gears, hopefully, toward radical change? This is a problem. Those who want to institute a black studies program must take into consideration all of these realities, because hopefully the black studies program will be used to speed positive social changes in our society; I think the program has to begin with careful consideration of the necessities of the present situation and with the ultimate possibilities for change in this society.

Leaving that question for the moment and getting back to the content of the program in general, I want to reiterate that the question of deciding upon the content of the program is very difficult to resolve. But we have to begin to pinpoint this in order to give some immediate direction to these efforts.

Black cultural nationalism has to be seen as an attempt, a necessarily historical attempt, to deal with another kind of cultural nationalism that is implied in our society, namely, the cultural nationalism of the dominant white group. You might call it a kind of cultural "particularism" which is found when you examine the cultural particularism of the Anglo-Saxon group or the WASP or whatever name you want to give to this stratum. I think we find that an ideology exists which *has* to deny the validity of other kinds of cultural values that might compete with its own standards—whether in the social sciences, the arts, literature, or economic activity. We find this particularism of the Anglo-American implicit in all that is done in our society, whether it is done unconsciously or consciously.

I think that this particularism provides a clue to the problem of the acceptance of the validity of the concept of black studies. It has been assumed in history that all that was required to make America attain its ideals was the confirmation and the extension of an Anglo-American political and economic creed. Today we see that this creed, unfortunately, has reached the point where it is seemingly unable to deal with the crises that beset the nation.

This failure demands that *another* set of cultural and political values be extended into our society to fill the void. Black studies must make the dominant particularism, the dominant racial creed, more capable of dealing with the internal crises facing us all. I think that this awareness is something that has to be cultivated meticulously by any black student movement. There must be a quality of intellectual clarity and intellectual patience in dealing with those tendencies in the intellectual world which would resist both the institution and the thrust of such a black studies program. I think that those who would institute the black studies program must not only understand their own particular black history but must also grapple with, and understand, the dual tradition that has been nurtured in this society and that has given our society its unique character. I think the question of a black studies program is intrinsically a two-way street: a black studies program—even if it expresses black particularism—is a kind of particularism which understands its own limits and its social function. Its social function is not to replace one particularism with another particularism but to counterbalance the historical effects and exaggeration of particularism toward a more racially balanced society, a society which would include expectations regarding the democratic creed.

Previously I mentioned certain particular aspects or approaches that I feel black studies must begin with. I mentioned the church, I mentioned economic activities, I mentioned institutions such as the theater, I mentioned criticism, literature, and the allied arts, and so forth. I believe this is an adequate starting point. I have also dealt with the overall ideology and with black cultural nationalism as the main intellectual spirit behind the increasing demands for the institution of black studies programs. However, I want to extend that concept into a discussion of how the academic thrust of black studies might begin to impinge upon and to modify the broader social structure.

Such considerations are necessary because, after all, we are not going to study black history in a vacuum. We are going to study black history with an eye toward its being socially functional. We are going to have black social studies with the understanding that this is a new social method of dealing with the infirmities of our society. I believe that a black studies program must at all times keep its eye on the broader manifestations of what I would call—and I mentioned this in my book—the functioning of America's "cultural apparatus" in all of its aspects. I believe that in terms of the society at large, whatever long-range effect black studies will have on the broader realities of America must first begin in the general area of our cultural apparatus.

For example, the university is part of our cultural apparatus. These are institutions of a special kind engaged in socially useful activities. But beyond that, in the broader society, we have other impactful and meaningful manifestations and functionings of the cultural apparatus. It is in this general area that black studies must direct its initial interest and attention. Black studies must begin to deal with the effects of the communications media on the society as a whole as well as with the effects of the communications media on the black community. It must also begin to examine the role of the film and the role of the theater in black society. It must begin to deal with the impact of the music world on the cultural life of the black community. In short, black studies must initiate a critical examination of, and a critical approach into, the manifestations of these aspects of the cultural apparatus.

To take one example, consider the Negro in the theater—one of my pet subjects. The theater, if one studies it very closely, reflects in many ways all of the successes, the failures, the ups and downs, the defaults, the want of criticism, and the adaptation of the black intellectual class and the black creative class to the larger society. If one examines the position of the Negro in the theater today, he will have an example, set apart from all other institutions, of the plight of the black intellectual, the black creator, in all aspects of American culture. The theater should become one of the prime laboratories of those who are going to use cultural nationalism as a basis for the creation of a black studies program.

As an institution, the theater reflects the failure of the integrationist ethic most uniquely and most glaringly, perhaps more clearly than any other institution that we can name in the cultural sphere. A historical examination of the black experience in the American theater will show that it is a good barometer of the rise and fall, the successes and failures, of all other black institutions. At one time Negroes had a thriving theater, particularly in New York. It was an autonomous institution. It was crowded with talent, creativity, and pioneering. This happened at the same historical moment that the American or white theater was beginning to make its debut in American society as a unique American institution.

There was a time when there was almost "democratic" collaboration between black and white in the development of American theater. Somewhere down the line, around World War I and thereafter, the manifestations of what I call the white cultural particularism began to assert itself in the American theater; and mind you, this trend has reference also to the plight or the status of the white theater today. From that point on, black creativity began to wane and the black performer and creator was, little by little, pushed out toward the fringes of the theater.

This development paralleled developments in other areas of black-white relations—this is why I claim that the theater should become a prime laboratory for a cultural approach to a black studies curriculum. In recent years, the Negro performer has raised the question of exclusion and discrimination in the American theater. These complaints continue unabated. Black complaints about discrimination come at a time when the American theater is in a crisis to the same degree that the nation itself is in a crisis. Therefore, at this moment, the Negro performer calling for integration echoes the contention of the black students who are questioning the integrationist ethic. Paradoxically, the Negro in the theater must—at this moment—maintain that the solution to his plight is more integration. However, he is losing sight of the fact that the theater is a sick institution and cannot accommodate the aims and desires and potentialities of the black presence in America.

This indicates, as far as I am concerned, why the black theater can and must become one of the prime exhibits here in dealing with the failure of the integrationist ethic. The Negro in the theater, as in all areas of American life, can only begin to regain or to win his rightful place within the American set-up through a retrenchment into self, a retrenchment into history. The creation of black studies must reflect his black history and an investigation into his past. These are the only ways in which the black student, the black intellectual, or the Negro of any calling or class can begin to re-examine his position in society as a whole, and then to begin to work from there toward a more equitable and democratic inclusion within American society.

Essay/Discussion Questions

1. What scholarly approach does Harold Cruse advocate in the establishment o African American Studies?

2. According to Cruse, what role should black cultural nationalism play in the development of African American Studies?

3. In Cruse's view, how does a critical examination of blacks in the theater contribute to African American Studies?

The Politics of Black Women's Studies

GLORIA T. HULL AND BARBARA SMITH

Merely to use the term "Black women's studies" is an act charged with political significance. At the very least, the combining of these words to name a discipline means taking the stance that Black women exist—and exist positively—a stance that is in direct opposition to most of what passes for culture and thought on the North American continent. To use the term and to act on it in a white-male world is an act of political courage.

Like any politically disenfranchised group, Black women could not exist consciously until we began to name ourselves. The growth of Black women's studies is an essential aspect of that process of naming. The very fact that Black women's studies describes something that is really happening, a burgeoning field of study, indicates that there are political changes afoot which have made possible that growth. To examine the politics of Black women's studies means to consider not only what it is, but why it is and what it can be. Politics is used here in its widest sense to mean any situation/relationship of differential power between groups or individuals.

Four issues seem important for a consideration of the politics of Black women's studies: (1) the general political situation of Afro-Ameri-can women and the bearing this has had upon the implementation of Black women's studies; (2) the relationship of Black women's studies to Black feminist politics and the Black feminist movement; (3) the necessity for Black women's studies to be feminist, radical, and analytical; and (4) the need for teachers of Black women's studies to be aware of our problematic political positions in the academy and of the potentially antagonistic conditions under which we must work.

The political position of Black women in America has been, in a single word, embattled. The extremity of our oppression has been determined by our very biological identity. The horrors we have faced historically and continue to face as Black women in a white-male-dominated society have implications for every aspect of our lives, including what white men have termed "the life of the mind." That our oppression as Black women can take forms specifically aimed at discrediting our intellectual power is best illustrated through the words of a "classic" American writer.

From *But Some of Us Are Brave: Black Women's Studies*, Gloria T. Hull, Patricia Bell Scott, and Barbara Smith, eds. Old Westbury, NY: The Feminist Press, 1982.

In 1932 William Faulkner saw fit to include this sentence in a description of a painted sign in his novel *Light in August*. He wrote:

> But now and then a negro nursemaid with her white charges would loiter there and spell them [the letters on the sign] aloud with *that vacuous idiocy of her idle and illiterate kind.*[1] [Italics ours.]

Faulkner's white-male assessment of Black female intellect and character, stated as a mere aside, has fundamental and painful implications for a consideration of the whole question of Black women's studies and the politics that shape its existence. Not only does his remark typify the extremely negative ways in which Afro-American women have been portrayed in literature, scholarship, and the popular media, but it also points to the destructive white-male habit of categorizing all who are not like themselves as their intellectual and moral inferiors. The fact that the works in which such oppressive images appear are nevertheless considered American "masterpieces" indicates the cultural-political value system in which Afro-American women have been forced to operate and which, when possible, they have actively opposed.

The politics of Black women's studies are totally connected to the politics of Black women's lives in this country. The opportunities for Black women to carry out autonomously defined investigations of self in a society which through racial, sexual, and class oppression systematically denies our existence have been by definition limited.

As a major result of the historical realities which brought us enslaved to this continent, we have been kept separated in every way possible from recognized intellectual work. Our legacy as chattel, as sexual slaves as well as forced laborers, would adequately explain why most Black women are, to this day, far away from the centers of academic power and why Black women's studies has just begun to surface in the latter part of the 1970s. What our multilayered oppression does not explain are the ways in which we have created and maintained our own intellectual traditions as Black women, without either the recognition or the support of white-male society.

The entry entitled "A Slave Woman Runs a Midnight School" in Gerda Lerner's *Black Women in White America: A Documentary History* embodies this creative, intellectual spirit, coupled with a practical ability to make something out of nothing.

> [In Natchez, Mississippi, there were] two schools taught by colored teachers. One of these was a slave woman who had taught a midnight school for a year. It was opened at eleven or twelve o'clock at night, and closed at two o'clock a.m. . . . Milla Granson, the teacher, learned to read and write from the children of her indulgent master in her old Kentucky home. Her number of scholars was twelve at a time and when she had taught these to read and write she dismissed them, and again took her apostolic number and brought them up to the extent of her ability, until she had graduated hundreds. A number of them wrote their own passes and started for Canada. . . .
>
> At length her night-school project leaked out, and was for a time suspended; but it was not known that seven of the twelve years subsequent to leaving Kentucky had been spent in this work. Much excitement over her night-school was produced. The subject was discussed in their legislature, and a bill was passed, that it should not be held illegal for a slave to teach a slave. . . . She not only [re]opened her night-school, but a Sabbath-school. . . . Milla Granson used as good language as any of the white people.[2]

This document illuminates much about Black women educators and thinkers in America. Milla Granson learned to read and write through the exceptional indulgence of her white masters. She used her skills not to advance her own status, but to help her fellow slaves, and this under the most difficult circumstances. The act of a Black person teaching and sharing knowledge was viewed as naturally threatening to the power structure. The knowledge she conveyed had a politically and materially transforming function, that is, it empowered people to gain freedom.

Milla Granson and her pupils, like Black people throughout our history here, made the greatest sacrifices for the sake of learning. As opposed to "lowering" educational standards, we have had to create our own. In a totally antagonistic setting we have tried to keep our own visions clear and have passed on the most essential kind of knowledge, that which enabled us to survive. As Alice Walker writes of our artist-thinker foremothers:

> They dreamed dreams that no one knew—not even themselves, in any coherent fashion—and saw visions no one could understand. . . . They waited for a day when the unknown thing that was in them would be made known; but guessed, somehow in their darkness, that on the day of their revelation they would be long dead.[3]

The birth of Black women's studies is perhaps the day of revelation these women wished for. Again, this beginning is not unconnected to political events in the world outside university walls.

THE ORIGINS OF BLACK WOMEN'S STUDIES

The inception of Black women's studies can be directly traced to three significant political movements of the twentieth century. These are the struggles for Black liberation and women's liberation, which themselves fostered the growth of Black and women's studies, and the more recent Black feminist movement, which is just beginning to show its strength. Black feminism has made a space for Black women's studies to exist and, through its commitment to all Black women, will provide the basis for its survival.

The history of all of these movements is unique, yet interconnected. The Black movement of the 1950s, '60s, and '70s brought about unprecedented social and political change, not only in the lives of Black people, but for all Americans. The early women's movement gained inspiration from the Black movement as well as an impetus to organize autonomously both as a result of the demands for all-Black organizations and in response to sexual hierarchies in Black- and white-male political groupings. Black women were a part of that early women's movement, as were working-class women of all races. However, for many reasons—including the increasing involvement of single, middle-class white women (who often had the most time to devote to political work), the divisive campaigns of the white-male media, and the movement's serious inability to deal with racism—the women's movement became largely and apparently white.

The effect that this had upon the nascent field of women's studies was predictably disastrous. Women's studies courses, usually taught in universities, which could be considered elite institutions just by virtue of the populations they served, focused almost exclusively upon the lives of white women. Black studies, which was much too often male-dominated, also ignored Black women. Here is what a Black woman wrote about her independent efforts to study Black women writers in the early 1970s:

> . . . At this point I am doing a lot of reading on my own of Black women writers ever since I discovered Zora Neale Hurston. *I've had two Black Lit courses and in neither were any women writers discussed.* So now I'm doing a lot of independent research since the Schomburg Collection is so close.[4] [Italics ours.]

Because of white women's racism and Black men's sexism, there was no room in either area for a serious consideration of the lives of Black women. And even when they have considered Black women, white women usually have not had the capacity to analyze racial politics and Black culture, and Black men have remained blind or resistant to the implications of sexual politics in Black women's lives.

Only a Black *and* feminist analysis can sufficiently comprehend the materials of Black women's studies; and only a creative Black feminist perspective will enable the field to expand. A viable Black feminist movement will also lend its political strength to the development of Black women's studies courses, programs, and research, and to the funding they require. Black feminism's total commitment to the liberation of Black women and its recognition of Black women as valuable and complex human beings will provide the analysis and spirit for the most incisive work on Black women. Only a feminist, pro-woman perspective that acknowledges the reality of sexual oppression in the lives of Black women, as well as the oppression of race and class, will make Black women's studies the transformer of consciousness it needs to be.

Women's studies began as a radical response to feminists' realization that knowledge of ourselves has been deliberately kept from us by institutions of patriarchal "learning." Unfortunately, as women's studies has become both more institutionalized and at the same time more precarious within traditional academic structures, the radical life-changing vision of what women's studies can accomplish has constantly been diminished in exchange for acceptance, respectability, and the career advancement of individuals. This trend in women's studies is a trap that Black women's studies cannot afford to fall into. Because we are so oppressed as Black women, every aspect of our fight for freedom, including teaching and writing about ourselves, must in some way further our liberation. Because of the particular history of Black feminism in relation to Black women's studies, especially the fact that the two movements are still new and have evolved nearly simultaneously, much of the current teaching, research, and writing about Black women is not feminist, is not radical,

and unfortunately is not always even analytical. Naming and describing our experience are important initial steps, but not alone sufficient to get us where we need to go. A descriptive approach to the lives of Black women, a "great Black women" in history or literature approach, or any traditional male-identified approach will not result in intellectually groundbreaking or politically transforming work. We cannot change our lives by teaching solely about "exceptions" to the ravages of white-male oppression. Only through exploring the experience of supposedly "ordinary" Black women whose "unexceptional" actions enabled us and the race to survive, will we be able to begin to develop an overview and an analytical framework for understanding the lives of Afro-American women.

Courses that focus on issues which concretely and materially affect Black women are ideally what Black women's studies/feminist studies should be about. Courses should examine such topics as the sexual violence we suffer in our own communities; the development of Black feminist economic analysis that will reveal for the first time Black women's relationship to American capitalism; the situation of Black women in prison and the connection between their incarceration and our own; the social history of Black women's domestic work; and the investigation of Black women's mental and physical health in a society whose "final solution" for us and our children is death.

It is important to consider also that although much research about these issues needs to be done, much insight about them can be arrived at through studying the literary and historical documents that already exist. Anyone familiar with Black literature and Black women writers who is not intimidated by what their reading reveals should be able to develop a course on rape, battering, and incest as viewed by Black female and male authors. Analysis of these patriarchal crimes could be obtained from the substantial body of women's movement literature on the subject of violence against women, some of which would need be criticized for its conscious and unconscious racism.

In addition, speakers from a local rape crisis center and a refuge for battered women could provide essential firsthand information. The class and instructor could work together to synthesize the materials and to develop a much-needed Black feminist analysis of violence against Black women. Developing such a course illustrates what politically based, analytic Black feminist studies can achieve. It would lead us to look at familiar materials in new and perhaps initially frightening ways, but ways that will reveal truths that will change the lives of living Black women, including our own. Black feminist issues—the real life issues of Black women—should be integral to our conceptions of subject matter, themes, and topics for research.

That politics has much to do with the practice of Black women's studies is perhaps most clearly illustrated by the lack of positive investigations of Black lesbianism in any area of current Black scholarship. The fact that a course in Black lesbian studies has, to our knowledge, yet to be taught has absolutely nothing to do with the "nonexistence" of Black lesbian experience and everything to do with fear and refusal to acknowledge that this experience does in fact exist.[5] Black woman-identified-women have existed in our communities throughout our history, both in Africa and in America. That the subject of Black lesbianism and male homosexuality is greeted with fearful silence or verbalized homophobia results, of course, from the politics of institutionalized heterosexuality under patriarchy, that is, the politics of male domination.

A letter written in 1957 by Black playwright and political activist Lorraine Hansberry to *The Ladder*, a pioneering lesbian periodical, makes clear this connection between homophobia and the sexual oppression of all women. She wrote:

I think it is about time that equipped women began to take on some of the ethical questions which a male-dominated culture has produced and *dissect and analyze them quite to pieces in a serious fashion.* It is time that 'half the human race' had something to say about the nature of its existence. Otherwise—without revised basic thinking—the woman intellectual is likely to find herself trying to draw conclusions— *moral conclusions*—based on acceptance of a social moral superstructure which has never admitted to the equality of women and is therefore immoral itself. As per marriage, as per sexual practices, as per the rearing of children, etc. *In this kind of work there may be women to emerge who will be able to formulate a new and possible concept that homosexual persecution and condemnation has at its roots not only social ignorance, but a philosophically active anti-feminist dogma.* But that is but a kernel of a speculative embryonic idea improperly introduced here.[6] [Italics ours.]

Hansberry's statement is an amazingly prescient anticipation of current accomplishments of lesbian-feminist political analysis. It is also amazing because it indicates Hansberry's feminist and lesbian commitments, which have previously been ignored and which will best be investigated through a Black feminist analysis of Black women's studies. Most amazing of all is that Hansberry was speaking, without knowing it, directly to us.

An accountable Black women's studies would value all Black women's experiences. Yet for a Black woman to teach a course on Black lesbians would probably, in most universities, spell career suicide, not to mention the personal and emotional repercussions she would inevitably face. Even to teach Black women's studies from a principled Black feminist perspective might endanger many Black women scholars' situations in their schools and departments. Given the difficulty and risks involved in teaching information and ideas which the white-male academy does not recognize or approve, it is important for Black women teaching in the white-male academy always to realize the inherently contradictory and antagonistic nature of the conditions under which we do our work. These working conditions exist in a structure not only elitist and racist, but deeply misogynist. Often our position as Black women is dishearteningly tenuous within university walls: we are literally the last hired and the first fired. Despite popular myths about the advantages of being "double-tokens," our salaries, promotions, tenure, and general level of acceptance in the white-male "community of scholars" are all quite grim. The current backlash against affirmative action is also disastrous for all Black women workers, including college teachers.

As Black women we belong to two groups that have been defined as congenitally inferior in intellect, that is, Black people and women. The paradox of Black women's position is well illustrated by the fact that white-male academics, like Schockley and Jensen—in the very same academy—are trying to prove "scientifically" our racial and sexual inferiority. Their overt or tacit question is, "How could a being who combines two mentally deficient biological identities do anything with her intellect, her nonexistent powers of mind?" Or to put it more bluntly, "How can someone who looks like my maid (or my fantasy of my maid) teach me anything?" As Lorraine Bethel succinctly states this dilemma:

> The codification of Blackness and female-ness by whites and males is seen in the terms "thinking like a woman" and "acting like a nigger" which are based on the premise that there are typically Black and female ways of acting and thinking. Therefore, the most pejorative concept in the white/male world view would be that of thinking and acting like a "nigger woman."[7]

Our credibility as autonomous beings and thinkers in the white-male-run intellectual establishment is constantly in question and rises and falls in direct proportion to the degree to which we continue to act and think like our Black female selves, rejecting the modes of bankrupt white-male Western thought. Intellectual "passing" is a dangerously limiting solution for Black women, a non-solution that makes us invisible women. It will also not give us the emotional and psychological clarity we need to do the feminist research in Black women's studies that will transform our own and our sisters' lives.

Black women scholars must maintain a constantly militant and critical stance toward the places where we must do our work. We must also begin to devise ways to break down our terrible isolation in the white-male academy and to form the kinds of support networks Black women have always formed to help each other survive. We need to find ways to create our own places—conferences, institutes, journals, and institutions—where we can be the Black women we are and gain respect for the amazing depth of perception that our identity brings.

To do the work involved in creating Black women's studies requires not only intellectual intensity, but the deepest courage. Ideally, this is passionate and committed research, writing, and teaching whose purpose is to question everything. Coldly "objective" scholarship that changes nothing is not what we strive for. "Objectivity" is itself an example of the reification of white-male thought. What could be less objective than the totally white-male studies which are still considered "knowledge"? Everything that human beings participate in is ultimately subjective and biased, and there is nothing inherently wrong with that. The bias of Black women's studies must consider as primary the knowledge that will save Black women's lives.

BLACK WOMEN'S STUDIES AS AN ACADEMIC AREA

Higher education for Black women has always been of serious concern to the Black community.[8] Recognition that education was a key mechanism for challenging racial and economic oppression created an ethic that defined education for women as important as education for men. Nearly 140 Black women attended Oberlin College between 1835 and 1865, prior to Emancipation, and Mary Jane Patterson, the first Afro-American woman to receive a B.A., graduated from Oberlin in 1862. The only two Black women's colleges still in existence, Spelman in Atlanta, Georgia, founded in 1881, and Bennett in Greensboro, North Carolina, founded in 1873, played a significant role in the education of Black women, as did those Black colleges founded as co-educational institutions at a time when most private white colleges were still single-sex schools.

Although Black women have long been involved in this educational work and also in creating self-conscious representations of ourselves using a variety of artistic forms, Black women's studies as an autonomous discipline only began to emerge in the late 1970s. At the moment, it is impossible to gauge definitely how much activity is going on in the field. There have been few statistical studies which have mapped the growth of women's studies generally, and there have been no surveys or reports to establish the breadth and depth of research and teaching on Black women.

One of the few sources providing some documentation of the progress of Black women's studies is *Who's Who and Where in Women's Studies,* published in 1974 by The Feminist Press. This book lists a total of 4,658 women's studies courses taught by 2,964 teachers. Approximately 45 (or less than 1 percent) of the courses listed focus on Black women. About 16 of these are survey courses, 10 are literature courses, 4 are history courses, and the rest are in various disciplines. The largest number of courses taught on Black women was in Afro-American and Black Studies departments (approximately nineteen) and only about three courses on Black women were being taught for women's studies departments. Approximately

nine Black colleges were offering women's studies courses at that time. None of the forty-five courses used the words "feminist" or "Black feminist" in the title.

More recent relevant comment can be found in Florence Howe's *Seven Years Later: Women's Studies Programs in 1976.* She states:

> . . . Like the social movement in which it is rooted, women's studies has tended to be predominantly white and middle-class, in terms of both faculty and curriculum, and there is a perceived need for a corrective. . . . The major strategy developed thus far is the inclusion of separate courses on Black Women, Chicanas, Third World Women, etc. Such courses, taught by minority women, have appeared on most campuses with the cooperation and cross-listing of various ethnic studies programs. For the most part, it is women's studies that has taken the initiative for this development.[9]

However, as Howe proceeds to point out, more seriously committed and fundamental strategies are needed to achieve a truly multiracial approach.

Clearly, then, if one looks for "hard data" concerning curriculum relating to Black women in the existing studies of academic institutions, we are seemingly nonexistent. And yet impressionistically and experientially it is obvious that more and more study is being done about Black women and, even more importantly, it is being done with an increasing consciousness of the impact of sexual-racial politics on Black women's lives. One thinks, for instance, of Alice Walker's groundbreaking course on Black women writers at Wellesley College in 1972, and how work of all sorts by and about Black women writers has since blossomed into a visible Black female literary "renaissance."

It seems that after survey courses (with titles like "The Black Woman in America") which provide an overview, most courses on Black women concentrate on literature, followed by social sciences and history as the next most popular areas. An early type of course that was taught focused upon "famous" individual Black women. Partly because at the beginning it is necessary to answer the basic question of exactly who there is to talk about, this is the way that materials on oppressed people have often been approached initially. Printed information written about or by successful individuals is also much more readily available, and analytical overviews of the field do not yet exist. Nevertheless, such focusing on exceptional figures is a direct outgrowth of centuries of concerted suppression and invisibility. When the various kinds of pedagogical resources which should exist eventually come into being, teachers will be able to move beyond this ultimately class-biased strategy.

The core of courses on Black women at colleges and universities has grown slowly but steadily during the 1970s. And increasing interest in Black feminism and recognition of Black women's experiences point to the '80s as the time when Black women's studies will come into its own. Perhaps this may be seen less in teaching than in the plethora of other activity in Black women's scholarship. Some essential books have begun to appear: the Zora Neale Hurston reader, *I Love Myself When I Am Laughing . . .* (Old Westbury, N.Y.: The Feminist Press, 1979), and Sharon Harley and Rosalyn Terborg-Penn's *The Afro-American Woman: Struggles and Images* (Port Washington, N.Y.: Kennikat, 1978), to name only two. Special issues of feminist magazines—like *Conditions* and *Heresies*—are being devoted to Black/Third World women. Workshop sessions and entire conferences on Black women (e.g., The Third World Lesbian Writers Conference in New York City and the National Council of Negro Women's national research conference on Black women held in Washington, D.C.—both in 1979) have been organized.

Other indications that Black/Third World women are talking to each other and carving out ways of thinking, researching, writing, and teaching include the founding of *Sojourner: A Third World Women's Research Newsletter,* in 1977, and the founding, in 1978, of the Association of Black Women Historians, which publishes the newsletter *Truth.* Finally, research and dissertations by young Black female scholars for whom the developments of the past few years have opened the option of studying Black women have begun to produce the knowledge that Black women's studies will continue to need. These scholars—many of them activists—are working on a wide range of subjects—including revising the Black woman's role in slavery, recovering Black female oral and popular culture, and revamping the reputations of earlier Black women authors.

At this point, we are on the threshold—still in our "Phase One," as it were. There are still far too few courses and far too few Black women employed in institutions where they might have the opportunity to teach them. Although people involved in women's studies are becoming increasingly aware of issues of race, the majority of white women teachers and administrators have barely begun the process of self-examination which must precede productive action to change this situation. The confronting of sexism in Black studies and in the Black community in general is a mostly unfought battle, although it is evident from recent Black publications—e.g., *Black Scholar's* Black Sexism Debate issue—that the opposing anti-Black-feminist and pro-Black-feminist forces are beginning to align.

Ideally, Black women's studies will not be dependent on women's studies, Black studies, or "straight" disciplinary departments for its existence, but will be an autonomous academic entity making coalitions with all three. Realistically, however, institutional support will have to come from these already established units. This will be possible only in proportion to the elimination of racism, sexism, and elitism.

Notes

1. William Faulkner, *Light in August* (New York: Modern Library, 1932), p. 53.
2. Laura S. Haviland, *A Woman's Life-Work, Labors and Experiences* (Chicago: Publishing Association of Friends, 1889; copyright 1881), pp. 300–301; reprinted in Gerda Lerner, ed., *Black Women in White America: A Documentary History* (New York: Vintage, 1973), pp. 32–33.
3. Alice Walker, "In Search of Our Mother's Gardens," *Ms.* (May 1974): 64–70, 105.
4. Bernette Golden, Personal letter, April 1, 1974.
5. J. R. Roberts, *Black Lesbians: An Annotated Bibliography* (Tallahassee, Fla.: Naiad, 1981) contains over three hundred entries of books, periodicals, and articles by and about Black lesbians and provides ample material for developing a variety of courses.
6. Quoted in Jonathan Katz, *Gay American History: Lesbians and Gay Men in the U.S.A.* (New York: T. Y. Crowell, 1976), p. 425.
7. Lorraine Bethel, "'This Infinity of Conscious Pain': Zora Neale Hurston and the Black Female Literary Tradition."
8. Most of the material in these first two paragraphs about Black women in higher education was gleaned from an unpublished paper by Patricia Bell Scott, "Issues and Questions in the Higher Education of Black Women: Taking a Brief Look Backwards."
9. This is a report of the National Advisory Council on Women's Educational Programs published in June 1977. Another study sponsored by the National Institute of Education, "Involvement of Minority Women in Women's Studies," promises additional data.

Essay/Discussion Questions

1. Why do Gloria Hull and Barbara Smith conceive of Black Women's Studies as a political project? According to them, what are the elements that make this a radical enterprise?
2. According to Hall and Smith, what twentieth-century political movements contributed to the rise of Black Women's Studies? Discuss the impact of these movements on Black Women's Studies.
3. What are some of the problems black women scholars face in higher educational institutions?

Black Studies, Multiculturalism and the Future of American Education

MANNING MARABLE

African-American Studies, broadly defined, is the systematic study of the black experience, framed by the socio-economic, cultural and geographical boundaries of sub-Saharan Africa and the black diaspora of North America, the Caribbean, Brazil and Latin America, and increasingly Europe itself. At its core, it is also the black intellectual tradition as it has assumed a complex burden over many generations, seeking to engage in a critical dialogue with white scholarship on a range of complex issues—most significantly, the definition and reality of race as a social construct, and the factors that explain the structures of inequality which greatly define the existence of black people across the globe. This definition was at the heart of W. E. B. Du Bois's assertion nearly a century ago that "the problem of the twentieth century is the problem of the color line."

From Du Bois's point of departure, we can assert that the problem of the twenty-first century is the challenge of "multicultural democracy": whether or not American political institutions and society can and will be radically restructured to recognize the genius and energy, the labor and aspirations of millions of people of color—Latinos, Asian Americans, American Indians, Arab Americans, African-Americans, and others.

I would like to explore three interrelated issues, which together provide a framework for discussing the study of the contemporary African-American experience, and questions of racial and ethnic diversity within democratic society. The first is the debate over Black Studies and, more generally, what has been termed "multiculturalism," especially in the context of higher education. The critics of both multiculturalism and Black Studies have linked the concepts with the concurrent controversy surrounding "political correctness" on campuses and in public-school curricula. However, to define "multiculturalism" properly we need to go beyond conservative rhetoric.

Second, what is the social context for a discussion of racial diversity and pluralism within American society as a whole? Because I am a social scientist of the African-American experience, my commentary will focus briefly on the disturbing trends away from equality within the national black community. These inequalities are leading us to two unequal Americas, divided not simply by racial identity but by sharply divergent levels of skills, learning and access to educational opportunities.

Finally, there is the larger issue of the future of race and ethnicity within American society itself. The question of difference within any society or culture is always conjunctural, ever-changing, and conditional. "Race" is not a permanent historical category, but an unequal relationship between social groups. We must rethink old categories and old ways of perceiving each other. We must define the issue of diversity as a dynamic, changing concept, leading us to explore problems of human relations and social equality in a manner which will expand the principles of fairness and opportunity to all members of society.

For any oppressed people, questions of culture and identity are linked to the structure of power and privilege within society. Culture is the textured pattern of collective memory, the critical consciousness and aspirations of a people. When culture is constructed in the context of oppression, it may become an act of resistance. This is why the national debate over "multiculturalism" assumes such critical significance within political discourse, as well as in the structure of the economy and society. With the demise of the Cold War, American conservatives have been denied the threat of communism as the ideological glue which could unify the voices of racism and reaction. Led by former Reagan secretary of education William Bennett and Republican presidential candidate Patrick Buchanan, conservatives have launched a "cultural war" against an unholy host of so-called new subversives, such as the proponents of "political correctness," affirmative action, Black Studies, gay and lesbian issues, feminism and, worst of all, "multiculturalism."

A working definition of "multiculturalism" begins with the recognition that our nation's cultural heritage does not begin and end with the intellectual and aesthetic products of Western Europe. Multiculturalism rejects the model of cultural assimilation and social conformity, which within the context of our schools has often relegated African-Americans, Latinos and other people of color to the cultural slums. The mythical "melting pot" in which a diverse number of ethnic antecedents were blended into a nonracist and thoroughly homogenized blend of cultures, never existed. Assimilation always assumed that the price for admission to America's cultural democracy for racial and ethnic minorities was the surrender of those things which truly made us unique: our languages and traditions, our foods and folkways, our religions, and even our names. The cultural foundations of the United States draw much of their creativity and originality from African, Latino, American Indian and Asian elements. Multiculturalism suggests that the cross-cultural literacy and awareness of these diverse groups is critical in understanding the essence of the American experience "from the bottom up."

Part of the general confusion about the concept of "multiculturalism" is that there are strikingly different and sometimes conflicting interpretations about its meaning. For example, in Western Europe, particularly in The Netherlands and the United Kingdom, a highly restrictive and regimented interpretation of multiculturalism exists. Different ethnic and racial minorities are, in effect, locked into their respective cultures, with an emphasis on the societal management of real or possible cultural, religious and social difference. "Tolerance" for diversity is the common denominator; all people are perceived as being equal, politically and socially—free to pursue their own unique rituals, collective traditions and creative arts without fear of discrimination or harassment. Within the parameters of this type of tolerance, there is an emphasis on the contours of difference, within the values, heritage and group behaviors of distinct cultural constituencies. Rarely is there any discussion linking culture to power, to a minority group's access to the resources, privileges and property which are concentrated within certain elites or classes. Institutional racism is hardly ever mentioned or even acknowledged.

Within the USA, there are at least four major interpretations of "multiculturalism," reflecting the widely diverse ethnic, racial and social-class composition of the nation. African-American Studies is an integral part of the multicultural debate. In very simplistic terms, these differing interpretations are "corporate multiculturalism," "liberal multiculturalism," "racial essentialism," and "radical democratic multiculturalism."

CORPORATE MULTICULTURALISM

Corporate multiculturalism seeks to highlight the cultural and social diversity of America's population, making managers and corporate executives more sensitive to differences such as race, gender, age, language, physical ability, and sexual orientation in the labor force. A number of major corporations regularly sponsor special programs honoring Martin Luther King, Jr.'s Birthday, or the Mexican-American holiday "Cinco de Mayo." Others hold "multi-cultural audits" for their staff and personnel, workshops and training sessions emphasizing awareness and sensitivity to people of color, women and others.

The major reasons for this multicultural metamorphosis among hundreds of America's largest corporations can be summarized in two phrases: "minority markets" and "labor force demographics." The value of the African-American consumer market in the USA exceeds $300 billion annually; the Spanish-speaking consumer market is not far behind, at $240 billion annually. Since the early 1960s there has been substantial evidence from market researchers indicating that African-Americans and Latinos have strikingly different buying habits from whites. To reach this growing consumer market, white corporations are now forced to do much more than produce advertisements featuring black, Asian American and Hispanic actors displaying their products. Multicultural marketing utilizes elements of minority cultures in order to appeal directly to nonwhite consumers.

As the overall labor force becomes increasingly Asian, Latino, Caribbean and African-American, the pressure increases on corporations to hire greater numbers of nonwhite managers and executives, and to distribute their product through minority-owned firms. Of course, nowhere in the discourse of corporate multiculturalism is there the idea that "racism" is not an accidental element of corporate social relations. Instead, the basic concept is to "celebrate diversity" of all kinds and varieties, while criticizing no one. Troubling concepts like "exploitation," "racism," "sexism" and "homophobia" are rarely mentioned.

LIBERAL MULTICULTURALISM

Liberal multiculturalism, by contrast, is explicitly anti-racist, and takes it for granted that educational institutions have a powerful social responsibility to deconstruct the ideology of human inequality. It is genuinely concerned with aesthetics, ideology, curriculum theory and cultural criticism. Liberal multiculturalism is broadly democratic as an intellectual approach for the deconstruction of the idea of race. But like corporate multiculturalism, it does not adequately or fully address the inequalities of power, resources and privilege which separate most Latinos, African-Americans and many Asian Americans from the great majority of white upper- and middle-class Americans. It does not adequately conceive of itself as a praxis, a theory which seeks to transform the reality of unequal power relations. It deliberately emphasizes aesthetics over economics, art over politics. It attempts to articulate the perceived interests of minority groups to increase their influence within the existing mainstream. In short, liberal multiculturalism is "liberalism" within the framework of cultural diversity and pluralism. The most articulate and influential proponent of this perspective is Professor Henry Louis Gates, Harvard University's Director of African-American Studies.

AFROCENTRISM

The third model of multiculturalism is racial essentialism. Here, advocates of diversity praise the artifacts, rituals and histories of non-Western Europe as "original," "unique," and even superior to those of Western Europe and white America. They juxtapose the destructive discrimination of "Eurocentrism" with the necessity to construct a counter-hegemonic ideological and cultural world-view. For many people of African descent, this has been translated into the cultural and educational movement called "Afrocentrism." First developed as a theoretical concept by Temple University scholar Molefi Asante, Afrocentrism has quickly inspired a virtual explosion of children's books; curriculum guides; cultural, historical, and educational textbooks; and literary works.

The strengths of the Afrocentric perspective and analysis are undeniable: the fostering of pride, group solidarity and self-respect among blacks themselves; a richer appreciation for African languages, art, music, ancient philosophies and cultural traditions; a commitment to unearth and describe the genius and creativity of blacks in the context of a racist and unforgiving America. As a paradigm for understanding and reinterpreting the contours of the African experience, Afrocentrism also advances an internationalist perspective, drawing correlations between black communities from Lagos to Los Angeles, from Brooklyn's Bedford-Stuyvesant to London's Brixton.

As many white Americans have retreated from an honest dialogue about the pervasiveness of racial inequality in American life, many black Americans are attracted to an Afrocentric perspective. In hundreds of communities where black parents are attempting to improve the quality of the education of their children, Afrocentrism has come to mean the demand to make curricula more culturally pluralistic. In dozens of social rituals of community life, from the kinte clothing used in weddings and ceremonial events, to the popularity of African art in private homes, Afrocentrism provides a coherent and logical oppositional framework to traditional Eurocentrism. In many ways, Afrocentrism has become broadly defined by many blacks outside the academy as simply the awareness of one's cultural heritage and recognition of the common destiny of all people of African descent. Afrocentrism draws upon the deep and very rich foundations of black nationalism within African-American civil society, which implicitly question the strategy and ideology of inclusion and assimilation. Because America's mainstream doesn't value or respect blackness, Afrocentrism provides the framework for an alternative world-view and oppositional consciousness.

The contradictions and weakness of Afrocentrism are just as striking. Although frequently discussed in the context of multiculturalism, in many respects Afrocentrism is theoretically and progammatically at odds with the larger trend toward pluralism and educational diversity. Conceptually, many Afrocentrists have absolutely no desire to engage in a critical discourse with white America, at any level. They frequently retreat into a bipolar model of racial relations, which delineates the contours of the black experience from a photographic negative of whiteness. In effect, this "freezes" the meaning of culture, reducing the dynamics and multiple currents of interpersonal and group interaction to a rigid set of ahistorical categories.

From a practical standpoint, an Afrocentric perspective perceives Black Studies as a unified discipline—that is, a distinct body of knowledge informed by a coherent methodology and a distinct body of literature which helps to define the field. William M. King, for example, characterized the "Afrocentric perspective" in scholarship as the application of that "world view, normative assumptions, and frames of reference [which] grow out of the experiences and folk wisdom of black people." But this approach raised a host of questions. As Delores P. Aldridge, long-time coordinator of Black Studies at Emory University observed, "Many Black Studies departments, originating as a result of pressure and flawed liberal consciences, lacked an agreed upon body of knowledge, disciplined frames of reference or bases of knowledge—the very characteristics that defined every other standard academic discipline." To create the character of a "discipline," Afrocentrists utilized various tactics, both administrative and political. In the case of the African-American Studies Department at Temple University, chairperson Molefi Asante insisted that all faculty hired adhere to an "Afrocentric perspective" as their primary commitment toward scholarly research and teaching. Asante was sophisticated enough not to insist that this meant that whites were "unqualified" to teach in his field. On the contrary: Asante strongly denies that Afrocentrism is in any way "separatist" or a theory of racial essentialism. The subtle theoretical distinctions Asante utilizes, however, are frequently missing in the arguments and analysis of many of his followers, who perceive Afrocentrism in more fundamentalist terms. All too often, Afrocentrism has been translated into its lowest common racial denominator, black vs. white.

It is certainly true that in most instances, the argument that white people are unqualified by their racial classification and identity to teach courses in the African-American experience is usually made inside universities by white administrators and faculty, not by blacks. The hidden assumption at work here is that no one who was not born black would have any reason to cultivate a scholarly interest or the proper dedication for the study of black life and history. Setting aside the example of Herbert Aptheker, and the hundreds of gifted and dedicated white intellectuals who disprove this hypothesis, the great danger in this argu-

ment is that it assumes that knowledge is grounded in racial, biological or even genetic factors. But if race itself is a social construct, an unequal relationship between social groups characterized by concentrations of power, privilege and authority of one group over another, then anyone of any ethnic, class or social background should be able to learn the complex experiences of another group. Membership or identity within an oppressed racial group often yields unique personal insights, which may be translated into texts and utilized in classroom teaching. The harsh reality of racial oppression yields experiences and insights which are extremely valuable tools for cross-cultural education. But our imaginations do not have to be imprisoned by the boundaries of our different identities—whether defined by race, gender, religious upbringing, physical impairment, or sexual orientation.

The more separatist and racially essentialist variety of Afrocentrism rarely explores the profound cultural dynamics of creolization and multiple identities of nationalism and ethnicity found throughout the black world, from the Hispanicized blackness of Dominicans, Puerto Ricans and Colombians, to the vast complexities of race in Cuba and Brazil, to the distinctions and tensions separating rural conservative Christian blacks in the Mississippi Delta and the cosmopolitan, urban, secular, hip-hop culture of young blacks in Watts, Harlem and Chicago's South Side. But the most serious weakness of Afrocentrism is its general failure to integrate the insights of cultural difference drawn from the perspectives of gender, sexual orientation, and class. It has no theory of power which goes beyond a racialized description of how whites, as a monolithic category, benefit materially, psychologically and politically from institutional racism. Thus rather than seeking allies to transform the political economy of capitalism across the boundaries of race, gender and class, most Afrocentrists approach the world as the main character in Ralph Ellison's classic novel *Invisible Man*: enclosed inside a windowless room filled with thousands of glowing light bulbs—illumination without vision.

RADICAL DEMOCRATIC MULTICULTURALISM

Finally, there is the insurgent movement toward "radical democratic multiculturalism," or what might be described more accurately as a transformationist cultural critique. These educators, artists, performers, writers and scholars are inspired by the legacy of W. E. B. Du Bois and Paul Robeson. They emphasize the parallels between the cultural experiences of America's minority groups with oppressed people throughout the world. Discussions of culture are always linked to the question of power, and the ways in which ideology and aesthetics are used to dominate or control oppressed people. The goal of the radical democratic multiculturalists is not the liberal inclusion of representative numbers of blacks, Latinos and others into the literary canon, media and cultural mainstream, but the radical democratic restructuring of the system of cultural and political power itself. It is to rethink the entire history of this country, redefining its heritage in order to lay claim to its future. It is to redefine "America" itself. Scholars in this current include Princeton University philosopher Cornel West; feminists bell hooks, Angela Davis and Patricia Hill Collins; legal scholars Patricia Williams and Lani Guinier; anthropologist Leith Mullings; political theorist James Jennings; historians Gerald Horne and Robin Kelley; and cultural critic Michael Eric Dyson.

The democratic multiculturalists approach Black Studies in a very different manner. They insist that African-American Studies is not a discipline, like physics or psychology, but a broad intellectual dialogue and exchange which incorporates divergent perspectives and concerns. Its intellectual anchor rests with a series of themes and questions which cut across individual disciplines. At the center of this exchange is the search for identity: who and what is the African-American—culturally, socially and in the oppressive context of racial domination and economic exploitation? How did the black community in America and elsewhere evolve over generations? What common cultural and social elements transcend geography and influence the construction of black reality in America, the Caribbean, Africa and elsewhere? By what strategies and means should we seek representation or empowerment? What is the future of African-American people within the context of a pluralistic democratic society which has yet to fulfill its promises of human equality and social justice? Such questions can be pursued through history, political science, religion, philosophy, sociology, anthropology, literature, economics, and a host of other disciplines.

This is not to say that the "radical democratic multiculturalists" agree with each other on all the essentials. Far from it. West is a powerful and articulate advocate of democratic socialism, and has expressed major reservations and criticisms about the term "multiculturalism." Hooks emphasizes the cultural dimensions of social change, and sharply dissents from a theoretical perspective which would place class as the singular or primary focus of her analysis of society. Guinier, the outstanding voice for challenging the problems inherent in "majority-rule democracy" of her generation, emphasizes the legal and policy dimensions of politics and empowerment, and is less concerned with cultural or ideological phenomena. Collins's analysis of black feminism is close conceptually to that of many Afrocentrists. Mullings and Davis, among others, approach social analysis from the vantage point of class relations, employing a Marxian methodology. One could argue that the differences between these public intellectuals of the multicultural left are just as significant as their similarities. Their "unity" is created to a great extent by the criticism of their opponents on the right, and by their common commitment to expand the definitions and boundaries of academic discourse and intellectual engagement to relate to the very real and practical problems of inequality which define urban America today.

THE FUTURE OF BLACK STUDIES

The quest for a unified theoretical framework and approach to the study of race and diversity has been elusive. For nearly half a century, we have pursued the goal of "diversity" in higher education, with at best mixed and uneven results. In the 1950s and early 1960s, liberal educators declared proudly that they were committed to the goal of a "color-blind environment." I distinctly recall professors saying to me that they "could not remember" whether this or that student was "a Negro." They fully embraced the liberal perspective of Dr. Martin Luther King, Jr., that individuals should be judged "not by the color of their skin but the content of their character." At the same time, we should assert that "color blindness," the eradication of white privilege and superiority and the abolition of all hierarchies which perpetuate black inferiority, should be our ultimate goal. As the great reggae artist Bob Marley of Jamaica once observed: "Until the color of a man's skin is of no greater consequence than the color of his eyes, there will be war."

But the question should be, how do we get here? How can we "deconstruct" race? We cannot get there by pretending that "race" and "color" no longer matter, that they have magically declined in significance since the 1960s. In a racist society, color symbolizes the inequality of power relations, the ownership of property and resources, between various groups and classes. To end racial prejudice, we must restructure the power relations between people of color and upper- to middle-income whites. This means that we must pursue a "color-conscious" strategy to create the conditions where color is one day irrelevant to determining the positions of power, educational access, health care, and other opportunities of daily life.

In the 1970s and 1980s, the ideal of color blindness gave way to what could be termed "symbolic representation." Liberal educators believed that the recipe for cultural diversity was to bring representatives of a new spectrum of interests into the academy—women, racial minorities, physically disabled people, lesbians and gays, and others. Programs were established to create new academic courses in Women's Studies, Black Studies, Chicano Studies, gay and lesbian studies, and Asian American Studies. Minorities and women were "symbolically represented" with their appointment as counselors and college recruiters. Multicultural student services centers were established to address perceived concerns of the students of color. These reforms should have represented the beginning, rather than the end, of a process of educational reconstruction on issues of social and cultural difference within the academy. Instead, somehow we have lost our way. And at many colleges and universities, we are actually moving backward. One reason is that women and racial minorities were usually hired and subsequently located in the bureaucratic margins of academic institutions, rather than within real centers of power. There were few deliberate programs which actually tried to identify scholars of color and/or female faculty with administrative abilities, to mentor and cultivate them, and to advance them. At some institutions, minority faculty occupied a revolving-door position, usually at the designated ranks of instructor or assistant professor never to be tenured or reappointed.

In some institutions, a conspiracy of silence developed between white conservative administrators and those few black or other minority faculty who had been hired during the initial wave of affirmative action and minority recruitment. Many conservative white administrators employed the discourse of diversity, but privately never really believed in its validity. They never accepted the academic rationale of African-American Studies, yet they adopted these programs on their campuses largely out of political necessity. To quell student unrest, to reduce criticism from minority educators and elected officials, they created such programs and departments on a ghetto-ized basis. Such programs, white conservative (and liberal) educators were convinced, would appeal to minority students. Moreover, all-white departments with traditional curricula would not be forced to alter their way of teaching or their discriminatory hiring policies. History departments wouldn't have to offer African-American history to students if the Black Studies program were deemed responsible for it. Music departments could ignore Duke Ellington. Literature departments could skip Alice Walker, Langston Hughes, Toni Morrison and James Baldwin.

The conspiracy of silence on the part of some second-rate yet politically astute black educators was expressed in construction of academic ghettos. Some African-American Studies programs actively discouraged the cross-listing of courses with traditional departments, on the grounds that this would undermine the unit's academic autonomy and integrity. Students received the dangerous and erroneous impression that only individuals who happened to be of African descent had the cultural background and intellectual training necessary to teach all things black.

Active, dedicated younger African-American scholars hired by such programs were frequently discouraged from interacting with colleagues trained in the same disciplines but affiliated to different academic departments. One example of this process is represented by the Black Studies Department under Professor Len Jeffries at the City College of the City University of New York. The controversy surrounding Professor Jeffries—his anti-Semitic speech in Albany, New York, in the summer of 1991; his subsequent hasty dismissal as chairman of Black Studies at City College; and his successful legal suit to reclaim his position and damages of $400,000— ignores the fundamental issue at stake. Jeffries had been reinstated as chair of Black Studies many times, going back over two decades, by the presidents of City College. His last rein-

statement as chair had occurred barely one month prior to his controversial speech, which had sparked alumni and public criticism calling for his immediate ousting. Yet the CUNY central administration knew full well about the major academic shortcomings within the department—the assertions that some students received grades for submitting absolutely no written work, or that Jeffries often skipped classes, or that an atmosphere of intimidation and harassment existed for other black faculty who disapproved of Jeffries' version of vulgar Afrocentrism. They ignored a mountain of student and faculty complaints because of their own institutional racism—the vast majority of white, middle-class students at CUNY were unaffected.

We must be honest and rigorous in our criticism of such programs. But we must also criticize the far more dangerous distortions of conservative intellectuals like Thomas Sowell, Shelby Steele, and William Bennett, who have concluded that multicultural studies have no relevance to higher education. On the contrary: the criteria for educational excellence must include a truly multicultural vision and definition. We must have African-American Studies programs and research institutes; Women's Studies and Ethnic Studies programs; academic programs reflecting the totality of the cultural and social diversity which is America. The challenge before us is to create such programs that are truly designed to impact the totality of the learning experience for all students. The challenge is to retrain our teachers and faculty so that they approach the art of instruction with a richer appreciation of the intricate factors of ethnicity and cultural diversity within their own disciplines. We must go beyond the traditional definitions of "diversity," the idea of cultural difference as a secondary feature of higher education's periphery, to redefine the core or the mainstream of the academy's central mission for itself. We must assert, for example, that the serious study of the African-American experience is important not just to black students for reasons of ethnic and racial pride, but for everyone; that all students, regardless of their ethnic background or heritage, can become intellectually enriched by explorations into the African-American experience.

In practical terms, this means that Black Studies scholars must go beyond the mere development of new courses to engage in a general discussion about faculty and staff development, and the use of racial diversity criteria in the promotion and tenure of teachers and in the evaluation of classroom instruction. Courses in Black Studies must be included among the general requirements for all students, regardless of their ethnic backgrounds. We need to initiate collaborative projects that link our research to the development of issues which impact blacks and other people of color not only inside the U.S. but across the globe. We must cultivate an internationalist perspective on education, recognizing that the solutions to the problems of learning in rapidly changing societies are not confined to any single country or culture.

Most importantly, Black Studies need to reassert the connections between academic excellence and social responsibility. The black community is faced with a series of economic, social and political problems, and scholarship must be the critical tool in analyzing the means for resolving and addressing contemporary issues. In the legacy of Du Bois and others, we must recognize that the struggle for liberation is linked to the best scholarly research. The next generation of Black Studies programs must recognize that "knowledge is power," and that the purpose of scholarly research is not merely to interpret but to change the world.

Compounding the challenges to the study of the black experience is the fact that the social composition of the African-American community has itself changed sharply since the 1960s. One cannot really speak about a "common racial experience" which parallels the universal opposition blacks felt when confronted by legal racial segregation. Moreover, the contemporary black experience can no longer be defined by a single set of socioeconomic, political and/or cultural characteristics. For roughly the upper third of the African-American population, the post-1960s era has represented real advancement in the quality of education, income, political representation and social status. Social scientists estimate that the size of the black middle class, for example, has increased by more than 400 percent in the past three decades. One out of every seven black households, as of 1990, had an annual gross income exceeding $50,000. The recent experience of the middle third of the African-American population, in terms of income, has been a gradual deterioration in its material, educational and social conditions. For example, between 1974 and 1990, the median income of black Americans compared to that of white Americans declined from 63 percent to 57 percent. However, it is the bottom one-third of the black community which in this past quarter of a century has experienced the most devastating social consequences: the lack of health care, widespread unemployment, inadequate housing, and an absence of opportunity.

The triumph of white conservatism; changes in public policy towards black America and our central cities; and the resultant divisions within the black community—all have contributed to a profound social and economic crisis within black households and neighborhoods. For example, the infant mortality rate for black infants is twice that for whites. Blacks, who represent only 13 percent of the total United States population, now account for approximately 80 percent of all "premature deaths" of individuals aged fifteen to forty-four—those who die from preventable diseases and/or violence. There are currently more than 650,000 African-American men and women who are incarcerated, and at least half of these prisoners are under the age of twenty-nine. In many cities the dropout rate for nonwhite high-school students exceeds 40 percent. The majority of urban homeless people are black and Latino, and, as of 1989, nearly half of all poor black families were spending at least 70 percent of their income on shelter alone.

Black America also faces a crisis in leadership. In 1964 there were 104 black elected officials in the United States, with only five members of Congress and not one black mayor. Though small, this group of leaders were immediately and intimately connected with those they represented, because they had largely grown up in and continued to live and work within their constituent communities. By 1994 there were more than 8,200 black officeholders throughout the nation, including forty members of Congress and four hundred mayors. This growing number of African-American leaders, with a broad influence in federal, state and local governments, is largely composed of individuals who have their roots in the middle class—the upper third of the income earners within the African-American community. Black leaders frequently lack organic connections with working-class and low-income communities; although they frequently "speak" for the interests of the entire black community, they lack a scientific or critical method for assessing or articulating mass public opinion. Organizations such as the NAACP, for example, do not have any scientific or quantitative measure of their own members' opinions. National black leaders rarely, if ever, interact with key African-American social-science scholars or show familiarity with recent research on the socioeconomic state of the black community.

Black America stands at a challenging moment in its history: a time of massive social disruption, class stratification, political uncertainty, and ideological debate. The objectives for black politics in the age of Jim Crow segregation were relatively simple: full social equality, voting rights, and he removal of "white" and "colored" signs from the doors of hotels and schools. Today's problems are fundamentally more complex in scope, character and intensity: the flight of capital investment from our central cities, with thousands of lost jobs: the deterioration of the urban tax base, with the decline of city services; black-on-black violence, homicide and crime; the decline in the quality of our public schools and the crisis of the community's values. To this familiar litany of problems one more must be added: the failure to identify, train and develop rising leaders within the African-American community who are informed by a critical and scientific understanding of the needs and perspectives of their own people.

This is the social-science challenge of Black Studies. In order to respond to this unique set of challenges, we must not only know the statistics; we must also acquire a concrete understanding of the views of black Americans. We must, furthermore, respond to the needs of African-Americans by encouraging the production of socially responsible scholarship and by nurturing the development of rising young leaders from within the black community. We need, with painful honesty and a clarity of vision, to engage in a dialogue concerning the real roots of the current economic, social, political and educational problems within African-American society. We must foster ideological and theoretical discussions which help to promote constructive discourse between and among Black Studies scholars. Equipped with this critical perspective, we may begin to implement long-term and comprehensive strategies for democratic empowerment and social change.

Essay/Discussion Questions

1. According to Manning Marable, what is the relationship between African American Studies and multiculturalism?

2. Discuss Marable's definitions of multiculturalism. What definition does he advocate, and why?

3. Discuss Marable's criticism of Afrocentricity.

4. What does Marable mean when he argues that the purpose of African American Studies is not only to interpret the world but also to change it?

Part I Key Terms

African American studies	*Cultural particularism*
Afrocentrism	*Racial essentialism*
Black cultural nationalism	*Black women's studies*
Corporate multiculturalism	*Radical democratic multiculturalism*
Talented tenth	*Black feminism*
Liberal multiculturalism	*Molefi K. Asante*

Part I Supplementary Readings

Alkalimat, Abdul, and Associates, *Introduction to Afro-American Studies: A Peoples College Primer,* Chicago: Twenty-first Century Books and Publications, 1986.

Anderson, Talmadge, *Introduction to African American Studies: Cultural Concepts and Theory,* Dubuque: Kendall/Hunt Publishing Company, 1993.

Asante, Molefi K., *The Afrocentric Idea,* Philadelphia: Temple University Press, 1987.

_____, *Afrocentricity,* Rev., Trenton: Africa World Press, Inc., 1988.

_____, *Kemet, Afrocentricity and Knowledge,* Trenton: Africa World Press, Inc., 1990.

Bailey, Ron, "Why Black Studies?" *The Education Digest,* Vol. 35, No. 9 (1970), pp. 46–48.

Ballard, Allen B., *The Education of Black Folk: The Afro-American Struggle for Knowledge in White America,* New York: Harper & Row, Publishers, 1973.

Cade, Toni, ed., *The Black Woman: An Anthology,* New York: New American Library, 1970.

Cruse, Harold, *The Crisis of the Negro Intellectual,* New York: William Morrow and Company, 1967.

Dill, Bonnie, "The Dialectics of Black Womanhood," *Signs: The Journal of Women in Culture and Society,* Vol. 3, 1979, pp. 543–555.

Ford, Nick Aaron, *Black Studies: Threat or Challenge?* Port Washington: Kennikat Press, 1973.

Hare, Nathan, "The Battle for Black Studies," *The Black Scholar,* Vol. 3, No. 9 (May 1972), pp. 32–37.

Hill-Collins, Patricia, *Black Feminist Thought: Knowledge, Consciousness, and the Politics of Empowerment,* Boston: Unwin Hyman, 1990.

hooks, bell, *Feminist Theory: From Margin to Center,* Boston: South End Press, 1984.

_____, *Talking Back, Thinking Feminist, Thinking Black,* Boston: South End Press, 1989.

_____, *Yearning: Race, Gender, and Cultural Politics,* Boston: South End Press, 1990.

Hudson-Weems, Clenora, *Africana Womanism: Reclaiming Ourselves,* Troy: Bedford Publishers, 1993.

Hull, Gloria T., Patricia Bell Scott, and Barbara Smith, eds., *All the Women Are White, All the Blacks Are Men, But Some of Us Are Brave: Black Women's Studies,* Old Westbury: The Feminist Press, 1982.

James, Stanlie M., and Abena P. A. Busia, eds., *Theorizing Black Feminisms: The Visionary Pragmatism of Black Women,* New York: Routledge, 1993.

Karenga, Maulana, *Introduction to Black Studies,* Inglewood: Kawaida Publications, 1982.

Ladner, Joyce A., ed., *The Death of White Sociology,* New York: Vintage Books, 1973.

Lorde, Audre, *Sister Outsider: Essays & Speeches,* Freedom: The Crossing Press, 1984.

McEvoy, James, and Abraham Miller, eds., *Black Power and Student Rebellion,* Belmont: Wadsworth Publishing Company, 1969.

Marable, Manning, *Beyond Black and White: Transforming African-American Politics,* New York: Verso, 1995.

_____, *How Capitalism Underdeveloped Black America: Problems in Race, Political Economy and Society*, Boston: South End Press, 1983.

Myers, Linda J., *Understanding the Afrocentric Worldview,* Dubuque: Kendall/Hunt, 1988.

Robinson, Armstead L., Craig C. Foster, and Donald H. Ogilvie, eds., *Black Studies in the University: A Symposium,* New Haven: Yale University Press, 1969.

Smith, Barbara, ed., *Home Girls: A Black Feminist Anthology,* New York: Kitchen Table, Women of Color Press, 1983.

Turner, James E., ed., *The Next Decade: Theoretical and Research Issues in Africana Studies,* Ithaca: Africana Studies and Research Center, 1984.

Welsing, Frances C. *The Isis Papers: The Keys to the Colors,* Chicago: Third World Press, 1991.

Woodson, Carter G., *The Mis-Education of the Negro,* Washington, D.C.: The Associated Publishers, Inc., 1933.

II

Africa and the Diaspora: Ties That Bind

The historical forces and events that gave rise to the populations of African-descended Americans constitute one of the most dramatic and complex developments in human history. The contact between Africa and the Americas has resulted in the emergence of a people, particularly in the United States of America, whose legacy has been a historic struggle for human rights, socioeconomic development, and collective survival. It was through the Atlantic slave trade and chattel slavery that the histories of Africa, Europe, and the Americas converged. These dehumanizing and exploitative economic institutions served as a foundation for the accumulation of capital and the industrial development of Western Europe and the United States of America.

Although the mid-fifteenth century exchange between Western Europe and West Africa began with trade in goods, European greed, lust for power, and drive for global expansion rapidly transformed that exchange into the capture and trade of African bodies. As a result, massive depopulation, social dislocation, and political disruption weakened the African continent and prepared the way for Western European imperialism and colonialism during the nineteenth and early twentieth centuries. The turbulent voyage of the "middle passage" from Africa to the Americas, which included the genocide of millions of Africans, resulted in one of the most dramatic population transplantations in human history. Africans from numerous nations—from different cultures and language groups—were crammed into slave ships and forced upon American shores. They were Bambara, Malinka, Fon, Dinka, Ewe, Bakongo, Igbo, Yoruba, Ashanti, Wolof, and hundreds more. The colonial American institution of chattel slavery was the context in which the members of this pan-African assembly fought back, improvised, and refashioned themselves into a new, yet very old, people—African Americans.

The Western European rape of Africa was accompanied by much distortion of African and African American history, necessary to rationalize the slavers' barbaric treatment of dark-skinned peoples. It is precisely the European and Euro-American construction of conventional negative images and stereotypes of African-descended peoples and their cultures that made African American Studies an urgent necessity in the first place. The African past is essential to African American Studies because it challenges Western cultural power and corrects what is traditionally presented as truth. Retrieving African history before the intervention of Europe links African-descended Americans to a human, geographical, temporal, and intellectual context beyond the confines of slavery and Western cultural domination in the Americas. African history, then, is part of the collective memory of African-descended Americans, and reclaiming that history has to be one of the vocations of African American Studies.

Whether we view the African experience in the Americas, or in the Western Hemisphere, as a continuation of African historical development, or whether we wish to construct the African American experience as discontinuous with that development, what is required is an ongoing intellectual struggle to overturn the falsifications of Western "scholarship" and to reconstruct a more accurate historical and contemporary image of African-descended people. The essays in this section lay a foundation for understanding the demand for reinterpreting African history, the slave trade, and chattel slavery as important linkages between Africa and her descendants in the Americas.

In his essay, "African History and Western Civilization," Boniface Obichere is concerned with the inadequate treatment of African history by European and African historians. Like Harold Cruse, Obichere also participated in the 1968 Black Studies Conference at Yale University. In many ways, Obichere's observations prefigure some of the contradictions in today's struggle between Afrocentrists and their enemies over the interpretation of the African and African American experience. For example, he points out how the bold new school of African history represented by the Senegalese scholar Cheikh Anta Diop, who argued that ancient Egyptian culture was at base African, angered French historian Raymond Mauny. Although Mauny had called for a new interpretation of African history, he clearly had problems with an interpretation with which he did not agree.

Obichere argues that controversies about the inadequate treatment and false interpretation of African history spring from what is commonly referred to today as Eurocentrism, a view in which the African experience is constructed as a footnote in a self-congratulatory portrait of Western civilization. Rejecting this approach and critical of both European and Europeanized African scholars, Obichere points out how the Eurocentric outlook and neo-colonial power characterized the study of African history in Africa during and after European colonial rule. He details the manner in which Western cultural domination affected the development of African universities—the curricula and course syllabi, dictatorial department heads, the continued use of European examinations and grading standards, the publication of scholarly research, the themes in African history, and the anonymity of important figures in African history. Rejecting this state of affairs, Obichere challenges black historians to decolonize their minds, reject conventional distortions, and reinterpret the history of the African experience. Finally, he points to the 1955 Bandung Conference, the gathering of colonized Afro-Asian peoples, as representative of how important the meaning of African history is to the dispossessed peoples of the Third World.

In the question and answer period following his formal presentation, Obichere elaborates on some of the themes previously mentioned. He points out the historic intellectual relationship among Africans, West Indians, and African Americans. He comments on the cultural contradictions between Africans and African Americans, and he notes his own experience with European cultural domination in the context of coming to appreciate black cultural expressions in America. Finally, Obichere asserts the importance of research that investigates the controversial issue of African contact with the Americas long before Columbus. For him, controversy and ongoing questioning can give rise to new knowledge.

The impact of the transatlantic slave trade and chattel slavery on European and American civilizations is the subject of C. L. R. James's article, "The Atlantic Slave Trade and Slavery: Some Interpretations of their Significance in the Development of the United States and the Western World." Noting that every human society has experienced slavery, James writes that in ancient times, although they were harshly treated, slaves were still considered human beings who could be educated and could hold governmental office. For example, in ancient Greece, slaves could exercise some democratic rights. According to James, the introduction of mechanical power into military conflict and the expansion of capitalism made the transatlantic slave trade and chattel slavery devastating. Moreover, James argues that the illicit trade of African flesh and the institution of chattel slavery set in motion Western Europe's Industrial Revolution. James shows that the enslavement of Africans was systemically cruel, which meant that slavers lived in constant fear of slave revolts. The late eighteenth-century Haitian Revolution and the overthrow of French slavocracy in the Western Hemisphere sent shock waves throughout the planter classes in the Americas. James goes on to examine the suppression of the slave trade, the movement to abolish chattel slavery, the Underground Railroad, and the emancipation of the slaves. Finally, he argues persuasively that the impact of chattel slavery became deeply embedded in the American personality, political culture, social vision, and institutional practices.

In "Reflections on the Black Woman's Role in the Community of Slaves," Angela Davis challenges the false image of the black woman, which has its foundation in the distorted history of the slave "family" in America. Pointing out that the term *matriarchy* is associated with power, Davis asserts that the white ruling class of slaveowners dominated the contours of the slave family. Hence, the brutalizing slave system precluded the formation of a black matriarchy. Nonetheless, Davis argues, slaves fought valiantly for the liberation of their families and communities. Her major purpose is to reclaim and recapture the significant role slave women played in fighting against the system of chattel slavery. Davis contends that the black woman, in her desperate struggle for existence, was indispensable to the survival of the community.

Davis points out that the exclusion of chattel slaves from the social and cultural institutions of white patriarchy and femininity rendered black men and women equal. That is, black males were largely powerless and could not play the role of dominant male; and black females, because they also were completely integrated into the economic production system of slave labor, could not play the role of the passive and bourgeois domestic female, which characterized the "cult of true womanhood." In Davis' words, both female and male slaves "shared in the deformed equality of equal oppression." Significantly, it was only in the slave quarters, away from the slaveowners' presence, that female and male slaves could experience a modicum of freedom and dignity among themselves.

However, even constrained by the dehumanizing institution of chattel slavery, black women and men were not totally powerless and hopeless. They fought constantly for their liberation. Relying heavily on historian Herbert Aptheker's book, *American Negro Slave Revolts,* Davis recounts the numerous recorded slave insurrections. She reveals how common it was for black women to resist their enslavement throughout both the southern and northern regions of America. Suggesting that slaveowners' oppressive violence gave rise to slaves' oppositional violence, Davis delineates the variety of methods slave women employed in order to resist chattel slavery: escape, poisoning, sabotage, murder, and insurrection. Indeed, even though they faced the reality of death like the men if caught, many rebel female slaves planned and led revolts against the system of slavery.

Davis notes that in addition to death and other punishments, slaveowners retaliated in a particularly vicious fashion against rebellious female slaves: rape. Sexual violence grew out of the white male supremacy of Southern culture. Davis argues that "the slave master's sexual domination of the black woman contained an unveiled element of counterinsurgency." In their attempts to deter slave insurrections, slaveowners raped black women, reducing them to the level of their biological existence. Treating slave women as female animals, slaveowners also became barbaric. Davis argues that the political dynamics of rape went beyond the assault on black women; they represented a sexual war against the slave community. The political dynamics of rape were designed to dishearten black men. Ultimately, rape failed as a deterrent to slave rebellions, as black warrior women fought valiantly with the men to overthrow the system. Even so, Davis notes that the legacy of racial oppression, economic exploitation, and sexual domination continues to constrain the life-chances of black women in their desperate struggle for existence.

The essay by Vincent Harding, "Symptoms of Liberty and Blackhead Signposts: David Walker and Nat Turner," examines the African American struggle to overturn chattel slavery in the first quarter of the nineteenth century. Harding focuses on the lives and times of David Walker, a free African American who strongly protested chattel slavery, and Nat Turner, a minister and a leader of one of the most significant slave rebellions in the American South. Born into a slave community in 1800, Nat Turner apparently possessed special gifts, which his family and the surrounding slave community recognized and encouraged. Harding notes that as a youth, Turner's religious development was nurtured by his grandmother; his father, who became a fugitive slave, taught Turner that chattel slavery must be resisted. Hence, Nat Turner grew into adulthood with a powerful religious zeal and an anti-slavery passion.

The violent oppression that was often part of the slavery system brought into existence its opposite, as slaves revolted and struggled for freedom throughout the Western Hemisphere. In an atmosphere of repression and rebellion, Nat Turner stepped forward on August 22, 1831, to lead a group of avengers in the slaughter of whites in Southhampton County, Virginia. Turner was later captured, tried in court, imprisoned, and put to death. Turner's insurrection, however, sent waves of fear throughout the slaveholding South. In reaction, frightened whites indiscriminately massacred hundreds of African Americans.

If Turner represented the radical tradition of slave revolt, David Walker exemplified the radical tradition of critical analysis and anti-slavery protest among free African Americans. Born legally free in 1785 in Wilmington, North Carolina, Walker later traveled throughout the South and witnessed the violent, degrading, and dehumanizing effects of chattel slavery. In 1826, he moved to Boston, Massachusetts, where he joined forces with other African American abolitionists as an organizer, lecturer, and writer. In 1827, *Freedom's Journal,* the first African American newspaper, was published in Boston; Walker became its agent. Harding observes that the almost simultaneous emergence of "David Walker and *Freedom's Journal* represented one of the earliest institutional manifestations of . . . the Great Tradition of Black Protest."

A fiercely religious and outspoken person, Walker denounced the twin evils of chattel slavery in the South and antiblack racism in the North. Harding thus demonstrates that Walker recognized and advocated, as did many other black abolitionists, a commonality of interest between the chattel slave and "free" African American. In 1829, Walker published a pamphlet, *Appeal,* which set in motion an African American tradition of radical analysis and criticism of white greed and racism and an advocacy of black solidarity and liberation. Clearly energized by Walker's religious zeal and sense of social justice, the *Appeal* combined the two major belief systems in early nineteenth-century America— Protestant Evangelical Christianity and natural rights philosophy. As Harding shows, Walker linked the struggle for African American freedom to God's justice: the fight for African American liberation was a holy crusade, and resistance to chattel slavery was obedience to God.

Walker's thoroughgoing criticism of chattel slavery, antiblack racism, and the white supremacist American government electrified and inspired African Americans but terrified and angered white Americans. Even though whites condemned and tried to suppress the *Appeal,* copies circulated through African American communities in the North and South. As copies reached the South, it was reported not only that some whites intended to kill Walker but also that a monetary reward had been offered for his death. Undaunted, Walker stood his ground, holding the view that in the struggle for African American freedom and justice, some would perish. On June 28, 1830, Walker became suddenly and mysteriously ill; he died on that day in his Boston store. It was believed throughout Boston's African American community that Walker had been poisoned.

For Vincent Harding, Nat Turner and David Walker represent an early tradition of African American radicalism and collective struggle against the structures of racial and cultural domination in America. One a slave and the other "free," both these men and their comrades fought for liberation and justice, providing a buoy of hope in America's racially troubled waters for the generations of African Americans who would follow.

Although not a new topic, as Gilberto Freyre's *The Masters and the Slaves: A Study in the Development of Brazilian Civilization* (1946) or Donald Pierson's *Negroes in Brazil: A Study of Race Contact at Bahai* (1942) indicate, the growing black consciousness movement among Afro-Brazilians has encouraged increasing attention to the African Diaspora in that part of the Western Hemisphere. Michael Mitchell examines the 1978 discovery of a black community in the rural Brazilian village of Cafundó, which is located near the cities of Sorocaba and São Paulo in the western part of Brazil. Much like the African community in the Sea Islands off the South Carolina coast, the Afro-Brazilians of Cafundó have preserved the African language and other Africanisms (i.e., African cultural survivals) of their nineteenth-century slave ancestors. What is significant about Cafundó is that Africanisms have been preserved in the most *modern* part of Brazil. Mitchell's purpose, therefore, is to explain how this development occurred.

Mitchell points out that the people of Cafundó are the descendants of two enslaved sisters who were eventually freed by their owner in the mid-1800s. Although the exact geographical origin of Cafundó's language is yet to be determined, Mitchell indicates that the language is similar to the Bantu family of languages spoken in southern Africa. In the late 1880s, Portuguese slave traders were still acquiring slaves from the interiors of Angola and Mozambique. Hence, Mitchell suggests that the Bantu language of Cafundó may have originated among the southern African Bantu-speaking people. He argues further that Cafundó's African language and culture were preserved, even as the region of Sorocaba shifted from an agricultural to an industrial-manufacturing economy, because (similar to the Sea Island communities), the people of Cafundó went from slaves to peasants. Mitchell points out that although white Northerners came to the Sea Islands, seeking to Westernize and Christianize them, black Sea Islanders resisted white intervention and fiercely held on to their rich African culture. Mitchell postulates a similar dynamic between Brazilian abolitionists and the Cafundistas in the late 1800s, when the Afro-Brazilian slave fought for their freedom.

Lydia Lindsey and Carlton Wilson examine the experiences of African and Caribbean immigrants to Western Europe, together with the situation of European-born blacks. Significantly, Lindsey and Wilson point out that, with a few exceptions, many black people from the United States historically have thought of Europe as free of racism, largely because there were no laws governing the conduct of the races. Moreover, many black Americans who visited Europe did not see segregated communities and other racist practices. Further, the authors indicate, black Americans generally have been treated as celebrities in Europe, which has prevented them from viewing the harsh realities of racial oppression there. Arguing against this misconception, Lindsey and Wilson probe the systematic racism that African, Caribbean, East Indian, and Pakistanis encounter in European nations.

Even though racial discrimination in Europe may not be readily visible in the law, Lindsey and Wilson argue that this evil exists in practice. Tracing European antiblack racism from the early twentieth century to the present, they maintain that European antiblack racism has operated quite similarly to its American version. What differentiates the European and American practices of antiblack racism is the European colonial experience, which remained entrenched in African and Caribbean nations for more than one hundred years after the termination of slavery. Yet, as the formerly colonized African, Caribbean, and even East Asian populations immigrated to European countries—and in many ways became *black* Europeans—their experiences in Europe let them know that they were a people apart with different a culture.

Because African Americans generally know very little, if anything, about the African European experience, Lindsey and Wilson suggest the development of Afrocentric European studies—the systematic study of African-descended peoples in Europe as a dimension of the African Diaspora. The authors argue that examining the African Diaspora in Europe from antiquity to the present would provide the opportunity to focus on African Europeans' experiences, achievements, and contributions to European civilization.

African History and Western Civilization

BONIFACE OBICHERE

What I want to do here is to examine the present inadequacies of treatment of African history in Africa and overseas, take a glance at what could be done to eliminate this sad state of affairs, and maybe share a few thoughts with you on African history and the Third World Movement.

Let me begin by narrating a personal experience. When I was living in the then Eastern Nigeria, now Biafra, I was in an English-style boarding school preparing for a London University examination, and of course one of my subjects was the History of the British Empire—and that included North America. In a textbook for this particular examination, which was a set of lectures written up in London at the time, it was very interesting to note that John Hancock was described, and I quote, as "the greatest smuggler in Boston." When I came to the United States a few years later, I was told as a student in a state university, if I wanted an honors degree in history, which I was in the process of getting, I had to do American history. So, I registered for American history for a whole year, and in that particular class I was taught that John Hancock was a very great patriot, and, of course, that his name appears first on the Declaration of Independence. This is a simple fact, but it affected me

profoundly later on in my college career, especially when I went back to Oxford. In this example you see the difference in thinking, the difference in attitude, the difference in prejudices and so on and so forth. What I have just said about John Hancock here seems to me to apply to the treatment of African history at the present time. Interpretations are polarized.

Writing in 1960, a Frenchman, Raymond Mauny, called on West African universities, those at Ibadan, Accra, and Dakar, and the American Negro universities to take up the challenge of the new school of African history.[1] I thought this was a good appeal by Raymond Mauny—whose treatment of African history is resented by many. This was eight years ago and it was a Frenchman speaking. What is significant here is that this Frenchman noticed or detected that Africa and the American universities had to cooperate in bringing out the material and in the interpretation of the new African history. The cause of Professor Mauny's statement was a book on African culture history written by an African, Cheikh Anta Diop, entitled *Nations Nègres et*

From *Black Studies in the University, A Symposium,* edited by Armstead L. Robinson, Craig C. Foster, Donald H. Ogilvie. Yale University Press, 1969.

Culture.[2] Mauny didn't like this book because it didn't follow the traditional interpretation of African history. It made bold claims based on evidence, including one that I think Mauny took issue with in his review of the book: that the bases of Egyptian culture were Negro before the invasion of Egypt by the Semitic-Greco-Roman world.

Taking this controversy a little farther, we see Margery Perham and Professor K. O. Dike, formerly of Ibadan University, entering into a similar controversy. Margery Perham was of the opinion that Africans weren't prepared for independence (she was writing in 1958, of course; she had no crystal ball to see what was going to happen in 1960) and Professor Dike responded very vehemently in a series of articles in *West Africa*. I think that the main theme of all Dike had to say was this (and I paraphrase him, I'm not quoting): that there were people who had a pathological unwillingness to accept evidence about African history and African contributions to world civilization. Professor Dike is a very great moderate, as you know; he is not of the nationalist school, and this coming from him is very strong indeed.

A few years later the battle was joined again, this time at England's premier university—at Oxford. The present Regius Professor of Modern History at Oxford, Hugh Trevor-Roper, expressed the opinion that he didn't think Africa and Asia had any history, except that history which began with European enterprise in these places. This time it was left to English people to do battle with Trevor-Roper. The first person who picked up the gauntlet was Basil Davidson, who countered Trevor-Roper in no uncertain terms. In fact, one of his questions was whether Trevor-Roper considered London a Roman city or an English city. And of course he asked him the origin of Oxford, Winchester, etc. Thomas Hodgkin joined battle also with Trevor-Roper, and we have seen that since then Mr. Trevor-Roper has been very quiet about African history.

These are a few things that will introduce you to the type of controversy that has been going on and is still raging about African history. I think that the basis of this controversy is the inadequacy of the treatment of African history and, secondly, the false interpretation that has hitherto been given to African history. That is, that the whole of African history was, in the words of Professors R. Robinson and J. A. Gallagher in *Africa and the Victorians*, "a gigantic footnote" to something that Britain was doing in Asia or in England, and so on. At the present time we have persons engaged in the study of African history who don't believe in the footnote theory and who think African history is a body of knowledge worth inquiring into in its own right, and for its own sake. Such men as Professors Roland Oliver and John D. Fage come to mind here.

Let us take the question of inadequacies of treatment of African history in the study of Western civilization. The textbook used for this course in History 1 under Professor Wolff at the University of Minnesota is that bible of the history of Western civilization by R. R. Palmer, which, incidentally, has acquired a workbook like Samuelson's in economics—and, of course, Joel Colton has added to the work. In here you are supposed to be studying the history of the "modern world"—but *that* modern world existed only in Europe and, partially, in the United States. I may be right in saying that about 33 1/3 percent of that book deals with German thinking—very little on Africa, and that on Africa deals with Englishmen and Frenchmen and Germans visiting Africa for a very short period of their lives. And I'm saying this very, very seriously. Now how many years did Cecil Rhodes spend in Africa? I think you could even exaggerate, or even be sensational, in saying that he spent more time in Oriel College, Oxford, than he spent in South Africa. Or what of Lugard? How many years of his life did he spend in Africa? Still these textbooks devote almost all of their treatment of Africa to these personalities.

MacKinnon for East Africa, and so on and so forth. Take the new text by Stromberg. What do we have on Africa?

I think the only real hope comes in the collectively *Civilization Past and Present,*[3] chaired by Professor Wallbank of the University of Southern California. It is in Volume I of *Civilization* that for the first time since I have been looking around I've seen an author devoting more pages to Africa than was devoted to China or India. Probably this kind of lopsided treatment is necessary: in the words of Oginga Odinga, if you've been leaning too much to the right, you have to make up for it by leaning very much to the left so that you'll gain an upright position in the process—because if you don't, you might continue leaning too much to the right.

In the classical world histories, what does one find on Africa? Take the best sellers of the early portion of this century: H. G. Wells' *Outline of History,* Van Loon's *World History,* H. G. Wells' *A Short History of the World.* Or take that American classic of William and Ariel Durant. What do we get on Africa? I would say, nothing, because to them the perspective is very different: African history has no appeal or they didn't want to bother about it. Toynbee's *A Study of History* is also to be included in this long list of inadequacies of treatment.

I'm not saying that Europeans and Americans are responsible, alone, for this type of situation. I think that Africans have contributed to this in a very large way and, with apologies to Harold Cruse,[4] the intellectuals especially. We have in West Africa an abundance of historians, more than in any other discipline, except for the recent generation of American-trained graduates who have gone into the sciences and nuclear physics and who have become experts in engineering and technology. Most of the old generation who were trained in London and Cambridge and Oxford were historians and lawyers. This was one thing to do to become a civil servant, get a house in the European section of town with stewards and gardeners and so on (I'm not going into this). The net result of this kind of "unreal" existence is that these gentlemen never bothered with *African* history.

I think this came up yesterday when somebody said that if black people pass through universities and go out and get jobs and buy a home in the hills, these black gentlemen are white in their thinking. And I would say that most educated Africans of the older generation, in fact, up to about 1956, were *Europeans.* There are terms in almost all the African languages calling them "Europeans": the Yorubas call them "Oyinbo dudu"—that's "black white man"; in Ibo they are called "Beke Ojii"—that is, a "black white man"; and the French-speaking countries have their expression for these people, such as *evolué.* So that it would be too much, taking their circumstances into consideration, to expect them to produce much in the way of African history.

Another reason for this statement that I'm making here is the nature of the curricula in African universities. First of all, feasibility studies had to be done, with grants from the British Colonial Office, to see if the Africans needed any university, that is, if the colonial power was to establish universities in Africa—forgetting that a very large percentage of the student population in England at that time was African. These study groups, such as the Ashby Commission, went around and looked at all possible factors and decided that commonwealth universities should be established. The Commonwealth Universities Act led to the establishment of Ibadan and Legon (Accra) in 1948. Of course, Fourah Bay College was in existence at this time, but as a college of Durham University. And Makerere College was in existence, but as a college of the University of London. In other words, it was very little different from, say, University College, or Bedford College, or King's College, London, because it had the same syllabus, it had the same examinations, which were given at the same times.

And here, again, I might interject a personal experience. I remember sitting in the examination hall in Owerri (Biafra) and the Education Officer, a rotund Englishman, showed us very clearly the envelope in which our examination questions were sent from England with the seal of the University Senate in London. The regulations were that these examinations had to be opened at a specified time so that they would start at the same time all over. This was to ensure that people wouldn't cable back and forth the questions from Nigeria to Britain. The Officer said, "Here are your examinations," undid the seal of the Senate, and then zip, we started off. It was just as simple as that, because I could have landed on the steps of London University and discussed those questions with the same degree of depth and ability as any honors student in England—because the questions were the same, the people who were going to mark and grade them were the same, living in the suburbs of Essex and Sussex or what have you. So, under these circumstances it would be too much to expect African universities to branch out into the investigation of African history, because only "European History," "English History," and "The History of the British Empire" were on the syllabus. There was no examination in American history as developed as it is today, though some of the British and African universities are changing their position because of pressure from the English-Speaking Union.

The universities in Africa have gained independence in the last few years and some of them have begun fundamental research on African history. But this is still very limited in scope. I take a dim view of this effort, in the light of the way in which it is being conducted. The chairmen of some of these programs and departments are ex-colonial officials or Europeans whom I wouldn't hesitate to accuse of the colonial administrator's mentality. They see the university as an extension of their secretariat during the colonial period. The universities in French-speaking Africa are notorious for this new role for ex-colonial officials.

For those who have no experience with African universities, the departments are not like the departments in American universities. The chairman of the department is a little despot. He decides what courses have to be taught, what books have to be used. Lecturers don't recommend textbooks, as is the case in America. As a matter of fact, lecturers have very little to say in the formulation of the contents of some of the courses they teach. This illustrates the degree to which the chairman affects the development of the curriculum and research in his department.

In Ibadan University especially we see this predicament in its fullest form. There is an Institute for Islamic Studies—run by a former British administrator, and the material coming out of the Institute reflects this. There was the African History Research Program in the University of Ife, which because of the local political situation became very parochial indeed. It is like the American history section of the History Department of Yale saying that American history was coterminous with the history of Connecticut. I think this would be ridiculous. I'm talking here about the Yoruba History Program initiated by Professor S. O. Biobaku at Ife. I'm not saying that the program is bad, but I am saying that the priorities are not right.

Now, let us go to the scholars on a different level—publications. Do you know that it was an American scholar of African history who told an African, a black African historian, that he should begin to look twice at the documents he reads in the Public Record Office? I'm talking here about the review by Professor Robert I. Rotberg of the book edited by Professor J. C. Anene and G. N. Brown where Rotberg was telling Anene in no uncertain terms to desist from calling Africans pirates simply because Sir John Kirk or Evan Smith writing from Zanzibar in the nineteenth century thought that these Africans were pirates. This goes a long way to illustrate what I'm driving at. Many black historians have not gone through what Dr. Nnamdi Azikiwe described as "mental emancipation," what Jomo Kenyatta talks about in his little volume of collected speeches, *Harambee,* as "dropping the colonial mentality." Of course, Evan Smith described some Zanzibari and Swahili and East African traders as pirates. But when in the 1960s one gets into the Public Record Office and reads these documents, doesn't one have a duty to oneself to question whether these were actually pirates or not?

The reason why I cited this example is that most of the material being published at present by African intellectuals is identical in tone with what was being published by Englishmen in London in the 1930s; in other words, it is a question of the old wine in a new jug. Professor Raymond Mauny's call for "the new school of African history" has not been heeded by some African historians. I think it is a professional thing: these men are tied to fledgling universities that are still subsidiaries of European universities, and therefore have to treat historical questions according to what the European universities require and demand. In Ibadan University, the University of Ife, and so on, it is still imperative to invite outside examiners from Cambridge or Oxford or London. Even Ahmadu Bello University, located in Northern Nigeria, has outside examiners from Oxford reading the examinations of their students, "to assure acceptable standards." Whose standards? Here, again, I have to knock at an old dead horse (I wouldn't mind flogging it again). It is the unrealistic colonial rule that degrees other than those obtained from England or Commonwealth universities are "worthless."

I think we have seen this colonial balloon punctured and deflated, but still the myth survives. American universities are excluded from the category of the selected, and those who hold degrees from them have a hard time getting jobs in Africa. If any African academics are not mature enough to know who's "fit to be licensed," in the words of Professor McWorter, I don't think they have a business in the university. Such men should end up in a little secretariat signing typed letters or answering phones. But if they think they have a business in the university, I think they should have the intellectual maturity and the honesty of purpose to know who is fit or unfit for university work. I don't think one needs an Englishman to decide that.

Also in this problem of intellectuals is the crisis of publication. Some African writers cannot get publishers because they don't toe the line. I mean this very seriously. Look at the example that I cited at the beginning of this presentation, Raymond Mauny versus Cheikh Anta Diop: if it hadn't been for *Présence Africaine,* Diop's book would never have been published. So, those Africans who write, maybe African history or any other type of cultural assessment of Africa, have to toe the line if they want to be published. I know a few cases and I wouldn't say that these cases are not representative. The question of publication, then, is a very serious one. Africa needs an indigenous press. We fool ourselves, saying we have an Ibadan University Press or we have a Dakar University Press, and so on. Most books are produced in England for Ibadan University: it's like a mother feeding Junior with processed food, because he can't eat on his own. Ibadan University should come of age one way or the other—grants, know-how, foreign aid, I don't care what—so that it could publish its own books just like the Indian universities and the American universities publish their own books.

Another fault of the intellectuals which has contributed to the inadequacy of treatment of African history—and I'm talking about both white and black intellectuals at this juncture—is the question of selection of non-important themes in African history. An Englishman told us in Los Angeles about three weeks ago (I'm talking here, in fact, about Professor Terence

Ranger of the University of East Africa in Dar es Salaam) that he visited Ibadan University a few months ago and he said that he was amazed to see Ibadan engrossed in a symposium on "Indirect Rule in Nigeria." For heaven's sake, what is "indirect rule" compared to other themes in Nigerian history? It is this kind of playing-the-ostrich which has led to the crisis in Nigeria. People neglect the issues. "Indirect rule"—so fine, because Lugard described this in his *Dual Mandate.*

During my research at Oxford one of my tasks, and it was an unpleasant task indeed, was reading through all the volumes of the Lugard Papers and discussing them with Dame Margery Perham and others. These papers have been pruned. Those things that people weren't expected to see have been destroyed, with the result that "p. 2" or "p. 6" of certain letters are missing, and so on and so forth. And in there I was privileged to read communications between Professor Reginald Coupland and Lugard when he was writing his *Dual Mandate.* After that I just changed my mind about the book, because Lugard wasn't saying what he did or what he wished to see done. He was trying to become "respectable," since he had retired in England and wanted to become "part of the society." This is my own view of what happened in there. So, for a university in West Africa at this time of the study of African history to spend months on "indirect rule" and to devote, in fact, an issue of the journal of the Nigerian Historical Society to the indirect rule question is, it seems to me, to be irrelevant, or to have the priorities wrong.

Now what has been the result of this concentration on non-important themes? It has been that we are accepting or relying very heavily on the histories of Africa written *outside.* I may say here that no African has produced a solid-type history of Africa up to this morning to my knowledge. The works that are in use are those that have recently come out of Prague, Paris, New York, and London.[5] I'm referring to Andre Sik and his *History of Africa*

(1966) in two volumes. This work has been translated into French and into English: then Hureck's two-volume study of *The History of Africa* also is being used, and people are begging for its translation into English and French as well. These studies we know are Marxist and lopsided, because their main theme is imperialism and how it exploited Africa and thwarted African history. It is the responsibility of Africans and "men of culture" in general, as St. Clair Drake said during the Congress of Africanists in Rome (1959), to destroy these myths and to produce the real facts of history.

African history should then be treated as African history and the important themes should be investigated. One would like to see studies of African political structures, structures of states; the functioning of these states should be studied in detail and the personalities should be studied. We were introduced—and I'm talking about my generation who went to school in Africa—to European history through a series of biographies ranging from Moses, Hammurabi, and Socrates down to Winston Churchill. There is nothing wrong with studying African biographies. G. Carter Woodson has a book on this, *African Heroes and Heroines* (1944). It is dated and needs revision.

This brings me to my crucial criticism at this point, and that is the question of *anonymity.* I think it was part of colonial policy to impose *anonymity.* I think it was part of colonial policy to impose anonymity on Africa and Africans. We don't have names. Our countries have no names. They are described by trade names—the Gold Coast, the Ivory Coast—and these stick. If you look at old maps, you'll see that these areas had other names, and some African politicians have revived these historical names. It might have been emotional of these politicians, but the names were worth reviving. Today "Ghana," for instance, is more meaningful than "Ivory Coast," because there are very few elephants left in Houphouet-Boigney's Ivory Coast. So the name itself is anachronistic.

Anonymity can be seen in the treatment of African heroes. Take the example I gave earlier, that Lugard made treaties with the King of Borgu in November 1894. Who was this man? He might have been a more important personality than Lugard, who was a freebooter in 1894. We want his name, Siré Torou, to enter into any historical treatment of that British expedition of 1894 into his kingdom of Borgu. This is one of the psychological problems that the black people in America and Africa have to face together. I think in the extreme version of the Muslim movement we see some people answering "X" because they think that the names they were given coincide with the anonymous treatment of the blacks and so they would rather be *completely* anonymous than go by the name of "Fine Face," or "Big Ears," or something like that. These names are from the Niger Delta states. We have "Jack Fine Face" and we have "Water-boy," and Bob Manuel. These are names that were foisted on the people of these areas in the seventeenth century by European slave dealers. These names still persist. So, it behooves us today to examine this question of anonymity, and in our writing of African history to make efforts to pinpoint the personalities who acted in Africa before the Europeans and after the Europeans arrived on the scene. In attacking this question of anonymity we should also endeavor to cleanse the historical record of Africa. We shouldn't look at Shaka only as a "bloodthirsty, nasty Zulu" because his European opponents described him that way. We should look at this famous man as a leader of his people; and we should look at him as an innovator in what we see our political scientists wrestling with today, the problem of state modernization. This is a problem which didn't start in the middle of the twentieth century.

To end up I want to look very briefly at African history and the Third World. Since the Bandung Conference (1955) the Afro-Asian world has been feeding on a new mental diet and that diet, whether it is in the extreme

form or in the mild form, reminds them that after all is said and done, despite poverty, despite segregation and discrimination, they are the *majority* of human beings, of what we have categorized as *homo sapiens*. I don't know the ramifications of this Bandung statement in the minds of our political leaders, but I think it is a very far-reaching point that was made at the Bandung Conference. Though Afro-Asian solidarity has not been a functional thing in many cases, I think it has been a fact, at least ideologically. Black history or the study of the black experience in America is one extension of this Afro-Asian consciousness. The black revolution in the United States and the political and social revolution going on in Africa and Asia[6] and, in fact, in Latin America cannot be completely segregated in water-tight compartments. George Shepperson of Edinburgh University has published an article showing the early intellectual contacts between the American blacks and Africans. The origins of the African political revolution have been linked to the American universities attended by African leaders. And of course there have been several of such studies.[7]

The Brazilians have come out with very many books and scholarly articles on the contributions of Africa to Brazilian life and culture. A Frenchman has come out with a study of Brazil and the West African trade. In the academic field, worthwhile endeavors are being made in the Third World, and the spokesmen of the Third World—"spokesmen" not by popular election, but probably by their arrogating this role to themselves—do drum this into the ears of the inhabitants of the Third World, to give them consolation, yes, but to elevate their spirits, I think, more than anything else. Therefore in the meaningful quest for identity in Africa and for identity in the United States by the blacks, African history has a role to play. People have argued that the blacks in America cannot point to where they came from. Well, this is as it might be; but they can point to Africa and say we originated there *some* time ago. Our forebears came from there. This fulfills an emotional need in the search for identity.

In considering the Third World, I think that certain vocabularies have been built up which are understood easily in Africa and in the black communities in the United States, Latin America, and in Asia. People are reading the same authors. Not only the quotations of Mao Tse-Tung are read, but also Frantz Fanon, Ernesto Che Guevara, and similar authors who think "the hard way" about what the black man has to do to pull himself up by his own bootstraps.

In conclusion, let me say that the inadequacies that I have examined are real. They exist, and I think they call for a remedy. Secondly, the curricula of African universities and black universities in America as well as the predominantly white universities should be brought in line with the needs of the day. If that includes the establishment of the study of the black experience, by all means do it. I would interject here that at UCLA we are now offering a course for credit on "The Black Man in the Changing American Context." This is a beginning and we hope to branch out by the fall quarter into other such courses. Thirdly, it seems to me that the study of the black experience, which includes African history in its broadest interpretation, is a worthwhile academic endeavor. It is enriching. In the words of Ron Karenga, it might "add some zest and some vim and some vigor" to the study of the bland "European experience." Fourthly, I would like to suggest that those engaged in the field of African history should try to redefine their purposes and their roles and try to tackle meaningful subjects, even though these may seem to be hard on the esophagus. Maybe they wouldn't be that hard when the various tools of research are employed in analyzing and interpreting these subjects.

Fifthly, I would call on those who have influence with publishers or those who can contribute to publications to see that all shades of opinion get exposure. It could be said that Africa is still living through the period of colonial censorship—very subtle, indeed, but very real. Even those Africans who have used all the current tools of the new history are still criticized adversely when their findings lead them to make interpretations different from the old ones. Finally then, I would say that African history has been neglected in the past. This realization has dawned suddenly on many universities, and several of them are trying to give prominence in African history, offering degrees up to the doctorate level in African history. This is really encouraging and I hope that this trend will continue at a faster rate and with broader perspectives and openness of mind.

Notes

1. *Bulletin de l'Institut Français d'Afrique Noire*, Vol. XXII, Series B (1960), p. 551.
2. Cheikh Anta Diop, *Nations Nègres et Culture* (Paris: Présence Africaine, 1955).
3. Walter T. Wallbank, Alastair M. Taylor, Nels M. Bailkey, *Civilization Past and Present*, Vol. I, 5th Edition (Chicago, 1965).
4. Harold Cruse, *The Crisis of the Negro Intellectual* (New York, 1967).
5. R. Oliver and J. D. Fage, *A Short History of Africa* (Penguin Book, 1966). R. I. Rotberg, *A Political History of Tropical Africa* (1964). R. Cornevin, *Histoire de l'Afrique*, 2 vols. (Vol. III in preparation). D. Westermann, *Geschichte Afrikas* (1952).
6. G. H. Jansen, *Non-Alignment and the Afro-Asian States* (New York, 1966). Brian Grozier, *Neocolonialism* (Philadelphia, 1964).
7. Kwame Nkrumah, *Ghana: The Autobiography of Kwame Nkrumah* (New York, 1957). E. W. Smith, *Aggrey of Africa* (London, 1929). Jones-Quartey, *A Life of Azikiwe* (New York, 1966). A. A. Nwafor Orizu, *Without Bitterness* (New York, 1944). Robert I. Rotberg, *The Rise of Nationalism in Central Africa* (Cambridge, 1965).

Question Period

Question: Professor Obichere, I was wondering if I could ask you three very short questions, possibly answered only "yes" or "no." If we grant that people who have to live in a country and have the experience of growing up in a particular environment may have a certain intrinsic advantage in working on their own society, I would ask, in reference to African history, Can *good* African history be done by non-Africans?

Obichere: The answer is yes.

Question: Do you feel that one must have a particular ideological stance with regard to contemporary African problems in order to do good African history, be the person African or not?

Obichere: The answer is no. By my own training—unless you are writing an official history, or unless you are a historian to a political party—I don't think that you could tie yourself down, in all honesty to your own endeavor, to any particular ideology. You're going to produce something that's very tendentious and lopsided. This is my criticism of Andre Sik's book. I've read that book through and through and the more I read it the more disgust I feel for parts of it. It is so lopsided. You can't see through the smoke of the continuous attack on "imperialism," and capitalism and so forth. This is what happens when you get so completely engrossed in an ideology that you want to subordinate everything else to it.

I think, as an African, I wouldn't hesitate to submit to a publisher a manuscript which finds that African history in a particular era is not what the politicians in Africa want it to be. I have to be honest to myself, first of all, before considering the other man. "To thine own self be true," said Shakespeare.

This brings me to what Professor Kilson said yesterday. In dealing with the slave trade, for instance, you think about the yo-ho-ho type of crewmen with handkerchiefs around their necks, drinking rum all night, who were rounded up in the streets of Bristol or Liverpool and taken to the West Coast. This is fine, it's historically true; one can go to the Public Record Office in England and see the bill of lading. These crewmen are as anonymous as the Africans that I mentioned, and objected to their anonymity. These crewmen were *anonymous,* they're "thirty crewmen, from such-and-such street in Bristol." That's what they *were* in that period in England, but when they got to Cape Coast or Whydah or Lagos, they had to deal with the Fanti chiefs or King Agaja or King Kosoko, who'd sell them the slaves. Even if this is not good for the feelings of those involved in practical politics or in building up ideologies and myths, it's still a historical fact. I prefaced my remarks with the story of John Hancock: as I see it, whether the people in Nantucket Sound believe that John Hancock is the greatest patriot America ever had or not, he still was a smuggler and a tax-evader.

Question: Eric Williams' book called *Capitalism and Slavery* discusses the economic importance of slavery as a revenue-producing institution. In it, he attempts to show that the slave trade may have produced much of the revenue necessary to kick off the industrial revolution in England. I wish you would comment on that.

Obichere: *Capitalism and Slavery* is a powerful book. To those who have been through graduate work at Oxford in Empire History, the development of that book is still a very lively issue. I don't think in all honesty that you could say that the slave trade alone produced the wealth that touched off the industrial revolution. This would be historically false, economically untrue, and a perversion of English history. There were other sources of revenue in England at that time besides the slave trade. It was a lucrative job, it was a lucrative business; you only need to see the books and diaries of the slave dealers and the companies in London and Liverpool and Bristol who fitted out the ships that went on this business. However, I don't think that if other factors had not been present, the wealth gained from the slave trade alone would have touched off the industrial revolution.

I'm not a one-factor interpreter of history, and this is why I run into problems with ideologues. Eric Williams' position is a valid one. The reason why I said that Williams' experience is still a live issue at Oxford is the fact that his drafts were rejected so many times by his supervisor. Eric Williams almost didn't make an Oxford D. Phil. because of the rigidity of his supervisor although he went on to All Souls after that—a great achievement! He ran into trouble and he had to rewrite and recant and revise. Where was that book published? Chapel Hill, North Carolina, wasn't it?—not Oxford University Press! There was an accumulation of capital as a result of the slave trade, but I don't think that one could in all intellectual honesty say that this was the primary and only source of the wealth which led to the industrial revolution.

Question: You chose to discuss the American black man under your section on the Third World and, I think I remember, your argument was that the relationship of Africa to Latin America was in some way similar to the relationship of the black man in America to Africa. I'm wondering, whether you're arguing that there is no special, no intimate, connection between black Americans and Africa, that the thing that's most common that one should look for and emphasize in the black studies view is the experience of colonialism, segregation, and oppression which is common to the Third World?

Obichere: Well, I think, what I intended to say, or what I did say, is that there is a relationship, *definitely*, between the black man in America and the black man in Africa, and, of course, the black man in Latin America. There is a special genetic relationship between the black man in America and the black man in Africa. A Senegalese friend of mine analyzed this for me in Paris. He said: "Look, both of you speak English." This is a simple fact, but it hasn't occurred to many of the analysts: the black man in America speaks English and the black man in West Africa, former British colonies, Central Africa, speaks English. Of course, the common experience of oppression is there.

I mentioned George Shepperson's article on the overwhelming influence of black Americans on the nationalist movement in Africa. This was a study done by an Englishman, or shall I say Scotsman, and it's a very valid study. In the African analysis of the Third World, the black American is definitely included. You hear some American militants talking about the situation of the black American as being that of colonialism; this may be very far from the truth—but that is how some African politicians look at it, and this is what is blared out from probably many local radio stations in Africa. It seems to me that this is how we have to look at it. It is a difficult thing, for instance, convincing an African politician whose only contact with Europe was through a cursory visit to London, who has never been a student in a university or, for that matter, a secondary school, that the situation the black Americans are fighting is not analogous or identical with the one that he fought in Africa. This is a very hard task. So, if I've answered your question, I'm saying that the special relationship exists, and in the wider context, of course, the overview is there.

Question: Does the special relationship depend on political issues or on cultural factors?

Obichere: I think maybe not on political issues, not necessarily on cultural factors as I see it, but on race-consciousness. We are black people. I was amazed a month ago, watching Paul Jacobs of San Francisco telling Louis Lomax just as it is, Louis Lomax put it to him this way, "Well, you are a Jew and I'm a black man, but I'm an American; I'm not Jewish, I'm Christian. I am an American first and a Negro second." Jacobs told Louis Lomax that he was living in a false world, that he wasn't facing reality. Jacobs asked him one question: "When the National Guard occupied Watts, if you had dared to leave your home in the hills and gone down to 103rd Street and Century Boulevard, would the Guards have said, "You are Louis Lomax, you are American!"—or would they have gunned you down at sight because you are black?"

This is a fact of life, the black American is *black*. And as long as he realizes that genetic relationship with Africa, I think this is where the ties are. Culturally, he may be different: it took me a while to start appreciating Ray Charles! This is culture. About a week ago I was out until 2 AM listening to LeRoi Jones and his theater group perform. But when I was green from Biafra where did I go? The Minneapolis Symphony, because I was taught in the boarding school that this was the ultimate in music. I went to the Guthrie Theater and watched Chekhov's *Three Sisters* and some Shakespeare. But today I can go to a black theater and enjoy it. So, culturally I wouldn't say that there is 100 percent harmony. One has to be acculturated, or "deculturated"—if I may coin that word.

Question: I'm still somewhat bothered by the same things that motivated an earlier question, and although I find your answers quite acceptable, I'm not sure I can rationalize them with some of the things I thought you were saying earlier. You have told us, I think quite well, how the historical record needs to be corrected. I'm reminded that black children in Surinam, the Netherlands Antilles, have a history book that begins telling them about when "the Germanic people came to our country"—not meaning Surinam, of course, but that part of Western Europe where Germanic peoples did come. I'm reminded that the geography texts in Jamaica, I think, have the first six sections on the different parts of England, Scotland, Wales, and Ireland, and finally at the back a very small map of India and the surrounding territories. There's a certain distortion of the world that was being taught to black people there.

I'm reminded of the Rebellion of 1865 in Jamaica where William Gordon was hanged by the neck until dead by Governor Edward J. Eyre at his orders. He was then a traitor, and now the nationalists and intellectuals have rewritten that and while the dates are the same and the names are the same, William Gordon is now a nationalist hero rather than a traitor and they named the new legislature after him. Yale, too, has been involved in rewriting history in Jamaica—over a different map, much to the chagrin of the Italian-American community. You mentioned Diop: in one of his books I think he also makes a claim for the discovery of America, only this time it's the sailors of Senegal who I think he claims also discovered America.

I'm not sure what you're calling for. Is it that we need 130 different versions of history, all viewed from the particular point of view of some particular nation-state? Herodotus wrote the history of the world from the point of view of the small nations, but it turned out that I think he had Greece in mind. That wasn't particularly useful. How can we proceed? Is there a possibility for a universal history on which we can all agree, a human history? Or must we be content with these different versions? I quite agree that the record needs to be corrected. I'm merely asking a question beyond that: Are we going to have to have different versions—national versions, perhaps sectional versions within a country, a black history, a white history, a Communist history, a capitalist history, and 130 nationalist histories? What is the alternative to that?

Obichere: The last portion of your statement brings out your question more clearly, and I'll address myself to that. It seems to me that you can have a universal history in a world history textbook, but I am persuaded to say that you must, of necessity, have 130 national histories and several histories of the same country *in* that particular country, written from different points of view. Empirical evidence proves this, and I'm not persuaded to think that human nature has changed very much. Rather, intellectual activity has diversified greatly, because there are more people involved. Take eighteenth-century England: There were official histories of England, there were handbooks of English history, and of course, with the age of the philosophes, there were things like David Hume's history of England. There is Macauley's *History of England*. It is nothing like Trevelyan's. H. Trevor-Roper is writing: he might come out with a history of England, of the upper classes, probably! A. J. P. Taylor interprets English history to you the way he sees it: his *England Since 1914* is an example. That's not the type of history that all the dons in Cambridge and Oxford will produce, but these are histories of England. I think it has been the age-old practice of historians to distill from the wealth of monographs and controversies the facts that seem to be the most salient ones. That seems to be indubitable.

Al Omari has said that the Africans discovered America in the fourteenth century, 180 years before Columbus set out—I cannot dismiss this as false, because it wasn't invented in the twentieth century. It is down there in the Arabic records right from the time of the 1310 Mali expedition sent out by King Bakary II of Mali. It behooves us today to question where that expedition *went*. Sailing in similar vessels out of the Iberian Sea and the Mediterranean, Columbus ended up not over the edge but in the New World; probably these Africans drifted on and those of them who survived landed on some island—which we don't know, but this is my hypothesis; and if historians can't use hypotheses, then they should be honest and say that there is no scientific approach to history. Incidentally whether it was the Mali sailors or not, Al Omari recorded that the second expedition sailed off and never came back, and there were two attempts. Well, this should be investigated. Why do we have to worry about the fact that the Vikings discovered America and not Co-

lumbus, simply because we see some runestones on the banks of the Mississippi in Minnesota? This is healthy inquiry. Once you become complacent, I think you write yourself off. Our knowledge of the past grows with controversy and continued inquiry and investigation.

Now, as for the latter part of the question, I really don't see what I could add to what I have already said—that I don't think history should be constructed around an ideology. It seems to me that this is not what good history ought to be. If a communist in Senegal living in Paris writes a history of Senegal, he will write it as he sees it. If the government of Senegal commissions people in the University of Dakar to write a history of Senegal, of course they are going to say what the Government wants to hear, not what they think. I may refer here to the history of Liverpool and Liverpool commerce—A *Century of Liverpool Commerce* by Martin W. A. Gibson, which you might have read. Immediately after that book was published, the Manchester Chamber of Commerce commissioned two professors at Manchester University, Arthur Redford and B. W. Clapp, to write *Manchester Merchants and Foreign Trade, 1850–1939* because they didn't want to be outdone by Liverpool. You can read these books with great profit and learn about Lancashire external trade and how it was organized, but I think it would be very erroneous and dangerous to think that this is the history of Lancashire. On the other hand, if you are writing a history of Lancashire you are going to find valid material in these monographs.

So, what I am calling for here is a continuation of the type of thing you were saying—a universal history that could be used for a universal history course, which gives the accepted views and opinions of the development of Africa, Asia, and Europe and America. And where there is controversy, by all means let the students be told that there is controversy over this point. Maybe they will be the ones to find out the answers.

Essay/Discussion Questions

1. According to Boniface Obichere, what was the basis for the inadequate examination of African history? What suggestions did he offer to correct the problem?

2. Why is African history important to African American Studies and to African-descended people outside of Africa?

3. Obichere states: "Our knowledge of the past grows with controversy and continued inquiry and investigation." In view of this statement, what might be the importance of investigating the African presence in the Americas before the arrival of Christopher Columbus?

The Atlantic Slave Trade and Slavery: Some Interpretations of Their Significance in the Development of the United States and the Western World

C. L. R. JAMES

Every people, every race, has passed through a stage of slavery. That which ought to be a commonplace of history has been obscured, corrupted and ignored by the injection of slavery into a modern and advanced society like the United States. It would be not only inextricably confusing but impossible to attempt any summary of the infinite varieties of slavery in past ages. However, it is useful to bear in mind two of these varieties. The first is the systematic breeding and selling of their own children into slavery by the backward peoples of Northern Europe. They traded with the highly developed civilization of Rome, even when Rome was ruled by the papacy. The second is the oft-repeated sneer that the magnificent civilization of ancient Greece was based on slavery. Slavery did not help to build the social order of Greece that laid the foundations of Western civilization in so many spheres. Rather, it was the growth of slavery which ruined ancient Greece.

Furthermore, the term "slave" did not then have the meaning it has had since the African slave-trade to the Americas. The slaves in the mines of Greece were cruelly exploited, but in Athens itself slaves could become educated and officials in the city administration, and could attend the ritual performances of the dramatic festivals. As late as the fourth century B.C., when the democracy was on the decline, Plato complained that the concept and practices of democracy were so deeply ingrained in Athenian society that not only the slaves, but the very horses and dogs walked about in the streets of Athens in a manner that proclaimed their democratic rights.

Today it would be impossible to examine the most important of all phases of slavery, African slavery in the American continents, without having some view of the slavery in

Reprinted, with permission, from John A. Williams and Charles F. Harris, eds., *Amistad: Writings in Black History and Culture*, Vintage Books, 1970.

Africa itself before the Europeans established the Atlantic slave-trade, and the African slavery which was the result of that trade. African slavery before the European slave-trade was internal For the most part it was also patriarchal. Thirty years ago, I summarized African civilization and the effects of the European slave-trade as follows:

> ... In the sixteenth century, Central Africa was a territory of peace and happy civilization. Traders travelled thousands of miles from one side of the continent to another without molestation. The tribal wars from which the European pirates claimed to deliver the people were mere sham fights; it was a great battle when half a dozen men were killed. It was on a peasantry in many respects superior to the serfs in large areas of Europe, that the slave trade fell. Tribal life was broken up and millions of detribalised Africans were let loose upon each other. The unceasing destruction of crops led to cannibalism; the captive women became concubines and degraded the status of the wife. Tribes had to supply slaves or be sold as slaves themselves. Violence and ferocity became the necessities for survival. The stockades of grinning skulls, the human sacrifices, the selling of their own children as slaves, these horrors were the product of an intolerable pressure on the African peoples, which became fiercer through the centuries as the demands of industry increased and the methods of coercion were perfected ...

Within recent decades an immense amount of research has been done on pre-European Africa. Not only does that analysis still hold its ground, but there has been added to it a conception of pre-European African history which stresses the intellectual achievements of the postwar world. In a study done for UNESCO on *Race and History,* Claude Lévi-Strauss, after a recognition of the "richness and audacity of the aesthetic invention" of primitive peoples turns to Africa:

> The contribution of Africa is more complex, but also more obscure, for it is only at a recent period that we have begun to suspect the importance of its role as a cultural melting pot of the ancient world: a place where all influences have merged to take new forms or to remain in reserve, but always transformed into new shapes. The Egyptian civilization, of which one knows the importance for humanity, is intelligible only as a common product of Asia and of Africa and the great political systems of ancient Africa, its juridical creations, its philosophical doctrines for a long time hidden from the West, its plastic arts and its music which explored methodically all possibilities offered by each means of expression are equally indications of an extraordinarily fertile past. The latter besides is directly attested to by the perfection of the ancient techniques of bronze and of ivory which surpass by far all that the West was practicing in those spheres in the same period.

Neolithic man tilled the soil, domesticated animals, invented and used tools, and lived a family life subject to certain social regulations. Claude Lévi-Strauss believed that this was the decisive moment in the history of human civilization. However, he is prepared to admit that there has been one other fundamental change in the life of civilized man. The Industrial Revolution, bringing mechanical power into use, altered the conditions of life and created a new type of society.

We can see this most dramatically in the two most important concerns of civilized man, war and revolution. Alexander the Great, Hannibal, Julius Caesar, and Napoleon each would have understood what the others were trying to accomplish on the field of battle; their strategy and tactics would have been much the same. But the moment we examine the American Civil War, military conflict breaks entirely out of the limits in which it had remained for thousands of years. The reason was the introduction of mechanical power—in the form of the railway—into war. Armies could now be five times as large as before. This larger army, with its rapidity of movement, upset the industrial and the social structure of the

nation. Today, a little more than a hundred years later, the development of industrial power imperils the very continuation of civilized life.

THE INDUSTRIAL REVOLUTION

It is the move to large-scale industry and the accumulation of great numbers of men in factories which is the starting point and the basis of Marx's theory of socialist revolution, and the contemporary nightmare of social destruction. There is no question today that the resources which initiated and established this epoch-making change in human life resulted from the Atlantic slave-trade and the enslavement of Africans in the Americas. Jean Léon Jaurès, in his history of the French Revolution, a work which is a landmark not only in the history of the Revolution, but in the writing of modern history, comments wistfully: "Sad irony of human history . . . The fortunes created at Bordeaux, at Nantes, by the slave-trade, gave the bourgeoisie that pride which needed liberty and contributed to human emancipation." But Jaurès, whose thought represented the quintessence of Social Democracy, was here limited by his preoccupation with parliamentary politics. Gaston-Martin, in his *L'Ere des*

Négriers, makes it clear that nearly all the industries which developed in France during the eighteenth century had their origin in goods or commodities destined either for the Coast of Guinea or for America. It was the capital gained from the slave trade which fertilized what became the Industrial Revolution. Though the bourgeoisie traded in many things, everything depended on the success or failure of the traffic in slaves. In *Capitalism and Slavery,* Eric Williams has demonstrated that it was in slavery and the slave trade that the power originated which created modern industry in England, making it the workshop of the world.

The overwhelming majority of historians show a curious disinclination to deal with the seminal role played by the slave trade and slavery in the creation of what distinguished Western civilization from all other civilizations. As far back as 1847, Karl Marx stated in very aggressive terms what modern civilization, and in particular the United States, owed to the enslavement of black people from Africa. Karl Marx, in 1846 in his polemical work *The Poverty of Philosophy,* made slavery in the United States the center of his comprehensive uncovering of the fires which stoked Western civilization.

> Direct slavery is just as much the pivot of bourgeois industry as machinery, credits, etc. Without slavery you have not cotton; without cotton you have no modern industry. It is slavery . . . and it is world trade that is the precondition of large-scale industry. Thus slavery is an economic category of the greatest importance.
>
> Without slavery North America, the most progressive of countries, would be transformed into a patriarchal country. Wipe North America off the map of the world, and you will have anarchy—the complete decay of modern commerce and civilization. Cause slavery to disappear and you will have wiped America off the map of nations.
>
> Thus slavery, because it is an economic category, has always existed among the institutions of the peoples. Modern nations have

been able only to disguise slavery in their own countries, but they have imposed it without disguise upon the New World.

Fifty years after Marx's statement, an American historian, a young man twenty-four years of age, tackled the question. In 1954, looking again at his doctoral dissertation written for Harvard University in 1896, *The Suppression of the African Slave Trade to the United States of America, 1638–1870,* Dr. W. E. B. Du Bois, in an apologia of two and a half pages, three times expressed his regret that when he was doing the work he had not had the benefit of any acquaintance with the works or theories of Karl Marx. Yet with his own independent, if youthful, judgment Dr. Du Bois here showed himself as far in advance of American historiography as he was to show himself in other spheres of American life.

First of all, the title of the book could be misleading. The actual attempt at suppression (1807–1825) is treated as late as Chapter Eight. What we have here is a history of the slave trade and slavery in the United States. It is true that the very first sentence of the monograph, as he calls it (197 pages of text and 98 pages of appendices), declares that he proposes to set forth the efforts from early colonial times until the present to limit and suppress the trade in slaves between Africa and America.

He first separates the Planting Colonies (the South) from the Farming Colonies (New Jersey), and then moves into the period of the Revolution. He notes that from about 1760 to 1787, there is a "pronounced effort to regulate, limit, or totally prohibit the traffic." Chapter Six deals with the Federal Convention and the spirit of compromise leading each state (i.e., in the South) to deal with the question of slavery as it pleased. Then comes a most interesting chapter where we see at work the same mind which in *Black Reconstruction in America* linked the emancipation of the slaves in 1865 to the Paris Commune in 1871, and the black struggle for freedom in 1935 to the world-wide struggle against fascism and for colonial emancipation.

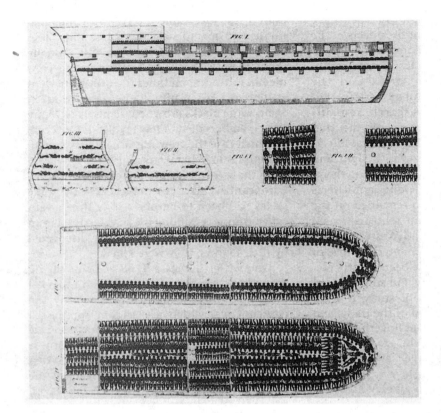

Detailed drawing of a slave ship, showing traders how to make the most efficient use of space in carrying their cargo.

Young Du Bois heads the chapter "Toussaint L'Ouverture and Anti-Slavery Effort, 1787–1807." The Haitian Revolt sharpens the debate for and against slavery in the U.S.A. It is "the main cause of two laws" and soon was "the direct instigation to a third." But despite the combined efforts of fear and philanthropy, the profits of trade won in the end.

Du Bois is pretty certain that it was the Haitian Revolution and its influence which was one of the main causes of the suppression of the slave trade by national law. But to the apathy of the federal government is now added "The Rise of the Cotton Kingdom 1820–1850." He concludes with a chapter on "The Lesson for Americans." The Constitutional Convention had avoided the issue when it had been possible to do something about it. "No American can study the connection of slavery with United States history and not devoutly pray

that his country will never have a similar social problem to solve, until it shows more capacity for such work than it has shown in the past." The last sentence of the text is even more clearly a product of moralistic thought. "From this we may conclude that it behooves nations, as well as men, to do things at the very moment when they ought to be done."

THE SOCIAL AND MORAL EFFECTS OF THE SLAVE TRADE

We can only estimate the numbers involved, but it is certain that the slave trade shifted many millions of Africans from their homeland. A conservative estimate is that 15,000,000 Africans landed after crossing the Atlantic; but some estimates give 50,000,000 and some go even higher. Further, the mortality rate on the voyage to the Americas was often high, and in addition some were killed in Africa in the raids and wars conducted to get slaves, and some died while waiting to be sold or shipped.

Effectively (and officially) the slave trade lasted three centuries, from about 1550 to 1850. Its period of greatest activity began after the middle of the seventeenth century. There have been many arguments about the effects of the trade on the African economy and population. We know it led directly to nineteenth-century colonialism in Africa and the accompanying degradation of the Africans. But an important area of research remains uninvestigated, which we can only mention here. What were the social and moral effects of slaving on the Africans who bought and sold slaves—what did they think of it themselves? What have been the long-term effects on the African peoples who remained on the continent? Our sources and scholarship are almost entirely Western, and Western thinking has governed our assessment, regardless of whether our standards have been overtly racist or antipathetic to slavery. But surely one of the most important areas of study is what Africans themselves thought of the trade, and what effect it had and perhaps lingeringly continues to have on Africa itself.

Scholars continue to argue about the effects on those taken into slavery. A plateau was reached in 1959, when Stanley Elkin examined the basis for what he called the "Sambo" stereotype of North American slave character. One of the most important bases of his argument is that the capture, voyage, sale, and adjustment to the new environment of the Africans may have created a "shock" that stripped them of their former personalities and rendered their cultural background meaningless.

Most revolts came either at the point of embarkation or between that time and actual sailing. Gaston-Martin catalogues several slave revolts on board ships, and says that he discovered fifty references to revolts, or about one every fifteen trips, in his studies of Nantes slaving. (Nantes is a French seaport.) He adds

that there were almost certainly many revolts which were never recorded, and he comments that they were very likely accepted as a normal hazard of the trade. Some revolts even took place at sea, where the slaves would perish even if they overcame the crew, for they had no idea of how to steer the ships. Ships' logs record the ferocity of these revolts. Usually they failed, with only a few slaves and crew members dead; sometimes the death toll went as high as forty or fifty. Rather than be taken again some blacks drowned themselves. Many crew members died. A few revolts did succeed, in which case the crew was usually massacred, sometimes merely taken captive.

In these revolts, captains accessed the most Europeanized slaves as the leaders—for some slaves had been to Europe at one time or another. Informers among the slaves existed from time to time; but when they were discovered by their fellows, they were killed.

One writer quotes a 1788 account saying the blacks were always on the lookout to rebel or escape. "Insurrections are frequently the consequence, which are seldom suppressed without much bloodshed. Sometimes these are successful and the whole ship's company is cut off." Basil Davidson himself adds, "When they failed to revolt before they reached the Americas, they revolted there." Of the slaves, he writes, "The best and strongest took the first or second chance to resist or revolt; the rest endured. But endurance did not mean acceptance."

Revolts might also take place in coordination with attacks by Africans on the ship or shore "warehouse." Around 1760, the *Diane* was attacked by Africans while the captives revolted. The French crew was captured and ransomed by Europeans who later handed them over to a French ship. The *Diane* was lost. The *Concorde* underwent two revolts. During the first, forty-five blacks disappeared; in the second a coordinated attack between revolting slaves and a party from land destroyed the ship and killed all the crew but one.

Death of Capt. Ferrer, the Captain of the Amistad, July, 1839.

Don Jose Ruiz and Don Pedro Montez, of the Island of Cuba, having purchased fifty-three slaves at Havana, recently imported from Africa, put them on board the Amistad, Capt. Ferrer, in order to transport them to Principe, another port on the Island of Cuba. After being out from Havana about four days, the African captives on board, in order to obtain their freedom, and return to Africa, armed themselves with cane knives, and rose upon the Captain and crew of the vessel. Capt. Ferrer and the cook of the vessel were killed; two of the crew escaped; Ruiz and Montez were made prisoners.

Once the ship had sailed, the danger of revolt was greatly diminished. Suicides were frequent among slaves who could not bear their misery or stand the idea of enslavement. Some slaves threw themselves overboard during the voyage, and there are many reports of slaves dying of nostalgia either en route or in the Americas. To combat nostalgia and simultaneously give the slaves an early recovery period from the first stage of the voyage, which was invariably the worst stretch for them, about one fifth of the Nantes slavers out of Guinea would stop off for four to six weeks at islands in the eastern Atlantic. Here the slaves could rest, get fresh food, and rebuild the strength they had lost during the first stage of the voyage. Sometimes a high rate of sickness would prompt a ship to make a stopover. "Already isolated from the continent, the Negroes, in spite of a few examples of revolts, seem less antagonistic than on land; returned to good physical condition, they better endure the two or three months at sea separating them from the American islands."

Epidemics were frequent and could kill up to half to two thirds of the cargo. The most common illnesses were scurvy, diarrhea, and various skin diseases. Insurrections, as we have seen, were still an occasional threat, and if the attempt failed masses of slaves might commit suicide together rather than submit to recapture. The mortality rate varied considerably from voyage to voyage and year to year. This is reflected in a list of mortality rates among slaves traded by Nantes shippers between 1715 and 1775. The rate ranged from 5 to 9 percent in sixteen years; from 10 to 19 percent in twenty-two years; 20 to 29 percent in fourteen years; and was 34 percent in 1733. In 1751, the year of the greatest slaving activity on the records, 10,003 Negroes were traded and 2,597 died, giving a mortality rate of 26 percent. For the total period from 1715 to 1775, 237,025 slaves were shipped and 35,727 died, giving a mortality rate of 15.1 percent.

After leaving the African coast and any stopovers, the "middle passage" began, lasting normally two or three months, though large ships might occasionally make the trip in forty days. The slaves could still die or commit suicide, though if there had been a stopover for "refreshment," the number of these deaths declined. But other dangers and the length of the middle passage eclipsed the earlier problems. Storms and calms were equally dangerous—the former because it could sink a ship, the latter because it could extend a voyage beyond the range of provisions. Pirates were a constant threat, and the frequent European wars put many enemy ships on the main sea lanes. As with the gathering of captives, a slaver's life, from his point of view, was not an easy one, and expenses could be disastrous. The degree of profit had to be calculated after several voyages, averaging out likely single losses against long-term gains. Whatever the problems, the trade was so extensive that it surely must have been profitable overall.

Treatment of the slaves on board depended a great deal on the captain. But if slavers were not systematically cruel, they were not at all benevolent.

A few writers emphasize that captains were normally not excessively cruel, for it was in their own interest to bring into port as large a live shipment as possible. but when we say "excessively," we are certainly speaking in relative terms. The slaves were never well treated; they were crowded into pens too small to stand up in. The slavers' basic doctrine was that the blacks would obey only in the face of force and terror. Fear of the slaves was the permanent psychological feature of slaver, slave trader, and slave owner. The captives were kept in irons throughout the voyages; the whips would be used for the most trivial purposes. And revolts were brutally punished. Normally only a few suspected ringleaders and examples were executed; but the manner of execution involved torture.

Upon arrival at his destination, the slaver first had to be cleared with health authorities. The inspectors were often bribable—indeed, they often refused clearance unless bribed. Sometimes they would demand that the captain disinfect his ship—buying the disinfectant in the colony, of course. A local governor who feared the captives might be dangerous could quarantine the ship under pretext of fearing a health problem. And genuine epidemics existed often enough to make genuine quarantine a necessity.

Next came port taxes. In the French colonies, Louis XV decreed that the island gover-

nors should receive a 2 percent ad valorem gratuity, half for themselves, half to be split by the two lieutenant governors. In fact this gratuity system was often used as the basis for extortion of much higher amounts. Captains who protested too much could find themselves in jail.

Official cheating of slaving captains was common, even when forbidden by royal edict. Large fees could be extorted for such things as anchorage, legal costs, registration of documents, and so on. And of course if the captain had to make calls at several ports, these expenses all were multiplied.

Captains normally tried to give their slaves refreshment to prepare them for sale. When they did not have time, they doped the slaves to give them as healthy an appearance as possible. Slavers would first get rid of their worst-looking slaves at a low price. Many speculators were prepared to take a chance on buying such slaves and hoping they would survive, reckoning a one-third survival rate as satisfactory. The slaver would receive about what he had originally paid for them.

Sometimes the sale might be held up until a propitious moment, especially if there was a glut on the slave market. Either the captain or the company's agent would handle the sale, sending out leaflets to announce the time and place, and the time when the "merchandise" could be inspected. The seller would divide his slaves up into lots of about three or four, grouping them in a way that would bring the highest bidding. The auction would either be done in the usual way—taking competing bids until the highest was reached; or else bidders would be allowed each to make one bid for an entire lot.

If the sales were transacted on board, there was a reasonable chance of suicide by some of the slaves; if on land, there was a reasonable chance of escape. Here, again, we have evidence that at least some of the slaves were not so shattered at this point that they had lost all sense of personality.

Slaves captured in raids were examined for fitness and hardiness (above). Depletion of Africans by slavers destroyed customs, cultures and mores to such an extent that Africa still has not recovered from its effects. This drawing (below) reveals the parting of mother and daughter, and a child at the breast of its mother. When the slave trade was drawing to a close, slave breeding became the method by which more slaves were propagated.

Payment was rarely in cash. Often it was on credit, and defaulted payments were frequent. Apparently noncash payments accounted for over half of the sales for Nantes slavers. At the start of the French and Indian War, they were owed 15,000,000 pounds. In order to stay on in the islands and collect their money, captains would frequently send their ships home under command of their first mates.

A second method of payment was either in merchandise or by deposit transfer at home. Most French planters kept bank accounts in France, and captains seem to have been good judges of which ones to trust. The most common method, certainly, was exchange of commodities. Either the buyer would give his goods to the seller directly, or else the buyer would write out I.O.U.'s which the captain would quickly spend on the island, buying up goods to bring home. The captains suffered some loss on the merchandise in this way—but presumably they more than made up for it when the commodities came to be sold in Europe, where they commanded very high prices.

This, then, was the slave trade. It was not easy on the slavers or on the slaves. It is notable that probably as many crew members as slaves died during the voyages. African leaders, if not ordinary free Africans, often willingly collaborated in the trade; and if they and the Europeans were out to get what they could from each other, and prepared to cheat each other where possible, it remains those who were actually enslaved who suffered the greatest miseries and hardships, and who died in vast numbers.

THE SLAVE'S LIFE

Who were the slaves? They came for the most part from West Africa, these slaves who had been stolen and taken from their homes and brought virtually nothing with them, except themselves. The slaves not only could not bring material objects with them, they could not easily bring over their older social institutions, their languages, and cultures. Coming from a large area of West Africa in which dozens upon dozens of distinct peoples lived, with their own languages, social relations, cultures, and religions, these Africans were jumbled together on board the slave ships, "seasoned" by the middle passage and then seasoned again in their first years in the New World.

For the slave brought himself; he brought with him the content of his mind, his memory. He thought in the logic and language of his people. He recognized as socially significant that which he had been taught to see and comprehend; he gestured and laughed, cried, and held his facial muscles in ways that had been taught him from childhood. He valued that which his previous life had taught him to value; he feared that which he had feared in

Africa; his very motions were those of his people and he passed all of this on to his children. He faced this contradictory situation in a context into which he was thrown among people of different African backgrounds. All Africans were slaves, slaves were supposed to act in a specific way. But what was this way? There was no model to follow, only one to build.

The slave from Africa was denied the right to act out the contents of his mind and memory—and yet he *had* to do this. How was this contradiction resolved? What were the new forms created in the context of slavery?

A new community was formed; it took its form in the slave quarters of the plantations and the black sections of the cities. In the United States, this community developed its own Christian church, one designed to meet the needs of slaves and Afro-American freedmen in the New World. It had its own system of communication based on the reality of the plantation. It had its own value system, reflective of the attitudes of African peasants, but at the same time owing its allegiance to dominant American modes. It had its own language patterns, because of the isolation of the plantation system from steady European linguistic influences. West African words and speech patterns were combined with the speech of the eighteenth-century Scotch-Irish.

This black community was the center of life for the slaves; it gave them an independent basis for life. The slaves did not suffer from rootlessness—they belonged to the slave community, and even if they were sold down the river they would find themselves on new plantations. Here, people who shared a common destiny would help them find a life in the new environment.

Each plantation was a self-sufficient unit. The slaves worked at all the skills necessary to maintain the plantation in working order and keep at a minimum the expense of importing necessary items from England. Slave blacksmiths manufactured everything from nails to plowshares. Coopers made the hoops around the tobacco barrels. The clothing they wore was turned out by slave shoemakers, dyers, tanners, and weavers. The slave artisan moved from one task to another as the need arose.

Skilled labor also took the slave off the plantation. Black pilots poled the rafts laden with tobacco from the tributaries of the river to its mouth, where the ship was anchored; black seamen conducted the ferries across Virginia's rivers to transport new settlers. Many planters found it more profitable to hire out their skilled black workmen for seventy-five to two hundred dollars a year. This black craftsman living away from the plantation was allowed seventy-five cents a week as his allowance for food and board. When the colonies engaged in their war with England for independence, all imports from the mother country ceased, Crude factories were started and slaves were used to work them; also, out of the mines they dug lead, a necessary ingredient in the manufacture of bullets.

The tedium of tobacco cultivation was worse than the exhaustion of simple physical labor. Cotton, which succeeded tobacco as the plantation's output, had to be chopped with great care when the young plant had no more than three or four leaves.

Overworked field hands would take off to the nearby weeds or swamps where they would lay out for a time. At night they would steal back to the slave quarters for food and information about what the master intended to do about their absence. In the swamps of the eastern section of North Carolina, runaways were employed by black lumbermen or the poor whites and could raise their own children for a time. The master, who didn't know the hideouts as well as the slaves did, let it be known through a word passed on to the slave quarters that he was prepared to negotiate for less work and no whippings if only his precious laborers would return.

The slaves fought to set their own tempo and rhythm of work. Says Frederick Douglass:

There is much rivalry among slaves, at times, as to which can do the most work and masters generally seek to promote such rivalry. But some of them were too wise to race each other very long. Such racing, we had the sagacity to see, was not likely to pay. We had times out for measuring each others strength, but we knew too much to keep up the competition so long as to produce an extra-ordinary days work. We knew that if by extra-ordinary exertion, a large quantity of work was done in one day, the face becoming known to the master, the same would be expected of us every day. This thought was enough to bring us to a dead halt whenever so much excited for the race.

There was very little of the slave's life that he could call his own. In the slave quarters at night there was a lowering of the mask that covered the day's labors. Bantering and mimicry, gossiping and laughter could be unrestrained. House servants regaled other members of the "row"—some of whom had never set foot in the big house—with tales of "master" and "missus," would "take them off" in speech and gesture so faithful that the less privileged would shake with laughter.

Besides the oppression of the master himself, his laws and his overseers, the slaves were oppressed by their limited knowledge of the world outside the plantation. Masters felt that a slave who learned how to read and write would lose his proficiency at picking worms off tobacco leaves or at chopping cotton, so thoroughly had slavery separated thought and feeling from work. But the capacities of men were always leaping out of the confinements of the system. Always with one eye cocked toward the door, the slaves learned how to read and write, thus they attained that standard—besides the accumulation of money, tobacco, cotton, and lands—by which society judged the standing of its members. The Bible was the most readily available book; its wide and varied use by the slave would have made the founders of Christianity proud. It was a course in the alphabet, a first reader, and a series of lessons in the history of mankind.

The capacities of men were always leaping out of the confinements of the system. Written passes, which slaves were required to carry on their person when away from the plantation, could be made up by those who had learned how to read and write. Deciphering the alphabet opened new avenues to the world. A primary achievement of the slaves as a class is that they fashioned a system of communication—an illegal, underground, grapevine telegraph which would stand the test of an emergency.

REBELLIONS AND ESCAPE

When hostilities broke out between the thirteen colonies and the King of England, the British field commander in the South offered freedom to every slave who would enter his army. In Virginia alone, thirty thousand fled their labors; the bitter comment of a slaveholder points up this situation: "Negroes have a wonderful art of communicating intelligence among themselves; it will run several hundred miles in a fortnight." There was such a large proportion of slaves in the state, that South Carolina did not even dare enter the War of Independence for fear of what its laboring force would do. It lost twenty-five thousand nevertheless. Across the South every fifth slave fled toward the British army.

An independent national state was being set up by an American Congress. The very air became filled with expressed passions of human rights, liberties, dignity, equality, and the pursuit of happiness. One of its effects on the slaves was seen on the night of August 30, 1800. Over one thousand slave rebels gathered some six miles from Richmond, capital city of Virginia, the state which was to produce four of the first five American Presidents. All through the spring of that year the slaves prepared their own arms, including five hundred bullets, manufactured in secret. Each Sunday

for months, Gabriel Prosser entered the city, noting its strategic points and possible sources of arms and ammunition. Their plan was to proclaim Virginia a Negro state. If the merchants of Richmond would yield their fortunes to the rebels their lives would be spared and they would be feted at a public dinner.

On the night appointed for the march a heavy rain had fallen, making the road into Richmond impassable. The delay gave the stunned authorities an opportunity to mobilize themselves. Some forty slaves were arrested and put on trial. They revealed no names of other participants. Some estimates placed the extent of the rebellion at ten thousand slaves, others put the figure as high as sixty thousand. The demeanor and remarks of the prisoners on trial—Gabriel: "I have nothing more to offer than what General Washington would have had to offer, had he been taken and put on trial by them. I have adventured my life to obtain the liberty of my countrymen . . ."

In this early period the slave who ran away was most often a skilled craftsman, a man with confidence of making his way in the world. As described by a newspaper advertisement of the day:

Run away from the subscriber's farm, about seven miles from Anapolis, on the 8th instant; two slaves Will and Tom; they are brothers. Will, a straight tall well-made fellow, upwards of six feet high, he is generally called black, but has a rather yellowish complexion, by trade a carpenter and a cooper, and in general capable of the use of tools in almost any work; saws well at the whip saw, about thirty years of age. When he speaks quick he stammers a little in his speech. Tom, a stout well-made fellow, a bright mulatto, twenty-four years of age, and about five feet nine or ten inches high; he is a complete hand at plantation work and can handle tools pretty well . . . they have a variety of clothing, and it is supposed they will not appear abroad in what they wear at home. Will writes pretty well, and if he and his brother are not furnished with passes from others they will not be lost for them, but upon proper examination may be discovered to be forged. These people it is imagined are gone for Baltimore as Tom has a wife there. . .

Except in a general way he could not be sure of the direction of his travels, guiding himself by the stars and by the moss which grew on the shady side of the trees. In earlier days the safest places of concealment were the nearby swamps, the neighboring Indian tribes and Spanish Florida. The long military arm of the slavocracy eventually reached into all these temporary outposts of freedom and incorporated them into slavery. Then soldiers returning from the War of 1812 brought the news that slavery was outlawed in Canada. The route of flight began to cut across the Kentucky mountain ranges and the Atlantic seacoast.

John Parker, a free black man from Ripley, Ohio, considered it below his dignity to ask any white man how to conduct slaves to freedom; he was responsible for the successful passage of one thousand runaways, but left no memoirs as to how he carried out his work.

In later years the work of the scout took him into the Deep South rather than await the knock on the door. On her expeditions, Harriet Tubman would take the precaution of starting on Saturday night so that they would be well along their journey before they were advertised. Harriet often paid another black person to follow the man who posted the descriptions of her companions and to tear them down. The risks of taking along different types of people in one group had to be considered. Babies were sometimes drugged with paregoric. She sometimes strengthened the fainthearted by threatening to use her revolver and declaring ". . . you go on or you die . . . dead (N)egroes tell no tales . . ."

As with practical people everywhere, everything was done with the materials at hand. An iron manikin in front of the home of Judge Piatt marked an interrupted station; the judge was hostile to the activity, but his wife was an enthusiastic undergrounder. A flag in the hand of the manikin signaled that the judge was not home and that his house had become a temporary station on the road. For disguise one runaway was provided simply with a gardening tool placed on his shoulder. He marched through town in a leisurely way like a man going to work somebody's garden, left the tool in a selected thicket at the edge of town, and proceeded on his way.

The Underground Railroad in the period of the 1840's grew so saucy that it advertised itself publicly as the only railroad guaranteed not to break down. Multiple routes were the key to the practical success of the railroad. It all came into being after the period of the Founding Fathers had definitively come to an end. The men of education, the leading figures of the Revolution, Washington, Jefferson, Adams, Hancock, Hamilton, Lafayette, and Kosciusko, all expressed opposition to slavery in their private conversations and correspondence. But their chief fear was that pushing antislavery to the fore might permanently divide the country into antagonistic sections.

Washington accurately described the sentiment in certain parts of the country after he himself had lost a slave in New England. "The gentleman in whose care I sent him has promised every endeavor to apprehend him; but it is not easy to do this when there are numbers who would rather facilitate the escape of slaves than apprehend them when they run away."

In the early formation of the Underground Railroad, another group whom the runaway touched with his fire was the Quakers. When they arrived in America to escape persecution, the prosperous trade in slaves corrupted even the most tender of consciences. Not being interested in politics, and prohibited by religious belief from being diverted by the theater, sports, or drink, the Quakers became highly successful businessmen and farmers. The Quakers were prominent and influential people and could afford to rely on the letter of the law which in Northern states had declared slavery illegal.

Having established the principle, effective organization for antislavery work came naturally to a group whose life had been drawn tightly together for hundreds of years as a religious sect. By 1820 there were some four thousand fugitive slaves in the Quaker stronghold of Philadelphia and all advertisements for runaways disappeared from Pennsylvania newspapers.

Free blacks, Quakers, and New Englanders, linked up to each other, conducted the Atlantic coast route of Underground Railroad operations Men of a different stamp initiated a section of the western route. At the turn of the century the back-country farmer of Virginia and the Carolinas suffered much from the poverty of his land. The state legislatures were in the control of coastal planters and their lawyers; new government taxes and old debts magnified his poverty. He freed himself of all these burdens by migrating westward into the wilderness.

The slaves who accompanied this first great tide of migration, which depopulated Virginia of two hundred thousand people, were as scattered as their masters. On the early frontier there was less consciousness of their slave status. They helped in the household chores, building cabins and protecting them from Indian attack. Often they were the boatmen, whose arrival was as welcome in the settlement as the ringing of a postman in a modern apartment house.

The runaway slave heightened the powers of the popular imagination. Here was a figure who not only fled oppressive institutions, but successfully outwitted and defied them. And his flight was to the heart of civilization, not away from it; he was a universal figure whose life was in turn adventurous, tragic, and humorous.

The runaway, freed from the disabilities of slavery, was in the second and third decades of the nineteenth century coming into close contact with another highly specialized group of people—the intellectuals. The thinking of intellectuals is characterized by the fact that they view matters whole and in general, however one-sidedly and abstractly. This jamming up of two diverse elements—the black man who supposedly had no civilization in the range of his existence, and the white intellectual in whom society had placed the whole heritage of civilization—produced those works that reminded people who gave thought to the slave held in bondage that they were themselves intimately bound with him for life.

THE ABOLITION MOVEMENT

The antislavery movement was produced by the specific relation of blacks and whites during the first third of the nineteenth century. It is a fantastic phenomenon climaxed by the central phenomenon of all American history, the Civil War. Writers offer various explanations, but after a certain amount of reflection it becomes clear that abolition must be seen as an absolutely necessary stage in making America a distinct civilization, rather than just one more piece of boundaried territory in the mosaic of the world's geography.

Abolition is the great indicator of parallel movements before the Civil War and after. History really moves when the traditionally most civilized section of the population— in this case New Englanders representing the longest American line of continuity with the English tradition of lawful sovereignty— joins as coequals with those without whose labor society could not exist for a day—in this case the plantation chattel. Otherwise, history stays pretty much the same, or worse yet, repeats itself. Such was the case of the independent lay preachers in the Great English Revolution, who joined with the apprentices and day laborers; the French intelligentsia in conjunction with peasants and slum proletarians of royalist France; the Russian intellectuals meeting on certain grounds with factory workers under a Czar. In all these instances history moved forward with lasting impress.

Abolition, itself an important instance of democracy, took upon itself the extension of a certain practice and mode of national behavior. Much of the mode of national behavior was based upon regional considerations—the great potential for abolition was the Southern slave in flight to freedom from plantation labor. Then there was the firmest base of abolition extant, the free black communities of Northern city and town. New York City, for a time, provided heavy financing. Garrison's Massachusetts was becoming an antislavery fortress and the rest of New England followed, in various degrees. Children of New England had settled in the fine agricultural flatlands of Ohio and upstate New York; a momentous development as "free soil" was prepared to clash with slave expansion appetites. Pennsylvania housed an antislavery diffused with Quakerized quietist feelings.

Without the self-expressive presence of the free blacks in the cities, embodying in their persons the nationally traumatic experience of bondage and freedom, antislavery would have been a sentiment only, a movement remote and genteel in a country known as impetuous and volatile. The bulk of subscribers to Garrison's *The Liberator* were blacks in New York, Boston, and Philadelphia. It was the publicity surrounding the revolt of Nat Turner which guaranteed that Garrison, the white advocate of immediate abolition, would become a household word. The independent conventions of free blacks were anterior to the rise of Garrison and his friends. The succession of slave personalities delivered by the Underground Railroad would eventually lead to black political independence from Garrison himself.

Ohio was the scene in the 1840's of the "Hundred Convention"—political life as daily fare, with regional figures turning into nationally representative ones: Douglass, the self-emancipated slave by way of Baltimore; Garrison, who hardly had left New England before except to visit neighboring New York or far-off merrie old England; these two together spoke themselves hoarse and into general exhaustion. This now-settled middle frontier, this venerable Old Northwest, was clamoring to hear about the state of the nation from true figures of national stature, since nothing more was heard from the doughfaces in Congress sitting on the hundreds of thousands of petitions pleading for justice to the slave, and discussing the role of free settlers in a democracy.

Impending war with Mexico was a spur to far-reaching conclusions. The revived National Negro Conventions listened to a proposal for a general strike by the slave laborers of the South, who would act as a human wall barring the United States Army from invading Mexican territory and turning it into a slave planting domain. The proposal lost by one vote.

Sophisticated prejudice tells us that *Uncle Tom's Cabin* by Harriet Beecher Stowe is another vast mistake! In impact and implications marking off the hour and the decade of its arrival it rang true; in universal aspect, clear. The average worker competing with the free black man for a job and a place to live, and wrestling with his prejudices all the while, went to see the play and wept upon his identification with the slave runaway. Where formal government failed on the slavery question, people reached for a government which the Greeks had introduced so very many years earlier: that of popular drama—which the city-state then made sure everyone could see for free—so that whatever they thought of politics they could see, through the form of dramatic representation, principles, conditions, and resolutions, and sense from that emotional experience where a whole society was going. Mere political representation was succeeded by a more intense social reproduction, a more popular accurate representation; in book form, *Uncle Tom's Cabin* circulated more widely through the whole of the nineteenth century than any other, with the sole exception of that book of books, the Bible.

And if it was the running debates with Stephen A. Douglas which elevated Abraham Lincoln from the legislator's semiobscurity to national star-fire, who or what besides abolition had initiated the debate, fixing free discussion of nearly obscured cruelties on a Mississippi cotton field as the nation's prime business; set forth the concrete choices, which no mere election could decide, on the future of mid-nineteenth-century America? And if the abolitionists' method had so elevated Lincoln, what shall we say of their achievement in turning each runaway slave, now threatened with kidnapping under a new and permanent sectional compromise, into a monument either to the American's love of liberty or acquiescence to captivity? Before abolition enabled Lincoln to hallow his name, it inscribed Shadrach and Anthony Burns and Dred Scott onto the heavens for the whole world to read the American future through them.

The leading charge against abolition in the 1850's was aimed at its nearly absolute trust in the uninterrupted processes of civilization. The main critique centered upon Garrison and Phillips' endorsing—before civil war broke out—the secession of the South, confident that slavery, separated from federal protection, must die.

THE CIVIL WAR

The Civil War was a corrective of the notorious nineteenth-century optimism which trusted free speech and free press and the industriousness of unchatteled labor to push authoritarianism of every familiar type over that same cliff where the vestiges of feudal relations had been shattered or left to hang for dear life.

Confronted by preslavery compromises which were a source of infinite corruption, abolition gave obeisance to certain eternal principles: themselves corollaries of the civilizing process at a certain stage. Growing transcending morality titled "the higher law" would overwhelm all momentary deviousness, nullify all expedients and prearrangements disguising themselves as pillars of the Federal Union.

Belief in the morality of "the higher law" was hardly an empty absolute, devoid of content and barren of result. It was a driving impetus separating democracy in politics from a growing "hunkerism," mere hankering after public office and governmental seat-warmings which dulled the very sense of social accountability and paled before the historical momentousness of American existence.

The years of Civil War show what might have been done much earlier during the War for Independence itself when this nation was first born, and egalitarian feelings were at a zenith. But then there had been no antislavery organization. The unity of the young nation, monarchies all, had taken a certain turn at the Constitutional Convention and elsewhere, indicating that the semblance of national solidity could be maintained only if the slave kept his back bent to his labor; the North and South, East and West would not divide, and foreign enemies would wait in vain for internal weakness as the signal to spring upon their prey, the New World as distinguished from the old. But national unity excluded the black from independence; national prosperity was guaranteed by subordinating the laborer to his labor. The very existence of abolitionists during the next climactic phase of this very same question—Civil War—simply insured that the slave would not be lost sight of no matter how much the government tried to lose sight of him.

The destruction of the Colonizationists earlier was the main factor staying the hand of the government which wanted to colonize blacks, freed men, even in the midst of, and because of, the tensions of Civil War to avoid disputations as to their American destiny.

On the universal effect of American abolition: it helped free the Russian serf on the other side of the world—but not directly. Indirectly, it is clear enough if we go by stepping-stone geography. Harriet Beecher Stowe's book was banned in Italy as an incitement to the peasantry. But the leading Russian publication of the intellectual exiles translated the whole work as a free supplement for all subscribers. Keep in mind, too, that from the time of Peter the Great, Russia had been trying to make its way through the front door of world civilization. Add to this a fact of international power politics: When England and France threatened to join the South, Russia shifted its weight to the North. In the middle of the Civil War the Russian fleet showed up in New York harbor, a great ball was thrown and a festive time was had by all. Abolition of serfdom there and of slavery here occurred almost simultaneously.

Something should be said about the white American worker in regard to abolition. Some were antislavery, some were not. Skilled workers, proud of their craft which brought them a measure of independence, were by and large antislavery. The unskilled, fearing possible competition from the blacks, inclined toward neutrality or gave in to caste prejudice. However, skilled or unskilled, the worker in America was an ardent democrat. No matter how much he suspected another man might take his job, he could not develop a great affection for plantation life as the prototype of American life as a whole.

Abolitionists were not only concerned with the rights of blacks, free and slave, they were concerned with their education. The abolitionist created the first integrated education in the United States—including higher education. And when they did not create integrated education they conducted classes and schools for the ex-slaves, schools partially staffed by black teachers. The abolitionists were at the center of the educational reforms and changes of this period in the United States. In schools for Negro children they experimented with improved methods of education.

But more. They fought not only for the emancipation of Negroes and the improvement of the lives of freedmen. They fought for the emancipation of women, their education, and their own self-development. Oberlin College, the first college to accept Negroes in the United States, was also the first college to accept women in the United States, becoming the first coeducational institution of higher learning.

In their struggle for women's rights, a struggle that went on inside and outside of the movement, abolitionists set in motion the liberation of women—and consequently of men. What Margaret Fuller and other great female abolitionists were trying to establish was their right to create relations with men in which they were not in effect the chattel of their husbands through the marriage contract, as slaves were chattel in the grip of property holders.

The abolitionists were involved in a crucial way in the most significant struggles for human emancipation that were going on in the United States: the abolition of capital punishment, prison reform, attacks on established religion in the name of purified religion, work for the rights of new waves of immigrants and better treatment of American Indians, and the movement to abolish war. Though they often differed among themselves, and were very often confused in the way that people are who are going forward, there is a very direct development from the Declaration of Independence to the abolitionists' efforts to Lincoln's understanding that the Civil War was about whether government of the people, by the people, and for the people would perish from the earth.

THE SLAVE COMMUNITY

It must be said that the slave community itself was the heart of the abolitionist movement. This is a claim that must seem most extraordinarily outrageous to those who think of abolitionism as a movement which "was unique, in the sense that, for symmetry and precision of outline, nothing like it had ever previously been seen." The element of order in the barbarism was this: the rationalization of a labor force upon which the whole process of colonization depended had the African at its most essential point. If he had not been able to work or sustain himself or learn the language or maintain cooperation in his social life, the whole question of America as a distinct civilization could never have arisen. We might be then talking about a sort of New Zealand or perhaps Canada.

The native American Indian was migratory in his habits and a hunter in his relation with nature. But the slave had to be an African laborer, a man accustomed to social life, before he could ever become a profitable grower of cotton or tobacco—the vital element required before America could claim that it had salvaged something from the wilderness. Something which could be extended to the point where it would win recognition as a landmark in man's emergence from subservience to any laws of nature.

The man who made it possible, and we do not know if he knew he was making it possible, was the transported African. Rationalization of the labor supply was tied in with rationalization of production itself. Planters in Louisiana would weigh the pros and cons of working slaves to death in the hazardous work of the rice paddies as against protecting the slave from excessive labor in order to maintain the interest in him as property. The long letters George Washington wrote on the organization of labor on his plantation represent merely one side. The exchange of letters between Thomas Jefferson and Benjamin Banneker, the surveyor of what was to become Washington, D.C., about the propensities and capacities of black people enslaved and otherwise is the other side of the same phenomenon: the recognition that for reasons both clear and obscure the fate of America had depended upon the blacks as laborers. This was to be argued out in the antislavery movement at a higher level, and in the midst of the Civil War and Reconstruction. It is also a seemingly

inescapable fact to everybody, but historians have managed to escape it. That is not altogether a surprise. The writing of history comes about at a period when men think about their activity so as to record it in a more permanent form. To give the slave his actual historical due is to alter one's notion about the course of civilization itself. If, for example, each plantation had to strive to be self-sufficient as a unit, it was the skilled and semi-skilled black who would make it so.

The runaway slave fled to the North without compass or definite point of destination, without being blessed like Columbus by Queen Isabella selling her jewels for the voyage, or like the pilgrims to Plymouth Rock—members of a church soon to make a revolution affecting all of England and Ireland; or like pioneers into the wilderness, trying to set a distance between themselves and civilization. If, as can be later demonstrated, the flight of the runaway slave from the South is seen as setting in motion a whole series of forces, which no other class of people, no mere party or political sect, no church or newspaper could succeed in animating, then the whole configuration of America as a civilization automatically changes before our eyes. The distinguishing feature of the slave was not his race but the concentrated impact of his work on the extensive cultivation of the soil, which eventually made possible the transition to an industrial and urban society.

The triumph of slavery, the negative recognition that the slave received in every work sphere shows how little the South or skilled workers themselves sometimes could tolerate the black as an artisan. In prebellum America he had to be driven out of trade after trade before the assertion could be demonstrated that the black man is fit for nothing more than brutish labor with its inevitable consequence.

Historically one can now begin almost anywhere to show what civilization meant to the slave as a preliminary to showing what the slaves meant to civilization. The natural form of organization was the work gang during the day and the slave quarters at night. The large scale of cultivation required for a profitable export crop guaranteed social connections for the slave even if he was isolated from the centers of "civilization" by the rural surroundings.

But the first specific form of slave organization was the fraternal association which was organized to accompany to their permanent resting place those caught up in life's mortal coils. Small coins were saved for accomplishing that occasion in at least minimal style. The slave was no more afraid to die than is or was any other mortal; he was fearful of dying unaccompanied by those with whom he had associated in the fullness of his life.

Given a holiday, that is, an occasion, the slave was, like most working humans up to this day, his own person. It was for naught that the defenders of the planter's way of life feared the effect of Fourth of July oratory. They might just as well have feared the Christianity in Christmas. It was not only intellectually that everything universal in sentiment panicked the "peculiar institution." It was the concentration of people all experiencing the unbridgeable gap between their arduous daily toil and the exceptional holiday from work—with the to-ing and the fro-ing from plantation to plantation, the arrival of guests and the spreading of news—which brought about the system of slave patrollers and written passes across the South.

We are dealing with matters of individual skill and social impulse. Small equivalents of the strike action took place at work. Flight to the neighboring woods, followed by messages trailed back to the work area showed that the blacks knew above all that, even if despised for race, they were necessary—vital to a labor process geared to the agricultural season. Feigning of illness was a commonplace; indeed, one simple definition of the abolition of slavery is that a man or woman need not go to work when incapacitated. This absenteeism may

seem of no great import by itself, but the diaries and records of the slavemasters show it to be a matter of grave concern. Everybody knew what was involved in the work process.

And the blacks knew what was involved in their day of rest. The growth of an autonomous black church draws up a balance sheet on historical Christianity. It is not finished yet, but if Christianity, as some assert, brought the principle of personality into a world that knew no such thing, and in the person of a simple carpenter who later recruited an equally simple fisherman and so on, the climax of that primitive church was the mass joining together of a population considered as so much flesh to be traded and hands to be worked and backs to be bent or broken under the lash. To the whites religion may have meant a buttress to conscience. To the blacks it meant a social experience out of which would come the active principle of personality: the black preacher.

In the more practical workings of the plantation, the slave owners themselves discovered that the position of foreman or driver was one which fewer and fewer whites measured up to in personal stature. So that in the decade before the Civil War there was a wholesale increase in the number of black overseers. Though it did not mean that race prejudice on the part of the slave owners had changed one whit, this problem of supervision was proof of the demoralizing effect black laborers had upon those who not only considered themselves superior to the slave's lot but had the weapons and the authority to put their superiority into momentary practice. Most white overseers went even before the slave system fell into the dust of Civil War. And by a healthy process of circularity, the fictional summations of the type, the Simon Legrees of the world, were portrayed with such effectiveness that it stimulated the movement toward that system which produced such monsters wholesale. The important point of the slave's contribution to civilization is that he recognized and did battle with the slavery system every day before, long before, white audiences would stare with horror at the representation on stage or in a book.

There is also the matter of the link-ups of the plantation to the outside world. Blacks were the boatmen and teamsters of that day in the South. They would have been the longshoremen as well, but were driven out. Simply by driving the master's coach around they learned of the outside world and brought back information to the slave community. It was known in some of the deepest haunts of the South that there was some kind of underground which would transport a runaway from one hiding place to another if he would but risk the trip.

Indeed, if by virtue of the brutishness and isolation of his situation the slave were himself a brute, how then could he make contact with such varying and even opposing sections of the population as he did? Harriet Tubman had a rapt listener in the philosopher Ralph Waldo Emerson, and Frederick Douglass in governor—and later Presidential candidate—William Seward. William Wells Brown could speak to all size groups, from two hundred to two hundred thousand people across Europe. It was not a matter of dispute about the capacity of the Negro; it was not even the great political debates about the future of America—slave or free. It was something so concrete, so easy to overlook and yet so broad in its consequences: The black man was a social being, in some senses the most highly social product of the United States. This was not necessarily due to skin color, but to the close relation between labor and society that he experienced more than did planters, ethnic immigrants, religious societies, pioneering settlements and their human products, political parties and their candidates.

THE EFFECTS OF BLACKS ON SOCIAL ISSUES

That link of labor and society took on national and even international proportions.

Starting from obscure places which nobody ever heard of or even wanted to hear, it became writ large as the experience of slavery intertwined with everything else—politics, diplomacy, commerce, migration, popular culture, the relation between the sexes, the question of labor and civilization in the future of America as a whole. The black man was not in any popularity contest as to who most represented this new man—this undefined American—who so intrigued the Europeans. He was something more: a self-appointed minister with nothing but experience, social experience, to guide him toward those qualities most universally recognizable in the ordinary people—some of whom are still tied to the land in Europe; some recently incorporated into proliferating industry; some hearkening to the American experience; some settling matters with crowns and courts in their Old World countries. The black man was the supreme example not just of how to rise in the world but of how to raise the world toward his own level. He inherited the Declaration of Independence which the plantation plutocracy mocked. In politics, Frederick Douglass took the Constitution as an antislavery document when his own abolition colleagues, Wendell Phillips and William Lloyd Garrison, set the match to it. The runaway slave, Dred Scott, threw the Chief Justice of the Supreme Court (and the country as a whole) into confusion on whether slavery was a national or regional issue. The black man was not afraid to declare war on war, for instance the conflict with Mexico over Texas in 1846. He could link himself to movements for temperance in drink or for the right of women to divorce or to the nonpayment of rents by upper New York State farmers.

It was training in social labor which gave blacks the opportunity to increasingly affect all social questions of their day. It was their concrete ability to turn from the faculties used in physical work to the powers of speech and other forms of self-expression which made certain of the ex-slaves the astonishing figures they were. After he drew two hundred thousand people to hear him in Europe, William Wells Brown then returned to a port near the Great Lakes, between America and Canada, to help fugitive slaves across the water, unite families, violating the mere boundaries of national existence. In addition he printed a paper announcing the uniting of families, the successes and sometimes failures of the underground travelers, their adventures and misadventures; and denouncing the "peculiar institution" and all those who would compromise with it, thinking they could thereby escape compromising themselves.

The startling challenge to current notions about civilization was presented by the slaves, as soon as they won the public's ear, on the familiar matter of conscience. The contribution of the blacks was that type of social experience—whether it was lyceum, church, or Underground Railroad—which challenged one set of social institutions with a social impact of a most original kind. Doomed by slavery to impersonality, the ex-slave responded with a personality and personal force that had the most obvious social implications and conclusions. Condemned to seasonal labor, and the rhythm and routine determined thereby, the blacks carried on agitation in and out of season until the body politic came to recognize that the country could no longer survive as it was; could survive only by embarking on an uncharted course of slave confiscation and Southern reconstruction. After having been isolated by slavery in provincial fixity, the runaway traversed national boundaries and oceanic waters. Graded by the abolition movement itself as fit only to tell slavery as an atrocity tale, Frederick Douglass and others insisted on publishing their own political policies. This is a long way from the reflex response to slavery by a disturbed conscience. It is a social impact on all media that distinguishes civilization from barbarism. The impact of the slave labor system upon the South

as a distinct region has a number of aspects clearly visible to this day.

THE UNIQUENESS OF THE SOUTHERN PLANTATION

The plantation was an organized community that was part of a larger regional configuration, but given the isolation concomitant with the rural character of slave society, the social stamp upon the individual, particularly the slave himself, guaranteed certain results. The internal economic principle of the plantation was self-sufficiency. To the slavemaster this meant insularity: foreign immigration mainly excluded; missionary society activity suspect (including the riding preachers who would as likely as not be antislavery); no lyceum or lecture circuit on any extensive scale; no compulsory elementary or secondary education; little exercise of the faculty of logical speculation. For a break in the routine of plantation life there were visits to the North, often no further than the river port city of Cincinnati; or politics in the state capital or in Washington, D.C., actually a Southern city.

To a large extent, certain of the above characteristics were true of America as a whole, or at least of its western part. Especially the smaller Southern planters had certain characteristics in common with the yeomanry of the American Northwest: the need to create isolated pockets of white habitation in a land belonging to the Indians, the establishment of paths into the wilderness, the harsh life for the women of the family, the backbreaking toil in wresting some socially productive result from the natural surroundings, and the independence of habit and speech that is the inevitable result in people living under these conditions.

The dialectical set of connections of the South to the old Northwest is both genuinely subtle and profound. Both were agrarian areas, with the Mississippi and other rivers serving as the turnstiles to ports and citified places.

Other similarities were the suspiciousness toward all those outside the isolated region where one's house and cultivated areas and perhaps hunting grounds were located; the tightness of the family and usually its patriarchal basis; the shortage of monies and credit, such that life frequently remained, generally according to the season, on a subsistence level, with only the holiday season to punctuate with some enjoyment above the everyday standard.

Further, there is the historical connection. All of American settlement, at its origins, proceeded in the same manner for both inland planters and Northern yeomanry, and their pioneering ways continued right up to the Civil War. In that sense Southern rural inhabitants were "these new men," the Americans who so intrigued the European observer often skeptical of America as (1) a civilization and (2) a viable nationality. Thus if the black man has been left out of so many history books, if the controversy over the significance of slavery to the South seemed until very recently a matter of no great moment, it is because a certain aspect of American historical continuity seemed to justify itself and no mere racist conspiracy of silence could accomplish what seems to have been imbedded within that historical aspect. To which must be added the fundamental matter of political organization and the effect of the South on certain basic institutions by which an organized society emerged out of the natural wilderness. The individual planter was conditioned not only by pioneering inland to new territories; he had to become an individualist with a social authority larger than the boundaries of his plantation. The reasons are as follows: The South had been originally colonized by British trading companies licensed by the Crown. The Northern settlements were more likely to be religious colonies or fur-trading outposts. So that from the very start the planter, who had to be in charge of the practical and hazardous work of founding some lasting economic basis

in the New World, was thrown into conflict with the concentrated mercantile capitalism of the metropolitan colonizing land. To put it succinctly, the anticapitalist bias of the Southerner was there from the day of his birth. It was no small thing. The former slave—the supposedly emancipated black—became, for lack of credit, a sharecropper. This happened because all of Southern history had prepared somebody for that role, and the people at the bottom of the social ladder fell into it and remained there, some unto this day. To make up for their embattlement as regards the shortage of capital, the Southerners would compensate with (a) their geography, strategically considered, (b) the fixed position of the main section of the laboring force—the slaves, and (c) a type of politics which would guarantee the viability of (a) and (b).

All these things add up to a "nativist" outlook that is not that of country bumpkins, but one characterized by a sophistication that was constantly changing by the very reason of its taking place in a nineteenth- and late eighteenth-century setting that was becoming rapidly modernized. Slavery is a peculiar institution not only because of its horrors but because it was something-unto-itself. The Southern attitude seems so often a matter of temperament—unformed character expressing itself against a general trend in worldly affairs which opposed the fixed investment of wealth in land and human chattel. In other words, the South produced "personality" rather than minds of singular or original power. But the personalities are of a similar and sustaining force: Patrick Henry, Jefferson, Jackson, Calhoun, Clay, Stonewall Jackson, Tom Watson, Huey Long are personages who will interest the public imagination until possibly they are surpassed by the characterization of the lives of the obscure slaves and indigent blacks. This tends to be the ongoing matter of interest in our own day.

There is a material basis for the Southern production of men and women of outstanding temperamental force. (The fictional Scarlett O'Hara or Blanche DuBois convey that the matter is not limited to the male gender.) Despite all geographical rationalizations, the commodity crops—tobacco, rice, sugar, cotton, and hemp—were not limited to the South by climate. The planters were a class capable of taking over matters of national interest: they had warred against nature, against the Indian; they had warred against the blacks on the plantation, against the British, the French, and the Spaniards. Their experience had a certain cast by virtue of the international nature of their products—human flesh and large-scale commodity crops. Such large-scale experiences do not lead to the production of small-minded men. So they participated in the formation of an original American nationality. The historical claim can be substantiated that they produced more figures of national distinction than did, say, by comparison, the robber barons. All this combines to make the controversy about the impact of slavery on American civilization such a pregnant and vital intellectual confrontation.

Certain mundane matters have to be mentioned at least in a preliminary way. It was the boredom and harshness of plantation life that ensured that not general activity, but politics was the only matter of universal interest and appeal. If the rural character of their life induced in the planters, or at least in some of them, a certain respect for plebeian democracy in other sections of the population, it had to be by the nature of the planter's own setting, an abridged version of popular participation in decision-making. The father of the political party of any mass status in American life was the planter-political philosopher, Thomas Jefferson. The father of popular participation in political office, apart from mere suffrage, was the planter Andrew Jackson. The head of an army having the popular militia as a section of its base was the planter George Washington. Yet the halfway houses to genuine democracy which each of these figures created

remain America's bones of contention unto this day.

What of social vision? The early accomplishments of these men corresponded to the formative period of American nationality. They could not go beyond. The results were imbedded in the American mentality but not anywhere in self-generating institutions. The popular militia is now the not-very-progressive National Guard. The political parties resting on mass suffrage are now in a state alternating between paralysis and crisis. The spoils of office distributed to members of the population are now a source of perpetual scandal and parasitism.

The Southern figures of the mid-nineteenth century vacillated between accommodation and hopeless fanaticism. Clay was a genius of the first order. He could never win actual leadership of the country as a whole, though he was persistent and colorful enough to engage the political attentions of his countrymen. Calhoun was a different sort. He sought to make the American Constitution a protector of the South's position in national life, invulnerable to changing national majorities. And of Jefferson Davis it can perhaps best be said that though he failed in the Southern rebellion, he was saved from hanging by the long tradition of Northern-Southern accommodation—a tradition punctured only by the actualities of the Civil War.

Some of the bobbling of the minds of the planters was due to the very fact that they stood on a tripod of vital revolutions in the then-known Western world: the Puritans in 1642, the War for Independence in 1776, and volatile France of 1789. The Clays and Calhouns lived to consider the realities of the continental-wide European Revolution of 1848. Their situation was one of Anglo-Saxon nativism turning against itself. Immigrant New York might celebrate 1848, Puritan New England might relate revolutionary antislavery sentiments to the wars between Cavaliers and Roundheads, the democratic yeomanry of the western territories might enjoy the sight of crowns falling all over Europe. The Southern planters had no comparable frame of reference. They stuck by Constitution and Compromise.

And when that did not last they went to war to protect geography. It was not all that simple. The border states which did not produce commodity crops but which had domestic slaves were the geniuses of accommodation right up to the last moment and beyond. The idyllic notion of domestic servitude, patriarchal chatteldom, originates from those Kentucky, Tennessee, upper Virginia, Maryland, and even Delaware manors. If American politics became entwined with a style of life rather than a manner of thought, we have no difficulties discovering why. In short, the Southern position was that of a provincialism entwined with American nationality as a whole, but defenseless against the universal trends of revolutionary democracy of the nineteenth century.

Nevertheless the effects of the planters were immense: The location of the nation's capital in the borderline South; the creation and manipulation of national political parties; the fielding of armies and the tradition of militant armed conflict; the specialization of the South in politics as maneuver and divagation; the bias in favor of the notion that agricultural wealth was real, and commercial wealth always fraudulent; the sense of the manor not as parasitic but as a center of human community; the assertion that the concreteness of the manorial community was superior to the impersonality of the large Northern city; the impulsiveness of the Southern personality as more appealing than the social discipline seemingly inherent in industry and commerce; the general linkup with the rural-romantic character of America's past—all of this seems irrevocable and untouchable by general intellectual argument.

The only way to deal with it is by taking up its foundations. The Southern planter could engage in politics on a much larger scale than many Northerners or Westerners because he was of a leisure class, born and bred—a commander of the fate of men, women, and children of a different color with a more permanently fixed status. Suckled by a black nurse, attended by black servants, often encouraged to sexual experiments in the slave quarters, accustomed to the sight of blacks caring for all business involving manual labor; encouraged, even inspired, by the succession of Southern Presidents, the ambitious Southerner could see politics, even statesmanship, as destiny's decision, and cast himself in the role of fortune's darling. Furthermore, for the isolated manorial communities, politics was the prime form of social communion, whereas in the North religious revivals swept all before them in periods in between political excitement. In today's parlance, the prebellum white planter gives the impression of having found an early answer to the problems of the "lonely crowd" in the solidity of his native tradition, the fixity of his social status and the values of an inherent and irrevocable individualism.

The availability and accessibility of having things always at hand extended itself to the vast virgin lands and the supply of slaves. If capital and credit were in short supply, then the curse was on the head of the mercantilists—be they tyrannical Englishmen or grasping Boston Yankees. Social status had taken on an overweening importance; but even greater was the display of public personality—elections as jousting contests, a codified individualism rather than the self-expansive effluvia of the Northern Transcendentalists.

The rationalizations for the Atlantic slave trade and American slavery, whether borrowed from the Bible or the instances of Greece and Rome, raise a compelling challenge to the whole matter of what indeed constitutes a civilization. It is safe to say that the majority of Western scholars seem to have placed a gloss on the manner and the matter of this case.

Essay/Discussion Questions

1. In reference to the system of chattel slavery, C. L. R. James states: "The capacities of men were always leaping out of the confinements of the system." What does he mean?

2. Discuss the ways in which African slaves resisted the dehumanizing process of chattel slavery. What roles did black women play in this struggle?

3. James argues that white historians largely ignored the contributions that African slaves made to the development of American civilization. In what ways did chattel slaves shape this process?

Reflections on the Black Woman's Role in the Community of Slaves

ANGELA DAVIS

I

The paucity of literature on the black woman is outrageous on its face. But we must also contend with the fact that too many of these rare studies must claim as their signal achievement the reinforcement of fictitious clichés. They have given credence to grossly distorted categories through which the black woman continues to be perceived. In the words of Nathan and Julia Hare, ". . . she has been labeled 'aggressive' or 'matriarchal' by white scholars and 'castrating female' by [some] blacks." *(Transaction,* November/December, 1970) Many have recently sought to remedy this situation. But for the time being, at least, we are still confronted with reified images of ourselves. And for now, we must still assume the responsibility of shattering them.

Initially, I did not envision this paper as strictly confined to the era of slavery. Yet, as I began to think through the issue of the black matriarch, I came to the conclusion that it had to be refuted at its presumed historical inception.

The chief problem I encountered stemmed from the conditions of my incarceration: opportunities for researching the issue I wanted to explore were extremely limited. I chose, therefore, to entitle this piece "Reflections . . ." It does not pretend to be more than a collection of ideas that would constitute a starting point—a framework within which to conduct a rigorous reinvestigation of the black woman as she interacted with her people and with her oppressive environment during slavery.

I would like to dedicate these reflections to one of the most admirable black leaders to emerge from the ranks of our liberation movement—to George Jackson, whom I loved and respected in every way. As I came to know and love him, I saw him developing an acute sensitivity to the real problems facing black women and thus refining his ability to distinguish these from their mythical transpositions. George was uniquely aware of the need to extricate himself and other black men from the remnants of divisive and destructive myths purporting to represent the black woman. If his life had not been so precipitously and savagely extinguished, he would have surely accomplished a task he had already outlined some time ago: a systematic critique of his past misconceptions about black women and of their roots in the ideology of the established order. He wanted to appeal to other black men, still similarly disoriented, to likewise correct themselves through self-criticism. George viewed this obligation as a revolutionary duty, but also, and equally important, as an expression of his boundless love for all black women.

II

The matriarchal black woman has been repeatedly invoked as one of the fatal by-products of slavery. When the Moynihan Report consecrated this myth with Washington's stamp of approval, its spurious content and propagandistic mission should have become apparent. Yet even outside the established ideological apparatus, and also among black people, unfortunate references to the matriarchate can still be encountered. Occasionally, there is even acknowledgement of the "tangle of pathology" it supposedly engendered. (This black matriarchate, according to Moynihan et al., defines the roots of our oppression as a people.) An accurate portrait of the African woman in bondage must debunk the myth of the matriarchate. Such a portrait must simultaneously attempt to illuminate the historical matrix of her oppression and must evoke her varied, often heroic, responses to the slaveholder's domination.

Lingering beneath the notion of the black matriarch is an unspoken indictment of our female forebears as having actively assented to slavery. The notorious cliché, the "emasculating female," has its roots in the fallacious inference that, in playing a central part in the slave "family," the black woman related to the slaveholding class as collaborator. Nothing could be further from the truth. In the most fundamental sense, the slave system did not—

and could not—engender and recognize a matriarchal family structure. Inherent in the very concept of the matriarchy is "power." It would have been exceedingly risky for the slaveholding class to openly acknowledge symbols of authority—female symbols no less than male. Such legitimized concentrations of authority might eventually unleash their "power" against the slave system itself.

The American brand of slavery strove toward a rigidified disorganization in family life, just as it had to proscribe all potential social structures within which black people might forge a collective and conscious existence.[1] Mothers and fathers were brutally separated; children, when they became of age, were branded and frequently severed from their mothers. That the mother was "the only legitimate parent of her child" did not therefore mean that she was even permitted to guide it to maturity.

Those who lived under a common roof were often unrelated through blood. Frederick Douglass, for instance, had no recollection of his father. He only vaguely recalled having seen his mother—and then on extremely rare occasions. Moreover, at the age of seven, he was forced to abandon the dwelling of his grandmother, of whom he would later say: "She was to me a mother and a father."[2] The strong personal bonds between immediate family members which oftentimes persisted despite coerced separation bore witness to the remarkable capacity of black people for resisting the disorder so violently imposed on their lives.

Where families were allowed to thrive, they were, for the most part, external fabrications serving the designs of an avaricious, profit-seeking slaveholder.

> The strong hand of the slave owner dominated the Negro family, which existed at his mercy and often at his own personal instigation. An ex-slave has told of getting married on one plantation: "When you married, you had to jump over a broom three times."[3]

This slave went on to describe the various ways in which his master forcibly coupled men and women with the aim of producing the maximum number of healthy child-slaves. In the words of John Henrik Clarke,

> The family as a functional entity was outlawed and permitted to exist only when it benefited the slave master. Maintenance of the slave family as a family unit benefited the slave owners only when, and to the extent that, such unions created new slaves who could be exploited.[4]

The designation of the black woman as a matriarch is a cruel misnomer. It is a misnomer because it implies stable kinship structures within which the mother exercises decisive authority. It is cruel because it ignores the profound traumas the black woman must have experienced when she had to surrender her childbearing to alien and predatory economic interests.

Even the broadest construction of the matriarch concept would not render it applicable to the black slave woman. But it should not be inferred that she therefore played no significant role in the community of slaves. Her indispensable efforts to ensure the survival of her people can hardly be contested. Even if she had done no more, her deeds would still be laudable. But her concern and struggles for physical survival, while clearly important, did not constitute her most outstanding contributions. It will be submitted that by virtue of the brutal force of circumstances, the black woman was assigned the mission of promoting the consciousness and practice of resistance. A great deal has been said about the black *man* and resistance, but very little about the unique relationship black women bore to the resistance struggles during slavery. To understand the part she played in developing and sharpening the thrust towards freedom, the broader meaning of slavery and of American slavery in particular must be explored.

Slavery is an ancient human institution. Of slave labor in its traditional form and of serfdom as well, Karl Marx had the following to say:

> The slave stands in absolutely no relation to the objective conditions of his labor; it is rather the *labor* itself, in the form of the slave as of the serf, which is placed in the category of *inorganic condition* of production alongside the other natural beings, e.g., cattle, or regarded as an appendage of the earth.[5]

The bondsman's existence as a natural condition of production is complemented and reinforced, according to Marx, by his membership in a social grouping which he perceives to be an extension of nature. Enmeshed in what appears to be a natural state of affairs, the attitude of the slave, to a greater or lesser degree, would be an acquiescence in his subjugation. Engels points out that, in Athens, the state could depend on a police force consisting entirely of slaves.[6]

The fabric of American slavery differed significantly from ancient slavery and feudalism. True, black people were forced to act as if they were "inorganic conditions of production." For slavery was "personality swallowed up in the sordid idea of property—manhood lost in chattelhood."[7] But there were no preexistent social structures or cultural dictates that might induce reconciliation to the circumstances of their bondage. On the contrary, Africans had been uprooted from their natural environment, their social relations, their culture. No legitimate sociocultural surroundings would be permitted to develop and flourish, for, in all likelihood, they would be utterly incompatible with the demands of slavery.

Yet another fact would militate against harmony and equilibrium in the slave's relation to his bondage: slavery was enclosed in a society otherwise characterized by "free" wage labor. Black men and women could always contrast their chains with the nominally free status of white working people. This was quite literally true in such cases where, like Frederick Douglass, they were contracted out as wage laborers. Unlike the "free" white men alongside whom they worked, they had no right to the meager wages they earned. Such were some of the many contradictions unloosed by the effort to forcibly inject slavery into the early stages of American capitalism.

The combination of a historically superseded slave labor system based almost exclusively on race and the drive to strip black people of all their social and cultural bonds would create a fateful rupture at the heart of the slave system itself. The slaves would not readily adopt fatalistic attitudes towards the conditions surrounding and ensnaring their lives. They were a people who had been violently thrust into a patently "unnatural" subjugation. If the slaveholders had not maintained an absolute monopoly of violence, if they had not been able to rely on large numbers of their fellow white men—indeed the entire ruling class as well as misled working people—to assist them in their terrorist machinations, slavery would have been far less feasible than it actually proved to be.

The magnitude and effects of the black people's defiant rejection of slavery have not yet been fully documented and illuminated. But there is more than ample evidence that they consistently refused to succumb to the all-encompassing dehumanization objectively demanded by the slave system. Comparatively recent studies have demonstrated that the few slave uprisings—too spectacular to be relegated to oblivion by the racism of ruling-class historians—were not isolated occurrences, as the latter would have had us believe. The reality, we know now, was that these open rebellions erupted with such a frequency that they were as much a part of the texture of slavery as the conditions of servitude themselves. And these revolts were only the tip of an iceberg: resistance expressed itself in other grand modes and also in the seemingly trivial forms of feigned illness and studied indolence.

If resistance was an organic ingredient of slave life, it had to be directly nurtured by the social organization that the slaves themselves improvised. The consciousness of their oppression, the conscious thrust towards its abolition, could not have been sustained without impetus from the community they pulled together through the sheer force of their own strength. Of necessity, this community would revolve around the realm which was furthermost removed from the immediate arena of domination. It could only be located in and around the living quarters, the area where the basic needs of physical life were met.

In the area of production, the slaves—pressed into the mold of beasts of burden—were forcibly deprived of their humanity. (And a human being thoroughly dehumanized has no desire for freedom.) But the community gravitating around the domestic quarters might possibly permit a retrieval of the man and the woman in their fundamental humanity. We can assume that in a very real material sense, it was only in domestic life—away from the eyes and whip of the overseer—that the slaves could attempt to assert the modicum of freedom they still retained. It was only there that they might be inspired to project techniques of expanding it further by leveling what few weapons they had against the slaveholding class whose unmitigated drive for profit was the source of their misery.

Via this path, we return to the African slave woman: in the living quarters, the major responsibilities "naturally" fell to her. It was the woman who was charged with keeping the "home" in order. This role was dictated by the male supremacist ideology of white society in America; it was also woven into the patriarchal traditions of Africa. As her biological destiny, the woman bore the fruits of procreation; as her social destiny, she cooked, sewed, washed, cleaned house, raised the children. Traditionally the labor of females, domestic work is supposed to complement and confirm their inferiority.

But with the black slave woman, there is a strange twist of affairs: in the infinite anguish of ministering to the needs of the men and children around her (who were not necessarily members of her immediate family), she was performing the *only* labor of the slave community that could not be directly and immediately claimed by the oppressor. There was no compensation for work in the fields; it served no useful purpose for the slaves. Domestic labor was the only meaningful labor for the slave community as a whole (discounting as negligible the exceptional situations where slaves received some pay for their work).

Precisely through performing the drudgery that has long been a central expression of the socially conditioned inferiority of women, the black woman in chains could help to lay the foundation for some degree of autonomy, both for herself and her men. Even as she was suffering under her unique oppression as female, she was thrust by the force of circumstances into the center of the slave community. She was, therefore, essential to the *survival* of the community. Not all people have survived enslavement; hence her survival-oriented activities were themselves a form of resistance. Survival, moreover, was the prerequisite of all higher levels of struggle.

But much more remains to be said of the black woman during slavery. The dialectics of her oppression will become far more complex. It is true that she was a victim of the myth that only the woman, with her diminished capacity for mental and physical labor, should do degrading household work. Yet, the alleged benefits of the ideology of femininity did not accrue to her. She was not sheltered or protected; she would not remain oblivious to the desperate struggle for existence unfolding outside the "home." She was also there in the fields, alongside the man, toiling under the lash from sunup to sundown.

This was one of the supreme ironies of slavery: in order to approach its strategic goal—to extract the greatest possible surplus from the labor of the slaves—the black woman had to be released from the chains of the myth of femininity. In the words of W. E. B. Du Bois, ". . . our women in black had freedom contemptuously thrust upon them."[8] In order to function as slave, the black woman had to be annulled as woman, that is, as woman in her historical stance of wardship under the entire male hierarchy. The sheer force of things rendered her equal to her man.

Excepting the woman's role as caretaker of the household, male supremacist structures could not become deeply embedded in the internal workings of the slave system. Though the ruling class was male and rabidly chauvinistic, the slave system could not confer upon the black man the appearance of a privileged position vis-à-vis the black woman. The man-slave could not be the unquestioned superior within the "family" or community, for there was no such thing as the "family provider" among the slaves. The attainment of slavery's intrinsic goals was contingent upon the fullest and most brutal utilization of the productive capacities of every man, woman, and child. They all had to "provide" for the master. The black woman was therefore wholly integrated into the productive force.

> The bell rings at four o'clock in the morning and they have half an hour to get ready. Men and women start together, and the women must work as steadily as the men and perform the same tasks as the men.[9]

Even in the posture of motherhood—otherwise the occasion for hypocritical adoration—the black woman was treated with no greater compassion and with no less severity than her man. As one slave related in a narrative of his life:

> . . . women who had sucking children suffered much from their breasts becoming full of milk, the infants being left at home; they therefore could not keep up with the other hands: I have seen the overseer beat them with raw hide so

that the blood and the milk flew mingled from their breasts.[10]

Moses Grandy, ex-slave, continues his description with an account of a typical form of field punishment reserved for the black woman with child:

> She is compelled to lie down over a hole made to receive her corpulency, and is flogged with the whip, or beat with a paddle, which has holes in it; at every stroke comes a blister.[11]

The unbridled cruelty of this leveling process whereby the black woman was forced into equality with the black man requires no further explanation. She shared in the deformed equality of equal oppression.

But out of this deformed equality was forged quite undeliberately, yet inexorably, a state of affairs that could unharness an immense potential in the black woman. Expending indispensable labor for the enrichment of her oppressor, she could attain a practical awareness of the oppressor's utter dependence on her—for the master needs the slave far more than the slave needs the master. At the same time she could realize that while her productive activity was wholly subordinated to the will of the master, it was nevertheless proof of her ability to transform things. For "labor is the living, shaping fire; it represents the impermanence of things, their temporality . . ."[12]

The black woman's consciousness of the oppression suffered by her people was honed in the bestial realities of daily experience. It would not be the stunted awareness of a woman confined to the home. She would be prepared to ascend to the same levels of resistance that were accessible to her men. Even as she performed her housework, the black woman's role in the slave community could not be identical to the historically evolved female role. Stripped of the palliative feminine veneer which might have encouraged a passive performance of domestic tasks, she was now uniquely capable of weaving into the warp and woof of domestic life a profound consciousness of resistance.

With the contributions of strong black women, the slave community as a whole could achieve heights unscalable within the families of the white oppressed or even within the patriarchal kinship groups of Africa. Latently or actively it was always a community of resistance. It frequently erupted in insurgency, but was daily animated by the minor acts of sabotage that harassed the slave master to no end. Had the black woman failed to rise to the occasion, the community of slaves could not have fully developed in this direction. The slave system would have to deal with the black woman as the custodian of a house of resistance.

The oppression of black women during the era of slavery, therefore, had to be buttressed by a level of overt ruling-class repression. Her routine oppression had to assume an unconcealed dimension of outright counterinsurgency.

III

To say that the oppression of black slave women necessarily incorporated open forms of counterinsurgency is not as extravagant as it might initially appear. The penetration of counterinsurgency into the day-to-day routine of the slave master's domination will be considered towards the end of this paper. First, the participation of black women in the overt and explosive upheavals that constantly rocked the slave system must be confirmed. This will be an indication of the magnitude of her role as caretaker of a household of resistance—of the degree to which she could concretely encourage those around her to keep their eyes on freedom. It will also confirm the objective circumstances to which the slave master's counterinsurgency was a response.

With the sole exceptions of Harriet Tubman and Sojourner Truth, black women of the slave era remain more or less enshrouded in unrevealed history. And, as Earl Conrad has demonstrated, even "General Tubman's" role has been consistently and grossly minimized. She was a far greater warrior against slavery than is suggested by the prevalent misconception that her only outstanding contribution was to make nineteen trips into the South, bringing over 300 slaves to their freedom.

> [She] was head of the Intelligence Service in the Department of the South throughout the Civil War; she is the only American woman to lead troops black and white on the field of battle, as she did in the Department of the South . . . She was a compelling and stirring orator in the councils of the abolitionists and the antislavers, a favorite of the antislavery conferences. She was the fellow planner with Douglass, Martin Delany, Wendell Phillips, Gerrit Smith, and other leaders of the antislavery movement.[13]

No extensive and systematic study of the role of black women in resisting slavery has come to my attention. It has been noted that large numbers of freed black women worked towards the purchase of their relatives' and friends' freedom. About the participation of women in both the well-known and more obscure slave revolts, only casual remarks have been made. It has been observed, for instance, that Gabriel's wife was active in planning the rebellion spearheaded by her husband, but little else has been said about her.

The sketch that follows is based in its entirety on the works of Herbert Aptheker, the only resources available to me at the time of this writing.[14] These facts, gleaned from Aptheker's works on slave revolts and other forms of resistance, should signal the urgency to undertake a thorough study of the black woman as antislavery rebel. In 1971 this work is far overdue.

Aptheker's research has disclosed the widespread existence of communities of blacks who were neither free nor in bondage. Throughout the South (in South and North Carolina, Virginia, Louisiana, Florida, Georgia, Mississippi, and Alabama), Maroon communities consisting of fugitive slaves and their descendants were "an ever present feature"—from 1642 to 1864—of slavery. They provided ". . . havens for fugitives, served as bases for marauding expeditions against nearby plantations and, at times, supplied leadership to planned uprisings."[15]

Every detail of these communities was invariably determined by and steeped in resistance, for their raison d'être emanated from their perpetual assault on slavery. Only in a fighting stance could the Maroons hope to secure their constantly imperiled freedom. As a matter of necessity, the women of those communities were compelled to define themselves—no less than the men—through their many acts of resistance. Hence, throughout this brief survey the counterattacks and heroic efforts at defense assisted by Maroon women will be a recurring motif.

As it will be seen, black women often poisoned the food and set fire to the houses of their masters. For those who were also employed as domestics, these particular overt forms of resistance were especially available.

The vast majority of the incidents to be related involve either tactically unsuccessful assaults or eventually thwarted attempts at defense. In all likelihood, numerous successes were achieved, even against the formidable obstacles posed by the slave system. Many of these were probably unpublicized even at the time of their occurrence, lest they provide encouragement to the rebellious proclivities of other slaves and, for other slaveholders, an occasion for fear and despair.

During the early years of the slave era (1708), a rebellion broke out in New York. Among its participants were surely many women, for one, along with three men, was executed in retaliation for the killing of seven whites. It may not be entirely insignificant that while the men were hanged, she was heinously burned alive.[16] In the same colony, women played an active role in a 1712 uprising in the course of which slaves, with their guns, clubs, and knives, killed members of the slaveholding class and managed to wound others. While some of the insurgents—among them a pregnant woman—were captured, others—including a woman—committed suicide rather than surrender.[17]

"In New Orleans one day in 1730 a woman slave received 'a violent blow from a French soldier for refusing to obey him' and in her anger shouted 'that the French should not long insult Negroes.'"[18] As it was later disclosed, she and undoubtedly many other women, had joined in a vast plan to destroy slaveholders. Along with eight men, this dauntless woman was executed. Two years later, Louisiana pronounced a woman and four men leaders of a planned rebellion. They were all executed and, in a typically savage gesture, their heads publicly displayed on poles.[19]

Charleston, South Carolina, condemned a black woman to die in 1740 for arson,[20] a form of sabotage, as earlier noted, frequently carried out by women. In Maryland, for instance, a slave woman was executed in 1776 for having destroyed by fire her master's house, his outhouses, and tobacco house.[21]

In the thick of the Colonies' war with England, a group of defiant slave women and men were arrested in Saint Andrew's Parish, Georgia, in 1778. But before they were captured, they had already brought a number of slave owners to their death.[22]

The Maroon communities have been briefly described; from 1782 to 1784, Louisiana was a constant target of Maroon attacks. When twenty-five of this community's members were finally taken prisoner, men and women alike were all severely punished.[23]

As can be inferred from previous examples, the North did not escape the tremendous impact of fighting black women. In Albany, New York, two women were among three slaves executed for antislavery activities in 1794.[24] The respect and admiration accorded the black woman fighter by her people is strikingly illustrated by an incident that transpired in York, Pennsylvania: when, during the early months of 1803, Margaret Bradley was convicted of attempting to poison two white people, the black inhabitants of the area revolted en masse.

> They made several attempts to destroy the town by fire and succeeded, within a period of three weeks, in burning eleven buildings. Patrols were established, strong guards set up, the militia dispatched to the scene of the unrest . . . and a reward of three hundred dollars offered for the capture of the insurrectionists.[25]

A successful elimination by poisoning of several "of our respectable men" (said a letter to the governor of North Carolina) was met by the execution of four or five slaves. One was a woman who was burned alive.[26] In 1810, two women and a man were accused of arson in Virginia.[27]

In 1811, North Carolina was the scene of a confrontation between a Maroon community and a slave-catching posse. Local newspapers reported that its members "had bid defiance to any force whatever and were resolved to stand their ground." Of the entire community, two were killed, one wounded, and two—both women—were captured.[28]

Aptheker's *Documentary History of the Negro People in the United States* contains a portion of the transcript of an 1812 confession of a slave rebel in Virginia. The latter divulged the information that a black woman brought him into a plan to kill their master and that yet another black woman had been charged with concealing him after the killing occurred.[29]

In 1816, it was discovered that a community of three hundred escaped slaves—men, women, children—had occupied a fort in Florida. After the United States Army was dispatched with instructions to destroy the community, a ten-day siege terminated with all but forty of the three hundred dead. All the slaves fought to the very end.[30] In the course of a similar, though smaller, confrontation between Maroons and a militia group (in South Carolina, 1826), a woman and a child were killed.[31] Still another Maroon community was attacked in Mobile, Alabama, in 1837. Its inhabitants, men and women alike, resisted fiercely—according to local newspapers, "fighting like Spartans."[32]

Convicted of having been among those who, in 1829, had been the cause of a devastating fire in Augusta, Georgia, a black woman was "executed, dissected, and exposed" (according to an English visitor). Moreover, the execution of yet another woman, about to give birth, was imminent.[33] During the same year, a group of slaves, being led from Maryland to be sold in the South, had apparently planned to kill the traders and make their way to freedom. One of the traders was successfully done away with, but eventually a posse captured all the slaves. Of the six leaders sentenced to death, one was a woman. She was first permitted, for reasons of economy, to give birth to her child.[34] Afterwards, she was publicly hanged.

The slave class in Louisiana, as noted earlier, was not unaware of the formidable threat posed by the black woman who chose to fight. It responded accordingly: in 1846, a posse of slave owners ambushed a community of Maroons, killing one woman and wounding two others. A black man was also assassinated.[35] Neither could the border states escape the recognition that slave women were eager to battle for their freedom. In 1850, in the state of Missouri, "about thirty slaves, men and women, of four different owners, had armed themselves with knives, clubs, and three guns and set out for a free state." Their pursuers, who could unleash a far more powerful violence than they, eventually thwarted their plans.[36]

This factual survey of but a few of the open acts of resistance in which black women played major roles will close with two further events. When a Maroon camp in Mississippi was destroyed in 1857, four of its members did not manage to elude capture, one of whom was a fugitive slave woman.[37] All of them, women as well as men, must have waged a valiant fight.

Finally, there occurred in October, 1862, a skirmish between Maroons and a scouting party of Confederate soldiers in the state of Virginia.[38] This time, however, the Maroons were the victors, and it may well have been that some of the many women helped to put the soldiers to death.

IV

The oppression of slave women had to assume dimensions of open counterinsurgency. Against the background of the facts presented above, it would be difficult indeed to refute this contention. As for those who engaged in open battle, they were no less ruthlessly punished than slave men. It would even appear that in many cases they may have suffered penalties that were more excessive than those meted out to the men. On occasion, when men were hanged, the women were burned alive. If such practices were widespread, their logic would be clear. They would be terrorist methods designed to dissuade other black women from following the examples of their fighting sisters. If all black women rose up alongside their men, the institution of slavery would be in difficult straits.

It is against the backdrop of her role as fighter that the routine oppression of the slave woman must be explored once more. If she was burned, hanged, broken on the wheel, her head paraded on poles before her oppressed brothers and sisters, she must have also felt the edge of this counterinsurgency as a fact of her daily existence. The slave system would not only have to make conscious efforts to stifle the tendencies towards acts of the kind described above; it would be no less necessary to stave off escape attempts (escapes to Maroon country!) and all the various forms of sabotage within the system. Feigning illness was also resistance as were work slowdowns and actions destructive to the crops. The more extensive these acts, the more the slaveholder's profits would tend to diminish.

While a detailed study of the myriad modes in which this counterinsurgency was manifested can and should be conducted, the following reflections will focus on a single aspect of the slave woman's oppression, particularly prominent in its brutality.

Much has been said about the sexual abuses to which the black woman was forced to submit. They are generally explained as an outgrowth of the male supremacy of Southern culture: the purity of white womanhood could not be violated by the aggressive sexual activity desired by the white male. His instinctual urges would find expression in his relationships with his property—the black slave woman, who would have to become his unwilling concubine. No doubt there is an element of truth in these statements, but it is equally important to unearth the meaning of these sexual abuses from the vantage point of the woman who was assaulted.

In keeping with the theme of these reflections, it will be submitted that the slave master's sexual domination of the black woman contained an unveiled element of counterinsurgency. To understand the basis for this assertion, the dialectical moments of the slave woman's oppression must be restated and their movement recaptured. The prime factor, it has been said, was the total and violent expropriation of her labor with no compensation save the pittance necessary for bare existence.

Secondly, as female, she was the housekeeper of the living quarters. In this sense, she was already doubly oppressed. However, having been wrested from passive, "feminine" existence by the sheer force of things—literally by forced labor—confining domestic tasks were incommensurable with what she had become. That is to say, by virtue of her participation in production, she would not act the part of the passive female, but could experience the same need as her men to challenge the conditions of her subjugation. As the center of domestic life, the only life at all removed from the arena of exploitation, and thus as an important source of survival, the black woman could play a pivotal role in nurturing the thrust towards freedom.

The slave master would attempt to thwart this process. He knew that as a female, this slave woman could be particularly vulnerable in her sexual existence. Although he would not pet her and deck her out in frills, the white master could endeavor to reestablish her femaleness by reducing her to the level of her *biological* being. Aspiring with his sexual assaults to establish her as a female *animal,* he would be striving to destroy her proclivities towards resistance. Of the sexual relations of animals, taken at their abstract biological level (and not in terms of their quite different social potential for human beings), Simone de Beauvoir says the following:

> It is unquestionably the male who *takes* the female—she is *taken.* Often the word applies literally, for whether by means of special organs or through superior strength, the male seizes her and holds her in place; he performs the copulatory movements; and, among insects, birds, and mammals, he penetrates . . . Her body becomes a resistance to be broken through . . .[39]

The act of copulation, reduced by the white man to an animal-like act, would be symbolic of the effort to conquer the resistance the black woman could unloose.

In confronting the black woman as adversary in a sexual contest, the master would be subjecting her to the most elemental form of terrorism distinctively suited for the female: rape. Given the already terroristic texture of plantation life, it would be as potential victim of rape that the slave woman would be most unguarded. Further, she might be most conveniently manipulable if the master contrived a ransom system of sorts, forcing her to pay with her body for food, diminished severity in treatment, the safety of her children, etc.

The integration of rape into the sparsely furnished legitimate social life of the slaves harks back to the feudal "right of the first night," the *jus primae noctis*. The feudal lord manifested and reinforced his domination over the serfs by asserting his authority to have sexual intercourse with all the females. The right itself referred specifically to all freshly married women. But while the right to the first night eventually evolved into the institutionalized "virgin tax,"[40] the American slaveholder's sexual domination never lost its openly terroristic character.

As a direct attack on the black female as potential insurgent, this sexual repression finds its parallels in virtually every historical situation where the woman actively challenges oppression. Thus, Frantz Fanon could say of the Algerian woman: "A woman led away by soldiers who comes back a week later—it is not necessary to question her to understand that she has been violated dozens of times."[41]

In its political contours, the rape of the black woman was not exclusively an attack upon her. Indirectly, its target was also the slave community as a whole. In launching the sexual war on the woman, the master would not only assert his sovereignty over a critically important figure of the slave community, he would also be aiming a blow against the black man. The latter's instinct to protect his female relations and comrades (now stripped of its male supremacist implications) would be frustrated and violated to the extreme. Placing the white male's sexual barbarity in bold relief, Du Bois cries out in a rhetorical vein:

> I shall forgive the South much in its final judgment day: I shall forgive its slavery, for slavery is a world-old habit; I shall forgive its fighting for a well-lost cause, and for remembering that struggle with tender tears; I shall forgive its so-called pride of race, the passion of its hot blood, and even its dear, old, laughable strutting and posing; but one thing I shall never forgive, neither in this world nor the world to come: its wanton and continued and persistent insulting of the black womanhood which it sought and seeks to prostitute to its lust.[42]

The retaliatory import of the rape for the black man would be entrapment in an untenable situation. Clearly the master hoped that once the black man was struck by his manifest inability to rescue his women from sexual assaults of the master, he would begin to experience deep-seated doubts about his ability to resist at all.

Certainly the wholesale rape of slave women must have had a profound impact on the slave community. Yet it could not succeed in its intrinsic aim of stifling the impetus towards struggle. Countless black women did not passively submit to these abuses, as the slaves in general refused to passively accept their bondage. The struggles of the slave woman in the sexual realm were a continuation of the resistance interlaced in the slave's daily existence. As such, this was yet another form of insurgency, a response to a politically tinged sexual repression.

Even E. Franklin Frazier (who goes out of his way to defend the thesis that "the master in his mansion and his colored mistress in her special house nearby represented the final triumph of social ritual in the presence of the deepest feelings of human solidarity")[43] could not entirely ignore the black woman who fought back. He notes: "That physical compulsion was necessary at times to secure submission on the part of black women . . . is supported by historical evidence and has been preserved in the tradition of Negro families."[44]

The sexual contest was one of many arenas in which the black woman had to prove herself as a warrior against oppression. What Frazier unwillingly concedes would mean that countless children brutally fathered by whites were conceived in the thick of battle. Frazier himself cites the story of a black woman whose great-grandmother, a former slave, would describe with great zest the battles behind all her numerous scars—that is, all save one. In response to questions concerning the unexplained scar, she had always simply said: "White men are as low as dogs, child, stay away from them." The mystery was not unveiled until after the death of this brave woman: "She received that scar at the hands of her master's youngest son, a boy of about eighteen years at the time she conceived their child, my grandmother Ellen."[45]

An intricate and savage web of oppression intruded at every moment into the black woman's life during slavery. Yet a single theme appears at every juncture: the woman transcending, refusing, fighting back, asserting herself over and against terrifying obstacles. It was not her comrade brother against whom her incredible strength was directed. She fought alongside her man, accepting or providing guidance according to her talents and the nature of their tasks. She was in no sense an authoritarian figure; neither her domestic role nor her acts of resistance could relegate the man to the shadows. On the contrary, she herself had just been forced to leave behind the shadowy realm of female passivity in order to assume her rightful place beside the insurgent male.

This portrait cannot, of course, presume to represent every individual slave woman. It is rather a portrait of the potentials and possibilities inherent in the situation to which slave women were anchored. Invariably there were those who did not realize this potential. There were those who were indifferent and a few who were outright traitors. But certainly they were not the vast majority. The image of black women enchaining their men, cultivating relationships with the oppressor, is a cruel fabrication that must be called by its right name. It is a dastardly ideological weapon designed to impair our capacity for resistance today by foisting upon us the ideal of male supremacy.

According to a time-honored principle, advanced by Marx, Lenin, Fanon, and numerous other theorists, the status of women in any given society is a barometer measuring the overall level of social development. As Fanon has masterfully shown, the strength and efficacy of social struggles—and especially revolutionary movements—bear an immediate relationship to the range and quality of female participation.

The meaning of this principle is strikingly illustrated by the role of the black woman during slavery. Attendant to the indiscriminate, brutal pursuit of profit, the slave woman attained a correspondingly brutal status of equality. But in practice, she could work up a fresh content for this deformed equality by inspiring and participating in acts of resistance of every form and color. She could turn the weapon of equality in struggle against the avaricious slave system that had engendered the mere caricature of equality in oppression. The black woman's activities increased the total incidence of antislavery assaults. But most important, without consciously rebellious black women, the theme of resistance could not have become so thoroughly intertwined in the fabric of daily existence. The status of black women within the community of slaves was definitely a barometer indicating the overall potential for resistance.

This process did not end with the formal dissolution of slavery. Under the impact of racism, the black woman has been continually constrained to inject herself into the desperate struggle for existence. She—like her man—has been compelled to work for wages, providing for her family as she was previously forced to provide for the slaveholding class. The infinitely onerous nature of this equality should never be overlooked. For the black woman has always also remained harnessed to the chores of the household. Yet, she could never be exhaustively defined by her uniquely "female" responsibilities.

As a result, black women have made significant contributions to struggles against the racism and the dehumanizing exploitation of a wrongly organized society. In fact, it would appear that the intense levels of resistance historically maintained by black people and thus the historical function of the black liberation struggle as harbinger of change throughout the society are due in part to the greater *objective* equality between the black man and the black woman. Du Bois put it this way:

> In the great rank and file of our five million women, we have the up-working of new revolutionary ideals, which must in time have vast influence on the thought and action of this land.[46]

Official and unofficial attempts to blunt the effects of the egalitarian tendencies as between the black man and woman should come as no surprise. The matriarch concept, embracing the clichéd "female castrator," is, in the last instance, an open weapon of ideological warfare. Black men and women alike remain its

potential victims—men unconsciously lunging at the woman, equating her with the myth; women sinking back into the shadows, lest an aggressive posture resurrect the myth in themselves.

The myth must be consciously repudiated as myth, and the black woman in her true historical contours must be resurrected. We, the black women of today, must accept the full weight of a legacy wrought in blood by our mothers in chains. Our fight, while identical in spirit, reflects different conditions and thus implies different paths of struggle. But as heirs to a tradition of supreme perseverance and heroic resistance, we must hasten to take our place wherever our people are forging on towards freedom.

Notes

1. It is interesting to note a parallel in Nazi Germany: with all its ranting and raving about motherhood and the family, Hitler's regime made a conscious attempt to strip the family of virtually all its social functions. The thrust of their unspoken program for the family was to reduce it to a biological unit and to force its members to relate in an unmediated fashion to the fascist bureaucracy. Clearly the Nazis endeavored to crush the family in order to ensure that it could not become a center from which oppositional activity might originate.

2. Herbert Aptheker, ed., *A Documentary History of the Negro People in the United States* (New York: Citadel Press, 1969), 272.

3. Andrew Billingsley, *Black Families in White America* (Englewood, NJ: Prentice-Hall, 1968), 61.

4. John Henrik Clarke, "The Black Woman: A Figure in World History," *Essence* (July 1971).

5. Karl Marx, *Grundrisse der Kritik der Politischen Oekonomie* (Berlin: Dietz Verlag, 1953), 389. [Davis's translation. *Ed.*]

6. Friedrich Engels, *Origin of the Family, Private Property and the State* (New York: International Publishers, 1942), 107.

7. Frederick Douglass, *Life and Times of Frederick Douglass* (New York: Collier Books, 1962), 96.

8. W. E. B. Du Bois, *Darkwater, Voices from Within the Veil* (New York: AMS Press, 1969), 185.

9. Lewis Clarke, *Narrative of the Sufferings of Lewis and Milton Clarke, Sons of a Soldier of the Revolution* (Boston: 1846), 127 [Quoted by E. Franklin Frazier, *The Negro Family in the United States*].

10. Moses Grandy, *Narrative of the Life of Moses Grandy; Late a Slave in the United States of America* (Boston: 1844), 18 [Quoted by Frazier].

11. Ibid.

12. Marx, *Grundrisse*, 266. [Davis's translation. *Ed.*]

13. Earl Conrad, "I Bring You General Tubman," *Black Scholar* I nos. 3–4 (January/February 1970): 4.

14. In February, 1949, Herbert Aptheker published an essay in *Masses and Mainstream* entitled "The Negro Woman." As yet, however, I have been unable to obtain it.

15. Herbert Aptheker, "Slave Guerrilla Warfare" in *To Be Free, Studies in American Negro History* (New York: International Publishers, 1969), 11.

16. Herbert Aptheker, *American Negro Slave Revolts* (New York: International Publishers, 1970), 169.

17. Ibid., 173.

18. Ibid., 181.
19. Ibid., 182.
20. Ibid., 190.
21. Ibid., 145.
22. Ibid., 201.
23. Ibid., 207.
24. Ibid., 215.
25. Ibid., 239.
26. Ibid., 241–242.
27. Ibid., 247
28. Ibid., 251.
29. Aptheker, *Documentary History,* 55–57.
30. Aptheker, *Slave Revolts,* 259.
31. Ibid., 277.
32. Ibid., 259.
33. Ibid., 281.
34. Ibid., 487.

35. Aptheker, "Guerrilla Warfare," 27.
36. Aptheker, *Slave Revolts,* 342.
37. Aptheker, "Guerrilla Warfare," 28.
38. Ibid., 29.
39. Simone de Beauvoir, *The Second Sex* (New York: Bantam Books, 1961), 18–19.
40. August Bebel, *Women and Socialism* (New York: Socialist Literature Co., 1910), 66–69.
41. Frantz Fanon, *A Dying Colonialism* (New York: Grove, 1967), 119.
42. Du Bois, *Darkwater,* 172.
43. E. Franklin Frazier, *The Negro Family in the United States* (Chicago: University of Chicago Press, 1966), 69.
44. Ibid., 53.
45. Ibid., 53–54.
46. Du Bois, *Darkwater,* 185.

Essay/Discussion Questions

1. Angela Davis examines critically the impact of chattel slavery on both black women and men. Discuss the similarities and differences in the slaveowners' treatment of female and male slaves.

2. What were Maroon communities, and why were they important?

3. Discuss the ways in which African slaves resisted the dehumanizing process of chattel slavery. What roles did female slaves play in the struggle to overturn chattel slavery?

I speak Americans for your good. We must and shall be free . . . in spite of you. You may do your best to keep us in wretchedness and misery, to enrich you and your children, but God will deliver us from under you. And wo, wo, will be to you if we have to obtain our freedom by fighting.

David Walker, 1829

I heard a loud voice in the heavens, and the Spirit instantly appeared to me and said . . . I should arise and prepare myself, and slay my enemies with their own weapons . . . for the time was fast approaching when the first should be last and the last should be first.

Nat Turner, 1831

Symptoms of Liberty and Blackhead Signposts: David Walker and Nat Turner

Vincent Harding

There was much about America in the 1820s that made it possible for white men and women, especially in the North, to live as if no river of struggle were slowly, steadily developing its black power beneath the rough surfaces of the new nation. Indeed, the newness itself, the busyness, the almost frenetic sense of movement and building which seized America, were all part of the comfortable cloud of unknowing that helped preserve a white sense of unreality. Nor was the incessant movement of the majority simply imagined. Every day hundreds of families were actually uprooting themselves from the more settled areas of the East and seeking their fortunes beyond the Appalachians, even beyond the Mississippi River. Other whites from Europe and the British Isles were landing regularly at the Eastern ports, making their way into the seaboard cities and across the country to the new West, providing an intimation of the waves of immigrants soon to come. Thus the sense of movement in America was based on a concrete, physical reality.[1]

Naturally, much attention and energy were invested in the political, economic, and social institutions being developed and refined to serve the new American society. The national government was defining its own sense of purpose and power. Courts, banks, corporations, systems of transportation, and religion—all were being molded, reshaped, and re-examined, set in motion to serve a nation of settlers intent on dominating a continent. Because of that goal, the natives of the land were receiving their share of attention, too—much to their regret. Relentlessly, the collective white behemoth pushed them from river to river, back into the wilderness, smashing the cultures of centuries as if the Anglo-Americans and their cousins were agents of some divine judgment in the land.[2]

As a matter of fact, major segments of white America were possessed by just such visions of divine action in their midst, saw America as a Promised Land, as a staging ground for the earthly manifestations of the coming (white) Kingdom of God. Such godly visions, built strangely on the deaths of significant portions of the nonwhite children of this Father, contributed their own peculiar busyness to the blurring of American vision. For from the stately church buildings of New England (many built on profits from the Trade), to the roughhewn meeting houses of the Northwest and the sprawling campgrounds of the South, men who considered themselves agents of God proclaimed the need of the people to prepare the way for His Coming. Whatever the differences in their theology or lack of it, from Unitarians to Hard-Shell Baptists, they were united in their sense that the God of Israel was among them in a special way, and busily announced the various implications of that presence among the (mostly white) people. Partly as a result of such holy activism and fervent conviction, various sections of the nation were periodically swept by paroxysms of religious ardor, and the enthusiastic style of evangelical Protestant revivalism set its mark on large sectors of American life.

It was a time for building, whether canals or corporations or Kingdoms of the Saints, a hectic time of new buildings when busy men and overworked women might understandably ignore certain dark and troubling movements among them. It was a time that some called the "Era of Good Feelings," when party strife among whites seemed less pronounced than during the earlier founding periods. But the harsh and bitter debate which was then being carried on in Congress and across the country over the expansion of slavery's territory spoke to a different reality, one which often seemed to break out and threaten all the white kingdoms.[3]

Meanwhile, down in the kingdom that cotton was building, there was just as much movement, building, and expansion, but of a somewhat different quality. Louisiana had become a state in 1812. Alabama entered the Union in 1817, and Mississippi two years later. Within the decade from 1810 to 1820, the population of the Alabama-Mississippi area

alone had increased from 40,000 to 200,000 persons, including more than 70,000 enslaved Africans. Since the official closing of the Atlantic slave trade to America, the internal traffic in human bondage had burgeoned; Virginia served as its capital, while the nearby slave markets of Washington, D.C., provided an appropriate commentary on the state of American democracy. With the rise of this domestic trade, which eventually took hundreds of thousands of black people from the seaboard breeding and trading grounds into the interior of the developing South, new sectional bonds were established across that entire area, helping to create a self-conscious South which was tied together in many ways by the chain of black lives.[4]

The nation had committed itself to slavery, and the South was the keeper. In the 1820s the Southern black population grew from 1.6 million to more than 2 million persons, comprising some 40 percent of the section's total population, and ranging as high as 70 to 90 percent in some plantation counties and parishes. In this kingdom that cotton was building, enslaved black people were everywhere, and it was at once harder and easier for white men and women to deceive themselves. But there was no escape from the realities represented by the radical black presence in America. Thus private and public writings from the South continually referred to deep levels of fear—fear of insurrection, fear of death at black hands, fear of black life, fear of blackness, fear of repressed and frightening white desires. Usually it came out in references to "an internal foe," or "the dangerous internal population," or "the enemy in our very bosom," perhaps revealing more than the writers ever knew.[5]

Yet even in the South, even there where all the busyness of America could not shield white men and women from the stark black reality, it was still possible not to see where the objective enemy really was. In the 1820s, in Virginia's Southhampton County, who would have chosen Nat Turner for the role?

NAT TURNER'S STORY

On the surface, Nat Turner appeared to represent much of that development which allowed men who called themselves masters to rest in the rightness of their ways. The ascetic Turner seemed to have imbibed deeply all the best elements of evangelical Southern white religion, all the proper anesthesia against the knowledge of who he had been, what he had lost, and what there was to regain. He did not use tobacco or liquor, he seemed to live a perfectly disciplined life among men as well as women (though not all owners would think well of *that* fruit of the Spirit); by and large, he caused no real trouble for the keepers of the status quo. Indeed, around 1821 the young black man had vividly demonstrated to whites the exemplary advantage of his high standing among the other Africans by returning voluntarily to Samuel Turner after having run away for about thirty days. Such a faithful black exhorter and singer of spiritual songs was of great value in the eyes of the white world. Of course the eyes of the white world did not see into the deepest level of Nat's real relationship to the black community, or into his real relationship to his God. Therefore whites could never have predicted that Nat, once harshened and honed in the burning river, would be possessed by a driving messianic mission to become God's avenging scourge against the slaveholders and their world.[6]

After his birth in 1800, the first community Nat Turner knew was that of his mother, father, and grandmother, a family not far removed from Africa but held in slavery by one Samuel Turner. Had they considered themselves or young Nat simply to be "slaves," he would never have become a Messenger. Rather, from the outset they taught him that he was meant for some special purpose (and therefore so were they), and they led him in that path. For instance, the immediate family and the surrounding black community were evidently convinced—as was Nat—that he had learned to read without instruction. Soon they were

fascinated by his experiments in the ancient crafts of Africa and Asia: pottery, papermaking, and the making of gunpowder. Perhaps this was seen as another manifestation of the esoteric knowledge the community was convinced that he possessed—knowledge that included events and times before his own birth. Meanwhile his grandmother Bridget, a "very religious" woman, instructed him in what she knew from the Scriptures and other sources, nurtured him in the songs of nighttime and sleep.[7]

We are not sure of all that Nat learned from his immediate family, but his father taught him at least one thing: slavery was not to be endured. While Nat was still a child his father had joined the ranks of the fugitives. (Who can imagine the conversation in that family before his father ran away into the shadows of history? How much of their substance did Nat carry to his own grave?) From the rest of the community of captives Nat learned the same lesson, which was often taught in the captives' own flight from slavery, in spite of the high costs involved. He knew of the injustices suffered by his community. He learned its ritual songs and prayers, and the stories of heroes like Gabriel. But Nat claimed that his most profound lessons came in his own lonely, personal struggles with the spirit, whom he identified as "the Spirit that spoke to the prophets."[8]

By the time he was twenty-five, Nat had wrestled many times in the night with the Spirit of his God, the God of his Fathers. He had been pressed especially hard by the words: "Seek ye first the Kingdom of God and all things shall be added unto you." As he attempted to plumb the meaning and mystery of that promise, he had been driven into his own month-long experience of the wilderness, but then had returned to the Turner farm. Steadily he became more convinced that the Kingdom he sought was not the one preached by most of the white men he had heard. Instead, he saw the promised Kingdom of righteousness as one which would somehow be realized on the very farms and fields of Virginia, a Kingdom in which the power of the slavemasters would be broken. What made the vision chilling and exhilarating was his vivid awareness of being a chosen instrument for the bringing in of this Kingdom.[9]

Still, the way forward was not yet really clear, and Nat Turner went about his life and work, waiting. By this time Turner was a familiar figure in Southhampton County and the surrounding areas. Of about average height, muscular in build, coffee-tan in complexion, with a wide nose and large eyes, he walked with a brisk and active movement among his people, marked within himself and among them as a special man. On Sundays and at midweek meetings he exhorted and sang in black Baptist gatherings. At one point, word spread that Nat Turner had cured a white man of some serious disease, and then had baptized the white believer and himself in a river. Such a story only added to his renown.[10]

None of these developments, none of this high regard, moved Turner from his central purpose and passionate search. He waited and worked and married, but knew that all these things were only a prelude. Then in 1825 a clearer vision came: "I saw white spirits and black spirits engaged in battle, and the sun was darkened—the thunder rolled in the Heavens, and blood flowed in streams—and I heard a voice saying, 'Such is your luck, such you are called to see, and let it come rough or smooth, you must surely bear it.'" Again, one day as he worked in the fields Nat claimed to have "discovered drops of blood on the corn as though it were dew from heaven." On the leaves of the trees he said he found "hieroglyphic characters, and numbers, with the forms of men . . . portrayed in blood." Through this African imagery the white and black fighters had appeared again, but this time the meaning was even clearer in his mind. What it signified to Nat was that "the blood of Christ had been shed on this earth . . . and was now returning to

earth." Therefore, he said, "it was plain to me that the Saviour was about to lay down the yoke he had borne for the sins of men, and the great day of judgement was at hand."[11]

On one level, Turner was obviously living within the popular nineteenth-century Euro-American millenarian religious tradition, marked by a belief in the imminent return of Christ to rule his earth. Often, for persons thus convinced, a terrible and sometimes beautiful urgency caught fire and burned within them, annealing and transforming their being.[12]

But the burning within Nat Turner came from an at once similar and very different fire. That became evident in the spring of 1828, when the fullest description of the Kingdom he sought, and of his own role in its coming, were spoken to Nat's third ear. With very rare exceptions, white American evangelical religion could not contain such a Word, had no ear for it. On May 12, 1828, Nat said, "I heard a loud voice in the heavens, and the Spirit instantly appeared to me and said the Serpent was loosened, and Christ had laid down the yoke he had borne for the sins of men, and that I should take it and fight against the serpent, for the time was fast approaching when the first should be last and the last should be first." As if to clear away any lingering doubt he might have had, Nat heard the spirit's clear instructions, that at the appearance of the proper sign "I should arise and prepare myself, and slay my enemies with their own weapons." After that he waited, he bided his time.[13]

> *Oh praised my honer, harshener*
> *till a sleep came over me,*
> *a sleep heavy as death. And when*
> *I awoke at last free*
>
> *And purified, I rose and prayed*
> *and returned after a time*
> *to the blazing fields, to the humbleness.*
> *And bided my time.*[14]

For twenty-eight years Nat Turner had been nurtured by the black community, instructed by signs on the leaves and in the skies. Now he was clear about who the enemy of righteousness was, and who were the servants of the devil; he had only to wait for the sign. But it may have been difficult to wait: about this time, it seems, Turner was whipped by Thomas Moore, his present owner, "for saying that the blacks ought to be free, and that they would be free one day or another."[15]

A bustling, growing, building white nation could miss the sign that such a man carried in his own flesh, but for persons who were willing to see, more obvious signs were available. These were the years of black insurrections in Martinique, Cuba, Antigua, Tortola, Jamaica, and elsewhere in the Western Hemisphere, and black people in the States were not oblivious of them or of their promise. This was demonstrated in the fall of 1826, when twenty-nine black people were being taken by sea from Maryland to Georgia on the *Decatur,* a vessel owned by one of the nation's largest slave traders. The black captives rebelled, killed two members of the crew, then ordered another crew member "to take them to Haiti" because they knew of the black struggle there. The boat was captured before they could reach their destination, but when the *Decatur* was taken to New York City, all but one of the captives escaped.[16]

Two years later a group of four black slave artisans were on a similar journey by ship from Charleston to New Orleans. Before leaving South Carolina, they vowed that they would never be slaves in New Orleans. By the time the boat docked, they all had committed suicide. At about the same time, fragmentary reports of rebellions and death on island plantations seeped out of other parts of Louisiana.[17]

There was no surcease. While Nat Turner saw visions and waited for signs, others continued to fight. In Mobile County, Alabama, a black man named Hal had led a group of outlyers for several years. By the spring of 1827 the fugitives were organized to the point where they were building a fort in the swamps.

One day while the construction was still going on, they were surprised, attacked, and defeated by a large group of whites. Later one of the white men reported: "This much I can say that old Hal . . . and his men fought like spartans, not one gave an inch of ground, but stood, was shot dead or wounded fell on the spot."[18]

DAVID WALKER'S STORY

While Nat Turner waited for the sign, and black people fought on ships, in forests, and on plantations, there were still other options and other signs, especially for those who could no longer bide their time. David Walker was one such man. He had been born legally free in 1785 in Wilmington, North Carolina, the child of a free mother, but he knew that he was not free, that his status ultimately depended upon the good will of white men. By the 1820s, while Nat waited for signs and saw visions, Walker had traveled across the South and into the trans-Appalachian West, had seen what America was doing to black people in slavery, and had become concerned about what slavery might yet do to him. Later, two scenes from those journeys stood out especially in his mind. He claimed to have watched the degradation of two black men: a son who was forced to strip his mother naked and whip her until she died; and a black husband forced to lash his pregnant wife until she aborted her child. Walker knew that, if faced with such savage choices, he would kill white men—and most likely be killed. "If I remain in this bloody land," he told himself, "I will not live long." By 1826, led by his own signs and visions, David Walker had moved to Boston.[19]

By then he was forty-one years old. A tall, slender, handsome man of dark complexion, Walker was a bachelor when he arrived. Perhaps he had thought it unwise to give too many hostages to white fortune while living and traveling in the South and West. Perhaps he wanted to be untrammeled in his passionate work on behalf of black freedom, a task he took up in very concrete ways soon after arriving in Boston. Almost immediately, the North Carolinian's house became a refuge for all black people in need of aid, especially the fugitives from slavery who came regularly into Boston. Walker was also an organizer and lecturer for the General Colored Association of Massachusetts, a black abolitionist organization, and when *Freedom's Journal,* the first black newspaper in America, began publication in 1827, Walker became an agent for the paper in Boston.[20]

The meeting of David Walker and *Freedom's Journal* in the Northern phase of the struggle raised a question of great moment: what is the role of the word—the spoken word, the preached word, the whispered-in-the-nighttime word, the written word, the published word—in the fight for black freedom?

In the slave castles and by the riversides of Africa, where our ancestors had gathered for the long journey into American captivity, the spoken word had many functions. It provided a bridge between and among them, to draw them together for the unity those first efforts demanded. On the ships the word was used to strengthen men and women and urge them toward the dangers of participation. It was often on the ships that the word, for the first sustained length of time, was directed toward the white captors. Early, in such a setting, the word was used in protest, in statements of black rights and white wrongs, of black people's determination to be men and women in spite of European attempts to dehumanize them. There, too, the word publicly spoken to white men often served as a rallying point for the Africans. For in many cases the word was openly uttered in spite of the rules and laws of the whites, spoken in the face of threats and punishment and even death. Such courageous speakers of the word understandably evoked strength and courage and hope in other captives.

Similar situations often prevailed when the black-white struggle moved from the prison

ships into the fields and forests of the New World prison state. In the South, the word was used as an organizing tool for the flight into the outlyers' camps or toward the North. In many such situations it spoke the truth about white oppression, black suffering, and the potential power of organized black will. Such a word strengthened and encouraged friends to continue to struggle to survive, to bide their time toward the struggle to overcome. And on many occasions, the prison states exacted the same cruel penalties as the prison ships for the honest, defiant, encouraging black word. For such words were radical acts.[21]

No less dangerous to white power in the South were the words spoken honestly from the Bible, the Word, telling men and women of a humanity no one could deny them, reminding a people that God opposed injustice and the oppression of the weak, encouraging believers to seek for messianic signs in the heavens, for blood on the leaves. On the tongues of black people—and in their hands—the Word might indeed become a sword.

On the other hand, in the antebellum North the role of the word developed somewhat differently, progressing less starkly but in the same essential direction. There, in situations where black men and women brought that word to bear against their oppressors, they usually addressed two intersecting realities: the bondage forced upon their brothers and sisters in the South, and the racist discrimination practiced against their own immediate community in the North. When they spoke or wrote against slavery, the fate of their word often depended upon where it was spoken and to what audience it was directed. Put forth among black people or white sympathizers, words from black speakers and writers denouncing slavery and its defenders usually did not present the same outright, abrasive challenge as in the South. However, such words could never be confined to those circles. They carried their own resonance and therefore their own dangers. No black critics, whatever their audiences, were suffered gladly, and it was not unusual—especially as the nation's argument over slavery grew more heated—for white mobs to break in on abolitionist meetings and especially attack the black men and women who dared stand as public judges of white law and order.[22]

As the debate over slavery intensified, the black word from the north became more provocative, more slashing in its condemnation, more daring in its encouragement to resistance. Then, when attempts were made to publish and distribute those words among the Afro-American captives of the South, radical words and deeds were clearly joined, and the challenge was explosive. In the same way, as black men and women pressed their fierce arguments against the conditions of Northern racism, they found increasing hostility in that section, too. For the word often called upon their brothers and sisters to struggle for changes in their status there, to resist, to fight back. Ultimately, the words against slavery in the South and discrimination in the North were joined, for the black community of the North was finally called upon to resist the laws which endangered the fugitive slaves who came among them. From pulpit, platform, and press the black word would urge them to take up the struggle of the enslaved on free ground, thereby proclaiming all American soil to be contaminated, unfree, and in need of the rushing, cleansing movement of the river.

So the word had many roles and many places in the Northern struggle. In 1827 the almost simultaneous appearance of David Walker and *Freedom's Journal* represented one of the earliest institutional manifestations of what we have called the Great Tradition of Black Protest. As such, it was in the mainstream of the river, closer to the surface than the churning depths. In its first issue this pioneer black periodical announced: "The civil rights of a people being of the greatest value, it shall ever be our duty to vindicate our brethren when oppressed, and to lay the cure before the public. We also urge upon our brethren (who are qualified by the laws of the different states) the expediency of using their elective franchise; and of making an independent use of the same. We wish them not to become the tools of party." For the *Journal,* the word meant quiet, sound advocacy of the black cause, an encouragement to acceptable black social and political development, and a source of information and advice for any whites who might be concerned about black needs. In 1827 the word of the Great Tradition was less strident than it had been on the slave ships, but it was the same tradition, and the time for its renewed stridency would come.[23]

By the following year, David Walker began his brief career as a goad to moderate voices like that of *Freedom's Journal.* For even as he moved within the Great Tradition, Walker's history, temperament, and commitments urged him toward deeper and more radical levels of struggle. In the fall of 1828 he delivered an address before the General Colored Association of his adopted state, calling on blacks to organize and act on their own behalf. In the address Walker first spoke of the need for political and social organization within the black community, identifying such structured, inner cohesion as a prerequisite to any effective struggle for freedom. "Ought we not to form ourselves into a general body to protect, aid, and assist each other to the utmost of our power?" Proceeding beyond this, he also said that "it is indispensably our duty to try every scheme we think will have a tendency to facilitate our salvation, and leave the final result to . . . God."

This last sentiment was not escapist. Rather, it suggested a certain affinity between Walker and the waiting Nat Turner. For David Walker was a staunch and faithful member of a black Methodist church in Boston, and he firmly believed that people—especially oppressed people—were called upon to act as well as pray, always placing their ultimate confidence in God. It was that context of active faith which illuminated the final words of Walker's speech to the Colored Association: "I verily believe that God has something in reserve for us, which when he shall have poured it out upon us, will repay us for all our suffering and misery."[24]

In February 1829, two months after the publication of Walker's December speech, a document which seemed to express certain elements of his thought more explicitly appeared in print. One Robert Young, a black New Yorker, published a pamphlet called *The Ethiopian Manifesto,* evidently intending to put forward a longer version later. It appears now that the larger statement never came, but the *Manifesto* picked up the themes from Walker's work and carried them forward. For Young, as for many Biblically oriented blacks of the time, the word Ethiopian was synonymous with African: where Walker had spoken generally of the need for political and social organization, Young seemed to advocate the establishment of a theocracy of Ethiopian people in America. Calling for the "convocation of ourselves into a body politic," Young said that "for the promotion of welfare of our order," it was necessary "to establish to ourselves a people framed into the likeness of that order, which from our mind's eye we do evidently discern governs the universal creation. Beholding but one sole power, supremacy, or head, we do of that head . . . look forward for succor in the accomplishment of the great design which he hast, in his wisdom, promoted us to its undertaking."[25]

Equally important, perhaps more so, was the *Manifesto*'s announcement to the black people of America and elsewhere that "the time is at hand, when, with but the power of words, and the divine will of our God, the vile shackles of slavery shall be broken asunder from you, and no man known shall dare to own or proclaim you as his bondsmen." This was a deliverance rather different from the kind Nat Turner pondered in Virginia, or that David Walker would soon propose. It depended solely on "the power of words" and the will of God. But according to Young, it would be manifested through a mulatto Messiah chosen by God from "Grenada's Island" in the West Indies. This Messiah would be the means whereby God would "call together the black people as a nation in themselves." Thus Young could say to white people: "Of the degraded of this earth, shall be exalted, one who shall draw from thee as though gifted of power divine, all attachment and regard of thy slave towards thee."[26]

Here was true messianic promise: divine intervention on behalf of the Ethiopian nation in America, to provide a savior to draw black people together as a nation, and somehow miraculously break the shackles of slavery. Its pan-Africanism, its sense of nationhood, its radical hope all marked this rather mysterious announcement as part of the stream of radical ideas in the struggle. But by then both David Walker and Nat Turner had heard other voices.

Not long after his arrival in Boston, David Walker had set up a new and used clothing shop on Brattle Street. That provided his living: but the freedom struggle of black people in America was his life. Not only did he regularly attend the abolitionist meetings and assist all the fugitives he could, but those who knew him noted that Walker was devoting very long, hard hours to reading and study. Driven by an urgency that he attributed to the spirit of God, his special role was taking shape, only faintly suggested by the speech near the end of 1828.

Sometime during this period Walker took time to get married, but there was no release of the internal pressure, no relaxation in the harsh schedule of reading and writing which he had set himself. Finally, having developed a series of notes and drafts, in September 1829 Walker supervised the printing of his explosive seventy-six-page pamphlet, *Walker's Appeal . . . to the Colored Citizens of the World But in Particular and very Expressly to those of the United States of America.* It read as if all the passion and commitment of his life had been poured into the document. In its pages, filled

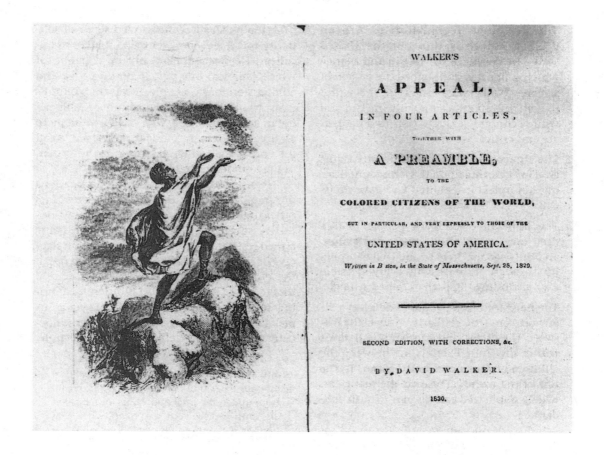

WALKER'S

APPEAL,

IN FOUR ARTICLES,

TOGETHER WITH

A PREAMBLE,

TO THE

COLORED CITIZENS OF THE WORLD,

BUT IN PARTICULAR, AND VERY EXPRESSLY TO THOSE OF THE

UNITED STATES OF AMERICA.

Written in B ston, in the State of Massachusetts, Sept. 28, 1829.

SECOND EDITION, WITH CORRECTIONS, &c.

BY DAVID WALKER.

1830.

with exclamations and pleas, with warnings and exhortations, one could almost hear the seething, roaring sounds of the black river, from the wailings of the African baracoons to the thundering declarations of Dessalines, and the quiet signals of the outlyers in Wilmington's swamps.[27]

Near the beginning of the work, Walker proclaimed it one of his major purposes "to awaken in the breasts of my afflicted, degraded and slumbering brethren, a spirit of inquiry and investigation respecting our miseries and wretchednesses in this REPUBLICAN LAND OF LIBERTY!!!!!" Essentially, he was demonstrating several of the major functions of radical teaching among dominated African peoples: to raise questions about the reasons for their oppression, to speak the truth concerning both oppressed and oppressor, to clarify as fully as possible the contradictions inherent in both communities, and to indicate the possible uses of these contradictions in the struggle for freedom. Actually, he accomplished even more than he set out to: for over a century, Walker's *Appeal* remained a touchstone for one crucial genre of black radical analysis and agitation. As such, its primary strength lay in the breadth and honesty of its analysis, in the all-consuming passion of its commitment to black liberation, and in the radical hope which lifted it beyond the familiar temptations to bitter despair. Understandably, then, David Walker's heirs, both conscious and unconscious, have been legion.[28]

In the pamphlet, which quickly went through three editions (with new material added to the later ones), ten major themes were addressed:

1. The profound degradation of African peoples, especially those in the United States, as a result of the racism and avarice which supported and shaped the system of slavery. (Walker was perhaps the first writer to combine an attack on white racism and white economic exploitation in a deliberate and critical way.)

2. The unavoidable judgment which a just God would bring upon the white American nation, unless it repented and gave up its evil ways of injustice and oppression.

3. The imperative for black people to face their own complicity in their oppression, and the need for them to end that complicity through resistance in every possible way, including the path of armed struggle.

4. The need for black people to develop a far greater sense of solidarity, especially between the "free" and captive populations within the United States, and between the children of Africa here and Africans in the rest of the world. (This was the first clear, widely publicized call for pan-African solidarity.)

5. The need to resist the attempts of the American Colonization Society to rid the country of its free black population.

6. The need to gain as much education as possible as a weapon in the struggle.

7. The possibility that a new society of peace and justice could come into being if white America were able to give up its malevolent ways, especially its racism and avarice.

8. The need for an essentially Protestant Christian religious undergirding for the black struggle for justice.

9. The likelihood that he, Walker, would be imprisoned or assassinated as a result of the *Appeal*.

10. The repeated statement of his own essential sense of solidarity with his brothers and sisters in slavery.

Actually, this last-mentioned sense of solidarity was the deepest source of Walker's radicalism. He was impelled not by a hatred of white America, but by a profound love and compassion for his people. It was this commitment to black people, and his unshakable belief in a God of justice, which led inevitably to an urgent statement of black radicalism, a call for uprooting and overturning of the system of life and death that was America.

Because of the nature and preoccupations of American society, the *Appeal,* in spite of its other urgent concerns, gained its greatest notoriety through advocacy of black messianic armed resistance to white oppression and slavery. Of course it was this advocacy which posed the most obvious, if not the most profound, threat to the American social order. Combining social, political, and economic religious messianism with the secular natural rights doctrine then current, Walker urged black people:

> Let your enemies go with their butcheries, and at once fill up their cup. Never make an attempt to gain our freedom or *natural right,* from under our cruel oppressors and murderers, until you see your way clear—when that hour arrives and you move, be not afraid or dismayed; for be you assured that Jesus Christ the king of heaven and of earth who is the God of justice and of armies, will surely go before you. And those enemies who have for hundreds of years stolen our *rights,* and kept us ignorant of him and his divine worship, he will remove.[29]

A black man had again taken products of white civilization and transmuted them for purposes of black freedom. In the *Appeal,* the two major systems of belief in early nineteenth-century America—Protestant evangelical Christianity and natural rights philosophy—were lifted up and bound in blood as a weapon in the struggle of black people toward justice. For Walker, the cause of freedom was the cause of God, and the cause of black justice was the cause of Jesus Christ; he readily promised the divine presence to all black people who would stand up and fight in that "glorious and heavenly cause" of black liberation.

Obviously such conclusions had never been dreamed of on the campgrounds of the South, in the churches of the North, or in the town halls, universities, and legislatures of the white nation. But whatever those white assumptions, Walker knew his own purposes, and his urging of a divinely justified armed struggle against oppression was relentless. Calling upon black people to fight openly against all who sought to maintain them in slavery, he wrote: "If you commence, make sure work—do not trifle, for they will not trifle with you—they want us for their slaves, and think nothing of murdering us in order to subject us to that wretched condition—therefore, if there is an *attempt* made by us, kill or be killed." He also added: "It is no more harm for you to kill a man who is trying to kill you, than it is for you to take a drink of water when thirsty; in fact the man who will stand still and let another man murder him is worse than an infidel."[30]

As he saw it, the fight for black freedom was in reality a holy crusade. Black resistance to slavery was sacred obedience to God; continued submission was sinful and risked God's judgment. Nor was Walker reticent about his own views on the need for such judgment: "The man who would not fight under our Lord and Master Jesus Christ, in the glorious and heavenly cause of freedom and of God . . . ought to be kept with all of his children or family, in slavery, or in chains, to be butchered by his cruel enemies."[31]

(Had Walker read the words of Dessalines? A quarter of a century before, calling for the blood of the white oppressors, the Avenger had asked: "Where is that Haytian so vile, Haytian so unworthy of his regeneration, who thinks he has not fulfilled the decrees of the Eternal by exterminating these blood-thirsty tyggers? If there be one, let him fly; indignant nature

discards him from our bosom . . . the air we breathe is not suited to his gross organs; it is the air of liberty, pure, august, and triumphant.")[32]

For those who needed a different kind of encouragement, Walker offered the promised Messiah, a figure first raised up by Robert Young and now militarized by Walker. Thus the passionate Boston radical promised the black nation that "the Lord our God . . . will send you a Hannibal," and urged black people to fight valiantly under his leadership, since "God will indeed deliver you through him from your deplorable and wretched condition under the Christians of America." There was no doubt about the warlike intentions of *this* Messiah, for under him, Walker said, "my colour will root some of the whites out of the very face of the earth." Indeed, David Walker was so certain of his God's judgment upon the evil of white American society that he foresaw the possibility of another route of judgment in case black people and their Hannibal-Messiah did not prove adequate. Here, his prediction was eventually and vividly confirmed: "Although the destruction of the oppressors God may not effect by the oppressed, yet the Lord our God will surely bring other destructions upon them—for not infrequently will he cause them to rise up against one another, to be split and divided, and to oppress each other, and sometimes to open hostilities with sword in hand."[33]

Did David Walker see signs and visions, as the waiting Nat Turner had seen them? Did such revelations explain the accuracy of his prophecies regarding the nation? Although he did not claim this sort of inspiration as explicitly as Nat Turner, Walker did reply to some of his critics by saying: "Do they believe that I would be so foolish as to put out a book of this kind without strict—ah! very strict commandments of the Lord? . . . He will soon show you and the world, in due time, whether this book is for his glory." So perhaps there really were visions; but there was something less esoteric as well. For it was obvious that Walker was driven to many of his conclusions not by kaleidoscopic images and voices whirring in the wind, but by a profound, unshakable belief in the justice of God, an element of faith which remained consistently present in the radical streams of black struggle. Confidence in that divine justice led to an assurance of divine retribution against America, which in turn encouraged black struggle in the cause of that justice and retribution. At one point in the *Appeal,* Walker asked: "Can the Americans escape God Almighty? If they do, can he be to us a God of justice?" To Walker the central answer was unmistakably clear: "God is just, and I know it—for he has convinced me to my satisfaction—I cannot doubt him."[34]

But even more than this lay behind Walker's fiercely accurate conclusions. Not for nothing had he spent years of travel, reading, and research examining white oppression in America, seeking to clarify his people's situation. For instance, his observations across the land led him to refer again and again to the economic motives behind white oppression. Early in the *Appeal* he said that, after years of observation and reading, "I have come to the immovable conclusion that [the Americans] have, and do continue to punish us for nothing else, but for enriching them and their country." This he called "avarice." Pursuing the theme of white avarice and greed, Walker moved to conclusions which would appear repeatedly in radical black analysis. Thus he continually referred to whites as "our *natural enemies.*" He conceded that "from the beginning [of international contacts between blacks and whites], I do not think that we were natural enemies to each other." But he quickly added that since the opening of the slave trade, the whites by their avarice and cruel treatment had made themselves the natural enemies of blacks. It was therefore logical for him not only to call for relentless struggle, but also to explore the possibility of emigration: he suggested Canada or Haiti.[35]

The use of such a term as "natural enemies" raised questions which continued to arise: precisely who were the enemies of black freedom, of black humanity, natural or otherwise? Were they all white Americans, thereby positing a struggle of white against black? Were some white Americans not the enemy? What was the role of the federal government in this conflict? Was it also the enemy? These were crucial questions, profoundly affecting the ways in which black people looked at whites as well as themselves, and the ways in which they organized themselves for struggle toward freedom.

In the *Appeal* it was not always clear where Walker was focusing his attack, and who was included among the "natural enemies." At times he mentioned "slave-holders and their advocates," but he also included Northern white racists, perhaps classifying them also as "advocates." On one occasion he pressed the issue to the critical point, saying, "Is this not the most tyrannical unmerciful and cruel government under Heaven?" Generally, the primary enemies that he identified—with sometimes more, sometimes less clarity—were these: the system of slavery and its advocates in North and South alike; the American government, which supported that system and other aspects of white supremacy; and the white citizens of the country at large who cooperated in any way in the degradation of black people. To identify the government, the system of slavery, and most of the people of white America as the enemies of black freedom, was to put forward a radical analysis in keeping with the slave-ship experience.[36]

His sound and basic analysis of the American situation and of the human condition led Walker also to explore further the matter of black self-government which he had originally raised in 1828, and which Robert Young had put forward in a more spiritualized form in February 1829. Now, in the fall of 1829, Walker found no inconsistency in advocating implacable struggle on these shores, and at the same time preparing for self-government here or elsewhere. In the course of the *Appeal*'s powerful attack on the racism of Thomas Jefferson's *Notes on Virginia,* Walker wrote: "Our sufferings will come to an end, in spite of all the Americans this side of eternity. Then we will want all the learning and talents among ourselves, and perhaps more, to govern ourselves."[37]

Whatever the future of black people in America, by 1829 Walker had also developed a mature and fascinating sense of pan-African identity, tying together past, present, and future. He not only identified black people with the past greatness of Egypt and the rest of Africa, but went on to identify the bonds of future struggle. He spoke to all black people in America, especially those who "have the hardihood to say that you are free and happy." For him there was no true freedom or happiness apart from his brothers and sisters in slavery; moreover, he insisted to black people that it was "an unshakable and forever immovable *fact* that your full glory and happiness, as well as that of all other coloured people under Heaven, shall never be fully consummated [without] the entire emancipation of your enslaved brethren all over the world. . . . I believe it is the will of the Lord that our greatest happiness shall consist in working for the salvation of our whole body." For those who doubted and said such pan-African liberation could never be accomplished, Walker spoke out of his profound faith in the God of our ancestors: "I assure you that God will accomplish it—if nothing else will answer he will hurl tyrants and devils into *atoms* [!] and make way for his people. But O my brethren! I say unto you again, you must go to work and prepare the way of the Lord."[38]

Everything in Walker's mind led back to "the way of the Lord," the way of justice for the Lord's oppressed African peoples. This way demanded harsh judgment upon white America. Or did it? In spite of Walker's passionate commitment to black freedom and God's justice, the *Appeal* shows a certain ambivalence toward white America and its future, as in this ambiguous warning: "I tell you

Americans! that unless you speedily alter your course, you and your *Country are gone*!!!! For God Almighty will tear up the very face of the earth!!!!" In his mind, then, there seemed to be some alternative: America might "speedily alter" its course. But was it really possible? He doubted it: "I hope that the Americans may hear, but I am afraid that they have done us so much injury, and are so firm in the belief that our Creator made us to be an inheritance to them for ever, that their hearts will be hardened, so that their destruction may be sure."[39] Nevertheless, in a tradition soon to be firmly set, Walker continued to speak to the hopeless white "Americans," continued to call them to new possibilities. Perhaps there was no other choice, since black people jointly occupied with the "Americans" the territory which was to be torn up by God's judgment. Who could be eager for a judgment on America, when its land was filled with Africa's children?

Thus he spoke as a kind of angry black pastor to white America: "I speak to Americans for your good. We must and shall be free . . . in spite of you. You may do your best to keep us in wretchedness and misery, to enrich you and your children, but God will deliver us from under you. And wo, wo, will be to you if we have to obtain our freedom by fighting." And what if the miracle occurred, and America decided that it wanted to change its ways, to seek justice and love misery, to let the oppressed go free? What would repentance require where black men and women (to say nothing of the natives of the land) were concerned?[40]

Here, as in the case of many of his later heirs, Walker was vague: "Treat us like men, and . . . we will live in peace and happiness together." What did that mean? What did justice and manhood require? Ending slavery was, of course, one obvious requirement, and Walker cited it. But beyond that, his answer was less clear: "The Americans . . . have to raise us from the condition of brutes to that of respectable men, and to make a national acknowledgment to us for the wrongs they have inflicted upon us." Perhaps that statement implied compensation to the African captives for the generations of unpaid labor. Perhaps it meant reparations in other forms. Perhaps it suggested some special role of honor in the society for those who had been so long humiliated by its racism and greed.[41]

At this point, we cannot be certain what David Walker saw as the proper acts of white repentance and restitution. Whatever he meant, his "Americans" did not care. As the three editions of the *Appeal* came rushing off the presses between October 1829 and June 1830, white men were in no way drawn to Walker's pastoral/prophetic calls to penance for the oppression of black people. What they reacted to in the *Appeal* were the sanguinary calls to black men, the ringing summonses to armed struggle against the white keepers of the status quo. For the "Americans," *that* was Walker's *Appeal,* and it constituted sedition.

Of course it was precisely because they were not interested in Walker's invitations to repentance that white people were forced to be frantically concerned with his summonses to divinely ordained rebellion. They were right to be concerned. In the months following publication there is some evidence that David Walker, in addition to distributing it among Northern blacks, made distinct attempts to see that his *Appeal* reached black captives of the South, sometimes sewing copies into the inner linings of coats he traded to Southern-bound black seamen, sometimes using other clandestine methods—including at least one white courier—to circulate it. Word came back from Georgia and Louisiana, from the Carolinas and Virginia (did it reach Southhampton County?) that the message was breaking through.[42]

Meanwhile white condemnation erupted from many sources. The governor of North Carolina, most likely mindful of the swamps around Walker's native Wilmington, denounced (and praised) the *Appeal.* He called it "an open appeal to [the black's] natural love

of liberty . . . and . . . totally subversive of all subordination in our slaves." He was, of course, totally correct. More unusual was the response from Benjamin Lundy, the best-known white antislavery publicist of the time: "A more bold, daring, inflammatory publication, perhaps, ever issued from the press of any country . . . I can do no less than set the broadest seal of condemnation on it." Thus conservatives who placed the preservation of their way of life before black freedom, and liberals who placed the validity of their own solutions before black-defined struggle, were equally dismayed.[43]

Some of Walker's "Americans" were more than dismayed. Shortly after whites in the South first gained access to the *Appeal,* it is said that "a company of Georgia men" not only vowed that they would kill David Walker, but offered a thousand-dollar reward for his death. When Walker's wife and friends heard of this, they frantically urged him to go to Canada at least for a time. It was useless advice to David Walker. He replied: "I will stand my ground. *Somebody must die in this cause.* I may be doomed to the stake and the fire, or to the scaffold tree, but it is not in me to falter if I can promote the work of emancipation."[44]

Nor was he alone in this determination. Walker's message electrified the black community of the North and provided new sources of courage for those among them who saw no ultimate solution apart from the sword of the Lord. Even more important, perhaps, scores of now anonymous black people throughout the South risked their lives to distribute the *Appeal.* In Savannah an unidentified "negro preacher" distributed it after it had reached the city by boat. In February 1830 four black men were arrested in New Orleans on charges of circulating the *Appeal.* That same winter, thirty copies of it were found on a free black man in Richmond, Virginia. Meanwhile black seamen carried it along the coast at similar peril.[45]

If he was able to follow the progress of the *Appeal* into the South, it is possible that David

Walker may have been most moved by its appearance in his home town of Wilmington, North Carolina. As a result of it, much "unrest and plotting" were noted in the black community. But there was also a great cost to pay. Early in 1830, a report from Wilmington announced that "there has been much shooting of negroes in Wilmington recently, in consequence of symptoms of liberty having been discovered among them."[46]

Walker had said it: "I will stand my ground. *Somebody must die in this cause.*" On the morning of June 28, 1830, in Boston's fair precincts of liberty, David Walker became suddenly and mysteriously afflicted, and fell dead in a doorway near his shop. Almost all of black Boston was convinced that the dauntless crusader had been poisoned.[47]

TURNER AND WALKER?

And what of Nat Turner? Did Walker's *Appeal* ever reach him as he waited for the proper sign in Southhampton County? No record exists of that contact, if it ever occurred. But the contact was not necessary, for Nat Turner had long been convinced that the God of Walker's *Appeal* had always been in Southhampton.

By the time of Walker's death, Turner had moved to a new home in the country, on the farm of Joseph Travis near Barrow Road. Legally, as such madness went, Nat was now owned by Putnam Moore, an infant. The child's father, Thomas Moore, Nat's last owner of record, had recently died, and in 1830 Moore's widow—Putnam's mother—married Joseph Travis. At that point she and the child moved with Nat to the Travis home and land. But wherever he was, working for whichever white person currently claimed to be his owner, Nat Turner knew that he had only one Master, who spoke in thunder and lightning and through the swaying, leafy trees. This was the Master who possessed his life, who had honed and harshened him in the wilderness, in the midst of the black community, in the movement of

black struggle. This was the leader of the black angels who would scourge the white oppressors and pour judgment like a red bloodtide over the land. So Nat did his temporary work and bided his time, watching for the sign.[48]

Green trees a bending
Poor sinner stands a tremblin'
The trumpet sounds within-a my soul
I ain't got long to stay here.

The sign came in February 1831, with an eclipse of the sun. White men seeking a sign may have thought it marked an end to their bleak season of economic suffering in Virginia and North Carolina, but Nat found a different message: the movement of the last into their proper place had begun. And so, soon after the eclipse, he told his closest comrades that the time of battle and blood was approaching. With him in the initial leadership cadre were four men: Henry Porter, Hark Travis, Nelson Williams, and Samuel Francis. Evidently there was a group of some twenty-five who would form the core of the fighting force at first, convinced that others would be recruited as the struggle was openly joined.[49]

The Fourth of July, that prime symbol of white American contradictions, was chosen as the date for the uprising. But as the time approached, Nat became ill (were there fears or premonitions?) and the date was abandoned. Another sign had to be sought. On August 13, 1831, there was "a day-long atmospheric phenomenon, during which the sun appeared bluish green," and Nat knew that he had found the way again. One week later he met with Hark and Henry to agree on a final plan. The next night they met again, this time with several others; they agreed on their work, and ate a final meal together. In the dark hours of the morning of August 22, Nat Turner's God pressed him forward at the head of his band of black avenging angels, drove him in search of what seemed the ultimate justice: that "the first should be last and the last should be first." According to a black tradition, Nat's final words to his followers were: "Remember, we do not go forth for the sake of blood and carnage; but it is necessary that, in the commencement of this revolution, all the whites we meet should die, until we have an army strong enough to carry out the war on a Christian basis. Remember that ours is not a war for robbery, nor to satisfy our passions; it is a *struggle for freedom."* Whatever the words, this was the goal, and the river now was churning.[50]

They began at the Travis household with hatchets and axes, and no life was spared. At that point, with very few exceptions, all whites were the enemy. It was not a matter of "good" and "bad" masters; all were involved in slavery. And the children—even Putnam Moore— were the heirs. Temporarily filled with such resolve, organized into rudimentary cavalry and infantry sections, Nat's men continued down the Barrow Road, storming house after house, destroying family after family: Francis, Reese, Turner, Peeples, Whitehead, each in its turn experienced the terrible slaughter, not alien to the children of Africa.

At the height of the advance, there were apparently some sixty men in Nat Turner's company, including several described as "free" Together, in a breathlessly brief period of solidarity, they were marching to Jerusalem, Virginia, and their leader was now "General Nat." Once again a captive black prophet, wresting the religion of white America out of its hands, had transformed it and had in turn been utterly changed. Now, as an insurrectionary commander carrying out the sanguinary vengeance of a just God, Nat Turner took up the spirit of David Walker's *Appeal* and burned its message into the dark and bloody ground of Virginia, streaking the black river with blood.[51]

Apparently, he had hoped to move so quickly and kill so thoroughly that no alarm would be given before his marchers reached Jerusalem, and had captured the cache of arms stored there. As in the case of Gabriel and Vesey, the steps beyond that action were not certain. Perhaps they planned to head toward the swamps. There were even rumors that they expected somehow to find their way to Africa. But in the brutal light of August, it was still Virginia, U.S.A. The skies had not broken open, the earth had not erupted in divine power and judgment—and they were not fully angels of light. Indeed, as time wore on that Monday there was a growing sense of confusion, disarray, and sometimes drunkenness among some of Nat's men. Often the prophet himself seemed distracted, and rode at the rear of his troops rather than at the front. Added to these internal problems was the tragic fact that General Nat's men "had few arms among them—and scarcely one, if one, that was fit for use." So it was still Virginia. They had not moved as rapidly, mobilized as effectively, transformed themselves as fully, nor destroyed as efficiently as Nat had expected. Before they reached the road to Jerusalem, the alarm had been spread, leaping like fire from one blanched and trembling set of lips to another, echoing in the clashing sound of church bells across the countryside. The alarm struck fear in the heart of some of Turner's band and they deserted. Others, still on plantations, decided that the struggle was now hopeless, and decided to remain with their masters, biding their time.[52]

Nevertheless, Nat had already challenged Virginia, the government of the United States, and all the fierce and chilling fears which raged within the depths of the white community everywhere. So vigilante groups, militia companies, and the ever-present military arm of the federal government were soon on their way to the battleground. By noon on Monday, in the blazing heat of a cornfield, Turner's insurrectionaries had their first encounter with the white militia and the volunteer companies which had rushed to organize. The blacks were heavily outgunned and, after suffering significant casualties among some of their best men, were forced to retreat. Still, with less than a third of his army remaining, General Nat maintained his resolve to reach Jerusalem.

But the path was blocked each way he moved, fear was rising among his decimated command, and night was now upon them. So they hid and prayed and hoped, while isolated members of their company were being trapped, captured, and sometimes murdered in the woods.

By the next day, Tuesday, August 23, it was hard to see how hopes or prayers would prevail. The countryside was swarming with hundreds of armed white men from surrounding counties, cities, and military bases in Virginia and North Carolina, and Turner had fewer than twenty rebels remaining. Even in the face of these odds, Nat and his men were determined to fight on, if only they could draw more blacks to their side. Before daybreak they moved to attack a large plantation near their encampment, daring to hope they would attract fresh recruits out of the slave quarters there. Instead, Turner's fighters were repulsed by a defending force made up of the owners and their enslaved blacks. At least one of the rebels was killed there and several were severely wounded, including Nat's close friend, Hark. That may have been the decisive experience of defeat. Soon after, in one last skirmish with the militia, three more of Nat's little band were killed; others were wounded and captured, becoming offerings to a fearful spirit of vengeance which raged through the white community. Only Prophet Nat and four followers managed to escape. Finally, before Tuesday was over, as the beleaguered black remnant force separated in desperate search for other possibly surviving companies, all save Nat were killed or captured.

The march to Jerusalem was over. The band of black avenging angels was crushed. Still, Nat Turner was not captured and was not defeated. That night he hid and hoped. As hundreds of men and animals searched him out he dug a hole in the ground and lay there, daring to nurture the dream that he might yet regroup his forces, refusing to believe that the promised time of judgment for Virginia's

slaveholders had not come (or had arrived in some form unrecognizable to him).[53]

In spite of Turner's desperate hope, there was no regrouping for his troops. Rather, while the residue of the black men hid or were rounded up, the outraged, terrified white forces struck back in overwhelming fury. Estimates range from scores to hundreds of black people slaughtered, most of whom evidently had no intimate connection with the uprising. Meanwhile, the prophet-turned-general was alone in the woods again, hiding, biding his time, most likely wondering if there would ever be another sign. He remained in hiding, avoiding capture for six weeks after the attempted revolution. But the signs were not propitious. His wife was found and lashed until she gave up those papers of his in her possession, papers "filled with hieroglyphical characters," characters which "appear to have been traced with blood."[54]

> *"The blood of Christ . . . was now returning to earth."*

His friends were being captured and killed. Perhaps, though, there may have been some comfort afforded him if Turner learned that many of them manifested an amazing spirit of courage and commitment, even in the face of death. Of some it was said that "in the agonies of Death [they] declared that they was going happy for that God had a hand in what they had been doing."[55]

While Nat was still hiding, another black preacher—this time one named David—attempted to enter the radical stream. In Duplin County, in southeastern North Carolina, far from Nat's place in the woods, David planned rebellion. With other enslaved Africans he plotted an insurrection for October 4, 1831, to culminate in a march on Wilmington. Were these some of David Walker's heirs, readers of the *Appeal,* marching on his native city in his honor? Or were they, as the authorities feared, part of Nat Turner's band of avengers? No one was certain, and the insurrection was blocked before it could demonstrate the direction of its flow. So even in Duplin County signs were not good, though the river was clearly in ferment.[56]

Out of that ferment, while Nat was still hiding, a fiery letter reached the town of Jerusalem, sounding almost as if the most stunning visions of Turner, Walker, and every other black insurrectionary leader had been put on paper and thrust into the Southern furnaces. Arriving from Boston, signed simply by "Nero," the missive proudly and provocatively announced to the white authorities that a paramilitary organization of black men was forming which would eventually lead hundreds of thousands of black people to take up arms in revenge for all the oppression of their people. According to Nero, their leader was even then traveling throughout the South, visiting "almost every Negro hut and quarters there." Key cadre members were training in Haiti, learning from the surviving leaders of that celebrated revolution. Everywhere in America they were recruiting, telling blacks "that if they are killed in this crusade that heaven will be their reward, and that every person they kill, who countenances slavery, shall procure for them an additional jewel in their heavenly crown." Had David Walker finally arrived in Southhampton County, vindicating the hidden Turner and his scores of dead companions? Or was this simply another of those radical, bloody visions which must soar wildly out of the river of a people's freedom struggle, expressing all the yearnings buried in the spirits of the mute sufferers?[57]

The silence which followed the letter offered no answers for the future and no concrete hope in the present, least of all for the fugitive insurrectionary. Then on October 30, 1831, Nat Turner was captured. His sign had not come; Nero's army had not appeared. Charged with "conspiring to rebel and making insurrection," he told his counsel that he wished to plead not guilty, because he "did not feel" that he was a guilty person. Guilt was not a relevant category for an instrument

of divine judgment—even if the last sign had not come.[58]

Perhaps he was sign in himself. Thomas Gray, a local slaveholding attorney who produced his own widely read version of Turner's confession, described Nat in prison as "clothed with rags and covered with chains, yet, daring to raise his manacled hand to heaven, with a spirit soaring above the attributes of man." Then Gray added, "I looked on him and my blood curdled in my veins." Turner's presence provoked similar terror and awe in other white observers, as well as deep levels of rage. Clearly some of that rage—and terror—had been spent in the postrebellion bloodletting, but lynching was still a possibility, so during the trial the court ordered the normal detachment of guards increased "to repel any attempt that may be made to remove Nat alias Nat Turner from the custody of the Sheriff." Nevertheless, when whites faced the reality of Nat Turner, other feelings and emotions seemed to overwhelm their rage. Indeed, there was something approaching fascination in the words of one contemporary: "During the examination, he evinced great intelligence and much shrewdness of intellect, answering every question clearly and distinctly, and without confusion or prevarication." Nat had no reason to be confused or to lie. Indeed, he did not hesitate to say that if he had another chance he would take the same bloody path to God again.[59]

It was on November 11, 1831, that Nat Turner went to the gallows, refusing to speak any final word to the crowd gathered to see him die, knowing that it was his living which had been his last, best testimony. Then, in its quiet, secret ways, the black community of Virginia and of the nation took his life into its own bosom and pondered it, just as some had done at the outset of his life. They continued to see signs, beginning with the day of his execution, for on that day, according to black tradition, "the sun was hidden behind angry clouds, the thunder rolled, the lightning flashed, and the most terrific storm visited that county ever known."[60]

> *My Lord He calls me, He calls me by the thunder*
> *The trumpet sounds within-a my soul*
> *I ain't got long to stay here.*

Perhaps, though, in keeping with all the irony of the history of our struggle, it was the terrified and ruthlessly driven white community which provided the ultimate sign of meaning for Nat Turner's movement. In the course of the massacre of blacks following the insurrection, the severed head of a black man had been impaled on a stake just where the Barrow Road, Nat's way of judgment, intersected the road to Jerusalem. The juncture became known as Blackhead Signpost and was meant, as usual, to be a warning against all future hope of black freedom [61]

In spite of the white world's intentions, that macabre roadmark, with its recollections of similar slave-ship rituals and other bloody American roads, may have been the awaited black sign, fraught with many meanings: the suffering and death continually interwoven with the black march toward the freedom of Jerusalem; the white force of arms forever placed in the way of the life-affirming black movement. But even that terrible sign may have been transmuted to mean much more, just as Nat Turner meant more. Perhaps above all else it was a statement of the way in which all black people were a collective Blackhead Signpost for America. By the time of Nat Turner, that possibility was clearer than ever before. For white America's response to the black struggle for freedom might well determine the ultimate destination of its own people, moving them toward greater, truer human freedom, or eventually closing all pathways into a dead end of tragic, brutish varieties of death. So black struggle and black radicalism had no choice but to continue as an active, moving, relentless sign, forcing the issue of the nation's future, never allowing any of our God-driven, freedom-seeking, Jerusalem-marching fathers to have died in vain, pointing the way.

Notes

1. The following overview of America in the late 1820s is based on many sources, including: Robert Baird, *Religion in America* (New York, 1844); Charles I Foster, *An Errand of Mercy: The Evangelical United Front, 1790–1837* (Chapel Hill: University of North Carolina Press, 1960); Sidney E. Ahlstrom, *A Religious History of the American People* (New Haven: Yale University Press, 1972); John B. McMaster, *A History of the People of the United States,* 8 vols. (New York: D. Appleton and Company, 1918–24), IV, V; Perry Miller, *The Life of the Mind in America* (New York: Harcourt, Brace & World, 1965); Alice Felt Tyler, *Freedom's Ferment: Phases of American Social History to 1860* (Minneapolis: University of Minnesota Press, 1944); George Dangerfield, *The Era of Good Feelings* (New York: Harcourt, Brace & World, 1963). Of course the interpretation is largely my own.

2. See for instance Helen Hunt Jackson, *A Century of Dishonor* (1885; rpt. Minneapolis: Scholarly Press, 1964), *passim;* Grant Foreman, *Indian Removal* (Norman: University of Oklahoma Press, 1953), *passim.* See also the excellent collection of documents on the dispossession in Virgil J. Vogel, ed., *This Country Was Ours: A Documentary History of the American Indian* (New York: Harper and Row, 1972).

3. On the Missouri Compromise debates, see Dangerfield, *The Era,* pp. 95–245; and Glover Moore, *The Missouri Controversy, 1819–1821* (Lexington: University of Kentucky Press, 1953), *passim.*

4. *Negro Population,* pp. 24–57. The internal slave trade is discussed fully in Frederic Bancroft, *Slave Trading in the Old South* (1931, rpt. New York: Frederic Ungar, 1959), pp. 19–66; also Robinson, *Slavery,* pp. 427–66.

5. *Negro Population,* pp. 24–57. Examples of the references are to be found, for instance, in Aptheker, *Slave Results,* pp. 18–45, and Tragle, *Southampton,* p. 17.

6. In dealing with the local attorney, Thomas Gray, and his version of Turner's *Confession* (Tragle, pp. 300–21), we are faced with many problems. Tragle offers a helpful analysis of the document and its authenticity in the course of his sharp and telling criticism of the novelist William Styron, pp. 401–09. I suspect that there is much truth in the *Confession,* that Gray inserts himself more than is helpful, and that Nat Turner conceals a good deal. Oates's biography, *The Fires of Jubilee,* is competent but flat, missing the mystery inherent in a man like Turner.

7. Tragle, *Southampton,* pp. 306–07.

8. *Ibid.,* p. 308.

9. *Ibid.*

10. Indeed, there soon developed a belief among many blacks that Nat was endowed with the gift of healing; others said he had power to control the clouds. Such stories, clearly drawing on the lively traditions of Africa, only added to the young man's renown. See Tragle, *Southampton,* pp. 222, 420–21, 100, 309–10; Oates, *Fires,* pp. 35–41; Aptheker, *Slave Revolts,* pp. 294–95.

11. On Nat Turner's marital status, the documents and suggestions provided by Tragle (*Southampton,* pp. 90, 281, 327) are valuable; also Oates, *Fires,* pp. 29, 162–63, 308–09.

12. The millenarian setting of early nineteenth-century Christianity is discussed in H. Shelton Smith, Robert T. Handy, Lefferts A. Loetscher, eds., *American Christianity,* 2 vols. (New York: Charles Scribner's Sons, 1960), II, 12, 16, 18; Nelson Burr, *A Critical Bibliography of Religion in America,* Vol. IV of James W. Smith and A. Leland Jamison, eds., *Religion in American Life,* 4 vols. (Princeton: Princeton University Press, 1961), I, 326–27; Ahlstrom, *Religious History,* pp. 474–78.

13. Tragle, *Southampton,* p. 310; Herbert Aptheker, Nat Turner's *Slave Rebellion* (New York: Humanities Press, 1966), pp. 137–38; Oates, *Fires,* p.41.

14. Robert Hayden, "Ballad of Nat Turner," *Selected Poems* (New York: October House, 1966), pp. 72–74.

15. Tragle, *Southampton,* p. 92; Oates, *Fires,* p. 42.

16. Aptheker, *Slave Revolts,* p. 265. On the subject of these other uprisings, there is a helpful bibliography in Eugene D. Genovese, *Roll, Jordan, Roll: The World the Slaves Made* (New York: Pantheon, 1974), pp. 709–11; an important, expanded version of his treatment and of his bibliography on the subject is available in *From Rebellion to Revolution: Afro-American Slave Revolts in the Making of the Modern World* (Baton Rouge: Louisiana State University Press, 1979). See also Aptheker, *Slave Revolts,* p. 278.

17. The story of the shipboard suicides is found in Austin Bearse, *Reminiscences of Fugitive-Slave Law Days in Boston* (1880; rpt. New York: Arno Press, 1969), p. 9.

18. Aptheker, *Slave Revolts,* pp. 279–80; a continued movement of rebellion and resistance by Alabama outlyers in this period is confirmed by James B. Sellers, *Slavery in Alabama* (University of Alabama Press, 1950), pp. 282–83. Also see Franklin, *From Slavery,* pp. 210–11.

19. Unfortunately, we still have nothing more comprehensive on David Walker's life than Henry Highland Garnet's "A Brief Sketch on the Life and Character of David Walker," first published in 1848 and reprinted in Herbert Aptheker, ed., *One Continual Cry: David Walker's Appeal to the Colored Citizens of the World* (New York: Humanities Press, 1965), pp. 40–44. A modern essay focusing especially on Walker's Boston years indicates a number of the pertinent questions about him: Donald M. Jacobs, "David Walker: Boston Race Leader, 1825–1830," *Essex Institute Historical Collections,* 107 (Jan. 1971), 94–107.

20. Garnet, "Brief Sketch," p. 41; *Freedom's Journal,* Mar. 16, 1827; Jacobs, "David Walker," pp. 95–97.

21. For examples of such words and their costliness, see Ira Berlin, *Slaves Without Masters* (New York: Pantheon, 1975), pp. 89–97, 336–38; Samuel Ringgold Ward, *Autobiography of a Fugitive Negro* (1855; rpt. Chicago: Johnson Publishing, 1970), p. 12; Robert S. Starobin, ed., *Blacks in Bondage: Letters of American Slaves* (New York: Franklin Watts, 1974), pp. 107–10. Moreover, persons like Nat Turner (above, p. 80) and Frederick Douglass (below, p. 103) could also testify to these realities.

22. For the dangers faced by black abolitionists in the North, see Aptheker, *Documentary,* I, 220; Dorothy Sterling, ed., *Speak Out in Thunder Tones* (New York: Doubleday, 1973), pp. 132–36; Ward, *Autobiography,* pp. 35–37.

23. Quoted in Bracey et al., *Black Nationalism,* p. 25.

24. The text of the speech appeared in *Freedom's Journal,* Dec. 19, 1828.

25. [Robert Alexander Young], *The Ethiopian Manifesto* (New York, 1829). The most readily available source of the full text is Sterling Stuckey, ed., *The Ideological Origins of Black Nationalism* (Boston: Beacon Press, 1972), pp. 30–38.

26. Stuckey, *Ideological Origins,* p. 30. In the light of Young's reference to Grenada as the source of the mulatto Messiah, a few alert twentieth-century black nationalists have noted that the mother of Malcolm X came to the United States from Grenada. However, internal evidence in the *Manifesto* suggests that Young was really pointing to himself as the promised deliverer. It is also important to note that, like so many similar manifestoes in the later black struggle, this one was addressed at least as fully to whites as to "Ethiopians."

27. There are several modern editions of the complete text of the *Appeal.* Among the most accessible are Charles M. Wiltse, *David Walker's Appeal* (New York: Hill and Wang, 1965), and Aptheker's *One Continual Cry.* Aptheker's introduction and footnotes are by far the most helpful; his text is used in this study.

28. Walker/Aptheker, pp. 64–65. Certainly the line of spiritual heirs reaches at least from Henry Highland Garnet (below, pp. 133–35, 140–43) to Malcolm X.

29. Walker/Aptheker, pp. 73–74.

30. *Ibid,* p. 89.

31. *Ibid.,* p. 75. It is fascinating to note how directly Walker is related to the traditions of religious/political revolution. For instance, very similar sentiments were expressed by the Anabaptist revolutionary Thomas Muntzer during the German Peasants' War of the sixteenth century; see Guenther Lewy, *Religion and Revolution* (New York: Oxford University Press, 1974), p. vii. Also, many concepts and even certain stylistic aspects of the *Appeal*

suggest that Walker had had access to the April 1804 proclamation by Jacques Dessalines, the Haitian liberator. See the Dessalines document in Drake, "Black Nationalism," pp. 28–35

32. Drake, "Black Nationalism," p. 30; above, pp. 58–59.

33. Walker/Aptheker, pp. 83–85, 65–66.

34. Confidence in God's retributive justice is a constant in the literature of black struggle. Many of its modern manifestations were most deeply lodged in the teachings of the Nation of Islam and their foremost heretic, Malcolm X. Compare Malcolm X, *The Autobiography of Malcolm X* (New York: Grove Press, 1964), pp. 246, 370; Elijah Muhammad, *The Fall of America* (Chicago: Muhammad's Temple of Islam No. 2, 1973), pp. 52–55, 108–11; and Louis E. Lomax, *When the Word Is Given* (New York: New American Library, 1964), pp. 175–76.

35. Walker/Aptheker, pp. 76, 126–28. Again, Walker seems very close to Dessalines. Indeed, his description of whites as the "natural enemies" of black people is precisely the same as Dessalines's in the 1804 proclamation: Drake, "Black Nationalism," p. 29.

36. Walker/Aptheker, pp. 139, 140, n.

37. *Ibid.,* pp. 77–78.

38. *Ibid.,* pp. 93–94. Consciously or not, Walker, the church member, introduced here a pan-African parallel to the New Testament concept of the Christian Church as the indivisible "body of Christ."

39. *Ibid.,* p. 104.

40. *Ibid.,* pp. 137–38.

41. *Ibid.* In our own post-Montgomery Boycott generation, we have seen leaders and institutions as varied as Martin Luther King, Jr., Malcolm X, James Forman, the Nation of Islam, and the Urban League, struggle mightily with the issue of what *would* be the appropriate restitution and reparations due to the black community.

42. Walker/Aptheker, pp. 45–50; William H. Pease and Jane H. Pease, "Document: Walker's Appeal Comes to Charleston: A Note and Documents," *JNH,* 59 July 1974), 287–92; H. E. Sterkx, *The Free Negro in Ante-Bellum Louisiana* (Rutherford, N.J.: Fairleigh Dickinson University Press, 1972), p. 98.

43. Quoted in Litwack, *North*, p. 234.
44. Walker/Aptheker, p.43. Eventually the bounty on Walker was raised to $3,000.
45. Ibid., pp. 45–50.
46. Aptheker, *Slave Revolts*, p. 290.
47. Walker/Aptheker, pp. 43–44. Jacobs, "David Walker," pp. 106–07, does not accept the poisoning theory, and raises an interesting question about Walker's age when he died.
48. Tragle, *Southampton*, p. xv. Oates, *Fires*, p. 51, identifies the marriage year as late 1829.
49. According to his *Confessions* (Tragle, p. 310), the four men named comprised the first group to whom Nat revealed his plans. By the time of the actual event, two more persons, Jack Reese and Will Francis, were included. See also Oates, *Fires*, pp. 52–53.
50. Tragle, *Southampton*, p. 310. The final words are quoted in G. Williams, *History of Negro Race*, II, 88. Williams knew and appreciated the oral traditions of the black community. This quotation may well have been reconstructed from such a source.
51. Tragle, *Southampton*, pp. 310–13. In addition, for all their lack of precision and accuracy, several contemporary newspaper reports suggest the impact of the event on the surrounding population. They are quoted in Tragle, pp. 31–72. See Oates, *Fires*, pp. 66–91.

52. On the poor supply of arms, see a contemporary statement quoted in Aptheker, *Nat Turner's Slave Rebellion*, p. 55.
53. On the involvement of the U.S. military, two different emphases appear in Aptheker, *Slave Revolts*, p. 300, and Tragle, *Southampton*, pp. 16–17. Also, note Oates, *Fires*, p. 97.
54. Tragle, pp. 34, 69, 74–75, 92; Aptheker, *Nat Turner's Slave Rebellion*, pp. 60–62.
55. Aptheker, *Nat Turner's Slave Rebellion*, pp. 37–38.
56. [Samuel Warner], *Authentic and Impartial Narrative of the Tragical Scene . . . in Southampton County* (New York, 1831), p. 23. The Warner document is also reproduced in Tragle, *Southampton*, pp. 279–300.
57. Ira Berlin, "Documents: After Nat Turner, A Letter from the North," *JNH*, 55 (Apr. 1970), 144–51.
58. The wording of the formal charge against Nat Turner is found in the Minute Book of the Court of Southampton County. The more familiar formulation: ". . . making insurrection, and plotting to take away the lives of divers free white persons," is evidently Gray's own version: Tragle, *Southampton*, pp. 221, 318.
59. Tragle, pp. 221, 132, 317; Oates, *Fires*, p. 119.
60. G. Williams, *History of Negro Race*, II, 90.
61. Tragle, p. 7.

Essay/Discussion Questions

1. Vincent Harding notes that David Walker's 1829 *Appeal* was one of the earliest radical statements in the great tradition of African American protest thought. It indicted white America, challenged the dehumanizing system of chattel slavery, and called for black solidarity and resistance. What impact did the *Appeal* have on black and white America?

2. It is often stated that Christianity was used to pacify African slaves in America. Yet Nat Turner and David Walker were highly religious men, strongly influenced by Christian theology, who played leadership roles in the struggle for African American liberation in the nineteenth century. Explain.

3. It can be argued that as a result of the Atlantic slave trade and chattel slavery, anti-black racism, in attitude and practice, became deeply embedded in the American personality, culture, and institutional arrangements. Discuss.

Cafundó: Counterpoint on a Brazilian African Survival*

MICHAEL MITCHELL

In March of 1978, a curious anthropological discovery took place in the state of São Paulo which was to have nationwide impact. Through extensive media coverage, Brazilians were made aware that, despite attempts to accomplish rapid modernization, their society remained one of sharp contrasts. The focus of attention was the rural community of Cafundó, located near the city of Sorocaba. There, for reasons that eluded and intrigued a Portuguese-speaking nation, the African language slaves, who had last arrived on Brazilian shores in the nineteenth century, had been preserved for more than a century.[1]

This discovery assumed the proportion of a celebrated event much like the "Roots" phenomenon in the United Slates: the media, the scholarly community, simple well-wishers and curiosity seekers toured the site offering gestures of respect for Cafundó's past and support for its continued survival. Afro-Brazilians, who were at the time experiencing a rejuvenation of their own collective consciousness, saw Cafundó as an especially fortuitous discovery because it made a common but remote history more accessible.[2]

The curiosity of the event quickly led to considerations with far-reaching implications. First, Cafundó promised to reshape understanding of Brazilian slavery, serving as a "living museum" that might uncover the mysteries of a past nearly destroyed; and second, Cafundó would raise questions about the nature of Brazilian development. How, it would be asked, could an Afro-Brazilian community clinging to the past through its African language be found to exist in the most "modern" part of Brazil? Could Cafundó suggest clues about the very nature of Brazilian development as well as enhance the fading colors of Brazil's cultural mosaic?

From *Centennial Review*, vol. 28, no. 3 (Summer 1984), pp. 185–203.

*The author wishes to acknowledge the help of the several colleagues who commented on an earlier draft of this article. Special thanks in particular go to Dr. Hugo Ferreira da Silva and Professor Peter Fry, who made available valuable research material on Cafundó. Special thanks also go to Professor Leslie Rout for his encouragement. Ms. Hattie Black and Ms. Carole Simmons provided generous assistance.

These and other questions comprise the major issues to be discussed in this essay. Particular attention will be given to the evolving political economy of the region surrounding Cafundó, and the impact of its conversion to a free peasant community on Cafundó's African survival.

I. CAFUNDÓ: A BRIEF DESCRIPTION

The village of Cafundó rests in a valley in the municipality of Salto de Pirapora, approximately 20 kilometers from the city of Sorocaba, and 130 kilometers from the city of São Paulo.[3] At First glance there is little to attest to the community's extraordinary character. In fact, it closely resembles a typical Paulista *caipira* community. (*Caipira* is a term generally used to refer to a person from the countryside or generally a rural way of life.) Its surroundings and resources are meager and only a battery-powered radio played throughout the day appears to link it with the outside world.

This community of roughly 70 people maintains itself through subsistence agriculture. Its inhabitants cultivate rice, beans, corn and manioc on just under 8 *alqueries** of land. Few draft animals are used in this endeavor, and generally their farming technology is rudimentary. Efforts to sustain themselves from their own plots are supplemented by hunting, and when the need dictates, work on neighboring fazendas as *agregados*. In the past, labor in the community was organized along cooperative lines but recent tensions have lessened the extent of cooperative labor. The ten or so houses which comprise the community are built of straw and mud and are in visible need of repair. Yet, contrary to the impression that a rudimentary life might suggest about its physical isolation, the Cafundistas are not completely cut off from the outside. In fact, a recently constructed road provides access to

Salto de Pirapora, where the Cafundistas occasionally socialize.

Family life in the village is organized around two patrilocal groups, the Caetanos and the Pires. (Although both are descendants from sisters, Antonia and Ifigenia, the two families bear little resemblance to one another, one being recognizably Afro-Brazilian, the other more closely *caboclo* in appearance. (*Caboclo* is a term to refer to a person of mixed indigenous and European backgrounds or the syncretic culture, composed of Amarindian and European elements.) Each has a spokesman for the respective families, but a Caetano, Sr. Octavio, is regarded as the leader of the community. Family ties are reinforced through a network of traditional fictive kinships (*compadrazco*).

According to oral tradition, Cafundó and a now extinct neighboring community, Caixambú, were established on land willed to Antonia and Ifigenia by one Antonio Almeida Leme Penteado in the 1860s. Along with the original inheritance, amounting to some 200 hectares of land (80 *alquires*), Antonia and Ifigenia also obtained their freedom. As a result of this inheritance the Cafundistas claimed legal title to their land.

Despite the attention brought to it for being an African relic, Cafundó is properly speaking a black caipira culture, that is, one made up of various syncretic elements common to rural communities throughout the São Paulo region. The Cafundistas, for instance, adhere to both Catholic and Afro-Brazilian rites, to *Umbanda* in particular, the most syncretic of the Afro-Brazilian religions. Their community celebrations are fixed to Christian and secular calendars, May 13, the date of abolition, being an especially celebrated event. Housing design and construction as well as farming techniques also approximate those found generally in rural São Paulo. In this regard Cafundó is less like Saramacan communities of Surinam, or the remnant of a classic *Quilombo*. (*Quilombo* is the name given the communities of runaway slaves in Brazil.) On the contrary, many

---

*1 *alqueire* = 2.1 hectares.

elements of Cafundó 's culture are shared generally with the black peasantry of the region.

II. THE LANGUAGE

Cafundó stands in relief against the cultural contours of rural Brazil because of a language of indisputable African origins. According to oral tradition the language was brought there by one Tio Alexandre, whose remarkable perseverance made it the special means of communication for the slaves of the Almeida Leme Penteado plantation.[4] Few existing details allow for a satisfying portrait of Tio Alexandre, and the uncertainty of his provenance lends a mythical character to the origins of Cafundó's language. However mythical the scant details may make its origins appear, they are not consistent with the known patterns of the Brazilian slave trade. Portuguese raiders were still menacing the interiors of Angola and Mozambique well into the 1880s, showing a preference for *Ladinos* or at least, those who could function in both Portuguese colonial and Brazilian settings.[5] (*Ladinos* is a term to describe acculturated slaves in Brazil.) Thus, Tio Alexandre could well have been one of the slave trade's last hapless victims.

The precise geographical origin of Cafundó's language has yet to be pinpointed. While it bears resemblance to several belonging to the Bantu family of languages, its extremely compact vocabulary makes its source difficult to locate with the exclusively Brazilian material available. Enough evidence exists, however, to place its source at least in Lusophone southern Africa.

The lexicon of the language is composed of some two hundred items of Bantu origin, primarily nouns, and fifteen or so verbs. These Bantu derivatives are used as word stems which are fitted into Portuguese grammatical and syntactical structures. "The fifteen verbs," Fry, Vogt, and Gnere explain, "[all have] Portuguese infinitive flexions of the first conjugation . . . For example, *Kwedá* [or *Kwedar*], to walk, *Kurtimá* [*Kurimar*], to work, *Kupopiá* [*Kupopiar*]; to talk, *Kukwerá* [*Kukwera*], to marry."[6] Moreover, Portuguese grammatical structures are fused with Bantu stems to form phrases and complete sentences, such as: "Vibudo *ta* Kupopjanui," the black man is speaking, or "Kosuba *O* Agutu Vavuru *No* Viso *Pra* Kwedá *Pra* Kukwerá," choosing a pretty girl with one's eyes to fall in love and marry (italics indicate Portuguese parts of speech).[7]

Even though it might appear that the limited vocabulary of Cafundó's language may not be sufficient to communicate a wide range of objects, ideas, and experiences, it easily suits the Cafundistas, who do not rely on it as the sole or even primary means of communication. Nor has the lexicon remained stagnant or shown signs of diminishing in use. in fact, the Iexicon seems to be evolving continually through the frequent use of circumlocutions to create expressions for which a need has been determined.

III. THE CRIME OF CAFUNDÓ

The vitality of Cafundó's language stems as much from the essential social functions it performs as from the semantical needs it fills. The language operates as a sort of shield to protect the community's integrity. Had it not been for the cohesion reinforced through their language, the Cafundistas might have been less vigorous in the defense of their community. In any event, their resolve to protect their community's integrity led to the so-called "crime of Cafundó," a story that deserves at least a brief telling.

No sooner had the publicity surrounding Cafundó's discovery subsided when a neighboring plantation owner attempted to press a legal claim against much of Cafundó's property. Frustrated with the pace of his litigation, the plantation owner ordered the territory he disputed fenced in by a gang headed by one Benedito Moreira de Souza. Immediately after Souza's arrival in the village for this purpose, the Cafundistas forced a confrontation with him, demanding that he show evidence of some legal authority. ("Reclamamos algum papei," explains Sr. Octavio when describing the incident himself.) Angered at the Cafundistas' courageous insistence on their rights, Souza began menacing the Cafundistas with a revolver. A struggle ensued and Souza was killed. Thus the so-called crime of Cafundó occurred. Shortly thereafter the three brothers of the Caetano family fled into the nearby forest to escape the vengeance sworn by Souza's relatives.[8]

Coincidentally, the victim, Souza, had been involved in a similar confrontation with the Cafundistas some ten years before. At that time, Souza had participated as the strong arm in a successful land swindle directed against the village of Caixambú, a community with familial and cultural ties to Cafundó, and located on the old Leme Penteado plantation as well (it is reported that the language was first spoken here). In that confrontation Souza had actually killed one of the Caetano brothers, a crime for which Souza was never brought to justice.

For months the Cafundistas lived in fear of retribution from Souza's relatives; they became virtual prisoners in their own community, posting sentries at the village's entrance and hardly daring to leave just for casual trips to the nearby town. Primarily through the efforts of a black lawyer, Hugo Fereira da Silva, who was sent to the community by the *United Black Movement* (Movimento Negro Unificado— M.N.U.), the Cafundistas were reassured that they would receive a competent and sympathetic defense.

According to Silva, a plea of self-defense should be heard favorably by the Brazilian courts. But besides making a case on the strict presentation of the facts, Silva intends to introduce a novel motion. He will argue that the defendants' bilingual status entitles them to the aid of interpreters through every stage of the judicial process. if accepted, this would invalidate much of the evidence on which the state's case can be made, since it comes mainly from depositions taken from the Cafundistas without benefit of translators. Although the facts of the case are such that a defense will not have to rest solely on this strategy, the implications of pursuing this line are not lost on Silva. He understands that it would force the Brazilian legal system to recognize, perhaps for the first time, the cultural pluralism created by Brazilian slavery and to acknowledge judicial responsibility for the legacy of slavery.[9]

IV. THE DEVELOPMENT OF SOROCABA

Notwithstanding the far-reaching legal implications of this case, what lends to the fascination of Cafundó is its location. Communities like this often are presumed to have been isolated by such overwhelming barriers as to make their integration into a national culture a seeming improbability. They are thought to have been somehow cut adrift from the main currents of social change, passed by or frozen into some insignificant frame of history, This of course is the popular conception of the *lombos* and *palenques* of the New World. Fugitive slaves, it is commonly asserted, sought refuge in otherwise impenetrable areas where they reconstructed virtually undisturbed cultures from the vague recollections of ancestral lands. Following this reasoning, one would expect a community like Cafundó to be located in the expanse of Brazil's unchartered territory. However, Cafundó quite simply defies this kind of explanation. In fact, its site suggests that it perhaps is the product of modernization and social change. The following is an effort to place the evolution of Cafundó in the context of the evolving political economy of the region of Sorocaba.

The history of the region surrounding Cafundó in many ways reflects the economic dynamism characteristic of the state. Sorocaba derived a relatively sustained prosperity and impetus for growth from a variety of economic sources encompassing livestock trading, manufacturing and the *grande lavora*. Located in the western part of the state, it assumed by the early to mid-eighteenth century a position as a gateway market center for interior cities north and south. With its rich endowments in pasture lands and fresh waters it achieved preeminence, particularly during the mineiro gold cycle, as a livestock center linking miners and farmers from Belo Horizonte with ranchers from Curitiba.

Sorocaba's *feiras* had grown to the point of widespread renown by the middle of the nineteenth century, so much so that the Portuguese traveler Augusto-Emilio Zaluar made special plans to see them. (*Feira* is a term for a fair or a market.) It was the human vitality of the *feira* with which Zaluar seems to have been especially taken. "It was worthy of marvel," Zaluar wrote. "One finds a population so varied that one can see all the elements which make us the popular classes here . . . as though all the provinces of the empire were represented, marked by their peculiarities of dress and the idiosyncrasies in their speech."[10] During the mid-nineteenth century, Sorocaba's *feiras* assumed military importance. Its *feiras* provided the major source of livestock supplies for the Brazilian army during the Paraguayan War.

Sorocaba might have succumbed to complacency in the flush of its livestock preeminence in the way that other regions of the state had so declined. Pinning their fortunes to a single economic cycle, some areas suffered the fate of Cunha, which, having squandered its coffee wealth, strangled indefinitely, never to recover its former prominence. Sorocaba on the other hand metered its economic dynamism to several rhythms and took full advantage of the capital accumulated from livestock trade to diversify its economy. Unlike Cunha, Sorocaba experienced continued economic vitality throughout the nineteenth century and well into the twentieth because of this.[11]

One direction which this diversification took was in the promotion of industry. During the nineteenth century, Sorocaba supported an assortment of industrial activities which ranged from iron works (that of the famed São Joào de Ipanema foundry established in 1813) to several light industries which had grown primarily out of the livestock trade. In the latter category there were factories which produced hats, textiles, leather and silver crafts. Silkworms also were cultivated commercially. These were the mainstays of nineteenth-century manufacturing in Sorocaba.[12]

Toward the end of the nineteenth century heavy industry was securely established in Sorocaba. By 1882, the Ipanema iron foundry was producing for the needs of both local and national clients. It provided, for example, iron goods for nearby *fezendas* as well as artifacts for the naval arsenal. With the completion of the Sorocaba extension in the state's railroad system, Sorocaba became the site of a regional locomotive maintenance and repair plant, which contained an impressive inventory of heavy machinery and a skilled labor force to operate it.[13]

The remaining piece of Sorocaba's nineteenth century economic triad was plantation agriculture. Sorocaba's inchoate incorporation into São Paulo's plantation economy, its *grande lavora*, was less rapid or surely less dramatic than that of other comparable municípios. When French botanist Auguste Saint Hilaire visited the area in 1818 he had occasion to remark about the underutilized lands in the city's environs.[14] Still, in the twilight of the colonial era, men of sugar were becoming the men of substance and this was no less so in Sorocaba than in, say, Campinas or Itu. Coffee too, was slow to arrive in Sorocaba. The scale of Sorocaba's coffee production in the mid-nineteenth century was considerably smaller than that of neighboring Itu, for example. Nevertheless, toward the end of the nineteenth century, Sorocaba contributed an increasingly greater part of the state's coffee economy, sufficient to make coffee a major item of freight shipped from here on the Sorocaban Railway. [15]

Cotton, grown by small farmers, and known as the poor man's crop for this reason, also enjoyed popularity in Sorocaba. Its boom, occasioned by the decline in North American cultivation during the Civil War, peaked in the 1860s. Attempts to capitalize on local supplies to establish textile factories foundered, however, on poor management, a situation which British promoters complained of in frustration. [16]

A sense of irony had to have escaped those who considered the plantation of the coffee culture as an improvements over similar socioeconomic units which perhaps were patrimonial and paternalistic. The coffee plantations of the nineteenth century were to presage new forms of commercial management, similar to those of industry, where enterprises operated according to unsentimental incentives of profit. Yet these institutions still required an ancient and brutal form of labor, human bondage.

Contemporary historiography has demonstrated that the treatment of slaves, especially during the coffee cycle, was uncompromisingly severe. [17] Slaves were driven without regard for the limits of their physical endurance. Harsh punishments for whatever infractions were the rule. Cafundó's own oral history, in fact, offers tales of the horrors of relentless beatings executed on the plantation on which their forefathers suffered. These conditions hardly left Sorocaba immune to slave revolts, two of which occurred early in the nineteenth century. One erupted in 1809 and the other in 1819. The 1809 revolt extended as far north as Campinas. [18]

Whether from an obsession with its own security, or from simple indifference, the slave regime in Sorocaba, as elsewhere, had to make certain adjustments in order to accommodate the African labor it imported to its plantations. This dictated the creation of a cultural space between the European elite and the slaves

who, according to one source at least, came from a variety of ethnic backgrounds besides that of the predominant Bantus of Angola and Mozambique. [19] Early on in the nineteenth century Sorocabans were becoming accustomed to the sounds of African languages spoken by field hands, domestic servants, and porters. Other "Africanisms" such as the religion of Macumba and the elite contrived Congadas, as well, thrived there. This was a cultural accommodation of no small degree and no short duration. [20]

V. FREEDOM AND THE LAND

Cafundó's origins can be plausibly linked to the particular circumstances surrounding the attenuation of slavery in Sorocaba. Nevertheless, there remains another important chapter in Cafundó's history. It is at the point when Cafundó received its grant of freedom and land that highly complex questions concerning the evolution of its culture arise.

The scarcity of detail regarding the manumission of the original residents and their grant of land lends itself inevitably to inconsistent interpretations, ones which future investigators possessing greater access to documentation will have to confirm or reject. Nevertheless, a brief review of some possible explanations of the facts, scant as they are, may be useful here.

In any event these are the facts which survive in Cafundó's oral tradition. Sometime in the 1860s Antonio Almeida Leme Penteado on his death left a will bequeathing his plantation to two sisters, the slaves Antonia and Ifigenia. The will stipulated, according to tradition, that Antonia and Ifigenia be set free on the condition that they neither sell the land nor marry anyone from outside the slave community of the old plantation. [21] Little else is known about the will or about the motives which led Almeida Leme Penteado to commit such an act, and here the discussion enters the realm of conjecture.

The most straightforward and flattering interpretation pictures Almeida Leme Penteado as a man of conscience extending a gesture of benevolence and affection to his slaves at his death. However, from what is known about master-slave relations on the entrepreneurial plantations of São Paulo, this seems highly unlikely. It does not stand to reason that a man who, according to oral tradition, dealt harshly with his slaves while alive would be moved by kindness to bequeath a fortune of considerable proportions to them. Perhaps a strong fit of conscience did overcome him. But there is no evidence reported of such profound remorse overwhelming the planter elite at the time.[22]

On the other hand, another interpretation might show that Almeida Leme Penteado's act was more consistent with the evolving political economy of his time. Carlos Vogt and Mauricio Gnere have been among the first to suggest a connection between changes in the structure of rural labor and the creation of Cafundó. Rather than an act of conscience, Vogt and Gnere contend that the intent of Penteado's will was to force his former slaves into becoming an economically dependent peasant caste, or to push them outright into debt peonage.[23]

While no documentary evidence has yet surfaced which would conclusively substantiate this interpretation, the Vogt-Gnere thesis possesses the merit of at least being consistent with the patterns of structural change taking place in nineteenth-century Sorocaba. And it would thus appear to be a more plausible explanation than one based on the questionable sentimentality of a hard-driving slave owner.

Vogt's and Gnere's line of argument runs along these general lines: The plantations which began springing up in Sorocaba in the mid-nineteenth century were vulnerable to the pressures of a volatile cash crop market. Cycles in the market caused widely varying prices for slaves. And to contend with these pressures planters continually sought ways to reduce the high cost of slave labor. Some planters like Nicolau Vergueiro experimented with European *colonos*.[24] Others tried the alternative of restructuring their slave labor through a new system of debt peonage. It should be pointed out, also, that this kind of structural change was extensive. Planters in the United States faced boom and bust price cycles which compelled them as well to experiment with different forms of plantation labor. Prior to the outbreak of the Civil War, North American planters had already created a caste of free but indebted black peasants, a caste which was intended to ease the pressures of an unstable commodities market on maintaining slaves.[25]

Useful and satisfying as the Vogt-Gnere thesis might be, it still leaves unresolved some of the more perplexing questions regarding the creation of Cafundó. While Vogt and Gnere have pointed to a fruitful line of argument to explore, their reliance on structural factors still leaves the motivation for the bequest of a planter's plantation to his former slaves to be explained. Did Almeida Leme Penteado for example possess such loyalty to the planter class to have resorted to a devise that would have benefited other planters but which would have been no direct benefit to him?

A clue to this puzzle might be found in the composition of the Sorocaban plantation elite and the political conflicts which enveloped it. The name Almeida Leme belonged to a notable plantation clan in Sorocaba which took an active part in the regional politics. In one important episode, that of the provincial revolt of 1842, the conservative Almeida Leme clan bitterly opposed the more liberal conspirators of Sorocaba. After the revolt was suppressed, the Almeida Leme clan found itself on the wrong side of a local conflict which formed support among many of Sorocaba's plantation elite.[26]

Political enmities are difficult to extinguish, and this axiom might help explain Almeida Leme Penteado's bequest. His will may have been a shrewd devise to keep his state intact against the designs of liberal rivals who may have had old scores to settle with the clan.

In any case, certain refinements in the original Vogt-Gnere thesis would have to be made in order to enhance its plausibility.

The Vogt-Gnere thesis even when refined also raises somewhat thorny questions regarding the continuity of the African language of Cafundó. In fact, the thesis contains an implicit but serious challenge to generally accepted theories about the persistence of Africanisms throughout the New World. On the whole, New World African cultures are thought to have developed along lines parallel to the institution of slavery. Where the institution survived, so too did African cultures, which, it is postulated, depended on the vitality brought to it by freshly imported slaves.[27] On the other hand, fragmented into a peasantry or atomized into debt peonage, former slaves would have been bereft of the institutional structure that would have allowed them to perpetuate a separate African culture. The collapse of the gold cycle in the eighteenth century, for instance, left the slaves of the Brazilian mining regions in situations almost identical to a subsistence peasantry. As a consequence of this, they were cut adrift from those institutions which gave them space to retain a collective identity and culture. In eighteenth century Sorocaba, where the network of mining economy extended, slaves undoubtedly found themselves in this situation. As Aluicio de Almeida reports, the majority of slaves found in and around Sorocaba in the latter half of the eighteenth century were almost completely creolized, possessing few traits of an African culture.[28] Thus, it might reasonably be asked how the culture of Cafundó could have survived a structural transition, such as their conversion into a free peasantry, which contained within it the dangers of cultural decomposition?

The case of the Sea Island communities located off the coast of South Carolina and Geor-

gia in the United States assumes a special interest here. These communities, similar to Cafundó with respect to the durability of their "Africanisms," also underwent the kind of structural transition which Vogt and Gnere hypothesize affected Cafundó. Both communities arrived at a particular stage in their evolution at which the structural supports for their culture, that is, the political economy of the plantation, were being radically altered by events. In fact, if anything can be said in comparing these communities it is that the Sea Islands underwent stronger, more direct threats to their cultural integrity than their Brazilian counterpart.

Encased in the traditions of the Sea Islands is the event which marks the transition from slavery to a peasantry. This is the so-called "gun shoot" of 1861, the Civil War encounter in which the Union forces, early during the course of the war, overran the Islands' Confederate fortifications, compelling the planters to flee in desperate haste. As a result of the "gun shoot" the occupying Union army was called on to assume jurisdiction over scores of thousands of field hands whose legal status the federal government was not to determine for some time later. These liberated slaves became, in an infelicitous phrase, "The Contrabands of War" for whom measures had to be devised to maintain them in an unredeemed state between legal bondage and still unattained unconditional freedom. Faced with the dilemma of formulating a policy of occupation, the Union government settled on a scheme, known as the Port Royal Experiment, which would inch "The Contrabands of War" toward actual freedom.[29]

Part of this experiment involved a restructuring of this former slave caste into both a rural wage proletariat and a class of small land holders. It also involved the participation of northern white volunteers sent to the Sea Islands to teach the skills that could ease the entry of the former slaves into a New social and economic order.

The Port Royal Experiment nevertheless assumed the proportions of a full-scale confrontation of cultures, pitting idealistic white Northerners against the black Sea Islanders. The white agents of western civilization were continually bewildered by what seemed to them an incomprehensible language (the Gullah dialect) and non-Christian atavism of the black Islanders' syncretic religion. And some were defeated by these cultural barriers, although others developed a sincere appreciation for the Sea Island culture and encouraged it to grow.[30] The results of the experiment were mixed, however. Humanitarian intentions and purposeful reforms foundered on government mismanagement and the corruption, land speculations, and tax dodging schemes of white opportunists. This failure just as quickly led to resentment, and, in an environment of mutual recriminations, few reforms actually took shape.

Despite the efforts of the Port Royal volunteers, the Sea Islanders held on to their rich African culture. Much of it in fact was being observed and celebrated in the twentieth century, decades after the experiment in Reconstruction had come to an end. During the 1930s and 1940s particularly, the Sea Islanders occasioned a degree of scholarly interest not unsurpassed by the attention given to Cafundó in Brazil. Scores of monographs carried a rather provocative debate on the Islanders' culture, and out of this came one especially prescient remark made by Linguist Lorenzo Turner that the Islanders' Gullah dialect might be best understood if compared to among other things the "Negro-Portuguese" dialects of Angola and Brazil.[31]

The Port Royal experience serves to highlight some interesting similarities between the Sea Islands and Cafundó. Even though their cultures, created in the harsh environment of slavery, were not completely unaffected by the transition from slavery to a free peasant caste, neither were they fully absorbed by overwhelming pressures into a wider, dominant white culture. Furthermore, both sets of communities apparently went about selectively absorbing elements into their culture in a fashion which reinforced their sense of collective identity and which later would enable them to be ranked as cultural aristocracies within a large black community.

Comparisons between the Sea Islands and Cafundó obviously have their limitations and should not be stretched too far. Nevertheless, this exercise points to still unanswered questions, loose ends, as it were, which should be attended before concluding this discussion.

For instance, it remains to be seen why in either the Sea Islands or Cafundó there occurred a process of selective acculturation more compatible with the shape of a larger black community than with a dominant white culture. In both cases these communities went about incorporating new experiences into their cultures in a manner which fell somewhere between the strict preservation of the African-slave cultures and the complete adoption of the ways of the new dominant order.

A suggestive illustration of this point is the commemoration of abolition. For the Sea Islanders it is celebrated on January 1, Emancipation Day; and for the Cofundistas it is observed on May 13. What is curious about these celebrations is that neither fits quite so neatly the historical experiences in these communities. While the Sea Islanders remained "Contrabands of War" even after the "gunshoot," they were at least the first to be set free from the bonds of traditional masters. Similarly, the Cafundistas received their freedom decades before the Brazilian decree of emancipation in 1888. In other words, both were set apart by peculiar circumstances from the course of national events and history. In light of this it seems appropriate to ask why these communities would celebrate the national dates of slavery's abolition instead of one more in keeping with their own respective histories.

At first glance this issue might be taken to be no more than quite normal and obvious commemorations of freedom. But, to accept this line of reasoning would mean attributing this fact to simply some structural transformation, that is, the reorganization of labor and land, and for reasons discussed previously this would be incomplete at best if not misleading. Thus the question remains, what accounts for the selective acculturation of these communities which are represented in the celebrations of slavery's abolition?

In the Sea Islands at any rate this structural transition involved a number of complex factors. It was triggered in no small way by an intra-elite struggle of grand proportions in which the liberation of a race figured as one of the central issues in dispute. The "gun-shoot" signaled the initial event in a protracted struggle and general emancipation marks the final moment of a long-awaited liberation. Racial vindication in this way assumed a high degree of salience for the Sea Islanders, who thus made their connection with a larger Afro-American community under the impact of the dramatic conflict of the war between the states. It would appear therefore that the dramatization of racial aspirations through intra-elite struggle can account for this instance of selective accumulation, that is the celebration of universal abolition. Structural factors alone are not as compelling. Thus, the case of Cafundó might be explained more fully if it could be shown that conditions similar to those in the Sea Islands prevailed at the time of Cafundó's conversion into a free peasant community. And in fact this could well have been the case here as in the Sea Islands.

It would fall well within recent interpretations of the Brazilian abolition campaign to assert that the Cafundistas had drawn on the visible intra-elite conflict over slavery to refashion their culture. As in the United States, the Brazilian abolitionist campaign provided dramatic expectations of an eventual racial redemption. Between the 1860s and the 1880s the conflict over abolition engulfed the major sectors of Brazilian society: city against coun-

tryside, monarch against the army, and master against slave. By the 1880s the conflict had grown to such proportions that it was not uncommon for fugitive slaves to engage openly in armed conflict to secure their freedom. Brazilian abolitionists, too, provocatively dispatched special agents to circulate anti-slave propaganda among slaves, even making provisions for the many who could not read.[32] The Cafundistas' efforts to link their culture to a larger community could plausibly have been the expression of expectations of racial vindication made salient by the protracted intra-elite struggle over abolition issues in Brazil.

VI. CONCLUSION

Among the several questions which spring from an analysis of Cafundó is one which to some may appear to be a recasting of an old controversy. Nevertheless it deserves restating. This concerns the significance of Cafundó. Few would deny that it is a rich source for scholarly reevaluations of Afro-Brazilian history and culture. But the crucial question concerning Cafundó's significance has to do with the symbolic purposes it serves. Cafundó derives its fame from the pride it has generated among many of its well-wishers in the recovering of a remote and otherwise neglected piece of the nation's history. Cafundó has allowed countless numbers of Brazilians, both black and white, to share in its cultural achievements, which for many symbolize the vitality of Brazilian popular culture. Yet however important its symbolic function may be, its value as an evocative symbol should not obscure a more immediate and perhaps more meaningful significance.

Frequently, and apparently with wide acceptance, Cafundó has come to be regarded as a "living museum." But, however rich the historical legacies of Cafundó may prove to be, its importance and its significance should not be confined to its symbolic value alone. To do so would be to commit a serious injustice, however unintended. Cafundó's supporters might be reminded that, whatever symbolic value Cafundó might hold for them, they may unwittingly lock it into a prison of history, preventing any alteration in its ecological or social circumstances, thus doing more harm than good. To regard Cafundó strictly as a living museum or worse, as an anarchistic throwback whose people have refused to conform to the inevitability of history, can lead to a romantic sentimentality that is indefensible in the face of Cafundó's more immediate social and economic problems. Cafundó instead should be taken to be an eminently contemporary drama of survival.

Notes

1. Reports on Cafundó appeared in several major Brazilian newspapers, among them *O Estado de São Paulo,* March 19, 1978; *Folha de São Paolo,* March 17, 1978; *Veja,* April 26, 1978; as well as the *Cruizeiro do Sul* (Sorocaba), March 18, 1978, March 21, 1978, and May 3, 1978.
2. Hugo Ferreira da Silva, "Cafundó: My People, My Folk, my Senzala, My Roots," *Journal of Black Studies,* vol. 11 no. 2 (December 1980), 223–229; Barbara Lavergue, "Quilombo Cafundó: Today's Cultural Resistance in Brazil," *Journal of Black Studies,* vol. 11 no. 2 (December 1980), 217–222.
3. The community has been ably described by a team of anthropologists from the Universidade Estadual De Campinas. Some of their work, the first serious descriptions of the community, have been published. See Carlos Vogt, Peter Fry, and Maurizio Gnere, "Las Lenguas Secetas de Cafundó," *Punto de Vista,* vol. 3, no. 9 (1980), 26–32; and Fry, Vogt, and Gnere, "Mafambura e Caxapura: Na Encruzilhada da Identidade," paper presented at the fourth meeting of the National Association of Social Science Research, Rio de Janeiro, October 28–30, 1980. The description of Cafundó is also based on the author's visit to the village in August 1979.
4. Vogt, Fry, and Gnere, "Las Lenguas Secetas de Cafundó," p. 30.
5. James Duffy, *Portuguese Africa* (Cambridge: Harvard University Press, 1959), p. 146.
6. Vogt, Fry, and Gnere, "Las Lenguas Secetas de Cafundó," p. 29.
7. Ibid.
8. *Cruizero do Sul,* July 20, 1978, July 30, 1978; *O Estado de São Paulo,* July 31, 1978.
9. Author's interview with Hugo Ferreira da Silva, August 1979; *Versus,* September 1978.
10. Augusto-Emilio Zaluar, *Peregrinçáo Pela Provincia de São Paulo* (São Paulo: Martins, 1954), p. 161.
11. On the economic decline of Cunha, see Robert Shirley, *The End of Tradition: Culture Change and Development in the Municipio of Cunha* (New York: Columbia University Press, 1971).
12. Zaluar, *Peregrinçáo Pela Provincia de São Paulo,* p. 161. Early industrialization, by the way, accommodated itself well to slavery in Sorocaba. The Ipanema Foundry, for example, initially operated with slave labor. See Aluicio Almeida, "Achegas A História de Sorocaba," *Revista Do Instituto Histórico e Geográfico de São Paulo* (São Paulo: Martins, 1939), p. 160; Auguste Saint-Hilaire, *Viagem A Provincia de São Paulo* (São Paulo: Martins, 1940), pp. 259–260.
13. José Oliviera de Barros, *Estrada De Ferra Sorocabana, Relatório, 1928* (São Paulo: Sociedade Impressora Paulista, 1939), p. 199; Almeida, "Achegas A História de Sorocaba," pp. 140, 153.
14. Saint-Hilaire, *Viagem A Provinicia de São Paulo,* pp. 248, 251.
15. Barros, *Estrada De Ferra Sorocabana,* p. 29.
16. Stanley Stein, *The Brazilian Cotton Manufacture* (Cambridge: Harvard University Press, 1957), pp. 45–46.
17. Suely Robles Reis Queiroz, *Escravidão Negra em São Paulo* (Rio de Janeiro: José Olympio, 1977).
18. Ernani Silva Bruno, *Viagem Ao Dos Paulistas* (Rio de Janeiro: José Olympio, 1966), p. 125.
19. Alfonso Freitas, "Sorocaba: Dos Temps Idos," *Revista do Instituto Histórico e Geográfico de São Paulo,* vol. 27 (1929), p. 115.
20. For other descriptions of African survivals in twentieth-century Sorocaba, see Florestan Fernandes, "Congadas e Batuques em Sorocaba," in *O Negro No Mundo dos Brancos* (São Paulo: Difel, 1972), pp. 239–255; and

"Contribuicao Para o Estudo De Um Lider Carismático," also in *O Negro No Mundo dos Brancos,* pp. 217–238.

21. Carlos Vogt and Maurizio Gnere, "Cafundó: Uma Comunidade Negra Que Fala Até Hoje Uma Lingua de Origem Africana," unpublished manuscript, Caminas, N.D., p. 9. See also various statements reported in *Cruzeiro do Sul,* March 19, 1978. Comments by Aluicio Almeida on the origins of Cafundó can be found in *O Estado de São Paulo,* March 19, 1978.

22. Suely Robles Reis Queiroz in *Veja,* April 26, 1978, pp. 71–72.

23. Vogt and Gnere, "Cafundó," pp. 7–10.

24. Warren Dean, *Rio Claro: A Brazilian Plantation System* (Stanford: Stanford University Press, 1976), pp. 83–103.

25. Eugene Genovese, *Roll Jordan Roll* (New York: Pantheon, 1974), pp. 400–401.

26. For references to the Almeida Leme family see Aluicio Almeida, *A Revolução Liberal de 1842* (Rio De Janeiro: José Olympio, 1944), pp. 64, 67–68, 72, 76–77.

27. See, for example, Marvin Alleyne, "Acculturation and the Cultural Matrix of Creolization," in Dell Hymes, ed., *Pidginization and Creolization of Languages* (Cambridge: Cambridge University Press, 1971), pp. 169–186.

28. Almeida, "Achegas A História de Sorocaba," pp. 110–118.

29. On the Port Royal experiment, see Willie Lee Rose, *Rehearsal for Reconstruction: The Port Royal Experiment* (New York: Vintage, 1964); William Pease and Jane Pease, *Black Utopia* (Madison: State Historical Society of Wisconsin, 1963), pp. 123–159; Guion Johnson, *A Social History of the Sea Islands* (New York: Negro University Press, 1969), pp. 154–208.

30. Rose, *Rehearsal for Reconstruction,* pp. 90–103.

31. Lorenzo Turner, *Africanisms in the Gullah Dialect* (New York: Arno Press, 1969), p. 13; see also William Bascome, "Acculturation Among the Gullah Negroes," in J. I. Dillard, ed., *Perspectives on Black English* (The Hague: Mouton, 1975), pp. 280–287, and J. I. Dillard, "The Writings of Herskovits on the Study of Language of the Negro in the New World," in *Perspectives on Black English,* pp. 288–295.

32. Robert B. Toplin, *The Abolition of Slavery in Brazil* (New York: Atheneum, 1972); Richard Graham, "Causes for the Abolition of Slavery in Brazil," *Hispanic American Historical Review,* vol. 46 (1966), pp. 123–136; see also Evaristo de Moraes, *A Campanha Abolicionista* (Rio de Janeiro: Leite Rioeiro, Frietas Bastos, Spicer, 1924).

Essay/Discussion Questions

1. Michael Mitchell examines the discovery of Africanisms in the rural Brazilian village of Cafundó. Why is this subject important?

2. The Cafundistas speak a language closely associated with what African language group?

3. Discuss the relationship between Brazilian abolitionists and the Cafundistas in the late nineteenth century.

Spurring a Dialogue to Place the African European Experience Within the Context of an Afrocentric Philosophy

Lydia Lindsey and Carlton E. Wilson

When Roi Ottley's *No Green Pastures* was being published in 1951, the racial attitudes and policies of Europe were not clearly evident to most Americans, but Ottley readily discerned that European societies did not offer any green pastures for Black people who yearn to become firmly rooted. Yet today many Americans still seem surprised to learn that there are people of African ancestry presently residing in European communities who are confronted daily with prejudice and discriminatory policies just as in the United States and South Africa. For the most part, African Europeans come from countries in Africa and the Caribbean. They make up about 3 percent of the population, share a common colonial, migratory, and racial experience, and tend to constitute a colony within the European countries.

The purpose of this article is to emphasize the importance of placing the African European experience within the context of an Afrocentric philosophy. The intent is to broaden the scope of world history and at the same time underscore the role of Africa and its people in shaping cultures and societies in Europe. A subsidiary purpose is to provide a better understanding of the African Diaspora (Asante, 1988, pp. vii-6).

Toward these ends the article focuses on the romanticized view of Americans toward Europe's facade of racial egalitarianism; the deep strain of racial prejudice that runs through the cultural fabric of Europe; the limitations of comparing the experiences of African Americans and African Europeans; and the benefits that can come to American society through the development and implementation of an African European studies curriculum for the 21st century.

Without a doubt, being Black and living in a White-dominated society, whether it be South

From *Journal of Black Studies,* vol. 25, no. 1 (September 1994), pp. 41–61. Copyright © 1994 by Sage Publications, Inc.

131

Africa, the United States, or Europe, is hardly an idyllic experience. "Racism is the problem of the world," says Mbongeni Ngena, South African playwright and author of *Sarafina*. He adds, "The only difference is that in South Africa, it is by law." As articulated by two African American patriots of freedom, W. E. B. Du Bois and Martin Luther King Jr., racism transcends national boundaries and degrades humanity wherever it flourishes (Lindsey, 1989b, p. 194). It is our contention that concerned Americans who seek to make a kinder and gentler world must become more keenly aware of human oppression throughout the world—even in Europe.

Europe has often served as a haven for African Americans seeking refuge from America's racial oppression and this has served to propagate the myth that racial prejudice and racism do not exist abroad. In 1851 when John Watkins, a fugitive slave from America, arrived in Liverpool, England, slavery had been abolished in England since 1834 and in France since 1848. Watkins noted that he was so overjoyed at the prospect of free soil that when he entered the docks at Liverpool he jumped for joy and thought of the words of the English writer William Cowper:

> Slaves cannot breathe in England. If their lungs receive our air that moment they were free. They touch our country their shackles fall. (Watkins, 1852, p. 37)

Frederick Douglass experienced similar emotions when he visited France in 1886; as Michel Fabre (1991) notes in his study on Black writers in France, Douglass was intent on seeing France and the embodiment of enlightened ideals of *liberte, egalite, fraternite*. Douglass approved of France because he did not feel any color prejudice (Fabre, 1991, p. 32). Indeed, as Douglass traveled throughout Europe he praised the Irish, English, and French for "measuring men according to their moral and intellectual worth, and not according to the color of their skin" (Meyer, 1984, pp. 233–237).

Watkins, Douglas, and many other African Americans who went to Europe before and after emancipation were the forebears of American visitors who would contribute to the creation of a myth of racial harmony that has characterized the Black experience in Europe. To these fugitive slaves and abolitionist speakers, and later to soldiers, writers, and entertainers, the position of Blacks in Europe was unlike their position in America. For example, whereas at the turn of the century Jim Crowism was still the norm in America, there was no legal color bar in England. Supposedly, Blacks could live where they wish and mix freely with Whites in hotels, pubs, and dance halls. In reality however, if not in law, there was a color bar. There was racial prejudice. It was not statutory; it was more covert and institutional, but it was no less damaging.

In France there likewise existed a certain liberalism toward race and color. Here it was a liberalism based upon the ideals of liberte, egalite, fraternite. Among the French, Blacks were known to have freedom of movement, and the French tended to judge Blacks based upon their personal worth (Ottley, 1951, p. 74). To be sure, France was far from being a racial utopia. As in England, racial prejudice has a long history in France, and Black immigrants have found it difficult to acquire housing and employment and have often been victims of racial hostility. Consequently, a few observers became convinced that the French only gave lip service to the idea of racial liberalism (McCloy, 1961, p. 244; Ottley, 1951, p. 75).

As a rule, racial prejudice in Europe did not affect American visitors, who were often celebrities or soldiers, but it had a significant effect on the Black population that lived in Liverpool, London, Paris, Marseilles, or Amsterdam. These Blacks, many of whom were born in these areas and others who migrated there from various colonies in Africa and the West Indies, were affected by a European attitude toward Blacks that had been created during the years of the slave trade, slavery, missionary zeal, and colonialism.

Europeans generally tended to view these Blacks as inferior beings who were only fit to serve them and be ruled by them. As the number of Blacks in the various mother countries began to increase, Whites began to perceive them as a threat to their economic and social order. Therefore, it became important to keep these people "in their rightful place" and at the same time cultivate the myth that the dominant White society was free of racial prejudice and discrimination. Meanwhile, the travel stories of Americans who visited European countries contributed, perhaps unknowingly, to the development of the misconception of the Black experience in Europe.

THE WORLD WAR I ERA

With the outbreak of war in 1914, thousands of African American soldiers eventually went to Europe; they were well received in most areas, although Jim Crowism was predominant in the American military. The Black soldiers who served under the French command were generally treated with equality, and many of them were rewarded for their courageous service. Away from the battlefield, too, as W. E. B. Du Bois reported, interracial fraternization was very common, as the French accepted Black soldiers (Fabre, 1991, p. 53). As a result of this intermingling, these soldiers felt that in France there was racial equality and true democracy. A young private wrote to Du Bois, telling him how Black soldiers were enjoying the blessing of true democracy in France. He also wrote that he and others regretted having to return home, where true democracy was "enjoyed only by white people—There is an air of liberty; equality; and fraternity here which does not blow in the black man's face— in liberty loving, democratic America . . . " (Aptheker, 1973, p. 234). These Black soldiers subsequently returned to America telling tales of their experiences in Europe that helped to promulgate the myth of racial parity in European societies.

Meanwhile, as African Americans were taking satisfaction in the belief that there were "green pastures" for Black people in Europe, indigenous European Blacks and colonials who served in the French and British armies continued to experience racial prejudice. The Senegalese who fought for the French were often ridiculed, placed in segregated units, and even used as cannon fodder (Fabre, 1991, p. 52). The British practiced similar policies toward their Black soldiers. The British officers who commanded the West African Frontier Force referred to their native soldiers as "apes" (Ba-Ture, 1918). The British West Indies regiment that was reorganized in 1915 saw only limited action, primarily in Egypt. because officialdom did not want them in Europe (Joseph, 1971, p. 122). At the end of the war many of the West Indian and African seamen who had served His Majesty's government were demobilized in various port cities, which included Liverpool, Cardiff, and London. Their presence, in addition to previous Black residents, created visible Black populations. In 1919 Liverpool had a Black population of 5,000. The overwhelming majority of these Blacks tended to congregate in Toxteth, an area near the docks. Their presence, in combination with the city's unemployment, housing shortage, and emotions aroused by the common sight of Black men associating with White women caused much anxiety among the White population and led to racial violence in 1919. During the disturbances, Blacks were randomly attacked and their property destroyed. The police reacted by charging and arresting many innocent Blacks. Charles Wootton, a 29-year-old ex-Naval Reserve fireman, was drowned by a White mob (Public Record Office, 1919). Similar violence occurred in Cardiff, London, and other seaport towns. It can safely be stated that there was anything but racial harmony in Britain in 1919. In fact, like the United States, Britain too experienced a "Red Summer of 1919."

During the interwar years many members of the "new Negro movement" or the "Black intelligentsia" visited Europe, especially France. These individuals wanted to live in a milieu that would nourish their cultural interest while turning a blind eye to racial prejudice. In France, they believed, they could live and work uninhibited by the racial prejudice that was woven into the fabric of American society. Many of them shared the views expressed by Johnson (1933) when he wrote:

> From the day I set foot in France I became aware of the working miracle within me. . . . I recaptured for the first time since childhood the sense of being just a human being. . . . I was suddenly free; free from a sense of impending discomfort, insecurity, danger; free from the conflict within the Man-Negro dualism and the innumerable maneuvers in thought and behavior that it compels; free from special scorn, special tolerance, special condescension, special commiseration; free to be merely a man. (p. 209)

Paul Robeson echoed Johnson's sentiments. For Robeson, Europe's air was his first breath of freedom (Hamilton, 1974, p. 5). Robeson's European experiences also served to validate the belief that European society was free of racial prejudice. He was firm in his position that life was better for Blacks in Europe because there were no statutory laws governing the behavior of the races. He did not see any all-Black, segregated communities, and there was no color bar in the first-class restaurants or hotels that he patronized (Duberman, 1988, pp. 87–88).

Frequently, in his own country he had been made to feel "alien among white people," but in Europe he was accepted for his talents. Robeson admitted that to many Europeans he was an oddity, but they, unlike White Americans, were willing to accept him as a Black artist (Hamilton, 1974, pp. 34, 42, 45). Although not all of the "Talented Tenth" who went to Europe shared Johnson's and Robeson's views, it is safe to state that the majority did, and that their sentiments played a role in projecting the misconception of the Black experience in Europe.

However, a dissenting view was voiced by Claude McKay, who was critical of race relations in many areas of Europe. McKay criticized the Black intelligentsia for being taken in by French liberalism and for what he considered a narrow, nationalistic view of race relations. He reminded them of the way the French treated their colonial population. He was livid in his response to public and press reaction to France stationing Black Moroccan and Senegalese soldiers in the Ruhr Valley after World War I. The stationing of Black soldiers in the Rhineland created a storm of protest in France, England, and Germany because people were horrified by the thought of Black soldiers being placed in an area where there were no Blacks, and particularly no Black women. Europeans maintained that this situation could only lead to miscegenation and moral decline.

In England, in line with this thinking, Edmund Dene Morel, the Secretary of the Union of Democratic Control, editor of *Foreign Affairs,* and Labor Member of Parliament, wrote an article in the *Daily Herald* titled, "Black Scourge in Europe Sexual Horror Let Loose by France on Rhine: Disappearance of Young German Girls." The article noted that,

> France was thrusting her Black savages . . . into the heart of Germany. These primitive African barbarian carriers of syphilis have become a terror and a horror to the Palatinate countryside. The barely restrainable bestiality of the Black troops has led to many rapes, an especially serious problem because Africans are the most developed sexually of any race, and for well-known physiological reasons, the raping of a white woman by a Negro is nearly always accompanied by serious injury and not frequently has fatal results. (*Daily Herald,* 1920, April 10)

Morel's views were so popular that he published a well-circulated pamphlet entitled *The Horror on the Rhine* (Reinders, 1968, p. 5).

In response, McKay wrote a letter of protest to the editor of the *Daily Herald*, George Lansbury. McKay challenged Morel on his racist views of the sexual prowess of Blacks. He maintained that his primary reason for protesting was because he did not want such propaganda to cause further strife and bloodshed among Blacks and Whites in England (McKay, 1920, p. 2). To be sure, McKay, unlike other members of the Black intelligentsia, did not observe a European society uninhibited by racial prejudice.

It should also be mentioned that Mary Church Terrell, president of the National Association of Colored Women, supported the use of Black soldiers in the Rhineland. Terrell was in Paris in 1919 as a delegate to the International Peace Conference (Fabre, 1991, p. 39). Later, in 1921, Terrell launched a protest when the French assured the Americans that they would only use White soldiers in the Rhineland. In a letter to the French Premier, Raymond Poincare, Terrell asserted that France had never discriminated against people on account of color, but that now France had placed a stigma on Black people. France had at last "publicly prostrated herself before the monster—Race Prejudice" (Terrell, 1940, pp. 364–365). Terrell's remarks to Premier Poincare were critical of French attitudes toward Blacks, but they too reveal certain misconceptions and misunderstandings about the Black experience in France.

For the most part, the Black intellectuals who visited Europe during the interwar years were removed from the day-to-day racism that affected those Blacks who were residents of Europe. For example, employment was a major issue for all during the 1920s and 1930s, but it appears that it was worse for Blacks. Evidence shows that Black factory workers were the first fired to make room for demobilized White workers. The British government even enacted laws that restricted the employment of Black seamen in favor of White seamen. Yet according to officialdom there was no color bar in England.

WORLD WAR II

As was true in America, World War II was a pivotal turning point in the dynamics of race relations in Europe. The war caused Britain to serve as host for nearly 1.5 million American soldiers, of whom 130,000 were Black (Smith, 1987, p. 4). It appears that the English reaction to the presence of Black soldiers should have exposed and destroyed the myth of racial harmony in Britain; instead, it further validated the myth.

For example, the myth of racial harmony was promoted by the way the general public received Black soldiers. In addition, Black soldiers themselves commented that they preferred the racial climate in England. Many of them wrote letters home noting that they were being treated well by the English, especially the women (National Archives, 1942–1944). The American press that followed the soldiers also applauded the way the Black soldiers were received by the British public. George W. Goodman, who was the executive secretary of the Washington Urban League, wrote that the "English proved beyond the shadow of a doubt that it is possible for people of different shades of skin to live side by side in peace and harmony" (1944, p. 10). And Ottley reported that the "British people are naturally hospitable. . . . They warmly greeted the Negro Troops. . . . Easy and friendly associations developed between the races" (1944, p. 4).

When the British public warmly welcomed Black soldiers, it helped to create an illusion that there was no prejudice. Black soldiers were treated well not because the British public was genuinely without prejudice but because they were viewed as temporary American visitors. They had been invited to Britain to fight a war and once the war was over they would leave. Britons and other Europeans were more tolerant of Blacks who were not coming to their countries to live, find housing, or search for jobs. To be sure, to some people the presence of Black soldiers was troubling, and they did not roll out the red carpet, but the soldiers were not a threat to their livelihood. Therefore, they could be tolerated for the duration of the war.

In contrast, however, West Indians and Black residents of Britain had a different experience during the war. West Indian workers and service personnel who came to England to labor in the munitions factories and serve in the Royal Air Force often experienced racial discrimination in employment, housing, and recreation. Concomitantly, long-term Black residents not only suffered from American racism, they also fell prey to homegrown racism. In June 1943, the popular West Indian cricketer and Ministry of Labor official Learie Constantine was denied accommodation at a West London hotel. In September 1943, Amelia King, a Black women whose family had been in England for generations and had traditionally served in His Majesty's Service, was denied the chance to serve in the Women's Land Army because she was Black.

POST–WORLD WAR II

The end of the war in 1945 brought additional visitors to Europe. Novelist William Gardner Smith in *Return to Black America* (1970) observed that after the war many American artists, writers, students, and just plain "Joes" went to settle in Europe. Many of these Americans were seeking a racial Shangri-la—a land of equality, a land of justice where no man would be penalized for the color of his skin (Smith, 1970, pp. 62–63). One of these settlers, Richard Wright, observed that American Blacks in France went about their daily routine with no anxiety about having to cope with arbitrary racial assaults directed against them on residential, occupational, or social grounds (Wright, 1951, p. 381). Smith asserted that the most obvious reason for this type of racial climate in Europe was that there were relatively few Black people in Europe. Furthermore, many of the Black Americans whom Europeans encountered were students, writ-

ers, entertainers, and the like, who presented no social problems. These individuals tended to mix with cosmopolitan Europeans who generally viewed themselves to be without prejudice, and they were not competing with the White indigenous population for jobs or housing. However, beyond the circle of the urban intellectuals lay the wider Europe of workers, clerks, civil servants, and shopkeepers. Among this wider European population, Black visitors were more likely to witness a less amenable racial climate (Smith, 1970, p. 65).

To be sure, there has never been a stringent system of racial restrictions in Europe such as South Africa's apartheid system or America's Jim Crow system. But a deep strain of prejudice against Blacks runs through the cultural fabric of Europe, a strain so subtle that it is not always easily perceived (Lindsey, 1989a, p. 146; 1989b, p. 194). Indeed, there are no green pastures in Europe for African Europeans. Although Europe has often served as a haven for African Americans seeking refuge from America's racial oppression, there is an institutional and structural system that keeps African Europeans in marginal positions and undermines their dignity and sense of personal worth. They languish on the fringes of European societies, and little is being done to move them closer to the core.

By 1958 a considerable number of West Indians, Indians, and Pakistanis had come to England (Fryer, 1984, p. 372; Lindsey, 1992, pp. 65–77). Later, other European nations witnessed similar colonial immigration from their African and West Indian colonies. The increase in the size of the Black population caused much concern among Europeans. In Britain there were outcries from various groups that Britain must be kept White or streams of blood would flow through the streets (Lindsey, 1992, p. 65). Racial prejudice and discrimination became more overt as these colonial immigrants, along with Blacks who were long-term residents, were denied adequate jobs, housing, and the rights of British citizenship (Kee, 1949, pp. 40–41). This was also the case for Blacks who came to Holland from Surinam, Aruba, or Curaçao, and for the *Gastarbeiter* (guest workers) in Germany (Essed, 1990, pp. 38–144). The Gastarbeiter helped to rebuild Germany, although they received low wages, were denied civil rights, and were always subject to the danger of being arrested and deported (Phillips, 1987, pp. 70, 84).

After the war it became increasingly difficult for officialdom to uphold the myth of racial harmony in Europe. In addition to the day-to-day racism that Blacks encountered, it is significant to mention that racial prejudice began to move into the mainstream of political affairs. Under the guise of immigration control, racist policies took on the illusion of respectability in many European nations. Politicians felt that limiting the Black population would improve race relations. This trend of thought led to such efforts in Britain as the 1962, 1968, and 1971 Commonwealth Immigrations Acts and the 1981 British Nationality Act, which were instrumental in bringing about changes in the legal status of Commonwealth immigrants from that of citizen to foreign aliens, thus effectively limiting their presence in Britain (Lindsey, 1992, p. 131). Unlike during the interwar years, after the war racism in certain areas gradually became institutionalized, legitimized, and nationalized (Fryer, 1984, p. 381). As a result there eventually emerged in European nations right-wing political groups that continually campaigned to keep their countries White. These various factions asserted that their country was unable to serve an influx of immigrants who placed a strain on goods and services and lowered the quality of life for all. These groups were attempting to expound a respectable brand of national interest that embodied the essence of racial prejudice. In Britain, Enoch Powell's racist remarks and actions condemned not only immigrants but long-term Black residents as well. Powell mobilized and popularized racism throughout the entire country (Fryer, 1984, p. 384). In

France after the war, small right-wing extremist organizations emerged that were, among other things, decidedly anti-Black. As more and more immigrants came to France, the popularity of such organizations increased, a trend that has continued until this very day.

ROOTLESSNESS

Africans who immigrated to Europe and those who were born there frequently feel unrooted and are riddled with identity anxieties. They are made to feel as though they are aliens in European societies. They fear repatriation. This is why it was so disconcerting to many Black Britons when Bernie Grant (Labour MP, Tottenham), one of the three Black members of Parliament who has a strong race stance, spoke out in favor of volunteer repatriation (Ford, 1993; Kogbara, 1993). His position appeared to validate the claims that African Europeans are not an integral part of European nations. Europeans have never fully conceded that Black people belong in their countries; yet the mere presence of Blacks suggests that they do belong. This is the riddle, the conundrum, which remains and continues to foster a sense of rootlessness in African Europeans.

Caryl Phillips, an African European writer, poignantly writes that African Europeans feel "like a transplanted tree that failed to take root in foreign soil" (1987, p. 9). They suffer from political, social, and cultural alienation, disorientation, and both flagrant and subtle racial problems. As a result, the sense of being firmly rooted in European society remains, more than ever, an elusive dream (Lindsey, 1989c, p. 113). Although it is probably the least recognized of human needs, the need to be rooted is important to the human soul; consequently, everything that has the effect of uprooting people, or of preventing them from becoming rooted, is enormously damaging to the psyche. It is, in essence, a crime against humanity.

By continuing to cover up and deny their own racism, Europeans perpetuate African Europeans' rootlessness. They have effected a shrewd style of racial realism that on the surface appears to be more liberal than that practiced in the United States and South Africa. The deceptions are calculatingly brutal, and because they are masked by the appearance of civility, only a few insightful people recognize the phenomenon. The treatment has been validated and popularized by the accounts of African American abolitionists, soldiers, entertainers, artists, and writers in France and England.

Liberal is the word most commonly used to describe Europeans' racial views, and it is certainly true that western European urban centers lack the hard-nosed aggression of racial antagonism of South Africa. But the lifestyles of African European people cause one to question the appropriateness of their liberal characterization when viewed in light of the increasing incidents and complaints of racial attacks; or is one to assume that liberal in European parlance means not attacking racism?

AFRICAN AMERICAN VISITORS

Frequently, otherwise sophisticated European Americans are deluded by the facade of racial egalitarianism in Europe, especially when that is compared to the racial inequities suffered by Blacks in South Africa and the United States. In addition, African Americans who have traveled in Europe generally do not notice the pervasiveness of Europe's racism and are inclined to believe that Europeans are considerably less prejudiced than White Americans. Indeed, they tend to acquire celebrationist views of Europeans during their visits. Their views can largely be attributed to the unique status they enjoy while abroad, where they are seen as captivating novelties. Europeans are able to appear tolerant just so long as Blacks are few in number and far away. Because only a limited number of African Americans go abroad, and because they usually have financial means, Europeans are less likely to display prejudices toward them (Lindsey, 1989b, p. 195).

African American tourists, students, soldiers, artists, writers, entertainers, and athletes are generally treated as celebrities because they carry the American dollar. Consequently, they are not in competition with the host population. Or to use a different frame of reference, they do not present a financial burden to the European economy. The prosperity of African Americans who have traveled abroad has enabled them to escape the degradation of racial prejudice in Europe. Furthermore, African American writers, musicians, artists, and entertainers make substantial contributions to the artistic community, and their talents are acknowledged. Such persons are indeed accepted for the content of their character and not the color of their skin.

Recently, in Diana Ross's sensitive and telling memoirs, *Secrets of a Sparrow* (1993) she, too, continues to propagate this myth of the absence of racial prejudice in Europe. She wrote:

> It was with the Supremes that I first had the chance to travel through Europe. It was a great opportunity for me then, and I have spent a lot of time there during the last ten years. I like how I feel when I'm there. I appreciate the sense of equality and freedom without the unspoken prejudice that is present in America. (pp. 130–131)

Further on, she writes that "Europe was an opportunity that I would never have had if I had not been a Supreme" (Ross, 1993, p. 131). But what she fails to capture in her memoirs is that because she was a Supreme, her experiences in Europe were qualitatively different from those of other people of African ancestry living in Europe. Indeed, at one point when she was working in Italy, she had her own private villa (Ross, 1993, p. 174). Her economic resources and celebrity status made it possible for her to rise above the negativity of color prejudice. The net effect of experiences such as Ross's is that both European Americans and African Americans tend to see Europe as a continent of civility and egalitarianism. All Americans should be ever mindful that even though the status of Black people in Europe may be less degrading than in South Africa, the scope of racial prejudice is no less pervasive. Europeans' racial tolerance and adherence to a multiracial equality have been greatly romanticized (Ottley, 1951, p. 5; Lindsey, 1989b, p. 195). There is much unspoken prejudice.

THE HARSH REALITY

As American observers who have traveled throughout Europe and studied its racial and social problems, we can say with utmost confidence that the racial inequities are real and cannot be denied. The problems are endemic. European governments have been slow, if not downright reluctant, to admit the magnitude of their racial problems. They have tended to label racial unrest as a mere domestic problem usually occurring concurrently with other social problems. In other words, any social problem is considered more acceptable than a race problem. Racial oppression in Europe is a harsh reality even if it is not readily discernible in the law. It exists in the lives of its Black citizens and cannot be wished away. Racial oppression in Europe must not continue to be ignored; it must be addressed by students, scholars, writers, entertainers, artists, and diplomats, as well as by the general public, irrespective of their race and ethnicity.

Similarities of Black people on both sides of the Atlantic are compelling, but so are the differences. One must be cautious not to oversimplify the similarities between American and European Blacks. In a structural sense, there are important differences in the position of Black people in the United States and Europe. For example, the enslavement of Blacks existed within the United States, whereas for most African Europeans slavery did not take place in Europe. There was no blatant system of racial restrictions in Europe, whereas in the United States segregation legally existed until 1964.

Consequently, Black people in the United States have a long tradition of struggle for liberation within a free democratic society, and African Americans appear to be more aware than African Europeans of the meanings and implications of being a member of an oppressed racial group within a supposedly egalitarian society. Conversely, in the Caribbean and Africa, colonialism remained entrenched for more than 100 years after the abolition of slavery. It was no less oppressive than segregation. Colonialism shaped a different form of social and economic stratification of society, and fueled independence movements in Africa and the Caribbean (Essed, 1990, pp. 232–233). However, colonial people never were under the illusion that they were operating within the context of an egalitarian free democratic society. Furthermore, one should be mindful of the various historical legacies, cultural patterns, and traditional practices of the Black population in Europe. At least 50% of the Black population living in Europe were born in Africa and the West Indies. The Black population is not a homogeneous entity. It is composed of various individuals and families from different classes and national backgrounds and with divergent ideologies and interests. It is a product of the African Diaspora. To be sure, the Black population is European, but it is also very conscious of its African and West Indian heritages. This should not be ignored!

An additional caveat is that in certain European countries, such as Britain and Holland, "Black" is sometimes used as an inclusive term to embrace all people of color, people who are descendants of immigrants from Asia, the Caribbean, and Africa. The term Black does not stand literally for black skin. Black is viewed as a political term rather than a characteristic of racial and ethnic identity. The term symbolizes the oppression of non-White people by the White ideology of racial purity (Lindsey, 1989b, p. 194; Essed, 1990, p. 29). Furthermore, all people with black skin do not consider themselves African European. Some people with a black phenotype call themselves mixed-race or take on the nationality of their European parent.

Despite these differences, African Americans and African Europeans share many comparable experiences in their history and in day-to-day interactions. Racism is expressed in many covert ways in the United States as well as in Europe. Subtle racism as described by Black people in the United States has striking similarities to that described by African Europeans. The similarities are so close that one group's thoughts on racism are readily echoed by the other.

The painful reality is that on both sides of the Atlantic a thorough approach to combating racism has yet to be evoked. There is a glimmer of an active movement toward antidiscrimination legislation and multiracial/ethnic education, and meager funds have been appropriated to carry them out. The result is a system of alienation that undermines the self-esteem and dignity of African Europeans and African Americans so that their condition of political and economic subjugation in White societies is virtually interminable. Everyday racism is embedded in the historical experiences of European and American societies and is manifested in situations, attitudes, and customs that produce racial inequality in the daily lives of people of African ancestry. The concept of everyday racism therefore includes practices at both institutional and personal levels, as experienced by Blacks in the workplace, in education, in public transportation, and in housing.

There is a need to shed light on the ignominy of national identity and racial expression experienced by Black people in Europe. There is a need to have a comparative examination of the role of racism in the daily lives of Black people in predominantly White societies. The examination needs to emphasize both the commonalties and differences in forms of racial oppression. There is a need to illuminate the diverse ways in which racism is woven into Black people's everyday contacts with Whites, which bring on the feelings of inferiority within White supremacist societies.

In the past, African European affairs have been overlooked or at best have been the subject of occasional media feature stories. However, as modern technology continues to shrink our world, there is an increasing need to understand the perceptions, behavior, and interests of all people on every continent. The basic needs and aspirations of ethnic and racial minorities are too often suppressed for so long that they erupt in violent outbursts, as in Britain's urban riots, or are used as political propaganda, as in the campaigns of the British National Front and Jean-Marie Le Pen's 1988 extreme-right campaign in France. More often than not, minority affairs are seen as mere domestic skirmishes, but we know all too well that skirmishes can escalate into large-scale conflicts such as Bosnia. It is incredibly ironic that African Americans have become a kind of aristocracy among the world's Black communities. Without a doubt America has not solved all of its racial problems, nor is the "American Dream" even close to a reality for all Americans, but America has surmounted some of the hurdles of its ugly past. For the most part, African Americans have made incomparable gains and their gains are coveted by other Black people throughout the world. Consequently, Blacks in other countries tend to regard African Americans as role models or pacesetters in the struggle for human equality. Yet African Americans are not sufficiently aware of the ongoing struggle for human equality by African peoples in European society.

TOWARD AN AFROCENTRIC CURRICULUM

A strategic step toward illuminating the Black experience in Europe would be to introduce an Afrocentric European studies curriculum. We are aware that the term *Afrocentric* is widely—and apparently intentionally—misused in the popular media and by some individuals. However, Afrocentricity, in this context, is simply the idea that Africa and people of African ancestry must be seen as proactive subjects within history rather than as passive objects in world history (Felder, 1993, p. 93). Thus, an Afrocentric European curriculum would explore the patterns of paternalism, hostility, and exclusion against people of color in Europe, and it would underscore African Europeans' achievements and contributions to European societies.

The central thrust of the curriculum would be that the Black experience has its historical link before the days of slavery and colonialism, and did not merely emerge with post–World War II immigration to Europe, which is so often thought to have marked the beginning of the nexus. For example, the study of Greek and Roman civilization should logically include the presence of Blacks in antiquity, and studies of European societies should recognize the presence of African European people and their communities (Wilson, 1990, p. 11). For many people, White and Black, a curriculum of this nature could be an eye-opener. They would learn a great deal by reflecting on the experiences of African peoples in Europe. It would liberate their minds from the blinkered perspectives, limited assumptions, and narrow visions of a single society. Also, the curriculum would open their eyes to a whole new world vision, through which they could view their futures (Small, 1989, p. 1).

Paul Gilroy's recent book, *The Black Atlantic: Modernity and Double Consciousness* (1993), takes a step in that direction. He argues that there is a culture that is not specifically African, American, Caribbean, or British, but all of these at once, a Black Atlantic culture whose themes and techniques transcend ethnicity and nationality to produce something new and, until now, unmarked. He brings together a whole range of issues in the study of Black Atlantic culture and situates them within the dynamics of the history of modernism. He inserts Black people as central participants in the creation of the modern world. Consequently, he has rewritten the history of modernity and modernism. He has put a comparative, transatlantic approach to studying culture and modernity firmly on the map.

To reiterate, we have discerned that there is a proclivity for denying the deep strain of racial prejudice that runs through the cultural fabric of Europe. In Europe, as in America, some African Europeans are successful, but the vast majority are not. Indeed, the celebrationist approach to learning about the African European experience would be reminiscent of articles that appeared during the 1950s in the magazine *Ebony*, which captured the all too few success stories of African Americans in the United States, whereas the greater part of the Black population remained in abject poverty. For this and related reasons, a curriculum in African European studies should reflect a balance between the celebrationist approach and the realities of Black life in Europe (Lindsey & Wilson, 1990, p. 9). Moreover, a genuine and sustained American interest in African European affairs can prove extremely valuable in formulating policies regarding European countries and developing nations for the 21st century.

Characteristically, African Europeans maintain close relationships with friends and relatives in their indigenous communities and have a substantial degree of influence in their homelands. If America would demonstrate greater appreciation of the concerns and culture of African Europeans, it would surely enhance the nation's role as a world leader in an multiracial/ethnic world and indeed validate claims that America is a "kinder and gentler nation." These people's lives have an impact on American interests both in Europe and in the countries of their origin. The American people need a greater understanding of problems faced by African Europeans and of the consequences of these problems. Our hope is that this article is a step toward this end and that it will encourage a dialogue. This could lead to a greater interest in an Afrocentric approach to European studies that underscores the African European experience in the African Diaspora.

References

Aptheker, H. (Ed.). (1973). *The correspondence of W. E. B. Du Bois, Vol. I, Selections, 1877–1934.* Amherst: University of Massachusetts Press.

Asante, M. K. (1988). *Afrocentricity.* Trenton, NJ: Africa World.

Ba-Ture. (1918, January–June). The apes at sea. *Blackwood's Magazine, 202,* pp. 539–548.

Duberman, M. B. (1988). *Paul Robeson.* New York: Knopf.

Essed, P (1990). *Everyday racism: Reports from women of two cultures.* Claremont, CA: Hunter House.

Fabre, M. (1991). *From Harlem to Paris: Black American writers in France, 1940–1980.* Urbana: University of Illinois Press.

Felder, C. H. (Ed.). (1993). *The original African heritage study bible.* Nashville, TN: James C. Winston.

Ford R. (1993, October 6). Black MP demands grants for repatriation of migrants. *The Times of London,* p. 3.

Fryer, P. (1984). *Staying Power: The history of Black People in Britain.* London: Pluto.

Gilroy, P. (1993). *The Black Atlantic: Modernity and double consciousness.* Cambridge, MA: Harvard University Press.

Goodman, G. W. (1944, Autumn). The Englishman meets the Negro. *Common Ground,* pp. 3–11.

Hamilton, V. (1974). *The life and times of a free Black man.* New York: Harper & Row.

Johnson, J. W. (1933). *Along this way.* New York: Viking.

Joseph, C. J. (1971, May). The British West Indies regiment. *Journal of Caribbean History. 2,* 94–124.

Kee, R. (1949, November 8). Is there a British color bar? *Negro Digest,* pp. 38–42.

Kogbara, D. (1993, October 10). I back Bernie on the right to go home. *The Sunday Times,* p. 7.

Lindsey, L. (1989a). An historical overview of the political status of Blacks in England since 1945. *Western Journal of Black Studies, 13,* 146–155.

Lindsey, L. (1989b). Black Britons rocked Britain's boat: An historical perspective on racial conflict in contemporary Britain. *Journal of Social and Behavioral Sciences, 35,* 189–206.

Lindsey, L. (1989c). [Review of *The European Tribe.*] *Journal of Black Studies, 20,* 113–115.

Lindsey, L. (1992). The role of immigration policy, race, class, and gender in shaping the status of Jamaican immigrant women workers in Birmingham England, 1948–1962. Unpublished doctoral dissertation, University of North Carolina at Chapel Hill.

Lindsey, L., & Wilson, C. (1990, May). Adjusting the scale. [Letter to the Editor]. *Black Enterprise,* p. 9.

McCloy, S. T. (1961). *The Negro in France.* Lexington: University of Kentucky Press.

McKay, C. (1920, April 24). A Black man responds [Letter to the editor of the *Daily Herald*]. *Workers Dreadnought,* p. 2.

Meyer, M. (1984). *Frederick Douglass: The narrative and selective writings.* New York: The Modern Library.

Morel, E. D. (1920 April 10). Black scourge in Europe sexual horror let loose by France on the Rhine: Disappearance of young German girls. *Daily Herald,* p. 1.

National Archives. (1942–1944). *Morale reports of Colored troops.* Record Group 332, 250.1. Suitland MD: Author.

Ottley, R. (1944, November). Dixie invades Britain. *Negro Digest, 3,* pp. 3–8.

Ottley, R. (1951). *The Negro in Europe today: No green pastures.* New York: Scribner.

Phillips, C. (1981). *The European tribe.* New York: Farrar Straus Giroux.

Public Records Office. (1919, November 15). *The race riots.* United Kingdom: Colonial Office, 318/382/137529 Hugh Burgess.

Reinders, R. (1968). Racialism on the left: E. D. Morel and the "Black Horror on the Rhine." *International Review of Social History, 13,* 1–28.

Ross, D. (1993). *Secrets of a sparrow: Memoirs.* New York: Villard.

Small, S. (1989, February 21). History of Blacks in British society. *Collegian,* p. 1.

Smith G. (1987). *When Jim Crow met John Bull: Black American soldiers in World War II Britain.* London: I. B. Tauris.

Smith, W. G. (1970). *Return to Black America.* Englewood Cliffs, NJ: Prentice-Hall.

Terrell, M. C. (1940). *A colored woman in a white world.* Washington, DC: Ransdell.

Watkins, J. (1852). Narrative of the life of James Watkins. Bolton, England: Kenyon & Abbott.

Wilson, C. (1990, December 10). Afrocentricity: Creating a balance. *Black Ink,* p. 11.

Wright, R. (1951, June–July). American Negroes in France. *The Crisis,* 381–383.

Essay/Discussion Questions

1. According to Lindsey and Wilson, the idea that Europe is much less racist than the United States is a myth. What has led to this myth?

2. Lindsey and Wilson propose that American universities institute an African European Studies curriculum. What are their reasons for this proposal? Do you support it? Why or why not?

Part II Key Terms

Abolitionist movement	*Industrial Revolution*
African Europeans	*Maroon communities*
Atlantic slave trade	*Mental emancipation*
Black matriarchy myth	*Middle passage*
Cafundó	*Nat Turner*
Cheikh Anta Diop	*Planter class*
Colonialism	*Rootlessness*
Civil War	*Sea Island communities*
David Walker	*Sexual domination of female slaves*
Fugitive slave	*Slave revolt*
Gabriel Prosser	*Underground Railroad*
Haitian Revolution	*White male supremacist ideology*
Harriet Tubman	

Part II Supplementary Readings

Ajayi, J. F. Ade, and Ian Espie, eds., *A Thousand Years of West African History: A Handbook for Teachers and Students,* Ibadan: Ibadan University Press, 1965.

Aptheker, Herbert, *A Documentary History of the Negro People in the United States: Vol. I, From Colonial Times through the Civil War,* New York: The Citadel Press, 1967.

_____, *One Continual Cry: David Walker's Appeal to the Colored Citizens of the World (1829–1830),* New York: Humanities Press, 1965.

Ben-Jochannan, Yosef, *Black Man of the Nile,* New York: Alkebu-Lan Books Associates, 1972.

_____, *Africa: Mother of Western Civilization,* New York: Alkebu-Lan Books Associates, 1971.

_____, *The African Origins of Major "Western Religions,"* New York: Alkebu-Lan Books Associates, 1970,

_____, *American Negro Slave Revolts,* New York: International Publishers, 1963.

Bernal, Martin G., *Black Athena: The Afro-Asiatic Roots of Classical Civilization, Vol. II: The Archaeological and Documentary Evidence,* New Brunswick: Rutgers University Press, 1991.

_____, *Black Athena: The Afro-Asiatic Roots of Classical Civilization, Vol. I: The Fabrication of Ancient Greece,* New Brunswick: Rutgers University Press, 1987.

Blackburn, Robin, *The Overthrow of Colonial Slavery, 1776–1848,* New York: Verso, 1988.

Blassingame, John W., ed., *Slave Testimony: Two Centuries of Letters, Speeches, Interviews, and Autobiographies,* Baton Rouge: Louisiana State University Press, 1977.

_____, *The Slave Community: Plantation Life in the Ante-Bellum South*, New York: Oxford University Press, 1972.

Boahen, Adu, *Topics in West African History,* Atlantic Highlands: Humanities Press, 1966.

Bovill, E. W., *The Golden Trade of the Moors,* New York: Oxford University Press, 1968.

Bradley, Keith R., *Slavery and Rebellion in the Roman World, 140 B.C.–70 B.C.,* Bloomington: Indiana University Press, 1989.

Cheek, William, and Aimee L. Cheek, *John Mercer Langston and the Fight for Black Freedom, 1829–1865,* Urbana: University of Illinois Press, 1989.

Clarke, John Henrik, ed., *New Dimensions in African History: The London Lectures of Dr. Yosef ben-Jochannan and Dr. John Henrik Clarke,* Trenton: Africa World Press, Inc., 1991.

Curtin, Philip D., *The Atlantic Slave Trade: A Census,* Madison: The University of Wisconsin Press, 1969.

Crowder, Michael, *West Africa Under Colonial Rule,* Evanston: Northwestern University Press, 1968.

Davidson, Basil, with F. K. Buah and the advice of J. F. Ade Ajayi, *A History of West Africa: To the Nineteenth Century,* Garden City: Anchor Books/ Doubleday and Company, 1966.

_____, *The African Slave Trade: Precolonial History, 1450–1850*, Boston: Little, Brown and Company, 1961.

_____, *The Lost Cities of Africa,* Boston: Little, Brown and Company, 1951.

Davis, David B., *Slavery and Human Progress,* New York: Oxford University Press, 1984.

_____, *The Problem of Slavery in the Age of Revolution,* Ithaca: Cornell University Press, 1975.

_____, *The Problem of Slavery in Western Culture,* Ithaca: Cornell University Press, 1966.

Davis, Ronald W., "Negro Contributions to the Exploration of the Globe," in Roucek, Joseph S., and Thomas Kiernan, eds., *The Negro Impact on Western Civilization,* New York: Philosophical Library Inc., 1970, pp. 33–50.

DeGraft-Johnson, J. C., *African Glory: The Story of Vanished Negro Civilizations,* New York: Walker and Company, 1966.

Diop, Cheikh Anta, *Civilization or Barbarism: An Authentic Anthropology,* New York: Lawrence Hill & Company, 1991.

_____, *Procolonial Black Africa: A Comparative Study of the Political and Social Systems of Europe and Black Africa, from Antiquity to the Formation of Modern States,* Trenton: Africa World Press and Westport: Lawrence Hill & Company, 1989.

_____, *The Cultural Unity of Black Africa,* Chicago: Third World Press, 1978.

_____, *The African Origin of Civilization: Myth or Reality,* Westport: Lawrence Hill & Company, 1974.

Douglass, Frederick, *My Bondage and My Freedom,* New York: Arno Press and the New York Times, 1969.

_____, *Life and Times of Frederick Douglass,* New York: Collier Books, 1962.

Drake, St. Clair, *Black Folk Here and There: An Essay in History and Anthropology,* Vol. II, Los Angeles: Center for Afro-American Studies/University of California, 1990.

_____, *Black Folk Here and There: An Essay in History and Anthropology,* Vol. I, Los Angeles: Center for Afro-American Studies/University of California, 1987.

Duberman, Martin, ed., *The Antislavery Vanguard: New Essays on the Abolitionists,* Princeton: Princeton University Press, 1965.

DuBois, W. E. B., *The Suppression of the African Slave Trade to the United States of America, 1638–1870,* New York: Russell & Russell, Inc., 1965.

_____, *The World and Africa: An Inquiry into the Part which Africa Has Played in World History,* New York: International Publishers, 1965.

_____, *Black Reconstruction in America, 1860–1880,* Cleveland: A Meridian Book/The World Publishing Company, 1964.

Edwards, Paul, ed., *Equiano's Travels: The Interesting Narrative of the Life of Olaudah Equiano or Gustavus Vassa, the African*, New York: Frederick A. Praeger, Publishers, 1967.

Foner, Eric, *Reconstruction: America's Unfinished Revolution, 1863–1877,* New York: Harper & Row, Publishers, 1988.

Forbes, Jack D., *Black Africans & Native Americans: Color, Race and Caste in the Evolution of Red–Black Peoples,* New York: Basil Blackwell Inc., 1988.

Frederickson, George M., *The Arrogance of Race: Historical Perspectives on Slavery, Racism, and Social Inequality,* Middletown: Wesleyan University Press, 1988.

Freyre, Gilberto, *The Masters and the Slaves: A Study in the Development of Brazilian Civilization,* New York: Alfred A. Knopf, 1956.

_____, *The Mansions and the Shanties: The Making of Modern Brazil,* New York: Alfred A. Knopf, 1968.

Greene, Lorenzo J., *The Negro in Colonial New England*, New York: Atheneum, 1968.

Harding, Vincent, *There Is a River: The Black Struggle for Freedom in America,* New York: Harcourt Brace Jovanovich, Publishers, 1981.

_____, *The Other American Revolution,* Los Angeles: Center for Afro-American Studies/University of California and Institute of the Black World, 1980.

Harris, Joseph E., *The African Presence in Asia: Consequences of the East African Slave Trade,* Evanston: Northwestern University Press, 1971.

Irwin, Graham W., *Africans Abroad: A Documentary History of the Black Diaspora in Asia, Latin America, and the Caribbean During the Age of Slavery,* New York: Columbia University Press, 1977.

Jackson, John G., *Man, God, and Civilization,* New Hyde Park: University Books, 1972.

_____, *Introduction to African Civilizations,* New Hyde Park: University Books, 1970.

Jacobs, Harriet, *Incidents in the Life of a Slave Girl,* New York: Harcourt, Brace, Jovanovich, 1973.

James, C. L. R., *The Black Jacobins: Toussaint L'Ouverture and the San Domingo Revolution,* New York: Vintage Books, 1963.

James, George G. M., *Stolen Legacy,* New York: Philosophical Library, 1954.

Jones, Edward L., *The Black Diaspora: Colonization of Colored People,* Seattle: Edward L. Jones, 1989.

_____, *Tutankhamon: Son of the Sun, King of Upper and Lower Egypt (XVII Dynasty),* Seattle: Edward L. Jones, 1978.

_____, *Profiles in African History,* Seattle: Edward L. Jones, 1972.

Jordan, Winthrop D., *White Over Black: American Attitudes Toward the Negro, 1550–1812,* Chapel Hill: The University of North Carolina Press, 1968.

Kanya-Forstner, A. S., *The Conquest of the Western Sudan: A Study in French Military Imperialism,* New York: Cambridge University Press, 1969.

Karenga, Maulana, *The Husia,* Los Angeles: University of Sankore Press, 1984.

Lane-Poole, Stanley, *The Story of the Moors in Spain,* New York: Putnam's Sons, 1886.

Lawrence, Harold G., "African Explorers of the New World," *The Crisis,* (June–July 1962), pp. 321–332.

Littlefield, David F., Jr., *Africans and Seminoles: From Removal to Emancipation,* Westport: Greenwood Press, 1977.

McPherson, James, *Battle Cry of Freedom: The Civil War Era,* New York: Oxford University Press, 1988.

Massey, Gerald, *A Book of the Beginnings,* 2 Vols., New Hyde Park: University Books, 1974.

_____, *Ancient Egypt: The Light of the World,* 2 Vols., New York: Samuel Weiser, Inc., 1970.

Montejo, Esteban, *The Autobiography of a Runaway Slave,* ed., Miguel Barnet, New York: The World Publishing Company, 1969.

Mullin, Gerald W., *Flight and Rebellion: Slave Resistance in Eighteenth-Century Virginia,* New York: Oxford University Press, 1972.

Nichols, Charles H., *Many Thousand Gone: The Ex-Slaves' Account of their Bondage and Freedom,* Bloomington: Indiana University Press, 1963.

Osae, T. A., and S. N. Nwabara, *A Short History of West Africa: A.D. 1000–1800,* London: University of London Press, 1968.

Patterson, Orlando, *Slavery and Social Death: A Comparative Study,* Cambridge: Harvard University Press, 1982.

Perdue, Theda, *Slavery and the Evolution of Cherokee Society, 1540–1866,* Knoxville: The University of Tennessee Press, 1979.

Phillips, William D. Jr., *Slavery from Roman Times to the Early Transatlantic Trade,* Minneapolis: University of Minnesota Press, 1985.

Piesterse, Jan Nederveen, *White on Black: Images of Africa and Blacks in Western Popular Culture,* New Haven: Yale University Press, 1992.

Postma, Johannes M., *The Dutch in the Atlantic Slave Trade, 1600–1815,* New York: Cambridge University Press, 1990.

Quarles, Benjamin, *Black Abolitionists,* New York: Oxford University Press, 1969.

Rodney, Walter, *How Europe Underdeveloped Africa,* London: Bogle-L'Ouverture Publications, 1972.

_____, "African Slavery and Other Forms of Social Oppression on the Upper Guinea Coast in the Context of the Atlantic Slave Trade," *Journal of African History,* Vol. 7 (1966), pp. 431–443.

Rogers, Joel A., *Sex and Race,* Vol. I, New York: J. A. Rogers, 1967.

_____, *Africa's Gift to America,* New York: Futuro Press, 1961.

_____, *Nature Knows No Color Line,* New York: J. A. Rogers, 1952.

Schama, Simon, *The Embarrassment of Riches: An Interpretation of Dutch Culture in the Golden Age,* New York: Alfred A. Knopf, 1987.

Stampp, Kenneth M., *The Peculiar Institution: Slavery in the Ante-Bellum South,* New York: Vintage Books, 1956.

Tannenbaum, Frank, *Slave and Citizen: The Negro in the Americas,* New York: Vintage Books, 1946.

Thompson, Lloyd, *Romans and Blacks,* Norman: University of Oklahoma Press, 1989.

_____, and J. Ferguson, eds., *Africa in Classical Antiquity,* Ibadan: Ibadan University Press, 1969.

Thompson, Vincent B., *The Making of the African Diaspora in the Americas, 1441–1900,* New York: Longman Inc., 1987.

Thornton, Archibald P., *The Imperial Idea and Its Enemies: A Study of British Power,* 2nd. Ed., New York: St. Martin's Press, 1985.

Tompkins, Peter, *Secrets of the Great Pyramids,* New York: Harper & Row, Publishers, 1971.

Van Sertima, Ivan, *They Came Before Columbus,* New York: Random House, 1976.

Von Wuthenau, Alexander, *The Art of Terracotta Pottery in Pre-Columbian Central and South America,* New York: Crown Publishers, Inc., 1970.

Weiner, Leo, *Africa and the Discovery of America,* Vol. I, Philadelphia: Innes & Sons, 1920.

_____, *Africa and the Discovery of America,* Vols. II & III, Philadelphia: Innes & Sons, 1922.

Webster, J. B., and A. A. Boahen, with H. O. Idowu, *History of West Africa: The Revolutionary Years—1815 to Independence,* New York: Praeger Publishers, 1967.

Welch, Galbraith, *Africa Before They Came: The Continent, North, South, East and West, Preceding the Colonial Powers,* New York: William Morrow and Company, 1965.

Williams, Chancellor, *The Destruction of African Civilizations: Great Issues of a Race from 4500 B.C. to 2000 A.D.,* Dubuque: Kendall/Hunt Publishing Company, 1971.

Williams, Eric, *Capitalism and Slavery,* Chapel Hill: The University of North Carolina Press, 1944.

Wiltse, Charles M., ed., *David Walker's Appeal,* New York: Hill and Wang, 1965.

III

Black Expressive Culture: Music and Literature

Although the oppressive and dehumanizing system of chattel slavery sought to destroy (and post-Emancipation America sought to deny) any remnants of African culture and to impose white European culture in its place, Africans and their American descendants preserved and transformed their own resilient culture. Significantly, it has been this African-based creative impulse that has largely energized and shaped what has emerged as American popular culture.

In the historic struggle to survive and resist Euro-American cultural domination (from the shock and chaos of chattel slavery to the contemporary period) African-descended Americans have refashioned themselves by transforming aspects of African culture. Through a tradition that included sacred and secular music, folktales, and autobiography, African American slaves were able to salvage a degree of self-esteem, dignity, and hope; in the process, they left a legacy that African American writers, singers, poets, and producers have taken and transformed.

The articles in this part depict aspects of African American expressive culture, particularly in the areas of music and literature. The purpose is not to ignore other areas of cultural expression, such as drama, dance, sculpture, painting, photography, or film-making, but to limit coverage to what is manageable.

Portia K. Maultsby's work "Africanisms in African American Music" skillfully examines the historic interaction between African and African American musical traditions. She points out that this African/African American cultural connection is not the retention of particular African songs but a conceptual framework that links these two dynamic traditions and clearly distinguishes them from Western European cultural forms. According to Maultsby, Africanisms were preserved in culture and music because African-descended Americans maintained ties to their African past, adapting to a hostile and changing environment by relying on familiar traditions and cultural practices.

Showing the development from the earliest African American sacred and secular musical forms to the most contemporary musical expressions, the author delineates the elements that characterize African and African American expressive culture. African and African American music-making, Maultsby says, is above all else communal and participatory.

In her essay, "'Wild Women Don't Have the Blues': Blues from the Black Woman's Perspective," Daphne Duval Harrison recounts the social history of the blues tradition in the 1920s, giving special attention to the variety of themes articulated by urban black female singers. Blues themes included infidelity, alienation, loneliness, despondency, death, poverty, injustice, love, and sex. These early blues women struggled with the fundamental issues of their existence and, as Harrison indicates, "brought to their lyrics and performances new meaning as they interpreted and reformulated the black experience from their unique perspective in American society as black females." Blues queens, like Ma Rainey, Bessie Smith, Sara Martin, Sippie Wallace, and Ida Cox, transformed their personal feelings into artistic expression by skillfully integrating the elements of disappointment and happiness to create the songs that made thousands of black people pack their shows and buy their records. The blues allowed these women to become major advocates for northern and southern black women.

Facing racial, class, and sexual oppression and exploitation, black female blues singers, very much like their male counterparts, used their music as an artform to demonstrate black people's toughness, resilience, and language versatility in the face of an absurd and vicious American world. Harrison shows that although black blues queens sang about the same issues that men did, they provided innovative interpretations. They sang openly about issues that were specific to urban black women—freedom from social and religious constraints, sexual and economic self-determination, alcoholism, and drugs. Like black singers of all ages, they lived the experiences that found articulation in their music. In the process, they raised the status of black women entertainers to a new height and were adored at home and abroad.

Nelson George in the essay "Black Beauty, Black Confusion (1965-70)" examines critically the interaction between the rise of soul music (an elaboration of rhythm and blues) and the political economy of the music world when the Civil Rights movement was declining and the Black Power movement was emerging. George explores the musical and business life and times of James Brown ("the hardest working man in show business") and Aretha Franklin ("the Queen of Soul"), who represent a period of volatile and creative African American cultural politics. In a moment when political activists were calling for African American self-determination and self-reliance, George shows that James Brown clearly exemplified a cultural and economic response. Hard working, audacious, innovative, versatile, and powerful on stage, Brown displayed these qualities on the business end as well; he controlled every aspect of his organization. George shows that during the late 1960s Brown was an important musical—and to some degree social—leader in the African American community because he exemplified African American pride and self-reliant development. Pointing out Brown's success, George also critically assesses Brown's ideological conservatism and the contradictions in his music's messages.

If James Brown was the godfather of rhythm and blues-soul, Aretha Franklin certainly was/is its undisputed queen. Emerging from the urban African American church, she integrated a sacred (gospel) ethos into her secular music-making with a unique and versatile style, a deeply emotional and meaningful message, and a hard-driving vocal power. This rendered Aretha heir to a long tradition of African American female blues, jazz, and rhythm-and-blues singers, which includes Dinah Washington, Ella Fitzgerald, Sarah Vaughn, Billie Holiday, Bessie Smith, and Ma Rainey. George traces Aretha's musical evolution from the restraining conditions at Columbia Records to her expressive freedom and blossoming at Atlantic Records. He reviews the wide range of her songs, showing how her uncompromising African American sound and musical versatility made her music accessible and acceptable to a broad spectrum of Americans—African American and white. Nelson George also talks about other developments in the music world during the late 1960s.

It is ironic that the African and African American literary tradition (that is, literary production in European languages) emerged during the eighteenth century largely so authors could contest Europeans' negative or distorted portrayal of African-descended people. From Phillis Wheatley's poetic efforts in the early 1770s to the present, African Americans active in the literary culture (including folklorists, essayists, novelists, poets, autobiographers, critics, playwrights, comedians, and screen-writers) have sought to tell their own stories about the African and African American experience. In the process, they have had to reject, refute, refashion, or improvise upon the literary conventions of the dominant Euro-American cultural establishment at particular historical moments.

The three remaining articles in this section focus on some of the trends and developments in twentieth-century African American literature, particularly literature as protest and challenge to white Euro-American cultural domination, economic exploitation, and political oppression. In his 1940 essay, "How 'Bigger' Was Born," Richard Wright discusses how he acquired the ideas about his tragic hero, Bigger Thomas, that went into his novel *Native Son*, published the same year. [Considered by some to be one of the greatest African American writers of all time, Wright authored an assortment of works, including *Uncle Tom's Children* (1938), *Twelve Million Black Voices* (1941), *Black Boy* (1945), *The Outsider* (1953), *Black Power* (1954), *The Color Curtain* (1956),

Pagan Spain (1957), *White Man, Listen!* (1957), *Eight Men* (1961), *Lawd Today* (1963), and *American Hunger* (1977).] For the radical intellectual Richard Wright—he was a Communist Party organizer and writer from 1934 to 1942—Bigger Thomas was the product of a dislocated social order. He was dispossessed and disinherited in a land of plenty. Capitalism and antiblack racism had long permeated every dimension of American life. The nation's culture, economy, politics, and psyche all were deeply penetrated. In America, the white ruling class was as powerful and hostile as ever; and poverty was rife, alienation rampant, and nihilism pervasive. As Wright constructed him, Bigger Thomas represents the failure of modern Western civilization.

Wright reveals that it was during his own childhood in the South that the literary representation of Bigger Thomas developed. Acknowledging that there were many Bigger Thomases, Wright describes five typifications. All of them were economically impoverished, culturally alienated, and politically dispossessed, which is why they were violent, angry, resentful, cynical, or even nihilistic. Wright's own development and social location helped him to sense the internal tensions of the people he encountered who came to embody the behavioral patterns of Bigger Thomas. As he matured in Chicago, Wright's voracious reading and evolving class consciousness allowed him to see that Bigger Thomas was not only black; there also were white Bigger Thomases (e.g., in Nazi Germany and Old Russia), who, because of their life experiences, reacted to the world in patterns very similar to those of black Bigger Thomas.

As a product of racist capitalist America himself, Wright wrestled with a concern about white America's reaction to his portrayal of Bigger Thomas; this slowed the writing process. Courageously, Wright concluded that he had to present a truthful image of Bigger Thomas— "resentful toward whites, sullen, angry, ignorant, emotionally unstable, depressed and unaccountably elated at times, and unable even, because of his own lack of inner organization which American oppression has fostered in him, to unite with the members of his own race." Wright also was aware of the black middle class's desire to conceal Bigger Thomas's truth from whites. The black bourgeoisie wanted to appease their white oppressors. What also slowed Wright's progress was his awareness of the necessity to portray Bigger Thomas's complex realities—his personal and private life, his double consciousness, his fear and dread, his political impulses, his relationship with white America, his reaction to oppression, and the impact of urban life on him. For Wright, *Native Son* would not be another piece of fiction (like his book of short stories, *Uncle Tom's Children*) that would cause liberal whites to cry, for "it would be so hard and deep that they would have to face it without the consolation of tears."

In many ways, Wright's powerful and angry protest writing prefigured the aggressive political and cultural insurgency of the late 1960s and

1970s—the Black Power and the Black Arts movements. Echoing yet going beyond Wright, these movements sought to challenge the very foundations of Western and Euro-American cultural domination in order to empower black people by transforming their self-consciousness. That is, if Wright spoke mainly to whites, hoping to encourage them to overturn their antiblack racism, the Black Arts movement spoke largely to black people, hoping to encourage them to take pride in the power of black culture. Black Arts advocates had no faith in the capacity of white moral transformation.

In his 1968 essay, "The Black Arts Movement," Larry Neal argues that Black Art is the cultural companion to the Black Power idea. He states that the central principle of both movements is for black people to define the world, politically and aesthetically, in their own interests. Hence, the creation and establishment of a black aesthetic was the necessary goal of Black Arts advocates, whose broader purpose was to transform American society. In order to accomplish these objectives, the Black Arts movement had to challenge and destroy the Euro-American aesthetic—its anti-human sensibility and its cultural domination. Hence, Black Arts advocates linked the ethical battle to demolish a declining Western cultural hegemony with the struggle to construct a new and powerful constellation of black cultural values and artistic expression.

In the remainder of his article, Neal describes the development of the Black Arts movement on the East and West coasts. He explores the influential work of some of the exemplars of the Black Arts movement—Maulana Karenga's cultural nationalist ideology, LeRoi Jones/Amiri Baraka's poetry and drama, and other important black playwrights of the period. According to Neal, what gave the Black Arts movement and its cultural expressiveness revolutionary significance—and where the Harlem Renaissance of the 1920s and 1930s failed—was the conscious effort to link art to the struggles of the black community.

Culture is an important way to construct, mobilize, and maintain power. In the field of American literary studies, the relationship between culture and power is most evident in the curriculum. Even after the 1960s assault by the Black Arts movement, the traditional course of study in high school and college continues to be dominated by a Eurocentric and male orientation, as if the field of important literature is the exclusive domain of dead white males. What is understood as the "classics" is composed of European and American authors and their literature. But how does literature become "classic"; who decides? On what basis is some literature included and other literature excluded from the "mainstream" curriculum or literary canon? The canon is the set of literary works, the grouping of significant philosophical, political, and religious texts, the particular accounts of history generally accorded cultural and intellectual weight within a society (Lauter, 1991). In recent years, the controversy surrounding the American literary canon has expanded, as African American and other scholars increasingly have contested the Eurocentric hegemony of American literature.

In "Unspeakable Things Unspoken: The Afro-American Presence in American Literature," Nobel Prize winner Toni Morrison focuses on the Western, or Euro-American, literary canon as a "protected preserve of the thoughts and works and analytical strategies of white men," and she investigates the impact of African American culture and literature on the study of literature in the United States of America. [Arguably one of the premier American writers of the contemporary period, Morrison is the author of a number of works, including *The Bluest Eye* (1970), *Sula* (1974), *Song of Solomon* (1977), *Tar Baby* (1981), *Beloved* (1987), *Playing in the Dark: Whiteness and the Literary Imagination* (1990), *Jazz* (1992), and *Race-ing Justice, En-gendering Power: Essays on Anita Hill, Clarence Thomas, and the Construction of Social Reality* (1992), which she edited.] Her subject is especially significant because in America, where every aspect of the culture historically has been racialized, contemporary defenders of the literary canon still seek to deny the relevance of "race" to writing. "Race," or blackness, becomes an unspeakable thing for the white literary establishment, even though it shapes the contours and content of American cultural and literary life. Morrison wants to know why it is that white male resistance to canonical change (i.e., to inclusion of a black presence in the construction of high literary art) is so virulent.

Morrison argues that this hostility stems from the seventeenth-century construction of Eurocentric hegemony and the sequence of arguments historically employed to justify black cultural exclusion: (1) there is no black or Third World art; (2) it exists but is inferior to Western European art; (3) it exists and is superior when it measures up to the "universal" criteria of Western European art; and (4) it is not so much art as it is a natural product that requires Eurocentric cultivation. Elaborating on the implications and consequences of each of these successive rationalizations of black exclusion, Morrison then offers three alternative strategies that would allow the inclusion of African American literature in the American literary canon: (1) develop a literary theory that accommodates African American literature; (2) examine and reinterpret the history of the American canon, searching for the manner in which the Africanist or black experience has influenced the language, structure, and meaning of American literature; and (3) examine contemporary and/or noncanonical literature for this Africanist presence.

Morrison argues that the nineteenth-century Eurocentric evasion of blackness by white American literature, while that literature celebrates itself as "universal," may well have reduced the quality of American literary expression. She then critically examines Herman Melville's novel *Moby Dick*, pointing out how an attentiveness to the black experience reveals deeper meanings in the text, especially about antiblack racism and the meaning of "whiteness" as ideology. Morrison then spends the remainder of her essay using her own writing to explain the literary and cultural ingredients that make a work of literature "Black." In this way, she suggests the impact of black culture on contemporary American literature. Morrison demonstrates that it is the particular manner in which she uses language as the expression of the cultural complexity of the African Americans that renders her work "Black."

As the study of African American expressive culture reveals, the Euro-American effort to silence and ignore it has been unsuccessful. Rather, that culture continues to demonstrate its resilience, power, and innovation. Derived from its African origins and retained by captured African slaves, an evolving and improvisational African American culture and style descended from the experience of black people. In the face of white America's dehumanization process, African American culture has formed the basis of black survival, resistance, and development.

Africanisms in African-American Music

PORTIA K. MAULTSBY

Since the first quarter of the twentieth century scholars have examined African-American history and culture in the context of an African past.[1] Their studies support the premise that the institution of slavery did not destroy the cultural legacy of slaves nor erase the memories of an African past. The survival of slaves in the New World depended on their ability to retain the ideals fundamental to African cultures. Although slaves were exposed to various European-derived traditions, they resisted cultural imprisonment by the larger society. Slaves adapted to life in the Americas by retaining a perspective on the past. They survived an oppressive existence by creating new expressive forms out of African traditions, and they brought relevance to European-American customs by reshaping them to conform to African aesthetic ideals.

The transformation of African traditions in the New World supports the position of Lawrence Levine that culture is a process rather than a fixed condition. Levine argues that culture is

the product of interaction between the past and present. Its toughness and resiliency are determined not by a culture's ability to withstand change, which indeed may be a sign of

stagnation not life, but by its ability to react creatively and responsively to the realities of a new situation.[2]

The continuum of an African consciousness in America manifests itself in the evolution of an African-American culture. The music, dance, folklore, religion, language, and other expressive forms associated with the culture of slaves were transmitted orally to subsequent generations of American blacks. Consequently, Levine adds, many aspects of African culture continue "to exist not as mere vestiges but as dynamic, living, creative parts of group life in the United States." This position contradicts that of earlier scholars who interpreted the fundamentals of African-American culture as distorted imitations of European-American culture.[3]

The music tradition established by slaves evolved over centuries in response to varying circumstances and environmental factors. Each generation of slaves and freeborn blacks created new musical genres and performance styles (see figure, p. 159). These forms are unique by-products of specific contexts and historical

Reprinted with permission, from Joseph E. Holloway, ed., *Africanisms in American Culture,* Indiana University Press.

periods. The purpose of this essay is to show that an identifiable conceptual framework links these traditions to each other and to African music traditions.

THE AFRICAN MUSICAL DIMENSION

The first scholars to examine customs and practices among blacks in the New World described the existence of African retentions in quantitative terms.[4] Although this practice of trait listing is valid, it does not account for changes that took place within the American context. Over the centuries specific African elements either have been altered or have disappeared from the cultures of New World blacks altogether. Yet the concepts that embody and identify the cultural heritage of black Americans have never been lost. The African dimension of African-American music is far-reaching and can be understood best when examined within this conceptual framework.

Early accounts of African performance in the New World, for example, document the existence of instruments clearly of African origin.[5] Eventually Western European musical instruments began to infiltrate and dominate African-American musical practice. Because the tempered tuning of these Western instruments differed from that of African instruments, black musicians were forced to deviate from certain African principles of melodic structure. Challenged to explore new means of melodic expression, blacks unconsciously created new ideas founded on existing African musical concepts. The result was the emergence of "blue notes" (flatted third and seventh degrees) and the production of pitches uncommon to Western scale structures.

Africanisms in African American music extend beyond trait lists and, as African ethnomusicologist J. H. Kwabena Nketia observes, "must be viewed in terms of creative processes which allow for continuity and change."[6] This point of view is shared by Olly Wilson, who concludes that African retentions in African American music are defined by the sharing of conceptual approaches to the music-making process and hence are "not basically quantitative but qualitative." Moreover, Wilson argues that the African dimension of African American music does not exist as

> a static body of something which can be depleted, but rather [as] a conceptual approach, the manifestations of which are infinite. The common core of this Africanness consists of the way of doing something, not simply something that is done.[7]

Music is integral to all aspects of black community life.[8] It serves many functions and is performed by individuals and groups in both formal and informal settings. The fundamental concept that governs music performance in African and African-derived cultures is that music-making is a participatory group activity that serves to unite black people into a cohesive group for a common purpose. This use of music in African-American communities continues a tradition found in African societies where, as Nketia observes,

> music making is generally organized as a social event. Public performances, therefore, take place on social occasions—that is, on occasions when members of a group or a community come together for the enjoyment of leisure, for recreational activities, or for the performance of a rite, ceremony, festival, or any kind of collective activity.[9]

The conceptualization of music-making as a participatory group activity is evident in the processes by which black Americans prepare for a performance. Since the 1950s, for example, black music promoters have advertised concerts as social gatherings where active audience involvement is expected. Promotional materials encourage potential concertgoers to "Come and be moved by" a gospel music concert or to "Come and jam with," "Come and get down with," or "Come and party with" a secular music concert. As Nketia notes, regardless of context—church, club, dance hall, or concert hall—public performance of black music serves

> a multiple role in relation to the community: it provides at once an opportunity for sharing in creative experience, for participating in music as a form of community experience, and for using music as an avenue for the expression of group sentiments.[10]

This communal approach to music-making is further demonstrated in the way contemporary performers adapt recorded versions of their songs for performance on the concert stage. Many begin their songs with ad lib "rapping" (secular) or "sermonettes" (sacred) to establish rapport with the audience. When the singing actually begins, the style of the performance complements the "we are here to jam" or "we are here to be moved" attitude of the audience/congregation. The audience/ congregation is encouraged to participate in any way, sometimes even to join performers on stage. Soul singer Sam Moore of the duo Sam and Dave recalls how he "would stop the band and get hand-clapping going in the audience [and] make them stand up."[11] Many black performers use this technique to ensure the active participation of audience members in the music event.

Music-making in Africa requires the active involvement of all present at the musical event. This approach to performance generates many of the cultural and aesthetic components that uniquely characterize music-making throughout the African diaspora. In a study of gospel music, ethnomusicologist Mellonee Burnim defines three areas of aesthetic significance in the black music tradition: delivery style, sound quality, and mechanics of delivery.[12] These categories are useful in examining qualities common to both African and African-derived music.

Style of Delivery

Style of delivery refers to the physical mode of presentation—how performers employ body movements, facial expressions, and clothing within the performance context. Burnim accurately asserts that music-making "in Black culture symbolizes vitality, a sense of aliveness."[13] This "aliveness" is expressed through visual, physical, and musical modes, all of which are interrelated in African musical performances. Olly Wilson defines the African musical experience as a

> multi-media one in which many kinds of collective human output are inextricably linked. Hence, a typical traditional [African] ceremony will include music, dance, the plastic arts (in the form of elaborate masks and/or costumes) and perhaps ritualistic drama.[14]

In African-American culture, the element of dress in musical performance is as important as the musical sound itself. When performers appear on stage, even before a musical sound is heard, audience members verbally and physically respond if costumes meet their aesthetic expectations. Performers establish an image, communicate a philosophy, and create an atmosphere of "aliveness" through the colorful and flamboyant costumes they wear. In the gospel tradition, Burnim observed that performers dress in "robes of bold, vivid colors and design." She also noted:

> At the 1979 James Cleveland Gospel Music Workshop of America in New Orleans, Louisiana, one evening's activities included a competition to select the best dressed male and female in gospel choir attire. The fashions ranged from brightly colored gowns and tuxedos to matching hooded capes lined in red.[15]

Ethnomusicologist Joyce Jackson, in her study of black gospel quartets, also observed that costumes are judged as part of the overall performance in gospel quartet competitions.[16]

The importance of dress in black music performances is demonstrated further in the popular tradition. In the film *That Rhythm . . . Those Blues,* vocalist Ruth Brown recalled how audiences expected performers to dress in the latest fashions. Responding to this expectation,

African-American Music: Its Development

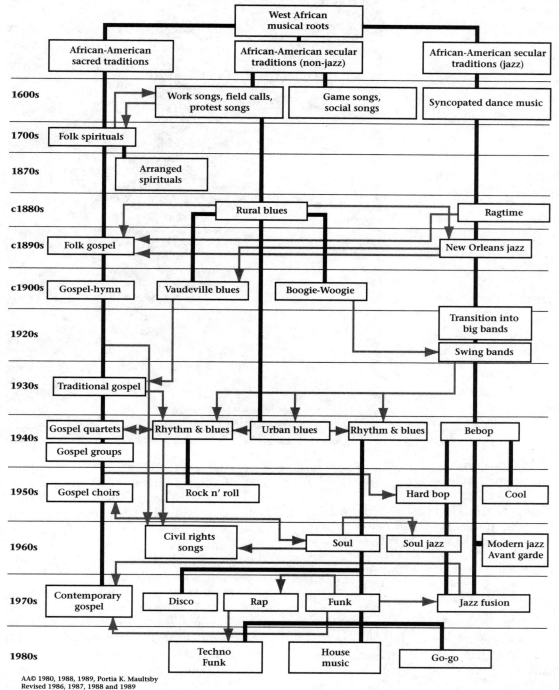

AA© 1980, 1988, 1989, Portia K. Maultsby
Revised 1986, 1987, 1988 and 1989

Early photograph of a young entertainer, in a splendidly rich gown and head covering.

Brown labeled herself as one of the first female singers

> that became known for the crinoline and multipetticoats and the shoes that matched the dresses. All of the singing groups [of the 1950s and 1960s] were impeccably dressed [in coordinated outfits] when they went on stage. If they wore white shoes . . . they were *white* shoes. Griffin shoe polish made all the money in the world.

The array of colors and fashions seen in concert halls, black churches, and other black performance sites is a vital part of the total visual experience. It is such a fundamental part of black cultural expression that these same principles of dress are observed by the audience. For example, audiences at Harlem's Apollo theater always wore the latest fashions. During the 1930s, the men "appeared in tight-belted, high-waisted coats" and the women "gracefully glided through the lobby in tight slinky dresses, high heels, and veils."[17]

The visual dimension of performance, according to Burnim's model, extends beyond dress to the physical behavior of musicians and their audiences. In communicating with their audiences, musicians display an intensity of emotion and total physical involvement through use of the entire body. Nketia points out that physical expression is part and parcel of music-making in African cultures:

> The values of African societies do not inhibit this. . . . it is encouraged, for through it, individuals relate to musical events or performing groups, and interact socially with others in a musical situation. Moreover, motor response intensifies one's enjoyment of music through the feelings of increased involvement and the propulsion that articulating the beat by physical movement generates.[18]

Accounts of religious services conducted by slaves illustrate the retention of these cultural values and attitudes in the New World. During the worship, slaves became active participants, freely responding verbally and physically to the sermon, the prayer, the music, and each other. This behavior prompted missionary Charles Colcock Jones to describe a revival meeting of slaves as a "confusion of sights and sounds!"

> Some were standing, others sitting, others moving from one seat to another, several exhorting along the aisles. The whole congregation kept up one loud monotonous strain, interrupted by various sounds: groans and screams and clapping hands. One woman specially under the influence of the excitement went across the church in a quick succession of leaps; now down on her knees with a sharp crack that smote upon my ear the full length of the church, then up again; now with her arms about some brother or sister, and again tossing them wildly in the air and clapping her hands together and accompanying the whole by a series of short, sharp shrieks. . . . Considering the mere excitement manifested in these disorderly ways, I could but ask: What religion is there in this?[19]

Observers of other religious gatherings of slaves noted that "there is much melody in their voices; and when they enjoy a hymn, there is a raised expression of the face. . . ." And "they sang so that it was a pleasure to hear, with all their souls and with all their bodies in unison; for their bodies wagged, their heads nodded, their feet stamped, their knees shook, their elbows and their hands beat time to the tunes and the words which they sing. . . ."[20]

The style of delivery that characterized musical performance during the seventeenth, eighteenth, and nineteenth centuries continues to be operative in both sacred and secular spheres of contemporary black America: black people consciously use their entire bodies in musical expression, and music and movement are conceived as a single unit. These concepts clearly are demonstrated in the presentation style of performers of popular music. Soul singer Al Braggs, for example, concluded his shows

> by pulling out all the vocal and choreographic stops . . . in the general manner of James Brown or Little Richard. He screams; he groans; he crawls rhythmically across the stage on his stomach dragging the microphone behind him; he leaps over, under, and around the microphone behind him; he lies on his back and kicks his feet in the air; he does some syncopated push-ups; he falls halfway over the edge of the stage and grabs the nearest hands; initiating a few unfinished dance steps, he does the limbo; he bumps and grinds; and gradually maneuvers himself off stage with a flying split or two, still twitching and shouting.[21]

This "unification of song and dance," as Burnim describes it, characterizes contemporary performances of black music. In the gospel tradition, choirs "march" in synchronized movements through the church during the processional and "step," "clap," and "shout" (religious dance) to the music performed during the worship.[22] This intrinsic relationship between music and movement is also seen during performances by popular music groups. Sam Moore commented that he and his partner, Dave Prater, "danced and moved around so much" during their performances that they lost "at least four or five pounds a night in sweat."[23] The accompanying musicians also danced in synchronized steps while playing their instruments, a concept patterned after black marching bands.

Sound Quality

The participatory dimension of music performance is only one aspect of the conceptual approach to music-making. Descriptions of black music performances over several centuries reveal that timbre is a primary feature that distinguishes this tradition from all others. The concept of sound that governs African-American music is unmistakably grounded in the African past. As Francis Bebey suggests,

> The objective of African music is not necessarily to produce sounds agreeable to the ear, but to translate everyday experiences into living sound. In a musical environment whose constant purpose is to depict life, nature, or the supernatural, the musician wisely avoids using beauty as his criterion because no criterion could be more arbitrary.
>
> Consequently, African voices adapt themselves to their musical contexts—a mellow tone to welcome a new bride; a husky voice to recount an indiscreet adventure; a satirical inflection for a teasing tone, with laughter bubbling up to compensate for the mockery—they may be soft or harsh as circumstances demand.[24]

In Africa and throughout the diaspora, black musicians produce an array of unique sounds, many of which imitate those of nature, animals, spirits, and speech. They reproduce these sounds using a variety of techniques, including striking the chest and maneuvering the tongue, mouth, cheek, and throat.[25] When arranged in an order and bound together by continuity of time, these sounds form the basis for musical composition.

The unique sound associated with black music results from the manipulation of timbre, texture, and shading in ways uncommon to Western practice. Musicians bring intensity to their performance by alternating lyrical, percussive, and raspy timbres; juxtaposing vocal and instrumental textures; changing pitch and dynamic levels; alternating straight with vibrato tones; and weaving moans, shouts, grunts, hollers, and screams into the melody.

The arbitrary notion of beauty has resulted in descriptions of black music as "weird," "strange," "noise," "yelling, " "hollering," "hooting," "screaming." The use of these words clearly indicates that the black music tradition does not adhere to European-American aesthetic values.

Instrumental sounds in African and African-derived music imitate timbres produced by the voice. Bebey observes that

> Western distinctions between instrumental and vocal music are evidently unthinkable in Africa where the human voice and musical instruments "speak" the same language, express the same feelings, and unanimously recreate the universe each time that thought is transformed into sound.[26]

Black instrumentalists produce a wide range of vocally derived sounds—"hollers," "cries," "grunts," "screams," "moans," and "whines," among others—by varying timbre, range, texture, and shading. They create these sounds by altering traditional embouchures, playing techniques, and fingerings and by adding distorting devices.[27] The vocal dimension of instrumental sounds is reflected in such phrases as "make it talk," "talk to me," and "I hear ya talkin'" used by black people to communicate that their aesthetic expectations have been met.

Mechanics of Delivery

The distinct sounds produced by black performers are combined with other aesthetic components to generate a pool of resources for song interpretation. Black audiences demand variety in music performances, and they expect musicians to bring a unique interpretation to each performance and to each song. Black performers meet these expectations in demonstrating their knowledge about technical aspects of performance. Within the African context, Bebey observes that "there is always plenty of scope for improvisation and ornamentation so that individual musicians can reveal their own particular talents and aptitudes. Thus, no two performances of any one piece will be exactly alike."[28] Improvisation is central to the category mechanics of delivery, which forms the third part of Burnim's aesthetic model.

Burnim convincingly argues that time, text, and pitch are the three basic components that form the structural network for song interpretation in black music. The element of time in black music is manipulated in both structural and rhythmic aspects of the performance. Time can be expanded by extending the length of notes at climactic points, by repeating words, phrases, and entire sections of songs, and by adding vocal or instrumental cadenzas. The density of textures can be increased "by gradually adding layers of handclaps, instrumental accompaniment, and/or solo voices."[29] This latter device, referred to as staggered entrances, characterized the improvised singing of slaves:

> With the first note of the hymn, began a tapping of feet by the whole congregation, gradually increasing to a stamp as the exercises proceeded, until the noise was deafening. . . . Then in strange contrast to this came the most beautiful melody the negroes have—a chant, carried by full bass voices; the liquid soprano of the melody wandering through and above it, now rising in triumphant swell, now falling in softened cadence. . . .[30]

The call-response structure is the key mechanism that allows for the manipulation of time, text, and pitch. The response or repetitive chorus provides a stable foundation for the improvised lines of the soloist. The use of call-response structures to generate musical change has been described many times in black music literature.

> These ditties [work songs sung by slaves], though nearly meaningless, have much music in them, and as all join in the perpetually recurring chorus, a rough harmony is produced. . . . I think the leader improvises the words . . . he singing one line alone, and the

whole then giving the chorus, which is repeated without change at every line, till the general chorus concludes the stanza. . . .[31]

The call-response structure also is used by jazz musicians to establish a base for musical change and rhythmic tension.

> [Count] Basie's men played short, fierce riffs. Their riff patterns were not even melodic elements, they were just repetitive rhythmic figures set against each other in the sections of the band. Against this sharp, pulsing background, Basie set his soloists, and they had free rein.[32]

Perhaps the most noticeable African feature in African-American music is its rhythmic complexity. Early descriptions of this tradition reveal that

> Syncopations . . . are characteristic of negro music. I have heard negroes change a well-known melody by adroitly syncopating it. . . . nothing illustrates the negro's natural gifts in the way of keeping a difficult tempo more clearly than his perfect execution of airs thus transformed from simple to complex accentuations.[33]

In both African and African-American music, rhythm is organized in multilinear forms. Different patterns, which are repeated with slight, if any, variation, are assigned to various instruments. The combination of these patterns produces polyrhythms.[34] Polyrhythmic structures increase the overall intensity of musical performances because each repetition produces added rhythmic tension. At the same time the repetition of patterns in one part allows for textual and melodic variation in another.

Many accounts of black music have described its repetitious form while noting the creative ways in which performers achieve variety. An example is this 1862 notice:

> Each stanza [of a song sung by slaves] contains but a single thought, set in perhaps two or three bars of music; and yet as they sing it, in alternate recitatives and choruses, with varying inflections and dramatic effect. . . .[35]

Under the mechanics of delivery category, the element of pitch is manipulated by "juxtaposing voices of different ranges or by highlighting the polar extremes of a single voice." Pitch is also varied through the use of "bends, slides, melismas, and passing tones" and other forms of melodic embellishment "in order to achieve the continuous changes, extreme latitude, and personalization"—an identifying trait of black musical expression.[36] "Playing" with pitch—or "worrying the line," as Stephen Henderson calls it[37]—is a technique integral to the solo style of many black performers, including blues singer Bobby Blue Bland.

> All the distinctive features of Bland's vocal style are in evidence, notably the hoarse cry and his use of melisma on key words. Bland's cry usually consists of a twisted vowel at the beginning of a phrase—going from a given note, reaching up to another higher one, and coming back to the starting point. . . . Almost without exception Bobby uses more than one note per syllable on the concluding word of each phrase. . . . In slower tempos he will stretch out syllables with even more melisma, using as many as ten or eleven notes over a two-syllable word.[38]

Time, text, and pitch are manipulated by black performers to display their creative abilities and technical skills and to generate an overall intensity within their performance.

When performers create and interpret songs within the aesthetic boundaries framed by black people, audiences respond immediately. Their verbal comments and physical gestures express approval of both the song being performed and the way it is performed. For example, performances by musicians in the popular idiom often are based on principles that govern black worship services. These principles are recognized and valued by black audiences, who respond in the same manner as they do to the presentations of black preachers and church choirs. Sam Moore recalled:

> When we performed, we had church. On Sundays the minister would preach and the people in the pews would holler and talk back to him. This is what we started doing. I arranged the parts between Dave and me so that one of us became the preacher and would say "Come on Dave" or "Come on Sam." The audience would automatically shout "Come on Sam" or "Sing Dave" or "Yes Sir." That was our style.[39]

Vocalist Deniece Williams believes that an audience actively participates in her performances because they identify with the gospel roots of her delivery style:

> You hear that [Church of God in Christ] in my music even though it is not the same deliverance of Aretha Franklin. But you feel it. A lot of people say to me "when you sing I feel it." I think that feeling comes from those experiences of church, gospel music and spirituality, which play a big part in my life.[40]

Audiences of Bobby Bland also respond in the character of the Sunday morning service:

> Women sprinkled throughout the audience yell back at him, shaking their heads and waving their hands [in response to Bland's melisma]. . . . Suddenly the guitarist doubles the tempo and repeats a particularly funky phrase a few times accompanied by "oohs," "aahs," and "yeahs" from the audience.[41]

When performers demonstrate their knowledge of the black musical aesthetic, the responses of audiences can become so audible that they momentarily drown out the performer. The verbal responses of audiences are accompanied by handclapping; footstomping; head, shoulder, hand, and arm movement; and spontaneous dance. This type of audience participation is important to performers; it encourages them to explore the full range of aesthetic possibilities, and it is the single criterion by which black artists determine whether they are meeting the aesthetic expectations of the audience. Songwriter-vocalist Smokey Robinson judges his concerts as unsuccessful if the audience is "not involved in what's happening on the stage."[42]

The concept of "performer-audience" as a single unit is even apparent in the way black people respond to music in nonpublic settings. Twentieth-century technological advances make music accessible twenty-four hours a day, every day. African-Americans often use recorded music as a substitute for live performances. While listening to recordings they become involved as active participants, singing along on familiar refrain lines and choruses, snapping their fingers, clapping their hands, moving to the beat, and verbally responding to especially meaningful words or phrases and sounds with "sing it baby," "tell the truth," "play your horn," "tickle them keys," and "get on down." This level of involvement, which replicates interaction at live performances, preserves an African approach to music-making in contemporary society.

Music-making throughout the African diaspora is an expression of life where verbal and physical expression is intrinsic to the process. This conceptual framework links all black music traditions together in the African diaspora while distinguishing these traditions from those of Western and Western-derived cultures. A salient feature of black music is the conceptualization of music-making as a communal-participatory activity. In addition, variation in timbre, song interpretation, and presentation style mirrors the aesthetic priorities of black people.

An African approach to music-making has been translated from one genre to the next throughout African-American musical history. Although these genres (see figure) are by-products of specific contexts and time frames, each genre is distinctly African American because it is governed by the conceptual framework already discussed. The remainder of this essay provides a chronology of African-American musical forms from slavery to the present.[43] The discussion presents evidence of how this conceptual unity has been transmitted from one African-American genre to the next since the first musics were created in the New World.

MUSIC IN THE SLAVE COMMUNITY

For more than 150 years slave traders and slaveholders unwittingly helped preserve an African identity in the African-American music tradition. Slave traders brought African instruments on board ships and encouraged slaves to sing and dance for exercise during the long voyage to the New World. These artifacts and creative expressions were among the cultural baggage slaves brought with them to the Americas.[44]

Studies of the institution of slavery point out that slave systems varied throughout the Americas and among colonies in the United States.[45] In situations where slaves had some measure of personal freedom they engaged in leisure activities that clearly reflected their African heritage.[46] In the United States, for example, slaves celebrated holidays for more than two centuries in African style. Two of the most spectacular and festive holidays, 'Lection Day and Pinkster Day celebrations, were observed from the mid-eighteenth through the mid-nineteenth centuries. On 'Lection Day slaves in the New England colonies elected a black governor or king and staged a big parade. Dressed in elaborate outfits, slaves celebrated by playing African games, singing, dancing, and playing African and European instruments in a distinctly African style. Pinkster Day was of Dutch origin, but slaves and free blacks in the North and South transformed it into an African-style festival.[47]

The unique character of the Pinkster Day celebration prompted James Fenimore Cooper to record his impressions:

> Nine tenths of the blacks of the city [New York], and of the whole country within thirty or forty miles, indeed, were collected in thousands in those fields, beating banjos [and African drums], singing African songs [accompanied by dancing]. The features that distinguish a Pinkster frolic from the usual scenes at fairs . . . however, were of African origin. It is true, there are not now [1845], nor were there then [1757] many blacks among us of African

birth; but the traditions and usages of their original country were so far preserved as to produce a marked difference between the festival, and one of European origin.[48]

The diaries of missionaries, travelers, and slaveholders and the accounts of slaves themselves further document that slaves continued to keep African traditions alive in the United States. In 1680 a missionary observed that slaves spent Sundays singing and dancing "as a means to procure Rain." An army general heard his slaves sing a war song in an African language during a visit to his plantation after the Revolutionary War. In another instance, a slave born in 1849 reported that African-born slaves sang their own songs and told stories about African customs during Christmas celebrations. And many observers noted the African flavor of the songs slaves sang while working.[49]

Slaveholders generally did not object to these and other African-derived activities provided they did not interfere with the work routine of slaves. Missionaries, on the other hand, objected to the singing and dancing, which they described as pagan and contrary to the teachings of Christianity. Committed to eliminating these activities, they mounted a campaign to proselytize slaves. Missionaries experienced success in the New England colonies but met resistance among slaveholders in the South, who feared that a change in religious status would alter the social status of slaves as chattel property.[50]

By the nineteenth century southern slaveholders had begun to support the activities of missionaries. Faced with the growing number of slaves who ran away, sabotaged plantation operations, and organized revolts, they believed that tighter control over slaves could be exercised through religion. Many slaveholders allowed their slaves to receive religious instruction, and some even facilitated the process by building "praise houses" on the farms and plantations.[51] Despite these and other efforts, the slaves' acceptance of Christianity was at best superficial. They interpreted

Christian concepts and practices through the filter of an African past, transforming the liturgy into an African ritual.

When slaves were allowed to conduct their own religious services, they defied all rules, standards, and structures established by the various denominations and sects. Their services were characterized by an unorthodox sermonizing style, unconventional behavior, and spontaneous musical expressions.[52] Missionaries frequently expressed disapproval of these services:

> The public worship of God should be conducted *with reverence and stillness on the part of the congregation;* nor should the minister— whatever may have been the previous habits and training of the people—encourage demonstrations of approbation or disapprobation, or exclamations, or response, or noises, or outcries of any kind during the progress of divine worship; nor boisterous singing immediately at its close. These practices prevail over large portions of the southern country, and are not confined to one denomination, but appear to some extent in all. I cannot think them beneficial.[53]

Missionaries were especially critical of the music they described as "short scraps of disjointed affirmations . . . lengthened out with long repetitious choruses."[54] The call-response structure and improvisatory style unique to musical performances of slaves did not adhere to European-American aesthetic values. These aesthetic differences prompted missionaries to include psalm and hymn singing in the religious instruction of slaves so that they would

> lay aside the extravagant and nonsensical chants, and catches and hallelujah songs of their own composing; and when they sing, which is very often while about their business of an evening in their houses [and in church], they will have something profitable to sing.[55]

In spite of these efforts, slaves continued to sing "songs of their own composing" while adapting psalms and hymns to conform to

African aesthetic principles. Henry Russell, an English musician who toured the United States from 1833 to 1841, described this process:

> When the minister gave out his own version of the Psalm, the choir commenced singing so rapidly that the original tune absolutely ceased to exist—in fact, the fine old psalm tune became thoroughly transformed into a kind of negro melody; and so sudden was the transformation, by accelerating the time, that, for a moment, I fancied that not only the choir but the little congregation intended to get up a dance as part of the service.[56]

One observer who witnessed the changing of a hymn into a "Negro song" commented that "Watts and Newton would never recognize their productions through the transformation they have undergone at the hands of their colored admirers."[57]

Other descriptions of religious services conducted by slaves confirm that they frequently fashioned Protestant psalms, hymns, and spiritual songs into new compositions by altering the structure, text, melody, and rhythm. They transformed the verse structure of the original song into a call-response or repetitive chorus structure; replaced the original English verse with an improvised text of African and English words and phrases; wove shouts, moans, groans, and cries into the melody of the improvised solo; substituted a faster tempo for the original one; and produced polyrhythmic structures by adding syncopated foot-stomped and hand-clapped patterns.[58] The body of religious music created or adapted by slaves and performed in a distinctly African style became known as "folk spirituals."

The religious tradition of slaves dominated the eighteenth- and nineteenth-century literature on African-American music. The scarcity of information on the secular tradition results in part from the reluctance of slaves to sing secular songs in the presence of whites. Missionaries discouraged slaves from singing secular songs, and slaves responded by going underground with these songs. The few accounts of secular music performances nevertheless confirm that this tradition shares the aesthetic qualities characteristic of folk spirituals:

> The negroes [a dozen stout rowers] struck up a song to which they kept time with their oars; and our speed increased as they went on, and became warmed with their singing. . . . A line was sung by a leader, then all joined in a short chorus; then came another [improvised] solo line, and another short chorus, followed by a longer chorus. . . . little regard was paid to rhyme, and hardly any to the number of syllables in a line; they condensed four or five into one foot, or stretched out one to occupy the space that should have been filled with four or five; yet they never spoiled the tune.[59]

As in the folk spiritual tradition, the call-response structure allowed for improvised solos and recurring refrain lines.

MUSIC IN THE FREE COMMUNITY

The northern states began to abolish slavery during the first half of the nineteenth century. Yet freed slaves were faced with discriminatory state legislation that once again placed restrictions on their mobility. The small percentage of freed slaves who lived in the South were in precarious positions because their "color suggested servitude, but [their] status secured a portion of freedom." Only a "portion of freedom" was theirs because legislation barred southern free blacks from participating in mainstream society.[60] Determined to create a meaningful life, freed blacks in the North and South established communities and institutions where they defined their own mode of existence and cultural frame of reference.[61] The black church became the center of community life, serving an array of functions— religious, cultural, social, educational, and political. Within this context, many blacks kept alive the cultural traditions and musical practices associated with the praise houses of the South.[62]

The abolition of slavery in the South temporarily disrupted the communal solidarity of the slave community. Individually and in small groups, African Americans attempted to establish new lives within the larger society. Some migrated from rural areas to cities and from South to North in search of social, political, and economic viability. Discriminatory practices, however, restricted their employment possibilities to such menial roles as domestic servants, janitors, chauffeurs, and delivery boys. Many could not find even menial jobs and, as a last resort, worked as sharecroppers on the land they had farmed as slaves. Others attempted to take advantage of educational opportunities to upgrade their social status. Despite these efforts toward "self-improvement," the broader society continued to control the mobility of blacks, forcing the masses to remain economically dependent on whites.[63]

The Fourteenth Amendment to the U.S. Constitution, ratified in 1868, guaranteed citizenship to freed slaves, and the Fifteenth Amendment of 1870 gave black men voting rights. Yet African-Americans became victims of discriminatory state legislation.[64] Many blacks survived as free persons in America because they relied on their traditional past for direction. They created a meaningful existence by preserving old values, fashioning new ones when necessary, and reestablishing the group solidarity they had known as slaves. For many decades following the Civil War, blacks continued to make music from an African frame of reference. White northerners who migrated south to assist blacks in their transition into mainstream society were especially critical of this practice among children at school:

> In the infant schoolroom, the benches were first put aside, and the children ranged along the wall. Then began a wild droning chant in a minor key, marked with clapping of hands and stamping of feet. A dozen or twenty rose, formed a ring in the centre of the room, and began an odd shuffling dance. Keeping time to this weird chant they circled round, one following the other, changing their step to quicker and wilder motion, with louder clapping of the hands as the fervor of the singers reached a climax. The words of their hymns are simple and touching. The verses consist of two lines, the first being repeated twice. . . . As I looked upon the faces of these little barbarians and watched them circling round in this fetish dance, doubtless the relic of some African rite, I felt discouraged. . . . However, the recollection of the mental arithmetic seemed a more cheerful view of the matter.[65]

Another observer concluded that common aesthetic features link the secular and religious traditions:

> Whatever they sing is of a religious character, and in both cases [performances of secular and religious music] they have a leader . . . who starts a line, the rest answering antiphonally as a sort of chorus. They always keep exquisite time and tune, and no words seem too hard for them to adapt to their tunes. . . . Their voices have a peculiar quality, and their intonations and delicate variations cannot be reproduced on paper.[66]

These descriptions confirm that African aesthetic concepts—of music and movement as a single unit, the varying timbres, the shadings, and the use of call-response structures to manipulate time, text, and pitch—remained vital to black musical expression in postbellum African-American culture.

Other accounts of postbellum black music reveal that both children and adults continued to sing songs from the past while creating new musical forms out of existing traditions.[67] As I wrote in an earlier essay, "The old form persisted alongside the new and remained a vital form of expression within specific contexts."[68] The new idioms, including blues, jazz, gospel, and popular music, became a unifying and sustaining force in the free black community. These and the older forms reaffirmed the values of an African past and simultaneously expressed a sense of inner strength and optimism about the future.

The secular music tradition became increasingly important. Even though missionaries had attempted to discourage slaves from singing secular songs, many free blacks asserted their independence by responding to the daily events in their lives through secular song. The secular form that became and remains particularly important to African-American culture is the blues.

The blues form shares general features and aesthetic qualities with past music traditions. It combines the musical structure and poetic forms of spirituals, work songs, and field cries with new musical and textual ideas. The improvisatory performance style emphasizes call-response (between the voice and accompanying instruments). Integral to the melody are slides, slurs, bends, and dips, and the timbres vary from moans, groans, and shouts to song-speech utterances.[69] The accompanying instruments—guitar, fiddle, piano, harmonica, and sometimes tub basses, washboards, jugs, a wire nailed to the side of a house, and other ad hoc instruments—are played in an African-derived percussive style.[70]

For more than a hundred years the essence of the blues tradition has remained the same. Amplified instruments added in the 1940s, rhythm sections in the 1950s, and horns in the 1960s are perhaps the only significant—yet in a sense only superficial—changes that have taken place in this tradition. In the twentieth century the "blues sound" crossed into the sacred world, giving life to an original body of sacred music called gospel.

Gospel music is a by-product of the late nineteenth- and early twentieth-century black "folk church." This church, associated with the Holiness and Pentecostal sects, is a contemporary version of plantation praise houses. Its character, as Pearl Williams-Jones has stated, "reflects the traditional cultural values of Black folk life as it has evolved since slave days, and is a cumulative expression of the Black experience."[71] The black folk church is distinguished from black denominational churches by the structure and nature of its service, religious practices, and philosophical concepts and the socioeconomic background of its members. The official doctrine of the folk church encourages spontaneous expressions through improvised song, testimonies, prayers, and praises from individuals.[72] Unlike other black churches, the folk church did not evolve from white Protestant denominations. Its musical repertoire, therefore, is distinctly different from that of mainline Protestant churches.

The music of the folk church, known as "church songs," has as its basic repertoire the folk spirituals and modified hymns sung by slaves in plantation praise houses. The new songs that became standards in the Black church were created spontaneously during the service by the preacher and congregation members, and they were performed in the style of folk spirituals. The only substantive change made in this tradition was the addition of musical instruments to the established accompaniment of hand-clapping and foot-stomping.[73] These instruments included tambourines, drums, piano, guitar, various horns and ad hoc instruments, and later the organ. The "bluesy," "jazzy," and "rockin'" sounds from these instruments brought a secular dimension to black religious music. The instrumental accompaniment, which became an integral part of religious music in the folk church, defined new directions for black religious music in the twentieth century.

During the first two decades of this century, the prototype for gospel music was established in the folk church. Horace Boyer noted, however, that members of this church "were not the first to receive recognition as gospel singers. Until the forties, Holiness churches did not allow their members to sing their songs before non-Holiness persons."[74] This policy did not confine the emerging gospel sound to the Holiness church. Members of the black community whose homes surrounded these churches were well aware of their existence.

Gospel music first reached the black masses as a "composed" form through the compositions of ministers and members of black Methodist and Baptist churches. Charles Albert Tindley, a Methodist minister in Philadelphia, created the prototype for a composed body of black religious music between 1900 and 1906. Some of these songs were hymnlike verses set to the melodies and rhythms of folk church songs; others were adaptations of spirituals and revival hymns.[75]

In the 1920s the Baptist songwriter Thomas Dorsey used Tindley's model to compose an identifiable and distinct body of black religious music called gospel. The former blues-jazz pianist organized his compositions around the verse-chorus form in which is embedded the call-response structure. Drawing from his blues background, he fashioned his melodies and harmonies using blues scale structures and developed a "rockin'" piano accompaniment in the boogie-woogie and ragtime traditions.

Unlike other black music genres, gospel songs often are disseminated as printed music. Yet the score provides only a framework from which performers interpret and improvise. Gospel music performances are governed by the same aesthetic concepts associated with the folk spiritual tradition. In interpreting the score, performers must demonstrate their knowledge of the improvisatory devices that characterize black music performances.

For more than eighty years the gospel tradition has preserved and transmitted the aesthetic concepts fundamental to music-making in Africa and African-derived cultures. Since its birth in the Holiness and Pentecostal churches it has found a home in storefront churches of various denominations and in many black middle-class Baptist, Methodist, Episcopal, and Catholic churches. The impact of gospel has been so great that its colorful African-derived kaleidoscope of oratory, poetry, drama, and dance and its musical style established a reservoir of cultural resources that contributed to the development of black popular music.

New secular forms of black musical expression were created in response to changes in society following World War II. The war years stimulated growth in the American economy, which in turn led to changes in the lives of black Americans. As I recounted in an earlier monograph, almost two million southern rural blacks abandoned "their low-paying domestic, sharecropping and tenant-farming jobs for work in factories located throughout the country. In cities, both Blacks and whites earned the highest wages in American history. So Americans, especially Black Americans, had much to celebrate during the postwar years."[76] The music to which they celebrated was termed rhythm and blues—a hybrid form rooted in the blues, gospel, and swing band traditions.

Blacks left the rural South with expectations of improving their economic, social, and political status. They soon discovered that opportunities for advancement in society were limited and that the segregated structure of cities restricted their mobility. Discriminatory housing laws, for example, forced many blacks to live and socialize in designated sections of cities—ghettos. These and other patterns of discrimination led to the reestablishment of familiar institutions, thereby continuing southern traditions and practices in the urban metropolis.

The ambiance of southern juke joints was transferred to blues bars, lounges, and clubs, which became the center of social gatherings in urban cities. Southern music traditions—blues and jazz—were central to the activity in these establishments. The segregated environment, the faster pace, the factory sounds, the street noises, and the technology of the metropolis gave a different type of luster, cadence, and sophistication to existing black musical forms. In response to new surroundings, the familiar sounds of the past soon were transformed into an urban black music tradition.

Blues, jazz, and gospel performers were among the millions of blacks who moved to the cities. They joined forces to create an urban-sounding dance music, rhythm and blues.

This music is characterized by a boogie bass line, "riffing" jazz-derived horn arrangements, blues-gospel piano, "honking" and "screaming" tenor sax, "whining" blues guitar, and syncopated drum patterns. The intensity of this sound was increased by the addition of blues and former gospel singers who "moaned" and "shouted" about life in the city. The rhythmic complexity and the performance style of rhythm and blues music preserved traditional values in the music of the city dwellers.

The spirit that captured the excitement of postwar city living began to fade in the mid-1950s. Conditions deteriorated, and life continued to be harsh for many African Americans, especially the inner-city dwellers. They responded by organizing a series of grass-roots protest activities that quickly gained momentum and attracted national attention. The spread of these political activities throughout the country was the impetus behind the civil rights and black power movements of the 1950s and 1960s. "Soul music" was a by-product of the 1960s movements.[77]

Leaders of the black power movement encouraged the rejection of standards and values of the broader society and a return to values of an African past. Many soul music performers became ambassadors for this movement. Through song they communicated its philosophy, advocating an awareness of an African heritage, encouraging the practice of African traditions, and promoting the concept of black pride. Their "soul message" was communicated in a style that captured the climate of the times and the spirit of a people. This style embraces all the aesthetic qualities that define the essence of the gospel tradition.[78]

The interrelatedness of soul and gospel music is illustrated through the interchangeability of the genres. For example, many gospel songs have been recorded under the label "soul" and vice versa. In some instances the text is the only feature that distinguishes one style from another. In others, genre identification may be determined only by the musical identity of the

artist who first recorded the song. Performances of soul and gospel music further illustrate that an aesthetic conceptual framework links the secular and sacred traditions to each other.

The era of soul music reawakened the consciousness of an African past. It sanctioned the new thrust for African exploration and simultaneously gave credence to an obscured heritage. This profound era also established new directions in black popular music that would continue to merge African expressions into new forms. The decade of the 1970s heralded this new music.

The 1960s ended with the anticipation of new opportunities for economic independence and full participation in mainstream life. Affirmative action, school desegregation, and other legislation was passed, and the early 1970s implied future changes in the structure of society. Such legislation cultivated a renewed sense of optimism among blacks, and many began to explore new economic, political, and social opportunities outside the black community.

By the mid-1970s this optimism had begun to fade with increased opposition to affirmative action legislation. The economic recession and the "reverse discrimination" concept of the 1970s led to a retrenchment of civil rights and economic opportunities designed to effect equality for blacks. Whites protested against busing and affirmative action policies. In response, the federal government retreated on earlier commitments to rights for blacks. The "gains" made in the early 1970s gave way to fiscal and social conservatism in the late 1970s and the 1980s. The general opposition to any social advantages for blacks fostered a return to the status quo where racism shaped the American ethos.[79]

Blacks responded to the realities of the 1970s and 1980s in diverse ways and with mixed feelings. Many assessed progress toward social, economic, and political equality as illusory at best. Some felt conditions had worsened, though a few privileged blacks believed the situation had improved.[80] The ambivalent feelings about social progress for blacks found its expression in new and diverse forms of black popular music—funk, disco, rap music, and personalized or trademark forms.

The song lyrics and music styles of funk, disco, and rap music epitomize the changing and sometimes conflicting viewpoints about progress. Although many performers continued to express optimism about the future, some introduced lyric themes of frustration, disillusionment, and distress. The "soul sound" dominated during the first half of the 1970s, but by the mid-1970s it had been transformed. Whereas soul carries the trademark of "message music," funk, disco, and rap music bore the stamp of "party" music.[81] It injected a new spirit of life into black communities and became a major unifying force for a core of African-Americans. This spirit is reflected in the lyric themes: "party," "have a good time," "let yourself go," and "dance, dance, dance." These themes suggest that the music had a therapeutic function. Rather than communicate political or intellectual messages, it encouraged blacks to release tension by simply being themselves. At the same time, the infectious beat of this music created an atmosphere that allowed for self-expression and unrestricted social interactions.

Funk, disco, and rap music are grounded in the same aesthetic concepts that define the soul music tradition. Yet the sound is distinguished from soul because emphasis is given to different musical components. These forms of the late 1970s are conceived primarily as dance music where melody plays a secondary role to rhythm. The African-derived polyrhythmic structures, the call-response patterns, and the quasi-spoken group vocals generate audience participation. The percussive sounds and timbrel qualities of synthesizers and other electronic devices add another dimension to the black sound. The musical and cultural features in 1970s and 1980s popular traditions continue to give credence to the vitality of an African past in contemporary forms of black music.

CONCLUSIONS

A study of African-American music from the seventeenth through the twentieth centuries reveals that African retentions in African-American music can be defined as a core of conceptual approaches. Fundamental to these approaches is the axiom that music-making is conceived as a communal/participatory group activity. Black people create, interpret, and experience music out of an African frame of reference—one that shapes musical sound, interpretation, and behavior and makes black music traditions throughout the world a unified whole.

The New World experiences of black people encouraged them to maintain ties to their African past. This unspoken association enabled them to survive and create a meaningful existence in a world where they were not welcomed. They adapted to environmental changes and social upheavals by relying on familiar traditions and practices. Music played an important role in this process. Although specific African songs and genres eventually disappeared from the culture of African Americans, Nketia points out that new ones were "created in the style of the tradition, using its vocabulary and idiom, or in an alternative style which combined African and non-African resources."[82] In essence, new ideas were recycled through age-old concepts to produce new music styles. The fundamentals of culture established by slaves persist in the twentieth century; they are reinterpreted as social times demand. African retentions in African-American culture, therefore, exist as conceptual approaches—as unique ways of doing things and making things happen—rather than as specific cultural elements.

Notes

1. Historical studies include Ira Berlin, *Slaves Without Masters: The Free Negro in the Antebellum South* (New York: Vintage, 1974); Eugene

D. Genovese, *Roll Jordan Roll: The World the Slaves Made* (New York: Pantheon, 1974); John Blassingame, *The Slave Community* (New York: Oxford University Press, rev. ed., 1979); Gerald W. Mullin, *Flight and Rebellion* (New York: Oxford University Press, 1972); and Robert Haynes, *Blacks in White America Before 1865* (New York: David McKay, 1972).

For cultural studies, see John W. Work, *Folk Song of the American Negro* (Nashville, Tenn.: Fisk University Press, 1915; reprinted by Negro Universities Press, New York, 1969); James Weldon and J. Rosamond Johnson, *American Negro Spirituals,* 2 vols. (New York: Viking Press, 1925 and 1926; reprinted in one volume by Da Capo Press, New York, 1969); Zora Neale Hurston, "Spirituals and NeoSpirituals" [1935], in *Voices from the Harlem Renaissance,* Nathan Huggins, ed. (New York: Oxford University Press, 1976), 344–47; Hall Johnson, "Notes on the Negro Spiritual" [1965], in *Readings in Black American Music,* Eileen Southern, ed. (New York: Norton, 2d ed., 1983), 273–80; Henry Krehbiel, *Afro-American Folksongs* (New York: Ungar, 1914); Melville J. Herskovits, *The Myth of the Negro Past* (Boston: Beacon Press, 1958); Lawrence Levine, *Black Culture and Black Consciousness* (New York: Oxford University Press, 1977); Dena Epstein, *Sinful Tunes and Spirituals* (Chicago: University of Chicago Press, 1977); Alan Dundes, ed., *Mother Wit from the Laughing Barrel* (Englewood Cliffs, NJ.: Prentice-Hall, 1973); Norman E. Whitten and John F. Szwed, eds., *Afro-American Anthropology* (New York: Free Press, 1970); Paul Oliver, *Savannah Syncopators: African Retentions in the Blues* (New York: Stein and Day, 1970); Albert J. Raboteau, *Slave Religion* (New York: Oxford University Press, 1978); Frederick Kaufman and John Guckin, *The African Roots of Jazz* (Alfred Publishing Company, 1979); Olly Wilson, "The Significance of the Relationship Between Afro-American Music and West African Music," *Black Perspective in Music* (Spring 1974) 2:3–22; and J. H. Kwabena Nketia, "African Roots of Music in the Americas: An African View," 82–88, Olly Wilson, "The Association of Movement and Music as a Manifestation of a Black Conceptual Approach to Music," 98–105, and David

Evans, "African Elements in Twentieth-Century United States Black Folk Music," 54–66, in Report of the 12th Congress, London, American Musicological Society.1981.

2. Levine, *Black Culture,* 5.
3. For a summary of theories advanced by these writers, see Herskovits, *Myth,* 262–69; Guy B. Johnson, *Folk Culture in St. Helena Island* (Chapel Hill: University of North Carolina Press, 1930); Lawrence Levine, "Slave Songs and Slave Consciousness." in *American Negro Slavery.* Allen Weinstein and Frank Otto Catell, eds. (New York: Oxford University Press, 2d ed., 1973), 153–82; and Dena Epstein, "A White Origin for the Black Spiritual? An Invalid Theory and How It Grew," *American Music* (Summer 1983) 1:53–59.
4. Richard Waterman, "African Patterns in Trinidad Negro Music," Ph.D. dissertation. Northwestern University, 1943, 26, 41–42; "Hot Rhythm in Negro Music," *Journal of the American Musicological Society* (1948) 1:24–37; and "On Flogging a Dead Horse: Lessons Learned from the Africanisms Controversy," *Ethnomusicology* (1963) 7:83–87. Alan Lornax, *Folk Song Style and Culture* (Washington, D.C.: American Association for the Advancement of Science, 1968). Herskovits, *Myth,* 261–69. Krebbiel, *Afro-American Folksong.*
5. For a summary of these accounts, see Epstein, *Sinful Tunes.* 19–99.
6. Nketia, "African Roots," 88.
7. Wilson, "Significance," 20.
8. For a discussion of the way music functions in African societies, see J. H. Kwabena Nketia, *The Music of Africa* (New York: Norton, 1974), 21–50, and Francis Bebey, *African Music: A People's Art,* Josephine Bennett, trans. (New York: Lawrence Hill, 1975), 1–38.
9. Nketia, *Music of Africa,* 21.
10. Ibid., 22.
11. Sam Moore, interview with author, 25 February 1983.
12. Mellonee Burnim, "The Black Gospel Music Tradition: A Complex of Ideology, Aesthetic, and Behavior," in *More than Dancing,* Irene V. Jackson, ed. (Westport, Conn.: Greenwood Press, 1985), 154.
13. Ibid., 159.
14. Wilson, "Association of Movement," 99.

15. Mellonee Burnim, "Functional Dimensions of Gospel Music Performance," *Western Journal of Black Studies* (Summer 1988) 12:115.

16. Joyce Jackson, "The Performing Black Sacred Quartet: An Expression of Cultural Values and Aesthetics," Ph.D. dissertation, Indiana University, 1988, 161–90.

17. Ted Fox, *Showtime at the Apollo* (New York: Holt, Rinehart and Winston, 1983), 69.

18. Nketia, *Music of Africa,* 206–7.

19. Letter from Rev. R. Q. Mallard to Mrs. Mary S. Mallard, Chattanooga, May 18, 1859, in *The Children of Pride,* Robert Manson Myers, ed. (New Haven, Conn.: Yale University Press, 1972), 483.

20. Andrew Reed and James Matheson, *A Narrative of the Visit to the American Churches* (London: Jackson and Walford, 1835), 219. Frederika Bremer, *Homes of the New World,* 1, trans. Mary Howitt (New York: Harper, 1854), 393.

21. Charles Kell, *Urban Blues* (Chicago: University of Chicago Press, 1966), 122.

22. Burnim, "Black Gospel Music Tradition," 160.

23. Sam Moore, interview with author, 25 February 1983.

24. Bebey, *African Music,* 115.

25. See Ruth M. Stone, "African Music Performed," in *Africa,* Phyllis M. Martin and Patrick O'Meara, eds. (Bloomington: Indiana University Press, 2d ed., 1986), 236–39, and Bebey, *African Music,* 119–24, for more in-depth discussions of musical sound in African cultures.

26. Bebey, *African Music,* 122.

27. Instrumental playing techniques of black musicians are discussed in Thomas J. Anderson et al., "Black Composers and the Avant-Garde," in *Black Music in Our Culture,* Dominique-Rene de Lerma, ed. (Kent, Ohio: Kent State University Press, 1970), 66, 68; David Evans, "African Elements," 61; Oliver, *Savannah Syncopators;* and Wilson, "Significance of the Relationship," 15–21.

28. Bebey, *African Music,* 30.

29. Burnim, "Black Gospel," 163.

30. [Elizabeth Kilham], "Sketches in Color," *Putnam's,* March 1870, 306.

31. Philip Henry Goose, *Letters from Alabama* (London: Morgan and Chase, 1859), 305.

32. Samuel B. Charters and Leonard Kunstadt, *Jazz: A History of the New York Scene* (New York: Da Capo Press, 1981), 288.

33. Quoted in Epstein, *Sinful Tunes,* 294–95.

34. For discussions of rhythmic structures in black music, see Wilson, "Significance of the Relationship," 3–15; Nketia, *Music of Africa,* 38; Evans,"African Elements," 17–18; Portia K. Maultsby, "Contemporary Pop: A Healthy Diversity Evolves from Creative Freedom," Billboard, June 9, 1979, BM-22; and Pearl Williams-Jones, "Afro-American Gospel Music in Development of Materials for a One Year Course," in *African Music for the General Undergraduate Student,* Vada Butcher, ed. (Washington, D.C.: Howard University Press, 1970), 211.

35. J[ames Miller] McKim, "Negro Songs," *Dwight's Journal of Music,* August 9, 1862, 148-49.

36. Burnim, "Black Gospel Music Tradition," 165.

37. Stephen Henderson, *Understanding the New Black Poetry* (New York: Morrow, 1973), 41.

38. Keil, *Urban Blues,* 124.

39. Sam Moore, interview with author, 25 February 1983.

40. Deniece Williams, interview with author, 22 April 1983.

41. Keil, *Urban Blues,* 124, 139.

42. Smokey Robinson, radio interview, WBLS, New York City, 16 January 1983.

43. My discussion in this limited space necessarily centers on selected genres, but a review of black music literature will show that the principles discussed are applicable to all genres of African-American music.

44. See Epstein, *Sinful Tunes,* 8-17.

45. See Laura Foner and Eugene D. Genovese, eds., *Slavery in the New World* (Englewood Cliffs, NJ.: Prentice-Hall, 1969), and Blassingame, *Slave Community.*

46. See Epstein, *Sinful Tunes.*

47. See Eileen Southern, *The Music of Black Americans* (New York: Norton, 2d ed., 1983), 53–59, and Epstein, *Sinful Tunes,* 66–68.

48. J[ames] Fenimore Cooper, *Satanstoe,* I (London: S.&L. Bentley, Wilson, and Fley, 1845), 122–23.

49. Descriptions are found in Morgan Godwyn, *The Negro's and Indian's Advocate, Suing for Their Admission into the Church* (London: F. D., 1680), 33; Jeanette Robinson Murphy, "The Survival of African Music in America," *Popular Science* (1899) 55:660–72; Epstein, *Sinful Tunes,* 41, 127–38,161–83; and Southern, ed., *Readings,* 71–121.

50. See Epstein, *Sinful Tunes,* 63-76, and Charles C. Jones, *Religious Instruction of the Negroes in the*

United States (New York: Negro Universities Press, 1969; reprint of 1842 edition), 21, for information on the proselytizing activities of missionaries.

51. Praise houses were places designated for the slaves' worship. For detailed information about the conver-sion of slaves, see Raboteau, *Slave Religion*; Milton Sernett, *Black Religion and American Evangelicalism* (Metuchen, NJ.: Scarecrow Press, 1975); John Lovell, *Black Song: The Forge and the Flame* (New York: Macmillan, 1972), 71-374; and Epstein, *Sinful Tunes*, 100-111, 191-216.

52. See Raboteau, *Slave Religion*; Sernett, *Black Religion*; Epstein, *Sinful Tunes*, 191-237; and Levine, *Black Culture*, 3-80.

53. Quoted in Epstein, *Sinful Tunes*, 201.

54. Southern, *Readings*, 63.

55. Jones, *Religious Instruction*, 266.

56. Henry Russell, *Cheer! Boys, Cheer! Memories of Men and Music* (London: John Macqueen, Hastings House, 1895), 85.

57. [Kilham], "Sketches," 309.

58. See Portia K. Maultsby, "Afro-American Religious Music 1619-1861," Ph.D. dissertation, University of Wisconsin-Madison, 1974, 182; Epstein, *Sinful Tunes*, 217-358; and Murphy, "Survival of African Music," 660-62. These aesthetic concepts may be heard on recordings: *Been in the Storm So Long*, recorded by Guy Carawan on Johns Island, South Carolina (Folkways Records FS 3842); *Afro-American Spirituals, Work Songs, and Ballads*, ed. by Alan Lomax, Library of Congress Music Division (AAPS L3); *Negro Religious Songs and Services*, ed. by B. A. Botkin, Library of Congress Music Division (AAFS L10).

59. Epstein, *Sinful Tunes*, 169-70. The secular musical tradition of slaves is discussed in Levine, *Black Culture*, 15; Harold Courlander, *Negro Folk Music U.S.A.* (New York: Columbia University Press, 1963), 80-88, 89-122, 146-61; and Epstein, 161-90.

60. Richard C. Wade, *Slavery in the Cities: The South 1820-1860* (New York: Oxford University Press, 1964), 249.

61. Leon F. Litwack, *North of Slavery* (Chicago: University of Chicago Press, 1961), 14, 64.

62. For descriptions of services associated with independent black churches, see Berlin, *Slaves Without Masters*, 284-303; Wade, *Slavery in the*

Cities, 160-76; Epstein, *Sinful Tunes*, 197, 223; Portia K. Maultsby, "Music of Northern Independent Black Churches During the Ante-Bellum Period," *Ethnomusicology*, September 1975, 407-18; Avrahm Yarmolinsky, ed., *Picturesque United States of America: 1811, 1812, 1813* (New York: William Edwin Rudge, 1930), 20; and Southern, *Readings*, 52–70.

63. Information about the status of blacks after the Civil War may be found in E. Franklin Frazier, *The Negro in the United States* (New York: Macmillan, 1949), 171-272; Levine, *Black Culture*, 136-70; C. Vann Woodward, *The Strange Career of Jim Crow* (New York: Oxford University Press, 2d rev. ed., 1966), 11–65; and Jeff Todd Titon, *Early Downhome Blues: A Musical and Cultural Analysis* (Urbana: University of Illinois Press, 1977), 3-15.

64. See Frazier, *Negro in the United States*, 123-68; Woodward, *Strange Career*, 11-65; and Michael Haralambos, *Right On: From Blues to Soul in Black America* (New York: Drake, 1975), 50-51.

65. Quoted in Epstein, *Sinful Tunes*, 281-82.

66. J[ames] W[entworth] Leigh, *Other Days* (New York: Macmillan, 1921), 156.

67. Ibid., 274-81, and Levine, *Black Culture*, 191-217, 239–70.

68. Portia K. Maultsby, "The Role of Scholars in Creating Space and Validity for Ongoing Changes in Black American Culture," in *Black American Culture and Scholarship* (Washington, D.C.: Smithsonian Institution, 1985), 11.

69. See Samuel Charters, *The Bluesmen* (New York: Oak Publications, 1967); Haralambos, *Right On*, 76-82; Titon, *Early Downhome Blues*; Levine, *Black Culture*, 217-24; Keil, *Urban Blues*, 50-68; Oliver, *Savannah Syncopators*, 36-66; and Evans, "African Elements," 57-62.

70. See William Ferris, *Blues from the Delta* (New York: Anchor Press, 1978), 37-38; David Evans, "Afro-American One Stringed Instruments," *Western Folklore* (October 1970) 29:229-45; Oliver, *Savannah Syncopators*, 37-38; and Evans, "African Elements," 59-60.

71. Pearl Williams-Jones, "The Musical Quality of Black Religious Folk Ritual," *Spirit* (1977) 1:21.

72. See ibid., 23, 25, and Melvin D. Williams, *Community in a Black Pentecostal Church* (Pittsburgh: University of Pittsburgh Press, 1974), for religious practices associated with this church.

73. See Pearl Williams-Jones, "Afro-American Gospel Music: A Crystallization of the Black Aesthetic," *Ethnomusicology* (September 1975) 19:374, 381, 383; Levine, *Black Culture,* 179-80; and Mellonee Burnim, "The Black Gospel Music Tradition: A Symbol of Ethnicity," Ph.D. dissertation, Indiana University, 1980. A variety of instruments used to accompany early gospel music may be heard on *An Introduction to Gospel Song,* compiled and edited by Samuel B. Charters (RBF Records RF5).

74. Horace Boyer, "Gospel Music," *Music Education Journal* (May 1978) 64:37.

75. Arna Bontemps, "Rock, Church, Rock!" *Ground* (Autumn 1942) 3:35-39. Bontemps gives the years 1901-6 as the period when Tindley wrote his first songs, whereas Boyer believes the period to be between 1900 and 1905.

76. Portia K. Maultsby, *Rhythm and Blues (1945–1955): A Survey of Styles* (Washington, D.C.: Smithsonian Institution, 1986), 6.

77. For a history of these movements, see Martin Luther King, Jr., *Why We Can't Wait* (New York: Signet, 1964), and Stokely Carmichael and Charles V. Hamilton, *Black Power: The Politics of Liberation in America* (New York: Vintage, 1967).

78. Portia K. Maultsby, "Soul Music: Its Sociological and Political Significance in American Popular Culture," *Journal of Popular Culture* (Fall 1983) 17:51-52. Many James Brown recordings released between 1969 and 1974 illustrated the black pride concept in soul music; also see Cliff White, "After 21 Years, Still Refusing to Lose," *Black World,* April 1977, 36. Other performers whose music reflected the social climate of the 1960s and early 1970s include the Impressions, "We're a Winner" and "This Is My Country";
Marvin Gaye, "Inner City Blues"; Staple Singers, "Respect Yourself" and "Be What You Are"; Gladys Knight and the Pips, "Friendship Train"; O'Jays, "Back Stabbers" and "Love Train"; Sly and the Family Stone, "Thank You for Talkin' to Me Africa," "Africa Talks to You," and "The Asphalt Jungle"; Temptations, "Cloud Nine"; and Diana Ross and the Supremes, "Love Child."

79. See Gerald R. Gill, *Meanness Mania: The Changed Mood* (Washington, D.C.: Howard University Press, 1980); Faustine Childress Jones, *The Changing Mood: Eroding Commitment?* (Washington, D.C.: Howard University Press, 1977); Harry C. Triandis, *Variations in Black and White Perceptions of the Social Environment* (Urbana: University of Illinois Press, 1976); Angus Campbell, *White Attitudes Toward Black People* (Ann Arbor: Institute for Social Research, University of Michigan, 1971); Charles Murray, *Losing Ground: American Social Policy 1950-1980* (New York: Basic Books, 1984); George Davis and Glenn Watson, *Black Life in Corporate America* (New York: Anchor, 1982); William Moore, Jr., and Lonnie H. Wagstaff, *Black Educators in White Colleges* (San Francisco: Jossey-Bass, 1974); Marvin W. Peterson, Robert T. Blackburn, et al., *Black Students on White Campuses: The Impact of Increased Black Enrollments* (Ann Arbor: Institute for Social Research, University of Michigan, 1978); and Janet Dewart, ed., *State of Black America* (New York: National Urban League, 1987).

80. See Gill, *Meanness Mania;* Jones, *Changing Mood;* and Dewart, ed., *State of Black America.*

81. Maultsby, "Role of Scholars," 19-21

82. Nketia, "African Roots," 83-84.

Essay/Discussion Questions

1. It is has been argued persuasively that the slave trade and chattel slavery did not destroy all aspects of African culture among African-descended Americans. Rather, slave populations retained Africanisms of various kinds. How does Portia Maultsby demonstrate this thesis in regard to African American music?

2. Describe the characteristics of African and African-derived music as discussed by Maultsby. What role did Africanisms play in the growth and development of African American expressive culture?

3. How have music and religion intersected in slave and free African American communities?

Now, when you've got a man don't ever be on the square,
If you do, he'll have a woman everywhere.
I never was known to treat one man right,
I keep 'em working hard both day and night.
Because wild women don't worry,
Wild women don't have the blues.
—IDA COX, "WILD WOMEN DON'T HAVE THE BLUES"

"Wild Women Don't Have the Blues": Blues from the Black Woman's Perspective

DAPHNE DUVAL HARRISON

These lines do not come from the southern black rural experience; rather, they depict the "new" city woman who had fled from medieval to modern America, in the words of E. Franklin Frazier, seeking the glamour of Harlem and other urban centers and the prospect of better jobs in factories. She had escaped the religious sanctions that had been imposed in her church down home and was eager to explore the outlets for leisure-time activities that were not approved by her elders. The dance hall, gay house, whiskey joint, and brothel offered unbridled pleasure and entertainment previously unavailable to the men and women who migrated North after World War I. The typical black woman emigrant left home at age fifteen or sixteen, around 1915–1920, seeking the better life that itinerant laborers and songsters described in their stories and songs about the cities. In those black odysseys, as Frazier called them, a life of good times, good living, and good money was to be had by anybody who dared to venture.[1] Hard times or abandonment required women to fend for themselves, armed with cynicism and an extraordinary drive to achieve economic and personal independence.

The blues women of Ida Cox's era brought to their lyrics and performances new meaning as they interpreted and reformulated the black experience from their unique perspective in American society as black females. They saw a world that did not protect the sanctity of black womanhood, as espoused in the bourgeois ideology; only white middle- or upper-class women were protected by it. They saw and experienced injustice as jobs they held were snatched away when white women refused to work with them or white men returned from war to reclaim them. They pointed out the pain of sexual and physical abuse and abandonment. They sought escape from the oppressive controls of the black church but they did not seek to sever their ties from home, family, and loved ones. They reorganized reality through surrealistic fantasies and cynical

From Daphne Duval Harrison, *Black Pearls: Blues Queens of the 1920s*, pages 63–111, 1988. Reprinted with permission from Rutgers University Press.

parodies such as "Red Lantern Blues," "Black Snake Moan," and "Stavin' Chain."

James Baldwin claims that while the blues express the pain of black experience they also bring relief, even joy.

> Now, I am claiming a great deal for the blues; I'm using them as a metaphor. . . . I want to talk about the blues, not only because they speak of this particular experience of life and this state of being, but because they contain the toughness that manages to make this experience articulate. . . . And I want to suggest that the acceptance of this anguish one finds in the blues, and the expression of it, creates also, however odd this may sound, a kind of joy.[2]

Baldwin does not see the contradictions as problematical because his life experiences as a black person in America often consisted of a joy born from pain.

The "bluesman, grappling with the fundamental issues of his existence, takes action against his fate by articulating his woes and thus, in effect, creating himself anew," according to Kimberly Benston.[3] In other words, the blues transcend conditions created by social injustice; and their attraction is that they express simultaneously the agony of life and the possibility of conquering it through the sheer toughness of spirit.[4] That is, the blues are not intended as a means of escape, but embody what Richard Wright calls "a lusty, lyrical realism, charged with taut sensibility."[5]

The blues, therefore, are a means of articulating experience and demonstrating a toughness of spirit by creating and re-creating that experience. Two qualities highly valued in the black community, articulateness and toughness, are thus brought together in this artform. Fluency in language is considered a powerful tool for establishing and maintaining status in the black community. Thus a man or woman who has mastered the art of signifying, rapping, or orating can subdue any challenger without striking a blow and is held in high esteem. (The present-day phenomenon of the grand masters of rap music demon-strate the continuation of this value among blacks in cities.) The resilience developed by black folks in the face of slavery and post-Reconstruction violence armed them with a will to survive against seemingly insurmountable odds. Those who did were the heroes and heroines of the black world—Frederick Douglass, Sojourner Truth, Harriet Tubman. Mary McLeod Bethune. John Henry, Marcus Garvey. and so on. To summarize, the blues are paradoxical in that they contain the expression of the agony and pain of life as experienced by blacks in America; yet, the very act and mode of articulation demonstrates a toughness that releases, exhilarates, and renews.

The blues singer evokes, matches, and intensifies the "blue" feeling of the listener in the act of singing the blues. Sterling Brown observed and recorded this in his poetry.

> *Dey comes to hear Ma Rainey from de little river*
> *   settlements*
> *From blackbottom cornrows and from lumber*
> *   camps*
> *Dey stumble in de halls, jes' a-laughin' an' a-*
> *   cacklin',*
> *Cheerin' lak roaring water, lak wind in river*
> *   swamps.*
> *An' some jokers keep deir laughs a-goin' in de crowded*
> *   aisles.*
> *An' some folk sits dere waiting wid deir aches an'*
> *   miseries*
> *Till Ma comes out before dem a-smilin' gold-toofed*
> *   smiles . . .[6]*

Neither the intent nor the result is escape but, instead, the artistic expression of reality. According to Roosevelt Sykes, blues pianist,

> "Blues is like a doctor. A blues player . . . plays for the worried people. . . . See, they enjoy it. Like the doctor works from the outside of the body to the inside of the body. But the blues works on the insides of the inside."[7]

The aesthetic quality depends upon the singer's ability to express deep feelings.

"You got to sing the blues with your soul. It looks like you hurt in the deep-down part of your heart. You really hurt when you sing the blues."[8]

The blues women expressed reality and enhanced the emotional impact of their experiences through the satire, irony, and drama of their individual performance styles. Variations in their experiences were often reflected in their treatment of themes. The underlying assumption is that content and style are an outgrowth of both the personal and professional experiences of these women. From these a new blues tradition evolved as the women incorporated existing practices—the break in the second half of each four bars of the first two lines of the standard twelve-bar blues; talking in breaks; improvising new verses for endless repetitions—into their own innovative styles.

These women expanded the realm of blues in several ways. They wedded blues to jazz through the interpolation of vocal melodies with accompanying instrumental rhythmic and melodic improvisation. They retained the spontaneity of live blues performance within the constraints of the new recording technology—limited recording time, censored lyrics, arrangers and composers imposing their views, and unfamiliar studio musicians—through the use of dramatic vocal techniques, serious and comedic ad libs, and references to current events. They voiced the experiences of the city women while demonstrating a common bond with southern rural women, and with men. They altered nonblues songs such as "He Used to Be Your Man But He's My Man Now," "Give Me That Old Slow Drag," and "Daddy Your Mama Is Lonesome for You," to fit the blues format and to evoke the blues feeling, thus expanding the blues market for songwriters.

Although most of the songs blues women sang were either composed or arranged by professional songwriters such as Clarence Williams, Chris Smith, Perry Bradford, and W. C. Handy, many wrote their own blues, too. They therefore were creative as well as interpretive artists. Among them were the country types such as Ma Rainey, city types, such as Bessie Smith, vaudeville-dance hall types, such as Ida Cox, and the sophisticated cabaret types, such as Alberta Hunter and Edith Wilson. Their vocal qualities ranged from light soprano to deep contralto, with varying degrees of soft, round, mellow tones to guttural, barrelhouse, razor-edged shouts. But all were blues singers, certified by the "millions of colored folks who [were] the principal buyers of 'blues' . . . written by born writers of 'blues' . . . sung by colored artists mostly girls whose training and natural sympathies enable[d] them to give an interpretation to 'blues' with such natural and telling effects."[9]

The southern country woman's life revolved around a peasant economy and was dependent upon the success or failure of crops. She was actively involved in sharecropping or tenant farming and worked in the fields with her family as a young child; she probably married in her early teens; she took in laundry or did domestic work; or moved to the city. Schooling was totally absent or ended after the primary grades. The early years of the blues women were also often spent in domestic or other service jobs. Hunter washed dishes in a whorehouse when she arrived in Chicago at age twelve; Wallace was a maid for a snakedancer in Texas; Lizzie Miles was a barmaid in New Orleans. According to Frazier, many southern black women's first exposure to town or city life was when they had temporary jobs as domestics. For the men, sawmills, turpentine, lumber, and road camps offered the first glimpse of town or city life. If they lived near the Mississippi River or the Gulf Coast, levee camps were a source of work.[10] Men who moved away from the plantations and farms often left their women behind. The southern country blues women understood the impact of crop failure, oppressive farmowners, cheating company stores, and the drudgery of working from sunup to sundown to make ends meet. They could express the hurt of women whose men left to find work and never returned, or were itinerant lovers who moved on when the jobs ran out, or were serving time on a prison farm or chain gang. Bessie Smith captured the feeling in "Long Road."

> It's a long old road, but I'm gonna find the end;
> It's a long old road, but I'm gonna find the end;
> And when I get back I'm gonna shake hands with a friend.[11]

Southern working-class women from cities such as Memphis, Houston, New Orleans, and Louisville were often no better off than their rural counterparts. They were directly exposed to the day-to-day inequities of racial politics and its economic consequences. The only dependable and consistent work available for them was domestic service as long as they knew how to keep their mouths shut and stay in line. Some took advantage of the new freedom and went to work in the cafés, honky-tonks, and dance halls where men from the lumber camps, foundries, and mills spent their money. They made alliances with the men that were usually as temporary and tenuous as the jobs the men held. When abandoned a few resorted to streetwalking to earn their keep; others joined the throng of migrants who headed to northern towns and cities. Alberta Hunter's "I Got a Mind to Ramble" and Sippie Wallace's "Up the Country Blues" both address that experience.

The tough, brutal life of the northern city began to take its toll on many black women in the early years of the twentieth century. Their realities were crowded tenements, poverty, disease, unemployment, marital conflict, and general despair. The "loose" women that some blacks preached about were outnumbered by the widows, divorcées, and single women who found city life to be harsh and unrelenting in its physical and mental stress. Indeed, the post–World War I boom not only stimulated additional migration to cities by black women, it

quickly pressed them into life in the "fast lane." Churches, social clubs, and fraternal societies blossomed alongside cabarets, whiskey joints, and brothels, and women were the mainstay of both types of institutions. Although complaints rose from church and temperance groups about the evils of alcohol, more blacks turned to whiskey for relief from social and emotional problems. The absence of family and community ties sometimes caused both men and women to move "from hand to hand" in Bessie Smith's words, straining marriages and relationships. The jealousy, discontent, and unhappiness created tensions that often erupted in domestic disturbances. Thus, jail and serving time are recurring themes in women's blues not only because of the bias in the legal system but because women in cities witnessed, were victims of, or sometimes resorted to violence to avenge mistreatment or infidelity. Women, at least in song, used violence, or the threat of violence, as one means of retaliation.

Therefore, the themes of women's blues lyrics are generally the same as those of the men's—infidelity, alienation, loneliness, despondency, death, poverty, injustice, love, and sex. But women responded to these concerns differently and dealt with certain themes more or less frequently. Some blues are a response to the hard times inflicted by society or nature. Flood blues by Rainey, Bessie Smith, and Wallace are a direct reaction to a natural phenomenon that wreaked havoc on thousands of poor rural southerners. Hard times for city and country folk are depicted not only in the prison blues, but in others that discuss unemployment, disease, and poverty. The current of morbidity that ripples through Spivey's "Blood Hound Blues" and "Red Lantern Blues" is also apparent in her "T.B. Blues" and "Dope Head Blues." She decries two problems that plagued the black community and castigates those who turned their backs on the victims. Her "New York Tombs," about the notorious prison, was written much later and continued to demonstrate the social consciousness of "T.B." and "Dope Head."[12]

Poverty was the omnipresent force which lurked in the black community, rural and urban, licking at the heels of those who were trying desperately to elude its stranglehold on their dreams. Bessie Smith's "Poor Man Blues" is an eloquent statement about the cruel irony of poverty in the land of riches. Though "Poor Man Blues" is post–World War I, its content is appropriate today.

> *Please listen to my pleading, 'cause I can't stand*
> *these hard times long.*
> *Please listen to my pleading, 'cause I can't stand*
> *these hard times long.*
> *They'll make an honest man do things you know is*
> *wrong.*

In the second stanza Smith reminds the listener that poor men served in the war and would do so again, if called, because they too are patriotic Americans.

> *Poor man fought all the battles, poor man would*
> *fight again today,*
> *Poor man fought all the battles, poor man would*
> *fight again today,*
> *He would do anything you ask him in the name of*
> *the U.S.A.*

Then, she challenges the rich to deny their exploitation of and dependence upon the labor and talent of the poor.

> *Now the war is over, poor man must live the same*
> *as you,*
> *Now the war is over, poor man must live the same*
> *as you,*
> *If it wasn't for the poor man, Mr. Rich Man what*
> *would you do?*[13]

There is no more powerful statement about the politics of poverty than in the concluding line.

Cox points the finger at Uncle Sam as the culprit who takes away her lover, husband, and "used to be" in "Uncle Sam Blues" and her source of income in "Pink Slip Blues." Both illustrate the tenuousness of life in the early

days of the Depression although Franklin D. Roosevelt's New Deal programs such as the Works Projects Administration had offered a new hope for thousands of low-skilled, unemployed Americans. This and social welfare programs promised an avenue out of poverty, but for many the expectation was greater than the outcome. The dreaded cutoff notice—the pink slip—was the central idea in Cox's wry rendition of a common scene among the poor in the 1930s.

In the first and second stanzas of "Pink Slip Blues," Cox shows how the welfare check becomes the controlling force in the life of a poor person.

> *One day every week I prop myself at my front door,*
> *One day every week I prop myself at my front door,*
> *And the police force couldn't move me 'fore that*
> *mailman blows.*
>
> *'Cause a little white paper Uncle Sam has done*
> *addressed to me,*
> *'Cause a little white paper Uncle Sam has done*
> *addressed to me,*
> *It meant one more week, one week of prosperity.*
>
> *But bad news got to spreading and my hair start to*
> *turning gray,*
> *But bad news got to spreading and my hair start to*
> *turning gray,*
> *'Cause Uncle Sam started chopping, cutting*
> *thousands off the WPA.*

The security of the weekly funds is ended and the person must go back to breadlines or begging to survive in a jobless world.

> *Just a little pink slip in a long white envelope,*
> *Just a little pink slip in a long white envelope,*
> *'Twas the end of my road, was the last ray of my*
> *only hope.*
>
> *After four long years, Uncle Sam done put me on*
> *the shelf,*
> *After four long years, Uncle Sam done put me on*
> *the shelf,*
> *'Cause that little pink slip means you got to go for*
> *yourself.*[14]

Uncle Sam personifies the men who control the quality of life for blacks in America, especially females. The paycheck is thus the sign of prosperity that can be taken away overnight. The ray of hope is dimmed by a pink slip: no more WPA job, no more money, no more prosperity. "Uncle Sam done put me on the shelf," could easily be translated as "my man or good daddy done put me on the shelf"; that "means you got to go for yourself," which most black women expected was inevitable. Although the mixed meaning found in blues poetry is often attributed to attempts to disguise sexual connotations, in "Hard Times Blues," Cox employs metaphors to describe the stress and conflict arising from two losses, job and money, and lover and provider. The dilemma of poverty is more painful because her man is not there to give her money or solace.

> *I never seen such a real hard time before,*
> *I never seen such a real hard time before,*
> *The wolf keeps walking all round my door.*
>
> *They howl all night and they mourn till the break*
>   *of day,*
> *They howl all night and they mourn till the break*
>   *of day,*
> *They seem to know my good man's gone away.*
>
> *I can't go outside to my grocery store,*
> *I can't go outside to my grocery store,*
> *I ain't got no money and my credit don't got no*
>   *more.*
>
> *Won't somebody please, try 'n' find my man for me,*
> *Won't somebody please, try 'n' find my man for me,*
> *Tell him I'm broke and hungry, lonely as I can be.*[15]

Note the stress words which capture the singer's feelings and verify their intensity and depth of despair. Such blues are timeless, not because of their musical uniqueness but because of the universality of their subject matter.

Most blues, however, express more personal, if still universal, themes. Love and sex, separately and together, occupy the greatest amount of attention but with varying intensity and seriousness. The tenuous nature of black male/female relationships lies at the core of blues literature. Lost love is universally agreed upon as the main cause of the blues and it is a theme with seemingly endless variations. Interestingly, women usually do not joke about loss, and are more likely to sing about their grief and its results: extreme depression, bad health, hallucinations and nightmares, suicide attempts, or violence. There are basically two causes for the loss of the lover sung about in women's blues—infidelity and death. Notable examples of loss due to death are the famous Graveyard series of blues recorded by Ida Cox: "Graveyard Dream Blues," "New Graveyard Dream Blues," "Coffin Blues," and "Death Letter Blues." These are superbly drawn scenarios of a woman tortured by visions of her lover's death or impending death. From the somber lyrics sung in traditional twelve-bar blues structure emerge images of a distraught woman unwilling to let go, even in the face of death. In "Death Letter Blues," the woman responds immediately when summoned to her dying lover's deathbed, a common scene for black women, even today, as disease, overwork, drug addiction, or violence snatch their men away prematurely.

> *I received a letter that my man was dying,*
> *I received a letter that my man was dying,*
> *I caught the first train and went back home flying.*

Having arrived too late she can only watch as his body is carried away for burial.

> *I followed my daddy to the burying ground,*
> *I followed my daddy to the burying ground,*
> *I watched the pallbearers slowly let him down.*

With matter-of-fact resignation, born of the constant struggle with fate, she accepts his departure with parting words of love, but her last words suggest that she is prepared to move on with her life:

> *That was the last time I saw my daddy's face,*
> *That was the last time I saw my daddy's face,*
> *Mama loves you, sweet papa, but I just can't take*
>   *your place.*[16]

The anguish of a bereaved woman at her man's wake is vividly portrayed in the dirgelike "Coffin Blues." Overcome by grief she calls out,

Daddy, oh Daddy, won't you answer me please,
Daddy, oh Daddy, won't you answer me please,
All day I stood by your coffin, trying to give my
*   poor heart ease.*

Unwilling to accept the reality of her loss she resorts to tender caresses and whispers in an attempt to communicate beyond the boundaries of death.

I rubbed my hands over your head, and whispered
*   in your ear,*
I rubbed my hands over your head. and whispered
*   in your ear,*
And I wonder if you know that your mama's here.

Reflecting on the pledge of love for her man, she expresses the desire to join him in death.

You told me that you loved me and I believed what
*   you said,*
You told me that you loved me and I believed what
*   you said,*
And I wish that I could fall here across your coffin
*   bed.[17]*

On the other hand, "Graveyard Dream Blues" could well be interpreted as a nightmare deriving from a love affair rife with conflict and infidelity.

Blues on my mind, blues all 'round my head,
Blues on my mind, blues all 'round my head,
I had a dream last night, the man I love was dead.

Lord, I went to the graveyard, fell down on my
*   knees.*
Lord, I went to the graveyard, fell down on my
*   knees,*
I asked the gravedigger to give me back my good
*   man, please.*

The gravedigger may well be a metaphor for the "other woman" or for fate lurking in the shadows to snatch the lover away, because his refusal to return her lover implies that he has the power to do so if he chooses.

The gravedigger looked me in the eye,
The gravedigger looked me in the eye,
Said, "I m sorry for you lady, your man said his
*   last goodbye."*

Refusing to believe her man is gone for good she is wretched with apprehension; relief floods through her being when she realizes it was a dream.

I was so worried, I wanted to scream,
I was so worried, I wanted to scream,
But when I woke up it was only a dream.[18]

Ironically, when the loss of a lover is due to betrayal or abandonment, then death is desired by the betrayed woman. "Death Sting Me Blues" by Sara Martin illustrates this theme in the final lines.

Blues, blues, blues, why did you bring trouble to
*   me?*
Blues, blues, blues, why did you bring trouble to
*   me?*
Oh, Death, please sting me and take me out of my
*   misery.[19]*

Other responses to abandonment and infidelity include depression, illness, flight, violent or nonviolent vengeance, invocation of the supernatural, and self-assertion. Bessie Smith's "Dying by the Hour" is the dramatic soliloquy of a woman whose depression about her man has driven her to promiscuity,

It's an old story, every time it's a doggone man
It's an old story, every time it's a doggone man
But when that thing is on you, you just drift from
*   hand to hand.*

to contemplation of suicide and hell,

I'd drink a bottle of acid, if it wouldn't burn me so
I'd drink a bottle of acid, if it wouldn't burn me so
And telephone the devil, that's the only place I'd go.

and extreme loss of weight,

Once I weighed 200, I'm nothing but skin and bones
Once I weighed 200, I'm nothing but skin and bones
I would always laugh but it's nothing but a moan
*   and groan.*

until she loses grip on herself and no longer has a will to live,

> *Lawd, I'm dying by the hour about that doggone man of mine*
> *Lawd, I'm dying by the hour about that doggone man of mine*
> *He said he didn't love me, that is why I'm dying and losing my mind.*[20]

The progressive despondency portrayed so dramatically by Smith sometimes took a different direction. Similar lines, "I used to weigh 200," appear in "Take Him off My Mind" by Ida Cox, but she does not consider suicide as a solution to her distress. Rather she contemplates murder but loses heart "when [her] love comes down."

> *I cried and I worried, all night lays and groan,*
> *I cried and I worried, all night lays and groan,*
> *I used to weigh 200, now I'm down to skin and bones.*
>
> *It's all about my man who has always kicked and dogged me 'round,*
> *It's all about my man who has always kicked and dogged me 'round,*
> *I tried my best to kill him but when I did my love comes down.*[21]

Cox and Smith both transport the listener to the somber nether regions of the broken spirit. A sense of resignation hangs on each note, which seems to take every ounce of strength that the singer can muster. Yet each responds to the same dilemma quite differently—Smith depicts complete resignation and lack of self-control; whereas Cox is ambivalent, holding on to her sanity by making verbal threats.

"Doggone men," were the bane of many a woman's existence, and solace was sought through audacious schemes which included signifying, going off with other men, or using gypsy magic or supernatural powers.

> *I've gone to the gypsy and begging on my bended knees,*

> *I've gone to the gypsy and begging on my bended knees,*
> *That man put something on me, Oh won't you take it off me please.*
>
> *Just fix him for me, gypsy, lay your money on the line,*
> *Just fix him for me, gypsy, lay your money on the line,*
> *Just fix him so he'll love me, but please take him off my mind.*[22]

The distraught woman's request is ambiguous, for she asks the gypsy to take the lover off her mind while fixing him so he will love her. The insoluble dilemma—the sweet pain of tormented love—is too good to let go completely.

"New Orleans Goofer Dust Blues" is a pithy lesson in the use of witchcraft for romantic security. The singer says, "Go to New Orleans, that's where you learn your stuff. / To keep your man now-a-days, / You got to use some goofer dust."[23] Louisiana was, and still is rich in the cultural mix that harbored and nurtured African voodoo, and the use of "goofer dust" was a commonly accepted remedy.

The strong belief that the supernatural had the power to affect love relationships underlies the examples above. In some cases, the blues are personified and are spoken of as having inherent powers which result in sickness, alcoholism, drug addiction, or death. Sara Martin's "Death Sting Me Blues" attributes "consumption of the heart," and her "uses of cocaine and whiskey" to the blues which "is like the devil" making her "hell-bound soon."

This supernatural persona is sometimes assigned to the blues to illustrate their power over the individual—to make you miserable; to haunt or to track you down; to aid you in getting your lover back; to enslave you. Bessie Smith's "In the House Blues" depicts the blues as a monstrous tormenter who disrupts her sleep and chases her about.

> *Catch 'em, don't let them blues in here,*
> *Catch 'em, don't let them blues in here,*

They shakes me in my bed, can't set down in my
*   chair.*

Oh, the blues has got me on the go,
Oh, the blues has got me on the go,
They runs around the house, in and out my front
*   door.*[24]

Similarly, Cox envisions the blues as a bearer of bad news each time they appear walking, talking, and smiling slyly.

Early this morning the blues came walkin' in my
*   room,*
Early this morning the blues came walkin' in my
*   room,*
I said, "Blues, please tell me what are you doing
*   here so soon.''*

They looked at me and smiled but yet they refused
*   to say,*
They looked at me and smiled but yet they refused
*   to say,*
I came again and they turned and walked away.

After disturbing her and arousing anxiety as the blues always aim to do, they confirm her suspicion that she will lose her man.

The first thing they told me. "Your man you're
*   going to lose."*
The first thing they told me. "Your man you're
*   going to lose.''*
At first I didn't believe it but I found out it was true.

Her final plea reminds the blues that they brought her pain and tears previously, and implicitly acknowledges that they are or will be a frequent visitor.

Blues, oh blues, you know you been here before.
Blues, oh blues, you know you been here before.
The last time you were here, you make me cry and
*   walk the floor.*[25]

Not only are the blues viewed as having physical attributes. which allow them to walk and run, talk to and shake the victim; but they can also predict the future and cause emotional reactions. They can even enslave the sufferer, according to Ma Rainey.

If I could break these chains and let my worried
*   heart go free,*
If I could break these chains and let my worried
*   heart go free,*
Well, it's too late now, the blues have made a slave
*   of me.*[26]

"Hoodoo Man Blues," "Spider Web Blues," "Red Lantern Blues," "Blood-Thirsty Blues," "Nightmare Blues," "Garter Snake Blues" are some of Spivey's blues with bloodcurdling, spooky images which call forth the conjurers, root doctors, and voodooism of southern black life. Yet they all deal with the conflict of torn love affairs or the aftermath of pain, as in "Blood Hound Blues," in which she describes how she poisoned her man, went to jail, escaped and was tracked by bloodhounds. The principle of this blues is vengeance by a woman who was abused: "Well, I know I done wrong, but he beat me and blacked my eye."[27] Spivey's "Blood Hound Blues" is typical of the blues that contain confessions of guilt and declarations of vindication and are a mixture of strength and weakness; the will to take corrective measures while admitting remorse or despair for the act committed.

Well, I poisoned my man, I put it in his drinking
*   cup,*
Well. I poisoned my man, I put it in his drinking
*   cup,*
Well, it's easy to go to jail, but lawd, they sent me
*   up.*

I know I've done wrong, but he beat me and
*   blacked my eye,*
I know I've done wrong, but he beat me and
*   blacked my eye,*
But, if the blood hounds don't get me, in the electric
*   chair I'll die.*[28]

The image of the vengeful woman who acted out her violence is often cast in a prison setting. "Court House Blues" by Clara Smith, "Sing Sing Prison" and "Jail House Blues" by Bessie Smith, and "Worried Jailhouse Blues" by Bertha "Chippie" Hill recount the horrid conditions of prison life and their toll on one's physical and mental well-being. Clara Smith considers a three-month sentence light compared to how the man she loved made her feel—ninety-nine years old. Though she was jailed "on account of one trifling man," the jurymen acquitted her.[29]

Bessie Smith unabashedly sang of killing her old man, and then made a bold plea for a fatal sentence in "Send Me to the Electric Chair." She describes in grisly detail how she "cut him with my barlow, I kicked him in his side, I stood there laughing over him while he wallowed round and died."[30] She begs the judge to "burn her" because she wants to reap what she sowed. This is a woman scorned who took the ultimate step with no regrets. Bessie Smith's own life was peppered with incidents of a violent nature, so the conviction she brought to this blues is authentic. She was known not to take any foolishness from anybody, male or female. In one fight with her husband she shot at him while he stood on the railroad tracks pleading his case. She and Clara Smith had words at a party in New York which allegedly ended with Bessie whipping Clara into submission.[31]

Mistreatment, whether philandering or physical abuse, is the source for many blues lyrics, and though actual violence to oneself or the perpetrator may result, it is more frequently threatened than carried out. In "Georgia Hound Blues," a womanizing, faithless mate is given fair warning by Cox. He is likened to a dog chasing after bitches in heat.

You don't want no one woman, you don't do
*   nothing but run around.*
You don't want no one woman, you don't do
*   nothing but run around.*
And chase after wild women, just a Georgia hound.

She castigates him for his lack of discretion and denigrates the fast women who are the source of community gossip.

Your love is like a radio, you are broadcasting
*   everywhere,*

Your love is like a radio, you are broadcasting
*   everywhere,*
You can locate the women clowning by listening in
*   the air.*

Fed up, she warns him that she may kill him if he does not straighten up.

Like a hound, you chase all night and you don't
*   come home till morn.*
Like a hound, you chase all night and you don't
*   come home till morn.*
Pretty daddy, the undertaker has got your last
*   [chase] on.*[32]

The hound, a familiar figure in southern life, was used for hunting coons, rabbits, and possums at night—a common occupation in the Georgia piney woods where Cox was born. During and after slavery the hounds' moonlight howls echoed as they chased their quarry—man or beast. By 1925 the radio was swiftly taking the place of the phonograph in American households, so it began to appear more and more in the lyrics of the music makers. And since blues singers also enjoyed the added popularity gained by their radio broadcasts, it was natural for their songs to incorporate advances in technology. The broadcasting simile, "your love is like a radio," refers to men's favorite locker room or barbershop sport—bragging about their conquests and exploits of women.

Martin's "Got to Leave My Home Blues" voices a different reaction—that of a woman who is admittedly promiscuous. At first, all of the woman's abuse and violence are directed toward herself, as she describes her descent into degradation.

I took morphine last night to ease my pain.
If it hadn't a been for the doctor I'd been in my
*   grave.*
I lost my job and almost lost my home,
'Cause I wouldn't let other women's men alone.

Then she shifts to a positive, aggressive position, shakes off her depression, and decides to eliminate the cause of her blues—her man.

Trials and tribulations are like a million pounds.
They ain't nothin' to what it'll be when I run my
  good man down.
I'm gonna shoot him and cut him just as long as I
  choose.
He's the cause of my having them, "Got to Leave
  My Home Blues."[33]

Her remorse derives from the recognition that promiscuity could plunge her into a downward spiral. It is short-lived as she plots a vicious attack on the man whom she blames for her wayward conduct. This blues has a message for both women and men: it points out the dangers of infidelity for married women, while reminding men that two-timing can be hazardous to their health.

Sometimes the ordeal of coping with an adulterous mate, poverty, and overwork proved too debilitating for a woman to retain her inner strength and determination. Thus we have a group of blues that depict the weariness, depression, disillusionment, and quiet rage that seethe below the surface when a woman has reached the end of her rope. Some have torturous opening lines which lead gradually toward an optimistic closing, as if the act of expressing the feeling is cathartic. Lizzie Miles, for instance, sang "I Hate a Man Like You." In her cynical rendition, she gradually draws forth an image of a woman who accepts, with resignation, the sorry state of her marriage to a philandering gambler. This bragging, arrogant, woman-chaser causes more trouble for her than he is worth. The sweet talk that attracted her has soured and turned into the poison that incites her to recite a litany about his shiftless behavior.

I hate a man like you, don't like the things you do,
When I met you, I thought you was right,
You married me and stayed out the first night.

She denounces him for gossiping about her,

Just like a woman you're always carrying tales,
Trying to make trouble, wanna get me in jail,
Then you can't find no one to go my bail.
Lawd, I hate a man like you.

and for gambling away all of his money, leaving the burden of their upkeep on her tired shoulders as a laundress.

Walkin' around with a switch and a rod, shootin'
  dice, always playing cards,
While I bring a pan from the white folks' yard.
Lawd, I hate a man like you.

Eatin' and drinkin', sittin' at the inn,
Grinnin' in my face and winkin' at my friends,
When my back is turned you're like a rooster at a
  hen,
Oh, I hate a man like you.[34]

Enmity has replaced love in this bitter relationship, yet there is no indication of intent to leave or do violence; only contempt remains, binding her vengefully to the spiteful end.

Rather than wallow in the pathos of broken or abusive love affairs, some women sang about leaving. "Oh now I'm leaving you, / Someday you'll understand, / 'Cause why? I can't go on loving a mistreating man."[35] Martin reminds her lover how she played the "game of love . . . on the square" but because he thought he could find a good woman anywhere he "never meant [her] no good."[36] The style of this blues is typical of the cabaret type. Clara Smith put it more bluntly in "Mama's Gone, Goodbye." She was "aching mighty long" because he had "dogged [her] around" for years but she woke up to tell him what was on her mind.

"Every Dog Has His Day," according to Sippie Wallace, even though "Love . . . have made many a girl wish that they were dead." She advised the mistreater to ". . . go on Baby, I'm gonna let you have yo' way / 'Cause every dog must have his day."[37] Not one to hold still for shabby treatment, Wallace strips her man of all the luxuries she gave him before she packs up and goes "Up the Country." She broadcasts to the neighborhood what her plans are, humiliating him in the process. "Up the Country Blues" puts the man's business "in the street," as she calls

Hey-ey, Mama, run tell your papa,
Go tell your sister, run tell your auntie,
That I'm going up the country, don't you wan-ta
go-o?
I need another husband to take me on my night
time stroll . . .

She sets the stage for a long rap that will be scathing, while demonstrating her power to put the shoe on the other foot. She continues,

When I was leaving, I left some folks a-grieving,
I left my friends a-moaning, I left my man a-
sighing,
'Cause he knew he had mistreat me and torn up all
my clothes . . .
I told him to give me that coat I bought him, that
shirt I bought him, those shoes I bought him,
socks I bought him,
'Cause he knew he did not want me, he had no
right to stall,
I told him to pull off that hat I bought him and let
his nappy head go bald.[38]

The power word in a rap is one that clearly denigrates one's kin or a man's looks. Wallace does both by calling "mama, papa, sister" and later makes derisive remarks about the lover's "nappy head," an absolute taboo during an era when blacks were striving to lighten their skin and straighten their hair so they could look more like whites. The object of such defamation probably wished he had been more discreet after this attack. Wallace captured a feeling experienced by many women—the desire for ultimate vengeance in a public arena. Under these circumstances, she would receive approval and support for this behavior and might even be joined by other women with a call-and-response chorus in a live performance.[39]

This is clearly an assertion of power and demonstrates that women began to use the blues as a positive means of retaliation. This tactic derives from a practice employed by African and Afro-Caribbean women to embarrass men who had either neglected or abused their women. Usually when black women "go

public," it is to negotiate respect, asserts anthropologist Roger Abrahams. One of the situations in which "talking smart" routines develop in male-female relationships occurs when "the two participants are deeply involved" and the woman uses it to "produce strategic advantages and to modify the man's behavior."[40] This is the goal implicit in Wallace's lyrics in which the silent, suffering woman is replaced by a loud-talking mama, reared-back with one hand on her hip and with the other wagging a pointed finger vigorously as she denounces the two-timing dude. Ntozage Shange, Alice Walker, and Zora Neale Hurston employ this scenario as the pivotal point in a negative relationship between the heroine/protagonists and their abusive men. Going public is their declaration of independence. Blues of this nature communicated to women listeners that they were members of a sisterhood that did not have to tolerate mistreatment.

Unlike the audacious mood exhibited by Wallace, melancholia pervades Clara Smith's version of "Freight Train Blues" as she contemplates her lover's mistreatment.

I hate to hear that engine blow, boo-hoo!
I hate to hear that engine blow, boo-hoo!
Every time I hear it blowing I feel like riding too.

I'm going away just to wear you off my mind,
I'm going away just to wear you off my mind,
And I may be gone for a doggone long, long time.

In the last stanza, Smith uses the traditional phrase, "I asked the brakeman let me ride," but when he refuses her the right to ride she retreats to her room.

When a woman gets the blues, she goes to her room
and hides,
When a woman gets the blues, she goes to her room
and hides,
When a man gets the blues, he catches a freight
train and rides.[41]

Thus, Smith's version points out the limitations on women's mobility as compared to men—women often have to conceal their pain and embarrassment behind closed doors or masked expressions.

Leaving a mistreating "daddy" was easier sung about than achieved, as indicated by the ambivalence expressed in Lottie Kimbrough's "Going Away Blues."

I'm going away it won't be long . . .
And then you know you must have done me wrong.

She loses her nerve and sobs:

My heart aches so I can't be satisfied.
I believe I'll take a train and ride,
I believe I'll take a train and ride,
'Cause I miss my cruel daddy from my side.

Finally, she reveals the source of some of her misery.

I've got Cadillac ways, got some super ideas.
I can't see what brought me here . . .
It must have been this new canned city beer.
I'm lame and blind can't hardly see,
My doggone daddy turned his back on me . . .[42]

We can deduce that alcohol was one of Kimbrough's devils, along with a thirst for the luxuries of high living in the city. It may well be that that combination clouded her judgment in the choice of men. The phrase, "lame and blind," may be alluding to venereal disease, another affliction that was rampant in northern cities.

Some women's blues acknowledged that their own infidelity was the cause of their troubles. In "Please Come Back and Love Me Like You Used to Do," Trixie Smith pledges to mend her wayward ways.

Once I had a dear sweet daddy,
But I didn't treat him right,
So he left this town with Mandy Brown,
That is why I'm blue tonight.
So I'm leaving here today
When I find him. he will hear me say,
Please come back and love me like you used to do
I think about you every day.

You reap just what you sow in the sweet by 'n' by,
And be sorry that you went away.

Although she makes the veiled threat that he may be sorry about leaving her, she quickly resorts to pleading for his return;

Oh baby, I'm crazy, almost dead,
I wish I had you here to hold my aching head.
I want you back and honest, baby I'll be true,
If you love me like you used to do.[43]

Sippie Wallace's "Mail Train Blues" is about a woman who is committed to traveling anywhere to find her man. In "K.C. Man's Blues," however, Clara Smith decides to stop roaming around, and wants to settle down with her K.C. Man who has white teeth, "two pretty gold crowns" (a sign of prosperity, as well as adornment popular among black men in those years), "poro hair" (a slicked back hairdo), and "coffee-color brown" skin. This man was the epitome of the high-stepping city dude who turned every woman's head when he glided down Hastings, State, or 33rd Street.[44]

Although she knows her man is in Chicago, Bessie Smith is too numbed by his departure to follow him.

Blues on my brain, my tongue refused to talk,
Blues on my brain, my tongue refused to talk,
I would follow my daddy, but my feet refuses to
*   walk.*

She even faults the "mean old firemen," and "cruel old engineer" for the loss, thus displacing the blame in order to ease the pain of her man's walking out on her. Her threat of suicide is hurled at them since no one else is there.

Big red headline, tomorrow's Defender news,
Big red headline, tomorrow's Defender news,
"Woman Dead Down Home with Those Chicago
*   Blues!"*
I said blues.[45]

Other traveling blues expressed the nostalgia of women who were homesick or tired of struggling for survival in the city; or who just had a "mind to ramble." Trixie Smith's "Railroad Blues" is truly a classic among the hundreds of train blues extant, and perhaps her best recording. She is joyful as she anticipates her arrival in Alabama for a reunion with her man. The faint sounds of the train rumbling toward the station set goose bumps shivering—"let it get here, let it get here, don't let it stop now, please, not before I get on." Smith captures that feeling of tingly anticipation tinged with apprehension as she shouts

> *Now if the train stays on the track I'm Alabama*
> *   bound.*
> *Now if the train stays on the track I'm Alabama*
> *   bound.*
> *Don't you hear that train coming, I'm Alabama*
> *   bound.*

Her elation abates temporarily when the sight of the train evokes the sad memory of her man's departure on an earlier train.

> *Now, the train went by with my Papa on the inside,*
> *Now, the train went by with my Papa on the inside,*
> *Lawd, I couldn't do nothing but hang my head and*
> *   cry.*

The feeling quickly subsides as her ride on the Seaboard and Airline train becomes imminent.

> *If you ever take a trip on the Seaboard and Airline,*
> *If you ever take a trip on the Seaboard and Airline,*
> *'Cause if you ride that train it will satisfy your*
> *   mind.*[46]

The shuffling back and forth from place to place characterized the restlessness of a people who were seeking relief from poverty, alienation, and discrimination. Mothers and fathers warned their children about the dangers of city life, two-timing men, dishonest employers, gambling, and whiskey, but they went anyway. At about nine years of age, Bertha "Chippie" Hill went with a circus and ended up singing blues in rough houses around New York's wharf. The Pratt City she sang about in "Pratt City Blues" was not her birthplace but she convinces the listener that it was. In a fine

traditional performance with Armstrong on cornet and Reuben Jones on piano, Hill demonstrates that she understands the nature of street life, a topic she sang about often. Her reason for traveling was to get away from a super-hot two-timer and to find good times on 18th Street, rather than in Sandusky [Ohio] where she had to hang her head in shame.

> *Get full of high-powered likker, it's down on 18th*
> *   Street.*
> *Get full of high-powered likker, it's down on 18th*
> *   Street.*
> *Going back to Pratt City, where it tastes nice and*
> *   neat.*[47]

Clara Smith's "L & N Blues" not only illustrates the "rambling bug" that afflicted women, but also gives an implicit message about segregated travel when she has to switch from the Pullman to coach on the trains below the Mason-Dixon line.

> *Got the travelin' blues, gonna catch a train and*
> *   ride,*
> *Got the travelin' blues, gonna catch a train and ride,*
> *When I ain't riding I ain't satisfied.*
>
> *I'm a ramblin' woman, I've got a ramblin' mind,*
> *I'm a ramblin' woman, I've got a ramblin' mind,*
> *I'm gonna buy me a ticket and ease on down the*
> *   line.*
>
> *Mason-Dixon line is down where the South begins,*
> *Mason-Dixon line is down where the South begins,*
> *Gonna leave a Pullman and ride the L & N.*[48]

The trains clickety-clacked down the East Coast from New York to Florida; from Chicago to Memphis, from Kansas City to Houston with numerous stops in between, winding their way in and out of some of this nation's most beautiful land—pretty little towns, greening tobacco farms, and railroad shanties—splitting the towns down the middle into a black-and-white checkerboard, exposing to its passengers the awful paradox of racism. Trains were the purveyors of hopeful black men and women who left the South for the "good life up North," or the North to go back home to friends and family "down South." They traveled with all their worldly goods in one battered suitcase or croaker sack, and a shoebox of tender, juicy fried chicken, biscuits and pork-chop sandwiches which added to the pungent aroma of warm bodies crowded in the coaches. Loud laughter and joking mixed with the cry of babies bounced to sleep by weary mothers as the train jostled its human cargo to its destination. And like Trixie, Clara, and Chippie they brought their hopes on board when they rode the train.

However, the cities, especially in the North, were not only symbols of hope; they were quagmires of human decay. As disease, alcoholism, drugs, and vice encroached on the black community, women introduced blues addressing these social concerns. Kimbrough's blues was not about an isolated case, for alcohol and dope and the diseases and afflictions that accompanied their use were just as destructive to women as to men. Bessie Smith's immortal "Gin Mill Blues" is probably the most famous. A recitation of the list of blues lyrics that discuss drinking, its causes and effects, could become a litany. The day-to-day struggle of black working-class people eventually turns into a depressive state in which alcohol is often sought as a pain reliever or "tonic." "My baby left me," "We had a fight," "My baby treats me mean," "My baby runs around," are recurrent phrases found in drinking blues sung by both women and men. Men sang about "Whiskey Headed Women," and "Juice Head Babies" and women sang about drinking to keep from worrying. Some boasted, others moaned. Margaret Johnson exhibits nonchalance about her habit in "Dead Drunk Blues." For her, drinking releases her from worry and frustration.

> *Oh give me Houston, that's the place I crave,*
> *Oh give me Houston, that's the place I crave,*
> *So, when I'm dry, I can drink whiskey (just the*
>   *same).*

> *Whiskey, whiskey, some folks' downfall,*
> *Whiskey, whiskey, some folks' downfall,*
> *But if I don't drink whiskey, I ain't no good at all.*

> *Lawd, can I get drunk papa, one mo', one mo'*
>   *time?*
> *Lawd, can I get drunk papa, one mo', one mo'*
>   *time?*
> *'Cause when I get drunk, nothin' worries my*
>   *mind.*[49]

There are two paradoxes in this blues, typical of the alcoholic: one is the belief that whiskey is a problem for some people but not for her; and the second is the contradiction that a drink will improve performance, sharpen the senses, while erasing worry or dulling the pain.

There is no evidence that Houston was the best city for whiskey-loving fun nor that women there were more likely to resort to drink. It just happened to be one of the cities where the blues was the staple of musical fare. In those smoky, crowded rooms the smell of barbecue, beer, whiskey, and sweaty bodies mingled into a delicious aroma rich with life. Johnson's performance exudes the good feeling derived from that carefree environment of momentary release from the pressures of life. With every drink, lost love, lost job, or mistreatment faded further into the background. Ma Rainey sang, "Reeling and rocking drunk as I can be," a blues about going to K.C. with her Gatling gun to bring her man back home.[50] Alcohol blues were big sellers for Bessie Smith and her peers because many people could identify with the problem.[51]

"Dope Head Blues" by Spivey was the first blues to openly address the drug problem, which was creeping into the black community in the twenties. Marijuana, or reefer as it was called then, and cocaine were sometimes mentioned by entertainment reporters though not explicitly: "Such and such dropped by and left us with a package that kept us smiling."[52] Studio sessions often began with drinks for all before laying the sound on wax. Sammy Price recalled that J. Mayo Williams made sure that his singers had plenty of liquor to loosen them up.[53] Unfortunately, alcohol and drugs soon spread like gangrene through the black community, infecting men and women, young and old, and the blues world added addiction to its repertoire of themes.

"Hustlin' Woman Blues" by Memphis Minnie and Lil Johnson's "Scuffling Woman Blues" voiced the grief of prostitutes who cannot "make it" on the streets either because the police are constantly hounding them or the pimp is pressuring for some more money.[54] In other instances, women are singing about their roles as sex objects and workhorses, whom men control and manipulate. An early Rainey blues, "Hustlin' Blues" captures that desperation and violence.[55] Chippie Hill's version of the same sordid story begins with a benign dialogue between her and the rent man, spoken by Richard Jones, pianist. But when she begins to sing about standing on the corner till her feet get soaking wet, you are jerked into the steamy dangerous world of hustling tricks. Caught between the desire to get out of the "business" and the immediate need to obtain funds for rent, food, and the omnipresent pimp, the streetwalker is the loser to a mean system with the odds stacked against her.

> Got the streetwalking blues, ain't gonna walk the
>   street no more,
> Got the streetwalking blues, ain't gonna walk the
>   street no more,
> 'Cause the cops is getting bad and the dough is
>   comin' slow.[56]

Sexual exploitation was not one-directional. Frazier observed that some of the homeless women sought associations with men simply to satisfy their desire for sex and companionship, but "younger more sophisticated types more adept at vice and crime . . . demand to be entertained by their daddies."[57] The more relaxed attitudes toward sex in the black working-class community was reflected in blues erotica. Women singers brought new twists to

such blues as they exploited and expanded the allusions used for double entendre.

"My Man-of-War," a double play on words, pairs the image of the famous racehorse Man-of-War with World War I battlefield language to paint a torrid, erotic scenario of sexual maneuvers.

> *My flat looks more like an armory,*
> *Takes his bugle when he calls me,*
> *At night he's drilling constantly,*
> *He's my man-of-war.*
>
> *When he advances, can't keep him back,*
> *So systematic is his attack,*
> *All my resistance is bound to crack,*
> *For my man-of-war.*
>
> *If I'm retreating, he goes around*
> *And gets me in the rear.*
> *He keeps repeating a flank attack*
> *Till victory is near.*
>
> *And when he turns his machine gun loose,*
> *Then I surrender, for there's no use,*
> *He makes me throw up my flag of truce,*
> *He's my man-of-war.*[58]

Some audiences expected raunchy lyrics and singers gave them what they wanted, from Rainey to Bessie Smith to Edith Wilson and Gladys Bentley. The difference was in degree just as with other themes: Wilson, Hunter, and Miles, for example, could use a feigned naiveté cultivated from their Paris cabaret experiences. However, they had originally emerged from the Chicago–New York cabaret scene, which preferred their spice less "refined." Rainey and Lucille Bogan responded to the demands of the tent show masses with raw, heavy-handed lyrics that were cleaned up for recordings.

A larger issue, often overlooked in such discussion, is how the women used these lyrics to project a new image of themselves as total beings with independent spirits. Garon, in his study of the psychological basis of blues poetry, points out the emergence of the black woman as a free-standing person who articulates the intent and desire to break away from sexual, as well as racial, oppression.[59] "Tired As I Can Be" by Bessie Jackson, also known as Lucille Bogan, is an eloquent illustration of that theory.

> *I'm a free-hearted woman, I let you spend my dough*
> *And you never did win, you kept on asking for more.*
> *And now I'm tired, I ain't gonna do it no more.*
> *And when I have you this time you won't know where to go.*
>
> *My house rent's due, they done put me outdoors*
> *And here you riding 'round her, in a V-8 Ford.*
> *I done got tired of your lowdown dirty ways*
> *And your sister say you been dirty, dirty all your days.*
>
> *. . . and now I'm tired, tired as I can be*
> *And I'm going back South, to my used to be.[60]*

The famous "Trouble in Mind Blues" as sung by Chippie Hill may begin with despair but the mood shifts to one of optimism as she gets going.

> *I'm alone every night and the lights are sinking low,*
> *I've never had so much trouble in my life before.*
> *My good man, he done quit me and there's talking all over town,*
> *And I know my baby, you can't keep a good woman down.*

And though suicide is mentioned, it is merely a fleeting thought because the confidence bred from coping with and successfully making it through myriad disappointments sustains her.

> *Now I'm blue, yes, I'm blue, but I won't be blue always,*
> *Because the sun is going to shine in my back door someday.[61]*

This optimistic audacity is a clear example of blues as life, identifying the source of the pain, acknowledging its effect, then taking a step to deal with it. In this instance, the blues is a purgative, or aesthetic therapy, as aptly de-scribed by black psychologists Alfred Pasteur and Ivory Toldson.[62] Hill captures the tone of the black woman who has grown up with the understanding that self-reliance is one of her most important tools for surviving in a male-dominated culture. In her rendition she articulates the anguish of a burdensome life, yet demonstrates that toughness of spirit which fuels the will to overcome despair and to wait for the better day that is on the horizon.

For some women self-reliance was not enough to fulfill their emotional and physical needs; distrust of men pushed some of them toward forms of antisocial behavior that isolated or alienated them from the group. As we have seen, violence was the most extreme of such reactions. Role reversal was another. Hence, the bragging, arrogant woman could fend for herself and make a fool of a man at the same time. Loving a man was for young women unschooled in the ways of the city. "I'll tell a king up on the throne, / That I don't love nobody, nobody under the sun, . . . so I don't have the blues," was advice given to the lovelorn in a dry, wry manner by Clara Smith, who changed from a loving woman to a vamping dame.[63] She doesn't "love nobody, need nobody, nor want nobody" and she wants the world to know that.

> *. . . When I'm with a feller, it's simply for making a show.*
> *I keep a feller spending till his money's gone*
> *And tell him that he's nothing but a pure breed hog.*
> *I don't love nobody, so I don't have no blues.*
>
> *I let a feller take me all around the town*
> *And if he ask me for a kiss, I will knock him down.*
> *I don't love nobody, so I don't have the blues.[64]*

Whether this declaration of cynicism should be taken literally is a matter of context. In a public arena the blues woman would receive an affirmative response from her audience because she had demonstrated that she was as bad as a man in mistreating a lover. For many of the women who identified with the singer and her song, however, that cynicism could give way to melancholia as memories of lost love or home and family welled up.[65] Another example of the same type of blues was Chippie Hill's "Charleston Blues," in which she puts down her old man in the female version of "Going to Chicago, sorry but I can't take you, / There's nothing in Chicago that a monkey-woman can do."

> I'm going to Charleston, honey, but I can't take you,
> I'm going down on King Street, baby, but I can't take you.
> Now, it ain't nothing on King Street, baby, that a crazy guy like you can do.
>
> I'm going back to the fish house, baby, and get me some shrimp,
> I'm going back to the fish house, baby, and get me some shrimp,
> I gotta feed, baby, two or three hungry old pimps.
>
> Now, I knowed you baby, when you did not even know yourself,
> Now, I knowed you baby, when you did not even know yourself,
> Now, you trying to give me the jive, baby, but you got to help yourself.[66]

Not only does she leave him but she impugns his masculinity by implying that he cannot take care of a woman or himself. Another sweet papa who couldn't take care of business had to hit the bricks in Bertha Idaho's "I Don't Care Where You Take It." After a year of listening to sweet talk that was followed by empty-handed excuses, he is advised to prearrange his visits so as to avoid running into the woman's new man.

> So, I don't care where you take it, sweet papa, just move it on out of here,
> 'Cause this ain't no filling station, or no parking space,
> If you looking for sweet doings, papa, find yourself another parking place,
> So, I don't care where you take it, sweet papa, just move it on out of here.[67]

Sex between men and women was not the only topic in women's sexual blues. Homosexuality, though generally frowned upon by the black community, was also sung about. The previously mentioned "Shave 'Em Dry," which had many versions by men and women, contains lines in the Rainey recording which may, according to Garon, refer to lesbianism. "Going downtown to spread the news / State Street women wearing brogan shoes / Eh-heh, daddy, let me shave 'em dry."[68] She also wrote and recorded "Prove It on Me," an explicit statement of her preference for women and willingness to be open about it.[69] Rainey's and Bessie Smith's episodes with women lovers are indicative of the independent stance they and other women blues singers took on issues of personal choice. By addressing the subject openly, they show other women that there are other options available—the same option that Shug, the blues woman, offers to Celie in a tender, powerful encounter in *The Color Purple.*

All of the sexual activities were not serious; many were fun and games, indulged in as diversions after long road-trips. Sex—with other women, young boys, whoever—could be found in the major cities where the women performed. Bertha Idaho's "Down on Pennsylvania Avenue" paints a vivid panorama of that famous Baltimore street, the center of nighttime activities for blacks during the 1920s, 1930s, and 1940s. Showpeople, pimps, prostitutes (male and female), gamblers, and numbers runners rubbed elbows with black businessmen and women. It was the place to be after dark if you were looking for action on the "freaky side."

> I want to tell you about a street I know,
> In the city of Baltimore.
> And every night about half past eight,
> The broads that [are] strolling just won't wait.
>
> Refrain: You'll find 'em every night on Pennsylvania Avenue.
>
> Let's take a trip down to that cabaret,
> Where they turn the night into day.

Some freakish sights you'll surely see,
You can't tell the he's from the she's.

Now if you want good loving, and want it cheap,
Just drop around about the middle of the week,
When the broads is broke and can't pay rent,
Get good loving, boys, for fifteen cents.[70]

Mary Dixon's swaggering encounters with all types of men did not prepare her for the kind she confronted in "All Around Mama." The first stanza shows that she was amenable to variety in her choice of men and that she was open to all kinds of lovemaking. Refrain:

I've had men of all sizes, had 'em tall and lean
Had 'em short had 'em flabby, had 'em in between,
I'm an all around mama, I'm an all around mama,
I'm an all around mama, with an all around mind.

She expresses her delight in finding a young man who can satisfy her sexual appetite; but drunkenness clouds her memory of another one-night stand.

Had a boy, young and tender, treated me so fine,
Never had nothing else but that thing on his mind.
Met a man in the gin-mill, we drank gin so fast,
Took me home, I remember, I said, "Oh my, yes!"

She draws the line when an effeminate man approaches.

I met a man, was a butler, when he spoke I ran,
Was too mannish for a woman, too girlish for a man.
Had a man, a good old sweetback, said that I
*   should know*
Said he didn't do no loving lest he had some dough.[71]

Yet she ends up spending her money on a sweetback.

Women also employed the bragging, signifying language of males to boast of fine physical attributes and high-powered sexual ability. In these blues are found metaphors that liken automobiles, foods, weapons, trains, and animals to the sex act or genitals. The prurient nature of many of these blues led to a spate of community activities seeking to ban them. Black newspapers waged the battle against per-

formers who included them in their repertoire and accused them of using lewd lyrics as a substitute for talent. This was clearly not the case because the best of the blues women sang sexual blues sometimes. Admittedly, some were openly lascivious and left little to the imagination. These red-hot mamas brag about sexual moves:

Men, they call me oven, they say I'm red-hot
Men, they call me oven, they say I'm red-hot
I can strut my pudding, spread my grease with ease
'Cause I know my onions, that's why I always
*   please.*[72]

or instruct women on how to and where to have sex.

Well, I'm goin' to Memphis, stop at [Satch's Hall]
Gonna tell you women how to cock it on the wall.[73]

She orders the man to move on because he is not a good sex partner.

Back your horse out my stable, back him out fast,
I got another jockey, get yourself another mare.
Now, you can't ride, honey, you can't ride this train,
I'm the chief engineer, I'm gone run it like Stavin'
*   Chain.*[74]

Only the most naive would miss the sexual implications of Bessie Smith's "I need a little sugar in my bowl, I need a little hotdog between my roll."[75]

The fun of some of these blues comes from their wonderful play on words, such as the sportscar metaphor of Hill's "Sports Model Mama." There is nothing sleazy nor sneaky in her bragging about her sexiness for this is a woman sure of herself and unashamed. Sex is her livelihood, hence her reference to daily "punctures"; and she claims that a small woman (sportscar) can do it as well as a large woman (limousine).

I'm just a plain little sport, have punctures every
*   day,*
I'm just a plain little sport, have punctures every day.
You may want a limousine, but they puncture the
*   same way.*

She does not hastily make love but takes her time, even though she may be criticized by her streetwalking cohorts.

> *I know you women don't like me because I speak*
> *my mind.*
> *I know you women don't like me because I speak*
> *my mind,*
>
> *I don't like to make speed, I'd rather take my time.*

She finally brags about men's preference for her brand of lovemaking.

> *When the men comes to buy you'll always hear*
> *them say,*
> *When the men comes to buy you'll always hear*
> *them say,*
> *Give me a sports model mama because they know*
> *the way.*[76]

Not only does she demonstrate that she can satisfy a man just as well as a more expensive or classier woman (limousine), but she also puts potential rivals at bay. Cleo Gibson uses the same automobile metaphors in "I've Got a Ford Engine": ". . . Ford engine movements in my hips / 10,000 miles guaranteed / . . . You can have your Rolls Royce / Your Packard and such / Take a Ford engine car to do your stuff."[77]

In "Rolls Royce Papa," Virginia Liston takes a different tack. She berates the man for his poor sexual performance with phrases like, "Your carburetor's rusty . . . your gas tank's empty . . . steering wheel wobbly."[78] Through these blues women called attention to the fact that some of the problems in relationships with men stemmed from men's sexual incompetence or impotence. Throaty growls, coy expressions, and sensuous movements lent a torrid atmosphere to the performances of these blues, which were intended to "titillate," according to Edith Wilson.[79] Singing lewd or raunchy blues provided a form of release of pent-up feelings which were repressed by social norms that prohibited open discussion of sex.[80] Consequently, they were usually performed only at parties, midnight rambles. bawdy houses, or clubs.

Sexy attributes as a threat to other women and a lure for men were flaunted in "Mean Tight Mama," by Sara Martin; "Mighty Tight Woman," a Sippie Wallace classic; "All Around Mama" by Mary Dixon. An "all around mama" could have men of "all sizes, . . . tall and lean, . . . short, . . . flabby, . . . in between . . . young and tender."[81] "Tightness" alluded to the female's closely built vaginal and pelvic area, which supposedly enhanced sexual pleasure. Clara Smith cloaks the activities of a promiscuous woman in a veiled display of innocence and pure-hearted virtue in her version of "Kitchen Mechanic."

> *Women talks about me and lies on me, calls me*
> *outta my name,*
> *They talks about me, lie about me, calls me outta*
> *my name.*
> *All their men come to see me just the same.*
>
> *I'm just a working girl, po' working gal, kitchen*
> *mechanic is what they say,*
> *I'm just a working girl, po' working gal, kitchen*
> *mechanic is what they say.*
> *But I'll have a honest dollar on that rainy day.*[82]

The dollar may be honest by the time the rainy day arrives but it will have to be laundered first, because the kitchen mechanic obviously is doing more than washing dishes.

Advice to other women is a staple among women's blues themes, especially how to handle your men. After her return to the stage in 1966, Sippie Wallace made "Women Be Wise, Don't Advertise Your Man," her theme song. The title and lyrics suggest that a good man is so rare, it is best for a woman who has one to keep quiet or someone will steal him. On the other hand, one should not invest all of one's affection in a single man, according to Clara Smith in "Every Woman's Blues."

> *Don't ever let no one man worry yo' mind,*
> *Don't ever let no one man worry yo' mind,*
> *Just keep you four and five, mess up all the time.*
>
> *You can read you' hymnbook, read your Bible, read*
> *your history, and spell on down,*

*You can read my letters, but you sho' can't read my
    mind.*
*When you think I'm crazy about you I'm leaving
    you all the time.*[83]

Not only is this woman sexually independent, but she is smart enough to know that book learning is merely one source of wisdom when making personal decisions. She asserts control over her own mind and refuses to be intimidated by her lack of education, a ploy often used to create a feeling of inferiority.

The best example, thematically and stylistically, of this genre is Ida Cox's "Wild Women Don't Have the Blues." She expresses disgust for women who brag about "their fighting husbands and no-good friends" in one breath and then "sit around all day and moan, wondering why their wandering papas don't come home."[84] Her advice is counter to the prevailing norms in the black community—monogamous relationships, fidelity, temperance, family, home, and health—yet it illustrates the urge for self-determination and expression.

I've got a disposition and a way of my own,
*When my man starts to kicking I let him find a
    new home,*
I get full of good liquor, walk the street all night,
Go home and put my man out if he don't act right.

Wild women don't worry,
Wild women don't have the blues.

The implication is that since men cannot be depended upon to be faithful, then a woman would be foolish to act like an angel in order to keep one.

You never get nothing by being an angel child,
You'd better change your way an' get real wild.
*I wanta' tell you something, I wouldn't tell you no
    lie,*
Wild women are the only kind that ever get by.
Wild women don't worry,
Wild women don't have the blues.[85]

Women's blues in the 1920s were often composed by others, usually men, but they represented a distinctly female interpretation. The choice of performing style, inflection, emphasis, and improvisation on certain aspects of the lyrics gave a perspective and expressiveness that had profound effect on their listeners. They introduced a new, different model of black women—more assertive, sexy, sexually aware, independent, realistic, complex, alive. Though the themes they addressed were universal, their renditions linked them to other women who identified with the realities of which they sang.

Notes

1 Frazier, *The Negro Family,* 210 and 212.
2 James Baldwin, "The Uses of the Blues," in *The Best from Playboy,* no. 6 (n.p., n.d.), 97.
3 Kimberly Benston, "Tragic Aspects of the Blues," *Phylon* 36:2 (1975), 169.
4 Ellison, *Shadow and Act,* 78.
5 Richard Wright, as quoted in *Woke up This Mornin': Poetry of the Blues,* ed. A. X. Nicholas (New York: Bantam Books, 1973), 6.
6 Brown, "Ma Rainey," in *Southern Roads.*
7 Quoted in Margaret McKee And Fred Chisenhall, *Beale Black and Blue: Life and Music on Black America's Main Street* (Baton Rouge: Louisiana State University Press, 1981), 170.

8 Lillie Mae "Big Mama Blues" Glover, quoted in ibid.
9 "Quality of the Blues," *The Metronome* 39 (September 1923), 140.
10 Frazier, *The Negro Family,* 210 and 224.
11 "Long Road," Bessie Smith quoted in Albertson, *Bessie Smith,* 36–37.
12 Victoria Spivey: "New York Tombs," Spivey EP101 1062; "T.B. Blues," Okeh 8494, 1927; and "Dopehead Blues," Okeh 8531, October 1927.
13 "Poor Man Blues," Bessie Smith, quoted in Albertson, *Bessie Smith,* 116.
14 "Uncle Sam Blues," Ida Cox, Columbia 12D-81253, 2 October 1923; and "Pink Slip Blues," Vocalian 05258, 1939.

15 "Hard Times Blues," Ida Cox, Vocalian 05298, 1939.

16 "Death Letter blues," Ida Cox, Paramount 12220, July 1924.

17 "Coffin Blues," Ida Cox, Paramount 12318-A, October 1923.

18 "Graveyard Dream Blues," Ida Cox, Paramount 12022-A, October 1923; Martin's version was recorded on Okeh 8099.

19 "Death Sting Me Blues," Sara Martin, Paramount 14025, 1928.

20 "Dying by the Hour," Bessie Smith, *Bessie Smith: The Empress,* Columbia G 30818.

21 "Take Him off My Mind," Ida Cox, Vocalian 05258, October 1939.

22 Ibid.

23 "New Orleans Goofer Dust Blues," Thelma LaVizzo, *I'm Coming from Seclusion,* Collectors Items 005.

24 Albertson, *Bessie Smith,* 47.

25 "Rambling Blues," Ida Cox, Paramount 12318-B, September 1925.

26 "Slave to the Blues," Ma Rainey, Paramount 12332, 1926.

27 "Blood Hound Blues," Victoria Spivey, RCA Victor V-38570, October 1929; reisued by RCA Victor on *Women of the Blues,* LP534, 1966.

28 Ibid.

29 "Court House Blues," Clara Smith, Columbia 14073-D, April 1925.

30 "Send Me to the Electric Chair," Bessie Smith, *Bessie Smith: The Empress,* Columbia G 30818.

31 See Albertson, *Bessie,* for accounts of these and other violent incidents.

32 "Georgia Hound Blues," Ida Cox, Paramount 12263, January 1925.

33 "Got to Leave My Home Blues," Sara Martin, Okeh 8146.

34 "I Hate a Man Like You," Lizzie Miles, RCA Victor LPV 508.

35 "Mistreating Man Blues," Sara Martin, Paramount 14025.

36 Ibid.

37 "Every Dog Has His Day," Sippie Wallace, Okeh 8205, February 1925.

38 "Up the Country Blues," Sippie Wallace, Okeh 8106, October 1923.

39 I vividly recall that the quiet of many Saturday nights, and sometimes a Sunday morning, was rent asunder when neighborhood women would scream epithets at their wayward husbands who came in drunk, too late, broke, or all these at once. There was always a tingle of excitement as my sister and I surreptitiously crept to our bedroom windows to hear every censored word. Although we relished the vicarious adventures, my fear that someone would be physically harmed was borne out at times. Miraculously, life resumed with its usual calm in a day or so and the philanderer often behaved better for a while.

40 Roger D. Abrahams, "Negotiating Respect: Patterns of Presentation among Black Women," *Journal of American Folklore* 88 (January 1975), 76.

41 "Freight Train Blues," Clara Smith, Columbia, September 1924.

42 Eric Sackheim, comp. *The Blues Line: A Collection of Blues Lyrics* (New York: Schirmer Books, 1969), 34.

43 "Please Come Back and Love Like You Used to Do," Trixie Smith, Paramount 12330, December 1925.

44 "K.C. Man Blues," Clara Smith, Columbia 12D-81222, October 1923.

45 "Chicago Bound Blues," Bessie Smith, Columbia, reissued on *Railroad Blues,* Rosetta Records RR1301, 1980.

46 "Railroad Blues," Trixie Smith, Paramount 12262, 1925.

47 "Pratt City Blues," Bertha "Chippie" Hill, Okeh 8420-A, 1926.

48 "L & N Blues," Clara Smith, Columbia 14073-D, March 1925. The "L & N" was the Louisville & Nashville Railroad.

49 "Dead Drunk Blues," Margaret Johnson, RCA Victor, 14 February 1927; reissued on *Women of the Blues,* RCA Victor LPV 534, 1966.

50 "Leaving This Morning," Ma Rainey, Paramount, September 1928; reissued on Riverside RLP 1003, Vol. 1.

51 Garon, *Blues and the Poetic Spirit,* 75.

52 See *The Afro-American,* and *Chicago Defender,* news-papers of the 1920s with bylines by "Gang" Tines.

53 Sammy Price, interview with the author, New York, 1977.

54 Oliver, *Aspects of the Blues Tradition,* 206.

55 Nicholas, *Woke Up This Mornin',* 22.

56 "Street Walker Blues," Bertha Hill, HJCA HC 102, June 1926.

57 Frazier, *The Negro Family,* 223.

58 "My Man-of-War," Lizzie Miles, reissued on *Women of the Blues,* RCA Victor LPV 534, 1966.

59 Garon, *Blues and the Poetic Spirit,* 78.

60 Sackheim, *Blues Line,* 45.

61 "Trouble in Mind," Bertha "Chippie" Hill, Circle J1003A, c. 1946.

62 Alfred Pasteur and Ivory Toldson, *Roots of Soul* (New York: Anchor Press/Doubleday, 1983), 128.

63 "I Don't Love Nobody," Clara Smith, Columbia 14016-D, January 1924.

64 Ibid.

65 Frazier, *The Negro Family,* 223.

66 "Charleston Blues," Bertha Hill, Circle J1004B, c. 1946.

67 "I Don't Care Where You Take It," Bertha Idaho, Rosetta Records RR 1300.

68 "Shave 'Em Dry," Ma Rainey, Paramount 1222A, August 1925.

69 Lieb, *Ma Rainey,* 124.

70 Oliver, *Aspects of the Blues Tradition,* 207.

71 Ibid., 206.

72 Sackheim, *Blues Line,* 40.

73 Ibid., 35.

74 "Stavin' Chain," Lil Johnson, *Copulating Blues.*

75 "Put a Little Sugar in My Bowl," Bessie Smith, *Copulating Blues.*

76 Oliver, *Aspects of the Blues Tradition,* 21.

77 Ibid., 214.

78 Ibid., 214 and 215.

79 Edith Wilson, speaking at a blues workshop at the Uni-versity of Maryland Baltimore County, October 1978.

80 According to Lucie G. Colvin, a historian, and Dr. W. B. Lamousé-Smith, a sociologist, the use of lewd songs in public is a tradition practiced on special occasions in some West African cultures. It allows women the opportunity to express otherwise taboo feelings. On a specified day, women vent against strict sexual norms without fear of reprisal. Thus the blues women continued that tradition.

81 "Mean Tight Mama," Sara Martin, Milestone MLP 2006, 1928; "I'm a Mighty Tight Woman," Sippie Wallace, Columbia 1442, 1926; "He May Be Your Man (But He Comes to See Me Sometimes)," Edith Wilson, Columbia A 3653, 9 June 1922.

82 "Kitchen Mechanic Blues," Clara Smith, Columbia 14097-D, August 1925.

83 "Every Woman's Blues," Clara Smith, Columbia 3943, June 1923.

84 "Wild Women Don't Have the Blues," Ida Cox, Paramount, 1924, reissued on Riverside RLP 9374.

85 Ibid.

Essay/Discussion Questions

1. According to Daphne Harrison, what are the meaning, purpose, and character of the blues?

2. Discuss the themes articulated by the blues queens of the 1920s and how they reflected these women's everyday life experiences.

3. How did singing the blues, as a form of expressive culture, reflect the individual and collective power of the blues queens? How did blues queens affect the special status of black women in an oppressive society?

Black Beauty, Black Confusion (1965–70)

NELSON GEORGE

Speaking at Howard University's 1965 commencement, Lyndon Baines Johnson pledged his total effort to bring blacks into the mainstream. His rhetoric was met with the cheers of the students and faculty of the prestigious black university in Washington, D.C. For, unlike so many speech-makers of the sixties, Johnson could, as president of the United States, back up what he promised. The legislative landmarks—the 1964 Civil Rights Act prohibiting racial segregation in public accommodations and the 1965 Voting Rights Act barring all forms of racial and religious discrimination in voting procedures—passed because Johnson, a white rural Southerner, believed in them enough to push them through. Johnson moved blacks into the heart of his government, naming five black ambassadors, the first black to a Cabinet-level position (Robert Weaver, director of the Department of Housing and Urban Development), and placed Thurgood Marshall on the Supreme Court.

Marshall's ascension to the nation's highest court was his just reward for successfully pursuing case after case for the NAACP—and black America—over his long career. Throughout the 1960s and into the 1980s Marshall would as a jurist, just as he had as a lawyer, fulfill the integrationist agenda of the "new Negro."

While Judge Marshall prospered and pressed on, two of his most important contemporaries stumbled. In 1965 Adam Clayton Powell, Jr., was one of Congress's most influential legislators. He'd been in the House of Representatives twenty years and, considering how loved he was in Harlem, it appeared he'd be there another twenty. In Chicago on March 28, 1965, he introduced a seventeen-point program, "My Black Position Paper for America's 20 Million Negroes," which was far from the assimilationist rhetoric of his peers. Powell spoke of blacks seeking "audacious power—the kind of power which cradles your head amongst the stars"—and fused the ideas of Washington and Du Bois by demanding that the civil-rights movement "shift its emphasis to the two-pronged thrust of the Black Revolution: economic self-sufficiency and political power." He felt the legislation of Johnson, particularly the 1964 Civil Rights

From *The Death of Rhythm and Blues* by Nelson George. Copyright © 1988 by Nelson George. Reprinted by permission of Pantheon Books, a division of Random House, Inc.

Act, meant nothing in the North without the economic component of "black power" to support it. More than any other leader of his generation, Powell articulated the dissatisfaction of young blacks with the traditional integrationist views of the civil-rights movement and the rising currents of black nationalism it fueled among activists.

Unfortunately, Powell never had a chance to pursue the vision put forward in his position paper. As reckless in his personal life as he was charismatic on the podium, Powell was a poor manager and had messy personal entanglements with women. Both made him vulnerable to attack. A lawsuit by a female constituent charging him with abuse led Powell, in 1967, to be stripped of his committee chairmanship and then his seat. Later that year Harlem would vote him back into Congress, but his colleagues refused to seat him. Finally, in 1969, after a suit to regain his seat was won in the Supreme Court, Powell was returned to Congress, but without his seniority. And by then, he was a broken man. He lost the 1970 congressional election and died two years later.

Martin Luther King, Jr., confronted a different barrier, but one that was almost as damaging to his effectiveness. In the fall of 1965 he announced that his Southern Christian Leadership Conference would begin an offensive in Chicago, hoping to use Southern civil-rights techniques in what King called the most "ghettoized" city of the North. He said, "The nonviolent movement must be as much directed against the violence of segregation . . . Egypt still exists in Chicago but the Pharaohs are more sophisticated and subtle."

Alas, King was right. Mayor Richard Daley, last of the big-city Irish power brokers of the North and a man as willful as any Pharaoh, was ready for Dr. King. So were a raft of complications he hadn't confronted during civil-rights triumphs in Birmingham and Selma. In Chicago, many local black leaders had intimate financial ties to Daley's white power structure. As a result, King never enjoyed the undivided support of Chicago's strong black establishment. Also, in contrast to their attitude during the Southern struggle, the national media weren't as supportive of the Chicago campaign and often suggested that the Nobel Peace Prize winner was now misguided. Daley outflanked King by shrewdly offering him a role in an existing antipoverty program. This offer allowed Daley to portray King as a disruptive force in the city. It didn't help that King had come out against the Vietnam War when that was still a radical stance, particularly for a civil rights leader dependent on the good will of government officials. Many Chicago whites who'd applauded King's victories in the South were uncomfortable when blamed for the economic disparities in their city. While the Southern Jim Crow barriers had presented easily identifiable (and distant) targets for reform, in Chicago it was difficult to convince whites that they had a responsibility to participate in rectifying economic discrimination. For white Chicagoans it was one thing to abolish racist laws. It was quite another to establish government policies ensuring blacks a chance at a life-style equivalent to whites.

Ultimately, after over a year of struggle and the threat of a potentially violent mass demonstration in nearby Cicero—the same city where that black family was almost lynched in the 1950s—King and Daley signed an open-housing agreement. It was a nice piece of writing, full of the right words and positions. But the bottom line was that King's energies had been wasted. Nothing had changed. Chicago was the same divided city the day he left as it had been before he arrived. King's only legacy to Chicago was an organization called Operation Breadbasket he left in the hands of an ambitious young minister named Jesse Jackson.

As King returned to the South, a leader clearly wounded by the lost Chicago struggle, black America bled into the streets. Watts and Chicago experienced black riots in 1965. Within two years, Tampa, Cincinnati, Atlanta, Newark, and Detroit all had similar explosions in the heart of their black communities, and would suffer even more unrest in 1968 when King was assassinated in Memphis. Because of the riots, "Black Main Street, U.S.A." became a series of before-and-after photographs, filled with businesses that in a blaze of anger became burnt-out shells. In place of stores came short-lived antipoverty programs. Once primarily the bane of jazzmen, heroin flooded the streets of black neighborhoods, infecting the children of the 1960s with a horrifying disease which eventually led them to crimes that debased their community and themselves. Civil rights, self-sufficiency, protest, politics . . . all of it faded for those trapped in the shooting galleries of the body and the mind.

The civil-rights struggle was not dead, but its energy was increasingly scattered. The Black Panthers embraced communism. Ron Karenga's U.S. organization advocated an Afrocentric cultural nationalism that saw African tradition as the cure for American ills. Powell's Black Power came to mean whatever its user needed it to. Of course, the assimilationists pressed on, encouraged by government support and antidiscrimination laws, though the leadership vacuum left by King's murder was immense.

But in the R&B world—known by then as "the world of soul" there was no such leadership gap, no energy scattered, no philosophical conflict. The most powerful individual on the scene had arrogance, black appeal, and a cultural integrity that was the envy of the young-blood political activists of the civil-rights center and the nationalist left. His name was James Brown.

THE GODFATHER

During the 1960s James Brown singlehandedly demonstrated the possibilities for artistic and economic freedom that black music could provide if one constantly struggled against its limitations. Brown was more than R&B's most dynamic performer. "J.B." used his prestige as a weapon to push through innovations in the sound and the marketing of black music. Though Berry Gordy's name tops the list of black music's great entrepreneurs, Brown's efforts—despite being directed in a single-minded celebration of self—are in some ways just as impressive. He was driven by an enormous ambition and unrelenting ego, making him a living symbol of black self-determination. White managers may have made all the business decisions for most black stars, but Brown maneuvered his white manager, Jack Bart, and later his son, Ben, into a co-managing situation, where no crucial decisions (and few minor ones) could be made without the singer's input. In the early sixties, when Brown's contemporaries (and rivals) Jackie Wilson and Sam Cooke traveled with, at best, a guitar and a bass player, Brown built a raucous revue backed by the preeminent big band of its era, one that performed with the flair of Louis Jordan's Tympany Five and the discipline of the Count Basie orchestra. Where booking agents and arena managers often dictated appearances to even the biggest R&B acts, Brown's organization used their clout to demand the best dates and biggest dollars. Eschewing national promoters, Brown handled the chore himself, cutting out the middlemen, which allowed him to offer black retailers and deejays a piece of the action in exchange for special promotional "consideration." Motown may have been the sound of young America, but Brown was clearly the king of black America. How he managed his kingdom illustrates his impact and remains his enduring legacy.

Brown was rightfully dubbed "the hardest-working man in show business" because of a work load of five to six one-nighters a week from the mid-sixties through the early seventies. Until 1973 he worked anywhere from nine to eleven months a year. The only breaks in his nonstop touring came when he played a lengthy stand at the Apollo, Howard, Uptown, or elsewhere. What isn't generally

James Brown, godfather of "soul."

known is that this rigorous schedule was very much of Brown's own making. Every two months or so Brown and his road managers (in the late 1960s it was Bob Patton and Alan Leeds) would pull out the Rand-McNally maps and decide the show's routing. A key city, "a money town" they called it, would be picked for the crucial Friday and Saturday night dates. Brown and company would then study the map and judge the next town they could reach comfortably by the next night. If they played Philadelphia's Uptown on Friday, maybe they'd hit Richmond, Virginia, Saturday, and Fayetteville, Arkansas, on Sunday. An ideal schedule would be laid out and then Brown's employees would call around the country to see if the show could be booked according to their plan. More often than not it was, since Brown was much loved by arena managers. For all the grit and earthiness of his music, Brown put on a clean show—no cursing, no gross sexuality—that brought in the entire family. Since arenas dealt directly with Brown's organization, instead of going through a local promoter, they never worried that Brown wouldn't show up or would be late—all consequences for such unprofessional conduct would fall directly on Brown. Brown's team was very sensitive to not overbooking a lucrative market and squeezing it dry. They tried to space dates in a "money town" between six to nine months apart and played slow markets once every year and a half

Since Brown controlled his always lucrative shows, he was able to use them to reward and penalize deejays or retailers who had or had not cooperated in promoting his material. In smaller cities, Brown often awarded deejays, notoriously underpaid as we've seen, a piece of the date, ensuring both their loyalty and the play of Brown's current release in the weeks prior to his appearance. In many cases these deejays became known in the market as "Mr. Brown's representatives"—a prestigious title in the black community—and were expected to provide Brown's organization with firsthand feedback on his records and supervise distribution of posters promoting the show.

The local deejays, in conjunction with Brown's national office, coordinated radio time buys and the purchase of advertising space in the black press beginning two months before Brown came to town. Usually two weeks before the appearance, Brown's office would monitor ticket sales to see if additional promotional efforts (radio spots, ticket give-aways, etc.) were needed.

Unlike today's tours, where tons of equipment are carried from city to city by a convoy of trucks, the entire James Brown Revue—forty to fifty people and all the gear—traveled in one truck and one bus. In the mid- to late 1960s the show's equipment consisted of two Supertrooper spotlights, one microphone, and an amplifier for the saxophones. The drum and rhythm section (bass, guitars) weren't mixed at all except for their own onstage amplifiers. Road manager Leeds remembers that in 1966, when Brown introduced a flickering strobe light into the act while dancing "the mashed potato, people in the audience were awestruck."

In 1985 it took the recording of "We Are the World" and the Live Aid concert to bring top stars and musicians together. In the R&B world twenty years before, it was customary for any other musicians in town to come around and say hello to the touring star. Backstage at a James Brown concert was a party, networking conference, and rehearsal studio all in one. Part of this was just professional camaraderie, though for many musicians these gatherings allowed them to bid for a spot in Brown's band. In the late 1960s, with Brown's low man making $400 a week and veteran players around $900, he was paying among the most generous rates in R&B.

Moreover, critics, deejays, and even other players generally acknowledged the band to be the best of its kind. Some thought Otis Redding's Bar-Kays were tough. So were the guys Sam and Dave used. Same for Joe Tex's band. But the JBs, as they came to be called, earned their reputation because they were as strong-willed and intense about their music as their boss. Under the guidance of Brown and superb mid-sixties bandleader Alfred (Pee Wee) Ellis, the JBs took the rhythm & blues basics laid down by Louis Jordan and his disciples and created a style, now known as funk, that inspired Sly Stone, George Clinton, and so many others to come.

Funk evolved while the JBs were on the road, on the tour bus, in hotels, backstage, and in hastily called recording sessions. A great many of Brown's pioneering dance jams were cut following concerts, including the early funk experiment from 1967, "Cold Sweat," and the landmark 1970 single "Sex Machine." Often a rare off-day would suddenly become a work day when the musical mood struck Brown. He liked to record his music as soon as he got an idea. The spark often came on the road, as Ellis and the players strove to keep the show fresh. With these rearrangements, new songs emerged from old.

For example, in January 1967, Brown's "Let Yourself Go," a two-and-a-half minute dance track now little recalled, reached number five on *Billboard's* soul chart. One reason it has faded from memory is that it was eventually overshadowed by a better song created from its chords. On the road that winter, "Let Yourself Go" became a ten-minute jam during which Brown displayed his mastery of several dances, including the camel walk and the mashed potato. While he was performing at the Apollo, someone pointed out that the jam was virtually a new tune. As a result, "There Was a Time," a song marked by one of the JBs' best horn lines, was recorded live and went on to become one of Brown's funkiest hits. As the melodies of Brown's songs became more rudimentary, and the interlocking rhythmic patterns grew more complex, the JBs began to use horns, guitar, and keyboards—usually melodic instruments—as tools of percussion. Short, bitter blasts of brass and reeds now punctuated the grooves and complemented Brown's harsh, declamatory vocals. Listening to recordings of the JBs from 1967 to 1969, the band's most innovative period, it is hard at times to distinguish the guitars from the congas because the band is so focused on rhythmic interplay.

As Robert Palmer wrote in the *Rolling Stone Illustrated History,* "Brown, his musicians, and his arrangers began to treat every instrument and voice in the group as if it were a drum. The horns played single-note bursts that were often sprung against downbeats. The bass lines were broken up into choppy two- and three-note patterns, a procedure common in Latin music since the forties but unusual in R&B." "Sheer energy" is what writer Al Young felt when he first heard Brown's classic "Cold Sweat." "James Brown was pushing and pulling and radiating in ultra-violent concentric circles of thermo-radiant funk," Young said. By the time of Brown's last great recording, "The Big Payback" in 1973, the JBs sounded as tense and sparse as a Hemingway short story, though admittedly a lot easier to dance to.

Brown's relentless flow of singles, many released in two parts, were products of an uncontrollable creative ferment. The grooves simply couldn't be contained by the three-minute 45 RPM format of the day. Unfortunately, the twelve-inch single was not yet in vogue; it would have been the perfect format for Brown's propulsive music. But today Brown's output would be constrained by other marketing strategies and corporate release patterns—the conventional wisdom that only so much product can be put out in any twelve-month period. At King Records, however, his recording home during his greatest years, Brown had carte blanche. It was a power he had fought for and won.

The sales of his 1962 *Live at the Apollo* were phenomenal. Even without wide white support, the record went gold at a time when most black studio albums sold only 200,000 copies; it stayed on *Billboard's* album chart for sixty-six weeks, and reached number two. Despite this success, Brown felt his singles weren't being marketed properly. So in an ambitious stab at gaining more control of his career, in 1964 Brown formed Fair Deal Productions, and, instead of delivering his next set of recordings to King, he sent them to Smash, a subsidiary of Chicago's Mercury Records. One of the records was "Out of Sight," a brilliant cut that in its use of breaks—sections where voices, horns, or guitars are heard unaccompanied—anticipated the work of disco deejays of the next decade. With Mercury's greater clout, the song became one of Brown's first records to reach whites.

Syd Nathan, King's feisty president and a charter member of the R&B indie old school, didn't hesitate to sue, and for almost a year, Brown, Nathan, and Mercury battled. The outcome: Brown stayed with King, but Nathan promised more aggressive promotion and gave Brown broader artistic control—similar to what Ray Charles enjoyed at Atlantic and ABC and Sam Cooke had with SAR and later at RCA. It was this control that would allow Brown to make the most controversial and important records of his career.

Dr. Martin Luther King, Jr., was assassinated in Memphis on April 4, 1968. Brown was booked for that night at the Boston Garden. Initially city officials were going to cancel the show, in light of the riots shaking Boston's black neighborhoods. Then the idea of broadcasting the show live on public television stations was suggested as a way to keep angry blacks off the streets. And so it was. Today, tapes of that performance are bootlegged and still treasured by black-music fans. At the time, it served its purpose, keeping the historically tense relations between whites and blacks in that "liberal" city cool, at least for the evening.

For Brown, never one lacking in self-esteem, this confirmed his power in black America, a power that the previous summer had led vice-president and presidential candidate Hubert Humphrey to give him an award for helping quell riots with public statements. A capitalist and a patriot (he played for troops in Vietnam and Korea), Brown was also genuinely moved by the black-pride movement. Seeking to fulfill his role as a leader, he cut "America Is My Home," and was branded an Uncle Tom by radical blacks. (His "Living in America" is the 1986 counterpart.) But he saw no contradiction, and shouldn't have, when he released "Say It Loud, I'm Black and I'm Proud" in the summer of 1968. Supported by the JBs' usual rhythmic intensity, Brown shouted out a testimonial to black pride that, like the phrase "Black Power," was viewed as a call to arms by many whites. For a time Brown's "safe" reputation with whites in the entertainment business suffered. In interviews, Brown has blamed resentful whites for his failure to enjoy another top-ten pop single until the 1980s. (In 1969 "Mother Popcorn" reached number eleven and "Give It Up or Turn It Loose" number fifteen.) Still, it didn't deter Brown from his newfound leadership role, and he went on to cut the message-oriented "I Don't Want Nobody to Give Me Nothing," the motivational "Get Up, Get Into It, Get Involved," the prideful "Soul Power," the cynical "Talking Loud and Saying Nothing," and the nondance rap record "King Heroin," a black

jail-house rhyme put to music. The irony of Brown's musical statements and public posturing as "Soul Brother #1" was that he became an embarrassingly vocal supporter of that notoriously antiblack politician, Richard Milhous Nixon.

Much of Nixon's appeal for Brown was the president's advocacy of "black capitalism," a seemingly fine philosophy that saw an increase in black-owned businesses as the key to black advancement. At the time, Brown owned several radio stations, much property, and a growing organization. He identified with black capitalism's self-reliant tone. Nixon, who understood the desire for power, made Brown feel he was a key example of black capitalism at work, which appealed to the singer's gigantic ego. Brown didn't understand the nuances of Nixon's plan—reach out to showcase some black business efforts while dismantling Johnson's Great Society programs, which for all their reputed mismanagement had helped a generation of blacks begin the process of upward mobility.

But naive though he might have been about Nixon, Brown did choose this juncture in his long career to assume some kind of leadership role in black America. It wasn't enough for him to be an artist anymore; he saw himself as a spokesman with as much right to articulate his world view as H. Rap Brown, Stokely Carmichael, Eldridge Cleaver, or any of the other more obviously political figures who professed authority. The "Godfather of Soul" had decided that he, too, could aggressively project his vision.

Looking back I find it is simply impossible to resolve all the contradictions in James Brown. As a businessman with a long and lucrative career based on astute self-management, he was a sterling example, and advocate, of black self-sufficiency. He was also as happy as he could be within the white-dominated system, buying diamond rings for his fingers with the profits from his white fans. A stone-cold assimilationist in the general political realm, he carried himself with an arrogant, superconfident demeanor that in fact wasn't far removed from the street-corner polemical style of other, far more radical sixties black spokesmen. In a way, it is these very contradictions—and Brown's own unbothered attitude about them—that make him a consummate American.

There is another aspect of Brown, though, that causes some unease if we try to hold him up as a kind of model. Given the unbridled machismo that was part and parcel of the energy driving him (as well as Carmichael, Cleaver, and others), black women were simply attached as a postscript to a male-directed message. As Michelle Wallace, with some overstatement but a lot of truth, observed in *Black Macho and the Myth of the Superwoman,* these men thought of women as mothers, cooks, and servants of the revolution, not as its leaders. It didn't have to be that way. Black women were, of course, as capable of leadership as any male. Fallout from this political patriarchy would be felt in black literature in the future, but in the late 1960s, feminist issues weren't overtly part of the agendas of the nationalist or even civil-rights movements.

THE QUEEN

Yet the one voice that spoke most directly to the aroused black psyche of the 1960s, though apolitical and preoccupied with struggles of the heart, was a woman's. If anyone wondered what "soul" was, all they had to do was play any of Aretha Franklin's Atlantic albums.

From 1967, when she joined Atlantic after six frustrating years at Columbia—when she recorded pop standards and traditional blues that didn't highlight her fiery gospel style—until about 1971, Aretha Franklin was not just indisputedly the best singer in the R&B-soul world but the focus for, to use a sixties cliché, the positive spiritual energy of her listeners. As daughter of Detroit's flamboyant and strong-voiced Reverend C. L. Franklin, Aretha was an heir to a legacy of redemption through music. At the same time, her widely publicized marital problems—*Time* made them an essential part of a June 1968 cover story—and her unmistakable voice made her the epitome of soul music, just as Ray Charles had been a decade before. Ah, that voice. One of the more cogent passages from the *Time* piece describes Franklin's approach as a "direct natural style of delivery that ranges over a full four octaves, and the breath control to spin out long phrases that curl sensuously around the beat and dangle tantalizingly from blue notes. But what really accounts for her impact goes beyond technique: it is her fierce, gritty conviction."

Jerry Wexler, in the wisest move of his long career, recorded Franklin at Fame Studio, in Muscle Shoals, Alabama, and at Criteria Studio in Miami, with Southern session men—white and black—who gave her voice the kind of complementary musical backing that had eluded her at Columbia. The songs were written by Aretha, or specifically written for her and chosen by her, with the rhythm arrangements usually built around her gospel-style piano. In a time when popular black, and then white, slang ("Do your thing!" "Sock it to me!") were admonitions to be loose, uninhibited, and natural, few things communicated these values better than Franklin's vocals. Despite singing love songs, many of them quite melancholy, Franklin's voice communicated so wide a range of emotion as to truly defy description.

"Intangible" is a word that music critics overuse daily, but listen to Franklin on "Dr. Feelgood" or "Ain't No Way" or "Say A Little Prayer" or "Think." One discovers not one Aretha Franklin but a cast of hundreds of women: some sweet, some mad, some cool, some sad, some angry, and a great many playful and sexy. Franklin expressed all a black woman could be, while her contemporaries (Diana Ross, Tina Turner, Dionne Warwick, Martha Reeves, even the underrated Gladys Knight) seemed trapped in one persona by the

Aretha Franklin, queen of "soul."

artistic decisions of male producers as well as by their own vocal limitations. Given her talent and the tenor of the times, it wasn't surprising that Franklin became a prime example of "natural crossover." Compared to Motown, Franklin's music made few concessions to "white" sensibilities. She and Atlantic found that white America was, at this point, more willing to accept "real" black music by blacks than at any time since World War II. Why?

The Western world, politically and culturally, was undergoing a profound upheaval. With the civil-rights movement and the Vietnam War as catalysts, traditional values of every kind—machismo, monogamy, patriotism—were being rejected, or at least questioned. The white teen market Alan Freed once cultivated had matured into a dynamic force for change; its interest in politics, drugs, and free love altered its music. "Rock & roll," that straightforward, unambitious consumer product, was now evolving into something more experimental, less categorizable, roughly dubbed "rock." White musicians were more explicitly articulating their cultural experience in pop music. And in 1967 the broader perspective rock represented was crystallized by the Beatles' *Sgt. Pepper's Lonely Hearts Club Band*.

This music had plain old rock & roll drumming, playing, and singing—the adaptation of black R&B—plus instrumentation and melodies from European classical music and English music halls. This was more ambitious than mere rock & roll. It was electronic. It was experimental. It sold albums instead of just 45s (and so got major labels interested). It was art. It was rock. It was white.

It was also liberal—probrotherhood and all that. The civil-rights movement's evolution into various forms of black nationalism and self-assertion had, in music as well as in Democratic politics, caused a breach. Into the late sixties, Motown was still selling itself as "The Sound of Young America," but it wasn't without critics, black and white, who now saw the label's aggressive upward mobility as an unnecessary attempt to escape blackness and sell out to the Establishment. So soul, with the uncompromising Aretha as its star, was enjoyed and purchased by whites and blacks. One of the most intense album-length explorations of soul ever recorded, *Aretha Live At the Fillmore,* with a guest appearance by Ray Charles, was cut at one of white promoter Bill Graham's temples of rock, San Francisco's Fillmore West.

In the 1950s rock & roll overshadowed R&B; in the sixties white musicians had difficulty synthesizing their own version of soul. This was primarily because white singers just couldn't match the intense vocal style of soul, though at the time the gap between white and black music was perceived differently, as less a musical than a political distinction. For example, in his introduction to the 1969 book *The Age of Rock,* Jonathan Eisen explained why only three of thirty-four essays dealt with black music by saying, "I have not placed as much emphasis on the music of the black community as I have on that of the white. The reasons, I trust, are evident. In recent years, young black musicians on the whole have been involved within an entirely different milieu, both social and musical, most of them concentrat-

ing on developing greater nationalistic self-consciousness."

In the late 1960s, with soul integral to the lives of black America, the white rock audience revived 1950s electric blues, a music which had been part of the R&B world but which, like rock & roll and straight doo wop, had been forsaken for soul. B. B. King, whose career had been in decline since the early sixties, was suddenly discovered in 1966 by the rock audience through the praise of white guitar heroes like the Electric Flag's Mike Bloomfield and Cream's Eric Clapton, and bookings at Graham's Fillmores East and West.

Muddy Waters, Howlin' Wolf, and Bobby (Blue) Bland were among the grand old electric bluesmen who found themselves getting paid better than at any time in their lengthy careers because they had suddenly started reaching that elusive white audience. Few blacks showed up at rock festivals and concert halls. Older black fans, who'd loved Muddy and company at the neighborhood bar, rarely came to these temples of youth culture partly because they didn't feel comfortable among middle-class white teens and college students, and partly because they didn't know about the gigs: advertising, in the underground press and progressive rock radio (the key media of ascendant rock culture), never reached them. To blacks who still valued the blues, it seemed these cultural heroes had been kidnapped by the younger brothers and sisters of the folks who'd led Chuck Berry astray. And to younger blacks—the soul children of the sixties—the blues just wasn't (remember this one?) "relevant" in a world of dashikis, Afro picks, and bell-bottoms. To paraphrase Ahmet Ertegun, black music is in constant flight from the status quo. Young blacks at the time abandoned the blues because it was "depressing," "backward," or "accommodating" to white values. This argument is crap—"relevancy" irrelevant itself—but then as now a lot of blacks believed it. In fact, blues was only suffering the same fate that, surprisingly, would soon befall soul.

CULTURE SHOCK

The black audience's consumerism and restlessness burns out and abandons musical styles, whereas white Americans, in the European tradition of supporting forms and style for the sake of tradition, seem to hold styles dear long after they have ceased to evolve.

The most fanatical students of blues history have all been white. These well-intentioned scholars pick through old recordings, interview obscure guitarists, and tramp through the Mississippi Delta with the determination of Egyptologists. Yet with the exception of Eric Clapton and maybe Johnny Winter, no white blues guitarist has produced a body of work in any way comparable to that of the black giants. Blacks create and then move on. Whites document and then recycle. In the history of popular music, these truths are self-evident.

But—and here's the paradox—all the great black musicians working in a pop idiom—be it rock & roll, R&B, or funk—become cultural curators or historical critics. By taking established black forms, preserving their essence but filtering these textures through an ambitious creative consciousness, they made astounding music that is in the tradition yet singular from it. For example, Jimi Hendrix used blues and R&B as his building blocks, and Sly Stone worked from gospel and soul. Yet black America's reaction to each was different: Hendrix was rejected, while Sly was viewed, before drug days, as a hero.

The difference was that Hendrix drew from a style blacks had already disposed of; Sly shrewdly stayed just a few steps ahead of the crowd. Both were children of the R&B world. Hendrix had been a sideman for numerous R&B bands after leaving Seattle in his teens, including the Isley Brothers. Sly, baptized as Sylvester Stewart, was reared in a roof-raising, sanctified church and worked as a popular deejay on several Bay Area stations. And both Sly and Jimi rebelled against the narrow-mindedness in which they grew up. It is not coincidental that they blossomed in environments removed from the traditions of black America, Hendrix in London and Sly in "free-love" San Francisco, where they each plunged into the hippie life-styles of those two countercultural centers, emerging with a black-based sound drenched in flower-power rhetoric that had little in common with the soul consciousness of James Brown or Aretha.

Unfortunately, Hendrix fatally damaged his connection with black audiences because of his innovative brilliance on the electric guitar, an instrument that, with the declining black interest in blues, fell into disfavor. At Motown, electric guitars, sometimes as many as four, were locked in intricate patterns. At Stax, Steve Cropper's lead lines were short, concise statements. But in rock, lead guitar extravagance was crucial to the music and the supporting culture. It was the perfect accompaniment to LSD and other chemicals of choice. Hendrix, once frustrated by R&B background work, greedily hogged every available space for his Stratocaster. In essence, Hendrix was the revenge of the R&B sideman, one with the ability to turn the voices inside his head into music—problem was, you just couldn't dance to it. Maybe if you were stoned at a light show the Jimi Hendrix Experience could be boogie fodder. Maybe if the grass was flowing at a local love-in you'd dance. However, to the audiences of Stax and Motown and James Brown, "Purple Haze" and "Hey Joe" just didn't do the do. Jimi's music was, if not from another planet, definitely from another country. In a weird symmetry, Hendrix, with his young white-teen audience, was a sixties equivalent of Chuck Berry. Like Berry, his success with guitar-based music made him an outcast on Black Main Street.

Sly was, alas, just as drug-crazed as Hendrix and just as enamored of "rock culture." He had an integrated band, not just racially but sexually, that looked as if the members had just wandered off the corner of Haight and Ashbury. No slick choreography around the

Family Stone. It was organized chaos or, as Dave Marsh wrote, "The women played, the men sang: the blacks freaked out, the whites got funky; everyone did something unexpected." Sly never worked the chitlin circuit. Like Hendrix, he played gigs with rock acts at rock revues almost from the beginning, working through contacts in the West Coast music scene.

But Sly always gave up the funk. His rhythm section, with bassist Larry Graham, drummer Greg Errico, and guitarist Freddie Stone, mirrored James Brown's jagged polyrhythms. On "I Want to Take You Higher," "Thank You (Falettinme Be Mice Elf Agin)," and "Sing A Simple Song," Sly brought Brown's funk to the rock masses almost uncut. Almost, because it would be inaccurate to say that Sly's music just allowed the mass dissemination of Brownish bottom. His memorable melodies and knack for sloganeering ("Hot Fun in the Summertime," "Stand!," "Everyday People," "Everybody Is a Star," "You Can Make It If You Try") were as infectious as the chant vocal approach he pioneered. In addition, and this is a crucial point, Sly was the first great R&B innovator raised to stardom on a corporate label.

Two years before the release of Sly's 1968 debut, "Dance to the Music," on Epic Records, its CBS corporate sister of the Columbia label had let Aretha's contract lapse and ended its affiliation with Carl Davis and the "Chicago sound." CBS was virtually out of the black music business. Things turned around at CBS, and the credit goes to its young president, Clive Davis. In 1965, CBS Records (Columbia, Epic, and its subsidiaries) had 11 percent of the overall market. By the end of 1968, CBS commanded 17 percent, and the figure was climbing due to Davis's aggressive signing of rock artists such as "white Negro" Janis Joplin; Chicago; Blood, Sweat and Tears; Simon and Garfunkel; and Sly and the Family Stone. Davis at first wasn't convinced that, in the age of Aquarius, Sly's glittery costumes could reach whites, which at the time was the only market

that concerned CBS. In his autobiography, Davis recalls a soul-searching meeting with Sly about his direction. According to Davis, the bandleader contended, "They will know what to make of it soon," he said. "I have a definite idea of what I am trying to do and I want to stay with it. Maybe the kids will be put off at first, but they'll get into it." Davis admitted he underestimated Sly's vision. But Sly's play worked; CBS backed the group all the way. This didn't mean, however, that Columbia had a fully developed strategy for exploiting black music. At the time, while Columbia was becoming a dominant force in rock music, a new entity was emerging as its chief foe in the youth market—the conglomerate Warner Bros., Elektra-Asylum, and (with its stellar black catalogue) Atlantic Records. Eventually, this combination, known today as WEA, would become CBS's chief rival in the industry.

Atlantic's absorption set Ahmet Ertegun and Jerry Wexler financially for life. The influx of dollars also solidified an ongoing sea change in the label's direction. In 1967, Atlantic's ATCO subsidiary signed one of rock's first supergroups, Cream (with guitarist Eric Clapton, bassist Jack Bruce, and drummer Ginger Baker), and the Beatlesque Australian vocal trio, the Bee Gees. In 1969, Led Zeppelin delivered two albums to Atlantic that laid the foundation for a new genre, heavy metal, while Ertegun personally wined and dined the Rolling Stones into a deal. Atlantic was now as closely identified with British rock as it had been with black music. After the late sixties, the balance at Atlantic would be tipped permanently to rock. It began with the death of Otis Redding in a plane crash on December 10, 1967. Then, during a bitter negotiation between Wexler and Stax's Jim Stewart, it was revealed that Atlantic, back in 1962 when the original distribution deal was made, had gained control of all the Stax masters. Taking advantage of a technicality in the contract, Atlantic held on to them. Apparently Wexler first mentioned them merely as a negotiating ploy. Embarrassed and stung, Stewart and Al Bell made a deal with Paramount Pictures Music Division, a subsidiary of Gulf + Western, for almost $3 million plus G + W stock. As part of this transaction, Bell was appointed executive vice-president of Stax and given a piece of the label's growing East Memphis catalogue.

So, unexpectedly, Stax became, just like Atlantic, a part of corporate America—though it was a relatively small acquisition for a huge oil company. Few observers at the time foresaw the negative impact these distribution shifts would have on the music and the institutions that made up the R&B world. It was simply assumed that the sudden influx of corporate dollars would allow everyone to do a better job at making, promoting, and distributing black music than ever before.

NARA

Sly's success at Columbia, and the Atlantic and Stax deals, signaled a significant realignment of power in the R&B world. At the same time, black radio was undergoing an internal political struggle and a stylistic evolution that brought revolutionary changes in how it sounded and was perceived.

The genesis of this change, according to Del Shields, then a jazz deejay at New York's WLIB, was the assassination of King. While James Brown was being broadcast on public TV in Boston, deejays across the country were on all night, sometimes against their owner's wishes, to stifle black backlash against this latest instance of American racism. Shields says, "Black radio came of age the night Dr. King was killed. Up until that time, black radio had never been tested nationally. No one ever knew its power. You knew the popularity of black disc jockeys, the power to sell various products. But on the night Dr. King was killed, all across America every black station was tested and everybody who was on the air at that time, including myself, told people to cool it. We tried to do everything possible to keep the

black people from just exploding even more than what they were.

"We were on WLIB, a daytime station that was supposed to go off at sunset. We stayed on till twelve, one o'clock at night. We went beyond the FCC ruling and, of course, had to answer to the FCC later with reports about why we stayed on. The oddity was that we, the black disc jockeys, made the decision to stay on. As a result, the station got the Peabody Award. The owner himself had called and told me I had no right to do that, but I told him I didn't have time to talk to him. When America looked at black radio in that particular period, it suddenly hit them that this was a potent force. If, in every major city, a black disc jockey had said, 'Rise up,' there would have been pandemonium. And that night was also the beginning of the end of black radio. It was never allowed to rise up again."

In the sixties, Shields was a highly politicized man who, before and after his jazz broadcast from Harlem's Lenox Avenue, hung out with a wide range of people, from Black Power advocate H. Rap Brown to his cousin, Bill Cosby, a rising comedian and costar of TV's first integrated action-adventure show, *I Spy*. Shields saw in the energy of both—a spokesman for radical black America and a mass-market symbol of upward mobility—the kind of mix that would fulfill black radio's potential. But for Shields's vision to become reality, several things had to happen: there had to be more black ownership (in the late sixties, fewer than ten stations had black owners); better trained disc jockeys who could demand higher salaries (Shields, a top deejay in New York, made only $250 a week; white counterparts earned $800); and black deejays needed some form of protection from abuse by station managers and manipulation by record-label executives. Because of the differences in job description and salary for deejays around the country, unionization was ruled out. An organization of some kind, with the committed leadership and membership of a civil-rights organization, was needed, and the framework for one existed.

The National Association for Radio Announcers (NARA) was an outgrowth of an old boy network of black deejays that Jack Gibson had helped establish in the fifties. In 1955, Gibson formally dubbed it an organization, though social club might have been a more apt description. NARA's parties were legendary. The deejays, many from small Southern stations, used the organization's annual gatherings to show off as flamboyantly as any recording star or pimp. Gibson recalls one gathering in St. Louis where NARA took over a hotel "and partied until it was time to go to church," which was typical of the organization. Well before the excesses of rock stars became common, NARA had a reputation for leaving an enduring impression on hotel managers. Much of this had to do with ego. Gather together four hundred men who make their living with glib tongues and jive, and you've got a hotel full of one-upmanship. Everyone wanted to know, who drank more? Who fucked more and longer? Who played the slyest poker? Who got the most payola? That competitiveness is of some importance to NARA's history since the biggest deejays controlled the organization and set the tone for its hell-raising. NARA and its members weren't oblivious of the civil-rights movement and the changes it brought to the fabric of black life. They gave money; they gave lip service. But their internal will for collective effort was weak. Business as usual was good for many; others feared reprisals from white bosses if they got too political.

In 1965, three years before King's assassination, Shields, then at Philadelphia's WDAS, had a fateful talk with Clarence Avante. Avante, the manager of jazz organist Jimmy Smith and soundtrack composer Lalo Schiffren, was viewed by whites and blacks as one of the most able dealmakers around, and he cultivated close ties with white record and TV executives at ABC, and within the CBS corporate

structure. He told Shields it was time to upgrade NARA and asked him to prepare an outline with ideas. Together with Ed Wright, program director of Cleveland's WABQ, and Jimmy Bishop, a deejay at WDAS, Avante and Shields began networking with other jocks around the country to prepare a coup d'état. At that year's convention in Houston, the group, known affectionately and pejoratively as the "new breed," surprised everyone by winning an election for control of NARA.

Suggestive of this new breed's perspective, they changed the organization's name from NARA to NATRA (National Association of Television and Radio Announcers), feeling that they needed to reach out beyond radio and records to all parts of the communications industry. An awards banquet, the first ever specifically for blacks in the broadcast industry, was held at the Waldorf Astoria. The choices were intriguing and revealing: Lena Horne, not a popular figure in black America at the time, and Sheldon Leonard, the white producer of *I Spy*, were respectively NATRA's woman and man of the year. Horne was chosen in a generous attempt to refurbish an image unfairly tarnished in black America by what many viewed as her career-long accommodation to whites; and Leonard, to emphasize to NATRA's membership that the world of communications encompassed more than hit records.

More ambitiously, political and social issues were introduced into the organization. Representatives of NATRA visited the Center for Study of Democratic Institutions in Santa Barbara, a liberal think tank, where they discussed strategies to politicize its membership. In 1968 a relationship was nurtured with Vice-President Hubert Humphrey resulting in NATRA's appointment to two presidential commissions on youth. If Humphrey was elected president, Shields thought he would help blacks acquire more broadcast outlets. At the same time, as executive vice-president, Shields began to lobby for increased advertising by Madison Avenue on black radio, meeting with advertising agencies and speaking to trade presses.

Through Shields, H. Rap Brown made an unscheduled speech at a NATRA meeting in Atlanta. The next year, after King's death and the unexpected power it revealed in black radio, meetings were organized by NATRA in New York between the white owners of these stations and their black deejays to discuss their differences for the first time ever. The owners were reluctant participants since they had the same respect for the jocks as the jocks had for them—none. It was testimony to NATRA's growing importance that any showed up at all.

Shields and Avante's boldest move was to propose that NATRA start its own school of broadcast science. In 1968 they found a failing college in Delaware and began negotiations to make it the site. Through Avante's contacts, CBS's and ABC's broadcast divisions promised equipment. Ten record companies at NATRA's 1968 convention said they would donate $25,000 each.

Shields recalls wistfully, "We were going to walk out of the Miami convention with a quarter of a million dollars [in donations] to build the NATRA School of Broadcast Science, and we blew it." He speculates that there were "certain people in the broadcast and TV industry who did not want to see black deejays gain the kind of responsibility and power we were talking about." It sounds like Shields thought some kind of Big Brother was watching—and he may not have been wrong. Someone was certainly on the prowl, jealous of the power NATRA was accumulating and looking for a way to get in on it, and they weren't afraid to use force. A series of violent events over the next few months involving both blacks and whites left the ambitious NATRA plan in shreds.

There was a lot of talk among people in the industry about "pressure" being applied—black activists were strong-arming white record-company owners for "reparations for past exploitation" (which many blacks applauded), but according to Shields, reprisals against black deejays too weren't unknown. For months before the 1968 convention, Shields recalls being the target of a series of threats from individuals who were after a cut of the new breed's action. "I'll never forget," says Shields, "Clarence Avante saying to me, 'Whatever you do, don't sell out.'" Just before the convention, the rumors in Harlem heated up—some dudes were out to hurt Shields—and one night, just after Shields left WLIB's offices on Lenox Avenue near 125th Street, three men beat him to the ground. The perpetrators were never caught.

It was only a prelude. At Miami, between August 14 and 18, white record men and black radio men were threatened, and some were beaten. Marshall Sehorn, Bobby Robinson's old New Orleans contact, was beaten. Phil Walden, Otis Redding's white manager, was threatened. So was Jerry Wexler. Shields spent only one day in Miami. When he arrived at the airport, members of NATRA warned him not to stay: "they" were after him. Meanwhile, members of NATRA's Southern branch complained in sessions that the organization wasn't responsive to the needs of the underpaid Southern jocks because its leadership was too busy politicking.

Once back in New York, Shields was visited by FCC head Nicholas Johnson, and the city's district attorney tapped his phone and put him under twenty-four-hour surveillance for two months—after the events at the Miami convention. After the violence and dissension of that gathering, the commitments to the school evaporated and the enthusiasm for the new breed waned. At the 1969 convention in Washington, D.C., Shields paid $10,000 to hire guards to protect himself and convention attenders. In fact, one of Shields's antagonists chided him for "stooping so low" as to hire his own thugs.

After 1969, the new breed pulled out of NATRA. Shields and Avante moved to Los Angeles in 1971 to fulfill one of their dreams by buying radio station KACE. NATRA's offices moved to Chicago and the organization quickly returned to its historic role as a movable feast for black deejays. Four years of attempted "relevance" proved to be a little too much for the brothers on the microphone. Instead of becoming a unified political force dedicated to raising professional standards, black deejays remained unorganized and unfocused. And even while they tried just to maintain their status quo, the radio industry was evolving in ways that would alter the role of black deejays forever.

GARY BYRD

Gary Byrd, a Buffalo native who grew up listening to Hound Dog Lorenz and Eddie O'Jay on WUFO, can be seen as a transitional figure in black radio. His career began in the era of the personality jock, continued into its period of decline, and then saw the birth of a new style of black radio that emphasized a rigidly defined professionalism.

Byrd's story begins in 1965 when, as a fifteen-year-old actor, he appeared in a "hip" school play called "The In Crowd," based on Dobie Gray's hit record. Hank Cameron, a schoolteacher and part-time WUFO jock, was impressed enough with Byrd's voice to ask the youngster if he had ever considered a career in radio. Byrd, who had aspirations to act and do comedy, thought radio announcing was close enough and said that he had. So Cameron arranged for Byrd to be trained at the station. He was given his own weekend air shift, where he initially concentrated on jazz, but quickly discovered that R&B was the people's choice. Moreover, the audience wanted the music presented with flair. Byrd had a lot to learn, but, as he explains, he developed ways to help himself catch up: "I was writing all this stuff down. I had a little notebook that I kept and I would write things down that seemed to be what you had to do as a personality deejay. Basically, when I came in, I was into jazz. I remember a guy cutting my hair and he said there was a lot of arguing about who could sing higher, Smokey

Robinson or Eddie Kendricks. I was like, 'Who's Smokey and Eddie?' I was into John Coltrane. That was what I was into because I had grown up in that side of Buffalo where there was always jazz around me. So when they started talking about these guys Smokey and Eddie, it was a year or so before I realized who they were talking about.

"When those records would come in, I made a little note that said, 'Pick your favorite records and present them big,' and I underlined 'big' to indicate you gotta do something. So I'd take 'Baby Do the Philly Dog' and some of those other records I really liked and I tried to work and build them up in my little primitive way as a teenage jock. And it worked for me, and stuff happened. And it was definitely part of a concept of personality radio which I came in on the last edges of."

By 1966, Byrd's on-air experience had made him a radio junkie, and he vowed one day to visit his favorite station, New York's WWRL. On junior day, a day set aside in Buffalo for juniors to celebrate their ascension to the senior class (students even saved money for it), Byrd informed his grandmother, who raised him, "I didn't really care about junior day. What I wanted to do was go to New York City." His grandmother asked, "New York City for what?" Byrd told her, "I want to hear this radio station, WWRL. I want to try to visit the station." His grandmother said he could stay with an aunt in the city, so Byrd, who'd never flown before, went to New York. "The first thing I did was turn RL on," he recalls. "The second was to call the station and tell them I wanted to visit." It's inconceivable today that at fifteen Byrd could land an on-air job at a station like WUFO, much less gain entry to an important New York radio station on the strength of a phone call. But not long after his call, Byrd was sitting in the WWRL studio with Rocky (G.) Groce. "I went and sat in and he asked me whether I was interested in radio. I said, 'I'm a jock.' Groce said, 'How you going to be a jock at seventeen?' I said, 'I'm a jock. I jock every day and I do a show on the weekends.' He said, 'Get outta here. You from Frankie Crocker's hometown Buffalo?' I said, 'Yeah.' He said, 'Well, what if I open this microphone and put you on. What will happen?' I said, 'What are you asking me to do?' He said, 'Introduce the record.' So the record was 'Shake, Rattle and Roll' by Arthur Cobbs. He opened the mike, and when he turned on the mike, it tuned off the cuing system, because you can't hear the speakers and I didn't have a headset on. But I hit the cue anyway. I just hit it blind. You hear the first two beats of a record and you kind of get a sense of it. I hit the cue and, of course, when it closed out, he was really surprised. So was Fred Barr, who was the big gospel jock, a white guy, who was there. The general manager came in and offered me a job at seventeen to come on RI. I was real blown out."

Byrd's grandmother, however, was perfectly willing to stand in the way of progress. She called him home to Buffalo where, not prepared to be your average kid, Byrd landed a spot on WYSL, a top-forty station in upstate New York utilizing a format that refined pop radio into a synthetic consistency that station owners loved and old-line deejays hated. Developed by Bill Drake, the format was initiated in 1965 at Los Angeles's KHJ, where Drake turned a money-losing outlet into the number-one station in the second-largest U.S. market. Drake did it by "tightening" the playlist, which meant playing the most popular records with frequency, limiting and shortening station identification, and holding commercials to below fourteen minutes per hour, four minutes under the FCC maximum. Playing two songs back to back, and beginning records under the deejay's introduction or as the news ended were Drake innovations that became American radio staples because they accelerated the pace of the broadcast. It also gave the deejays very little time to talk, for Drake believed that a uniform station sound was more important than cultivating star deejays. From KHJ, Drake went on to consult on the formats

of all RKO-owned stations and rose to a vice-presidency at the chain before forming his own very lucrative consulting firm. Byrd describes the Drake format as, "Time, temperature, artist, title of the record. 'It's 4:07 on CKLW. I'm Gary Byrd. Here are the Temptations.' On comes 'Ain't Too Proud to Beg.'"

In Byrd's analysis, the Drake format "started to take over the country because it shut up jocks who basically may have had nothing to say in an entertaining way. And white jocks at the time were more into wacky humor. I'm not saying all the black jocks were doing something great, but it was a different sense of relationship. It wasn't like the craziness kind of stuff. That was the basic thing it did. It equalized the formats. It meant that if a guy didn't have talent, he could still come in and do the format if he had a nice voice and could control himself. He could give the station a uniform sound. If he blows, take him out, put another jock on. It was that simple. Because it was no longer the jock, it was the station."

And this philosophy, to Byrd's chagrin, was being brought into black radio. Looking back, Byrd cites two reasons the R&B world embraced Drake's format. Like Shields, Byrd puts much of the blame for the demise of the black personality deejay on white management's fear of their power. "It was a plantation mentality we're talking about," he says. "What black radio had along this time was powerful personalities who were built through rapping and an ability to relate to the community and then became very popular. Well, again, the station managers were white. They didn't want to see a black jock become bigger than the station."

The other reason was the changing psychology of black America. To a wide cross section of the community—from those who identified with Dr. King's uplifting cadences to those who pursued Ron Karenga's nationalism, from those who embraced the Panther's socialism to the many seeking to prove they were as all-American as any white—the rapid ramblings of the black deejays were embarrassments. At a time when Sidney Poitier was America's number one box-office star, black folks of every description had no patience with the Eddie (Rochester) Andersons of the airwaves. Drake's format was the leash that reined them in.

As Byrd remembers ruefully, "What I'll say about integration is it was a kind of period where you learn to put on your suit, put on this shirt, and get a job, now. Suddenly management is saying, 'We have white people listening. Let's be careful. Don't talk too ethnically. Talk proper. Pronounce your *-ings.*' It was this sort of thing. What it did was take jocks who were doing that and made them symbolic of all jocks. So even the jock who was doing a very hip personality thing in a hip way got wiped out. He was lumped with the rest."

In the view of Byrd and others, the era of the black personality jock ended in 1967, when the Drake format seeped into black radio. That seems premature. As we know from NATRA, many of the best-known R&B deejays retained their power to move audiences and influence record companies past that point. In addition, there were many stations, including WWRL from 1969 to 1971, that, while adopting a modified top-forty format, didn't sound radically different to the untrained ear from a few years before. Byrd was on the air there in the evening in 1970 when WWRL went to number five in New York City, the highest Arbitron rating in its history.

What finally ended the old era and ushered in a new one was FM radio, a technological development that wouldn't take hold in black America until the 1970s. When it hit, tradition went out the window, taking with it a great many careers.

Notes

Between talking at length with Alan Leeds, now a member of Prince's organization, and reading James Brown's autobiography, *The Godfather of Soul* (Macmillan, 1986), I found out more about the hardest working man in show business than I wanted to know. Clive Davis's *Clive* (Morrow, 1974), Jonathan Eisen's *The Age of Rock* (Vintage, 1969), and Guralnick's *Sweet Soul Music* (Harper & Row, 1986) talk not just about the mechanics of selling music but about the attitudes toward that side of the business. *Time* magazine's 1968 cover story on Aretha Franklin is a collector's item. Gary

Byrd, when not broadcasting or songwriting, gives great interviews. Del Shields, now a reverend, though still a radio broadcaster, gave me access not just to his memories but many of his papers and articles outlining the changes NARA-NATRA underwent. Stephen Oates's biography of Dr. King, *Let the Trumpet Sound* (Harper & Row, 1982), Landess and Quinn's antagonistic look at the head of the Rainbow, *Jesse Jackson and the Politics of Race* (Jamerson Books, 1985), and E. Curtis Alexander's self-published Adam Clayton Powell celebration (1983) helped with the politics.

Essay/Discussion Questions

1. Nelson George argues that in the 1960s, the black-pride movement and black capitalism strongly influenced rhythm and blues performer James Brown's artistic and economic practices. Discuss.

2. According to Nelson George, Queen of Soul music Aretha Franklin delivered uncompromisingly a powerful musical sound and social message that emerged from the life experiences of the African American woman, yet she was able to transcend the boundaries of race, class, and gender and to appeal to a broad public. Explain.

3. In a critical statement, George declares: "Blacks create and then move on. Whites document and then recycle. In the history of popular music, these truths are self-evident." What does he mean? Do you agree or disagree with this observation?

How "Bigger" Was Born

Richard Wright

I am not so pretentious as to imagine that it is possible for me to account completely for my own book, *Native Son*. But I am going to try to account for as much of it as I can, the sources of it, the material that went into it, and my own years' long changing attitude toward that material.

In a fundamental sense, an imaginative novel represents the merging of two extremes; it is an intensely intimate expression on the part of a consciousness couched in terms of the most objective and commonly known events. It is at once something private and public by its very nature and texture. Confounding the author who is trying to lay his cards on the table is the dogging knowledge that his imagination is a kind of community medium of exchange: what he has read, felt, thought, seen, and remembered is translated into extensions as impersonal as a worn dollar bill.

The more closely the author thinks of why he wrote, the more he comes to regard his imagination as a kind of self-generating cement which glued his facts together, and his emotions as a kind of dark and obscure designer of those facts. Always there is something that is just beyond the tip of the tongue that could explain it all. Usually, he ends up by discussing something far afield, an act which incites skepticism and suspicion in those anxious for a straight-out explanation.

Yet the author is eager to explain. But the moment he makes the attempt his words falter, for he is confronted and defied by the inexplicable array of his own emotions. Emotions are subjective and he can communicate them only when he clothes them in objective guise; and how can he ever be so arrogant as to know when he is dressing up the right emotion in the right Sunday suit? He is always left with the uneasy notion that maybe any objective drapery is as good as *any* other for any emotion.

And the moment he does dress up an emotion, his mind is confronted with the riddle of that "dressed up" emotion, and he is left peering with eager dismay back into the dim reaches of his own incommunicable life. Reluctantly, he comes to the conclusion that to account for his book is to account for his life, and he knows that that is impossible. Yet,

Originally published in the *Saturday Review of Literature*, June 1, 1940. Reprinted in Richard Wright, *Native Son*, New York: Harper and Row, 1966.

some curious, wayward motive urges him to supply the answer, for there is the feeling that his dignity as a living being is challenged by something within him that is not understood.

So, at the outset, I say frankly that there are phases of *Native Son* which I shall make no attempt to account for. There are meanings in my book of which I was not aware until they literally spilled out upon the paper. I shall sketch the outline of how I *consciously* came into possession of the materials that went into *Native Son,* but there will be many things I shall omit, not because I want to, but simply because I don't know them.

The birth of Bigger Thomas goes back to my childhood, and there was not just one Bigger, but many of them, more than I could count and more than you suspect. But let me start with the first Bigger, whom I shall call Bigger No. 1.

When I was a bareheaded, barefoot kid in Jackson, Mississippi, there was a boy who terrorized me and all of the boys I played with. If we were playing games, he would saunter up and snatch from us our balls, bats, spinning tops, and marbles. We would stand around pouting, sniffling, trying to keep back our tears, begging for our playthings. But Bigger would refuse. We never demanded that he give them back; we were afraid, and Bigger was bad. We had seen him clout boys when he was angry and we did not want to run that risk. We never recovered our toys unless we flattered him and made him feel that he was superior to us. Then, perhaps, if he felt like it, he condescended, threw them at us and then gave each of us a swift kick in the bargain, just to make us feel his utter contempt.

That was the way Bigger No. 1 lived. His life was a continuous challenge to others. At all times he *took* his way, right or wrong, and those who contradicted him had him to fight. And never was he happier than when he had someone cornered and at his mercy; it seemed that the deepest meaning of his squalid life was in him at such times.

I don't know what the fate of Bigger No. 1 was. His swaggering personality is swallowed up somewhere in the amnesia of my childhood. But I suspect that his end was violent. Anyway, he left a marked impression upon me; maybe it was because I longed secretly to be like him and was afraid. I don't know.

If I had known only one Bigger I would not have written *Native Son.* Let me call the next one Bigger No. 2; he was about seventeen and tougher than the first Bigger. Since I, too, had grown older, I was a little less afraid of him. And the hardness of this Bigger No. 2 was not directed toward me or the other Negroes, but toward the whites who ruled the South. He bought clothes and food on credit and would not pay for them. He lived in the dingy shacks of the white landlords and refused to pay rent. Of course, he had no money, but neither did we. We did without the necessities of life and starved ourselves, but he never would. When we asked him why he acted as he did, he would tell us (as though we were little children in a kindergarten) that the white folks had everything and he had nothing. Further, he would tell us that we were fools not to get what we wanted while we were alive in this world. We would listen and silently agree. We longed to believe and act as he did, but we were afraid. We were Southern Negroes and we were hungry and we wanted to live, but we were more willing to tighten our belts than risk conflict. Bigger No. 2 wanted to live and he did; he was in prison the last time I heard from him.

There was Bigger No. 3, whom the white folks called a "bad nigger." He carried his life in his hands in a literal fashion. I once worked as a ticket-taker in a Negro movie house (all movie houses in Dixie are Jim Crow; there are movies for whites and movies for blacks), and many times Bigger No. 3 came to the door and gave my arm a hard pinch and walked into the theater. Resentfully and silently, I'd nurse my bruised arm. Presently, the proprietor would come over and ask how things were going. I'd

Richard Wright, one of
America's finest novelists.

point into the darkened theater and say: "Bigger's in there." "Did he pay?" the proprietor would ask. "No, sir," I'd answer. The proprietor would pull down the corners of his lips and speak through his teeth: "We'll kill that goddamn nigger one of these days." And the episode would end right there. But later on Bigger No. 3 was killed during the days of Prohibition: while delivering liquor to a customer he was shot through the back by a white cop.

And then there was Bigger No. 4, whose only law was death. The Jim Crow laws of the South were not for him. But as he laughed and cursed and broke them, he knew that some day he'd have to pay for his freedom. His rebellious spirit made him violate all the taboos and consequently he always oscillated between moods of intense elation and depression. He was never happier than when he had outwitted some foolish custom, and he was never more melancholy than when brooding over the impossibility of his ever being free. He had no job, for he regarded digging ditches for fifty cents a day as slavery. "I can't live on that," he would say. Ofttimes I'd find him reading a book; he would stop and in a joking, wistful, and cynical manner ape the antics of the white folks. Generally, he'd end his mimicry in a depressed state and say: "The white folks won't let us do nothing." Bigger No. 4 was sent to the asylum for the insane.

Then there was Bigger No. 5, who always rode the Jim Crow streetcars without paying and sat wherever he pleased. I remember one morning his getting into a streetcar (all streetcars in Dixie are divided into two sections: one section is for whites and is labeled—FOR WHITES; the other section is for Negroes and is labeled—FOR COLORED) and sitting in the white section. The conductor went to him and said: "Come on, nigger. Move over where you belong. Can't you read?" Bigger answered: "Naw, I can't read." The conductor flared up: "Get out of that seat!" Bigger took out his knife, opened it, held it nonchalantly in his hand, and replied: "Make me." The conductor turned red, blinked, clenched his fists, and walked away, stammering: "The goddamn scum of the earth!" A small angry conference of white men took place in the front of the car and the Negroes sitting in the Jim Crow section overheard: "That's that Bigger Thomas nigger and you'd better leave 'im alone." The Negroes experienced an intense flash of pride and the streetcar moved on its journey without incident. I don't know what happened to Bigger No. 5. But I can guess.

The Bigger Thomases were the only Negroes I know of who consistently violated the Jim Crow laws of the South and got away with it, at least for a sweet brief spell. Eventually, the whites who restricted their lives made them pay a terrible price. They were shot, hanged, maimed, lynched, and generally hounded until they were either dead or their spirits broken.

There were many variations to this behavioristic pattern. Later on I encountered other Bigger Thomases who did not react to the locked-in Black Belts with this same extremity and violence. But before I use Bigger Thomas as a springboard for the examination of milder types, I'd better indicate more precisely the nature of the environment that produced these men, or the reader will be left with the impression that they were essentially and organically bad.

In Dixie there are two worlds, the white world and the black world, and they are physically separated. There are white schools and black schools, white churches and black churches, white businesses and black businesses, white graveyards and black graveyards, and, for all I know, a white God and a black God. . . .

This separation was accomplished after the Civil War by the terror of the Ku Klux Klan, which swept the newly freed Negro through arson, pillage, and death out of the United States Senate, the House of Representatives, the many state legislatures, and out of the public, social, and economic life of the South. The motive for this assault was simple and urgent. The imperialistic tug of history had torn the Negro from his African home and had placed him ironically upon the most fertile plantation areas of the South; and, when the Negro was freed, he outnumbered the whites in many of these fertile areas. Hence, a fierce and bitter struggle took place to keep the ballot from the Negro, for had he had a chance to vote, he would have automatically controlled the richest lands of the South and with them the social, political, and economic destiny of a third of the Republic. Though the South is politically a part of America, the problem that faced her was peculiar and the struggle between the whites and the blacks after the Civil War was in essence a struggle for power, ranging over thirteen states and involving the lives of tens of millions of people.

But keeping the ballot from the Negro was not enough to hold him in check; disfranchisement had to be supplemented by a whole panoply of rules, taboos, and penalties designed not only to insure peace (complete submission), but to guarantee that no real threat would ever arise. Had the Negro lived upon a common territory, separate from the bulk of the white population, this program of oppression might not have assumed such a brutal and violent form. But this war took place between people who were neighbors, whose homes adjoined, whose farms had common boundaries. Guns and disfranchisement, therefore, were not enough to make the black neighbor keep his distance. The white neighbor decided to limit the amount of education his black neighbor could receive; decided to keep him off the police force and out of the local national guards; to segregate him residentially; to Jim Crow him in public places; to restrict his participation in the professions and jobs; and to build up a vast, dense ideology of racial superiority that would justify any act of violence taken against him to defend white dominance; and further, to condition him to hope for little and to receive that little without rebelling.

But, because the blacks were so *close* to the very civilization which sought to keep them out, because they could not *help* but react in some way to its incentives and prizes, and because the very tissue of their consciousness received its tone and timbre from the strivings of that dominant civilization, oppression spawned among them a myriad variety of reactions, reaching from outright blind rebellion to a sweet, other-worldly submissiveness.

In the main, this delicately balanced state of affairs has not greatly altered since the Civil War, save in those parts of the South which have been industrialized or urbanized. So volatile and tense are these relations that if a Negro rebels against rule and taboo, he is lynched and the reason for the lynching is usually called "rape," that catchword which has garnered such vile connotations that it can raise a mob anywhere in the South pretty quickly, even today.

Now for the variations in the Bigger Thomas pattern. Some of the Negroes living under these conditions got religion, felt that Jesus would redeem the void of living, felt that the more bitter life was in the present the happier it would be in the hereafter. Others, clinging still to that brief glimpse of post–Civil War

freedom, employed a thousand ruses and stratagems of struggle to win their rights. Still others projected their hurts and longings into more naïve and mundane forms—blues, jazz, swing—and, without intellectual guidance, tried to build up a compensatory nourishment for themselves. Many labored under hot suns and then killed the restless ache with alcohol. Then there were those who strove for an education, and when they got it, enjoyed the financial fruits of it in the style of their bourgeois oppressors. Usually they went hand in hand with the powerful whites and helped to keep their groaning brothers in line, for that was the safest course of action. Those who did this called themselves "leaders." To give you an idea of how completely these "leaders" worked with those who oppressed, I can tell you that I lived the first seventeen years of my life in the South without so much as hearing of or seeing one act of rebellion from *any* Negro, save the Bigger Thomases.

But why did Bigger revolt? No explanation based upon a hard and fast rule of conduct can be given. But there were always two factors psychologically dominant in his personality. First, through some quirk of circumstance, he had become estranged from the religion and the folk culture of his race. Second, he was trying to react to and answer the call of the dominant civilization whose glitter came to him through the newspapers, magazines, radios, movies, and the mere imposing sight and sound of daily American life. In many respects his emergence as a distinct type was inevitable.

As I grew older, I became familiar with the Bigger Thomas conditioning and its numerous shadings no matter where I saw it in Negro life. It was not, as I have already said, as blatant or extreme as in the originals; but it was there, nevertheless, like an undeveloped negative.

Sometimes, in areas far removed from Mississippi, I'd hear a Negro say: "I wish I didn't have to live this way. I feel like I want to burst." Then the anger would pass; he would go back to his job and try to eke out a few pennies to support his wife and children.

Sometimes I'd hear a Negro say: "God, I wish I had a flag and a country of my own." But that mood would soon vanish and he would go his way placidly enough.

Sometimes I'd hear a Negro ex-soldier say: "What in hell did I fight in the war for? They segregated me even when I was offering my life for my country." But he, too, like the others, would soon forget, would become caught up in the tense grind of struggling for bread.

I've even heard Negroes, in moments of anger and bitterness, praise what Japan is doing in China, not because they believed in oppression (being objects of oppression themselves), but because they would suddenly sense how empty their lives were when looking at the dark faces of Japanese generals in the rotogravure supplements of the Sunday newspapers. They would dream of what it would be like to live in a country where they could forget their color and play a responsible role in the vital processes of the nation's life.

I've even heard Negroes say that maybe Hitler and Mussolini are all right; that maybe Stalin is all right. They did not say this out of any intellectual comprehension of the forces at work in the world, but because they felt that these men "did things," a phrase which is charged with more meaning than the mere words imply. There was in the back of their minds, when they said this, a wild and intense longing (wild and intense because it was suppressed!) to belong, to be identified, to feel that they were alive as other people were, to be caught up forgetfully and exultingly in the swing of events, to feel the clean, deep, organic satisfaction of doing a job in common with others.

It was not until I went to live in Chicago that I first thought seriously of writing of Bigger Thomas. Two items of my experience combined to make me aware of Bigger as a meaningful and prophetic symbol. First, being free of the daily pressure of the Dixie environment, I was able to come into possession of my own feelings. Second, my contact with the labor movement and its ideology made me see Bigger clearly and feel what he meant.

I made the discovery that Bigger Thomas was not black all the time; he was white, too, and there were literally millions of him, everywhere. The extension of my sense of the personality of Bigger was the pivot of my life; it altered the complexion of my existence. I became conscious, at first dimly, and then later on with increasing clarity and conviction, of a vast, muddied pool of human life in America. It was as though I had put on a pair of spectacles whose power was that of an x-ray enabling me to see deeper into the lives of men. Whenever I picked up a newspaper, I'd no longer feel that I was reading of the doings of whites alone (Negroes are rarely mentioned in the press unless they've committed some crime!), but of a complex struggle for life going on in my country, a struggle in which I was involved. I sensed, too, that the Southern scheme of oppression was but an appendage of a far vaster and in many respects more ruthless and impersonal commodity-profit machine.

Trade-union struggles and issues began to grow meaningful to me. The flow of goods across the seas, buoying and depressing the wages of men, held a fascination. The pronouncements of foreign governments, their policies, plans, and acts were calculated and weighed in relation to the lives of people about me. I was literally overwhelmed when, in reading the works of Russian revolutionists, I came across descriptions of the "holiday energies of the masses," "the locomotives of history," "the conditions prerequisite for revolution," and so forth. I approached all of these new revelations in the light of Bigger Thomas, his hopes, fears, and despairs; and I began to feel far-flung kinships, and sense, with fright and abashment, the possibilities of *alliances* between the American Negro and other people possessing a kindred consciousness.

As my mind extended in this general and abstract manner, it was fed with even more vivid and concrete examples of the lives of Bigger Thomas. The urban environment of Chicago, affording a more stimulating life, made the Negro Bigger Thomases react more violently than even in the South. More than ever I began to see and understand the environmental factors which made for this extreme conduct. It was not that Chicago segregated Negroes more than the South, but that Chicago had more to offer, that Chicago's physical aspect—noisy, crowded, filled with the sense of power and fulfillment—did so much more to dazzle the mind with a taunting sense of possible achievement that the segregation it did impose brought forth from Bigger a reaction more obstreperous than in the South.

So the concrete picture and the abstract linkages of relationships fed each other, each making the other more meaningful and affording my emotions an opportunity to react to them with success and understanding. The process was like a swinging pendulum, each to and fro motion throwing up its tiny bit of meaning and significance, each stroke helping to develop the dim negative which had been implanted in my mind in the South.

During this period the shadings and nuances which were filling in Bigger's picture came, not so much from Negro life, as from the lives of whites I met and grew to know. I began to sense that they had their own kind of Bigger Thomas behavioristic pattern which grew out of a more subtle and broader frustration. The waves of recurring crime, the silly fads and crazes, the quicksilver changes in public taste, the hysteria and fears—all of these had long been mysteries to me. But now I looked back of them and felt the pinch and pressure of the environment that gave them their pitch and peculiar kind of being. I began to feel with my mind the inner tensions of the people I met. I don't mean to say that I think that environment *makes* consciousness (I sup-

pose God makes that, if there is a God), but I do say that I felt and still feel that the environment supplies the instrumentalities through which the organism expresses itself, and if that environment is warped or tranquil, the mode and manner of behavior will be affected toward deadlocking tensions or orderly fulfillment and satisfaction.

Let me give examples of how I began to develop the dim negative of Bigger. I met white writers who talked of their responses, who told me how whites reacted to this lurid American scene. And, as they talked, I'd translate what they said in terms of Bigger's life. But what was more important still, I read their novels. Here, for the first time, I found ways and techniques of gauging meaningfully the effects of American civilization upon the personalities of people. I took these techniques, these ways of seeing and feeling, and twisted them, bent them, adapted them, until they became *my* ways of apprehending the locked-in life of the Black Belt areas. This association with white writers was the life preserver of my hope to depict Negro life in fiction, for my race possessed no fictional works dealing with such problems, had no background in such sharp and critical testing of experience, no novels that went with a deep and fearless will down to the dark roots of life.

Here are examples of how I culled information relating to Bigger from my reading:

There is in me a memory of reading an interesting pamphlet telling of the friendship of Gorky and Lenin in exile. The booklet told of how Lenin and Gorky were walking down a London street. Lenin turned to Gorky and, pointing, said: "Here is *their* Big Ben." There is *their* Westminster Abbey." "There is *their* library." And at once, while reading that passage, my mind stopped, teased, challenged with the effort to remember, to associate widely disparate but meaningful experiences in my life. For a moment nothing would come, but I remained convinced that I had heard the meaning of those words sometime, somewhere before. Then, with a sudden glow of satisfaction of having gained a little more knowledge about the world in which I lived, I'd end up by saying: "That's Bigger. That's the Bigger Thomas reaction."

In both instances the deep sense of exclusion was identical. The feeling of looking at things with a painful and unwarrantable nakedness was an experience, I learned, that transcended national and racial boundaries. It was this intolerable sense of feeling and understanding so much, and yet living on a plane of social reality where the look of a world which one did not make or own struck one with a blinding objectivity and tangibility, that made me grasp the revolutionary impulse in my life and the lives of those about me and far away.

I remember reading a passage in a book dealing with old Russia which said: "We must be ready to make endless sacrifices if we are to be able to overthrow the Czar." And again I'd say to myself: "I've heard that somewhere, sometime before." And again I'd hear Bigger Thomas, far away and long ago, telling some white man who was trying to impose upon him: "I'll kill you and go to hell and pay for it." While living in America I heard from far away Russia the bitter accents of tragic calculation of how much human life and suffering it would cost a man to live as a man in a world that denied him the right to live with dignity. Actions and feelings of men ten thousand miles from home helped me to understand the moods and impulses of those walking the streets of Chicago and Dixie.

I am not saying that I heard any talk of revolution in the South when I was a kid there. But I did hear the lispings, the whispers, the mutters which some day, under one stimulus or another, will surely grow into open revolt unless the conditions which produce Bigger Thomases are changed.

In 1932 another source of information was dramatically opened up to me and I saw data of a surprising nature that helped to clarify the personality of Bigger. From the moment that Hitler took power in Germany and began to oppress the Jews, I tried to keep track of what was happening. And on innumerable occasions I was startled to detect, either from the side of the Fascists or from the side of the oppressed, reactions, moods, phrases, attitudes that reminded me strongly of Bigger, that helped to bring out more clearly the shadowy outlines of the negative that lay in the back of my mind.

I read every account of the Fascist movement in Germany I could lay my hands on, and from page to page I encountered and recognized familiar emotional patterns. What struck me with particular force was the Nazi preoccupation with the construction of a society in which there would exist among all people (*German* people, of course!) *one* solidarity of ideals, *one* continuous circulation of fundamental beliefs, notions, and assumptions. I am not now speaking of the popular idea of regimenting people's thought; I'm speaking of the implicit, almost unconscious, or pre-conscious, assumptions and ideals upon which whole nations and races act and live. And while reading these Nazi pages I'd be reminded of the Negro preacher in the South telling of a life beyond this world, a life in which the color of men's skins would not matter, a life in which each man would know what was deep down in the hearts of his fellow man. And I could hear Bigger Thomas standing on a street corner in America expressing his agonizing doubts and chronic suspicions, thus: "I ain't going to trust nobody. Everything is a racket and everybody is out to get what he can for himself. Maybe if we had a true leader, we could do something." And I'd know that I was still on the track of learning about Bigger, still in the midst of the modern struggle for solidarity among men.

When the Nazis spoke of the necessity of a highly ritualized and symbolized life, I could hear Bigger Thomas on Chicago's South Side saying: "Man, what we need is a leader like

Marcus Garvey. We need a nation, a flag, an army of our own. We colored folks ought to organize into groups and have generals, captains, lieutenants, and so forth. We ought to take Africa and have a national home." I'd know, while listening to these childish words, that a white man would smile derisively at them. But I could not smile, for I knew the truth of those simple words from the facts of my own life. The deep hunger in those childish ideas was like a flash of lightning illuminating the whole dark inner landscape of Bigger's mind. Those words told me that the civilization which had given birth to Bigger contained no spiritual sustenance, had created no culture which could hold and claim his allegiance and faith, had sensitized him and had left him stranded, a free agent to roam the streets of our cities, a hot and whirling vortex of undisciplined and unchannelized impulses. The results of these observations made me feel more than ever estranged from the civilization in which I lived, and more than ever resolved toward the task of creating with words a scheme of images and symbols whose direction could enlist the sympathies, loyalties, and yearnings of the millions of Bigger Thomases in every land and race. . . .

But more than anything else, as a writer, I was fascinated by the similarity of the emotional tensions of Bigger in America and Bigger in Nazi Germany and Bigger in old Russia. All Bigger Thomases, white and black, felt tense, afraid, nervous, hysterical, and restless. From far away Nazi Germany and old Russia had come to me items of knowledge that told me that certain modern experiences were creating types of personalities whose existence ignored racial and national lines of demarcation, that these personalities carried with them a more universal drama-element than anything I'd ever encountered before; that these personalities were mainly imposed upon men and women living in a world whose fundamental assumptions could no longer be taken for granted: a world ridden with national and

class strife; a world whose metaphysical meanings had vanished; a world in which God no longer existed as a daily focal point of men's lives; a world in which men could no longer retain their faith in an ultimate hereafter. It was a highly geared world whose nature was conflict and action, a world whose limited area and vision imperiously urged men to satisfy their organisms, a world that existed on a plane of animal sensation alone.

It was a world in which millions of men lived and behaved like drunkards, taking a stiff drink of hard life to lift them up for a thrilling moment, to give them a quivering sense of wild exultation and fulfillment that soon faded and let them down. Eagerly they took another drink, wanting to avoid the dull, flat look of things, then still another, this time stronger, and then they felt that their lives had meaning. Speaking figuratively, they were soon chronic alcoholics, men who lived by violence, through extreme action and sensation, through drowning daily in a perpetual nervous agitation.

From these items I drew my first political conclusions about Bigger: I felt that Bigger, an American product, a native son of this land, carried within him the potentialities of either Communism or Fascism. I don't mean to say that the Negro boy I depicted in *Native Son* is either a Communist or a Fascist. He is not either. But he is product of a dislocated society; he is a dispossessed and disinherited man; he is all of this, and he lives amid the greatest possible plenty on earth and he is looking and feeling for a way out. Whether he'll follow some gaudy, hysterical leader who'll promise rashly to fill the void in him, or whether he'll come to an understanding with the millions of his kindred fellow workers under trade-union or revolutionary guidance depends upon the future drift of events in America. But, granting the emotional state, the tensity, the fear, the hate, the impatience, the sense of exclusion, the ache for violent action, the emotional and cultural hunger, Bigger Thomas, conditioned as his organism is, will not become an ardent, or even a lukewarm, supporter of the *status quo*.

The difference between Bigger's tensity and the German variety is that Bigger's, due to America's educational restrictions on the bulk of her Negro population, is in a nascent state, not yet articulate. And the difference between Bigger's longing for self-identification and the Russian principle of self-determination is that Bigger's, due to the effects of American oppression, which has not allowed for the forming of deep ideas of solidarity among Negroes, is still in a state of individual anger and hatred. Here, I felt, was *drama!* Who will be the first to touch off these Bigger Thomases in America, white and black?

For a long time I toyed with the idea of writing a novel in which a Negro Bigger Thomas would loom as a symbolic figure of American life, a figure who would hold within him the prophecy of our future. I felt strongly that he held within him, in a measure which perhaps no other contemporary type did, the outlines of action and feeling which we would encounter on a vast scale in the days to come. Just as one sees when one walks into a medical research laboratory jars of alcohol containing abnormally large or distorted portions of the human body, just so did I see and feel that the conditions of life under which Negroes are forced to live in America contain the embryonic emotional prefigurations of how a large part of the body politic would react under stress.

So, with this much knowledge of myself and the world gained and known, why should I not try to work out on paper the problem of what will happen to Bigger? Why should I not, like a scientist in a laboratory, use my imagination and invent test-tube situations, place Bigger in them, and, following the guidance of my own hopes and fears, what I had learned and remembered, work out in fictional form an emotional statement and resolution of this problem?

But several things militated against my starting to work. Like Bigger himself, I felt a mental censor—product of the fears which a Negro feels from living in America—standing over me, draped in white, warning me not to write. This censor's warnings were translated into my own thought processes thus: "What will white people think if I draw the picture of such a Negro boy? Will they not at once say: 'See, didn't we tell you all along that niggers are like that? Now, look, one of their own kind has come along and drawn the picture for us!'" I felt that if I drew the picture of Bigger truthfully, there would be many reactionary whites who would try to make of him something I did not intend. And yet, and this was what made it difficult, I knew that I could not write of Bigger convincingly if I did not depict him as he *was:* that is, resentful toward whites, sullen, angry, ignorant, emotionally unstable, depressed and unaccountably elated at times, and unable even, because of his own lack of inner organization which American oppression has fostered in him, to unite with the members of his own race. And would not whites misread Bigger and, doubting his authenticity, say: "This man is preaching hate against the whole white race"?

The more I thought of it the more I became convinced that if I did not write of Bigger as I saw and felt him, if I did not try to make him a living personality and at the same time a symbol of all the larger things I felt and saw in him, I'd be reacting as Bigger himself reacted: that is, I'd be acting out of *fear* if I let what I thought whites would say constrict and paralyze me.

As I contemplated Bigger and what he meant, I said to myself: "I must write this novel, not only for others to read, but to free *myself* of this sense of shame and fear." In fact, the novel, as time passed, grew upon me to the extent that it became a necessity to write it; the writing of it turned into a way of living for me.

Another thought kept me from writing. What would my own white and black comrades in the Communist party say? This thought was the most bewildering of all. Politics is a hard and narrow game; its policies represent the aggregate desires and aspirations of millions of people. Its goals are rigid and simply drawn, and the minds of the majority of politicians are set, congealed in terms of daily tactical maneuvers. How could I create such complex and wide schemes of associational thought and feeling, such filigreed webs of dreams and politics, without being mistaken for a "smuggler of reaction," "an ideological confusionist," or "an individualistic and dangerous element"? Though my heart is with the collectivist and proletarian ideal, I solved this problem by assuring myself that honest politics and honest feeling in imaginative representation ought to be able to meet on common healthy ground without fear, suspicion, and quarreling. Further, and more importantly, I steeled myself by coming to the conclusion that whether politicians accepted or rejected Bigger did not really matter; my task, as I felt it, was to free myself of this burden of impressions and feelings, recast them into the image of Bigger and make him *true*. Lastly, I felt that a right more immediately deeper than that of politics or race was at stake; that is, a *human* right, the right of a man to think and feel honestly. And especially did this personal and human right bear hard upon me, for temperamentally I am inclined to satisfy the claims of my own ideals rather than the expectations of others. It was this obscure need that had pulled me into the labor movement in the beginning and by exercising it I was but fulfilling what I felt to be the laws of my own growth.

There was another constricting thought that kept me from work. It deals with my own race. I asked myself: "What will Negro doctors, lawyers, dentists, bankers, school teachers, social workers and business men, think of me if I draw such a picture of Bigger?" I knew from long and painful experience that the Negro middle and professional classes were the people of my own race who were more than others ashamed of Bigger and what he meant. Having narrowly escaped the Bigger Thomas reaction pattern themselves—indeed, still retaining traces of it within the confines of their own timid personalities—they would not relish being publicly reminded of the lowly, shameful depths of life above which they enjoyed their bourgeois lives. Never did they want people, especially *white* people, to think that their lives were so much touched by anything so dark and brutal as Bigger.

Their attitude toward life and art can be summed up in a single paragraph: "But, Mr. Wright, there are so many of us who are *not* like Bigger. Why don't you portray in your fiction the *best* traits of our race, something that will show the white people what we have done in *spite* of oppression? Don't represent anger and bitterness. Smile when a white person comes to you. Never let him feel that you are so small that what he has done to crush you has made you hate him! Oh, above all, save your *pride!*"

But Bigger won over all these claims; he won because I felt that I was hunting on the trail of more exciting and thrilling game. What Bigger meant had claimed me because I felt with all of my being that he was more important than what any person, white or black, would say or try to make of him, more important than any political analysis designed to explain or deny him, more important, even, than my own sense of fear, shame, and diffidence.

But Bigger was still not down upon paper. For a long time I had been writing of him in my mind, but I had yet to put him into an image, a breathing symbol draped out in the guise of the only form of life my native land had allowed me to know intimately, that is, the ghetto life of the American Negro. But the basic reason for my hesitancy was that another and far more complex problem had risen to plague me. Bigger, as I saw and felt him, was a snarl of many realities; he had in him many levels of life.

First, there was his personal and private life, that intimate existence that is so difficult to snare and nail down in fiction, that elusive core of being, that individual data of consciousness which in every man and woman is like that in no other. I had to deal with Bigger's dreams, his fleeting, momentary sensations, his yearning, visions, his deep emotional responses.

Then I was confronted with that part of him that was dual in aspect, dim, wavering, that part of him which is so much a part of *all* Negroes and *all* whites that I realized that I could put it down upon paper only by feeling out its meaning first within the confines of my own life. Bigger was attracted and repelled by the American scene. He was an American, because he was a native son; but he was also a Negro nationalist in a vague sense because he was not allowed to live as an American. Such was his way of life and mine; neither Bigger nor I resided fully in either camp.

Of this dual aspect of Bigger's social consciousness, I placed the nationalistic side first, not because I agreed with Bigger's wild and intense hatred of white people, but because his hate had placed him, like a wild animal at bay, in a position where he was most symbolic and explainable. In other words, his nationalist complex was for me a concept through which I could grasp more of the total meaning of his life than I could in any other way. I tried to approach Bigger's *snarled* and *confused* nationalist feelings with *conscious* and *informed* ones of my own. Yet, Bigger was not nationalist enough to feel the need of religion or the folk culture of his own people. What made Bigger's social consciousness most complex was the fact that he was hovering unwanted between two worlds—between powerful America and his own stunted place in life—and I took upon myself the task of trying to make the reader feel this No Man's Land. The most that I could say of Bigger was that he felt the *need* for a whole life and *acted* out of that need; that was all.

Above and beyond all this, there was that American part of Bigger which is the heritage of us all, that part of him which we get from our seeing and hearing, from school, from the hopes and dreams of our friends; that part of him which the common people of America never talk of but take for granted. Among millions of people the deepest convictions of life are never discussed openly; they are felt, implied, hinted at tacitly and obliquely in their hopes and fears. We live by an idealism that makes us believe that the Constitution is a good document of government, that the Bill of Rights is a good legal and humane principle to safeguard our civil liberties, that every man and woman should have the opportunity to realize himself, to seek his own individual fate and goal, his own peculiar and untranslatable destiny. I don't say that Bigger knew this in the terms in which I'm speaking of it; I don't say that any such thought ever entered his head. His emotional and intellectual life was never that articulate. But he knew it emotionally, intuitively, for his emotions and his desires were developed, and he caught it, as most of us do, from the mental and emotional climate of our time. Bigger had all of this in him, dammed up, buried, implied, and I had to develop it in fictional form.

There was still another level of Bigger's life that I felt bound to account for and render, a level as elusive to discuss as it was to grasp in writing. Here again, I had to fall back upon my own feelings as a guide, for Bigger did not offer in his life any articulate verbal explanations. There seems to hover somewhere in that dark part of all our lives, in some more than in others, an objectless, timeless, spaceless element of primal fear and dread, stemming, perhaps, from our birth (depending upon whether one's outlook upon personality is Freudian or non-Freudian!), a fear and dread which exercises an impelling influence upon our lives all out of proportion to its obscurity. And, accompanying this *first fear,* is, for the want of a better name, a reflex urge toward ecstasy, complete submission, and trust. The springs of religion are here, and also the origins of rebellion. And in a boy like Bigger, young, unschooled, whose subjective life was clothed in the tattered rags of American "culture," this primitive fear and ecstasy were naked, exposed, unprotected by religion or a framework of government or a scheme of society whose final faiths would gain his love and trust; unprotected by trade or profession, faith or belief; opened to every trivial blast of daily or hourly circumstance.

There was yet another level of reality in Bigger's life: the impliedly political. I've already mentioned that Bigger had in him impulses which I had felt were present in the vast upheavals of Russia and Germany. Well, somehow, I had to make these political impulses felt by the reader in terms of Bigger's daily actions, keeping in mind as I did so the probable danger of my being branded as a propagandist by those who would not like the subject matter.

Then there was Bigger's relationship with white America, both North and South, which I had to depict, which I had to make known once again, alas; a relationship whose effects are carried by every Negro, like scars, somewhere in his body and mind.

I had also to show what oppression had done to Bigger's relationships with his own people, how it had split him off from them, how it had baffled him; how oppression seems to hinder and stifle in the victim those very qualities of character which are so essential for an effective struggle against the oppressor.

Then there was the fabulous city in which Bigger lived, an indescribable city, huge, roaring, dirty, noisy, raw, stark, brutal; a city of extremes: torrid summers and sub-zero winters, white people and black people, the English language and strange tongues, foreign born and native born, scabby poverty and gaudy luxury, high idealism and hard cynicism! A city so young that, in thinking of its short history, one's mind, as it travels backward in time, is stopped abruptly by the barren stretches of wind-swept prairie! But a city old enough to have caught within the homes of its long, straight streets the symbols and images of man's age-old destiny, of truths as old as the mountains and seas, of dramas as abiding as the soul of man itself! A city which has become the pivot of the Eastern, Western, Northern, and Southern poles of the nation. But a city whose black smoke clouds shut out the sunshine for seven months of the year; a city in which, on a fine balmy May morning, one can sniff the stench of the stockyards; a city where people have grown so used to gangs and murders and graft that they have honestly forgotten that government can have a pretense of decency!

With all of this thought out, Bigger was still unwritten. Two events, however, came into my life and accelerated the process, made me sit down and actually start work on the typewriter, and just stop the writing of Bigger in my mind as I walked the streets.

The first event was my getting a job in the South Side Boys' Club, an institution which tried to reclaim the thousands of Negro Bigger Thomases from the dives and the alleys of the Black Belt. Here, on a vast scale, I had an opportunity to observe Bigger in all of his moods, actions, haunts. Here I felt for the first time that the rich folk who were paying my wages did not really give a good goddamn about Bigger, that their kindness was prompted at bottom by a selfish motive. They were paying me to distract Bigger with ping-pong, checkers, swimming, marbles, and baseball in order that he might not roam the streets and harm the valuable white property which adjoined the Black Belt. I am not condemning boys' clubs and ping-pong as such; but these little stopgaps were utterly inadequate to fill up the centuries-long chasm of emptiness which American civilization had created in these Biggers. I felt that I was doing a kind of dressed-up police work, and I hated it.

I would work hard with these Biggers, and when it would come time for me to go home

I'd say to myself, under my breath so that no one could hear: "Go to it, boys! Prove to the bastards that gave you these games that life is stronger than ping-pong. . . . Show them that full-blooded life is harder and hotter than they suspect, even though that life is draped in a black skin which at heart they despise. . . ."

They did. The police blotters of Chicago are testimony to how *much* they did. That was the only way I could contain myself for doing a job I hated; for a moment I'd allow myself, vicariously, to feel as Bigger felt—not much, just a little, just a *little*—but, still, there it was.

The second event that spurred me to write of Bigger was more personal and subtle. I had written a book of short stories which was published under the title of *Uncle Tom's Children*. When the reviews of that book began to appear, I realized that I had made an awfully naïve mistake. I found that I had written a book which even bankers' daughters could read and weep over and feel good about. I swore to myself that if I ever wrote another book, no one would weep over it; that it would be so hard and deep that they would have to face it without the consolation of tears. It was this that made me get to work in dead earnest.

Now, until this moment I did not stop to think very much about the plot of *Native Son*. The reason I did not is because I was not for one moment ever worried about it. I had spent years learning about Bigger, what had made him, what he meant; so, when the time came for writing, *what had made him and what he meant* constituted my plot. But the far-flung items of his life had to be couched in imaginative terms, terms known and acceptable to a common body of readers, terms which would, in the course of the story, manipulate the deepest held notions and convictions of their lives. That came easy. The moment I began to write, the plot fell out, so to speak. I'm not trying to oversimplify or make the process seem oversubtle. At bottom, what happened is very easy to explain.

Any Negro who has lived in the North or the South knows that times without number he has heard of some Negro boy being picked up on the streets and carted off to jail and charged with "rape." This thing happens so often that to my mind it had become a representative symbol of the Negro's uncertain position in America. Never for a second was I in doubt as to what kind of social reality or dramatic situation I'd put Bigger in, what kind of test-tube life I'd set up to evoke his deepest reactions. Life had made the plot over and over again, to the extent that I knew it by heart. So frequently do these acts recur that when I was halfway through the first draft of *Native Son* a case paralleling Bigger's flared forth in the newspapers of Chicago. (Many of the newspaper items and some of the incidents in *Native Son* are but fictionalized versions of the Robert Nixon case and rewrites of news stories from the *Chicago Tribune*.) Indeed, scarcely was *Native Son* off the press before Supreme Court Justice Hugo L. Black gave the nation a long and vivid account of the American police methods of handling Negro boys.

Let me describe this stereotyped situation: A crime wave is sweeping a city and citizens are clamoring for police action. Squad cars cruise the Black Belt and grab the first Negro boy who seems to be unattached and homeless. He is held for perhaps a week without charge or bail, without the privilege of communicating with anyone, including his own relatives. After a few days this boy "confesses" anything that he is asked to confess, any crime that handily happens to be unsolved and on the calendar. Why does he confess? After the boy has been grilled night and day, hanged up by his thumbs, dangled by his feet out of twenty-story windows, and beaten (in places that leave no scars—cops have found a way to do that), he signs the papers before him, papers which are usually accompanied by a verbal promise to the boy that he will not go to the electric chair. Of course, he ends up by being executed or sentenced for life. If you think I'm telling tall tales, get chummy with some white cop who works in a Black Belt district and ask him for the lowdown.

When a black boy is carted off to jail in such a fashion, it is almost impossible to do anything for him. Even well-disposed Negro lawyers find it difficult to defend him, for the boy will plead guilty one day and then not guilty the next, according to the degree of pressure and persuasion that is brought to bear upon his frightened personality from one side or the other. Even the boy's own family is scared to death; sometimes fear of police intimidation makes them hesitate to acknowledge that the boy is a blood relation of theirs.

Such has been America's attitude toward these boys that if one is picked up and confronted in a police cell with ten white cops, he is intimidated almost to the point of confessing anything. So far removed are these practices from what the average American citizen encounters in his daily life that it takes a huge act of his imagination to believe that it is true; yet, this same average citizen, with his kindness, his American sportsmanship and good will, would probably act with the mob if a self-respecting Negro family moved into his apartment building to escape the Black Belt and its terrors and limitations. . . .

Now, after all of this, when I sat down to the typewriter, I could not work; I could not think of a good opening scene for the book. I had definitely in mind the kind of emotion I wanted to evoke in the reader in that first scene, but I could not think of the type of concrete event that would convey the motif of the entire scheme of the book, that would sound, in varied form, the note that was to be resounded throughout its length, that would introduce to the reader just what kind of an organism Bigger's was and the environment that was bearing hourly upon it. Twenty or thirty times I tried and failed; then I argued that if I could not write the opening scene, I'd start with the scene that followed. I did. The

actual writing of the book began with the scene in the pool room.

Now, for the writing. During the years in which I had met all of those Bigger Thomases, those varieties of Bigger Thomases, I had not consciously gathered material to write of them; I had not kept a notebook record of their sayings and doings. Their actions had simply made impressions upon my sensibilities as I lived from day to day, impressions which crystallized and coagulated into clusters and configurations of memory, attitudes, moods, ideas. And these subjective states, in turn, were automatically stored away somewhere in me. I was not even aware of the process. But, excited over the book which I had set myself to write, under the stress of emotion, these things came surging up, tangled, fused, knotted, entertaining me by the sheer variety and potency of their meaning and suggestiveness.

With the whole theme in mind, in an attitude almost akin to prayer, I gave myself up to the story. In an effort to capture some phase of Bigger's life that would not come to me readily, I'd jot down as much of it as I could. Then I'd read it over and over, adding each time a word, a phrase, a sentence until I felt that I had caught all the shadings of reality I felt dimly were there. With each of these rereadings and rewritings it seemed that I'd gather in facts and facets that tried to run away. It was an act of concentration, of trying to hold within one's center of attention all of that bewildering array of facts which science, politics, experience, memory, and imagination were urging upon me. And then, while writing, a new and thrilling relationship would spring up under the drive of emotion, coalescing and telescoping alien facts into a known and felt truth. That was the deep fun of the job: to feel within my body that I was pushing out to new areas of feeling, strange landmarks of emotion, tramping upon foreign soil, compounding new relationships of perceptions, making new and—until that very split second of time!—unheard-of and unfelt effects with words. It had a buoying and tonic impact upon me; my senses would strain and seek for more and more of such relationships; my temperature would rise as I worked. That is writing as I feel it, a kind of significant living.

The first draft of the novel was written in four months, straight through, and ran to some 576 pages. Just as a man rises in the mornings to dig ditches for his bread, so I'd work daily. I'd think of some abstract principle of Bigger's conduct and at once my mind would turn it into some act I'd seen Bigger perform, some act which I hoped would be familiar enough to the American reader to gain his credence. But in the writing of scene after scene I was guided by but one criterion: to tell the truth as I saw it and felt it. That is, to objectify in words some insight derived from my living in the form of action, scene, and dialogue. If a scene seemed improbable to me, I'd not tear it up, but ask myself: "Does it reveal enough of what I feel to stand in spite of its unreality?" If I felt it did, it stood. If I felt that it did not, I ripped it out. The degree of morality in my writing depended upon the degree of felt life and truth I could put down upon the printed page. For example, there is a scene in *Native Son* where Bigger stands in a cell with a Negro preacher, Jan, Max, the State's Attorney, Mr. Dalton, Mrs. Dalton, Bigger's mother, his brother, his sister, Al, Gus, and Jack. While writing that scene, I knew that it was unlikely that so many people would ever be allowed to come into a murderer's cell. But I wanted those people in that cell to elicit a certain important emotional response from Bigger. And so the scene stood. I felt that what I wanted that scene to say to the reader was *more important than its surface reality or plausibility.*

Always, as I wrote, I was both reader and writer, both the conceiver of the action and the appreciator of it. I tried to write so that, in the same instant of time, the objective and subjective aspects of Bigger's life would be caught in a focus of prose. And always I tried to *render, depict,* not merely to tell the story. If a thing was cold, I tried to make the reader *feel* cold, and not just tell about it. In writing in this fashion, sometimes I'd find it necessary to use a stream of consciousness technique, then rise to an interior monologue, descend to a direct rendering of a dream state, then to a matter-of-fact depiction of what Bigger was saying, doing, and feeling. Then I'd find it impossible to say what I wanted to say without stepping in and speaking outright on my own; but when doing this I always made an effort to retain the mood of the story, explaining everything only in terms of Bigger's life and, if possible, in the rhythms of Bigger's thought (even though the words would be mine). Again, at other times, in the guise of the lawyer's speech and the newspaper items, or in terms of what Bigger would overhear or see from afar, I'd give what others were saying and thinking of him. But always, from the start to the finish, it was Bigger's story, Bigger's fear, Bigger's flight, and Bigger's fate that I tried to depict. I wrote with the conviction in mind (I don't know if this is right or wrong; I only know that I'm temperamentally inclined to feel this way) that the main burden of all serious fiction consists almost wholly of character-destiny and the items, social, political, and personal, of that character-destiny.

As I wrote I followed, almost unconsciously, many principles of the novel which my reading of the novels of other writers had made me feel were necessary for the building of a well-constructed book. For the most part the novel is rendered in the present; I wanted the reader to feel that Bigger's story was happening *now,* like a play upon the stage or a movie unfolding upon the screen. Action follows action, as in a prize fight. Whenever possible, I told of Bigger's life in close-up, slow-motion, giving the feel of the grain in the passing of time. I had long had the feeling that this was the best way to "enclose" the reader's mind in a new world, to blot out all reality except that which I was giving him.

Then again, as much as I could, I restricted the novel to what Bigger saw and felt, to the limits of his feeling and thoughts, even when I was conveying *more* than that to the reader. I had the notion that such a manner of rendering made for a sharper effect, a more pointed sense of the character, his peculiar type of being and consciousness. Throughout there is but one point of view: Bigger's. This, too, I felt, made for a richer illusion of reality.

I kept out of the story as much as possible, for I wanted the reader to feel that there was nothing between him and Bigger; that the story was a special *première* given in his own private theater.

I kept the scenes long, made as much happen within a short space of time as possible; all of which, I felt, made for greater density and richness of effect.

In a like manner I tried to keep a unified sense of background throughout the story; the background would change, of course, but I tried to keep before the eyes of the reader at all times the forces and elements against which Bigger was striving.

And, because I had limited myself to rendering only what Bigger saw and felt, I gave no more reality to the other characters than that which Bigger himself saw.

This, honestly, is all I can account for in the book. If I attempted to account for scenes and characters, to tell why certain scenes were written in certain ways, I'd be stretching facts in order to be pleasantly intelligible. All else in the book came from my feelings reacting upon the material, and any honest reader knows as much about the rest of what is in the book as I do; that is, if, as he reads, he is willing to let his emotions and imagination become as influenced by the materials as I did. As I wrote, for some reason or other, one image, symbol, character, scene, mood, feeling evoked its opposite, its parallel, its complementary, and its ironic counterpart. Why? I don't know. My emotions and imagination just like to work that way. One can account

for just so much of life, and then no more. At least, not yet.

With the first draft down, I found that I could not end the book satisfactorily. In the first draft I had Bigger going smack to the electric chair; but I felt that two murders were enough for one novel. I cut the final scene and went back to worry about the beginning. I had no luck. The book was one-half finished, with the opening and closing scenes unwritten. Then, one night, in desperation—I hope that I'm not disclosing the hidden secrets of my craft!—I sneaked out and got a bottle. With the help of it, I began to remember many things which I could not remember before. One of them was that Chicago was overrun with rats. I recalled that I'd seen many rats on the streets, that I'd heard and read of Negro children being bitten by rats in their beds. At first I rejected the idea of Bigger battling a rat in his room; I was afraid that the rat would "hog" the scene. But the rat would not leave me; he presented himself in many attractive guises. So, cautioning myself to allow the rat scene to disclose *only* Bigger, his family, their little room, and their relationships, I let the rat walk in, and he did his stuff.

Many of the scenes were torn out as I reworked the book. The mere rereading of what I'd written made me think of the possibility of developing themes which had been only hinted at in the first draft. For example, the entire guilt theme that runs through *Native Son* was woven in *after* the first draft was written.

At last I found out how to end the book; I ended it just as I had begun it, showing Bigger living dangerously, taking his life into his hands, accepting what life had made him. The lawyer, Max, was placed in Bigger's cell at the end of the novel to register the moral—or what *I* felt was the moral—horror of Negro life in the United States.

The writing of *Native Son* was to me an exciting, enthralling, and even a romantic experience. With what I've learned in the writing of this book, with all of its blemishes, imperfections, with all of its unrealized potentialities, I am launching out upon another novel, this time about the status of women in modern American society. This book, too, goes back to my childhood just as Bigger went, for, while I was storing away impressions of Bigger, I was storing away impressions of many other things that made me think and wonder. Some experience will ignite somewhere deep down in me the smoldering embers of new fires and I'll be off again to write yet another novel. It is good to live when one feels that such as that will happen to one. Life becomes sufficient unto life; the rewards of living are found in living.

I don't know if *Native Son* is a good book or a bad book. And I don't know if the book I'm working on now will be a good book or a bad book. And I really don't care. The mere writing of it will be more fun and a deeper satisfaction than any praise or blame from anybody.

I feel that I'm lucky to be alive to write novels today, when the whole world is caught in the pangs of war and change. Early American writers, Henry James and Nathaniel Hawthorne, complained bitterly about the bleakness and flatness of the American scene. But I think that if they were alive, they'd feel at home in modern America. True, we have no great church in America; our national traditions are still of such a sort that we are not wont to brag of them; and we have no army that's above the level of mercenary fighters; we have no group acceptable to the whole of our country upholding certain humane values; we have no rich symbols, no colorful rituals. We have only a money-grubbing, industrial civilization. But we do have in the Negro the embodiment of a past tragic enough to appease the spiritual hunger of even a James; and we have in the oppression of the Negro a shadow athwart our national life dense and heavy enough to satisfy even the gloomy broodings of a Hawthorne. And if Poe were alive, he would not have to invent horror; horror would invent him.

New York, March 7, 1940.

Essay/Discussion Questions

1. According to Richard Wright, what was the origin of Bigger Thomas, the victim-rebel in his novel *Native Son*?

2. What factors stalled Wright's initial efforts to start writing *Native Son*?

3. In his novel of ideas, *Native Son,* Wright focused on the social outlook and life experiences of dispossessed urban black people. Why did he write about this sector of the black population, and what was the response from the black middle class?

The Black Arts Movement

LARRY NEAL

I

The Black Arts Movement is radically opposed to any concept of the artist that alienates him from his community. Black Art is the aesthetic and spiritual sister of the Black Power concept. As such, it envisions an art that speaks directly to the needs and aspirations of Black America. In order to perform this task, the Black Arts Movement proposes a radical reordering of the western cultural aesthetic. It proposes a separate symbolism, mythology, critique, and iconology. The Black Arts and the Black Power concept both relate broadly to the Afro-American's desire for self-determination and nationhood. Both concepts are nationalistic. One is concerned with the relationship between art and politics; the other with the art of politics.

Recently, these two movements have begun to merge: the political values inherent in the Black Power concept are now finding concrete expression in the aesthetics of Afro-American dramatists, poets, choreographers, musicians, and novelists. A main tenet of Black Power is the necessity for Black people to define the world in their own terms. The Black artist has made the same point in the context of aesthetics. The two movements postulate that there are in fact and in spirit two Americas—one black, one white. The Black artist takes this to mean that his primary duty is to speak to the spiritual and cultural needs of Black people. Therefore, the main thrust of this new breed of contemporary writers is to confront the contradictions arising out of the Black man's experience in the racist West. Currently, these writers are reevaluating western aesthetics, the traditional role of the writer, and the social function of art. Implicit in this reevaluation is the need to develop a "Black aesthetic." It is the opinion of many Black writers, I among them, that the Western aesthetic has run its course: it is impossible to construct anything meaningful within its decaying structure. We advocate a cultural revolution in art and ideas. The cultural values inherent in western history must either be radicalized or destroyed, and we will probably find that even radicalization is impossible. In fact, what is needed is a whole new system of ideas. Poet Don L. Lee expresses it:

> . . . We must destroy Faulkner, dick, jane,
> and other perpetuators of evil. It's time for

Reprinted with permission from *The Drama Review*, 12:4 (1968).

DuBois, Nat Turner, and Kwame Nkrumah. As Frantz Fanon points out: destroy the culture and you destroy the people. This must not happen. Black artists are culture stabilizers; bringing back old values, and introducing new ones. Black Art will talk to the people and with the will of the people stop impending "protective custody."

The Black Arts Movement eschews "protest" literature. It speaks directly to Black people. Implicit in the concept of "protest" literature, as Brother Knight has made clear, is an appeal to white morality:

> Now any Black man who masters the technique of his particular art form, who adheres to the white aesthetic, and who directs his work toward a white audience is, in one sense, protesting. And implicit in the act of protest is the belief that a change will be forthcoming once the masters are aware of the protestor's "grievance" (the very word connotes begging, supplications to the gods). Only when that belief has faded and protestings end, will Black art begin.

Brother Knight also has some interesting statements about the development of a "Black aesthetic":

> Unless the Black artist establishes a "Black aesthetic" he will have no future at all. To accept the white aesthetic is to accept and validate a society that will not allow him to live. The Black artist must create new forms and new values, sing new songs (or purify old ones); and along with other Black authorities, he must create a new history, new symbols, myths and legends (and purify old ones by fire). And the Black artist, in creating his own aesthetic, must be accountable for it only to the Black people. Further, he must hasten his own dissolution as an individual (in the Western sense)—painful though the process may be, having been breast-fed the poison of "individual experience."

When we speak of a "Black aesthetic" several things are meant. First, we assume that there is already in existence the basis for such an aesthetic. Essentially, it consists of an African-American cultural tradition. But this aesthetic is finally, by implication, broader than that tradition. It encompasses most of the useable elements of Third World culture. The motive behind the Black aesthetic is the destruction of the white thing, the destruction of white ideas, and white ways of looking at the world. The new aesthetic is mostly predicated on an Ethics which asks the question: whose vision of the world is finally more meaningful, ours or the white oppressors? What is truth? Or more precisely, whose truth shall we express, that of the oppressed or of the oppressors? These are basic questions. Black intellectuals of previous decades failed to ask them. Further, national and international affairs demand that we appraise the world in terms of our own interests. It is clear that the question of human survival is at the core of contemporary experience. The Black artist must address himself to this reality in the strongest terms possible. In a context of world upheaval, ethics and aesthetics must interact positively and be consistent with the demands for a more spiritual world. Consequently, the Black Arts Movement is an ethical movement. Ethical, that is, from the viewpoint of the oppressed. And much of the oppression confronting the Third World and Black America is directly traceable to the Euro-American cultural sensibility. This sensibility, anti-human in nature, has, until recently, dominated the psyches of most Black artists and intellectuals; it must be destroyed before the Black creative artist can have a meaningful role in the transformation of society.

It is this natural reaction to an alien sensibility that informs the cultural attitudes of the Black Arts and the Black Power movement. It is a profound ethical sense that makes a Black artist question a society in which art is one thing and the actions of men another. The Black Arts Movement believes that your ethics and your aesthetics are one. That the contradictions between ethics and aesthetics in western society is symptomatic of a dying culture.

The term "Black Arts" is of ancient origin, but it was first used in a positive sense by LeRoi Jones:

> We are unfair
> And unfair
> We are black magicians
> Black arts we make
> in black labs of the heart
>
> The fair are fair
> and deathly white
>
> The day will not save them
> And we own the night

There is also a section of the poem "Black Dada Nihilismus" that carries the same motif. But a fuller amplification of the nature of the new aesthetics appears in the poem "Black Art":

> Poems are bullshit unless they are
> teeth or trees or lemons piled
> on a step. Or black ladies dying
> of men leaving nickel hearts
> beating them down. Fuck poems
> and they are useful, would they shoot
> come at you, love what you are,
> breathe like wrestlers, or shudder
> strangely after peeing. We want live
> words of the hip world, live flesh &
> coursing blood. Hearts and Brains
> Souls splintering fire. We want poems
> like fists beating niggers out of Jocks
> or dagger poems in the slimy bellies
> of the owner-jews . . .

Poetry is a concrete function, an action. No more abstractions. Poems are physical entities: fists, daggers, airplane poems, and poems that shoot guns. Poems are transformed from physical objects into personal forces:

> . . . Put it on him poem. Strip him naked
> to the world. Another bad poem cracking
> steel knuckles in a jewlady's mouth
> Poem scream poison gas on breasts in green berets . . .

Then the poem affirms the integral relationship between Black Art and Black people:

> . . . Let Black people understand
> that they are the lovers and the sons
> of lovers and warriors and sons
> of warriors Are poems & poets &
> all the loveliness here in the world

It ends with the following lines, a central assertion in both the Black Arts Movement and the philosophy of Black Power:

> We want a black poem. And a
> Black World.
> Let the world be a Black Poem
> And let All Black People Speak This Poem
> Silently
> Or LOUD

The poem comes to stand for the collective conscious and unconscious of Black America—the real impulse in back of the Black Power movement, which is the will toward self-determination and nationhood, a radical reordering of the nature and function of both art and the artist.

II

In the spring of 1964, LeRoi Jones, Charles Patterson, William Patterson, Clarence Reed, Johnny Moore, and a number of other Black artists opened the Black Arts Repertoire Theatre School. They produced a number of plays including Jones' *Experimental Death Unit # One, Black Mass, Jello,* and *Dutchman.* They also initiated a series of poetry readings and concerts. These activities represented the most advanced tendencies in the movement and were of excellent artistic quality. The Black Arts School came under immediate attack by the New York power structure. The Establishment, fearing Black creativity, did exactly what it was expected to do—it attacked the theatre and all of its values. In the meantime, the school was granted funds by OEO through HARYOU-ACT. Lacking a cultural program itself, HARYOU turned to the only organization which addressed itself to the needs of the community. In keeping with its "revolutionary" cultural ideas, the Black Arts Theatre took its programs into the streets of Harlem. For three months, the theatre presented plays, concerts, and poetry readings to the people of the community. Plays that shattered the illusions of the American body politic and awakened Black people to the meaning of their lives.

Then the hawks from the OEO moved in and chopped off the funds. Again this should have been expected. The Black Arts Theatre stood in radical opposition to the feeble attitudes about culture of the "War On Poverty" bureaucrats. And later, because of internal problems, the theatre was forced to close. But the Black Arts group proved that the community could be served by a valid and dynamic art. It also proved that there was a definite need for a cultural revolution in the Black community.

With the closing of the Black Arts Theatre, the implications of what Brother Jones and his colleagues were trying to do took on even more significance. Black Art groups sprang up on the West Coast and the idea spread to Detroit, Philadelphia, Jersey City, New Orleans, and Washington, D.C. Black Arts movements began on the campuses of San Francisco State College, Fisk University, Lincoln University, Hunter College in the Bronx, Columbia University, and Oberlin College. In Watts, after the rebellion, Maulana Karenga welded the Black Arts Movement into a cohesive cultural ideology which owed much to the work of LeRoi Jones. Karenga sees culture as the most important element in the struggle for self-determination:

> Culture is the basis of all ideas, images and actions. To move is to move culturally, i.e. by a set of values given to you by your culture.
>
> Without a culture Negroes are only a set of reactions to white people.

The seven criteria for culture are:

1. Mythology
2. History
3. Social Organization
4. Political Organization
5. Economic Organization
6. Creative Motif
7. Ethos

In drama, LeRoi Jones represents the most advanced aspects of the movement. He is its prime mover and chief designer. In a poetic essay entitled "The Revolutionary Theatre," he outlines the iconology of the movement:

> The Revolutionary Theatre should force change: it should be change. (All their faces turned into the lights and you work on them black nigger magic, and cleanse them at having seen the ugliness. And if the beautiful see themselves, they will love themselves.) We are preaching virtue again, but by that to mean NOW, toward what seems the most constructive use of the word.

The theatre that Jones proposes is inextricably linked to the Afro-American political dynamic. And such a link is perfectly consistent with Black America's contemporary demands. For theatre is potentially the most social of all of the arts. It is an integral part of the socializing process. It exists in direct relationship to the audience it claims to serve. The decadence and inanity of the contemporary American theatre is an accurate reflection of the state of American society. Albee's *Who's Afraid of Virginia Woolf?* is very American: sick white lives in a homosexual hell hole. The theatre of white America is escapist, refusing to confront concrete reality. Into this cultural emptiness come the musicals, an up-tempo version of the same stale lives. And the use of Negroes in such plays as *Hello Dolly* and *Hallelujah Baby* does not alter their nature; it compounds the problem. These plays are simply hipper versions of the minstrel show. They present Negroes acting out the hang-ups of middle-class white America. Consequently, the American theatre is a palliative prescribed to bourgeois patients who refuse to see the world as it is. Or, more crucially, as the world sees them. It is no accident, therefore, that the most "important" plays come from Europe—Brecht, Weiss, and Ghelderode. And even these have begun to run dry.

The Black Arts theatre, the theatre of LeRoi Jones, is a radical alternative to the sterility of the American theatre. It is primarily a theatre of the Spirit, confronting the Black man in his interaction with his brothers and with the white thing.

> Our theatre will show victims so that their brothers in the audience will be better able to understand that they are brothers of victims, and that they themselves are blood brothers. And what we show must cause the blood to rush, so that prerevolutionary temperaments will be bathed in this blood, and it will cause their deepest souls to move, and they will find themselves tensed and clenched, even ready to die, at what the soul has been taught. We will scream and cry, murder, run through the streets in agony, if it means some soul will be moved, moved to actual life understanding of what the world is, and what it ought to be. We are preaching virtue and feeling, and a natural sense of the self in the world. All men live in the world, and the world ought to be a place for them to live.

The victims in the world of Jones' early plays are Clay, murdered by the white bitch-goddess in *Dutchman,* and Walker Vessels, the revolutionary in *The Slave.* Both of these plays present Black men in transition. Clay, the middle-class Negro trying to get himself a little action from Lula, digs himself and his own truth only to get murdered after telling her like it really is:

> Just let me bleed you, you loud whore, and one poem vanished. A whole people neurotics, struggling to keep from being sane. And the only thing that would cure the neurosis would be your murder. Simple as that. I mean if I murdered you, then other white people would understand me. You understand? No, I

guess not. If Bessie Smith had killed some white people she wouldn't needed that music. She could have talked very straight and plain about the world. Just straight two and two are four. Money. Power. Luxury. Like that. All of them. Crazy niggers turning their back on sanity. When all it needs is that simple act. Just murder. Would make us all sane.

But Lula understands, and she kills Clay first. In a perverse way it is Clay's nascent knowledge of himself that threatens the existence of Lula's idea of the world. Symbolically, and in fact, the relationship between Clay (Black America) and Lula (white America) is rooted in the historical castration of black manhood. And in the twisted psyche of white America, the Black man is both an object of love and hate. Analogous attitudes exist in most Black Americans, but for decidedly different reasons. Clay is doomed when he allows himself to participate in Lula's "fantasy" in the first place. It is the fantasy to which Frantz Fanon alludes in *The Wretched Of The Earth* and *Black Skins, White Mask:* the native's belief that he can acquire the oppressor's power by acquiring his symbols, one of which is the white woman. When Clay finally digs himself it is too late.

Walker Vessels, in *The Slave,* is Clay reincarnated as the revolutionary confronting problems inherited from his contact with white culture. He returns to the home of his ex-wife, a white woman, and her husband, a literary critic. The play is essentially about Walker's attempt to destroy his white past. For it is the past, with all of its painful memories, that is really the enemy of the revolutionary. It is impossible to move until history is either re-created or comprehended. Unlike Todd, in Ralph Ellison's *Invisible Man,* Walker cannot fall outside history. Instead, Walker demands a confrontation with history, a final shattering of bullshit illusions. His only salvation lies in confronting the physical and psychological forces that have made him and his people powerless. Therefore, he comes to understand that the world must be restructured along spiritual imperatives. But in the interim it is basically a question of *who* has power.

> *Easley.* You're so wrong about everything. So terribly, sickeningly wrong. What can you change? What do you hope to change? Do you think Negroes are *better* people than whites . . . That they can govern a society better than whites? That they'll be more judicious or more tolerant? Do you think they'll make fewer mistakes? I mean really, if the Western white man has proved one thing . . . it's the futility of modern society. So the have-not peoples become the haves. Even so, will that change the essential functions of the world? Will there be more love or beauty in the world . . . more knowledge . . . because of it?
>
> *Walker.* Probably. Probably there will be more . . . if more people have a chance to understand what it is. But that's not even the point. It comes down to baser human endeavor than any social-political thinking. What does it matter if there's more love or beauty? Who the fuck cares? Is that what the Western ofay thought while he was ruling . . . that his rule somehow brought more love and beauty into the world? Oh, he might have thought that concomitantly, while sipping a gin rickey and scratching his ass . . . but that was not ever the point. Not even on the Crusades. The point is that you had your chance, darling, now these other folks have theirs. *Quietly.* Now they have theirs.
>
> *Easley:* God, what an ugly idea.

This confrontation between the black radical and the white liberal is symbolic of larger confrontations occurring between the Third World and Western society. It is a confrontation between the colonizer and the colonized, the slavemaster and the slave. Implicit in Easley's remarks is the belief that the white man is culturally and politically superior to the Black Man. Even though Western society has been traditionally violent in its relation with the Third World, it sanctimoniously deplores violence or self assertion on the part of the enslaved. And the Western mind, with clever rationalizations, equates the violence of

the oppressed with the violence of the oppressor. So that when the native preaches self-determination, the Western white man cleverly misconstrues it to mean hate of *all* white men. When the Black political radical warns his people not to trust white politicians of the left and the right, but instead to organize separately on the basis of power, the white man cries: "racism in reverse." Or he will say, as many of them do today: "We deplore both white and black racism." As if the two could be equated.

There is a minor element in *The Slave* which assumes great importance in a later play entitled *Jello*. Here I refer to the emblem of Walker's army: a red-mouthed grinning field slave. The revolutionary army has taken one of the most hated symbols of the Afro-American past and radically altered its meaning. This is the supreme act of freedom, available only to those who have liberated themselves psychically. Jones amplifies this inversion of emblem and symbol in *Jello* by making Rochester (Ratfester) of the old Jack Benny (Penny) program into a revolutionary nationalist. Ratfester, ordinarily the supreme embodiment of the Uncle Tom Clown, surprises Jack Penny by turning on the other side of the nature of the Black man. He skillfully, and with an evasive black humor, robs Penny of all of his money. But Ratfester's actions are "moral." That is to say, Ratfester is getting his back pay; payment of a long overdue debt to the Black man. Ratfester's sensibilities are different from Walker's. He is *blues people* smiling and shuffling while trying to figure out how to destroy the white thing. And like the blues man, he is the master of the understatement. Or in the Afro-American folk tradition, he is the Signifying Monkey, Shine, and Stagolee all rolled into one. There are no stereotypes any more. History has killed Uncle Tom. Because even Uncle Tom has a breaking point beyond which he will not be pushed. Cut deeply enough into the most docile Negro, and you will find a conscious murderer. Behind the lyrics of the blues and the shuffling porter looms visions of white throats being cut and cities burning.

Jones' particular power as a playwright does not rest solely on his revolutionary vision, but is instead derived from his deep lyricism and spiritual outlook. In many ways, he is fundamentally more a poet than a playwright. And it is his lyricism that gives body to his plays. Two important plays in this regard are *Black Mass* and *Slave Ship*. *Black Mass* is based on the Muslim myth of Yacub. According to this myth, Yacub, a Black scientist, developed the means of grafting different colors of the Original Black Nation until a White Devil was created. In *Black Mass,* Yacub's experiments produce raving White Beast who is condemned to the coldest regions of the North. The other magicians implore Yacub to cease his experiments. But he insists on claiming the primacy of scientific knowledge over spiritual knowledge. The sensibility of the White Devil is alien, informed by lust and sensuality. The Beast is the consummate embodiment of evil, the beginning of the historical subjugation of the spiritual world.

Black Mass takes place in some prehistorical time. In fact, the concept of time, we learn, is the creation of an alien sensibility, that of the Beast. This is a deeply weighted play, a colloquy on the nature of man, and the relationship between legitimate spiritual knowledge and scientific knowledge. It is LeRoi Jones' most important play mainly because it is informed by a mythology that is wholly the creation of the Afro-American sensibility.

Further, Yacub's creation is not merely a scientific exercise. More fundamentally, it is the aesthetic impulse gone astray. The Beast is created merely for the sake of creation. Some artists assert a similar claim about the nature of art. They argue that art need not have a function. It is against this decadent attitude toward art—ramified throughout most of Western society—that the play militates. Yacub's real crime, therefore, is the introduction of a meaningless evil into a harmonious universe. The evil of the Beast is pervasive, corrupting everything and everyone it touches. What was beautiful is twisted into an ugly screaming thing. The play ends with destruction of the holy place of the Black Magicians. Now the Beast and his descendants roam the earth. An offstage voice chants a call for the Jihad to begin. It is then that myth merges into legitimate history, and we, the audience, come to understand that all history is merely someone's version of mythology.

Slave Ship presents a more immediate confrontation with history. In a series of expressionistic tableaux it depicts the horrors and the madness of the Middle Passage. It then moves through the period of slavery, early attempts at revolt, tendencies toward Uncle Tom-like reconciliation and betrayal, and the final act of liberation. There is no definite plot (LeRoi calls it a pageant), just a continuous rush of sound, groans, screams, and souls wailing for freedom and relief from suffering. This work has special affinities with the New Music of Sun Ra, John Coltrane, Albert Ayler, and Ornette Coleman. Events are blurred, rising and falling in a stream of sound. Almost cinematically, the images flicker and fade against a heavy backdrop of rhythm. The language is spare, stripped to the essential. It is a play which almost totally eliminates the need for a text. It functions on the basis of movement and energy—the dramatic equivalent of the New Music.

III

LeRoi Jones is the best known and the most advanced playwright of the movement, but he is not alone. There are other excellent playwrights who express the general mood of the Black Arts ideology. Among them are Ron Milner, Ed Bullins, Ben Caldwell, Jimmy Stewart, Joe White, Charles Patterson, Charles Fuller, Aisha Hughes, Carol Freeman, and Jimmy Garrett.

Ron Milner's *Who's Got His Own* is of particular importance. It strips bare the clashing attitudes of a contemporary Afro-American family. Milner's concern is with legitimate manhood and morality. The family in *Who's Got His Own* is in search of its conscience, or more precisely its own definition of life. On the day of his father's death, Tim and his family are forced to examine the inner fabric of their lives; the lies, self-deceits, and sense of powerlessness in a white world. The basic conflict, however, is internal. It is rooted in the historical search for black manhood. Tim's mother is representative of a generation of Christian Black women who have implicitly understood the brooding violence lurking in their men. And with this understanding, they have interposed themselves between their men and the object of that violence—the white man. Thus unable to direct his violence against the oppressor, the Black man becomes more frustrated and the sense of powerlessness deepens. Lacking the strength to be a man in the white world, he turns against his family. So the oppressed, as Fanon explains, constantly dreams violence against his oppressor, while killing his brother on fast weekends.

Tim's sister represents the Negro woman's attempt to acquire what Eldridge Cleaver calls "ultrafemininity." That is, the attributes of her white upper-class counterpart. Involved here is a rejection of the body-oriented life of the working class Black man, symbolized by the mother's traditional religion. The sister has an affair with a white upper-class liberal, ending in abortion. There are hints of lesbianism, i.e. a further rejection of the body. The sister's life is a pivotal factor in the play. Much of the stripping away of falsehood initiated by Tim is directed at her life, which they have carefully kept hidden from the mother.

Tim is the product of the new Afro-American sensibility, informed by the psychological revolution now operative within Black America. He is a combination ghetto soul brother and militant intellectual, very hip and slightly flawed himself. He would change the world, but without comprehending the particular history that produced his "tyrannical" father. And he cannot be the man his father was—not until he truly understands his father. He must understand why his father allowed himself to be insulted daily by the "honky" types on the job; why he took a demeaning job in the "shit-house"; and why he spent on his family the violence that he should have directed against the white man. In short, Tim must confront the history of his family. And that is exactly what happens. Each character tells his story, exposing his falsehood to the other until a balance is reached.

Who's Got His Own is not the work of an alienated mind. Milner's main thrust is directed toward unifying the family around basic moral principles, toward bridging the "generation gap." Other Black playwrights, Jimmy Garrett for example, see the gap as unbridgeable.

Garrett's *We Own the Night* takes place during an armed insurrection. As the play opens we see the central characters defending a section of the city against attacks by white police. Johnny, the protagonist, is wounded. Some of his Brothers intermittently fire at attacking forces, while others look for medical help. A doctor arrives, forced at gun point. The wounded boy's mother also comes. She is a female Uncle Tom who berates the Brothers and their cause. She tries to get Johnny to leave. She is hysterical. The whole idea of Black people fighting white people is totally outside of her orientation. Johnny begins a vicious attack on his mother, accusing her of emasculating his father—a recurring theme in the sociology of the Black community. In Afro-American literature of previous decades the strong Black mother was the object of awe and respect. But in the new literature her status is ambivalent and laced with tension. Historically, Afro-American women have had to be the economic mainstays of the family. The oppressor allowed them to have jobs while at the same time limiting the economic mobility of the Black man. Very often, therefore, the woman's aspirations and values are closely tied to those of the white power structure and not to those of her man. Since he cannot provide for his family the way white men do, she despises his weakness, tearing into him at every opportunity until, very often, there is nothing left but a shell.

The only way out of this dilemma is through revolution. It either must be an actual blood revolution, or one that psychically redirects the energy of the oppressed. Milner is fundamentally concerned with the latter and Garrett with the former. Communication between Johnny and his mother breaks down. The revolutionary imperative demands that men step outside the legal framework. It is a question of erecting *another* morality. The old constructs do not hold up, because adhering to them means consigning oneself to the oppressive reality. Johnny's mother is involved in the old constructs. Manliness is equated with white morality. And even though she claims to love her family (her men), the overall design of her ideas are against black manhood. In Garrett's play the mother's morality manifests itself in a deep-seated hatred of Black men; while in Milner's work the mother understands, but holds her men back.

The mothers that Garrett and Milner see represent the Old Spirituality—the Faith of the Fathers of which DuBois spoke. Johnny and Tim represent the New Spirituality. They appear to be a type produced by the upheavals of the colonial world of which Black America is a part. Johnny's assertion that he is a criminal is remarkably similar to the rebel's comments in Aimé Césaire's play, *Les Armes Miraculeuses* (*The Miraculous Weapons*). In that play the rebel, speaking to his mother, proclaims: "My name—an offense; my Christian name—humiliation; my status—a rebel; my age—the stone age." To which the mother replies: "My race—the human race. My religion—brotherhood." The Old Spirituality is

generalized. It seeks to recognize Universal Humanity. The New Spirituality is specific. It begins by seeing the world from the concise point-of-view of the colonialized. Where the Old Spirituality would live with oppression while ascribing to the oppressors an innate goodness, the New Spirituality demands a radical shift in point-of-view. The colonialized native, the oppressed must, of necessity, subscribe to a *separate* morality. One that will liberate him and his people.

The assault against the Old Spirituality can sometimes be humorous. In Ben Caldwell's play, *The Militant Preacher,* a burglar is seen slipping into the home of a wealthy minister. The preacher comes in and the burglar ducks behind a large chair. The preacher, acting out the role of the supplicant minister begins to moan, praying to De Lawd for understanding.

In the context of today's politics, the minister is an Uncle Tom, mouthing platitudes against self-defense. The preacher drones in a self-pitying monologue about the folly of protecting oneself against brutal policemen. Then the burglar begins to speak. The preacher is startled, taking the burglar's voice for the voice of God. The burglar begins to play on the preacher's old time religion. He *becomes* the voice of God insulting and goading the preacher on until the preacher's attitudes about protective violence change. The next day the preacher emerges militant, gun in hand, sounding like Reverend Cleage in Detroit. He now preaches a new gospel—the gospel of the gun, an eye for an eye. The gospel is preached in the rhythmic cadences of the old Black church. But the content is radical. Just as Jones inverted the symbols in *Jello,* Caldwell twists the rhythms of the Uncle Tom preacher into the language of the new militancy.

These plays are directed at problems within Black America. They begin with the premise that there is a well defined Afro-American audience. An audience that must see itself and the world in terms of its own interests. These plays, along with many others, constitute the basis for a viable movement in the theatre—a movement which takes as its task a profound reevaluation of the Black man's presence in America. The Black Arts Movement represents the flowering of a cultural nationalism that has been suppressed since the 1920s. I mean the "Harlem Renaissance"—which was essentially a failure. It did not address itself to the mythology and the lifestyles of the Black community. It failed to take roots, to link itself concretely to the struggles of that community, to become its voice and spirit. Implicit in the Black Arts Movement is the idea that Black people, however dispersed, constitute a *nation* within the belly of white America. This is not a new idea. Garvey said it and the Honorable Elijah Muhammad says it now. And it is on this idea that the concept of Black Power is predicated.

Afro-American life and history is full of creative possibilities, and the movement is just beginning to perceive them. Just beginning to understand that the most meaningful statements about the nature of Western society must come from the Third World of which Black America is a part. The thematic material is broad, ranging from folk heroes like Shine and Stagolee to historical figures like Marcus Garvey and Malcolm X. And then there is the struggle for Black survival, the coming confrontation between white America and Black America. If art is the harbinger of future possibilities, what does the future of Black America portend?

Essay/Discussion Questions

1. What was the connection between the Black Arts Movement and the Black Power Movement of the late 1960s and 1970s?

2. What was the purpose of the Black Arts Movement? To what extent does contemporary African American popular culture—for example, rap music, urban black films, or black theatre—reflect contributions of the Black Arts Movement?

3. According to Neal, what is the black aesthetic?

Unspeakable Things Unspoken: The Afro-American Presence in American Literature (1990)

Toni Morrison

I planned to call this paper "Canon Fodder," because the terms put me in mind of a kind of trained muscular response that appears to be on display in some areas of the recent canon debate. But I changed my mind (so many have used the phrase) and hope to make clear the appropriateness of the title I settled on.

My purpose here is to observe the panoply of this most recent and most anxious series of questions concerning what should or does constitute a literary canon in order to suggest ways of addressing the Afro-American presence in American literature that require neither slaughter nor reification—views that may spring the whole literature of an entire nation from the solitude into which it has been locked. There is something called American literature that, according to conventional wisdom, is certainly not Chicano literature, or Afro-American literature, or Asian-American, or Native American, or . . . It is somehow separate from them and they from it, and in spite of the efforts of recent literary histories, restructured curricula and anthologies, this

separate confinement, be it breached or endorsed, is the subject of a large part of these debates. Although the terms used, like the vocabulary of earlier canon debates, refer to literary and/or humanistic value, aesthetic criteria, value-free or socially anchored readings, the contemporary battle plain is most often understood to be the claims of others against the whitemale origins and definitions of those values; whether those definitions reflect an eternal, universal and transcending paradigm or whether they constitute a disguise for a temporal, political and culturally specific program.

Part of the history of this particular debate is located in the successful assault that the feminist scholarship of men and women (black and white) made and continues to make on traditional literary discourse. The male part of the whitemale equation is already deeply engaged, and no one believes the body of literature and its criticism will ever again be what it

This essay first appeared in *Michigan Quarterly Review* (Winter 1989), 1–34.

was in 1965: the protected preserve of the thoughts and words and analytical strategies of whitemen.

It is, however, the "white" part of the question that this paper focuses on, and it is to my great relief that such terms as "white" and "race" can enter serious discussion of literature. Although still a swift and swiftly obeyed call to arms, their use is no longer forbidden.[1] It may appear churlish to doubt the sincerity, or question the proclaimed well-intentioned self-lessness of a nine-hundred-year-old academy struggling through decades of chaos to "maintain standards." Yet of what use is it to go on about "quality" being the only criterion for greatness knowing that the definition of quality is itself the subject of much rage and is seldom universally agreed upon by everyone at all times? Is it to appropriate the term for reasons of state; to be in the position to distribute greatness or withhold it? Or to actively pursue the ways and places in which quality surfaces and stuns us into silence or into language worthy enough to describe it? What is possible is to try to recognize, identify and applaud the fight for and triumph of quality when it is revealed to us and to let go the notion that only the dominant culture or gender can make those judgments, identify that quality or produce it.

Those who claim the superiority of Western culture are entitled to that claim only when Western civilization is measured thoroughly against other civilizations and not found wanting, and when Western civilization owns up to its own sources in the cultures that preceded it.

A large part of the satisfaction I have always received from reading Greek tragedy, for example, is in its similarity to Afro-American communal structures (the function of song and chorus, the heroic struggle between the claims of community and individual hubris) and African religion and philosophy. In other words, that is part of the reason it has quality for me—I feel intellectually at home there. But that could hardly be so for those unfamiliar with my "home," and hardly a requisite for the pleasure they take. The point is, the form (Greek tragedy) makes available these varieties of provocative love because it is masterly—not because the civilization that is its referent was flawless or superior to all others.

One has the feeling that nights are becoming sleepless in some quarters, and it seems to me obvious that the recoil of traditional "humanists" and some postmodern theorists to this particular aspect of the debate, the "race" aspect, is as severe as it is because the claims for attention come from that segment of scholarly and artistic labor in which the mention of "race" is either inevitable or elaborately, painstakingly masked; and if all of the ramifications that the term demands are taken seriously, the bases of Western civilization will require rethinking. Thus, in spite of its implicit and explicit acknowledgement, "race" is still a virtually unspeakable thing, as can be seen in the apologies, notes of "special use" and circumscribed definitions that accompany it[2]—not least of which is my own deference in surrounding it with quotation marks. Suddenly (for our purposes, suddenly) "race" does not exist. For three hundred years black Americans insisted that "race" was no usefully distinguishing factor in human relationships. During those same three centuries every academic discipline, including theology, history, and natural science, insisted "race" was *the* determining factor in human development. When blacks discovered they had shaped or become a culturally formed race, and that it had specific and revered difference, suddenly they were told there is no such thing as "race," biological or cultural, that matters and that genuinely intellectual exchange cannot accommodate it.[3] In trying to come to some terms about "race" and writing, I am tempted to throw my hands up. It always seemed to me that the people who invented the hierarchy of "race" when it was convenient for them ought not to be the ones to explain it away, now that it does not suit their purposes for it to exist. But there is culture and both gender and "race" inform and are informed by it. Afro-American culture exists and though it is clear (and becoming clearer) how it has responded to Western culture, the instances where and means by which it has shaped Western culture are poorly recognized or understood.

I want to address ways in which the presence of Afro-American literature and the awareness of its culture both resuscitate the study of literature in the United States and raise that study's standards. In pursuit of that goal, it will suit my purposes to contextualize the route canon debates have taken in Western literary criticism.

I do not believe this current anxiety can be attributed solely to the routine, even cyclical arguments within literary communities reflecting unpredictable yet inevitable shifts in taste, relevance or perception. Shifts in which an enthusiasm for and official endorsement of William Dean Howells, for example, withered; or in which the legalization of Mark Twain in critical court rose and fell like the fathoming of a sounding line (for which he may or may not have named himself); or even the slow, delayed but steady swell of attention and devotion on which Emily Dickinson soared to what is now, surely, a permanent crest of respect. No. Those were discoveries, reappraisals of individual artists. Serious but not destabilizing. Such accommodations were simple because the questions they posed were simple: Are there one hundred sterling examples of high literary art in American literature and no more? One hundred and six? If one or two fall into disrepute, is there space, then, for one or two others in the vestibule, waiting like girls for bells chimed by future husbands who alone can promise them security, legitimacy—and in whose hands alone rests the gift of critical longevity? Interesting questions, but, as I say, not endangering.

Nor is this detectable academic sleeplessness the consequence of a much more radical shift, such as the mid-nineteenth century one heralding the authenticity of American literature itself. Or an even earlier upheaval—receding now into the distant past—in which theology and thereby Latin, was displaced for the equally rigorous study of the classics and Greek to be followed by what was considered a strangely arrogant and upstart proposal that English literature was a suitable course of study for an aristocratic education, and not simply morally instructive fodder designed for the working classes. (The Chaucer Society was founded in 1848, four hundred years after Chaucer died.) No. This exchange seems unusual somehow, keener. It has a more strenuously argued (and felt) defense and a more vigorously insistent attack. And both defenses and attacks have spilled out of the academy into the popular press. Why? Resistance to displacement within or expansion of a canon is not, after all, surprising or unwarranted. That's what canonization is for. (And the question of whether there should be a canon or not seems disingenuous to me—there always is one whether there should be or not—for it is in the interests of the professional critical community to have one.) Certainly a sharp alertness as to *why* a work is or is not worthy of study is the legitimate occupation of the critic, the pedagogue and the artist. What is astonishing in the contemporary debate is not the resistance to displacement of works or to the expansion of genre within it, but the virulent passion that accompanies this resistance and, more importantly, the quality of its defense weaponry. The guns are very big, the trigger-fingers quick. But I am convinced the mechanism of the defenders of the flame is faulty. Not only may the hands of the gun-slinging cowboy-scholars be blown off, not only may the target be missed, but the subject of the conflagration (the sacred texts) is sacrificed, disfigured in the battle. This canon fodder may kill the canon. And I, at least, do not intend to live without Aeschylus or William Shakespeare, or James or Twain or Hawthorne, or Melville, etc., etc., etc. There must be some way to enhance canon readings without enshrining them.

When Milan Kundera, in *The Art of the Novel*, identified the historical territory of the novel by saying "The novel is Europe's creation" and that "The only context for grasping a novel's worth is the history of the European novel," the *New Yorker* reviewer stiffened. Kundera's "personal 'idea of the novel,'" he wrote,

> is so profoundly Eurocentric that it's likely to seem exotic, even perverse, to American readers. . . . *The Art of the Novel* gives off the occasional (but pungent) whiff of cultural arrogance, and we may feel that Kundera's discourse . . . reveals an aspect of his character that we'd rather not have known about. . . . In order to become the artist he now is, the Czech novelist had to discover himself a second time, as a European. But what if that second, grander possibility hadn't been there to be discovered? What if Broch, Kafka, Musil—all that reading—had never been a part of his education, or had entered it only as exotic, alien presence? Kundera's polemical fervor in *The Art of the Novel* annoys us, as American readers, because we feel defensive, excluded from the transcendent 'idea of the novel' that for him seems simply to have been there for the taking. (If only he had cited, in his redeeming version of the novel's history, a few more heroes from the New World's culture.) Our novelists don't discover cultural values within themselves; they invent them.[4]

Kundera's views, obliterating American writers (with the exception of William Faulkner) from his own canon, are relegated to a "smugness" that Terrence Rafferty disassociates from Kundera's imaginative work and applies to the "sublime confidence" of his critical prose. The confidence of an exile who has the sentimental education of, and the choice to become, a European.

I was refreshed by Rafferty's comments. With the substitution of certain phrases, his observations and the justifiable umbrage he takes

can be appropriated entirely by Afro-American writers regarding their own exclusion from the "transcendent 'idea of the novel.'"

For the present turbulence seems not to be about the flexibility of a canon, its range among and between Western countries, but about its miscegenation. The word is informative here and I do mean its use. A powerful ingredient in this debate concerns the incursion of third-world or so-called minority literature into a Eurocentric stronghold. When the topic of third world culture is raised, unlike the topic of Scandinavian culture, for example, a possible threat to and implicit criticism of the reigning equilibrium is seen to be raised as well. From the seventeenth century to the twentieth, the arguments resisting that incursion have marched in predictable sequence: (1) there is no Afro-American (or third world) art. (2) it exists but is inferior. (3) it exists and is superior when it measures up to the "universal" criteria of Western art. (4) it is not so much "art" as ore—rich ore—that requires a Western or Eurocentric smith to refine it from its "natural" state into an aesthetically complex form.

A few comments on a larger, older, but no less telling academic struggle—an extremely successful one—may be helpful here. It is telling because it sheds light on certain aspects of this current debate and may locate its sources. I made reference above to the radical upheaval in canon-building that took place at the inauguration of classical studies and Greek. This canonical rerouting from scholasticism to humanism, was not merely radical, it must have been (may I say it?) savage. And it took some seventy years to accomplish. Seventy years to eliminate Egypt as the cradle of civilization *and* its model and replace it with Greece. The triumph of that process was that Greece lost its own origins and became itself original. A number of scholars in various disciplines (history, anthropology, ethnobotany, etc.) have put forward their research into cross-cultural and intercultural transmissions with varying degrees of success in the reception of their work. I am reminded of the curious publishing history of Ivan van Sertima's work, *They Came Before Columbus,* which researches the African presence in Ancient America. I am reminded of Edward Said's *Orientalism,* and especially the work of Martin Bernal, a linguist, trained in Chinese history, who has defined himself as an interloper in the field of classical civilization but who has offered, in *Black Athena,* a stunning investigation of the field. According to Bernal, there are two "models" of Greek history: one views Greece as Aryan or European (the Aryan Model); the other sees it as Levantine—absorbed by Egyptian and Semitic culture (the Ancient Model). "If I am right," writes Professor Bernal, "in urging the overthrow of the Aryan Model and its replacement by the Revised Ancient one, it will be necessary not only to rethink the fundamental bases of 'Western Civilization' but also to recognize the penetration of racism and 'continental chauvinism' into all our historiography, or philosophy of writing history. The Ancient Model had no major 'internal' deficiencies or weaknesses in explanatory power. It was overthrown for external reasons. For eighteenth and nineteenth century Romantics and racists it was simply intolerable for Greece, which was seen not merely as the epitome of Europe but also as its pure childhood, to have been the result of the mixture of native Europeans and *colonizing* Africans and Semites. Therefore the Ancient Model had to be overthrown and replaced by something more acceptable."[5]

It is difficult not to be persuaded by the weight of documentation Martin Bernal brings to his task and his rather dazzling analytical insights. What struck me in his analysis were the *process* of the fabrication of Ancient Greece and the *motives* for the fabrication. The latter (motive) involved the concept of purity, of progress. The former (process) required misreading, predetermined selectivity of authentic sources, and—silence. From the Christian theological appropriation of Israel (the Levant),

to the early nineteenth-century work of the prodigious Karl Müller, work that effectively dismissed the Greeks' own record of their influences and origins as their "Egyptomania," their tendency to be "wonderstruck" by Egyptian culture, a tendency "manifested in the 'delusion' that Egyptians and other non-European 'barbarians' had possessed superior cultures, from which the Greeks had borrowed massively,"[6] on through the Romantic response to the Enlightenment, and the decline into disfavor of the Phoenicians, "the essential force behind the rejection of the tradition of massive Phoenician influence on early Greece was the rise of racial—as opposed to religious—anti-semitism. This was because the Phoenicians were correctly perceived to have been culturally very close to the Jews."[7]

I have quoted at perhaps too great a length from Bernal's text because *motive,* so seldom an element brought to bear on the history of history, is located, delineated and confronted in Bernal's research, and has helped my own thinking about the process and motives of scholarly attention to and an appraisal of Afro-American presence in the literature of the United States.

Canon building is Empire building. Canon defense is national defense. Canon debate, whatever the terrain, nature and range (of criticism, of history, of the history of knowledge, of the definition of language, the universality of aesthetic principles, the sociology of art, the humanistic imagination), is the clash of cultures. And *all* of the interests are vested.

In such a melee as this one—a provocative, healthy, explosive melee—extraordinarily profound work is being done. Some of the controversy, however, has degenerated into *ad hominem* and unwarranted speculation on the personal habits of artists, specious and silly arguments about politics (the destabilizing forces are dismissed as merely political; the status quo sees itself as not—as though the term "*a*political" were only its prefix and not the most obviously political stance imaginable since one of the functions of political ideology is to pass itself off as immutable, natural and "innocent"), and covert expressions of critical inquiry designed to neutralize and disguise the political interests of the discourse. Yet much of the research and analysis has rendered speakable what was formerly unspoken and has made humanistic studies, once again, the place where one has to go to find out what's going on. Cultures, whether silenced or monologistic, whether repressed or repressing, seek meaning in the language and images available to them.

Silences are being broken, lost things have been found and at least two generations of scholars are disentangling received knowledge from the apparatus of control, most notably those who are engaged in investigations of French and British Colonialist Literature, American slave narratives, and the delineation of the Afro-American literary tradition.

Now that Afro-American artistic presence has been "discovered" actually to exist, now that serious scholarship has moved from silencing the witnesses and erasing their meaningful place in and contribution to American culture, it is no longer acceptable merely to imagine us and imagine for us. We have always been imagining ourselves. We are not Isak Dinesen's "aspects of nature," nor Conrad's unspeaking. We are the subjects of our own narrative, witnesses to and participants in our own experience, and, in no way coincidentally, in the experience of those with whom we have come in contact. We are not, in fact, "other." We are choices. And to read imaginative literature by and about us is to choose to examine centers of the self and to have the opportunity to compare these centers with the "raceless" one with which we are, all of us, most familiar.

II

Recent approaches to the reading of Afro-American literature have come some distance;

have addressed those arguments, mentioned earlier (which are not arguments, but attitudes), that have, since the seventeenth century, effectively silenced the autonomy of that literature. As for the charge that "there is no Afro-American art," contemporary critical analysis of the literature and the recent surge of reprints and rediscoveries have buried it, and are pressing on to expand the traditional canon to include classic Afro-American works where generically and chronologically appropriate, and to devise strategies for reading and thinking about these texts.

As to the second silencing charge, "Afro-American art exists, but is inferior," again, close readings and careful research into the culture out of which the art is born have addressed and still address the labels that once passed for stringent analysis but can no more: that it is imitative, excessive, sensational, mimetic (merely), and unintellectual, though very often "moving," "passionate," "naturalistic," "realistic" or sociologically "revealing." These labels may be construed as compliments or pejoratives and if valid, and shown as such, so much the better. More often than not, however, they are the lazy, easy brand-name applications when the hard work of analysis is deemed too hard, or when the critic does not have access to the scope the work demands. Strategies designed to counter this lazy labeling include the application of recent literary theories to Afro-American literature so that noncanonical texts can be incorporated into existing and forming critical discourse.

The third charge, that "Afro-American art exists, but is superior only when it measures up to the 'universal' criteria of Western art," produces the most seductive form of analysis, for both writer and critic, because comparisons are a major form of knowledge and flattery. The risks, nevertheless, are twofold: (1) the gathering of a culture's difference into the skirts of the Queen is a neutralization designed and constituted to elevate and maintain hegemony. (2) circumscribing and limiting the literature to a mere reaction to or denial of the Queen, judging the work solely in terms of its referents to Eurocentric criteria, or its sociological accuracy, political correctness or its pretense of having no politics at all, cripple the literature and infantilize the serious work of imaginative writing. This response-oriented concept of Afro-American literature contains the seeds of the next (fourth) charge: that when Afro-American art is worthy, it is because it is "raw" and "rich," like ore, and like ore needs refining by Western intelligences. Finding or imposing Western influences in/on Afro-American literature has value, but when its sole purpose is to *place* value only where that influence is located it is pernicious.

My unease stems from the possible, probable, consequences these approaches may have upon the work itself. They can lead to an incipient orphanization of the work in order to issue its adoption papers. They can confine the discourse to the advocacy of diversification within the canon and/or a kind of benign coexistence near or within reach of the already sacred texts. Either of these two positions can quickly become another kind of silencing if permitted to ignore the indigenous created qualities of the writing. So many questions surface and irritate. What have these critiques made of the work's own canvas? Its paint, its frame, its framelessness, its spaces? Another list of approved subjects? Of approved treatments? More self-censoring, more exclusion of the specificity of the culture, the gender, the language? Is there perhaps an alternative utility in these studies? To advance power or locate its fissures? To oppose elitist interests in order to enthrone egalitarian effacement? Or is it merely to rank and grade the readable product as distinct from the writeable production? Can this criticism reveal ways in which the author combats and confronts received prejudices and even creates *other terms* in which to rethink one's attachment to or intolerance of the material of these works? What is important in all of this is that the critic not be engaged in laying claim on behalf of the text to his or her own dominance and power. Nor to exchange his or her professional anxieties for the imagined turbulence of the text. "The text should become a problem of passion, not a pretext for it."

There are at least three focuses that seem to me to be neither reactionary nor simple pluralism, nor the even simpler methods by which the study of Afro-American literature remains the helpful doorman into the halls of sociology. Each of them, however, requires wakefulness.

One is the development of a theory of literature that truly accommodates Afro-American literature: one that is based on its culture, its history, and the artistic strategies the works employ to negotiate the world it inhabits.

Another is the examination and reinterpretation of the American canon, the founding nineteenth-century works, for the "unspeakable things unspoken"; for the ways in which the presence of Afro-Americans has shaped the choices, the language, the structure—the meaning of so much American literature. A search, in other words, for the ghost in the machine.

A third is the examination of contemporary and/or noncanonical literature for this presence, regardless of its category as mainstream, minority, or what you will. I am always amazed by the resonances, the structural gearshifts, and the *uses* to which Afro-American narrative, persona and idiom are put in contemporary "white" literature. And in Afro-American literature itself the question of difference, of essence, is critical. What makes a work "Black"? The most valuable point of entry into the question of cultural (or racial) distinction, the one most fraught, is its language—its unpoliced, seditious, confrontational, manipulative, inventive, disruptive, masked and unmasking language. Such a penetration will entail the most careful study, one in which the impact of Afro-American presence on modernity becomes clear and is no longer a well-kept secret.

I would like to touch, for just a moment, on focuses two and three.

We can agree, I think, that invisible things are not necessarily "not there"; that a void may be empty, but is not a vacuum. In addition, certain absences are so stressed, so ornate, so planned, they call attention to themselves; arrest us with intentionality and purpose, like neighborhoods that are defined by the population held away from them. Looking at the scope of American literature, I can't help thinking that the question should never have been "Why am I, an Afro-American, absent from it?" It is not a particularly interesting query anyway. The spectacularly interesting question is "What intellectual feats had to be performed by the author or his critic to erase me from a society seething with my presence, and what effect has that performance had on the work?" What are the strategies of escape from knowledge? Of willful oblivion? I am not recommending an inquiry into the obvious impulse that overtakes a soldier sitting in a World War I trench to think of salmon fishing. That kind of pointed "turning from," deliberate escapism or transcendence may be lifesaving in a circumstance of immediate duress. The exploration I am suggesting is, how does one sit in the audience observing, watching the performance of Young America, say, in the nineteenth century, say, and reconstruct the play, its director, its plot and its cast in such a manner that its very point never surfaces? Not why. How? Ten years after Tocqueville's prediction in 1840 that "'Finding no stuff for the ideal in what is real and true, poets would flee to imaginary regions . . .' in 1850 at the height of slavery and burgeoning abolitionism, American writers chose romance."[8] Where, I wonder, in these romances is the shadow of the presence from which the text has fled? Where does it heighten, where does it dislocate, where does it necessitate novelistic invention; what does it release; what does it hobble?

The device (or arsenal) that serves the purpose of flight can be Romanticism versus verisimilitude; new criticism versus shabbily disguised and questionably sanctioned "moral uplift"; the "complex series of evasions," that is sometimes believed to be the essence of modernism; the perception of the evolution of art; the cultivation of irony, parody; the nostalgia for "literary language"; the rhetorically unconstrained textuality versus socially anchored textuality, and the undoing of textuality altogether. These critical strategies can (but need not) be put into service to reconstruct the historical world to suit specific cultural and political purposes. Many of these strategies have produced powerfully creative work. Whatever *uses* to which Romanticism is put, however suspicious its origins, it has produced an incontestably wonderful body of work. In other instances these strategies have succeeded in paralyzing both the work and its criticism. In still others they have led to a virtual infantilization of the writer's intellect, his sensibility, his craft. They have reduced the meditations on theory into a "power struggle among sects" reading unauthored and unauthorable material, rather than an outcome of reading *with* the author the text both construct.

In other words, the critical process has made wonderful work of some wonderful work, and recently the means of access to the old debates have altered. The problem now is putting the question. Is the nineteenth century flight from blackness, for example, successful in mainstream American literature? Beautiful? Artistically problematic? Is the text sabotaged by its own proclamations of "universality"? Are there ghosts in the machine? Active but unsummoned presences that can distort the workings of the machine and can also *make* it work? These kinds of questions have been consistently put by critics of Colonial Literature vis-à-vis Africa and India and other third world countries. American literature would benefit from similar critiques. I am made melancholy when I consider that the act of defending the Eurocentric Western posture in literature as not only "universal" but also "race-free" may have resulted in lobotomizing that literature and in diminishing both the art and the artist. Like the surgical removal of legs so that the body can remain enthroned, immobile, static—under house arrest, so to speak. It may be, of course, that contemporary writers deliberately exclude from their conscious writerly world the subjective appraisal of groups perceived as "other," and whitemale writers frequently abjure and deny the excitement of framing or locating their literature in the political world. Nineteenth-century writers, however, would never have given it a thought. Mainstream writers in Young America understood their competition to be national, cultural, but only in relationship to the Old World, certainly not vis-à-vis an ancient race (whether Native American or African) that was stripped of articulateness and intellectual thought, rendered, in D. H. Lawrence's term, "uncreate." For these early American writers, how could there be competition with nations or peoples who were presumed unable to handle or uninterested in handling the written word? One could write about them, but there was never the danger of their "writing back." Just as one could speak to them without fear of their "talking back." One could even observe them, hold them in prolonged gaze, without encountering the risk of being observed, viewed, or judged in return. And if, on occasion, they were themselves viewed and judged, it was out of a political necessity and, for the purposes of art, could not matter. Or so thought Young America. It could never have occurred to Edgar Allan Poe in 1848 that I, for example, might read *The Gold Bug* and watch his efforts to render my grandfather's speech to something as close to braying as possible, an effort so intense you can see the perspiration—and the stupidity—when Jupiter says "I knows," and Mr. Poe spells the verb "nose."*

Yet in spite or because of this monologism there is a great, ornamental, prescribed absence in early American literature and, I sub-

mit, it is instructive. It only seems that the canon of American literature is "naturally" or "inevitably" "white." In fact it is studiously so. In fact these absences of vital presences in Young American literature may be the insistent fruit of the scholarship rather than the text. Perhaps some of these writers, although under current house arrest, have much more to say than has been realized. Perhaps some were not so much transcending politics, or escaping blackness, as they were transforming it into intelligible, accessible, yet artistic modes of discourse. To ignore this possibility by never questioning the strategies of transformation is to disenfranchise the writer, diminish the text and render the bulk of the literature aesthetically and historically incoherent—an exorbitant price for cultural (whitemale) purity, and, I believe a spendthrift one. The reexamination of founding literature of the United States for the unspeakable unspoken may reveal those texts to have deeper and other meanings, deeper and the power, deeper and other significances.

One such writer, in particular, it has been almost impossible to keep under lock and key is Herman Melville.

Among several astute scholars, Michael Rogin has done one of the most exhaustive studies of how deeply Melville's social thought is woven into his writing. He calls our attention to the connection Melville made between American slavery and American freedom, how heightened the one rendered the other. And he has provided evidence of the impact on the work of Melville's family, milieu, and, most importantly, the raging, all-encompassing conflict of the time: slavery. He has reminded us that it was Melville's father-in-law who had, as judge, decided the case that made the Fugitive Slave Law law, and that "other evidence in *Moby Dick* also suggests the impact of Shaw's ruling on the climax of Melville's tale. Melville conceived the final confrontation between Ahab and the white whale some time in the first half of 1851. He may well have written his last chapters only after returning from a trip to New York in June. [Judge Shaw's decision was handed down in April, 1851]. When New York antislavery leaders William Seward and John van Buren wrote public letters protesting the *Sims* ruling, the New York *Herald* responded. Its attack on "The Anti-Slavery Agitators" began: "Did you ever see a whale? Did you ever see a mighty whale struggling?"[9]

Rogin also traces the chronology of the whale from its "birth in a state of nature" to its final end as commodity.[10] Central to his argument is that Melville in *Moby Dick* was being allegorically and insistently political in his choice of the whale. But within his chronology, one singular whale transcends all others, goes beyond nature, adventure, politics and commodity to an abstraction. What is this abstraction? This "wicked idea"? Interpretation has been varied. It has been viewed as an allegory of the state in which Ahab is Calhoun, or Daniel Webster; an allegory of capitalism and corruption, God and man, the individual and fate, and most commonly, the single allegorical meaning of the white whale is understood to be brute, indifferent Nature, and Ahab the madman who challenges that Nature.

But let us consider, again, the principal actor, Ahab, created by an author who calls himself Typee, signed himself Tawney, identified himself as Ishmael, and who had written several books before *Moby Dick* criticizing missionary forays into various paradises.

Ahab loses sight of the commercial value of his ship's voyage, its point, and pursues an idea in order to destroy it. His intention, revenge, "an audacious, immitigable and supernatural revenge," develops stature—maturity—when we realize that he is not a man mourning his lost leg or a scar on his face. However intense and dislocating his fever and recovery had been after his encounter with the white whale, however satisfactorily "male" this vengeance is read, the vanity of it is almost adolescent. But if the whale is more than blind, indifferent Nature unsubduable by masculine aggression,

if it is as much its adjective as it is its noun, we can consider the possibility that Melville's "truth" was his recognition of the moment in America when whiteness became ideology. And if the white whale is the ideology of race, what Ahab has lost to it is personal dismemberment and family and society and his own place as a human in the world. The trauma of racism is, for the racist and the victim, the severe fragmentation of the self, and has always seemed to me a cause (not a symptom) of psychosis—strangely of no interest to psychiatry. Ahab, then, is navigating between an idea of civilization that he renounces and an idea of savagery he must annihilate, because the two cannot coexist. The former is based on the latter. What is terrible in its complexity is that the idea of savagery is not the missionary one: it is white racial ideology that is savage and if, indeed, a white, nineteenth-century, American male took on not abolition, not the amelioration of racist institutions or their laws, but the very concept of whiteness as an inhuman idea, he would be very alone, very desperate. and very doomed. Madness would be the only appropriate description of such audacity, and "he heaves me," the most succinct and appropriate description of that obsession.

I would not like to be understood to argue that Melville was engaged in some simple and simple-minded black/white didacticism, or that he was satanizing white people. Nothing like that. What I am suggesting is that he was overwhelmed by the philosophical and metaphysical inconsistencies of an extraordinary and unprecedented idea that had its fullest manifestation in his own time in his own country, and that that idea was the successful assertion of whiteness as ideology.

On the *Pequod* the multiracial, mainly foreign, proletariat is at work to produce a commodity, but it is diverted and converted from that labor to Ahab's more significant intellectual quest. We leave whale as commerce and confront whale as metaphor. With that interpretation in place, two of the most famous chapters of the book become luminous in a completely new way. One is Chapter 9, The Sermon. In Father Mapple's thrilling rendition of Jonah's trials, emphasis is given to the purpose of Jonah's salvation. He is saved from the fish's belly for one single purpose, "To preach the Truth to the face of Falsehood! That was it!" Only then the reward "Delight"—which strongly calls to mind Ahab's lonely necessity. "Delight is to him . . . who against the proud gods and commodores of this earth, ever stand forth his own inexorable self. . . . Delight is to him whose strong arms yet support him, when the ship of this base treacherous world has gone down beneath him. Delight is to him who gives no quarter in the truth and kills, burns, and destroys all *sin* though he pluck it out from under the robes of Senators and Judges. Delight—top-gallant delight is to him who acknowledges no law or lord, but the Lord his God, and is only a *patriot to heaven*" [italics mine]. No one, I think, has denied that the sermon is designed to be prophetic, but it seems unremarked what the nature of the sin is—the sin that must be destroyed, regardless. Nature? A sin? The terms do not apply. Capitalism? Perhaps. Capitalism fed greed, lent itself inexorably to corruption, but probably was not in and of itself sinful to Melville. Sin suggests a moral outrage within the bounds of man to repair. The concept of racial superiority would fit seamlessly. It is difficult to read those words ("destruction of sin," "patriot to heaven") and not hear in them the description of a different Ahab. Not an adolescent male in adult clothing, a maniacal egocentric, or the "exotic plant" that V. S. Parrington thought Melville was. Not even a morally fine liberal voice adjusting, balancing, compromising with racial institutions. But another Ahab: the only white male American heroic enough to try to slay the monster that was devouring the world as he knew it.

Another chapter that seems freshly lit by this reading is Chapter 42, The Whiteness of the Whale. Melville points to the do-or-die significance of his effort to say something unsayable in this chapter. "I almost despair," he writes, "of putting it in a comprehensive form. It was the whiteness of the whale that above all things appalled me. But how can I hope to explain myself here; and yet in some dim, random way, explain myself I must, *else all these chapters might be naught*" [italics mine]. The language of this chapter ranges between benevolent, beautiful images of whiteness and whiteness as sinister and shocking. After dissecting the ineffable, he concludes: "Therefore . . . symbolize whatever grand or gracious he will by whiteness, no man can deny that in its profoundest *idealized significance* it calls up a peculiar apparition to the soul." I stress "idealized significance" to emphasize and make clear (if such clarity needs stating) that Melville is not exploring white *people*, but whiteness idealized. Then, after informing the reader of his "hope to light upon some chance clue to conduct us to the hidden course we seek," he tries to nail it. To provide the key to the "hidden course." His struggle to do so is gigantic. He cannot. Nor can we. But in nonfigurative language, he identifies the imaginative tools needed to solve the problem: "subtlety appeals to subtlety, and without imagination no man can follow another into these halls." And his final observation reverberates with personal trauma. "This visible [colored] world seems formed in love, the invisible [white] spheres were formed in fright." The necessity for whiteness as privileged "natural" state, the invention of it, was indeed formed in fright.

"Slavery," writes Rogin, "confirmed Melville's isolation, decisively established in *Moby Dick,* from the dominant consciousness of his time." I differ on this point and submit that Melville's hostility and repugnance for slavery would have found company. There were many white Americans of his acquaintance who felt repelled by slavery, wrote journalism about it, spoke about it, legislated on it and were active in abolishing it. His attitude to slavery alone would not have condemned him to the almost autistic separation visited upon him. And if he felt convinced that blacks were worthy of being treated like whites, or that capitalism was dangerous—he had company or could have found it. But to question the very notion of white progress, the very idea of racial superiority, of whiteness as privileged place in the evolutionary ladder of humankind, and to meditate on the fraudulent, self-destroying philosophy of that superiority, to "pluck it out from under the robes of Senators and Judges," to drag the "judge himself to the bar,"—that was dangerous, solitary, radical work. Especially then. Especially now. To be "only a patriot to heaven" is no mean aspiration in Young America for a writer or the captain of a whaling ship.

A complex, heaving, disorderly, profound text is *Moby Dick,* and among its several meanings it seems to me this "unspeakable" one has remained the "hidden course," the "truth in the Face of Falsehood." To this day no novelist has so wrestled with its subject. To this day literary analyses of canonical texts have shied away from that perspective: the informing and determining Afro-American presence in traditional American literature. The chapters I have made reference to are only a fraction of the instances where the text surrenders such insights, and points a helpful finger toward the ways in which the ghost drives the machine.

Melville is not the only author whose works double their fascination and their power when scoured for this presence and the writerly strategies taken to address or deny it. Edgar Allan Poe will sustain such a reading. So will Nathaniel Hawthorne and Mark Twain; and in the twentieth century, Willa Cather, Ernest Hemingway, F. Scott Fitzgerald, and William Faulkner, to name a few. Canonical American literature is beggmg for such attention.

It seems to me a more than fruitful project to produce some cogent analysis showing instances where early American literature identifies itself, risks itself, to assert its antithesis to blackness. How its linguistic gestures

prove the intimate relationship to what is being nulled by implying a full descriptive apparatus (identity) to a presence-that-is-assumed-not-to-exist. Afro-American critical inquiry can do this work.

I mentioned earlier that finding or imposing Western influences in/on Afro-American literature had value provided the valued process does not become self-anointing. There is an adjacent project to be undertaken—the third focus in my list: the examination of contemporary literature (both the sacred and the profane) for the impact Afro-American presence has had on the structure of the work, the linguistic practice, and fictional enterprise in which it is engaged. Like focus two, this critical process must also eschew the pernicious goal of equating the fact of that presence with the achievement of the work. A work does not get better because it is responsive to another culture; nor does it become automatically flawed because of that responsiveness. The point is to clarify, not to enlist. And it does not "go without saying" that a work written by an Afro-American is automatically subsumed by an enforcing Afro-American presence. There is a clear flight from blackness in a great deal of Afro-American literature. In others there is the duel with blackness, and in some cases, as they say, "You'd never know."

III

It is on this area, the impact of Afro-American culture on contemporary American literature, that I now wish to comment. I have already said that works by Afro-Americans can respond to this presence (just as non-black works do) in a number of ways. The question of what constitutes the art of a black writer, for whom that modifier is more search than fact, has some urgency. In other words, other than melanin and subject matter, what, in fact, may make me a black writer? Other than my own ethnicity—what is going on in my work that makes me believe it is demonstrably inseparable from a cultural specificity that is Afro-American?

Please forgive the use of my own work in these observations. I use it not because it provides the best example, but because I know it best, know what I did and why, and know how central these queries are to me. Writing is, *after* all, an act of language, its practice. But *first* of all it is an effort of the will to discover.

Let me suggest some of the ways in which I activate language and ways in which that language activates me. I will limit this perusal by calling attention only to the first sentences of the books I've written, and hope that in exploring the choices I made, prior points are illuminated.

The Bluest Eye begins "Quiet as it's kept, there were no marigolds in the fall of 1941." That sentence, like the ones that open each succeeding book, is simple, uncomplicated. Of all the sentences that begin all the books, only two of them have dependent clauses: the other three are simple sentences and two are stripped down to virtually subject, verb, modifier. Nothing fancy here. No words need looking up; they are ordinary, everyday words. Yet I hoped the simplicity was not simple-minded, but devious, even loaded. And that the process of selecting each word, for itself and its relationship to the others in the sentence, along with the rejection of others for their echoes, for what is determined and what is not determined, what is almost there and what must be gleaned, would not theatricalize itself, would not erect a proscenium—at least not a noticeable one. So important to me was this unstaging, that in this first novel I summarized the whole of the book on the first page. (In the first edition, it was printed in its entirety on the jacket.)

The opening phrase of this sentence, "Quiet as it's kept," had several attractions for me. First, it was a familiar phrase familiar to me as a child listening to adults; to black women conversing with one another, telling a story, an anecdote, gossip about some one or event within the circle, the family, the neighborhood. The words are conspiratorial. "Shh, don't tell anyone else," and "No one is allowed to know this." It is a secret between us and a secret that is being kept from us. The conspiracy is both held and withheld, exposed and sustained. In some sense it was precisely what the act of writing the book was: the public exposure of a private confidence. In order fully to comprehend the duality of that position, one needs to think of the immediate political climate in which the writing took place, 1965–1969, during great social upheaval in the life of black people. The publication (as opposed to the writing) involved the exposure; the writing was the disclosure of secrets, secrets "we" shared and those withheld from us by ourselves and by the world outside the community.

"Quiet as it's kept," is also a figure of speech that is written, in this instance, but clearly chosen for how speakerly it is, how it speaks and bespeaks a particular world and its ambience. Further, in addition to its "back fence" connotation, its suggestion of illicit gossip, of thrilling revelation, there is also, in the "whisper," the assumption (on the part of the reader) that the teller is on the inside, knows something others do not, and is going to be generous with this privileged information. The intimacy I was aiming for, the intimacy between the reader and the page, could start up immediately because the secret is being shared, at best, and eavesdropped upon, at the last. Sudden familiarity or instant intimacy seemed crucial to me then, writing my first novel. I did not want the reader to have time to wonder "What do I have to do, to give up, in order to read this? What defense do I need, what distance maintain?" Because I know (and the racer does not—he or she has to wait for the second sentence) that this is a terrible story about things one would rather not know anything about.

What, then, is the Big Secret about to be shared? The thing we (reader and I) are "in" on? A botanical aberration. Pollution, perhaps.

A skip, perhaps, in the natural order of things: a September, an autumn, a fall without marigolds. Bright common, strong and sturdy marigolds. When? In 1941, and since that is a momentous year (the beginning of World War II for the United States), the "fall" of 1941, just before the declaration of war, has a "closet" innuendo. In the temperate zone where there is a season known as "fall" during which one expects marigolds to be at their peak, in the months before the beginning of U.S. participation in World War II something grim is about to be divulged. The next sentence will make it clear that the sayer, the one who knows, is a child speaking, mimicking the adult black women on the porch or in the back yard. The opening phrase is an effort to be grown-up about this shocking information. The point of view of a child alters the priority an adult would assign the information. "We thought it was because Pecola was having her father's baby that the marigolds did not grow" foregrounds the flowers, backgrounds illicit, traumatic, incomprehensible sex coming to its dreaded fruition. This foregrounding of "trivial" information and backgrounding of shocking knowledge secures the point of view but gives the reader pause about whether the voice of children can be trusted at all or is more trustworthy than an adult's. The reader is thereby protected from a confrontation too soon with the painful details, while simultaneously provoked into a desire to know them. The novelty, I thought, would be in having this story of female violation revealed from the vantage point of the victims or could-be victims of rape—the persons no one inquired of (certainly not in 1965)—the girls themselves. And since the victim does not have the vocabulary to understand the violence or its context, gullible, vulnerable girl friends, looking back as the knowing adults they pretended to be in the beginning, would have to do that for her, and would have to fill those silences with their own reflective lives. Thus, the opening provides the stroke that announces something more than a secret shared, but a silence broken, a void filled, an unspeakable thing spoken at last. And they draw the connection between a minor destabilization in seasonal flora with the insignificant destruction of a black girl. Of course "minor" and "insignificant" represent the outside world's view—for the girls both phenomena are earthshaking depositories of information they spend that whole year of childhood (and afterwards) trying to fathom, and cannot. If they have any success, it will be in transferring the problem of fathoming to the presumably adult reader, to the inner circle of listeners. At the least they have distributed the weight of these problematical questions to a larger constituency, and justified the public exposure of a privacy. If the conspiracy that the opening words announce is entered into by the reader, then the book can be seen to open with its close: a speculation on the disruption of "nature," as being a social disruption with tragic individual consequences in which the reader, as part of the population of the text, is implicated.

However, a problem, unsolved, lies in the central chamber of the novel. The shattered world I built (to complement what is happening to Pecola), its pieces held together by seasons in childtime and commenting at every turn on the incompatible and barren white-family primer, does not in its present form handle effectively the silence at its center. The void that is Pecola's "unbeing." It should have had a shape—like the emptiness left by a boom or a cry. It required a sophistication unavailable to me, and some deft manipulation of the voices around her. She is not *seen* by herself until she hallucinates a self. And the fact of her hallucination becomes a point of outside-the-book conversation, but does not work in the reading process.

Also, although I was pressing for a female expressiveness (a challenge that resurfaced in *Sula*), it eluded me for the most part, and I had to content myself with female personae because I was not able to secure throughout the work the feminine subtext that is present in the opening sentence (the women gossiping, eager and aghast in "Quiet as it's kept"). The shambles this struggle became is most evident in the section on Pauline Breedlove where I resorted to two voices, hers and the urging narrator's, both of which are extremely unsatisfactory to me. It is interesting to me now that where I thought I would have the most difficulty subverting the language to a feminine mode, I had the least: connecting Cholly's "rape" by the whitemen to his own of his daughter. This most masculine act of aggression becomes feminized in my language, "passive," and, I think, more accurately repellent when deprived of the male "glamor of shame" rape is (or once was) routinely given.

The points I have tried to illustrate are that my choices of language (speakerly, aural, colloquial), my reliance for full comprehension on codes embedded in black culture, my effort to effect immediate co-conspiracy and intimacy (without any distancing, explanatory fabric), as well as my (failed) attempt to shape a silence while breaking it are attempts (many unsatisfactory) to transfigure the complexity and wealth of Afro-American culture into a language worthy of the culture.

In *Sula,* it's necessary to concentrate on *two* first sentences because what survives in print is not the one I had intended to be the first. Originally the book opened with "Except for World War II nothing ever interfered with National Suicide Day." With some encouragement. I recognized that it was a false beginning. "*In medias res*" with a vengeance, because there was no *res* to be in the middle of—no implied world in which to locate the specificity and the resonances in the sentence. More to the point, I knew I was writing a second novel, and that it too would be about people in a black community not just foregrounded but totally dominant; and that it was about black women—also foregrounded and dominant. In 1988, certainly, I would not need (or feel the

need for) the sentence—the short section—that now opens *Sula.* The threshold between the reader and the black-topic text need not be the safe, welcoming lobby I persuaded myself it needed at that time. My preference was the demolition of the lobby altogether. As can be seen from *The Bluest Eye,* and in every other book I have written, only *Sula* has this "entrance." The others refuse the "presentation"; refuse the seductive safe harbor; the line of demarcation between the sacred and the obscene, public and private, them and us. Refuse, in effect, to cater to the diminished expectations of the reader, or his or her alarm heightened by the emotional luggage one carries into the black-topic text. (I should remind you that *Sula* was begun in 1969, while my first book was in proof, in a period of extraordinary political activity.)

Since I had become convinced that the effectiveness of the original beginning was only in my head, the job at hand became how to construct an alternate beginning that would not force the work to genuflect and would complement the outlaw quality in it. The problem presented itself this way: to fashion a door. Instead of having the text open wide the moment the cover is opened (or, as in *The Bluest Eye,* to have the book stand exposed before the cover is even touched, much less opened, by placing the complete "plot" on the first page—and finally on the cover of the first edition), here I was to posit a door, turn its knob and beckon for some four or five pages. I had determined not to mention any characters in those pages, there would be no people in the lobby—but I did, rather heavy-handedly in my view, end the welcome aboard with the mention of Shadrack and Sula. It was a craven (to me, still) surrender to a worn-out technique of novel writing: the overt announcement to the reader whom to pay attention to. Yet the bulk of the opening I finally wrote is about the community, a view of it, and the view is not from within (this is a door, after all) but from the point of view of a stranger—

the "valley man" who might happen to be there on some errand, but who obviously does not live there and to and for whom all this is mightily strange, even exotic. You can see why I despise much of this beginning. Yet I tried to place in the opening sentence the signature terms of loss: "There used to be a neighborhood here; not any more." That may not be the world's worst sentence, but it doesn't "play," as they say in the theater.

My new first sentence became "In that place, where they tore the nightshade and blackberry patches from their roots to make room for the Medallion City Golf Course, there was once a neighborhood." Instead of my original plan, here I am introducing an outside-the-circle reader into the circle. I am translating the anonymous into the specific, a "place" into a "neighborhood," and letting a stranger in through whose eyes it can be viewed. In between "place" and "neighborhood" I now have to squeeze the specificity and the *difference;* the nostalgia, the history, and the nostalgia for the history; the violence done to it and the consequences of that violence. (It took three months, those four pages, a whole summer of nights.) The nostalgia is sounded by "once"; the history and a longing for it is implied in the connotation of "neighborhood." The violence lurks in having something torn out by its roots—it will not, cannot grow again. Its consequences are that what has been destroyed is considered weeds, refuse necessarily removed in urban "development" by the unspecified but no less known "they" who do not, cannot, afford to differentiate what is displaced and would not care that this is "refuse" of a certain kind. Both plants have darkness in them: "black" and "night." One is unusual (nightshade) and has two darkness words: "night" and "shade." The other (blackberry) is common. A familiar plant and an exotic one. A harmless one and a dangerous one. One produces a nourishing berry, one delivers toxic ones. But they both thrived here together, *in that place when it was a neighborhood.* Both are gone now, and the description that follows is of the other specific things, in this black community, destroyed in the wake of the golf course. Golf course conveys what it is not, in this context: not houses, or factories, or even a public park, and certainly not residents. It is a manicured place where the likelihood of the former residents showing up is almost nil.

I want to get back to those berries for a moment (to explain, perhaps, the length of time it took for the language of that section to arrive). I always thought of Sula as quintessentially black, metaphysically black, if you will, which is not melanin and certainly not unquestioning fidelity to the tribe. She is new world black and new world woman extracting choice from choicelessness, responding inventively to found things. Improvisational. Daring, disruptive, imaginative, modern, out-of-the-house, outlawed, unpolicing, uncontained and uncontainable. And dangerously female. In her final conversation with Nel she refers to herself as a special kind of black person woman, one with choices. Like a redwood, she says. (With all due respect to the dream landscape of Freud, trees have always seemed feminine to me.) In any case, my perception of Sula's double-dose of *chosen* blackness and *biological* blackness is in the presence of those two words of darkness in "nightshade" as well as in the uncommon quality of the vine itself. One variety is called "enchanter," and the other "bittersweet" because the berries taste bitter at first and then sweet. Also nightshade was thought to counteract witchcraft. All of this seemed a wonderful constellation of signs for Sula. And "blackberry patch" seemed equally appropriate for Nel: nourishing, never needing to be tended or cultivated, once rooted and bearing. Reliably sweet but thorn-bound. Her process of becoming, heralded by the explosive dissolving of her fragilely-held-together ball of string and fur (when the thorns of her self-protection are removed by Eva), puts her back in touch with the complex, contradictory, evasive, independent, liquid modernity

Sula insisted upon. A modernity which overturns pre-war definitions, ushers in the Jazz Age (an age *defined* by Afro-American art and culture), and requires new kinds of intelligences to define oneself.

The stage-setting of the first four pages is embarrassing to me now, but the pains I have taken to explain it may be helpful in identifying the strategies one can be forced to resort to in trying to accommodate the mere fact of writing about, for and out of black culture while accommodating and responding to mainstream "white" culture. The "valley man's" guidance into the territory was my compromise. Perhaps it "worked," but it was not the work I wanted to do

Had I begun with Shadrack, I would have ignored the smiling welcome and put the reader into immediate confrontation with his wound and his scar. The difference my preferred (original) beginning would have made would be calling greater attention to the traumatic displacement this most wasteful capitalist war had on black people in particular, and throwing into relief the creative, if outlawed, determination to survive it whole. Sula as (feminine) solubility and Shadrack's (male) fixative are two extreme ways of dealing with displacement—a prevalent theme in the narrative of black people. In the final opening I replicated the demiurge of discriminatory, prosecutorial racial oppression in the loss to commercial "progress" of the village, but the references to the community's stability and creativeness (music, dancing, craft, religion, irony, wit all referred to in the "valley man's" presence) refract and subsume their pain while they are in the thick of it. It is a softer embrace than Shadrack's organized, public madness—his disruptive remembering presence which helps (for a while) to cement the community, until Sula challenges them.

"The North Carolina Mutual Life Insurance agent promised to fly from Mercy to the other side of Lake Superior at 3:oo."

This declarative sentence is designed to mock a journalistic style; with a minor alteration it could be the opening of an item in a smalltown newspaper. It has the tone of an everyday event of minimal local interest. Yet I wanted it to contain (as does the scene that takes place when the agent fulfills his promise) the information that *Song of Solomon* both centers on and radiates from.

The name of the insurance company is real, a well known black-owned company dependent on black clients, and in its corporate name are "life" and "mutual"; *agent* being the necessary ingredient of what enables the relationship between them. The sentence also moves from North Carolina to Lake Superior—geographical locations, but with a sly implication that the move from North Carolina (the south) to Lake Superior (the north) might not actually involve progress to some "superior state"—which, of course it does not. The two other significant words are "fly," upon which the novel centers and "Mercy," the name of the place from which he is to fly. Both constitute the heartbeat of the narrative. Where is the insurance man flying to? The other side of Lake Superior is Canada, of course, the historic terminus of the escape route for black people looking for asylum. "Mercy," the other significant term, is the grace note; the earnest though, with one exception, unspoken wish of the narrative's population. Some grant it; some never find it; one, at least, makes it the text and cry of her extemporaneous sermon upon the death of her granddaughter. It touches, turns and returns to Guitar at the end of the book—he who is least deserving of it—and moves him to make it his own final gift. It is what one wishes for Hagar; what is unavailable to and unsought by Macon Dead, senior; what his wife learns to demand from him, and what can never come from the white world as is signified by the inversion of the name of the hospital from Mercy to "no-Mercy." It is only available from within. The center of the narrative is flight; the springboard is mercy.

But the sentence turns, as all sentences do, on the verb: promised. The insurance agent does not declare, announce, or threaten his act. He promises, as though a contract is being executed—faithfully—between himself and others. Promises broken, or kept; the difficulty of ferreting out loyalties and ties that bind or bruise wend their way throughout the action and the shifting relationships. So the agent's flight, like that of the Solomon in the title, although toward asylum (Canada, or freedom, or home, or the company of the welcoming dead), and although it carries the possibility of failure and the certainty of danger, is toward change, an alternative way, a cessation of things-as-they-are. It should not be understood as a simple desperate act, the end of a fruitless life, a life without gesture, without examination, but as obedience to a deeper contract with his people. It is his commitment to them, regardless of whether, in all its details, they understand it. There is, however, in their response to his action, a tenderness, some contrition, and mounting respect ("They didn't know he had it in him.") and an awareness that the gesture enclosed rather than repudiated themselves. The note he leaves asks for forgiveness. It is tacked on his door as a mild invitation to whomever might pass by, but it is not an advertisement. It is an almost Christian declaration of love as well as humility of one who was not able to do more.

There are several other flights in the work and they are motivationally different. Solomon's the most magical, the most theatrical and, for Milkman, the most satisfying. It is also the most problematic—to those he left behind. Milkman's flight binds these two elements of loyalty (Mr. Smith's) and abandon and self-interest (Solomon's) into a third thing: a merging of fealty and risk that suggests the "agency" for "mutual" "life," which he offers at the end and which is echoed in the hills behind him, and is the marriage of surrender and domination, acceptance and rule, commitment to a group *through* ultimate isolation.

Guitar recognizes this marriage and recalls enough of how lost he himself is to put his weapon down.

The journalistic style at the beginning, its rhythm of a familiar, hand-me-down dignity is pulled along by an accretion of detail displayed in a meandering unremarkableness. Simple words, uncomplex sentence structures, persistent understatement, highly aural syntax—but the ordinariness of the language, its colloquial, vernacular, humorous and, upon occasion, parabolic quality sabotage expectations and mask judgments when it can no longer defer them. The composition of red, white and blue in the opening scene provides the national canvas/flag upon which the narrative works and against which the lives of these black people must be seen, but which must not overwhelm the enterprise the novel is engaged in. It is a composition of color that heralds Milkman's birth, protects his youth, hides its purpose and through which he must burst (through blue Buicks, red tulips in his waking dream, and his sisters' white stockings, ribbons and gloves) before discovering that the gold of his search is really Pilate's yellow orange and the glittering metal of the box in her ear.

These spaces, which I am filling in, and can fill in because they were planned, can conceivably be filled in with other significances. That is planned as well. The point is that into these spaces should fall the ruminations of the reader and his or her invented or recollected or misunderstood knowingness. The reader as narrator asks the questions the community asks, and both reader and "voice" stand among the crowd, within it, with privileged intimacy and contact, but without any more privileged information than the crowd has. That egalitarianism which places us all (reader, the novel's population, the narrator's voice) on the same footing reflected for me the force of flight and mercy, and the precious, imaginative yet realistic gaze of black people who (at one time, anyway) did not mythologize what or whom it mythologized. The "song" itself contains this unblinking evaluation of the miraculous and heroic flight of the legendary Solomon, an unblinking gaze which is lurking in the tender but amused choral-community response to the agent's flight. Sotto (but not completely) is my own giggle (in Afro-American terms) of the proto-myth of the journey to manhood. Whenever characters are cloaked in Western fable, they are in deep trouble; but the African myth is also contaminated. Unprogressive, unreconstructed, self-born Pilate is unimpressed by Solomon's flight and knocks Milkman down when, made new by his appropriation of his own family's fable, he returns to educate her with it. Upon hearing all he has to say, her only interest is filial. "Papa? . . I've been carryin' Papa?" And her longing to hear the song, finally, is a longing for balm to die by, not a submissive obedience to history—anybody's.

The opening sentence of *Tar Baby,* "He believed he was safe," is the second version of itself. The first, "He thought he was safe." was discarded because "thought" did not contain the doubt I wanted to plant in the reader's mind about whether or not he really was—safe. "Thought" came to me at once because it was the verb my parents and grandparents used when describing what they had dreamed the night before. Not "I dreamt," or "It seemed" or even "I saw or did" this or that—but "I thought." It gave the dream narrative distance (a dream is not "real") and power (the control implied in *thinking* rather than *dreaming*). But to use "thought" seemed to undercut the faith of the character and the distrust I wanted to suggest to the reader. "Believe" was chosen to do the work properly. And the person who does the believing is, in a way, about to enter a dream world, and convinces himself, eventually, that he is in control of it. He believed; was convinced. And although the word suggests his conviction, it does not reassure the reader. If I had wanted the reader to trust this person's point of view I would have written "He was

safe." Or, "Finally, he was safe." The unease about this view of safety is important because safety itself is the desire of each person in the novel. Locating it, creating it, losing it.

You may recall that I was interested in working out the mystery of a piece of lore, a folk tale, which is also about safety and danger and the skills needed to secure the one and recognize and avoid the other. I was not, of course, interested in retelling the tale; I suppose that is an idea to pursue, but it is certainly not interesting enough to engage me for four years. I have said, elsewhere, that the exploration of the Tar Baby tale was like stroking a pet to see what the anatomy was like but not to disturb or distort its mystery. Folklore may have begun as allegory for natural or social phenomena; it may have been employed as a retreat from contemporary issues in art, but folklore can also contain myths that reactivate themselves endlessly through providers—the people who repeat, reshape, reconstitute and reinterpret them. The Tar Baby tale seemed to me to be about masks. Not masks as covering what is to be hidden, but how masks come to life, take life over, exercise the tensions between itself and what it covers. For Son, the most effective mask is none. For the others the construction is careful and delicately borne, but the masks they make have a life of their own and collide with those they come in contact with. The texture of the novel seemed to want leanness, architecture that was worn and ancient like a piece of mask sculpture: exaggerated, breathing, just athwart the representational life it displaced. Thus, the first and last sentences had to match, as the exterior planes match the interior, concave ones inside the mask. Therefore "He believed he was safe" would be the twin of "lickety split, lickety split, lickety lickety split." This close is (1) the last sentence of the folk tale. (2) the action of the character. (3) the indeterminate ending that follows from the untrustworthy beginning. (4) the complimentary meter of its twin sister [u u / u u / with u u u / u u u /], and (5) the wide and marvelous space between the contradiction of those two images: from a dream of safety to the sound of running feet. The whole mediated world in between. This masked and unmasked; enchanted, disenchanted; wounded and wounding world is played out on and by the varieties of interpretation (Western and Afro-American) the Tar Baby myth has been (and continues to be) subjected to. Winging one's way through the vise and expulsion of history becomes possible in creative encounters with that history. Nothing, in those encounters, is safe, or should be. Safety is the foetus of power as well as protection from it, as the uses to which masks and myths are put in Afro-American culture remind us.

"124 was spiteful. Full of a baby's venom."

Beginning *Beloved* with numerals rather than spelled out numbers, it was my intention to give the house an identity separate from the street or even the city; to name it the way "Sweet Home" was named; the way plantations were named, but not with nouns or "proper" names—with numbers instead because numbers have no adjectives, no posture of coziness or grandeur or the haughty yearning of arrivistes and estate builders for the parallel beautifications of the nation they left behind, laying claim to instant history and legend. Numbers here constitute an address, a thrilling enough prospect for slaves who had owned nothing, least of all an address. And although the numbers, unlike words, can have no modifiers, I give these an adjective—spiteful (There are three others). The address is therefore personalized, but personalized by its own activity, not the pasted on desire for personality.

Also there is something about numerals that makes them spoken, heard, in this context, because one expects words to read in a book, not numbers to say, or hear. And the sound of the novel, sometimes cacaphonous, sometimes harmonious, must be an inner ear sound or a sound just beyond hearing, infusing the text with a musical emphasis that words can do sometimes even better than music can. Thus

the second sentence is not one: it is a phrase that properly, grammatically, belongs as a dependent clause with the first. Had I done that, however (124 was spiteful, comma, full of a baby's venom, or 124 was full of a baby's venom), I could not have had the accent on *full* [/ u u / u / u pause/ u u u u / u].

Whatever the risks of confronting the reader with what must be immediately incomprehensible in that simple, declarative authoritative sentence, the risk of unsettling him or her, I determined to take. Because the *in medias res* opening that I am so committed to is here excessively demanding. It is abrupt, and should appear so. No native informant here. The reader is snatched, yanked, thrown into an environment completely foreign, and I want it as the first stroke of the shared experience that might be possible between the reader and the novel's population. Snatched just as the slaves were from one place to another, from any place to another, without preparation and without defense. No lobby, no door, no entrance—a gangplank, perhaps (but a very short one). And the house into which this snatching—this kidnapping—propels one, changes from spiteful to loud to quiet, as the sounds in the body of the ship itself may have changed. A few words have to be read before it is clear that 124 refers to a house (in most of the early drafts "The women *in the house* knew it" was simply "The women knew it." "House" was not mentioned for seventeen lines), and a few more have to be read to discover why it is spiteful, or rather the source of the spite. By then it is clear, if not at once, that something is beyond control. but is not beyond understanding since it is not beyond accommodation by both the "women" and the "children." The fully realized presence of the haunting is both a major incumbent of the narrative and sleight of hand. One of its purposes is to keep the reader preoccupied with the nature of the incredible spirit world while being supplied a controlled diet of the incredible political world.

The subliminal, the underground life of a novel is the area most likely to link arms with the reader and facilitate making it one's own. Because one must, to get from the first sentence to the next, and the next and the next. The friendly observation post I was content to build and man in *Sula* (with the stranger in the midst), or the down-home journalism of *Song of Solomon* or the calculated mistrust of the point of view in *Tar Baby* would not serve here. Here I wanted the compelling confusion of being there as they (the characters) are; suddenly, without comfort or succor from the "author," with only imagination, intelligence, and necessity available for the journey. The painterly language of *Song of Solomon* was not useful to me in *Beloved*. There is practically no color whatsoever in its pages, and when there is, it is so stark and remarked upon, it is virtually raw. Color seen for the first time, without its history. No built architecture as in *Tar Baby,* no play with Western chronology as in *Sula;* no exchange between book life and "real" life discourse—with printed text units rubbing up against seasonal black childtime units as in *The Bluest Eye.* No compound of houses, no neighborhood, no sculpture, no paint, no time, especially no time because memory, prehistoric memory, has no time. There is just a little music, each other and the urgency of what is at stake. Which is all they had. For that work, the work of language is to get out of the way.

I hope you understand that in this explication of how I practice language is a search for and deliberate posture of vulnerability to those aspects of Afro-American culture that can inform and position my work. I sometimes know when the work works, when *nommo* has effectively summoned, by reading and listening to those who have entered the text. I learn nothing from those who resist it, except, of course, the sometimes fascinating display of their struggle. My expectations of and my gratitude to the critics who enter, are great. To those who talk about how as well as what; who identify the workings as well as the work; for whom the study of Afro-American literature is neither a crash course in neighborliness and tolerance, nor an infant to be carried, instructed or chastised or even whipped like a child, but the serious study of art forms that have much work to do, but are already legitimatized by their own cultural sources and predecessors—in or out of the canon—I owe much.

For an author, regarding canons, it is very simple: in fifty, a hundred or more years his or her work may be relished for its beauty or its insight or its power; or it may be condemned for its vacuousness and pretension—and junked. Or in fifty or a hundred years the critic (as canon builder) may be applauded for his or her intelligent scholarship and powers of critical inquiry. Or laughed at for ignorance and shabbily disguised assertions of power—and junked. It's possible that the reputations of both will thrive, or that both will decay. In any case, as far as the future is concerned, when one writes, as critic or as author, all necks are on the line.

Notes

1. See *"Race," Writing, and Difference,* ed. Henry Louis Gates (Chicago, 1986).
2. Among many examples, Ivan van Sertima, *They Came Before Columbus, The African Presence in Ancient America* (New York, 1976), xvi–xvii.
3. Tzvetan Todorov, "'Race,' Writing, and Culture," translated by Loulou Mack, in Gates, *"Race," Writing, and Difference,* 370–80.
4. Terrence Rafferty, "Articles of Faith," *The New Yorker,* 16 May 1988, 110–18.
5. Martin Bernal, *Black Athena: The Afroasiatic Roots of Classical Civilization, volume I: The Fabrication of Ancient Greece 1785–1985* (Rutgers, N.J., 1987), 2.
6. Ibid., 310.
7. Ibid, 337.

8. See Michael Paul Rogin, *Subversive Genealogy: The Politics and Art of Herman Melville* (Berkeley, 1985), 15.
9. Ibid., 107 and 142.
10. Ibid., 112.

* Author's Note: Older America is not always distinguishable from its infancy. We may pardon Edgar Allan Poe in 1848 but it should have occurred to Kenneth Lynn in 1986 that some young Native American might read his Hemingway biography and see herself described as "squaw" by this respected scholar, and that some young men might shudder reading the words "buck" and "half-breed" so casually included in his scholarly speculations.

Essay/Discussion Questions

1. According to Toni Morrison, why is "race" or the African American experience the "unspeakable thing unspoken" in American literature? Why do the defenders of the American literary canon refuse to include African American literature? What has been the historic rationalization for this practice?

2. According to Morrison, what contributions can African American literature make to the study of American literature?

3. Morrison states: "The spectacularly interesting question is, "What intellectual feats had to be performed by the author or his critic to erase me from a society seething with my presence, and what effect has that performance had on the work?' What are the strategies of escape from knowledge?" What do these questions mean, and why does Morrison ask them?

Part III Key Terms

Africanism	*Harlem Renaissance*
Aretha Franklin	*Improvisation*
Bigger Thomas	*James Brown*
Black power	*LeRoi Jones/Amiri Baraka*
Black Arts Movement	*Literary canon*
Blues	*NARA*
The Bluest Eye	*Richard Wright*
Gary Byrd	*Toni Morrison*

Part III Supplementary Readings

Abrahams, Roger D., *Deep Down in the Jungle: Negro Narrative Folklore from the Streets of Philadelphia,* Chicago: Aldine Publishing Company, 1970.

Awkard, Michael, *Inspiriting Influences: Tradition, Revision, and Afro-American Women's Novels,* New York: Columbia University Press, 1989.

Badger, Reid, *A Life in Ragtime: A Biography of James Reese Europe,* New York: Oxford University Press, 1995.

Baker, Houston A. Jr., *Workings of the Spirit: The Poetics of Afro-American Women's Writing,* Chicago: The University of Chicago Press, 1991.

_____, *Afro-American Poetics: Revisions of Harlem and the Black Aesthetic,* Chicago: The University of Chicago Press, 1988.

_____, *Modernism and the Harlem Renaissance,* Chicago: The University of Chicago Press, 1987.

_____, *Blues, Ideology, and Afro-American Literature: A Vernacular Theory,* Chicago: The University of Chicago Press, 1984.

_____, *The Journey Back: Issues in Black Literature and Criticism,* Chicago: The University of Chicago Press, 1980.

_____, and Patricia Redmond, ed., *Afro-American Literary Study in the 1990s,* Chicago: The University of Chicago Press, 1989.

Baldwin, James, *The Price of the Ticket: Collected Nonfiction, 1948-1985,* New York: St. Martin's Press, 1985.

_____, *The Devil Finds Work,* New York: The Dial Press, 1976.

_____, *The Fire Next Time,* New York: Dell Publishing Company, 1962.

_____, *Nobody Knows My Name: More Notes of a Native Son,* New York: Dell Publishing Company, 1961.

_____, *Notes of a Native Son,* Boston: Beacon Press, 1955.

Baraka, Amiri, *Selected Plays and Prose of Amiri Baraka/LeRoi Jones,* New York: William Morrow and Company, Inc., 1979.

_____ and Fundi, *In Our Terribleness,* Indianapolis: The Bobbs-Merrill Company, Inc., 1970.

Barksdale, Richard and Kenneth Kinnamon, eds., *Black Writers of America: A Comprehensive Anthology,* New York: The Macmillan Company, 1972.

Bell, Roseann P., Bettye J. Parker, and Beverly Guy-Sheftall, eds., *Sturdy Black Bridges: Visions of Black Women in Literature*, Garden City: Anchor Books/Doubleday, 1979.

Berliner, Paul F., *Thinking Jazz: The Infinite Art of Improvisation*, Chicago: The University of Chicago Press, 1994.

Braxton, Joanne M. and Andree N. McLaughlin, eds., *Wild Women in the Whirlwind: Afra-American Culture and the Contemporary Literary Renaissance*, New Brunswick: Rutgers University Press, 1990.

Brown, Sterling A., *The Collected Poems of Sterling A. Brown*, New York: Harper & Row, Publishers, 1980.

Cain, George, *Blueschild Baby*, New York: McGraw-Hill Book Company, 1970.

Carby, Hazel V., *Reconstructing Womanhood: The Emergence of the Afro-American Woman Novelist,* New York: Oxford University Press, 1987.

Charters, Samuel B. and Leonard Kunstadt, *Jazz: A History of the New York Scene*, New York: Da Capo Press, 1981.

Chinweizu, Onwuchekwa Jemie, and Ichechukwu Madubuike, *Toward the Decolonization of African Literature*, Washington, D. C.: Howard University Press, 1983.

Christian, Barbara, *Black Women Novelists: The Development of a Tradition, 1892-1976*, Westport: Greenwood Press, 1980.

Clarke, Donald, *Wishing on the Moon: The Life and Times of Billie Holiday*, New York: Viking, 1994.

Cole, Bill, *John Coltrane*, New York: Schirmer Books, 1976.

Collier, James L., *The Making of Jazz: A Comprehensive History*, Boston: Houghton Mifflin Company, 1978.

Corbin, Steven, *No Easy Place to Be*, New York: Simon and Schuster, 1989.

Craige, Betty J., ed., *Literature, Language, and Politics*, Athens: The University of Georgia Press, 1988.

Culler, Jonathan, *Framing the Sign: Criticism and Its Institutions*, Norman: University of Oklahoma Press, 1988.

Dance, Stanley, *The World of Count Basie*, New York: Charles Scribner's Sons, 1980.

Davis, Lennard J., and M. Bella Mirabella, eds., *Left Politics and the Literary Profession*, New York: Columbia University Press, 1990.

Davis, Miles, *Miles: The Autobiography,* New York: Simon and Schuster, 1989.

Diawara, Manthia, ed., *Black American Cinema*, New York: Routledge, 1993.

Dillard, Joey L., *Black English: Its History and Usage in the United States*, New York: Vintage Books, 1973.

Eagleton, Terry, *Literary Theory: An Introduction,* Minneapolis: University of Minnesota Press, 1983.

Ellison, Ralph W., *Flying Home and Other Stories*, ed., John F. Callahan, New York: Random House, 1996.

_____, *Going to the Territory*, New York: Random House, 1986.

_____, *Shadow and Act*, New York: A Signet Book/The New American Library, 1966.

_____, *Invisible Man,* New York: Random House, Inc., 1952.

Evans, Mari, ed., *Black Women Writers (1950-1980): A Critical Evaluation*, Garden City: Anchor Books/Doubleday, 1994.

_____, *I am a Black Woman*, New York: William Morrow and Company, Inc., 1970.

Fisher, Miles M., *Negro Slave Songs in the United States,* New York: The Citadel Press, 1963.

Floyd, Samuel A., Jr., *The Power of Black Music: Interpreting Its History from Africa to the United States*, New York: Oxford University Press, 1995.

Foley, Barbara, *Radical Representations: Politics and Form in U. S. Proletarian Fiction, 1929-1941,* Durham: Duke University Press, 1993.

Gabbard, Krin, ed., *Jazz Among the Discourses.* Durham: Duke University Press.

_____, ed., *Representing Jazz.* Durham: Duke University Press.

Garland, Phyl, *The Sound of Soul*, Chicago: Henry Regnery Company, 1969.

Gayle, Addison Jr., *Richard Wright: Ordeal of a Native Son*, Garden City: Anchor Press/Doubleday, 1980.

_____, *The Way of the New World: The Black Novel in America*, Garden City: Anchor Press/Doubleday, 1975.

_____, ed., *The Black Aesthetic*, Garden City: Anchors Books, 1972.

Gates, Henry L. Jr., *The Signifying Monkey: A Theory of Afro-American Literary Criticism*, New York: Oxford University Press, 1988.

_____, *Figures in Black: Words, Signs, and the "Racial" Self*, New York: Oxford University Press, 1987.

George, Nelson, *Blackface: Reflections on African-Americans and the Movies*, New York: HarperCollins Publishers, 1994.

_____, *Buppies, B-Boys, Baps & Bohos: Notes on Post-Soul Black Culture*, New York: HarperCollins Publishers, 1992.

_____, *The Death of Rhythm & Blues*, Pantheon Books, 1988.

Goss, Linda and Marian E. Barnes, eds., *Talk That Talk: An Anthology of African-American Storytelling*, New York: Simon & Schuster Inc., 1989.

Graff, Gerald, *Beyond the Cultural Wars: How Teaching the Conflicts Can Revitalize American Education*, New York: W. W. Norton and Company, 1992.

_____, *Professing Literature: An Institutional History*, Chicago: The University of Chicago Press, 1987.

Gwaltney, John L., *Drylongso: A Self-Portrait of Black America*, New York: Random House, 1980.

Hakutani, Yoshinobu, *Richard Wright and Racial Discourse*, Columbia: University of Missouri Press, 1996.

Harrison, Daphne D., *Black Pearls: Blues Queens of the 1920s*, New Brunswick: Rutgers University Press, 1988.

Hay, Samuel A., *African American Theatre: An Historical and Critical Analysis*, New York: Cambridge University Press, 1994.

Hazzard-Gordon, Katrina, *Jookin': The Rise of Social Dance Formations in African-American Culture*, Philadelphia: Temple University Press.

Henderson, Stephen, *Understanding the New Black Poetry: Black Speech and Black Music as Poetic References*, New York: William Morrow and Company, Inc., 1973.

Herskovits, Melville J., *The Myth of the Negro Past*, Boston: Beacon Press, 1958.

Himes, Chester, *The Third Generation*, New York: Thunder's Mouth Press, 1989.

_____, *Black on Black*, Garden City: Doubleday & Company, Inc., 1973.

Holloway, Joseph E., ed., *Africanisms in American Culture*, Bloomington: Indiana University Press, 1990.

Hughes, Langston, ed., *The Book of Negro Humor*, New York: Dodd, Mead & Company, 1966.

_____, and Arna Bontemps, eds., *The Book of Negro Folklore*, New York: Dodd, Mead & Company, 1958.

Huggins, Nathan I., *Harlem Renaissance*, New York: Oxford University Press, 1971.

Hurston, Zora Neale, *Their Eyes Were Watching God*, Urbana: University of Illinois Press, 1978.

Jackson, Blyden, *A History of Afro-American Literature, Vol. I, The Long Beginning, 1746-1895*, Baton Rouge: Louisiana State University Press, 1989.

Jones, LeRoi/Amiri Baraka, *The Autobiography of LeRoi Jones/Amiri Baraka*, New York: Fruendlich Books, 1984.

_____, *Black Music*, New York: William Morrow and Company, 1968.

_____, *Blues People*, New York: William Morrow and Company, 1963.

_____ and Larry Neal, eds., *Black Fire: An Anthology of Afro-American Writing*, New York: William Morrow & Company, 1968.

Joyce, Joyce A., *Richard Wright's Art of Tragedy*, Iowa City: University of Iowa Press, 1986.

Lauter, Paul, *Canons and Contexts*, New York: Oxford University Press, 1991.

Leitch, Vincent B., *American Literary Criticism: From the 30s to the 80s*, New York: Columbia University Press, 1988.

Levine, Lawrence W., *Black Culture and Black Consciousness: Afro-American Folk Thought from Slavery to Freedom*, New York: Oxford University Press, 1977.

Lewis, David L., *When Harlem was in Vogue*, New York: Alfred A. Knopf, Inc., 1981.

Locke, Alain, *The New Negro*, New York: Atheneum, 1969.

_____, *The Negro and His Music*, Port Washington: Kennikat Press, Inc., 1968.

Long, Richard A. and Eugenia W. Collier, eds., *Afro-American Writing: An Anthology of Prose and Poetry*, 2 Vols., Washington Square: New York University Press, 1972.

Kamp, Louis, and Paul Lauter, eds., *The Politics of Literature: Dissenting Essays on the Teaching of English*, New York: Pantheon Books, 1970.

Keil, Charles, *Urban Blues*, Chicago: The University of Chicago Press, 1966.

Kofsky, Frank, *Black Nationalism and the Revolution in Music*, New York: Pathfinder Press, 1970.

McDowell, Deborah E. and Arnold Rampersad, eds., *Slavery and the Literary Imagination*, Baltimore: The Johns Hopkins University Press, 1989.

McMillan, Terry, *Waiting to Exhale*, New York: Viking, 1992.

_____, ed., *Breaking Ice: An Anthology of Contemporary African-American Fiction*, New York: Penguin Books, 1990.

_____, *Disappearing Acts*, New York: Viking, 1989.

Miller, Eugene, *Voice of a Native Son: The Poetics of Richard Wright*, Jackson: University Press of Mississippi, 1990.

Miller, R. Baxter, *The Art and Imagination of Langston Hughes*, Lexington: The University Press of Kentucky, 1989.

Naylor, Gloria, *Mama Day*, New York: Ticknor & Fields, 1988.

_____, *Linden Hills*, New York: Ticknor & Fields, 1985.

_____, *The Women of Brewster Place*, New York: Viking Books, 1982.

Neal, Larry, *Visions of a Liberated Future: Black Arts Movement Writings,* New York: Thunder's Mouth Press, 1989.

Nicholson, Stuart, *Billie Holiday*, Boston: Northeastern University Press, 1995.

Nisenson, Eric, *Ascension: John Coltrane and His Quest*, New York: St. Martin's Press, 1993.

O'Meally, Robert, *Lady Day: The Many Faces of Billie Holiday*, New York: Arcade Publishing, 1991.

Reed, Ishmael, *Terrible Threes*, New York: Atheneum, 1989.

_____, *Writin' Is Fightin': Thirty-Seven Years of Boxing on Paper*, New York: Atheneum, 1988.

_____, *Reckless Eyeballing*, New York: St. Martin's Press, 1986.

_____, *Terrible Twos,* New York: Atheneum, 1982.

_____, *Mumbo Jumbo*, New York: Avon Books, 1972.

Roberts, John W., *From Trickster to Badman: The Black Folk Hero in Slavery and Freedom,* Philadelphia: University of Pennsylvania Press, 1989.

Rose, Phyllis, *Jazz Cleopatra: Josephine Baker in Her Time*, New York: Doubleday, 1989.

Rose, Tricia, *Black Noise: Rap Music and Black Culture in Contemporary America*, Hanover: Wesleyan University Press, 1994.

Said, Edward W., *The World, the Text, and the Critic*, Cambridge: Harvard University Press, 1983.

_____, *Orientalism*, New York: Random House, 1978.

Scruggs, Charles, *Sweet Home: Invisible Cities in the Afro-American Novel*, Baltimore: The Johns Hopkins University Press, 1993.

Sernett, Milton C., ed., *Afro-American Religious History: A Documentary Witness*, Durham: Duke University Press, 1985.

Simpkins, Cuthbert O., *Coltrane: A Biography*, New York: Herndon House Publishers, 1975.

Smith, Valerie, *Self-Discovery and Authority in Afro-American Narrative*, Cambridge: Harvard University Press, 1987.

Smitherman, Geneva, *Talkin and Testifyin: The Language of Black America*, Boston: Houghton Mifflin Company, 1972.

Soitos, Stephen F., *The Blues Detective: A Study of African American Detective Fiction*, Amherst: The University of Massachusetts Press, 1996.

Sollors, Werner, *Amiri Baraka/LeRoi Jones: The Quest for a "Populist Modernism,"* New York: Columbia University Press, 1978.

Southern, Eileen, *The Music of Black Americans: A History*, New York: W. W. Norton & Company, Inc., 1971.

Spencer, Jon M., *Blues and Evil*, Knoxville: The University of Tennessee Press, 1993.

Stuckey, Sterling, *Going Through the Storm: The Influence of African American Art in History*, New York: Oxford University Press, 1994.

_____, *Slave Culture: Nationalist Theory and the Foundations of Black America*, New York: Oxford University Press, 1987.

_____, "Through the Prism of Folklore: The Black Ethos in Slavery," *The Massachusetts Review*, Vol. 3 (Summer 1968), pp. 416–437.

Tate, Claudia, ed., *Black Women Writers at Work*, New York: The Continuum Publishing Corporation, 1988.

Thomas, J. C., *Chasin' the Trane: The Music and Mystique of John Coltrane*, New York: Da Capo Press, 1976.

Tirro, Frank, *Jazz: A History*, New York: W. W. Norton & Company, 1977.

Turner, Lorenzo, *Africanisms in the Gullah Dialect*, Chicago: The University of Chicago Press, 1949.

Walker, Margaret, *Richard Wright: Daemonic Genius*, New York: Warner Books, 1988.

_____, *Jubilee*, Boston: Houghton Mifflin, 1966.

Wall, Cheryl A., ed., *Changing Our Own Words: Essays on Criticism, Theory, and Writing by Black Women*, New Brunswick: Rutgers University Press, 1989.

Washington, Helen M., ed., *Memory of Kin: Stories About Family by Black Writers*, New York: Anchor Books/Doubleday, 1991.

_____, ed., *Black-Eyed Susans/Midnight Birds: Stories by and About Black Women*, New York: Anchor Books/Doubleday, 1990.

_____, *Invented Lives: Narratives of Black Women, 1860–1960*, New York: Anchor Books/Doubleday, 1987.

Watts, Jerry G., *Heroism & the Black Intellectual: Ralph Ellison, Politics, and Afro-American Intellectual Life*, Chapel Hill: The University of North Carolina Press, 1994.

Whitten, Norman E. Jr., and John F. Szwed, eds., *Afro-American Anthropology: Contemporary Perspectives*, New York: The Free Press, 1970.

Wideman, John E., *Philadelphia Fire*, New York: Henry Holt and Company, 1990.

_____, *The Lynchers*, New York: Henry Holt and Company, 1973.

Williams, Sherley A., *Dessa Rose*, New York: William Morrow and Company, Inc., 1986.

Willis, Susan, *Specifying: Black Women Writing the American Experience*, Madison: The University of Wisconsin Press, 1987.

Wilmore, Gayraud S., ed., *African American Religious Studies: An Interdisciplinary Anthology*, Durham: Duke University Press, 1989.

Wood, Forrest G., *The Arrogance of Faith: Christianity and Race in America from the Colonial Era to the Twentieth Century*, New York: Alfred A. Knopf, 1990.

Wright, Ellen and Michel Fabre, eds., *Richard Wright Reader*, New York: Harper & Row, Publishers, 1978.

Discovering the Meaning of Black Identity: Psychic Dimensions of Oppression

More than thirty years ago, in *The Wretched of the Earth*, the revolutionary West Indian psychiatrist Frantz Fanon stated: "Because it is a systematic negation of the other person and a furious determination to deny the other person all attributes of humanity, colonialism forces the people it dominates to ask themselves the question constantly: 'In reality, who am I?'" Brought to the Americas by European slave-traders, and held in captivity as chattel slaves for more than three hundred years, black people had to fashion a collective consciousness of themselves based on a fusion of Africanisms they brought with them and the conditions of European cultural domination and economic exploitation they faced in the Americas. To whites, Africans' blackness came to symbolize all that was frightening, dangerous, and evil in Western culture and civilization; this blackness, and ultimately African bodies, had to be violently constrained, disfigured, and despised. Fanon thus argued, in *Black Skin, White Masks*, that black people are in every sense of the word oppressed by Western—white—civilization.

Cultural domination constitutes the social relations of power between the oppressor and the oppressed. In the situation of anti-black racist tyranny, white supremacy so depersonalizes its victims that they often experience a fragmenting of their consciousness. This splitting produces what Fanon calls "psychic alienation"—the estrangement or separating of a person from some of the essential qualities of personhood. It is experienced as a form of individual and collective self-contempt or self-loathing. Internalizing the oppressor's mystification of the world, many oppressed people come to regard themselves as uniquely unable to satisfy normal criteria of psychological health or moral adequacy. Believing in their own inferiority, the victims of psychic tyranny often oppress and exploit each other. It is within the cauldron of the historic dynamic of Euro-American cultural hegemony that black people have both struggled against and internalized the long nightmare of psychic assault.

The essays in this section probe aspects of the psychological and cultural transformation of black people from Africans to black Americans. The purpose here is to examine the continuing psychological reactions of many black people to the historic regime of white supremacy. This section seeks to answer the following question: How has anti-black racism affected African American psychological development?

In his article, "African Philosophy: Foundations for Black Psychology," Wade N. Nobles seeks to construct a black psychology on the basis of understanding the meaning of West African philosophical and cultural traditions of spiritual and community life. By examining the ethos, or guiding beliefs, of preslavery and precolonial West Africa, Nobles hopes to get at the heart of a West African philosophical system that will serve as a foundation for developing a black psychology distinctly different from white psychology.

Nobles' investigation of the West African philosophical principles of life, or ethos, focuses on religion and philosophy, the notion of unity, the concept of time, death and immortality, and kinship. Relying largely on John Mbiti's research in *African Religions and Philosophies* (1970), Nobles finds that the traditional West African ethos is based fundamentally on communal, rather than individual, concerns. This is the fundamental distinction between traditional African culture and the modern Western philosophical tradition. Noting the importance of oral tradition for understanding the meaning of African religion and philosophy, Nobles observes that spirituality was the essence of traditional African identity and existence. Collectively and individually, traditional Africans lived their religion; spiritual beliefs interacted with social and personal conduct. Similarly, traditional Africans believed in the unity of the universe, with God as the creator and sustainer of all life. Hence, traditional Africans understood themselves to be not separate from the natural environment but an essential part of it. From unity as a guiding principle came a sense of collective responsibility.

Nobles notes that in traditional West African thinking, the concept of time referred to lived experiences both of communities and individuals. Hence, time contained two dimensions, the past and the present, which often overlapped. This meant that traditional West Africans calculated time by reflecting on present events and relating them to the past; in this manner of looking back, communities and individuals maintained a strong sense of historical time through remembering past generations. As a consequence, traditional Africans understood time and human events as part of the natural rhythm of nature—birth, puberty, initiation, marriage, procreation, old age, death, and immortality. In traditional African philosophy, the natural rhythm of nature, to which human existence belonged, was everlasting.

On the basis of traditional West African philosophical principles, Nobles seeks to reconstruct a black American psychology. He argues that because the oppressive chattel slave experience rigidly isolated them, captured African were able to retain elements of their cultural and philosophical traditions. Nobles points out that African populations throughout the Americas have retained a variety of traditional cultural elements, which have continued to influence their psychological development at different stages of their American experience. Referring to black people in the United States, Nobles delineates three experiential stages and argues that alien Euro-American philosophical positions did not destroy all elements of African cultural and philosophical traditions. Indeed, he maintains that core aspects of these traditions have survived and continue to play an important role in the psychological development of black Americans. According to Nobles, the challenge of black psychology is to examine the mechanism by which African cultural and philosophical traditions have survived and contributed to the development of black people in America.

Other commentators on the black experience suggest that slave-owners made a conscious and systematic effort to dehumanize and depersonalize their captives. This historical interpretation argues that slave-owners sought to create the perfect slave—one who was docile, obedient, and afraid—by means of control, management, and violence. Here is the source of black Americans' psychological oppression or, in the words of Frantz Fanon, psychic alienation—the estrangement or separating of a person from some of the essential attributes of personhood.

In the excerpt contained in this section from his classic text, *The Peculiar Institution: Slavery in the Ante-Bellum South*, historian Kenneth M. Stampp recounts the psychological and physical violence slave-owners employed in order to create a good slave. Stampp collected material for this discussion primarily from the manuals and other documents slave-owners prepared on the system of managing and training slaves. Stampp pointed out five recurring tactics of this dehumanizing system.

First, those who managed the slaves had to maintain strict discipline. One slave-owner said, "Unconditional submission is the only footing upon which slavery should be placed." Another said, "The slave must know that his master is to govern absolutely and he is to obey implicitly, that he is never, for a moment, to exercise either his will or judgment in opposition to a positive order." Second, slave-owners thought that they had to implant in the slave a consciousness of personal inferiority. They deliberately extended this sense of personal inferiority to the slave's past. Slave-owners believed that in order to control black people, the slaves "had to feel that African ancestry tainted them, that their color was a badge of degradation." The third step in the training process was to awe the slaves with a sense of the slave-owner's enormous power. It was essential, various slave-owners declared, "to make them stand in fear." The fourth aspect was the attempt to "persuade the bondsman to take an interest in the master's enterprise and to accept his standards of 'good conduct'." Thus the slave-owner sought to train slaves to accept unquestioningly his value system or criteria of what was good and true and beautiful. The final step, according to Stampp's documents, was "to impress Negroes with their helplessness: to create in them a habit of perfect dependence upon their masters."

Here, then, was the system of dehumanization and depersonalization designed and practiced by slave-owners to produce the perfect slave. To be sure, all chattel slaves were not submissive, frightened, weak, and dependent. Many were defiant, angry, resentful, and rebellious, as historian John Blassingame demonstrates in his book, *The Slave Community: Plantation Life in the Ante-Bellum South* (1972). Nevertheless, the psychic alienation and slave mentality that resulted during the terroristic and oppressive system of chattel slavery—followed by Euro-America's practice of segregation and anti-black racism—have had lasting effects on the psychological and personality development of black Americans.

W. E. B. Du Bois' essay, "Of Our Spiritual Strivings," is a classic statement of the psychological and existential condition of the African American in the absurd situation of anti-black racism. In particular, his observations constitute a black man's point of view and reaction to the psychology of racist oppression. Written on the eve of the twentieth century, it is a deeply moving essay in which Du Bois seeks to reveal, as much as his rationalist orientation will allow, his innermost soul as an African American. He uses the veil as his essential metaphor and theme, symbolizing white American imposition of physical separation (segregation) and psychological separation (racism). For Du Bois, white power, as a form of tyrannical domination, excludes and dehumanizes black Americans and turns them into a "problem." And since whites do not recognize black peoples' essential humanity, whites speak to and act unintelligently toward black people; this reinforces how thoroughly all African Americans are pushed to the margins of the American social order.

Significantly, a veil is a single entity possessing two sides. In the moment that it separates people, it also links them. Hence, African Americans also are intricately woven into America's social fabric. The black people are both excluded from and included in the American social dynamic, and this is the source of their psycho-social predicament. The situation produces a divided self. In Du Bois' words, African Americans experience double consciousness, an identity crisis, in which they are burdened with the clash between their African cultural heritage and social outlook and the values promulgated by white American cultural domination. For African Americans, the struggle for self-consciousness is interrupted and shaped by their oppressors' consciousness, so even when African Americans look at themselves or each other, they do so, according to Du Bois, from the negative standpoint or world view of white American cultural hegemony.

Since it is this clash of African and American cultures that constitutes African Americans' psychological and cultural dilemma, the resultant "spiritual striving" is the struggle to blend the two dimensions of the divided self. Du Bois seems to be suggesting that black Americans' search for self-understanding—in his words, "to attain self-conscious manhood"—is a search for psycho-social wholeness; it also is a historic struggle for black people's humanity within an anti-black American social dynamic.

African Philosophy: Foundations for Black Psychology

WADE W. NOBLES

African Americans derive their most fundamental self-definition from several cultural and philosophical premises which we share with most West African "tribes."[1] In exploring the character of these premises, which are basic conceptions of the nature of man and his relation to other men and his environment, we hope to establish a foundation upon which a black psychology can be constructed. Thus, it will be contended that black psychology is something more than the psychology of so-called underprivileged peoples, more than the experience of living in ghettoes or of having been forced into the dehumanizing condition of slavery. It is more than the "darker" dimension of general psychology. Its unique status is from the positive features of basic African philosophy which dictate the values, customs, attitudes, and behavior of Africans in Africa and the New World.

The notion of common experience or common ethos seems almost fictional if one accepts uncritically the research finding of many so-called Africanists who argue that the territory of the Western region of Africa held and still does hold within its boundaries many different "tribes," each having its own language, religion, and customs. However, one must note the orientation of these many Africanists whose incidental whiteness colors much of what they have to say. One must, therefore, be conscious of the inherent social dialectic. That is to say, while most foreign students of Africa have maintained that the Western "tribes" have little shared experience because each has a distinct language and religion and many unique customs, they have overlooked "the similarities of the forest for the differences between the trees." In this view, it is suggested that the overemphasis given tribal differences by white investigators is the anthropological or scientific version of the imperialist strategy of "divide and conquer." Hence, it is likely that many white ethnographers are predisposed by conscious or unconscious racist assumptions to focus upon superficial differences and are thus "blinded" to underlying similarities in the experiential communality of African peoples. Fortunately, however, this anthropological analog of the

Reprinted from *Black Psychology*, 3rd ed., Reginald L. Jones, ed., Berkeley, California: Cobb & Henry, Publishers, 1991.

"divide and conquer" strategy has been re-dressed by black (and even by a few white) scholars (Mbiti, 1970; Herskovits, 1958). These scholars maintain that "tribal" differences in Africa were minor compared to the binding quality of their communality. This author suggests that what supported this regional communality was a set of guiding beliefs—an ethos. Closer examination of the region indicates that the ethos determined two operational orders. The first is the notion that the people were part of the natural rhythm of nature: They were one with nature. The second order is the notion of the survival of one's people—that is, the "tribe." Hence, the African experience defines man's place (role) in nature's scheme.

However, unlike a written constitution, the ethos is more akin to a spiritual disposition and probably could best be described a collective unconsciousness. Although the ethos cannot be scientifically (i.e., empirically) examined with current methodology, it is believed that one way to understand the essential and pervasive nature of the African (black) ethos is to explore and understand African philosophy.[2] It follows therefore that insofar as the African (black) ethos is distinct from that of the prevailing white ethos (upon which traditional psychology was founded) then a black psychology based upon the black ethos must also be uniquely different from white psychology. It is this principle that allows African philosophy to take its place as the foundation for black psychology.

AFRICAN PHILOSOPHY

Religion and Philosophy

John Mbiti (1970) defines African philosophy as "the understanding, attitude of mind, logic, and perception behind the manner in which African peoples think, act, or speak in different situations of life." What is central to Brother Mbiti's definition is the "spiritual disposition," the "collective consciousness,"—in a word, the ethos. At this point, it should be made very explicit that when talking about the ethos one is talking about it in the context of African philosophy. In a sense, the ethos can be considered the operational definition of African philosophy. More specifically, this "collective consciousness" can be described as a *vita attitude*. That is to say, a kind of faith in a transcendental force and a sense of vital solidarity.

Examination of preslavery Africa suggests that there were hundreds of African peoples, or tribes, and some would suggest that each had its own philosophical system. More sophisticated scholarship indicates that for West Africa in general, philosophy was the essence of the people's existence, and that the many tribes shared one overriding philosophical system. It was through religion, however, that this philosophical system was expressed. In this sense religion and philosophy are the same phenomenon. Hence, to understand the essence of these peoples' existence one must examine their religion, proverbs, oral traditions, ethics, and morals—keeping clearly in mind that underlying the differences in detail is a general philosophical system which prevailed in Africa. Religion, however, is the more observable phenomenon and as such it permeated every aspect of the African's life. It was, in a very real sense, not something for the betterment of the individual, but rather something for the community of which the individual was an integral part. For the traditional African, to be human was to belong to the whole community (Mbiti, 1970, p. 5). Curiously enough, many African languages did not have a word for religion as such. Religion was such an integral part of man's existence that it and he were inseparable. Religion accompanied the individual from conception to long after his physical death.

As most scholars of African religion will attest, one of the greatest difficulties in studying African religion and philosophy is that there are no sacred scriptures or texts. A great number of beliefs and practices were and can be found in African society. However, these beliefs and/or traditions were handed down from father to son for generation upon generation. As such, and in accordance with the prevailing *oral tradition,* the beliefs were corporate and the acts were communal. Traditional religion in Africa was not proselytized. The people were their religion. Thus, individuals could not "preach" their religion to "others." As was noted above, religion was the observable phenomenon and, for the most part, the tribes seemingly were observably different. For instance, the Dogon conception of the universe is based, on the one hand, on the principle of vibrations of matter, and on the other hand, on a general movement of the universe as a whole (Forde, 1954, p. 84). For the Dogon, proliferation of life was directed by a perpetual alternation of opposites—right-left, high-low, odd-even, male-female—all reflecting the principle of twinness (no mention of right-wrong). Like all creatures, these twin beings, living images of the fundamental principle of twinness in creation, were each (i.e., both opposites) equipped with two spiritual principles of opposites. That is, each of them was himself a pair. This notion of man's unity with the universe is reflected in the Dogon belief that "man is the seed of the universe" (Forde, 1954). Hence, the organization of the earth's system is reproduced in every individual.

The Fon of Dahomey believed that at the beginning of the present world there were the pair (twins) Mawu-Lisa—Mawu the female, Lisa the male. They were "regarded as twins and their union was the basis of the organization of the world" (Forde, 1954, p. 219). The Mende, also of West Africa, believed that each parent gave to their offspring some aspect of its (the child's) unified constitution. For instance, the Mende believed that the physical part of an individual (i.e., bones, flesh, etc.) is provided by the father through the semen he puts into the mother. The child's spirit (Ngafa) is contributed by its mother. The Ashanti believed that the human being is formed from the blood (Mogya) of the mother and the spirit (Ntoro) of the father (Forde, 1954, p. 196). Both peoples nevertheless believed that the spirit and the physical body and blood unite as one in making the new human being. In this sense each tribe had its own religious (life) system, and for one to have propagated his religion would have involved propagating the entire life of the people concerned. However, the substance of each tribal life system was not different.

Traditional Africans made no distinction between the act and the belief. "What people do is motivated by what they believe, and what they believe springs from what they do and experience" (Mbiti, 1970, p. 5). Action and belief in traditional West African society were not separated. They belonged to a single whole. Accordingly, traditional beliefs made no concrete distinction between the spiritual and the physical. Note that the Mende perceived physical and spiritual components as uniting to make the human. Life after death is found in all African societies. However, belief in the continuation of life after death did not represent a hope for the future or possibly a better life when one dies. For the African, once dead, there was neither Heaven to be hoped for nor Hell to be feared. Again, this reflects the idea of vital force.

The whole of one's existence was an ontological religious phenomenon. The African was a deeply religious being living in a religious universe (Mbiti, 1970). For him to live was to be involved in, to be part of, a religious drama. As noted, traditional African religion was a religious ontology. As such, the ontology was characteristically very anthropocentric—everything was seen in terms of its relation to man.

Notion of Unity

The anthropocentric ontology was a complete unity which nothing could break up or destroy. Everything was functionally connected; to destroy one category completely would cause the destruction of the whole of existence, including the Creator. God was viewed as the originator and sustainer of man. The spirits explained man's destiny. Man was the center of the ontology. The animals, plants, and natural phenomena constituted the environment in which man lived. In addition to the five categories, *there existed a force, a power, or energy which permeated the whole universe.* In this kind of natural order (i.e., unity), God was the source and ultimate controller of the energy, but the spirits also had access to it. A few human beings—the Shaman (i.e., medicine men, priest, and rainmakers)—possessed the knowledge and ability to tap, manipulate, and use to a limited degree this energy. For the Dogon the social order was projected in the individual. An indivisible cell which, on the one hand, is a microcosm of the whole, and on the other hand has a circumscribed function. Not only was a person the product of his institutions, he also was their motive power. Lacking, however, any special power in himself, he was the representative of the whole. The individual affected the cosmic order which he also displayed (Forde, 1954). As stated earlier, a prevailing belief (Dogon) was that the organization (unity) of the earth's system was reproduced in every individual. This notion of the unity of things was so ingrained that the Mende, for instance, had developed a sense of collective responsibility. Also ingrained in the notion of unity is a particular conception of time.

Concept of Time

African philosophy concerned itself with two dimensions of time—the past and the present; and this conception of time helped to explain the general life system of traditional Africans.[3] The direction of one's life system was from the present dimension backward to the past dimension. For the people, time itself was simply a composition of past events. Very little concern was given to time in and of itself. It existed, but the African time concept was (is) very elastic. It encompassed events that had already occurred, those that are taking place, and those that will occur immediately (Mbiti, 1970). What had no possibility of occurring immediately or had not taken place fell into the category of "no time" (Mbiti, 1970). Time as reckoned by phenomena. "Actual time" was what (events) was present or past and, because time essentially moved backward rather than forward, the traditional African set his mind not on future things but chiefly on what had taken place. Thus, the West African's understanding of all things—that is, the individual, the tribe (community), and the five characters of the universe—was governed or dominated by these two dimensions (past and present) of time. In order to make sense, or be real, to the West African, time had to be experienced; and the way in which one experienced time was partly through one's own individual life and partly through the life of the tribe which went back many generations before one's birth. Because time was reckoned by phenomena, "instead of numerical calendars, there were what one would call phenomenon calendars, in which the events or phenomena which constituted time were reckoned or considered in their relation with one another as they take place" (Mbiti, 1970). The Mandingo for instance had (have) a distinct "seasonal" calendar which reflected the changing of the seasons. Hence, the phenomenal changes of the environment constituted time. For most Africans, time was meaningful at the point of the event and not at the mathematical moment. Thus, in traditional life, any period of time was reckoned according to its significant events.

Recognizing the associations and connotations that the English words *past, present,* and *future* have, Brother Mbiti uses two Swahili words (Sasa and Zamani) to represent present and past. Sasa has the sense of immediacy, nearness, nowness (Mbiti, 1970). It is the period of immediate concern for the people because that is *where* or *when* they exist. The Sasa period is not mathematically or numerically constant. Each member of the tribe has his own and, hence, the older the person, the longer his Sasa period. Each tribe (society, nation) also has its own Sasa period.

The Zamani period is not limited to what Europeans call the past. It overlaps or encompasses the Sasa and the two are not separable. The Sasa feels or disappears into the Zamani. However, before events become incorporated into the Zamani, they have to be realized or actualized within the Sasa dimension. Thus, events (people) move backward from the Sasa dimension to the Zamani dimension. In a sense, Zamani is the graveyard of time (Mbiti, 1970). The Sasa dimension binds individuals and their immediate environment together. As such, it determines the experiential communality, encompassing the conscious limits of the tribe. The Zamani dimension, however, encompasses the Sasa dimension in a sort of spiritual medium and thus gives a common foundation to the universal reality and binds together all created things. All is embraced within the Zamani.

Everything has its center of gravity in the Zamani period, with nothing ever ending. West African peoples expect human history to continue forever, because it is part of the natural rhythm moving from Sasa to Zamani. The Mende apparently have a belief in rebirth or reincarnation. Children are sometimes named after a particular ancestor, especially when they bear a resemblance to him. This behavior inevitably seems to suggest that the Mende, like other West African peoples, have a notion that the life cycle is renewable. Human life is part of the rhythm of nature, and just as the days, months, seasons, and years have no end, there is no end to the rhythm of birth, puberty, initiation, marriage, procreation, old age, death, entry in the community of the departed (the living dead), and

entry into the company of the spirits. Life is an ontological rhythm, and abnormality or the unusual is what disrupts the ontological harmony.

Death and Immortality

In many African tribes, a person was not considered a full human being until he had gone through the whole rhythmic process of physical birth, naming ceremony, puberty, initiation rites (sometimes in the form of ceremonial rebirth), and finally marriage and procreation. Then, and only then, was one fully "born"—a complete person. Similarly, death initiated the systematic rhythmic process through which the person gradually was removed from the Sasa to the Zamani period. Hence, death and immortality have especial significance in West African traditions. After physical death, as long as a person was remembered and recognized (by name) by relatives and friends who knew him (i.e., remembered his personality, character, and words and incidents of his life), he would continue to exist in the Sasa period. When, however, the last person who knew him also died, then the former passed out of the horizon of the Sasa period and, in effect, became completely dead. He no longer had any claims to family ties. He entered the Zamani period; that is, he became a member in the company of spirits.

The departed person who was remembered (recognized) by name was what Brother Mbiti calls the living-dead. He was considered to be in a state of personal immortality. The Mende believed that a person survives after death and that his surviving personality goes to the land of the dead (Forde, 1954). Those in personal immortality were treated symbolically like the living. The cycle of an individual ancestor, the Mende believed, lasted as long as the dead person was remembered in prayers and sacrifices (Forde, 1954). Hence, they were respected, given food and drink in the form of libations, and listened to and obeyed. Being remembered (recognized) and respected while in personal immortality was important for the traditional African, a fact which helps one to understand the religious significance and importance of marriage and procreation in West African societies. Procreation was the surest way to insure that one would not be cut off from personal immortality. In a kind of multiplicative fashion, polygamy reinforced one's insurance.

Inevitably, as stated earlier, the point was reached when there was no longer anyone alive who would recognize and give respect to the (living-dead) person. At this point, the process of dying was completed. However, he did not vanish out of existence. He now entered into the state of collective immortality. Now in the company of the spirits, he had at last entered the Zamani period. From this point on, the departed became nameless spirits who had no personal communication or ties with human families.

In terms of the ontology, entrance into the company of the spirits is man's final destiny. Paradoxically, death lies "in front" of the individual; it is a "future" event of sorts. But, when one dies, one enters the state of personal immortality and gradually "goes back" into the Zamani period. It should be emphasized that the African ontology was endless; such a view of man's destiny should not be construed to mean the end. Nothing ever ends.

Kinship: Collective Unity

Before concluding this brief and cursory review of African philosophy, a few words should be devoted to West African kinship, especially because kinship tied together the personal life system. Before they had carved up and colonized West Africa, Europeans could not say where one tribe ended and another tribe began. The number of people who made up what might be considered a tribe varied greatly. Depending upon the enumerator or ethnographer, many tribes were classified as unique and distinctly separate or simply as one.

Studies of African religious beliefs and practices demonstrate that among the many so-called distinct tribes there were more similarities (communalities) than differences (Mbiti, 1970). This author contends that all tribes shared basic beliefs—in the "survival of the tribe" and in the fact that the tribe was an integral and indispensable part of nature. Belief in tribal survival was reflected in and sustained by a deep sense of kinship—probably one of the strongest cohesive devices in traditional life. Kinship controlled all relationships in the community (Mbiti, 1970). It included animals, plants, and nonliving objects. In effect, kinship bound together the entire life system of the tribe.

The kinship system stretched laterally (horizontally) in every direction as well as vertically. Hence, each member of the tribe was related not only to the tribal ancestors (both living-dead and spirits) but also to all those still unborn. In addition, each was a brother or sister, father or mother, grandmother or grandfather, cousin or brother-in-law, uncle or aunt, or some relation to everybody else. Africans still have many kinship terms which define the precise relationship binding any two people. Knowledge of one's tribal genealogy, vertical and horizontal, was extremely important. It imparted a sense of sacred obligation to extend the genealogical line. Through genealogies, persons (individuals) in the Sasa period were firmly linked to those who had entered the Zamani period.

To summarize: "In traditional life, the individual did not and could not exist alone" (Mbiti, 1970). The individual owed his very existence to other members of the "tribe," not only those who conceived and nourished him but also those long dead and still unborn. The individual did not exist unless he was corporate or communal; he was simply an integral part of the collective unity. Africans believed that the community (tribe) made, created, or produced the individual; thus, the existence of the community was not imagined to be dependent on individual ingression.

Unlike Western philosophical systems, the African philosophical tradition does not place heavy emphasis on the "individual." Indeed one might say that in a sense it does not allow for individuals. It recognizes that "only in terms of other people does the individual become conscious of his own being" (Mbiti, 1970). Only through others does one learn his duties and responsibilities toward himself and others. Most initiation rites were designed to instill a sense of corporate responsibility and collective destiny. Thus, when one member of the tribe suffered, the entire tribe suffered; when one member of the tribe rejoiced, all of his kinsmen—living, dead, and still unborn— rejoiced with him. When one man got married, he was not alone, nor did his wife "belong" to him alone. The children from all unions belonged to the collective body.

Whatever happened to the individual happened to the corporate body, the tribe, and whatever happened to the tribe, happened to the individual. A concept the Ashanti share with all other Akan peoples is that "the dead, the living, and those still to be born of the 'tribe' are all members of one family." A cardinal point in understanding the traditional African's view of himself; his self-concept is that he believes: "I am because we are; and because we are, therefore, I am" (Mbiti, 1970).

EXPERIENTIAL COMMUNALITY

Cultural Configuration

Any basic cultural anthropology text will give one a general feeling about why and how man began to live in groups. However, what is not discussed in most texts is the interaction between man—in the group—and man's particular environment. The notion of particular environment is an important one for this pre-

sentation because it determines the common elements of the group's living experiences. For instance, primitive people living in the Sahara Desert respond differently to their environment than inhabitants of the frigid zones or polar regions.[4] And those living in the tropic regions of the Congo would respond still another way to the elements in their environment. A more pointed example is provided by the differences between people living in postindustrial and preindustrial environments. It can be said that the uniqueness of one's environment determines the parameters of one's experience.

Experiential communality is defined here as the sharing of a particular experience by a group of people. It helps to determine what the people will ultimately be like, and, congruently, what ethos, or set of guiding beliefs, a people will follow. These guiding beliefs, in turn, dictate the creation and adoption of the values and customs which in the final analysis determine what social behavior a people will express in *common*—their cultural configuration. Thus, experiential communality is important in determining society's fundamental principles—its beliefs about the nature of man and what kind of society man should create for himself.

The peoples of Africa have traditionally lived in units or clusters commonly referred to as "tribes." For centuries West Africa has characteristically consisted of rolling stretches of tall grassy plains with intermittent bush country and scattered tropical rain forest (Bohannan, 1964). Within this region, the traditional peoples (tribes) were closely related to each other, yet distinct. Each tribe had its own distinct language which was related to the languages of all the other tribes in the region. African languages have been classified as of the Sudanic family (Werner, 1930) and the Niger-Congo stock (Bohannan, 1964). The closely related Bantu languages, the most well known of the Niger-Congo group, ranged from the west coast to most of central and southern

Africa (Bohannan, 1964). Clearly, just as there was a common geographical flavor to the region, so, too, did its inhabitants develop and maintain common behaviors.[5]

The physical nature of the experiential communality is important mainly in that the more unique or distinct it is, the higher the probability that the physical boundaries hinder the influx of neighboring cultural elements. Likewise, it also allows for the development and protective maintenance of indigenous cultural elements. Just as important, however, is the interaction of communal man with his unique environment. The quintessence of this phenomenon is that it results in a set of guiding beliefs which dictate the values and customs the people adopt. Ultimately, this set (or sets) of values determines man's social behavior.

As noted earlier, close examination of the African ethos suggests two operational orders—survival of the tribe and oneness with nature. It was also suggested then that the ethos is probably the focal point of black psychology. The remainder of this paper will be devoted to offering evidence pointing to the continuing functioning of an African ethos.

African Reality and Psychological Assumptions

Black psychology is more than general psychology's "darker" dimension. African (Black) psychology is rooted in the nature of black culture which is based on particular indigenous (originally indigenous to Africa) philosophical assumptions. To make black psychology the dreaded darker dimension of general psychology would amount to distorting African reality so that it will fit Western psychological theories and/or assumptions. For example, a study of the history of general psychology reveals that the controversial mind-body problem stems from the set of early Greek myths known as the Orphic Mysteries. One myth recounts how Dionysus was killed by the *evil* Titans and Zeus saved Dionysus' heart

and killed the Titans. Zeus then created man from the "evil" Titan ashes and Dionysus' heart. Hence, man has a dual nature: He is both *evil* and *divine*. However, the assumptions arising from these early myths caused a problem. There had to be an evaluation of what was "good" and what was "bad." Assuming a dichotomy of the mind and the body, the early philosophers suggested that the body was the "bad" and the mind was the "good"—beliefs accepted unquestioningly during the early period of general psychology's emergence as a "science." Not surprisingly, psychology chose the mind (good) as the domain of its inquiry.

The African concept of man is fundamentally different. Dogon, Mende, and Ashanti all assume man's dual nature but do not attempt to *divide* "mind" from "body" or refer to or imply an inherent good or evil in either aspect of the duality. The propositions of "the notion of unity," "one with nature," and "survival of the people" deny the possibility of such an artificial and arbitrary dichotomy. What is seemingly dualistic is the concept of "twinness." However, as stated earlier, the twin components unite to make the unified man. For Africans, who believed that man, like the universe, is a complicated, *integrated,* unified whole, concerns such as the mind-body controversy would never arise and theoretical developments and/or analysis based solely on the explication of the "mind" or the "body" as separate entities would be useless.

Although the mind-body issue is a single example, it is believed sufficient to demonstrate how philosophical assumptions determined the scientific investigation of psychology. Certainly particular people cannot be meaningfully investigated and understood if *their* philosophical assumptions are not taken into account.

TOWARD BLACK PSYCHOLOGY

This brings us closer to black psychology's evolution from African philosophy. The remaining question is how does one know or how can one "prove" that Africans living in the Western world, and in contemporary times, still have or maintain an African philosophical definition. Black psychology's development is contingent first upon analysis of the linkages between distinct experiential periods in the lives of Africans, and second upon the demonstration of the particular ways in which African philosophy, interacting with alien (particularly Euro-American) philosophies, has determined contemporary African (black) people's perception of reality.

On the Question of Proof

> History is an endeavor toward better understanding, and, consequently, a thing in movement. To limit oneself to "describing science as it is," will always be to betray it. . . . (Bloch, 1953)

For black psychology—and the many other social science areas which are attempting to "blackenize" themselves in order to "explain" contemporary African peoples—the question of proof centers around more than determining whether a particular cultural element (e.g., an artifact) has been retained. The focus must be on the philosophical-psychological linkages between Africans and African Americans (or Americanized Africans).

To determine whether—and to what extent—African orientation has persisted, one must ask "How could it have been maintained?" "What mechanism or circumstances allowed it to be maintained?" An orientation stemming from a particular indigenous African philosophy could only be maintained when its cultural carriers were isolated (and/or insulated) from alien cultural interaction and if their behavioral expression of the orientation did not openly conflict with the cultural-behavioral elements of the "host" society. If the circumstances of the transplantation of New World blacks met one or both of these

conditions, then it is highly probable that the African orientation was retained. This writer maintains that a factor that often facilitated the retention of the African orientation was the particular region's physical features. And the slaves' accessibility to Western indoctrination was probably directly related to the degree of the retention of the African orientation. The rigidly enforced isolation of blacks allowed New World Africans to retain their definition (orientation). Thus, the oppressive system of slavery indirectly encouraged the retention, rather than the destruction, of the African philosophical orientation.

Throughout the New World, large numbers of Africans lived, segregated in given areas. Lorenzo Turner (1958) notes that "wherever Negroes were in the United States, the policy of racial segregation must have often aided in keeping alive the African influence." It is proposed here that a comparative historical analysis of such areas as Brazil, Jamaica, Dutch Guiana, the rural South, and the northern ghetto would reveal a striking and direct correlation between (1) ecological and geographic factors and accessibility of interaction with Westerners and (2) maintenance of the African orientation. Not until the television "explosion" of the early 1950s did the African orientation come fully into contact with Western (Euro-American) styles of behavior and the American way of life.

Expressive behavior and cultural modalities are determined by philosophical definition. One can observe "Africanisms" throughout the New World because the orientation that allows a people to develop or continue to utilize particular cultural elements was not interfered with. Thus, the statement "We are an African people" is valued because, for the most part, New World conditions did not permit the enculturation of the African orientation.

Considerations for Black Psychology

The experiential communality of African peoples can be subdivided into periods. For

Africans living in the Western world, particularly in North America, the breakdown used here is (1) the African experience (prior to 1600), (2) the slavery experience (1600 to 1865), and (3) contemporary black America (1865 to present).

However, rather than treat a few specific behavioral transitions, the discussion will focus on several major philosophical positions and correlative behavioral modalities. The first is survival of the people. From this philosophical position an extended definition of self evolved. That is to say, the self was by philosophical definition the "we" instead of the "I." Tribal membership became the most important identity. One's identity was thus rooted in being an Ashanti, or an Ibo rather than the person, Lodagaa Nyakyusi, who just happened to be an Igbira. Thrust into an alien culture, the "we" notion seemingly came under severe attack. Many scholars note, for example, the prevalent practice during slavery (second distinct experiential communality period) of purposely separating members of the same tribe in order to break down the collective reinforcement of a common definition. However, additional information suggests that in North America the system of slavery was extremely unstructured in its beginning. Nevertheless, the system eventually came to define itself in terms of black people.

During this same period, the notion of tribe or peoplehood which is crucial to the "we" notion underwent a particular modification. Clearly, Africans recognized and respected the distinctions of the tribe. The understanding that one was an Igbira or an Ibo suggested many things. However, the philosophical position within each tribe was the set of guiding beliefs which prescribed the survival of the tribe as a first order. As the system of American slavery began to define slavery in terms of Africans, tribe was more broadly defined in the minds of the Africans. Hence, one sees Africans no longer giving the Ibo or Igbira distinction its former level of importance but

rather adopting broader categories. Thus, as slavery was moving closer and closer to its final definition, the slaves themselves were moving closer to African or black as the final definition of tribe. Thus, the notion of survival of the tribe was not changed or modified during the slavery experience. In fact, one could suggest that the slavery experience allowed the underlying communality of West Africa to surface and define itself as African. Hence, in slavery, the cardinal point, "I am because we are; and because we are, therefore, I am," was not destroyed. In contemporary times, one can note the prevalence of benevolent societies and the role of the Negro church as expressing clear concern for the survival of the tribe.

The second philosophical position that has survived the effects of different experiential periods is the idea of man being an integral part of the "natural rhythm of nature," or, one with nature. Clearly, this can be seen within the African experience in terms of the anthropocentric ontology. The expression of this natural rhythm in the initiation rites gave definition to many of the periods within a person's Sasa dimension. This notion of rhythm also was expressed in the "talking drums."

In traditional African society, the living setting was the community and the emphasis was placed on living in the community not living in a particular household. Even in contemporary times, the "community" seems to manifest this same perception. One could propose that seeing oneself as an integral part of a community is the contemporary definition of man being an integral part of the natural rhythm of nature.

The oral tradition has clearly been transmitted throughout the three experiential periods. As indicated earlier, beliefs and traditions were handed down from father to son for generations upon generations. This tradition gave tremendous importance to the mind or the memory. Remembering phenomenal events in one's Sasa period was very important if not crucial. The slavery tradition seemingly allowed this tradition to continue. That is, because oral communication was the only acceptable system—laws prohibited slaves from being taught to read and write—slavery unknowingly permitted the cultural transmission of the African traditional emphasis on oration and its consequent effects on the mind or memory to remain pretty much intact. Brother Dr. Joseph White (1970) suggests that playing the "dozens" as part of the oral tradition is a game used by black youngsters to teach themselves to keep cool, think fast under pressure, and not say what is really on their minds. Things like rapping and the dozens could also be viewed as *initiation rites* or possibly instances where the "power" of the word is used to make the "individual" psychologically feel better. For example, the Avogan and the Lobi Singi (Herskovits, 1966) are ritualized orations and dance ceremonies where the offended is afforded release of suppressed emotions by ridiculing another. The Dogon have a very interesting circumstance in which certain relations are characterized by exchanges of often obscene insults and gestures (Forde, 1954). Is this the dozens in African form, or better yet are the dozens an African tribalism that has been maintained throughout the different experiential communalities? Another aspect of the oral tradition is the naming ritual. In traditional times, a child was named after an ancestor to symbolize his (the ancestor's) return (Forde, 1954). Often the name typifies a special event in the child's life. Hence, because a person acquired names as he associated with different special experiences, one person may have many names. One need only examine the names of black people to reveal historical tenacity in this orientation—for example, Bo Jangles, Brown Bomber, Stepin Fetchit, Wilt-the-Stilt, Muddy Waters, Iceberg Slim.

With certain modifications, tribalisms have been transmitted in the form of Africanisms throughout the New World experiential periods. Cooperative effort (tribalism) was expressed in the slavery experience. The "Knights of Wise" symbolize that notion and the notion of the survival of the tribe. Funerals in contemporary black America are very symbolic of the custom of reaffirming the bonds of kinship. Distinct motor habits also have been maintained up to the present. Photographic analysis of a particular dance in the Ashanti Kwaside rite illustrates a perfect example of the Charleston. Morality was taught in traditional times via the use of animal tales. Parables were widely prevalent during slavery—the most notable being the "Brer Fox, Brer Rabbit Tales." In contemporary times, one simply notes the use of animal names to denote certain qualities. In the black communities (villages) throughout this country, women and men are referred to as "foxes," "cows," "bears," "buzzards," "dogs," and so forth. The style of talking (dramatic pauses, intonation, and the like), are all reminiscent of a people in tune with the natural rhythm of nature—in tune with the oneness of nature.

The concept of time clearly is illustrative. The attitude that time is phenomenal rather than mathematical can be demonstrated to persist throughout the suggested experiential periods. The notion of CPT (colored people's time) has been translated to mean thirty minutes to an hour later than the scheduled meeting time. However, in the minds of Africans (blacks), time is flexible and the event begins when one gets there. This author thus suggests that a more appropriate enunciation of CPT is "communal potential time."

Black psychology must concern itself with the question of "rhythm." It must discuss, at some great length, "the oral tradition." It must unfold the mysteries of the spiritual energy now known as "soul." It must explain the notion of "extended self" and the "natural" orientation of African peoples to insure the "survival of the tribe." Briefly, it must examine the elements and dimensions of the experiential communalities of African peoples.

It is my contention, therefore, that black psychology must concern itself with the mechanism by which our African definition has been maintained and what values its maintenance has offered black people. Hence, the task of black psychology is to offer an understanding of the behavioral definition of African philosophy and to document what, if any, modifications it has undergone during particular experiential periods.

Notes

1. Like most words that refer to things African, the English usage of the word "tribe" has mixed connotations. In addition, one must recognize that the defining characteristic for a tribe was completely alien and arbitrary. As British and American anthropologists changed their definitions of what constituted a tribe, so changed the physical size of a tribe's membership.

   Although Africa can be considered a cultural entity, most African Americans came from West Africa. While there is diversity, the author assumes that there are unifying cultural themes. For a rather different point, however, see R. A. Lavine, "Personality and Change" in J. N. Padden and E. W. Soja, *The African Experience, Vol. 1.* (Evanston, Ill.: Northwestern University Press, 1970). For present purposes, West Africa is seen as extending from Senegal to Angola.

2. Note that given African philosophy is for the most part unwritten and has no conceptual terms as we know them. The understanding of African philosophy is accomplished by analyzing the traditional structures reflected in tales, proverbs, myths, and such. It is these which in turn reflect the structural concepts of the philosophy.

3. Africa is a very large continent and there are some differences in the concept of time in different areas. For example, hunters have a different conception of time than those in farming communities. In the present paper, the author is making certain simplifying assumptions for purposes of exposition.

4. Primitive is used here in the original sense (without negative connotations)—that is, primary, first, early.

5. In this case, behavioral tools—that is, languages.

References

Abraham, W. W. (1962). *The Mind of Africa.* Chicago: University of Chicago Press.

Bloch, M. (1953). *Historians Craft.* New York: Knopf. (Translated by Peter Putnam).

Bohannan, P. (1964). *Africa and Africans.* New York: American Museum of Science Books.

Forde, D. (1954). *African Worlds.* London: Oxford University.

Gamble, D. P. (1957). *The Wolof of Senegambia.* New York: International Publication Service.

Herskovits, M. J. (1958). *The Myth of the Negro Past.* Boston: Beacon Press.

Jahn, J. (1961). *Muntu.* New York: Grove Press.

Kenyatta, J. (1938). *Facing Mr. Kenya.* London: Vintage Books.

Mbiti, J. S. (1970). *African Religions and Philosophies.* Garden City, NY: Anchor Books, Doubleday.

McCall, D. F. (1969). *Africa in Time-Perspective.* New York: Oxford University Press.

Murdock, G. P. (1959). *Africa: Its Peoples and Their Cultural History.* New York: McGraw-Hill.

Oliver, R., & Fage, J. D. (1962). *A Short History of Africa.* Baltimore: Penguin.

Parrinder, G. (1969). *Religion in Africa.* Baltimore: Penguin.

Radcliff-Brown, A., & Forde, D. (Eds.). (1967). *African Systems of Kinship and Marriage.* New York: Oxford University Press.

Taylor, J. V. (1963). *The Primal Vision.* Philadelphia: Fortress Press.

Temples, P. (1959). *Bantu Philosophy.* Paris: Presence Africaine.

Turner, L. (1958). African Survivals in the New World with Special Emphasis on the Arts. *Africans Seen by American Negroes.* Paris: Presence Africaine.

Werner, A. (1925). *Structure and Relationship of African Languages.* London: Kegan Paul.

White, J. (1970). Guidelines for Black Psychologists. *The Black Scholar,* I(5), 52-57.

White, J. (1970a, August). Toward a Black Psychology. *Ebony,* pp. 25, 44-45, 48–50, 52.

Essay/Discussion Questions

1. What are the cultural and philosophical premises used by Wade Nobles to construct an argument for a black psychology?

2. According to Nobles, how does black psychology differ from white psychology?

3. According to Nobles, what contribution does African conception of humanity make to understanding black psychology?

To Make Them Stand in Fear

KENNETH M. STAMPP

"It is a pity," a North Carolina planter wrote sadly, "that agreeable to the nature of things Slavery and Tyranny must go together and that there is no such thing as having an obedient and useful Slave, without the painful exercise of undue and tyrannical authority." The legislatures and courts of the ante-bellum South recognized this fact and regulated the relationship of master and slave accordingly. "The power of the master must be absolute, to render the submission of the slave perfect," a southern judge once affirmed.[1] Short of deliberately killing or maliciously maiming them, the owner did have almost absolute power over his chattels.

If a bondsman ran away, if he stole the goods, injured the property, or disobeyed the commands of the master, he was guilty of a private and not a public offense; and the state left the prevention and punishment of such offenses to the owner.[2] In governing his bondsmen, therefore, the master made the law, tried offenders, and administered penalties. Whether he exercised his despotic authority benevolently or malevolently depended upon his nature.

Masters were not all alike. Some governed their slaves with great skill and induced them to submit with a minimum of force. Others, lacking the personal qualities needed to accomplish this, governed inefficiently. For example, an Alabama woman with an undisciplined temper found it nearly impossible to control her domestics. Two of them, Alex and Hampton, obeyed her commands only when they found it agreeable to do so; the rest of the time they treated her orders with "the utmost contempt." Hampton "has often laughed in my face and told me that I was the only mistress he ever failed to please, on my saying he should try another soon, he said he could not be worsted, and was willing to go." During a dinner with a friend this mistress was astonished to see how smoothly his household ran. His servants were perfectly trained: "you hear no noise, see no confusion, . . . and their master has no need to point them to their duty. By what secret does he manage all this? The contrast with me is mortifying, truly."[3]

Slaves were not all alike either. They reacted to a particular master or overseer in different ways, some acquiescing in his authority

Reprinted from *The Peculiar Institution: Slavery in the Ante-Bellum South* by Kenneth M. Stampp. New York: Vintage Books, 1956.

and others rebelling against it. Some, because of their temperaments, found it impossible to get along with even a humane master. Ephraim, the property of a kind and pious small Virginia slaveholder, was in trouble so frequently that his master labeled him a "bad negro." After running away Ephraim was sold to a New Orleans slave trader; according to his owner, it was "his wish . . . to be sold."[4] Sometimes a restless slave became passive when transferred to another owner.

A master valued each slave not only on the basis of his physical condition and proficiency as a worker but also in terms of mutual compatibility. For this reason southern courts repeatedly ruled that it was impossible to give any slave an objective valuation. "One man will give or take fifty or one hundred dollars more or less in the purchase of one [bondsman] than another man will," declared a judge. Two prospective purchasers might come to opposite conclusions about the character of a slave: "A habit that would render him useless to one man, would scarcely be considered a blot upon his character in the hands of another." Indeed, the value of slaves depended "upon a thousand things"; it was in the "wretched market of the mere slave trader" that they were rated only "by pound avoirdupois."[5]

The successful master was often a keen student of human psychology. Those who discussed the problem of managing slaves advised owners to study carefully the character of each chattel. "As . . . some negroes are greater offenders than others, so does it require different management for differently disposed negroes. You should *not* 'treat them all alike.'" Too many masters did not understand this. Some bondsmen, warned a Virginian, required "spurring up, some coaxing, some flattery, and others nothing but good words." Many a valuable slave had been "broken down by injudicious management."[6]

It was within this framework of human relationships that the peculiar institution had to operate. To achieve the "perfect" submission of his slaves, to utilize their labor profitably, each master devised a set of rules by which he governed. These were the laws of his private domain—and the techniques which enabled him to minimize the bondsmen's resistance to servitude. The techniques of control were many and varied, some subtle, some ingenious, some brutal. Slaveholders generally relied upon more than one.

A wise master did not take seriously the belief that Negroes were natural-born slaves. He knew better. He knew that Negroes freshly imported from Africa had to be broken in to bondage; that each succeeding generation had to be carefully trained. This was no easy task, for the bondsman rarely submitted willingly. Moreover, he rarely submitted completely. In most cases there was no end to the need for control—at least not until old age reduced the slave to a condition of helplessness.

Masters revealed the qualities they sought to develop in slaves when they singled out certain ones for special commendation. A small Mississippi planter mourned the death of his "faithful and dearly beloved servant" Jack: "Since I have owned him he has been true to me in all respects. He was an obedient trusty servant. . . . I never knew him to steal nor lie and he ever set a moral and industrious example to those around him. . . . I shall ever cherish his memory." A Louisiana sugar planter lost a "very valuable Boy through an accident: His life was a very great one. I have always found him willing and obedient and never knew him to fail to do anything he was put to do."[7] These were "ideal" slaves, the models slaveholders had in mind as they trained and governed their workers.

How might this ideal be approached? The first step, advised those who wrote discourses on the management of slaves, was to establish and maintain strict discipline. An Arkansas master suggested the adoption of the "Army Regulations as to the discipline in Forts." "They must obey at all times, and under all circumstances, cheerfully and with alacrity," affirmed a Virginia slaveholder. "It greatly impairs the happiness of a negro, to be allowed to cultivate an insubordinate temper. Unconditional submission is the only footing upon which slavery should be placed. It is precisely similar to the attitude of a minor to his parent, or a soldier to his general." A South Carolinian limned a perfect relationship between a slave and his master: "that the slave should know that his master is to govern absolutely, and he is to obey implicitly. That he is never for a moment to exercise either his will or judgment in opposition to a positive order."[8]

The second step was to implant in the bondsmen themselves a consciousness of personal inferiority. They had "to know and keep their places," to "feel the difference between master and slave," to understand that bondage was their natural status. They had to feel that African ancestry tainted them, that their color was a badge of degradation. In the country they were to show respect for even their master's nonslaveholding neighbors; in the towns they were to give way on the streets to the most wretched white man. The line between the races must never be crossed, for familiarity caused slaves to forget their lowly station and to become "impudent."[9]

Frederick Douglass explained that a slave might commit the offense of impudence in various ways: "in the tone of an answer; in answering at all; in not answering; in the expression of countenance; in the motion of the head; in the gait, manner and bearing of the slave." Any of these acts, in some subtle way, might indicate the absence of proper subordination. "In a well regulated community," wrote a Texan, "a negro takes off his hat in addressing a white man. . . . Where this is not enforced, we may always look for impudent and rebellious negroes."[10]

The third step in the training of slaves was to awe them with a sense of their master's enormous power. The only principle upon which slavery could be maintained, reported a group of Charlestonians, was the "principle of fear." In his defense of slavery James H. Hammond admitted that this, unfortunately, was true but put the responsibility upon the abolitionists. Antislavery agitation had forced masters to strengthen their authority: "We have to rely more and more on the power of fear. . . . We are determined to continue masters, and to do so we have to draw the reign tighter and tighter day by day to be assured that we hold them in complete check." A North Carolina mistress, after subduing a troublesome domestic, realized that it was essential "to make them stand in fear."[11]

In this the slaveholders had considerable success. Frederick Douglass believed that most slaves stood "in awe" of white men; few could free themselves altogether from the notion that their masters were "invested with a sort of sacredness." Olmsted saw a small white girl stop a slave on the road and boldly order him to return to his plantation. The slave fearfully obeyed her command. A visitor in Mississippi claimed that a master, armed only with a whip or cane, could throw himself among a score of bondsmen and cause them to "flee with terror." He accomplished this by the "peculiar tone of authority" with which he spoke. "Fear, awe, and obedience . . . are interwoven into the very nature of the slave."[12]

The fourth step was to persuade the bondsmen to take an interest in the master's enterprise and to accept his standards of good conduct. A South Carolina planter explained: "The master should make it his business to show his slaves, that the advancement of his individual interest, is at the same time an advancement of theirs. Once they feel this, it will require but little compulsion to make them act as it becomes them"[13] Though slaveholders induced only a few chattels to respond to this appeal, these few were useful examples for others.

The final step was to impress Negroes with their helplessness, to create in them "a habit of perfect dependence" upon their masters.[14] Many believed it dangerous to train slaves to be skilled artisans in the towns, because they tended to become self-reliant. Some thought it equally dangerous to hire them to factory owners. In the Richmond tobacco factories they were alarmingly independent and "insolent." A Virginian was dismayed to find that his bondsmen, while working at an iron furnace, "got a habit of roaming about and *taking care of themselves*." Permitting them to hire their own time produced even worse results. "No higher evidence can be furnished of its baneful effects," wrote a Charlestonian, "than the unwillingness it produces in the slave, to return to the regular life and domestic control of the master."[15]

A spirit of independence was less likely to develop among slaves kept on the land, where most of them became accustomed to having their master provide their basic needs, and where they might be taught that they were unfit to look out for themselves. Slaves then directed their energies to the attainment of mere "temporary ease and enjoyment." "Their masters," Olmsted believed, "calculated on it in them—do not wish to cure it—and by constant practice encourage it."[16]

Here, then, was the way to produce the perfect slave: accustom him to rigid discipline, demand from him unconditional submission, impress upon him his innate inferiority, develop in him a paralyzing fear of white men, train him to adopt the master's code of good behavior, and instill in him a sense of complete dependence. This, at least, was the goal.

But the goal was seldom reached. Every master knew that the average slave was only an imperfect copy of the model. He knew that some bondsmen yielded only to superior power—and yielded reluctantly. This complicated his problem of control.

Notes

1. Charles Pettigrew to Ebenezer Pettigrew, May 19, 1802, Pettigrew Family Papers; Catterall (ed.), *Judicial Cases*, II, p. 57.
2. Catterall (ed.), *Judicial Cases*, I, p. 382; V, p. 249.
3. Sarah A. Gayle Ms. Journal, entries for March 24, September 15, November 10, 1833.
4. Walker Diary, entry for October 5, 1846.
5. Catterall (ed.), *Judicial Cases*, II, pp. 97, 318, 530.
6. *Southern Cultivator*, XVIII (1860), p. 287; *Farmers' Register*, I (1834), pp. 564–65; IV (1836), p. 115.
7. Baker Diary, entry for July 1, 1854; Alexander Franklin Pugh Ms. Plantation Diary, entry for June 21, 1860.
8. *Southern Cultivator*, IV (1846), pp. 43–44; XVIII (1860), pp. 304–305; *Farmers' Register*, V (1837), p. 32.
9. *Southern Planter*, XII (1852), pp. 376–79; *Southern Cultivator*, VIII (1850), p. 163; *Farmers' Register*, I (1834), pp. 564–65.
10. Douglass, *My Bondage*, p. 92; Austin *Texas State Gazette*, October 10, 1857.
11. Phillips (ed.), *Plantation and Frontier*, II, pp. 108–11; *De Bow's Review*, VII (1849), p. 498; Mary W. Bryan to Ebenezer Pettigrew, October 20, 1835, Pettigrew Family Papers.
12. Douglass, *My Bondage*, pp. 250–51; Olmsted, *Back Country*, pp. 444–45; [Ingraham], *South-West*, II, pp. 260–61.
13. *Farmers' Register*, IV (1837), p. 574.
14. *Southern Cultivator*, IV (1846), p. 44.
15. *Southern Planter*, XII (1852), pp. 376–79; Olmsted, *Seaboard*, pp. 58–59; Charleston *Courier*, September 12, 1850.
16. Olmsted, *Seaboard*, pp. 128–29.

Essay/Discussion Questions

1. According to Kenneth Stampp, what systematic mechanisms did slave-owners use to create good slaves?

2. The late Caribbean revolutionary psychiatrist Frantz Fanon once argued that black people are in every way the victims of Western

civilization. Using chattel slavery as an example, develop an essay that sustains Fanon's claim.

3. In view of the overall purpose(s) of chattel slavery, is it reasonable to refer to some slaveowners as benevolent?

O water, voice of my heart, crying in the sand,
All night long crying with a mournful cry,
As I lie and listen, and cannot understand
The voice of my heart in my side or the voice of the sea,
O water, crying for rest, is it I, is it I?
All night long the water is crying to me.
Unresting water, there shall never be rest
Till the last moon droop and the last tide fail,
And the fire of the end begin to burn in the west;
And the heart shall be weary and wonder and cry like the sea,
All life long crying without avail,
As the water all night long is crying to me.
ARTHUR SYMONS

Of Our Spiritual Strivings

W. E. B. DU BOIS

Between me and the other world there is ever an unasked question: unasked by some through feelings of delicacy; by others through the difficulty of rightly framing it. All, nevertheless, flutter round it. They approach me in a half-hesitant sort of way, eye me curiously or compassionately, and then, instead of saying directly, How does it feel to be a problem? they say, I know an excellent colored man in my town; or, I fought at Mechanicsville; or, Do not these Southern outrages make your blood boil? At these I smile, or am interested, or reduce the boiling to a simmer, as the occasion may require. To the real question, How does it feel to be a problem? I answer seldom a word.

And yet, being a problem is a strange experience,—peculiar even for one who has never been anything else, save perhaps in babyhood and in Europe. It is in the early days of rollicking boyhood that the revelation first bursts upon one, all in a day, as it were. I remember well when the shadow swept across me. I was a little thing, away up in the hills of New England, where the dark Housatonic winds between Hoosac and Taghkanic to the sea. In a wee wooden schoolhouse, something put it into the boys' and girls' heads to buy gorgeous visiting-cards—ten cents a package—and exchange. The exchange was merry, till one girl, a tall newcomer, refused my card,—refused it peremptorily, with a glance. Then it dawned upon me with a certain suddenness that I was different from the others; or like, mayhap, in heart and life and longing, but shut out from their world by a vast veil. I had thereafter no desire to tear down that veil, to creep through; I held all beyond it in common contempt, and lived above it in a region of blue sky and great wandering shadows. That sky was bluest when I could beat my mates at examination-time, or beat them at a foot-race, or even beat their stringy heads. Alas, with the years all this fine contempt began to fade; for the worlds I longed

From *Souls of Black Folk* by W. E. B. Du Bois, Penguin Books, 1989. (First published by A. C. McClurg & Co., 1903.)

for, and all their dazzling opportunities, were theirs, not mine. But they should not keep these prizes, I said; some, all, I would wrest from them. Just how I would do it I could never decide: by reading law, by healing the sick, by telling the wonderful tales that swam in my head,—some way. With other black boys the strife was not so fiercely sunny: their youth shrunk into tasteless sycophancy, or into silent hatred of the pale world about them and mocking distrust of everything white; or wasted itself in a bitter cry, Why did God make me an outcast and a stranger in mine own house? The shades of the prison-house closed round about us all: walls strait and stubborn to the whitest, but relentlessly narrow, tall, and unscalable to sons of night who must plod darkly on in resignation, or beat unavailing palms against the stone, or steadily, half hopelessly, watch the streak of blue above.

After the Egyptian and Indian, the Greek and Roman, the Teuton and Mongolian, the Negro is a sort of seventh son, born with a veil, and gifted with second-sight in this American world,—a world which yields him no true self-consciousness, but only lets him see himself through the revelation of the other world. It is a peculiar sensation, this double-consciousness, this sense of always looking at one's self through the eyes of others, of measuring one's soul by the tape of a world that looks on in amused contempt and pity. One ever feels his twoness,—an American, a Negro; two souls, two thoughts, two unreconciled strivings; two warring ideals in one dark body, whose dogged strength alone keeps it from being torn asunder.

The history of the American Negro is the history of this strife—this longing to attain self-conscious manhood, to merge his double self into a better and truer self. In this merging he wishes neither of the older selves to be lost. He would not Africanize America, for America has too much to teach the world and Africa. He would not bleach his Negro soul in a flood of white Americanism, for he knows that Ne-

gro blood has a message for the world. He simply wishes to make it possible for a man to be both a Negro and an American, without being cursed and spit upon by his fellows, without having the doors of Opportunity closed roughly in his face.

This, then, is the end of his striving: to be a co-worker in the kingdom of culture, to escape both death and isolation, to husband and use his best powers and his latent genius. These powers of body and mind have in the past been strangely wasted, dispersed, or forgotten. The shadow of a mighty Negro past flits through the tale of Ethiopia the Shadowy and of Egypt the Sphinx. Throughout history, the powers of single black men flash here and there like falling stars, and die sometimes before the world has rightly gauged their brightness. Here in America, in the few days since Emancipation, the black man's turning hither and thither in hesitant and doubtful striving has often made his very strength to lose effectiveness, to seem like absence of power, like weakness. And yet it is not weakness,—it is the contradiction of double aims. The double-aimed struggle of the black artisan—on the one hand to escape white contempt for a nation of mere hewers of wood and drawers of water, and on the other hand to plough and nail and dig for a poverty-stricken horde—could only result in making him a poor craftsman, for he had but half a heart in either cause. By the poverty and ignorance of his people, the Negro minister or doctor was tempted toward quackery and demagogy; and by the criticism of the other world, toward ideals that made him ashamed of his lowly tasks. The would-be black *savant* was confronted by the paradox that the knowledge his people needed was a twice-told tale to his white neighbors, while the knowledge which would teach the white world was Greek to his own flesh and blood. The innate love of harmony and beauty that set the ruder souls of his people a-dancing and a-singing raised but confusion and doubt in the soul of the black artist; for the beauty revealed to him was the soul-beauty of a race which his larger audience despised, and he could not articulate the message of another people. This waste of double aims, this seeking to satisfy two unreconciled ideals, has wrought sad havoc with the courage and faith and deeds of ten thousand thousand people,—has sent them often wooing false gods and invoking false means of salvation, and at times has even seemed about to make them ashamed of themselves.

Away back in the days of bondage they thought to see in one divine event the end of all doubt and disappointment; few men ever worshipped Freedom with half such unquestioning faith as did the American Negro for two centuries. To him, so far as he thought and dreamed, slavery was indeed the sum of all villainies, the cause of all sorrow, the root of all prejudice; Emancipation was the key to a promised land of sweeter beauty than ever stretched before the eyes of wearied Israelites. In song and exhortation swelled one refrain—Liberty; in his tears and curses the God he implored had Freedom in his right hand. At last it came, suddenly, fearfully, like a dream. With one wild carnival of blood and passion came the message in his own plaintive cadences:—

> *"Shout, O children!*
> *Shout, you're free!*
> *For God has bought your liberty!"*

Years have passed away since then,—ten, twenty, forty; forty years of national life, forty years of renewal and development, and yet the swarthy spectre sits in its accustomed seat at the Nation's feast. In vain do we cry to this our vastest social problem:—

> *"Take any shape but that, and my firm nerves*
> *Shall never tremble!"*

The Nation has not yet found peace from its sins; the freedman has not yet found in freedom his promised land. Whatever of good may have come in these years of change, the shadow of a deep disappointment rests upon the Negro people,—a disappointment all the more bitter because the unattained ideal was unbounded save by the simple ignorance of a lowly people.

The first decade was merely a prolongation of the vain search for freedom, the boon that seemed ever barely to elude their grasp,—like a tantalizing will-o'-the-wisp, maddening and misleading the headless host. The holocaust of war, the terrors of the Ku-Klux Klan, the lies of carpet-baggers, the disorganization of industry, and the contradictory advice of friends and foes, left the bewildered serf with no new watch-word beyond the old cry for freedom. As the time flew, however, he began to grasp a new idea. The ideal of liberty demanded for its attainment powerful means, and these the Fifteenth Amendment gave him. The ballot, which before he had looked upon as a visible sign of freedom, he now regarded as the chief means of gaining and perfecting the liberty with which war had partially endowed him. And why not? Had not votes made war and emancipated millions? Had not votes enfranchised the freedmen? Was anything impossible to a power that had done all this? A million black men started with renewed zeal to vote themselves into the kingdom. So the decade flew away, the revolution of 1876 came, and left the half-free serf weary, wondering, but still inspired. Slowly but steadily, in the following years, a new vision began gradually to replace the dream of political power,—a powerful movement, the rise of another ideal to guide the unguided, another pillar of fire by night after a clouded day. It was the ideal of "book learning"; the curiosity, born of compulsory ignorance, to know and test the power of the cabalistic letters of the white man, the longing to know. Here at last seemed to have been discovered the mountain path to Canaan; longer than the highway of Emancipation and law, steep and rugged, but straight, leading to heights high enough to overlook life.

Up the new path the advance guard toiled, slowly, heavily, doggedly; only those who have watched and guided the faltering feet, the misty minds, the dull understandings, of the dark pupils of these schools know how faithfully, how piteously, this people strove to learn. It was weary work. The cold statistician wrote down the inches of progress here and there, noted also where here and there a foot had slipped or some one had fallen. To the tired climbers, the horizon was ever dark, the mists were often cold, the Canaan was always dim and far away. If, however, the vistas disclosed as yet no goal, no resting-place, little but flattery and criticism, the journey at least gave leisure for reflection and self-examination; it changed the child of Emancipation to the youth with dawning self-consciousness, self-realization, self-respect. In those sombre forests of his striving his own soul rose before him, and he saw himself,—darkly as through a veil; and yet he saw in himself some faint revelation of his power, of his mission. He began to have a dim feeling that, to attain his place in the world, he must be himself, and not another. For the first time he sought to analyze the burden he bore upon his back, that dead-weight of social degradation partially masked behind a half-named Negro problem. He felt his poverty; without a cent, without a home, without land, tools, or savings, he had entered into competition with rich, landed, skilled neighbors. To be a poor man is hard, but to be a poor race in a land of dollars is the very bottom of hardships. He felt the weight of his ignorance,—not simply of letters, but of life, of business, of the humanities; the accumulated sloth and shirking and awkwardness of decades and centuries shackled his hands and feet. Nor was his burden all poverty and ignorance. The red stain of bastardy, which two centuries of systematic legal defilement of Negro women had stamped upon his race, meant not only the loss of ancient African chastity, but also the hereditary weight of a mass of corruption from white adulterers, threatening almost the obliteration of the Negro home.

A people thus handicapped ought not to be asked to race with the world, but rather allowed to give all its time and thought to its own social problems. But alas! while sociologists gleefully count his bastards and his prostitutes, the very soul of the toiling, sweating black man is darkened by the shadow of a vast despair. Men call the shadow prejudice, and learnedly explain it as the natural defence of culture against barbarism, learning against ignorance, purity against crime, the "higher" against the "lower" races. To which the Negro cries Amen! and swears that to so much of this strange prejudice as is founded on just homage to civilization, culture, righteousness, and progress, he humbly bows and meekly does obeisance. But before that nameless prejudice that leaps beyond all this he stands helpless, dismayed, and well nigh speechless; before that personal disrespect and mockery, the ridicule and systematic humiliation, the distortion of fact and wanton license of fancy, the cynical ignoring of the better and the boisterous welcoming of the worse, the all-pervading desire to inculcate disdain for everything black, from Toussaint to the devil,—before this there rises a sickening despair that would disarm and discourage any nation save that black host to whom "discouragement" is an unwritten word.

But the facing of so vast a prejudice could not but bring the inevitable self-questioning, self-disparagement, and lowering of ideals which ever accompany repression and breed in an atmosphere of contempt and hate. Whisperings and portents came borne upon the four winds: Lo! we are diseased and dying, cried the dark hosts; we cannot write, our voting is vain; what need of education, since we must always cook and serve? And the Nation echoed and enforced this self-criticism, saying: Be content to be servants, and nothing more; what need of higher culture for half-men? Away with the black man's ballot, by force or fraud,—and behold the suicide of a race! Nevertheless, out of the evil came something of good,—the more careful adjustment of education to real life, the clearer perception of the Negroes' social responsibilities, and the sobering realization of the meaning of progress.

So dawned the time of *Sturm und Drang:*

storm and stress today rocks our little boat on the mad waters of the world-sea; there is within and without the sound of conflict, the burning of body and rending of soul; inspiration strives with doubt, and faith with vain questionings. The bright ideals of the past,—physical freedom, political power, the training of brains and the training of hands,—all these in turn have waxed and waned, until even the last grows dim and overcast. Are they all wrong,—all false? No, not that, but each alone was over-simple and incomplete,—the dreams of a credulous race-childhood, or the fond imaginings of the other world which does not know and does not want to know our power. To be really true, all these ideals must be melted and welded into one. The training of the schools we need to-day more than ever,—the training of deft hands, quick eyes and ears, and above all the broader, deeper, higher culture of gifted minds and pure hearts. The power of the ballot we need in sheer self-defence, else what shall save us from a second slavery? Freedom, too, the long-sought, we still seek,—the freedom of life and limb, the freedom to work and think, the freedom to love and aspire. Work, culture, liberty,—all these we need, not singly but together, not successively but together, each growing and aiding each, and all striving toward that vaster ideal that swims before the Negro people, the ideal of human brotherhood, gained through the unifying ideal of Race; the ideal of fostering and developing the traits and talents of the Negro, not in opposition to or contempt for other races, but rather in large conformity to the greater ideals of the American Republic, in order that some day on American soil two world-races may give each to each those characteristics both so sadly lack. We the darker ones come even now not altogether empty-handed: there are to-day no truer exponents of the pure human spirit of the Declaration of Independence than the American Negroes; there is no true American music but the wild sweet melodies of the Negro slave; the American fairy tales and folklore are Indian and African; and, all in all, we black men seem the sole oasis of simple faith and reverence in a dusty desert of dollars and smartness. Will America be poorer if she replace her brutal dyspeptic blundering with light-hearted but determined Negro humility? or her coarse and cruel wit with loving jovial good-humor? or her vulgar music with the soul of the Sorrow Songs?

Merely a concrete test of the underlying principles of the great republic is the Negro Problem, and the spiritual striving of the freedmen's sons is the travail of souls whose burden is almost beyond the measure of their strength, but who bear it in the name of an historic race, in the name of this the land of their fathers' fathers, and in the name of human opportunity.

And now what I have briefly sketched in large outline let me on coming pages tell again in many ways, with loving emphasis and deeper detail, that men may listen to the striving in the souls of black folk.

Essay/Discussion Questions

1. According to W. E. B. Du Bois, African Americans are burdened with an agonizing double consciousness that affects their self-image and their historic struggle for freedom. What is the nature of this duality? Why does oppression give rise to some form of duality? How can this contradiction be resolved?

2. Does double consciousness afflict all black people?

3. Does Du Bois appear to accept the view of whites that either he is or black Americans are a problem? White supremacy and anti-black racism certainly pose problems for black people, but do these evil ideologies and practices make black people a problem people or a people with problems?

Part IV Key Terms

Black psychology   *Identity crisis*

Double consciousness   *Psychic alienation*

Part IV Supplementary Readings

Banks, James A., and Jean D. Grambs, eds., *Black Self-Concept: Implications for Education and Social Science*, New York: McGraw-Hill Book Company, 1972.

Bartky, Sandra Lee, *Femininity and Domination: Studies in the Phenomenology of Oppression*, New York: Routledge, 1990.

Blassingame, John W., *The Slave Community: Plantation Life in the Ante-Bellum South*, New York: Oxford University Press, 1972.

Bulhan, Hussein A., *Frantz Fanon and the Psychology of Oppression*, New York: Plenum Press, 1985.

Cross, William E., Jr., *Shades of Black: Diversity in African-American Identity*, Philadelphia: Temple University Press, 1991.

Du Bois, W. E. B., *The Souls of Black Folk*, New York: Dodd, Mead & Company, 1961.

Early, Gerald, ed., *Lure and Loathing: Essays on Race, Identity, and the Ambivalence of Assimilation*, New York: Allen Lane/Penguin Press, 1993.

Ellison, Ralph, *Invisible Man*, New York: Random House, 1952.

Fanon, Frantz, *The Wretched of the Earth*, New York: Grove Press, 1963.

_____, *Black Skin, White Masks*, New York: Grove Press, 1967.

Foucault, Michel, *Madness and Civilization: A History of Insanity in the Age of Reason*, New York: New American Library.

Glass, James M., *Delusion: Internal Dimensions of Political Life*, Ithaca: Cornell University Press, 1985.

_____, *Private Terror/Public Life: Psychosis and the Politics of Community*, Ithaca: Cornell University Press, 1989.

_____, *Shattered Selves: Multiple Personality in a Postmodern World*, Ithaca: Cornell University Press, 1993.

_____, *Psychosis and Power: Threats to Democracy in the Self and the Group*, Ithaca: Cornell University Press, 1995.

Gordon, Lewis R., *Bad Faith and Antiblack Racism*, Atlantic Highlands: Humanities Press, 1995.

_____, *Fanon and the Crisis of European Man: An Essay on Philosophy and the Human Sciences*, New York: Routledge, 1995.

_____, ed., *Existence in Black: An Anthology of Black Existential Philosophy*, New York: Routledge, 1997.

_____, T. Denean Sharpley-Whiting, and Renee T. White, eds., *Fanon: A Critical Reader*, Cambridge: Blackwell Publishers, 1996.

Haley, Alex, and Malcolm X, *The Autobiography of Malcolm X*, New York: Grove Press, 1964.

Hodge, John L., Donald K. Struckmann, and Lynn D. Trost, *Cultural Bases of Racism and Group Oppression: An Examination of Traditional "Western" Structures Which Support Racism, Sexism and Elitism*, Berkeley: Two Riders Press, 1975.

Holloway, Joseph E., ed., *Africanism in American Culture*, Bloomington: Indiana University Press, 1990.

Irele, Abiola, "In Praise of Alienation," in V. Y. Mudimbe, ed., *The Surreptitious Speech: Presence Africaine and the Politics of Otherness, 1947–1987*, Chicago: The University of Chicago, 1992, pp. 201–224.

Jones, Reginald L., ed., *Black Psychology*, 3rd. ed., Berkeley: Cobb & Henry Publishers, 1991.

Kovel, Joel, *White Racism: A Psychohistory*, New York: Pantheon Books, 1970.

Laing, R. D., *The Divided Self: An Existential Study of Sanity and Madness*, New York: Pantheon Books, 1962.

_____, *The Politics of Experience*, New York: Ballantine Books, 1967.

_____, *Self and Others*, New York: Pantheon Books, 1969.

_____, and A. Esterson, *Sanity, Madness and the Family: Families of Schizophrenics*, Baltimore: Penguin Books, 1968.

Levin, David M., ed., *Pathologies of the Modern Self: Postmodern Studies of Narcissism, Schizophrenia, and Depression*, New York: New York University Press, 1987.

Mbiti, John S., *African Religions and Philosophies*, Garden City: Doubleday Books, 1970.

Memmi, Albert, *The Colonizer and the Colonized*, Boston: Beacon Press, 1967.

_____, *Dominated Man: Notes towards a Portrait*, Boston: Beacon Press, 1968.

Morrison, Toni, *The Bluest Eye*, New York: Holt, Rinehart and Winston, 1970.

_____, *Beloved*, New York: Alfred A. Knopf, 1987.

Mudimbe, V. Y., *The Invention of Africa: Gnosis, Philosophy, and the Order of Knowledge*, Bloomington: University of Indiana Press, 1988.

Naylor, Gloria, *The Women of Brewster Place*, New York: Penguin Books, 1983.

Patterson, Orlando, *Slavery and Social Death: A Comparative Study*, Cambridge: Harvard University Press, 1982.

Poussaint, Alvin F., "The Mental Status of Blacks," *The State of Black America*, New York: The National Urban League, pp. 187-239.

Sass, Louis A., *Madness and Modernism: Insanity in the Light of Modern Art, Literature, and Thought*, Cambridge: Harvard University Press, 1992.

Stampp, Kenneth M., *The Peculiar Institution: Slavery in the Ante-Bellum South*, New York: Random House, 1956.

Thomas, Charles W., *Boys No More*, Beverly Hills: Glencoe Press, 1971.

Walker, Alice, *The Color Purple*, New York: Washington Square Press, 1982.

Wright, Richard, *Native Son*, New York: Harper & Row, 1940..

_____, *Black Boy: A Record of Childhood and Youth*, New York: Harper & Row, 1945.

_____, *The Outsider*, New York: Harper & Row, 1953.

_____, *White Man, Listen!*, Garden City: Doubleday & Company, Inc., 1957.

PART V COMMENTARY

The Black Family: Historical and Policy Issues

Shaken by the chaos, dislocation, and dehumanization of enslavement, the African American family has played a major role in the collective survival and social development of African-descended Americans. Drawing from their disrupted but not destroyed cultural traditions, African slaves from diverse ethnic backgrounds (for example, Wolof, Bambara, Igbo, Yoruba, Akan, Fon) who were transported to America had to recreate family and community life in the crucible of economic exploitation and racial oppression. These circumstances set in motion a historical process that required the adaptation and refashioning of African American family dynamics in the midst of harsh and changing circumstances. Today, racial and economic discrimination continue to dictate the conditions under which the contemporary African American family will survive.

The articles collected in this section provide discussion about some trends in the historical development of the African American family and a debate about the cultural and socioeconomic conditions that are influencing the contemporary African American family. Among observers and analysts of the African American situation, there is much agreement on the facts of African American family instability: rising rates of broken marriages, out-of-wedlock births, female-headed households, teenage pregnancies, and welfare dependency among economically impoverished urban African Americans. Where there is considerable disagreement is about the causes of and alternatives to the mounting African American family predicament.

The essay by Andrew Billingsley, "Historical Backgrounds of the Negro Family," examines structures and processes of traditional West African family and communal culture and the effects of chattel slavery on the development of African American family and community life in the United States. By comparing and contrasting the cultural patterns of different and highly complex West African societies, Billingsley illus-

305

trates the central importance of the family. He surveys different kinship relations, patterns of residence, and family organization, and he points out the roles of fathers, mothers, and other significant adults in the love and care of children. However, the slave trade and slavery massively disrupted these regularities of social life both among West African societies and among the West Africans who were involuntarily and brutally transported to the Americas.

Billingsley then turns to the impact of chattel slavery on the emergence of the African American family and its life in the community. Transforming free human beings into unfree commodities, the dynamic process of enslavement forcefully reshaped and deformed the development of the African American personality, culture, and family and community life. It is the dehumanizing experience of enslavement, according to Billingsley, that distinguishes African Americans from those groups of people who voluntarily immigrated to America.

Billingsley contrasts patterns of slavery in the United States and Latin America, particularly Brazil. Although noting that both institutions of enslavement were cruel and inhuman, he suggests that the "closed" system of slavery in the United States was more brutal and its negative consequences more enduring than was the "open" system of slavery in Latin America. Billingsley finds that the institution of chattel slavery in the United States denied to the enslaved the most fundamental rights, even the recognition of the slave's humanity. In contrast, the influence of the Catholic Church and other Spanish and Portuguese cultural and legal traditions resulted in a Latin American system of enslavement that generally protected the physical and personal integrity of slaves, encouraged their manumission, and allowed more stable marriages between slaves and free people of color.

In the American South, however, slave families were denied the protection of the law; slaveowners generally held supreme power over all aspects of their slaves' family and community life. Significantly, male slaves and husbands were relatively powerless to protect their wives, children, and other family members from the violent and/or sexual aggression of slaveowners. Billingsley employs slave narratives to depict the difficulty slaves experienced in their efforts to establish and maintain family ties. The narratives show that when slaves escaped, even the so-called favorite and trusted ones expressed anger toward their former slaveowners about the exploitation, cruelty, and the indignity of being enslaved. The narratives also illustrate the intense love between members of enslaved families and their determination to sustain some form of family life, even as slaveowners sought to destabilize and break up this institution.

Billingsley charges that when the slaves were freed following the Civil War, America never compensated them or their descendants for the more than two centuries of cultural, economic, and political exploitation under chattel slavery. Therefore, during the years immediately after Emancipation, freedom from chattel slavery for thousands of African Americans meant freedom to die of starvation or illness. Indeed, Reconstruction and its aftermath proved to be a monumental disaster for the great mass of African Americans, as the white South reconstituted its regime of violent domination and reinstated the disenfranchisement of former slaves and their descendants. Therefore, African Americans and their families continued a virtual struggle for survival long after chattel slavery had ended.

In his article "The Negro Family," sociologist E. Franklin Frazier skillfully examines the social and economic forces that helped to shape the structure and dynamic of African American families from slavery to freedom. Like Billingsley, Frazier points out that the plantation organization had a major impact on the development of the African American family during the period of chattel slavery. The enslaved family was subject to the changing conditions of the slave system. Since the father might be sold away, the African American mother came to represent the most dependable and important member of the enslaved family. Additionally, the enslaved family was shaped by the practice of slaveowners, some of whom sexually violated their female slaves, producing racially mixed children. Some white men acknowledged and cared for these children, but many did not.

Frazier goes on to analyze the social forces affecting the internal structure and composition of African American families in rural and urban areas. He points out that by the 1940s, economic and social conditions contributed to an increasing tendency toward female heads of household among African Americans in the rural South. The tendency was greater among sharecroppers than among homeowners, resulting from women who were widowed, divorced, or unmarried. Out of this development, which had its ultimate origin in chattel slavery, emerged a pattern of maternal family organization in which the grandmother came to play a dominant role. Frazier observes that the "matriarchal" pattern of family life actually developed in the form of an extended family structure, including several generations of biologically related and adopted children. Additionally, in upper-class African American communities in the rural South, semipatriarchal and extended family patterns developed. In Southern cities, emerging class and geographical differentiation among African Americans also shaped family organization: increasingly stable and semipatriarchal family patterns characterized middle- and upper-class homeowners, while the opposite was the case for lower-class families.

Frazier indicates that the migration from Southern rural to Northern urban areas, beginning at the turn of the century, dislodged many African American families. Yet, he notes, by the 1940s the impact of urban living and emerging socioeconomic class distinctions gave rise to different patterns of African American family and community organization. Frazier observes that the tendency toward family instability was greater in the less well-off center of African American communities, while patterns of family stability and homeownership were greater among middle- and upper-class families who resided on the periphery of these communities.

In recent years, it has become increasingly evident that the African American family is facing a major crisis. Of course, there seems to be a general American trend toward increased divorce, and the increase in out-of-wedlock births among whites just twenty years ago was popularized by the use of such terms as "love child" to refer to the newborn babies. Moreover, Americans seem to be marrying at a later age, and more couples are living together without having gone through a marriage ceremony. Hence, the growing crisis of African American family destabilization needs to be seen in the context of a general alteration of American family arrangements. But that is not the complete story.

The last two articles in this section represent the kind of ideological debate underway among African American policy analysts about the character of the catastrophe confronting the African American family and the future challenge to the African American community posed by a rapidly changing American society. Conservative and Marxian perspectives appear here; the liberal approach is not represented. The conservative perspective tends to find the problem within the individual; it is a matter of moral and value development or change. Because the conservative tends to be critical of government's role, even calling government the cause of many social problems, the conservative advocates a minimal or limited role for government in handling social difficulties. The liberal perspective tends to place the problem within the structural impediments of the existing society. Hence, liberals tend to advocate a more active role for government in managing social problems within existing societal arrangements. The Marxian perspective tends to locate problems at the level of the social order, or its changing character, and in the social relations of power and domination between ruling and subordinate classes. Hence, Marxists tend to view social problems as coming out of the ruling class's exploitation of subordinate classes in a particular social order. In the view of Marxists, problems can either be better handled or be exacerbated by a fundamental change in the existing social order.

In his article, "The Black Family: A Critical Challenge," conservative Glenn C. Loury argues that the catastrophic problem of African American family dislocation (i.e., the rise in rates of teenage pregnancy and out-of-wedlock births) is largely a result of the prevailing and confused values, attitudes, and behavior of young African American women and men. He says that many poor inner-city African American youngsters lack self-esteem and produce children for whom they cannot care in a desperate effort to gain social status. He charges that government welfare policy reinforces and even rewards this behavior by making public assistance easily available and free of stigma. Declaring that government cannot solve the African American family crisis, Loury challenges the African American middle class and its social and religious institutions to take the initiative and provide the leadership necessary to promote more positive moral values and virtuous behavior among impoverished inner-city African American youth.

William Darity, Jr., et al. offer a neo-Marxian analysis of the African American family predicament in their article, "The Dependent Status of Black Families." They suggest that the declining condition of the African American family is related to a contemporary social transformation of major proportions—the winding down of capitalism and the winding up of managerialism. The traditional Marxist outlook states that capitalist society is to be overtaken not by a managerialist but by a socialist society. The declining capitalist society has been energized by money and manufacturing; in contrast, the rising managerial society increasingly is driven by mental capacity and managerial skill. In the emerging social order, a new class of intellectuals and technical intelligentsia is struggling to claim political and cultural dominance from its initial benefactor, the old business class. Hence, in light of contemporary trends and developments, Darity et al. provide a neo-Marxian perspective by refashioning the traditional Marxist analysis in order to explain the black family situation in an emerging post-capitalist order.

Tracing trends and developments relative to the black family back to the age of chattel slavery and emergent capitalism in America, the authors argue that the dependent condition of the black family is rooted in the historical oppression of captured Africans by Euro-Americans. Under the dehumanizing system of chattel slavery, buttressed by the ideology of white supremacy, whites exploited slaves economically and sexually, totally indifferent to the sanctity of the black families. Indeed, as slave-owners' property, slave families had no legal status, as Darity and his colleagues contend by examining the 1857 Supreme Court decision in the Dred Scott case. Even after chattel slavery ended, the courts found ways to negate the original intent of the Reconstruction Amendments, which was to improve the material conditions of former slaves. By the nineteenth century's end, the courts helped usher in an era of American apartheid, punctuated by the 1896 *Plessy v. Ferguson* Supreme Court decision—segregation, lynching, political disenfranchisement, economic exploitation, black male imprisonment, and anti-black terrorism. According to Darity et al., these trends and developments conspired to deprive many black families of supportive male spouses.

Midway through the twentieth century, the courts of law again appeared to be supportive of rights of black Americans. However, as Darity et al. argue, this was a hollow gesture. They demonstrate that both public policies and court decisions in the managerial era converged to destabilize and destroy black and poor families; low-income fathers were marginalized and imprisoned while growing numbers of female-headed families became increasingly impoverished. While the labor-intensive industrial-capitalist system required the working class, the emerging knowledge-intensive postindustrial-managerial society deems working-class skills as unnecessary. In large part, working-class people of all nationalities become superfluous in the managerial age. As more working-class black males are pushed into unemployment, black families become further impoverished and fall apart. The managerial courts often force poor black men into prison, so black females and their children become increasingly destitute.

As a case study of court-sponsored family dissolution, Darity et al. examine the important mid-1960s divorce case of *Mazique v. Mazique*. In this instance, the managerial courts helped to destroy a prominent Washington, D. C., black family; the decision signaled future legal challenges to the family as such in the emerging age of managerialism. This was a case that clearly involved corruption and collusion among the various segments of the legal system—e.g., police, lawyers, and judges. Although she had assisted her husband in obtaining his medical degree and in establishing his medical practice, Mrs. Mazique was the target of the court's brutality. In the final analysis, the courts ruled that Dr. Mazique need pay only a pittance in support of his two sons and former wife. Mrs. Mazique tried courageously but unsuccessfully to appeal her case to the Supreme Court. As a result, Mrs. Mazique lost her human rights, reminiscent of the Dred Scott experience, as she and her children were pauperized. *Mazique v. Mazique* thus pointed the way to future challenges, trends, and developments related to the sanctity of the American family in the managerial age.

To know the possibilities of a race
An appraisal of its past is necessary.
CARTER G. WOODSON

Historical Backgrounds of the Negro Family

ANDREW BILLINGSLEY

In their study of the major ethnic groups in New York, Glazer and Moynihan concluded their discussion of the Negro family with the observation that: "The Negro is only an American, and nothing else. He has no values and culture to guard and protect."[1] This statement could not possibly be true. And yet, it represents the prevailing view among liberal intellectuals who study the Negro experience from the outside. Nat Hentoff, who holds a different view, has pointed out that not one of the critical reviewers of Glazer and Moynihan's book took them to task for this generalization.[2] The implications of the Glazer-Moynihan view of the Negro experience are far-reaching. To say that a people have no culture is to say that they have no common history which has shaped them and taught them. And to deny the history of a people is to deny their humanity.

If, on the other hand, the Negro people constitute in some important respects an ethnic subsociety with a distinct history, what are the essential elements of this history? Three facts stand out above all others. The first is that the Negro people came to this country from Africa and not from Europe. The second is that they came in chains and were consequently uprooted from their cultural and family moorings. The third is that they have been subjected to systematic exclusion from participation and influence in the major institutions of this society even to the present time. Because of these three factors, "the Jews, Irish, Italians, Poles or Scandinavians who see no difference between their former plight and that of Negroes today are either grossly uninformed or are enjoying an unforgiveable false pride."[3]

At the same time, it needs saying that the Negro experience has not been uniform. It has varied according to time, place, and other conditions. The consequences of these experiences have also been varied and complex. Furthermore, not all the history of the Negro people has been negative. There is much in the historical backgrounds of the Negro people which has helped them survive in the face of impossible conditions. This history has produced a most resilient and adaptive people with a strong appreciation for the realities of existence, as reflected in the ability of Negroes to "tell it like it is," and to "get down to the nitty-gritty" in talking about their life circumstances, at least among their friends, if not always when among their enemies. (Perhaps the increasing ability of Negroes of all social classes to speak out to the wider society about their conditions and "tell it like it is" also indicates a feeling, or at least a precarious hope, that we are indeed among friends.)

In this chapter, we will set forth some highlights of the historical backgrounds of the Negro people which have helped to shape both the structure and the functioning of Negro families The family is at once the most sensitive, important, and enduring element in the culture of any people. Whatever its structure, its most important function is everywhere the same—namely, to insure the survival of its people.

Two aspects of Negro history will be considered, their African backgrounds and the impact of slavery. Each of these topics could and should be the subject of full-length books. We can only sketch some of the highlights to show their relevance for a more general understanding of Negro families, and a more comprehensive strategy for the reconstruction of Negro family and community life.

AFRICAN BACKGROUNDS

Negroes, under the tutelage of white Americans, have long viewed their African background with a sense of shame. To be called an African when I was growing up in Alabama was much worse than being called a "nigger." And, to be called a "black African" was a sign of extreme derision.

Later, when I was a student in a Negro college, we were more sophisticated, but we were no less ambivalent about our heritage. The two or three African students on campus were isolated. They were viewed and treated with great disdain, while the two or three white students were the objects of adulation. The African students represented the deep, dark past, while the Caucasians represented the great white hope of the future. In spite of vast changes which have occurred in the world since World War II, with respect to Africa and

its place in the world, large numbers of Negroes still feel just a twinge of inferiority associated with their African heritage. How could it be otherwise, considering the sources of our knowledge about ourselves and our past? Yet the image is changing radically and rapidly. Negroes are taking seriously the questions posed by Lincoln Lynch, formerly of the Congress on Racial Equality: "It is a question of who are we, and where do we come from, and where are we going?"

A careful reading of history and ethnographic studies reveals a pattern of African backgrounds which are ancient, varied, complex, and highly civilized. The evidence suggests that far from being rescued from a primitive savagery by the slave system, Negroes were forcibly uprooted from a long history of strong family and community life every bit as viable as that of their captors. It was a very different type of society from the European-oriented society in the new world.

Several general features of African family life showed great viability. First, family life was not primarily—or even essentially—the affair of two people who happened to be married to each other. It united not simply two people, but two families with a network of extended kin who had considerable influence on the family, and considerable responsibility for its development and well-being. Marriage could neither be entered into nor abandoned without substantial community support. Secondly, marriage and family life in pre-European Africa, as among most tribal people, was enmeshed in centuries of tradition, ritual, custom, and law. "When the Arabs swept into North and West Africa in the Seventh Century," writes John Hope Franklin, "they found a civilization that was already thousands of years old."[4] Thirdly, family life was highly articulated with the rest of the society. The family was an economic and a religious unit which, through its ties with wider kinship circles, was also a political unit. Family life, then, was strong and viable, and was the center of the

African civilization. "At the basis even of economic and political life in Africa was the family, with its inestimable influence over its individual members."[5]

Patterns of Family Life

The most striking feature of African family and community life was the strong and dominant place in family and society assigned to and assumed by the men. This strong, masculine dominance, however, far from being capricious authoritarianism, was supported, guided, and limited by custom and tradition, which also provided a substantial role for the women. The children were provided a quality of care and protection not common in modern societies, for they belonged not alone to their father and mother, but also, and principally, to the wider kinship group.

Family life in West Africa was patterned along several dimensions, including descent, type of marriage, type of family (nuclear, extended), residential pattern, and patterns of child care and protection.

There were three basic patterns of descent or kinship in Africa. The most common was patrilineal descent, in which kinship ties are ascribed only through the father's side of the family. The next most common pattern was matrilineal, in which kinship was reckoned through the mother's side of the family. A third pattern present in only a small part of Africa, mostly in the southern portion of the continent, was double descent, in which kinship was reckoned through both the male and female. This pattern, the only one recognized in America, was virtually unknown in the part of West Africa from which American Negroes came.

The Ibo of Eastern Nigeria, the Yoruba of Western Nigeria, and their neighbors the Dahomeans were patrilineal societies.[6] The Ashanti of Ghana were matrilineal.[7] The Yako people (of Nigeria) practiced double descent.[8] Lineage carried with it distinct rights and ob-

ligations. Certain responsibilities of relatives for the care of the family, and especially the children followed the ascription of lineage, as did legal rights and inheritance. In the patrilineal societies, only one's father's relatives were legally and socially responsible for one's welfare. Inheritance was confined to the father's line. Even in patrilineal situations, however, certain informal courtesies were extended to the mother's relatives. Marriage among mother's relatives was generally forbidden, and other relatives often took on major responsibilities in helping with the care of children even though not legally required to do so.

Even in double descent societies there were norms providing for orderly functioning. According to Daryll Forde, the Yako managed rather well.

> The rights and obligations which derive from matrilineal kinship do not formally conflict with those derived patrilineally. . . . Matrilineal kinship should take precedence over patrilineal in the inheritance of transferable wealth, especially livestock and currency . . . and payments made to a wife's kin at the time of her marriage. . . . On the other hand, patrilineal rights and obligations. . . largely relate to the use of land and houses and to the provision of cooperative labor.[9]

Marriage in Africa was rarely an informal matter between two consenting partners and their relatives. Ceremony and exchange of property were important aspects of an elaborate process which consisted of two basic types: those marriages based on the initiation of the two consenting partners and those based on the initiative of their parents and kin.[10] In either case, both the relevant partners and their parents had to give their consent. While there were more than a dozen specific forms which mating and marriage took in one West African tribe alone, they nevertheless followed these two basic patterns. Those initiated by the principals were less elaborate than those initiated by their parents.

A central feature of marriage in West Africa, as among other non-Western peoples, was the bride price, the requirement of some property or material consideration on the part of the bride to legitimize the marriage contract. The bride price might be paid in goods, money such as native beverages, foodstuffs, livestock, and the like. Or it might be paid in the form of services, such as the bridegroom agreeing to help his prospective father-in-law in the fields, or bringing firewood for his mother-in-law. Thirdly, the bride price might be a payment in kind, in which the bridegroom delivers to his bride's relatives a sister, daughter, or other female relative in exchange for the one he is taking away from them.

The bride price not only was a symbol of the serious and communal nature of marriage, but also served to compensate the parents for a real loss.

Once a couple was married, there were several possible patterns of residence they might follow. The pattern most common in Europe and America is referred to by anthropologists as "neolocal" residence. This pattern involves both partners leaving their homes and taking up residence together in a household not determined by parental ties. This pattern was present, but not common, in Africa. It was almost nonexistent in that portion of West Africa from which American Negroes came.

Another pattern which also had restricted use in Africa was "duolocal" residence, in which neither partner left his parental home after marriage; both partners continued to live among their relatives while visiting each other for brief periods and perhaps working together in the fields. This was a rare custom in Africa, but in Ghana a few tribes practiced this arrangement for the first few years of marriage. Duolocal residence had certain economic advantages for newlyweds who had not had time to establish their economic viability.

Much more common in Africa was a third residential pattern referred to as "unilocal," in which one partner left his or her home and

kin to live with the other, who remained in or near the household of his or her parents. There were three varieties of unilocal residence. One pattern was of matrilocal residence, which involved the man leaving his home and taking up residence with his wife in her family home. This pattern, while common in other parts of the world where matrilineal societies predominate, had very limited currency in West African societies. Common in West Africa was another pattern of unilocal residence referred to as "avunculocal" residence, in which the wife left her home to live with her husband who lived, not in the household of his parents, but in that of his maternal uncle. This happened most often in those matrilineal societies where the man had already left home at the time of adolescence and gone to live with or near his maternal uncle, who was primarily responsible for him. A third pattern was patrilocal, in which the wife went to live in the home and compound of her husband and his relatives. This patrilocal residential pattern corresponds with the patrilineal rule of descent, and was the most common residential pattern for families in all of West Africa.

Of the three basic forms of marriage, monogamy, which unites one man with one woman, was the most common throughout West Africa. Polyandry, which unites one woman with two or more husbands, was almost unknown in this part of the world. But polygyny, which unites one man with two or more wives, was common, though not dominant, throughout that portion of Africa from which slaves were brought to America. Murdock found, as late as 1957, that polygyny was still practiced and sanctioned in 88 per cent of the 154 African societies he studied.

Household organization followed two basic patterns, the nuclear family and the extended family. These two forms of residence existed side by side. Under the nuclear residential pattern, a man and his wife or wives and their children lived together in his house or compound. Often, each woman, along with her small children, occupied a small hut within the husband's compound. Either the man visited them in turn or they took turns coming to spend two or three nights in his hut while doing the cooking and housekeeping. In the extended family household, two or more families, related to each other, lived in the house or compound of a single head. In a typical patrilocal, polygamous extended family, the household might include a patriarchal head, his several wives, and their children, his older sons and their wives and children, plus his younger brothers and their wives and children.

Among the Dahomeans, for example, a senior man in the community may preside over a compound in which live himself and his wives, his younger brothers and their wives, his grown sons and their wives, and the children of all these women.

> There were many instances where a first wife welcomed her second, and where both joined to make a place for the third. Indeed, a woman who, caring for her husband, wishes to further his position in society will . . . make it possible with her own savings for him to obtain another wife. Similarly, when the four day week assigned to a given wife to cohabit with a common husband comes while she is menstruating, her co-wives arrange their time so that this conflict does not deprive her of her opportunity to be with him. And it is far from unusual for a woman to be kind to her husband's children by other women, and for a man to be as close to his children as to their mother. In essence, the great mass of Dahomean matings, either because of complacency or of human ability to make the best of a situation, are permanent ventures which, in terms of human adjustment, cannot be called failures.[11]

The Care and Protection of Children

The father played a very important role in the care and protection of the children in all these West African societies. The strong bonds that bind both fathers and mothers to their children are suggested by the experience of the Ashanti:

> In terms of personal behavior and attitudes, there is often no apparent difference between the relations of mother and children and those of father and children. The warmth, trust, and affection frequently found uniting parents and offspring go harmoniously with the respect shown to both.[12]

Legally, however, an Ashanti father had no authority over his children. In this matrilineal society, the children belonged to the mother's family. Her oldest brother, therefore, carried out the legal responsibilities assigned, in other societies, to the father. Nevertheless, by custom, the children grow up in their father's house, and it was both his obligation and privilege to "feed, clothe, and educate them, and later to set them up in life."[13] The father was responsible for their moral and civic, as well as their economic training. "If anything, Ashanti fathers (unlike mothers) tend to be overly strict in exacting obedience, deference, and good behavior from their children."[14] The following excerpt from Fortes shows the nature of this relationship:

> Ashanti say that a man has no hold over his children, except through their love for him and their conscience. A father wins his children's affection by caring for them. They cannot inherit his property, but he can and often does provide for them by making them gifts of property, land, or money during his lifetime or on his deathbed.[15]

The children reciprocate the affection and respect of their father. Fortes continues:

> To insult, abuse, or assault one's father is an irreparable wrong, one which is bound to bring ill luck. While there is no legal obligation on a son or daughter to support a father in his old age, it would be regarded as a shame and an evil if he or she did not do so.[16]

A father was responsible for the moral behavior of his sons. He, as well as the mother, must give the consent for his son to marry. He is responsible to find his son a wife and to make sure that the suitor of his daughter is able to support her.

Among the Ibo, who were patrilineal, the father's authority was so strong that it was felt his curse would render a child useless for life.[17] Even among the Yako, who recognized double descent, the father was the paramount authority unless the mother and her small children left the compound. Then, as in the case of the matrilineal groups, the mother's brother took up the father's authority.

In all of West African society, whether patrilineal or matrilineal, the relationship between mother and child was primary and paramount. Until he was weaned at the age of one or two, a child was almost never without his mother. "The Ashanti regard the bond between mother and child as the keystone of all social relations."[18] Among the Dahomeans, in spite of their patrilineal descent, the relationship between mother and child was especially strong.

Fortes has described the role of the Ashanti mother:

> An Ashanti woman stints no labour or self-sacrifice for the good of her children. It is mainly to provide them with food, clothing and shelter that she works so hard, importunes her husband, and jealously watches her brother to make sure that he discharges the duties of legal guardian faithfully. No demands upon her are too extreme for a mother. Though she is loathe to punish, and never disowns a child, an Ashanti mother expects obedience and affectionate respect from her children.[19]

The strong attachment to the mother carries over into adulthood for both men and women:

> Ashanti say that throughout her life, a woman's foremost attachment is to her mother, who will always protect and help her. A woman grows up in daily and unbroken intimacy with her mother, learns all feminine skills from her, and above all, derives her character from her. . . . For a man, his mother is his most trusted confidante, especially in

intimate personal matters. A man's first ambition is to gain enough money to be able to build a house for his mother if she does not own one. To be mistress of her own home, with her children and daughters' children around her, is the highest dignity an ordinary woman aspires to.[20]

Herskovitz has observed that among the Dahomeans, children are much more relaxed with their mother than in their father's presence. He continues, "An outstanding instance of the closeness of the relationship between mother and child in this patrilineal society was had in connection with the recording of songs." On one such occasion, he observed of a chief that "though when he commanded his wives and subordinates, he was imperious and his slightest desire was promptly gratified, he was both gentle and affectionate with his mother."[21]

In a matrilineal society, sole legal authority over a child was vested in his mother's oldest living brother. A man's sister's children, and not his own children, were his legal heirs. The rights and obligations associated with this relationship were especially likely to be brought into play in the case of divorce. The mother's brother then assumed the duties and obligations of a father to the children, in addition to his duties to his own children. In general, however, this relationship was more legal than actual, except in regard to inheritance. In this respect, it was sometimes said that the nephew was the enemy of the mother's brother, waiting for him to die.

The father's sister also assisted in the care and protection of his children. She received respect and affection similar to that offered the father, but the attachment was not so deep as to the father and his brothers. She referred to her brother's children as her own, and would discipline and scold them if necessary. His children felt at home in her house and often ate and slept there. This relationship, while not legally binding, was functional and reciprocal. The father's sister could count on her brother's kindness and helpfulness with her own children. They were, after all, his potential heirs.

> Men say that it is to his sister that a man entrusts weighty matters, never to his wife. He will discuss confidential matters, such as those that concern property, money, public office, legal suits, and even the future of his children, or his matrimonial difficulties with his sister, secure in the knowledge that she will tell nobody else.[22]

In the matrilineal society, the strongest bond, next to that between mother and child, was that between siblings by the same mother.

> An older sibling is entitled to punish and reprimand a younger sibling and must be treated with deference. He is, conversely, obliged to help his younger sisters and brothers if they get into trouble. In all other matters, however, equality and fraternity are the governing norms of siblings. It is often said among the Ashanti, for example, "Your brother or your sister, you can deny them nothing."[23]

Among the Ashanti, the relationship between sisters was particularly close.

> Sisters try to live together all their lives. A woman treats her sister's children so much like her own that orphan children often do not know whether their apparent mother is their true mother or their mother's sister. This holds, though to a lesser degree, for the brother's.

Siblings borrowed from each other freely, as if their property were joint. "Borrowing between siblings cannot create debts." The strong relationship between siblings was supported by law and custom.

> The pivot of the Ashanti kinship system in its function as a system of legal relationship is the tie between brother and sister. A brother has legal power over his sister's children because he is her nearest male equivalent and legal power is vested in males (even in a matrilineal society). A sister has claims on her brother because she is his female equivalent and the only source of the continuity of his descent line (in a matrilineal society).[24]

It is sometimes said that "men find it difficult to decide what is more important to them—to have children or for their sisters to have children." If there is a conflict between the need to care for one's sister's children or producing one's own, men generally concluded, according to Fortes, that "sad as it may be to die childless, a good citizen's first anxiety is for his lineage to survive."

If the position of mother and child was the closest, and that of brother and sister the most fraternal, that between a person and his grandparents was the most revered in all of West African society. In Ashanti, for example, "The grandparents on both sides are the most honored of all one's kinfolk." Their position and status were of the greatest importance for the whole social system, in part because they stood between ordinary citizens and the ancestors. If the ancestors got their status because they stood between man and god, the grandparents got theirs because they stood only a little lower on the ladder of infinity. Among the Yoruba, it was the duty and privilege of grandparents to name newborn children. Among the Ashanti, grandmothers—both maternal and paternal—exercised great influence and responsibility in the care and protection of children. "It is from the grandparents of both sexes that children learn family history, folklore, proverbs, and other traditional lore. The grandparents are felt to be the living links with the past."[25]

Family life in the West Africa of our forebears was heavily influenced by geographic, historical, and cultural conditions in that part of the world. A preliterate people, the West Africans nevertheless had a highly complex civilization. Their patterns of family life were closely knit, well organized, highly articulated with kin and community, and highly functional for the economic, social, and psychological life of the people.

Thus the men and women who were taken as slaves to the New World came from societies every bit as civilized and "respectable" as those of the Old World settlers who mastered them. But the two were very different types of society, for the African family was much more closely integrated with the wider levels of kinship and society. The simple transition of millions of persons from Africa to America would in itself have been a major disruption in the lives of the people, even if it had proceeded on a voluntary and humane basis. As we shall see presently, however, this transition was far from simple, voluntary, and humane.

THE IMPACT OF SLAVERY ON NEGRO FAMILY LIFE

The Negro family in the United States began with Anthony and Isabella, who were among the original twenty Negroes landed at Jamestown in 1619, one year before the Mayflower. Later Anthony and Isabella were married, and in 1624 their son William became "the first Negro child born in English America."[26] These first Negroes were treated essentially as indentured servants. However, after 1690 the bulk of Negroes were brought into the country and sold as slaves.

We have shown that the Negroes brought to the United States were the descendants of an ancient and honorable tradition of African family life. While scholars are still in considerable dispute about the relative influence of this heritage on Negro family life today, particularly in the United States, there is no doubt that the breaking up of that tradition by the slave trade has had a major impact on both the form and substance of the Negro family. African slavery, stretching over a period of four centuries and involving the capture of more than 40 million Africans, was, for the European countries, a colossal economic enterprise with effects not unlike those of the discovery of gold. But for the African Negroes, it was a colossal social and psychological disruption.

The transportation of slaves from Africa to the New World completely disrupted the cultural life of the Africans and the historical development of the Negro people. This total discontinuity had a particular impact on the Negro family, because the family is the primary unit of social organization. Some of the ways in which this culture was disrupted may be briefly stated.

First, moving as they did from Africa to the New World, the Negroes were confronted with an alien culture of European genesis. Thus, unlike some of the later migrants, including the Germans, Irish, and Italians, they were not moving into a society in which the historical norms and values and ways of life were familiar and acceptable. Secondly, they came from many different tribes with different languages, cultures, and traditions. Thirdly, they came without their families and often without females at all. In the fourth place, they came in chains. These are all major distinctions between the Negro people and all the other immigrants to this country. Therefore, whatever the nature of the two cultural systems from which they came and to which they arrived, and whatever their capacity for adaptation, they were not free to engage in the ordinary process of acculturation. They were not only cut off from their previous culture, but they were not permitted to develop and assimilate to the new culture in ways that were unfettered and similar to the opportunities available to other immigrant groups.

The Negro slaves in the United States were converted from the free, independent human beings they had been in Africa, to property. They became chattel. This process of dehumanization started at the beginning of the slave-gathering process and was intensified with each stage along the way. It should not be difficult to discern that people who, having been told for 200 years—in ways more effective than words—that they are subhuman, should begin to believe this themselves and internalize these values and pass them on to their children and their children's children. Nor is it difficult to imagine how the history and current status of the Negro people might

Early photograph of a slave couple outside their cabin.

be different if, for all those 200 years, our ancestors had been paid a decent wage for their labor, taught how to invest it, and provided all the supports, privileges, and responsibilities which the New World offered its immigrants of Caucasian ancestry. Conversely, the process of Negro dehumanization provided superior opportunities, privileges, and status to the white majority at the expense of the black minority, and deeply ingrained within white people a crippling sense of superiority.

These are the dynamics of the slave system which must have been in the mind of President Lyndon Johnson when he spoke so eloquently of the need of our society to "heal our history." But the dehumanizing experience of slavery did not come all at once; it came in stages. "Slavery," says Lerone Bennett,

was a black man who stepped out of his hut [in Africa] for a breath of fresh air and ended up

ten months later in Georgia with bruises on his back and a brand on his chest.[27]

It was that and more. At every stage of this process, the Negroes became progressively more disengaged from their cultures, their families, and their humanity. This transition from freedom to slavery has been captured graphically in personal accounts of the experience

One such account comes directly from the pen of an African who was captured and sold into slavery. Olaudah Equiano, who was later known as Gustavus Vassa, was born in Africa in 1745. When he was eleven years old, he was kidnapped, sold into slavery, and transported to the New World. After being sold and resold several times, he finally was given an opportunity by a Philadelphia merchant to work and buy his freedom. He became educated and in 1791 wrote his autobiography. He tells of his early experience with slavery.

The first object which saluted my eyes when I arrived on the coast was the sea, and a slave ship, which was then riding at anchor, and waiting for its cargo. These filled me with astonishment, which was soon connected with terror, when I was carried on board. I was immediately handled, and tossed up to see if I were sound, by some of the crew; and I was now persuaded that I had gotten into a world of bad spirits, and that they were going to kill me. Their complexions too differing so much from ours, their long hair, and the language they spoke (which was very different from any I had ever heard), united to confirm me in this belief.

. . . When I looked round the ship too and saw a large furnace or copper boiling, and a multitude of black people of every description chained together, every one of their countenances expressing dejection and sorrow, I no longer doubted of my fate; and, quite overpowered with horror and anguish, I fell motionless on the deck and fainted.

. . . I was soon put down under the decks, and there I received such a salutation in my nostrils as I had never experienced in my life: so that with the loathsomeness of the stench and crying together, I became so sick and low that I was not able to eat, nor had I the least desire to taste anything.

I now wished for the last friend, death, to relieve me; but soon, to my grief; two of the white men offered me eatables; and, on my refusing to eat, one of them held me fast by the hands, and laid me across, I think, the windlass, and tied my feet, while the other flogged me severely.

. . . I would have jumped over the side, but I could not; and, besides, the crew used to watch us very closely who were not chained down to the decks, lest we should leap into the water; and I have seen some of these poor African prisoners most severely cut for attempting to do so, and hourly whipped for not eating. This indeed was often the case with myself.

In a little time after, amongst the poor chained men, I found some of my own nation, which in a small degree gave ease to my mind. I inquired of these what was to be done with us? They gave me to understand we were to be carried to these white people's country to work for them. I then was a little revived, and thought, if it were no worse than working, my situation was not so desperate.[28]

These episodes capture the essence of the several stages of the slave trade. These consisted first of gathering slaves in Africa, principally as a result of intertribal warfare, but sometimes by simple barter with the chiefs. Premium was placed on young males. The disruptive elements in this practice to family life are apparent. The preponderance of men was so great until, in later years, it was necessary for the European government to require that at least a third of the slaves sold in the New World should be female. In spite of this practice, on many of the plantations, men outnumbered women by nine to one. After capture the slaves were marched to the seaports, a walk often requiring weeks or months of travel. While most of the slaves were gathered on the West Coast of Africa, sometimes they were gathered as many as one thousand miles inland. These slave marches were essentially human caravans, guarded by armed men "with the leaders of the expedition carried in hammocks." The situation has been described by Tannenbaum as follows:

> Little Negro villages in the interior of Africa were frequently attacked in the middle of the night, the people were either killed or captured by Europeans themselves or. . . by Africans acting [for profit] and the victims left alive were shackled with a collar about the neck, men, women and children, and driven for hundreds of miles to the coast.[29]

The rate of sickness and death of the Africans along the slave march was very high. Du Bois has said, "Probably every slave imported represented on the average 5 corpses in Africa or on the high seas."[30] On reaching the coast, the Africans were there sold to the European traders, branded, and put aboard ship for the next phase, which consisted of the celebrated "middle passage." During this passage across the ocean, the slaves were kept in holds like cattle, with a minimum of room and sanitation facilities. When they died, which was frequent, or became seriously ill, which was more frequent, they were cast overboard. The fourth stage consisted of the seasoning of the slaves on the plantations of the West Indies, where they were taught the rudiments of New World agriculture. They were also taught the rudiments of communication in English so as to be able to carry out the instructions of the slave owners and overseers on the plantations. The next stage consisted of the transportation of the slaves to the ports on the mainland, where they were sold to local slave traders, who in turn auctioned them off to the highest bidder, without special regard to their families or tribal connections. The final stage consisted of their disbursal to the plantations in North and South America. The whole process, from the time of a person's capture in Africa until he was settled on a plantation in the New World, sometimes took six months to a year.

Slavery, then, was a massive disruption of the former cultural life of the Africans, which at the same time, by its very nature, prevented the adequate assimilation of the slaves into the New World culture. The crass commercialism of the slave system dominated every phase of this process.

In summary, the Africans came from a vastly different cultural and social system than was known in Europe and the New World. They came in chains under brutal conditions. Whatever their capacity for adaptation, they were not permitted to adapt. They were often sold to plantations and scattered without regard for their former tribal or family connections. The difficulty of reestablishing and maintaining their cultural systems was as apparent in this process as it was appalling. The small number of slaves distributed on each plantation prevented their developing a reliable set of new cultural forms. And finally, the absence of powerful institutions for the protection of

the slaves and their humanity accounted for both the destruction of the previous cultural forms and the prevention of the emergence of new ones as a free and open human development. No other immigrant group can make these statements.

Dominant Patterns of Slavery

While slavery everywhere was cruel and inhuman, it did not everywhere take the same pattern. There were important variations and degrees of cruelty, with differing consequences for the family life of the slaves. Slavery was very different in the United States from what it was in the Latin American countries.

All the major historians who have treated slavery in the New World agree that it was a vastly different and much more oppressive institution in the United States than in Latin America. The essential distinction was that in Latin America slavery was an "open" institution, whereas in the United States it was "closed." These are relative rather than absolute distinctions, but the evidence supporting these general differences is striking.

If historians are agreed on the nature of slavery on the two New World continents, they are not completely agreed on the causes. The major distinction seemed to lie in the structure of the societies and economies of the United States and Brazil, with their different historical and cultural approaches to slavery. Stanley Elkins has pointed to the institutional nature of some of these social forces:

> In Latin America, the very tension and balance among three kinds of organizational concerns—the church, crown, and plantation agriculture—prevented slavery from being carried by its planting class to its ultimate logic. For the slave, this allowed for the development of men and women as moral beings, the result was an "open system"; a system of contacts with free society through which ultimate absorption into that society could and did occur with great frequency.[31]

Tannenbaum has laid heavy stress on the role of the church as an institution and on the Portuguese and Spanish slave laws, which helped to make the slave system in Brazil more humane. The legal system protecting the slaves in this area, and the strong intervention of the church on behalf of the slaves were absent in the United States, which accounts, in part, for the severity of the slave system here. The French slaveholding systems had the active interest of the Catholic church, but not the slave legal tradition.[32]

While not discounting completely the influence of the Catholic church and of the legal traditions protecting slaves, Marvin Harris lays much more stress on the third factor—the types of plantation agriculture involved.[33] In addition, he introduces a fourth factor, the demographic distribution of the population. The Negro slaves in Latin America significantly outnumbered the white settlers, in part because Spain, and probably also Portugal, had a permanent manpower shortage. Since England had a population surplus, the English colonies had many more white settlers. Still a fifth social factor which helps to explain the differences in the two systems of slavery is that the Spanish and the Portuguese both had a history of racial assimilation, while the English and other Northern European people had a history and tradition of racial homogeneity and exclusion of other peoples. A sixth factor is that the Spanish and Portuguese men came to the New World alone in large proportions, while the English brought their wives and families.

In our view, all these forces operated together in the Latin American countries to produce a kind of slave system which helped to generate the social, economic, and political climate for three basic conditions which were absent in the United States: (1) the protection of the physical and personal integrity of slaves; (2) the open, sanctioned, and actual encouragement of manumission; (3) the open, sanctioned, and actual encouragement of stable marriages among slaves and free Negroes.

Physical and Personal Integrity

Slavery in Latin America was a matter of a contract between the bondsman and his master, focused essentially on the master's ownership of the bondsman's labor under certain restricted conditions, with protections of the slave built into the law. In the United States, on the contrary, without such history of legal protections, slavery was allowed to reach its logical extreme of complete ownership of the slave by the master, who was free, depending on his needs, resources, and conscience, to do with his slave as he wished.

The Brazilian law provided for the physical protection and integrity of the slaves as it did for free citizens. For example, in Spanish and Portuguese colonies, it was illegal to kill a slave. In the United States, to kill or not to kill a slave was up to the conscience of the master, and he could beat, injure, or abuse a slave without just cause. In Brazil, if the owner did any of these things, the slave had access to the court, and the judge, if he found the owner guilty, required him to sell the slave to another and kinder owner, pay the original owner a fair price, and forbade the resale of the slave to that owner. This protection for the life and limb of the slave, so crucial to the maintenance and development of both physical and mental health, was completely absent from the legal system of the United States. In the United States, this legacy of the white man's prerogatives to mistreat the Negro man has myriad ramifications in the behavior and the personality structures of both white and Negro men today. For white men, even among liberals and radicals, there is a pervasive sense of condescension toward Negroes which is sometimes reflected in paternalism, sometimes in arrogant disregard, and often in both. Rarely does the sense of true fraternity exist. For the Negro, the chronic sense of inferiority, vulnerability, and submission is sometimes expressed in hostility and, at other times, in dependence. The dominance-submission pattern of white-Negro interrelationships, which often pervades interracial efforts, is a legacy of this slave tradition, in which the Negro slave in the United States was so completely at the mercy of the white man for his very life and physical safety. Elkins has likened the absolute authority of slavery to that of the Nazi concentration camps, in which Jews became dehumanized in a few years.

> The new adjustment, to absolute power in a closed system, involved infantilization, and the detachment was so complete that little trace of prior (and thus alternative) cultural sanctions for behavior and personality remained for the descendants of the first generation.... We do not know how generally a full adjustment was made by the first generation of fresh slaves from Africa. But we do know—from a modern experience—that such an adjustment is possible, not only within the same generation, but within two or three years. This proved possible for people in a full state of complex civilization, for men and women who were not black and not savages.[34]

Legal protections for slaves were not systematic; rather, they were sporadic and unevenly enforced. Every slave state had slave codes, but they differed according to time, place, and manner of enforcement.[35] A slave rebellion could set off a new pattern of enforcement. The essential feature of all the codes was, of course, the same. They were not designed to protect the slaves, but to protect the master in the exercise or use of his property.

The very essence of the slave codes was the requirement that slaves submit to their masters and other white men at all times.[36] They controlled his movements and communications with others and they forbade all persons, including the master, to teach a slave to read and write.

In the United States slaves accused of committing some act of misbehavior were dealt with, for the most part, directly and swiftly by the master or his overseers. If they were brought into court, it was most likely to be one of the informal slave courts with one Justice of the Peace or three to five slave owners sitting as judge and jury. Occasionally, for serious felonies, slaves might be tried in a regular court. The consequences for the slaves were pretty much the same whatever the form of adjudication. Only rarely, for example, did courts enforce laws against the killing of a slave.[37] Neither slaves nor free Negroes could testify against white people. White prosecutors, juries, and judges were not predisposed to provide justice for the slaves. This orientation, fortified by the legal system, was designed to protect the master and other white persons from the slaves and other Negroes.

In a chapter of his book entitled, "To Make Them Stand in Fear," Kenneth Stampp has described the six processes slavemasters used and recommended to each other in their common goal of reducing the slave to subhuman status and perpetuating that status.

> Here, then, was the way to produce a perfect slave: accustom him to rigid discipline, demand from him unconditional submission, impress upon him his innate inferiority, develop in him a paralyzing fear of white men, train him to adopt the master's code of good behavior, and instill in him a sense of complete dependence.[38]

All these efforts at suppression and submission of the slaves worked most of the time and exacted their heavy toll on the personality and behavior of the slaves and their descendants. It was not all smooth sailing for the masters, however. Numerous efforts on the part of the Negroes to fight back included runaways, fights with and murders of cruel masters, and actual insurrections. For all these acts of outrage, the penalties were as swift as they were harsh.

The most notable rebellion was led by Nat Turner on August 22 and 23, 1831. It lasted only forty-eight hours, killed only sixty whites, actively involved only seventy slaves. But it has been described as the most fateful of the slave revolts. It sent fear through the hearts of both whites and Negroes, and its multiple consequences were reflected in the loss of white lives, the retaliation of the whites, and the fear it engendered, in part, because Nat Turner had been such a model slave, deeply religious and obedient. He was sheltered by slaves for two months before he was caught, tried, and hanged.[39]

Manumission

A second respect in which the political, legal, religious, economic, and demographic forces combined to produce a different slave system in Latin America involved manumission. Not only were slaves treated with certain limited, though specified, degrees of humanity, but the very system of slavery in Latin America encouraged the freeing of slaves. There were hundreds of ways in which slaves could earn their freedom, and slave owners were often rewarded for freeing their slaves.

Slaves could purchase their own freedom or the freedom of a wife or of a child at birth for money which they could earn from work performed on Sundays or any of the other numerous holidays in these Catholic countries. In Brazil, the Negroes had altogether 84 days a year in which they could work for themselves, save their money, and do with it as they wished. They could even purchase their own freedom on the installment plan. Each installment provided certain liberties. On paying the first installment, for example, a slave was free to move out of his master's house, provided that he continued working for him. The practice was so widespread that slaves often paid all but the final installment, so that they remained technically a slave while in most respects free, and thus avoided the taxes and military service imposed on citizens. Freedom societies sprang up; these were savings associations for the purchase of the freedom of their fellow members. A man would often purchase the freedom of his wife while he remained a slave, and thus their children would

be free because their status followed their mother's. For the most part, the original purchasing price of the slave was the price a slave had to pay for himself, though he might actually be worth more on the open market.

In addition to purchasing his freedom, there were a myriad of other ways in which a slave in Latin America could become free. His master could simply free him of his own accord, provided that he did it in the church or before a judge or by some solemn and explicit procedure, such as making a statement to that effect in writing. If a slave was owned by two people— say husband and wife—and one wanted to free him, the other was bound to accept a just price fixed by a local judge and accede to the freedom. A slave could become free against his master's will for doing heroic deeds for the community, such as reporting disloyalty against the king, or by denouncing a forced rape or murder in the community. Under some circumstances, a slave could become free even against his master's will by becoming a minister. If a slave became heir to his master, or was appointed guardian of his master's children, he was automatically freed. A parent having ten children could automatically claim freedom. In addition, freeing of one's slaves became an honorable tradition. Masters often would free a slave or two on the occasion of their daughter's wedding or the birth of the first son in the family. Favorite house slaves were often freed on the occasion of their birthdays or weddings.

These measures, in which the law itself facilitated manumission, had far-reaching consequences in the whole social structure of Latin America, setting up social expectations and values favorable to the freeing of slaves, but totally absent in the system of laws, norms, and social values of the plantation South in the United States A man wanting to free his slave in Latin America was encouraged by the system. A man wanting to free his slave in the United States had to go against prevailing norms. For the Negro slaves, slavery in Latin

America was a burning caldron with a ladder and an open top. In the United States, there was no ladder, and though people sometimes found their way out by the aid of kindly masters, their own daring escapes, or the aid of abolitionists, including especially the underground railroad, the top of the caldron was not to any significant extent open. There merely were holes in it which served as "screens of opportunity," through which only a few were allowed to escape.

In Brazil, fully two-thirds of the Negroes had already been freed through various procedures by the time of general emancipation in 1888. In the United States, on the other hand, never more than 10 per cent of the Negroes were free. In Brazil, once the slave had been freed, he enjoyed all the ordinary civil rights of other citizens; in fact, if a Negro was not known to be a slave in Brazil, he was presumed to be a free man. A completely different culture existed in the United States. Freed Negroes had only limited and circumscribed privileges and almost no legal rights. And a Negro in the United States South, prior to emancipation, was presumed to be a slave unless he could prove his free status.

Among the most far-reaching consequences of the two different slave systems were the manner of their dissolution and the status of the masses of freed men after emancipation. Brazil managed to escape the bloody holocaust which ended slavery in this country and produced a crisis in the social order which has not yet been healed. Slavery was actually abolished gradually and in stages in Brazil. In 1871, the Portuguese government promulgated the "doctrine of the free womb." This doctrine held that since slavery in Brazil was ownership of a person's labor and not of his innermost parts, the womb of a slave woman was free, and consequently any issue from that womb was also free. In view of this practice of freeing all newborn babies, it was only a matter of time till slavery would have died a natural death in Brazil. In 1885, a law was passed declaring that all slaves should become free on reaching the age of sixty. And finally, on May 13, 1888, "The Golden Law" was passed, abolishing slavery and freeing all slaves in Brazil.[40]

There were, of course, exceptional men in the United States who violated the slave codes because of self-interest, paternalism, humanitarianism, or a combination of all three. Slaves were sometimes freed for such "meritorious" service as reporting a planned slave insurrection. Among the very rare instances of outright manumission for apparently humanitarian reasons, a man in the upper South who willed that his slaves be freed on his death gave four reasons for such unusual, if still cowardly behavior:

> Reason the first. Agreeably to the rights of man, every human being, be his or her color what it may, is entitled to freedom. . . . Reason the second. My conscience, the great criterion, condemns me for keeping them in slavery. Reason the third. The golden rule directs us to do unto every human creature as we would wish to be done unto. . . . Reason the fourth and last. I wish to die with a clear conscience.[41]

Another major distinction between the United States and Latin America is that while the emancipated Negroes in the United States were "freedmen," in Brazil they were for the most part simply "free men." They were accepted into the free society, not only of the other ex-slaves, but of the whites as well. The closed system of slavery in the United States had produced a caste-like set of relations between white and Negro unknown in Brazil, where a person was considered to be inferior only if he was a slave—a condition that could be remedied. In the United States, on the other hand, it was considered that a person was a slave because he was innately inferior, and both conditions were associated with his blackness. Consequently, it has proved, even after emancipation, much more difficult for our society to shake off the badge of inferiority associated with color and the caste-like qualities which confound the socioeconomic distinctions between the races. In Latin America, the distinction is primarily socioeconomic.

The Family

A third respect in which the Latin American legal system protected the slaves was by providing for the creation and preservation of the family.

In Latin America, the law and the Church provided certain protections for the family life of the Negro slaves. Slaves were free to marry, even against the will of their masters, provided only that they keep serving him as before. They were free to intermarry with free persons, provided only that their slave status

not be concealed. Slaves who were married could not be sold apart from each other unless it was guaranteed that they could continue to live together as man and wife. None of these minimum protections of the family were built into the system of slavery in the United States, where slaves were often permitted to marry, but only at the discretion of the master. In the United States, the slave husband was not the head of his household; the white owner was the head. The family had no rights that the slave owner was bound to respect. The wholesale disregard for family integrity among the slaves may be suggested by the following quotation from an actual advertisement in a New Orleans newspaper: "A Negro woman, 24 years of age, and her two children, one eight and

Early photograph of a slave family, posing outside their dwelling.

the other three years old. Said Negroes will be sold separately or together as desired."[42] Another, in South Carolina in 1838, offered 120 slaves for sale of both sexes and every description, including "several women with children, small girls suitable for nurses, and several small boys without their mothers."[43]

The official records of shipping companies also reflected this family disruption "Of four cargoes, making a total of 646 slaves, 396 were apparently owned by Franklen and Armfield. Among these there were only two full families. . . . There were 20 husbandless mothers with 33 children."[44]

Perhaps the cruelest of all the forms of emasculation of the Negro family was the very widespread practice, perhaps in all the slave states, of breeding slaves for sale as if they were cattle. An enterprising slave master, then, could enjoy not only the emotional advantages accrued from sex relations with his female slaves, but also the economic advantage which accrued from selling his offspring in the open market. Such decadence was much too common to have been confined to a few undesirable or emotionally disturbed white citizens. It was widespread and normative, though of course not all planters engaged in such practices More common, perhaps, was the practice of breeding slaves among each other. One advertisement of a shipment of slaves claimed that

> they are not Negroes selected out of a larger gang for the purpose of a sale, but are prime. Their present owner, with great trouble and expense, selected them out of many for several years past. They were purchased for stock and breeding Negroes and to any planter who particularly wants them for that purpose, they are a very choice and desirable gang.[45]

In the United States, then, contrary to Latin America, the legal system made no provision for, and took no special recognition of, marriage and family life among the Negro slaves. In addition, the slave owners and other whites took frequent sexual advantage of the slave women. Even if she were the wife of a slave, her husband could not protect her. The Attorney General of Maryland observed in one of his reports that "a slave never has maintained an action against the violator of his bed."[46] This statement apparently would apply in other states as well, regardless of whether the violator was slave or citizen. The powerlessness of the Negro man to protect his family for two and a half centuries under slavery has had crippling consequences for the relations of Negro men and women to this very day.

Slavery and Family Life in the United States

Marriage among slaves was not altogether absent in the United States, and was probably more common than has been generally recognized. It was, however, a far different institution with much less structural and institutional support in this country than in Latin America. The strong hand of the slave owner dominated the Negro family, which existed only at his mercy and often at his own personal instigation. An ex-slave has told of getting married on one plantation:

> When you married, you had to jump over a broom three times. Dat was de license. If master seen two slaves together too much he would tell 'em dey was married. Hit didn't make no difference if you wanted to or not; he would put you in de same cabin ant make you live together. . . . Marsa used to sometimes pick our wives fo' us. If he didn't have on his place enough women for the men, he would wait on de side of de road till a big wagon loaded with slaves come by. Den Marsa would stop de ole nigger-trader and buy you a woman. Wasn't no use tryin' to pick one, cause Marsa wasn't gonna pay but so much for her. All he wanted was a young healthy one who looked like she could have children, whether she was purty or ugly as sin.[47]

The difficulties Negro men had in establishing, protecting, and maintaining family ties, together with the strong values they placed on family life and responsibilities, are graphically depicted in the correspondence between ex-slaves and their ex-masters. It often happened that the slaves who escaped into freedom by the underground railroad were those who had been treated relatively well by their owners, and who even had been taught to read and write. Often they were the "favorite" slaves of the owners, highly trusted and considered dependable and grateful. Thus, it was not uncommon that when a slave holder found out the whereabouts of an ex-slave, he would write to him, imploring him to return. Three letters by ex-slaves written in response to such appeals will illustrate the damaging consequences slavery had for Negro family life. The first was written by Henry Bibb in 1844, after he had escaped into Canada by way of the underground railroad.

Dear Sir:—I am happy to inform you that you are not mistaken in the man whom you sold as property, and received pay for as such. But I thank God that I am not property now, but am regarded as a man like yourself, and although I live far north, I am enjoying a comfortable living by my own industry. If you should ever chance to be traveling this way, and will call on me, I will use you better than you did me while you held me as a slave. Think not that I have any malice against you, for the cruel treatment which you inflicted on me while I was in your power. As it was the custom of your country, to treat your fellow men as you did me and my little family, I can freely forgive you.

I wish to be remembered in love to my aged mother, and friends; please tell her that if we should never meet again in this life, my prayer shall be to God that we may meet in Heaven, where parting shall be no more.

You wish to be remembered to King and Jack. I am pleased, sir, to inform you that they are both here, well, and doing well. They are both living in Canada West. They are now the owners of better farms than the men are who once owned them.

You may perhaps think hard of us for running away from slavery, but as to myself, I have but one apology to make for it, which is this: I have only to regret that I did not start at an earlier period. I might have been free long before I was. But you had it in your power to have kept me there much longer than you did. I think it is very probable that I should have been a toiling slave on your property today, if you had treated me differently.

To be compelled to stand by and see you whip and slash my wife without mercy, when I could afford her no protection, not even by offering myself to suffer the lash in her place, was more than I felt it to be the duty of a slave husband to endure, while the way was open to Canada. My infant child was also frequently flogged by Mrs. Gatewood, for crying, until its skin was bruised literally purple. This kind of treatment was what drove me from home and family, to seek a better home for them. But I am willing to forget the past. I should be pleased to hear from you again, on the reception of this, and should also be very happy to correspond with you often, if it should be agreeable to yourself. I subscribe myself a friend to the oppressed, and Liberty forever.[48]

Another letter was written in 1860 by J. W. Loguen who escaped to New England:

Mrs. Sarah Logue: Yours of the 20th of February is duly received, and I thank you for it. It is a long time since I heard from my poor old mother, and I am glad to know that she is yet alive, and, as you say, "as well as common." What that means, I don't know. I wish you had said more about her.

You are a woman; but had you a woman's heart, you never could have insulted a brother by telling him you sold his only remaining brother and sister, because he put himself beyond your power to convert him into money.

You sold my brother and sister, Abe and Ann, and twelve acres of land, you say, because I ran away. Now you have the unutterable meanness to ask me to return and be your miserable chattel, or, in lieu thereof, send you $1000 to enable you to redeem the land, but not to redeem my poor brother and sister! If I were to send you the money, it would be to get my brother and sister, and not that you should get land. You say you are a cripple, and doubtless you say it to stir my pity, for you knew I was susceptible in that direction. I do pity you from the bottom of my heart. Nevertheless, I am indignant beyond the power of words to express, that you should be so sunken and cruel as to tear the hearts I love so much all to pieces; that you should be willing to impale and crucify us all, out of compassion for your foot or leg. Wretched woman! Be it known to you that I value my freedom, to say nothing of my mother, brothers, and sisters, more than your whole body; more, indeed, than my own life; more than all the lives of all the slaveholders and tyrants under heaven.

You say you have offers to buy me, and that you shall sell me if I do not send you $1000, and in the same breath and almost in the same sentence, you say, "You know we raised you as we did our own children." Woman, did you raise your own children for the market? . . .

. . . But you say I am a thief, because I took the old mare along with me. Have you got to learn that I had a better right to the old mare, as you call her, than Manasseth Logue had to me? Is it a greater sin for me to steal his horse, than it was for him to rob my mother's cradle, and steal me? If he and you infer that I forfeit all my rights to you, shall not I infer that you forfeit all your rights to me? Have you got to learn that human rights are mutual and reciprocal, and if you take my liberty and life, you forfeit your own liberty and life? Before God and high heaven, is there a law for one man which is not a law for every other man?

If you or any other speculator on my body and rights, wish to know how I regard my rights, they need but come here, and lay their hands on me to enslave me. Did you think to terrify me by presenting the alternative to give my money to you, or give my body to slavery? Then let me say to you, that I meet the proposition with unutterable scorn and contempt. The proposition is an outrage and an insult. I will not budge one hair's breadth. I will not breathe a shorter breath, even to save me from your persecutions. I stand among a free people, who, I thank God, sympathize with my rights,

and the rights of mankind; and if your emissaries and venders come here to re-enslave me, and escape the unshrinking vigor of my own right arm, I trust my strong and brave friends, in this city and State, will be my rescuers and avengers.[49]

A third letter is from Jourdon Anderson, who was freed by the Union Army Forces during the Civil War.

Sir: I got your letter, and was glad to find that you had not forgotten Jourdon, and that you wanted me to come back and live with you again, promising to do better for me than anybody else can. . . .

. . . I want to know particularly what the good chance is you propose to give me. I am doing tolerably well here. I get twenty-five dollars a month, with victuals and clothing; have a comfortable home for Mandy,—the folks call her Mrs. Anderson—and the children—Milly, Jane, and Grundy—go to school and are learning well. The teacher says Grundy has a head for a preacher. They go to Sunday School, and Mandy and me attend church regularly. We are kindly treated. Sometimes we overhear others saying, "Them colored people were slaves" down in Tennessee. The children feel hurt when they hear such remarks; but I tell them it was no disgrace in Tennessee to belong to Colonel Anderson. Many darkeys would have been proud, as I used to be, to call you master. Now if you will write and say what wages you will give me, I will be better able to decide whether it would be to my advantage to move back again.

. . . Mandy says she would be afraid to go back without some proof that you were disposed to treat us justly and kindly; and we have concluded to test your sincerity by asking you to send us our wages for the time we served you. This will make us forget and forgive old scores, and rely on your justice and friendship in the future. I served you faithfully for thirty two years, and Mandy twenty years. At twenty-five dollars a month for me, and two dollars a week for Mandy, our earnings would amount to eleven thousand six hundred and eighty dollars. Add to this the interest for the time our wages have been kept back, and deduct what you paid for our clothing, and three doctor's visits to me, and pulling a tooth for Mandy, and the balance will show what we are in justice entitled to.

... In answering this letter, please state if there would be any safety for my Milly and Jane, who are now grown up, and both goodlooking girls. You know how it was with poor Matilda and Catherine. I would rather stay here and starve—and die, if it come to that—than have my girls brought to shame by the violence and wickedness of their young masters. You will also please state if there has been any schools opened for the colored children in your neighborhood. The great desire of my life is to give my children an education, and have them form virtuous habits.

Say howdy to George Carter, and thank him for taking the pistol from you when you were shooting at me.[50]

The Negro family existed during slavery in the United States, but it was a most precarious existence, dependent wholly on the economic and personal interests of the white man, and the grim determination and bravery of the black man.

Interracial Marriage

A fourth respect in which the slave system in the United States differed markedly from that in Latin America relative to family life was in the area of interracial marriage. Marriage between white persons and black persons, particularly between European men and African women, was common, sanctioned, and encouraged in Latin America even under slavery. It was forbidden by law in the United States, not only during slavery, but in modern times as well. Not until 1967 were the last legal supports for such bans struck down by the U. S. Supreme Court. Even now, however, despite the lack of legal support for such bans on interracial marriage, the customs and norms of the white majority in the country, and to some extent the black minority, make interracial marriage a rare and deviant sort of behavior.

Marriage among peoples of different cultural backgrounds is considered, by many students of assimilation, to be the ultimate test of the process of integration, as well as of whether a caste system exists, separating two peoples into superior and inferior beings. In these respects, then, the question of interracial marriage is more than a matter of personal choice; it is an index of the view and place of different peoples in the national life.

It is not, of course, that miscegenation and other forms of interracial contact have been absent in the United States. In fact, they have been persistent. But they have been more or less illicit, unsanctioned by the wider society. Consequently, the white men who have been the chief exploiters of Negro women in such relationships have escaped the responsibilities associated with these relationships. The manner in which Negro women were exploited by white men during slavery, and the damage these relationships caused to the stability of Negro family life can be seen from two personal accounts provided us by two remarkable Negro women writers, Pauli Murray and Margaret Walker. Both accounts are taken from actual family histories.

Pauli Murray tells of her own great-grandmother, Harriet, who was born a slave in 1819. She was the product of miscegenation and described as mulatto. When she was fifteen, she was sold to a medical doctor in North Carolina who bought her as a housemaid for his own eighteen-year-old daughter. These two women, the slave and the mistress, grew into the most intricate of relationships filled with all the human drama of love, envy, and hate imaginable.[51]

When Harriet was twenty years old, she asked her owner for permission to marry a young mulatto man who was born free, and who lived and worked in the town. It is said that Dr. Smith, her owner, readily agreed. "It was good business. He had no obligation to the husband, and every child by the marriage would be his slave and worth several hundred dollars at birth." Harriet and her husband were not permitted to live together permanently, but he was permitted to visit her in the evenings after she had finished her work in the "big house." After three years, in about 1842, they had a child. Of course, this son became a slave like his mother, and was the property of Dr. Smith.

Sometime after this, Dr. Smith's two grown sons came home from college, and both took a special interest in Harriet. "Before long," Miss Murray tells us, "everybody in the house knew that a storm was brewing between the brothers, and that Harriet was the cause of it." The author then describes an encounter between Sydney, one of the Smith sons, and Reuben, Harriet's free Negro husband.

Sydney Smith informed Reuben that he could not be legally married to a slave, and that if he were ever caught visiting Harriet again he would be whipped and thrown in jail. The author continues: "Reuben had to leave without a word to Harriet. That was the last she ever saw of him." It is not, however, that Reuben abandoned his wife, his child, and his rights so easily; he came back to see them one time, but the two Smith brothers saw him.

> The brothers beat Reuben with the butt end of a carriage whip and when they finally let him go, they told him if he ever came back on the Smith lot, they'd shoot him on sight. He disappeared from the county and nothing was heard of him again.

Shortly after Reuben was banished from his wife's cabin, Sydney Smith "had his way with her" in the presence of her little boy.

> He raped her again, again, and again in the weeks that followed. Night after night he would force open her cabin door and nail it up again on the inside so that she could not get out. Then he would beat her into submission.

Sydney's brother Frank was furious at the turn of events. One night he accosted Sydney on his way from Harriet's cabin.

The brothers had it out once and for all, and there was a terrible fight. Early the next morning, one of the slaves found Sydney lying unconscious in the yard, his clothes soaked with blood and an ugly hole in his head. . . . He learned his lesson. He never touched Harriet again.

But already Harriet was pregnant with Sydney's child. This child, born on the Smith lot in February 1844, was Pauli Murray's grandmother. After the baby was born, Sydney's brother Frank "had his way" with Harriet. This time she did not fight back.

This relationship was long and enduring. Over the course of five years, Harriet bore to Francis Smith three daughters. Harriet was now the mother of five children by three different fathers, all growing up on the same plantation but treated according to their father's positions. Julius, the oldest, was almost ignored by the Big House, and his mother was almost a stranger to him. When he was around thirteen, he got lost in the woods during a heavy snowstorm. They found him almost frozen to death. He was severely crippled for the rest of his life.

The girls lived lives of crippling ambivalence.

> The Smiths were as incapable of treating the little girls wholly as servants as they were of recognizing them openly as kin. At times the Smiths' involuntary gestures of kinship were so pronounced, the children could not help thinking of themselves as Smith grandchildren. At other times, their innocent overtures of affection were rebuffed without explanation and they were driven away with cruel epithets.

In *Jubilee* Margaret Walker tells a similar story[52] of her own grandmother Vyry, and her great-grandmother Hetta. Several generations before the Civil War, Hetta, a slave girl, had borne fifteen children by the time she was twenty-nine She died in childbirth with the sixteenth. Many of them, including Vyry, were by the son of her owner. Vyry is the center of a most fascinating account of the pre-Civil War period in the life of the slaves, freedmen, and masters. Randall Ware, a young freedman, who loved, courted, married, and lost her, is a most remarkable example of black manhood, who, despite the efforts of the system to crush him, managed to survive. There was a man, if only for one brief season! He insisted on exercising his freedom in the plantation South, which conspired to make slaves of all black people. He almost rescued his wife and family from slavery. He escaped to the North by way of the underground railroad and returned to fight in the Civil War. This is not, however, a story of essential triumph. It is a vivid illustration of the tragedy of slavery and the crippling consequences it had for Negro family life.

In summary, it may be said that the slave system had a crippling effect on the establishment, maintenance, and growth of normal patterns of family life among the Negro people. This impact was cruel in all the Americas. It was exceedingly vicious in the United States. There were several facets of this process of personal, family, and social emasculation First, the family was broken up at the very beginning of the slave trade in the manner in which the slaves were gathered, the disregard the captors showed to family and kinship ties, the preference they showed for selecting young men in the prime of their life, and the consequent underrepresentation of females for hundreds of years, and the inhumane conditions under which the slaves were quartered, worked, and treated.

All these conditions were found everywhere in the slave system, although some evidence suggests that the living conditions were worse in the United States. The particular factors which characterize the impact of slavery on the Negro family in the United States include, in addition to the above, the absence of legal foundation, sanction, and protection of marriage as an institution among the slaves; the exploitation of slave women by white owners and overseers for both pleasure and profit; the systematic denial of a role for the man as husband and father; the willful separation of related men, women, and children and selling them to different plantations. In short, there was the absence, in the United States, of societal support and protection for the Negro family as a physical, psychological, social, or economic unit. This crippled the development, not only of individual slaves, but of families, and hence of the whole society of Negro people. The consequences these conditions wrought for generations of Negroes under the slave system were direct and insidious. The consequences for succeeding and even modern generations of Negroes are, perhaps, less direct, but no less insidious. At no time in the history of this country have Negroes experienced, systematically and generally, the kind of social supports from the society which would even approach the intensity of the negative impact of slavery. Not only has the society not made any massive efforts to undo the damages of slavery and actively integrate the Negro people into the society on the basis of equality, but many of the explicit conditions of slavery still exist at the present time.

The Failures of Reconstruction After the Civil War

It is often said that slavery was a long time ago; that surely the freedom and opportunity granted to the Negro people by emancipation has been sufficient to overcome the ravages of slavery; and that, surely, contemporary white people and institutions bear no responsibility for slavery and reap no benefit from this dark chapter in human history.

But the historical facts are otherwise. The Negro people have never been indemnified, either economically, or politically, or socially, or psychologically for two centuries of bondage. And furthermore, the wider society has not reconstructed itself to any substantial degree in any of these areas of life.

The end of slavery with the Civil War in the United States brought a certain freedom to the slave and the free Negro alike, but it was also a crisis of major proportions. For tens of thousands of Negroes, emancipation meant the freedom to die of starvation and illness. In some communities, one out of every four Negroes died. The destitution and disease among the Negroes, who were now uncared for and had no facilities to care for themselves, was so great that the editor of a famous newspaper observed with considerable glee that "The child is already born who will behold the last Negro in the State of Mississippi."[53] And Mississippi had more Negro slaves than any other state. Nor were such dire straits and predictions confined to one state. The eminent southern scholar, Dr. C. K. Marchall, expressed a similar and more general hypothesis: "In all probability New Year's Day on the morning of the 1st of January, 1920, the colored population in the South will scarcely be counted."[54]

The survival of the Negro people after such a holocaust can be attributed primarily to the resiliency of the human spirit. It most certainly cannot be attributed in large measure to the efforts of his society to help him survive. For the ingredient most absent to make freedom meaningful was the ingredient which has been most useful to other depressed people, namely opportunity.

There were no national, regional, or other large-scale plans for dealing with the ex-slaves. How could they be integrated into the life of the embattered republic as free men? Uncertainty abounded. There were enlightened voices who put forward suggestions. The most rational package suggested that the nation should give each ex-slave forty acres of land, a mule, the ballot, and leave him alone. Charles Sumner of Massachusetts plugged hard for the ballot, Thaddeus Stevens of Pennsylvania plugged even harder for the forty acres. And several generations before Justice Louis D. Brandeis was to expound his famous doctrine of the freedom to be let alone, Frederick Douglass, the ex-slave, echoed the same sentiment.

> The Negro should have been let alone in Africa. . . . If you see him plowing in the open field, leveling the forest, at work with a spade, a rake, a hoe, a pick-axe, or a bill, let him alone;. . . If he has a ballot in his hand, let him alone.[55]

But the nation's response was to be much more limited and temporary. The Freedman's Bureau, probably the first national social welfare administration, during six short years with severely limited funds, administrative imagination and courage, and in the face of apathy in the North and hostility in the South, strove to feed and clothe ex-slaves and poor whites, and to establish hospitals and schools. It did a commendable job under the circumstances, but much too little and over too short a time. President Andrew Johnson's heart was not in the efforts of the Freedman's Bureau, and despite certain efforts of Congress he crushed this program.

John Hope Franklin has summed up the period of reconstruction as follows:

> Counter reconstruction was everywhere an overwhelming success. In the face of violence

the 14th and 15th Amendments provided no protection for the Negro citizen and his friends. The federal enforcement laws of 1870 and 1871 proved wholly inadequate, especially when enforcement was left to the meager forces that remained in the South at the time of their enactment. Negroes could hardly be expected to continue to vote when it cost them not only their jobs but their lives. In one state after another, the Negro electorate declined steadily as the full force of the Klan came forward to supervise the elections that federal troops failed to supervise. . . . The federal government was, more and more, leaving the South to its own devices. Even more important was the enormous prestige that the former Confederates enjoyed. In time they were able to assume leadership in their communities without firing a shot or hanging a single Negro. What they lacked in political strength they made up in economic power. By discharging or threatening to discharge Negro employees who persisted in participating in politics, they could reduce the Negro electorate to a minimum. By refusing to pay taxes to support the expanded and inflated functions of the new governments, they could destroy Radical Reconstruction in a season. But the former Confederates relied on no one method. By political pressure, economic sanctions, *and* violence they brought Radical Reconstruction crashing down almost before it began.[56]

Of course, Emancipation had some advantages for the Negro family. Although family members could be whipped, run out of town, or murdered, they could not be sold away from their families. Marriages were legalized and recorded. The hard work of farming, even sharecropping, required all possible hands—husband, wife, and children.

Emancipation, then, was a catastrophic social crisis for the ex-slave, and Reconstruction was a colossal failure. At the same time, there were some "screens of opportunity" which did enable large numbers of families to survive, some to achieve amazingly stable and viable forms of family life, and a few to achieve a high degree of social distinction.

Notes

1. Nathan Glazer and Daniel P. Moynihan, *Beyond the Melting Pot* (Cambridge, Mass.: The M.I.T. Press and The Harvard University Press, 1963), p. 51.
2. Nat Hentoff, "The Other Side of the Blues," in *Anger and Beyond: The Negro Writer in the United States,* ed. Herbert Hill (New York: Harper & Row, Publishers, 1966), p. 76.
3. Harold L. Sheppard and Herbert E. Striver, *Civil Rights, Employment, and the Social Status of American Negroes* (Kalamazoo, Mich.: The W. E. Upjohn Institute for Employment Research, June, 1966), p. 47.
4. John Hope Franklin, *From Slavery to Freedom* (New York: Alfred A. Knopf, Inc., 1956), p. 11.
5. *Ibid.,* p. 28.
6. Melville J. Herskovits, *Dahomey: An Ancient West African Kingdom* (New York: J. J. Augustin, 1938), I; and Francis I. Nzimiro, "Family and Kinship in Ibo Land: A Study in Acculturation Process" (Ph. D. dissertation, University of Cologne, 1962).
7. Melville J. Herskovits, *The Myth of the Negro Past* (Boston: Beacon Press, 1958); Robert A. Lystad, *The Ashanti: A Proud People* (New Brunswick, N.J.: Rutgers University Press, 1958); and Meyer Fortes, "Kinship and Marriage Among the Ashanti," in *African Systems of Kinship and Marriage,* eds. A. R. Radcliffe-Brown and Daryll Forde (New York: Oxford University Press, Inc., 1950), pp. 207–51. Future quotations from this source reprinted by permission of Oxford University Press, Inc.
8. Daryll Forde, "The Yako of Nigeria," in A. R. Radcliffe-Brown, *op. cit.*
9. *Ibid.,* p. 306.
10. George P. Murdock, *Africa: Its People and Their Culture History* (New York: McGraw Hill Book Company, 1959).
11. Herskovits, *Dahomey,* p. 341.
12. Meyer Fortes, "Kinship and Marriage Among the Ashanti," *op. cit.,* p. 270.
13. *Ibid.,* p. 268.
14. *Ibid.,* p. 268.
15. *Ibid.,* p. 268.
16. *Ibid.,* p. 268.
17. Nzimiro, *op. cit.*
18. Fortes, p. 262.
19. *Ibid.,* p. 263.
20. *Ibid.,* p. 263.
21. Herskovits, *Dahomey,* p. 155.
22. Fortes, p. 275.
23. *Ibid.,* p. 273.
24. *Ibid.,* p. 274.
25. *Ibid.,* p. 276.
26. Lerone Bennett, Jr., *Before the Mayflower: A History of the Negro in America* (Chicago: Johnson Publishing Co., 1964), p. 30.
27. *Ibid.,* pp. 30–31.
28. Milton Meltzer, ed., In *Their Own Words: A History of the American Negro 1619–1865,* copyright (© 1964 by Milton Meltzer (New York: Thomas Y. Crowell Company, 1954; Apollo Edition, 1967), pp. 3–5. Reprinted by permission of Thomas Y. Crowell Company, and Harold Ober Associates, Inc.
29. Frank Tannenbaum, *Slave and Citizen: The Negro in the Americas* (New York: Random House, Inc., 1946), p. 21.
30. W. E. B. Du Bois, *The Negro* (New York: Holt, Rinehart & Winston, Inc., 1915), pp. 155– 56.
31. Stanley Elkins, *Slavery: A Problem in American Institutional and Intellectual Life* (New York: Grosset & Dunlap, Inc., 1963), p. 81.
32. Tannenbaum, p. 65.
33. Marvin Harris, *Patterns of Race in the Americas* (New York: Walker and Co., 1964), p. 81.
34. Elkins, pp. 88–89.
35. Kenneth M. Stampp, *The Peculiar Institution: Slavery in the Ante-Bellum South* (New York: Vintage Books, 1956), p. 206.
36. *Ibid.,* p. 207.
37. *Ibid.,* p. 222.
38. *Ibid.,* p. 148.
39. Meltzer, pp. 33–34.
40. E. Bradford Burns, *A Documentary History of Brazil* (New York: Alfred A. Knopf, Inc., 1966), p. 278.
41. Stampp, pp. 235–36.
42. Tannenbaum, p. 77.
43. *Ibid.,* pp. 77–78.
44. *Ibid.,* p. 78.
45. *Ibid.,* p. 80.
46. *Ibid.,* pp. 76–77.
47. Meltzer, pp. 46–47.
48. *Ibid.,* pp. 100–101.
49. *Ibid.,* pp. 120–22.

50. *Ibid.*, pp. 170–72.
51. Pauli Murray, *Proud Shoes: The Story of an American Family* (New York: Harper & Row, Publishers, 1956), quotes from pp. 38–48.
52. Margaret Walker, *Jubilee* (Boston: Houghton Mifflin Company, 1966).

53. Bennett, p. 188.
54. *Ibid.*, p. 188.
55. *Ibid.*, pp. 186–87.
56. John Hope Franklin, *Reconstruction After the Civil War* (Chicago: University of Chicago Press, 1961), pp. 172–73.

Essay/Discussion Questions

1. According to Andrew Billingsley, the slave trade and chattel slavery disrupted patterns of traditional African family and community life. Even so, slaves retained aspects of traditional African culture and values and then refashioned them within the context of American chattel slavery. Discuss some dimensions of traditional African family and community life; then indicate some aspects of that tradition retained and refashioned by African slaves and their descendants.

2. Slaveowners and the dehumanizing system of chattel slavery powerfully influenced the development of slave families and communi-ties; yet, African slaves were able to create families and communities of their own even under conditions of cultural domination, political oppression, and economic exploitation. First, discuss the character of the slaveowner's power over slaves. Second, probe those conditions of culture and of limited autonomy that enabled slaves to develop their own patterns of family and community life.

3. If the slave trade and chattel slavery represented savage assaults on emerging African American family and communal life, what impact did Emancipation and Reconstruction have on black families and communities?

The Negro Family

E. FRANKLIN FRAZIER

Throughout its development, the Negro family has been influenced in its inter nal social and psychological organiza- tion as well as in its formal structure by the economic and social forces which have deter- mined the character of Negro communities.

THE NEGRO FAMILY DURING SLAVERY

In a previous chapter we have seen how diffi- cult it is to establish upon a factual basis any connection between the development of the Negro family in the United States and the African family system.[1] The attempts to ex- plain the sex behavior and familial life of American Negroes by reference to African cul- ture traits rest upon speculation and specious analogies. Among some isolated groups of Ne- groes in the New World, as for example in Haiti and Jamaica, it appears that elements of African culture have been retained in the Ne- gro family.[2] But even in Brazil, where condi- tions were more favorable for the survival of the African family system, one can scarcely find traces of the African family system to- day.[3] Therefore, in tracing the development of the Negro family we shall simply analyze the known economic and social factors in the

American environment which offer a suffi- cient explanation of the past development and present character of the Negro family.[4]

During the early development of the plan- tation system the excess of males in the Negro population resulted in casual associations for satisfaction of sexual hunger.[5] But soon there was no lack of women, and mating ranged from purely physical contacts, sometimes en- forced by the masters, to permanent associa- tions in which deep sentiment between spouses and parental affection toward children created a stable family group. At the same time the character of the sexual contacts and family life of the slaves was determined to some extent by the master's attitudes toward his slaves. Some masters with no regard for the prefer- ence of their slaves mated them as they did their stock. There were instances where Negro males were used as stallions.[6] In a world where patriarchal traditions were firmly established, even less consideration was shown for the wishes of the female slaves. But this was not the whole story, for the majority of masters either through necessity or because of their humanity showed some regard for the wishes of the slaves in their mating.

Since African mores and traditions ceased to control the sexual impulses and determine the forms of mating, their behavior in this regard was subject to individual impulse and sexual attraction. It appears that from the beginning spontaneous attraction played an important part in mating. Moreover, there was rivalry among the males for the sexual favors of the females. This rivalry was kept under control by the master in the interest of order on the plantation. But rivalry did not manifest itself solely in the display of brute force. There came into existence a form of courtship in which tender feelings and attention to the wishes of the woman played an important part in winning her favors. In addition to these psychological factors there were social forces within the plantation organization that tended to humanize the sexual impulses of the slaves and place moral restraints upon their mating. The plantation, as we have seen, was a social as well as an industrial institution in which there was a division of labor and an opportunity for the expression of the individual talents.[7] Within the social world of the plantation, there were social distinctions, involving obligations and expectations in regard to behavior. Consequently the sexual conduct and mating of the slaves were not without moral restraints.

Where slavery became a settled way of life and the plantation organization acquired a patriarchal character, the slave family achieved some degree of permanence. The master's concern for the moral welfare of the slaves included a close supervision of their sex behavior and marital relations. On some plantations there were slave families including three generations that had "married" according to slave customs under the close supervision of their mistresses. Such family groups generally included the father and husband as well as the mother and her children. This was especially true where the father was, for example, a skilled mechanic and had acquired a responsible position in the plantation organization.[8] The solidarity and permanence of such families were due to a number of factors. Habitual association in the same household played some part. But, in addition, genuine affection often developed between the spouses and between the parents and children. Where the family was permitted privacy and permitted to cultivate its own gardens and engage in other common activities, family unity was given substantial basis in common interests. Thus under the most favorable conditions of slavery the Negro family did among certain elements of the slave population acquire considerable stability. But very often the exigencies of the slave system, such as the settlement of an estate, might destroy the toughest bonds of conjugal affection and parental love.

Because of the conditions imposed by the slave system, the mother was the most dependable and the most important member of the Negro family. The idealized picture of the Negro mother during slavery has represented her as a devoted nurse of the master's children.[9] But there is also plenty of evidence of the devotion of the slave mother to her own offspring. Despite the hardships and suffering which pregnancy and childbirth often involved, the slave mother often exhibited a fierce devotion to her children. In the case of young children, masters were compelled in their own interest to recognize the biological dependence of the child upon the mother. But, in addition, they were forced to recognize the affectional and sentimental ties between the Negro mother and her offspring. A Negro father might be sold and separated from his family, but when the Negro mother was sold the master was forced to take into account her relation to her children. The bonds of affection between mother and offspring were generally developed in the slave cabin where the Negro mother nurtured her brood and was mistress. Even if she were separated from her children she often visited them at night to care for them and find affection and solace from her cares. On the other hand, the father was often a visitor to the cabin two or three times a week, while his interest in his children might only be adventitious. He was compelled not only to recognize the mother's more fundamental interest in the children but her authority in the household. Thus there developed among the slaves a type of family that was held together principally by the bonds of blood and feeling existing between the mother and her offspring and the sentimental ties that often developed between the children in the same household.

Although it is difficult to estimate the extent to which members of the slaveholding class had sexual relations with the slaves, there is sufficient evidence of widespread concubinage and even polygyny on the part of the white masters. The maternal family organization, i.e., the family in which the mother was the head and main source of support, was fostered partly by the sexual association between the males of the white race and the slave women on the plantation. In the cities where the slaves were released from the plantation discipline and there were free Negroes, the associations between white men and Negro and mulatto women were generally casual.[10] Mulatto children resulting from these relationships were often neglected and became public charges. The sexual relations between the white men and colored women, slave and free, were undoubtedly due at times to physical compulsion on the part of white men. Moreover, mutual attraction also played some part in securing the compliance of the colored woman. But, it appears from available evidence, that the prestige of the white race and the advantages resulting from these associations were generally sufficient to secure the acquiescence of the colored woman. The character of the family groups resulting from the association of the men of the master race and the women of the subordinate race varied considerably.

At the bottom of the scale was the Negro woman who was raped and became separated from her mulatto child without any violence to her maternal feelings; or the slave woman who submitted dumbly or out of animal feeling to sexual relations that spawned a nameless and unloved half-white breed over the South. . . . Sexual attraction gave birth at times to genuine affection; and prolonged association created between white master and colored mistress enduring sentiment. There were instances where white fathers sold their mulatto children; but more often they became ensnared by their affection for their colored offspring.[11]

There were white men who acknowledged their offspring and gave them an education and a start in the world. There were white slaveholders who neglected their wives and gave their affection and their worldly goods to their colored mistress and their mulatto offspring.[12] In some cases the white masters even separated themselves from white society and lived entirely with their colored mistresses and mulatto offspring. But since such unions were rare and without the legal and moral support of the communities, the black or mulatto woman was generally the head of the household.

FAMILY LIFE AMONG THE FREE NEGROES

The family life of many of the Negroes who were free before the Civil War was less stable than that of the better situated slaves. This was especially true of the impoverished Negroes who crowded the slums of the cities of the North as well as the South. Among these elements in the free Negro population there was much sexual promiscuity and family relationships were loose and uncertain. Though there was less moral degradation in the rural areas, nevertheless, the family life of the free Negroes in the poorer regions of the South rested upon a precarious basis. On the other hand, there was emerging among the free Negro workers a class of skilled artisans whose family life conformed to the family pattern of the white laboring class. In some cases the tradition of stable family life had been built up during several generations of freedom and economic security. Or the tradition of stable family life might even have its roots in slavery. Very often the male head of the family had bought his freedom and that of his wife and some of his children. This class continued to increase in areas where slavery was becoming less profitable up to the Civil War.

However, it was chiefly in Charleston, South Carolina, New Orleans, and a few other areas that the free Negro families acquired to a marked degree an institutional character. Marriage as a legal relationship became a part of the mores of this group as they took over the familial behavior of the whites and the stability and continuity of their family life became rooted in property as well as traditions. Moreover, members of these families were accorded a superior social status by the community. In Charleston as well as in New Orleans a number of the free colored families were descended from the mulatto refugees who fled from San Domingo during the revolution in the latter part of the eighteenth century. The community of free mulattoes in New Orleans was much larger and had a longer history than the free colored people of Charleston. When thousands of well-to-do and cultured mulatto refugees from Haiti poured into New Orleans in the latter part of the eighteenth century the government found it necessary to relax the laws restricting the freedom of this class in regard to dress or to move about at will. At the time of the Louisiana Purchase this class had become an important element in the population and formed an intermediate social stratum between the whites and the slaves. Since these families were of mulatto origin they had taken over the culture of the whites. Moreover, their white forebears had frequently given them educational advantages as well as property. The imprint of this cultural heritage was apparent in the personalities of the mem-

bers of these free families. They were dignified and undertook to support a literary and artistic culture. They took pride in their white ancestry, which included many whites of distinction. They were intensely conscious of their superior status in a society where Negro blood was the badge of slavery. In New Orleans the traditions of a large number of the free mulatto families went back to the role of the mulattoes in the defense of the city against the British in 1814. Many of them sent their children to France to be educated, thus preserving a mode of life that was similar to that of their French neighbors but alien to their Anglo-Saxon neighbors as well as the mass of black slaves.

The patterns of family life developed in this group were as different from that of the great mass of the Negro population as the type of family life which developed among those isolated communities of Negro, Indian, and white descent scattered in various parts of the country.[13] In some cases these communities originated in the eighteenth century.[14] In such communities patriarchal family traditions were firmly established during the pioneer days. These families generally cherished their white and Indian ancestry. But sometimes the Indian character of these communities has been completely effaced and they are classified as Negro communities.[15] Therefore, in tracing the roots of the Negro family in the United States it is necessary to take account of the role of these families in the development of Negro family life.

DISORGANIZATION AND REORGANIZATION OF NEGRO FAMILY LIFE AFTER EMANCIPATION

The immediate effect of the Civil War and Emancipation upon the family life of the slaves was to disrupt the customary relationships and destroy whatever control the master exercised over the sex and family life of the slaves. When the invading armies disrupted the plantation organization, thousands of Negroes were set adrift and began to wander footloose about the country. Not only were the sentimental and habitual ties between spouses severed but even Negro women often abandoned their children. Among the demoralized elements in the newly emancipated Negroes promiscuous sexual relationships and frequent changing of spouses became the rule. The northern missionaries who came South during and following the Civil war were often perplexed by the confusion in marital relations. On the other hand, the disorders arising from the Civil War and Emancipation often provided a proof of the strength of marital and family ties that had developed during slavery. Many mothers kept their children with them and cared for them at a tremendous sacrifice. Describing the fleeing refugees, Higginson wrote, "Women brought children on their shoulders; small black boys carried on their backs little brothers equally inky, and gravely depositing them, shook hands."[16] Moreover, it was noted by the missionaries and others who were in a position to observe the newly emancipated blacks that there was a general disposition on the part of the Negroes to search for their kinfolk.

The development of the Negro family following the confusion which ensued as the result of Emancipation was influenced by a number of social and economic factors. The heroic efforts of the northern missionaries, who attempted to place marriage on a legal and institutional basis, bore fruits wherever they labored. They were supported in their efforts by the Negro church organizations with intelligent ministers and a core of stable families. Moreover, the schools in which the missionaries labored became centers in which sexual mores were taught and enforced and institutionalized family relations were cultivated. Despite the important contributions which the missionaries made to stabilizing family relations, the operation of more fundamental social and economic forces in the life of the Negro were to determine the character of his family life.

The family life of the emancipated Negro was influenced to a large extent by his social development under slavery. Even during slavery some of the freedmen had engaged in semifree economic activities in order to support their families. Among the better situated slaves, the family had acquired considerable stability and the transition to freedom did not result in disorganization. The father had developed a deep and permanent attachment to his wife and an interest in his children. As a freedman he remained on the plantation as a tenant and assumed responsibility for his family.[17] The more ambitious freedmen were not willing to continue as tenants but began to acquire land.

In acquiring land the Negro husband and father laid foundation for patriarchal authority in the family. His interest in his wife and children no longer rested upon a purely sentimental or habitual basis but on an economic tie. In some cases the interest of the father in his wife and children began when he bought them from their owners before Emancipation. But it was only after the Emancipation when the former slave established himself as a freedman that this phase of the development of masculine authority in family relations became important. Even among the freedmen who were tenants, it was customary for the father and husband to make contracts with the landowners and assume responsibility for their families.

This development of the family was associated with the development of other phases of the institutional life of the Negroes. The churches were under the control of men and the control which it exercised tended to confirm the man's interest and authority in the family. Moreover, in the Bible, which for the freedmen was the highest authority in such matters, they found a sanction for masculine authority. The families that had been free before the Civil War played an important role in consolidating masculine authority in the Negro family. Although in some localities the prejudice of this group toward the newly emancipated blacks prevented intermarriage at first, gradually the more successful freedmen married into the families that had been free before Emancipation.

During the latter part of the nineteenth century and the first decade of the present century, two general tendencies were apparent in the development of the Negro family. First, there was an ever increasing number of stable families with a pattern of family organization similar to the American pattern. These families, which were to be found in both rural and urban communities throughout the country, were sharply differentiated from the Negro masses. The emergence of this group of stable families is roughly indicated in the growth of homeownership up to 1910. By 1910 a fourth of the Negroes in rural areas and 22 per cent of the Negroes in cities were homeowners.[18] A part of the homeowning families formed an upper class in Negro communities, while the remaining homeowning families represented the slow emergence of a middle class. The second general tendency is represented in the development of family life on a habitual and sentimental basis among the Negro masses in the rural South. The migration of Negroes to cities, especially the mass migrations to northern cities during and following World War I, has affected both of these developments. In the discussion which follows, we shall consider the changes which have occurred between the two World Wars and the present status of the Negro family.

HIGH PROPORTION OF FAMILIES WITH FEMALE HEADS

As we have seen there has been an excess of females in the Negro population since 1840.[19] However, the excess of females has been characteristic of the cities rather than the rural areas. In fact, the excess of males in the rural-farm Negro population has been increasing during the past two decades.[20] At the same time, there has been a decrease in the ratio of males to females in the rural-nonfarm Negro population to the point that there was a slight excess of females in 1940. It is not possible to determine the effect of these changes in the sex ratio on the marital status of the rural Negro population over the past fifty years. As has been shown in a number of studies, there is considerable uncertainty concerning the real marital status of the Negroes in the rural South.[21]

In Table XIX, we have the proportion of nonwhite (Negro) families in the rural and farm areas of the South with female heads and the marital status of the female heads of families.[21a] Women are heads of more than a fifth of the Negro families in the South. In the rural nonfarm areas the proportion of Negro families with female heads is about the same as that for the South as a whole. But in the rural farm areas the proportion of families with female heads is only one-half as great as that for the entire region, and one-third as great as the proportion in urban areas. The larger proportion of families with female heads among owners than among tenants in rural areas is most likely due to the fact that landlords prefer to have tenant families with male heads or in the absence of legal marriage, families with a male who plays the role of husband. In view of the uncertainty concerning the real marital status of Negroes in rural regions, several facts should be noted in regard to the marital status of female heads of families. First, the husband is absent in a fifth of the families of tenants as compared with a tenth of the families of owners. Secondly, a much larger percentage of the female heads of owner families than of tenant families are described as widowed. Widowhood is the real marital status of a larger proportion of owners than of tenant women who are returned in the federal census as widows. Then, the greater proportion of divorced women among the tenant families with female heads is indicative of the greater instability of the tenants. Finally, the larger proportion of single women who are head of tenant fami-

TABLE XIX PERCENTAGE OF NONWHITE FAMILIES WITH FEMALE HEADS AND MARITAL STATUS OF FEMALE HEADS OF FAMILIES BY TENURE FOR URBAN AND RURAL SOUTH: 1940*

Tenure	Percentage of Families with Female Heads	Families with Female Heads				
		Total	Husbands Absent	Widowed	Divorced	Single
Total	21.7	100.0	21.6	62.2	4.9	11.3
Owner	24.5	100.0	11.5	77.4	3.4	7.7
Tenant	20.9	100.0	25.4	56.5	5.4	12.7
Urban	31.0	100.0	24.6	57.9	5.1	12.4
Owner	29.5	100.0	12.4	76.0	3.2	8.4
Tenant	31.5	100.0	27.9	53.0	5.6	13.5
Rural—Nonfarm	22.7	100.0	18.2	65.6	5.1	11.1
Owner	27.5	100.0	11.7	76.7	3.7	7.9
Tenant	20.1	100.0	22.8	57.6	6.1	13.5
Rural—Farm	11.6	100.0	16.7	70.9	3.9	8.5
Owner	16.4	100.0	16.7	70.9	3.9	8.5
Tenant	10.3	100.0	19.7	66.5	4.2	9.6

*Based on *Sixteenth Census of the United States: 1940. Population and Housing Families.* "Ceneral Characteristics," p. 31.

lies undoubtedly reflects the large amount of illegitimacy in these rural communities.

THE NEGRO FAMILY ON THE PLANTATION

Among a large proportion of the Negroes in the plantation South, courtship begins at an early age through mutual attraction and often involves sexual relations. Where sex relations result in pregnancy, the young people may or may not marry.[22] The birth of a child imposes certain obligations upon the mother because the mores of the Negro community make the relation between mother and child the most sacred of human relations. In fact, a certain distinction attaches to being fruitful or the fulfillment of one's function as a woman. On the other hand, marriage has not become a part of the mores. The father of the child may suggest "marriage" because he wants a woman to provide a home for him and he in turn is willing to provide subsistence for his family. The woman's response to his offer of "marriage" depends upon the attitude of her parents or her desire to start a new family. In the isolated rural communities where this type of

so-called "sexual freedom" is permitted there are, nevertheless, certain restraints placed upon sex relations. During a period of courtship a girl is supposed to have one man only. Since in becoming pregnant she imposes economic burdens upon her family, she is obligated out of consideration for her parents to keep this in mind. The father of her child is likewise under obligation to help take care of the child. But in such communities the moral restraints of the larger community are absent. The women generally do not have a sense of guilt in regard to having children outside of marriage. When the couple decide upon marriage, which is generally of the common-law type, they enter into a cooperative relationship. The permanence of the "marriage" depends not only upon affection and sentiment but often upon the extent to which they can "work together" on the farm. Moreover, even after the men and women have entered "marriage," they may not have a sense of guilt when they have outside affairs. They seem to have fulfilled their obligation to their mates by giving him or her preference in their affections.

In the isolated rural communities, especially among the lower classes, these courtships and

TABLE XX PERCENTAGE DISTRIBUTION OF POPULATION IN PRIVATE HOUSEHOLDS BY
HEADS AND RELATION TO HEAD AND BY COLOR AND SEX FOR THE SOUTH: 1940*

	Nonwhite Head	White Male	Female	Male
	39.5	10.3	44.4	6.5
Relationship to Head				
Wife	—	31.9	—	40.9
Child	41.5	38.2	45.2	40.8
Grandchild	5.4	4.8	2.1	1.9
Parent	0.6	2.4	0.9	2.5
Other Relative	6.3	6.7	4.1	4.3
Lodger	6.2	4.8	3.1	2.3
Servant or Hired Hand	0.5	0.9	0.2	0.5

*Sixteenth Census of the United States: 1940. Population. Vol. IV. "Characteristics by Age."
Part 1, p. 114.

forms of marriage do not result in personality conflicts or in social disorganization. In the less isolated communities there are personality conflicts because of the influence of the dominant mores and the control exercised by those conventional family groups that attempt to enforce American family mores. Moreover, outside of the plantation region where there are communities of rural Negroes who have assimilated American standards of family behavior and there are schools and other agencies of communication, the family behavior described is confined largely to the lower classes. In the upper-class families there is supervision of the behavior of young people and legal marriage is a prerequisite to the founding of a family. Throughout the rural South these upper-class families place great value upon morality in sex and family relations and the father is recognized as the head.[23]

As the result of the sex and marital practices which we have described, the Negro family in the rural areas assumes certain peculiar forms of organization. It is not possible to secure a measure of the extent of the various forms in the Negro rural population. However, for the South as a whole, we have statistics on the distribution of the population in private households with relation to the head of the household (See Table XX). Since there is a much higher percentage of families with female heads among nonwhites (Negroes) than

among whites, a smaller proportion of Negro women than of white women is in the relationship of wife to the head of the family. There are, however, other differences which reflect divergences in family organization and practices, such as the larger proportion of "grandchildren," "other relatives," and "lodgers" in Negro families. The larger proportion of "servants or hired hands" is also indicative of certain features of the Negro family rather than of the greater employment of servants in the household. The significance of these statistical differences will become clear as we study the organization of the Negro family.

The maternal Negro family, or the family in which the mother is the head, functions in its most primitive form as a natural organization in the rural areas of the South.[24] Historically, it had its origin as we have seen during the slavery period when the mother was the most dependable element in the family. Since Emancipation the maternal family has been supported by the folkways and mores of the rural communities. The matricentric family grows into a type of matriarchate in which the grandmother is the dominant figure. The mother acquires the status of a grandmother when her daughters become mothers and bring their children into the household.[25] Because of her age and experience the grandmother exercises authority over the members of the family and assumes responsibility for their welfare. The

TABLE XXI PERCENTAGE OF NONWHITE FAMILIES WITH EMPLOYED HEAD THAT
WERE HOMEOWNERS IN EACH OCCUPATION GROUP IN THE SOUTH: 1940*

Occupation	Group Total	Urban	Rural Nonfarm	Rural Farm
Professional and Semiprofessional	49.3	49.6	45.1	56.7
Farmers and Farm Managers	23.1	54.7	45.9	22.4
Proprietors, Managers, etc.	48.0	42.5	62.2	75.0
Clerical, Sales, etc.	41.4	37.3	62.4	68.8
Craftsmen, Foremen, etc.	34.7	29.7	46.2	41.5
Operatives	21.6	20.7	21.9	29.6
Domestic Service	17.3	13.9	28.5	15.6
Service Workers	27.9	25.0	43.6	37.9
Farm Laborers	10.2	20.0	25.6	5.0
Laborers	20.5	16.1	25.8	29.1
Total	21.9	21.3	29.6	19.3

*Based upon *Sixteenth Census of the United States: 1940. Population and Housing Families.*
"General Characteristics," p. 43.

grandmother is a repository of folk wisdom and is called upon during the major crises of life. She attends the sick and the dead; but her superior wisdom and authority are recognized chiefly in matters concerning childbirth. She is often the "granny" or midwife who supplies young mothers with knowledge concerning babies and attends them during the crisis of childbirth. In 1940 four-fifths of the live births of Negroes in Mississippi and South Carolina were attended by midwives as compared with a fourteenth of white live births in these states.[26] In Virginia and Tennessee the percentage of live births attended by midwives was 58.6 and 26.1 respectively.

The "matriarchal" type of family among rural Negroes in the South is an extended family in that it includes several generations and nephews and nieces and adopted children. This is indicated to some extent by the statistics in Table XX in the larger percentage of grandchildren and "other" relatives in Negro private households than in white households. There is not, however, a larger percentage of "parents" in Negro private households because the persons who would normally be in the relationship of "parent" to the head of the household are themselves the grandparents, who are often the heads of the household.

The extended Negro families are not all matriarchal in organization. Among the upper-class families in the rural South there are semipatriarchal families of the extended type. The development of the semipatriarchal type of family has been related to the acquisition of land. Moreover, the extent of homeownership in the rural farm area of the South is related to the socioeconomic status of the inhabitants of the rural area. More than a fifth (Table XXI) of the farm families, including farmowners and renters, owned their homes, while among the farm laborers only one family in twenty was a homeowner. Landowners and homeowners often exercise authority over their married sons as well as their unmarried daughters. But generally their sons are "emancipated" upon reaching maturity and establish their own families on an independent basis.

THE NEGRO FAMILY IN SOUTHERN TOWNS AND CITIES

In the towns and smaller cities of the South, these various forms of family organization tend to persist with certain modifications. The maternal family plays a larger role because of the opportunities for the employment of women in domestic service and the grandmother con-

TABLE XXII PERCENTAGE OF NONWHITE FAMILIES WITH EMPLOYED HEAD THAT WERE HOMEOWNERS IN EACH OCCUPATION GROUP IN FOUR SOUTHERN CITIES: 1940*

Professional and Semiprofessional	46.4	35.7	53.3	32.3
Proprietors, Managers, etc.	29.3	36.4	33.3	36.4
Clerical, Sales, Etc.	33.3	19.0	50.0	23.9
Craftsmen, Foremen, etc.	10.1	17.9	30.2	17.8
Operatives	9.6	20.1	19.1	7.1
Domestic Service	8.0	8.5	14.9	3.2
Service Workers	14.5	7.9	22.0	8.4
Laborers	9.1	10.5	16.9	7.7
Total	12.7	14.0	21.1	9.4

*Based upon Sixteenth Census of the United States: 1940. Population and Housing Families, p. 290.

tinues to be the head of a large proportion of Negro families. On the other hand, the extended family tends to disintegrate and the growth of the semipatriarchal type of family is encouraged as the chance for homeownership is increased. It is, however, in the larger cities of the South that the effects of urbanization and the occupational differentiation of the Negro population are manifested in the organization of family life. There is, first, a decline in the size of the family or the number of children to women of childbearing age. For example, the number of children under five years of age to 1,000 Negro women 15 to 49 years of age in Atlanta, Birmingham, and Memphis was 170, 177, and 163 respectively as compared with 472 for Negro women in the rural-farm South.[27] In the cities of the South a much larger proportion—nearly a third as compared with a tenth for rural areas—of Negro families have female heads. As one may observe in Table XIX the proportion of families with female heads is slightly higher among tenants in urban areas than among owners. There are even more striking differences between female heads of families who are owners and tenants in regard to marital status. In the tenant families with female heads over a fourth of the husbands are absent as compared with an eighth of the owner families; and three-fourths of the owners are widowed as compared with a little more than half of the renter families.

There is a tendency for the upper- and middle-class families to become segregated into the better areas of the Negro community. These families are distinguished from the lower-class families in regard to the extent of homeownership. In Table XXII, we have the amount of homeownership among the different occupational groups in four southern cities with Negro communities numbering over 100,000. In New Orleans where homeownership is comparatively low, the difference in pattern of homeownership among the various occupational classes is most pronounced. Homeownership is lowest for the domestic workers with low incomes and considerable family disorganization. It is higher for laborers and unskilled workers in industry and even higher for service workers among whom there are many stable and ambitious families. Among the skilled workers or craftsmen, homeownership is twice as high as among the service workers. It is among the white-collar workers—professional and clerical workers and proprietors—that homeownership assumes considerable importance and that the most stable families with a semipatriarchal organization are found.

THE NEGRO FAMILY IN BORDER CITIES

In the border cities, as in the cities of the South, the various types of family organization described above tend to persist. There has been, however, in the border cities a comparatively

TABLE XXIII PERCENTAGE OF NONWHITE FAMILIES WITH EMPLOYED HEAD THAT WERE HOMEOWNERS IN EACH OCCUPATIONAL GROUP IN THREE BORDER CITIES, 1940*

Occupational Group	Baltimore	Washington, D.C.	St. Louis, Mo.
Professional and Semiprofessional	53.1	59.6	35.1
Proprietors, Managers, etc.	18.2	23.1	9.3
Clerical, Sales, Etc.	30.0	37.0	19.4
Craftsmen, Foremen, etc.	9.0	19.5	10.4
Operatives	12.2	20.6	4.2
Domestic Service	8.0	7.4	6.5
Service Workers	11.9	18.5	8.1
Laborers	5.3	14.6	7.1
Total	11.1	20.4	8.8

*Based upon *Sixteenth Census of the United States: 1940. Population and Housing,* "General Characteristics," pp. 290–291.

large group of stable families with a semi-patriarchal organization over a long period. Many of these families have their roots among the Negroes who were free in these cities before the Civil War. Moreover, the constant migration of Negroes from the South has brought to the border cities many stable families. There is a tendency for the various patterns of family life to correspond to the class structure of the Negro communities in border cities.[28] Although among the lower class there is considerable family disorganization and many families have only a mother or grandmother as head, there is a core of stable families even in this class. It is, however, among the middle class, embracing about a fourth of the Negro community, that one finds the largest group of stable families of a semipatriarchal type. In border cities as in southern cities the extent of homeownership in the various occupational groups provides a rough indication of family stability in the different classes (See Table XXIII). In the district of Columbia, where Negro women of this class have an opportunity for desirable employment, some of these families tend to become equalitarian in their organization, that is, the husband and wife have equal status in the family.

However, it is among the upper-class families that the equalitarian type of family is most pronounced. Unlike the wives in upper-class Negro families in the South, many of the wives in the upper-class families in the border cities are employed in professional and clerical occupations. This not only gives the wives a certain degree of independence but enables the family to maintain certain standards of consumption. Because of their standards of consumption and their values upper-class families have few children and there are many childless couples. A study in 1937 of 114 colored faculty members of Howard University revealed that those who had been married ten years or more had an average of 1.1 children per family. Of the entire group studied, 60 per cent indicated that they had voluntarily restricted their families.[29] Likewise, in a study of 65 families among the Washington colored elite it was found that 36 of the 65 families had no children and that in the remaining 29 families there were only 43 children or an average of less than 0.7 of a child per family for the entire group.

THE NEGRO FAMILY IN NORTHERN CITIES

The effects of urban living upon the character and organization of Negro family life are most pronounced in the large cities of the North.[30] The mass migration of Negroes to the cities of the North resulted in considerable family dis-

TABLE XXIV PERCENTAGE OF NEGRO MALES AND FEMALES FIFTEEN YEARS OF AGE AND OVER, SINGLE, MARRIED, WIDOWED, AND DIVORCED, IN THE FIVE ZONES OF THE HARLEM NEGRO COMMUNITY, NEW YORK CITY, 1930*

Marital Status	Sex	Zone I	Zone II	Zone III	Zone IV	Zone V
Single	M	42.6	38.5	35.3	34.0	31.1
	F	30.9	27.6	26.3	25.6	23.5
Married	M	49.8	56.0	60.3	62.3	64.2
	F	50.5	54.8	57.6	59.8	60.1
Widowed	M	7.3	4.7	3.6	2.9	3.8
	F	17.6	16.4	15.0	13.0	14.4
Divorced	M	0.2	0.5	0.4	0.6	0.5
	F	0.6	0.8	0.7	1.1	1.6

*Reproduced with the permission of The University of Chicago Press, from *The Negro Family in the United States,* p. 318.

organization. In a later chapter this phase of Negro family life will be considered among the problems of the adjustment of the Negro to American civilization. Here we are concerned primarily with the forms of family organization which have evolved in the urban areas of the North. In the Negro community in the northern city, as we have seen, there is a selection and segregation of various elements in the Negro population.[31] There is a selection and segregation on the basis of age and sex, a process which is related to the marital and family status of the population. The proportion of females and children in the population increases in the successive zones of the cities as one moves from the center outward, marking the expansion of the Negro community.[32] There is a selection and segregation of the population on the basis of marital status. This can be seen in the case of the Harlem Negro community in New York City (See Table XXIV). The decrease in the percentage of men and women single from the first to the fifth zone is associated with a progressive increase in the proportion of men and women married. The progressive increase in the proportion married is correlated with a decrease in the proportion widowed. This reflects not so much a difference in the death rates of men and women as a difference in the institutional character of the family. Because of the increasing importance of legal marriage, there are proportionately fewer deserted women and unmarried mothers who call themselves widows and there is an increase in the percentage of women divorced. The small percentage of divorced persons in the zones in and near the center of the community does not mean greater stability of family life in these areas but rather that separations are irregular and without legal sanctions as probably were also the unions in the first place.

The differences in marital status in the successive zones of expansion of the Negro community are indicative of the selective effects of urban life on the Negro family. In Zone I, which is the business and recreational center of the Negro community, family life tends to disappear as in the center of American cities.[33] Although the concentric zones marking the expansion of the Negro population are not homogeneous in culture, they nevertheless reflect the growing influence of family life in the successive zones. Not only is this indicated in the increase in the proportion married but in the birth rates and in the number of children (See Table XXV). In the first zone only 66 children were born in 1930 to each 1,000 Negro women of childbearing age and there were only 115 children under five to each 1,000 women 20 to 44 years of age. The birth rates and the ratio of children to women of childbearing age increase regularly in the successive zones. In the fifth zone on the periphery of the Harlem community the ratio of children to women of childbearing age is almost equal to the ratio in the rural-farm South.

TABLE XXV Number of Children Under Five Born to 1,000 Negro Women, 20 to 44 Years of Age, and Number of Children Born to 1,000 Negro Married Women, 15 to 44 Years of Age, in the Negro Harlem Community, New York City: 1930*

Zone	Women 20–44	Children Under 5	Ratio of Children to Women	Married Women, 15–44 (Estimated)	Number of Births	Births per 1,000 Married Women 15–44
I	4,141	476	115	2,495	165	66.1
II	23,612	4,160	176	15,087	1,230	81.5
III	21,107	4,749	225	13,883	1,276	91.9
IV	12,498	3,940	315	8,552	1,211	141.6
V	3,872	1,790	462	2,833	477	168.4

*Reproduced with permission from *The Negro Family in the United States* by E. Franklin Frazier, pp. 321 and 322. Copyright 1939 by The University of Chicago Press.

The progressive stabilization of family life in the zones marking the expansion of the Negro is indicated in some cities by the regular increase of the rate of homeownership in the successive zones. In the District of Columbia the rates of homeownership among Negroes for the five zones in 1940 were: 2.5, 9.3, 17.3, 27.9, and 51.2.[34] The same phenomenon was observable in Chicago in 1930, where the rates for the seven zones were: 0.0, 1.2, 6.2, 7.2, 8.3, 11.4, and 29.8.[35] These increases in the rate of homeownership are related to the tendency for the higher occupational classes to become concentrated in the areas on the periphery of the Negro community. This is seen in Table XXVI, where the percentage of homeownership for the different occupational classes is given. Higher rates of homeownership for the higher occupational groups are most marked in Chicago, Detroit, and Philadelphia. Although it is not so pronounced in New York City with its numerous apartment houses, homeownership there too is higher among the higher occupational classes.

FAMILY LIFE AMONG THE VARIOUS CLASSES

Because of the extent to which class differentiation has evolved in the large northern cities, the organization of Negro family life must be studied in relation to the class structure in these communities. It may be well to begin at the bottom of the class structure, since as one considers the higher levels the effects of urban living from the standpoint of reorganization of the family in the urban environment become more pronounced. The lower-class families are physically segregated to a large extent in the deteriorated areas where Negroes first secure a foothold in the community. It is among this class that one finds the large proportion of families with female heads. This is the result of the economic insecurity of the men and illegitimacy. Because of the precarious hold which women of this class have on men, their attitudes alternate between one of subordination to secure affection and one of domination because of their greater economic security than their spouses.[36] But there is in the lower class a "church centered" core of families that endeavor to maintain stable family relations despite their economic insecurity and other exigencies which make family life unstable. Even during periods of comparative prosperity the employment of women may prove a disintegrating factor since these families lack a deeply rooted tradition.

The occupational differentiation of the Negro population in the northern city, as we have seen, has made possible the emergence of a substantial middle class.[37] The middle class is comprised largely of clerical workers and persons in the service occupations, though there are professional workers and some business persons in this class.[38] But, perhaps, the most important accession to the middle class in the northern cities has been the families of

TABLE XXVI PERCENTAGE OF NONWHITE FAMILIES WITH EMPLOYED HEAD THAT WERE HOMEOWNERS IN EACH OCCUPATION GROUP IN FOUR NORTHERN CITIES: 1940*

Occupational Group	New York	Chicago	Philadelphia	Detroit
Professional and Semiprofessional	6.5	20.6	32.4	30.8
Proprietors, Managers, etc.	7.1	22.9	10.3	26.7
Clerical, Sales, Etc.	8.6	18.1	33.3	50.0
Craftsmen, Foremen, etc.	9.6	6.8	6.8	21.1
Operatives	3.3	3.7	10.2	17.9
Domestic Service	2.6	4.0	14.3	5.6
Service Workers	4.1	7.1	12.9	19.1
Laborers	5.0	5.5	5.9	11.1
Total	4.9	7.9	20.4	19.2

*Based upon *Sixteenth Census of the United States: 1940. Population and Housing,* "General Characteristics," pp. 290–291.

industrial workers, especially the skilled workers. It is among this occupational class that the male head of the family has sufficient economic security to play the conventional role of provider for his family without the aid of the wife. This was indicated in a study of the industrial employment of Negro men and the employment of Negro married women in 75 northern and southern cities with a total population of 100,000 or more in 1930. It was found that the proportion of married women employed declined as the proportion of employed Negro males in industry increased.[39]

Although the husband or father in the middle-class Negro family is generally recognized as the head of the family, the wife or mother is not completely subordinated. There is often a division of labor in the management of the household and a spirit of democracy in the family. The dignified and respected position of the wife and mother is due partly to the tradition of independence among Negro women. The spirit of democracy often springs from the fact that there is considerable cooperation in order that the family may purchase a home or that the children may obtain an education. The education of children means that the family is "getting up" in the world. To be respectable and to "get up" in the world are two of the main ambitions of middle-class families. Therefore, it is not unusual that parents in middle-class families make tremendous

sacrifices to enable their children to get a college education.[40] At the same time the children of the middle class are not as a rule spoiled as are often the children in the upper class. They are generally subjected to strict discipline but they are not treated with the harshness which is often found in the case of children in lower-class families. The boys who begin at any early age to earn money in such jobs as running errands and selling newspapers generally develop a sense of responsibility and habits of industry. Consequently, the ambitious and thrifty middle-class families are the mainstay of the Baptist and Methodist churches and other institutions in the Negro community.

We come finally to the upper-class families in the large cities of the North. The upper-class Negro families do not derive their support from invested wealth but rather from professional and other kinds of services. Yet because of their class position, their outlook is often that of a wealthy leisure class. Many heads of upper-class families can tell success stories of their rise in the world, but these stories are very seldom concerned with becoming heads of business enterprises. As a rule the stories tell of their struggle to achieve a professional education. Moreover, the wives of these upper-class men like upper-class wives in the border cities are sometimes employed in professional occupations.

Where the wife is employed the upper-class family is generally equalitarian in its organization. But even where the wife is not employed, the wife in the upper-class family enjoys considerable equality in the family and freedom in her activities and contacts in the community. In some upper-class families, where the wife is economically dependent, she nevertheless determines to a large extent the manner in which the family income is spent. She herself may be the object of much conspicuous consumption since she becomes the symbol of her husband's economic position. Whether engaging in "social life" or aiding in "civic" activities, she behaves according to the expectations of her class position. Since respectability is taken for granted in this class, the unconventional behavior of husband or wife is not allowed to become a matter of public knowledge. When unconventional behavior of husband or wife becomes public, it generally means the divorce court. An important feature of the expectations of her class is that while respectability is taken for granted, the wife is supposed to appear as "refined" and "cultured."[41]

Among the upper class in the northern city there are many childless couples and relatively few children in families with children. Men and women who have struggled to achieve a high position in the Negro community are not inclined to have the standards which they attempt to maintain lowered by the burden of children. Moreover, since these men have often experienced many privations to achieve an education, they want to spare their children similar hardships. As a consequence the children of the upper class are often spoiled. The parents attempt to satisfy their children's wishes and try often to maintain them in the manner of the children of the rich. Upper-class parents in border and southern cities often send their children to the colleges in the North that represent, in their opinion at least, a certain exclusiveness. There is some evidence to support the rumors which have often circulated in Negro communities that mulatto women sometimes have refused to have children by their black husbands. A sampling of Negro families in three southern cities, secured from the unpublished data of the 1910 federal census, revealed that couples in which the husband was black and the wife was a mulatto had fewer children on the average than either the couples in which both husband and wife were black or both husband and wife were mulatto.[42] In contemplating marriage, upper-class Negroes in the North as well as in the South take into consideration the color of their prospective mates, especially its effect upon the color of their children.

Among upper-class families there is much individualism. Husbands, wives, and children insist as a rule upon the right to follow their own interests. This individualism becomes very conspicuous among the so called "emancipated" and "sophisticated" elements in the upper class. Many of these "families" are really childless couples. Their outlook on life is not only individualistic but secular. They represent a new type of intelligentsia in the Negro group. They are acquainted with the latest and best literature; they are concerned with movements within and without the Negro group. They associate freely with white middle-class intellectuals. Among this group may be found many of the "interracial" couples, since the intelligentsia does not exhibit the same hostility to intermarriage as the more conservative and isolated elements in the upper class. Thus they provide a bridge for the complete integration of the Negro in the northern city.

In this chapter we have traced the development of the Negro family and its organization in relation to the emerging class structure of rural and urban communities. It was shown how the family acquired a stable character during slavery as the result of the social and economic organization of the plantation. Then, it was shown how the family first became established on an institutional basis among the Negroes that were free before the Civil War. The analysis revealed the disorganizing effects of the Civil War and Emancipation and the subsequent reorganization in the rural South. Then we saw how the migrations to cities, especially the mass migrations to northern cities, produced a new crisis in the family life of the Negro. The experience with city life, it was seen, has not resulted simply in the disorganization of the family, held together chiefly by

habit and sentiment, but in the reorganization according to middle-class patterns, thus reflecting the new class structure in urban communities. The family has been, thus, not only the most important form of organized social life among Negroes, but it has been the means by which the new forms of adjustment have been mediated to succeeding generations. . . .

Notes

1. See Chapter 1, pp. 10–14.
2. See Melville J. Herskovits, *Life in a Haitian Valley* (New York, 1937), pp. 81–121; and Martha W. Beckwith, *Black Roadways: A Study of Jamaican Folk Life* (Chapel Hill, 1929), p. 54.
3. E. Franklin Frazier, "The Negro Family in Bahia, Brazil," *The American Sociological Review*, Vol. VII, pp. 465–78.
4. The discussion which follows is based almost entirely upon E. Franklin Frazier, *The Negro Family in the United States* (Chicago, 1939), which contains a detailed analysis, supported by documents and statistics, of the points presented in this chapter.
5. A visitor to America made the following observations: "Those [slaves] who cannot obtain women (for there is a great disproportion between the number of the two sexes) traverse the woods in search of adventures, and often encounter those of an unpleasant nature. They often meet a patrol of whites, who tie them up and flog them, and then send them home." Berguin Duvallon, "Travels in Louisiana and the Floridas, in the Year 1802," pp. 79–94, in *Journal of Negro History*, II, 172.
6. See, for example, Edward Kimber, *Itinerant Observations in America*. Reprinted from the *London Magazine*, 1745–46 (Savannah, Ga., 1878), pp. 37–38.
7. See Chapter III above.
8. See for example J. W. C. Pennington, *The Fugitive Blacksmith: or Events in the History of J. W. C. Pennington* (London, 1850).
9. Writers on Negro slavery, especially apologists for the system, have represented the Negro mother or "Mammy" as a devoted nurse of the children of the master and as indifferent to her own children. The attitude of the Negro

woman toward the children of the master was conditioned by her association with the white children and the rewards which her role as substitute mother brought her. Likewise, her attitude toward her own children was determined by what pregnancy and childbearing meant to her. See Frazier, *The Negro Family in the United States*, pp. 42–57, for a full discussion of this point.
10. In Charleston and more especially in New Orleans associations between white men and mulatto women often developed into stable alliances.
11. *The Negro Family in the United States* by E. Franklin Frazier, p.85. Copyright 1939 by The University of Chicago Press.
12. Although many white women in the South, accepting masculine prerogatives in a patriarchal system, resigned themselves to the situation, others gave vent to their jealousy and displeasure by acts of cruelty to the slave women and their mulatto offspring. The same reaction on the part of white women occurred in Brazil. See Gilberto Frevre, *Casa Grande & Senzala* (Rio de Janeiro, 1943), Vol. 2, pp. 53940.
13. See Frazier, *The Negro Family in the United States*, Chapter XI, "Racial Islands."
14. See, for example, William and Theophilus G. Steward, *Gouldtown: A Very Remarkable Settlement of Ancient Date* (Philadelphia, 1913).
15. For the origin of some of these communities we have historical evidence; but for others one must depend upon the traditions which have been preserved concerning the pioneers. See *Legislative Petitions, Archives of Virginia, King William County, 1843*. Quoted in J. H. Johnston, "Documentary Evidence of the

Relations of Negroes and Indians," *Journal of Negro History,* XIV, pp. 29–30.

16. Thomas Wentworth Higginson, *Army Life in a Black Regiment* (New York, 1900), p. 235.

17. As a rule the freedmen were unwilling to continue to work in gangs as during slavery; but insisted upon having the land divided so that each family could work as an independent unit.

18. See Frazier, *The Negro Family in the United States,* pp. 246–47.

19. See pp. 180–81.

20. See *Sixteenth Census of the United States, 1940. Population* "Characteristics of the Population," 2, Part I, pp. 19–20.

21. See Frazier, *The Negro Family in the United States,* pp. 108 ff; Hortense Powdermaker, *After Freedom* (New York, 1939), pp. 152 ff; Charles S. Johnson, *Shadow of the Plantation* (Chicago, 1934), pp. 40–44.

21a. A female head of a family is a woman—single, widowed, divorced, or if married her husband is not living with the family—who is regarded as head of the family.

22. Early sex relations account for the high birth rates among young Negro families. For the age group, 10 to 14, the birth rate for Negro women is 3.1 as compared with 0.2 for white women; and for the age group, 15 to 19, 102.7 for Negro women as compared with 42.1 for white women. Bureau of the Census. *Vital Statistics of the United States: 1940.* Part I, p. 9.

23. See Frazier, *The Negro Family in the United States,* Chapter XII, "The Black Puritans."

24. Ernest W. Burgess and Harvey J. Locke, *The Family. From Institution to Companionship* (New York, 1945), p. 161, use the term "matricentric" to designate the type of family organization described here.

25. See Frazier, *op. cit.,* Chapter VIII.

26. Burgess and Locke, op. cit., p. 165.

27. *Sixteenth Census of the United States: 1940. Population* "Differential Fertility 1940 and 1910," pp. 78, 231, 233.

28. See pp. 285–89 above.

29. See Frazier, *The Negro Family in the United States,* p. 442.

30. It appears, however, that increases in the sex ratio among Negroes in southern cities has a greater influence on marriage rates than in northern cities. See Oliver C. Cox, "Sex Ratio and Marital Status Among Negroes," *American Sociological Review,* Vol. 5, p. 942.

31. See pp. 257 ff. above.

32. See E. Franklin Frazier, *The Negro Family in Chicago* (Chicago, 1932), pp. 117–18; and Frazier, *The Negro Family in the United States,* pp. 315–16.

33. See Burgess and Locke, *op. cit.,* pp. 118–19.

34. An interesting aspect of this process is that the rates for white homeownership closely paralleled the rates for Negroes. They were for the five zones; 2.2, 9.7, 20.7, 31.9, and 53.9.

35. Frazier, *The Negro Family in Chicago,* p. 127.

36. St. Clair Drake and Horace R. Cayton, *Black Metropolis, A Study of Negro Life in a Northern City* (New York, 1945), pp. 583–84.

37. See pp. 300–02 above.

38. Cf. Drake and Cayton, *op. cit.,* p. 661. See also pp. 300–01 above.

39. The coefficient of correlation was—0.67. See Frazier *The Negro Family in the United States,* pp. 461 and 616–18.

40. *Ibid.,* pp. 473–74.

41. Cf. Drake and Cayton, *op. cit.,* p. 531.

42. The samples were taken from Birmingham, Alabama, Charleston, South Carolina, and Nashville, Tennessee. See Frazier, *The Negro Family in the United States,* Appendix B, Table 26, p. 603.

Essay/Discussion Questions

1. E. Franklin Frazier seems to argue that African American family and community life experienced cycles of instability and stability as a result of changing social and economic forces. Discuss.

2. To what extent do regional (urban and rural or southern and northern) and socioeconomic differences affect patterns of African American family and community life?

3. In Frazier's analysis, what impact did the Great Migrations of the late nineteenth and early twentieth centuries have on the black family?

The Black Family: A Critical Challenge

GLENN C. LOURY

The nuclear family, whether European or Oriental, socialist or bourgeois, modern or traditional is the center of social life in all cultures. Societies rely on the family, in one form or another, to accomplish the essential tasks of producing and socializing children. The continued prosperity—indeed the survival—of any society depends on how adequately families discharge this responsibility.

TRENDS IN AMERICAN FAMILY LIFE

There is now enormous concern in many quarters that the American family has weakened, and that this weakening is implicated in an array of social problems from criminal participation to declining academic achievement. Measures to strengthen the family have been proposed and enacted in the Congress and the need to restore family values is widely discussed. Private foundations and government agencies are spending millions of dollars annually on research and demonstration projects that seek to understand how changes now occurring in family life can be dealt with best.

The basis for this concern is reflected in recent demographic trends. Compared to a generation ago, the American family of today has changed dramatically: Older and younger single adults are more likely to live alone (Fuch, 1983). Marriage seems to have become less popular. Divorce is a much more prevalent phenomenon today than it was thirty years ago (Cherlin, 1981). The age at which women first marry has been rising, the fraction of first children conceived prior to marriage has been increasing and the proportion of these women who marry by the time their child is born has been falling. O'Connell and Moore (1980) estimate that among white teens (15–19) who had a first birth between 1959 and 1962, less than one-third of the births were premaritally conceived, though slightly more than two-thirds of these were legitimated by marriage. Whereas among white teens who experienced first births between 1975 and 1978, nearly two-thirds had conceived prior to marriage and slightly more than half of these births were subsequently legitimated.

The traditional relationship between child bearing and marriage is also undergoing dramatic change. The fertility of married women

TABLE I BIRTHS TO UNMARRIED WOMEN PER THOUSAND WOMEN, BY RACE AND AGE OF MOTHER, SELECTED YEARS

	Whites			Nonwhites		
	15–19	20–24	25–29	15–19	20–24	25–29
1940	3.3	5.7	4.0	42.5	46.1	32.5
1950	5.1	10.0	8.7	68.5	105.4	94.2
1955	6.0	15.0	13.3	77.6	133.0	125.2
1960	6.6	18.2	18.2	76.5	166.5	171.8
1965	7.9	22.1	24.3	75.8	152.6	164.7
1970	10.9	22.5	21.1	90.8	120.9	93.7
1975	12.0	15.5	14.8	86.3	102.1	73.2
1980	16.0	22.6	17.3	83.0	109.2	79.1

Source: Adapted from Wilson and Neckerman, 1984, Tables 3 & 4.

TABLE II PERCENT OF BIRTHS WHICH OCCUR OUT-OF-WEDLOCK, BY RACE AND AGE OF MOTHER, SELECTED YEARS

	Whites			Nonwhites		
	15–19	20–24	25–29	15–19	20–24	25–29
1955	6.4	1.9	0.9	40.1	18.9	13.3
1960	7.1	2.2	1.1	42.1	20.0	14.1
1965	11.4	3.8	1.9	49.2	23.0	16.3
1970	17.1	5.2	2.1	61.3	29.5	18.1
1975	23.0	6.1	2.6	74.7	39.9	22.7
1979	30.3	9.5	3.7	82.5	50.1	28.7

Source: Adapted from Wilson and Neckerman, 1984, Tables 3 & 4.

is falling, and that of most groups of unmarried women is rising (see the tables above). The incidence of teenage sexuality and childbearing has risen sharply in recent years. Between 1971 and 1979 the fraction of American teenage girls who were sexually active rose from 30% to 50% (Zelnick and Kanter, 1980). A recent Planned Parenthood report comparing teenage fertility rates in the U.S. with those in other industrialized countries shows that in 1980 the number of pregnancies per 1,000 women aged 15–19 was nearly twice as high in the U.S. as in the closest Western European country (Elise Jones, et al., "Teenage Pregnancy in Developed Countries: . . .").

As a result of these trends, there has been an increase in family instability—i.e., a growing number of families which break up or never form, leaving children to be raised by one of the parents, almost always the mother. This is a phenomenon affecting whites, blacks and

Hispanics alike, though it is by far most significant among blacks (Wilson and Neckerman, 1984). Divorce, separation and widowhood are the principal means by which single-parent families arise among whites (Cherlin, 1981; Bane and Ellwood, 1984), but the most important source of such families among blacks is the high rate of out-of-wedlock births. Among black women aged 15–24 the fraction of births which occurred outside of marriage rose from 41% in 1955 to 68 % in 1980. Out-of-wedlock births have also risen to unprecedented levels for white women. This has occurred in part because of the growing fertility of unmarried women, but an even more important reason is the recent, sharp decline in marital fertility.

It is clear from Tables I & II that, while the fertility of unmarried women (with the exception of white teens) held steady or declined between 1970 and 1980 (note the decline by more than 50% in fertility of unmarried nonwhite women ages 25–29 from 1960–1980), birth rates among married women fell sufficiently faster than the fraction of births occurring to unmarried women of all ages and races rose notably over this period. Indeed between 1960 and 1979 fertility among both white and nonwhite married women fell by roughly one-third (*Vital Statistics of the United States, 1979*). In addition, the fraction of women who are unmarried has been rising dramatically in recent years. Among white women 20–24 years of age, the percent single rose from 32.2% to 47.2% between 1965 and 1980, while the rise for comparable black women was from 34.3% to 68.7%! For women 25–29 the fraction unmarried more than doubled among white (8.0% to 18.3%) and more than tripled among blacks (11.6% to 37.2%) between 1965 and 1980 (Wilson and Neckerman, 1984).

Also important for the rise of out-of-wedlock births among young and black women has been the trend in the fraction of women who never marry, which, according to Census data, rose from 9% to 23% of black women aged 25–44 between 1950 and 1979, while staying constant at roughly 10% over this period for whites (Cherlin, 1981). This racial difference in the increased fraction of never married women has also been observed in the Panel Study of Income Dynamics by Bane and Ellwood, who report a widening black-white difference in the fraction never married, and claim that ". . . in 1982 four times as large a proportion of black as white women were never married, separated, divorced or widowed mothers (Bane and Ellwood, 1984:33).

Thus, female family heads have become both more numerous and younger among blacks and whites, but especially among blacks. The increasing prevalence of female-headed families is illustrated by the experience of the last decade (see Table III).

These trends have significant implications for the living arrangements of children, and therefore for the incidence of childhood poverty, as has been emphasized by recent observ-

TABLE III PERCENT OF FAMILIES WITH FEMALE HEADS BY RACE 1974–1983

	White	Black	Hispanic
1974	9.9	34.0	17.4
1975	10.5	35.3	18.8
1976	10.8	35.9	20.9
1977	10.9	37.1	20.0
1978	11.5	39.2	20.3
	White	Black	Hispanic
1979	11.6	40.5	19.8
1980	11.6	40.2	19.2
1981	11.9	41.7	21.8
1982	12.4	40.6	22.7
1983	12.2	41.9	22.8

Source: Adapted from Wilson and Neckerman, 1984, Table 2.

ers (Moynihan, 1985; Wilson and Neckerman, 1984; Bane and Ellwood, 1984). For obvious reasons the incidence of poverty is substantially greater among female-headed households; the poverty rate of female-headed families was 36.3% in 1982, compared to a rate for married couple families of 7.6%. Female headed families made up 45.7% of the poverty population in 1982, and 71 % of the black poor (U.S. Bureau of the Census, 1983).

Young, never-married mothers, though likely to be living at home when they have their children, are also likely to change households before their child reaches the age of six. Bane and Ellwood estimate (using the PSID) that two-thirds of black and white unwed mothers who give birth while living at home will move into different living arrangements prior to their child's sixth birthday. Among blacks, though, two-thirds of these moves are into independent female-headed families, while for whites two-thirds of the moves are into two-parent families. They further estimate that, independent of the original living arrangements of the mother, among children born out of wedlock, less than 10% of whites but more than 50% of blacks will remain in female-headed families for their entire childhood (Bane and Ellwood, 1984).

The consequences of early pregnancy for both mother and child can be quite severe.

Teenage motherhood has been shown to be associated with prolonged poverty and welfare dependency (Wilson and Neckerman, 1984; Bane and Ellwood, 1983; Hofferth and Moore, 1979), low achievement in education by the mother (Hofferth and Moore, 1979), and increased subsequent fertility and the closer spacing of births (Trusser and Menken, 1978). A careful longitudinal study of inner city black children in Chicago raised under alternative family circumstances has found that the children growing up in households where their mother is the only adult are significantly more likely to exhibit difficulty adapting to the social environment of the classroom, as measured by their first and third grade teachers' descriptions of the child's behavior in school (Kellam, et al., 1977).

CONCERN FOR THE BLACK FAMILY

Thus, these trends in adolescent and out-of-wedlock child-bearing should occasion the most serious public concern. This is especially so for the black population, in which the extent of the problem is vastly greater than for whites, for the decay of black family life is an awesome barrier to economic and social progress for blacks. It is directly implicated in the continued extent of poverty among black children. In 1980, nearly three of every five female-headed black families lived below the poverty line, compared to only about one of every six two-parent black families (U.S. Bureau of the Census, Current Population Reports, Series P 60, 1981). Even though the poverty rate fell during the 1970s for both male and female-headed black families, the fraction of black families below the poverty line increased, due to the higher rate of poverty among female-headed families, together with their growing number. This is a circumstance which deserves serious public attention.

A discussion of this sort can hardly avoid recalling the experience surrounding the controversial "Moynihan Report" (U.S. Dept. of Labor, 1965). There Moynihan had made two arguments: one regarding the causes of the (then only recently noticed) trend in family instability among blacks, and the other concerning the policy implications of this trend for the pursuit of equality of opportunity. His causal argument derived from the earlier work of E. Franklin Frazier (Frazier, 1939) and held that the black population was plagued by a "matri-focal family structure" deriving from the experience of slavery, during which the role of black men within the family had been severely circumscribed. His policy argument was that, in light of the deleterious economic consequences of this family instability, a national policy of racial equality should attempt to directly promote alternative family behaviors among blacks. He concluded that "The Negro family in the urban ghettos is crumbling. . . . So long as this situation persists, the cycle of poverty and disadvantage will continue to repeat itself."

The last two decades of history has shown that Moynihan had been remarkably accurate in his forecast. Today, the fraction of black children in single-parent homes is twice that of when his report was released. Moreover, there is now a consensus, among blacks and whites, liberals and conservatives alike, that the birth of children to young, unwed teens is a critical element of the cycle of ghetto poverty. But at the time of its release, his report occasioned a firestorm of political protest, making it impossible that his policy recommendations be adopted. Prominent black intellectuals and politicians attacked Moynihan as a racist, and dismissed his report as an attempt to impose white, middle-class values on poor blacks whose behavior was simply different from, not inferior to, the norm. (For a discussion of the reactions to the "Moynihan Report" see Rainwater and Yancy, 1967.) As a result, plans by the Johnson Administration to develop a national initiative to assist the black family were abandoned, and many years passed before public officials dared to broach the subject again.

357

This tragic error must not be repeated. Never again should we refuse to acknowledge grave social problems facing any segment of our society. Still, there is the need to maintain a delicate balance when discussing these issues. It is not the proper role of government to mandate the morals of its citizens. Nor should public officials label specific groups of citizens as exhibiting "deviant" or "pathological" behavior. But this does not mean that social norms and community values have no role to play in restraining individuals' antisocial and dysfunctional behavior. Nor does it rule out the possibility that the problems are sometimes more severe for some groups than for others.

Though correct in his emphasis on the problem and his recommendation that public action was necessary, recent historical research has demonstrated that Moynihan's explanation of family problems among blacks as having derived from the slave experience is almost certainly wrong. Racial differences of the extent discussed above are a post-World War II phenomenon, and are not to be found in the earlier historical record; they therefore cannot be explained by reference to the experience of black slavery. Although national information on family structure first became available only with the 1940 decennial census, examination of early manuscript census forms for individual cities and counties clearly demonstrates that most women heading families in the late nineteenth and early twentieth centuries were widows; that even among the very poor, a substantial majority of the families were intact; and that, for the most part, the positive association between intact family structure and social class was due to the higher rate of mortality among poor men (Furstenberg et al., 1975).

The evidence also demonstrates that among northern, urban black migrant communities in the early twentieth century, the intact family was also the norm. Approximately 85% of black families living in Harlem in 1925 were intact,

and the teenage mother raising her children alone was virtually unknown; comparable findings were noted for blacks in Buffalo in 1910 (Gutman, 1976). In 1940 10.1% of white families and 14.9% of black families were female headed; and though single-parent families were more common among city dwellers, census data from that year indicate that fully 72% of urban black families with children were headed by men (Wilson and Neckerman, 1984). By 1960 the proportion of single-parent families had begun to increase sharply for blacks, rising from 21.7% in 1960, to 28.3% by 1970, and reaching 41.9% in 1983. Among whites the proportion also rose, from 8.1% in 1960 to 12.2% in 1983.

BLACK TEENAGE PREGNANCY: TRENDS AND RESPONSES

We may ask then, if Moynihan's (and Frazier's) sociology was wrong, what accounts for the current group disparity in family instability? Given the higher rate of teenage childbearing among urban blacks, investigators have explored a number of hypotheses to explain this phenomenon. Beginning in the mid-1960s, a series of ethnographic studies involving close observation of specific communities have been undertaken (Clark, 1965; Rainwater, 1970; Stack, 1974; Gilder, 1978). These studies have called attention to cultural and normative factors operative in poor urban communities, deriving from the severe economic hardship of inner-city life, but interacting with governmental income support systems (Gilder, 1978; Murray, 1984) and evolving in such a way as to feed back onto individual behavior and exacerbate this hardship.

Wilson and Neckerman (1984), citing evidence from a survey of black female teens undertaken in 1979 by the Urban League of Chicago and compiled by Dennis Hogan of the University of Chicago, argue that there is an insufficient aversion to unwed pregnancy in this population. The aforementioned data are said to show that black teen mothers reported far fewer pregnancies to be unwanted than their white counterparts (among whom Zelnick and Kanter, 1980, report finding 82% of pre-marital pregnancies to 15–19 year olds to have been unwanted). Stack, 1974, observing an unnamed midwestern inner-city community, notes "People show pride in all their kin, and particularly new babies born into their kinship networks. Mothers encourage sons to have babies, and even more important, men coax their 'old ladies' to have their baby" (p. 121).

Observation of participants in Project Redirection, a two-year planned intervention with teenagers who had already borne one child out-of-wedlock, which had the objective of preventing the additional pregnancy, confirms that prevailing values and attitudes among these young women and their boyfriends constitute a critical part of the teen pregnancy story (Branch et al., 1984). There it was observed that "Participants who lack self-esteem often find it difficult to resist pressure from boyfriends. . . . Participants tolerate (being beaten by their boyfriends, or exploited economically) believing that, because of their children, other men will not want them" (p. 39). Moreover, concern at the Harlem site of this project regarding the issue of welfare dependency led to the following observation:

> Staff initially took an activist stance in their efforts to intercede with the welfare system on behalf of participants . . . This pattern changed, however when . . . (certain) behavior patterns were beginning to emerge . . . It seemed that many were beginning to view getting their own welfare grants as the next stage in their careers . . . (I)t became apparent that some participants' requests for separate grants and independent households were too often a sign of manipulation by boyfriends, in whose interest it was to have a girlfriend on welfare with an apartment of her own . . . (S)taff realized that these attitudes and behaviors were . . . counterproductive to the goal of promoting self-sufficiency. (Branch et al., p. 60)

Project Redirection involved the use of "community women," older women who befriended and advised the teen mothers over the course of the first year of the study. It is noteworthy that these community women ". . . have come out strongly against emancipated minor status for participants (which allows 15 and 16 year old mothers to obtain public aid, including housing, independently of their parents), feeling that it is better that teens remain under family guidance, no matter how difficult the family situation or conflict may be" (Branch et al., 1984:60). This project had a very limited impact on the sexual behavior and subsequent additional pregnancies of the young women enrolled. Commenting on this outcome Branch et al. (1984) observed: "The major finding is that members of this target group . . . hold a constellation of attitudes and values about boyfriends, sexual relationships, pregnancy and childbearing that are extremely resistant to change. Against the tenacity of these values, the presentation of factual information alone is inadequate to bring about substantial behavioral improvement" (p. 103). These findings lend credence to the view that peer group and community behavioral norms in the inner city play a substantial role in the explosion of young single parents.

In seeking an appropriate response to these developments we must understand two things: (1) the forces that have caused the teen pregnancy and illegitimate birth rates to be so high in poor black communities; and (2) the manner in which governmental policies and private actions within black communities can combine to counteract these forces. What was missing in 1965, and what remains scarce now, is *combined* public and private actions that can effectively attack the problem. The confusion of values, attitudes and beliefs of black youngsters who produce children for whom they cannot provide must be addressed; and, those aspects of government policy which reinforce, or reward such values must be publicly questioned. It is the job of black civic, political and religious leaders to do the former, and the task of public leadership at the local, state and federal levels to undertake the latter.

It should be stated at the outset that some of the factors influencing the behavior of young people do not lie within anyone's control. Our youth are engaging in sexual activity outside of marriage at a higher rate, and at a younger age than did their parents. Social taboos that exercised some restraint on extramarital sexuality a generation ago have become passé. Yet, though yesterday's moral climate cannot be restored, teaching our young people to behave responsibly in the face of today's social pressures and temptations should be within our grasp. It has traditionally been the role of the family and of religious institutions to instill this sense of responsibility, and so it remains. For blacks, this issue is especially critical.

The National Urban League has taken the lead with its Male Responsibility Campaign. The program objective is to reach young black males through a national advertising effort of print ads, posters and a radio commercial. Its theme: "Don't make a baby if you can't be a father." With the voluntary cooperation of black newspapers, music associations, and broadcasters it is geared to reach a mass audience. Several aspects of the program deserve special emphasis. First, it illustrates the opportunity for traditional civil rights organizations to provide leadership for the black community on important social issues too sensitive for public agencies. Second, it focuses on the male. Too often intervention is directed exclusively at the teen mother—helping her to return to school and trying to prevent further pregnancies. Third, it harnesses the creative talents and notoriety of prominent blacks to improve the quality of life for ordinary black people.

One often hears the argument that nothing significant can be done about "children having children" until something is done about the lack of economic options for poor ghetto youngsters. Some commentators have suggested that the unemployment of black men is

mainly responsible for the family problems observed in this population (Norton, 1985; Wilson and Neckerman, 1984). In their interesting and valuable paper, Wilson and Neckerman note that the numbers of employed black men relative to the numbers of black women of comparable age has declined sharply for every age group of blacks since 1960, with the decline being particularly precipitate for younger men. The low employment of black men is presumed to reduce their propensity to marry, without having a comparable negative effect on the propensity to reproduce. The result is an increasing out-of-wedlock birth rate, with comparable increases in the percentage of families headed by women.

There is, to be sure, a great need to expand employment among poor young people, but more is involved here than limited economic opportunity. The foregoing argument is far from satisfactory, because it presumes what in part needs to be explained—that young men will continue to father children though they know they cannot support them. The link between employment and family responsibilities for men is very complex, and the direction of causality is far from clear. It is arguable, for example, that a man's effort to find and keep work would be greater to the extent that he feels himself primarily responsible for the maintenance of his family.

The fact that so many young black men are fathers but not husbands, and that they do not incur the financial obligations of fatherhood, might then be taken as an explanation of their low levels of employment. A more serious kind of unemployment plagues young men in poor black communities. There many women struggle to raise their children without financial or emotional support from fathers who have jobs, but make no effort to see their children. These men are unemployed with respect to their most important adult responsibility. Yet unlike the hardship caused by a lost job and income, this kind of unemployment can be cured by an act of will. Every means of persuasion should be used to see that both parents take full responsibility for their children.

Unfortunately, some of the crippling social problems evident in poor black communities have been exacerbated by the way public programs and agencies have chosen to treat those problems. Easy and stigma-free availability of public assistance, and the financial penalty imposed when a welfare family takes a job and thereby loses its public housing and medical benefits along with its welfare payments, may discourage responsible behavior by young men and women who bring children into the world without the means to support them. This concern, expressed by Charles Murray in his recent, much debated book *Losing Ground* (Murray, 1984), is of particular significance to blacks, because such a large fraction of our community depends on state and federal assistance.

It is clear from statistical evidence that, while conditions have worsened for the low-income central city black population since the 1960s, the status of blacks with good educations and marketable skills has improved significantly. Increasingly, the black community is becoming divided into a relatively prosperous middle class and a desperately poor underclass. Though problems of discrimination continue to exist for middle-class blacks, they are minor when compared to the life-threatening conditions and dwindling opportunities poor blacks face. It has become evident that the problems of poor black communities are greater than simply a lack of resources—that the norms and behaviors of residents in these communities contribute to their difficulty. Thus, the question becomes whether government efforts to help have, in any way, served to undermine the normative base of poor black communities.

Murray believes that they have, and his argument deserves the most serious attention. He charges that aspects of the conventional wisdom which has dominated thinking about public policy in the social sciences and allied helping professions since the sixties have con-

tributed to the decline in living standards among inner city blacks, one aspect of which is the growth of female-headed families. He holds that a complex and delicately balanced system of values and norms regulates the behavior of individuals in poor (and all other) communities, that adverse change in these behavioral norms has occurred in recent decades, and that ideological precepts particular to the liberal wisdom on social policy (e.g., that those in need of public assistance were in no way to be held accountable for the behavior which may have led to their dependency) may have played a key role in abetting this change.

Yet, in our effort to avoid the sin of "blaming the victim," we sacrificed the ability to reward those persons who, though perhaps of modest financial means, conducted themselves in such a way as to avoid falling into the trap of dependency. The status and dignity that people derive from conducting their lives honorably—working to support themselves and their children, raising their sons to stay out of trouble with the law, and their daughters to avoid early unwed pregnancy—was undermined by the idea that poverty is everywhere and always the result of a failure in the system, not the individual. For if those who fail are seldom at fault, those who succeed can only have done so by their good fortune, not their virtue.

This points to what I consider to be the most critical element of any strategy to confront the current black family crisis—the need to promote virtuous behavior among the inner-city poor. This is inevitably a sensitive, controversial matter, one which public officials will often seek to avoid. But it is a crucial aspect of the problem which concerned private leaders in the black community must confront head-on. Among those many black families who have attained middle-class status in the last two decades, there is a keen sense of the importance of instilling in their children values and norms consistent with success. It would seem then that there is a responsibility for successful blacks, through religious and civic organizations and personal contacts internal to the black community, to transmit the norms that have proved so useful in shaping their own lives to the black poor who have fallen behind the rest of society (Loury, 1985). One might refer to such an activity as supplying "moral leadership." No one else can do it; the matter is urgent.

Community organizations, public housing resident management associations, churches and the rest must deal with this matter. Mutually concerned people who trust one another enough to be able to exchange criticism must seek to establish and enforce norms of behavior that lie beyond the capacity of the state to promulgate. Government has, after all, limited coercive resources (incarceration, or the denial of financial benefits being the main ones). Communities can invoke more subtle and powerful influences over the behavior of their members. The expectations of people about whom we care constitutes an important source of such influence. Yet to employ these means requires that people be willing to come forward and say: "This is what we believe in; this is what we stand for; yet, look at where we now are."

References

Bane, Mary Jo, and David Ellwood (1984), "Single Mothers and their Living Arrangements," unpublished paper, Harvard University.

Branch, Alvia, James Riccio and Janet Quint (1984), *Building Self-Sufficiency in Pregnant and Parenting Teens,* Final Implementation Report of Project Redirection, New York: Manpower Demonstration Research Corporation (April).

Cherlin, Andrew (1981), *Marriage, Divorce and Remarriage,* Cambridge, Ma.: Harvard Univ. Press.

Clark, Kenneth B. (1965), *Dark Ghetto,* New York: Harper & Row.

Frazier, E. Franklin (1939), *The Negro Family in the United States,* Chicago; University of Chicago Press.

Fuch, Victor (1983), *How We Live: An Economic Perspective on Life and Death,* New York: Basic Books.

Furstenberg, Frank (1976), *Unplanned Parenthood: The Social Consequences of Teenage Childbearing,* New York, Free Press.

Gilder, George (1978), *Visible Man: A True Story of Post Racist America,* New York: Basic Books.

Gutman, Herbert G. (1976), *The Black Family in Slavery and Freedom, 1750–1925,* New York: Pantheon Books.

Hofferth, Sandra L., and Kristin A. Moore (1979), "Early Childbearing and Later Economic Well-Being," *American Sociological Review,* 44:784–815 (October).

Kellam, Sheppard, Margaret Ensminger and R. Jay Turner (1977), "Family Structure and the Mental Health of Children," *Archives of General Psychiatry* 34:1012–22.

Loury, Glenn C. (1985), "The Moral Quandary of the Black Community," *The Public Interest,* No. 79 (Spring).

Moynihan, Daniel P. (1985), "Family and Nation," *The Godkin Lectures, Harvard University,* Harvard Univ. Press).

Murray, Charles (1984), *Losing Ground: American Social Policy 1950–1980,* New York: Basic Books.

O'Connell, Martin, and Maurice J. Moore (1980), "The Legitimacy Status of First Births to U.S. Women Aged 15–24,1939–1978," *Family Planning Perspectives* 12(1): 16–25.

Rainwater, Lee (1970), *Behind Ghetto Walls: Black Families in a Federal Slum,* Chicago: Adeline Publishing Co.

Rainwater, Lee, and William Yancey (1967), *The Moynihan Report and the Politics of Controversy,* Cambridge, Mass.: MIT Press.

Stack, Carol (1974), *All Our Kin: Strategies for Survival in a Black Community,* New York: Harper and Row.

Trussel, J., and J. Menken (1978), "Early Childbearing and Subsequent Fertility," *Family Planning Perspectives* 10(4):209–218.

U.S. Bureau of the Census (1983), "Characteristics of the Population Below Poverty Level: 1982," *Current Population Reports,* P 60, No. 144, Washington, D.C.: Government Printing Office.

U.S. Department of Labor (1965), *The Negro Family: The Case for National Action,* Washington, D.C.: Government Printing Office.

Wilson, William J., and Katherine M. Neckerman (1984), "Poverty and Family Structure; The Widening Gap Between Evidence and Public Policy Issues," University of Wisconsin-Madison, Institute for Research on Poverty Conference Paper, December 1984.

Zelnick, Melvin, and John Kanter (1980), "Sexual Activity, Contraceptive Use and Pregnancy Among Metropolitan-Area Teenagers: 1971–1979," *Family Planning Perspectives* 12:230–237 (September/October).

Essay/Discussion Questions

1. As a conservative black policy analyst, what is Glenn Loury's explanation for the crisis of contemporary black family instability? Is it a result of a pattern of impoverished individual culture and behavior, or is it a result of impediments within the structural dynamics of American society and its economy?

2. For Loury, does poverty result in out-of-wedlock births, or does the occurrence of unwed mothers cause poverty?

3. Loury challenges what sector of the black population to find solutions to black urban poverty. Why?

The Dependent Status of Black Families: A Structural Framework II

WILLIAM DARITY, JR., AND SAMUEL L. MYERS, JR.,
WITH EMMETT D. CARSON AND WILLIAM SABOL

9.1. THE COURTS AND THE BLACK FAMILY UNDER CAPITALISM

In slavery times blacks were property. Statutory law linking black skin to perpetual servitude dated at least to the mid-17th century, well before the founding of the republic (Wax, 1973, 371–2). A judiciary in step with its age would have been expected to acquiesce in and/or to reinforce this tendency, to have issued decisions that maintained the lack of humanity of these human items of property.

But the situation was not so straightforward, particularly in the antebellum period (1800–1860). Debate still rages among southern legal scholars over whether southern courts took a largely ameliorative stance toward the slave system and toward the statutory law that provided the legal basis for the system, or whether southern courts were merely another instrument in the slave master's arsenal of oppression. Among those scholars who take the ameliorator's tack there is a further debate over whether the judges in southern lower courts and appellate courts acted out of sincere opposition to the excesses of the slave system and recognized the moral personality of the slave, or if their actions stemmed from an expedient and "'paternalistic' desire to protect slavery—whether to protect the master's property interest to disprove abolitionists' calumnies, or to discourage the worst white repressiveness that could, if not judicially restrained, encourage slave unrest or uprising" (Nash, 1979, 11).

Southern legal historian A. E. Keir Nash (1979) has claimed that there was no such thing as a unified Southern legal code with respect to slavery, nor was there a consistent pattern of Southern legal jurisprudence. He places a strong emphasis on variability in the decisions reached by judges from state to state, contingent in part on variation in the statu-

From *The Black Underclass: Critical Essays on Race and Unwantedness*, by William A. Darity, Jr., and Samuel L. Myers, Jr., *with* Emmett D. Carson, and William Sabol. Reprinted by permission of Garland Publishing, Inc., New York, 1994.

tory law before them and in part on variation in the attitudes of the judges themselves. He observes that there even was substantial variability in which slave-holding states had courts that treated freed blacks differentially or in the same fashion as whites.

But even Nash, who has advanced the strongest amelioratory interpretation of some southern judicial actions under slavery, never has claimed that the courts were other than an arena where the contradictions of the slave system could find verbal expression. Southern courts did not become agencies of abolition nor extensive manumission. Southern courts did not deign to address the sexual subjugation of black female slaves to white masters and overseers. Nor did they endeavor to keep slave families intact. Of course, as Nash observes, neither did northern courts for that matter. Aside from supporting certain static protections for blacks, northern courts did little more.[1] Their judges did not actively support the free status of runaways from the southern plantation system.

The national Constitution of the United States adopted in 1787 formalized and sustained the legal foundation of slavery. At no juncture did the courts seek to advance an interpretation of the Constitution that would have undermined slavery. Indeed, slavery became more oppressive and legalistic following the adoption of the Constitution, a pattern of events that culminated in the Dred Scott decision of 1857. With Dred Scott the U.S. Supreme Court's majority gave full vent to philosophical white supremacy in a renewed endorsement of the slave system, the spirit of which resounds to this day.

Central to the implications of Dred Scott was the denigration of the black family, of the offspring of black parents, of employment options for the black workers, and of the opportunity for political participation by blacks. Specifically the case denied any customary rights and privileges to the institution of marriage among blacks:

It is important to recognize the significance of the message the *Dred Scott* decision relayed for the position of the black family. The minority opinion presented by Justice Curtis rested heavily on the argument that [Dred and Harriet] Scott's legal act marriage provided the basis for declaring the black family free of slavery. . . . The *Dred Scott* decision, in effect, repudiated the notion clearly stated by Justice Curtis that an especial legal protection was to be ascribed to the act of marriage, the official formation of families, if the consenting parties were black. Not only were the parents condemned to slavery but so were their offspring. (Darity, 1980, 22)

The Dred Scott decision is best known for its explicit denial of rights of citizenship "to a member of the 'the Negro African race,' even though free in the state of his residence" (Waite, 1946, 222). What is less well understood is the comprehensive denial of the protections of the U.S. Constitution toward the family of a member of "the Negro African race." The highest court in the land had issued for the first time a majority decision that declared that, like cattle or beasts of burden, the children of slaves were themselves chattel and their parents had no rights over them. Blacks were placed officially in the category of America's "unelect." A further implication is that the decision maintained the practice of counting slaves for legislative purposes as two-thirds of a person, a notion that carried over into human relations and constitutional protections.

It should be added that Dred Scott decision was only the second instance in the Court's history, up until that time, in which it exercised its authority to engage in judicial review to overturn an Act of Congress. It had not done so since the Marshall Court first asserted the doctrine of judicial review in the *Marbury v. Madison* case in 1803. In Dred Scott the Court also declared "unconstitutional and void . . . the so-called 'Missouri Compromise' of 1820; thereby denying the power of Congress to prohibit slavery in any of the states or territories of the Union" (Waite, 1946, 222). The Court moved on behalf of southern white men of property to obstruct legislative intent. In addition, the Dred Scott decision effectively defined a slave-like status for free blacks in any state or territory of the United States. The Tawney Court's majority had uncompromisingly staked out a pro-slavery posture.[2]

In the interregnum represented by Reconstruction, the Freedman's Bureau became the *de facto* lawmakers for blacks in the South, monitoring contract labor arrangements between ex-slaves and farmers (Waite, 1946, 223). With the termination of Reconstruction, the key facets of judicial action affecting blacks involved the Constitutional amendments intended to end slavery and to give blacks citizenship—Constitutional amendments that overturned the thrust of *Dred Scott v. Sandford*. The Court's subsequent handling of these amendments had indirect implications for the black family, particularly in terms of the effects on the adult male presence within the family.

The 13th Amendment abolished slavery everywhere in the United States except in the prisons. This was a concession to southern landowners who were incapable of reaping their harvests without a readily available workforce. The abolition of slavery was accompanied by "black males increasingly [refusing] to work sunup to sundown hours and substantially fewer black women and children worked at all, [so that] landowners spoke bitterly about the blacks' inability to work in a free system and demanded the power to regulate the former slaves" (Haws and Namorato, 1979, 311-2).

The mechanism of regulation was the structure of vagrancy and debtor laws with a scheme of fines such that, if unpaid, led to the freedman being sent to the lock-up facility. Leasors of labor could agree to pay off the fines to obtain workers for an indefinite period of time. Black males who were objects of the more important bonded labor or prison-lease system could be removed from proximity to their families, potential spouses, and communities for long periods of time and at great distances. The judiciary as the sentencing institution in the imposition of fines bore a strong instrumental role in the operation of both the bonded labor and convict labor systems. Misdemeanors were transformed into felonies. Sentences for minor crimes were lengthened calculatedly. The intent was to maintain a supply of cheap and passive black labor. The courts also enforced the legal validity of credit schemes where landowners placed black families in debt peonage by their arbitrary selection of interest rates on the value of goods or funds advanced to black workers (Jaynes, 1986, 301-16). Thus the judiciary served to reinforce tendencies toward a greater incidence of female family headship and poverty among black families.

Southern labor needs dictated some stabilization of the black family, without the male head, in slavery times. This necessity carried over into the postbellum period. But today the courts even attack the matriarchate structure, since black labor is no longer viewed as useful. The reintroduction of a form of involuntary servitude through the penal apparatus was dictated by the labor requirements of the southern landowners. Black males were necessary—as manual laborers. The Southern scheme of property rights was to be reestablished despite the Civil War.

The overrepresentation of blacks in southern prisons must be viewed in light of the paradoxical finding that *northern* prisons are also disproportionately black, and have been so for more than a century. Significantly, from 1870 to 1900 black overrepresentation in northern prisons was almost twice that of black overrepresentation in southern prisons. In the very period during which Southern prisons were becoming black as a direct consequence of legal changes affecting blacks' newly-won status as freedmen, northern prisons maintained a sizeable and disproportionate number of blacks, raising questions about the equanimity of northern "justice" as well (Myers and Sabol, 1985).

The 13th Amendment was not used until 1911 (*Bailey v. Alabama*) and 1914 (*US v. Reynolds*) by the Supreme Court to strike down debt-peonage. But these decisions were handed down by the White Court (1910–1921) which took, in Benno Schmidt's (1982, 444–524) estimation, a more progressive stance on racial matters than the courts that preceded or followed it. It was an unusual interlude, according to Schmidt, the possible exception that proves the rule of Supreme Court complicity in Jim Crow arrangements.[3] In fact, Schmidt (1982, 474) suggests that the highest court's earlier support for segregation statutes spurred passage of even more Jim Crow legislation at the state level.

The 14th Amendment's equal protection clause was intended to strike down the Black Codes—the existence of separate laws for blacks—and to bring blacks under the uniform coverage of the U.S. Constitution. But again the judiciary operated to undercut legislative intent. Significantly, the 14th Amendment soon was transformed by the Supreme Court into a device to protect business interests from adverse regulation:

> The Fourteenth Amendment, one of three antislavery amendments, soon became a shield for corporate business. The former slaves were forgotten, as the Justices blandly and blithely 'amended' the Amendment.[4]

Such an ingenious construction and manipulation of the 14th Amendment to serve ends other than the provision of human rights for blacks foreshadowed the contemporary dilution of anti-discrimination measures via an ever-expanding definition of "minorities" to include white females, homosexuals, and political refugees who recently have immigrated to the United States.

With respect to the 15th Amendment the "grandfather clause" was the device adopted by several states to block blacks from exercising the vote. The White Court did declare such clauses inconsistent with the 15th Amendment in two cases in 1915 (Waite, 1946, 268–9).[5] But these cases came relatively late in the day, so to speak, and despite the indication of a gradual movement of the Court toward support for "Negro rights" such statutory restrictions on black voting rights probably were the tip of the iceberg.

In general, the judiciary moved to support the *de facto* restoration of the pre-Civil War order in the South. At the apex of the judiciary, support for apartheid in America reached its height with *Plessy vs. Ferguson* (1896), which enunciated the separate but equal doctrine. In fact, *Plessy v. Ferguson* (the Fuller Court) sanctioned the reality of separate but unequal conditions and facilities for blacks and whites. The Supreme Court was among the leaders of what Robert Cover (1982, 1295) describes as "the massive retreat from protecting Black rights between the 1870s and 1920s. . . ."

Again Schmidt (1982, 445) identifies the White Court as an exception during the latter part of the period, but he acknowledges that "The White Court did not repudiate the essential principles of Jim Crow laid down by the Fuller Court. . . ." Its significance lay in its resistance to the "radical spread of apartheid" throughout the nation. Schmidt's (1983, 1402) ultimate assessment of the White Court seems decisive. "In no sense did the White Court mount a serious constitutional challenge to the legal structure of racism in American society."

Postbellum lynch laws in the South, which the courts generally failed to repudiate, never mind retard, represents the most visibly horrifying instances of judicial complicity in neoslavery. The companion acts of castration constitute violent symbols of continued assertion of control over the black male. But the substantive assertion of that control came through a penal system which deprived numerous black families of a male spouse and breadwinner.

9.2 THE COURTS AND THE BLACK FAMILY IN THE MANAGERIAL AGE

The "massive retreat" from defense of black rights apparently reversed in the managerial era, but the reversal only has been apparent. "Negro rights" cases became the centerpiece of the decisions of the Warren Court. But there were peculiarities here. The shift in the court's stance vis-a-vis civil rights for blacks came precisely at a juncture in which the crucial litigation from the standpoint of the well-being of the black family was *not* civil rights cases. Second, the civil rights cases can be interpreted as instruments for managerial class advancement rather than cases solely beneficial to blacks. After all, in an earlier era the 14th Amendment was utilized to insulate corporate America from regulation; "the former slaves were forgotten."

In a population beset by a continuously high incidence of female-headed and impoverished families, litigation governing the rights of families that have suffered from divorce, separation, or desertion would have special relevance. Here is where we find the outlines for the shape of things to come for non-black families. For the most part:

> Court decisions have preserved a dependent condition for black families as well as families headed by women regardless of race. As the two categories converge, judicial activism fits the mold of the twin tendencies of pushing women out of homemaking and men out of familial responsibilities. Divorced husbands have with impunity been able to avoid making child support payments. Moreover, the level of payments set by the courts has been inadequate to prevent a sharp drop in the standard of living for the newly single women and their children even when divorced husbands have actually made the payments. . . . The Court stance has been, in general, to reduce the responsibilities of the now absent father, thereby pushing the mother into the labor force, or onto the welfare rolls, or both (Darity and Myers, 1984b, 180–1)[6]

In addition, when child support collection efforts have been enforced they have concentrated primarily on males least able to pay. They have been targeted "on collections from low-income fathers who have never been married to the mothers of their children. [Such collections are motivated by the desire] to reduce the costs of the welfare system rather than to sustain the financial security of the mother and the child . . . "(Darity and Myers, 1984b. 181).

The dramatic increase in the cost of welfare and the significant increase in the size of the welfare rolls in the decade of the 1970s prompted policy makers and legislators to seek means for shifting the burden of child support from the state to the delinquent father. The state found a willing ally in the court. Both because many child support awards originally had been determined by the courts, and because the court traditionally has had jurisdiction over the determination of paternity, many fathers of children receiving welfare benefits found themselves unwilling defendants with welfare agencies as plaintiffs.

The objective was simple. Delinquent fathers, when faced with the prospect of going to jail or perhaps paying a fine for nonsupport of their children on welfare, would provide their offspring with the court-mandated support and thereby reduce the fiscal burden on the local welfare agency. This deterrence strategy follows the logic of much of the reasoning of America's criminal justice system. And, like the criminal justice system, racially uneven outcomes have emerged.

Richard Lempert (1981–2) has detailed the lengths that the courts will go to collect child support payments. He finds wage assignments and imprisonment as popular sanctions. The choice of sanction, unsurprisingly, is not racially neutral. Compared to those who receive warning from the court, blacks and low-income fathers are more likely to receive the sanction of imprisonment. When there are wages to assign, moreover, the money goes not to the mother or the child, but to the welfare agency, the real plaintiff in the case.

Lempert's data provide clear support for the hypothesis that the court in child support awards is far more interested in collection and punishing delinquency than it is in the well-being of mothers and their children. The deterrence strategy, moreover, clearly works against the objective of creating stable and economically viable two-parent households. Given the threat of imprisonment or wage assignment, fathers who are unable to make regular payments have a greater incentive to flee, to disappear, and to break off ties completely with their children and their children's mothers. It seems unlikely that judges honestly believe such punitive sanctions will help families stay together; but what seems clear is that whatever chance there may be for separated parents to reunite or for fathers of children born out of wedlock to marry and/or support those children's mothers vanishes when the court adopts its punitive sanctions.

That this evidence points to a bias against blacks and against the black family seems apparent from the emphasis on wage assignments. Black males earn lower wages than white males. Black males also are less likely to have a job or to be in the labor market looking for a job. The penalty that the court imposes, presumably color blind, falls hardest upon blacks without any apparent benefit to either black children or their mothers (Hill, 1988). When the father, unable to pay or to produce wages that can be assigned, is imprisoned, the result is neither revenues to the state, to reduced the welfare burden, nor payments to the welfare recipients. Whether this bias can be attributed to intentional or unintentional racial discrimination is not material. The result is that the court, through its power to enforce child support laws, makes the black family still more vulnerable.

Furthermore, the courts have not been protective of female-headed families regardless of the origin of such families—whether by marital splits or their formation by never-married women who have children. While granting "civil rights" to blacks, notwithstanding a spate of negative decisions throughout the 1980s, the managerial courts' "family law" decisions consistently have been destructive of black family rights. Families of never-married women are afforded illusory protections at best. The courts seek to establish paternity, ostensibly with an eye toward having the father of the woman's child provide financial support. But any funds so obtained typically are merely transferred to state agencies to reduce the expenses of the welfare system, rather than going directly to mother and child (Hill, 1988, 40–2).

Even the civil rights cases now appear to have dimensions that go far beyond protection of blacks in the managerial age. Minority rights just as easily can mean protection for non-black minorities. There is an inherent arbitrariness with respect to whom the courts identify as suspect classes to be protected by the judiciary's paternalistic supervision through application of the equal protection clause. Under the Burger court the groups whom the Supreme Court identified as meriting protection appeared to be shrinking, but at any time, the Court could ride a new ideological wave that directs it toward a more expansive interpretation. Charles Clarke (1982, 201–52), for one, would like to see the Court identify the poor as a suspect class. Judicial ingenuity could, for example, make it possible for blacks to cease being a suspect class while women might become such a class. Any configuration is possible, once more diluting the intent of the 14th Amendment. It gives the managerial class, through the auspices of the Court, the capacity to determine, at its whim, who is the favored group of the moment.

From the standpoint of the courts' role in the administration of the penal system, it no longer services the convict labor system through its sentencing decisions, since that system no longer exists. The advanced development of "prison yard" industries was blocked by labor union opposition to an institution that could produce commodities at costs well below conventional market prices. What diversification and consolidation of prison production has taken place represents a shift from brooms and license plates to refinishing desks and paper production. But the prison no longer serves an important labor supply function in the North or South. If anything the major function of the contemporary prison system is to house part of the managerial estate's surplus population (Jankovic, 1977, 17–31).

Not only is this surplus population disproportionately comprised of black males, the prisons serve as a breeding ground for drug abuse and homosexuality. Thus the process of criminal justice depletes the availability of marriageable men for black women. Variations in the male-female sex ratio have significant effects on the incidence of female-headship in any population. The sex-ratio problem among blacks is aggravated by the system of criminal justice.

To compound matters, judicial "liberalism" throughout the 1970s and most of the 1980s with regard to reproductive rights reinforces anti-natalism and even prospects for "voluntary" genocide among the black underclass. The Court's decree of the legal availability of abortion opened the door for greater exercise of the option to terminate pregnancies among women who could anticipate impoverished single parenthood futures. The vise tightened on black families, as the legality of abortion accompanied a deepening economic struggle to support children.

9.3 *MAZIQUE VS. MAZIQUE:* A CASE STUDY

When it took place, the divorce of Edward and Jewell Mazique was the object of protracted media attention, particularly in the black press.[7] Both parties to the divorce were prominent in Washington's black elite and talented individuals in their own respective rights. Edward Mazique was perhaps the most well-known physician in the District of Columbia, known not only for being an outstanding practitioner but also for his outspoken positions on social problems, especially those involving health and medical issues. Jewell Mazique had established a reputation as a scholar-journalist, as a leader in human rights activity in the nation's capital, and as a crusader for quality education. She was one of the organizers of the first march on Washington in the 1930s, a march directed against unfair employment practices in the District government. As a journalist she took powerful and provocative stands on controversial issues concerning race relations and international affairs.[8] Public interest in the divorce was largely voyeuristic at the time.

But the case had substantive implications that could not have been obvious at the time. The decision in *Mazique v. Mazique* at the D.C. Court of Appeals level became precedent-setting not only in several future divorce cases, but also in a wide variety of cases where individuals sought to act as their own lawyers when unable to obtain satisfactory legal service from lawyers.[9] The case had a chilling effect on Congressional efforts to design legislation to provide additional protections for families headed by women who had experienced either divorce or desertion (Darity 1982, 22). The decision came in the midst of a period of intense struggle over personal property rights and the conditions of women and children, reflected, in particular, by Congressional attempts to "modernize" the District's dower law between 1961 through 1965.[10]

It also signalled, in retrospect, the absence of any consistent judicial efforts to preserve at least the material well-being of even well-to-do families—black or white—subjected to marital dissolution. Indeed, this case shows clearly how the courts actively can declass a partner to a marriage. Most important, *Mazique v. Mazique* is a case that stands at the threshold of the winding down of capitalism and the winding up of the managerial estate. On the surface what appears to be an ordinary divorce case, *Mazique v. Mazique* revealed how narrow a distance has been traveled by the courts since *Dred Scott v. Sandford* with respect to the black family.

This divorce settlement involving a black couple originally was handed down by the D.C. General Sessions Court in 1964, and the lower court's disposition was upheld at every level of appeal.[11] Finally, in 1966 the Supreme Court denied the petition for *writ of certiorari* altogether.[12] This was, of course, the same Supreme Court that had given the nation *Brown vs. Board of Education* and a growing body of minority rights decrees that ostensibly would uplift "the Negro." It is also noteworthy that it was Thurgood Marshall, Solicitor General of the United States between 1965 and 1967, and "the first known descendant of Africans to sit on the Supreme Court" who was responsible for the denial of petition for appeal (Darity 1982, 23).

There were numerous oddities—even mysterious elements—to these proceedings. First, Mrs. Mazique never could find a lawyer who could commit to her defense without urging her to agree to a rapid and meager settlement over the division of the couple's substantial wealth. This despite the fact that the couple been married for more than twenty years, and the wife had purchased their first real estate property while working two jobs when her husband was enrolled as a medical student. She had not only supported her husband through medical school, but she had assisted him in opening his medical practice. But the Judge at the Municipal Court of Appeals never requested documents detailing Dr. Mazique's income sources or property holdings in arriving at his decision. Nor were they requested at higher levels of appeal.

Second, Mrs. Mazique sought to subpoena materials to establish that she had sought police protection from her husband as early as November 7, 1961 and that Dr. Mazique had been summoned to the District Attorney's office. She sought to demonstrate that when she "deserted" her home it was out of fear for her life. But the subpoena was quashed by the US Attorney, indicating an unusual interest in a divorce by the federal government, an unusual interest that may have had a suppressed political backdrop.[13] Without such evidence, it looked like Mrs. Mazique had committed an act of unwarranted desertion rather than being an endangered victim.

Third, the Judge at the General Sessions Court assigned to the Mazique case, John Burnett, was criticized by the US Court of Appeals in mid-1964 "for what the court felt was an excessive preoccupation with the lurid details of a custody case" Burnett had heard in 1962. Still the D.C. Court of Appeals upheld Burnett's decision in 1963, as did the US Court of Appeals, although both appeals courts chided Burnett for his "injudicious behavior and intemperate language."[14]

His behavior at the Mazique case remained injudicious and his language remained intemperate. The transcript of the hearing reveals that he was intimidating throughout, telling Mrs. Mazique—despite her inability to find a supportive attorney—"So here you are without an attorney, without any judgment as to how to try the case, and you have just got to stand up and face the music." Later he was to observe "I believe that most [of] what Mrs. Mazique has said is made out of whole cloth . . . . I don't think Mrs. Mazique is entitled to one red cent of the property or any share whatsoever therein. I'll give it all to Dr. Mazique."[15] Despite Mrs. Mazique's alleged propensity for fabrication, she was given uncontested custody of the Maziques' two sons. Nevertheless, Burnett's decision again was upheld at higher levels of appeal in this case, with no criticism of his performance.

But there were others who found the pattern of Burnett's actions clearly suspect. In August

1965, Senator Bartlett from Alaska went to the floor of Congress to protest the judge's "outrageous conduct in reaction to another case where Burnett had ordered a child removed from her heartbroken mother."[16] Immediately before impeachment proceedings were to get underway, Burnett died suddenly in what was ruled an apparent suicide. But the capacity of the judiciary to act like the slave-owners of old at the trading block in splintering families was an authority that went unaltered.

Although Burnett was particularly obnoxious in his actions from the bench, his judgments were infrequently overturned. Nor were his judgments substantively different from those of his more dignified colleagues on the bench. Custody of the children usually was uncontested and awarded to the mothers—even when they were accused by their husbands of having psychiatric problems—while wealth was awarded to the fathers. One of the victims of the General Sessions Court-style of executing family law, Clara Newkirk Dawson, charged that the pattern was far more than coincidental. "Criticism is rampant that there is selected collusion among colored members of the bar, frat brothers, poker partners, transcending professional clients and traditional ethics reaching far into the police department, private detectives and even the judgeship."[17] Indeed, when Mary Alice Brown appeared in the same court in divorce proceedings in 1964 her husband was represented by his own brother, Charles K. Brown, the same attorney who represented Edward Mazique. By March 1964 John Thornton, chairman of the National Capital Voters Association, had called for an investigation by the U.S. Attorney's office of charges of "collusion, intimidation, explanation [sic: exploitation] and extortion in an alleged divorce racket . . . in Domestic Relations Court. . . ."[18]

Of course, there were some exceptions to the general pattern. With characteristic arbitrariness in late 1965 the Domestic Relations Court of the D.C. Court of General Sessions ordered one of the largest alimony payments

recorded until that time—$12,500 in alimony in addition to $16,000 in child support for 4 minor children to be paid annually by Donald Kahn, grandson of the late Moses L. Annenberg, to Marian C. Kahn. The husband's attorney described the judge's action, in this case Judge Joseph Ryan, as being "'fair and reasonable' considering the economic backgrounds of the parties involved."[19]

Equally striking is a case adjudicated in 1964 that had an antithetical outcome from *Mazique v. Mazique*. The case, *De Witt v. De Witt*, involved a husband who was a physician with an established practice, the couple had been married 20 years, the wife had worked about six years to put him through medical school, and they had two sons. Ruling "that the wife is entitled to [more than] bare subsistence but to maintenance in the manner which the station of life of the parties makes appropriate," the appeals court denied the husband's appeal of a General Sessions Court ruling by Judge Joseph Waddy, that the husband must pay the wife $1,300 a month as separate maintenance and as child support.[20] In this instance the court had decided that the wife's social class status was to be maintained.

In contrast, Judge Burnett had directed Dr. Mazique to pay $400 per month in child support to Mrs. Mazique. And Waddy was the same judge who ordered payments of $400 per month for support and maintenance of wife and child in the case of *Doerfler v. Doerfler*, where the husband was an affluent professional.[21] Burnett was white; Waddy was black. An integrated bench developed a consistent pattern of sustaining the break-up and devastation of families.

Examination of cases going before the District Court of Appeals from General Sessions court between 1957 and 1969 reveals the typical child support award was under $500 per month, *regardless* of the race and economic status of the families before divorce. The courts frequently perpetuated the poverty of the poor or pauperized the middle-income spouse and her children, precisely as was done to Jewell Mazique. Men were coddled for abandoning their responsibilities to their families; women were left to struggle to preserve a decent life for their children.

It was not until the mid-1970s that the fair division of wealth became commonplace in lower court decisions. Indeed by 1981, in *In re Marriage of Smith*, the principle of commingling of property had moved the premises of the division of property far from *Mazique vs. Mazique*.[22] The possibility of equitable division of property after separation regardless of marital status of a couple and *regardless of title to property* emerges in the cohabitation cases of the late 1970s also.[23] By 1985 the New York Supreme court even declared that a doctor's license can be considered marital property.[24] This new trend emerges too late for the families that faced the destructive cyclone of court activity in 1950s and 1960s. Whether the change has arisen because of egalitarian sentiments associated with the extension of feminist ideology or because of a conservative attempt to push mothers back into the home, or, finally, because of growing recognition of the implications of cases like *Mazique v. Mazique* for white families, the courts have changed their posture. But again the families of never-married women (*now* who do not cohabit) do not enter into the courts' web of "protection" at all. How firm that protection has become also remains an open question.

Although the managerial elite expresses a certain agnosticism over the "correct" family type, managerial policies largely have militated against the two-parent, male-female family or, at minimum, a constructive and responsible role for ex-husbands. Judicial action has been a major element spearheading

this thrust of contemporary social policy (Darity and Myers, 1948b, 178–80).

9.4 CONCLUSION

The managerial courts represent a vast discontinuity with respect to the capitalist courts that preceded them. With respect to the black family, despite the ongoing negative impact of judicial decision making, there is a comparable discontinuity. Capitalist courts upheld a social order in which blacks were perceived as useful for their physical labor. Removal of the black male from the black family came about precisely because of that necessity. Managerial courts uphold a social order in which blacks are often viewed as socially unnecessary by much of the rest of society. Destruction of the black family is permitted because of that lack of necessity.

The deepest irony is, given this history, that broad elements of the black middle class continue to believe that the judiciary is potentially an agency of relief. In the new age, it is perhaps the courts—courts of unlimited reach and jurisdiction—that pose a major ongoing threat to the restoration of the husband-wife family in general and for the black husband-wife family specifically.

The black middle class displayed a pattern of increasingly solid and stable family life until the late 1950s and early 1960s. But thereafter the pattern of marital dissolution and instability that had characterized the black underclass also penetrated the black middle class. A maelstrom had hit associated with the ascension of managerial society. The dissolution of the marriage between Edward and Jewell Mazique seems to be a paradigm case revealing those trends and developments.

Notes

1. Also on the questionable degree of justice offered to blacks by Northern courts see George Washington Williams' classic discussion in his

History of the Negro Race in America from 1619 to 1880, Vol. 2 (New York: G. P. Putnam's Sons, 1883), 111–119, 142–146, and also Leon

Litwack, *North of Slavery: The Negro in the Free States 1790–1860* (Chicago: University of Chicago Press, 1961).

2. Waite (1946, 223) reported that two more cases came before the Supreme Court prior to the Civil War: "In *Ableman v. Booth,* a controversy between the State of Wisconsin and the Federal Government, arising under the Fugitive Slave Law, Chief Justice Tawney, without dissent, sustained the constitutionality of that statute 'in all its provisions,' and declared the supremacy of the Court in all matters of interpretation and execution of powers claimed under the Constitution and Acts of Congress. *Ex parte Kentucky vs. Dennison* came up in March, 1861. A Kentucky statute made it a crime to assist a slave to escape. One Lago was indicted under this statute and took refuge in Ohio. On demand of the State of Kentucky that he be surrendered for trial the Governor of Ohio refused. Thereupon an application was made to the Supreme Court for a writ of mandamus, on the ground that the Constitution made it the duty of the Governor of Ohio to comply. The Court, by Tawney, C. J., recognized the obligation but held that it was only a moral one which could not be enforced by mandamus." Both of these cases reveal the Supreme Court in a more ameliorative mood but plainly far from a path to reversal of the substantive defense of the slave system evident in *Dred Scott v. Sandford.*

3. Randall Kennedy, however, has challenged Schmidt's interpretation of the performance of the White Court, arguing that Schmidt has produced an apologetic tract. See Randall Kennedy, "Race Relations Law and the Tradition of Celebration: The Case of Professor Schmidt," *Columbia Law Review* 86 (1986): 1622–1661.

4. This was, of course, the notorious Slaughter House Case. Miller, *The Supreme Court,* op. cit., 75 Also see Waite, 1946, pop. 228–30.

5. The relevant cases were *Guinn vs. U.S.,* 238 U.S. 347, and *Myers vs. Anderson* 238 U.S. 368 (1915).

6. For a detailed examination of racial differences in child support assignments and payments see Robert B. Hill, "The Impact of Child Support Policies on Black Families," Report prepared for the Black Family Resource Center of the Baltimore Urban League, June 2, 1888. See pp. 40–2 especially. White noncustodial fathers on average pay more child support but *not* relative to their incomes, since they "are overrepresented among middle-income and employed men." (42)

7. See, e.g. "Physician Wins Divorce, But Wife Plans to Appeal," *The Washington Afro-American*, 5 September 1964, 2; "Famed D.C. Medic, Mazique, Wins Hot Divorce Battle," *Jet Magazine* September 24, 1964, 23; "Mrs. Mazique Hits Divorce, Claims Need of Welfare Aid," *The Washington Afro-American* 7 November 1964, 1–2; "Mazique Divorce Case Near End, appeal Tues.," *The Washington Afro-American*, 27 November 1965, 1–2; "Political Pressures Charged in Mazique Divorce Appeal," *The Washington Afro-American*, 4 December 1965, 4; "Mrs. Mazique Asks Top Court to Review Divorce: Irregularities Cited," *Journal and Guide* (Norfolk, Va.), 21 May 1966, 1; "Supreme Court Action Closes Mazique Case," *The Washington Afro-American*, 25 June 1966, 1.

8. Jewell Mazique was the author of a remarkable column that appeared regularly, primarily in the *Washington Afro-American* newspaper. Her essays included "Leave 'Late-Blooming Liberals' to Fend for Selves in Africa" (September 6, 1960), "Lumumba's Case Saddens Americans But Remedy Looms at United Nations" (September 17, 1960), "South Africa as a Republic Raises Questions of Political Significance" (October 15, 1960), and "An Open Letter: Africans Urged to Beware of Trade Union Imperialism" (October 29, 1960). Her essays displayed a fervent pan-Africanist sentiment and a hard-hitting objectivity as she stripped away illusions about the actions and motives of South Africa's liberals, African trade unionists seeking to establish links with the AFL-CIO with a center in Israel, and the contradictory positions of the white financiers of major civil rights organizations. The latter topic was taken up in her hard-hitting column "White Liberals Seek 'Silver Rights'; We Seek Civil Rights," *Herald-Dispatch (Los Angeles)* (July 29, 1961).

9. See *Sebold v. Sebold,* 444 F.2d 864, D.C. Ct.App. (1971), *King v. King,* 286A.2d 234, D.C. (1972),

Johnson v. Johnson, 257 A.2d 402, D.C. (1969), *Dickson v. Dickson* 263, D.C. A.2d 640 (1970). *Mumma v. Mumma* 280, D.C. A.2d 73 (1971), *Campbell v. Campbell* ,353, D.C. A.2d 276 (1976), *Mazique vs. Mazique* also has been cited as a precedent to establish that a litigant seeking to represent himself or herself will be expected to perform like a trained attorney, i.e., the plaintiff will not be afforded any special exceptions. In effect the court's message is "You'd better hire a lawyer." See *Parker v. Wallace*, 473 SW 2.d 767 (1972), *Stebbins v. Keystone Insurance*, 481, D.C. Ct.App. F.2d 501 (1973), *Genson v. Ripley*, 544 F. Supp. ARIZ 251 (1981), and *Dozier v. Ford Motor Co.*, 702, D.C. Ct.App. F.2d 1189 (1983).

10. The District of Columbia Law Revision Commission, "A Statutory History of Dower in the District of Columbia Prepared for the Public Forum on the Repeal of the District's Law on Dower," mimeo 1989, especially 7–12.

11. 206 A.2d 577, D.C. Ct.App. (1964), 356 F.2d 801 (1966). The appeal at the federal court level was heard by a panel that included Warren Burger, who later would serve as Chief Justice.

12. 384 U.S. 981.

13. See the document "Motion to Quash Subpoena Duces Tecum," Civil Action No. D-2502–63, July 1964 signed by David C. Acheson, US Attorney, and Tim Murphy, Assistant US Attorney.

14. "Judge Burnett Chided for Interest in Lurid Details," *The Washington Post*, 10 July 1964, 36.

15. *"Mazique v. Mazique,"* Civil Action No. 2502–63, 2422–61, D.C. Court of General Sessions, Civil Division-Domestic Relations Branch, 2 July 1964, 200–201.

16. *Congressional Record*, 20 August 1965, 21241–2. Also see "The Attack on Judge Burnett," *Washington Daily News*, 18 August 1965, 30.

17. Clara Newskirk Dawson "Voice of the People Says Domestic Relations Court Is Rationing Justice for Colored," *The Washington Afro-American* 10 August 1963.

18. "Voters Groups Says Divorce Racket Here," *The Washington Afro-American*, 31 March 1964, 20.

19. "$28,500 Yearly Set as Payment in Divorce Case," *The Washington Star*, 15 December 1965, E3.

20. 201 A.2d 527.

21. 196 A.2d 90.

22. On the emergence of the commingling principle in the late 1970s and early 1980s, see Farber, *op. cit.*, 974–80.

23. Mendel and Sloan, *op. cit.*, 81–6.

24. See the O'Brien case discussed in "Sharing the Spoils of Divorce," *The New York Times*, 31 December 1985, A14.

Essay/Discussion Questions

1. Public policy analysts with differing ideological persuasions agree that the problems associated with the instability within the contemporary African American family have reached crisis proportions. Describe at least three indicators of current black family instability that analysts specify.

2. William Darity, Jr. and his colleagues argue that the destabilization of the African American family is related to the changing character of American society. According to them, what is the nature of the current social transformation in America?

3. According to Darity et al., what role have the courts of law played in the dissolution of the black American family? Examine their argument with respect to *Mazique v. Mazique*.

Part V Key Terms

Aid to Families with Dependent Children	*Marital status*
	Matrilineal descent
Double descent	*Miscegenation*
Extended family	*Monogamy*
Female-headed family	*Nuclear family*
Fertility rate	*Patrilineal descent*
Freedman's Bureau	*Polygamy*
Kinship system	*Slave code*
Managerial class	

Part V Supplementary Readings

Billingsley, Andrew, "Black Families and White Social Science," in Joyce A. Ladner, ed., *The Death of White Sociology*, New York: Vintage Books, 1973, pp. 431–450.

_____, *Black Families in White America*, Englewood Cliffs: Prentice-Hall, Inc., 1968.

Blassingame, John, *The Slave Community: Plantation Life in the Ante-Bellum South*, New York: Oxford University Press, 1972.

Clark, Reginald M., *Family Life and School Achievement: Why Poor Black Children Succeed or Fail*, Chicago: The University of Chicago Press, 1983.

Darity, William A., Jr., "The Class Character of the Black Community: Polarization Between the Black Managerial Elite and the Black Underclass," *Black Law Journal,* Vol. 7, No. 1 (1981), pp. 21–31.

Darity, William A., Jr., and Samuel L. Myers, Jr., with Emmett D. Carson, and William Sabol, *The Black Underclass: Critical Essays on Race and Unwantednness,* New York: Garland Publishing, Inc., 1994.

DuBois, W. E. B., ed., *The Negro America Family,* Cambridge: MIT Press, 1970.

Frazier, E. Franklin, *The Negro Family in the United States*, Chicago: The University of Chicago Press, 1939.

_____, "The Negro Slave Family," *Journal of Negro History*, Vol. 15 (April 1930), pp. 198–259.

Gary, Lawrence, E., *Black Men*, Beverly Hills: Sage Publications, 1981.

Gutman, Herbert G., *The Black Family in Slavery and Freedom, 1750–1925,* New York: Pantheon Books, 1976.

Gwaltney, John L., *Drylongso: A Self-Portrait of Black America*, New York: Random House, 1971.

Hill, Robert B., *The Strength of Black Families*, New York: The National Urban League, 1971.

Johnson, Charles S., *Growing Up in the Black Belt: Negro Youth in the Rural South*, Washington, D. C.: The American Council on Education, 1941.

_____, *Shadow of the Plantation*, Chicago: The University of Chicago Press, 1934.

Ladner, Joyce A., *Tomorrow's Tomorrow: The Black Woman*, Garden City: Doubleday and Company, Inc., 1971.

Lightfoot, Sara, *Worlds Apart: Relationships Between Family and Schools*, New York: Basic Books, 1978.

McAdoo, Harriet P., ed., *Black Families*, Beverly Hills: Sage Publications, 1981.

Madhubuti, Haki R., *Black Men: Obsolete, Single, Dangerous?—The Afrikan American Family in Transition*, Chicago: Third World Press, 1990.

Malson, Micheline R, Elisabeth Mudimbe-Boyi, and Jean F. O'Barr, eds., *Black Women in America: Social Science Perspectives*, Chicago: The University of Chicago Press, 1988.

Moynihan, Daniel P., *Family and The Nation*, New York: Harcourt Brace Jovanovich, 1986.

_____, *The Negro Family: The Case for National Action*, Washington, D. C.: Office of Planning and Research, U. S. Department of Labor, 1965.

Nobles, Wade, "Africanity and Black Families," *The Black Scholar*, Vol. 5 (1974), pp. 10–17.

Powdermaker, Hortense, *After Freedom: A Cultural Study in the Deep South,* New York: The Viking Press, 1939.

Rainwater, Lee, *Behind Ghetto Walls: Black Life in a Federal Slum*, Chicago: Aldine, 1970.

Rainwater, Lee and William L. Yancey, *The Moynihan Report and the Politics of Controversy*, Cambridge: The MIT Press, 1967.

Rodgers-Rose, La Frances, ed., *The Black Woman*, Beverly Hills: Sage Publications, 1980.

Scanzoni, John H., *The Black Family in Modern Society,* Chicago: The University of Chicago Press, 1971.

Scott v. Sandford, 60 U.S. (19 How.) 393 (1856).

Stack, Carol, *All Our Kin: Strategies for Survival in a Black Community*, New York: Harper and Row, Publishers, 1974.

Staples, Robert, *The World of Black Singles: Changing Patterns of Male Female Relations*, Westport: Greenwood Press, 1981.

_____, *Introduction to Black Sociology*, New York: McGraw-Hill Book Company, 1976.

_____, *The Black Woman in America: Sex, Marriage, and the Family*, Chicago: Nelson-Hall Publishers, 1973.

_____ ed., *The Black Family: Essays and Studies,* Belmont: Wadsworth Publishing Company, 1971.

Watkins, Mel, and Jay David, ed., *To Be a Black Woman: Portraits in Fact and Fiction,* New York: William Morrow and Company, Inc., 1970.

Wilkinson, Doris Y., and Ronald L. Taylor, eds., *The Black Male in America: Perspectives on His Status in Contemporary Society,* Chicago: Nelson-Hall Inc., 1977.

Willie, Charles V., *The Family Life of Black People,* Columbus: Charles E. Merrill, 1970.

Wilson, William J., *The Truly Disadvantaged: The Inner City, The Underclass, and Public Policy,* Chicago: The University of Chicago Press, 1987.

_____, *When Work Disappears: The World of the New Urban Poor,* New York: Alfred A. Knopf, 1996.

VI

The African American Struggle for Literacy and Quality Education

The struggle for literacy and quality education has been a major dimension of the historic battle for African American human rights and social development. It is a struggle that began with the slave trade and continues into the 1990s. Chattel slaves were denied literacy and formal education because whites feared that literate slaves would become enlightened, communicate with each other, and plan slave rebellions. The tradition of denying formal education to African-descended Americans became deeply embedded in the nation's culture.

Yet within the slave quarters Africans and their American descendants came to believe in the power of knowledge as a tool for liberation. The body might be shackled but the mind could be free; a free mind often could struggle to free the body. As early as the 1830s, slaves and free African Americans established secret schools in homes and churches, even under threats of legal punishment and white terrorism. Indeed, Union soldiers during the Civil War were surprised to find many literate slaves, their literacy carefully kept from the slaveowner's knowledge. As early as the eve of Emancipation, then, education as a pathway to freedom had emerged as a strong tradition among African Americans. It was this tradition that motivated southern African American legislators during Reconstruction to advocate public education; it was this tradition that encouraged African Americans to establish their own schools and colleges during the nineteenth and early twentieth centuries; and it was this same tradition that galvanized the African American struggle to overthrow segregated educational institutions and practices in the Old South during the mid-1950s.

Segregation, which rested on the ideological foundation of chattel slavery, was the post-emancipation theory and practice of white American oppression of African-descended Americans. Based on assumptions of white supremacy and black inferiority, segregation denied African Americans full citizenship rights and privileges, deprived them of equal protection of the laws, and excluded them from using first-class public accommodations. The 1896 *Plessy v. Ferguson* Supreme Court decision had established the "separate but equal" doctrine, which resulted in the effective legalization of separate public schools for black and white Americans throughout the South. Educational segregation in practice also continued outside the South even though it was not legally sanctioned. Although separate, the two sets of schools were hardly equal; educational apartheid in America generally denied effective schooling to former slaves and their descendants.

The landmark 1954 Supreme Court decision of *Brown v. Board of Education* outlawed dual public school systems throughout the South. The decision raised the hopes of African Americans across the country, for they interpreted *Brown* as providing the means to achieve equal educational opportunity and excellence in education. But the l955 Supreme Court *Brown* decision, which directed the implementation of the earlier ruling, was a disappointment to African Americans and a joy to white segregationists. It provided no precise time frame for instituting desegregated school systems; rather, the justices allowed the South to move "with all deliberate speed."

Even with the Supreme Court's moderation, many public school systems sought to evade the Court's ruling. In some southern communities white parents flatly refused to send their children to schools with African American children, choosing instead to enroll them in white private academies, which sprouted overnight. Other public school systems developed policies and programs, such as tracking, that channeled large numbers of African American youngsters into educational dead-ends. Many African American spokespersons labelled these strategies "programmed retardation" and charged that they were worse than segregation in the Old South.

The *Brown* ruling resuscitated the Civil Rights movement, whose main thrust was racial desegregation. In the mid-1960s, the interests of the Civil Rights elite and educational experts converged. Unfortunately, their emphasis on racial integration seemed to overshadow a concern for good education. It was the 1966 Coleman Report, an example of educational expertise, that contributed significantly to the transition from desegregation to integration by encouraging busing to achieve racial balance in public schools. This approach was given effective legitimacy by the courts and supported strongly by the Civil Rights establishment. Although many educators, lay persons, and some experts initially opposed the Coleman Report (James Coleman himself later repudiated the report's major findings), busing for racial balance was proclaimed the dominant solution to the problem of public school segregation. The fact that the *Brown* decision was intended to foster education seemed to be forgotten.

By the late 1970s and early 1980s, it was becoming increasingly clear that many of nation's public schools were failing to educate their students. In many cases, the limitations of such integration strategies as busing for racial balance were becoming evident as urban demographic changes transformed big city school districts into enclaves of African American and Hispanic American students. To bus African American or Hispanic American students from one school where they are the majority population across town to another school where they also are a majority population is redundant and meaningless. Another strategy, the magnet school, was instituted to attract white students into predominantly African American or Hispanic American schools. To the consternation of African American and Hispanic American parents and students, magnet schools became two schools within a school. White youngsters are enrolled in the magnet curriculum, but resident African American or Hispanic American students attending the school because it is in their district generally are excluded from this curriculum. Therefore, the 1980s witnessed growing tensions in America's politics of urban education.

The educational dilemmas emerging in the last three decades have caused many African American observers to ask how well current educational theory and practice serve the interests of most African American children. Many have become skeptical about the existing system's ability to meet the scholastic needs of African American children.

The articles in this section provide an examination of major historical trends in the development of African American education, some contemporary contradictions and dilemmas in the provision of equal educational opportunity and quality education to African Americans.

"Learning to Read" and "Growing in Knowledge" come from Frederick Douglass's autobiography, *Life and Times of Frederick Douglass*, published in 1892, three years before his death. Douglass, born into slavery, escaped and later became an abolitionist, a renowned orator, an advisor to President Abraham Lincoln, a diplomatic representative of the United States to Haiti and the Dominican Republic, and a newspaper publisher. He was one of the major African American leaders of the nineteenth century. His autobiography is considered a classic work within the slave narrative genre.

In the two chapters included here, Douglass recalls his childhood experiences in learning to read and write. In the first, Douglass describes a brief moment when his new mistress in Baltimore, Mrs. Auld, unwittingly and in her husband's absence began to teach him to read. He notes that her constant reading aloud from the Bible prompted him to ask for her assistance. Informed by his wife of young Douglass's developing success at learning the alphabet, Mr. Auld apparently chastised her and forbade her educating Douglass further. The slaveowner pointed out to his wife how the slave management system depended upon keeping slaves illiterate. This episode made Douglass even more determined to learn how to read and write.

In the second chapter included here, Douglass recounts the shrewd and ingenious strategies he employed to become literate and gain information. The acquisition of knowledge allowed him to grasp the underlying character of the slave management system and its dehumanizing process. He asserted: "Slaveholders . . . are only a band of successful robbers, who, leaving their own homes, went into Africa for the purpose of stealing and reducing my people to slavery." Douglass's autobiography indicates his hatred of chattel slavery and its attempt to keep him ignorant. His narrative also represents Douglass's absolute determination to learn.

In the late 1960s, community activist Jewell R. C. Mazique wrote an impassioned attack on public school systems' increasing inability to provide educational excellence. In her essay, "Betrayal in the Schools: As Seen by an Advocate of Black Power," Mazique argues that the growing problem of public school decline resulted from the ideas, policies, and programs of a liberal coalition of educational experts, behavioral specialists, political policy makers, business elites, and black civil rights elites. She asserts that because black and white liberals insisted on imposing busing and other integrationist policies before all else, public schools abandoned educational fundamentals (reading, writing, and computational skills), subverted academic motivation, and perverted positive character development. Educational professionals increasingly excluded black and working class white parents from the policymaking process, which resulted in growing parental frustration and anger. Whites continued their massive migration to the suburbs, and urban public school systems were being transformed into failure factories. According to Mazique, the alternative to an emerging educational disaster, for both black and white youngsters, would be the incorporation of quality education into public schools: educational basics, academic motivation, and positive character development. The collapse of effective public schooling in the 1990s and its dire consequences for the nation make Mazique's analysis foresighted. However, the necessary educational redevelopment entails a struggle for power. As Mazique concludes: "The constant in all of this is power. Power determines the denial of the fundamental tools of knowledge, and power can determine the nature and extent of the education meted out."

The general problem of communities facing a powerful political force bent on integration is particularized by Floyd Hayes, as he recounts the struggle of citizens in Washington, D.C., to have a say in their school policies. His article, "Race, Urban Politics, and Educational Policy-making in Washington, D.C.: A Community's Struggle for Quality Education," examines the politics of public school desegregation in the nation's capital during the late 1950s and 1960s. Using an in-depth interview with one of the key community participants in the city's early educational politics, as well as official reports and documents of the District of Columbia public school system, Hayes chronicles the community's struggle against the central administration's tracking policy, one that many community participants viewed as racially discriminatory and more damaging to African American children than was school segregation in the Old South. Hayes focuses on the community's challenge to educational professionals and their expertise. Although the tracking system ultimately was terminated by U.S. Court of Appeals Judge J. Skelly Wright in the *Hobson v. Hansen* (1967) case, the local community lost the battle to establish quality education in the public school system as local and national policymakers and professional experts advanced busing and other integration strategies as alternative policy solutions.

A powerful dimension of the 1960s youth uprising witnessed black college students struggling to expand their numbers, establish Black Studies, and increase the size of black faculty and staff at historically white universities. Accompanying the growing black presence at these institutions were struggles by many to change both the university's curriculum and pedagogy, or theory and practice of teaching. Black Studies was multidisciplinary, student-centered, and community-oriented; clearly, the emerging field went against the grain of the academy's tradition. For the young black faculty members, the problem became to hold onto their new faculty positions by legitimizing their scholarship and obtaining tenure, or job security.

Joy James's essay, "Teaching Theory, Talking Community," represents the continuation of the struggle for legitimacy and recognition in the academy into the current period. She speaks from the standpoint of the young black female professor's struggle to teach in the interest or service of collective black liberation. Her subject matter is political theory or philosophy; her pedagogy is liberationist; her focus is community-based. In this way, James clearly teaches against the grain of conventional Eurocentric intellectual hegemony, which is grounded in white supremacy, by recapturing and elevating the African and African American philosophical experience and its significance for understanding political philosophy and theory, as such. In the process, she draws heavily on the philosophical and theoretical experiences of African and African American women.

The revolutionary or liberatory dimension of James's work is rooted in an ethical theory of teaching and knowing that facilitates her students' learning through the process of validating their personal experience, self-reflection, judgment, and community action. That is, James consciously encourages her students to be not mere passive learners but ethically engaged agents of social change and community liberation—against racial oppression, sexual violence, economic exploitation, and other forms of cultural domination. For James, the teaching of theory and philosophy against the grain of Eurocentric domination is an aspect of progressive political practice whose objective is collective black liberation specifically, and human emancipation generally.

Learning to Read and Growing in Knowledge

FREDERICK DOUGLASS

Established in my new home in Baltimore, I was not very long in perceiving that in picturing to myself what was to be my life there, my imagination had painted only the bright side, and that the reality had its dark shades as well as its light ones. The open country which had been so much to me was all shut out. Walled in on every side by towering brick buildings, the heat of the summer was intolerable to me, and the hard brick pavements almost blistered my feet. If I ventured out on to the streets, new and strange objects glared upon me at every step, and startling sounds greeted my ears from all directions. My country eyes and ears were confused and bewildered. Troops of hostile boys pounced upon me at every corner. They chased me, and called me "eastern-shore man," till really I almost wished myself back on the Eastern Shore. My new mistress happily proved to be all she had seemed, and in her presence I easily forgot all outside annoyances. Mrs. Sophia was naturally of an excellent disposition—kind, gentle, and cheerful. The supercilious contempt for the rights and feelings of others, and the petulance and bad humor which generally characterized slaveholding ladies, were all quite absent from her manner and bearing toward me.

She had never been a slaveholder—a thing then quite unusual at the South—but had depended almost entirely upon her own industry for a living. To this fact the dear lady no doubt owed the excellent preservation of her natural goodness of heart, for slavery could change a saint into a sinner, and an angel into a demon. I hardly knew how to behave towards "Miss Sophia," as I used to call Mrs. Hugh Auld. I could not approach her even as I had formerly approached Mrs. Thomas Auld. Why should I hang down my head, and speak with bated breath, when there was no pride to scorn me, no coldness to repel me, and no hatred to inspire me with fear? I therefore soon came to regard her as something more akin to a mother than a slaveholding mistress. So far from deeming it impudent in a slave to look her straight in the face, she seemed ever to say, "Look up, child; don't be afraid." The sailors belonging to the sloop esteemed it a great privilege to be the bearers of parcels or

Reprinted from *Life and Times of Frederick Douglass*, written by himself. Collier Books, 1962.

messages for her, for whenever they came, they were sure of a most kind and pleasant reception. If little Thomas was her son, and her most dearly loved child, she made me something like his half-brother in her affections. If dear Tommy was exalted to a place on his mother's knee, "Freddy" was honored by a place at the mother's side. Nor did the slave-boy lack the caressing strokes of her gentle hand, soothing him into the consciousness that, though motherless, he was not friendless. Mrs. Auld was not only kindhearted, but remarkably pious, frequent in her attendance at public worship and much given to reading the Bible and to chanting hymns of praise when alone.

Mr. Hugh was altogether a different character. He cared very little about religion, knew more of the world and was more a part of the world, than his wife. He doubtless set out to be, as the world goes, a respectable man and to get on by becoming a successful shipbuilder, in that city of shipbuilding. This was his ambition, and it fully occupied him. I was of course of very little consequence to him, and when he smiled upon me, as he sometimes did, the smile was borrowed from his lovely wife, and like borrowed light, was transient, and vanished with the source whence it was derived. Though I must in truth characterize Master Hugh as a sour man of forbidding appearance, it is due to him to acknowledge that he was never cruel to me, according to the notion of cruelty in Maryland. During the first year or two, he left me almost exclusively to the management of his wife. She was my lawgiver. In hands so tender as hers, and in the absence of the cruelties of the plantation, I became both physically and mentally much more sensitive, and a frown from my mistress caused me far more suffering than had Aunt Katy's hardest cuffs. Instead of the cold, damp floor of my old master's kitchen, I was on carpets; for the corn bag in winter, I had a good straw bed, well furnished with covers; for the coarse corn meal in the morning, I had good bread and mush occasionally; for my old tow-linen shirt, I had good clean clothes. I was really well off. My employment was to run of errands, and to take care of Tommy, to prevent his getting in the way of carriages, and to keep him out of harm's way generally.

So for a time everything went well. I say for a time, because the fatal poison of irresponsible power, and the natural influence of slave customs, were not very long in making their impression on the gentle and loving disposition of my excellent mistress. She at first regarded me as a child, like any other. This was the natural and spontaneous thought; afterwards, when she came to consider me property, our relations to each other were changed, but a nature so noble as hers could not instantly become perverted, and it took several years before the sweetness of her temper was wholly lost.

The frequent hearing of my mistress reading the Bible aloud, for she often read aloud when her husband was absent, awakened my curiosity in respect to this *mystery* of reading, and roused in me the desire to learn. Up to this time I had known nothing whatever of this wonderful art, and my ignorance and inexperience of what it could do for me, as well as my confidence in my mistress, emboldened me to ask her to teach me to read. With an unconscious and inexperience equal to my own, she readily consented, and in an incredibly short time, by her kind assistance, I had mastered the alphabet and could spell words of three or four letters. My mistress seemed almost as proud of my progress as if I had been her own child, and supposing that her husband would be as well pleased, she made no secret of what she was doing for me. Indeed, she exultingly told him of the aptness of her pupil and of her intention to persevere, as she felt it her duty to do, in teaching me, at least, to read the Bible. And here arose the first dark cloud over my Baltimore prospects, the precursor of chilling blasts and drenching storms. Master Hugh was astounded beyond measure and, probably for the first time, proceeded to unfold to his wife the true philosophy of the slave system, and the peculiar rules necessary in the nature of the case to be observed in the management of human chattels. Of course he forbade her to give me any further instruction, telling her in the first place that to do so was unlawful, as it was also unsafe, "for," said he, "if you give a nigger an inch he will take an ell. Learning will spoil the best nigger in the world. If he learns to read the Bible it will forever unfit him to be a slave. He should know nothing but the will of his master, and learn to obey it. As to himself, learning will do him no good, but a great deal of harm, making him disconsolate and unhappy. If you teach him how to read, he'll want to know how to write, and this accomplished, he'll be running away with himself." Such was the tenor of Master Hugh's oracular exposition, and it must be confessed that he very clearly comprehended the nature and the requirements of the relation of master and slave. His discourse was the first decidedly anti-slavery lecture to which it had been my lot to listen. Mrs. Auld evidently felt the force of what he said, and, like an obedient wife, began to shape her course in the direction indicated by him. The effect of his words *on me* was neither slight nor transitory. His iron sentences, cold and harsh, sunk like heavy weights deep into my heart, and stirred up within me a rebellion not soon to be allayed.

This was a new and special revelation, dispelling a painful mystery against which my youthful understanding had struggled, and struggled in vain, to wit, the white man's power to perpetuate the enslavement of the black man. "Very well," thought I. "Knowledge unfits a child to be a slave." I instinctively assented to the proposition, and from that moment I understood the direct pathway from slavery to freedom. It was just what I needed, and it came to me at a time and from a source whence I least expected it. Of course I was greatly saddened at the thought of losing the assis-

tance of my kind mistress, but the information so instantly derived, to some extent compensated me for the loss I had sustained in this direction. Wise as Mr. Auld was, he underrated my comprehension, and had little idea of the use to which I was capable of putting the impressive lesson he was giving to his wife. He wanted me to be a slave; I had already voted against that on the home plantation of Col. Lloyd. That which he most loved I most hated, and the very determination which he expressed to keep me in ignorance only rendered me the more resolute to seek intelligence. In learning to read, therefore, I am not sure that I do not owe quite as much to the opposition of my master as to the kindly assistance of my amiable mistress. I acknowledge the benefit rendered me by the one, and by the other, believing that but for my mistress I might have grown up in ignorance.

• • •

I lived in the family of Mr. Auld, at Baltimore, seven years, during which time, as the almanac makers say of the weather, my condition was variable. The most interesting feature of my history here was my learning, under somewhat marked disadvantages, to read and write. In attaining this knowledge I was compelled to resort to indirections by no means congenial to my nature, and which were really humiliating to my sense of candor and uprightness. My mistress, checked in her benevolent designs toward me, not only ceased instructing me herself, but set her face as a flint against my learning to read by any means. It is due to her to say, however, that she did not adopt this course in all its stringency at first. She either thought it unnecessary, or she lacked the depravity needed to make herself forget at once my human nature. She was, as I have said, naturally a kind and tender-hearted woman, and in the humanity of her heart and the simplicity of her mind, she set out, when I first went to live with her, to treat me as she supposed one human being ought to treat another.

Nature never intended that men and women should be either slaves or slaveholders, and nothing but rigid training long persisted in, can perfect the character of the one or the other.

Mrs. Auld was singularly deficient in the qualities of a slaveholder. It was no easy matter for her to think or to feel that the curly-headed boy, who stood by her side, and even leaned on her lap, who was loved by little Tommy, and who loved Tommy in turn, sustained to her only the relation of a chattel. I was more than that; she felt me to be more than that. I could talk and sing; I could laugh and weep; I could reason and remember; I could love and hate. I was human, and she, dear lady, knew and felt me to be so. How could she then treat me as a brute, without a mighty struggle with all the noblest powers of her soul? That struggle came, and the will and power of the husband were victorious. Her noble soul was overcome, and he who wrought the wrong was injured in the fall no less than the rest of the household. When I went into that household, it was the abode of happiness and contentment. The wife and mistress there was a model of affection and tenderness. Her fervent piety and watchful uprightness made it impossible to see her without thinking and feeling that "that woman is a Christian." There was no sorrow nor suffering for which she had not a smile. She had bread for the hungry, clothes for the naked, and comfort for every mourner who came within her reach.

But slavery soon proved its ability to divest her of these excellent qualities, and her home of its early happiness. Conscience cannot stand much violence. Once thoroughly injured, who is he who can repair the damage? If it be broken toward the slave on Sunday, it will be toward the master on Monday. It cannot long endure such shocks. It must stand unharmed, or it does not stand at all. As my condition in the family waxed bad, that of the family waxed no better. The first step in the wrong direction was the violence done to nature and to conscience in arresting the benevolence that would have enlightened my young mind. In ceasing to instruct me, my mistress had to seek to justify herself *to* herself, and once consenting to take sides in such a debate, she was compelled to hold her position. One needs little knowledge of moral philosophy to see where she inevitably landed. She finally became even more violent in her opposition to my learning to read than was Mr. Auld himself. Nothing now appeared to make her more angry than seeing me, seated in some nook or corner, quietly reading a book or newspaper. She would rush at me with the utmost fury, and snatch the book or paper from my hand, with something of the wrath and consternation which a traitor might be supposed to feel on being discovered in a plot by some dangerous spy. The conviction once thoroughly established in her mind, that education and slavery were incompatible with each other, I was most narrowly watched in all my movements. If I remained in a separate room from the family for any considerable length of time, I was sure to be suspected of having a book, and was at once called to give an account of myself. But this was too late—the first and never-to-be-retraced step had been taken. Teaching me the alphabet had been the "inch" given, I was now waiting only for the opportunity to "take the ell."

Filled with the determination to learn to read at any cost, I hit upon many expedients to accomplish that much desired end. The plan which I mainly adopted, and the one which was the most successful, was that of using as teachers my young white playmates, with whom I met on the streets. I used almost constantly to carry a copy of *Webster's Spelling-Book* in my pocket, and when sent on errands, or when playtime was allowed me, I would step aside with my young friends and take a lesson in spelling. I am greatly indebted to these boys—Gustavus Dorgan, Joseph Bailey, Charles Farity, and William Cosdry.

Although slavery was a delicate subject and, in Maryland, very cautiously talked about among grown-up people, I frequently talked with the white boys about it, and that very freely. I would sometimes say to them, while seated on a curbstone or a cellar door, "I wish I could be free, as you will be when you get to be men." "You will be free, you know, as soon as you are twenty-one, and can go where you like, but I am a slave for life. Have I not as good a right to be free as you have?" Words like these, I observed, always troubled them, and I had no small satisfaction in drawing out from them, as I occasionally did, that fresh and bitter condemnation of slavery which ever springs from natures unseared and unperverted. Of all consciences, let me have those to deal with, which have not been seared and bewildered with the cares and perplexities of life. I do not remember ever while I was in slavery, to have met with a *boy* who defended the system, but I do remember many times, when I was consoled by them, and by them encouraged to hope that something would yet occur by which I would be made free. Over and over again, they have told me that "they believed I had as good a right to be free as *they* had," and that "they did not believe God ever made any one to be a slave." It is easily seen that such little conversation with my playfellows had no tendency to weaken my love of liberty, nor to render me contented as a slave.

When I was about thirteen years old, and had succeeded in learning to read, every increase of knowledge, especially anything respecting the free states, was an additional weight to the almost intolerable burden of my thought—*"I am a slave for life."* To my bondage I could see no end. It was a terrible reality, and I shall never be able to tell how sadly that thought chafed my young spirit. Fortunately or unfortunately, I had, by blacking boots for some gentlemen, earned a little money with which I purchased of Mr. Knight, on Thames street, what was then a very popular school book, viz., *The Columbian Orator,* for which I paid fifty cents. I was led to buy this book by hearing some little boys say that they were going to learn some pieces out of it for the exhibition. This volume was indeed a rich treasure, and, for a time, every opportunity afforded me was spent in diligently perusing it. Among much other interesting matter, that which I read again and again with unflagging satisfaction was a short dialogue between a master and his slave. The slave is represented as having been recaptured in a second attempt to run away, and the master opens the dialogue with an upbraiding speech, charging the slave with ingratitude, and demanding to know what he has to say in his own defense. Thus upbraided and thus called upon to reply, the slave rejoins that he knows how little anything that he can say will avail, seeing that he is completely in the hands of his owner, and with noble resolution, calmly says, "I submit to my fate." Touched by the slave's answer, the master insists upon his further speaking, and recapitulates the many acts of kindness which he has performed toward the slave, and tells him he is permitted to speak for himself. Thus invited, the quondam slave made a spirited defense of himself, and thereafter the whole argument for and against slavery is brought out. The master was vanquished at every turn in the argument, and, appreciating the fact, he generously and meekly emancipates the slave, with his best wishes for his prosperity.

It is unnecessary to say that a dialogue with such an origin and such an end, read by me when every nerve of my being was in revolt at my own condition as a slave, affected me most powerfully. I could not help feeling that the day might yet come when the well-directed answers made by the slave to the master, in this instance, would find a counterpart in my own experience. This, however, was not all the fanaticism which I found in *The Columbian Orator.* I met here one of Sheridan's mighty speeches on the subject of Catholic Emancipation, Lord Chatham's speech on the American War, and speeches by the great William Pitt, and by Fox. These were all choice documents to me, and I read them over and over again, with an interest ever increasing, because it was ever gaining in intelligence, for the more I read them the better I understood them. The reading of these speeches added much to my limited stock of language, and enabled me to give tongue to many interesting thoughts which had often flashed through my mind and died away for want of words in which to give them utterance. The mighty power and heart-searching directness of truth, penetrating the heart of a slaveholder and compelling him to yield up his earthly interests to the claims of eternal justice, were finely illustrated in the dialogue, and from the speeches of Sheridan I got a bold and powerful denunciation of oppression and a most brilliant vindication of the rights of man.

Here was indeed a noble acquisition. If I had ever wavered under the consideration that the Almighty, in some way, had ordained slavery and willed my enslavement for His own glory, I wavered no longer. I had now penetrated to the secret of all slavery and of all oppression, and had ascertained their true foundation to be in the pride, the power, and the avarice of man. With a book in my hand so redolent of the principles of liberty, and with a perception of my own human nature and of the facts of my past and present experience, I was equal to a contest with the religious advocates of slavery, whether white or black, for blindness in this matter was not confined to the white people. I have met, at the South, many good, religious colored people who were under the delusion that God required them to submit to slavery and to wear their chains with meekness and humility. I could entertain no such nonsense as this, and I quite lost my patience when I found a colored man weak enough to believe such stuff. Nevertheless, eager as I was to partake of the tree of knowledge, its fruits were bitter as well as sweet. "Slaveholders," thought I, "are only a band of successful robbers, who, leaving their own homes, went into Africa for the purpose

of stealing and reducing my people to slavery." I loathed them as the meanest and the most wicked of men. And as I read, behold! the very discontent so graphically predicted by Master Hugh had already come upon me. I was no longer the light-hearted, gleesome boy, full of mirth and play, that I was when I landed in Baltimore. Light had penetrated the moral dungeon where I had lain, and I saw the bloody whip for my back and the iron chain for my feet, and my good, kind master was the author of my situation. The revelation haunted me, stung me, and made me gloomy and miserable. As I writhed under the sting and torment of this knowledge I almost envied my fellow slaves their stupid indifference. It opened my eyes to the horrible pit, and revealed the teeth of the frightful dragon that was ready to pounce upon me, but alas, it opened no way for my escape. I wished myself a beast, a bird, anything rather than a slave. I was wretched and gloomy beyond my ability to describe. This everlasting thinking distressed and tormented me, and yet there was no getting rid of this subject of my thoughts. Liberty, as the inestimable birthright of every man, converted every object into an asserter of this right. I heard it in every sound, and saw it in every object. It was ever present to torment me with a sense of my wretchedness. The more beautiful and charming were the smiles of nature, the more horrible and desolate was my condition. I saw nothing without seeing it, and I heard nothing without hearing it. I do not exaggerate when I say that it looked at me in every star, smiled in every calm, breathed in every wind and moved in every storm.

I have no doubt that my state of mind had something to do with the change in treatment which my mistress adopted towards me. I can easily believe that my leaden, downcast, and disconsolate look was very offensive to her. Poor lady! She did not understand my trouble, and I could not tell her. Could I have made her acquainted with the real state of my mind and given her the reasons therefor, it might have been well for both of us. As it was, her abuse fell upon me like the blows of the false prophet upon his ass; she did not know that an angel stood in the way. Nature made us friends, but slavery had made us enemies. My interests were in a direction opposite to hers, and we both had our private thoughts and plans. She aimed to keep me ignorant, and I resolved to *know*, although knowledge only increased my misery. My feelings were not the result of any marked cruelty in the treatment I received; they sprung from the consideration of my being a slave at all. It was *slavery*, not its mere *incidents* that I hated. I had been cheated.

I saw that slaveholders would have gladly made me believe that, in making a slave of me and in making slaves of others, they were merely acting under the authority of God, and I felt to them as to robbers and deceivers. The feeding and clothing me well could not atone for taking my liberty from me. The smiles of my mistress could not remove the deep sorrow that dwelt in my young bosom. Indeed, this came, in time, but to deepen the sorrow. She had changed, and the reader will see that I too, had changed. We were both victims to the same overshadowing evil, she as mistress, I as slave. I will not censure her harshly.

Essay/Discussion Questions

1. Why did slaveowners deny literacy and formal education to their slaves?
2. According to Douglass, why was learning to read and write so important to slaves?

3. Throughout the slave states, educating slaves was often punishable by law. Yet slaves often used extreme and dangerous measures to obtain formal education. Discuss Douglass's strategy for learning how to read and write.

Betrayal in the Schools

Jewell R. C. Mazique

The problem in the public schools is not exclusively racial anymore, if indeed it ever was. Rather, the shutdown in New York City and the predictions of more to come in Philadelphia, Washington, Detroit, Chicago and other cities represent a clash of cultures, a conflict of interests, a struggle for power. While the discord is clearly evident in the area of education, the coming community breakdown will not be limited to school shutdowns. Rather, as is already occurring in New York, there will be a chain reaction spilling over into other areas of the community, black and white, igniting everything touched. In the meantime, the white masses will come to identify with struggling blacks—for white children, too, have gradually become victims of a system which destroys rather than builds. This is why the New York situation is being watched nationally by questioning parents and community leaders who face similar problems.

The children of the masses, black and white, in the United States are not learning to read, write, spell and figure because these indisputable fundamentals have been getting less and less attention while budgets, school plants, cafeterias, projectors and other academic paraphernalia, to say nothing of administrative staff (including psychologists, counselors, paraprofessionals and drivers for "balancing and bussing") have been accepted as standard equipment for educating the young. The fashionable and passionate emphasis on fads, frills and fun is such that the profound significance and proficient art of teaching have been lost on many younger teachers, themselves more and more the product of the modern system of education without literacy. It is not unusual to hear a "liberal" instructor assure a parent disturbed by her child's lack of reading progress that poor spelling is no deterrent to learning and should not be a source of worry—after all, the teacher herself never could spell. Besides, "What do we have dictionaries for?"

But the further along in school such pupils advance, the harder it becomes to "guess" words, and harder still to stop every minute of an assignment to seek out proper spelling from a dictionary. Disgust, loss of interest, declining motivation soon follow, and eventually a turning away from school entirely. The personality of the student is thus subverted, the character of the community changes as radical

Reprinted from the January 1969 issue of *Triumph*.

deterioration of the learning institution takes place, and the school, as a learning institution, finally dies.

Consequently, legislation and judicial decisions directing programs against "de facto" segregation and racial discrimination are outdated and self-defeating not alone for the masses of blacks, but for the masses of whites as well. Like Alice in Wonderland, the faster the blacks have run in the last several years (since the Supreme Court's momentous school desegregation decision) the "behinder" they have gotten in education; while the faster the white masses have run to stay ahead, the more they have locked themselves, with their children, into a well-fashioned but ill-conceived trap.

The subversion of the public school system is as tragic for the white masses as it is for the blacks; but neither the subversion nor its significance has been recognized by whites, for several reasons. The rapid decline in the mastery of basic skills by the offspring of whites has unfortunately been attributed to "the revolution" in education and the advent of blacks in their midst—a necessary evil, in other words, if the world's leading democracy is to be truly democratic. Second, the importance of literacy and computation, traditionally recognized by slaves and ex-slaves as essential for securing freedom against re-enslavement, is not so fresh in the minds of whites as it is in the consciousness of blacks. To the latter, therefore, any school that fails to distribute the "tools of knowledge" "ain't no school at all," it is an institution preparing our offspring for slavery again in this technological age or, worse still, perhaps preparing them for more advanced, more implacable institutions—incarceration in mental institutions or criminal penitentiaries, for example. Once the trick is recognized for what it is—the imposition of a handicap on youngsters in the name of education—no amount or variety of foods to substitute for a deficient mental diet served at two-hour intervals, coupled with programs of entertainment and "sustained excitement," will placate black parents.

THE ELECT AND THE UNELECT

Our forebears were enslaved for 250 years not because they were "savages" and "uncivilized" as claimed, but rather, because there was born in those days in the Western World a new form of government founded largely on the Judaeo-Calvinist concept of "the elect and the unelect"—a pre-Christian doctrine based on the premise that some men are born outside salvation. Actually this form of government arose in response to a desire on the part of a select minority to dominate the majority. Later, that minority of whites could reenforce its position with the profits, power and pleasure to be derived from enslaved blacks. Since no man, black or white, willingly submits to slavery, it became necessary, in order to institutionalize the system, to break up the family, tribe and clan as fast as blacks debarked from the slave ship. The second essential for guaranteed control over blacks was to deny them literacy while educating them for service on the plantation lands and in the "Big House." Thus, in the larger sense, it cannot be asserted honestly that Africans were denied education, for they were taught weaving and sewing, cooking and housekeeping, carpentry and numberless skills, but teaching the alphabet and numbers was immediately frowned upon, then finally barred completely. (Literate slaves would have been able to pick up knowledge of their heritage and the outside world; they could also communicate in writing, plot up-risings and plan escape through the underground railroad, as Frederick Douglass did following his "boot-leg" instruction in reading, writing and arithmetic.)

Since World War I, when we fought "to make the world safe for democracy," emphasis on that political ideal steadily rose. But strangely, as the ideal came closer and closer to realization in other areas, the development of youth through mass education to fulfill the objective shifted into reverse—exactly in proportion to the vast outlay of money, the expanding school staff and startling development of educational "innovations." For ours is a heritage that adheres, in spite of it all, to the Judaeo-Calvinist concept of an "elect-elite"—a concept that was applied to our educational system through the philosophy of John Dewey. That philosophy, unfortunately, provides a means of keeping the disadvantaged in a disadvantaged position.

Beginning in the twenties the revolution in public education spread rapidly from Columbia University and New York City to the smallest hamlet in the United States. This was so effectively accomplished through teacher's colleges, workshops and seminars on teaching methods, the mass media and public relations channels, that functional illiteracy soon became widespread among the American masses.

Just as blacks began questioning the American system of "education without literacy" two things happened. With the introduction of TV, "looking at the idiot's box" became the "thing" (as possession of the television set as a piece of furniture conferred status), offering hope to youth for effortless development. Secondly, educational theorists introduced a proliferation of new interpretations, assumptions, and evaluations of pupils and parents necessitating radical changes in "groupings," eating habits, transportation, parent-child relations, etc. which had little or no bearing on the quality of education. In fact, black parents could eventually protest that as the budget went up, educational achievement went down, that as "innovations" were introduced, youngsters became frustrated, until finally the new techniques became so suspect among black parents that they would charge the school system with *programmed retardation.*

Silence on the effects of modern mass education was broken in 1955 with the publication of Rudolph Flesch's enlightening work,

Why Johnny Can't Read, suggesting a kind of conspiracy at work, cataloguing the ravages of Dewey's revolution.

What Flesch had noted about the effect of education on children in general was more true of blacks. Many southern black fathers and mothers, who had never got beyond eighth grade, managed to send their children to college even during the Depression. Although these young students' experiences were limited and the books and libraries available were in short supply, most became quite literate in English and many went on to master other languages. Moreover, the dialect handicaps and speech difficulties of black children, so often complained about by educational theorists and teachers in northern cities and "integrated" schools, were readily overcome in the Ole South as fast as pupils learned to read, spell and master grammar and sentence structure. These same blacks, parents now, residing in big cities, cannot understand the reason for today's pervasive functional illiteracy and its accompanying loss of motivation, but they do know that it is a terrible thing which is undermining their most precious dreams and aspirations. More and more they have become suspicious of the various forces at work—politically astute and financially well-equipped—and always blaming them for little Johnny's inability to read, write, spell and compute, and consequently his restlessness in the classroom and trouble making.

HOW TO GROW CRIMINALS

In the early fifties, Flesch pleaded with the educational theorists and school administrators to mend their ways so that the 33 million babies born between 1945 and 1953 might fare better than the immediately preceding generation of children. But where are these black and white children today, now ranging in ages from twenty-three to fifteen, who were never taught to read, never developed the responsibility to carry out an assignment, to follow directions, never learned to respect knowledge or the purveyors of knowledge, never became masters of their own souls with the self-discipline that separates the civilized from the savage, the criminal from the contained? They are the drop-outs, juvenile delinquents and dope addicts of our time using their energies toward destructive ends and applying their talents to bank robberies and con games—to bringing down the nation which allowed them to be betrayed.

Why did Mr. Flesch's brilliant work, which hit the academic terrain like a thunderstorm on the desert sands, die aborning? Why did he lose so soon the ear of questioning, anxious parents? Because overnight the Supreme Court's *Brown* decision had deflected the full energies of the nation to ending school segregation and racial discrimination. For the small businessman or would-be businessman, blockbusting became the most profitable of the early community innovations following "desegregation" of schools. It was to become a source of quick profits for these speculators both in terms of housing turnover and of "mechanizing" the classroom. White parents leap-frogged over "integrated" communities to suburbia, seeking new schools for their own children. At the same time black parents were running so fast in search of acceptance and better education for their children, that few stopped long enough to observe what was happening to these children. It was too late when blacks discovered that schools were being "integrated" but that education was being taken out of them. The whites were running so fast to suburbia to escape it all that they did not notice that they had left education behind and that once in suburbia they had to start from scratch, building a whole new system of education from plant to curriculum. By the time they questioned the new arrangement, the issue of "balancing and bussing" broke.

Balancing and bussing now became the thing in public school education, based on the premise that homogeneous neighborhood schools limit education, especially when their charges are "culturally deprived" low-income blacks. Liberals explained to doubting black parents that school district boundary changes and zigzag zoning were necessary to eliminate "tracking," or "ability grouping," an earlier desegregation scheme.

Soon, black parents in the big cities were complaining that the new district boundaries removed their children further from their local communities and a normal school atmosphere, alienating them from their natural environment. Moreover, it made parental participation in the educational process more difficult both because of geographical distance, and because of their strange and strained relations with other parents in far-away communities with whom they had nothing in common.

Interestingly, far-out innovations like balancing and bussing were the exclusive creation of white liberals, although black Anglo-Saxons often executed the plans. Regardless of the declining situation in public schools—in education itself—the white masses have continued running to suburbia with their children, while blacks, under the direction of white liberal educational theorists, opportunistic politicians, engaging psychologists and enterprising businessmen, push them out. Seldom has it occurred to anxious black and white parents that such issues as interracial mixing, seating arrangements, ability grouping, balancing and bussing, or even "blackfaces" in history books, are really issues of organization, mobility, transportation, individual comfort and such like, and have little bearing on the acquisition of literacy. Moreover, these non-academic issues affected many black pupils more adversely than segregation had, while paralyzing public education for the masses of whites. But the dust had to settle before black and white masses were to comprehend the direction of a social revolution which consisted of one step forward and two steps backward.

THE FREUDIAN ETHIC

Education theorists, with their quackish prescriptions based on misleading misdiagnosis of pupil problems, would have been exposed in the fifties in spite of all the confusions accompanying the "civil rights movement" and "race-mixing," if the "mental health movement" and related idiocies had not been flourishing at the same time. Mythological tradition, now representing itself as a science (in the form of the "Freudian Ethic") demanded the abandonment of allegiance to God, and consequently to man as the center of things, making of all men mere objects subject to political manipulation.

Thus, when pupils could not read after not being taught how, it was explained that "non-reading" was a condition due to Oedipus complexes, lack-love mothers, parental anxieties, family conflicts, poverty, hunger, cultural deprivation, nervous stomachs, heredity, parental interferences, matriarchal homes, unwed or broken homes, sibling rivalries, "bookless homes." The school thus became, in fact, a failure clinic to which anxious parents, black and white, periodically reported to receive futility reports on their children. The school system of Washington, D.C. could report to the House Committee on Education and Labor in 1965 that in some of the District's public schools as many as 85 percent of the pupils were reading below normal, if reading at all. Today, the heart of the New York struggle over decentralization is the fact that last year's Regents' test revealed that 85 percent of black and Puerto Rican pupils were reading below grade level. The District of Columbia senior high school teachers have reported being assigned twelfth grade students reading on the first grade level. One high school teacher has reported a section of senior nonreaders rated minus one—that is, they did not know even the alphabet.

Flesch had protested the instruction of children by "guessing or gambling" reading techniques. These techniques, I believe, became the persistent habit pattern of the young as the way to approach the problems of the world. Rather than digging in for mastery and understanding of the complexities of life and human development, which requires hard work, group action and collective concern, a generation of black youth has been sacrificed in the battle for "civil rights." However talented and worthy a student may be, if he cannot read, write or spell in his native tongue, how can he major in languages, history or philosophy? If he has never learned the multiplication tables and how to calculate square roots, how can he enter engineering and physics?

Flesch had predicted it all: "I say, therefore, that the word method is gradually destroying democracy in this country; it returns to the upper middle class the privileges that public education was supposed to distribute evenly among the people. The American Dream is, essentially, equal opportunity through free education for all. This dream is beginning to vanish in a country where the public schools are falling down on the job."

In the breeze we can still hear Martin Luther King romanticize "I had a dream" for the benefit of black children. But it will remain a dream unfulfilled as long as the fundamental tools of knowledge are denied to inquiring tender black minds when they come to the first grade searching for it. As long as the manipulators, masquerading as psychologists, counselors, educational philosophers and theoreticians, are allowed to function as an "elect-elite," the masses they are dehumanizing will be left intellectually and spiritually naked in an age of automation and cybernation.

Tragically, the gates of the highest academic citadels, sealed tight for centuries against blacks, now swing open; but the "comers" from the ranks of blacks are few and far between, for the public schools are such that their products never qualify. The liberal educator-class, which controls these schools, financed, marched and otherwise participated in the "civil rights movement"; but what they

Betrayal in the Schools

gave with one hand—desegregation of schools and "decovenanting" of housing—they took with the other, all the while being regarded as the greatest, most charitable and philanthropic liberals the world has ever known.

In this connection, Patrick J. Moynihan argues that racism is destined to overcome the handicaps imposed by liberals, and that blacks will eventually qualify for places in first rate universities and colleges. This movement would certainly be getting under way right now, as the calls go out from Yale, MIT, Brown and other universities, had black youth been taught the fundamentals in the public schools where their poor parents were forced to enroll them while they struggled to make ends meet.

THE CULTURAL CLASH

For some of the black masses, at least until recently, the parochial schools have provided a sort of "hot-house" situation where the indigenous strain of black worth, creativity and individual dignity could survive, while other blacks were being victimized by the Protestant-Freudian ethic and the drive for "civil rights" and "mental health." In these Catholic schools many children who had been written off as uneducable before transfer from the public schools learned to read, write, spell and compute in spite of race and economic circumstances. And recently black children who transferred from public to Muslim schools in New York, Chicago, Washington and elsewhere have achieved similar gains.

Some may argue the motives of the desegregation theoreticians and politicians, but none can dispute results: hundreds of thousands of blacks have lost hope for the first time since Emancipation. The struggle in New York is one result—and there will be others. But if the real issues underlying declining literacy and undermining achievement had been aired, the tragic New York debacle, which threatens a cultural conflict such as was never experienced in the South or for that matter in the whole

history of the United States, might have been avoided.

The lines of democracy, the rights and wrongs, the good and the bad have gotten so tangled that the country, at least a significant segment of it, may find itself re-examining its whole historical role in servicing the masses, especially the education of their children. It may also find itself thinking seriously about the charges by John F. Hatchett, a black nationalist teacher in New York, who maintains that Jewish teachers were poisoning the minds of black children, even while Albert Shanker, in the name of the teachers' union which he heads, blasted blacks in general as anti-Semites and even "Nazis."

Had the trouble in New York merely reflected issues related to the race problem, we might look forward to a relatively prompt and happy solution. But the cultural clash, accompanied by a conflict of interest and a struggle for power in New York City and elsewhere in the nation is cutting sharply across lines of religion and race, polarizing the United States in a most unexpected fashion.

Behind the facade of school desegregation and the emphasis on racial discrimination and civil rights, serious trouble has been brewing for some time. But many black intellectuals who wish "to tell it as it is" have not been able to be heard. They could have warned—and the nation would have been the better for it—that by providing the public schools with ever-increasing federal funds (Title I, Title II and so on) the government was literally planting the seeds of its own destruction. Programs turning the school into a service station providing amply for everything from food to "sustained excitement," everything except a steady diet of fundamental education, drills and homework, were destined to do for the growing child what food and entertainment does for an untrained animal: make him big and strong, the better to turn on his keeper.

But St. Luke says "I tell you, if these are silent [or silenced] the rocks will cry out." The rocks have not cried out in recent years without reason. Young people of the District of Columbia did not turn out and turn on the community without cause last April 5. Vandalism of school buildings in recent years by betrayed and disappointed young people represents the logical development of a cold war directed against a system which has betrayed and alienated youth, and which is steadily becoming worse.

THE "INNOVATION" RACKET

Failure factories supported and fed by a system of programmed retardation, and promoted by the change racketeers, is what has stirred blacks to revolt. The schemes, the machines, the tests on materials untaught, the change agents—these are the persons and forces serving to make blacks and growing numbers of the white masses feel more and more estranged from their institutions and their culture. We cannot alienate black youth, deculturize, and dehu-

manize them, and simultaneously develop them for positive citizenship.

While disappointed youngsters are smashing display cases and breaking school windows, looting and burning in disgust within the exploited areas, change agents are locked up in "innovation" shops cooking up other schemes, tactics and excuses for failing to distribute the tools of knowledge which have been promised to all the children of the black and white masses in this democracy of ours.

Blacks, as do whites wherever they reside, want their children to enjoy the advantages of effective education. These advantages are rooted in the basic fundamentals of knowledge—reading, writing and arithmetic. Education begins with a mastery of the lingua franca—literacy—in any country for any people. The constant in all of this is power. Power determines the denial of the fundamental tools of knowledge and power can determine the nature and extent of the education meted out.

Essay/Discussion Questions

1. Jewell Mazique argues that the great educational betrayal in the late 1960s was the denial of quality education to public school students. According to her, what were the causes and consequences of this betrayal?

2. According to Mazique, why did black parents accuse urban school systems of programmed retardation?

3. What strategies did many big city public school systems use in order to avoid the *Brown* decision to desegregate?

Race, Urban Politics, and Educational Policy-making in Washington, D.C.: A Community's Struggle for Quality Education

FLOYD W. HAYES III

In the 1950s and 1960s, the movement for public school desegregation came to a head in the context of a convergence of a budding challenge to educational progressivism's theory and practice of societal guidance and the emerging struggle for African-American civil rights. Both efforts challenged the administrative authority of education professionals, experts, and theorists. At the turn of the century, a coalition of educational reformers, local business elites, and the educated middle class succeeded in establishing urban school bureaucracies headed by professional educational managers. The Progressive Era of educational reform is best distinguished by its enthusiasm for a "science" of education, which emphasized expertise, efficiency, and a growing organizational complexity of urban school systems. Since administrative progressives believed that people could manage their own destiny through the conscious application of science to social difficulties, applied educational research—expert knowledge rather than common sense—came to be viewed as a foundation for social engineering

(Tyack and Hansot 1982). These arrangements, however, severely restricted popular participation in the urban educational policy-making process.

By the 1950s, public discontent mounted with educational professionals and theorists who were accused of lowering educational standards and introducing into the public school curriculum courses that many parents and citizen groups interpreted as replacing reading, writing, and arithmetic with fun, fads, and frolicking (Washington 1969). Many concerned parents were encouraged and sustained by such widely read and discussed books as *Why Johnny Can't Read,* by Rudolf Flesch (1955), and *Education and Freedom,* by Hyman Rickover (1959). The authors of these texts harshly criticized the limitations of educational progressivism and school professionals and experts.

The Supreme Court's epic 1954 *Brown* decision, outlawing public school segregation, and

Reprinted from *Urban Education,* Vol. 25, No. 3, October 1990, pp. 237–257. Copyright © 1990 Sage Publications, Inc. Reprinted by permission of Sage Publications, Inc.

the intensifying civil rights movement of the 1950s and 1960s, helped to set in motion forces in many urban African-American communities that, in turn, came to challenge fundamentally the prerogatives and intent of educational professionals and the exclusionary bureaucratic policymaking process of urban public school systems. For example, in Washington, D.C., African-American community organizations and activists clashed with educational professionals over the implementation of the school system's desegregation policy of tracking. In opposition to this policy strategy, citizen groups and participants demanded traditional quality education: the distribution and mastery of the fundamental tools of knowledge, academic motivation, and good character building.

The broad goal of this article is to examine the politics of educational policymaking in Washington, D.C., during the 1950s and 1960s. More specifically, the aim is to chronicle the community struggle against the central administration's tracking-policy strategy, a policy strategy that many community participants saw as more damaging to African-American children than school segregation in the Old South was. Until 1968, when Washington's first elected school board took office, the city's public schools were the only major federally controlled educational system in the nation. Hence the politics of school desegregation in Washington are significant because, as the nation's capital, the city generally was considered a bellwether for the rest of the country (LaNoue and Smith 1973). Moreover, the specific events recounted in this article have been largely overlooked in the scholarly literature on educational politics in Washington, D.C.

Primary data sources for the research presented here include official reports and documents of the District of Columbia public school system. A further step in the process includes an in-depth interview with a key participant in the city's early educational politics examined in this study.[1]

DEMOGRAPHIC TRANSFORMATION

Changing demographic trends in the nation's capital help to explain the politicization of educational policymaking as the desegregation process unfolded. From 1930 to 1950, while the proportion of the African-American population in the Washington metropolitan area as a whole decreased slightly (from 24.9 percent to 23.6 percent), the proportion of African-Americans in the District of Columbia itself increased from 27.1 percent to 35.7 percent. However, percentages can be deceiving. In actual numbers, the African-American population for the Washington metropolitan area increased from 167,409 to 345,954 persons, and the actual numbers of African-American District residents rose from 132,068 to 289,600 persons during that twenty-year period. A more dramatic population change occurred over the next decade. By 1960, although the proportion of African-Americans for the Washington metropolitan area only increased 25.0 percent, this represented an increase in actual numbers to 502,546 persons. Significantly, the proportion of the District's African-American population rose to 55.2 percent, or to 427,100 persons (Passow 1967). Over the next two decades, the proportion and number of Washington's African-American residents would continue to mount as increasing numbers of whites relocated to surrounding suburban areas.

The transformation of Washington's racial composition, begun twenty years before the schools were desegregated, set in motion changes in the racial makeup of the city's public school enrollment. A more dramatic transformation took place following school desegregation. Between 1949 and 1953, white enrollment had declined by about 4,000 students; between 1954 and 1958, that enrollment fell by nearly 12,000 students. Overwhelmingly members of a rising middle class of professionals and managers employed chiefly in the burgeoning federal bureaucracy, many whites left Washington to enroll their children in predominantly white public schools

TABLE 1 ENROLLMENTS BY RACE, WASHINGTON, D.C., PUBLIC SCHOOLS, 1951–1981

Year	Total Enrollment	Afro-American Enrollment	White Enrollment	Percentage Afro-American	Percentage White
1951	95,932	50,250	45,682	52.4	47.6
1956	107,312	72,954	34,358	68.0	32.0
1961	127,268	103,804	23,464	81.6	18.4
1966	146,644	133,275	13,369	90.9	9.1
1971	142,899	136,256	6,643	95.4	4.6
1976*	125,908	119,814	4,406	95.2	3.5
1981	94,425	89,160	3,321	94.4	3.5

SOURCE: ADAPTED FROM WOLTERS (1984, 16).

*Percentages do not add up to 100 after 1973 because Indians, Asians, and Hispanics are counted separately.

in the nearby affluent suburbs of Maryland and Virginia.

The growth of African-American enrollment in the District's public schools also was striking. As Table 1 portrays, from 1951 to 1956, African-American enrollment rose from 52.4 percent to 68.0 percent, or from 50,250 to 72,954 students. Five years later, African-American students constituted 81.6 percent of the public school enrollment. There were then 103,804 African-American students in a total public school enrollment of 127,268.

DESEGREGATION AND THE STRUGGLE AGAINST TRACKING

In the aftermath of the Supreme Court's decisions on 17 May 1954 in *Brown and Bolling* v. *Sharpe* (which terminated the dual-school system in Washington, D.C.), and along with some pressure from the White House, the District government moved to desegregate its public schools. Because of the city's unique political history, its schools were the only major federally controlled public educational system in the nation, and the Eisenhower administration expected Washington to serve as a "showcase" to the nation in making an orderly and prompt transition to a desegregated school system (LaNoue and Smith 1973).

In 1957, following the departure of Superintendent Hobart Corning, the Washington school board appointed Associate Superintendent Carl Hansen as the new superintendent

to lead the school desegregation campaign. Hansen was a Nebraska native who had graduated from the state's university in Lincoln; he had obtained an education doctorate at the University of Southern California and had been a high school teacher and later a high school principal in Omaha before coming to Washington. Thus Hansen was an experienced educator who blended managerial expertise with a strong commitment to desegregated schooling. Indeed, he became one of the nation's foremost spokespersons for school desegregation (Wolfers 1984).

At the commencement of the 1956 school year, the district's educational administration instituted a new program of tracking high school students. Hansen, then associate superintendent responsible for high schools, played a major role in the new policy's implementation. The stated objective of the tracking policy was to allow students with similar academic ability to work together regardless of racial or economic background. Based upon motivation, teachers' evaluation of students' past classroom performance, and scores on achievement and aptitude tests given by educational researchers in the school system's pupil appraisal department, students were steered into one of four separate curriculum tracks: honors, college preparatory, general, and basic (remedial). High-performing students with IQ scores above 120 were to be placed in a special honors course of study; students with IQ scores between 120 and 75 were assigned either to the college preparatory or the general track if they were performing near grade level; students with IQ scores below 75 were put in the remedial or basic track. This latter track included mentally retarded students and those performing three years below grade level with IQ scores between 85 and 75 (U.S. Congress 1966; Wolters 1984).

While the tracking system did result in a modicum of racial and social class mixture in the honors and college preparatory categories, the general and basic tracks, which at the outset consisted overwhelmingly of African-American pupils from economically poor families, came increasingly to include African-American youngsters from professional classes as well. From the beginning, the tracking system was the target of numerous critics who expressed the view that students were being labeled and channeled by educational professionals and researchers into a narrow groove from which they would never exit (Mazique 1986; LaNoue and Smith 1973; Wolters 1984).

Starting with the 1959 school year, upon Superintendent Hansen's recommendation the Washington school board extended the tracking system by including elementary and junior high schools. The new policy established three tracks. Beginning with the fourth grade, youngsters with low IQ scores and a significant level of mental retardation were channeled into the basic track. Students ranking normal on aptitude tests and classroom performance were steered into the general track. Students with IQ scores above 125 and high classroom performance were directed to the honors track (Wolters 1984).

From its inception, the administratively driven policy of tracking elementary and junior high school students caused conflict. And, as the negative consequences of the tracking strategy became more and more apparent, broad community opposition increased precipitously into the 1960s. Three school board members expressed the apprehension that categorizing youngsters in the basic and general tracks at the beginning of their educational careers was premature and might retard normal and later academic growth and development (Wolters 1984). Community groups protested that the tracking system was a new tactic for labeling students and for reinstating a structure of dominance and African-American subordination more harmful than racial segregation in the Old South. Many charged that when educational managers, experts, and researchers applied to African-American students such terms as *culturally deprived, economically disadvantaged, victims of developmental disability, or permanently handicapped by degenerative evolution,* the implication of inherent racial inferiority would result. Moreover, community participants held the view that these characterizations helped to legitimize a theory and practice of withholding basic education from African-American students labeled *uneducable*. Critics charged, then, that the tracking system early excluded African-American youngsters from academic preparation and the educational specialists and managers then tested these students on what they had not been taught. This process allowed educational professionals to achieve a self-fulfilling prophecy (Mazique 1986).

In the early 1960s, community discontent continued to mount as citizen groups and activists charged that tracking denied African-American children a quality education or even a basic one. Community spokespersons intensified their criticism of the tracking system, arguing that steering children into low and middle tracks during elementary school would thwart subsequent educational growth. Additionally, it was reported that in some cases African-American children were summarily defined as mentally retarded without being examined and then automatically channeled into the low track (U.S. Congress 1966; Mazique 1986). Finally, angry African-American District residents demanded that all elementary school students, regardless of racial and class backgrounds, be given a basic education.

In the fall of 1960, the central administration responded to community concerns by establishing the Amidon School, an experiment in integrated quality education (Hansen 1960). The Amidon Plan proved to be a controversial undertaking. Superintendent Hansen announced that the new school, located in the extensively redeveloped quadrant of southwest Washington, was to be an integrated school that provided a program of educational fundamentals. Students from all over the District were admitted on a first-come, first-served basis. Superintendent Hansen stated bluntly the guiding assumptions of the Amidon Plan:

> If you teach children directly and in a highly organized way, they will learn better and faster and will, if teaching is consistent with what is known about the nature of learning, grow wholesomely, developing confidence as they acquire competence and gaining in self-respect as they accomplish difficult objectives. (Hansen 1960, 6)

Starting with the first grade, Amidon's curriculum stressed basic subjects—spelling, penmanship, arithmetic, and reading (taught by the traditional phonic method). Grammar, normally taught in the sixth grade, was introduced in the third grade, together with French and Spanish. History and geography were taught individually and not included in "social studies." While students were grouped together on the basis of similar academic achievement, tracking was not implemented in the Amidon Plan. There were no school parties, no orchestra, and no student government; field excursions also were minimized. In this academically demanding program, homework was the rule (Hansen 1960).

Controversy, however, could not be avoided. Many liberal educational reformers and theorists condemned the Amidon School as a capitulation to conservatism. Some charged that the new school might succeed only as a result of selecting students from middle-class families who prized quality education and were willing to transport their children personally to and from the school. Other liberal educational reformers attacked the Amidon School's subject-centered curriculum and the institution's emphasis on structured student activity. However, when Hansen later announced that a staggering 94 percent of Amidon's students—a substantial number of whom came from low-income and working-class families—scored above the national average in both reading and mathematics, many educational experts were put on the defensive (U.S. Congress 1966). A growing number of parents and community groups argued that the Amidon model of quality education should be implemented throughout the Washington public school system.

By the mid-1960s, the issue of public school integration polarized the District and the nation. Many angry African-American parents and community organizations charged that as public school integration was pushed forward at all costs as the primary goal of education by educational professionals and even civil rights proponents, good classroom teaching, academic motivation, and positive character development in the public schools increasingly were set aside. Since the federal government controlled the Washington public school system, many African-American and white community groups and civic activists lobbied various congressional committees, appealing for improvement in the quality of education for all students in the District's schools.

The League for Universal Justice and Goodwill was one of the community organizations most critical of the tracking system. A grassroots organization headed by the Reverend Walter A. Gray, the League consisted mainly of Baptist and Methodist ministers, African-American parents, and an assortment of African-American civic groups, including the National Capital Voters Association and the University Neighborhoods Council. The League's primary goal was not particularly racial integration but rather enhancement of the quality of education in Washington's schools. From its founding in 1960 to 1965, the League continually lobbied local and national policymakers to institute effective measures to stem the tide of educational decline and decay in the District's public schools (Mazique 1986).

In 1965, the League petitioned the U.S. House of Representatives Committee on Education and Labor, then chaired by Congressman Adam Clayton Powell, to investigate racial discrimination and the tracking system in the Washington public schools. One hundred twenty-five leaders of civic, religious, professional, and fraternal organizations signed the 13 September 1965 petition. As a direct result of the League's petition, the House Committee on Education and Labor's Task Force on Antipoverty in the District of Columbia held a series of public hearings in October 1965 and January 1966, to look into the condition of the Washington public schools. Significantly, the League's important petition (a formal request by a local community organization) cannot be found in the early pages of the congressional report of the hearings; rather, it is deeply embedded in the more than 850-page document (U.S. Congress 1966, 260–261).

The petitioners leveled a general accusation of racial discrimination against the District's public school system. Additionally, the petitioners made four specific charges: (1) the tracking system denied equal educational opportunity; (2) school funds were allocated inversely proportional to needs; (3) there was a growing trend toward establishing an all-white administration in the areas of curriculum development and educational policymaking; and (4) the District school system flagrantly attacked the personal dignity of African-American students, which resulted in rising community hostility and increasing dropouts and delinquency. In addition to urging that the congressional committee undertake a fuller study of the petitioners' complaints, the petition contained a detailed description and elaboration of the petitioners' four major charges against the school system (U.S. Congress 1966).

The Reverend Gray appeared before the congressional task force and submitted a lengthy written statement, which contained a powerful indictment of the tracking system and Superintendent Hansen. The Reverend Gray labeled the tracking system "programmed retardation" and called Hansen a "promoter of educational colonialism and cultural supremacy, the manager of the unfair distribution of funds, violator of public trust and inaugurator of the mass destruction of [the] self-image" of Washington's African-American students (U.S. Congress 1966, 266). Gray denounced the tracking system and predicted the progressive deterioration of the District's schools if authoritative measures were not taken to reverse trends he considered disastrous.

The Reverend Gray concluded his statement with a strong recommendation for the immediate abolition of the tracking system and the dismissal of Superintendent Hansen. In addition, he called for a prime emphasis on quality education; a uniform curriculum; annual performance ratings for teachers; the encouragement and promotion of qualified African-American teachers; a system of public financial accountability to ensure against discriminatory school-funding policies favoring more affluent schools; the termination of the policy of assigning staff personnel and other professionals to non-teaching services (e.g., testers and counselors), resulting in a spiraling school budget; and the end of the school system's theories and practice of racial and cultural supremacy and attacks on the personal dignity of African-American students (U.S. Congress 1966).

Other League members also spoke during the hearings and directly challenged the administrative hegemony of the District's public schools. Significantly, Mrs. Jewell Mazique, a parent and consultant to the League, expressed the views of many ordinary citizens when she exposed the limits of professional expertise and stated the lay public's role in educational policymaking. She asserted:

> Mr. Chairman and members of this committee, we believe that conditions in our local

schools, where moral development has declined, and where the quality of education obtained has deteriorated (in spite of rising budgets and federal aid), command a public airing and an honest investigation of what is wrong. *If the administrators, educational theorists and other professionals cannot supply the answer, then it becomes the public's duty to assist* [italics in original]. We cannot continue indefinitely the downward trend toward imminent collapse of public education and expect our country to maintain its place in the sun [emphasis added]. (U.S. Congress 1966, 266).

In her lengthy statement, Mrs. Mazique provided a critical analysis of the tracking system. She, too, referred to tracking as a system of "programmed retardation," exposing the fact that through a kind of unwritten law, children were placed in tracks at the end of kindergarten following the administration of "readiness" tests and evaluation by the school principal, teachers, and counselors. Mrs. Mazique attacked the practice of using the terms *ability grouping* and *tracking* interchangeably, pointing out that the former term allowed for parental choice while the latter concept denied parental decision making in children's educational development. Charging that the tracking system was grounded in theories of "cultural deprivation," which assumed that African-American children were uneducable or lacked sufficient motivation to learn, Mrs. Mazique pointed out that the African-American traditional yearning for knowledge dated back to the emancipation of the slaves. If something had occurred in recent years to interrupt that motivation, Mrs. Mazique observed, the problem should be placed at the door of the tracking-policy makers who systematically retarded the educational development of African-American and poor white children in Washington, D.C. Mrs. Mazique concluded with a demand for the end of the tracking system and the institutionalization of an educational program of excellence throughout the District's schools (U.S. Congress 1966).

Some educational experts also condemned Washington's public school tracking system, observing that the policy discriminated against students on the basis of race and class. For example, Howard University education professor Elias Blake presented a statistical analysis that showed that low track assignment correlated with low family income. Marvin Cline, a Howard University psychology professor, attacked the tracking system as racially discriminatory. He advocated a policy strategy of racial balance in the schools to improve educational quality. For Cline, desegregation was merely a step in the direction of complete racial integration (U.S. Congress 1966).

Significantly, neither Blake nor Cline had plugged into the network of community groups and concerns set in motion earlier by the Reverend Gray and the League for Universal Justice and Goodwill. When they eventually learned of Blake and Cline and their presentations before the Education and Labor Committee task force, many community participants felt sabotaged. As many community leaders later asserted, Blake's charge that the tracking system targeted low-income families and Cline's emphasis on racial integration and busing subtly shifted the issues away from community hopes and aspirations for enhancing quality education (Mazique 1986).

Following an extensive set of hearings, the House Committee on Education and Labor's task force recommended the termination of the District's tracking system. However, nothing resulted from the recommendation, as most congressmen considered it advisable to leave educational matters in the hands of local school officials. Since the majority of the District's judicially appointed school board members were loyal to Superintendent Hansen, the tracking system remained unchanged, for a time (Wolters 1984).

What led ultimately to the abolition of tracking in the District's public schools was a lawsuit filed by Julius Hobson, Sr. Hobson, a civil rights activist and government employee, was also one of the District's most vocal critics of the tracking system and Superintendent Hansen. Hobson, too, had testified before the Education and Labor Committee's task force, where he assailed the tracking system for racial and class bias. In the aftermath of the hearings, Hobson took legal action against the District's school officials, challenging the constitutionality of their educational policies, including tracking. However, the resulting legal policy decisions contrasted sharply with the hopes and aspirations of the District's African-American community for the institutionalization of quality education throughout the schools. In effect, traditional community leaders and organizations lost control of the issues as new persons like Hobson emerged to play major roles and put forward alternative issues. A discussion of these issues follows.

HOBSON V. HANSEN AND THE ABOLITION OF TRACKING: CONTRADICTIONS AND DILEMMAS

In July 1966, Hobson filed a class action suit in federal district court against Superintendent Hansen, the school board, and the Washington judges who appointed the board. He complained that Washington's public schools unconstitutionally denied African-American and impoverished students equal educational opportunities provided to more well-off and white students. Additionally, Hobson charged that these educational disparities were the consequences of the tracking system, the principle of neighborhood schools, unfair teacher appointments to schools, and optional school zones for some students. Hobson questioned the constitutionality of the congressional act giving federal district court judges the power to appoint school board members. The last complaint was separated from the others, and a three-judge district court heard it. The nature of Hobson's challenge required that the three-judge panel be composed of circuit judges unrelated to the appointment process. In a decision from which

Judge J. Skelly Wright dissented, the panel upheld the constitutionality of the statute, ruling that Congress could delegate appointive authority to federal judges in Washington, D.C. However, a request of the Judicial Conference of the District of Columbia Circuit resulted in a subsequent congressional amendment of the statute to allow for an elected school board (Horowitz 1977; LaNoue and Smith 1973).

Judge J. Skelly Wright of the U.S. Court of Appeals heard Hobson's remaining charges. Judge Wright sustained Hobson in *Hobson* v. *Hansen* (1967). The judge held a lengthy hearing and wrote a far-reaching opinion and decree, ordering the school board to: abolish the tracking system, develop a student assignment policy in harmony with the court's order and not based completely on the neighborhood-school principle, provide transportation to African-American students wishing to transfer to white schools, terminate optional school zones, and design a program of "color-conscious" faculty assignments to effect teacher integration (Horowitz 1977; LaNoue and Smith 1973).

The *Hobson* v. *Hansen* ruling did not put an end to controversy surrounding the assortment of major educational issues in Washington. Indeed, some dilemmas emerged as a result of the decision. However, the case is important to Washington's public school history because it set in motion future challenges to educational policymaking by accentuating the major issues. The leading actors in the District's educational politics from 1967 to 1971 also emerged as a result of the case and its late effect on the school system (LaNoue and Smith 1973). These new issues and leaders effectively supplanted goals and struggles of traditional community leaders and organizations, like the Reverend Gray and the League for Universal Justice and Goodwill, which had fought for quality education since the late 1950s and early 1960s.

Stated in brief, it might be suggested that the *Hobson* v. *Hansen* decision sought to achieve three objectives: integration, quality education, and equality of educational opportunity. Three prominent actors in Washington's educational politics became publicly associated with each of these objectives. Judge Wright came to represent an ongoing allegiance to integration; Hobson came to represent equal educational opportunity; and Mrs. Anita Allen, recently appointed to the school board, came to represent the quest for quality education. Allen, as a member of Washington's first predominantly African-American school board, helped carry the vote to effectuate Judge Wright's decision and to direct Superintendent Hansen not to challenge the ruling. This occurred on 1 July 1967—the day Allen took office. Hansen promptly resigned and joined a dissenting board member in an unsuccessful suit to appeal the *Hobson* decision. Several ineffective superintendents followed Hansen, resulting in the school system's lack of strong executive authority. Moreover, the school board could not provide vigorous leadership because it was embroiled in internal squabbles and faced with community discontent (LaNoue and Smith 1973).

Although Hobson became Washington's first elected official in more than a century when he was a member of the school board for one year in 1968, he generally played the role of an agitator and outside critic of the school system. Similar to many middle-class reformers, however, Hobson failed to establish strong linkages with the community he was supposed to represent. In his reelection bid in 1969, Hobson lost to Exie Mae Washington, a former domestic worker who was promoted to community leadership status through the poverty program. Hobson also had been damaged in his attempt to encourage educational change because of a weakened school bureaucracy and the lack of strong administrative leadership to respond to his demands (LaNoue and Smith 1973).

In the final analysis, the three major objectives of the Wright decision in the *Hobson* case

could not be accomplished all at once. Judge Wright had strongly emphasized racial integration and set in motion policies and practices that contradicted the Washington African-American community's original goal of quality education. As a result of the judge's decree, coupled with the research findings of educational policy entrepreneurs (particularly, the Coleman report of 1966), the goal shifted from quality education to racial balancing and busing. This was not the policy strategy desired by Washington's African-American community, although racial balancing and busing fit well within the social management policy agenda of educational reform's liberal professional-managerial elites and many civil rights advocates. The African-American community had demanded quality education: the distribution and mastery of the fundamental tools of knowledge (reading, writing, and computational skills), academic motivation, and good character building. For many African-American community participants, emphasis on racial balancing and busing set aside the concern for achieving quality education. One community observer flatly characterized the result as a "betrayal in the schools" (Washington 1969).

Judge Wright's decision in the *Hobson* case also contributed to the continuation of white flight from Washington and its public schools. By the time the decree was handed down, the city's public schools were 92 percent African-American, and with the continued growth in the proportion of African-American students, integration became impossible. Even the school board seemed to realize the declining possibility and importance of integration when it released the findings of the Passow report, an exhaustive study and analysis of Washington's schools. One section of the report stated bluntly that it was pointless to speak of racial integration or racial balance in a school system with a student enrollment of more than 90 percent African-American (Passow 1967).

CONCLUSION

Prior to the 1950s, American educational politics and policy were largely dominated by the legacy of the turn-of-the-century Progressive Era of school reform. That earlier reform movement sought to remove politics from urban education by centralizing executive power in the person of professional educational managers; establishing bureaucratically organized school systems; and using the rhetoric of "science," expertise, and efficiency as the guiding principles of the educational enterprise. Indeed, both lay officials on urban school boards and the lay public largely were deferential to educational professionals, managers, and their expert knowledge.

However, a managerial style, organizational form, and educational ideology operative in one period can frequently become impediments in the next. An inherent problem with the managerial decision-making process, organizational complexity, and scientistic rhetoric of the educational reform period was that they severely restricted public participation in the urban educational policymaking process. Thus, in the 1950s and 1960s, these arrangements gave rise to a popular challenge to the prerogatives of educational professionals and their exclusive bureaucratic policymaking process. Moreover, ordinary citizens began to confront the hegemonic role of expert knowledge in educational decision making.

In the case of Washington, the introduction of the tracking system into the public schools is an example of managerial-bureaucratic policymaking that effectively excluded popular participation. Moreover, the strategy of channeling children into different curricular tracks—based upon "scientific" IQ test scores as interpreted by educational experts and classroom performance evaluations by principals and teachers—exemplified educational reformers' rhetoric and practice of social management. In addition, the policy had racial overtones, as it directed a large proportion of African-American children to the low track. As a result of being constrained from influencing decisions affecting their interest in protecting their children's future educational development, parental and community groups became increasingly angry and directly challenged the District's educational professionals and specialists. The efforts of the League for Universal Justice and Goodwill and other grassroots organizations to attack politically the formulators and implementors of the tracking system represented a shift from the past era of public school politics when educational professionals largely commanded popular deference to an emerging politics of education distinguished by increased community challenge to public school professionals. This new brand of open and aggressive community politics would come to characterize the politics of urban educational policymaking in the 1970s and 1980s (Hayes 1985).

The present study of the historical trends and developments in the politics of public schooling in the District of Columbia exposes a transition from segregation with parental and community concern for quality education to integration with official emphasis on tracking and later racial busing and balancing, ultimately newer forms of racial discrimination that denied quality education to African-American youngsters. The District's public school officials advocated the tracking system as a means of complying with the *Brown* and *Bolling* Supreme Court decisions. In contrast, the African-American community attacked this policy, seeking the institutionalization of quality education throughout the public school system. The League and its members defined quality education as the distribution and mastery of the basic tools of knowledge, academic motivation, and positive character development. They characterized the tracking system as "programmed retardation," charging that this policy strategy was worse than segregation in the Old South. Community spokespersons argued forcefully that tracking would result in the eventual deterioration of public education in Washington.

Asserting that tracking early on retarded a child's later academic growth and development, legitimized a practice of withholding educational fundamentals from African-American students, and denied African-American children a quality education or even a basic one, the District's African-American residents demanded a basic education in all of the city's schools. Indeed, the success of the District's Amidon Plan and its subject-centered curriculum served as proof then and now that a return to the basics in public schools would lead to quality education for all students regardless of race or class background. Recognizing the value of Amidon's curriculum, Washington's community leaders called in vain for similar plans to be implemented throughout the District.

Because of the District's unique political history as the nation's capital, the city public schools were controlled by Congress. Therefore, as community frustration and discontent with public school officials grew, the League petitioned the House Committee on Education and Labor to investigate charges of racial and class discrimination in the District's schools. The hope was that Congress would abolish the tracking system.

Congress did not abolish the tracking policy, maintaining the collective opinion that educational matters should remain in the hands of local officials. The community was defeated in its struggle for quality education, even though community leaders had initiated an effective challenge to Washington's public school professionals and the tracking system. Judge J. Skelly Wright's ruling in the *Hobson* case did terminate tracking in the District's schools; however, he ignored the community's cry for quality education as a priority for Washington's schools. Thus, with Wright's decision, the issues shifted from the community's concern for enhancing quality education to the educational professionals' and experts' policy agenda and debate (at the national and local levels) regarding racial balancing and

busing. This was the "great betrayal" and represented a regrouping and continuation of educational reform's goal of social management into the 1960s and 1970s. While racial balancing and busing could not be achieved in Washington's schools, whose students were more than 90 percent African-American, racial balancing and busing did command the attention of educational professionals and community participants in the surrounding suburban jurisdictions of the greater Washington metropolitan area (see Hayes 1985). Moreover, in the 1970s, an increasingly active judiciary came to sanction and enforce various forms of racial balancing and busing in metropolitan areas across the nation (Kirp 1982; Willie and Greenblatt 1981). Such judicial activism may have been the single most significant factor in the ultimate decline of public education.

Although the District's African-American community lost its struggle for quality education, its leaders' earlier predictions of the dire consequences of the tracking system's "programmed retardation" cannot be ignored today (see Oakes 1985). Moreover, Mrs. Mazique's warning before the 1966 congressional task force regarding "the downward trend toward imminent collapse of public education" is confirmed by the contemporary national anxiety and debate about America's current educational predicament (for example, see Altbach, Kelly, and Weis 1985; National Commission on Excellence in Education 1983). As in many other urban school systems, the number of National Merit scholars graduating from Washington's high schools is minuscule, and a substantially large proportion of them require remedial assistance upon entering college. Washington's public schools are faced with an assortment of educational and social difficulties: dropouts and continued enrollment decline since 1970, drug-related activities, teenage pregnancies, school closings, and growing parental discontent (Sanchez 1990; Vassell 1990). There are recent indications that many African-American parents are withdrawing their children from the public schools and enrolling them in private and parochial schools. Commenting on the progressive deterioration of public trust in the District's schools, one researcher has observed that "a permanent lack of confidence has now replaced the 'crisis of confidence'" (Diner 1990). For the Washington, D.C. public school system, and for urban public school systems throughout America, the great challenge of the future will be to reinstate quality education and thereby rebuild confidence in public education.

Note

1. This study benefited from in-depth interviews with Mrs. Jewell R. Mazique conducted in 1986. She is one of the few, if not the only, remaining key community participants in the events chronicled in this article. I am grateful to her for sharing with me her wealth of historical knowledge and personal experience regarding educational politics in Washington, D.C., since the 1950s.

References

Altbach, P. G., G. P. Kelly, and L. Weis, eds. 1985. *Excellence in education. Perspectives on policy and practice.* Buffalo NY: Prometheus.

Bolling v. *Sharpe,* 347 U.S. 497 (1954).

Brown v. *Board of Education,* 347 U.S. 483 (1954).

Coleman, J., E. Campbell, C. J. Hobson, J. McPartland, A. M. Mood, F. D. Weinfeld, and R. L. York. 1966. *Equality of educational opportunity.* 2 vols. (Report no. OE-38001, Office of Education.) Washington, DC: GPO.

Diner, S. J. 1990. Crisis of confidence: Public confidence in the schools of the Nation's capital in the twentieth century. *Urban Education* 25:112–37.

Flesch, R. 1955. *Why Johnny can't read.* New York: Harper & Row.

Hansen, C. F.1960. *The Amidon Plan: For education in the sixties in the D.C. Public Schools.* Washington, DC: D.C. Government.

Hayes. F. W., III. 1985. Division and conflict in postindustrial politics: Social change and educational policymaking in Montgomery County, Maryland. Ph.D. diss., University of Maryland.

Hobson v. *Hansen,* 265 F. Supp. 902 (1967).

Horowitz, D. F. 1977. *The courts and social policy.* Washington, DC: Brookings Institute.

Kirp, D. L. 1982. *Just schools: The idea of racial equality in American education.* Berkeley: University of California Press.

LaNoue, G. R., and B. L. R. Smilh. 1973. *The politics of school decentralization.* Lexington: Lexington Books.

Mazique, J. R. 1986. Interview. 5 March.

National Commission on Excellence in Education. 1983. *A nation at risk: The imperative for educational reform.* Washington, DC: GPO.

Oakes, J. 1985. *Keeping track: How schools structure inequality.* New Haven, CT: Yale University Press.

Passow, A. H. 1967. *Toward creating a model urban school system: A study of the Washington D.C. public schools.* New York: Teachers College, Columbia University.

Rickover, H. C. 1959. *Education and freedom.* New York: E. P. Dutton.

Sanchez, R. 1990. New D.C. school figures show large declines. *Washington Post* (7 March): A1, A12.

Tyack, D. B., and E. Hansot. 1982. *Managers of virtue: Public school leadership in America 1820–1980.* New York: Basic Books.

U.S. Congress. House. Committee on Education and Labor. *Investigation of the schools and poverty in the District of Columbia: Hearings before the Task Force on Antipoverty in the District of Columbia.* 89th Cong., 1st and 2d sess., 1965–1966. Y4.

Vassell, O. 1990. Parents group wants board booted. *Washington Post* (14 April): A1, A2.

Washington, M. W.1969. Betrayal in the schools: As seen by an advocate of African-American power. *Triumph Magazine* (January): 16–19.

Willie, C. V., and S. L. Greenblatt, eds. 1981. *Community politics and educational change: Ten school systems under court order.* New York: Longman.

Wolters, R. 1984. *The burden of Brown: Thirty years of school desegregation.* Knoxville: University of Tennessee Press.

Essay/Discussion Questions

1. In the aftermath of the *Brown v. Board of Education* (1954) and *Bolling v. Sharpe* (1954) Supreme Court decisions, the Washington D.C. public school system implemented what policy strategy in order to evade desegregation? How did black community leaders and organizations respond?

2. Hayes argues that a coalition of educational policy specialists and civil rights leaders interrupted the Washington, D.C. black community's struggle for quality education and redirected the movement toward racial integration—racial balancing and busing. What have been the long-term effects of this policy strategy throughout America's big city school systems? How has the implementation of racial balancing and busing affected many urban African American (and Latino) communities?

3. Discuss the *Hobson v. Hansen* (1967) case and its impact on the Washington, D.C. public school system.

People of color have always theorized—but in forms quite different from the Western form of abstract logic . . . our theorizing (and I intentionally use the verb rather than the noun) is often in narrative forms, in the stories we create . . . [in] dynamic rather than fixed ideas. . . . How else have we managed to survive with such spiritedness the assault on our bodies, social institutions, countries, our very humanity? And women. at least the women I grew up around, continuously speculated about the nature of life through pithy language that unmasked the power relations of their world. . . . My folk, in other words, have always been a race for theory—though more in the form of the hieroglyph, a written figure which is both sensual and abstract, both beautiful and communicative.

BARBARA CHRISTIAN, "THE RACE FOR THEORY"[1]

Teaching Theory, Talking Community

JOY JAMES

THE ERASURE OF AFRICANA WOMEN IN ACADEMIC THEORY

Contemporary African American theorists such as Barbara Christian, who writes that theory not rooted in practice is elitist, think within an African and community-centered tradition in which the creativity of a people in the race for theory sustains humanity. However, teaching theory as nonelitist, and intending the liberation and development of humanity, specifically African communities, contradicts much of academic theory,[2] which is Eurocentric.

All philosophy and theory, Eurocentric or Afracentric, is political. Academic "disciplines," when sexualized and racialized, tend to reproduce themselves in hierarchically segregated forms. To confront segregation means recognizing that current academic or educational standards have never worked, and were never intended to work, for us as a people. Our tenuous presence in (White) universities and colleges speaks to the fact that individuals, but not the community, may attain some success in an educational process centered on the marginalization of all but the "European" (socially constructed as White, propertied heterosexuals).

In academia many philosophy or theory courses may emphasize logic and memorizing the history of "Western" philosophy, rather than the activity of philosophizing or theorizing. When the logic of propositions is the primary object of study, how one argues becomes more important than for what one argues. The exercise of reason may take place within an illogical context. Catechizing academic canons obscures the absurdity of their claims to universal supremacy and the massive flaws in legacies, such as Platonic and

Reprinted from Joy James and Ruth Farmer, eds., *Spirit, Space, and Survival: African American Women in (White) Academe*, New York: Routledge, 1993, pp. 118–135.

Aristotelian "universal" principles derived from the hierarchical splintering of humanity; and/or the European Enlightenment's deification of scientific rationalism.

Some thinkers canonized in academia have argued that theory and philosophy are open to the "everyday" person and intend the good of humanity. However, few identify African people as both equal partners in that humanity and important theorists in its behalf. Fewer still connect the "life of the mind" to the understanding that "Black people have to a disproportionate extent supplied the labor which has made possible the cultivation of philosophical inquiry."[3] We have also disproportionately cultivated the philosophies that provide nonabstract meanings of freedom and justice: surviving genocidal oppression allows insights into (in)humanity and (in)justice that transcend the abstractions of academic philosophy and theory. The root knowledge of African living thinkers, of democratic power and philosophy, is not often practiced inside ivory towers where provincial thinking, itself almost a universal in academia, reflects rather than critiques Eurocentrism.

"Eurocentrism" is not synonymous with European. In a society and culture where the White European represents both the ideal and universal manifestation of civilization, unsurprisingly, "Black" as well as "White" people adopt or adapt this icon as worldview. My schooling in White-dominated institutions has painfully impressed on me the depth of indoctrination and the difficulty of deprogramming myself from "truths" formulated under the tutelage of institutional bigotry which relegated "Blackness" and "femaleness" to savage superstition, invisibility or exotica and "Whiteness" and "maleness" to a paragon and the sublime.

Samir Amin defines Eurocentrism as:

a culturalist phenomenon in the sense that it assumes the existence of irreducibly distinct cultural invariants that shape the historical paths of different peoples. Eurocentrism is

therefore anti-universalist, since it is not interested in seeking possible general laws of human evolution. But it does present itself as universalist, for it claims that imitation of the Western model by all peoples is the only solution to the challenges of our time.[4]

White supremacy rationalizes Eurocentrism's anti-universalist stance. It has shaped and misshapened European philosophy, with destructive effects on the material lives of the majority of the world's people and the spiritual and intellectual lives of all. Cornel West's description of White supremacy applies to the Eurocentric, academic mindset:

the idea of white supremacy emerges partly because of the powers within the structure of modern discourse—powers to produce and prohibit, develop and delimit, forms of rationality, scientificity, and objectivity which set perimeters and draw boundaries for the intelligibility, availability, and legitimacy of certain ideas.[5]

Adhering to the tastes of White supremacy, "white solipsism"[6] masquerades as philosophy within the myth of European "racial," therefore intellectual, superiority. As legitimizing a world order of domination becomes an intellectual mandate, Eurocentrism, like the carnival house of mirrors, projects what it distorts. Its solipsistic reflections racialize (and sexualize) theory, "whitening" thinkers indispensable to its canons: the Egyptian philosophers, Aesop, Jesus of Nazareth, Augustine. Given the broad paintbrush of White supremacy, it is a tragicomedy that historical African or Semitic figures are depicted in illustrated academic texts as physically "White," some with blond hair, or taught paradoxically as if they had no ethnicity or race (in which case their racial identities are assumed to be "White"). With or without illustrations falsifying historical identities, students receive theory with the bias that philosophy is the product of the minds of "great" White men, and in Women's Studies of "great" White women, respectively beneficent patriarchs or matriarchs. (In African American studies the prioritizing of African American men as theorists produces its own distortions.)

With the European centered as "universal" or normative, all else, by default, becomes marginal. When Eurocentric bias is seen as incidental rather than endemic to academic thinking, "indiscretions" are thought to be containable if cauterized to allow the work to retain its status.[7] Consequently critiques of (hetero)sexism, racism, and classism failing to analyze individual writers as representatives of a collective consciousness reinforce Eurocentrism's hegemony as a metaparadigm, albeit as a flawed one.

Philosophical traditions, such as those of service to ancestors and community, challenge the authoritarian, authoritative voice of this metaparadigm. Living thinkers[8] operate, outside the worldview of "scientific" materialism and "objective" rationalism, within paradigms which hold the nonduality and interpenetration of reality—the sacred and secular, the political and spiritual, the individual and community. Presenting community as the foundation of reality and knowledge, these paradigms reject the elitism of academic thinking. They are consequently heresies; academia discredits indigenous cosmologies, and their concepts of nonlinear time, nonduality and commitments to community, as exotic aberrations and primitive thought. Since academia recognizes neither the intellectual nor moral authority of the (African) communities it dissects, and African communities do not determine how African people are to be "studied," our misrepresentation seems the rule.[9] Dismissing the centrality of African ancestral and living thinkers creates a catastrophic loss of realities and commitments present in traditional African cosmology.

The designation of academia, with its biases, as *the* legitimate intellectual realm for philosophy and theory deflects attention from traditional cosmologies and living thinkers. Theorizing within a tradition for liberated communities presents a worldview centered in spirituality, community survival, and human development. The devaluation of community and African thinking overlooks the universal aspects of the philosophy and theorizing of African "traditionalists," particularly women. Academic thinking promotes not only obscurantism but also the erasure of Africana women from theory.

Playing by its house rules, academia can set standards which no African American woman can meet *as an African American woman*. If it is assumed that we only speak as "Black women"— not as *women*—or "Black people"—not as *human beings*—our stories and theorizing are considered irrelevant or not applicable to women or people in general; they are reduced to descriptions of a part rather than analyses of a whole (humanity). When teaching about our lives as Africana women is viewed as a descent to the particular (*everything* African) from the "universal norm" (*anything* European), biology becomes destiny, with European biology as manifest destiny. Receiving recognition as "theorists" or "intellectuals" because of the "Westernization" and masculinization of our thinking (and lives) as Africana women still leave us "unqualified" as *Africana* women. Acknowledging "theory" only from those in transmutation in an Eurocentric form, reduces theory to technique. If it is only legitimized when communicated in "academese," then we must be trained out of traditional, communal communication to do theory.

If style or technical language determines much of what is recognized as theory, voguing is subjectless "objective" writing which claims to be without desires or interests.[10] Although desire and interest are not obliterated by proclamation, under the apotheosis of academic thinking, rationalism as "theory" vanquishes desire. Its technocratic jargon and writing, which "explore" or "probe" the lives of Africana women, lend themselves, like all colonial interventions and invasions, to misrepresentation and falsification. The objectification of

African American women through the "expert" voice of "trained" speakers, including the voices of African American women academics who attempt to "re-articulate" knowledge,[11] is often a distorting interference. Since academese as an alien language is not designed to respectfully or adequately communicate African experiences,[12] using it we may appropriate and disrespect our own voices and people.

Appropriation requires abstractions. When we are stripped, or strip ourselves, of our context in community, caricatures incompatible with theory or philosophy deepen our intellectual alienation. The categorization of Black women in bipolar stereotypes—the "Mammy-Sapphire" swing of suffering or angry victims, without the ashé or power as ancestors and living thinkers,[13] is the prerequisite for relocation to some ghetto in an academic mind. Ghettoized in our own minds, and those of others, prevents a serious encounter with Africana women and blocks meeting ourselves as theorists. By demanding recognition for a community that theorizes, we can turn our extreme location into an advantage. The vantage point to being out on a ledge of institutional alienation is the ken of the view. Out there one can see the ways in which time, space, and people are strung up and strung out. Artificial timelines manipulate space and thought. In academic theory time is European time; space is that occupied by Europeans; great thinkers are their mythologized ancestors.

I find that people who routinely accept that European-Whites competently critique and teach African (American) thought may find it incongruous (or racial heresy) to accept that Africans-Blacks competently analyze and teach, and therefore contribute to, European (American) thought. The complaints of White European American students who rebelliously argue when assigned the writings of people of color that they "thought this was supposed to be a course on 'theory or women's studies'" are logical in this context. Their grievances are based on unmet expectations set by the false advertising of departments and programs which reduce theory to Eurocentric thought and Women's Studies to White women's studies. Attempting to bring more realism to our program, I jettison the Eurocentric paradigm in teaching my section of "Feminist Theory," renaming the course "Womanist/Feminist theory" and teaching Native American, Africana, Latina, Asian and European (American) women thinkers. My language has also changed. I more often say "Theory" without the qualifiers "Womanist" or "Black Feminist" when referring to the work of African American women theorists. (I take a cue from White men who do not title their works "*White Masculinist* Theory"; White women who do not preface their writings with "*White* Feminist Theory"; and, African American men who do not identify their publications as "Afrocentric *Masculinist* Theory."[14])

Attempts to recognize African contributions to understandings of philosophy and cosmology have focused on integration in spaces dominated by Europeans. Perhaps the most overworked decoy in academe's intellectual apartheid is curriculum "integration." Integration and "inclusivity" as new forms of segregation can act as a subterfuge for racist, (hetero)sexist and classist education. Curriculum integration, an easy home remedy to a racist canon, lends itself to the creation of more sophisticatedly segregated academic departments, programs, and courses. "Special interest" or "diversity" courses simultaneously integrate and segregate. They fail to transform disciplines which view racism as a problem of excess or indiscretion in the hegemony and not as the cornerstone of the hegemony itself. Disciplines seek to ameliorate exclusion through integration rather than struggle for new meanings and philosophies; the panacea becomes paradigmatic reform rather than a revolution of paradigms. Not the African community but academe determines the meaning, intent, and degree of "integration" of "Whites

Only" disciplines; under these conditions, the reproduction of segregation is unsurprising.

In reform, the axis of the universe remains the same. Although academia bestows degrees and grants tenure, it does not necessarily produce philosophers and theorists. Eurocentric-academic theory is hardly an honorable participant in the race for theory. The purveyors of philosophy and theory retain their prerogatives to introduce anonymous, interchangeable satellites as mirrors for their own reflections: Black women are viewed as cosmetic aides to those holding firmly to their place at the center of the mirror. What does it mean that "academic theory" presents African American women thinkers as generic satellites in White star-studded galaxies? What would it mean to revolutionize the teaching of theory in academe in order to present African American women thinkers as builders of the shared universe, within African cosmology?

MAKING OUR PRESENCE KNOWN

Before I can even teach theory, given its current biological construction in academia, I am continuously challenged to "prove" that I am qualified. Comparing my work experiences with those of other African American women academics, I notice that despite our having been hired through a highly competitive process, we seem to be asked more routinely, almost reflexively, if we have Ph.Ds. We could attribute this, and have, to our 'diminutive' height, youngish appearance or casual attire. Yet I notice that White women about our height, unsuited, and under 60, seem not to be interrogated as frequently about their qualifications. Continuously asked my "qualifications" as a "theorist" I cited to the inquisitive or inquisition: my *training*—a degree in political philosophy; *my research*—a dissertation on a European theorist; or my *employment*—teaching theory courses in academe. These are prerequisites for institutional membership but not measurements of competency.

I accept that nothing will qualify me to students and faculty who do not struggle with their racism, fear, and hostility towards African people, philosophy, and theorizing centered on liberation. For me, teaching theory courses on the praxis of African American women permits me to claim that I think. Connecting my teaching to community organizing allows me to say I theorize. Service in African liberation qualifies me.

These qualifications make me a suspicious character if not "unqualified" for academe. A hydra for teachers and students who do not set them, criteria established without our input are shrouds. The issue is not whether there should be standards and qualifications; there always are. The issue is who sets and will set them, and for whose benefit they function. The reward of transgressing conventional academic standards is reestablishing connections to community wisdom and practice. The specter of failing to meet institutional standards and "qualifications" inhibits the search for new models of knowledge and teaching.

In teaching, I try to learn and share more about the history of social thought. Teaching about the origins of the "academy," "philosophy" and "theory" as predating the "Greek ancestors" of "Western civilization" broadens the scope of both the time and space in which theory takes place; it expands academia's concept of who theorizes. Changing the concept of time or the timeline changes the context for philosophy and theory.[15] Philosophy extends beyond the appearance of Europeans (and their designated ancestors) in history; so theory extends beyond the spaces they occupy or rule. To restrict our discussions of the contributions of African cosmology and philosophy to the "contemporary" period implies that we have no "ancient" or "modern" history in philosophizing. Without a history philosophy is not indigenous to us as a people; and "contemporary" theorizing becomes disconnected from its tradition. That is why we must reinsert ourselves in time and history on the continuum, and confront academic disciplines attempting to erase us from that line. The ways in which I approach theory are changing.

Extending time to find other origins of theory, I encounter more comprehensive spaces and thoughts. Hypaetia, the (Egyptian or Greek) woman philosopher, sits with the "Ancient" philosophers of academic masculinist theory. The Kongo women kings theorize in a unique cosmology coexisting with the space occupied by Locke, and Rousseau and other philosophs of the European Enlightenment. Angela Davis and African revolutionary theorizing coexist with the European (American) liberalism of Rawls, Arendt, and Bentham in contemporary political theory. In "essential feminist writings," Ida B. Wells is taught alongside Mary Wollstonecraft and Susan B. Anthony; Virginia Woolf and Mary Daly are placed beside Assata Shakur and Audre Lorde.

The ways in which I teach theory are changing. Cultivating respectfulness in myself and seeking it in my students, I ask my classes: "Who are you? Do you know your personal and political relationship to the knowledge studied?" I find that autobiographical theorizing discourages appropriation and objectification, while encouraging students to identify themselves as potential theorists and embark in self-reflections that include critiques of racist, classist and (hetero)sexist assumptions (a "backlash" usually follows any sustained critique of entrenched, dominant biases). I urge students to carefully consider the claim by revolutionary African American women who write that the roles of living thinkers are open to all and that they are not "exceptional" (those who participate in a legacy follow rather than deviate from the normative).

Students encounter the women's images and voices through video and audio tapes that supplement readings for discussions on women's contributions to and roles in liberation struggles. These images, along with exploring our relationships and responsibilities to writers, stories, and theories, pull us off the sidelines as "spectators" and consumers of Africana "performance" towards our own roles as actors. Contending with my own "consumerism," I find that progressive Africana activists give me more than subject matter for courses; they also provide instruction in philosophy and democratic pedagogy. I am pushed most as a teacher-student when wrestling with the implications of philosophy and theorizing in the autobiographies of revolutionary African American women. More than any other type of writing, this form prods me to confront my personal and political responsibilities to ancestors, youth, and future generations. Attempting to share what I learn, the internal obstacles appear. They emerge out of my physical and sometimes intellectual alienation from work for community liberation and the philosophers and theorists of the community. They coexist with the ever-present external obstacles of indifference and hostility towards Black liberation theorizing. Despite the internal and external obstacles, I begin to fear less being dismissively ignored by academics and fear more my own ignorance about the faltering ties to our ancestors' loving, radical traditions. Although it grates the academic norm, responsibility means that legitimacy and authority come from the humanity of my communities.[16] If respect and recognition mean communicating our wisdom and humanity in struggle, regardless, then pedagogy will be the transport.

TALKING THEORY: ACTIVISM IN PEDAGOGY

Pedagogy rooted in ethical concerns and an epistemology based on a four part process of experience, reflection, judgment, and action,[17] organize my courses. Readings stimulate and challenge students to expand their experiential base. They then enter their reflections in journals, essay papers and compare their insights in small student work groups. Judging dominant norms, students design activities or projects to demystify and challenge economic and racial-sexual oppression, and evaluate their own ideologies. Through organizing, they obtain a greater experimental base to reflect on philosophy and theorizing, cosmologies, freedom and liberation struggles. The last step in this epistemological framework is action. Ethical action expands experiences, stimulates self-reflections, and judging. A pedagogy that denies the validity of personal experiences, that makes no space for self-reflection, that discourages judgment, and severs action from insight confuses fragmented thinking with knowledge. Guided by ethical concerns to think and organize to resist oppression, we walk closer to the place where humanist political thinkers stand. There, hopefully with a less distant and more substantial awareness of their theorizing, we begin to comprehend and critique.

To respectfully teach about theorizing by African American women activists requires such a pedagogy based on ethics and active commitment to community liberation. So, I reject the concept of education as value-neutral and use "extracurricular" activities as a lab component (for instance, the hands-on experience of "applied" knowledge or "labs" to supplement "book" knowledge is indispensable in disciplines such as chemistry or architecture). These activities, encouraging students to take an active rather than passive role in their self-development, advance critical analyses of: child abuse; sexual violence; adultism; racism; (hetero)sexism; and classism.

For example, in my senior seminar on "Women and the State," students wrote papers and organized educational forums for the campus and local community on relevant topics. Their educationals in the campus center, held on Tuesday afternoons in March during Women's History Month, were: "Women and Militarization," "Women and Occupation," and "Women Political Prisoners." "Women and Militarization" occurred around the time of

the U.S. bombing of Iraq. Over 100 people attended this educational, which students organized as a tribunal or mock trial in which African American, Caribbean and Native American and European American women activists and teachers testified on U.S. crimes against humanity, specifically violence resulting from racism and sexism in U.S. domestic and foreign policies. The students performed-educated as poets, defense and prosecution lawyers, judge, and witnesses. They staged guerilla theatre to disrupt their mock trial: dressed in mourning garb, the "ghosts" of several women murdered by their male companions in domestic violence interrupted the proceedings, bitterly denouncing the court for ignoring their desperate petitions, as living women, to stop their batterers.

Although the majority of students in the "Women and the State" seminar stated that they found organizing their forum and attending and critiquing the others as one of their most difficult and most rewarding educational experiences, interrelating doing and knowing for ethical-political action is not a popular practice in academe. White students have told me that they resent not the request to engage in activities outside the classroom (they do for other classes), but the request to act against racism, believing it unjust to require, as proper and necessary, that students (staff and faculty) confront adultism, classism, racism, and (hetero)sexism in their courses and themselves. (Other more liberal advocates of multiculturalism have argued that critiques of texts are the only *responsible action* in academic classes.)

I argue for activism as an indispensable component in learning. Action promotes consciousness of one's own political practice; such self-consciousness is a prerequisite to literacy. "Interest" in the lives of Black women and democratic struggles is superficial and the "knowledge" acquired specious if one remains illiterate in the language of community and commitment spoken by the women activists.

Activism promotes literacy. It is usually the greatest and most difficult learning experience, particularly if it is connected to communities and issues broader than the parameters of academic life.

Theory and philosophy "born in struggle" carry extremely difficult lessons. Activism concretizing ethical ideals in action, allows us to better comprehend a form of thinking unfamiliar in abstract academic thought—theorizing under fire or under conditions of confrontation or repression. Thinking to stay alive and be free is the heart of liberation praxis. For half a millenium, Indigenous and African peoples in the Americas and Africa have theorized for their individual lives and the life of the community. Theorizing as a life and death endeavor rather than leisured, idle speculation, embodies revolutionary praxis. As faculty we may find ourselves in positions where living by our beliefs and theory carries the hazards of not receiving grants, promotion or tenure; students may lose scholarships and higher grades. We rarely though find ourselves in positions where living by our ideals carries the possibility that we may die for them. We generally never have to risk our lives to claim our ideals and freedom, as have radical thinkers and activists such as: Harriet Tubman; Ann Moody; Assata Shakur; Martin Luther King, Jr.; Malcolm X; and, Fred Hampton.[18]

Several years ago, while a visiting scholar at a midwestern university, I was able to learn more about how risk-taking and radical organizing test ideas, ideologies and commitments. During my semester tenure, the Ku Klux Klan based in its national headquarters in Indiana decided to march and stage a rally in the local campus town. The general response against the march and rally centered on individual comments of fear and anger. There was little collective, organized response until one night, as part of a woman's film festival, a small number of students viewed William Greaves' video, "A Passion for Justice," on the life of Ida B. Wells. An African American woman senior

facilitated the discussion session that followed the video during which students shared how they were impressed by Ida B. Wells' courageous and influential activism, which began at such a young age, their age. They were silent when asked about the relationship between their feelings of inspiration for the story of Miss Wells' resistance and their feelings of anger and fear about the upcoming Klan march. Exploring these issues later that night in their dorm rooms, students began strategy sessions: they decided to allow their admiration for Miss Wells to lead them to organize a counter-educational critiquing racism, homophobia, sexism, and antisemitism in response to the impending KKK march.

African American women students led the organizing and formed a coalition with European Americans, European Jewish Americans and gay and lesbian activists. Some of these African American women students had experienced the most violent racial/sexual assaults on campus. At an early organizing meeting, one African American senior spoke of being dragged off a catwalk into bushes as her White male assailant yelled "nigger bitch" while repeatedly punching her. As she struggled away she noticed White student spectators who made no effort to assist or intervene. The woman student stated that the university's investigation and handling of the attack were equally unresponsive.

Faculty criticisms and complaints about White dominated universities did not translate into support for the student initiated organizing. Most African American faculty and administrators, like their White counterparts, were reluctant to publicly support a student "speakout" against racist, sexist, and homophobic violence critical of the university. University employees mirrored the divisions among African American students in which more cautious or conservative students dismissed student organizers as "radical" and ridiculed them for "overreacting." Political differences among African American students, faculty and administration were exacerbated during the KKK organizing.

Fear of criticizing the administration or faculty, along with homophobia, sexism and caste elitism allowed faculty and more conservative African American students to distance themselves from student activists. Yet students and youth face the greatest dangers from racial-sexual violence on campus and in society. Alongside community women and men, only two European American women and I as faculty actively organized with students educating against, in the wake of the Klan rally, increasing racist/antisemitic verbal abuse and physical violence on campus. The Klan rally highlighted faculty ambivalence and refusal to support student organizing and the university administration's unwillingness to publicly take an uncompromised stance against and responsible action for diminishing racist, antisemitic, homophobic, and sexual violence on campus.

It seemed that we faculty and administrators believed our class and caste status in academe granted us immunity from the violence assaulting many African American youth, women, and gay and lesbian students. My own inabilities, with others, to always speak and talk to community in the midst of organizing conflicts, were compounded by my impatience and frustration with the political rhetoric and passivity of nonactivists. The confusion and strains impressed on me the precarious balance of teaching and talking for justice and my own uncertainty and anger, with others, about the terrain of struggle and community.

COMMUNITY

Individual changes in classroom teaching to deconstruct racist-heterosexist curricula and build community are marginal if not supported by the department or program and other instructors. Often the struggles for more accuracy and accountability in education are labeled and depoliticized as personal (personnel) whims of faculty rather than responsible action. I have found that personalizing my confrontations with eurocentric thinkers or academic careerists is a form of depoliticization that contributes to my own isolation and ineffectualness. Supporting progressive curricula and pedagogies demands political change. Yet, my experiences show that few are willing to engage in the type of activism and restructuring necessary to supplant tokenism.

I share Toni Morrison's observations in "Rootedness: The Ancestor As Foundation," applying her thoughts on writing to teaching, another art form:

> If anything I do in the way of writing . . . isn't about the village or the community or about you, then it is not about anything. I am not interested in indulging myself in some private, closed exercise of my imagination that fulfills only the obligation of my personal dreams—which is to say, yes, the work must be political. It must have that as its thrust. That's a pejorative term in critical circles now: if a work of art has any political influence in it, somehow it's tainted. My feeling is just the opposite: if it has none, it is tainted.[19]

Academics and students, if not always content, seem comparatively "safe" from the political-economic conditions destroying African communities and villages. Educational status and economic "stability" grant us space to move about the world as if our survival were guaranteed, despite the increasing impoverishment and death of Africans worldwide.[20] Privilege may reduce our primary preoccupation in academia to struggles for accreditation and legitimacy from the intellectual representatives of the "new" old world order.

I am paid to, and so I pay my bills and taxes to the military, by teaching "theory" in a White university's White Women's Studies program in a White suburb called "Amherst." On my better days, I think freely about a people loving and theorizing for liberation. I try to think in the traditions in which philosophy and theory are the tools of initiates and "slaves"[21] to the community, rather than the techniques of academic employees; this is problematic in places where people talk and write about life and death in and to abstraction. Although at times afraid to forget and to always remember my indebtedness to the militant Black praxis that forced open the doors of White academia, I am grateful to the call to be in a tradition of midwifery to philosophizing and theorizing, a tradition that intends community and respect for African ancestors, the living, and future born.

Notes

1. Barbara Christian, "The Race for Theory," reprinted in *Making Face, Making Soul; Haciendo Caras,* edited by Gloria Anzaldua (San Francisco: Aunt Lute Foundation, 1990), 336.

2. Native American writer Lee Maracle notes the circular logic of academic theory: "Theory: If it can't be shown, it can't be understood. Theory is a proposition, proven by demonstrable argument. Argument: Evidence, proof. Evidence: demonstrable testimony, demonstration. . . . Argument is defined as evidence; proof or evidence is defined by demonstration or proof; and theory is a proposition proven by demonstrable evidence. None of these words exist outside of their inter-connectedness. Each is defined by the other." Lee Maracle, *Oratory: Coming to Theory.* North Vancouver, B.C. Gallerie Women Artists' Monographs, Issue 1 (September 1990), 3.

3. European American feminist Elizabeth Spelman cites this quote from a journal issue on African Americans and philosophy in her work *Inessential Woman: Problems of Exclusion in Feminist Thought.* (Boston: Beacon Press, 1988).

4. Amin continues: "Eurocentrism is a specifically modern phenomenon, the roots of which go back only to the Renaissance, a phenomenon that did not flourish until the nineteenth century. In this sense, it constitutes one dimension of the culture and ideology of the modern capitalist world." Samir Amin, *Eurocentrism* (New York: Monthly Review Press, 1989), vii.

5. Cornel West, "A Genealogy of Modern Racism," *Prophesy Deliverance* (Philadelphia: Westminster Press, 1982).

6. The phrase "White solipsism" comes from White lesbian feminist Adrienne Rich's article "Disloyal to Civilization: Feminism, Racism, Gynephobia," *On Lies, Secrets, and Silence* (New York: Norton, 1979). Solipsism is the belief that only one's self is knowable or constitutes the world.

7. Racist, classist, and (hetero)sexist thinking routinely garner the title of "philosophy" or universally true—even when Eurocentric studies decree a new universal truth that there is no "universal truth." Although Europeans and European thought were not and are not the center of the universe, "civilization," or "theory," what tends to accompany "de-centering" the European, as Barbara Christian notes in "The Race for Theory," is the claim that there is no center. That traditional African cosmology, or Native American cosmology, might contain a center is rarely raised in academic theory. The relativist claim of "no center," backed by the hegemony of White supremacy, is like the claims of being "color-blind" or "raceless" in a racist system. It is blindness by convenience to deny domination and struggles for equality.

8. See Chapter 3, "African Philosophy, Theory, and 'Living Thinkers'" in this anthology.

9. Generally in Women's Studies, White women choose the Black feminist/womanist scholars. Recently, I found myself in the odd position of comforting a White woman on her difficulty in securing a position as a professor in African American women's literature. All her interviews had been with European Americans who controlled the hiring process. White women decided which black woman they would hire for their "Black Women's Studies" line, based on their definition of Black feminism; since they decided on me, I'm working. I try to define and shape a program that respects rather than objectifies African people. The WORCC

proposal in the appendix is one such attempt. However, the Center for Teaching committee rejected it, reportedly as "controversial," and "something you would do anyway" without institutional support.

10. Patricia Hill Collins describes the ideology of this worldview where "research methods generally require a distancing of the researcher as a 'subject' with full human subjectivity and objectifying the "object" of study . . . the absence of emotions from the research process . . . ethics and values [as] inappropriate in the research process . . . adversarial debates . . . [as] the preferred method of ascertaining truth. . . ." See: Patricia Collins, "Learning from the Outsider Within: The Sociological Significance of Black Feminist Thought," *Social Problems* 33:6 and *Black Feminist Thought* (Boston: Unwin Hyman, 1990, reprint Routledge).

11. Patricia Hill Collins uncritically argues for such "rearticulation" in "Learning from the Outsider Within: The Sociological Significance of Black Feminist Thought," *Social Problems* 33:6 and *Black Feminist Thought.*

12. "When alien voices attempt to convey the African center, everything is lost in translation." K. Kia Bunseki Fu Kiau in a talk at the Caribbean Cultural Center in New York, January 1991, spoke of four different levels of language: level 1 of everyday life, level 2 of the esoteric or philosophical traditions of a people, and level 3 of those who mediate and translate between both levels. The fourth level came with colonization and conquest. Level 4, alien language, is where Europeans interrogated African people on level 1, the non-initiated. Foreigners believed they had encountered a whole people and their cosmology or lack of cosmology by speaking only with those on the level of everyday life.

13. For examples of ashé or power of African women see: *Gelede: Art and Female Power Among the Yoruba,* edited by Henry and Margaret Drewal (Bloomington: Indiana University Press), 74.

14. Eurocentric masculinist theory centers on White men while Eurocentric feminist theory (responding to the "gender," not race/class/heterosexual bias of masculinist Eurocentrism)

focuses on White women. This cohabitation reflects obedience to academic houserules: Eurocentric feminist theory courses are also taught within a White canon of "essential writings." The increasing role of European-american women in teaching Africanamerican women writers may merely signal increasing appropriation. Without a paradigmatic shift from Eurocentrism, appropriation features colorized reruns: the paradigm of White middle class women's victimization in blackface. Without an African centered paradigm from which to teach writings by women of color critiquing racist feminism, the center remains "White," and the works remain criticism of the prevailing hegemony not theorizing from African philosophy.

15. Academia's presentation of time and consequently the history of thought promotes the delusion that philosophy (and civilization) began with "the Greeks" rather than the African scholars who preceded and taught them, and the African civilizations which predate Athens. Voids in timelines manufacture artificial "origins" which, legitimizing European rule, deny the African ancestral lineage in European philosophy. "Ancient" becomes the 'sui generis' thinking of "Europeanized" Greeks; "Medieval" the European Christian Church, with a de-Africanized Augustine; "Modern" European Enlightenment philosophs; and "Contemporary" European (American) writers and thinkers." "Ancient," "Medieval," "Modern," and "Contemporary" as categories for time also become categories of space and "race," denoting geography and ethnicity. Theorists assigned in each category are invariably "White" men in masculinist theory (where Hannah Arendt qualifies as the "exceptional ("White") woman) and "White" women in feminist theory.

16. Bernice Johnson Reagon argues this about the work of Martin Luther King, Jr., see "Nobody Knows the Trouble I See"; or "By and By I'm Gonna Lay Down My Heavy Load," *Journal for American History* (Vol. 78, No. 1, June 1991).

17. Theologian Bernard Lonergan discusses in *INSIGHT: An Understanding of Human Knowing* (New York: Harper and Row, 1957) an

epistemology similar to the African (Afro-centric) ethical paradigm in which knowledge exists for the sake of communal good and individual human liberation (which are not presented as oppositional). Experience, reflection, judgment, and action are part of the process by which people (knowingly or unknowingly) learn. Action is indispensable to the learning process: you know how to ride a bicycle or drive a car not from merely reading books about bicycles or cars, but from riding or driving one as well (building furthers your knowledge). One knows how to live, learn and teach without patriarchal, White supremacist, or classist elitist assumptions by doing activities that confront and diminish racism, sexism, heterosexism, and classism.

18. Prior to his assassination by the FBI and Chicago police in 1971, Fred Hampton prophesied: "I'm going to die for the people because I live for the people." Quoted in "A Nation of Law? (1968–71)," *Eyes on the Prize, Part II* which documents Hampton's political work for the African American community, the FBI's disruption of the Black liberation movement and its eventual assassination of Fred Hampton and Mark Clark. This segment of *Eyes on the Prize, Part II* also covers the Attica uprising for prisoners' human rights and its violent repression by the New York State government.

19. Morrison, 344–45.

20. The U.S. dominates international financial institutions such as the World Bank and International Monetary Fund (IMF). These institutions have underdeveloped Africa, Latin America and the Caribbean so that we as a people are poorer in the 1990s than we were in the 1960s. According to UNICEF's 1988 report, *State of the World's Children,* the "Third World" is in debt to the U.S. and Western European nations/financial institutions for over $1000 billion (U.S. currency). People in the most impoverished countries in the world pay to the West more in interest and capital than they receive in new aid and loans: each year African, Caribbean, and Latin American nations transfer $20+ billion to historical colonizers. UNICEF estimates that over half a million young children died in 1988 because of these economic policies in which 14% of the world's population—U.S. and other "Western" elites—consumes 70% of its resources. While IMF austerity programs decimate lives and autonomy of regions, U.S./Western European based multinational or transnational corporations exacerbate dislocation, labor and sexual exploitation of women and children—the "docile" labor supply. In this economic crisis of contemporary colonialism, modern day vampirism of the Black World enriches foreign and native elites. At "home" the situation is not very different.

In the U.S. "austerity programs" against the poor take on a new dimension as the World Bank and IMF implement "development" projects for what remains of indigenous people's lands. African American people are poorer today than we were a generation ago: the "poverty draft" provides "equal opportunity employment" in military "service" or prison industries. Here, two out of three adults in poverty are women; with women of color twice as likely to be poor as White women. Here, an estimated 33 million people live below the whimsically set "poverty line." Millions live on the line and over one million do not even "register" because they are homeless. Ten percent of the U.S. people own 83% of the wealth and resources while twenty million are jobless. In some cities, up to 80% of the 16–19 year old African American youth have "dropped out" of the labor force; 70–80% are driven out of high schools. The National Urban League's 14th annual "State of Black America" (1988) report quantifies the results of the dominant U.S. philosophy and theory in practice: from 1984–1986, the life expectancy for Whites increased (from 75.3 years to 75.4), while the life expectancy for African Americans decreased (from 69.7 to 69.4 years); an African American infant is twice as likely to die in her/his first year as a White infant.

21. According to Bunseki Fukia, in Kongo philosophy the Nganga—the initiated elders and teachers—are "slaves" to the community (lecture, Caribbean Cultural Center, New York City, February 1991).

Essay/Discussion Questions

1. Joy James argues for a practice of teaching philosophy and theory that is rooted in black women's experiences and that is committed to social change and black community liberation. Can teaching avoid being political in an American society in which racial, class, and gender oppression and exploitation are deeply embedded?

2. According to James, what is a pedagogy of activism and liberation?

3. What are the benefits and burdens of a pedagogy of activism and liberation?

Part VI Key Terms

Basic skills

Brown v. Board of Education

Cultural clash

Desegregation

Hobson v. Hansen

Integration

League for Universal Justice and
Goodwill

Literacy

Pedagogy

Programmed retardation

Quality education

Tracking

Part VI Supplementary Readings

Anderson, James D., *The Education of Blacks in the South, 1860–1935*, Chapel Hill: The University of North Carolina Press, 1988.

Arons, Stephen, and Charles Lawrence III, "The Manipulation of Consciousness: A First Amendment Critique of Schooling," in Robert B. Everhart, ed., *The Public School Monopoly: A Critical Analysis of Education and the State in American Society*, Cambridge: Ballinger Publishing Company, 1982, pp. 225–268.

Barber, Benjamin R., *The Aristocracy of Everyone: The Politics of Education and the Future of America*, New York: Ballantine Books, 1992.

Bell, Derrick, "Brown v. Board of Education and the Interest-Convergence Dilemma," *Harvard Law Review*, Vol. 93 (January 1980), pp. 518–532.

Bond, Horace M., *The Education of the Negro in the American Social Order*, New York: Prentice-Hall, 1934.

Brazziel, William F., *Quality Education for All Americans*, Washington, D.C.: Howard University Press, 1974.

Bullock, Henry A., *A History of Negro Education in the South, from 1619 to the Present*, New York: Praeger Publishers, 1967.

Clark, Kenneth B., *Dark Ghetto: Dilemmas of Social Power*, New York: Harper and Row, Publishers, 1965.

Clark, Reginald M., *Family Life and School Achievement: Why Poor Black Children Succeed or Fail*, Chicago: The University of Chicago Press, 1983.

Coleman, James S., Ernest Q. Campbell, Carol J. Hobson, James McPartland, Alexander Mood, Frederic D. Weinfeld, and Robert L. York, *Equality of Educational Opportunity*, 2 Vols., Washington, D.C.: U. S. Government Printing Office, 1966.

Corson, William R., *Promise or Peril: The Black College Student in America*, New York: W. W. Norton and Company, Inc., 1970.

Dreyfuss, Joel, and Charles Lawrence III, *The Bakke Case: The Politics of Inequality*, New York: Harcourt Brace Jovanovich, 1979.

DuBois, W. E. B., *The Education of Black People: Ten Critiques, 1906–1960*, ed. Herbert Aptheker, New York: Monthly Review Press, 1973.

_____, "The Field and Function of the American Negro College," in Andrew G. Paschal, ed., *A W. E. B. DuBois Reader*, New York: Macmillan Publishing Co., Inc., 1971, pp. 51–69.

_____, "Does the Negro Need Separate Schools?" *Journal of Negro Education,* Vol. 4 (July 1935), pp. 328–335.

Edmonds, Ronald R., "Improving the Effectiveness of New York City Public Schools," in *The Minority Student in Public Schools: Fostering Academic Excellence*, Princeton: Educational Testing Service, Office for Minority Education, 1981, pp. 23–30.

Edwards, Harry, *Black Students*, New York: The Free Press, 1970.

Fleming, John E., Gerald R. Gill, and David H. Swinton, *The Case for Affirmative Action for Blacks in Higher Education*, Washington, D.C.: Howard University Press, 1978.

Foster, Michele, *Black Teachers on Teaching*, New York: The New Press, 1997.

The 14th Admendment and School Busing, Hearings Before the Subcommittee on the Constitution of the Committee on the Judiciary, United States Senate, Washington, D.C.: U. S. Government Printing Office, 1972.

Franklin, Vincent P., *The Education of Black Philadelphia: The Social and Educational History of a Minority Community, 1900–1950*, Philadelphia: University of Pennsylvania Press, 1979.

Franklin, Vincent P., and James D. Anderson, eds., *New Perspectives on Black Educational History*, Boston: G. K. Hall and Company, 1978.

Freire, Paulo, *Pedagogy of the Oppressed*, New York: Herder and Herder, 1972.

Garibaldi, Antoine, ed., *Black Colleges and Universities: Challenges for the Future*, New York: Praeger Publishers, 1984.

Giroux, Henry A., *Postmodernism, Feminism, and Cultural Politics: Redrawing Educational Boundaries*, Albany: State University of New York Press, 1991.

_____, *Theory & Resistance in Education: A Pedagogy for the Oppressed*, South Hadley: Bergin and Garvey Publishers, 1983.

Giroux, Henry A., and Peter McLaren, eds., *Critical Pedagogy, the State, and Cultural Struggle*, Albany: State University of New York Press, 1989.

Gurin, Patricia, and Edgar Epps, *Black Consciousness, Identity, and Achievement: A Study of Students at Historically Black Colleges*, New York: John Wiley and Sons, Inc., 1975.

Hale-Benson, Janice, *Black Children: Their Roots, Culture, and Learning Styles*, Baltimore: The Johns Hopkins University Press, 1982.

Hayes, Floyd W. III, "Politics and Education in America's Multicultural Society: An African American Studies' Response to Allan Bloom," *The Journal of Ethnic Studies*, Vol. 17, No. 2 (Summer 1989), pp. 71–88.

_____, *Retreat from Quality: Policy Intellectuals, Education Policymaking and Politics in a Changing Society*, Washington, D.C.: Institute for Independent Education, Inc., 1989.

_____, *Structures of Domination and the Political Economy of Black Higher Education in a Technocratic Era: A Theoretical Framework*, Occasional Papers, No. 3, Washington, D.C.: Institute for the Study of Educational Policy, 1981.

Henig, Jeffrey R., *Rethinking School Choice: Limits of the Market Metaphor*, Princeton: Princeton University Press, 1994.

Hochschild, Jennifer L., *Thirty Years After Brown*, Washington, D.C.: Joint Center for Political Studies, 1985.

_____, *The New American Dilemma: Liberal Democracy and School Desegregation*, New Haven: Yale University Press, 1984.

Investigation of the Schools and Poverty in the District of Columbia, Hearings Before the Task Force on Antipoverty in the District of Columbia of the Committee on Education and Labor, House of Representatives, Washington, D.C.: U. S. Government Printing Office, 1966.

James, Joy, *Resisting State Violence: Radicalism, Gender, and Race in U.S. Culture*, Minneapolis: University of Minnesota Press, 1996.

_____, *Transcending the Talented Tenth: Black Leaders and American Intellectuals*, New York: Routledge, 1996.

James, Joy, and Ruth Farmer, eds., *Spirit, Space, and Survival: African American Women in (White) Academe*, New York: Routledge, 1993.

Jones, Faustine C., *A Traditional Model of Educational Excellence: Dunbar High School of Little Rock, Arkansas*, Washington, D.C.: Howard University Press, 1981.

Katznelson, Ira, and Margaret Weir, *Schooling for All: Class, Race and the Decline of the Democratic Ideal*, Berkeley: University of California Press, 1985.

Kirp, David L., *Just Schools: The Idea of Racial Equality in American Education*, Berkeley: University of California Press, 1982.

Kluger, Richard, *Simple Justice: The History of Brown v. Board of Education and Black America's Struggle for Equality*, New York: Alfred A. Knopf, 1975.

Kozol, Jonathan, *Amazing Grace: The Lives of Children and the Conscience of a Nation*, New York: Crown Publishers, Inc., 1995.

_____, *Savage Inequalities: Children in America's Schools*, New York: Crown Publishers, Inc., 1991.

Lieberman, Myron, *Public Education: An Autopsy*, Cambridge: Harvard University Press, 1993.

Lightfoot, Sara, *The Good School: Portraits of Character and Culture,* New York: Basic Books, Inc., Publishers, 1983.

Lomotey, Kofi, ed., *Going to School: The African-American Experience*, Albany: State University of New York Press, 1990.

Lukas, J. Anthony, *Common Ground: A Turbulent Decade in the Lives of Three American Families*, New York: Alfred A. Knopf, 1985.

McLaren, Peter, *Critical Pedagogy and Predatory Culture: Oppositional Politics in a Postmodern Era*, New York: Routledge, 1995.

McNeil, Linda M., *Contradictions of Control: School Structure and School Knowledge*, New York: Routledge and Kegan Paul, 1986.

Meier, Kenneth J., Joseph Stewart, Jr., and Robert E. England, *Race, Class, and Education: The Politics of Second-Generation Discrimination,* Madison: The University of Wisconsin Press, 1989.

Misgeld, Dieter, "Education and Cultural Invasion: Critical Social Theory, Education as Instruction, and the 'Pedagogy of the Oppressed'," in John

Forester, ed., *Critical Theory and Public Life,* Cambridge: The MIT Press, 1985, pp. 77–118.

Moore, William, Jr., and Lonnie H. Wagstaff, *Black Educators in White Colleges,* San Francisco: Jossey-Bass Publishers, 1974.

Mosteller, Frederick, and Daniel P. Moynihan, eds., *On Equality of Educational Opportunity,* New York: Vintage Books, 1972.

National Commission of Excellence in Education, *A Nation at Risk: The Imperative for Educational Reform,* Washington, D.C.: U. S. Department of Education, 1983.

Nkomo, Mokubung, ed., *Pedagogy of Domination: Toward a Democratic Education in South Africa,* Trenton: Africa World Press, Inc., 1990.

Oakes, Jeanne, *Keeping Track: How Schools Structure Inequality,* New Haven: Yale University Press, 1985.

Orfield, Gary, *School Desegregation Patterns in the United States, Large Cities and Metropolitan Areas, 1968–1980,* Washington, D.C.: Joint Center for Political Studies, 1983.

_____, *Desegregation of Black and Hispanic Students from 1968 to 1980*, Washington, D.C.: Joint Center for Political Studies, 1982.

Persell, Caroline H., *Education and Inequality: The Roots of Stratification in America's Schools,* New York: The Free Press, 1977.

Peterson, Marvin W., Robert T. Blackburn, Zelda F. Gamson, Carlos H. Arce, Roselle W. Davenport, and James R. Mingle, *Black Students on White Campuses: The Impacts of Increased Black Enrollments,* Ann Arbor: Institute for Social Research/The University of Michigan, 1978.

Pride, Richard A., and J. David Woodard, *The Burden of Busing: The Politics of Desegregation in Nashville, Tennessee,* Knoxville: The University of Tennessee Press, 1985.

Rist, Ray C., *The Invisible Children: School Integration in American Society,* Cambridge: Harvard University Press, 1978.

_____, *The Urban School: A Factory for Failure—A Study of Education in American Society,* Cambridge: The MIT Press, 1973.

Rubin, Lillian B., *Busing and Backlash: White Against White in an Urban School District,* Berkeley: University of California Press, 1972.

Schapiro, Svi, *Between Capitalism and Democracy: Educational Policy and the Crisis of the Welfare State,* New York: Bergin and Garvey Publishers, 1990.

School Desegregation, Hearings Before the Subcommittee on Civil and Constitutional Rights of the Committee on the Judiciary, House of Representatives, Washington, D.C.: U. S. Government Printing Office, 1982.

Schere, Robert G., *Subordination or Liberation?: The Development and Conflicting Theories of Black Education in Nineteenth-Century Alabama,* The University of Alabama Press, 1977.

Shujaa, Mwalimu J., ed., *Too Much Schooling, Too Little Education: A Paradox of Black Life in White Societies,* Trenton: African World Press, Inc., 1994.

Scott, Hugh J., *The Black School Superintendent: Messiah or Scapegoat?* Washington, D.C.: Howard University Press, 1980.

Sowell, Thomas, *Inside American Education: The Decline, The Deception, The Dogmas*, New York: The Free Press, 1993.

_____, *Black Education: Myths and Tragedies*, New York: David McKay Company, Inc., 1972.

Thomas, Gail E., ed., *Black Students in Higher Education: Conditions and Experiences in the 1970s*, Westport: Greenwood Press, 1981.

Thompson, Daniel C., *Private Black Colleges at the Crossroads*, Westport: Greenwood Press, Inc., 1973.

U. S. Commission on Civil Rights, *Racial Isolation in the Public Schools*, Vol. I, Washington, D.C.: U. S. Government Printing Office, 1967.

Webber, Thomas L., *Deep Like the Rivers: Education in the Slave Quarter Community, 1831–1865*, New York: W. W. Norton and Company, Inc., 1978.

Willie, Charles V., ed., *The Sociology of Urban Education: Desegregation and Integration*, Lexington: Lexington Books, 1978.

Willie, Charles V., and Susan L. Greenblatt, eds., *Community Politics and Educational Change: Ten School Systems Under Court Order*, New York: Longman, 1981.

Willie, Charles V., and Ronald R. Edmonds, eds., *Black Colleges in America: Challenge, Development, Survival,* New York: Teachers College Press/ Columbia University, 1978.

Wolters, Raymond, *The Burden of Brown: Thirty Years of School Desegregation,* Knoxville: The University of Tennessee Press, 1984.

_____, *The New Negro on Campus: Black College Rebellions of the 1920s,* Princeton: Princeton University Press, 1975.

VII

Political Economy of the African American Situation

In colonial America, the African American struggle for collective survival and secular and spiritual salvation began under the most extreme conditions of economic exploitation—chattel slavery. Concomitantly, the governing white financial elite accumulated enormous wealth by means of the slave trade and from chattel slaves' free and exploited labor; this capital served as the basis of a rapidly growing American economy.

After slavery's abolition, the former bondspeople had to fight a continuous battle against geographical, socioeconomic, cultural, and political obstacles to improve their economic situation. At the dawn of the twentieth century, African Americans embarked on a historic journey from rural to urban and from southern to northern regions, seeking better life chances. In the process, they gradually refashioned themselves from mainly rural agricultural laborers to largely urban industrial workers. In the last quarter of the twentieth century, which is witnessing the decline of America's industrial manufacturing economy and the rise of a postindustrial-managerial economy, the trajectory of the African American economic predicament appears increasingly ambivalent. Impoverished inner-city enclaves are growing rapidly, yet there is also a class of college-educated and professional suburbanites and urban gentry.

The articles in this part profile the African American participation in the changing American political economy from chattel slavery to the contemporary period. In "The Demand for Black Labor: Historical Notes on the Political Economy of Racism," Harold M. Baron analyzes critically the manner in which America's capitalist economic exploitation and racist political oppression constrained African American economic development from the colonial period to the mid-1960s. Baron argues that African slave labor in colonial America contributed to the large-scale accumulation of wealth during the early stages of American capitalist development. But he reveals that the enslavement and exploitation of African labor could not have existed if it had depended on a market-oriented system alone. Baron suggests that white Europeans subordinated Africans and their American descendants by means of an elaborate culture of racial control, which became woven deeply into the fabric of American ideology, culture, and social and political institutional practices. Hence, the ideologies of profit maximization and white European supremacy, together with the institutional practices of the slave trade and chattel slavery, resulted in a veritable culture of domination that uniquely characterized the new American nation-state.

Baron points out that after slavery was abolished, the economic condition of the former bondspeople did not change substantially. Although international war and the rise of a new European middle class undercut chattel slavery in the Americas, the culture of racial control continued to operate in the American South. In the years from 1860 to World War I, Baron points out, African Americans' labor shifted from slavery to sharecropping and other forms of agrarian labor, which brought in barely subsistence wages. Slavery may have ended but the great mass of African Americans remained economically and politically powerless.

After the nation's transition from agrarian to industrial capitalism, Baron shows, skilled factory work initially went to white workers, while African American workers were either excluded or given unskilled menial jobs. Hence, white workers were not required to compete with African American workers for employment in the emerging industrial manufacturing sector of the economy. World War I set in motion the African American penetration into America's industrial labor force. Migrating to northern urban areas, African Americans initially entered such industries as steel, meat packing, and automobile manufacturing as strike breakers. Even then, there were particular jobs, usually the hardest and most dangerous, designated for African American workers. Especially during the Great Depression of the 1930s, white labor unions fought hard to maintain preferential employment practices for white workers and to institute racially discriminatory and exclusionary practices directed at African American industrial workers.

Baron shows that from World War II to the mid-1960s, African Americans made the transition to a largely urban working class population. African American organizations and leadership—for example, Marcus Garvey's black nationalist mass movement, the liberal National Association for the Advancement of Colored People, and A. Phillip Randolph's socialist Brotherhood of Sleeping Car Porters labor union— represented in various ways a new stage in the self-conscious, collective struggle of African American working masses to confront racially based political and economic oppression in America. Although economic conditions for the northern urban African American working class improved over those of their southern peasant counterparts, Baron argues that in America's metropolitan centers there arose a dual labor-market system—a primary market into which white workers were recruited and hired and a secondary one in which African American workers were recruited and hired. These conditions resulted in lower wages, higher job turnover, and higher unemployment for blue-collar urban African American workers. It was within this context that African American frustration with economic and racial subordination exploded into urban rebellions across America in the mid-1960s.

The work by Daniel R. Fusfeld and Timothy Bates, "Black Economic Well-Being Since the 1950s," investigates closely the African American economic situation since World War II. The authors describe areas of improvement and decline, suggesting that trends indicate a growing economic polarization within the African American community: younger and better-educated persons show improved income and occupational status; those persons with less education but with average skills experience the ups and downs associated with fluctuating economic conditions; and those at the bottom of the economic ladder are getting worse off, even experiencing conditions of semipermanent impoverishment. These changing employment trends coincide with shifts in regional patterns of industrial employment. The authors also suggest a pessimistic future for many urban African American industrial workers.

Fusfeld and Bates argue that indicators of African American economic progress since World War II are complicated. On the one hand and in comparison to whites, there was general improvement in individual income, education, white-collar employment, high visibility occupations (e.g., entertainment and professional sports) and professional-managerial positions in private enterprise. On the other hand, the authors show that conditions for many non-southern urban African Americans worsened, particularly among teenagers and adult males. These trends also have contributed to other patterns of social dislocation and represent a progressive deterioration of urban African American communities: increased female-headed households, out-of-wedlock births, teenage pregnancy, violent death among African American males, and imprisonment.

The authors closely analyze economic trends and developments during the 1950s, 1960s, 1970s, and 1980s. In the decade of the 1950s, the continuing northern and urban migration, together with ongoing racial discrimination in the industrial labor market, resulted in rising unemployment and underemployment for African Americans. This pattern was somewhat offset by some African American penetration into the white-collar occupational force. During the 1960s, improvements in African American economic and employment conditions resulted from better economic conditions generally, more opportunities in white-collar occupations, and anti-discriminatory civil rights activism. In the 1970s, general deterioration of industrial manufacturing cities (snowbelt) and a decline in the number of blue-collar jobs generally hurt African American employment. In the 1980s, shifting economic conditions were apparent as economic growth and development continued in cities and regions whose economies were based on human services and government (sunbelt). Under these conditions, young and well-educated African Americans experienced gains in professional, technical, and managerial occupations. Fusfeld and Bates suggest that in the new economy, the employment future for professionals is brighter than that for less-educated industrial workers; however, employment prospects for the uneducated are bleak.

Finally, Fusfeld and Bates comment on the emergence of big-city African American political executives and administrations. This is generally taking place in older, larger cities that are experiencing economic trauma and decline. The authors point out that election or appointment of African American political executives and administrators does not necessarily translate into general economic advancements for the great multitude of African American city residents.

The Demand for Black Labor: Historical Notes on the Political Economy of Racism

HAROLD M. BARON

The economic base of racism would have to be subjected to intensive analysis in order to get at the heart of the oppression of black people in modern America. If we employ the language of Nineteenth Century science, we can state that the economic deployment of black people has been conditioned by the operation of two sets of historical laws: the laws of capitalist development, and the laws of national liberation. These laws were operative in the slave era as well as at present. Today the characteristic forms of economic control and exploitation of black people take place within the institutional structure of a mature state capitalist system and within the demographic frame of the metropolitan centers. The economic activities of blacks are essentially those of wage (or salary) workers for the large corporate and bureaucratic structures that dominate a mature capitalist society. Thus today racial dynamics can be particularized as the working out of the laws of the maintenance of mature state capitalism and the laws of black liberation with the metropolitan enclaves (rather than a consolidated territorial area) as a base.

This essay places major emphasis on capitalist development. While attention will be paid to aspects of national liberation, it would be a very-different essay if that were the main point of concentration. Further, in order to make the inquiry manageable, it concentrates on the key relationship of the demand for black labor.

A backward glance at certain factors in the evolution of racism will help establish the cogency of the major categories that we employ in the analysis of the present day. Historically, the great press for black labor as the work force for plantation slavery simultaneously supplied the momentum for the formation of institutional racism and set the framework for the creation of the black community in the United States. The strength of this demand for black slaves, in regard to both the vast numbers of persons involved and its duration over centuries, was based on the dialectics of the relationship between slavery in the New World and the development of capitalism in Europe: Each provided necessary conditions for the other's growth.

A large-scale accumulation of capital was a prerequisite for the emergence of capitalism as the dominant system in Europe. Otherwise capitalism was doomed to remain basically a mercantile operation in the interstices of a primarily manorial economy. From the Sixteenth Century on, the strength of developing nation-states and their ability to extend their tentacles of power beyond the limits of Europe greatly accelerated the process that Marx called "the primitive accumulation of capital."

> The discovery of gold and silver in America, the extirpation, enslavement, and entombment in the mines of the aboriginal population, the beginning of the conquest and looting of the East Indies, the turning of Africa into a warren for the hunting of black skins, signalized the rosy dawn of the era of capitalist production. These idyllic proceedings are the chief momenta of primitive accumulation. This phase of the accumulation process was accomplished not only by domestic exploitation, but also by the looting of traditional stores of non-European peoples and the fostering of a new system of slavery to exploit their labor.[1]

In a sense European capitalism created, as one of the pre-conditions for its flourishing, a set of productive relations that was antithetical to the free-market, wage-labor system which characterized capitalist production in the metropolitan countries. English capitalism at home was nurturing itself on a proletariat created through the dispossession of the peasantry from the land, while at the same time accumulating much of the capital necessary to command the labor of this proletariat through the fixing of African deportees into a servile status in the colonies. "In fact, the veiled slavery of the wage-earners of Europe needed for its pedestal slavery pure and simple in the New World."

Slaves from Africa, at first in the mines and then on the plantations of the New World, produced goods that enlarged the magnitude of the circulation of commodities in international trade—a process that was essential to the mercantilist phase of capitalist history. Although this slavery was not capitalist in the form of production itself, that is was not based on the purchase of alienated wage labor,[2] the plantation system of the New World composed an integral part of the international market relations of the growing capitalist system. The demand for slaves was subject to mercantile calculations regarding production costs and market prices:

> Long before the trans-Atlantic trade began, both the Spanish and the Portuguese were well aware that Africa could be made to yield up its human treasure. But in the early part of the Sixteenth Century the cost of transporting large numbers of slaves across the Atlantic was excessive in relation to the profits that could be extracted from their labor. This situation changed radically when, toward the middle of the century . . . sugar plantings were begun in Brazil . . . and by the end of the Sixteenth Century sugar had become the most valuable of the agricultural commodities in international trade. Importation of Negroes from Africa now became economically feasible.[3]

Once in the world market, a commodity lost all the markings of its origin. No distinction could be made as to whether it was produced by free or slave labor. It became just a good to be bought and sold.

Production from the slave plantations greatly increased the volume of commodities in circulation through trade, but the social relations of slavery and racism rendered the black producers so distinctly apart that it was possible to appropriate a greater proportion of their product as surplus than it was through any other established mechanism that defined lowly social status. Two sets of conditions combined to make the exploitation of the New World slaves particularly harsh. First, the production of plantation goods for the impersonal needs of the rapidly expanding international market removed many of the restraints and reciprocities that had inhered in patriarchal forms of slavery in which production was essentially for home use. Second, since West Africa was outside of Christendom or Mediterranean civilization, there were few existing European cultural or political limitations that applied to the treatment of black chattels.

The economics of slavery could not have existed over an extended period as just a set of shrewd market-oriented operations. Elaboration of a whole culture of control—with political, social, and ideological formulations—was necessary to hold dominance over the black slaves and to keep the non-slave-holding whites in line. Given that the white Europeans were subjugating the black Africans, the culture of control became largely structured around a color-oriented racialism. "Slavery could survive only if the Negro were a man set apart; he simply had to be different if slavery were to exist at all." The development of a rationale regarding the degradation of all blacks and the formation of conforming institutional practices were necessary to maintain a social order based on enslavement of some blacks. Accordingly, this culture of racial control rapidly diffused throughout the whole of North Atlantic civilization and all the American colonies of its various nations. In the United States, racism—that is, subjugation based on blackness rather than on servitude alone—was more sharply defined than in most other places in the Americas.

When the European powers extended their influence down the African coast, they did not have sufficient military and economic advantage to establish sovereignty over the lands. They could only set up trading outposts. However first on islands off the coast of Africa and then on the islands and coastal lowlands of the Americas, the Europeans were able to gain control of the land, often exterminating the indigenous population. In such distant territories black workers from Africa could be driven in the mines and plantations free from any constraints that could be imposed by the states, tribes, and traditions of Africa. Set apart by their servitude and their blackness, they were

also removed from any rights that low-status groups within the metropolitan country might have had. Laboring on the American plantations came to embody the worst features of ancient slavery and the cash nexus.

Black chattel slavery, with the concomitant elaboration of institutional and ideological racism as its socio-political corollary, became a new type of societal formation. True, as David Brion Davis has pointed out, the institutions of New World slavery grew out of the forms of the late Middle Ages' Mediterranean slavery. Regarding racism, Winthrop Jordan has shown that the pre-existing derogatory imagery of darkness, barbarism, and heathenism was adapted to formulate the psychology and doctrines of modern racism.[4] While the adaptation of these available institutional and ideological materials provided the original forms for New World slavery, as a whole the system was something distinctly novel. This novelty was chiefly conditioned by the developing capitalist relations that provided the seemingly insatiable demand for plantation products. Accordingly, the demand for black labor under circumstances like these had to be different from any slavery that was indigenous to West Africa or had operated earlier in Europe.

Capitalism's stamp on New World slavery was sharply revealed via the slave trade that supplied the demand for black labor. Alongside the marketing of the output of slave labor, the trade in the bodies which produced these goods became a major form of merchant capitalistic enterprise in itself. Down into the Nineteenth Century the purchase of black slaves frequently was a constant cost of production. This held in extreme for parts of Brazil where it was considered more economical to work slaves to death within five to ten years and replace them with fresh purchases than to allow enough sustenance and opportunity for family living so that the slave force could be maintained by natural reproduction. The latest and most careful estimate of the total deportation of black slaves to the Americas is between 9,000,000 and 10,000,000. Up to 1810 about 7,500,000 Africans were imported—or about three times the number of Europeans immigrating in the same period.[5]

Slave trade and slave production brought wealth and power to the bourgeois merchants of Western Europe. As C. L. R. James has summed up the situation for France: "Nearly all the industries which developed in France during the Eighteenth Century had their origin in goods or commodities destined for either the coast of Guinea or America. The capital from the slave trade fertilized them. Though the bourgeois traded in other things than slaves, upon the success or failure of the (slave) traffic everything else depends." In the case of England, Eric Williams, in *Capitalism and Slavery*, has detailed in terms of manufacturing, shipping, and capital accumulation how the economic development of the mother land was rooted in New World Slavery.[6] But it is more dramatic to let a contemporary Eighteenth Century economist speak for himself:

> The most-approved judges of the commercial interest of these kingdoms have ever been of the opinion that our West Indian and African trades are the most nationally beneficial of any carried on. It is also allowed on all hands that the trade to Africa is the branch which renders our American colonies and plantations so advantageous to Great Britain; that traffic only affording our planters a constant supply of Negro servants for the culture of their lands in the produce of sugar, tobacco, rice, rum, cotton, pimento, and all plantation produce; so that the extensive employment of our shipping into and from our American colonies, the great brook of seamen consequent thereupon, and the daily bread of the most considerable part of our British manufacturers, are owing primarily to the labor of Negroes. . . .

WITHIN THE BOUNDARIES OF THE UNITED STATES

In the colonial period of the United States the commercial basis of all the colonies rested largely on the Atlantic trade in slave-produced commodities. The Southern colonies directly used a slave population to raise tobacco and rice for export. While the Northern colonies all had slave populations, their major links were auxiliaries to the Atlantic trade—growing provisions for the Caribbean plantations, developing a merchant marine to carry slaves to the islands and sugar to Europe. After Independence the slave production of cotton provided the base for the pre-Civil War economic take-off and industrial revolution:

> It was cotton which was the most important influence in the growth in the market size and the consequent expansion of the economy: . . . In this period of rapid growth, it was cotton that initiated the concomitant expansion in income, in the size of the domestic markets, and in the creation of social overhead investment (in the course of its role in marketing cotton) in the Northeast which were to facilitate the subsequent rapid growth of manufactures. In addition, cotton accounted for the accelerated pace of westward migration, as well as for the movement of people out of self-sufficiency into the market economy.

In the territory of the United States, the elaboration of plantation slavery had some distinctive features that are worthy of attention for the light that they shed on the present. For one thing the slave system here tended to become a self-contained operation in which the demand for new slaves was met by natural increase, with the slave deficit areas of the Lower South importing black bondsmen from the Upper South. Self-containment was also defined in that there were few possibilities that a black man could achieve any other status than that of slave—involuntary servitude and blackness were almost congruent. Plantations operating under conditions of high prices for manufactured goods and easy access to their own land holdings for whites had been forced to train black slaves as artisans and craftsmen. As one scholar concluded:

Indeed, it is hard to see how the Eighteenth Century plantation could ever have survived if the Negro slave had not made his important contribution as an artisan in the building and other trades calling for skill in transforming raw materials into manufactured articles. The self-sufficiency of the Southern colonies necessitated by the Revolution was more successful than it could have been if the Negro slave artisan had not been developing for generations before.

But skills only exceptionally led to freedom. Even the relatively small number of what John Hope Franklin calls "quasi-free Negroes" tended to lose rights, both in the North and in the South, after the adoption of the Constitution. By way of contrast, in Latin America an extensive free black population existed alongside a large number of freshly imported slaves.

The position of the "quasi-free Negro" is one of the most important keys to understanding later developments. Sheer economic conditions operated to prevent him from developing a secure social status. The flourishing of the cotton culture sustained a high demand for slaves at the same time that state and federal illegalization of the slave trade reduced the importation of Africans. Therefore limitations on both the numbers and prerogatives of non-slave blacks functioned to maintain the size of the slave labor force. The completeness with which race and slavery became merged in the United States is revealed by a review of the status of blacks on the eve of the Civil War. About 89% of the national black population was slave, while in the Southern states the slave proportion was 94%. The status of the small number of quasi-free Negroes was ascribed from that of the mass of their brothers in bondage. Nowhere did this group gain a secure economic position; only a few of them acquired enough property to be well off. In the countryside, by dint of hard work, a few acquired adequate farms. Most, however, survived on patches of poor soil or as rural laborers. Free blacks fared the best in Southern cities,

many of them being employed as skilled artisans or tradesmen. The ability of free blacks to maintain a position in the skilled trades was dependent on the deployment of a larger number of slaves in these crafts and industrial jobs. Slave-owners provided a defense against a color bar as they protected their investment in urban slaves. However the rivalry from a growing urban white population between 1830 and 1860 forced blacks out of many of the better jobs, and in some cases out of the cities altogether. "As the black population dropped, white newcomers moved in and took over craft after craft. Occasionally to the accompaniment of violence and usually with official sanction, slave and free colored workers were shunted into the most menial and routine chores."

Basic racial definitions of the slave system also gained recognition in the North, through the development of a special servile status for blacks. During the colonial era, Northern colonies imported slaves as one means of coping with a chronic labor shortage. While most blacks were employed in menial work, many were trained in skilled trades. "So long as the pecuniary interests of a slave-holding class stood back of these artisans, the protests of white mechanics had little effect. . . ." With emancipation in the North, matters changed. As Du Bois further noted concerning Philadelphia, during the first third of the Nineteenth Century, the blacks, who had composed a major portion of all artisans, were excluded from most of the skilled trades. Immigrants from Europe soon found out that, although greatly exploited themselves, they could still turn racism to their advantage. The badge of whiteness permitted even the lowly to use prejudice, violence, and local political influence to push blacks down into the lowest occupations. In 1850, 75% of the black workers in New York were employed in menial or unskilled positions. Within five years the situation had deteriorated to the point at which 87.5% were in these categories. Northern states did not compete with slave states for black workers, even when labor shortages forced them to encourage the immigration of millions of Europeans. Through enforcement of fugitive slave laws and discouragement of free black immigration, through both legal and informal means, the North reinforced slavery's practical monopoly over blacks.

For the pre-Civil War period, then, we can conclude that there was no significant demand for black labor outside the slave system. The great demand for black workers came from the slave plantations. No effective counterweight to plantation slavery was presented by urban and industrial employment. As a matter of fact, in both North and South the position of the urban skilled black worker deteriorated during the generation prior to the Civil War. In the South the magnitude of cities and industries was limited by the political and cultural imperatives inherent in hegemony of the planter class. Whatever demand there was for black labor in Southern cities and industries was met essentially by adapting the forms of slavery to these conditions, not by creating an independent pressure for free blacks to work in these positions.

To a large extent the more-heightened form of racism in the United States grew out of the very fact that the USA was such a thoroughgoing bourgeois society, with more bourgeois equalitarianism than any other nation around. Aside from temporary indenture, which was important only through the Revolutionary era, there were no well-institutionalized formal or legal mechanisms for fixing of status among whites. Up to the Civil War the ideal of an equalitarian-yeoman society was a major sociopolitical factor in shaping political conditions. Therefore if the manumitted slave were not marked off by derogation of his blackness, there was no alternative but to admit him to the status of a free-born enfranchised citizen (depending on property qualifications prior to the 1830s).

Under these circumstances the planter class made race as well as slavery a designation of condition. A large free black population that had full citizens' rights would have been a threat to their system. They therefore legislated limitations on the procedures for manumission and placed severe restrictions on the rights of free blacks. Low-status whites who did have citizens' rights were encouraged by the plantocracy to identify as whites and to emphasize racial distinctions so as to mark themselves off from both slave and free blacks precisely because this white group did have a legitimate place in the political process. Fear of competition from blacks, either directly or indirectly through the power of large planters, also gave the large class of non-slave-holding whites a real stake in protecting racial distinctions. In Latin America, by contrast, the remnants of feudal traditions regarding the gradations of social ranks already provided well-established lowly positions into which free Negroes or half-castes could step without posing a threat to the functional hegemony of the slave-master class. Further, given the small number of Europeans and the great labor shortage, ex-slaves provided ancillary functions, such as clearing the frontier or raising food crops, that were necessary for the overall operation of the slave system.[7]

This absoluteness of racial designation, so intimately related to the character of bourgeois order in this nation, meant that racism became intertwined in the entire state system of rule. That is to say that not only were the procedures of slave control and racial derogation of the blacks embodied in the Constitution and other fundamental features of state action, but these mechanisms soon interpenetrated the general state operations for the control of certain classes of whites over other whites. Therefore, while racism was as American as apple pie, and was subscribed to in some form even by most white abolitionists, it also became a special weapon in the regional arsenal of the Southern plantocracy in their contention for a dominant position in determination of national policy. The planters' employment of racist appeals proved effective on a national basis, especially in the generation prior to the Civil War, only because an underlying acceptance of their assumptions existed in all regions. Domestically within the South, racism operated to cement the solidarity of all whites under the hegemony of the planter class—even though slavery provided the power base from which the plantocracy were able to subordinate the white yeomanry. This strategy met with success, for the intensification of racist propaganda during the ante-bellum period was accompanied by a slackening of attacks on the plantation system. In return for the security granted to the base of their power, the planters had to make some concessions to the poor whites regarding formal rights of citizenship such as extension of the franchise and legislative reapportionment; but alterations in form did not change the fundamental power relations. The racialist culture of control merged into both the political apparatus and the social forms of hegemony by which white class rule was sustained. White rule was not identical with, but did mediate, the rule of the plantocracy over all of Southern society.

THE TRANSITION ERA, FIRST PHASE: 1860 TO WORLD WAR I

So far we have been establishing a comprehension of some of the underlying contradictions that frame the control of black labor by examining their origins in the slave era. Before we turn to the present period there is another set of relationships that will provide further conceptual illumination: the conditions that underlay the abolition of slavery. One set of factors lay in the world development of capitalism itself. The bourgeoisie's seizure of power in the French Revolution destabilized that nation's colonial regime and undermined the slave system by promulgating the doctrine of the rights of man as a universal dictum. In England, the expansion of its capitalist might into Asia gave rise to a powerful political inter-

est counter to that of the West Indian planters; plus, the success of the industrial revolution created the material base for envisioning a liberal bourgeois order with thorough formal equality. In the United States, the demise of slavery occurred in the midst of a war that established the further course of capitalist development—whether it would proceed on a "Prussian model," with the planters playing the role of the Junkers, or the industrialists and little men on the make would independently establish their hegemony through an entrepreneurially oriented state.

The other source of abolition lay in the role of the black people in the Americas. Denied the right to reconstruct their African societies, they strove to survive and reconstitute themselves as a people. Amidst the plantations and the black quarters of the cities, a new community was formed. At crucial points these black communities transcended the need for survival and struck out for liberation. While sabotage, escapes, and uprisings were consistent themes of New World slavery, the key move was the successful revolt of the black Jacobins in Haiti under the leadership of Toussaint L'Ouverture, which set an example for black and other oppressed people from that time on. By winning their freedom and defeating the most powerful armies in the world, these revolutionaries not only forced changes in the relative relations of the forces in Europe, but also undermined much essential confidence in the continuing viability of the slave system as a whole. It was little accident that both the British and the U.S. abolition of the slave trade followed shortly on the heels of the Haitian revolution.

In the United States, where a large white population was always close at hand, there were few important slave revolts, and even those were invariably put down before they could become well established. Black self-determination took the form of day-to-day slave resistance, and the development of an independent political line within the abolitionist movement. Most important, the role of black people in the Civil War converted it into a struggle for their own freedom. As Du Bois cogently summarizes:

> Freedom for the slave was a logical result of a crazy attempt to wage war in the midst of four million black slaves, trying the while sublimely to ignore the interests of those slaves in the outcome of the fighting. Yet these slaves had enormous power in their hands. Simply by stopping work, they could threaten the Confederacy with starvation. By walking into the Federal camps, they showed to doubting Northerners the easy possibility of using them as workers and as servants, as spies, as farmers, and finally as fighting soldiers. And not only using them thus, but by the same gesture depriving their enemies of their use in just these fields. It was the fugitive slave who made the slaveholders face the alternative of surrendering to the North or to the Negroes.

The Civil War destroyed the Southern plantocracy as a major contender for the control of national power. For a decade during Reconstruction, the freedmen struggled to establish themselves as an independent yeomanry on the lands they had worked for generations. However both South and North agreed that blacks were to be subservient workers—held in that role now by the workings of "natural" economic and social laws rather than the laws of slavery. The Compromise of 1877 was the final political blow to black Reconstruction, remanding to the dominant white Southerners the regulation of the black labor force.

Abolition of slavery did not mean substantive freedom to the black worker. He was basically confined to a racially-defined agrarian labor status in which he was more exploited than any class of whites, even the landless poor. White land-owners extracted an economic surplus from the labor of blacks through a variety of arrangements, including peonage, wage labor, sharecropping, and rent tenancy. Even the black owners of land were often dependent on white patronage for access to the small plots of inferior soil to which they usually held title. Profits predicated on low wages or onerous share arrangements were often augmented by long-term indebtedness at usurious rates of interest for advances of provisions and supplies. Many a sharecropper and laborer would not realize any appreciable money income for years on end.

The methods of labor control over the black peasantry did not greatly raise net labor costs over those of the slavery era. In both eras the black masses received only enough to survive and reproduce. Pressure on profits came from falling commodity prices rather than from rising labor costs. "The keynote of the Black Belt is debt. . . ." wrote W. E. B. Du Bois at the turn of the century. "Not commercial credit, but debt in the sense of continued inability of the mass of the population to make income cover expenses." Of conditions in Dougherty County, Georgia he wrote:

> In the year of low-priced cotton, 1898, of 300 tenant families 175 ended their year's work in debt to the extent of $14,000; 50 cleared nothing; and the remaining 75 made a total profit of $1600. . . . In more prosperous years the situation is far better—but on the average the majority of tenants end the year even or in debt, which means they work for board and clothes.

From the obverse side white planters in racist language gave their supporting testimony to this extra economic exploitation of the black peasants. One Alabama landlord declared: "White labor is totally unsuited to our methods, our manners, and our accommodations. No other laborers (than the Negro) of whom I have any knowledge would be so cheerful or so contented on four pounds of meat and a peck of meal a week, in a little log cabin 14 by 16 feet, with cracks in it large enough to afford free passage to a large-size cat." From Mississippi a planter spoke to the same theme: "Give me the nigger every time. The nigger will never 'strike' as long as you give him plenty to eat and half clothe him: He will live on less and do more hard work, when properly managed, than any other class or race of people."[8]

Black agriculturists were important to the economic development of the South and the nation. Raw cotton production tripled between 1870 and 1910. Consumption of cotton by domestic manufacturers increased six-fold from 800,000 bales in 1870 to 4,800,000 bales in 1910. Cotton continued to be the United States' leading export commodity in global trade, still accounting for a quarter of the value of all merchandise exports on the eve of World War I—in spite of the fact that prices had decreased greatly through international competition as the European powers encouraged cotton production in the overseas areas in which they were augmenting their imperial power. Such rapid growth of cotton production (and that of other farm commodities) implied a great demand for black workers in the fields. Characteristically blacks were engaged on the cotton plantations, especially those with richer lands. The form of engagement was roughly divided between sharecropping, wage labor, and rental tenancy. Between 1890 and 1910 the number of black men in agriculture increased by over half a million, or 31%. During this entire period three out of five black men were employed in agriculture.

Maintaining the semi-servile status of the black labor force required the augmentation of colorcaste distinctions. Southern slavery, after all, had been more than just an economic arrangement: it was a cultural system that provided a wide range of norms congruent with plantation discipline. Slave status had served as a line of demarcation throughout the society. Therefore emancipation not only changed the economic form of planter control, but also left gaps in the social superstructure that reinforced it. Under these conditions the strengthening of racialism per se in all cultural arrangements became an imperative for any hope of continuance of the planters' hegemony over Southern society. Since racism had pervaded all major facets of social and political control, much of the further elaboration of colorcaste distinctions arose in the course of the Southern ruling class's struggles to keep the rest of the whites in line.

The road to the establishment of this new system of order in the South was by no means a smooth one. Abrogation of the slave system had made possible some new types of mobility among both blacks and whites, bringing about changes in the forms of inter-racial conflict and class conflict. Blacks were now able to move geographically, even in the face of continued legal and extralegal restraints. The migration that took place was mainly a westerly one within the South. Inside the black community class mobility developed through the emergence of a small middle class. At the same time, there now opened up to poorer whites areas that had formerly been the preserve of slavery. During the pre-Civil War era no white would compete with a slave for his position on the plantation. Albeit when planters and slaveless small farmers did contend for land, as frequently occurred, the black slave was indirectly involved. With emancipation, racial rivalry for the soil became overt. Freedmen struggled to gain land, sometimes as owners but more frequently as indebted tenants. At the same time, many white small-holders, forced out from infertile and worn soil, sought many of the same lands. After the Civil War the white farmers increased in numbers at a greater rate than the blacks. By 1900, even as tenants, the whites were in the majority. Blacks moved from a noncompetitive status in slavery (or perhaps better "concealed competition between the bond and the free"), as Rupert Vance has pointed out, to a condition of overt interracial competition. "As slaves Negroes were objects of race prejudice; as a new competitive group struggling for status and a place on the land Negroes found themselves potential objects of mass pressure and group conflict."

Transformations also took place within the Southern ruling class. Ownership of land tended to shift out of the hands of the old planter class into those of merchants, lawyers, and in some cases Northern interests, removing many of the impediments to land-owners' making their decisions more markedly, on the basis of pure entrepreneurial calculations. This partial unfreezing of labor and capital resources provided some important preconditions for the industrialization of the South. Nevertheless, the ideal for black labor in the eyes of dominant white groups was that of a contented agrarian peasantry. Paternalistic members of the Southern elite spoke of satisfied workers controlled by fair but rigidly enforced rules. "Let the Negro become identified with and attached to the soil upon which he lives, and he himself, the landowner, and the country alike will be advanced by his labor."

In the social and political realms the conflicts inherent in the black peasantry's subjugation became intertwined with the conflicts inherent in the subordination of any potential political power in the hands of the white smallholders and landless. As things turned out, blacks were to suffer both from the control of the propertied and from the competition of the poor. The political process provided a major means by which this was carried out. "It is one of the paradoxes of Southern history," writes C. Vann Woodward, "that political democracy for the white man and racial discrimination for the black were often products of the same dynamics." The imperatives of preserving class rule supplied the basis of the paradox: "It took a lot of ritual and Jim Crow to bolster the rule of white supremacy in the bosom of a white man working for a black man's wage." Functionally the poorer whites were permitted to influence the formal political process only under conditions that would not undermine the essential power and economic control of the ruling class. The execution of this strategy was completed during the defeat of the Populist movement in the 1890s by excluding the black people from politics and by heightening the color-caste distinctions through an extension of Jim Crow laws

and customs. Since the black people had already been defeated through Redemption 20 years before, the moves to disfranchise black people at the turn of the century had as "the real question . . . which whites would be supreme." Ruling circles channeled disfranchisement to their own ends "as they saw in it an opportunity to establish in power 'the intelligence and wealth of the South' which could of course 'govern in the interests of all classes.'"[9] Many whites as well as blacks were denied the ballot, and the substantive differences expressed in the political process were delimited to a narrower range. Inter-class conflicts among whites were much displaced by inter-racial conflicts, and the hegemony of larger property interests was secured.

The agrarian designation of the black masses was reinforced by the lack of competition for their labor from other sectors of the economy. The Southern demand for factory help, except for unskilled work, was essentially a demand for white labor. The textile industry, the primary industry of the New South, was marked off as a preserve of the white worker. The mythology that black workers were incapable of measuring up to the conditions in the textile mills was reinforced by the rationale that the domestic peace required that white poor have some kind of economic preserve, free from competition.

> Thus when the industrialization of the South began about 1880 and attained remarkable proportions by the outbreak of the (First) World War, it had comparatively little significance for the Negro agricultural workers. . . . The poor whites took the cotton mills as their own; and with the exception of sweeping, scrubbing, and the like in cotton factories, there was virtually no work for the Negroes in the plants. They were, therefore, compelled to labor on the farms, the only other work that was available.

The rather-considerable increase in industrial employment of blacks between 1890 and 1910 was concentrated in railroading, lumbering, and coal mining—that is, in non-factory-type operations with these three industries often located in rural areas. Lumbering and allied industries could almost have been considered an extension of agriculture, as the workers shifted back and forth from one to the other. Outside of agriculture the vast bulk of black workers were to be found either in domestic and personal service or in unskilled menial fields that were known in the South as "Negro jobs." In the cities the growth occupations were chiefly porters, draymen, laundresses, seamstresses. However non-propertied whites did begin to crowd into many skilled positions that had been the black man's preserve under slavery. Black mechanics and artisans, who had vastly outnumbered Southern whites as late as 1865, fought a losing battle for these jobs down to 1890, when they were able to stabilize a precarious minority position in some of the construction trades.

Exclusion of black workers from industry was not based on rational calculation regarding the characteristics of the labor supply. Contrary to all the racist rationales about incapacity and lack of training, most industrial firms considered blacks good workers. When the employers were questioned specifically about the comparative quality of black and white workers in their plants, the majority held that they were equally satisfactory. The Chattanooga Tradesman in 1889 and 1891, on its own, and again in 1901 in cooperation with the Atlanta University Sociology Department, made surveys of firms employing skilled and semi-skilled blacks. The Tradesman's editor concluded from the results that "the Negro, as a free laborer, as a medium skilled and common worker, is by no means a 'failure' . . . he is a remarkable success." In the 1901 survey over 60% of the employers held that their black workers were as good as or better than their white workers.

Northern ruling classes were quick to accept those conditions in the South that stabilized the national political system and provided

the raw commodities for their mills and markets. Therefore they supported the establishment of a subservient black peasantry, the regional rule of the Southern propertied interests, and the racial oppression that made both of these things possible. The dominant Northern interests shared the ideal of the smooth kind of racial subjugation projected by the paternalistic Southern elite, but they went along with what proved necessary. "Cotton brokers of New York and Philadelphia, and cotton manufacturers of New England . . . knew full well the importance of bringing discipline to the Southern labor force. When theories of Negro equality resulted in race conflict, and conflict in higher prices of raw cotton, manufacturers were inclined to accept the point of view of the Southern planter rather than that of the New England zealot." Northern businessmen who supported black education in the South had in mind a system that would encourage the students to stay in rural areas and would train them for hard work and menial positions.[10]

Thus, through a process that Harvard's Paul Buck approvingly called *The Road to Reunion* and Howard's Rayford Logan scathingly labeled *The Betrayal of the Negro,* national political, business, and intellectual elites came to define race as a Southern question for which they would not assume any leadership. By 1900 Southern sympathizer and Northern anti-slavery man alike agreed on the rightfulness of the subjugation of the black man. It was accepted as a necessary condition for order in the American state. And order was most essential to the extraordinary expansion of the industrial system. Beyond that point the black man was ignored and considered a "nothing," especially on Northern ground. Reasons of state and racism had combined to legitimize the new form of agrarian thralldom.

In the North itself during this period there was minimal work for blacks, even though the Northern economy was labor-starved to the extent that it promoted and absorbed a European immigration of over 15,000,000 persons. Blacks were not only shut off from the new jobs, but lost many of the jobs they had traditionally held. The Irish largely displaced them in street paving, the Slavs displaced them in brickyards, and all groups moved in on the once-black stronghold of dining-room waiting. Study the chapters on economic life in Leon Litwack's *North of Slavery: The Negro in the Free States, 1790–1860* and Leslie Fishel's unfortunately unpublished dissertation "The North and the Negro, 1865–1900: A Study in Race Discrimination."[11] They both read as if they are describing the same situation. If there is a difference, it is that Fishel describes a greater decline in status.

The reasons for this displacement of black workers in the North are complex. Northern capital engaged Southern workers, both black and white, by exporting capital to the South rather than by encouraging any great migration, thus enabling itself to exploit the low wage structure of the economically backward South while avoiding any disturbance in its precarious political or economic balance. Sometimes racism would operate directly, as when the National Cash Register Company (Dayton, Ohio) laid off 300 black janitors because the management wanted to have white farm boys start at the bottom and work their way up.[12] In addition, job competition often led white workers to see blacks, rather than employers, as the enemy. At least 50 strikes, North and South, in which white workers protested the employment of blacks have been recorded for the years 1881 to 1900.[13] There was a minor counter-theme of class solidarity which existed to a certain extent in the Knights of Labor and was reaffirmed by the Industrial Workers of the World, but as the job-conscious American Federation of Labor gained dominance over the union movement, racial exclusion became the operative practice, with the only major exception occurring among the United Mine Workers. (It was actually more common in the South than in the North for black workers to hold a position so strong in particular industries that unions had to take them into account; in these instances they were generally organized in separate locals.) Episodes in which blacks were used as strikebreakers contributed to the unions' hostility toward blacks, but it should be added that racism seriously distorted the perceptions of white workers. Whites were used as scabs more frequently and in larger numbers, but the saliency of racial categories was able to make the minority role of blacks stand out more sharply, so that in many white workers' minds the terms "scab" and "Negro" were synonymous.[14]

The course of national development of black people was set within the framework of their concentration in the Southern countryside. During Reconstruction a truly heroic effort was made by the black masses to establish a self-sufficient yeomanry on the land. Smashing of this movement set back the progression of independent black militancy more than a generation. New forms of embryonic nationalism emerged or re-emerged. Exodus groups tried with a certain success to establish themselves on the land in Kansas, Oklahoma, and Indiana. Pan-Africanism appeared once again with interest in colonization. But the major expression took place in a muted form through the role of Booker T. Washington, who, as August Meier has shown so well, had his base in the black people's desire for racial solidarity, their struggle for land and for the preservation of crafts, and the aspirations of a rising bourgeoisie in the cities which derived its livelihood from the black masses. Washington's social and political accommodations allowed the movement to exist and even gain support from Northern and Southern ruling circles. At the same time Washington's withdrawal from socio-political struggle reflected the weak post-Reconstruction position of black people in the agrarian South. Militant forms of black national liberation would not re-emerge until a black proletariat had developed in the urban centers.

THE TRANSITION ERA, SECOND PHASE: WORLD WAR I TO WORLD WAR II

The new equilibrium of racial regulation that had stabilized around tenancy agriculture as the dominant force of black exploitation received its first major disturbance from the impact of World War I. A certain irony inheres in the condition that imperialism's cataclysm should begin the break-up of agrarian thralldom within the United States. The War's effect on black people took place through the mediation of the marketplace, rather than through any shake-up of political relations. Hostilities in Europe placed limitations on American industry's usual labor supply by shutting off the flow of immigration at the very time the demand for labor was increasing sharply due to a war boom and military mobilization. Competition with the Southern plantation system for black labor became one of the major means of resolving this crisis of labor demand.

The black labor reserve in the countryside that had existed essentially as a *potential* source of the industrial proletariat now became a very *active* source. Whereas in the past this industrial reserve had not been tapped in any important way except by rural-based operations such as lumbering, with the advent of the War the industrial system as a whole began drawing on it. This new demand for black workers was to set in motion three key developments: first, the dispersion of black people out of the South into Northern urban centers; second, the formation of a distinct black proletariat in the urban centers at the very heart of the corporate capitalist process of production; third, the break-up of tenancy agriculture in the South. World War II was to repeat the process in a magnified form and to place the stamp of irreversibility upon it.

Migration out of the countryside started in 1915 and swept up to a human tide by 1917. The major movement was to Northern cities, so that between 1910 and 1920 the black population increased in Chicago from 44,000 to 109,000; in New York from 92,000 to 152,000;

in Detroit from 6,000 to 41,000; and in Philadelphia from 84,000 to 134,000. That decade there was a net increase of 322,000 in the number of Southern-born blacks living in the North, exceeding the aggregate increase of the preceding 40 years. A secondary movement took place to Southern cities, especially those with shipbuilding and heavy industry.

Labor demand in such industries as steel, meat-packing, and autos was the key stimulant to black migration. The total number of wage-earners in manufacturing went from 7,000,000 in 1914 to around 9,000,000 in 1919—an increase twice that of any preceding five-year period. A survey of the experience of the major employers of black labor in Chicago reported that "Inability to obtain competent white workers was the reason given in practically every instance for the large number of Negroes employed since 1914." A contemporary U.S. Government report stated:

> All of these employment managers and the higher executives of Northern industry are sadly worried by their labor problem. They feel that things are going from bad to worse; that even wage increases can avail little; they hope for national labor conscription for the period of the War as the only adequate solution to their problem, and are eager for Federal aid. . . . The majority of executives interviewed were favorable to the experiment with Negro employment in the North, and were sympathetic to suggestions concerning selection, training, housing, and recreation for the newcomer.[15]

The profit-maximization imperatives of Northern capitalist firms for the first time outweighed the socio-political reasons for leaving the Southern planters' control over black labor undisturbed and without any serious competition.

Labor agents sent South by railroad and steel companies initiated the migration by telling of high wages and offering transportation subsidy. In some cases whole trainloads of workers were shipped North. Though American firms had employed labor recruiters for work among

(Upper left) A tenant farmer and his wife, photographed in 1941. (Upper right) The son of a family of migrant strawberry pickers sits in the doorway of the family's quarters, 1939. (Bottom left) A family of sharecroppers is forced to move from their farm in Missouri during the depth of the Great Depression, 1939.

the European peasantries for decades, this was the first time they went forth in any strength to bring black peasants to the city. Many Southern localities tried to protect their labor stocks by legislating proscriptions on labor agents and charging them prohibitive license fees, but on the whole recruiters played only a secondary role. A more important impetus to migration came from the Northern-based black press, most notably the *Chicago Defender,* and above all from the letters and the reports of blacks who had already moved north. Successful employment served as its own advertisement, and better wages outside the South proved very attractive. During the summer of 1917 male wage-earners in the North were making $2.00 to $2.50 a day while the money wages on Mississippi farms ranged from 75¢ to $1.25.[16] Early migrations to Northern cities had been from the Upper South. Now blacks came in from all over, with the Deep South having the heaviest representation. In many cotton areas boll-weevil invasions destroyed the crop, acting as a push off the land at the same time Northern industry was providing a pull.

There was a temporary slackening of the demand for black labor when post-war demobilization caused heavy unemployment. In Chicago, where as many as 10,000 black laborers were out of work, the local Association of Commerce wired to Southern chambers of commerce: "Are you in need of Negro labor? Large surplus here, both returned soldiers and civilian Negroes ready to go to work."[17] In Detroit in 1921, black unemployment rates were five times as great as those of native white workers, and twice as great as those of the foreign born. But a strong economic recovery at the very time that restrictive immigration laws went into effect brought a second great migration out of the South in the years 1922 to 1924. The magnitude of this second movement has been estimated at slightly under a half-million persons, and may have been greater than that of the wartime movement.[18] The employers who already had a black sector in their work force

were able to tap this supply with much less trouble and cost than had been incurred a few years before. As William Graves, personal assistant to Julius Rosenwald, told the Chicago Union League Club: "The Negro permanency in industry was no longer debatable."[19]

The tremendous social dislocations created by the mobilization and the wartime economic boom heightened inter-racial tensions and laid the groundwork for over 20 race riots that occurred on both sides of the Mason-Dixon Line. Careful studies of the two major race riots in Northern industrial centers (East Saint Louis in 1917 and Chicago in 1919) reveal the tremendous friction that had developed between white and black workers.[20] These hostilities were not simply an outgrowth of race prejudice, for in both cases employers had fostered competition for jobs, especially by employing blacks as strikebreakers. Conflict between working-class whites and working-class blacks was analogous in a way to the previously-discussed racial competition among tenants and smallholders for land in the South. When the conflict erupted into mass violence, the dominant whites sat back and resolved the crises in a manner that assured their continued control over both groups.

The first feature of the program that Northern industry developed in relation to the inter-racial conflicts that the riots evidenced was that the permanency of black workers in the North was conclusively established. Management accepted its interest in guaranteeing minimal survival conditions of housing, education, et cetera to perpetuate this labor force. Even during slack times business had to maintain a certain continuity of employment, especially in those jobs that functionally became Negro jobs. Economically, even in a recession, long-run costs are reduced if something of a permanent work force is retained, for when good times return the recruitment and training of an entirely new labor force can require a great monetary outlay. Thus, as the 1920s wore on, while there was a virtual cessation of articles regarding the employment of blacks in business-oriented and welfare publications, the fact that blacks *would* be employed was now accepted. The shifting of racial stereotypes to fit the new situation was indicated by a business spokesman who reported that the black man "has lost his slovenliness, lazy habits, gambling, and liquor-drinking propensities." He noted that plant superintendents in heavy industry had come to consider black workers especially tractable. "They found Negroes on the whole far more adjustable than the foreign-born. They used a common language, were loyal in times of stress, and were more cooperative in matters such as stock purchases, buying insurance, et cetera."

At the same time, it has to be understood that black workers were employed on management's own terms. Sometimes these terms would involve the deliberate use of blacks to divide the work force. As a case in point, International Harvester integrated the hiring of blacks into its open-shop policies. Part of its strategy was to keep any nationality group from becoming too numerous in any one plant lest they become cohesive in labor conflicts. The decision on hiring was left up to the individual plant superintendents, some keeping their shops lily-white, others hiring large numbers of black workers. Harvester's management was caught up in a contradiction between its need for black workers, especially in the disagreeable twine mill and foundry, and its desire to keep them below 20% at any one plant.

A somewhat different approach was taken by Ford Motor Company. In the 1921 depression Henry Ford decided to maintain the black work force at the gigantic River Rouge plant in the same proportion as blacks in the total population of the Detroit area. The great majority of blacks at the River Rouge plant were employed in hot, heavy jobs in the rolling mills and foundry, but it was company policy to place a few in every major production unit and even allow a certain amount of upgrading to skilled positions. At the other Ford

plants, as at the other major auto companies, black workers were confined to hard unskilled jobs. But the job concessions at Rouge became a mechanism by which Ford was able to gain considerable influence over Detroit's black community. Hiring was channeled through some preferred black ministers who agreed with Henry Ford on politics and industrial relations. Company black personnel officials were active in Republican politics and in anti-union campaigns. Ford had learned early a racial tactic that is widely employed today— that of trading concessions, relaxing economic subordination in order to increase political subordination.

In industry generally the black worker was almost always deployed in job categories that effectively became designated as "Negro jobs" This classification, openly avowed in the South, was often claimed in the North to be merely the way things worked out through application of uniform standards. The superintendent of a Kentucky plough factory expressed the Southern view:

> Negroes do work white men won't do, such as common labor; heavy, hot, and dirty work; pouring crucibles; work in the grinding room; and so on. Negroes are employed because they are cheaper. . . . The Negro does a different grade of work and makes about 10¢ an hour less.

There was not a lot of contrast in the words of coke works foremen at a Pennsylvania steel mill: "They are well fitted for this hot work, and we keep them because we appreciate this ability in them." "The door machines and the jam cutting are the most undesirable; it is hard to get white men to do this kind of work." The placement of workers in separate job categories along racial lines was so marked in Detroit that in response to a survey many employers stated that they could not make a comparison between the wages of whites and blacks because they were not working on the same jobs.[21] In the North there was some blurring of racial distinctions, but they remained strong enough to set the black labor force off quite clearly. While the pay for the same job in the same plant was usually equivalent, when blacks came to predominate in a specific job classification, the rate on it would tend to lag. White and black workers were often hired in at the same low job classification; however for the whites advancement was often possible, while the blacks soon bumped into a job ceiling. In terms of day-to-day work, white labor was given a systematic advantage over black labor and a stake in the racist practices.

Northern management's public equal-opportunity posture to preserve their black work force was expressed with clarity at a 1920 conference of officials from five Chicago firms, employing over 6,000 workers, and an official of the Chicago Urban League:

> All of these labor managers expressed the opinion that there would be no reduction in the force of Negro employees. They cited the shortage of men for heavy labor, due to the lack of immigration from abroad, and all said that their companies were eager to employ more Negroes. Equal pay for the same work to whites and to Negroes was given as general practice. General satisfaction with Negro labor was expressed, and the ability of their Negro workers is equal, they said, to that of white workers of corresponding education. All mentioned the advantage, as compared with various immigrant groups, of a common language, enabling all foremen and officers to speak directly with the men. No discrimination in use of restaurants, sanitary facilities, et cetera was reported. All testified that Negroes were given the same opportunities as white workers for advancement to higher positions. The fact that a smaller percentage of Negroes are to be found in the higher positions is due, they said, to the fact that a smaller proportion are as well educated.

The amazing thing about this meeting is that if the references to the immigrants are deleted it has the sound of similar sessions that are held today—half a century later.[22]

In the South, where four-fifths of the nation's black population still lived at the end of the 1920s, the situation of black labor was to all appearances essentially unchanged. The number of black men engaged in Southern industry grew during this decade only 45% as fast as the number of whites. Black workers were concentrated in stagnant or declining plants, such as sawmills, coal mines, and cigar and tobacco factories. The increased hiring of blacks in such places was chiefly a reflection of the fact that the jobs had no future and the employers were not able to attract white workers. Black employment in textiles was severely limited, as in South Carolina, where state law forbade blacks to work in the same room, use the same stairway, or even share the same factory window as white textile workers. Industry in the South, as far as black workers were concerned, still offered little competition to the dominance of agrarian tenancy.

Beneath the surface, however, significant changes were taking place in the rural South. While as late as the mid-1930s Charles S. Johnson could write of a cotton county in Alabama that "The plantation technique on the side of administration was most effective in respect to discipline and policing, and this technique has survived more or less despite the formal abolition of slavery," this state of affairs was then being undermined. Cotton cultivation was moving westward, leaving many blacks in the Southeast without a market crop. Out in the new cotton lands in Texas and Oklahoma whites provided a much larger proportion of the tenants and sharecroppers. By 1930 a slight decrease was seen in the number of black farm operators and laborers. Later, the great depression of the 1930s accelerated this trend as the primary market for agricultural commodities collapsed and the acreage in cotton was halved. Black tenants were pushed off land in far greater proportions than whites. New Deal agricultural programs were very important in displacing sharecroppers and tenants, since they subsidized reductions in acreage. In the early government-support programs landlords tended to monopolize subsidy payments, diverting much of them out of tenants' pockets. When the regulations were changed in the tenants' favor, the landowner had an incentive to convert the tenants to wage laborers or dismiss them altogether so as to get the whole subsidy.[23] The great depression marked the first drastic decline in the demand for black peasants since their status had been established after the Civil War.

In 1940 there were 650,000 fewer black farm operators and laborers than there had been a decade earlier—representing a one-third drop in the total. The push out of the countryside helped maintain a small net rate of migration to the North. More significantly, however, during the depression decade a high rate of black movement to the city kept on while the rate of white urbanization slackened greatly.

Although the great majority of black people remained in the rural South, we have dealt primarily with the character of the demand for black workers in the course of their becoming established directly in the urban industrial economy. This initial process was to form the matrix into which the ever-increasing numbers of black workers were to be fitted. As the size of the black population in big cities grew, "Negro jobs" became roughly institutionalized into an identifiable black sub-labor market within the larger metropolitan labor market. The culture of control that was embodied in the regulative systems which managed the black ghettos, moreover, provided an effective, although less-rigid, variation of the Jim Crow segregation that continued with hardly any change in the South. Although the economic base of black tenancy was collapsing, its reciprocal superstructure of political and social controls remained the most powerful force shaping the place of blacks in society. The propertied and other groups that had a vested interest in the special exploitation of the black peasantry were still strong enough to maintain their hegemony over matters concerning race. At the same time, the variation of Jim Crow that existed in the North was more than simply a carry-over from the agrarian South. These ghetto controls served the class function for industrial society of politically and socially setting off that section of the proletariat that was consigned to the least desirable employment. This racial walling off not only was accomplished by direct ruling-class actions, but also was mediated through an escalating reciprocal process in which the hostility and competition of the white working class was stimulated by the growth of the black proletariat and in return operated as an agent in shaping the new racial controls.

The prolonged depression of the 1930s that threw millions out of work severely tested the position of blacks in the industrial economy. Two somewhat contradictory results stood out for this period. First, whites were accorded racial preference as a greatly disproportionate share of unemployment was placed on black workers. Second, despite erosion due to the unemployment differential, the black subsectors of the urban labor markets remained intact.

In the first years of the slump, black unemployment rates ran about two-thirds greater than white unemployment rates. As the depression wore on, the relative position of the black labor force declined so that by the end of the decade it had proportionately twice as many on relief or unemployed in the Mid-Atlantic States, and two and a half times as many in the North Central States. In the Northern cities only half the black men had regular full-time employment. In the larger cities, for every four black men in full-time regular employment there was one engaged in government-sponsored emergency relief. The differential in the South was not as great, for much of the unemployment there was disguised by marginal occupations on the farms.

The rationing out of unemployment operated in such a way as to reinforce the demarcation of "Negro jobs." Blacks were dismissed in higher proportions from the better positions. In Chicago they were displaced from professional and managerial occupations at a rate five times that of whites. The displacement rate from clerical, skilled, and semiskilled jobs was three times larger, while from unskilled and service jobs it was down to twice that of whites. As a result the total percentage of skilled and white-collar workers in the black labor force declined to half its former proportion, and the servant and personal service sector expanded again. Nationally, blacks lost a third of the jobs they had held in industry, declining from 7.3% to 5.1% of the total manufacturing employment. In the South the continuous unemployment even made white workers bid for those jobs in the tobacco industry that for generations had been recognized as "Negro jobs." An example from Northern industry: International Harvester no longer had a dire need for black workers, and the company let them slip off from 28% to 19% in the twine mill, and 18% to 10% at the McCormick Works.

The limited openings available to black job-seekers were in precisely those fields that were defined as "Negro jobs." Therefore, in the urban areas, young white workers with less than a seventh-grade education had a higher rate of unemployment than blacks. With grade-school and high-school diplomas, however, the whites' chances for jobs increased markedly while blacks' chances actually declined. In general increased age and experience did not improve the black worker's position in the labor market.

On the eve of World War II, when defense production really began to stimulate the economy, the number of jobs increased rapidly. At first, however, it was almost as if the black unemployed had to stand aside while the whites went to work. In April 1940, 22% of the blacks (about 1,250,000 persons) were unemployed, as were 17.7% of the white labor force. By October, employment had increased by 2,000,000 jobs, and white unemployment had declined to 13%, while black unemployment remained at the same level. Firms with tremen-

dous labor shortages still abided by their racial definitions of jobs and refused to take on available black workers. In September 1941 a U.S. Government survey found that of almost 300,000 job openings, over half were restricted to whites. In Indiana, Ohio, and Illinois, 80% of the openings were thus restricted.

Military mobilization of much of the existing labor force and an almost 20% growth in non-farm employment from 32,000,000 in 1940 to 40,000,000 in 1942 were the preconditions necessary to enlarge the demand for black labor. While the President's creation of the Fair Employment Practices Committee (FEPC) under pressure from black organizations helped open up some doors, it was the logic of the labor market that shook the racial status quo. By 1942, management-oriented publications were dealing with the question of employing black workers—a topic they had not considered since the mid-1920s.

The American Management Association told its members: "As some shortages develop for which there is no adequate supply of labor from the usual sources, management is forced to look elsewhere. It is then that the Negro looms large as a reservoir of motive power—a source which management has hitherto given only a few furtive, experimental pokes with a long pole." Once more surveys were conducted which showed that most employers consider black workers as efficient as whites. Management reiterated statements about nondiscrimination when production conditions forced them to change their racial hiring practices. *Fortune* magazine consoled its executive readers that their personal racism need not be violated: "Theoretically, management should have fewer objections to hiring colored labor than any other part of the industrial team. The employer seldom has social contact with his workers anyway, and his primary concern is production efficiency and satisfactory investment return."

Nationally, the demand for black labor was tremendous. In the spring of 1942 it composed 2.5% to 3% of the war-production work force, and by the fall of 1944 this proportion had risen to 8.3%. These million and a half black war workers were concentrated in the areas of the most stringent labor shortage. Fourteen industrial centers accounted for almost half of these war workers, and of these centers only one was located in the South and only two were border cities. In areas of acute labor shortage, the absence of any white reserve of labor gave blacks much greater access to war work than in labor surplus areas. Black migration was a necessary condition for this employment, and the movement of the families out of the Southern countryside and small towns was accelerated.

The vast demand for labor in general, that had to turn itself into a demand for black labor, could only be accomplished by way of a great expansion of the black sectors of metropolitan labor markets. Training programs for upgrading to skilled and semi-skilled jobs were opened up, at first in the North and later in the South. By 1943-1944, 35% of preemployment trainees in shipbuilding courses and 29% in aircraft were blacks. World War I had established a space for black laborers as unskilled workers in heavy industry. During World War II this space was enlarged to include a number of semi-skilled and single-skilled jobs in many industries.

World War II marked the most dramatic improvement in economic status of black people that has ever taken place in the urban industrial economy. The income of black workers increased twice as fast as that of whites. Occupationally, blacks bettered their positions in all of the preferred occupations. The biggest improvement was brought about by the migration from South to North (a net migration of 1,600,000 blacks between 1940 and 1950). However within both sections the relative proportion of blacks within skilled and semi-skilled occupations grew. In clerical and lower-level professional work, labor shortages in the government bureaucracies created a necessity for

a tremendous black upgrading into posts hitherto lily-white.

During the era between the two World Wars the national aspirations of blacks worked themselves out on the base of their new material conditions—that is, those of their becoming an urban people whose masses were proletarians. Conflicting tendencies beset this movement at every stage. The dominant white society usually followed the strategy of denying the very existence of its peoplehood. The black community was considered a pathological form rather than something valid in itself. Whenever the black community did thrust itself forward, the tactics of management shifted to a balance of naked repression with co-optive channeling. Within the community there was a constant contention as to which of the class forces would dominate—the black bourgeoisie, that sector of the black working class operating under the dominance of white trade-union organizations, or a nationally-based black working class.

The greatest organized expression of black nationalism occurred in the Garvey Back-to-Africa Movement after 1920. As Harry Haywood has so trenchantly characterized this broad mass development, it was conditioned by the convergence of two class developments:

> On the one hand it was the trend of the recent migrants from the peasant South. . . . The membership of these organizations by and large was composed of the new, as yet non-integrated Negro proletarians; recent migrants from the cotton fields, who had not yet shaken the dust of the plantation from their heels and remained largely peasants in outlook. Embittered and disillusioned by postwar terror and unemployment, they saw in the Garvey scheme of a Negro nation in Africa a way out to the realization of their deep-grounded yearnings for land and freedom. . . . On the other hand, Garveyism reflected the ideology of the Negro petty bourgeoisie, their abortive attempt at hegemony in the Negro movement. It was the trend of the small property-holder: the shopkeepers, pushed to the wall, ruined or threatened with

ruin by the ravages of the crisis; the frustrated and unemployed Negro professionals—doctors and lawyers with impoverished clientele, storefront preachers, poverty-stricken students—in sum those elements of the middle class closest to the Negro laboring people and hence affected most keenly by deterioration of their conditions.

When the migration of black peasants to the Northern cities dropped off in the mid-1920s, the Garvey movement began to lose out, and the US Government was able to move in with prosecutions to break it up.

The more-successful entrepreneurial types, such as the bankers, insurance executives, and newspaper publishers, were able now to seize the lead in the cities. They generated an optimism about the future of black capitalism that has never been recaptured. This group, which provided services chiefly to a black clientele, lost out when the depression brought wholesale bankruptcy, and this experience smashed illusions about the future of black business.

Proletarian leadership now re-emerged on a firmer foundation of having assimilated its new conditions of existence. From the masses themselves there was a surge of battles in the cities for emergency relief and against housing evictions. This intervention of the working class and unemployed inserted a new vigor into the "Don't Buy Where You Can't Work" campaigns that bourgeois leadership had initiated to win jobs from white firms operating in the ghetto. In 1935 a riot broke out in Harlem, and for the first time blacks moved from a defensive posture in such a situation and employed violence on a retaliatory basis against the white store-owners. As concessions were gained, part of the energy was channeled into the New Deal relief bureaucracy and Democratic Party politics, where patronage and paternalism took the edge off much independent thrust. Nevertheless, important struggles for jobs, government-supported housing, and more territory for living space helped consolidate an institutional infrastructure for the black community and gave an urban definition to its national consciousness, or race pride, as it was called in those days.

The trade-union organizing drives of the CIO which actively sought out black workers in heavy and mass-production industry provided a new focus. From 1937 to World War II the CIO conducted the most massive working-class campaign that has ever taken place in America. Its dynamism was so great that it reset the direction of the political activity of the working class, the black community, and the Left. Even the bourgeois-led organizations, like the NAACP, came to accept the decisive leadership role of the CIO. While black workers played an integral part in this organizing campaign, with over 200,000 members in the CIO ranks by 1940, the black working class did not develop an independent program or organization that dealt with the national oppression of their people.

Only after the outbreak of World War II, when blacks were still being excluded from much of the rapidly expanding economy, did a black movement set out independently from the New Deal-labor coalition and take the initiative in defining a race position on the national level. In January 1941 A. Philip Randolph, President of the Brotherhood of Sleeping Car Porters, an all-black AFL union, issued a call for a massive march on Washington to demand of the Government a greater share in the defense effort. The March on Washington Movement expressed the mood of the black community and received an upswelling of support sufficient to force President Roosevelt to establish a Fair Employment Practices Committee in return for the calling off of the projected march. Although this movement was not able to establish a firmly organized working-class base or sustain itself for long, it foreshadowed a new stage of development for a self-conscious black working class with the appeal that "An oppressed people must accept the responsibility and take the initiative to free themselves."

Sleeping car porter on trains was a job exclusively given over to blacks. The porters joined together in a union, the Brotherhood of Sleeping Car Porters, and were able to mount effective labor actions.

CURRENT CONDITIONS OF DEMAND—
AN OUTLINE

(A full examination of the present-day political economic conditions regarding the demand for black labor requires a whole separate essay. We are limited here to indicating some of the most essential features.)

The changes that took place in the economic deployment of black labor in World War II were clearly an acceleration of developments that had been under way since World War I. In a process of transition, at a certain point the quantity of change becomes so great that the whole set of relationships assume an entirely different character. Such a nodal point took place during World War II, and there resulted a transformation in the characteristic relations of institutional racism from agrarian thralldom to a metropolitan ghetto system.

Within a generation, few of the concrete economic or demographic forms of the old base remained. In 1940, over three-fourths of all blacks lived in the South, close to two-thirds lived in rural areas there, and just under half were still engaged in agriculture. By 1969, almost as many blacks lived outside the South as still resided in that region, and only 4% of the black laborers remained in agriculture, as they had left the farms at a much more rapid rate than whites. Today, only about a fifth of the total black population live in the rural areas and small towns of the South.

The United States, during the Twentieth Century, has become a distinctively urban nation—or, more accurately, a metropolitan nation with its population centered in the large cities and their surrounding configurations. The first three decades of this century witnessed the rapid urbanization of whites; the next three decades saw an even more rapid urbanization of blacks. In 1940 the proportion of the country's black population living in urban areas (49%) was the same as that proportion of whites had been in 1910. Within 20 years, almost three fourths of all blacks were urban dwellers, a higher proportion than the corresponding one for whites. More specifically, the black population has been relocated into the central cities of the metropolitan areas—in 1940, 34% of all blacks resided in central cities; in 1969, 55%. The larger cities were the points of greatest growth. In 1950 black people constituted one out of every eight persons in the central cities of the metropolitan areas of every size classification, and one out of every twenty in the suburbs. By 1969, black people constituted one out of every four in the central city populations of the large metropolitan areas (1,000,000 plus), and about one out of six in the medium-size metropolitan areas (250,000 to 1,000,000), while in the smaller-size metropolitan areas (below 250,000) and the suburbs the proportions remained constant. Today black communities form major cities in themselves, two with populations over 1,000,000, four between 500,000 and 1,000,000, and eight between 200,000 and 500,000. Newark and Washington DC already have black majorities, and several other major cities will most likely join their ranks in the next 10 years.

The displacement of blacks from Southern agriculture was only partially due to the pull of labor demand in wartime. Technological innovation, being a necessary condition of production, acted as an independent force to drive the tenants out of the cotton fields. The push off the land occurred in two phases. Initially, right after the war, the introduction of tractors and herbicides displaced the cotton hands from full-time to seasonal work at summer weeding and harvest. The now part-time workers moved from the farms to hamlets and small towns. During the 1950s mechanization

of the harvest eliminated most of the black peasantry from agricultural employment and forced them to move to the larger cities for economic survival.

Elimination of the Southern black peasantry was decisive in changing the forms of racism throughout the entire region, for it meant the disappearance of the economic foundation on which the elaborate superstructure of legal Jim Crow and segregation had originally been erected. Not only did this exploited agrarian group almost vanish, but the power of the large landholders who expropriated the surplus it had produced diminished in relation to the growing urban and industrial interests. While the civil-rights movement and the heroic efforts associated with it were necessary to break the official legality of segregation, it should be recognized that in a sense this particular form of racism was already obsolete, as its base in an exploitative system of production had drastically changed. The nature of the concessions made both by the ruling class nationally and by the newer power groups of the South can be understood only in terms of this fuller view of history.

For the United States as a whole, the most important domestic development was the further elaboration and deepening of monopoly state capitalism. As the political economy has matured, technological and management innovation have become capital-saving as well as labor-saving. Capital accumulation declines as a proportion of the gross national product, and a mature capitalist economy enters into a post-accumulation phase of development. Under these conditions the disposal of the economic surplus becomes almost as great a problem as the accumulation of it. Corporations promote consumerism through increased sales effort, planned obsolescence, and advertising. The State meets the problem by increasing its own expenditures, especially in non-consumable military items, by providing monetary support to consumption through subsidies to the well-off, and by spending a certain amount on welfare for the working class and the poor. Markedly lower incomes would add to the surplus disposal problems and would create economic stagnation as well as risking the most-disruptive forms of class struggle.

Working-class incomes have two basic minimum levels, or floors. One is that which can be considered the level of the good trade union contract which has to be met even by non-union firms that bid in this section of the labor market. State intervention is usually indirect in the setting of these incomes, but has grown noticeable in the last few years. The other income floor is set by direct government action via minimum-wage and welfare legislation. In the Northern industrial states where trade unions are stronger, both these income floors tend to be higher than in rural and Southern states.

Although in the mature capitalist society both economic and political imperatives exist for a certain limiting of the exploitation of the working class as a whole, each corporation still has to operate on the basis of maximizing its profits. The fostering of a section of the working class that will have to work at the jobs that are paid at rates between those of the two income floors works to meet the needs of profit maximization. Other jobs that fall into this category are those that might pay at the collective bargaining contract level but are subject to considerable seasonal and cyclical unemployment, and those from which a high rate of production is squeezed under hard or hazardous conditions. In all the developed Western capitalist states, there exists a group of workers to fill the jobs that the more politically established sectors of the working class shun. These marginal workers generally are set apart in some way so that they lack the social or the political means of defending their interests. In Western Europe usually they are noncitizens coming from either Southern Europe or Northern Africa. In England they are colored peoples coming from various parts of the Empire. In the urban centers of the United States race serves to mark black and brown workers for filling in the undesirable slots.

Further, in the distribution of government transfer payments each class and status group strives to maximize its receipts. Therefore the powerless tend to receive a smaller proportion of these funds, and those that are delivered to them come in a manner which stigmatizes and bolsters political controls.

Specifically, in the metropolitan centers in America, there is a racial dual labor-market structure. Side by side with the primary metropolitan job market in which firms recruit white workers and white workers seek employment, there exists a smaller secondary market in which firms recruit black workers and black workers seek jobs. In the largest metropolitan areas this secondary black market ranges from one-tenth to one-quarter of the size of the white market. For both the white and black sectors there are distinct demand and supply forces determining earnings and occupational distribution, as well as separate institutions and procedures for recruitment, hiring, training, and promotion of workers.

The distinctiveness of these two labor forces is manifested by many dimensions—by industry, by firm, by departments within firms, by occupation, and by geographical area. Within all industries, including government service, there are occupational ceilings for blacks. In a labor market like that of the Chicago metropolitan area, there are a number of small and medium-size firms in which the majority of the workers are black. However about two-thirds of the small firms and one-fifth of the medium ones hire no blacks at all. In larger firms a dual structure in the internal labor market marks off the position of the black worker along the same lines that exist in the metropolitan labor market.

A review of black employment in Chicago in 1966 finds that blacks tend to work in industries with lower wages, higher turnover, and higher unemployment. Further, they are also over-represented in the industries which exhibit sluggish growth and obviously less chance for advancement. Black men provide a third of the blue-collar workers in such industries as textiles, retail stores, primary metals, and local transportation, while in utilities, advertising, and communication they constitute less than 6%. Black women are even more concentrated in furnishing over half the blue-collar women workers in five industries—personal services, education, retail stores, hotels, and railroads.

In terms of internal labor market segregation, one of the Chicago firms best known as a fair-practice employer has a major installation located in the black community in which blacks constitute 20% of the blue-collar workers and less than 5% of the craftsmen and white-collar workers. A General Motors plant with 7500 workers is reported to have 40% black semi-skilled operatives, but only between 1% and 2% black craftsmen. A foundry firm will have one black clerk out of nearly 100 white-collar workers, while 80% of its blue-collar operators will be black.

The most-detailed information we have on racial dualism for an internal labor market is for the Lackawanna plant of Bethlehem Steel Company near Buffalo. The Lackawanna plant is a major employer of black workers in the Buffalo labor market. In 1968 it employed 2600 out of a total black labor force of about 30,000 for the area. Within the plant blacks constituted about 14% of the work force, which runs in the neighborhood of 19,000. The majority of black employees were assigned to only five of the plant's departments, while only 15% of the whites were in the same units. Within the individual units, blacks were given either the hardest or the lowest-paying jobs. In the plant's Coke Oven Department blacks held 252 out of 343 of the labor jobs, while whites held 118 out of 119 craft jobs. Blacks predominated in the battery and coal-handling units, where the top job paid $3.12 an hour. Whites made up the bulk of the work force in the better-paying by-products and heating units, which had hourly pay rates ranging up to $3.42 and $3.65.

Basic Steel is a high-labor-turnover industry. From April 1, 1966 to December 31, 1967 the Lackawanna plant hired about 7000 workers. Black job-seekers obviously identified the firm as being active in this labor market. Although 30% to 50% of the job applicants were black, the initial screening ended up with only 20% blacks among those newly hired. Prospects were screened by a general-aptitude test the passing score for which was not validated by any measure of performance. As the labor market tightened, the passing score lowered. About an eighth of those hired were hired without taking a test, and 96% of this category were whites. The Supervisor of Employment also gave clear preference to residents of Angola, a nearly all-white suburb. Once on the payroll, a majority of the newly hired blacks were assigned to one of the five departments in which most of the black workers already were placed. Only 20% of newly hired whites were assigned to these departments, all of which were among the hotter and dirtier locations in the plant.

The dual labor market operates to create an urban-based industrial labor reserve that provides a ready supply of workers in a period of labor shortage and can be politically isolated in times of relatively high unemployment. In a tight labor market the undesirable jobs that whites leave are filled out of this labor reserve so that in time more job categories are added to the black sector of the labor market. If the various forms of disguised unemployment and sub-employment are all taken into account, black unemployment rates can run as high as three or four times those of whites in specific labor markets in recession periods. The welfare and police costs of maintaining this labor reserve are high, but they are borne by the State as a whole and therefore do not enter into the profit calculations of individual firms.

This special exploitation of the black labor force also leads to direct economic gains for the various employers. Methodologically it is very difficult to measure exactly the extra surplus extracted due to wage discrimination, although in Chicago it has been estimated that unskilled black workers earn about 17% less on similar jobs than unskilled white workers of comparable quality. While in a historical sense the entire differential of wage income between blacks and whites can be attributed to discrimination, the employer realizes only that which takes place in the present in terms of either lesser wage payments or greater work output. Estimates of this realized special exploitation range on the order of 10% to 20% of the total black wage and salary income.

The subordinate status of the black labor market does not exist in isolation, but rather is a major part of a whole complex of institutional controls that constitute the web of urban racism.[24] This distinctive modern form of racism conforms to the 300-year-old traditions of the culture of control for the oppression of black people, but now most of the controls are located within the major metropolitan institutional networks—such as the labor market, the housing market, the political system. As the black population grew in the urban centers a distinctive new formation developed in each of these institutional areas. A black ghetto and housing market, a black labor market, a black school system, a black political system, and a black welfare system came into being—not as parts of a self-determining community, but as institutions to be controlled, manipulated, and exploited. When the black population did not serve the needs of dominant institutions by providing a wartime labor reserve, they were isolated so that they could be regulated and incapacitated.

This model of urban racism has had three major components with regard to institutional structures: (1) Within the major institutional networks that operate in the city there have developed definable black subsectors which operated on a subordinated basis, subject to the advantage, control, and priorities of the dominant system. (2) A pattern of mutual reinforcement takes place between the barriers that define the various black subsectors. (3) The controls over the lives of black men are so pervasive that they form a system analogous to colonial forms of rule.

The history of the demand for black labor in the post-war period showed the continued importance of wartime labor scarcities. The new job categories gained during World War II essentially were transferred into the black sectors of the labor market. Some war industries, like shipbuilding, of course, dropped off considerably. In reconversion and the brief 1948–1949 recession blacks lost out disproportionately on the better jobs. However the Korean War again created an intense labor shortage, making black workers once more in demand, at least until the fighting stopped. The period of slow economic growth from 1955 to the early 1960s saw a deterioration in the relative position of blacks as they experienced very high rates of unemployment and their incomes grew at a slower rate than those of whites. The civil-rights protests had generated little in the way of new demand. Only the coincidence of the rebellions of Watts, Newark, and Detroit with the escalation of the Vietnam War brought about a sharp growth in demand for black labor.

All the available evidence indicates that there has been no structural change of any significance in the deployment of black workers, most especially in private industry. Certain absolute standards of exclusion in professional, management, and sales occupations have now been removed, but the total growth in these areas has been slight except where a black clientele is serviced, as in the education and health fields. The one significant new demand in the North has been that for women clerical workers. This arises from a shortage of this particular kind of labor in the central business districts, which, being surrounded by the black community, are increasingly geographically removed from white supplies of these workers. About 90% of Chicago's black female white-collar workers work either in their own communities or in the central business districts, and are not employed in the rapidly growing outlying offices. In the South the whole pattern of racial regulation in the major cities is shifting over to a Northern model, so that the basic situation of black workers in Atlanta or Memphis is approaching that of the North about a decade ago.

Until the uprisings in the mid-60s, management of racial affairs was carried out either by the unvarnished maintenance of the status quo (except when black workers were needed) or by an elaborate ritual of fair practices and equal employment opportunity. The latter strategy operated as a sort of sophisticated social Darwinism to make the rules of competition for the survival of the fittest more equitable. Actually it blurred institutional realities, channeling energies and perceptions into individualized findings of fact. The black protest movement finally forced a switch to a policy of affirmative action that is supported by legal encouragement. In either case no basic structures have actually been transformed. As a review of studies on the current racial status in several industries finds: "Over the long haul, however, it is apparent that the laws of supply and demand have exercised a greater influence on the quantitative employment patterns of blacks than have the laws of the land."

In the Cold War era the trade-union movement lost its innovative dynamism and became narrowly wage-oriented. Overwhelmingly, the net racial effect of the collective-bargaining agreements was to accept the given conditions in a plant. Only a very few unions, usually from the CIO, conducted any fights for the upgrading of black workers. More usual was the practice of neglecting shop grievances. Within union life itself the black officials who arose as representatives of their race were converted into justifiers of the union administration to the black workers. On the legislative and judicial fronts—that is, away from their day-to-day base of operations—national unions supported the programs of civil-rights

organizations and the fair-employment symbolism. In fact by the early 1960s the racial strategies of national trade unions and those of the most sophisticated corporate leadership had converged.

The actions of the black community itself were destined to become the decisive political initiator, not only in its own liberation struggles but on the domestic scene in general. From World War II through the Korean War the urban black communities were engaged in digesting the improvements brought about by the end of the depression and by the wartime job gains. Both bourgeois and trade-union leadership followed the forms of the New Deal-labor coalition, but the original substance of mass struggle was no longer present.

The destabilization of the whole agrarian society in the South created the conditions for new initiatives. The Montgomery bus boycott was to re-introduce mass political action into the Cold War era. The boldness of the civil-rights movement, plus the success of national liberation movements in the Third World, galvanized the black communities in the major cities. At first the forms of the Southern struggle were to predominate in pro-integration civil-rights actions. Then youth and workers were swept into the movement and re-defined its direction toward black self-determination. The mass spontaneity in the ghetto rebellions revealed the tremendous potential of this orientation.

The ghetto systems and the dual labor markets had organized a mass black proletariat, and had concentrated it in certain key industries and plants. In the decade after World War II the most important strategic concentration of black workers was in the Chicago packing houses, where they became the majority group. United Packinghouse Workers District I was bold in battles over conditions in the plants and supplied the basic leadership for militant protest on the South Side. Even though the UPW was the most advanced of all big national unions on the race question, a coalition of black officials and shop stewards had to wage a struggle against the leadership for substantive black control. This incipient nationalist faction was defeated in the union, and the big meat packers moved out of the city, but before it disappeared the movement indicated the potential of black-oriented working-class leadership. The Packinghouse Workers' concrete struggles contrasted sharply with the strategy of A. Philip Randolph, who set up the form of an all-black Negro American Labor Council and then subordinated its mass support to maneuvers at the top level of the AFL-CIO.

After the ghetto uprisings workers were to reassert themselves at the point of production. Black caucuses and Concerned Workers' Committees sprang up across the country in plants and installations with large numbers of blacks.[25] By this time the auto industry had created the largest concentration of black workers in the nation on its back-breaking production lines in Detroit. Driven by the peculiarities of the black labor market, the "big three" auto companies had developed the preconditions for the organization of the Dodge Revolutionary Union Movement (DRUM) and the League of Revolutionary Black Workers. The insertion onto this scene of a cadre that was both black-conscious and class-conscious, with a program of revolutionary struggle, forged an instrument for the militant working-class leadership of the Black Liberation Movement. The League also provides an exemplary model for proletarians among other oppressed groups, and might even be able to stimulate sections of the white working class to emerge from their narrow economistic orientation.

The ruling class is caught in its own contradictions. It needs black workers, yet the conditions of satisfying this need compel it to bring together the potential forces for the most effective opposition to its policies, and even for a threat to its very existence. Amelioration of once-absolute exclusionary barriers does not eliminate the black work force that the whole web of urban racism defines. Even if the capitalists were willing to forgo their economic and status gains from racial oppression, they could not do so without shaking up all of the intricate concessions and consensual arrangements through which the State now exercises legitimate authority. Since the ghetto institutions are deeply intertwined with the major urban systems, the American Government does not even have the option of decolonializing by ceding nominal sovereignty that the British and French empires have both exercised. The racist structures cannot be abolished without an earthquake in the heartland. Indeed, for that sophisticated gentleman, the American capitalist, the demand for black labor has become a veritable devil in the flesh.

Notes

1. Karl Marx: Capi*tal* (Kerr Edition), Volume 1, Page 823.
2. Ibid., Page 833.
3. "As is well known, commodity production preceded (capitalist) commodity production, and constitutes one of the conditions (but not the sole condition) of the rise of the latter." V. I. Lenin: *Development of Capitalism in Russia* (Moscow, Foreign Languages Publishing House, 1956), Page 606.
4. Eugene D. Genovese: *The Political Economy of Slavery* (New York, 1967) contends that the plantation slave system was the base of a social order in the American South that essentially was pre-capitalist and quasi-aristocrat.
5. Marvin Harris: *Patterns of Race in the Americas* (New York, 1964), Page 13.
6. Winthrop Jordan: *White Over Black* (Chapel Hill, 1968), Page 184.
7. *The Problem of Slavery in Western Culture* (Ithaca, 1966), Pages 41–46.
8. *White Over Black,* Pages 3–43.
9. Carl N. Degler: "Slavery in the United States and Brazil: An Essay in Comparative History,"

American Historical Review (April 1970), Pages 1019–1021; Davis: *The Problem of Slavery,* Pages 232–233.

10. Philip Curtin: *The Atlantic Slave Trade* (Madison, 1969), Page 269; A. M. Carr Saunders, *World Population* (Oxford, 1936), Page 47.

11. *The Black Jacobins* (Second Edition, New York, 1963), Page 48. See also Gaston Martin: *Nantes au XVIII Siecle: L'Ere des Negriers* (Paris, 1931), Pages 422–433.

12. *Capitalism and Slavery* (Chapel Hill, 1944), Pages 50–84.

13. Malachi Postlethwayt: *The Advantage of the African Trade* (1772), quoted in Abram L. Harris: *The Negro as Capitalist* (Philadelphia, 1936), Pages 2–3.

14. Douglas North: *The Economic Growth of the United States, 1790–1860* (Englewood Cliffs, New Jersey, 1961), Pages 68–69.

15. Marcus Wilson Jernegan: *Laboring and Dependent Classes in Colonial America, 1607–1763* (Chicago, 1931), Page 23.

16. By this time free blacks constituted between 40% and 60% of the black population in Brazil and 35% in Cuba: Herbert S. Klein: "The Colored Freedmen in Brazil," *Journal of Social History* (Fall 1969), Pages 30–54.

17. Richard Wade: *Slavery in the Cities* (New York, 1964), Page 275.

18. W. E. B. Du Bois: *The Philadelphia Negro* (1967 Edition, New York), Page 33. See also Herman Bloch: *The Circle of Discrimination* (New York, 1969), Pages 21–26.

19. Robert Ernst: "The Economic Status of New York Negroes, 1850–1863," reprinted in August Meier and Elliot Rudwick (editors): *The Making of Black America* (New York, 1969), Volume 1, Pages 250–261.

20. This statement is not meant to imply that there were not some important class distinctions or inequalities in income or wealth, but it does claim that the social and political means of defining status along these lines were not as clear-cut as they were in Europe or in Latin America.

21. Harris: *Patterns of Race,* Chapter 7. A modern analogy to the Latin American status situation is evidenced in the US Army's ability to be one of the very first major American institutions to desegregate. "Placement of white adult males in a subordinate position within a rigidly-stratified system, that is, appears to produce behavior not all that different from the so-called personality traits commonly held to be an outcome of cultural or psychological patterns unique to Negro life. Indeed, it might be argued that relatively little adjustment on the part of the command structure was required when the infusion of the Negroes into the enlisted ranks occurred as the military establishment was desegregated. It is suggested, in other words, that one factor that contributed to the generally smooth racial integration of the military might be the standard treatment—like 'Negroes' in a sense—that was accorded to all lower-ranking enlisted personnel." Charles C. Moskos Junior: "Racial Integration in the Armed Forces," *American Journal of Sociology* (September 1966), reprinted in Raymond Mack: *Race, Class, and Power* (Second Edition, New York, 1968), Pages 436–455.

22. C. L. R. James: "The Atlantic Slave Trade and Slavery," *Amistad I* (New York, 1970), Pages 133–134. The possibility of a bourgeois mode of development of the black community in the US was cut off, although valiant efforts were made in this direction by black professional men, entrepreneurs, and craftsmen. Nineteenth Century Pan-Africanism and black nationalism most likely had significant roots in this phenomenon.

23. W. E. B. Du Bois: *Black Reconstruction in America, 1860–1880* (1962 Edition, Cleveland), Page 121.

24. "The Compromise of 1877 did not restore the old order in the South, nor did it restore the South to parity with other sections. It did assure the dominant whites political autonomy and non-intervention in matters of race policy, and promised them a share in the blessings of the new economic order. In return the South became . . . a satellite of the dominant region. . . . Under the regime of the Redeemers the South became a bulwark instead of a menace to the new order." C. Vann Woodward: *Reunion and Reaction* (Second Edition, New York, 1956), Pages 266–267.

25. *The Souls of Black Folk,* Chapter 8.

26. Quoted in Woodward: *Origins of the New South,* Page 208.

27. Rupert Vance: "Racial Competition for Land," in Edgar T. Thompson (editor): *Race Relations and the Race Problem* (Durham, 1939), Pages 100–104.

28. J. B. Killebrew: *Southern States Farm Magazine* (1898), Pages 490–491, cited in Nolen (previously cited), Page 170. For a concrete explication of this approach, see Alfred Holt Stone: *Studies in the American Race Problem* (New York, 1909), Chapter 4.

29. Woodward: *Origins of the New South,* Page 211.

30. Ibid., Pages 328–330.

31. Charles H. Wesley: *Negro Labor in the United States, 1850-1925* (New York, 1927), Pages 238–239; Claude H. Nolen: *The Negro's Image in the South* (Lexington, Kentucky, 1968), Page 190.

32. Lorenzo J. Greene and Carter G. Woodson: *The Negro Wage Earner* (Washington, 1930), Pages 49–50.

33. Wesley: *Negro Labor,* Page 142; W. E. B. Du Bois: *The Negro Artisan* (Atlanta, 1902), Pages 115–120.

34. Du Bois: *The Negro Artisan,* Pages 180–185. However, when the *Manufacturer's Record of Baltimore* conducted its own survey in 1893, the majority of manufacturers held that blacks were unfitted for most employment, but admitted that with training they could be used—an opinion they also held of the "primitive white man." One big difference in this latter survey was the inclusion of the cotton mills, a line that had already been declared a "white man's industry." Cited in Wesley: *Negro Labor,* Pages 244–248.

35. Paul H. Buck: *The Road to Reunion* (Boston, 1937), Pages 154–155.

36. Carter G. Woodson: "Story of the Fund," Chapter 2, typescript, Julius Rosenwald Papers, University of Chicago Library; Louis Harland: *Separate and Unequal* (Chapel Hill, 1958), Page 77.

37. Department of History, Harvard University, 1953.

38. Frank U. Quillan: *The Color Line in Ohio* (Ann Arbor, 1913), Page 138.

39. W. E. B. Du Bois: *The Negro Artisan,* Pages 173–175.

40. Spero and Harris: *The Black Worker* is still essential on this. Also see: Bernard Mandel: "Samuel Gompers and the Negro Workers, 1886–1914," *Journal of Negro History* (January 1955), Pages 34–60; Herbert G. Gutman: "The Negro and the United Mine Workers of America," in Julius Jacobson (editor): *The Negro and the American Labor Movement* (New York, 1968), Pages 49–127; and the entire issue of *Labor History* (Summer 1969).

41. William M. Tuttle Junior: "Labor Conflict and Racial Violence: The Black Worker in Chicago, 1894–1919," *Labor History* (Summer 1969), Pages 406–432; Spero and Harris: *The Black Worker,* Pages 131–134. For a national survey on strikebreaking see Fishel: *The North and the Negro,* Pages 454–471.

42. August Meier: *Negro Thought in America, 1880–1915* (Ann Arbor, 1963).

43. Chicago Commission on Race Relations: *The Negro in Chicago* (Chicago, 1922), Pages 362–363.

44. US Labor Department: *Negro Migration in 1916–17* (Washington 1919), Page 124.

45. Ibid., Pages 22–23, 27–33, 118–122; Spear: *Black Chicago,* Pages 33–38.

46. Wesley: *Negro Labor,* Pages 293–294; US Labor Department: *Negro Migration,* Pages 125–126.

47. William M. Tuttle Junior: *Race Riot: Chicago in the Red Summer of 1919* (New York, 1970), Pages 130–132.

48. Herman Feldman: *Racial Factors in American Industry* (New York and London, 1931), Pages 42–43.

49. Louise V. Kennedy: *The Negro Peasant Moves Cityward* (New York, 1930), Pages 35–36.

50. William C. Graves: "Memorandum of Address Made June 17th Before the Inter-racial Committee of the Union League Club," Julius Rosenwald Papers, University of Chicago Library.

51. Elliot M. Rudwick: *Race Riot at East Saint Louis, July 2,1917* (Carbondale, 1964); Tuttle: *Race Riot.*

52. Spero and Harris: *The Black Worker,* Pages 167–168.

53. Graves: "Memorandum of Speech Made June 17th."

54. Robert Ozanne: *A Century of Labor-Management Relations at McCormick and International Harvester* (Madison, 1967), Pages 183–187.

55. Bailer: "The Negro Automobile Worker," Pages 416–419; Herbert Northrup: *Organized Labor and the Negro* (New York, 1944), Pages 189–195.

56. Spero and Harris: *The Black Worker,* Page 169.

57. Cayton and Mitchell: *The Black Worker,* Page 31.

58. Kennedy: *The Negro Peasant Moves Cityward,* Page 98; Feldman: *Racial Factors in American Industry,* Pages 57–58.

59. "Conference on the Negro in Industry Held by the Committee on Industry, Chicago Commission on Race Relations, April 23, 1920," typescript, Julius Rosenwald Papers, University of Chicago Library.

60. This writer gave such a reading to several hundred management officials at a session sponsored by the Graduate School of Management of the University of Chicago in 1969. It was an ironic success.

61. Erwin D. Hoffman: "The Genesis of the Modern Movement for Equal Rights in South Carolina, 1930–1939," *Journal of Negro History* (October 1959), Page 347.

62. Charles S. Johnson: *The Shadow of the Plantation* (Chicago, 1934), Page 210. For a good review of the situation of blacks in the rural South during this period, see E. Franklin Frazier: *The Negro in the United States* (New York, 1949), Chapter 10.

63. Gunnar Myrdal: *An American Dilemma* (1964 Edition, New York, two volumes), Volume 1, Pages 256–269.

64. One indication that the current pattern was established by 1930 is given by Herman Feldman's *Racial Factors in American Industry,* published the following year. Feldman was able to prescribe and to concretely illustrate a set of industrial-relations practices that sound amazingly similar to what today are called equal-opportunity programs. The major difference is that in 1930 the firms did not have to take into account the political strength of the black community.

65. Drake and Cayton: B*lack Metropolis,* Volume 1, Pages 215–217 and 226–227; Richard Sterner: *The Negro's Share* (New York, 1934), Pages 39–46 and 219–291, providing a useful compilation of material used in this and the following paragraph; Ozanne: *A Century of Labor Management Relations,* Page 187; Charles S. Johnson: "The Conflict of Caste and Class in an American Industry," *American Journal of Sociology* (July 1936), Pages 55–65.

66. "The Negro's War," *Fortune* (June 1942), Pages 76–80.

67. Ibid.; American Management Association: *The Negro Worker* (Research Report Number 1, 1942), Pages 3–4 and 27–28; Nicholas S. Falcone: *The Negro Integrated* (New York, 1945).

68. Robert Weaver: *Negro Labor, A National Problem* (New York, 1946), Pages 78–93.

69. Harry Haywood: *Negro Liberation* (New York, 1948), Pages 198–199.

70. A few years after the collapse of 1929 Abram Harris surveyed this flourishing of black capitalism and concluded: The limits of a separate economy are precariously narrow within the confines of the present industrial system. How the independent black economy is to develop and function in the face of persistent industrial integration, business combinations, the centralization of capital control, and the concentration of wealth none of the advocates of the plan can explain. . . . As long as capitalism remains, however, it is reasonably certain that the main arteries of commerce, industry, credit, and finance will be controlled by white capitalists. Under the circumstances, the great mass of black and white men will continue to be dependent on these capitalists for their livelihood, and the small white capitalist in turn will continue to be subordinate to these larger financial and industrial interests. Thus it is obvious that the independent black economy—whether it develops on the basis of private profit or on the basis of co-operation—cannot be the means of achieving the Negro's economic salvation. (The *Negro as Capitalist,* Page x)

71. Cayton and Mitchell: *Black Workers and the New Unions;* Drake and Cayton: *Black Metropolis,* Volume 1, Pages 312–341; James Olsen: "Organized Black Leadership and Industrial Unionism: The Racial Response, 1939–1945," *Labor History* (Summer 1969), Pages 475–486.

72. The standard work on the MOW movement is Herbert Garfinkel: *When Negroes March* (Glencoe, 1959). The MOW movement actually presaged two forms of future tactics. In its appeal to the masses for a black-defined program of struggle it summarized all of the decade's action for jobs on a local level and impelled them forward on a national basis. On the other hand, in that the movement failed to develop an organized working-class constitu-

ency, it foretold tactics of maneuver without mass struggle—of legislative lobbying, judicial procedures, and jockeying within the Democratic Party—which were to be pursued by the bourgeois and trade-union organizations until demonstrations and civil disobedience finally arose from below out of the civil-rights movement.

73. These estimates are as of 1969. Data from the 1970 census were not available at the time of writing.

74. Richard H. Day: "The Economics of Technological Change and the Demise of the Sharecropper," A*merican Economic Review* (June 1967), Pages 427–449; Seymour Melman: "An Industrial Revolution in the Cotton South," *Economic History Review,* Second Series (1949), Pages 59–72.

75. Analysis of the relation of economic and class shifts in the South to the civil-rights movement and the nature of its limited victories from 1954 to 1965 has been seriously neglected. Anyone undertaking such a study should keep in mind V. I. Lenin's fundamental law of revolution: "It is not enough for revolution that the exploited and oppressed masses should understand the impossibility of living in the old way and demand changes, it is essential for revolution that the exploiters should not be able to live and rule in the same way." (Left Wing Communism)

76. David J. Smyth and Peter D. Lowe: "The Vestibule to the Occupational Ladder and Unemployment: Some Econometric Evidence on United Kingdom Structural Unemployment," *Industrial and Labor Relations Review* (July 1970), Pages 561–565.

77. This and following paragraphs on the dual labor market are basically a summary of Harold M. Baron and Bennett Hymer: "The Negro Worker in the Chicago Labor Market," in Julius Jacobson (editor): *The Negro and the American Labor Movement* (New York, 1968), Pages 232–285.

78. The following facts come from the *United States of America Versus Bethlehem Steel Company and Associates,* US District Court, Western District of New York, Civ-1967-436, Stipulation of Facts, July 1, 1968 and Second Stipulation of Facts, September 20, 1968.

79. D. Taylor: "Discrimination and Occupational Wage Differences in the Market for Unskilled Labor," *Industrial and Labor Relations Review* (April 1968), Pages 375–390.

80. For a recent estimate see Lester Thurow: *The Economy of Poverty and Discrimination* (Washington 1969). He finds the gains to wage discrimination were $4,600,000,000 in 1960. Advantages to white workers due to higher employment rates were $6,500,000,000.

81. For an extended treatment of the institutionalization of racism in the metropolis see Harold Baron: "The Web of Urban Racism," in Louis Knowles and Kenneth Prewitt (editors): *Institutional Racism in America* (New York, 1969), Pages 134–176.

82. Vernon M. Briggs Junior: "The Negro in American Industry: A Review of Seven Studies," *Journal of Human Resources* (Summer 1970), Pages 371–381.

83. William Kornhauser: "The Negro Union Official: A Study of Sponsorship and Control," *American Journal of Sociology* (March 1952), Pages 443–452; Scott Greer: "Situational Pressures and Functional Role of the Ethnic Labor Leader," *Social Forces* (October 1953), Pages 41–45.

84. The writer has the records of the Chicago chapter of the NALC in his possession.

85. For a description of some of these organizations see Herbert Hill: "Black Protest and Struggle for Union Democracy," *Issues in Industrial Society* (1969), Pages 19–24 and 48.

Essay/Discussion Questions

1. How did the demand for African labor as the unpaid workforce for plantation slavery simultaneously provide the motivation for the development of institutional racism and set in motion the formation of the black community in the United States?

2. Because both governmental laws and business interests sanctioned chattel slavery, should black Americans now be compensated for over 350 years of free labor?

3. The slave trade and chattel slavery provided the foundations for America's developing colonial political economy, which has resulted in the contemporary American corporate state. Discuss.

4. How did the white planter class control poor and non-slave-holding whites in the South?

5. Baron argues that chattel slavery was more than an economic arrangement; it was a system of cultural domination and control. Discuss.

6. As black people migrated from the agrarian South to the industrial North around the turn of the century, they were confronted with the racism, fear, and terrorism of urban working-class whites. Discuss the causes and consequences of racial antagonism within America's emerging urban industrial economy. How was this racism an extension of America's slave past, and how did both of these conditions help to shape an emerging black working class and economic instability within urban black communities?

Black Economic Well-Being Since the 1950s

Daniel R. Fusfeld and Timothy Bates

Has black economic well-being improved since World War II? There are no simple answers. This chapter will document areas of improvement as well as deterioration, and we will explore the causes of these diverse trends. Overall, the evidence points to polarization within the black community: the younger and better-educated are registering strong and sustained gains in income and occupational status; those who are not highly educated—yet not below average in skills and years of schooling—continue to ride the cyclical roller coaster, prospering in periods of labor shortage and suffering during prolonged recessions; those on the bottom appear to be positively worse off, perhaps representing a semipermanent lumpenproletariat facing very uncertain prospects for future job market upgrading. Regional trends, interacting with major shifts in industry employment patterns—the decline of automobile industry employment for example—complicate all generalizations about trends in black well-being.

Future income and employment prospects for black workers are assessed rather pessimistically in this chapter. Particularly among black male workers the future may bring about an affluent elite of white-collar workers, a greatly diminished number of middle-income blue-collar workers, and a large and growing number of low-income unemployed and underemployed workers whose labor force attachment is quite marginal.

THE EVIDENCE FOR MAJOR ECONOMIC PROGRESS

Black progress in education and occupational status has been quite pronounced in recent decades. Income trends are less clear-cut, but evidence that incomes of blacks have been rising relative to incomes of whites, summarized in table 9.1, has been widely cited to demonstrate long-term, sustained improvements in the well-being of blacks. Although black family incomes have fallen relative to white incomes in the 1970s (table 9.1), long-term improvement is still apparent. Furthermore, there are a number of valid reasons for using incomes of individuals, as opposed to families, as the "more accurate" measure of trends in relative black income position. For

Reprinted, with permission, from *The Political Economy of the Urban Ghetto*, by Daniel R Fusfeld and Timothy Bates, Southern Illinois University Press, 1984.

TABLE 9.1 INCOMES OF BLACK INDIVIDUALS AND FAMILIES, STATED AS PERCENTAGES OF WHITE INDIVIDUAL AND FAMILY INCOMES

Year	Black Families*	Black Males†	Black Females†
1947	51	–	–
1948	53	54	43
1949	51	48	46
1950	54	54	45
1951	53	55	42
1952	57	55	39
1953	56	55	59
1954	56	50	54
1955	55	53	52
1956	51	52	57
1957	53	53	58
1958	51	50	59
1959	52	47	62
1960	55	53	62
1961	53	52	67
1962	53	49	67
1963	53	52	67
1964	56	57	70
1965	55	61	73
1966	60	59	79
1967	59	57	80
1968	60	61	81
1969	61	59	85
1970	61	60	92
1971	60	60	90
1972	59	62	96
1973	58	63	93
1974	60	64	92
1975	61	63	92
1976	60	63	95
1977	57	61	88
1978	59	64	92
1979	57	65	93
1980	58	63	96
1981	56	63	92

Sources: U. S. Bureau of the Census, *Current Population Reports*, ser. P.60, no. 137, table 15 (Washington, D.C.: Government Printing Office, Mar. 1983), pp. 39-42. Ibid., table 16, pp. 43-46.

*Figures prior to 1967 include blacks and other races; figures since 1967 include blacks only.
†Figures for blacks refer to blacks and other races.

example, much of the decline in black family incomes since 1970 is directly related to the rise of single-parent families rather than changes in labor market status. Table 9.1 clearly shows that black male incomes improved dramatically during the prosperous 1960s (the relevant black-white income ratio rose from .47 in 1959 to .59 in 1969); furthermore, some additional improvement occurred during the recessionary 1970s—black male incomes rose from 59 percent of white incomes in 1969 to 65 percent in 1979. An even more clear-cut improvement in relative incomes is apparent in data describing relative black female incomes in table 9.1. In each of the last three decades, black female incomes (expressed as a percentage of white female incomes) have increased dramatically. Whereas black females

TABLE **9.2** TRENDS IN BLACK EDUCATIONALATTAINMENT

A. Median Years of School Completed by Persons 25 and Older

	Nonwhite	Black	White	Difference
1940	5.8	—	8.7	2.9
1960	8.2	—	10.9	2.7
1980	—	12.0	12.5	0.5

B. Number of Blacks Enrolled in Colleges and Universities

1965	274,000
1970	522,000
1975	948,000
1980	1,007,000

Source: Census of population data, cited in John Reid, "Black America in the 1980s," *Population Bulletin* 37, no. 5 (1982):25; U.S. Bureau of the Census, *Current Population Reports,* ser. P-20, no. 373, table 3 (Washington, D.C.: Government Printing Office, Feb. 1983), p. 5.

received only 46.3 percent as much as their white female counterparts in 1949, their 1979 relative incomes were 93.1 percent of white incomes. By 1979, black females actually exceeded white cohort incomes in every area of the United States except the South. Now that's progress. Or is it? We will argue that nationwide black relative income comparisons (or black-white income ratios) are severely flawed measures of black economic well-being. Essentially, data such as those summarized in table 9.1 obscure more than they reveal, actually setting back our understanding of complex issues by relying upon overly simplistic measures of black income position.

The issue of black educational gains since World War II is much more straightforward than a comparison of relative incomes. Progress in the education realm has been widespread, as shown in table 9.2. Among black adults, median years of school completed in 1980 was 12.0 years, only slightly behind the 12.5 years reported by the white adult population. The incidence of teenagers (16 through 19 years of age) out of school with no high school diploma in 1981 was 13.6 percent for blacks, 11.7 percent for whites. The incidence of black college enrollment for those eighteen to twenty-four years old rose from 10.3 percent in 1965 to 19.4 percent in 1981; the corresponding enrollment rate for whites was roughly 26 percent through-

out this period. Although college enrollment of black students peaked at 1,103,000 in 1977, 1,080,000 were enrolled in 1981 which suggests approximate stability rather than enrollment declines. Available evidence indicates black educational gains throughout the 1960s and 1970s, with no trend towards backsliding emerging to date in the 1980s.

Educational achievements have translated into occupational gains for many black workers, especially among young college graduates. Black male college graduates twenty-five to thirty-four years old earned in 1959 only 59 percent as much as their white college graduate cohorts; by 1979 this figure had jumped to 84 percent. In the case of students holding MBA degrees, black-white parity has apparently been achieved. The Association of MBA Executives reports MBA degree holders hired in 1980 started out with average salaries of $24,259, with blacks and whites receiving approximately equal pay.

Penetration into white-collar occupations has been prevalent among younger black women. In 1980, 49.4 percent of the black females who worked during the year were employed in white-collar jobs. The incidence of white-collar employment for black males was 23.9 percent; over 17 percent were employed as skilled craftsmen, however, while another 25.2 percent worked as operatives—which is

TABLE **9.3** GROWTH IN THE NUMBER OF BLACK ELECTED OFFICIALS

	1970	1982
Federal	10	18
State, Regional	169	397
County	92	465
City	623	2,451
Judicial, Law Enforcement	213	563
Education	362	1,266
Total number of elected black officials	1,469	5,160

Source: E.R. Shipp, "'63 Marcher sees gains but a 'Long Way to Travel,'" *New York Times* 28 Aug. 1983, p.30.

commonly well-paid factory work. These occupational figures must be interpreted with one important qualification in mind: those not working are excluded. Similarly, income figures such as those summarized in table 9.1 include only those persons having income. Of course, the incidence of blacks working in any given time period is lower than the incidence of employed whites; the same pattern applies to income recipients. Nonetheless, real occupational gains have been realized by black workers since the 1950s, and this is especially true for females.

One final piece of evidence indicating black progress in recent decades is the increase of blacks in highly visible, prestigious positions. The traditional areas of high visibility—entertainment and professional sports—are now overshadowed by blacks serving in top elected offices. Since the 1960s, blacks have also served at very high levels in government bureaucracies: the presidential cabinet, the Supreme Court, major state government positions. In fact, increased representation of blacks is apparent at all levels of government (table 9.3).

In the private sector, blacks account for rapidly growing numbers of younger executives at major corporations. In the media, black stereotypes of thirty years ago have been largely relegated to the dustbin of history; blacks now appear in authoritative roles such as newscasters.

In light of all the above—relative income gains, narrowing the educational gap, upward occupational mobility, including penetration of society's most prestigious positions—it is not surprising that most respondents to a 1980 Gallup poll felt that the quality of life for blacks had improved during the 1970s.

THE EVIDENCE SUGGESTING THAT BLACK ECONOMIC WELL-BEING IS DECLINING

Most of the respondents to the Gallup poll mentioned above were whites. Among black respondents, the majority felt that their quality of life had stayed the same or gotten worse during the 1970s. The broad generality of the question—How have blacks fared over time?—is apt to produce oversimplified answers supported by simplistic evidence. Some are better off; others are worse off. While widespread economic and social progress was clearly the norm during the 1960s, much evidence indicates regression in black economic status in the 1970s. According to Vernon Jordan, former president of the Urban League, "For Black Americans the decade of the 1970s was a time in which many of their hopes, raised by the civil rights victories of the 1960s, withered away."

The economic well-being of black Americans has traditionally improved during periods of labor scarcity: World War I, the 1920s, World War II, and the Vietnam War. Relative income gain has also accompanied the twentieth-century residential shift from the rural South to northern and southern urban areas.

471

TABLE 9.4 INCOME OF BLACKS* BY REGION AND SEX STATED AS PERCENTAGES OF WHITE INCOMES (*CALCULATIONS BASED ON MEDIANS*)

A. North, West	Black Males	Black Females
1953	74	85
1959	73	106
1964	75	110
1969	78	120
1974	75	113
1979	70	105
1981	66	103

B. South	Black Males	Black Females
1953	46	45
1959	33	42
1964	46	53
1969	54	62
1974	54	74
1979	60	81
1981	58	74

Sources: U.S. Bureau of the Census, *Current Population Reports*, ser. P 23, no. 80, table 30 (Washington, D.C.: Government Printing Office, 1979) p. 46. Ibid., ser. P-60, no. 129, table 47 (Nov. 1981), pp. 183–193. Ibid., ser. P 60, no. 137, table 43 (Mar. 1983), pp. 133–40.

*Data for 1964 and earlier refer to black and other races; post-1964 data refer to blacks only.

But aside from boom periods that have drawn black workers into better-paying jobs, how widespread and enduring are the black income and occupational gains of recent decades? Has the change from a predominantly southern rural to a predominantly urban America drastically lessened racial discrimination, or have new forms of racial inequality arisen in the cities? Long-term occupational gains appear to endure, particularly for black females, but other labor force trends are ominous. Abstracting from the cyclical ups and downs, blacks since World War II have experienced rising unemployment rates and falling labor force participation rates; the labor force status of urban black males shows signs of long-run deterioration. By 1980, 15 percent of all black males twenty-five to sixty-four years of age were telling the Census Bureau that they had earned absolutely nothing during 1979. In 1969, median black family incomes in the north central states were $19,182 (in 1981 dollars); by 1981 the comparable median figure had plummeted to $15,474.

Relative incomes of urban blacks have not risen dramatically in the post-World War II era. Incomes of blacks in the cities still ride the cyclical roller coaster: up in the 1940s, down in the 1950s, up in the 1960s, down in the 1970s. Numerous studies that argue otherwise invariably fail to sort out the one-time-only income gains accompanying urbanization, labor market cyclical swings, and the income gains of the highly educated.[1] Gains of migration, of boom periods, and of a fortunate few are incorrectly interpreted as evidence of overall black economic uplifting.

The simplest way to clarify trends in black economic status is to segment blacks geographically into those residing in southern states, and northern and western states.[2] Blacks residing in the nonsouthern states are overwhelmingly urban, and table 9.4 shows that their relative incomes—for both males and females—fell between 1959 and 1979. The drop was particularly pronounced for black males, whose incomes, stated as a percentage of median white male incomes, fell from 78 percent in

TABLE 9.5 NET MIGRATION OF BLACKS BY REGION (*IN THOUSANDS*)

	South	Northeast	North Central	West
1940–1950	—1,599	+463	+618	+339
1950–1960	—1,473	+496	+541	+293
1960–1970	—1,380	+612	+382	+301
1970–1980	+209	—239	—103	+132
Total	—4,243	+1,332	+1,438	+1,065

Sources: U.S. Bureau of the Census, *Current Population Reports,* ser. P 23, no. 80, Tables 8 and 9 (Washington, D.C.: Government Printing Office, 1979), pp. 15–16. Ibid., ser. P 20, no. 368, table 42 (Dec, 1981), p. 130.

1969 to 66 percent in 1981. Recall that this *excludes* all zero income earners, thereby understating the extent of relative black income decline for the entire population.[3] The picture in the South was entirely different. Agricultural transformation . . . increased the impoverishment of many southern blacks during the 1950s. This is reflected in table 9.4: the ratio of black to white incomes fell from .46 to a rock bottom .33 for males between 1953 and 1959, and the female ratio fell from .45 to .42. Starting from a position of widespread southern poverty and deprivation in 1959, steady and sustained improvement took place in the next two decades. During this period of transition, blacks residing in the South shifted from being predominantly rural to largely urban in residence. Their shift from agriculture to the urban job market was facilitated by strong southern urban economic expansion, . . . which continued in the 1970s despite recessionary national conditions. In other words, the large relative income gains of southern blacks (table 9.4) reflect the one-time-only gains accompanying urbanization and integration into non-agricultural lines of work.

Rural to urban migration was, of course, part of a nationwide redistribution of black population. Table 9.5 shows that, in addition to rural to urban migration within the South, the net migration out of the South was nearly 4.5 million for blacks from 1940 to 1970. This, too, reflected a movement that was predominantly rural to urban. Nationwide gains in relative black incomes (table 9.1) that accom-

panied this population shift, however, did not produce proportionate increases in black economic well-being. Rural areas of the South have the lowest cost of living of any region of the United States, much lower than comparable living costs in urban areas.[4] In fact, black migrants of this era disproportionately moved to large cities where living costs are among the highest in the nation. The 1980 census reported that 34 percent of all blacks resided in just seven urban centers: New York, Chicago, Los Angeles, Philadelphia, Detroit, Baltimore, and Washington, D.C. A rural South Carolina family subsisting on $2,500 a year may or may not be better off subsisting on $7,500 a year in Harlem. Rural South Carolina housing rental rates are certainly dwarfed by the cost of comparable housing in big city ghettos. Higher living costs obviously consume a share of the gains realized by rural to urban migrants, significantly offsetting relative black-white median income gains.

The validity of black-white income ratio comparisons over time is suspect for many reasons. Forms of noncash compensation, for example, have augmented white real incomes faster than that of blacks in recent decades. Especially in the professional and managerial occupations (disproportionately white), compensation in such forms as educational stipends, pensions, insurance premiums, and expense account living has increased more rapidly than actual wages and salaries. One study showed that black employees were much less likely than whites to participate in private pension plans, and those who did participate were eligible for or receiving pensions that were far smaller than those of white recipients.

Another severe conceptual problem for black-white income comparisons concerns exclusion of some forms of income—such as capital gains and undistributed profits—from the census income definition. Nor are the wealthy the only ones receiving such uncounted income; families at the other end of the spectrum are often recipients of food stamps, Medicaid, and other forms of uncounted income. The list of biases goes on and on. The rich, for example, disproportionately receive property income, and income from property is systematically under-reported to the government on a much larger scale than wage income.

Do the corporate elite, with their company cars, country club memberships, dining and entertainment expense allowances, generous pensions, etc. bias the reported income statistics more or less than poor blacks who receive free school lunches and subsidized housing? We really have no idea. Black-white income comparisons lose their validity increasingly as such forms of uncounted income expand over time. Reported income is a crude measure of actual income, and long-term comparisons of black-white income ratios should be viewed as even cruder measures of relative black well-being.

In summary, the evidence cited in table 9.1 does not show that blacks as a group are relatively better off than they were in the early 1950s.

1. A large share of reported income gains is negated by the shift from low cost of living areas in the rural South to high cost of living urban areas.

2. Income figures include only those earning income; the proportion of black males with zero income rose absolutely from 1953 to 1981 and it rose relative to whites. In contrast, the proportion of black women with zero income fell in absolute terms, but rose relative to whites.

3. Black-white income ratios obscure trends in income distribution within the black community. Black incomes could, for example, be a constant percentage of white incomes during a time period when rapid gains by the well-educated are forcing up this percentage, and income losses by the less-educated are pulling down relative black incomes. When one abstracts from the rural to urban shift (which produced major gains for low-income blacks), it turns out that the post-World War II period is indeed characterized by rising income inequality within the black community.

4. Differences in reported versus actual income are present due to income concealment, income measurement peculiarities, as well as conceptual problems as to what is and is not income. These problems tend to make the precision of black-white income comparisons highly uncertain.

Among less-educated and less-skilled black Americans, absolute improvement in economic well-being may indeed be absent. Our inability to adjust accurately for cost of living differences between rural southern and urban areas alone makes it impossible to compare the well being of less skilled blacks in the 1950s with that of the 1980s. Measures of unemployment and labor force participation, however, suggest deterioration among less-skilled male workers. The proportion of black males employed full-time for the entire year of 1955 was 56.6 percent. During the prosperous year of 1969 this percentage had fallen to 51.7 percent, and by 1980 only 45.0 percent of those who worked were employed full-time year-round.

Black teenagers face employment problems that dwarf those of older black workers. Black teenagers have closed most of the education gap with their white cohorts, suggesting that their labor force status should begin to resemble more closely that of white teenagers. The opposite has in fact occurred (table 9.6). Indeed, education advances may be having a perverse effect on the labor force status of

Table 9.6 Civilian Labor Force Participation Rate *(Percentage)*

	Male		Female	
	Black*	White	Black*	White
A. Participation Rate for Persons Age 16 or older				
1969	75.0	78.7	48.0	40.5
1971	75.5	79.7	47.4	42.7
1973	71.3	78.7	47.6	42.8
1975	72.1	78.7	48.2	45.7
1977	70.9	77.8	49.3	47.0
1979	71.7	78.5	52.3	49.9
1981	70.4	77.8	52.7	51.4
1983	69.5	76.2	53.6	52.2
B. Participation Rate for Persons 18–19 Years Old				
1969	62.3	59.6	41.8	48.1
1971	54.0	65.5	33.5	52.6
1973	59.7	69.3	41.0	53.9
1975	54.2	71.8	38.4	58.5
1977	55.5	71.4	40.6	58.7
1979	58.6	73.8	42.3	63.7
1981	59.0	72.8	43.0	61.6
1983	49.1	65.6	41.0	60.8

Sources: U.S. Bureau of Labor Statistics, "Employment and Earnings" (Washington, D.C. Government Printing Office), various issues.

*Includes all nonwhites

young blacks. Stronger educational credentials often create an unwillingness to accept jobs to which particularly low status is attached.[5]

The most disturbing statistics on black well-being are not directly related to the labor market. Signs of breakdown in the social fabric of low-income urban black communities, although poorly understood, are undoubtedly exacerbated by labor market problems. In 1979, for example, 15 percent of all deaths among black men were attributable to accidents, homicide, and suicide. Black males twenty-five to thirty-four years of age experienced death rates two and one-half times higher than whites in the same age group. The age-adjusted black death rate from homicide was over six times higher than the corresponding white rate. Throughout the 1970s, the incidence of imprisonment of young black males rose dramatically. On an entirely different matter, black families of the form "single-parent female with her own children" increased in number 91.6 percent from 1970 to 1980. During the same time period,

married couple families with their own children decreased in number by 5.9 percent.[6]

The proportion of black families living in poverty has increased since 1970, from 9.5 percent to 30.8 percent in 1981. This development is related to the increasing incidence of households headed by females; 52.9 percent of all such black families were below the poverty level in 1981. High rates of out-of-wedlock births exacerbate the trend of more black children being raised in households whose income is sub-poverty level. Rates of out-of-wedlock childbearing are particularly high among black teenagers. Childbearing typically terminates the education of young mothers, resulting in limited job access. Young single women with small children, little education, and few skills often end up on welfare. A recent study found that approximately 40 percent of all black families with children under 18 are getting AFDC (Aid to Families with Dependent Children) benefits, compared to 6.8 percent for white families.

Causes of all the above, from violent death to the rising incidence of female-headed households living in poverty, are only dimly understood, but they do not suggest a pattern of widespread, across-the-board increases in black well-being. Rather, they suggest the sort of deterioration in community cohesion that would accompany declining labor market opportunities. High and rising unemployment rates among the young, falling labor force participation rates, a rising incidence of violent death and of incarceration in prisons—these are traits of an emerging class of disaffected young urban blacks. They are the emerging lumpenproletariat.

THE UNANSWERED QUESTIONS

The progress portrayed in the first section, "The Evidence For Major Economic Progress," is the picture that dominates existing social science literature. It is so filled with over-generalizations and so reliant upon one analytical tool—the black-white income ratio—that its message is largely wrong. And yet, very real educational gains do exist and it is important to understand why they have not resulted in more enduring and widespread income gains. Racial discrimination in the labor market along with more sophisticated forms of statistical discrimination . . . account for part of the problem. Many of the mysteries about trends in black economic welfare, though, can be clarified by putting them in the context of other social events. Changing patterns in the demand for labor have simultaneously improved female labor force status and undermined male prospects. The role of organized labor has shaped black occupational access, as has civil rights activism. Trends in major industries that employ blacks disproportionately—manufacturing, government, services—determine the value of educational credentials and thus shape black occupational access and earnings. These factors have varied greatly from decade to decade, producing diverse trends in black earnings. Furthermore, these are the factors that will shape black economic status in the years ahead.

THE 1950S

In several important ways, the 1950s reflected the beginnings of trends that were to become dominant determinants of urban black well-being in the 1980s—gains in white-collar occupations for the more educated and an increasingly tenuous employment situation for the less educated. During the decade, rural to urban migration continued at a brisk pace and the largest black population gains were registered by major industrial cities. Most of the employed black males worked in the major blue-collar occupations—operative, general laborer, craftsmen, and foremen—and the majority of these were employed in manufacturing. Black females were concentrated primarily in low-wage service occupations and secondly, in the operative category. The frequency of white city residents in the white-collar occupations—professional, manager, clerical, and sales—was three to four times greater proportionally than the incidence of blacks in white-collar jobs.

Factory jobs were the highest paying type of employment that was widely available to urban blacks. They provided the route to upward mobility for the less skilled, and the early 1950s, spurred by the Korean War, brought sustained gains in manufacturing employment. Nationwide unemployment rates for non-whites stood at 4.1 percent in 1953, and the teenage unemployment incidence was 7.3 percent. In this era of 20 percent plus unemployment rates (early 1983 figures) for prime working age black males, it is useful to recall that in the 1950s, blacks with fewer skills and much less education experienced full employment in urban America.

The 1950s decade was not, however, a period of uninterrupted black economic gain. While blacks were being ejected en masse from southern agriculture, their economic fortunes in the cities ebbed and flowed along with the uneven demands for their labor services.

There were two very distinct sides to the coin of black economic prospects in northern and western cities: opportunities were more diverse and the pay was generally higher, but black unemployment in the North was much higher than it had been traditionally in the rural South. After the Korean War, an ominous new trend developed: 1953 was the last year of relatively low black unemployment—4.4 percent for males and 3.7 percent for females. The corresponding rates for prosperous years in the 1960s were typically more than double the 1953 black unemployment rates. These were years of retrogression rather than progress. Whereas nonwhite unemployment rates as a percentage of white rates averaged around 170 percent during the late 1940s and early 1950s, in 1955 the nonwhite unemployment rate was more than double the corresponding white rate. After 1955, black unemployment rates were consistently more than twice as high as white unemployment rates. During the 1950s, the relative income of black males declined significantly in every major region of the country. For the entire United States, though, the black-white income ratio for males declined only moderately, attributable solely to black migration from low-income rural southern areas to higher-income northern states.

Black migration in the 1950s was heavily responsible for the decline in relative black economic well-being experienced in northern and western states. As machinery displaced men on a large scale in the most backward areas of the rural South, a northward stream of black migrants engulfed inner cities in the North and West. The migrants of the 1950s found a different situation in the cities than did their counterparts of earlier periods. There were few jobs available for them in the northern cities. The reasons were chiefly to be found in labor market structural difficulties as well as national economic trends. Briefly, the migrants were moving to the big city at the wrong point in history.

First, the southern refugees of the 1950s were among the least-skilled and the worst-educated of all Americans. The skills that they had were largely agricultural; the little education that they had was obtained in rural southern schools of poor quality. Their few skills and talents were not widely demanded by urban employers.

Second, the mass production industries in northern cities were hiring few blue-collar workers. Many large employers of earlier black migrants—automobile, steel, and electrical equipment—were actually reducing their unskilled and semiskilled labor forces. Job availability in manufacturing was greatest for white-collar workers such as engineers and technicians, but blacks generally lacked the skills required for entry into these jobs. Manufacturing growth no longer required vast numbers of unskilled workers.

Third, black migrants from the South faced competition in the labor market from whites displaced from farms, particularly in the Midwest. Technological transformation of agriculture was a national phenomenon. When the decline in farm employment began in 1920, some 11.5 million persons were employed in agriculture. By 1940, the figure had fallen to 9.5 million, but by 1964 it had dropped to 4.7 million. The white workers displaced from agriculture also moved into urban areas. Since they were better educated and more highly skilled than the southern black migrants (and were not black), they tended to get the more desirable jobs.

Fourth, national economic growth had slowed down. The nation's gross national product increased at a rate of only 2.4 percent annually between 1953 and 1960, as compared to 4 percent per year from 1946 to 1953. Unemployment rose throughout the economy, and a substantial amount of economic slack developed. Under these conditions, the un-

TABLE 9.7 OCCUPATION OF EMPLOYED BLACKS BY SEX, FOR CENTRAL-CITY RESIDENTS OF CHICAGO, BALTIMORE, CLEVELAND, DETROIT, AND PHILADELPHIA *(PERCENTAGE)*

	1950	1960	1970
A. Male			
Professional, Technical	2.3	4.0	5.8
Manager, Proprietor	2.7	2.4	3.0
Sales	1.9	2.4	2.6
Clerical	6.4	9.7	10.0
Craftsmen, Foremen, and Kindred	11.4	13.0	16.0
Operative	30.9	33 9	34.4
Laborer	26.3	18.5	12.5
Service	16.5	15.6	15.2
Private Household	1.0	0.5	0.4
(% White Collar)	(13.3)	(18.5)	(21.4)
B. Female			
Professional, Technical	4.8	8.4	11.1
Manager, Proprietor	1.4	1.3	1.6
Sales	2.3	2.9	3.4
Clerical	7.5	16.9	30.8
Craftsmen, Foreman, and Kindred	1.2	1.2	1.7
Operative	27.6	22.9	18.3
Laborer	2.5	1.3	1.8
Service	21.1	23.6	22.9
Private Household	32.6	21.5	8.4
(% White Collar)	(16.0)	(29.5)	(46.9)

Source: U.S. Census of Population.

educated black migrant was not only the last hired, but in many instances he or she was not hired at all.

Fifth, what economic expansion there was took place on the fringes of metropolitan areas. Jobs created in suburban locations were often not easily accessible to the poorest of the black migrants who settled mainly in the central cities.[7]

The economic experience of black migrants after the Korean War was often one of unemployment and underemployment. By 1958, nonwhite unemployment had reached 12.6 percent nationwide, and it stayed between 10 and 13 percent until the escalation of the Vietnam War in 1964. The unemployment rates do not include those involuntarily restricted to part-time work or those employed at very low wages—the subemployed. The ranks of the subemployed typically exceeded the ghetto unemployed, often by wide margins. Ghetto

joblessness had always been widespread during recessions and depressions. Since the 1950s, however, high rates of black unemployment have been a permanent feature of ghetto life—in boom times as well as during recessionary periods. This is entirely a post-Korean War phenomenon.

The decade of the 1950s was not entirely bleak for urban blacks. The brunt of increased unemployment and underemployment was absorbed by recent migrants and young people. The more educated, long-term ghetto dwellers made occupational gains in the white-collar fields, particularly in clerical work (table 9.7). Increased penetration into clerical occupations was particularly beneficial to black females in the 1950s, and it helped to boost black female incomes relative to their white female counterparts. Many of the older industrial cities that had experienced heavy black in-migration were, during the 1950s, experiencing CBD expansion; a number of large-scale employers of clerical labor—corporate headquarters, banks, insurance companies, and government agencies—were expanding their central-city operations.

Aside from gains in certain white-collar areas, though, the dominant features of black labor market involvement in the 1950s were rising unemployment and underemployment, restricted opportunities in manufacturing after 1953 (the traditional route of upward mobility for unskilled blacks), and deteriorating incomes of black males relative to their white counterparts.

Problems in manufacturing employment were exacerbated by discriminatory policies concerning layoff and job upgrading. . . . [U]nion concern for black worker rights fell rather dramatically during the 1950s, and unions were often supportive of unfair treatment of black employees. The seniority system was a particular irritant. There are a number of seniority system designs, each with its own set of problems for black workers. During full employment periods, blacks benefit from the widest possible seniority base (one that is commonly plant-wide in scope). Seniority may then be a basis for maximum upgrading and promotion opportunities if the system is applied in an impartial manner. But, during periods of employment contraction, blacks benefit most from a narrow-based seniority system (departmental or occupational) since their high concentration in several occupations and departments provides protection from being bumped by whites who have greater seniority. In fact, plants often used departmental seniority for job upgrading and plant-wide seniority for layoffs. This arrangement clearly favored white workers over blacks, and it directly reflected the balance of racial power in the unions. While the job upgrading opportunities went mainly to white workers, black workers were most likely to be laid off during recessions. These discriminatory practices were widespread in such supposedly progressive

unions as the United Auto Workers. Although blacks accounted for 8 to 9 percent of all auto workers in the 1950s, they never accounted for as much as one-half of 1 percent of skilled craftsmen. General Motors had over 11,000 skilled workers in the Detroit area; fewer than 100 were black.[8]

THE 1960S

During periods of labor shortage, the swollen ranks of unemployed and underemployed urban blacks are drawn off to staff more stable and remunerative jobs. Black workers often find it possible to move from low-wage competitive sector jobs into higher-wage work with large corporations or the government. Second, job upgrading invariably becomes an issue during boom periods, and barriers to black occupational advancement are challenged. It is no coincidence that concern about racially discriminatory employment practices always appears to be most prevalent during periods of rapid economic expansion and job creation. This was the situation in the 1960s: jobs were available in areas where black penetration had traditionally been minimal, and discriminatory hiring practices were reduced, allowing black employment gains in skilled and white-collar lines of work.

In important ways the World War II era provided the model for 1960s black employment gains. . . . [T]he federal government led the way to expanded job access in the early 1940s. Executive Order 8802, signed by President Roosevelt in 1941, required that all defense contractors adopt nondiscriminatory employment practices. The federal government reformed its own hiring practices during World War II and employed hundreds of thousands of black workers in white-collar jobs. Hiring black females as clerical workers on a large scale thus began in the 1940s. One important difference between World War II and the 1960s, however, was the role of organized labor as a champion of black rights. While the CIO unions played this role in the early 1940s, blacks themselves—via the civil rights movement—won many victories in the struggles of the 1960s for improved job access.

Two major themes dominate the improvement in black economic well-being during the 1960s. First, this long period of sustained economic growth created strong labor demands that translated into widespread income and occupational gains for black workers (tables 9.4 and 9.7). Second, civil rights activism produced an outpouring of legislation designed to curb racial discrimination as well as an avalanche of court rulings that advanced the cause of equal rights. All of this produced a reshaping of public attitudes about the roles of minority groups in U.S. society: black willingness to assume subservient economic, social, and political roles fell, and whites increasingly accepted the notion that equality of opportunity should apply to blacks as well as to themselves.

Trends in the Demand for Labor

In the urban labor markets (particularly the big city job markets) where most black workers compete for jobs, long-run trends toward expanding white-collar employment accelerated, while trends toward stagnant or declining manufacturing employment were reversed during the 1960s. Even in the older northeastern and midwestern cities, the long-term loss of manufacturing jobs was actually halted. Cleveland, for example, is an old industrial city that has lost well over 50 percent of its manufacturing production jobs since 1947. Between 1963 and 1967, Cleveland manufacturing employment actually grew slightly— from 168,900 to 171,300 jobs. Baltimore typified the employment trends of many snowbelt cities. This city experienced a net increase of nearly 9,000 manufacturing jobs between 1962 and 1967. Bennett Harrison and Edward Hill estimated that, in those lines of Baltimore manufacturing offering high-wage blue-collar

work, employment had declined by 19 percent between 1953 and 1959, stabilized from 1959 to 1962, and then increased by 5 percent between 1962 and 1970. In the suburban areas of snowbelt cities, manufacturing production jobs were typically growing in availability, inducing the more mobile elements of the ghetto labor force to commute to suburban jobs. Black males in Detroit made particularly large gains in numbers of jobs held in high-wage manufacturing employment. By 1970, over 33 percent of the employed central city black male Detroit residents were commuting to suburban jobs.

Declining manufacturing employment after the Korean War severely reduced black employment prospects during the mid- to late 1950s. Rapidly increasing unemployment was the result. The long 1960s boom partially reversed this situation, predictably bringing falling black male unemployment rates and rising real incomes. For the snowbelt cities, however, the prosperous 1960s were merely an interlude; manufacturing production work had already resumed its long-term decline by 1970, and the trend has been straight downhill ever since. Furthermore, the suburban periphery is no longer a source of growing manufacturing employment for blue-collar workers. This long-term decline is one of the key factors behind the sharp drop since 1969 (table 9.4) in the relative incomes of black males who reside in northern and western states.

. . . [L]ong-term growth patterns in major urban areas favor the white-collar worker over his blue-collar counterpart. During the prosperous 1960s, both blue- and white-collar job holders progressed, but opportunities were greatest in the white-collar occupations. Ghettos are usually located near central city CBDs, where white-collar employment is most heavily concentrated. For those black urban residents having the educational background necessary to compete for these jobs, expanding CBDs in the 1960s offered numerous possibilities. Younger, better-educated black females benefited most from this situation, moving heavily into clerical occupations while also registering some gains in the professions. In 1950, "cleaning lady" had been the most common job title among urban black females. By 1970, private household employment was a distant fourth, and clerical work was in first place. In cities such as Chicago during the 1960s, it was commonplace to observe tripling and even quadrupling of black female clerical employment in industries like banking.

Rapidly expanding government employment probably provided the greatest opportunities for black female gains. Over half of all government jobs are clerical or professional and these are the two occupations that black females have penetrated most rapidly since 1950. Indeed, most of the employed black women who work as professionals are employed by the government; among them, teaching is the most common profession. In many northern cities such as Baltimore and Chicago, over 25 percent of all employed black females in 1970 worked for the government.

The shift in black female occupational structure has been profound since 1950. While black males were still overwhelmingly employed in blue-collar and service occupations, black women were in the 1960s rapidly narrowing differences in occupational structure with white females by moving into white-collar jobs. Like whites, black females have been steadily shifting away from the operative occupational category but black male operative employment grew in both absolute and relative terms after 1950, following a trend that dates back to World War I. Black men remain heavily employed in manufacturing, which is a highly cyclical sector of the economy that is shrinking in significance, while black women rely increasingly on administrative and professional work that is both less cyclical and growing. Although blue-collar manufacturing jobs for men and white-collar clerical work for women provided important gains for blacks in the 1960s, low-wage work continued to be a major

employer of ghetto labor. Services and retail trade are major low-wage employers. Even in manufacturing, certain sectors such as apparel offer poor-paying, dead-end, unstable work of the least desirable sort. Employment growth in these low-wage sectors during the 1960s was particularly prevalent in the sunbelt cities.

Civil Rights Activism

Comprehensive treatment of the civil rights movement would require more than a chapter; it requires a separate volume. Here we simply highlight those aspects that are most directly relevant to the employment status of blacks. The Civil Rights Act of 1964 is one obvious landmark. Title VII of that act outlawed discrimination based on race, sex, or national origin by private employers, unions, and employment agencies; the Equal Employment Opportunity Commission (EEOC) was set up to investigate charges of discrimination. In 1972, the Commission's powers were expanded, allowing it to file suits on behalf of those injured by employment discrimination. Another major piece of the fair employment infrastructure grew out of Executive Order 11246, issued in 1965, which prohibits employment discrimination by recipients of federal contracts. The Office of Federal Contract Compliance (OFCC) was created to monitor compliance with the order. Given the subjective nature of much employment discrimination, actual government policy in this realm has varied from year to year, and numerous court cases have been necessary to define boundaries between discrimination, nondiscrimination, and affirmative action.

The EEOC and OFCC lack the personnel necessary to enforce adequately their legislative mandates, but the effectiveness of antidiscrimination efforts in the employment realm is not totally dependent upon these two agencies. Quite aside from the EEOC and the OFCC, the law permits injured parties to seek redress through the courts. Nonetheless, the

EEOC's record has been disappointing. In 1973, for example, nearly fifty thousand individuals filed complaints with the EEOC alleging discrimination, many more than the approximately one thousand EEOC professional staff could handle. By 1977, the backlog of cases had grown to 130,000. The OFCC has the power to cancel or suspend government contracts and it sometimes exerts strong pressure on government contractors. In 1969, for example, the OFCC issued the Philadelphia Plan for affirmative action by federal construction contractors in that city: contractors were ordered to increase their employment of minority craftsmen from the current 2 percent to goals of 4 to 9 percent within one year, and 19 to 26 percent within four years. Thus affirmative action plans became part of civil rights law.

Aggressive use of EEOC and OFCC powers is rare. The OFCC debarred no contractors between 1965 and 1970 and debarred an average of two per year between 1971 and 1977. All EEOC litigation through 1977 resulted in estimated back pay settlements of only $65 million. Nonetheless, a few well-publicized settlements have induced many employers to hire at least a few blacks for better-paying jobs. In 1973, American Telephone and Telegraph signed a consent decree that included a multimillion dollar package providing back pay and future promotions for women and minorities. Large firms in general have established minority hiring plans and, at a minimum, pay lip service to minority hiring and promotion.

Estimating the exact impact of anti-discrimination laws on black employment and earnings is quite impossible, but several conclusions are warranted. First, blatant discrimination as formerly practiced by such unions as the AFL building trades has been sharply curtailed. Second, it is now the norm for large companies to employ at least a few blacks in both skilled blue-collar ranks and managerial white-collar jobs. Third, fair employment laws depend upon

active enforcement for much of their effectiveness. Proponents of these laws face a constant battle to insure that the enforcement agencies possess the resources and the willingness to combat employment discrimination. The record to date suggests that comprehensive enforcement has never been attempted. Fourth, employers are most likely to adhere to the spirit of anti-discriminatory laws during periods of economic expansion. Tough questions such as racial implications of various seniority systems need not arise when black employees are being hired and upgraded. During economic downturns, however, the last hired are most apt to be the first fired; these are black workers disproportionately.

One difficulty in assessing the impact of measures as controversial and subjective as anti-discrimination laws is the fact that they are inseparable from overall attitudes on the status of minorities. One major impact of civil rights activism is that black workers themselves are less likely to tolerate discrimination on the job in a milieu where equal rights concerns are paramount. In the 1920s, blacks were grateful for access to any kind of position in better-paying industries. In contrast, the charged environment in the 1960s encouraged black workers to speak out against discrimination in the work place, in unions, and in society in general. Most employers, especially those large enough to attract the attention of the EEOC or OFCC, wanted to avoid the publicity that was apt to accompany allegations of discrimination in hiring and promotion. Firms hiring numerous blacks for several occupations (such as clerical or operative) often improved promotion opportunities and upgraded at least a few blacks. Creating the perception of better job opportunities helped to legitimize employment practices, thus perhaps lessening black disenchantment in all ranks. Less discriminatory hiring practices were widely adapted as pragmatic business practices: an expanding economy generated the need to hire additional workers, and greater access to job openings for blacks not only helped to avoid government scrutiny, it was also a wise public relations gesture.

THE 1970S

The three major industry groups employing black workers were manufacturing, services, and government. Job growth in manufacturing was moderate during the 1960s, while employment creation in government and services was quite rapid and widespread. Black employees benefited from these strong labor demands. But the 1960s also created job gains in traditionally discriminatory industries such as construction, which lessened racial barriers because of government scrutiny and declining public acceptance of racist hiring and training policies. Similar pressure, plus growing clerical worker needs, caused industries traditionally employing few blacks—finance, communications, utilities—to recruit black workers actively during the 1960s. Rapid educational gains also helped to deepen the industry-occupational mix open to black job seekers. In the more rapidly growing sunbelt regions of the United States, this 1960s pattern of improved job access continued well into the 1970s. Declining labor demands in the slower growing, more recession-prone snowbelt economy set the stage for losses in black economic well-being during the 1970s. Job losses in manufacturing were heavily concentrated in several high-paying, unionized industries where black male employment gains of the 1960s had been particularly strong. Job losses in government were much less widespread, but they were concentrated heavily in areas such as New York City and Cleveland, where black employment in government had risen substantially in the 1960s.

The impact of manufacturing sector decline upon black workers is shown clearly by the situation in motor vehicles. Blacks prospered disproportionately from auto industry pros-

perity in the 1960s. The proportion of all motor vehicle industry employees who were black rose from 9.1 percent in 1960 to 13.4 percent in 1970; 138,609 blacks worked in this one industry at the end of the 1960s.[9] The rule of thumb that the auto companies employ at least one million workers during a good year—valid as late as 1978 when employment reached 977,000—is no longer applicable. The industry in the 1980s is investing heavily in labor-saving equipment and use of foreign-made parts is increasing. Researchers for the United Auto Workers Union estimate that 1985 auto industry employment may be as low as 527,000, only 54 percent of the 1978 total. Future industry employment, of course, depends upon the market share of imported autos: the 527,000 job estimate assumes a 30.9 percent import share of the U.S. car market. The U.S. Chamber of Commerce estimates that communities lose, on average, two service jobs for every three manufacturing jobs that disappear.

A study of workers displaced from manufacturing industries in the early 1970s found that average annual percentage earnings losses, during the first two years after job loss, were: autos, 43.4%; steel, 46.6%; aerospace, 23.6%; electronic components, 8.3%; shoes, 11.3%; and women's clothes, 13.3%.

Re-employment was the norm for workers displaced in the early 1970s, and the severity of earnings loss is associated with two obvious factors: wages before displacement, and alternative opportunities for employment. Since autos and steel are both high-wage industries heavily concentrated in slow-growth snowbelt states, their displaced workers predictably experienced high earnings losses. Displacement from lower-wage manufacturing industries produced the smallest earnings losses, especially in instances such as electronic components where employment is concentrated in the healthier sunbelt states. These patterns of earnings losses may actually be accentuated in the 1980s, due to the severity of regional employ-

TABLE 9.8 RATIO OF NONWHITE TO WHITE FAMILY MEDIAN INCOMES IN SELECTED STATES, 1959–1979

	1959	1969	1979	Change: 1959–1979
A. Snowbelt Industrial States				
Illinois	.68	.70	.60	—.08
Ohio	.70	.74	.67	—.03
Michigan	.68	.75	.69	+.01
Pennsylvania	.71	.74	.62	—.09
B. Sunbelt Southeastern States				
Alabama	.42	.49	.55	+.13
Georgia	.44	.52	.56	+.12
North Carolina	.43	.57	.63	+.20
Virginia	.50	.59	.62	+.12

Sources: U.S. Bureau of the Census, *Advance Estimates of Social, Economic, and Housing Characteristics—Supplementary Report: Counties and Selected Places* (by State) Alabama ser. PHC80-S2-2 (Washington, D.C.: Government Printing Office, 1983), p. 39; ibid., Georgia S2–12, p. 79; ibid., Illinois S2-15, p. 75; ibid., Michigan S2–24, p. 67; ibid., North Carolina S2–35, p. 55; ibid., Ohio S2-37, p 67; ibid., Pennsylvania S2-40, p. 63; ibid., Virginia S2-48, p. 75. U.S. Bureau of the Census, *Census of Population: 1970, General Social and Economic Characteristics, Final Report PC (1)-C2, Alabama* (Washington, D.C.: Government Printing Office,1972), pp. 2–164; ibid., *Georgia*, pp.12–238; ibid., *Illinois*, pp. 15–336; ibid., *Michigan*, pp. 24–246; ibid., *North Carolina*, pp. 35–201; ibid., *Ohio*, pp. 37–327; ibid., *Pennsylvania*, pp. 40–308; ibid., *Virginia*, pp. 48–209.

Assumptions:

1983–88 3.4 percent average annual increase in GNP, 2.1 percent average annual increase in nonfarm employment.

1988–93 2.7 percent average annual increase in GNP, 1.2 percent average annual increase in nonfarm employment.

Source: Data Resources, Inc.

ment declines in the Midwest, where steel-making and auto manufacturing and assembly are so heavily concentrated.

Industrial cities like Cleveland, Chicago, and Pittsburgh no longer provide the route to upward mobility via manufacturing employment for less-skilled workers. The massive losses of blue-collar manufacturing jobs in the 1970s and 1980s, interacting with local government fiscal difficulties, are effectively reversing many of the employment gains captured by blacks in the 1960s. Yet these are the same cities in which highly educated blacks continued in the 1970s to gain jobs in the expanding management and administrative sectors. It is precisely in these older industrial cities where the contrast between the haves and the have nots is sharpening most rapidly: a portion of the smaller white-collar group prospers while the larger blue-collar urban black workforce is undermined. In the aggregate regional statistics (table 9.8), the

misfortune of the many swamps the progress of the few, and the income gains of the 1960s are decisively erased. The severity of the losses recorded in table 9.8 undoubtedly reflects, too, weakening local government employment, which reduced the ranks of the more affluent white-collar group. The fact that Michigan is the only state registering a gain since 1959 in relative black family incomes partially reflects the superior unemployment compensation benefits received by auto workers.

The situation in the South was altogether different in the 1970s. A stronger regional economy has created blue-collar as well as white-collar jobs, and local government fiscal difficulties were less severe than in the snow-belt cities. Relative black incomes continued their 1960s trajectory. Regional differences are particularly apparent in the unemployment data. In March 1980, black male unemployment rates in Illinois and Ohio exceeded 16 percent; the corresponding rates in Georgia and North Carolina were 8.7 and 8.3 percent. The differential in female unemployment rates for blacks was less pronounced: 13.6 and 13.2 percent in Illinois and Ohio, versus 11.2 and 11.1 percent in Georgia and North Carolina. The female differential pattern reflects the fact that sunbelt black women workers have penetrated white-collar jobs to a much lesser degree than their snow-belt counterparts. Continued black economic gains in the South were brought to a halt, however, by the severe recession of the early 1980s, as shown in table 9.4.

THE 1980S

Has the twentieth-century transition of blacks from a predominantly southern rural to a predominantly urban America drastically lessened racial discrimination, or have new forms of racial inequality arisen in the cities? Black economic progress in the sunbelt cities sheds the most light on this question. Table 9.8 shows a trend toward convergence in snow-belt and sunbelt black-white income ratios. Relative black incomes were still slightly higher in most of the northern states in 1979, but the continued 1980s decline of blue-collar jobs in high-wage manufacturing industries pulled the regional wage ratios into closer alignment. Briefly, the labor market in northern cities is increasingly resembling the southern job scene: blacks in both regions face most rapid job growth at the higher and lower ends of the market, and least opportunity in the middle occupational echelons.

Harrison's study of sunbelt cities shows that blacks there have traditionally had a much higher proportion of low-wage and part-time jobs than their snowbelt counter parts. . . . [S]outhern and southwestern cities were more service and trade oriented, while snowbelt cities and SMSAs were more manufacturing oriented. Declining snowbelt manufacturing along with growth in services is lessening these differences in industrial composition as well as wage structure; service work is very low in pay relative to manufacturing. Furthermore, the sunbelt manufacturing production jobs, relatively low paying, are frequently in those fields that are most likely to be growing nationwide in coming years. Electronics, for example, is expected to expand in snowbelt as well as sunbelt regions, but it rarely offers blue-collar workers the wages paid by such traditional employers as the metal shaping and manufacturing industries. . . . [T]he expanding lines of manufacturing tend to produce jobs for highly trained, technical, scientific, and professional personnel, and production jobs staffed by low-wage workers. Rapidly rising productivity per worker also characterizes this sector, minimizing high tech industry's ability to create new jobs (fig. 9.1) Data Resources Incorporate (DRI) estimates that output per high tech worker will rise by 46 percent between 1983 and 1993, double the projected increase for services (23 percent) and manufacturing (24 percent). The manufacturing sector lost roughly three million jobs between 1980 and 1982. Neither a cyclical upswing in manufacturing industries nor continued growth in high tech areas is predicted to replace, by 1990, the production jobs lost during the early 1980s.

Those industries where job growth is most rapid, services and trade (fig. 9.1), are primarily low-wage industries; high-wage sectors—construction, transportation, public utilities, government, and manufacturing—have been stagnant since the 1960s, with available job openings concentrated in white-collar, skilled fields. Aside from the 1960s, these trends in job growth have actually been apparent since the end of the Korean war. In Baltimore, for example, 31 percent of all private sector jobs in 1953 were found in the low-wage non-manufacturing industries; by 1974, 43 percent of the jobs were found in this sector. During this same time period, high-wage manufacturing work fell from 32 percent to 25 percent of Baltimore's private sector employment. While

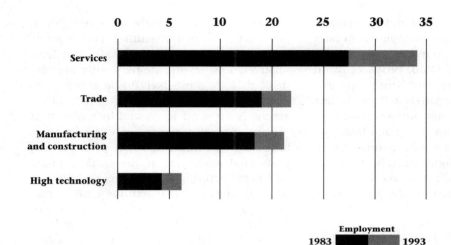

Figure 9.1
Employment by Industry: 1983 and 1993 *(in millions of workers).*

Employment
1983   1993

Assumptions:
1983–88 3.4 percent average annual increase in GNP, 2.1 percent average annual increase in nonfarm employment.
1988–93 2.7 percent average annual increase in GNP, 1.2 percent average annual increase in nonfarm employment.

Source: Data Resources, Inc.

high-wage sectors tend to offer full-time year-round work predominantly, low-wage industries such as services and retail trade more frequently offer only part-time work to their employees.

Sources of future income gains for black workers in urban America are not readily apparent. Even in the best paying occupations the outlook for gains is not altogether bright. In the professional and technical occupations for example, most blacks are employed as teachers, nurses, health care technicians, social workers, and counselors.[10] These represent the lowest paying types of jobs available in this heterogeneous occupational grouping, and they are largely lines of work where career opportunities for upgrading in pay and responsibilities are minimal. Furthermore, black professionals rely heavily on government, particularly city government, for employment and they are concentrated in older, larger cities where fiscal problems are most severe. Not

only are future employment gains unlikely, but outright employee reductions are the norm in cities such as Chicago and Detroit.

The situation in the clerical occupations is brighter, since long-term employment growth in this line of work is expected to continue into the foreseeable future. While government workforce reductions have a negative impact on clerical job opportunities, this has been offset by growing private sector demand for workers in this field. Jobs in computer-related fields, such as data entry, should continue to grow rapidly. Clerical work, however, offers few opportunities for occupational advancement, and pay is below average relative to wage and salary levels in the overall economy. While the large-scale shift of black workers into clerical occupations does represent a long-term upgrading in labor force status, it certainly does not represent a move towards long-term equality in labor force status. In fact, the social status and remuneration associated with clerical work have been steadily declining, relative to the other occupations, throughout the twentieth century.

Nonetheless, prospects in clerical and professional occupations are brighter than those facing blue-collar workers. Advances in education and training can lead to further gains in growth areas such as the managerial and nongovernment professional occupations, and younger black workers are increasing their penetration in these lines of employment. Yet it is among the young that polarization appears to be most pronounced: rapid income gains for the best educated coexist with very high unemployment rates and falling labor force participation rates for the majority of young blacks. Long-term economic trends suggest that the latter group is most likely to find work in low-paying but growing industries, particularly services. Night-watchman, dishwasher, janitor—these are the types of low-wage, unstable work that will increasingly typify job opportunities for ghetto residents.

High unemployment and low labor force participation rates among black teenagers are often cited as evidence of declining job prospects. The unemployment problems of this group are indeed staggering—the unemployment rate for blacks sixteen to nineteen years of age actually topped 50 percent in August 1981—but we feel that teenagers are not an appropriate group for illustrating labor market trends. Part of the black teenage employment problem reflects improved education and training opportunities. These opportunities have induced many young blacks to substitute schooling or military service for work. Because those with better than average employment prospects are most likely to pursue advanced education and training, the attractiveness to employers of the remaining out-of-school civilian black youth population is reduced. This process partially explains both the rising incidence of black youth unemployment and the occupational and income gains realized by educated young blacks.

To illustrate the polarization process we focus not upon black teenagers but upon those twenty to twenty-four years of age. Trends in their labor market status are documented utilizing data from the Census of Population Public Use Samples for Illinois and Ohio. Similar data for North Carolina and Georgia are used below to explain differences in snowbelt/sunbelt employment situations facing young black males. The labor force participation rate of black males twenty to twenty-four years old in Ohio and Illinois resembles that of all adult black males in those states—70.3 percent for the former versus 70.7 percent for the latter—but the similarities end there. These younger blacks are better educated than the overall black workforce and they have entered the labor force during the time when all of the forces promoting polarization discussed above were fully operative. Census data yield the following information: (1) the labor force participation rate of black males twenty to twenty-four years of age fell from 76.5 percent in 1970 to 70.3 percent in 1980; (2) their unemployment rate rose from 12.5 percent in 1970 to 29.3 percent in 1980; (3) they were heavily concentrated in manufacturing employment in both 1970 and 1980, and the majority of those in manufacturing worked in three high-wage sectors: metal (predominantly steel mills), machinery, and transportation equipment; (4) 43.8 percent of this group worked in manufacturing in 1970, versus 31.1 percent in 1980; (5) their incidence of white-collar employment rose from 23.6 percent in 1970 to 28.1 percent in 1980; (6) their incidence of employment in service occupations rose from 10.4 percent in 1970 to 20.1 percent in 1980.

Overall, the proportion of black males twenty to twenty-four years of age in Ohio and Illinois who held jobs fell precipitously between 1970 and 1980. Whereas 63 percent were working in 1970 on the date when they filled out their census forms, only 41 percent were employed in 1980. Job loss in the tradi-

TABLE 9.9 SELECTED DATA ON BLACK MALE EMPLOYEES IN OHIO AND ILLINOIS IN 1979 *(MEANS ONLY)**

	Manufacturing	Services	All Employees
Total wage and salary income	$14,263	$8,137	$12,346
Total income from all sources	$14,742	$8,609	$12,882
Weeks worked in 1979	44.4	37.2	42.0
Average number of hours worked per week	40.0	35.8	38.4
Weeks unemployed in 1979	3.6	5.6	4.2
Total number of observations	4,723	2,282	13,285

SOURCE: SAMPLE A OF THE 1980 CENSUS OF POPULATION AND HOUSING: PUBLIC USE MICRODATA SAMPLE.

*This table represents a 2.5 percent random sample of the population of Ohio and Illinois. According to the data source, 2.5 percent of the universe of black male employees 16 years of age or older in 1980 in these two states constituted 15,079 observations. In performing the mean calculations, 1,794 of the observations were excluded because they had not worked as employees during 1979. Unpaid workers in family businesses were excluded from the sample of 13,285 observations.

tional manufacturing sector was partially offset by growth of white-collar employment, but it was in the low-wage service sector where job expansion was most pronounced. Table 9.9 compares earnings and employment stability in the manufacturing and service areas. Relative to manufacturing, service work is low paying. In 1979, mean wage and salary incomes for black male service workers in Ohio and Illinois reached only $8,137; mean wage incomes of their cohorts employed in manufacturing stood 75.3 percent higher, at $14,263. The service workers receive low hourly wages, but they are also handicapped by their higher incidence of part-time work. According to table 9.9, average weeks worked in 1979 was 37.2 for service workers and 44.4 for manufacturing employees. Similarly, the average number of hours worked per week was a lower 35.8 hours in services, versus 40.0 hours in manufacturing. Finally the typical service worker portrayed in table 9.9 spent 5.6 weeks unemployed in 1979 (versus 3.6 in manufacturing) and he spent 9.2 weeks as a nonparticipant in the labor force (versus 4.0 weeks in manufacturing). The educational credentials of black workers employed in manufacturing and services were quite similar overall: 23.0 percent of those in services had attended school beyond the high school level, as had 22.8 percent of those in manufacturing. Both groups, however, lagged behind the average educational credentials of black males employed outside of the service and manufacturing areas.

Rising unemployment rates and declining labor participation of blacks twenty to twenty-four years of age are partially caused by the nature of the service jobs that increasingly typify their employment alternatives. Many service industries do not offer full-time, year-round work. Employment in services frequently entails enduring bouts of unemployment and labor force nonparticipation. Seven specific types of industries employed nearly 81 percent of the black male service workers summarized in table 9.9. In order of importance they were: restaurant (employing 20.3 percent of the service workers), public administration, hospital, education, service to building firms, real estate, and hotel. Restaurants and hotels that cater to tourists are normally seasonal employers, and educational institutions often have reduced needs for service workers in the summertime. Other major service employers such as hospitals often provide stable work, but wage rates for their service employees are typically very low. Employment in hospitals has grown quite rapidly for all blacks in Ohio and Illinois in the last two decades. It was the largest single industry in which black females in these two states worked in 1980; over 16 percent of all black working women listed hospitals as their industry of employment in 1980, and while most were service workers, 27.2 percent worked as professionals, primarily nurses.

While younger snowbelt black males shifted rapidly out of high-wage manufacturing work in the 1970s and toward unemployment as well as low-wage service jobs (and white-collar employment), their sunbelt cohorts experienced no such tumultuous changes in labor force status. Southern blacks are protected from the trauma of losing high-wage manufacturing jobs because they had few of them in the first place. Among the black males working in manufacturing in North Carolina and Georgia, three lines—textiles, wood products, and food processing—provide over one-half of the jobs. These three low-wage industries employed 54.2 percent of the Georgia and North Carolina black males working in manufacturing in 1970, versus 55.2 percent of those in manufacturing in 1980. Among those twenty to twenty-four years of age, black males in these two states relied on manufacturing for 38.6 percent of their jobs in 1970, and 36.7 percent of them in 1980. White-collar and service work did increase in incidence over the 1970s decade, but the changes were minor ones. Black males twenty to twenty-four years old saw the incidence of service employment rise from 13.4 percent to 15.7 percent while the percentage of those in white-collar jobs rose from 15.7 percent in 1970 to 17.1 percent in 1980. Their incidence of unemployment did rise slightly over the decade, but the 2.4 percent rise from 12.6 to 15.0 percent in the unemployment rate was dwarfed in magnitude by the 16.8 percentage points (from 12.5 to 29.3 percent) that were tacked on to the unemployment rate of their northern cohorts.

The changes in labor force status among twenty- to twenty-four-year-old black males of course reflect changes that in varying degrees shape the economic well-being of all black male workers. Thus, the declining incidence of employment in manufacturing is undercutting the job status of all snowbelt black workers. Among all employed Ohio and Illinois black male employees, 40.1 percent worked in manufacturing in 1970 versus 34.4 percent in 1980. Rising unemployment and falling rates of labor force participation typify black male workers from twenty-five to fifty-four years of age. For those in Illinois and Ohio, the incidence of unemployment rose from 4.4 to 13.5 percent between 1970 and 1980, while their labor force participation rate fell from 87.4 to 82.7 percent. In contrast, their cohorts in Georgia and North Carolina experienced stable labor force participation rates and an increase in the incidence of unemployment from 3.1 to 6.8 percent. During the recessionary early 1980s, snowbelt black workers fell further behind their sunbelt counterparts because of their greater dependence upon the most cyclical segments of manufacturing—steel, autos, and related durables. Indeed, in 1982, the North Central region actually surpassed the South for the first time in history as the region having the highest rate of black poverty (39.8 percent). It would be incorrect, however, to conclude that southern black economic well-being is surpassing that of northern blacks precisely because of the highly cyclical nature of much northern durable goods manufacturing. Although the long-term outlook for employment in snowbelt heavy industry is dim, upturn phases in the business cycle are still capable of alleviating (partially) the large cyclical component of black unemployment.

INCREASING GOVERNMENT REPRESENTATION MAY NOT IMPROVE BLACK ECONOMIC WELL-BEING

History suggests that strong and sustained economic growth periods improve black labor force status in both absolute and relative terms. Overall health of the economy will continue to be a vital determinant of black economic well-being in the future. A strong political voice, typified by 1960s civil rights activism, may also produce economic dividends for the black community. Gains in local government, though, may offer little potential unless the fiscal crises of the older, larger cities are alleviated.

Black political goals in central cities have been city hall power, improved city services for black neighborhoods, and a larger proportion of city government jobs. Winning city hall, though, is increasingly a hollow political prize. Facing constant job loss, disinvestment, and tax base deterioration, black leaders in cities like Detroit, Gary, and Newark are increasingly dependent upon state and federal funds. The early 1980s has produced a rising indifference to the fiscal problems of declining central cities by state and particularly national government bodies. Black mayors can thus do little to alter the well-being of their constituents because they lack control over the economic resources needed to do the job.

Private capital can be induced to invest in America's aging cities if the terms are right: enter CBD renovation, convention centers, "favorable" tax climates, and the like. Leveraged by federal dollars, multibillion dollar urban renewal programs have transformed or are transforming downtown areas in cities as diverse as Boston and Pittsburgh. Urban renewal often removes "blight" from the periphery of the CBD, freeing potentially valuable property for use as infrastructure that complements CBD interests, and sites for private sector expansion, ranging from high-rise apartments to corporate office buildings. Blight typically consists of low-cost housing for blacks; it is replaced by parking facilities, sports stadiums, convention centers, freeway interchanges, and high-cost apartments. Urban renewal thus becomes urban removal, with the displaced minority population squeezed into a diminished stock of rental housing.

Although urban renewal policies do indeed seem to be renovating downtown areas in many large cities, their political feasibility is increasingly being undermined by an obvious contradiction. How can black politicians be elected when they espouse CBD renovation projects, especially when these projects have traditionally destroyed black neighborhoods? How can scarce local government services be concentrated on downtown areas when the social needs of ghettos are so astoundingly high? Some ghetto blacks, of course, expect to benefit from the jobs generated by downtown expansion. Because these jobs are largely administrative, however, the highly educated segment of the labor force, managers and the professionals, are likely to benefit disproportionately from CBD job growth. Successful downtown renovation increasingly attracts young white professionals into inner-city neighborhoods, and a process of gentrification often results. Rents are invariably driven up in black neighborhoods adjacent to gentrified districts, further reducing the accessible housing supply for low-income blacks.

The resultant political unpopularity of urban renewal programs in black communities makes it difficult for black mayors to pursue the types of policies most apt to attract private capital to the central city. Equitable redistribution of city services and property tax burdens is similarly fraught with political dangers. Envision a mayor who successfully reallocates city services from the haves to the have-nots: educational resources are assigned to ghetto schools to bring them up to par with the city's best schools; police are transferred from the CBD to high-crime, inner-city neighborhoods, and so forth. Does the quality of life subsequently improve for the lower-income residents of this equitably governed metropolis? The answer is unclear. A city government that offers higher taxes and fewer services to the resident wealthy and local business interests is perceived as a threat to their well-being. If this threat appears to be more than transitory, the powerful and the prosperous will react in ways that may destroy much of the city's economic base. If local government does not cater to the interests of the business community, firms will cut back drastically on their local investment plans. Financial institutions, fearing a contraction in business activity, tighten up on their local lending activities. Firms that had contemplated moving job-generating activities into this locality will be inclined to locate in "friendlier" environs. Many higher-income residents will respond to service cuts and tax increases by moving to suburbia. Outward migration of both residents and economic activity, combined with tight local money markets, will generate declining property values. Declining property values create a need for higher local taxes and/or cuts in services. The city economy spirals downward; local employment opportunities diminish. Thus, even in cities where blacks have achieved political power, improvement programs become hostages to the economic interests of the corporate elite.

Notes

1. The increasing incidence of two-earner families among whites is partially responsible for the downward trend in relative black family incomes. See Charles Brown, "The Federal Attack on Labor Market Discrimination: The Mouse That Roared?" National Bureau of Economic Research Working Paper no. 669 (Cambridge, Mass., Apr. 1981) pp. 2–14, for a discussion of this question.
2. John Reid, "Black America in the 1980s," *Population Bulletin* 37, no. 5:24–25.
3. Cited in Christopher Jencks, "Discrimination and Thomas Sowell," *New York Review of Books* 3 Mar. 1983, p. 36.
4. Occupational figures were taken from U.S. Bureau of the Census, *Current Population Reports,* ser. P-60, 132, table 55 (Washington, D.C.: Government Printing Office, July 1982), pp. 192–99. These figures refer to persons eighteen years of age and older as of Mar. 1981; occupation was recorded for all who worked during the 1980 calendar year.
5. Results of this Gallup poll were cited in "Black Statistics: A Look at the Figures on Social Change," *Focus* (Spring 1981):1. A good overview of the employment gains of better-educated blacks appears in Richard Freeman, *Black Elite: The New Market for Qualified Black Americans* (New York: McGraw, 1976), chaps. 6 and 9.
6. National Urban League report, *The State of Black America 1980,* cited in ibid., p. 4.
7. U.S. Bureau of the Census, *Current Population Reports,* ser. P 60, no. 137, table 16 (Washington, D.C.: Government Printing Office, Mar. 1983), pp. 43–46.
8. See, for example, Richard Freeman, "Black Economic Progress Since 1964: Who Has Gained and Why" in *Studies in Labor Markets,* ed. Sherwin Rosen (Cambridge, Mass.: National Bureau of Economic Research, 1981), pp. 247–94.
9. Regional breakdowns of relative income trends over time must be done with caution because of incomparability problems between the two groupings, "nonwhite" and "black." Nonwhite and black are often used interchangeably as groupings for describing black income trends; this procedure is invalid when applied to the western United States because trends in nonwhite incomes differ sharply from black income trends. This bias rises due to rapid income gains realized by the sizeable Asian population that resides in the West. Smaller Asian populations in other regions of the United States decrease this bias substantially.
10. Studies showing substantial progress in black economic well-being typically focus upon wage and salary earnings only. This approach further distorts trends in *overall* black status, particularly among males, because it neglects the high and rising incidence of zero-wage and salary earners which is much higher than the incidence of black zero-income earners. See, for example, James Smith and Finis Welch, "Race Differences in Earnings: A Survey and New Evidence," in *Current Issues in Urban Economics,* ed. Peter Mieszkowski and Mahlon Straszheim (Baltimore: Johns Hopkins Univ. Pr., 1979), pp. 40–69.

    Severe biases arising in relative income studies that exclude the zero-income (or wage) individuals are analyzed in William Darity "Illusions of Black Economic Progress," *Review of Black Political Economy* 10, no. 4 (1980):153–67, and Charles Brown, "Black-White Earnings Ratios Since the Civil Rights Act of 1964: The Importance of Labor Market Drop-outs," National Bureau of Economic Research Working Paper no. 617 (Cambridge, Mass.: National Bureau of Economic Research, Jan. 1981).

11. Michael Reich, *Racial Inequality* (Princeton, NJ.: Princeton Univ. Pr., 1981), p. 65. By 1970, the proportion of southern blacks residing in urban areas had risen to 67.4 percent.

12. Sar Levitan, William Johnson, and Robert Taggert, *Still A Dream. The Changing Status of Blacks Since 1960* (Cambridge, Mass: Harvard Univ. Pr., 1975), p. 24.

13. Ibid., p.26.

14. Improved social security disability benefits have contributed to falling labor force participation rates among black males 45 and older. Older people who have not yet reached retirement age opt for these benefits, because they are poor and unhealthy—not because they are black—according to a study by Donald Parsons, "Racial Trends in Male Labor Force Participation," *American Economic Review* 70, no. 5 (1980):912–14. Blacks disproportionately are recipients of disability benefits. Parsons found, however, that black-white differences in the incidence of benefit recipients were eliminated when health and economic circumstances were controlled for.

15. Before 1970, black teenage labor force participation rates were falling nationally but this was caused largely by the shift out of southern, agricultural work. In nonsouthern areas, participation rates were stable between 1950 and 1970, although unemployment rates were rising. See John Cogan, "The Decline in Black Teenage Employment: 1950–1970," *American Economic Review* 72, no. 4 (1982):621–35.

16. Michael J. Piore, *Birds of Passage* (Cambridge: Cambridge Univ. Pr., 1979), pp. 79–80, 162–63.

17. Reid, "Black America in the 1980s," p. 16.

18. Ibid., p. 21.

19. Ibid., pp. 11–12

20. Arthur Ross, "The Negro in the American Economy," in *Employment, Race, and Poverty,* ed. Arthur Ross and Herbert Hill (New York: Harcourt, 1967), p. 30.

21. Alan Batchelder, "Decline in the Relative Income of Negro Men," *Quarterly Journal of Economics* 78, no. 4, (1964):525–48.

22. In the Chicago SMSA, for example, white-collar jobs in manufacturing increased from 1950 to 1960, while production jobs decreased in number; on balance, total manufacturing employment declined by approximately three thousand. Black employment in manufacturing declined by about two thousand between 1950 and 1960 in the Chicago SMSA. See John Kain and John Quigley, *Housing Markets and Racial Discrimination: A Microeconomic Analysis* (New York: National Bureau of Economic Research, 1975), p. 89.

23. See Walter Butcher, "Productivity, Technology and Employment in U.S. Agriculture," in *The Employment Impact of Technology Change, Appendix, Vol. II, Technology and the American Economy,* Report of the National Commission on Technology, Automation, and Economic Progress (Washington, D.C. Government Printing Office, 1966), pp. 135–52.

24. Evidence on this issue is highly conflicting but it points, on balance, to limited suburban job access for the younger and poorer (least mobile) ghetto residents. See Mahlon Straszheim, "Discrimination and Transportation Accessibility in Urban Labor Markets for Black Workers," University of Maryland Project on the Economics of Discrimination (College Park, Md.: Mimeograph, 1979), pp. 10–15, for a good summary of the controversy surrounding this issue.

25. See Batchelder, "Decline in Relative Income," p. 544. A more comprehensive survey known as the "Wirtz Survey" revealed shockingly high rates of ghetto subemployment in 1966. This survey is discussed in Francis Fox Piven and Richard A. Cloward, *Regulating the Poor: The Functions of Public Welfare* (New York: Pantheon, 1971), pp. 215–17.

26. James Geschwender, *Class, Race, and Worker Insurgency* (Cambridge: Cambridge Univ. Pr., 1977), pp. 32–34.

27. Ibid., pp. 41–42.

28. U.S. Bureau of the Census, *Census of Manufacturers 1967*, vol. 3, *Area Statistics* Part 2, Nebraska-Wyoming, (Washington, D.C.: Government Printing Office, 1971), pp. 36–37.

29. Bennett Harrison and Edward Hill, "The Changing Structure of Jobs in Older and Younger Cities," Joint Center for Urban Studies of MIT and Harvard University Working Paper no. 58 (Cambridge, Mass.: Joint Center for Urban Studies of MIT and Harvard University, Mar. 1979), p. 21.

30. Occupation data cited in this section have been calculated from the public use samples of the U.S. Census of Population.

31. Harrison, "Changing Structure," pp. 12–19.

32. Brown, "Federal Attack," p. 9.

33. Levitan, Johnson, and Taggert, "Still a Dream," p. 272.

34. Peter Eisinger, "The Economic Conditions of Black Employment in Municipal Bureaucracies," Institute for Research on Poverty Discussion Paper no. 661–81 (Madison, Wis.: Institute for Research on Poverty, 1981), p.16.

35. Geschwender, *Class, Race, and Worker Insurgency*, p. 43.

36. Mark Dodosh, "Auto Industry's Moves Jolt Many in Midwest and More Jolts Loom," *Wall Street Journal*, 26 May 1981, p. 1.

37. Barry Bluestone and Bennett Harrison, *The Deindustrialization of America* (New York: Basic Books, 1982), pp. 69–71.

38. Ibid., p. 57.

39. U.S. Bureau of the Census, *Advance Estimates of Social, Economic, and Housing Characteristics—Supplementary Report: Counties and Selected Places* (by state), ser. PHC80-S2 (Washington, D.C.: Government Printing Office, 1983).

40. Harrison and Hill, "Changing Structure," pp. 16–32.

41. "America Rushes to High Tech for Growth," *Business Week* 28 Mar. 1983, p. 86.

42. Total manufacturing employment declined from 26,382,000 in Jan. 1979 to 23,133,000 in Jan. 1983. The emerging consensus on this decline is summarized by Audrey Freeman, senior research associate at the Conference Board: "Employment is going to recover somewhat among production workers, simply because output is going to rise again, but I don't think it will ever reach its former level," in Henry Myers, "Recession Ripples: Economists Say Slump Hastened Some Trends but Spawned Very Few," *Wall Street Journal,* 25 May 1983, p. 1.

43. Harrison and Hill, "Changing Structure," pp. 20–26.

44. Reich, *Racial Inequality,* p. 30.

45. Harry Braverman, *Labor and Monopoly Capital* (New York: Monthly Review Pr., 1974), chap. 15.

46. This is documented in Robert Mare and Christopher Winship, "Racial Socioeconomic Convergence and the Paradox of Black Youth Joblessness: Enrollment, Enlistment, and Employment, 1964–1981," University of Chicago Economics Research Center Discussion Paper 83–14, (Chicago, July 1983).

47. Timothy Schellhardt, "North Central U.S. Surpasses South in Black Poverty Rate," *Wall Street Journal* 9 Aug. 1983, p. 35.

48. Richard Child Hill, "Fiscal Collapse and Political Struggle in Decaying Central Cities in the United States," in *Marxism and the Metropolis,* ed. William Tabb and Larry Sawers (New York: Oxford Univ. Pr., 1978) pp. 226–28.

49. For an excellent case study of this phenomenon, see Chester Hartman and Rob Kessler, "The Illusion and Reality of Urban Renewal: San Francisco's Yerba Buena Center," in *Marxism and the Metropolis,* ed. William Tabb and Larry Sawers (New York: Oxford Univ. Pr., 1978), pp. 153–78.

Essay/Discussion Questions

1. Daniel Fusfeld and Timothy Bates suggest that a major trend in the last few decades has been the economic polarization of the African American community. What is the nature of this polarization, and what are some of its causes and possible consequences?

2. What factors seem to be contributing to a growing discontent among many young urban African Americans? What role should government play to improve the life chances of low-income urban African Americans? What are some of the historical and contemporary

societal forces that prevent or hinder large-scale black entrepreneurial efforts?

3. The American economy is experiencing a transition from an industrial-manufacturing (physical labor) base in the first half of the twentieth century to a service-knowledge (mental work) base in the second half and into the twenty-first century. What are possible implications of this economic transformation for different classes of African Americans? What is the significance of education in the emerging economy?

Part VII Key Terms

Capitalism

Culture of control

Culture of Poverty thesis

Economic exploitation

Equal Employment Opportunity
Commission

Fair Employment Practice
Committee

"Negro Jobs"

Patriarchal

Planter class

Poor whites

Racism

A. Phillip Randolph

Sharecropping

Urban migration

Urban underclass

Working class

Part VII Supplementary Readings

Anderson, Elijah, "Race and Neighborhood Transition," in Paul E. Peterson, ed., *The New Urban Reality*, Washington, D. C.: The Brookings Institution, 1985, pp. 99–127.

Braddock, Jomillis H. II, and James M. McPartland, "How Minorities Continue to Be Excluded from Equal Employment Opportunities: Research on Labor Market and Institutional Barriers," *Journal of Social Issues*, Vol. 43, No. 1 (1987), pp. 5–39.

Brown, Michael K., and Stephen P. Erie, "Blacks and the Legacy of the Great Society: The Economic and Political Impact of Federal Social Policy," *Public Policy*, Vol. 29 (Summer 1981), pp. 299–330.

Bunche, Ralph J., "A Critique of New Deal Social Planning As It Affects Negroes," *Journal of Negro Education*, Vol. 5 (January 1936), pp. 59–65.

Clark, Kenneth B., *Dark Ghetto: Dilemmas of Social Power*, New York: Harper and Row, Publishers, 1965.

Danziger, Sheldon H., and Daniel H. Weinberg, eds., *Fighting Poverty: What Works and What Doesn't*, Cambridge: Harvard University Press, 1986.

Darity, William A., Jr., ed., *Labor Economics: Modern Views*, Boston: Kluwer Nijhoff, 1984

_____, "Reaganomics and the Black Community," in Sidney Weintraub and Marvin Goodstein, eds., *Reaganomics in the Stagflation Economy*, Philadelphia: University of Pennsylvania Press, 1983, pp. 59–77.

Darity, William A., Jr., and Samuel Myers, Jr., "Does Welfare Dependency Cause Female Headship?: The Case of the Black Family," *Journal of Marriage and the Family*, Vol. 46 (November 1984), pp. 765–780.

Drake, W. Avon, and Robert D. Holsworth, *Affirmative Action and the Stalled Quest for Black Progress*, Urbana: University of Illinois Press, 1996.

Du Bois, W. E. B., *The Philadelphia Negro: A Social Study*, New York: Benjamin Blom, 1967.

Erie, Steven P., "Public Policy and Black Economic Polarization," *Policy Analysis*, Vol. 6 (Summer 1980), pp. 305–318.

Farley, Reynolds, *Blacks and Whites: Narrowing the Gap?* Cambridge: Harvard University Press, 1984.

Foner, Philip S., *Organized Labor and the Black Worker, 1619–1973,* New York: International Publishers, 1974.

Franklin, Raymond, and Solomon Resnik, *The Political Economy of Racism*, New York: Holt, Rinehart and Winston, Inc., 1973.

Gill, Gerald, *Meanness Mania: The Changed Mood*, Washington, D. C.: Howard University Press, 1980.

Glasgow, Douglas G., *The Black Underclass: Poverty, Unemployment, and Entrapment of Ghetto Youth,* San Francisco: Jossey-Bass Publishers, 1980.

Gould, William B., *Black Workers in White Unions: Job Discrimination in the United States*, Ithaca: Cornell University Press, 1977.

Greene, Lorenzo, and Carter G. Woodson, *The Negro Wage Earner*, Washington, D. C.: Associated Publishers, 1930.

Grossman, James R., *Land Of Hope: Chicago, Black Southerners, and the Great Migration*, Chicago: The University of Chicago Press, 1989.

Hayes, Floyd W. III, "The Political Economy, Reaganomics, and Blacks," *The Western Journal of Black Studies*, Vol. 6, No. 2 (Summer 1982), pp. 89–97.

_____, "Government Retreat, the Dispossessed, and the Politics of African American Self-Reliant Development in the Age of Reaganism," in Marilyn E. Lashley and Melanie Njeri Jackson, eds., *African Americans and the New Policy Consensus: Retreat of the Liberal State?* Westport: Greenwood Press, 1994, pp. 99–120.

Hill, Robert B., "The Illusion of Black Economic Progress," *Social Policy*, Vol. 9, No. 3 (November-December 1978), pp. 14–25.

Hochschild, Jennifer L., *Facing Up to the American Dream: Race, Class, and the Soul of the Nation*, Princeton: Princeton University Press, 1995.

Jones, Barbara A., "Black Women and Labor Force Participation: An Analysis of Sluggish Growth Rates," *Review of Black Political Economy*, Vol. 14, No. 2–3 (Fall-Winter, 1985–1986), pp. 11–31.

Jones, Faustine C., *The Changing Mood in America: Eroding Commitment?* Washington, D. C.: Howard University Press, 1977.

Jones, Jacqueline, *The Dispossessed: America's Underclasses from the Civil War to the Present,* New York: Basic Books, 1992.

Kasarda, John D., "Urban Change and Minority Opportunities," in Paul E. Peterson, ed., *The New Urban Reality*, Washington, D. C.: The Brookings Institution, 1985, pp. 33–67.

Kerner, Otto, *Report of the National Advisory Commission on Civil Disorders*, Washington, D. C.: U. S. Government Printing Office, 1968.

Kotlowitz, Alex, *There Are No Children Here*, New York: Doubleday, 1991.

Landry, Bart, *The New Black Middle Class*, Berkeley: University of California Press, 1987.

Lemann, Nicholas, *The Promised Land: The Great Migration and How It Changed America*, New York: Alfred A. Knopf, 1991.

Lusane, Clarence, *Pipe Dream Blues: Racism and the War on Drugs*, Boston: South End Press, 1991.

Marable, Manning, *How Capitalism Underdeveloped Black America: Problems in Race, Political Economy and Society*, Boston: South End Press, 1983.

Maxwell, Joan P., *No Easy Answers: Persistent Poverty in the Metropolitan Washington Area*, Washington, D. C.: Greater Washington Research Center, 1985.

Mead, Lawrence M., *The New Politics of Poverty: The Nonworking Poor in America*, New York: Basic Books, 1992.

_____, *Beyond Entitlement: The Social Obligations of Citizenship*, New York: The Free Press, 1986.

Meier, August and Elliott M. Rudwick, *From Plantation to Ghetto: An Interpretive History of American Negroes*, New York: Hill and Wang, 1966.

Murray, Charles, *Losing Ground: American Social Policy 1950–1980*, New York: Basic Books, 1984.

Ofari, Earl, *The Myth of Black Capitalism*, New York: Monthly Review Press, 1970.

Perlo, Victor, *Economics of Racism: Roots of Black Inequality*, New York: International Publishers, 1975.

Pinkney, Alphonso, *The Myth of Black Progress*, New York: Cambridge University Press, 1984.

Quincey, Richard, *Class, State, and Crime*, New York: Longman Inc., 1977.

Ransom, Roger L. and Richard Sutch, *One Kind of Freedom: The Economic Consequences of Emancipation*, New York: Cambridge University Press, 1977.

Reich, Michael, *Racial Inequality: A Political-Economic Analysis*, Princeton: Princeton University Press, 1981.

Reich, Robert, *The Work of Nations: Preparing Ourselves for 21st-Century Capitalism*, New York: Alfred A. Knopf, 1991.

Reiman, Jeffrey, *The Rich Get Richer and the Poor Get Prison: Ideology, Class, and Criminal Justice*, New York: John Wiley and Sons, 1979.

Shulman, Steven, and William Darity, Jr., eds., *The Question of Discrimination: Racial Inequality in the U. S. Labor Market*, Middletown: Wesleyan University Press, 1989.

Smith, James P., and Finis R. Welch, *Closing the Gap: Forty Years of Economic Progress for Blacks*, Santa Monica: The RAND Corporation, 1986.

Sowell, Thomas, *Knowledge and Decisions*, New York: Basic Books, 1980.

Spero, Sterling D., and Abram L. Harris, *The Black Worker: The Negro and the Labor Movement*, New York: Columbia University Press, 1931.

Starobin, Robert S., *Industrial Slavery in the Old South*, New York: Oxford University Press, 1970.

Steidlmeier, Paul, *The Paradox of Poverty: A Reappraisal of Economic Development Policy*, Cambridge: Ballinger Publishing Company, 1987.

Tidwell, Billy J., *Playing to Win: A Marshall Plan for America*, New York: National Urban League, Inc., 1991.

Tonry, Michael, *Malign Neglect: Race, Crime, and Punishment in America*, New York: Oxford University Press, 1995.

Valentine, Charles A., *Culture and Poverty: Critique and Counter-Proposals*, Chicago: The University of Chicago Press, 1968.

Westcott, Diane N., "Blacks in the 1970s: Did They Scale the Job Ladder?" *Monthly Labor Review,* Vol. 105, No. 6 (June 1982), pp. 29–38.

Wilhelm, Sidney, *Who Needs the Negro?* Cambridge: Schenkman Publishing Company, Inc., 1970.

Williams, Eric, *Capitalism and Slavery,* Chapel Hill: University of North Carolina Press, 1944.

Willie, Charles V., ed., *The Caste and Class Controversy,* New York: General Hall Inc., 1979.

Wilson, William J., *When Work Disappears: The World of the New Urban Poor,* New York: Alfred A. Knopf, 1996.

_____,*The Truly Disadvantaged: The Inner City, the Underclass, and Public Policy,* Chicago: The University of Chicago Press, 1987.

_____, *The Declining Significance of Race: Blacks and Changing American Institutions,* Chicago: The University of Chicago Press, 1978.

Yette, Samuel, *The Choice: The Issue of Black Survival,* New York: G. P. Putnam's Sons, 1971.

VIII

Racism, Resistance, and Radicalism

The American experiment historically has been defective because of the contradiction between the theory and practice of democracy. The establishment of the American nation-state was flawed because the American revolution was superficial, leaving the colonial society fundamentally unchanged. The founders of the American political system and the U. S. Constitution wrote about liberty and justice, but they protected the slave trade and chattel slavery. Moreover, fear, economic necessity, and imperialist desires encouraged Euro-Americans to develop and use racist ideologies in order to justify wars of annihilation against Native American Indians, the capture and subordination of Africans, the removal of Mexicans from their land, the importation of Asians as cheap laborers, and the establishment of racial segregation. Thus, as forms of cultural domination, racial oppression and economic exploitation have been America's longest hatreds—deeply embedded in all aspects of American civilization. Yet, in each historical era, black and other oppressed nationalities improvised ways to resist the forces of dehumanization.

The dialectical relationship between oppression and opposition continues, and the essays in this section examine the complex character of this conflict in a time of mounting racism and growing economic division in America. The essays focus on antiblack racism and its evasion; the Civil Rights and Black Power Movements of the 1960s, including the leadership roles of black women; the 1992 multiethnic rebellion in Los Angeles; police brutality against blacks; and the failure of black middle-class leadership.

In his essay "Racist Ideology," Lewis R. Gordon argues that the current Racist Age is marked by a will to deny racism's existence. Racism is based on the fundamental assumption of categories of superior and inferior human beings. In the United States, racism means antiblack racism. For Gordon, racism is a form of bad faith or lying to oneself; racists refuse to recognize the humanity of black people. Indeed, the debate about racial justice is merely a rhetorical tactic that seeks to evade the truth of racial injustice. Hence, the discussion about racial justice is delusional. Gordon states that antiblack racism and its denial penetrate the core of the American social order, whether the issue is equal-opportunity discrimination against blacks or social scientific explanations of black behavior. In racist America, black people generally are not viewed as having valid problems; they are viewed as problems themselves. Moreover, since whites deny their own racism and reject black people's humanity, whites fiercely oppose the issue of racial justice. Gordon argues that they may call for the end of race as a category of identification, but this only means looking at all humanity as white. In the antiblack racist predicament, Gordon notes that black people are confronted with the absurdity of constantly justifying their existence. Thus, in employment or other institutional arrangements, whites "see" too many black people on the scene ostensibly there to take away some "white" privilege, position, or possession.

If antiblack racism is deeply embedded in the American culture of domination, then black resistance to racial injustice also is part of the American tradition of freedom. In his "Letter from Birmingham City Jail," the celebrated civil rights leader Martin Luther King, Jr., responded to eight liberal white Alabama clergymen who had written an open letter criticizing the nonviolent civil disobedience movement. In his famous jail cell letter, King rebutted their claims. Citing Birmingham's system of racial injustice, King asserted that "Injustice anywhere is a threat to justice everywhere." He reviewed the four fundamental elements of the civil disobedience struggle and rejected white liberals' call for patience in the face of vicious racism. He challenged the black middle class to overcome its indifference to the racial and economic difficulties of the black masses; he likewise urged the black masses to repudiate the resentment and anger of black nationalists, declaring that the civil disobedience struggle represented his alternative to both extremes. Noting white church leaders' indifference to black people's struggle for liberation but their support for Birmingham's racist police, King criticized the city's police brutality. King concluded his letter by asserting that black people's destiny—their search for freedom—is intertwined with America's destiny.

For many black people, America's intransigent antiblack racism made Martin Luther King's integrationist civil disobedience movement seem submissive and impractical. Naming white racism as a permanent feature of America, black nationalist leaders called for black solidarity in the struggle against white terrorism. The most powerful and eloquent black nationalist leader of the early 1960s was Malcolm X. In one of his most famous speeches, "The Ballot or the Bullet," Malcolm X's central theme is black unity as a basis for social and political action—electoral politics or defensive violence. In this 1964 talk, Malcolm X character-ized white America's treatment of black people as political oppression, economic exploitation, and social degradation. Pointing out how the U.S. Constitution and its amendments failed to confer on black people any concrete citizenship rights, Malcolm X declared that black people are the victims of American democracy. Moreover, he rejected the American dream, calling it an American nightmare.

Malcolm X then examined critically the character of America's gov-ernmental and political structure, asserting the hypocrisy of American democracy. In the face of a powerful conspiracy between segregationists and liberals to deny black voting rights, Malcolm X recommended that black people's struggle for human rights should be more expansive than the limited movement for civil rights. This would allow black people to take their demands to the United Nations like other oppressed nation-alities. Malcolm X concluded by discussing guerrilla warfare and by defining the elements of black nationalism. He believed that if the American government refused to protect black Americans against white violence, then black people had the right to defend themselves.

In "Sister Act," former Black Panther Party Central Committee mem-ber and now law professor Kathleen Cleaver reviews three recently published stories about black female leadership during the civil rights and black power struggles in the 1960s. She examines *In My Place*, TV news commentator Charlayne Hunter-Gault's memoir of her struggle to integrate the University of Georgia; *This Little Light of Mine*, Kay Mills' thorough biography of the Mississippi civil rights activist Fannie Lou Hamer; and *A Taste of Power: A Black Woman's Story*, Elaine Brown's account of her Black Panther Party experience. Cleaver distinguishes these three women on the basis of their leadership styles—symbolic leadership, grass-roots leadership, and leadership by default. Charlayne Hunter-Gault's courageous battle in 1961 to be one of the first black students enrolled at the historically white and racist University of Georgia symbolized southern black people's determination to struggle against vicious segregation with dignity and pride. Her efforts helped to galvanize an emerging black youth movement that was to become a major arm of the civil rights struggle. As a former sharecropper, Fannie Lou Hamer's grass-roots leadership included working with the Student Nonviolent Coordinating Committee on voter registration efforts among black poor and ordinary Mississippians. A powerful orator, Mrs. Hamer was an embodiment of self-determination as she fought segregation, helped to organize the Mississippi Freedom Democratic Party, and successfully challenged the national Democratic Party to seat an inte-grated delegation from Mississippi at the party's 1968 convention in Chicago.

As a Black Panther Party Central Committee member in the 1960s, Kathleen Cleaver probes Elaine Brown's testament with a critical eye. She characterizes Brown's style as leadership by default, stating that by the time Brown captured the reins of organizational power in the early 1970s, the Black Panther Party was fragmented and in disarray—caught between the crossfires of internal chaos and external governmental assault. Cleaver soundly criticizes Brown's authoritarian rule of the party. Moreover, Cleaver convincingly challenges Brown's accuracy in the interpretation and actual recounting of events in the party's history, literally calling Brown's attempt little more than an angry pack of lies presented as "a black woman's story." Indeed, Cleaver argues that Brown's infatuation with a declining Huey P. Newton—who had been one of the party's founders but now was no longer able to lead the party—distorted her understanding and appreciation of the meaning, significance, history, and dynamics of the Black Panther Party and the black power movement.

In "All Power to the People: The Political Thought of Huey P. Newton and the Black Panther Party," Hayes and Kiene discuss trends, developments, and contradictions related to the emergence and transformation of the Black Panther Party's ideology and social practice in the 1960s. Founded in 1966 by Huey P. Newton and Bobby Seale in Oakland, California, as the Black Power Movement took flight, the Panthers represented a generation of courageous young urban men and women who sought to defy America's racist and capitalist state. Hayes and Kiene employ a stages-of-development approach to analyze Newton's and the Panthers' changing political ideas—black nationalism, revolutionary nationalism, revolutionary internationalism, and revolutionary intercommunalism—as well as the importance of armed struggle and the role of the lumpenproletariat within that struggle. Hayes and Kiene argue that Newton's and the Panthers' attempts to merge aspects of race and class perspectives for the purpose of advancing revolutionary theory and practice were constrained by both the internal contradictions and the external pressures the party faced. Rapid ideological shifts and conflict with cultural nationalist groups, as well as United States governmental infiltration and repression, led to the party's decline and decay.

"Anatomy of a Rebellion: A Political-Economic Analysis," by Oliver, Johnson, and Farrell examines the causes of the 1992 Los Angeles revolt that followed the acquittal of four police officers accused of brutally beating Rodney King. The authors argue that the multiethnic rebellion resulted from years of police and criminal-justice abuse, the demographic transformation of South Central Los Angeles from a largely black population to a mixture of blacks and Central Americans, ethnic succession in the local business environment from Jewish to Korean, and Los Angeles' economic transition from industrial-manufacturing to high-tech and advanced service employment. According to the authors, these changing conditions gave rise to jobless poor blacks and working poor Latinos. Looking at federal government policy dynamics in Los Angeles, the authors point out that the Reagan administration contributed to the urban rising by facilitating a laissez-faire business climate, dismantling the structure of community-based organizations, and weakening urban school systems. Hence, rather than work toward the social, economic, and human revitalization and redevelopment of South Central Los Angeles, the effort was to employ the police-state tactics of incarcerating a growing impoverished and criminalized black and Latino population. What the people of South Central Los Angeles need, the authors suggest, is an infusion of federal funds in order to develop a comprehensive public works service-employment program, an effective job-training and job placement program, the creation of meaningful employment opportunities, and an urban transportation system that reconnects South Central Los Angeles to the other viable economic, social, and cultural sectors of the entire city's multicultural area. Although the authors are not optimistic about its possibility, they call for effective national and local leadership that must go beyond reacting to the symptoms of mounting impoverishment. Leaders need to attack the concrete sources of increasing urban poverty, anger, and resentment.

At least since the 1960s, African American and Latino communities in big cities across America have complained constantly about police brutality and repression. The 1965 Watts rebellion, like many other urban revolts in the 1960s, resulted from the abuse of local state power in the form of excessive police coercion. Yet affluent and middle-class white Americans largely ignored these charges of racialized police tyranny until the 1991 videotaped assault of Rodney King by Los Angeles' gang in blue. That tape revealed to the world how racial (in)justice actually is practiced in the "City of Angels."

Even so, the Simi Valley jury could find the cops not guilty of beating a black man with a savagery and viciousness comparable to slave owners' dehumanizing sadism during the period of chattel slavery. This is because the criminalized image of black people (along with that of their brown and red brothers and sisters) is so fixed in America's racist and violent culture—these racialized outsiders are always already guilty of something in the white American mind—that the most degrading and unjustified police assault on their bodies is accepted as legally justifiable. Since an antiblack society places little or no value on the black body, cries of racialized police terrorism largely go unheard.

In his essay, Judson Jeffries takes a critical look at the issue of the San Diego police execution of former Tampa Bay Buccaneer football player Demetrius DuBose. Indeed, this is a public health issue, as the subtitle of his essay states. Jeffries goes on to suggest that African Americans need to view and assert the police brutality and murder of black people as a public policy issue. Through an assessment of the circumstances surrounding DuBose's death, other cases of police brutality, as well as his own personal experiences with the Los Angeles police, Jeffries argues that African American males' murder by urban police in cities across this nation has reached epidemic proportions. He sees this as a form of repression and intimidation designed to preempt any form of unity among the oppressed masses of black Americans necessary for revolutionary action against America's ruling establishment.

In the face of America's deepening culture of racism and violence, once again there is an urgent necessity for competent, courageous, committed, and credible black leadership. However, both popular black opinion and scholarly research seem to support the argument that black people have had no effective leadership in the post–Civil Rights era. Maulana Karenga examines the crisis in black middle-class leadership following the Reagan Administration's seizure of the national government. Karenga suggests a socio-historical approach to analyzing the crisis of black leadership, pointing out that this problem stems from a generalized economic, political, and cultural crisis in America—a rightward and racist societal shift signaled by the Reagan ascendancy.

Karenga asserts that the crisis of black leadership is plagued by the problems of theory and practice. For him, the theoretical problem entails the lack of a clear definition of leadership necessary for selecting and evaluating the performance of black leadership. Often people use such false or flawed criteria as status, visibility, or style in trying to define or assess black leadership. Karenga points out that the ideological deficiency of black middle-class leadership and its ambivalence about social acceptance into the American middle class prevented a systematic and thoroughgoing criticism of the Reagan regime. In terms of the problem of practice, Karenga argues that black middle-class leadership is overly dependent on the federal government, that black middle-class leadership was preempted by the rise of black neo-conservatives during the Reagan era, and that black middle-class leadership relied too heavily on coalition politics. To these problems, Karenga argues for the need of black intellectuals to develop an effective liberational theory and practice of leadership and struggle based on black people's human worth and possibilities. Hence, Karenga defines leadership as "the self-conscious capacity to provide vision and values, and produce structures, programs, and practice which satisfy human needs and aspirations and transform persons and society in the process."

Racist Ideology

Lewis R. Gordon

Perhaps the most dominant feature of racist ideology is the extent to which it is premised upon a spirit of evasion. The very supposition of a superior segment of humanity—a primary theme requiring a designated *inferior* humanity, which stands as the sine qua non of racism—demands the recalcitrant attitude of looking in the face of human beings and failing to see them. In this regard, racism stands fundamentally as a form of bad faith, wherein one lies to oneself in an effort to hide from freedom and responsibility. Since responsibility is an ever-present feature of human relationships, bad faith involves the effort to evade the responsibility incumbent upon the recognition of human beings. Such evasion hides one, ultimately, from oneself.[1]

I open with these remarks primarily because of the extent to which such evasion is not only a feature of race discourse, particularly in the United States, but also a feature of the naiveté that accompanies a great deal of "popular" responses to racist ideology. There is, for instance, in the current hoopla of "multicultural" discourse, a full-fledged self-bewitchment which confuses antiracial rhetoric with the achievement of antiracial reality.

What is submerged in the ecstasy of self-delusion is the extent to which the quest for denial may be premised upon the continued reality of racial injustice. This circumstance is in part premised upon the fact that racial justice is no more than a verbal aim of a society that depends so much on racial injustice. Thus, mystification is the usual response. For instance, it has become popular to treat racism as an equal opportunity affair. If racial discrimination can be leveled out, then racial responsibility and racial "privilege," the argument goes, can be rendered truly anonymous.

The problem is that demographical reality says otherwise. Take, for example the case of affirmative action. Although blacks have been getting laid off at up to five times the rate of whites, affirmative action guidelines continue to be met in various sectors of American society. How is that possible? The obvious answer is that the cat has been let out of the bag: affirmative action guidelines can be met through hiring white women and designated non-black minorities. What both private and public sectors show in this regard is that, given the opportunity to hire or admit any other

Reprinted from *Social Text*, No. 42, Spring 1995, pp. 40–45.

ethnic or racial group besides blacks, the hiring of blacks would fall low on the priority list. In fact, blacks may even be fired or laid off for the purposes of hiring more "acceptable" groups—groups, that is, who in fact have greater possibility of identification/assimilation within the United States' racist status quo, such as, for example, white women and Latinos and Latinas who can "pass."[2]

What this suggests, then, is that in the context of the United States, the black/white dichotomy functions in a far more determining way than is acknowledged in the current rhetoric of equal-opportunity discrimination. This is because, in the United States, *racism* means *antiblack racism*. All other groups are assessed and ultimately discriminated against or favored in terms of the extent to which they carry residues of whiteness or blackness. Thus, to articulate the racial situation in the United States without focusing on blacks leads, ultimately, to *evading* American racism.

Blackness as a marker of racial ideology permeates not only the structures of employment and opportunity, but also the directions of social scientific *explanations* as well. Choose any social phenomenon and simply make a black subject its bearer. Suddenly, race-causal explanations would emerge. There are people out there studying black subjects in experiments to see if blacks are predisposed to violence against each other, as though millions of people crammed into small geographical domains have never been violent to each other throughout the course of history, or as though a crime-dominated, segregated society like the United States doesn't result in people killing those to whom they have the most access. There are people out there studying blacks' disposition to crime as though police officers and many Americans do not tend to "see" crime only in the form of the black body. There are also people studying the supposed promiscuity of black working-class teenagers without accounting for whether the assault on the poor in this country leaves simi-

lar teenage-pregnancy rates among white working-class teenagers. W. E. B. Du Bois said it well at the turn of the century when he pointed out that, in the American context, black people are not often seen as having legitimate problems. They are seen as the problems themselves.

There is a Manichaean element to racism. Under Manichaeism, one treats problems of value like problems of pollution; one need only clean away a vice and injustice as one would sterilize bacteria from water. We find this dimension of Manichaeism ironically presented in the form of purported anti-Manichaeism today, in the popular rhetoric of eliminating race itself instead of dealing with conditions that militate against treating members of "races" as respected members of the human community. This approach is misguided because it fails to account for how race functions in a racist society to begin with. Only people who are designated as inferior are regarded ultimately as races. In the U.S. context, this means that whites have the luxury of bare-human designation.

Thus, we find whites who are indignant in a world in which they are expected to regard blacks as their equal. The demand for equality drags them down from their godly status into the realm of staring the possibility of humanity in the face. The problem is that they've never taken seriously the possibility that the humanity that stares them back in the face may be a black one. Finding themselves in such a situation, they find themselves suddenly *racialized* and have, with the ready aid of black cohorts, unleashed the familiar war on racial identity.[3]

Yet, there is a reason why, in the face of the demand for racial justice, there exists so much resistance to the very question of racial justice itself. If whites do in fact benefit from an antiblack world, how can it be possible that racial justice should be an issue for whites? There is a reason why in various parts of the country hate groups are preparing themselves for a race war by training in paramilitary techniques. There is a reason why, in spite of its well know terrorist activity, the Ku Klux Klan maintains "legal" status in the U.S. It is fear of an implication of just decisions made in "favor" of blacks, and that is this: racial justice is not designed for *whites*. It is absurd to articulate whites as an historically oppressed group, and it is because of that absurdity that there have been efforts to decenter the discourse on racial justice from its focus on race to ethnic groups and individuals. Thus, one hears about historically oppressed white ethnics and then *Bakke* who was supposedly discriminated against by policies that favored *blacks*.

The discussion is then "loosened up" in a form purporting to respond to everyone's "difference." But we know what lurks in the background of current "cultural differences" discourse. It has been suggested in the context of this symposium on the current state of the debates on race, for instance, that race may still matter because racism endures. An assumption here, however, is that racism itself is not the primary target as much as the accompanying assertion of race. If so, I don't see how the following conclusion can be avoided: Why not simply give up race?

At this point, blacks more than any other group have reason to be suspicious, since such a quest often translates into a call for blacks to turn their faces away from reality. Whites have nothing to lose in a world in which one no longer sees race precisely because they are the already-assumed standpoint of humanity and the group by which race is conditioned. Not to see race means not only to "see" only white people or see all other people as white, but also to act as if the conditions that govern the distribution of racial reality were in the hands of blacks and other people of color. While whites can act as though there were no such realities as race and racism, any black that chooses to do so acts at his or her peril.[4]

It is not my wish to disappear. The rhetoric of eliminating race as a category of discussion—usually in virtue of its status as a constructed phenomenon—misses the fundamental ethical issue. One doesn't deal with racism by evading its subject matter. The arduous ethical task of forging a relationship of respect toward black people in U.S. society cannot be addressed by pretending they no longer exist. In other words, the bottom line is: Do black people have a right to exist?

Since I don't know of any group of human beings who can make a viable response to such a loaded question, a question loaded in the sense of playing on the bare fact that existence in itself justifies nothing save that one faces either the choice to go on or the self-defeating resort of suicide, we can then see the oppressive nature of the demand. Yet, black people face this demand every day. To be black in the United States is the ever-present call to justify still being around.

I spoke earlier of affirmative action. The year I entered the university in which I now work, there were sixteen black faculty members out of two thousand white ones. I was the only black hired that year in my division. There were forty hires. I am in a profession in which my group, blacks, comprises two percent. Throughout the year, the school paper published a constant stream of dribble about the displacement of workers by blacks and the lowering of "standards" at the institution. There was even a Ku Klux Klan march, in which the major rallying cry was against the displacement of whites by blacks in what were presumed to be white jobs.

It is amazing how many mediocre white folks and misguided black folks in the United States gullibly pursue such rubbish. How often do resentment and concern for standards emerge among such whites when only whites have been hired in such positions? Apparently, they are only displaced when blacks are hired. So, apparently, whites don't have to justify being hired over other whites but blacks have to justify such apparent "injustice." I wonder how many white academics, for instance, would like to trade the two percent probability with their black colleagues, given that hiring rates persist at well over ninety percent in favor of whites. If there is anyone "taking jobs" away from white people, the demographics show that it is, in some cases nine times out of ten, other white people.

Yet whites "see" too many black people out there, too many black people ever alert to get their bit of whiteness. Why? If we return to our disgruntled white individual in a world of black opportunity, it becomes obvious. If he doesn't have a cause for alarm until a black is either hired or admitted, then the basic assumption on which his reasoning is based becomes clear. How many black people are too many in an antiblack racist's world? The answer is simple: one.

To be black, then, means to live in a world in which one is always superfluous. The significance of this phenomenon is what is denied on the current effort to deny racism itself. The one-is-one-too-many motif enables, of course, the illusion of a proliferation of racial "mixing." The black man who stands in supposedly "integrated" advertisements constitutes black presence. The tiny cadre of black faculty in universities is treated as the accomplishment of racial justice. In fact, a special kind of rhetorical device holds the day. Institutions boast about "having" blacks as though one can have black people through the "possession" of one or two. The representative dimension of such "possessing" comes to the fore, however, when we think of them as "representing" blacks who are absent. In a world of having blacks, there is the evasion of black inclusion itself. Responsibility is sanitized in a protective wrapping that keeps many blacks out through profiling the few who are presented as being "in." This move renders the excluded to a form of invisibility in which even their cries are rendered mute.

Representative blackness also affords the familiar devices of Booker T. Washington-ism through which blackness is presented to white America in a filtered, acceptable form. We have witnessed this phenomenon emerge in full force over the past decade and a half with the ascendence of a black pseudo-intelligentsia/pseudo-bourgeoisie that ultimately takes the heat off of whites in race politics in the United States, with rhetoric that relegates the experience of black people to paranoia, illusion, pathology, nihilism, self-hatred, and intellectual deficiency. They are pseudo-powerful because their only source of capital is the intermediary role they play between powerful white communities and economically comfortable but alienated segments of black communities, which encourages their tendency to work amid the illusion of technique premised on a philosophical position that judges, while rejecting the conditions of being judged. They constitute a pseudo-intelligentsia because of the extent to which, when all is said and done, the only political organizing they are engaged in has more impact on the linings of their pockets than on the forces of misrepresentation and dehumanization in their specializations and communities. The players are well known and the falsehoods they spread are popular ultimately because they have an audience who accepts fiction as fact and regards fact as fiction.

There is a great deal of fiction being spread out there about black folks. But in the past two decades, there has been a destabilization of intellectual disciplinary techniques with which to respond to such tales of the crypt. Today, anyone can publish any falsehood about black people without worry, precisely because the *responses* won't be aired within the media contexts in which the damaging assertions were first made, and the people who make them never go on record as acknowledging their falsehoods. Worse, we are dealing here with individuals who are scholars and high-ranking public officials who encourage a population already without good will to accept as fact what is said. For a time, I thought this was a problem of gullible white people. But more and more, it seems to me that the situation stems from an unwillingness to seek information that may prove otherwise.[5]

Søren Kierkegaard said it best when he asked: "Which deception is most dangerous? Whose recovery is more doubtful, that of him who does not see or of him who sees and still does not see? Which is more difficult, to awaken one who sleeps or to awaken one who, awake, dreams that he is awake?"[6] Kierkegaard wrote in the context of what he saw as the comfortable scandal of the Present Age. His remarks work very well also amid the comfortable sleeping awakenness of the current Racist Age.

Notes

1. For more discussion of this phenomenon, see Lewis R. Gordon, *Bad Faith and Antiblack Racism* (Atlantic Highlands, N.J.: The Humanities Press, 1995).
2. For a discussion, see Anthony Monteiro, "Toward a Program for African-American Equality," *Political Affairs* 73 (February 1994): 19–25.
3. For a discussion of the "racialization"of whites, see Robert Westley, "White Normativity and the Racial Rhetoric of Equal Protection," in *Black Texts and Black Textuality: Constructing and De-Constructing Blackness,* ed. Lewis R. Gordon and Renee T. White (forthcoming). The *cohorts* here refers to the phenomenon of "elite" cultural studies, wherein there is the ongoing evasion, for the most part, of serious confrontation with race issues through focus on the red herring and often strawman of "modernism."
4. Think of Frantz Fanon's concerns throughout his classic *Black Skin, White Masks,* trans. Charles Lamm Markmann (New York: Grove, 1967).
5. For a discussion of the circumstances alluded to here, see the provocative issue of *Black Studies Bulletin: Words Work, A Periodic Journal of Black Culture* 16 (Winter 1993–1994), subtitled "Blacks, Jews, and Henry Louis Gates, Jr.: A Response."
6. Søren Kierkegaard, *Works of Love,* trans. Howard and Edna Hong (New York: Harper Torchbooks, 1962), 23.

Essay/Discussion Questions

1. According to Lewis Gordon, why is white Americans' denial of anti-black racism so significant?
2. In Gordon's view, why is racism synonymous with anti-black racism?
3. Gordon argues that in a racist context, the black person becomes superfluous. What does he mean?

Letter from Birmingham City Jail

MARTIN LUTHER KING, JR.

D *r. King wrote this famous essay (written in the form of an open letter) on 16 April 1963 while in jail. He was serving a sentence for participating in civil rights demonstrations in Birmingham, Alabama. He rarely took time to defend himself against his opponents. But eight prominent "liberal" Alabama clergymen, all white, published an open letter earlier in January that called on King to allow the battle for integration to continue in the local and federal courts and warned that King's nonviolent resistance would have the effect of inciting civil disturbances. Dr. King wanted Christian ministers to see that the meaning of Christian discipleship was at the heart of the African American struggle for freedom, justice, and equality.*

My dear Fellow Clergymen,

While confined here in the Birmingham city jail, I came across your recent statement calling our present activities "unwise and untimely." Seldom, if ever, do I pause to answer criticism of my work and ideas. If I sought to answer all of the criticisms that cross my desk, my secretaries would be engaged in little else in the course of the day, and I would have no time for constructive work. But since I feel that you are men of genuine good will and your criticisms are sincerely set forth, I would like to answer your statement in what I hope will be patient and reasonable terms.

I think I should give the reason for my being in Birmingham, since you have been influenced by the argument of "outsiders coming in." I have the honor of serving as president of the Southern Christian Leadership Conference, an organization operating in every southern state, with headquarters in Atlanta, Georgia. We have some eighty-five affiliate organizations all across the South—one being the Alabama Christian Movement for Human Rights. Whenever necessary and possible we share staff, educational and financial resources with our affiliates. Several months ago our local affiliate here in Birmingham invited us to be on call to engage in a nonviolent direct-action program if such were deemed necessary. We readily consented and when the hour came we lived up to our promises. So I am here, along with several members of my staff, because we were invited here. I am

From *Why We Can't Wait* (New York: Harper & Row, 1963, 1964). The American Friends Committee first published this essay as a pamphlet. It has probably been reprinted more than anything else Dr. King wrote.

here because I have basic organizational ties here.

Beyond this, I am in Birmingham because injustice is here. Just as the eighth century prophets left their little villages and carried their "thus saith the Lord" far beyond the boundaries of their hometowns; and just as the Apostle Paul left his little village of Tarsus and carried the gospel of Jesus Christ to practically every hamlet and city of the Graeco-Roman world, I too am compelled to carry the gospel of freedom beyond my particular hometown. Like Paul, I must constantly respond to the Macedonian call for aid.

Moreover, I am cognizant of the interrelatedness of all communities and states. I cannot sit idly by in Atlanta and not be concerned about what happens in Birmingham. Injustice anywhere is a threat to justice everywhere. We are caught in an inescapable network of mutuality, tied in a single garment of destiny. Whatever affects one directly affects all indirectly. Never again can we afford to live with the narrow, provincial "outside agitator" idea. Anyone who lives in the United States can never be considered an outsider anywhere in this country.

You deplore the demonstrations that are presently taking place in Birmingham. But I am sorry that your statement did not express a similar concern for the conditions that brought the demonstrations into being. I am sure that each of you would want to go beyond the superficial social analyst who looks merely at effects, and does not grapple with underlying causes. I would not hesitate to say that it is unfortunate that so-called demonstrations are taking place in Birmingham at this time, but I would say in more emphatic terms that it is even more unfortunate that the white power structure of this city left the Negro community with no other alternative.

In any nonviolent campaign there are four basic steps: (1) collection of the facts to determine whether injustices are alive, (2) negotiation, (3) self-purification, and (4) direct action. We have gone through all of these steps in Birmingham. There can be no gainsaying of the fact that racial injustice engulfs this community.

Birmingham is probably the most thoroughly segregated city in the United States. Its ugly record of police brutality is known in every section of this country. Its injust treatment of Negroes in the courts is a notorious reality. There have been more unsolved bombings of Negro homes and churches in Birmingham than any city in this nation. These are the hard, brutal and unbelievable facts. On the basis of these conditions Negro leaders sought to negotiate with the city fathers. But the political leaders consistently refused to engage in good faith negotiation.

Then came the opportunity last September to talk with some of the leaders of the economic community. In these negotiating sessions certain promises were made by the merchants—such as the promise to remove the humiliating racial signs from the stores. On the basis of these promises Rev. Shuttlesworth and the leaders of the Alabama Christian Movement for Human Rights agreed to call a moratorium on any type of demonstrations. As the weeks and months unfolded we realized that we were the victims of a broken promise. The signs remained. Like so many experiences of the past we were confronted with blasted hopes, and the dark shadow of a deep disappointment settled upon us. So we had no alternative except that of preparing for direct action, whereby we would present our very bodies as a means of laying our case before the conscience of the local and national community. We were not unmindful of the difficulties involved. So we decided to go through a process of self-purification. We started having workshops on nonviolence and repeatedly asked ourselves the questions, "Are you able to accept blows without retaliating?" "Are you able to endure the ordeals of jail?" We decided to set our direct-action program around the Easter season, realizing that with the exception of Christ-

511

mas, this was the largest shopping period of the year. Knowing that a strong economic withdrawal program would be the by-product of direct action, we felt that this was the best time to bring pressure on the merchants for the needed changes. Then it occurred to us that the March election was ahead and so we speedily decided to postpone action until after election day. When we discovered that Mr. Connor was in the run-off, we decided again to postpone action so that the demonstrations could not be used to cloud the issues. At this time we agreed to begin our nonviolent witness the day after the run-off.

This reveals that we did not move irresponsibly into direct action. We too wanted to see Mr. Connor defeated; so we went through postponement after postponement to aid in this community need. After this we felt that direct action could be delayed no longer.

You may well ask, "Why direct action? Why sit-ins, marches, etc.? Isn't negotiation a better path?" You are exactly right in your call for negotiation. Indeed, this is the purpose of direct action. Nonviolent direct action seeks to create such a crisis and establish such creative tension that a community that has constantly refused to negotiate is forced to confront the issue. It seeks so to dramatize the issue that it can no longer be ignored. I just referred to the creation of tension as a part of the work of the nonviolent resister. This may sound rather shocking. But I must confess that I am not afraid of the word tension. I have earnestly worked and preached against violent tension, but there is a type of constructive nonviolent tension that is necessary for growth. Just as Socrates felt that it was necessary to create a tension in the mind so that individuals could rise from the bondage of myths and half-truths to the unfettered realm of creative analysis and objective appraisal, we must see the need of having nonviolent gadflies to create the kind of tension in society that will help men to rise from the dark depths of prejudice and racism to the majestic heights of understanding and brotherhood. So the purpose of the direct action is to create a situation so crisis-packed that it will inevitably open the door to negotiation. We, therefore, concur with you in your call for negotiation. Too long has our beloved Southland been bogged down in the tragic attempt to live in monologue rather than dialogue.

One of the basic points in your statement is that our acts are untimely. Some have asked, "Why didn't you give the new administration time to act?" The only answer that I can give to this inquiry is that the new administration must be prodded about as much as the outgoing one before it acts. We will be sadly mistaken if we feel that the election of Mr. Boutwell will bring the millennium to Birmingham. While Mr. Boutwell is much more articulate and gentle than Mr. Connor, they are both segregationists, dedicated to the task of maintaining the status quo. The hope I see in Mr. Boutwell is that he will be reasonable enough to see the futility of massive resistance to desegregation. But he will not see this without pressure from the devotees of civil rights. My friends, I must say to you that we have not made a single gain in civil rights without determined legal and nonviolent pressure. History is the long and tragic story of the fact that privileged groups seldom give up their privileges voluntarily. Individuals may see the moral light and voluntarily give up their unjust posture; but as Reinhold Niebuhr has reminded us, groups are more immoral than individuals.

We know through painful experience that freedom is never voluntarily given by the oppressor; it must be demanded by the oppressed. Frankly, I have never yet engaged in a direct action movement that was "well-timed," according to the timetable of those who have not suffered unduly from the disease of segregation. For years now I have heard the words "Wait!" It rings in the ear of every Negro with a piercing familiarity. This "Wait" has almost always meant "Never." It has been a tranquilizing thalidomide, relieving the emotional stress for a moment, only to give birth to an ill-formed infant of frustration. We must come to see with the distinguished jurist of yesterday that "justice too long delayed is justice denied." We have waited for more than 340 years for our constitutional and God-given rights. The nations of Asia and Africa are moving with jetlike speed toward the goal of political independence, and we still creep at horse and buggy pace toward the gaining of a cup of coffee at a lunch counter. I guess it is easy for those who have never felt the stinging darts of segregation to say, "Wait." But when you have seen vicious mobs lynch your mothers and fathers at will and drown your sisters and brothers at whim; when you have seen hate-filled policemen curse, kick, brutalize and even kill your black brothers and sisters with impunity; when you see the vast majority of your twenty million Negro brothers smothering in an airtight cage of poverty in the midst of an affluent society; when you suddenly find your tongue twisted and your speech stammering as you seek to explain to your six-year-old daughter why she can't go to the public amusement park that has just been advertised on television, and see tears welling up in her little eyes when she is told that Funtown is closed to colored children, and see the depressing clouds of inferiority begin to form in her little mental sky, and see her begin to distort her little personality by unconsciously developing a bitterness toward white people; when you have to concoct an answer for a five-year-old son asking in agonizing pathos: "Daddy, why do white people treat colored people so mean?"; when you take a cross-country drive and find it necessary to sleep night after night in the uncomfortable corners of your automobile because no motel will accept you; when you are humiliated day in and day out by nagging signs reading "white" and "colored"; when your first name becomes "nigger" and your middle name becomes "boy" (however old you are) and your last name becomes "John," and when your wife and mother are never given the respected title "Mrs."; when you are harried by day and haunted by night by the fact that you are a Negro, living constantly at tiptoe stance never quite knowing what to expect next, and plagued with inner fears and outer resentments; when you are forever fighting a degenerating sense of "nobodiness"; then you will understand why we find it difficult to wait. There comes a time when the cup of endurance runs over, and men are no longer willing to be plunged into an abyss of injustice where they experience the blackness of corroding despair. I hope, sirs, you can understand our legitimate and unavoidable impatience.

You express a great deal of anxiety over our willingness to break laws. This is certainly a legitimate concern. Since we so diligently urge people to obey the Supreme Court's decision of 1954 outlawing segregation in the public schools, it is rather strange and paradoxical to find us consciously breaking laws. One may well ask, "How can you advocate breaking some laws and obeying others?" The answer is found in the fact that there are two types of laws: there are *just* and there are *unjust* laws. I would agree with Saint Augustine that "An unjust law is no law at all."

Now what is the difference between the two? How does one determine when a law is just or unjust? A just law is a man-made code that squares with the moral law or the law of God. An unjust law is a code that is out of harmony with the moral law. To put it in the terms of Saint Thomas Aquinas, an unjust law is a human law that is not rooted in eternal and natural law. Any law that uplifts human personality is just. Any law that degrades human personality is unjust. All segregation statutes are unjust because segregation distorts the soul and damages the personality. It gives the segregator a false sense of superiority, and the segregated a false sense of inferiority. To use the words of Martin Buber, the great Jewish philosopher, segregation substitutes an "I-it" relationship for the "I-thou" relationship, and ends up relegating persons to the status of things. So segregation is not only politically, economically and sociologically unsound, but it is morally wrong and sinful. Paul Tillich has said that sin is separation. Isn't segregation an existential expression of man's tragic separation, an expression of his awful estrangement, his terrible sinfulness? So I can urge men to disobey segregation ordinances because they are morally wrong.

Let us turn to a more concrete example of just and unjust laws. An unjust law is a code that a majority inflicts on a minority that is not binding on itself. This is difference made legal. On the other hand a just law is a code that a majority compels a minority to follow that it is willing to follow itself. This is sameness made legal.

Let me give another explanation. An unjust law is a code inflicted upon a minority which that minority had no part in enacting or creating because they did not have the unhampered right to vote. Who can say that the legislature of Alabama which set up the segregation laws was democratically elected? Throughout the state of Alabama all types of conniving methods are used to prevent Negroes from becoming registered voters and there are some counties without a single Negro registered to vote despite the fact that the Negro constitutes a majority of the population. Can any law set up in such a state be considered democratically structured?

These are just a few examples of unjust and just laws. There are some instances when a law is just on its face and unjust in its application. For instance, I was arrested Friday on a charge of parading without a permit. Now there is nothing wrong with an ordinance which requires a permit for a parade, but when the ordinance is used to preserve segregation and to deny citizens the First Amendment privilege of peaceful assembly and peaceful protest, then it becomes unjust.

I hope you can see the distinction I am trying to point out. In no sense do I advocate evading or defying the law as the rabid segregationist would do. This would lead to anarchy. One who breaks an unjust law must do it *openly, lovingly* (not hatefully as the white mothers did in New Orleans when they were seen on television screaming, "nigger, nigger, nigger"), and with a willingness to accept the penalty. I submit that an individual who breaks a law that conscience tells him is unjust, and willingly accepts the penalty by staying in jail to arouse the conscience of the community over its injustice, is in reality expressing the very highest respect for law.

Of course, there is nothing new about this kind of civil disobedience. It was seen sublimely in the refusal of Shadrach, Meshach and Abednego to obey the laws of Nebuchadnezzar because a higher moral law was involved. It was practiced superbly by the early Christians who were willing to face hungry lions and the excruciating pain of chopping blocks, before submitting to certain unjust laws of the Roman Empire. To a degree academic freedom is a reality today because Socrates practiced civil disobedience.

We can never forget that everything Hitler did in Germany was "legal" and everything the Hungarian freedom fighters did in Hungary was "illegal." It was "illegal" to aid and comfort a Jew in Hitler's Germany. But I am sure that if I had lived in Germany during that time I would have aided and comforted my Jewish brothers even though it was illegal. If I lived in a Communist country today where certain principles dear to the Christian faith are suppressed, I believe I would openly advocate disobeying these anti-religious laws. I must make two honest confessions to you, my Christian and Jewish brothers. First, I must confess that over the last few years I have been gravely disappointed with the white moderate. I have almost reached the regrettable conclusion that the Negro's great stumbling block in the stride toward freedom is not the White Citizen's Counciler or the Ku Klux Klanner, but the white moderate who is more devoted to "order" than to justice; who prefers a negative peace which is the absence of tension to a positive peace which is the presence of justice; who constantly says, "I agree with you in the goal you seek, but I can't agree with your methods of direct action"; who paternalistically feels that he can set the timetable for another man's freedom; who lives by the myth of time and who constantly advised the Negro to wait until a "more convenient season." Shallow understanding from people of good will is more frustrating than absolute misunderstanding from people of ill will. Lukewarm acceptance is much more bewildering than outright rejection.

I had hoped that the white moderate would understand that law and order exist for the purpose of establishing justice, and that when they fail to do this they become dangerously structured dams that block the flow of social progress. I had hoped that the white moderate would understand that the present tension of the South is merely a necessary phase of the transition from an obnoxious negative peace, where the Negro passively accepted his unjust plight, to a substance-filled positive peace, where all men will respect the dignity and worth of human personality. Actually, we who engage in nonviolent direct action are not the creators of tension. We merely bring to the surface the hidden tension that is already alive. We bring it out in the open where it can be seen and dealt with. Like a boil that can never be cured as long as it is covered up but must be opened with all its pus-flowing ugliness to the natural medicines of air and light, injustice must likewise be exposed, with all of the tension its exposing creates, to the light of human conscience and the air of national opinion before it can be cured.

In your statement you asserted that our actions, even though peaceful, must be condemned because they precipitate violence. But can this assertion be logically made? Isn't this like condemning the robbed man because his possession of money precipitated the evil act

of robbery? Isn't this like condemning Socrates because his unswerving commitment to truth and his philosophical delvings precipitated the misguided popular mind to make him drink the hemlock? Isn't this like condemning Jesus because His unique God-consciousness and never-ceasing devotion to His will precipitated the evil act of crucifixion? We must come to see, as federal courts have consistently affirmed, that it is immoral to urge an individual to withdraw his efforts to gain his basic constitutional rights because the quest precipitates violence. Society must protect the robbed and punish the robber.

I had also hoped that the white moderate would reject the myth of time. I received a letter this morning from a white brother in Texas which said: "All Christians know that the colored people will receive equal rights eventually, but it is possible that you are in too great of a religious hurry. It has taken Christianity almost two thousand years to accomplish what it has. The teachings of Christ take time to come to earth." All that is said here grows out of a tragic misconception of time. It is the strangely irrational notion that there is something in the very flow of time that will inevitably cure all ills. Actually time is neutral. It can be used either destructively or constructively. I am coming to feel that the people of ill will have used time much more effectively than the people of good will. We will have to repent in this generation not merely for the vitriolic words and actions of the bad people, but for the appalling silence of the good people. We must come to see that human progress never rolls in on wheels of inevitability. It comes through the tireless efforts and persistent work of men willing to be co-workers with God, and without this hard work time itself becomes an ally of the forces of social stagnation. We must use time creatively, and forever realize that the time is always ripe to do right. Now is the time to make real the promise of democracy, and transform our pending national elegy into a creative psalm of brotherhood. Now is the time to lift our national policy from the quicksand of racial injustice to the solid rock of human dignity.

You spoke of our activity in Birmingham as extreme. At first I was rather disappointed that fellow clergymen would see my nonviolent efforts as those of the extremist. I started thinking about the fact that I stand in the middle of two opposing forces in the Negro community. One is a force of complacency made up of Negroes who, as a result of long years of oppression, have been so completely drained of self-respect and a sense of "somebodiness" that they have adjusted to segregation, and, of a few Negroes in the middle class who, because of a degree of academic and economic security, and because at points they profit by segregation, have unconsciously become insensitive to the problems of the masses. The other force is one of bitterness and hatred, and comes perilously close to advocating violence. It is expressed in the various black nationalist groups that are springing up over the nation, the largest and best known being Elijah Muhammad's Muslim movement. This movement is nourished by the contemporary frustration over the continued existence of racial discrimination. It is made up of people who have lost faith in America, who have absolutely repudiated Christianity, and who have concluded that the white man is an incurable "devil." I have tried to stand between these two forces, saying that we need not follow the "do-nothingism" of the complacent or the hatred and despair of the black nationalist. There is the more excellent way of love and nonviolent protest. I'm grateful to God that, through the Negro church, the dimension of nonviolence entered our struggle. If this philosophy had not emerged, I am convinced that by now many streets of the South would be flowing with floods of blood. And I am further convinced that if our white brothers dismiss us as "rabble-rousers" and "outside agitators" those of us who are working through the channels

of nonviolent direct action and refuse to support our nonviolent efforts, millions of Negroes, out of frustration and despair, will seek solace and security in black nationalist ideologies, a development that will lead inevitably to a frightening racial nightmare.

Oppressed people cannot remain oppressed forever. The urge for freedom will eventually come. This is what happened to the American Negro. Something within has reminded him of his birthright of freedom; something without has reminded him that he can gain it. Consciously and unconsciously, he has been swept in by what the Germans call the Zeitgeist, and with his black brothers of Africa, and his brown and yellow brothers of Asia, South America and the Caribbean, he is moving with a sense of cosmic urgency toward the promised land of racial justice. Recognizing this vital urge that has engulfed the Negro community, one should readily understand public demonstrations. The Negro has many pent-up resentments and latent frustrations. He has to get them out. So let him march sometime; let him have his prayer pilgrimages to the city hall; understand why he must have sit-ins and freedom rides. If his repressed emotions do not come out in these nonviolent ways, they will come out in ominous expressions of violence. This is not a threat; it is a fact of history. So I have not said to my people "get rid of your discontent." But I have tried to say that this normal and healthy discontent can be channelized through the creative outlet of nonviolent direct action. Now this approach is being dismissed as extremist. I must admit that I was initially disappointed in being so categorized.

But as I continued to think about the matter I gradually gained a bit of satisfaction from being considered an extremist. Was not Jesus an extremist in love—"Love your enemies, bless them that curse you, pray for them that despitefully use you." Was not Amos an extremist for justice—"Let justice roll down like waters and righteousness like a mighty stream." Was not Paul an extremist for the gospel of Jesus Christ—"I bear in my body the marks of the Lord Jesus." Was not Martin Luther an extremist—"Here I stand; I can do none other so help me God." Was not John Bunyan an extremist—"I will stay in jail to the end of my days before I make a butchery of my conscience." Was not Abraham Lincoln an extremist—"This nation cannot survive half slave and half free." Was not Thomas Jefferson an extremist—"We hold these truths to be self-evident, that all men are created equal." So the question is not whether we will be extremist but what kind of extremist will we be. Will we be extremists for hate or will we be extremists for love? Will we be extremists for the preservation of injustice—or will we be extremists for the cause of justice? In that dramatic scene on Calvary's hill, three men were crucified. We must not forget that all three were crucified for the same crime—the crime of extremism. Two were extremists for immorality, and thusly fell below their environment. The other, Jesus Christ, was an extremist for love, truth and goodness, and thereby rose above his environment. So, after all, maybe the South, the nation and the world are in dire need of creative extremists.

I had hoped that the white moderate would see this. Maybe I was too optimistic. Maybe I expected too much. I guess I should have realized that few members of a race that has oppressed another race can understand or appreciate the deep groans and passionate yearnings of those that have been oppressed and still fewer have the vision to see that injustice must be rooted out by strong, persistent and determined action. I am thankful, however, that some of our white brothers have grasped the meaning of this social revolution and committed themselves to it. They are still all too small in quantity, but they are big in quality. Some like Ralph McGill, Lillian Smith, Harry Golden and James Dabbs have written about our struggle in eloquent, prophetic and understanding terms. Others have marched with us down nameless streets of the South. They have languished in filthy roach-infested jails, suffering the abuse and brutality of angry policemen who see them as "dirty nigger-lovers." They, unlike so many of their moderate brothers and sisters, have recognized the urgency of the moment and sensed the need for powerful "action" antidotes to combat the disease of segregation.

Let me rush on to mention my other disappointment. I have been so greatly disappointed with the white church and its leadership. Of course, there are some notable exceptions. I am not unmindful of the fact that each of you has taken some significant stands on this issue. I commend you, Rev. Stallings, for your Christian stance on this past Sunday, in welcoming Negroes to your worship service on a non-segregated basis. I commend the Catholic leaders of this state for integrating Springhill College several years ago.

But despite these notable exceptions I must honestly reiterate that I have been disappointed with the church. I do not say that as one of the negative critics who can always find something wrong with the church. I say it as a minister of the gospel, who loves the church; who was nurtured in its bosom; who has been sustained by its spiritual blessings and who will remain true to it as long as the cord of life shall lengthen.

I had the strange feeling when I was suddenly catapulted into the leadership of the bus protest in Montgomery several years ago that we would have the support of the white church. I felt that the white ministers, priests and rabbis of the South would be some of our strongest allies. Instead, some have been outright opponents, refusing to understand the freedom movement and misrepresenting its leaders: all too many others have been more cautious than courageous and have remained silent behind the anesthetizing security of the stained-glass windows.

In spite of my shattered dreams of the past, I came to Birmingham with the hope that the white religious leadership of this community would see the justice of our cause, and with deep moral concern, serve as the channel through which our just grievances would get to the power structure. I had hoped that each of you would understand. But again I have been disappointed. I have heard numerous religious leaders of the South call upon their worshippers to comply with a desegregation decision because it is the *law,* but I have longed to hear white ministers say, "Follow this decree because integration is morally *right* and the Negro is your brother." In the midst of blatant injustices inflicted upon the Negro, I have watched white churches stand on the sideline and merely mouth pious irrelevancies and sanctimonious trivialities. In the midst of a mighty struggle to rid our nation of racial and economic injustice, I have heard so many ministers say, "Those are social issues with which the gospel has no real concern," and I have watched so many churches commit themselves to a completely otherworldly religion which made a strange distinction between body and soul, the sacred and the secular.

So here we are moving toward the exit of the twentieth century with a religious community largely adjusted to the status quo, standing as a taillight behind other community agencies rather than a headlight leading men to higher levels of justice.

I have traveled the length and breadth of Alabama, Mississippi and all the other southern states. On sweltering summer days and crisp autumn mornings I have looked at her beautiful churches with their lofty spires pointing heavenward. I have beheld the impressive outlay of her massive religious education buildings. Over and over again I have found myself asking: "What kind of people worship here? Who is their God? Where were their voices when the lips of Governor Barnett dripped with words of interposition and nullification? Where were they when Governor Wallace gave the clarion call for defiance and hatred? Where were their voices of support when tired, bruised and weary Negro men and women decided to rise from the dark dungeons of complacency to the bright hills of creative protest?"

Yes, these questions are still in my mind. In deep disappointment, I have wept over the laxity of the church. But be assured that my tears have been tears of love. There can be no deep disappointment where there is not deep love. Yes, I love the church; I love her sacred walls. How could I do otherwise? I am in the rather unique position of being the son, the grandson and the great-grandson of preachers. Yes, I see the church as the body of Christ. But, oh! How we have blemished and scarred that body through social neglect and fear of being nonconformists.

There was a time when the church was very powerful. It was during that period when the early Christians rejoiced when they were deemed worthy to suffer for what they believed. In those days the church was not merely a thermometer that recorded the ideas and principles of popular opinion; it was a thermostat that transformed the mores of society. Wherever the early Christians entered a town the power structure got disturbed and immediately sought to convict them for being "disturbers of the peace" and "outside agitators." But they went on with the conviction that they were "a colony of heaven," and had to obey God rather than man. They were small in number but big in commitment. They were too God-intoxicated to be "astronomically intimidated." They brought an end to such ancient evils as infanticide and gladiatorial contest.

Things are different now. The contemporary church is often a weak, ineffectual voice with an uncertain sound. It is so often the arch-supporter of the status quo. Far from being disturbed by the presence of the church, the power structure of the average community is consoled by the church's silent and often vocal sanction of things as they are.

But the judgment of God is upon the church as never before. If the church of today does not recapture the sacrificial spirit of the early church, it will lose its authentic ring, forfeit the loyalty of millions, and be dismissed as an irrelevant social club with no meaning for the twentieth century. I am meeting young people every day whose disappointment with the church has risen to outright disgust.

Maybe again, I have been too optimistic. Is organized religion too inextricably bound to the status quo to save our nation and the world? Maybe I must turn my faith to the inner spiritual church, the church within the church, as the true *ecclesia* and the hope of the world. But again I am thankful to God that some noble souls from the ranks of organized religion have broken loose from the paralyzing chains of conformity and joined us as active partners in the struggle for freedom. They have left their secure congregations and walked the streets of Albany, Georgia, with us. They have gone through the highways of the South on tortuous rides for freedom. Yes, they have gone to jail with us. Some have been kicked out of their churches, and lost support of their bishops and fellow ministers. But they have gone with the faith that right defeated is stronger than evil triumphant. These men have been the leaven in the lump of the race. Their witness has been the spiritual salt that has preserved the true meaning of the gospel in these troubled times. They have carved a tunnel of hope through the dark mountain of disappointment.

I hope the church as a whole will meet the challenge of this decisive hour. But even if the church does not come to the aid of justice, I have no despair about the future. I have no fear about the outcome of our struggle in Birmingham, even if our motives are presently misunderstood. We will reach the goal of freedom in Birmingham and all over the nation, because the goal of America is freedom. Abused and scorned though we may be, our destiny is tied up with the destiny of America. Before the Pilgrims landed at Plymouth we were here. Before the pen of Jefferson etched across the pages of history the majestic words of the Declaration of Independence, we were here. For more than two centuries our foreparents labored in this country without wages; they made cotton king; and they built the homes of their masters in the midst of brutal injustice and shameful humiliation—and yet out of a bottomless vitality they continued to thrive and develop. If the inexpressible cruelties of slavery could not stop us, the opposition we now face will surely fail. We will win our freedom because the sacred heritage of our nation and the eternal will of God are embodied in our echoing demands.

I must close now. But before closing I am impelled to mention one other point in your statement that troubled me profoundly. You warmly commended the Birmingham police force for keeping "order" and "preventing violence." I don't believe you would have so warmly commended the police force if you had seen its angry violent dogs literally biting six unarmed, nonviolent Negroes. I don't believe you would so quickly commend the policemen if you would observe their ugly and inhuman treatment of Negroes here in the city jail; if you would watch them push and curse old Negro women and young Negro girls; if you would see them slap and kick old Negro men and young boys; if you will observe them, as they did on two occasions, refuse to give us food because we wanted to sing our grace together. I'm sorry that I can't join you in your praise for the police department.

It is true that they have been rather disciplined in their public handling of the demonstrators. In this sense they have been rather publicly "nonviolent." But for what purpose? To preserve the evil system of segregation. Over the last few years I have consistently preached that nonviolence demands that the means we use must be as pure as the ends we seek. So I have tried to make it clear that it is wrong to use immoral means to attain moral ends. But now I must affirm that it is just as wrong, or even more so, to use moral means to preserve immoral ends. Maybe Mr. Connor and his policemen have been rather publicly nonviolent, as Chief Pritchett was in Albany, Georgia, but they have used the moral means of nonviolence to maintain the immoral end of flagrant racial injustice. T. S. Eliot has said that there is no greater treason than to do the right deed for the wrong reason.

I wish you had commended the Negro sit-inners and demonstrators of Birmingham for their sublime courage, their willingness to suffer and their amazing discipline in the midst of the most inhuman provocation. One day the South will recognize its real heroes. They will be the James Merediths, courageously and with a majestic sense of purpose facing jeering and hostile mobs and the agonizing loneliness that characterizes the life of the pioneer. They will be old, oppressed, battered Negro women, symbolized in a seventy-two-year-old woman of Montgomery, Alabama, who rose up with a sense of dignity and with her people decided not to ride the segregated buses, and responded to one who inquired about her tiredness with ungrammatical profundity: "My feet is tired, but my soul is rested." They will be the young high school and college students, young ministers of the gospel and a host of their elders courageously and nonviolently sitting-in at lunch counters and willingly going to jail for conscience's sake. One day the South will know that when these disinherited children of God sat down at lunch counters they were in reality standing up for the best in the American dream and the most sacred values in our Judeo-Christian heritage, and thusly, carrying our whole nation back to those great wells of democracy which were dug deep by the Founding Fathers in the formulation of the Constitution and the Declaration of Independence.

Never before have I written a letter this long (or should I say a book?). I'm afraid that it is much too long to take your precious time. I can assure you that it would have been much shorter if I had been writing from a comfortable desk, but what else is there to do when you are alone for days in the dull monotony of a narrow jail cell other than write long letters, think strange thoughts, and pray long prayers?

If I have said anything in this letter that is an overstatement of the truth and is indicative of an unreasonable impatience, I beg you to forgive me. If I have said anything in this letter that is an understatement of the truth and is indicative of my having a patience that makes me patient with anything less than brotherhood, I beg God to forgive me.

I hope this letter finds you strong in the faith. I also hope that circumstances will soon make it possible for me to meet each of you, not as an integrationist or a civil rights leader, but as a fellow clergyman and a Christian brother. Let us all hope that the dark clouds of racial prejudice will soon pass away and the deep fog of misunderstanding will be lifted from our fear-drenched communities and in some not too distant tomorrow the radiant stars of love and brotherhood will shine over our great nation with all of their scintillating beauty.

Yours for the cause of Peace and Brotherhood,
Martin Luther King, Jr.

Essay/Discussion Questions

1. What is the distinction that Martin Luther King, Jr. made between just and unjust laws? Shouldn't all laws be obeyed? On what basis did King argue for disobeying some laws? Is his argument justifiable? Why or why not?

2. In the face of violent white assault, was the tactic of nonviolent direct action an act of courage or cowardice? Why?

3. In his letter, King strongly criticized white religious leaders' indifference to anti-black racism in the South. Discuss.

The Ballot or the Bullet

MALCOLM X

en days after Malcolm X's declaration of independence, the Muslim Mosque, Inc., held the first of a series of four Sunday night public rallies in Harlem, at which Malcolm began the job of formulating the ideology and philosophy of a new movement. In the opinion of many who heard these talks, they were the best he ever gave. Unfortunately, taped recordings of these meetings were not available in the preparation of this book. Simultaneously, however, Malcolm began to accept speaking engagements outside of New York—at Chester, Pennsylvania; Boston; Cleveland.; Detroit; etc.—and tapes of some of these were available.

In the Cleveland talk, given at Cory Methodist Church on April 3, 1964, Malcolm presented many of the themes he had been developing in the Harlem rallies. The meeting, sponsored by the Cleveland chapter of the Congress of Racial Equality, took the form of a symposium entitled "The Negro Revolt— What Comes Next?" The first speaker was Louis E. Lomax, whose talk was in line with CORE doctrine and was well received by the large, predominantly Negro audience. Malcolm's talk got even more applause, although it differed in fundamental respects from anything ever said at a CORE meeting.

"The Ballot or the Bullet," Malcolm's own title for his speech, was notable, among other things, *for its statement that elements of black nationalism were present and growing in such organizations as the NAACP and CORE. For various reasons, the black nationalist convention which in this talk he projected for August, 1964, was not held.*

Mr. Moderator, Brother Lomax, brothers and sisters, friends and enemies: I just can't believe everyone in here is a friend and I don't want to leave anybody out. The question tonight, as I understand it, is "The Negro Revolt, and Where Do We Go From Here?" or "What Next?" In my little humble way of understanding it, it points toward either the ballot or the bullet.

Before we try and explain what is meant by the ballot or the bullet, I would like to clarify something concerning myself. I'm still a Muslim, my religion is still Islam. That's my personal belief. Just as Adam Clayton Powell is a Christian minister who heads the Abyssinian Baptist Church in New York, but at the same time takes part in the political struggles to try

Reprinted from *Malcolm X Speaks: Selected Speeches and Statements*, George Breitman, ed. New York: Pathfinder Press, 1965/1989.

and bring about rights to the black people in this country; and Dr. Martin Luther King is a Christian minister down in Atlanta, Georgia, who heads another organization fighting for the civil rights of black people in this country; and Rev. Galamison, I guess you've heard of him, is another Christian minister in New York who has been deeply involved in the school boycotts to eliminate segregated education; well, I myself am a minister, not a Christian minister, but a Muslim minister; and I believe in action on all fronts by whatever means necessary.

Although I'm still a Muslim, I'm not here tonight to discuss my religion. I'm not here to try and change your religion. I'm not here to argue or discuss anything that we differ about, because it's time for us to submerge our differences and realize that it is best for us to first see that we have the same problem, a common problem—a problem that will make you catch hell whether you're a Baptist, or a Methodist, or a Muslim, or a nationalist. Whether you're educated or illiterate, whether you live on the boulevard or in the alley, you're going to catch hell just like I am. We're all in the same boat and we all are going to catch the same hell from the same man. He just happens to be a white man. All of us have suffered here, in this country, political oppression at the hands of the white man, economic exploitation at the hands of the white man, and social degradation at the hands of the white man.

Now in speaking like this, it doesn't mean that we're antiwhite, but it does mean we're anti-exploitation, we're anti-degradation, we're anti-oppression. And if the white man doesn't want us to be anti-him, let him stop oppressing and exploiting and degrading us. Whether we are Christians or Muslims or nationalists or agnostics or atheists, we must first learn to forget our differences. If we have differences, let us differ in the closet; when we come out in front, let us not have anything to argue about until we get finished arguing with the man. If the late President Kennedy could get together with Khrushchev and exchange some wheat, we certainly have more in common with each other than Kennedy and Khrushchev had with each other.

If we don't do something real soon, I think you'll have to agree that we're going to be forced either to use the ballot or the bullet. It's one or the other in 1964. It isn't that time is running out—time has run out! 1964 threatens to be the most explosive year America has ever witnessed. The most explosive year. Why? It's also a political year. It's the year when all of the white politicians will be back in the so-called Negro community jiving you and me for some votes. The year when all of the white political crooks will be right back in your and my community with their false promises, building up our hopes for a letdown, with their trickery and their treachery, with their false promises which they don't intend to keep. As they nourish these dissatisfactions, it can only lead to one thing, an explosion; and now we have the type of black man on the scene in America today—I'm sorry, Brother Lomax—who just doesn't intend to turn the other cheek any longer.

Don't let anybody tell you anything about the odds are against you. If they draft you, they send you to Korea and make you face 800 million Chinese. If you can be brave over there, you can be brave right here. These odds aren't as great as those odds. And if you fight here, you will at least know what you're fighting for.

I'm not a politician, not even a student of politics; in fact, I'm not a student of much of anything. I'm not a Democrat, I'm not a Republican, and I don't even consider myself an American. If you and I were Americans, there'd be no problem. Those Honkies that just got off the boat, they're already Americans; Polacks are already Americans; the Italian refugees are already Americans. Everything that came out of Europe, every blue-eyed thing, is already an American. And as long as you and I have been over here, we aren't Americans yet.

Well, I am one who doesn't believe in deluding myself. I'm not going to sit at your table and watch you eat, with nothing on my plate, and call myself a diner. Sitting at the table doesn't make you a diner, unless you eat some of what's on that plate. Being here in America doesn't make you an American. Being born here in America doesn't make you an American. Why, if birth made you American, you wouldn't need any legislation, you wouldn't need any amendments to the Constitution, you wouldn't be faced with civil-rights filibustering in Washington, D.C., right now. They don't have to pass civil-rights legislation to make a Polack an American.

No, I'm not an American. I'm one of the 22 million black people who are the victims of Americanism. One of the 22 million black people who are the victims of democracy, nothing but disguised hypocrisy. So, I'm not standing here speaking to you as an American, or a patriot, or a flag-saluter, or a flag-waver—no, not I. I'm speaking as a victim of this American system. And I see America through the eyes of the victim. I don't see any American dream; I see an American nightmare.

These 22 million victims are waking up. Their eyes are coming open. They're beginning to see what they used to only look at. They're becoming politically mature. They are realizing that there are new political trends from coast to coast. As they see these new political trends, it's possible for them to see that every time there's an election the races are so close that they have to have a recount. They had to recount in Massachusetts to see who was going to be governor, it was so close. It was the same way in Rhode Island, in Minnesota, and in many other parts of the country. And the same with Kennedy and Nixon when they ran for president. It was so close they had to count all over again. Well, what does this mean? It means that when white people are evenly divided, and black people have a bloc of votes of their own, it is left up to them to determine who's going to sit in the White House and who's going to be in the dog house.

It was the black man's vote that put the present administration in Washington, D.C. Your vote, your dumb vote, your ignorant vote, your wasted vote put in an administration in Washington, D.C., that has seen fit to pass every kind of legislation imaginable, saving you until last, then filibustering on top of that. And your and my leaders have the audacity to run around clapping their hands and talk about how much progress we're making. And what a good president we have. If he wasn't good in Texas, he sure can't be good in Washington, D.C. Because Texas is a lynch state. It is in the same breath as Mississippi, no different; only they lynch you in Texas with a Texas accent and lynch you in Mississippi with a Mississippi accent. And these Negro leaders have the audacity to go and have some coffee in the White House with a Texan, a Southern cracker—that's all he is—and then come out and tell you and me that he's going to be better for us because, since he's from the South, he knows how to deal with the Southerners. What kind of logic is that? Let Eastland be president, he's from the South too. He should be better able to deal with them than Johnson.

In this present administration they have in the House of Representatives 257 Democrats to only 177 Republicans. They control two-thirds of the House vote. Why can't they pass something that will help you and me? In the Senate, there are 67 senators who are of the Democratic Party. Only 33 of them are Republicans. Why, the Democrats have got the government sewed up, and you're the one who sewed it up for them. And what have they given you for it? Four years in office, and just now getting around to some civil-rights legislation. Just now, after everything else is gone, out of the way, they're going to sit down now and play with you all summer long—the same old giant con game that they call filibuster. All those are in cahoots together. Don't you ever think they're not in cahoots together, for the man that is heading the civil-rights filibuster is a man from Georgia named Richard Russell. When Johnson became president, the first man he asked for when he got back to Washington, D.C., was "Dicky"—that's how tight they are. That's his boy, that's his pal, that's his buddy. But they're playing that old con game. One of them makes believe he's for you, and he's got it fixed where the other one is so tight against you, he never has to keep his promise.

So it's time in 1964 to wake up. And when you see them coming up with that kind of conspiracy, let them know your eyes are open. And let them know you got something else that's wide open too. It's got to be the ballot or the bullet. The ballot or the bullet. If you're afraid to use an expression like that, you should get on out of the country, you should get back in the cotton patch, you should get back in the alley. They get all the Negro vote, and after they get it, the Negro gets nothing in return. All they did when they got to Washington was give a few big Negroes big jobs. Those big Negroes didn't need big jobs, they already had jobs. That's camouflage, that's trickery, that's treachery, window-dressing. I'm not trying to knock out the Democrats for the Republicans, we'll get to them in a minute. But it is true— you put the Democrats first and the Democrats put you last.

Look at it the way it is. What alibis do they use, since they control Congress and the Senate? What alibi do they use when you and I ask, "Well, when are you going to keep your promise?" They blame the Dixiecrats. What is a Dixiecrat? A Democrat. A Dixiecrat is nothing but a Democrat in disguise. The titular head of the Democrats is also the head of the Dixiecrats, because the Dixiecrats are a part of the Democratic Party. The Democrats have never kicked the Dixiecrats out of the party. The Dixiecrats bolted themselves once, but the Democrats didn't put them out. Imagine, these lowdown Southern segregationists put the Northern Democrats down. But the Northern Democrats have never put the Dixiecrats

down. No, look at that thing the way it is. They have got a con game going on, a political con game, and you and I are in the middle. It's time for you and me to wake up and start looking at it like it is, and trying to understand it like it is; and then we can deal with it like it is.

The Dixiecrats in Washington, D.C., control the key committees that run the government. The only reason the Dixiecrats control these committees is because they have seniority. The only reason they have seniority is because they come from states where Negroes can't vote. This is not even a government that's based on democracy. It is not a government that is made up of representatives of the people. Half of the people in the South can't even vote. Eastland is not even supposed to be in Washington. Half of the senators and congressmen who occupy these key positions in Washington, D.C., are there illegally, are there unconstitutionally.

I was in Washington, D.C., a week ago Thursday, when they were debating whether or not they should let the bill come onto the floor. And in the back of the room where the Senate meets, there's a huge map of the United States, and on that map it shows the location of Negroes throughout the country. And it shows that the Southern section of the country, the states that are most heavily concentrated with Negroes, are the ones that have senators and congressmen standing up filibustering and doing all other kinds of trickery to keep the Negro from being able to vote. This is pitiful. But it's not pitiful for us any longer; it's actually pitiful for the white man, because soon now, as the Negro awakens a little more and sees the vise that he's in, sees the bag that he's in, sees the real game that he's in, then the Negro's going to develop a new tactic.

These senators and congressmen actually violate the constitutional amendments that guarantee the people of that particular state or county the right to vote. And the Constitution itself has within it the machinery to expel any representative from a state where the voting rights of the people are violated. You don't even need new legislation. Any person in Congress right now, who is there from a state or a district where the voting rights of the people are violated, that particular person should be expelled from Congress. And when you expel him, you've removed one of the obstacles in the path of any real meaningful legislation in this country. In fact, when you expel them, you don't need new legislation, because they will be replaced by black representatives from counties and districts where the black man is in the majority, not in the minority.

If the black man in these Southern states had his full voting rights, the key Dixiecrats in Washington, D.C., which means the key Democrats in Washington, D.C., would lose their seats. The Democratic Party itself would lose its power. It would cease to be powerful as a party. When you see the amount of power that would be lost by the Democratic Party if it were to lose the Dixiecrat wing, or branch, or element, you can see where it's against the interests of the Democrats to give voting rights to Negroes in states where the Democrats have been in complete power and authority ever since the Civil War. You just can't belong to that party without analyzing it.

I say again, I'm not anti-Democrat, I'm not anti-Republican, I'm not anti-anything. I'm just questioning their sincerity, and some of the strategy that they've been using on our people by promising them promises that they don't intend to keep. When you keep the Democrats in power, you're keeping the Dixiecrats in power. I doubt that my good Brother Lomax will deny that. A vote for a Democrat is a vote for a Dixiecrat. That's why, in 1964, it's time now for you and me to become more politically mature and realize what the ballot is for; what we're supposed to get when we cast a ballot; and that if we don't cast a ballot, it's going to end up in a situation where we're going to have to cast a bullet. It's either a ballot or a bullet.

In the North, they do it a different way. They have a system that's known as gerrymandering, whatever that means. It means when Negroes become too heavily concentrated in a certain area, and begin to gain too much political power, the white man comes along and changes the district lines. You may say, "Why do you keep saying white man?" Because it's the white man who does it. I haven't ever seen any Negro changing any lines. They don't let him get near the line. It's the white man who does this. And usually, it's the white man who grins at you the most, and pats you on the back, and is supposed to be your friend. He may be friendly, but he's not your friend.

So, what I'm trying to impress upon you, in essence, is this: You and I in America are faced not with a segregationist conspiracy, we're faced with a government conspiracy. Everyone who's filibustering is a senator—that's the government. Everyone who's finagling in Washington, D.C., is a congressman—that's the government. You don't have anybody putting blocks in your path but people who are a part of the government. The same government that you go abroad to fight for and die for is the government that is in a conspiracy to deprive you of your voting rights, deprive you of your economic opportunities, deprive you of decent housing, deprive you of decent education. You don't need to go to the employer alone, it is the government itself, the government of America, that is responsible for the oppression and exploitation and degradation of black people in this country. And you should drop it in their lap. This government has failed the Negro. This so-called democracy has failed the Negro. And all these white liberals have definitely failed the Negro.

So, where do we go from here? First, we need some friends. We need some new allies. The entire civil-rights struggle needs a new interpretation, a broader interpretation. We need to look at this civil-rights thing from another angle—from the inside as well as from the outside. To those of us whose philosophy is black nationalism, the only way you can get involved in the civil-rights struggle is give it a new interpretation. That old interpretation excluded us. It kept us out. So, we're giving a new interpretation to the civil-rights struggle, an interpretation that will enable us to come into it, take part in it. And these handkerchief-heads who have been dillydallying and pussyfooting and compromising—we don't intend to let them pussyfoot and dillydally and compromise any longer.

How can you thank a man for giving you what's already yours? How then can you thank him for giving you only part of what's already yours? You haven't even made progress, if what's being given to you, you should have had already. That's not progress. And I love my Brother Lomax, the way he pointed out we're right back where we were in 1954. We're not even as far up as we were in 1954. We're behind where we were in 1954. There's more segregation now than there was in 1954. There's more racial animosity, more racial hatred, more racial violence today in 1964, than there was in 1954. Where is the progress?

And now you're facing a situation where the young Negro's coming up. They don't want to hear that "turn-the-other-cheek" stuff, no. In Jacksonville, those were teenagers, they were throwing Molotov cocktails. Negroes have never done that before. But it shows you there's a new deal coming in. There's new thinking coming in. There's new strategy coming in. It'll be Molotov cocktails this month, hand grenades next month, and something else next month. It'll be ballots, or it'll be bullets. It'll be liberty, or it will be death. The only difference about this kind of death—it'll be reciprocal. You know what is meant by "reciprocal"? That's one of Brother Lomax's words, I stole it from him. I don't usually deal with those big words because I don't usually deal with big people. I deal with small people. I find you can get a whole lot of small people

and whip hell out of a whole lot of big people. They haven't got anything to lose, and they've got everything to gain. And they'll let you know in a minute: "It takes two to tango; when I go, you go."

The black nationalists, those whose philosophy is black nationalism, in bringing about this new interpretation of the entire meaning of civil rights, look upon it as meaning, as Brother Lomax has pointed out, equality of opportunity. Well, we're justified in seeking civil rights, if it means equality of opportunity, because all we're doing there is trying to collect for our investment. Our mothers and fathers invested sweat and blood. Three hundred and ten years we worked in this country without a dime in return—I mean without a dime in return. You let the white man walk around here talking about how rich this country is, but you never stop to think how it got rich so quick. It got rich because you made it rich.

You take the people who are in this audience right now. They're poor, we're all poor as individuals. Our weekly salary individually amounts to hardly anything. But if you take the salary of everyone in here collectively it'll fill up a whole lot of baskets. It's a lot of wealth. If you can collect the wages of just these people right here for a year, you'll be rich—richer than rich. When you look at it like that, think how rich Uncle Sam had to become, not with this handful, but millions of black people. Your and my mother and father, who didn't work an eight-hour shift, but worked from "can't see" in the morning until "can't see" at night, and worked for nothing, making the white man rich, making Uncle Sam rich.

This is our investment. This is our contribution—our blood. Not only did we give of our free labor, we gave of our blood. Every time he had a call to arms, we were the first ones in uniform. We died on every battlefield the white man had. We have made a greater sacrifice than anybody who's standing up in America today. We have made a greater contribution and have collected less. Civil rights, for those of us whose philosophy is black nationalism, means: "Give it to us now. Don't wait for next year. Give it to us yesterday, and that's not fast enough."

I might stop right here to point out one thing. Whenever you're going after something that belongs to you, anyone who's depriving you of the right to have it is a criminal. Understand that. Whenever you are going after something that is yours, you are within your legal rights to lay claim to it. And anyone who puts forth any effort to deprive you of that which is yours, is breaking the law, is a criminal. And this was pointed out by the Supreme Court decision. It outlawed segregation. Which means segregation is against the law. Which means a segregationist is breaking the law. A segregationist is a criminal. You can't label him as anything other than that. And when you demonstrate against segregation, the law is on your side. The Supreme Court is on your side.

Now, who is it that opposes you in carrying out the law? The police department itself. With police dogs and clubs. Whenever you demonstrate against segregation, whether it is segregated education, segregated housing, or anything else, the law is on your side, and anyone who stands in the way is not the law any longer. They are breaking the law, they are not representatives of the law. Any time you demonstrate against segregation and a man has the audacity to put a police dog on you, kill that dog, kill him, I'm telling you, kill that dog. I say it, if they put me in jail tomorrow, kill—that—dog. Then you'll put a stop to it. Now, if these white people in here don't want to see that kind of action, get down and tell the mayor to tell the police department to pull the dogs in. That's all you have to do. If you don't do it, someone else will.

If you don't take this kind of stand, your little children will grow up and look at you and think "shame." If you don't take an uncompromising stand—I don't mean go out and get violent; but at the same time you should never be nonviolent unless you run into some nonviolence. I'm nonviolent with those who are nonviolent with me. But when you drop that violence on me, then you've made me go insane, and I'm not responsible for what I do. And that's the way every Negro should get. Any time you know you're within the law, within your legal rights, within your moral rights, in accord with justice, then die for what you believe in. But don't die alone. Let your dying be reciprocal. This is what is meant by equality. What's good for the goose is good for the gander.

When we begin to get in this area, we need new friends, we need new allies. We need to expand the civil-rights struggle to a higher level—to the level of human rights. Whenever you are in a civil-rights struggle, whether you know it or not, you are confining yourself to the jurisdiction of Uncle Sam. No one from the outside world can speak out in your behalf as long as your struggle is a civil-rights struggle. Civil rights comes within the domestic affairs of this country. All of our African brothers and our Asian brothers and our Latin-American brothers cannot open their mouths and interfere in the domestic affairs of the United States. And as long as it's civil rights, this comes under the jurisdiction of Uncle Sam.

But the United Nations has what's known as the charter of human rights, it has a committee that deals in human rights. You may wonder why all of the atrocities that have been committed in Africa and in Hungary and in Asia and in Latin America are brought before the UN, and the Negro problem is never brought before the UN. This is part of the conspiracy. This old, tricky, blue-eyed liberal who is supposed to be your and my friend, supposed to be in our corner, supposed to be subsidizing our struggle, and supposed to be acting in the capacity of an adviser, never tells you anything about human rights. They keep you wrapped up in civil rights. And you spend so much time barking up the civil-rights tree, you don't even know there's a human-rights tree on the same floor.

When you expand the civil-rights struggle to the level of human rights, you can then take the case of the black man in this country before the nations in the UN. You can take it before the General Assembly. You can take Uncle Sam before a world court. But the only level you can do it on is the level of human rights. Civil rights keeps you under his restrictions, under his jurisdiction. Civil rights keeps you in his pocket. Civil rights means you're asking Uncle Sam to treat you right. Human rights are something you were born with. Human rights are your God-given rights. Human rights are the rights that are recognized by all nations of this earth. And any time anyone violates your human rights, you can take them to the world court. Uncle Sam's hands are dripping with blood, dripping with the blood of the black man in this country. He's the earth's number-one hypocrite. He has the audacity—yes, he has—imagine him posing as the leader of the free world. The free world!—and you over here singing "We Shall Overcome." Expand the civil-rights struggle to the level of human rights, take it into the United Nations, where our African brothers can throw their weight on our side, where our Asian brothers can throw their weight on our side, where our Latin-American brothers can throw their weight on our side, and where 800 million Chinamen are sitting there waiting to throw their weight on our side.

Let the world know how bloody his hands are. Let the world know the hypocrisy that's practiced over here. Let it be the ballot or the bullet. Let him know that it must be the ballot or the bullet.

When you take your case to Washington, D.C., you're taking it to the criminal who's responsible; it's like running from the wolf to the fox. They're all in cahoots together. They all work political chicanery and make you look like a chump before the eyes of the world. Here you are walking around in America, getting ready to be drafted and sent abroad, like a tin soldier, and when you get over there, people ask you what are you fighting for, and you have to stick your tongue in your cheek. No, take Uncle Sam to court, take him before the world.

By ballot I only mean freedom. Don't you know—I disagree with Lomax on this issue—that the ballot is more important than the dollar? Can I prove it? Yes. Look in the UN. There are poor nations in the UN; yet those poor nations can get together with their voting power and keep the rich nations from making a move. They have one nation—one vote, everyone has an equal vote. And when those brothers from Asia, and Africa and the darker parts of this earth get together, their voting power is sufficient to hold Sam in check. Or Russia in check. Or some other section of the earth in check. So, the ballot is most important.

Right now, in this country, if you and I, 22 million African-Americans—that's what we are—Africans who are in America. You're nothing but Africans. Nothing but Africans. In fact, you'd get farther calling yourself African instead of Negro. Africans don't catch hell. You're the only one catching hell. They don't have to pass civil-rights bills for Africans. An African can go anywhere he wants right now. All you've got to do is tie your head up. That's right, go anywhere you want. Just stop being a Negro. Change your name to Hoogagagooba. That'll show you how silly the white man is. You're dealing with a silly man. A friend of mine who's very dark put a turban on his head and went into a restaurant in Atlanta before they called themselves desegregated. He went into a white restaurant, he sat down, they served him, and he said, "What would happen if a Negro came in here?" And there he's sitting, black as night, but because he had his head wrapped up the waitress looked back at him and says, "Why, there wouldn't no nigger dare come in here."

So, you're dealing with a man whose bias and prejudice are making him lose his mind, his intelligence, every day. He's frightened. He looks around and sees what's taking place on this earth, and he sees that the pendulum of time is swinging in your direction. The dark people are waking up. They're losing their fear of the white man. No place where he's fighting right now is he winning. Everywhere he's fighting, he's fighting someone your and my complexion. And they're beating him. He can't win any more. He's won his last battle. He failed to win the Korean War. He couldn't win it. He had to sign a truce. That's a loss. Any time Uncle Sam, with all his machinery for warfare, is held to a draw by some rice-eaters, he's lost the battle. He had to sign a truce. America's not supposed to sign a truce. She's supposed to be bad. But she's not bad any more. She's bad as long as she can use her hydrogen bomb, but she can't use hers for fear Russia might use hers. Russia can't use hers, for fear that Sam might use his. So, both of them are weaponless. They can't use the weapon because each's weapon nullifies the other's. So the only place where action can take place is on the ground. And the white man can't win another war fighting on the ground. Those days are over. The black man knows it, the brown man knows it, the red man knows it, and the yellow man knows it. So they engage him in guerrilla warfare. That's not his style. You've got to have heart to be a guerrilla warrior, and he hasn't got any heart. I'm telling you now.

I just want to give you a little briefing on guerrilla warfare because, before you know it, before you know it—It takes heart to be a guerrilla warrior because you're on your own. In conventional warfare you have tanks and a whole lot of other people with you to back you up, planes over your head and all that kind of stuff. But a guerrilla is on his own. All you have is a rifle, some sneakers and a bowl of rice, and that's all you need—and a lot of heart. The Japanese on some of those islands in the Pacific, when the American soldiers landed, one Japanese sometimes could hold

the whole army off. He'd just wait until the sun went down, and when the sun went down they were all equal. He would take his little blade and slip from bush to bush, and from American to American. The white soldiers couldn't cope with that. Whenever you see a white soldier that fought in the Pacific, he has the shakes, he has a nervous condition, because they scared him to death.

The same thing happened to the French up in French Indochina. People who just a few years previously were rice farmers got together and ran the heavily-mechanized French army out of Indochina. You don't need it—modern warfare today won't work. This is the day of the guerrilla. They did the same thing in Algeria. Algerians, who were nothing but Bedouins, took a rifle and sneaked off to the hills, and de Gaulle and all of his highfalutin' war machinery couldn't defeat those guerrillas. Nowhere on this earth does the white man win in a guerrilla warfare. It's not his speed. Just as guerrilla warfare is prevailing in Asia and in parts of Africa and in parts of Latin America, you've got to be mighty naive, or you've got to play the black man cheap, if you don't think some day he's going to wake up and find that it's got to be the ballot or the bullet.

I would like to say, in closing, a few things concerning the Muslim Mosque, Inc., which we established recently in New York City. It's true we're Muslims and our religion is Islam, but we don't mix our religion with our politics and our economics and our social and civil activities—not any more. We keep our religion in our mosque. After our religious services are over, then as Muslims we become involved in political action, economic action and social and civic action. We become involved with anybody, anywhere, any time and in any manner that's designed to eliminate the evils, the political, economic and social evils that are afflicting the people of our community.

The political philosophy of black nationalism means that the black man should control the politics and the politicians in his own community; no more. The black man in the black community has to be re-educated into the science of politics so he will know what politics is supposed to bring him in return. Don't be throwing out any ballots. A ballot is like a bullet. You don't throw your ballots until you see a target, and if that target is not within your reach, keep your ballot in your pocket. The political philosophy of black nationalism is being taught in the Christian church. It's being taught in the NAACP. It's being taught in CORE meetings. It's being taught in SNCC (Student Nonviolent Coordinating Committee) meetings. It's being taught in Muslim meetings. It's being taught where nothing but atheists and agnostics come together. It's being taught everywhere. Black people are fed up with the dillydallying, pussyfooting, compromising approach that we've been using toward getting our freedom. We want freedom now, but we're not going to get it saying "We Shall Overcome." We've got to fight until we overcome.

The economic philosophy of black nationalism is pure and simple. It only means that we should control the economy of our community. Why should white people be running all the stores in our community? Why should white people be running the banks of our community? Why should the economy of our community be in the hands of the white man? Why? If a black man can't move his store into a white community, you tell me why a white man should move his store into a black community. The philosophy of black nationalism involves a re-education program in the black community in regards to economics. Our people have to be made to see that any time you take your dollar out of your community and spend it in a community where you don't live, the community where you live will get poorer and poorer, and the community where you spend your money will get richer and richer. Then you wonder why where you live is always a ghetto or a slum area. And where you and I are concerned, not only do we lose it

when we spend it out of the community, but the white man has got all our stores in the community tied up; so that though we spend it in the community, at sundown the man who runs the store takes it over across town somewhere. He's got us in a vise.

So the economic philosophy of black nationalism means in every church, in every civic organization, in every fraternal order, it's time now for our people to become conscious of the importance of controlling the economy of our community. If we own the stores, if we operate the businesses, if we try and establish some industry in our own community, then we're developing to the position where we are creating employment for our own kind. Once you gain control of the economy of your own community, then you don't have to picket and boycott and beg some cracker downtown for a job in his business.

The social philosophy of black nationalism only means that we have to get together and remove the evils, the vices, alcoholism, drug addiction, and other evils that are destroying the moral fiber of our community. We ourselves have to lift the level of our community, the standard of our community to a higher level, make our own society beautiful so that we will be satisfied in our own social circles and won't be running around here trying to knock our way into a social circle where we're not wanted.

So I say, in spreading a gospel such as black nationalism, it is not designed to make the black man re-evaluate the white man—you know him already—but to make the black man re-evaluate himself. Don't change the white man's mind—you can't change his mind, and that whole thing about appealing to the moral conscience of America—America's conscience is bankrupt. She lost all conscience a long time ago. Uncle Sam has no conscience. They don't know what morals are. They don't try and eliminate an evil because it's evil, or because it's illegal, or because it's immoral; they eliminate it only when it threatens their existence.

So you're wasting your time appealing to the moral conscience of a bankrupt man like Uncle Sam. If he had a conscience, he'd straighten this thing out with no more pressure being put upon him. So it is not necessary to change the white man's mind. We have to change our own mind. You can't change his mind about us. We've got to change our own minds about each other. We have to see each other with new eyes. We have to see each other as brothers and sisters. We have to come together with warmth so we can develop unity and harmony that's necessary to get this problem solved ourselves. How can we do this? How can we avoid jealousy? How can we avoid the suspicion and the divisions that exist in the community? I'll tell you how.

I have watched how Billy Graham comes into a city, spreading what he calls the gospel of Christ, which is only white nationalism. That's what he is. Billy Graham is a white nationalist; I'm a black nationalist. But since it's the natural tendency for leaders to be jealous and look upon a powerful figure like Graham with suspicion and envy, how is it possible for him to come into a city and get all the cooperation of the church leaders? Don't think because they're church leaders that they don't have weaknesses that make them envious and jealous—no, everybody's got it. It's not an accident that when they want to choose a cardinal [as Pope] over there in Rome, they get in a closet so you can't hear them cussing and fighting and carrying on.

Billy Graham comes in preaching the gospel of Christ, he evangelizes the gospel, he stirs everybody up, but he never tries to start a church. If he came in trying to start a church, all the churches would be against him. So, he just comes in talking about Christ and tells everybody who gets Christ to go to any church where Christ is; and in this way the church cooperates with him. So we're going to take a page from his book.

Our gospel is black nationalism. We're not trying to threaten the existence of any organization, but we're spreading the gospel of black nationalism. Anywhere there's a church that is also preaching and practicing the gospel of black nationalism, join that church. If the NAACP is preaching and practicing the gospel of black nationalism, join the NAACP. If CORE is spreading and practicing the gospel of black nationalism, join CORE. Join any organization that has a gospel that's for the uplift of the black man. And when you get into it and see them pussyfooting or compromising, pull out of it because that's not black nationalism. We'll find another one.

And in this manner, the organizations will increase in number and in quantity and in quality, and by August, it is then our intention to have a black nationalist convention which will consist of delegates from all over the country who are interested in the political, economic and social philosophy of black nationalism. After these delegates convene, we will hold a seminar, we will hold discussions, we will listen to everyone. We want to hear new ideas and new solutions and new answers. And at that time, if we see fit then to form a black nationalist party, we'll form a black nationalist party. If it's necessary to form a black nationalist army, we'll form a black nationalist army. It'll be the ballot or the bullet. It'll be liberty or it'll be death.

It's time for you and me to stop sitting in this country, letting some cracker senators, Northern crackers and Southern crackers, sit there in Washington, D. C., and come to a conclusion in their mind that you and I are supposed to have civil rights. There's no white man going to tell me anything about my rights. Brothers and sisters, always remember, if it doesn't take senators and congressmen and presidential proclamations to give freedom to the white man, it is not necessary for legislation or proclamation or Supreme Court decisions to give freedom to the black man. You let that white man know, if this is a country of freedom, let it be a country of freedom; and if it's not a country of freedom, change it.

We will work with anybody, anywhere, at any time, who is genuinely interested in tackling the problem head-on, nonviolently as long as the enemy is nonviolent, but violent when the enemy gets violent. We'll work with you on the voter-registration drive, we'll work with you on rent strikes, we'll work with you on school boycotts—I don't believe in any kind of integration; I'm not even worried about it because I know you're not going to get it anyway; you're not going to get it because you're afraid to die; you've got to be ready to die if you try and force yourself on the white man, because he'll get just as violent as those crackers in Mississippi, right here in Cleveland. But we will still work with you on the school boycotts because we're against a segregated school system. A segregated school system produces children who, when they graduate, graduate with crippled minds. But this does not mean that a school is segregated because it's all black. A segregated school means a school that is controlled by people who have no real interest in it whatsoever.

Let me explain what I mean. A segregated district or community is a community in which people live, but outsiders control the politics and the economy of that community. They never refer to the white section as a segregated community. It's the all-Negro section that's a segregated community. Why? The white man controls his own school, his own bank, his own economy, his own politics, his own everything, his own community—but he also controls yours. When you're under someone else's control, you're segregated. They'll always give you the lowest or the worst that there is to offer, but it doesn't mean you're segregated just because you have your own. You've got to control your own. Just like the white man has control of his, you need to control yours.

You know the best way to get rid of segregation? The white man is more afraid of separation than he is of integration. Segregation means that he puts you away from him, but not far enough for you to be out of his jurisdiction; separation means you're gone. And the white man will integrate faster than he'll let you separate. So we will work with you against the segregated school system because it's criminal, because it is absolutely destructive, in every way imaginable, to the minds of the children who have to be exposed to that type of crippling education.

Last but not least, I must say this concerning the great controversy over rifles and shotguns. The only thing that I've ever said is that in areas where the government has proven itself either unwilling or unable to defend the lives and the property of Negroes, it's time for Negroes to defend themselves. Article number two of the constitutional amendments provides you and me the right to own a rifle or a shotgun. It is constitutionally legal to own a shotgun or a rifle. This doesn't mean you're going to get a rifle and form battalions and go out looking for white folks, although you'd be within your rights—I mean, you'd be justified; but that would be illegal and we don't do anything illegal. If the white man doesn't want the black man buying rifles and shotguns, then let the government do its job. That's all. And don't let the white man come to you and ask you what you think about what Malcolm says—why, you old Uncle Tom. He would never ask you if he thought you were going to say, "Amen!" No, he is making a Tom out of you.

So, this doesn't mean forming rifle clubs and going out looking for people, but it is time, in 1964, if you are a man, to let that man know. If he's not going to do his job in running the government and providing you and me with the protection that our taxes are supposed to be for, since he spends all those billions for his defense budget, he certainly can't begrudge you and me spending $12 or $15 for a single-shot, or double-action. I hope you understand. Don't go out shooting people, but any time, brothers and sisters, and especially the men in this audience—some of you wearing Congressional Medals of Honor, with shoulders this wide, chests this big, muscles that big—any time you and I sit around and read where they bomb a church and murder in cold blood, not some grownups, but four little girls while they were praying to the same god the white man taught them to pray to, and you and I see the government go down and can't find who did it.

Why, this man—he can find Eichmann hiding down in Argentina somewhere. Let two or three American soldiers, who are minding somebody else's business way over in South Vietnam, get killed, and he'll send battleships, sticking his nose in their business. He wanted to send troops down to Cuba and make them have what he calls free elections—this old cracker who doesn't have free elections in his own country. No, if you never see me another time in your life, if I die in the morning, I'll die saying one thing: the ballot or the bullet, the ballot or the bullet.

If a Negro in 1964 has to sit around and wait for some cracker senator to filibuster when it comes to the rights of black people, why, you and I should hang our heads in shame. You talk about a march on Washington in 1963, you haven't seen anything. There's some more going down in '64. And this time they're not going like they went last year. They're not going singing "We Shall Overcome." They're not going with white friends. They're not going with placards already painted for them. They're not going with round-trip tickets. They're going with one-way tickets.

And if they don't want that non-nonviolent army going down there, tell them to bring the filibuster to a halt. The black nationalists aren't going to wait. Lyndon B. Johnson is the head of the Democratic Party. If he's for civil rights, let him go into the Senate next week and declare himself. Let him go in there right now and declare himself. Let him go in there and denounce the Southern branch of his party. Let him go in there right now and take a moral stand—right now, not later. Tell him, don't wait until election time. If he waits too long, brothers and sisters, he will be responsible for letting a condition develop in this country which will create a climate that will bring seeds up out of the ground with vegetation on the end of them looking like something these people never dreamed of. In 1964, it's the ballot or the bullet. Thank you.

Essay/Discussion Questions

1. Malcolm X argued that since the American government failed to protect black people against violent white assaults, black people should defend themselves. Is his argument reasonable and defensible?

2. Why did Malcolm X suggest that black Americans expand the character of their struggle from one of civil rights to one of human rights?

3. What did Malcolm X mean by "the ballot or the bullet"?

Sister Act

KATHLEEN NEAL CLEAVER

The image of Charlayne Hunter, holding her head high and wearing a stylish leopardskin coat, beside Hamilton Holmes, both escorted by a tall black attorney, the three of them striding across the University of Georgia campus in 1961, is a snapshot of the sixties that I cannot forget. The memory remains so vivid, in part, because Holmes had once lived in my hometown in Alabama, but also because in that moment the collective destiny of our race was being advanced, propelled by lawsuits that forced segregated institutions of learning to admit black students. A few years earlier, it had taken the National Guard and a thousand paratroopers to escort nine black students through hostile mobs into Central High School in Little Rock, Arkansas. A few years later, police swarmed around the University of Alabama in Montgomery where Governor George Wallace vowed he would "stand in the door" to stop black students from enrolling, proclaiming himself a champion of segregation "forever." In the wake of the earthshaking Supreme Court decision in *Brown v. Board of Education* that declared separate but equal schools unconstitutional, the entrance of black students into formerly all white schools became the vortex of social transformation.

On that January morning Charlayne and Hamilton became the first black students ever admitted into the University of Georgia. The court order that permitted them to register was living testimony that we had just seized an almost magical power, and one, we were persuaded, that would repeal the awful legacy of slavery enshrined within the laws enforcing segregation. We were transfixed by the drama . . . and besides, Charlayne was stunningly beautiful.

* * * *

As were thousands upon thousands of others, I was also transfixed by Fannie Lou Hamer's radical challenge to the 1964 Democratic National Convention in Atlantic City, where she demanded that the Mississippi Freedom Democratic Party she represented replace the segregationist delegation from Mississippi. Mississippi at that time was synonymous with the bloody horrors of lynching. It was where the body of Emmett Till, a black teenager from Chicago, was found floating in the Tallahatchie river in the summer of 1955 after he

Reprinted from *Transition, An International Review,* 60 (1993), 84–100.

had spoken to a white girl; it was where, in the summer of 1964, three civil rights workers—Goodman, Chaney, and Schwerner—who had gone to investigate a church bombing were murdered; it was a desolate, poverty-stricken land where unchecked terrorism perpetuated white supremacy at any cost.

After the Atlantic City convention, Mrs. Hamer became nationally known, and throughout her life she continued in her plain-talking way to galvanize attention, polarize attitudes, and popularize the struggles of America's poorest and most exploited folks. "I'm sick and tired of being sick and tired," was a saying she made famous. Mrs. Hamer was no fair-skinned coed like Charlayne; she was a stocky, uneducated sharecropper who was thrown in jail, beaten, and kicked off her plantation because she tried to register to vote. To me and thousands who supported the movement, Mrs. Hamer was a beacon of heroism, unshakable courage, and innate dignity.

I cannot recall any corresponding dramatic incident that focused my attention on Elaine Brown, who had joined the Los Angeles chapter of the Black Panther Party some time before I first saw her. Our first meeting may have been in the packed church where we held the funeral for Alprentice "Bunchy" Carter. He was the leader of the Los Angeles Panthers, who was shot to death on the campus of UCLA by members of a rival organization—Ron Karenga's US, or United Slaves—in January 1969 after attending a student meeting. I think she sang at the funeral.

By that time Charlayne Hunter's daring entrance into the University of Georgia and Mrs. Hamer's defiant insistence on a principled acceptance by the Democratic Party had been submerged by hundreds of other inspiring and infuriating events. My own consciousness had been seared by the billowing smoke, unending bloodshed, and incipient rebellions that were raging across our cities like a forest fire. The entire country had mourned not only the assassination of a president, but in one year the

tragedy of seeing Rev. Martin Luther King, Jr., and Bobby Kennedy shot down by calculating killers. The ever-mounting carnage of the war in Vietnam was engendering a depth of alienation, dissension, and confusion without precedent in this century.

I myself had moved from cheering civil rights victories from the sidelines to serving the cause of black liberation on the frontlines. By then I was a member of the Central Committee of the Black Panther Party, and I wondered how and when I would be reunited with Eldridge, my husband of one year. Not only was he Bunchy Carter's closest friend, but he was the information minister of the Black Panther Party; two months earlier he had fled the country to avoid being returned to prison on charges of assaulting three Oakland police officers in a shoot-out with the Panthers that spring.

In My Place, Charlayne Hunter-Gault's memoir of that era, *This Little Light of Mine,* Kay Mills' comprehensive biography of Fannie Lou Hamer, and *A Taste of Power: A Black Woman's Story,* Elaine Brown's account of her years with the Panthers, all poignantly bring into focus the varied terrain I and many others traveled—or at least watched others travel—in those years. But these authors do more than revisit our recent past. Through the way they both complement and contradict each other, they illuminate the often unexamined beliefs we hold about leadership.

For each of these stories tells us about a woman whose life was in part defined by the movement for black self-determination that rocked this nation out of its cold war complacency during the sixties. Each in its own way presents a style of leadership that helps explain that complex movement. And understanding these styles of leadership may hold a key to the mystery of American renewal, a key that seems to elude us.

Hunter-Gault's charming memoir, Mills's richly detailed biography of Mrs. Hamer, and Brown's near surreal account of her rise to control of the Black Panther Party tell stories,

VIII Racism, Resistance, and Radicalism

respectively, about symbolic leadership, grass-roots leadership, and leadership by default. Of course, these modes of leadership merely delineate clusters of conduct that may share much in common, even overlap in various ways. But the importance of symbolic and grass-roots leadership in the formative phases of the civil rights movement was crucial. The role of leadership by default is less clear. But we know that in any organization or movement there are individuals who do not possess the innate skills or characteristics of leadership, but whom unforeseen events place in a position of authority.

The movement, in fact, cultivated these various styles of individual leadership and individual action in order to mobilize the popular energy it needed to transform the closed southern society. Much of the earliest effort was devoted to generating the confidence people needed to confront a brutal power structure that denied even the slightest sense of personal dignity to blacks.

For example, Rosa Parks's refusal to give up her seat on the Montgomery bus to a white man who demanded it, and her subsequent arrest, were necessary to start the chain reaction that led to the Montgomery bus boycott in 1956. She was, to be sure, neither the first nor the only woman to refuse to move when ordered by the bus driver to do so, or to be arrested for her resistance. What's significant is that she was arrested at a moment when community sensitivity was rubbed raw by the frequency of such arrests and the repeated indignities that occurred on the city buses; that she was a respected community figure who was active in the NAACP Youth Council; and that her neighbors and friends were ready to launch a protest boycott in response to her arrest because a combination of socially secure and financially successful ministers, teachers, and working people could identify with her. Parks's gesture symbolized the defiance that the larger community wanted to express at the degrading treatment meted out to every black bus rider daily, and thus her individual protest

sparked a community protest that, in turn, sparked a mass movement. The symbolic leadership Parks exhibited, when combined with the grass-roots leadership of E. D. Nixon—a longtime union activist who pulled together attorneys, ministers, the women's groups, and the NAACP to respond to her arrest—helped provide the social context in which the brilliant leadership talents of Rev. Martin Luther King, the new pastor of Montgomery's Dexter Avenue Baptist Church, could be displayed.

The exigencies of leadership by default were something the Black Panther Party had frequent opportunities to contend with. The harsh repression that the emerging Black Panther Party in Oakland, California, faced in the form of constant arrests, harassment, and armed attacks by the police was a deliberate tactic adopted by the government to destroy its leadership. The arrest, imprisonment, or exile of the early founders and leaders of the Black Panther Party left the direction of the floundering movement in the hands of David Hilliard, the chief of staff, by late 1969. The movement's centrifugal energy made it dependent upon a charismatic, authoritarian style of leadership that Hilliard could not provide. Yet he was tenaciously loyal and determined, and despite his lack of sufficient preparation or personal ability, he exercised formal leadership of the party, although not without considerable internal disgruntlement and disruption. In short, it fell to Hilliard to exercise leadership by default. After all, no mechanism was in place for choosing the officers, as the Black Panthers had not yet stopped being a dynamic movement and become a stable organization. At the same time, grass-roots and symbolic leadership were also profoundly significant in mobilizing the popular support the Black Panther Party depended upon to survive and grow in the face of the police attempts to weaken and destroy it.

* * * *

Johnetta Cole, the president of Spelman College, has said that leadership is about service, about what one is able to do in the interests of others. In the context of a movement, as opposed to a traditional organizational structure, leadership is not so much a matter of giving orders as it is about winning support: it works through persuasion, not coercion. The stories of these three women link them to the broader destiny of their people; and their distinct styles of leadership give us insight into the means by which they persuaded others to act in the interests of their community.

The symbolic leadership Charlayne Hunter exercised as a college freshman was both awe-inspiring and onerous. She writes that "the Movement had endowed me with a sense of mission that was bigger than myself, and I felt I had to lose my public self in order to find my place in that new world," and she described feeling concern over whether "I would ever be able to establish an identity as anything other than a symbol." It was important to her that she was known, but "I wanted it to be through the efforts of my ability," she writes, "rather than through something that but for the time and the place should have been an ordinary, routine occurrence. I wanted to be famous one day, but not simply for going to college."

Kay Mills points out that when Mrs. Hamer entered the voter registration movement as a middle-aged sharecropper, "in many communities women stepped into movement leadership because it was simply too dangerous for a black man to stand up to the system. He would lose his job, possibly his life." And she explains that because the Student Nonviolent Coordinating Committee (SNCC), rather than Martin Luther King's Southern Christian Leadership Council, was the most visible organization in Mississippi, the movement in Mississippi was not dominated by ministers but "relied on grass-roots people. Where there were grass roots, there were women."

Mrs. Hamer was one of the first people to get involved in SNCC's voter registration campaign in Sunflower County, the bastion of the notorious Senator James O. Eastland. After be-

ing kicked off the plantation in retaliation for her attempts to register to vote, Mrs. Hamer became a full-time movement organizer, dependent for her livelihood on the $10-a-week stipend SNCC provided its staff. Mills quotes from a letter Hamer sent to SNCC:

> My family and I have suffered greatly since I started working with the movement. Although we've suffered greatly, we have not suffered in vain. I am determined to become a first-class citizen. Some people will say that we are satisfied with the way in which we are living because we've always worked hard for little or nothing. So if registering to vote means becoming a first-class citizen and changing the structure of our state government, I am determined to get every Negro in the State of Mississippi registered. By doing this we can get the things we've always been denied the rights to. I can say this, we need a change in Mississippi; I'm sick of being hungry, naked, and looking at my children and so many other children crying for bread.

This statement of simple conviction was typical of Mrs. Hamer's fierce strength of character.

Elaine Brown's style of leadership was entirely different. Her story opens with her ascension to the role of chairman of the Black Panther Party in the wake of Huey Newton's hasty departure to Cuba. The year was 1974, by which time the internal dissension, external repression, and the exhaustion of that underlying momentum that had generated the mass movements for social change for the past twenty years had left the party decimated. It had shrunk from a national organization with over fifty chapters into a small body with only a few branch offices outside of Oakland. She addressed the assembled Panthers from the stage, saying: "Specifically, as we had begun to do before Comrade Huey's forced exile, we're going to continue the consolidation of our efforts in one city, *this* city. *Oakland* is the birthplace of this party. Oakland will be the birthplace of revolution in the United States." She also asserted her personal dominance in this speech:

I repeat, I have control over all the guns and all the money of this party. There will be no external or internal opposition I will not resist and put down. I will deal resolutely with anyone or anything that stands in the way. So if you don't like it, if you don't like the fact that I am a woman, if you don't like what we're going to do, here is your chance to leave. You'd better leave because you won't be tolerated.

Brown describes her feelings in that moment as "baptismal. There was something in that moment that seemed a reparation for all the rage and pain in my life." What she does not relate is that the gang-boss style she adopted from Huey Newton had already driven out almost all the individuals who were capable of contributing anything significant to a revolutionary movement; the ones that remained were those who were willing to accept being insulted, intimidated, and threatened into following orders.

Stewart Albert, a journalist who wrote about the Black Panthers for numerous underground newspapers during that era and coauthored the book *The Sixties Papers,* has described the process by which the Panther Party fell "prey to a siege mentality. The Party was racked by harmful purges, distrust, and political splits. By 1972 the Black Panther Party had ceased functioning as a national organization." Elaine Brown's authoritarian leadership style helps explain why it never would again attain national significance.

* * * *

A connection between the type of leadership these women display and the relationships that form their personal experiences can be discerned in these stories. Charlayne Hunter-Gault, a journalist who is now famous, as she had hoped, for her ability, has a big smile that fills her face. The cover photograph on her memoir shows that radiant, mischievous, beautiful smile as she delivered the commencement address at the University of Georgia in 1988, twenty-five years after her own gradua-

tion. Even then, her presence was symbolic, because she was the first black person in the 203-year history of the school ever to be the commencement speaker. She reminded the assembled parents and students that day how "no one would pretend that the Old South is dead and buried, that the events of the past twenty-five years, even my presence here today, have transformed our peculiar world into one that is beyond recognition." But despite the failures and the fact that the Confederate flag still flies on the campus today, she and Hamilton Holmes lit a watch fire. The watch fire, she said, celebrated "the revelation that amid misunderstanding and confusion—and hate—the good fortune of one curious, inquisitive Black girl who once dreamed of being Brenda Starr and found the University of Georgia the place to fulfill that dream, and one gifted young Black man who wanted to be a healer could be attained." She concluded her remarks with the acknowledgment that she celebrated the joyous moment with the class of 1988 "in a way that few others can" and asked them to join her "in what Zora Neale Hurston called our continuing 'journey to the horizon in search of people,' justice, equity and love."

Ms. Hunter-Gault's memoir gives us a moving, funny, and lyrical child's-eye view of her youth, for her book ends with her graduation from college in 1963, its final chapter being her 1988 commencement address. Although it covers a short time period, the memoir reveals a journalist's eye for the connection of her story to a larger context. The memoir weaves together local lore, family history, world affairs, and the naivete of a young girl's outlook on life. And yet for all its complexity, it reads swiftly, like a novella.

Her endearing story describes a young girl who deeply admired her mother and wanted more than anything to grow up to be like her: smart and strong, creative and feminine. Charlayne's father, an army chaplain, frequently lived away from the family, which consisted at first of grandmother, mother, Charlayne, and eventually two younger brothers. There were sporadic times when they all lived together on military bases, but the experience that gave her such a strong sense of place was growing up within extended family networks in South Carolina and Georgia. It was within that stable pyramid of family, church, and school that her sense of security was nurtured. It sustained her in the face of every adversity and sheltered her as the family moved from Due West, South Carolina, to Covington, Georgia, to the sophisticated metropolis of Atlanta, which black people then called "L.A." for "Lovely Atlanta."

Both her grandfather and father were ministers of the African Methodist Episcopal Church, the independent black denomination that spearheaded much of the civil rights movement. Her strong family, her teachers, and her friends continually nourished a sense of self-esteem, pride, and commitment to the black community in young Charlayne. Yet the time came when the cocoon of segregation in which she had grown up was cast aside, as a group of black college students in Atlanta joined the direct action campaign against segregation and issued the Atlanta Statement on Human Rights in 1960.

She describes her response to the change that she felt in that moment, when the community was no longer willing to remain silent. She writes

> Something had changed in us. We had been protected and privileged within the confines of our segregated communities. But now that we students had removed the protective covering, we could see in a new light both our past and our future. We could see that past—the slavery, the segregation, the deprivation and denial—for what it was: a system designed to keep us in our place and convince us, somehow, that it was our fault, as well as our destiny. Now, without ambivalence or shame, we saw ourselves as the heirs to a legacy of struggle, but struggle that was as Martin Luther King taught, ennobling; struggle that was enabling us to take control of our destiny. And as a result, we did not see ourselves or the other young people demonstrating in one way or another throughout the South as heroes to be praised, celebrated, or fretted over. We were simply doing what we were born to do.

Fannie Lou Hamer distinguished herself precisely because she did not do what she was born to do. After her first attempt to register to vote at the age of 45 was discovered, the owner of the plantation where she and her family lived and worked told her that she had better go back there and take her name off that book. "Mr. Dee," she answered him, "I didn't go down to register for you. I went down to register for myself." That defiance meant not only that she had to leave the plantation, but that she might be shot. After staying with relatives in a neighboring county for a few days, she came back and said, "Killing or no killing, I'm going to stick with civil rights." That was in the summer of 1962.

Mills describes Fannie Lou Hamer then as one of the few converts to the movement in Sunflower County, a place where most people were "too fearful, too dependent on whites to challenge their power." The three families who did participate, either by housing SNCC workers or registering to vote, had shots fired into their homes, which put an abrupt end to local interest in the movement. The tactic that SNCC then adopted was to begin to provide for the rural families' needs for food and services, and, with Mrs. Hamer's eloquence and encouragement, once again to stimulate interest in registering to vote.

SNCC workers took Mrs. Hamer to citizenship training sessions and helped develop her considerable leadership abilities. She soon became the featured speaker at their own training sessions, and was essential in introducing SNCC recruits and students to the realities of Mississippi. She would talk openly about her life experience, her arrest and beating in jail in Winona, and then give her own analysis of the way political and economic power operated in the United States. According to Eleanor Holmes Norton, she was an orator without equal. Norton marveled at Fannie Lou Hamer's ability to "put together a mosaic of coherent thought about freedom and justice, so that when it was all through, you knew what you had heard because it held together with wonderful cohesion. . . . Her speeches had themes. They had lessons. They had principles. . . . She had put her finger on something truly important that all of us felt but she had said. . . . You never needed to hear anybody else speak again."

Mrs. Hamer's ability to capture the essence of the struggle in compelling language that all could understand made her a favored speaker, as Mills tells us. SNCC soon expanded the range of her travels. Mrs. Hamer's energies were unflagging. She regularly raised money for SNCC; she helped SNCC stage mock elections. She helped organize the Mississippi Freedom Democratic Party. She cajoled and persuaded northerners to send food, clothing, and money to black Mississippians who were struggling to resist the retaliation visited upon them by plantation bosses. She organized surplus food giveaways and registration campaigns.

Mrs. Hamer was never concerned with whether the source of funds or the students who came to Mississippi to help were white or black. "If we're trying to break down this barrier of segregation," she told an SNCC meeting in 1963, "we can't segregate ourselves." As SNCC organizer Hollis Watkins is quoted as saying, "She was about justice. She was not just about blacks. She was about justice wherever it came down."

As the years went by, Mrs. Hamer continued to be active in political campaigns, efforts to elect black officials once the Voting Rights Act became law, efforts to get federal registrars into Sunflower County, efforts to create a new integrated delegation from Mississippi to the Democratic Party convention, in which she was finally seated during the 1968 convention at Chicago. By then, however, the national focus was no longer on what happened inside but what was happening in the streets outside the convention, as the Chicago police and the antiwar protestors confronted each other. She also worked with the Child Development Group, became active in efforts to establish Head Start programs, and worked to organize food cooperatives and Freedom Farm, as well as provide low-cost housing for Sunflower County residents. She was a plaintiff in lawsuits challenging the denial of voting rights, election fraud, and school desegregation. Mrs. Hamer worked unceasingly to create a more just social and political world until her death of heart failure in 1977.

Mills is an experienced journalist whose chronicle of Mrs. Hamer's career is thickly supported with observations from numerous people who knew Mrs. Hamer and the movement to which she devoted her life. Mrs. Hamer—that "indomitable untutored philosopher from Jim Eastland's county," as one historian called her—emerges in this account as a tireless, selfless woman who became involved in politics because she knew what "politicians and the press so often forget: that in a true democracy, people are politically active not to achieve celebrity or money but to change their own lives."

But beyond that she was a caring person whom one former Mississippi summer student worker remembers as "funny" and "loving," "a very endearing person. Everybody felt special about Mrs. Hamer. Everybody had that connection with her, and she obviously gave it back to you. . . . It was that kind of love connection that was her trademark." Douglas Wynn, a Mississippi attorney closely aligned with Lyndon Johnson and the Democratic Party, described Mrs. Hamer as "a woman of great integrity" although "not a political realist," and said that "she supported her convictions with every ounce of energy she had, and my God, that woman had some energy." Her commitment made it possible for other people to resist, to register, to sacrifice, to demand a voice in running their lives, and to alter the closed society of Mississippi.

At her funeral, Stokely Carmichael said that Mrs. Hamer represented "the very best of us." Andrew Young also spoke at her funeral, telling the huge crowd that she "shook the foundations of this nation, and everything I learned about preaching, politics, life and death I learned in your midst. There are many people who are now elected officials who would not be where they are had we not stood up then. And there is not one of those that was not influenced and inspired by the spirit of this one woman, Mrs. Hamer."

* * * *

Elaine Brown's portrayal of her family and upbringing—centered on a bleak childhood in Philadelphia—is absorbing, but it is her relation to the Black Panther Party that dominates most of the story. Certainly her account bears little resemblance to the sort of detailed chronicle Mills presents of Mrs. Hamer's forceful leadership; nor does it show the kind of more personal reflection Charlayne Hunter-Gault conveys in her look back at her youth. Despite an apparently sensational subject matter, recounted in the style of a fast-paced novel, Brown's narrative suffers from a certain myopia. Because she rarely connects the events of her own life with what is going on in the larger world, and infrequently supplies dates to the incidents she describes, her story has a pervasive sense of unreality.

Brown expresses so little reflection on the episodes she recounts that they remain in a perpetual present, like music. Music was what first brought Elaine to California, when she dropped out of Temple University in Philadelphia and took a plane to Los Angeles in 1965. She never says how the Watts riot affected her; it's as if it had never occurred. She came to California to make it as a songwriter and singer. It was a career that never took off, but music seemed to remain her refuge, and she continued to write songs and to sing while in the Panthers.

After an awful beating at the hands of one of her transitory lovers in Los Angeles, she muses about her upcoming meeting with a Motown executive about a record contract. "As I thought about those songs, all my songs, it occurred to me that most of them had been written to men for men. That realization made me wonder what exactly there was in my life that had made me come to rely so on the power of men. I began to wonder if that was why I was really in the Black Panther Party, with its men and guns."

> People were oppressed, and I was one of them. The party held some solution to that, and I was part of it. Huey was the best of men, and I was part of him. It was a perfect formulation for my life—except that in those three hours of pain I had endured, I felt more than physical pain. I had felt the weight of my aloneness. And I had seen the core of my fear, which was loneliness. This was the deepest truth of why I was in the Black Panther Party, of why I smothered my life with Huey Newton.

The central theme of *A Taste of Power*, in fact, is Elaine's obsession with Huey Newton, a self-destructive obsession apparently more erotic than political, and one so consuming it distorted her entire understanding of how the Black Panther Party came into being and what it represented.

In the bleak Mississippi poverty that Fannie Lou Hamer was born into and the more comfortable circumstances that young Charlayne Hunter knew, both women learned early in life to respect their race. In an incident Mills describes, Fannie Lou Hamer once asked her mother, "How come we are not white? Because white people have clothes, they can have food to eat, and we work all the time and don't have anything." Her mother answered, "I don't ever want to hear you say that again, honey. You respect yourself as a little child, a little black child. And as you grow older, respect yourself as black woman. Then one day other people will respect you." For her part, Charlayne Hunter describes "all the positive reinforcement I had gotten from my father and the rest of my family [that] white people were not superior, just *different.*"

But no such reinforcement ever came to the young Elaine, by her own account. As a child, she was determined, in her words, "to join those white people" that she met in the school for gifted children she attended. She tells us that she became convinced in elementary school that she was not really like the other colored girls. "My mother had told me that. White people were telling me that . . . I belonged in their world. I had not only learned to talk white and act white, I could do white things." It was not until after she moved to Los Angeles and became the mistress of Jay Kennedy (a novelist and executive with Sinatra Enterprises who years earlier had been Harry Belafonte's manager) that, with his encouragement, she began to appreciate herself as a black woman. "I did not mind listening to him discuss the merits of the civil rights movement or the Black Power Movement, and the like," she writes. "Issues concerning black people, however, were not personally relevant to me."

By 1967, all this changed, we learn. Jay Kennedy reneged on his promise to leave his wife and marry her, and an encounter in a Watts housing project with a group of little girls she agreed to teach piano melted her former indifference to the plight of poor blacks. She repudiated her white lover and his white world, and became Black with a capital B. She was soon in the center of Los Angeles's black nationalist community, working on a newspaper at the Black Congress.

Her first association with the Black Panther Party came through meeting Earl Anthony, who was then representing the Huey Newton Defense Fund. And soon she was in the thick of a revolutionary movement. The accuracy of Brown's narrative comes repeatedly into question as her story progresses. At times Brown

reports untrue statements she attributes to other characters. But her own credibility suffers because of carelessness about dates. To choose a relatively trivial instance, she claims to have bought and read *Soul on Ice* in late 1967 when it was not published until February of 1968. Other lapses are more worrying, involving either omissions that distort reality or outright fabrications of conversations and events. 1 am left wondering whether the cause of her reckless disregard for truth is due to emotional fatigue, the inevitable weakness of memory unaided by documents, a pathological compulsion to lie, or a less benign impulse, like deliberate disinformation.

For example, she attributes phrases to individual Panthers at a time when they were not yet part of the contemporary rhetoric—putting the words "ready to die for the people" in Bunchy Carter's mouth when such words were not used until after he was killed. Other such errors plague her account. While the name of the "Black Panthers" was actually taken from the Lowndes County Freedom Organization in Alabama, which used the Panther as its logo, Brown depicts the name as having originated with the Deacons for Defense in Louisiana, a group she incorrectly describes as the only armed civil rights organization in the country. She incorrectly refers to the writings of Marx as mandatory reading at a period in which the required reading list included Franz Fanon, Kwame Nkrumah, Malcolm X, and Mikhail Bakunin, but not Karl Marx.

Inaccurate details aside, Brown shows a propensity to substitute the stale phraseology of the Panther newspaper for coherent explanation. For example, instead of a straightforward description of how the Breakfast for Children program was begun, she writes, "The more the party sharpened the discrepancies between haves and have-nots, between the powerful and the powerless, the oppressor and the oppressed, the more the people would seek to resolve them. That, and the desire to temporarily alleviate the pain of poverty, was precisely the purpose of the party's Free Breakfast for Children program." In fact, the program came from an idea Bobby Seale proposed, as a means of both helping poor inner-city children get a good breakfast before they went to school and helping deflect the mounting harassment of the police. In Brown's account, the program was a response to J. Edgar Hoover's proclamation that the Black Panthers were the greatest threat to the internal security of the United States. Yet Hoover's remark was made almost two years after the breakfast program was started. Evidently because of Brown's personal antipathy toward Seale—she maliciously attacks him in her book, calling him "an idiot"—she misrepresents entirely the nature of the breakfast program.

But her flair for misrepresentation extends beyond careless mistakes, a flawed memory for dates, and personal vendettas. As editor of the Black Panther newspaper during the height of the purges that led to the so-called split in the party in February 1971, Brown wrote several vicious articles attacking or expelling some of the most respected leaders from the organization, articles that were examples of calculated deceit. In particular, the order—written by Brown and signed by Newton—expelling Geronimo Pratt in December 1970 went so far as to accuse him of being a CIA agent. What makes their denunciation so ironic is that Pratt is a classic victim of the COINTELPRO (Counter Intelligence Program) that the FBI launched against the Black Panthers. Framed by the FBI on a murder charge, Pratt has remained for 21 years behind bars serving a life sentence.

Brown was also the author of the incoherent article accusing Eldridge Cleaver, who at the time was living in exile in Algiers, of "defecting" from the party—this, after he and the entire International Section had been *expelled* by Newton in 1971. Perplexingly enough, she adopts this analysis in her current account of that period, as if time has stood still for her. In an effort to shore up her accusation, she even

invents a discussion she claims to have had, during a trip to Moscow, with a delegation Cleaver and Robert Sheer organized to travel to Asia, a discussion foreshadowing the eventual split, attributing to Cleaver views he did not hold at the time. She also neglects to report that her own views were ferociously critical of Hilliard's leadership.

Other facts she excludes—especially ones that would help explain those she includes—are staggering. For example, in the wake of the split in the Panthers, Newton dispatched hit men who shot down Robert Webb, a refugee from the San Francisco chapter, in broad daylight on 125th Street in Harlem. In retaliation, Sam Napier, who was in charge of the distribution of the Panther newspaper for the entire country, was killed in a New York Panther office. While Brown includes a description of Napier's death, she curiously omits the murder of Webb that precipitated it, thus giving a distorted account of what was happening to the party.

But what I found even more disturbing was the nature of her own leadership, which she presents as manipulative, authoritarian, and prone to fits of rage. She acknowledges that she had no friends but shows no insights about why. What, finally, are we to make of her expressed devotion to the organization when she plainly had no genuine understanding—beyond the stale and secondhand rhetoric of socialism—of what a popular movement was all about? Thus she refers at times to the Black Panther Party as a "terrorist" organization, a term used by FBI agents to justify their destruction of such groups.

The author's selective memory severely mars *A Taste of Power*. There is, for instance, her startling disclaimer concerning the death of Betty Van Patten, a bookkeeper, whose body was found floating in the San Francisco Bay shortly after the Panthers hired her. According to Brown, she hired her and fired her, but she didn't kill her. Whatever the real story was, Brown glosses over it. Again, describing her campaign for a seat on the Oakland City Council, Brown mentions in passing that she was at the top of a prison gang's hit list. What gang? Why? She refers to individuals, such as Earl Anthony or Melvin Cotton Smith, who have subsequently been identified as police informants or FBI agents—but makes no acknowledgment that their infiltration of the party is now public knowledge.

Her evasiveness about the successes of COINTELPRO is even more peculiar, in my view. While she identifies the FBI in general terms as an enemy, she never acknowledges its calculated efforts to generate internal dissent, disruption, and distrust through its COINTELPRO operations, efforts that ultimately succeeded in splitting the leadership of the Black Panther Party. Instead, she blames the split in the party on Cleaver, who was at the time isolated in northern Africa. I can only guess why she was so reluctant to discuss the FBI's counterintelligence operations, especially after so much information has been made available about the program's remarkable success.

Clearly, there is a story to be told about Elaine Brown's rise to a position of leadership of the Black Panther Party, but it is not in this book. In its place we are given a pastiche of half-truths, self-dramatizing confessions, fabrications, and falsehoods presented as "a black woman's story."

Ironically, her story ends in the same way as the story told in *A Lonely Rage* by the former Black Panther Party chairman, Bobby Seale, whom she repudiates so energetically. Both fled Huey Newton's madness by secretly rushing to the airport and flying away from Oakland, never to return. For all Brown's energy, duplicity, aggression, and devotion, she was left with nothing but a daughter, with whom she rarely spent time, and the oppressive burden of memories—memories of that moment of leadership she seized by default. Despite it all, however, she affirms her undimmed love for the Black Panther Party, like a battered

wife reluctantly fleeing from her husband. Did the organization she abandoned still have anything of value to offer the Oakland community? This is a question she never gets around to asking. But the madness she valiantly tried to conceal supplies the answer, because she herself was forced to flee. By the time she fled—in fact, even years before—the Panthers offered nothing but destruction.

The bloodstained conflicts that wrecked the Black Panther Party and permitted Brown to end up in a position of power are not explained in her book. Instead, she seeks to project a myth of leadership that she claims to have inherited from Newton. By that time, however, he was so tormented by paranoia, drug addiction, alcoholism, and outbursts of sadistic violence that his own potential for leadership was perverted beyond recognition.

In *A Taste of Power*, the deterioration of the Panthers is glorified, while the origin of the movement in the community's radical struggle with endemic powerlessness in the face of police, state, and economic domination is left unexamined. No attention is given to the symbolic leadership and grass-roots leadership that Newton, Seale, and others provided in the early years of the Black Panther Party. No analysis is offered of how the early leadership of the Black Panther Party captivated the imagination of thousands of black youths. As a result, the relationship between Brown and the evolving Panther organization cannot be realistically understood. Ultimately, the account she writes of her sexual adventures, confrontations with the police, and arm twisting with the political establishment reads like a tale full of sound and fury, signifying nothing.

To recognize the weakness of her individual claim to leadership is not, of course, to deny the movement in which she participated its profound significance. The underlying social challenge that was mounted in fits and starts, by mass action as well as single acts of heroism, demanded a complex mixture of many types of leaders and participants. True leadership recognized no monopoly on gender or race, and the urgent insistence that our conditions be changed called forth the strengths of an entire generation.

Bravery, commitment, and a willingness to sacrifice propelled many young people, some whose names we recall and others whose names have been forgotten, past jeering mobs and brutal rejection in order to fulfill the long-frustrated longings black people felt for equal treatment and equal access to the ballot, the school house, and the material fruits of labor. The military, the courtroom, and the ugly ghetto streets as well became battlegrounds for black advancement. All the dreams and all the energy and all the deeds added up to major changes for masses of people.

What these books give us that is important is a way, I think, to learn to recognize the type of conduct and belief that promotes this bravery, commitment, and willingness to sacrifice. When we can better cultivate that spirit of leadership that brought us the advances of the sixties, we can once again see our sisters and brothers and friends persuading each other to serve each other's interests as well as their own. Therein lies our abiding hope for American renewal.

Essay/Discussion Questions

1. Historically, writers largely ignored the roles of black women in the Civil Rights and Black Power Movements of the 1950s and 1960s. How does Kathleen Cleaver seek to correct this contradiction?

2. What are the reasons for Kathleen Cleaver's severe criticism of Elaine Brown's book, *A Taste of Power*?

3. What leadership principles and practices does Cleaver bring to light in her examination of the experiences of Fannie Lou Hamer, Charlayne Hunter-Gault, and Elaine Brown?

All Power to the People: The Political Thought of Huey P. Newton and the Black Panther Party

FLOYD W. HAYES III AND FRANCIS A. KIENE III

Recent events have rekindled interest in the Black Panther Party and the significance of its legacy. The absurd murder of Huey P. Newton in 1989 by a young black man signifies the mounting despair and rage in urban black America, resulting from the dehumanizing forces of economic impoverishment and popular indifference. It was the concrete situation of dispossession that brought the Black Panther Party into existence in the first place. Indeed, the circumstances under which Newton died demonstrate persuasively that urban black America's economic and social conditions have continued to decline since the 1960s.

The appearance of three new books has encouraged many to re-examine and reconsider the importance of the Black Panther Party. In *A Taste of Power: A Black Woman's Story*,[1] Elaine Brown writes persuasively, but not always accurately, about her experiences in the Black Panther Party. It is a statement about her personal development and later rise to power within the Party. The memoir also portrays the role of women in the organization. In another memoir, *This Side of Glory: The Auto-biography of David Hilliard and the Story of the Black Panther Party*,[2] the former Black Panther Party chief of staff writes a courageous and sensitive account of his life inside and outside of the Party. He recounts personal and political triumph, defeat, and redemption. Both books provide insider views of the Black Panther Party's dynamics, successes, contradictions, and decline.

Hugh Pearson's text, *The Shadow of the Panther: Huey Newton and the Price of Black Power in America*,[3] in effect chronicles the underside of the Black Panther Party. Pearson attempts a cold-blooded, objective analysis of the Party, but his anger and disillusionment with some shadowy aspects of the Panthers seem to cause him to focus unevenly on Newton's and the Panthers' destructive and militaristic tendencies.

All three recent books describe and analyze the social conditions of the 1960s that gave rise to angry groups of urban black youths who

For inclusion in Charles E. Jones, ed., *The Black Panther Party Reconsidered: Reflections and Scholarship*, Baltimore: Black Classics Press, 1999.

came together to form the Black Panther Party. It is significant that since the end of the 1960s, the social conditions of urban black America have progressively worsened. America's continued indifference to its urban dispossessed now has produced a generation that is more disillusioned, isolated, angry, and understandably cynical and nihilistic than ever were the generation that joined the Black Panther Party.

Many of today's inner-city black residents have no hope in America nor in themselves; hence, urban areas increasingly are becoming predatory communities where residents prey on each other in a desperate struggle to survive in a dreadful environment. Similar to the Black Panthers a generation ago, today's urban black dwellers continue to resist police brutality, racism, and harassment as they engage in angry discourse about the absurdity and despair of living in urban impoverished conditions that make inner-city residents the outsiders of the American social order. Significantly, the Panthers sought to educate, provoke, and transform American society. Contemporary urban black youth, inspired by the emerging significance of Malcolm X, appear to have abandoned any expectation of a better future; hence, they direct mounting rage against each other as well as toward the evolving racialization of power and privilege in America.[4]

In the late 1960s the Black Panther Party gained national attention as an organization of defiant young black men and women committed to resisting by any means necessary what Malcolm X had called America's white power structure. Emerging within the crucible of the Black Power Movement, these urban revolutionaries symbolized the rejection of Martin Luther King, Jr., and the Civil Rights establishment's sterile theorizing and ineffectual strategies of nonviolent civil disobedience.[5] Viewing urban black communities as colonies occupied by a system of white, hostile police, the Panthers fearlessly contested the power of the state to brutalize black citizens.

Huey P. Newton became the Party's chief theoretician. As such, Newton and the Black Panther Party were central figures in the Black Power Movement and major contributors in the 1960s and 1970s to the debate over the condition of and proper goals and strategies for the black population in America. Yet little scholarly work has concentrated on Newton's and the Panthers' political ideas. Therefore, the broad purpose of this paper is to examine, critically but sympathetically, some of the main currents of Newton's political thought and the Black Panther Party's ideology. More specifically, our aim is to probe the evolution of their political ideas.

As a dimension of Black Power ideology, Newton's thinking and the Black Panther Party's outlook are significant because they represent the continuation of a tradition of radical African American political thought, dating back at least to W. E. B. Du Bois, that attempts to view the black struggle through the prism of race and class. Historically, American scholars have struggled with the relationship between the concepts of race and class in trying to understand and explain the changing character of their society.[6] So it was with Huey P. Newton and the Black Panther Party, for they also exhibited the ongoing tension regarding the proper balance between race and class analyses. Through an examination of the development of Newton's and the Panthers' political utterances—black nationalism, revolutionary nationalism, revolutionary internationalism, and revolutionary intercommunalism—as well as the importance of armed struggle and the role of the lumpenproletariat within that struggle, we demonstrate that Newton and the Black Panther Party's efforts to merge aspects of race and class perspectives in an attempt to develop revolutionary theory and practice were hampered by both the internal problems and external pressures facing the Panthers.

Significantly, we recognize the difficulty of dividing the Panthers' political discourse into stages of development. Indeed, we try to show that the Party's rapidly evolving ideas were not fundamental breaks but shifts in degrees of emphasis, especially with respect to the concepts of race and class. Although we employ a stages-of-development model for analyzing Newton's and the Panthers' political ideas, it is important not to view this process merely as a linear progression. Rather, the evolving character of their political perspectives is better understood as a dialectical interaction—between black nationalism and revolutionary nationalism or between revolutionary nationalism and revolutionary internationalism or between revolutionary internationalism and revolutionary intercommunalism—resulting from the changing social conditions the Panthers confronted. Each transition to a new set of political views represented an attempt to resolve contradictions inherent in the previous system of ideas.

FOUNDING OF THE BLACK PANTHER PARTY

Although the Civil Rights Movement was mainly a southern phenomenon, its middle-class orientation and nonviolent integrationist ideology became sources of increasing frustration and disillusionment for a broad segment of the black population in America's northern and western cities. It was the perceived ineffectiveness of the Civil Rights Movement in the face of an intransigent anti-black power structure that served as a catalyst for the development of the more radical Black Power Movement out of which the Black Panther Party emerged. Huey Newton recalls in his autobiography, *Revolutionary Suicide:*

> We had seen Martin Luther King come to Watts in an effort to calm the people and we had seen his philosophy of nonviolence rejected. Black people had been taught nonviolence; it was deep in us. What good, however, was nonviolence when the police were determined to rule by force?[7]

Thus, Newton deemed it necessary to create an organization that would focus on the needs of ordinary people and involve members of the lower class. Influenced by Malcolm X's nationalism, Mao Tse-Tung's axiom of "picking up the gun," and Frantz Fanon's and Che Guevara's theories of revolutionary violence, Huey Newton and Bobby Seale founded the Black Panther Party for Self-Defense in Oakland, California, in 1966. Newton and Seale planned the Party's platform and program, which Newton actually wrote, delineating "What We Want" and "What We Believe." The program's elements included: self-determination for the black community; decent housing, critical education, and full employment for black people; self-defense and the end of police brutality in black communities; and the freedom of black prisoners.[8]

Marx and Engels were skeptical that the lumpenproletariat—the rogues, prostitutes, thieves, hustlers, murderers, gamblers, and paupers—could assist in the revolutionary transformation of capitalist society. However, the Panthers took a different position on the lumpenproletariat's role, which proved to be one of the most controversial aspects of their political ideology and practice. On this issue, Huey Newton and Bobby Seale drew heavily from a reading of Frantz Fanon's discussion of the colonized lumpenproletariat's revolutionary potential in his book, *The Wretched of the Earth.*[9] Although employing a Marxian theory of revolutionary change, Fanon pointed out that it had to be sufficiently refashioned to fit the colonial situation. Hence, Fanon argued that the anti-colonial insurrection emerged in the countryside and filtered into the cities by means of the peasantry or the lumpenproletariat who resided on the urban periphery. Fanon wrote:

> It is within this mass of humanity, this people of the shanty towns, at the core of the *lumpen-proletariat* that the rebellion will find its urban spearhead. For the *lumpen-proletariat,* that horde of starving men, uprooted from

their tribe and from their clan, constitutes one of the most spontaneous and the most radically revolutionary forces of a colonized people.[10]

After introducing Huey Newton to Fanon's text, Bobby Seale saw that Newton grasped the significance of Fanon's view of the lumpenproletariat for organizing the brothers off the street. That is, if the Panthers did not mobilize them, they would become an organized threat to the Panthers. Seale wrote:

> Huey understood the meaning of what Fanon was saying about organizing the lumpenproletariat first, because Fanon explicitly pointed out that if you didn't organize the lumpenproletariat and give a base for organizing the brother who's pimping, the brother who's hustling, the unemployed, the downtrodden, the brother who's robbing banks, who's not politically conscious—that's what lumpenproletariat means—that if you didn't relate to these cats, the power structure would organize these cats against you.[11]

Therefore, Newton sought to reach and recruit into the Black Panther Party young men who were disaffected and dispossessed. He often talked about the collective significance of "street brothers," and his responsibility to and affinity with them. In Newton's view, they all shared the same alienation from the American system of oppression:

> The street brothers were important to me, and I could not turn away from the life shared with them. There was in them an intransigent hostility toward all those sources of authority that had such a dehumanizing effect on the community. In school the "system" was the teacher, but on the block the system was everything that was not a positive part of the community. My comrades on the block continued to resist that authority, and I felt that I could not let college pull me away, no matter how attractive education was. These brothers had the sense of harmony and communion I needed to maintain that part of myself not totally crushed by the schools and other authorities.[12]

Moreover, in advocating the importance of the urban black lumpenproletariat, Newton arrived at another significant conclusion. He explained that although the development of technology initially expands the middle and working classes, the perpetual specialization and sophistication of the oppressor's technology will ultimately diminish the need for a large labor force.[13] The rise of computers and the increasing requirement for expertise necessary to operate the new machinery in the age of advanced technology threatens the survival and social development of those who lack the proper knowledge and skills. This understanding led Newton to consider the possibility that the working class could be transformed out of existence; their numbers would continue to decline, increasing the size of the lumpenproletariat.[14] Thus, as a matter of survival, Newton believed it logical for the lumpenproletariat to initiate revolutionary struggle.

One of the Party's initial activities was the armed patrol of the Oakland police to ensure that black residents were not brutalized and were informed of their rights. According to Newton, this effort was key to the Panther's ability to recruit members during the organization's early stages of development. Panthers would talk to the "street brothers" about their right to arm themselves, and the Party's application of this practice through patrolling the police impressed many in the community.[15] One of the most important functions of the Black Panther Party was to provide a number of community programs which included free breakfast for children, free health clinics, and liberation youth schools. Although the Panthers sought to portray an image of revolutionary urban guerrillas, it has been argued by some scholars that the Panthers' objectives, as stated in the platform and program, were actually more reformist than revolutionary.[16] Newton pointed out, however, that the Party's community programs were neither revolutionary nor reformist; rather, they were survival programs. He argued that for revolutionary transformation to occur in America, the people had to first possess a fundamental and supportive groundwork that maintained their potential for existence.[17] Therefore, Newton admitted that when the Party started in 1966, it maintained basically what were considered self-defense and black nationalist philosophies.[18] Significantly, Newton's and the Party's ideological perspectives continued to evolve rapidly through several stages, each of which was accompanied by external and internal tensions.

BLACK NATIONALISM

Beginning in October 1966, the Black Panther Party initially stressed more of a race than a class analysis of the black situation in America. However, it is important to observe that even at this early stage of development Newton's and the Party's ideas did not correspond exactly to the black nationalist standpoint as did other Black Power organizations of this period, such as Maulana Karenga's US Organization in Los Angeles.

Nowhere in the Panther platform and program is there a call for a black nation; rather, they evaded this issue. In 1968, when Newton was in jail, he had added to Point Ten of the Party's platform, "What We Want," statement related to the issue of a black nation. Point Ten originally read: "We want land, bread, housing, education, clothing, justice and peace." To that, Newton added the following:

> And as our major political objective, a United Nations–supervised plebiscite to be held throughout the black colony in which only black colonial subjects will be allowed to participate, for the purposes of determining the will of black people as to their national destiny.[19]

This addition was prompted by the thinking of the Panthers' Minister of Information, Eldridge Cleaver, who himself was inspired by Malcolm X's enunciation of this idea. Regarding the issue of whether the Party supported

racial integration or separation, Cleaver stated in July 1968 that the Party thought it "too premature" to decide which side it was on.[20] This seeming ambivalence on a basic element of black nationalism does not, however, contradict the Party's black nationalist orientation at this time.

The language and content of the October 1966 Black Panther Party Platform and Program essentially was based on a black nationalist perspective, for it emphasized the importance of racial solidarity. The document dealt solely with the problems, grievances, and demands of the dispossessed black population. In this way, it acknowledged black people's unique identity, which is the primary principle of black nationalism. The first point of the Program proclaims: "We believe that black people will not be free until we are able to determine our destiny." Self-determination is the essence of the concept of a nation.

In their implementation of the Community Action Patrol during this period, the Panthers were concerned exclusively with defending Oakland's black community from police harassment. This again encouraged a view of the black community's unique and separate identity, which resulted from their oppression and dehumanization by a racialized system and process of power. Other programs of the Party during this period were largely black nationalist also. For example, the Junior Panther Program for the younger children in the Oakland community taught black history and revolutionary principles so that these youngsters would "grow up to be men and defend their people in the black community."[21]

Additionally, black nationalist themes clearly were predominant in Huey Newton's early thinking. On the issue of black insurrection, which characterized the nationalist aspirations of black leaders during slavery, such as Denmark Vesey and Nat Turner, Newton stated:

> Black people must now move, from the grassroots up through the perfumed circles of

the black bourgeoisie, to seize by any means necessary a proportionate share of the power vested and collected in the structure of America. We must organize and unite to combat by long resistance the brutal force used against us daily.[22]

Here again, it is important to note that at this time Newton spoke exclusively of black self-determination and of solidarity across class lines—a traditional black nationalist theme.

In another essay, Newton acknowledged two historic black nationalist leaders, when he wrote: "Marcus Garvey and Malcolm X were the two black men of the twentieth century who posed an implacable challenge to both the oppressor and the endorsed spokesmen that could be dealt with in any other way than precisely the foul manner recorded by history."[23] Newton then went on to point out how the Black Panther Party picked up the gun and how other black people should also.

In yet another essay, Newton focused on the black male psyche. He argued that the black man's life is "built on mistrust, shame, doubt, guilt, inferiority, role confusion, isolation, and despair." With such a life, the black man "is dependent upon the white man ('THE MAN') to feed his family, to give him a job, educate his children, serve as the model that he tries to emulate. . . . He hates 'The Man' and he hates himself . . . What did he do to be so black and blue?"[24] Again, the white man's emasculation of the black man is a common and historic black nationalist representation, and black nationalist groups historically have stressed the rehabilitation and revitalization of black manhood. This image of black aggressiveness and masculinity was the hallmark of the Panthers during the early stage of their development.

What are we to make of the Black Panther Party's early nationalist orientation as adumbrated in its October 1966 Ten-Point Program? One writer viewed this early statement as naive and reformist.[25] Another argued that the program was "more a statement of grievances and concessions demanded from the white power structure than it is a program to mobilize black people in escalating struggle for control and power."[26]

Perhaps it would be better not to view the Ten Point Program as the singular guide for understanding the ideological basis of Black Panther actions, even though it consistently was printed on the next to the last page of the Party's weekly newspaper, *Black Panther*. The Panthers themselves acknowledged the unfinished character of the document. For instance, slain Chicago Black Panther leader Fred Hampton once stated: "Our ten point program is in the midst of being changed right now, because we used the word 'white' when we should have used the word 'capitalist'."[27] Therefore, in order to discover and evaluate the ideological basis for the Panthers' actions, it is necessary to look beyond the Ten-Point Program to other writings and speeches, especially after the Panthers recognized, in 1968, that their seemingly nationalist outlook was not sufficient to overturn the historic structures and processes of black dehumanization, oppression, and dispossession. As a result of this realization, the Panthers re-analyzed their ideology and moved to embrace a revolutionary nationalist position, renouncing any type of black nationalism. As Bobby Seale once stated: "Our ideology is to be constantly moving, doing, solving, and attacking the real problems and the oppressive conditions we live under, while educating the masses of the people."[28]

In this early period, the Black Panthers' repudiation of black nationalism was based on the continuing tensions between race and class analyses of the black situation. As their reading of and thinking about revolutionary literature evolved, Newton and the Panthers saw the increasing importance of class analysis and the limits of the narrow nationalist perspective for understanding the condition of black and other oppressed people. Thus, the Panthers' disillusionment with what they perceived as reactionary nationalism prompted a transition to revolutionary nationalism.

REVOLUTIONARY NATIONALISM

Newton asserted that the Party adopted a nationalist ideology because it was believed that some form of nationhood was the solution.[29] Analyzing history, the Party concluded that colonized people had fought off the yoke of oppression and exploitation in the past by establishing a nation comprising their own racial, ethnic, or cultural group. However, because black people lacked the power to become a dominant faction in America, thereby making nationhood problematic, Newton was forced to reassess the Panther's nationalist position. This led to the development of revolutionary nationalism, which meant nationalism with socialism.

In *Revolutionary Suicide*, Newton explained that his transformation from black nationalism to socialism was a long and arduous process. While a student at Merritt College in Oakland, Newton supported Castro's Cuban revolution and was thus criticized by others and labeled a socialist. Nevertheless, he believed that if this was socialism, then socialism must be a cogent system of ideas. He was introduced to Marxism around the time of the Black Panther Party's founding through reading Lenin's *Materialism and Empirio-Criticism*.[30] Later, after finishing several volumes of Mao Tse-Tung, Newton embraced the socialist perspective. Summarizing his ideological transformation, he stated: "It was my life plus independent reading that made me a socialist—nothing else."[31]

In a 1968 interview with *The Movement*, a white radical periodical, while he was in prison, Newton defined the Black Panther Party as a revolutionary nationalist organization. According to Newton, revolutionary nationalism depended upon "a people's revolution with the end goal being the people in power. Therefore, to be a revolutionary nationalist you would by necessity have to be a socialist." This perspective included a definite role for white radicals, which as Newton defined it was "to first choose his friend and his enemy and after doing this,

which it seems he's already done, then to not only articulate his desires to regain his moral standard and align himself with humanity, but also to put this into practice by attacking the protectors of the institutions."[32]

Extremely opposed to the Panthers' rapidly developing revolutionary nationalist perspective was the largely dominant cultural nationalist position, which the Party called "pork chop nationalism." In Newton's words cultural nationalism was

> a reaction instead of responding to political oppression. The cultural nationalists are concerned with returning to the old African culture and thereby regaining their identity and freedom. In other words, they feel that the African culture will automatically bring political freedom. Many times cultural nationalists fall into line as reactionary nationalists.[33]

According to Newton, an excellent example of reactionary nationalism was Haitian President Francois Duvalier. After kicking out the colonizers, he inserted himself into the role of the oppressor. A clear example of revolutionary nationalism, Newton declared, was the Algerian revolution that Frantz Fanon described and analyzed in *The Wretched of the Earth*.[34] Significantly then, cultural nationalists view white people and racist oppression as the main enemies, while socialists see the capitalist class and economic exploitation as the primary antagonists. Therefore, as revolutionary nationalists, Newton and the Panthers maintained that their struggle centered on destroying the conditions that generated the twin evils of capitalism and racism.

As a developing revolutionary nationalist, Newton proposed that the Black Panther Party unite with the world's oppressed people who struggle for decolonization and liberation. In the 1960s, Newton, as did numerous other theorists, advanced the position that black people in America were colonized in much the same way as the people of Africa, Asia, and Latin America whom the Western Europeans had taken over in the 19th century. Further,

Newton argued that the urban police force occupied black communities in the same fashion that the United States military occupied areas of Vietnam. This was the legacy of the formation of the American political and economic system, which was established largely by the violent appropriation of Native American lands and the exploitation of African slave labor. The dislocation and relocation of Africans and their American descendents, along with the dehumanization and exploitation of their labor, represented a form of colonialism—domestic or internal colonialism.[35] It was from a sense of solidarity with other colonized peoples that Newton determined that the Panthers should work with white leftists, a significant departure from cultural nationalism.

THE PANTHERS AND WHITE LEFTISTS

The Black Panther Party's initial alliance with a white leftist group was with the Peace and Freedom Party in 1967. This association began in the narrow interest of seeking support to free imprisoned Huey Newton, but it then expanded to include the larger issue of black liberation within the ideological context of class struggle. The alliance between the Black Panther Party and the Peace and Freedom Party marked the first definite move of the Panthers from a quasi-nationalist to a revolutionary socialist position. As Anthony observed, the controversial alliance with the Peace and Freedom Party also "marked the end of our honeymoon in the black community in general, and the black liberation movement in particular. Since '66, the *modus operandi* of the movement had been to exclude whites. The coalition came in for sharp criticism, publicly and privately, from many quarters."[36]

The alliance, nevertheless, seemed to serve the purposes of the Black Panther Party well. It provided the necessary financial and administrative resources to mount and support the Free Huey Movement, and it appears doubtful that the Panthers would have been able to

make the Free Huey Movement a *cause célèbre* around the country if it had not been for the supportive machinery and resources of the Peace and Freedom Party. Most importantly, the Black Panther Party never was co-opted by its alliance with the Peace and Freedom Party. Most black nationalists feared co-optation in dealing with white organizations. Indeed, if anyone was co-opted in this alliance, perhaps it was the Peace and Freedom Party rather than the Panthers. The influence the Black Panther Party had over the Peace and Freedom Party is suggested by the fact that many of the Panther leaders became Peace and Freedom Party candidates for elective office.

Other white leftist groups with which the Panthers had alliances included the Students for a Democratic Society (SDS), Women's Liberation, and the Gay Liberation Front. At an SDS national council meeting in Austin, Texas, on March 30, 1969, it declared support for the Black Panther Party and passed resolutions to implement that support—formation of Newton-Cleaver Defense Committees, printing and distribution of information about the history and development of Black Panther Party programs, and the development and/or strengthening of informal and formal relations with the Panthers.[37]

In a special "Letter from Huey to the Revolutionary Brothers and Sisters about the Women's Liberation and Gay Liberation Movements," Newton called for the formation of a working coalition with these two groups. To those who opposed the full participation of these groups at revolutionary conferences, rallies, and demonstrations, Newton admonished:

> Remember, we haven't established a revolutionary value system; we're only in the process of establishing it. I don't remember us ever constituting any value that said that a revolutionary must say offensive things towards homosexuals, or that a revolutionary should make sure that women do not speak out about their own particular kind of oppression. Matter of fact, it's just the opposite: we

say that we recognize the women's right to be free. We haven't said much about the homosexual at all, and we must relate to the homosexual movement because it's a real thing. And I know through reading and through my life experience, my observations, that homosexuals are not given freedom and liberty by anyone in the society. Maybe they might be the most oppressed people in the society.[38]

The Panthers organized these and other radical groups into a National Committee to Combat Fascism. Organized at a three-day conference in Oakland, California, in July 1969 this association became the most important mechanism for Panther alliances with white groups. There were some 2,500 participants, led by the Panthers and including SDS, the Young Patriots, Latino groups, and the Communist Party. The principal proposal of the conference was community control of the police—an issue that dated back to the early days of the self-defense activities of the Panthers against police harassment. At this conference, the Panthers had definitely moved beyond a black nationalist orientation to a class position.[39]

Although not without some contradictions, these various alliances were valuable to the Panthers as far as providing an assortment of financial and material resources that were otherwise unobtainable. However, as has been indicated, these alliances cost the Panthers a significant loss of credibility within many black communities, particularly among those who maintained a black nationalist orientation. Moreover, the Panthers' relations with white leftists often were turbulent and even conflictual. Some white radicals disrespected the intellectual power and theoretical leadership of the Panthers, while others literally betrayed them.[40] In some quarters, it seemed that the Panthers were overly concerned with gaining white allies, which drove away some black allies, whereas they needed both black and white allies alike.

Many Black Panther Party rallies were attended largely by white radicals and their sup-

porters. Although the black community embraced the Panthers in times of crisis and in their survival programs—the Los Angeles black community's support following the shootout at UCLA is a good example—black community residents generally did not turn out in great numbers at Panther rallies. This application of the Panthers' revolutionary nationalist orientation, alliances with white leftists, engendered negative reactions in some sectors of the black community.

CLASHES WITH CULTURAL NATIONALISM

Perhaps most influential in their strong critical reaction to cultural nationalism were the often deadly conflicts and rivalries the Panthers had with various other black nationalist formations. In establishing their power in the Bay Area during the early days, the Panthers neutralized the influence of other black nationalist organizations. The first group the Panthers clashed with was the black nationalist association at the Black House in San Francisco. Originally, Eldridge Cleaver had been one of the co-founders of the Black House, which was basically culturally oriented. Prominent figures at the Black House were the two black playwrights, Amiri Baraka and Ed Bullins. According to Earl Anthony, the Black House "was not predisposed to the politics of the Black Panther Party for Self-Defense and had been most critical of the actions of the Party." In response, the Panthers entered the Black House armed and gave notice that its members were evicted. "They left the premises, and the Black House was then occupied by the Black Panther Party for Self-Defense."[41]

In addition to the cultural nationalists of the Black House, the Panthers confronted another black political organization in San Francisco, who also called themselves the Black Panther Party. This San Francisco-based group accused the Oakland Panthers of being prematurely paramilitary, maintaining that the political struggle was the first priority. In contrast, the Newton group believed, following the maxim of Chairman Mao Tse-Tung of China, that "Political power grows out of the barrel of the gun." By the end of 1967, the San Francisco-based Panthers had faded from the scene, unable to compete with the more colorful and provocative Oakland Panthers.[42]

Perhaps the most serious and deadliest conflict between the Panthers and a black nationalist formation was with Los Angeles community leader Maulana Karenga and US organization.[43] In search of more support for the Party and the Free Huey Movement, the Panthers in 1968 established an office in the area of Los Angeles where Karenga's organization flourished. US was a black cultural nationalist organization, which emerged after the 1965 Watts insurrection under the leadership of Maulana Karenga. His members were highly disciplined, with a strong commitment to his nationalist ideas. The leading cadre of his organization was the Simba Wachuka (Swahili for Young Lions), an army of skillfully trained young men.[44] Earl Anthony, then the Party's Minister of Education, observed what was destined to be a tragic development:

> At that time the Los Angeles "turf" was almost the exclusive domain of US, since there were no organization or individual within or without the Black Congress which was strong enough to be its equal politically or militarily. But the Panthers soon began to gain strength and challenge its power, and the first signs of bad blood developed. This rivalry was to develop into a power struggle of tragic proportions.[45]

Disagreements between the Black Panther Party and US did indeed reach horrifying dimensions in January 1969. A collision occurred in the context of the campus-based Black Student Union's participation in the selection of a director for the new Black Studies Program at the University of California at Los Angeles. Members of both the Panthers and US were students in UCLA's High Potential Program— a special entry enterprise for African American, Latino, Asian American, and Native American students who were bright but underachievers in past educational pursuits. The "turf" conflict between the Panthers and US spilled over onto UCLA's campus, as both organizations sought to influence the Black Student Union and its agenda.

As a member of the Black Student Union's Community Advisory Committee, Maulana Karenga had participated in the early stages of planning and discussion regarding the selection of the Black Studies Program's director. There was no Panther representation. Yet, as a result of their own struggle for a power base at UCLA, both US and the Panthers came to have substantial stakes in who was chosen as director. John Huggins and Alprentice (Bunchy) Carter, both students in the High Potential Program, headed the Panther contingent at UCLA. A change in the leadership of the Black Student Union resulted in Huggins' later involvement in the Black Studies Program selection process. As the relative influence of the Panthers on the UCLA campus increased in proportion to that of US, the ongoing tension between these two organizations exploded into an unrelenting power struggle. It all culminated in a bloody gun-fight on January 17, 1969, when three US members shot and killed Huggins and Carter following a Black Student Union meeting.[46] In the ensuing years at least two other Panthers were killed in confrontations with members of US organization.

The conflict with US organization strengthened the Panthers' practical and ideological hostility to cultural nationalism and reinforced the commitment to Marxist-Leninism. Hence, the Panthers sought to create a strong Marxist-Leninist vanguard party that went well beyond the black nationalist worldview. As this development proceeded, social conditions and the character of their overall struggle encouraged the Panthers to embrace a more global view of social revolution.

TOWARD REVOLUTIONARY INTERNATIONALISM

Although the Panthers retained their revolutionary nationalist views fairly intact during Huey Newton's imprisonment, that changed upon his release in August 1970. Representing the impact of an increasingly global consciousness on his thinking, Newton once again transformed the Black Panther Party ideology, maintaining the basic elements of revolutionary nationalism as far as coalition politics was concerned. The new Panther ideology represented a transition to revolutionary internationalism.

Newton's new thinking was based on the view that the United States was no longer a nation, but an empire that dominated the entire world. Accordingly, the bourgeoisie that Marxist-Leninist adherents sought to defeat was international in character, and Newton believed that "the only way we can combat an international enemy is through an international strategy, unity of all people who are exploited, who will overthrow the international bourgeoisie, and replace it with a dictatorship by the proletariat, the workers of the world."[47]

Under this view, national movements for liberation were to be supported as long as they also were internationalist. Newton declared: "If they are nationalist alone then they are chauvinist. If they are both nationalist and international, they realize that they need liberated territory but they also realize that their interests are the same as every other people's interests who are fighting against imperialism."[48]

On the issue of the nationalist aspirations of black people, Newton believed that their history contradicted any demand for nationhood:

> We feel that black people in America have a moral right to claim nationhood because we are a colonized people. But history won't allow us to claim nationhood, because it has bestowed an obligation upon us; to take socialist development to its final stage, to rid the world of the imperialist threat, the threat of the

capitalist and the warmonger. Once he is destroyed then there will be no need for nationhood, because the nations won't need to defend themselves against imperialism.[49]

Thus, Newton's concept of revolutionary internationalism suggested the ultimate destruction of nationhood itself so that humankind would develop a sense of mutual friendship throughout the world. To the extent that it called for the solidarity of the "Third World" against Western imperialism, the Black Panthers' internationalist ideas were compatible with other internationalist views, such as those advocated by Pan-Africanist Stokely Carmichael. The basic difference was that Pan-Africanism did not discount nationalism, even though Pan-Africanism too incorporated an appreciation of Marxist theory and had a global outlook. Moreover, the Panthers interpreted the Pan-Africanist emphasis on nationalism as synonymous with racial chauvinism, a perspective the revolutionary internationalist Panthers sought to discredit.

The Party took some steps to implement the theory of revolutionary internationalism. Newton offered to the National Liberation Front and Provisional Revolutionary Government of South Vietnam "an undetermined number of troops to assist you in your fight against American imperialism." Nguyen Thi Dinh, Deputy Commander of the South Vietnamese People's Liberation Armed Forces, accepted the offer in the following manner: "With profound gratitude, we take notice for your enthusiastic proposal; when necessary, we shall call for your volunteers to assist us."[50]

Newton came under heavy criticism in the United States from such people as Roy Wilkins, veteran civil rights leader, who questioned Newton's commitment to the advancement of poor urban and rural black Americans. Newton responded by explaining his ideology of internationalism: "We are internationalist because our struggle must proceed on many fronts. While we feed and clothe the poor at home, we must meet and attack the oppressor wherever he may be found."[51]

In a further attempt to put into practice their theory of revolutionary internationalism, the Panthers officially opened an International Section of the Black Panther Party in the Algerian capital of Algiers on September 13, 1970. Algiers had become somewhat of a refuge for fugitive Panthers ever since Eldridge Cleaver surfaced there in June 1969 and was subsequently joined by his wife Kathleen. They, and other Panthers there, sought to communicate with and issue statements supporting liberation movements in North Korea, North Vietnam, and China.

REVOLUTIONARY INTERCOMMUNALISM: A HIGHER PHASE OF MARXIST UTOPIANISM

In the face of changing world dynamics, the Panthers sought to refine the concept of internationalism, which resulted in a transition to revolutionary intercommunalism. This was put forward at the turbulent September 1970 Revolutionary People's Constitutional Convention in Philadelphia.

Intercommunalism drew upon the fundamental ideological thrust of internationalism, that the United States was not a nation, but an empire that exploited and dominated the world. However, intercommunalism went on to suggest that United States imperialism had transformed other nations into oppressed communities: "If a nation cannot protect its boundaries and prevent the entry of an aggressor, if a nation cannot control its political structure and its cultural institutions, then it is no longer a nation, it must be something else." According to the Panthers, this something else—oppressed communities of the world—pointed out serious limitations of both the nationalist and internationalist perspectives. Therefore, the Panthers said: "We must place our future hopes upon the philosophy of intercommunalism."[52]

Like internationalism, the oppressed peoples of the world needed to work together to overthrow United States capitalism and imperialism, under the banner of revolutionary intercommunalism. As with other Panther ideas, the shift to intercommunalism seemed more of a change in degrees of emphasis, rather than a complete departure from or break with the Party's earlier internationalist position. That is, revolutionary intercommunalism stressed the existence of exploited and oppressed global communities and their need for collective revolutionary emancipation.

With a flourish of Marxian utopianism, the end goal of intercommunalism was idealistic—nothing short of a global socialism was sought. Going beyond revolutionary internationalism, the new ideological position stressed egalitarian elements and looked forward, in theory at least, to the abolition of invidious social class distinctions. Reminiscent of Marx's 1875 *Critique of the Gotha Program*, each and every person would be able to take up his or her position in the general division of labor. The Panthers wrote: "We pledge ourselves to end imperialism and distribute the wealth of the world to all the people of the world. We foresee a system of true communism where all people produce according to their abilities and all receive according to their needs."[53]

If there was a cultural lag between the destruction of the oppressive state apparatus and the erection of the new world order based on revolutionary intercommunalism, the Panthers called for "all people in the communities throughout the world to be represented in decision making and participation in direct proportion to their presence in the population under consideration."[54] This call seemed to be a somewhat disguised assent to nationalism in the aftermath of a global socialist revolution.

In perspective, then, revolutionary intercommunalism was the Panthers' attempt to adapt Marxism to fit the dynamics of the rapidly changing world of the 1970s. Global class struggle by the world's lumpenproletariat against the world's bourgeoisie and its managerial apparatus (United States imperialism and capitalism) was the means to bringing about a new world order—a global, egalitarian community based on socialism. Given this set of circumstances, Newton saw the role of the Black Panther Party to expose imperialist antagonisms and to raise the people's consciousness to the point of undertaking revolutionary social action.[55]

CONCLUSION

As this essay has shown, the Black Panther Party was an organization whose ideas and activities were in constant motion as a result of confronting the dynamic character of local, national, and international change and development. The progressive development of Huey P. Newton's and the Panthers' political thought—black nationalism, revolutionary nationalism, revolutionary internationalism, revolutionary intercommunalism, and the revolutionary role of the lumpenproletariat—represented an effort by a generation of young, dispossessed, and defiant black Americans to formulate a theory and practice of fundamental social transformation. As their assessment and analysis evolved with respect to black oppression, specifically, and social domination, generally, Newton's and the Panthers' political ideas changed accordingly.

In some ways, however, the rapidly advancing character of Newton's and the Panthers' thinking proved problematic. Often ideological shifts were not accompanied by sufficient political education so that rank-and-file Panthers could understand fully the new set of ideas.[56] This organizational weakness contributed in some respects to the Party's internal instability. Additionally, the content of ideological changes contributed to problems the Panthers had with rival organizations, especially black nationalist. As discussed in this paper, the Panthers' repudiation of national-

ism and embrace of socialism added to mounting ideological conflicts with Maulana Karenga's US organization and other nationalist groups. It needs to be pointed out, however, that the Black Power Movement witnessed hard-line ideological positions taken by nearly all politically militant and insurgent theorists, activists, and organizations. Almost everyone despised ideological deviation. This undermined the larger struggle for social justice and human liberation.

The decline and destruction of the Black Power Movement and the Black Panther Party—this resulted from internal fissures and governmental infiltration and repression—interrupted and redirected the thinking and actions of one of the major black insurgent formations of the last half of the twentieth century.[57] Emerging in urban areas of a nation that was largely indifferent to the historic structures and processes of cultural domination, anti-black racism, and economic dispossession, idealistic and angry young men and women of the Black Panther Party represented a serious threat, if only for a short time, to the American social order and its system of governance. Viewing themselves as a revolutionary vanguard organization of oppressed urban black communities, the Panthers seized the political space in order to speak audaciously to the people and to the powerful about justice, liberation, self-determination, and revolution. The Panthers demanded the transformation of power relationships within American society and throughout the world, arguing that in order to destroy the conditions that produced and maintained ignorance and poverty, the dispossessed themselves needed to take hold of the reins of power.

Yet, two decades after the Panthers fearlessly championed a system of radical social change, the inequitable socio-economic conditions against which they struggled continue and, indeed, are worsening for many urban communities. These trends and developments are the result of the winding down of the industrial-capitalist society of money and manufacturing and the winding up of the postindustrial-managerial order of knowledge, science, and technology.[58] Experiencing growing cynical disillusionment, increasing hopelessness, intensifying meaninglessness, and mounting rage, many urban communities are becoming predatory zones as their residents turn on each other in a desperate and self-destructive attempt to survive in a society that is indifferent to their impoverishment. This dispiriting and often anarchical situation—much worse than the one from which the Panthers emerged nearly thirty years ago—cries out for a positive alternative. Hence, the question: Can Huey Newton's and the Panthers' legacy of radical and emancipatory political ideas and the struggle for survival be retrieved at the edge of the 21st century? For those suffering on the heights of alienation and despair, the effort to resist social pessimism becomes supreme.

Notes

1. Elaine Brown, *A Taste of Power: A Black Woman's Story*, New York: Pantheon Books, 1992.
2. David Hilliard and Lewis Cole, *This Side of Glory: The Autobiography of David Hilliard and the Story of the Black Panther Party*, Boston: Little, Brown and Company, 1993.
3. Hugh Pearson, *The Shadow of the Panther: Huey Newton and the Price of Black Power in America*, Reading: Addison-Wesley Publishing Company, 1994.
4. See Mark Baldassare, ed., *The Los Angeles Riots: Lessons for the Urban Future*, Boulder: Westview Press, 1994; Dhoruba Bin Wahad, Mumia Abu-Jamal, and Assata Shakur, *Still Black, Still Strong: Survivors of the U. S. War Against Black Revolutionaries*, New York: Semiotext(e), 1993; Leon Bing, *Do or Die*, New York: HarperCollins, 1991; Kody Scott, *Monster: The Autobiography of an L.A. Gang Member*, New York: Penguin Books, 1993; Robert Gooding-Williams, ed., *Reading Rodney King, Reading Urban Uprising*, New York: Routledge, 1993.
5. For a recent analysis of the Black Power Movement, see William L. Van Deburg, *New Day in Babylon: The Black Power Movement and American Culture*, Chicago: The University of Chicago Press, 1992.
6. See Oliver C. Cox, *Caste, Class, and Race: A Study in Social Dynamics*, New York: Monthly Review Press, 1948; Harold Cruse, *The Crisis of the Negro Intellectual*, New York: William Morrow & Company, Inc., 1967.
7. Huey P. Newton, *Revolutionary Suicide*, New York: Harcourt Brace Jovanovich, Inc., 1973, p. 110.
8. See Philip S. Foner, ed., *The Black Panthers Speak*, Philadelphia: J. B. Lippincott Company, 1970; August Meier, Elliott Rudwick, and Francis L. Broderick, eds., "Interview with Huey Newton," *Black Protest Thought in the Twentieth Century*, New York: Macmillan Publishing Company, 1971, pp. 495–515.
9. Frantz Fanon, *The Wretched of the Earth*, New York: Grove Press, Inc., 1963.
10. Ibid., p. 103.
11. Bobby Seale, *Seize the Time: The Story of the Black Panther Party and Huey P. Newton*, New York: Random House, Inc., 1970, p. 30.
12. Newton, *Revolutionary Suicide*, pp. 73–74.
13. Newton, *To Die for the People: The Writings of Huey P. Newton*, New York: Random House, Inc., 1972; Newton and Erik H. Erikson, *In Search of Common Ground: Conversations with Erik H. Erikson and Huey P. Newton*, New York: W. W. Norton and Company, Inc., 1973.
14. Ibid.
15. Newton, *Revolutionary Suicide*.
16. See Manning Marable, "The Legacy of Huey P. Newton," *The Crisis of Color and Democracy*, Monroe: Common Courage Press, 1992, pp. 202–206; for a similar critique of the Black Power Movement as a whole, see Harold Cruse, *Rebellion or Revolution*, New York: William Morrow and Company, Inc., 1968.
17. Newton, *To Die for the People*.
18. Newton and Erikson, *In Search of Common Ground*.

19. Black Panther Party, "What We Want, What We Believe," in Foner, ed., *The Black Panthers Speak*, pp. 3–4.
20. Seale, *Seize the Time*, p. 63; Gene Marine, *The Black Panthers*, New York: New American Library , 1969, p. 185.
21. Seale, *Seize the Time*, p. 105.
22. *The Black Panther*, June 20, 1967, p. 2.
23. *The Black Panther*, July 3, 1967, p. 10.
24. *The Black Panther*, May 15, 1967, p. 18.
25. Marable, *The Crisis of Color and Democracy*.
26. James Boggs, *Racism and the Class Struggle: Further Notes from a Black Worker's Notebook*, New York: Monthly Review Press, 1970, p. 183.
27. Foner, ed., *The Black Panthers Speak*, p. 143.
28. Seale, *Seize the Time*, p. 426.
29. Newton, *To Die for the People*.
30. See Henry Hampton and Steve Fayer, *Voices of Freedom: An Oral History of the Civil Rights Movement from the 1950s through the 1980s*, New York: Bantam Books, 1990.
31. Newton, *Revolutionary Suicide*, p. 70.
32. Foner, ed., *The Black Panthers Speak*, pp. 50 and 55.
33. Newton, *To Die for the People*, p. 92; Foner, ed., *The Black Panthers Speak*, p. 50.
34. See Newton, *To Die for the People*; Foner, ed., *The Black Panthers Speak*; Meier, Rudwick, and Broderick, "Interview with Huey Newton."
35. See Robert L. Allen, *Black Awakening in Capitalist America: An Analytic History*, Garden City: Doubleday & Company, Inc., 1969; Robert Blauner, "Internal Colonialism and Ghetto Revolt," *Social Problems*, Vol. 16, No. 4 (Spring 1969), pp. 393–408; Stokely Carmichael and Charles Hamilton, *Black Power: The Politics of Liberation in America*, New York: Random House, Inc., 1967; John O'Dell, "A Special Variety of Colonialism," *Freedomways*, Vol. 7, No. 7 (Winter 1967), pp. 7–15.
36. Earl Anthony, *Picking Up the Gun: A Report on the Black Panthers*, New York: The Dial Press, 1970.
37. See *Guardian*, April 19, 1969, reprinted in Foner, ed., *The Black Panthers Speak*, pp. 228–229.
38. *The Black Panther*, August 21, 1970, p. 5.
39. *Newsweek*, August 4, 1969, p. 35.
40. See Hilliard, *This Side of Glory*.
41. Anthony, *Picking Up the Gun*, p. 21; Amiri Baraka, interview with Floyd W. Hayes III, September 28, 1994.
42. Anthony, *Picking Up the Gun*.
43. Maulana Karenga, *The Roots of the US-Panther Conflict: The Perverse and Deadly Games Police Play*, San Diego: Kawaida Publications, 1976.
44. Van Deburg, *New Day in Babylon*.
45. Anthony, *Picking Up the Gun*, p. 73. David Hilliard and Elaine Brown also describe the Panthers' tension-filled experiences with Maulana Karenga and US organization; see Hilliard, *This Side of Glory* and Brown, *A Taste of Power*.
46. Gail Sheehy, "Black Against Black: The Agony of Panthermania," *New York*, November 16, 1970, pp. 45–50.
47. *The Black Panther*, January 16, 1971, p. 10.
48. Ibid.
49. Ibid.
50. *The Black Panther*, January 19, 1971, pp. 10–11.
51. *The Black Panther*, September 26, 1970, pp. 12–13.
52. *The Black Panther*, December 5, 1970, pp. 7–8. Hilliard also discusses the meaning and significance of revolutionary intercommunalism in *This Side of Glory*.
53. Ibid., p. 8.
54. Ibid.
55. Newton and Erikson, *In Search of Common Ground*.
56. See Hilliard, *This Side of Glory*.
57. See Charles E. Jones, "The Political Repression of the Black Panther Party, 1966–1977: The Case of the Oakland Bay Area," *Journal of Black Studies*, Vol. 18, No. 4 (June 1988), pp. 415–434; Karenga, *The Roots of the US-Panther Conflict*; Newton, "War Against the Panthers: A Study of Repression in America," unpublished dissertation for the Ph.D., University of California at Santa Cruz, 1980; Kenneth O'Reilly, *Racial Matters: The FBI's Secret File on Black America, 1960–1972*, New York: The Free Press, 1989.
58. William A. Darity, Jr., and Samuel L. Myers, Jr., with Emmett D. Carson, and William Sabol, *The Black Underclass: Critical Essays on Race and Unwantedness*, New York: Garland Publishing, Inc., 1994.

Essay/Discussion Questions

1. Discuss the changing character of the Black Panther Party's political ideology. According to Hayes and Kiene, what impact did the changes have on party organization and action?

2. It can be argued that the Black Power movement erupted as a result of frustrations with the Civil Rights movement. Compare and contrast the two movements by examining their leaders, ideologies, and organizations. What were the strengths and weaknesses of each movement?

3. A variety of contemporary rap groups refer in their music to Black Power figures and themes. To what extent has the Black Power movement contributed to rap music? Provide specific examples.

4. In the late 1960s, impoverished urban economic conditions and racial discrimination throughout American society contributed to the rise of the revolutionary Black Panther Party, which had an impact on national and international communities. Similar, if not worse, economic, political, and cultural conditions exist today; yet no radical or revolutionary social and political movement seems to have captured the hearts and minds of America's youth on a scale that comes close to the 1960s Black Power movement or the Black Panther Party. Discuss the reasons for this situation.

Anatomy of a Rebellion:
A Political-Economic Analysis

MELVIN L. OLIVER, JAMES H. JOHNSON, JR.,
AND WALTER C. FARRELL, JR.

It is quite impossible to understand the events surrounding the acquittal of the four police officers accused of brutally beating Rodney King without placing them within the local and national circumstances and forces that have deepened class and racial inequalities over the past two decades. Both at the local and national level, the trajectory of economic, political, and social trends has exacerbated the ever-so-fragile social fabric of our nation's cities, making ripe the conditions that kindled the social explosion that occurred in Los Angeles on 29 April 1992.

In this essay, we reflect on the Los Angeles civil disorder of 1992 from an urban political economy perspective. It is our contention that the course and magnitude of changes in the urban political economy of American cities in general, and Los Angeles in particular, were crucial in bringing to the forefront the contradictions underlying the Los Angeles urban rebellion. Thus, this essay is an anatomy of the civil unrest that seeks to unravel its relationship to rebellions of the past, highlighting both the ever-changing and unchanging nature of the relationship of black Americans to the economic and political order, and the consequences

of the introduction of new actors into the sociopolitical mix of large American cities. In order to accomplish this, we situate the civil unrest within the broader context of the recent demographic, social, and economic changes occurring in the Los Angeles milieu. The object of this analysis is to ground the rebellion in the context of a political system that is frayed at the edges in its attempt to integrate new voices into the body politic and, at the same time, is incapable of bringing into the economic mainstream significant portions of the African-American community (traditionally one of the most economically marginal segments of American society). Can the efforts that have been spawned as a consequence of the urban rebellion achieve a modicum of success in confronting these difficult challenges? We address this issue in a brief but critical review of existing policies and proposals that have been advanced to "rebuild" Los Angeles. Finally, we

This chapter is based on a previous analysis of the civil disorder in Los Angeles entitled "The Los Angeles Rebellion: A Retrospective View," which appeared in *Economic Development Quarterly* 6 (1992): 356–372 and was co-authored by James H. Johnson, Jr., Cloyzelle K. Jones, Walter C. Farrell, Jr., and Melvin L. Oliver.

TABLE 1 TOLL FROM SELECTED REBELLIONS

City/State	Date	Number Arrested	Number Injured	Number Dead	Property Damage	Other Characteristics
Newark, NJ	12–17 July 1967	n.a.	1,500	26	$ 58,796,605	300 fires set
Detroit, MI	23–28 July 1967	7,000	2,000	43	162,396,707	—
Los Angeles, CA	11–17 August 1965	n.a.	1,032	34	182,565,079	—
Washington, DC	4–9 April 1968	6,036	1,202	9	45,292,079	—
Los Angeles, CA	29–30 April 1992	16,291	2,383	52	785 million –1 billion	500 fires set

Source: "Toll from Other Riots," *USA Today,* 5 May 1992, 4A, and Timothy Noah and David Wessel, "Urban Solutions: Inner City Remedies Offer Novel Plans—and Hope, Experts Say," *Wall Street Journal,* 4 May 1992, A1, A16.
NOTE: n.a. = not available.

TABLE 2 LAW ENFORCEMENT PERSONNEL ON DUTY

Los Angeles Police and County Sheriff's Department	3,720
California Highway Patrol	2,300
Fire	2,700
National Guard	10,000
Army	2,500
Marines	1,500

Source: "L.A. Aftermath at a Glance," *USA Today,* 6 May 1992, 3A.

TABLE 3 LOS ANGELES REBELLION, 1992: ARREST BY RACE/ETHNICITY (30 APRIL THROUGH 4 MAY 1992)

	LAPD	Sheriff's Department	Total	Percent
Latino	2,764	728	3,492	36.9
Black	2,022	810	2,832	29.9
White	568	72	640	6.8
Other/Unknown	84	2,408	2,492	26.4
Total	5,438	4,018	9,456	100

Source: Virginia I. Postrel, "The Real Story Goes Beyond Black and White," *Los Angeles Times,* 8 May 1992, A11.

outline our own strategy for redeveloping South Central Los Angeles, one which is designed to address the real "seeds" of the civil unrest.

ANATOMY OF THE REBELLION

The recent civil unrest in Los Angeles was the worst such event in recent U.S. history. None of the major civil disorders of the 1960s, including the Watts rebellion of 1965, required a level of emergency response or exacted a toll—in terms of loss of life, injuries, and property damage and loss—comparable to the Los Angeles rebellion of 1992 (table 1). The burning, looting, and violence that ensued following the rendering of a not-guilty verdict in the police-brutality trial required the deployment

of not only the full forces of the Los Angeles Police Department (LAPD) and the Los Angeles County Sheriff's Department, but also 10,000 National Guardsmen and 3,500 military personnel (table 2). The Fire Department received 5,537 structure fire calls and responded to an estimated 500 fires. An estimated 4,000 businesses were destroyed. Fifty-two people died and 2,383 people were injured, including 20 law-enforcement and fire personnel. Property damage and loss have been estimated at between $785 million and $1 billion (table 1).

In contrast to the civil disorders of the 1960s, this was a multiethnic rebellion. The diversity is reflected in table 3, which depicts, for the period 30 April through 4 May, arrests

TABLE 4 LOS ANGELES REBELLION, 1992: ILLEGAL ALIENS ARRESTED
AND DEPORTED BY COUNTRY OF ORIGIN

Mexico	360
El Salvador	62
Guatemala	35
Honduras	14
Jamaica	2
Other Countries	4
Total	477

Source: George Ramos and Tracy Wilkinson, "Unrest Widens Rifts in Latino
Populations," *Los Angeles Times,* Washington edition, 8 May 1992, 1.

by race/ethnicity. It has been estimated that
1,200 of the 16,000 plus arrested were illegal
aliens, roughly 40% of whom were handed
over to INS officials for immediate deportation
(table 4). Also in contrast to the civil disorders
of the 1960s, the burning and looting were
neither random nor limited to a single neighborhood; rather, the response was targeted,
systematic, and widespread, encompassing
much of the legal city. This fact has led us to
purposefully and consistently refer to the civil
unrest as a rebellion as opposed to a riot.

THE VERDICT AND THE REBELLION IN
RETROSPECT

We think it is safe to say that both the verdict
rendered in the police-brutality trial, and the
widespread burning, looting, and violence
which ensued after the jury issued its decision,
shocked most Americans. In retrospect, however, we would like to suggest that both the
verdict and the subsequent rebellion were quite
predictable. The treatment of black suspects
by the police and black defendants by the
courts represents a continuity in the experience of blacks in relationship to the criminal-
justice system.

The outcome of the trial, in our view, was
predictable for two reasons. The first pertains to
the defense attorneys' successful bid for a change
of venue for the trial. Simi Valley, the site of the
trial, and Ventura County more generally, is a
predominantly white community known for
its strong stance on law and order, as evidenced

by the fact that a significant number of LAPD
officers live there.[1] Thus, the four white police
officers were truly judged by a jury of their
peers.[2] Viewed in this context, the verdict should
not have been unanticipated.

The second development that made the
outcome of the trial predictable, in retrospect,
was the defense attorneys' ability to put Mr.
King, instead of the four white police officers,
on trial. (We should note here, parenthetically,
that the media is also guilty in this regard, as
evidenced by its consistent characterization of
the case as "the Rodney King trial.") The defense attorneys, in effect, played the so-called
"race card"; they painted Mr. King as unpredictable, dangerous, and uncontrollable, much
as Mr. Bush, in the 1988 presidential campaign, used Willie Horton, the convicted rapist
released on a temporary work furlough only to
commit another heinous crime, to paint Mr.
Dukakis as being soft on crime.[3]

In today's society, the Willie Horton stereotype, recent surveys tell us, is often applied
categorically to black males, irrespective of
their social and economic status, but especially if they reside in the inner city.[4] It is our
contention that the jury agreed with the defense attorneys' portrayal of Mr. King as dangerous and uncontrollable, and thus rendered
a verdict in favor of the four white police
officers, notwithstanding the seemingly irre-
futable videotaped evidence.

Why do we think, in hindsight, that the
civil unrest following the verdict in the police-
brutality trial was predictable? We believe that

the response was not about the verdict in the police-brutality trial per se; rather, the civil unrest reflected the high degree of frustration and alienation that had built up among the citizens of South Central Los Angeles over the last 20 years. The rebellion as we view it in retrospect, was a response not to a single but rather to repeated acts of what is widely perceived in the community to be blatant abuse of power by the police and the criminal-justice system more generally.[5]

The civil unrest was also a response to a number of broader, external forces which have increasingly isolated the South Central Los Angeles community, geographically and economically, from the mainstream of the Los Angeles society.[6] These forces include: recent structural changes in the local (and national) economy; wholesale disinvestment in the South Central Los Angeles community by banks and other institutions, including the local city government; and nearly two decades of conservative federal policies which have simultaneously affected adversely the quality of life of the residents of South Central Los Angeles and accelerated the decline and deterioration of their neighborhoods.

Moreover, these developments were occurring at a time when the community was experiencing a radical demographic transformation, an unprecedented change in population accompanied by considerable tensions and conflict between long-term residents and the more recent arrivals.[7] Viewed from this perspective, the verdict in the police-brutality trial was merely the proverbial straw that broke the camel's back.[8]

SEEDS OF THE REBELLION

The videotaped beating of Mr. Rodney King was only the most recent case in which there were serious questions about whether LAPD officers used excessive force to subdue or arrest a black citizen. For several years, the City of Los Angeles has had to pay out millions of

taxpayers' dollars to settle the complaints and lawsuits of citizens who were victims of LAPD abuse. Moreover, the black citizens of the city of Los Angeles have been disproportionately victimized by the LAPD's use of the choke hold, a tactic employed to subdue individuals who are perceived to be uncooperative. During the 1980s, 18 citizens of Los Angeles died as a result of LAPD officers' use of the choke hold; 16 of them reportedly were black.[9]

Accordingly, the not-guilty verdict rendered in the police-brutality trial was also only the most recent in a series of cases in which the decisions emanating from the criminal-justice system were widely perceived in the black community to be grossly unjust. This decision came closely on the heels of another controversial verdict in the Latasha Harlins case. A videotape revealed that Ms. Harlins—an honor student at a local high school—was fatally shot in the back of the head by a Korean shopkeeper following an altercation over a carton of orange juice. The shopkeeper received a six month suspended sentence and was ordered to do six months of community service.[10]

These and related events have occurred in the midst of drastic demographic change in South Central Los Angeles. Over the last two decades, the community has been transformed from a predominantly black to a mixed black and Latino area (Figure 1). Today, nearly one-half of the South Central Los Angeles population is Latino. In addition, there also has been an ethnic succession in the local business environment, characterized by the exodus of many of the Jewish shopkeepers and a substantial influx of small, family-run Korean businesses. This ethnic succession in both the residential environment and the business community has not been particularly smooth. The three ethnic groups—blacks, Latinos, and Koreans—have found themselves in conflict and competition with one another over jobs, housing, and scarce public resources.[11]

Part of this conflict stems from the fact that the Los Angeles economy has undergone a

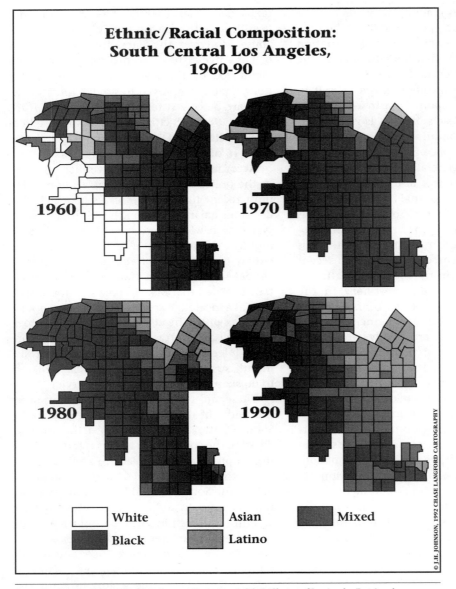

Ethnic/Racial Composition: South Central Los Angeles, 1960-90

1960 1970 1980 1990

White   Asian   Mixed
Black   Latino

© J.H. JOHNSON, 1992 CHASE LANGFORD CARTOGRAPHY

Figure I Ethnic Change in South Central Los Angeles, 1960–80, and Locations of Korean Businesses, 1987

Source: Los Angeles Community Development Department, *Ethnic Clusters of Los Angeles* (Los Angeles, Community Development Department 1977, 1982), and Korean Chamber of Commerce of Los Angeles, *Directory of Korean Business* (Los Angeles, Korean Chamber of Commerce of Los Angeles, 1987).

fairly drastic restructuring over the last two decades.[12] This restructuring includes, on the one hand, the decline of traditional, highly unionized, high-wage manufacturing employment; and on the other, the growth of employment in the high-technology-manufacturing, the craft-specialty, and the advanced-service sectors of the economy. As Figure 2 shows, South Central Los Angeles—the traditional industrial core of the city—bore the brunt of the

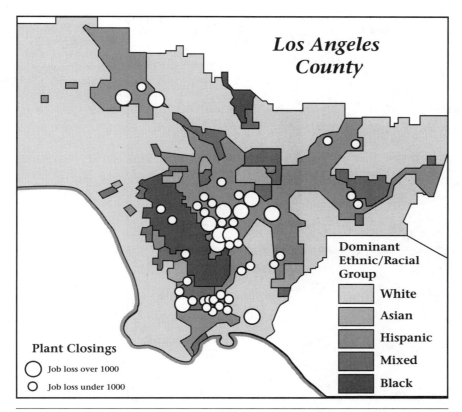

Figure 2 Plant closings in L.A. County, 1978–82

Source: Maya Blum, Kathryn Carlson, Estela J. Morales, Ross Nussbaum, and Patricia J. Wilson, "Black Male Joblessness, Spatial Mismatch, and Employer Preferences: A Case Study of Los Angeles," unpublished paper, Center for the Study of Urban Poverty, University of California, Los Angeles, May 1992.

decline in manufacturing employment, losing 70,000 high-wage, stable jobs between 1978 and 1982.[13]

At the same time these well-paying and stable jobs were disappearing from South Central Los Angeles, local employers were seeking alternative sites for their manufacturing activities. As a consequence of these seemingly routine decisions, new employment growth nodes or "technopoles" emerged in the San Fernando Valley, in the San Gabriel Valley, and in El Segundo near the airport in Los Angeles County, as well as in nearby Orange County (Fig 3).[14] In addition, a number of Los Angeles-based employers established production facilities in the Mexican border towns of Tijuana, Ensenada,

and Tecate. Between 1978 and 1982, over 200 Los Angeles-based firms, including Hughes Aircraft, Northrop, and Rockwell, as well as a host of smaller firms, participated in this deconcentration process.[15] Such capital flight, in conjunction with the plant closings, has essentially closed off to the residents of South Central Los Angeles access to what were formerly well-paying, unionized jobs.[16]

It is important to note that, while new industrial spaces were being established elsewhere in Los Angeles County (and in nearby Orange County as well as along the U.S.-Mexico border), new employment opportunities were emerging within or near the traditional industrial core in South Central

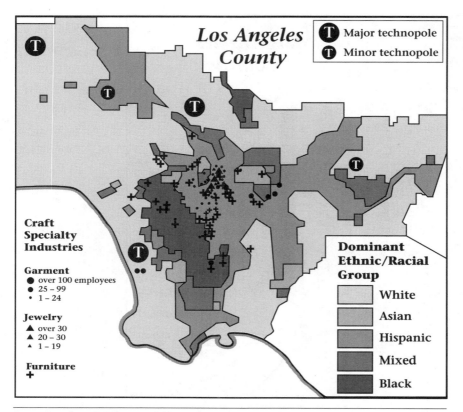

Figure 3 Locations of craft specialty industries and job growth techno-poles in L.A. County, 1990

Source: Data from U.S. Bureau of the Census, *1990 Census of Population* (Washington, DC: U.S. Department of Commerce, 1991), and the Data Center, *Plant Shutdown Directory* (Oakland, CA: The Data Center, 1978–1982).

Los Angeles (Figure 3). But, unlike the manu-facturing jobs that disappeared from this area, the new jobs are in competitive sector indus-tries, which rely primarily on undocumented labor and pay, at best, minimum wage.

In part as a consequence of these develop-ments, and partly as a function of employers' openly negative attitudes toward black work-ers, the black-male jobless rate in some resi-dential areas of South Central Los Angeles hovers around 50%. Whereas joblessness is the central problem for black males in South Central Los Angeles, concentration in low-paying, bad jobs in competitive sector indus-tries is the main problem for the Latino residents of the area. Both groups share a com-mon fate: incomes below the poverty level

(Figure 4). Whereas one group is the working poor (Latinos), the other is the jobless poor (blacks).[17]

In addition to the adverse impact of struc-tural changes in the local economy, South Central Los Angeles also has suffered from the failure of local institutions to devise and imple-ment a plan to redevelop and revitalize the community. In fact, over the last two decades, the local city government has consciously pur-sued a policy of downtown and westside rede-velopment at the expense of South Central Los Angeles. One needs only to look at the skyline of downtown and the so-called Wilshire corri-dor—that twenty-mile stretch extending along Wilshire Boulevard from downtown to the Pacific Ocean—to see the impact of this policy.[18]

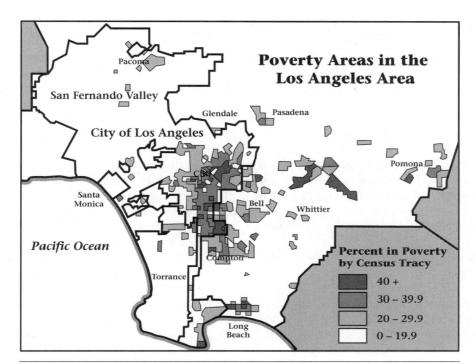

Figure 4
Poverty Areas in
Los Angeles Area

Source: Data from U.S. Bureau of the Census, *1980 Census of Population and Housing, Census Tracts* (Washington, DC: U.S. Department of Commerce, 1981).

Finally, the seeds of the rebellion are rooted in nearly two decades of conservative policy making and implementation at the federal level. Many policy analysts talk about the adverse impact on minorities and their communities of Democratic president Lyndon Johnson's "War on Poverty" programs of the 1960s, but we must not lose sight of the fact that the Republicans have been in control of the White House for all but four (the Carter years) of the past 20 years.[19] A number of public policies implemented during this period, and especially during the years when Mr. Reagan was president, we contend, served as sparks for the recent civil unrest. Three of these policy domains are worthy of note here.

The first pertains to the federal government's establishment of a laissez-faire business climate in order to facilitate the competitiveness of U.S. firms. Such a policy, in retrospect, appears to have facilitated the large number of plant closings in South Central Los Angeles and capital flight to the U.S./Mexico border and various Third World countries. Between 1982 and 1989 there were 131 plant closings in Los Angeles, idling 124,000 workers. Fifteen of these plants moved to Mexico or overseas.[20]

The second involved the federal government's dismantling of the social safety net in minority communities. Perhaps most devastating for the South Central Los Angeles area has been the defunding of community-based organizations (CBOs). Historically, CBOs were part of that collectivity of social resources in the urban environment which encouraged the inner-city disadvantaged, especially disadvantaged youth, to pursue mainstream avenues of social and economic mobility and discouraged dysfunctional or antisocial behavior. In academic lingo, CBOs were effective "mediating" institutions in the inner city.[21]

During the last decade or so, however, CBOs have become less effective as mediating institutions. The reason for this is that the federal support they received was substantially reduced. In 1980, when Mr. Reagan took office, CBOs received an estimated 48% of their funding from the federal government.[22] As part of the Reagan Administration's dismantling of the social safety net, many CBOs were forced to reduce substantially programs that benefited the most disadvantaged in the community. Inner-city youth have been most adversely affected by this defunding of community-based initiatives and other safety-net programs

It should be noted, moreover, that the dismantled social safety net has been replaced with a criminal dragnet. That is, rather than allocate support for social programs that discourage or prevent disadvantaged youth from engaging in dysfunctional behavior, over the past decade or so, the federal government has pursued a policy of resolving the problems of the inner city through the criminal-justice system.

Given this shift in policy orientation, it should not be surprising that, nationally, 25% of prime-working-age young black males (ages 18–35) are either in prison, in jail, on probation, or otherwise connected to the criminal-justice system.[23] Although reliable statistics are hard to come by, the anecdotal evidence suggests that at least 25% of the young black males in South Central Los Angeles have had a brush with the law. What are the prospects of landing a job if you have a criminal record? Incarceration breeds despair and in the employment arena, it is the scarlet letter of unemployability.[24]

Educational initiatives enacted during the late 1970s and early 1980s, which were designed to address the so-called "crisis" in American education, constitute the third policy domain. There is actually a very large body of social-science evidence which shows that such policies as tracking by ability group,

grade retention, and the increasing reliance on standardized tests as the ultimate arbiter of educational success have, in fact, disenfranchised large numbers of black and brown youth. In urban school systems, they are disproportionately placed in special-education classes and are more likely than their white counterparts to be subjected to extreme disciplinary sanctions.[25]

The effects of these policies in the Los Angeles Unified School District (LAUSD) are evident in the data on school-leaving behavior. For the Los Angeles Unified School district as a whole, 39.2% of all of the students in the class of 1988 dropped out at some point during their high-school years. However, for high schools in South Central Los Angeles, the dropout rates were substantially higher, between 63% and 79%. It is important to note that the dropout problem is not limited to the high-school population. According to data compiled by LAUSD, approximately 25% of the students in the junior high schools in South Central Los Angeles dropped out during the 1987–88 academic year.

Twenty years ago it was possible to drop out of school before graduation and find a well-paying job in heavy manufacturing in South Central Los Angeles. Today, however, those types of jobs are no longer available in the community, as we noted previously. Juxtaposing the adverse effects of a restructured economy and the discriminatory aspects of education reforms, what emerges is a rather substantial pool of inner-city males of color who are neither at work nor in school. These individuals are, in effect, idle; and previous research shows us that it is this population which is most likely to be in gangs, to engage in drug trafficking, and to participate in a range of other criminal behavior.[26] Moreover, we know that it is this population of idle, minority males that experiences the most difficulty forming and maintaining stable families, which accounts, at least in part, for the high percentage of female-headed families with incomes below the poverty level in South Central Los Angeles.

EXPLAINING THE SOURCES OF A MULTIETHNIC REBELLION

The most distinctive aspect of the Los Angeles rebellion was its multiethnic character. While blacks were the source of the disturbances as they broke out on the first night of the rebellion, by the second evening it was clear that the discontent that emerged initially was shared by many of the city's largest racial group, the Latino community. As we have just pointed out, the economically depressed Latinos in Los Angeles are comprised of a working-poor population, characterized by a large and significant core of Mexican and Central American immigrants. But what is interesting is that the rebellion did not encompass the traditional Mexican-American community of East Los Angeles. Indeed, the fires and protest were silent in these communities as political leaders and local residents ardently cautioned residents against "burning your own community."[27] Nevertheless, Latinos in South Central Los Angeles did not hesitate to participate in looting, particularly against Korean merchants. How do we explain this pattern?[28]

One important element necessary to explain the uneven participation of Latinos in the rebellion is to place the Latino experience into the context of struggles to incorporate that community politically into the electoral system in Los Angeles city and county. With the largest Latino population outside of Mexico City, Latinos have been severely underrepresented in city and county governments. In a struggle emanating from the 1960s, Latinos, particularly Mexican Americans, have been involved in protesting this situation, in ways ranging from street-level, grass-roots activity to highly coordinated court challenges to racially biased redistricting schemes that have unfairly diluted Latino voting strength.[29] That struggle has just recently begun to bear fruit. In the important court case *Garza et al. v. County of Los Angeles,* Los Angeles County was found guilty of racial bias in the redistricting process and ordered to accept an alternative redistricting plan that led to the election of Gloria Molina as the first Latino(a) to serve on the powerful five-person Los Angeles County Board of Supervisors.[30] Recent maneuvering at the city level will ensure significant representation of Latinos on the Los Angeles City Council, but not without considerable conflict between entrenched black and Latino City Council leaders over communities that are racially mixed.[31] Los Angeles is a city in flux politically.

While it is clear that an emerging Latino majority will assume greater political power over time, the political-empowerment process has left several portions of the Latino population behind. In particular, Mexican Americans in Los Angeles, who have a longer history there and are more likely to constitute greater portions of the voting-age-citizen population, are the key recipients of the political spoils that have come in the Latino struggle for electoral power. All the elected officials to come into power as a consequence of these struggles are Mexican, and while they articulate a "Latino" perspective on the issues, they also tend to represent a narrow "Mexican" nationalism.[32] The growing Central American population, which is residentially based in South Central Los Angeles and not in the traditional core of East Los Angeles, has not benefited for the most part from the political empowerment of Mexicans in Los Angeles. They are recent immigrants, not able to vote, and thus have become the pawns in negotiations with the county and city over the composition of political districts. Black and white politicians now represent districts with up to 50% of the population being Latino. But because they are unable to vote, a declining black or white population of 25% to 35% can maintain control over these districts without addressing the unique needs of a majority of the community. The upshot has been the political neglect of a growing community whose problems of poverty have been just as overlooked as those of the black poor.

This contrast was easily observed during the rebellion as traditional Mexican-American community leaders were either silent or negative toward the mass participation of Latinos in the rebellion. Those Latinos in South Central had little stake in the existing political and economic order while East Los Angeles was riding the crest of a successful struggle to incorporate their political demands into the electoral system. Just as the black community is divided into a middle and a working class that are connected to the system by way of their political and economic ties, the Latino community in Los Angeles is increasingly divided by income, ethnicity, and citizenship.

The second element necessary to understand the involvement of Latinos, particularly Central American and Mexican immigrants, in the rebellions is the existence of interethnic hostilities between these groups and Korean Americans. While much is made of African-American and Korean-American conflict, little is said about an equally and potentially more volatile conflict between Latinos and Koreans.[33] While the crux of African-American and Korean-American conflict is based on the uneasy relationship between merchant and customer, the Latino-Korean conflict has the added dimensions of residential and workplace conflict. Latino involvement in the rebellion was most intense in Koreatown. Koreatown is an ethnic enclave demarcated by both the Korean control of businesses and a dwindling Korean residential presence. The community, in fact, is residentially mixed, with large portions of Latinos and Koreans. Latinos in this community come into contact with Koreans on multiple levels and, from all we know from current research, experience considerable hostility in each level.[34] First, in terms of residence, Latinos complain of discrimination on the part of Korean landlords as buildings and apartments are rented according to racial background.

Second, as customers in Korean establishments, Latinos complain of forms of disrespectful treatment similar to that about which black customers complain. Third, as employees in Korean small businesses, Latinos point to high levels of exploitation by their employers. Thus, in this context, it was not surprising to see the vehemence and anger that the Latino community in South Central Los Angeles expressed, especially toward the Korean community.

THE FEDERAL BLUEPRINT

How do we simultaneously deal with the seeds of the rebellion, as we have characterized them above, and rebuild the physical infrastructure of South Central Los Angeles? In attempting to answer this question, we shall limit the discussion here to the federal government's blueprint, as the local "Rebuild L.A." initiative remains somewhat vague in both scope and content.[35]

Table 5 highlights the Bush administration's plan to revitalize the South Central Los Angeles community. In actuality, the main elements of the plan constitute what Secretary of Housing and Urban Development Jack Kemp termed, prior to the Los Angeles rebellion, his blueprint for a "Conservative War on Poverty."[36]

Mr. Kemp promotes enterprise zones, as table 5 shows, as being the key to job creation and retention in the inner cities. He proposes to eliminate capital-gains taxes and reduce levies for business that will locate in specified inner-city areas. However, there is no history of success of such strategies in poor communities like South Central Los Angeles.

Moreover, recent research has indicated, as we noted earlier, that those white businesses in the inner city are especially reluctant to hire black males. Employer responses to a field survey in Chicago showed that they generally embrace the prevailing racial stereotypes about this group—that they are lazy, lack a good work ethic, are ineducable, and perhaps most important, dangerous.[37]

TABLE 5 THE FEDERAL BLUEPRINT

Program	Description	$ Allocation
Emergency Aid	To address immediate needs of citizens impacted by the crisis.	$600 million
"Weed and Seed"	Beef up law enforcement and social services (Headstart, Job Corps, WIC, Safe Haven Program) in the inner city.	$500 million
"Project HOPE"	Encourage home ownership among residents of public-housing projects.	$1 billion
"Move to Opportunity"	Five-city plan to subsidize welfare families that move from depressed inner-city areas, using housing vouchers and providing advice.	$20 million
Welfare reform	Raise to $10,000 from $1,000 the amount of assets that welfare recipients may accumulate without losing benefits. Builds on Wisconsin Plan to discourage welfare mothers from having more babies.	
Urban Enterprise Zones	Establishment of specifically designated areas where investment and job creation would be encouraged through incentives such as tax breaks and regulation relief.	

Source: Jessica Lee, "Bush Presents His Urban Policy," *USA Today,* 6 May 1992, 8A.

Couple this social reality with the fact that the major priorities for businesses when making locational decisions are access to markets, access to a quality labor force (code words for no blacks), infrastructure, and crime rates. These business factors are considered to be much more important in site selection than tax rates. And where enterprise zones have been successful, employers have brought their work force with them rather than employing community residents, or they have used these enterprise locations as warehouse points where there is a need for few workers.[38]

Secretary Kemp has had a long-term commitment to empowering the poor by making them homeowners—the theory being that individuals will have a stronger commitment to maintaining that which they own and to joining in other efforts to enhance their general neighborhood environment. Project HOPE, as it is called, would make home ownership affordable (table 5). This idea had languished in the Bush administration for the last four years, until the Los Angeles rebellion pushed it to center stage.[39]

However, this program would lock poor people into communities that are isolated, socially and economically, from mainstream employment and educational opportunities. And it would do nothing to expand the housing stock. Project HOPE is analogous to the reservation status provided to Native Americans in the government's effort to empower them. As a result, in part, of their isolation over time, Native Americans currently have some of the highest rates of unemployment, alcoholism, and domestic abuse of any American ethnic or racial group.

The federal blueprint, as table 5 shows, also includes monies to give the poor, inner-city residents of South Central Los Angeles greater choice in deciding what school their children will attend. The encouragement of educational choice among public and private schools—using public dollars—needs to be carefully monitored. Although promoted as the solution to the crisis in public education, poor parents are at risk of being losers in a system where choice is "unchecked." The much-heralded Wisconsin Parental Choice Plan has achieved a modicum of success because this public/private initiative was carefully designed to meet the educational needs of poor children.

The Wisconsin legislature structured this plan to mandate that private educational providers develop their recruitment strategies and curricular offerings specifically to accommodate poor students. Since nonpoor youngsters already had a wide range of educational choice, it was appropriate that poor children—who are the least well served in our educational system—have their interests served. Educational choice should be driven by the needs of the poor if we are to revitalize education in inner cities.[40]

Finally, the Bush administration proposes to spend $500 million on a "Weed and Seed Program," which is designed to rid the community of the violent criminal element and to provide support for programs like Headstart and the Job Corps which are known to benefit the urban disadvantaged and their communities (table 5). As it is currently envisioned, however, the program places too much emphasis on the "weed" component and not enough on the "seed" component. Of the $500 million proposed for the program, only $109 million is targeted for "seed" programs like Headstart. With nearly 80% of the proposed funding targeted for the "weed" component, the primary goal of the program is, clearly, to continue the warehousing of large numbers of poor inner-city youth in the penal system.[41]

This, in our view, is a misplaced programmatic focus, as it is ever so clear that harsher jail and prison terms are not deterrents to crime in inner-city areas like South Central Los Angeles. What is needed in South Central Los Angeles, instead, is more "seed" money; to the extent that increased police power is deployed in South Central Los Angeles, it should be via a community policing construct where officers are on the street, interfacing with community residents prior to the commission of a crime.

We are, quite frankly, dubious of the so-called conservative war on poverty and, in particular, of its likely impact in South Central Los Angeles. The federal blueprint, and apparently the local "Rebuild L.A." initiative headed by Mr. Peter Ueberroth as well, is built on the central premise that, if the proper incentives are offered, the private sector will, in fact, play the leading role in the revitalization and redevelopment of South Central Los Angeles. We do not think this is going to happen for the reasons stated earlier: the types of governmental incentives currently under consideration in Washington are not high on private businesses' locational priority lists.

In view of these facts, and the social-science evidence is clear on the ineffectiveness of enterprise-zone legislation both in Britain and in 36 states in this country,[42] we firmly believe that what is needed to rebuild South Central Los Angeles is a comprehensive public-works service-employment program, modeled on President Roosevelt's Works Progress Administration program of the 1930s. Jobs to rebuild the infrastructure of South Central Los Angeles can provide meaningful employment for the jobless in the community, including the hard-core disadvantaged, and can be linked to the skilled trades' apprenticeship-training programs.

To incorporate the hard-core disadvantaged into such a program would require a restructuring of the Private Industry Council's Job Training Partnership Act Program (JTPA). The program must dispense with its performance-based approach in training where funding is tied to job placement. This approach does not work for the hard-core disadvantaged because training agencies, under the current structure, have consistently engaged in creaming—recruiting the most "job-ready" segment of the inner-city population—to ensure their continued success and funding. Meanwhile, the hard-core unemployed have received scant attention and educational upgrading.[43]

We are now convinced that a WPA-type initiative, combined with a restructured JTPA program, will go a long way toward resolving the chronic jobless problem, especially among young males of color in the community, and toward rebuilding the infrastructure of South Central Los Angeles.

Such a program would have several goals that would enhance the social and economic viability of South Central Los Angeles. First, it would create meaningful jobs that could provide the jobless with skills transferable to the private sector. Second, it would rebuild a neglected infrastructure, making South Central Los Angeles an attractive place to locate for business and commerce. Finally, and most important, by reconnecting this isolated part of the city to the major arteries of transportation, by building a physical infrastructure that could support the social and cultural life of this richly multicultural area (e.g., museums, public buildings, housing), and by enhancing the ability of community and educational institutions to educate and socialize the young, this plan would go far in providing a sustainable "public space" in the community. For it is our contention, that only when South Central Los Angeles is perceived as a public space that is economically vibrant and socially attractive will the promise of this multicultural community be fulfilled. Thus far, private-sector actions and federal-government programs and proposals have done nothing to bring us nearer to reaching this goal.

CONCLUSION

The fires have been extinguished in South Central Los Angeles and other cities, but the anger and rage continue to escalate, and they are likely to reemerge over time to the extent that the underlying political and economic causes are left to fester. While political, business, and civic leaders have rushed to advance old and new strategies and solutions to this latest urban explosion, much of what is being proposed is simply disjointed and/or déjà vu.

Clearly there is a need for additional money to resolve the underlying causes of this urban despair and devastation, but money alone is not enough. Government is constitutionally mandated to ensure "domestic tranquillity," but government alone cannot empower poor communities. And although blacks and other people of color have a special role and obligation to rebuild their neighborhoods because they are the majority of the victims and the vandals, they cannot solely assume this burden of responsibility.

What is needed, in our view, is a reconceptualization of problem solving where we meld together, and invest with full potential, those strategies offered from liberals and conservatives, from Democrats and Republicans, and from whites and people of color. Three cities (Milwaukee, Los Angeles, and Detroit, respectively) have served, individually and collectively, as urban laboratories where we have engaged in action research and proffered solutions to the urban problems which have generated violent outbursts.

The contentious state of police/minority-community relations has served as the linchpin of urban unrest in each instance. While relations have improved in several large cities in recent years, the Los Angeles Police Department has been frozen in time. Black and Hispanic males have been particularly brutalized in their encounters with police, the majority of whom are white males. But more disconcerting is the fact that poor, central-city minority communities have become more crime-ridden of late. Thus, minorities find themselves in the ambiguous situation of needing greater police service on the one hand and protection from the excesses of those same services on the other. This contradictory situation has kept relations between these groups at a race/class boiling point.

More police officers are desperately needed in high-crime communities that are disproportionately populated by the poor. Local, state, and federal dollars (federal funds for this initiative are in the crime bill before Congress) need to be allocated quickly toward this end.

At present, violent felons are beginning to outnumber police officers in many of our urban centers.[44] As we noted previously, this increase in police power should be deployed via a community policing program. Such an effort can serve to control minor offenses and to build trust between police and community residents. Community policing has evidenced positive results in Detroit and Philadelphia and is showing encouraging signs in Milwaukee and numerous other large and small cities. In addition, the intensive recruitment of minority officers and specific, ongoing (and evaluated) diversity training will further reduce police/minority community tensions. But most important in this effort is enlightened, decisive leadership from the office of the chief, a position of abysmal failure in Los Angeles.

The national administration's initial response to the rebellion was to blame it on deficiencies among the urban poor, particularly on the supposed lack of "family values" and the predominance of female-headed households.[45] This jaundiced view ignores the real sources of the conflict and concentrates instead on the symptomatology of growing up in concentrated-poverty communities where the social resources and assistance necessary to negotiate mainstream society successfully are either totally lacking or insufficient.[46] Thus, the policy implication that needs to be drawn from the rebellion is that, in order to bring the poor and disenfranchised into mainstream society, in order to enhance their acceptance of personal responsibility, and in order to promote personal values consistent with those of the wider society, we must find a way to provide a comprehensive program of meaningful assistance to this population. But clearly, a change in personal values alone, as suggested by some right-wing analysts, will not substitute for job training, job creation, and the removal of racial stereotypes and discrimination.[47] The spatial concentration of contemporary poverty presents significant challenges to policy makers and human-service providers

alike. Although numerous programs and initiatives have been instituted to combat these problems, they suffer from three important weaknesses.

First, there is a lack of coordination among programs aimed at improving the life chances of citizens in poor communities. Second, no systematic steps have been taken to evaluate existing efforts, to ensure that the programs are effectively targeting the "hardest to serve," adults with low skills and limited work history, and youth who are teen parents or school dropouts. Third, there is no comprehensive strategy for planning future resource allocations as needs change and as these communities expand in size.

A recent national study of training and employment programs, under the Job Training Partnership Act, revealed that little has been done to address the remedial educational needs of high-school drop-outs and that those with the greatest need for training and employment services are not targeted. However, overcoming these and other program weaknesses is not sufficient to solve these complex problems. A strategic plan is needed to alleviate the social ills associated with concentrated poverty

There is a need to conduct a comprehensive inventory of agencies and institutions that provide services to populations in poverty areas. We also need to assess and evaluate the service providers' performance in an attempt to identify strengths, weaknesses, and missing links in their service-delivery systems. On the basis of these findings, a strategy should be devised for a more effective and coordinated use of existing resources and for generating new resources to address unmet needs. Finally, we need to propose a plan of action that would encourage development in the 1990s that links together the various program initiatives.

And, most important, representatives of the affected ethnic and racial groups must be in key decision-making roles if these efforts are to achieve success.[48] Citizens of color, individually and through their community, civic and religious institutions, bear a responsibility to promote positive values and lifestyles in their communities and to socialize their youth into the mainstream. But they cannot do this alone.

They cannot be held accountable for the massive plant closings, disinvestments, and exportation of jobs from our urban centers to Third World countries. There must be an equality in status, responsibility, and authority across race and class lines if we are to resolve our urban crises. Government, in a bipartisan fashion, must direct its resources to those programs determined to be successful with the poor, the poor must be permitted to participate in the design of programs for their benefit, and society at all levels must embrace personal responsibility and a commitment to race and gender equity.

How likely are these reforms to be implemented? If one were to analyze the prospects of these changes from the perspective offered in this paper, the answer would not be an optimistic one. However, an important consequence of the rebellion was to shake the very foundation of the taken-for-granted quality of our discourse and practice about race and class in American society. It opens up the opportunity for reassessing positions, organizing constituencies, and collectively engaging issues that have been buried from sight until now. Given these new openings, the Los Angeles urban rebellion of 1992 gives us all the opportunity to work on building a society in which "we can all get along."

Notes

1. See Jane Gross, "In Simi Valley, Defense of a Shared Way of Life," *New York Times,* 4 May 1992, A9.
2. See David Margolick, "As Venues Are Changed, Many Ask How Important a Role Race Should Play," *New York Times,* 23 May 1992, Al.
3. See Walter C. Farrell, Jr., James H. Johnson, Jr., and Cloyzelle K. Jones, "Field Notes from the Rodney King Trial and the Los Rebellion," 28 and 29 April and 2, 3, and 4 May 1992.
4. See, for example, Jolene Kirschenman and Kathryn Neckerman, "We'd Love to Hire Them But . . . : The Meaning of Race For Employers," *The Urban Underclass,* ed. Christopher Jencks and Paul Peterson (Washington, DC: The Brookings Institution, 1990), 203–24; R. J. Struyk, M. A. Turner, and M. Fix, *Opportunities Denied, Opportunities Diminished: Discrimination in Hiring* (Washington, DC: The Urban Institute, 1991).
5. See Jason De Parle, "Year-Old Study on Police Abuse Is Issued by U.S.," *New York Times,* 20 May 1992, A1 and A10; Joseph D. MacNamara, "When the Police Create Disorder," *Los Angeles Times,* May 1992, Ml and M6; Melvin L. Oliver, Walter C. Farrell, Jr., and James H. Johnson, Jr., "A Quarter-Century of Slipping Backward," *Los Angeles Times,* 10 August 1990, B7; Dennis Schatzman, "50–60 Percent of Riot Arrestees Had No Prior Contact with the Law," *Los Angeles Times,* 28 May 1992, Al and A16; David K. Shipler, "Khaki, Blue, and Blacks," *New York Times,* 26 May 1992, 15.
6. See Ed Soja, Rebecca Morales, and Goetz Wolff, "Urban Restructuring: An Analysis of Social and Spatial Change in Los Angeles," *Economic Geography,* 58 (1983): 221–35: Melvin L. Oliver and James H. Johnson, Jr., "Interethnic Conflict in an Urban Ghetto: The Case of Blacks and Latinos in Los Angeles," *Research in Social Movements, Conflicts and Change* 6 (1984): 57–94; James H. Johnson, Jr., and Melvin L. Oliver, ''Interethnic Minority Conflict in Urban America: The Effects of Economic and Social Dislocations," *Urban Geography* 10 (1989): 449–56; James H. Johnson, Jr., and Melvin L. Oliver, "Economic Restructuring and Black Male Joblessness: A Reassessment," *Urban Labor Market and Job Opportunity,* ed. George Peterson and Wayne Vrohman (Wahington, DC: The Urban Institute, 1992), 113–147.
7. See Oliver and Johnson, "Interethnic Conflict in an Urban Ghetto," and Johnson and Oliver, "Interethnic Minority Conflict in Urban America."

8. See Melvin L. Oliver, "It's the Fire Every Time, and We Do Nothing," *Los Angeles Times,* 1 May 1992, B7.

9. See Farrell, Johnson, and Jones, "Field Notes.

10. See Elaine Kim, "They Armed in Self-Defense," *Newsweek,* 18 May 1992, 10, and Seth Mydans, "Jury Acquits Los Angeles Policemen in Taped Beating," *New York Times,* 29 April 1992, A1 and A8.

11. See Oliver and Johnson, "Interethnic Conflict in an Urban Ghetto"; Johnson and Oliver, "Interethnic Minority Conflict in Urban America"; and James H. Johnson, Jr., and Curtis C. Roseman, "Increasing Black Outmigration from Los Angeles: The Role of Household Dynamics and Kinship Systems," *Annals of the Association of American Geographers* 80 (1990): 205–222.

12. See Soja, Morales, and Wolff, "Urban Restructuring"; Johnson and Oliver, "Economic Restructuring and Black Male Joblessness" *Urban Geography* 12, no. 6, pp. 542–562; and Johnson and Oliver, "Economic Restructuring and Black Male Joblessness: A Reassessment."

13. See Soja, Morales, and Wolff, "Urban Restructuring."

14. See A. J. Scott, "Flexible Production Systems and Regional Development: The Rise of New Industrial Spaces in North America and Western Europe," *International Journal of Urban and Regional Research* 12 (1988): 61–113, and A. J. Scott, *Metropolis: From Division of Labor to Urban Form* (Berkeley: University of California Press, 1986).

15. See Soja, Morales, and Wolff, "Urban Restructuring."

16. See Johnson and Oliver, "Economic Restructuring and Black Male Joblessness."

17. See Johnson and Oliver, "Economic Restructuring and Black Male Joblessness"; Soja, Morales and Wolff, "Urban Restructuring"; and Ed Luttwak, "The Riots: Underclass vs. Immigrants," *New York Times,* 15 May 1992, A15.

18. See Robert Beauregard and H. Braviel Holcomb, *Revitalizing Cities, Resource Publication in Geography* (Washington, DC: Association of American Geographers, 1981).

19. See Gary Orfield and Carole Ashkinaze, *The Closing Door: Conservative Policy and Black Opportunity* (Chicago: University of Chicago Press, 1991).

20. These statistics for the years 1982–1989 were extracted from *The Data Center's Plant Shutdowns Monitor Directory* (Oakland, CA: The Data Center, 1978–1982).

21. See P. L. Berger and R. J. Newhaus, *To Empower People: The Role of Mediating Structures in Public Policy* (Washington, DC: American Enterprise Institute, 1977), and Melvin L. Oliver, "The Urban Black Community as Network: Toward a Social Network Perspective," *Sociological Quarterly* 29 (1988): 623–45.

22. See L. M. Salamon, "Non-Profit Organizations: The Lost Opportunity," *The Reagan Record,* ed. John L. Palmer and Isabel V. Sawhill (Cambridge, MA: Ballinger Publishing Co., 1984), 261–85.

23. See Marc Mauer, "Americans Behind Bars," *Criminal Justice* (Winter 1992): 12–18 and 38.

24. See Johnson and Oliver, "Economic Restructuring and Black Male Joblessness."

25. See Gary Orfield, "Exclusion of the Majority: Shrinking College Access and Public Policy in Metropolitan Los Angeles," *The Urban Review* 20 (1988): 147–163.

26. See W. K. Viscusi, "Market Incentives for Criminal Behavior," *The Black Youth Employment Crisis,* ed. R. B. Freeman and H. J. Holzer (Chicago: University of Chicago Press, 1986).

27. George Ramos and Tracy Wilkinson, "Unrest Widens Rifts in Latino Population," *Los Angeles Times,* 5 June 1992, 1.

28. See Peter Kwong, "The First Multicultural Riots," *Inside the L.A. Riots,* ed. Don Hazen (Los Angeles: Institute for Alternative Journalism, 1992), 88–93.

29. See James Regalado, "Conflicts over Redistricting in Los Angeles County: Who Wins? Who Loses?" *Racial and Ethnic Politics in California,* ed. Byran O. Jackson and Michael B. Preston (Berkeley: I.G.S. Press, 1991), 373–93.

30. See J. Morgan Krousser, "How to Determine Intent: Lesson from L.A.," *Social Science Working Paper* 741 (1992), California Institute of Technology.

31. See James A. Regalado, ed., *Political Battles over L.A. County Board Seats: A .Minority Perspective* (Los Angeles: Edmund G. "Pat" Brown Institute, 1989).

32. See Ramos and Wilkinson, "Unrest Widens Rifts in Latino Population."

33. See Kwong, "The First Multicultural Riots."

34. In focus groups conducted immediately following the rebellion, Spanish-speaking, mostly immigrant respondents spoke eloquently of their interactions with Koreans in terms of housing, business, and work. While none of the participants condoned the violence, and only one respondent admitted participating in the looting, many expressed in graphic terms incidents of being harassed by Korean-American shopkeepers because of the assumption they would steal, or of being turned down for housing because the Korean-American landlord wanted to keep the apartment complex all Korean-American, or of being forced to work overtime for a Korean-American employer. This form of interethnic conflict has rarely surfaced, but we believe it is central to understanding the multi-ethnic character of the L.A. rebellion.

35. See Richard Stevenson, "With Few Tools, Ueberroth Begins Mission in Riot Areas," *New York Times,* 5 May 1991, A23.

36. Marshall Ingwerson, "Radical Intent: HUD Chief Wants Poverty to Top Conservative Agenda," *Christian Science Monitor,* 11 October 1991, 9.

37. See Kirschenman and Neckerman, "We'd Love to Hire Them But . . ."

38. See David Osborne, "The Kemp Cure-All," *New Republic,* 3 April 1989, 21–25, and Neal R. Peirce, "Kemp's Enterprise Zones: Breakthrough or Chimera," *Nation's Cities Weekly,* 5 June 1989, 4.

39. See Kathleen Decker, "Kemp Champions Blacks and Poor: Secretary Preaches Theme of Hope in Squalor of Ghettos," *Los Angeles Times,* 19 April 1989, A1.

40. See Walter C. Farrell, Jr., and Jacquelyn E. Mathews, "School Choice and the Educational Opportunities of African American Children," *Journal of Negro Education* 59 (1990): 526–37, and Gary George and Walter C. Farrell, Jr., "School Choice and African American Students: A Legislative View," *Journal of Negro Education* 59 (1990): 521–25.

41. See Terry Eastland, "'Weed and Seed': Root Out Crime, Nurture Poor," *Wall Street Journal,* 14 May 1992, A1.

42. See Osborne, "The Kemp Cure-All."

43. See Susan B. Garland, "90 Days to Learn to Scrub? Sure, If Uncle Sam's Paying," *Business Week,* 20 January 1992, 70.

44. See "Put Police before Prisons," editorial, *New York Times,* 23 May 1992, A10.

45. See "Excerpts from Vice President's Speech on Cities and Poverty," *New York Times,* 19 May 1992, A12; Lawrence M. Mead, "Job Programs and Other Bromides," *New York Times,* 19 May 1992, A15; and James Q. Wilson, "How to Teach Better Values in Inner Cities," *Wall Street Journal,* 18 May 1992, A14.

46. See William Julius Wilson, *The Truly Disadvantaged* (Chicago: University of Chicago Press, 1987), 198, and James H. Johnson, Jr., and Melvin L. Oliver, "Modeling Urban Underclass Behavior," *Center for the Study of Urban Poverty, Occasional Paper 3,* UCLA Institute for Social Science Research, 1990-1991.

47. See John D. Kasarda, "Why Asians Can Prosper Where Blacks Fail," *Wall Street Journal,* 28 May 1992, A20; Mead, "Job Programs and Other Bromides"; and James Q. Wilson, "How to Teach Better Values in Inner Cities."

48. See Robert Woodson, "Transform Inner Cities from the Grassroots Up," *Wall Street Journal,* 1 June 1992, A12.

Essay/Discussion Questions

1. According to Melvin Oliver and his colleagues, what factors contributed to the Los Angeles rebellion of 1992?

2. Oliver et al. demonstrate that the 1992 rebellion was a multicultural event. Discuss the changing demographic character of South Central Los Angeles and its relationship to the uprising.

3. Historically, African American and Latino urban citizens have constantly complained about police brutality; yet white American largely denied and disbelieved these charges. What impact did the videotape of Rodney King's beating by Los Angeles police have on the national consciousness regarding police brutality?

If police hassling is part of a larger process of different surveillance by race—a process in which African Americans are exposed to greater scrutiny not only by police but across many social domains, for example, by teachers, shopkeepers, and fellow pedestrians—such hassling may exact a personal cost by not granting minorities the status of a trusted, equal citizen.
—ANDREW HACKER

There's never been a case where a Black officer shot and killed a white person by error. These things don't happen to white people.
—AN ANONYMOUS WHITE POLICE OFFICER

Police Brutality as a Major Public Health Issue: The Tragic Shooting of Former Tampa Bay Buccaneer Demetrius DuBose

JUDSON L. JEFFRIES

On the evening of August 4th, I sat at my desk reading the Purdue University *Exponent* as the fatigue from a day that began at 6:00 A.M. was forcing my eyelids shut. I had nearly finished the less than 15-page publication when suddenly my eyes became fixated on a headline that read, "Slain Player's Family Files Suit." Being the sports enthusiast that I am, I read on anxiously and admittedly, very nervously. When I got to the second paragraph it read: Demetrius DuBose, previously of the Tampa Bay Buccaneers and former co-captain of the Notre Dame football team, was shot several times by two white San Diego police officers on July 24, after he allegedly charged at them with nunchakus sticks, a martial arts weapon he had taken from one of the officers.

Oh my God I blurted out in disbelief. I don't believe this, I uttered as I arose from my desk in disgust. As I paced back and forth I began to experience a myriad of emotions. I was stunned and angry. Stunned because of what I assumed to be a senseless killing and eventual cover-up, angry because DuBose had been shot on the 24th of July and here I was just learning of his death darn near two weeks later. How could this be?, I wondered. Was it because I had not been paying attention to the news of late? Or was it because much of the media coverage had been saturated with stories about the Kennedy/Bissette tragedies? Maybe it was a combination of the two, as I had been extremely busy recently putting together the final version of my first book, soon to be released.

In any event it was reported that the officers were investigating a burglary in the athlete's neighborhood when they happened upon the Notre Dame graduate and began to question him. The family's preliminary findings show DuBose was calm and cooperated with the officers' investigation until they began to "intimidate, harass," and subsequently handcuff him. What happened in the ensuing melee is still somewhat murky. What is clear is that the two San Diego police officers fired several shots into the young man's body. Said District Attorney Paul Pfingst: "The officers really didn't have a choice, they had to shoot." The officers claimed they feared for their lives. Ironically, the same justification was given by two Los Angeles police officers exactly twenty years ago when they embarked on Eula Love's house in response to a complaint about an unpaid utility bill—and ended up killing her. The officers claimed that Love too had charged at them, with knife in hand.[1]

According to Brian Watkins, a lawyer for the family, after shooting DuBose the officers stood over the young man's body for more than 10 minutes before an ambulance was called. Officers claim DuBose resisted attempts to question him and appeared to be under the influence of alcohol or other drugs. Now where have I heard that before? San Diego City Councilman George Stevens said some passersby saw DuBose bending over when he was shot, while others said he was shot in the back as he turned away from the officers. An autopsy revealed that DuBose was shot twelve times in all. Twelve times.

The San Diego police department's propensity for harassing blacks did not begin with DuBose. The department was first thrust into the national spotlight for its treatment of blacks during the mid- to late 1970s. Between March 1975 and January 1977 Edward Lawson was arrested fifteen times by the San Diego police.[2] He was prosecuted twice, convicted once; the second charge was dismissed. Lawson supposedly fit the stereotype of a burglar. Tall, angular, energetic, black with an athletic build, Lawson could have been taken for a guard or small forward for a college basketball team, except for one thing. Lawson had let his hair grow out naturally into long, coiled "dreadlocks."

When Lawson took long walks at night in lily-white San Diego neighborhoods, he would often be stopped by police, who would ask for his ID. Lawson refused to identify himself on grounds that there was no reason to stop him since he was engaged in no criminal activity and was not planning to commit a crime. Nevertheless he was subjected to numerous arrests. Lawson sued to have the California statute requiring that persons provide "credible and reliable" identification to police declared unconstitutional. Lawson, who himself undertook and completed much of the legal research, won his case and later collected substantial civil damages from the City of San Diego. Justice Sandra Day O'Connor found that the statute Lawson had challenged was too broad and vested police with "virtually complete discretion . . . . to determine whether the suspect has satisfied the statute." In the end Lawson capitalized on his understanding of the police assignment to protect property, plus his realistic assumptions about how the police would respond to a black man with dreadlocks strolling in a white neighborhood after dark.[3]

In reality, the legal rules stemming from cases like Lawson's have an effect on only a small part of the normative climate of policing. Unfortunately, even after the Lawson case, police were not prohibited from asking a citizen for identification, but if he refused, they could not arrest him for refusing.

At any rate the DuBose killing is but one of a long list of men of color, especially black men, who have experienced brutality at the hands of those who are sworn to serve and protect. That black Americans are the least satisfied (of all racial groups) with police performance is not surprising. One of the major problems facing blacks today is that of police brutality, or more specifically, police murder. Although the role of race in police use of excessive force may be empirically indeterminate to many researchers, for African Americans the relationship is more obvious.[4] Inci-

TABLE 1 INCOMPLETE LIST OF BLACK AND LATINO DEATHS RESULTING FROM EXCESSIVE POLICE FORCE SINCE THE RODNEY KING INCIDENT

Name	Place	Type of Brutality
Malice Green	Detroit	Beaten to death by flashlight-wielding police
Johnny Gammage	Pittsburgh	Beaten and choked to death by 5 policemen
Lebert Folkes	New York	Shot in face for suspected stealing of a car
Timmie Sinclair	Atlanta	Clubbed with tactical baton as his wife and children looked on
Tracy Mayberry	Hollywood, CA	Beaten and kicked to death
Annie Rae Dixon	Tyler, Texas	84-year-old shot as she lay in bed
Charles Bush	Las Vegas	Killed by police who entered home without warrant
Philip Pannell	Teaneck, N.J.	Fatally shot in back as he ran away from officers who were frisking youth in a schoolyard
Amadou Diallo	New York	Shot 20 times by police in his own home
Tyisha S. Miller	Riverside, CA	Shot as she sat in a disabled car
Robert Russ	Evanston, IL	Northwestern football player shot to death while he sat in his car
Anthony Baez	New York	Choked to death after his football accidentally hit a squad car
Alex Rivera	New York	Shot to death because he was believed to have a gun in a paper bag (actually a soda can)
Federico Pereria	New York	Choked to death as police removed him from a car

dents of terror and violence perpetuated by law enforcement officials against people of color, particularly blacks, have become almost commonplace. So much so that some blacks would like to see police brutality placed on the national agenda as a major public health issue. Indeed, from 1986 to 1991 the Department of Justice received nearly 8,000 complaints each year concerning criminal civil rights violations by police officers. It should be noted that this number represents only a fraction of the actual police abuse cases.[5] Investigations of police departments in Los Angeles, New York, Chicago, Philadelphia, Baltimore, Houston, and other cities reveal that racism and brutality are widespread and often tolerated by department commanders.[6] A recent study of the Los Angeles Police Department supports this finding. From 1986 through 1990, allegations of excessive force or improper tactics were filed against approximately 1,800 officers, more than 1,400 of who had one or more previous complaints; 183 officers had four or more allegations, 44 had six or more, 16 had eight or more, and one officer had sixteen complaints.[7]

Police kill individuals throughout the country, and blacks, being the most widely dispersed group, are more likely than other minorities to be targets of police killings. Some African Americans like Abner Louima, Timmie Sinclair, and Rodney King live to tell of their experiences; others like Demetrius DuBose, Robert Russ, Lebert Folkes, Johnny Gammage and Malice Green were not as fortunate (see table). In October 1995, Gammage was pulled over while driving his Jaguar through a predominantly white Pittsburgh suburb, only to be beaten and choked to death after allegedly attacking five white police officers. The following year Lebert Folkes, while parked in front of his house, was pulled from behind the wheel of a car mistakenly reported to be stolen and shot in the face at point blank range. Some argue that excessive police force against blacks is not motivated by racial animus. That New York City police officers shouted racial slurs while they beat and sodomized Abner Louima shows that such a belief deserves much rethinking.

The fact that young black males are more likely to meet a violent death than their white counterparts is well known, so well known that the numbers have reached epidemic proportions without much fanfare. Apparently this grim reality was not lost on young

DuBose. While filling out a questionnaire for the 1990 Notre Dame media guide, he gave a somber yet rather prophetic response. Asked to complete the phrase, "When I'm 35, I want to be . . . ," the sophomore student-athlete wrote simply, "alive."

To say I was looking forward to watching this undersized linebacker's career unfold is an understatement. I had recently once again started rooting for the Tampa Bay Buccaneers. That my renewed interest in the Bucs' success coincided with the hiring of Tony Dungy is no accident. My initial infatuation with the Bucs began as a kid in 1978 when the team drafted a black quarterback named Doug Williams out of historically black Grambling State University. Indeed, I was looking forward to seeing DuBose's talent develop along the lines of other past and present Tampa Bay greats like Dewey Selmon, David Lewis, Cecil Johnson, Hugh Green, and Hardy Nickerson.

The execution of DuBose makes one wish aloud for the resumption of the Deacons for Defense and Justice and the Black Panther Party—the 1966 version. Armed with guns, cameras, tape recorders, and law books the Panthers would monitor the actions of police to ensure that the rights of pedestrians and motorists were not infringed upon when detained by police. In 1999 there is no such group. Consequently, there will most likely be no recourse. And if there is no video there may be no fiduciary restitution, God forbid.

Many years ago Vernon Johns, the militant southern Baptist preacher who pastored Dexter Avenue Baptist Church before giving way to Dr. Martin Luther King, Jr., once offered a sermon titled, "It's Safe to Murder Negroes."[8] This statement still holds true. Why? As Johns put it, "because black folk stand idly by and allow it to happen."[9] And because the justice system usually administers little more than a "slap on the wrist" by way of punishment when the defendant is white and the victim is black. This is especially true when the perpetrator is a white police officer.

The murder of hundreds of black people each year by the police illustrates that institutional racism is the order of the day. Charles W. Mills put it best when he wrote: "Whites have entered into a contract where they have agreed not to recognize blacks as equals."[10] Case in point: John Brabham, a college student was murdered by William Walker, a white policeman.[11] Brabham ran a traffic light in Brooklyn. He stopped the car, ran, and was pursued by the officer. Walker claimed that he ordered the youth to "freeze," an order that was ignored according to the officer. Walker said he noticed a pistol in the young man's hand, and because of this fired twice, killing Brabham. A pistol was found near Brabham's body. Later testimony by fellow officers indicated that Walker had done what is so widely practiced in major cities through the U.S. He had planted the pistol beside the youth's body. Predictably, officer Walker was acquitted by an all-white jury.

Police brutality is but one form of oppression that blacks are consigned to endure on a daily basis in this country. A most telling study of police behavior in the 1960s by Paul Takagi revealed that 51 percent of the people killed by police were black even though blacks made up less than 10 percent of the population.[12] One study of the use of fatal force by police conducted in the 1970s revealed that blacks were seven times more likely to be killed by the police than whites.[13] A similar study conducted in the 1980s found that blacks were nine times more likely than whites to be killed by police.[14]

It appears that as blacks become more incorporated in American political, economic, and social life the more hostile law enforcement behaves toward them. There are about 23 million African Americans in this country, maybe more. The establishment knows that the unity of these 23 million or so African Americans would spell the death of the status quo. So, at all costs, the establishment seeks to preclude these African Americans from uniting, keep them from becoming bold and revolutionary. The powers that be know that they must keep these 23 million African Americans apprehensive and intimidated. The thought of 23 million revolutionary-minded African Americans is more terrifying to the establishment than any band of long-haired right-wing militia groups scattered about the country. One way the establishment has been able to keep blacks reticent is by making an example of those who attempt to defy their second-class citizenship. Police violence has replaced lynching as the method for keeping so-called uppity and disobedient blacks in their place. Such was the case with Move in Philadelphia.

On Mother's Day in 1985 Philadelphia police attempted to evict Move, a black back-to-nature socially conscious outfit, from a house in West Philadelphia. Move refused to leave and allegedly threatened the police with guns.[15] The police surrounded the house and attempted to force Move out of it with high-pressure water hoses. After several hours of spraying and 750,000 tons of water proved unable to do the job, police conducted an air raid. Using a helicopter, they dropped an incendiary device composed of TOVEX mining explosive on the roof of the house.[16] The blaze that followed killed seven Move members and four of their children and leveled a city block, destroying sixty homes and leaving 240 people homeless.[17] Ironically, Daryl Gates, Los Angeles Chief of Police, would tell a national audience on CBS's *Face the Nation* that approving the bombing had made Philadelphia's Mayor Wilson Goode a "hero" who "should run for national office" because he had shown "some of the finest leadership I've ever seen from a politician."[18]

Police brutality has been a long-standing issue in the black community that stretches as far back as the arrival of Blacks to the new world. Huey P. Newton used to say that the police patrol the black community like a military unit occupies a foreign territory. This statement still holds true. Via a sophisticated

military-prison industrial complex certain orders are given to the Chief of Police, who passes them on to his men, the Gestapo, the foot soldiers in the trenches of the ghetto. For generations after, the formal, officially approved role of police, both in the South and often in the Northern "free" states, was that of oppressor—keeping slaves in their place and capturing and returning runaways to their owners and later, enforcing Jim Crow segregation laws.[19] In fact, the early role of many Southern police in the "slave patrols" formally included inflicting corporal punishment on offenders (runaways or disobedient slaves) without prior judicial process.[20]

While corporal punishment of Blacks—by today's standards excessive force—may have been a formal police function in the slave states, history has recorded the attitudinal climate that prevailed toward Blacks in many Northern communities. When Alexis de Tocqueville traveled throughout the U.S. in the 1830s he discovered that there was more overt hostility and hatred toward blacks in the North, where slavery did not exist, than in the South, where it did.[21]

It seems little has changed. Despite America's ignominious racist past, before the graphic 1991 videotape of the Rodney King beating and the savage attack on Sandra Antor by a white South Carolina state trooper (also caught on videotape) most whites refused to believe or feigned that police harassment of blacks was and is not a pressing social ill. For them instances like these are aberrations, anomolies, exceptions to the rule, rather than any established habitual pattern of behavior on the part of law enforcement.

As a resident of Los Angeles for several years I experienced police harassment on several occasions. During one two-year period (1992–1994) I was detained and questioned a total of seven times. I recall one night near the corner of 30th Street and Figueroa a police cruiser with spotlight shining drove onto the sidewalk thus blocking my path. I immediately raised my hands in full view. With the spotlight pointed toward my face, the two white officers leaped from the vehicle, one with nightstick in hand, the other standing by the car with his service revolver pointed at me. As the nightstick-wielding officer made his way toward me I informed him that I was a USC student. When the officer noticed the University of Southern California identification card I was strategically holding in my hand he turned to the gun-brandishing officer and yelled out, "Is this the guy?" The officer focusing to get a good look at my face replied, "No, that's not him." The nightstick-wielding officer then retreated back to the car and the two sped off. No apology, no nothing. I am convinced that the only thing that saved me that night was that seemingly fluorescent gold and crimson ID card.

On another night that same year, exhausted from studying all evening I decided to take a short break. As I was standing in front of a donut shop (no kidding) three police cruisers drove by slowly with the officer in the lead car leering at me for some odd reason. Now, my mother has a saying, "You wouldn't know someone was staring at you if you weren't staring at them." Point well taken, so I looked away to avoid the officer's face. But you know how, even though you are not looking at someone, with the benefit of peripheral vision you know that person is staring at you. As the squad cars drove past exiting the parking lot, I breathed a sigh of relief. When the light turned green the officers made a right turn, giving the impression they were headed toward the Los Angeles Coliseum. Then all of a sudden the officers made another right turn back into the parking lot where I was standing. As the lead car approached I remember saying to myself, "mutherf___er, what do you want now?" As the lead car drove toward me the driver rolled down his window and asked incredulously, "What are you doing?" No good evening, no nice night tonight isn't it, no nothing. I replied, "Getting a breath of fresh air." He then

shot back, "Well, move along." Admittedly, I looked at him with all the contempt I could muster as I complied with his order. Anyway, apparently I did not disperse as quickly as this officer would have liked because the next thing I knew the car door swung open and the officer jumped out, whereupon he barked, "I thought I told you to move along." What transpired next would be considered unnecessary by any reasonable person's standards. The officer ordered me to put my hands on my head and spread my legs, whereupon the officer frisked me and asked, "What gang do you belong to?" I ignored him. By this time a small crowd had formed a considerable distance away. Among those assembled was a USC athlete who I was currently tutoring as part of my responsibilities as an academic mentor in the athletic department. Upon seeing this officer attempt to manhandle me in an obvious effort to humiliate and degrade me, the athlete shouted to the officers, "That's my mentor at USC." After the officer found my ID card he then said rather sarcastically to another officer, "Check to see if there are any warrants out on this guy." When the report came back clean, the officer returned my belongings and ordered me to go home before he arrested me for loitering.

Again, I complied with the officer's directive but admittedly not until I spoke of his manhood in a way that would have made both Malcolm X and Huey P. Newton proud. As the officer lunged at me another officer restrained him. The irony is that particular officer was black. That night I decided to go to the police station and file a complaint. Not surprisingly, nothing ever came of it. At a very young age I had been told by older black men that there are some black officers who will treat other blacks just as harshly if not more harshly than a white officer when that black officer is in the presence of a white policeman. Here, the black officer overcompensates for his race as a way of being accepted by his white colleagues. The number of black police officers and black mayors has doubled since 1972; however, whether these increases will result in more equitable treatment of blacks from law enforcement remains to be seen.[22]

For many years those whites that were aware of police brutality argued that it was a problem experienced by a small segment of the population—the black poor. Suffice it to say, the incidences of excessive force involving track star Al Joyner, Hall of Fame baseball player Joe Morgan, Dwight (Doc) Gooden, and former Los Angeles Laker Jamal Wilkes weakens this argument.[23] Even if it was a problem that affected only poor blacks, that would not make it any less despicable. The fact is, police brutality transcends class and to some extent race.

As irony would have it, the 28-year-old millionaire Demetrius DuBose is detained and questioned about a *burglary* in his own *neighborhood* no less, and what follows is an unfathomable cold-blooded killing at the hands of the police that conjures up images of James Chaney. "Nigger, how dare you question our authority" is what probably ran through the minds of those officers when DuBose refused to genuflect. If this was the case, this type of behavior coincides with what Richard Sykes and John Clark have termed "deference exchange."[24] They argue that police expect acknowledgment by the citizen that police-citizen interactions are governed by an asymmetrical status norm—the police are the boss. The authors contend that those individuals who reject this norm are more likely to be victimized by excessive force than those who adhered to this tacit understanding.[25] As of this writing, neither the police department's nor the city's investigation has been completed. An aberration, I imagine Chief David Bejarano will say once the department's investigation is concluded. That the sun rises in the east and sets in the west is also an aberration, and by design.

Notes

1. Hubert G. Locke, "The Color of Law and the Issue of Color: Race and the Abuse of Police Power," *Police Violence: Understanding and Controlling Police Abuse of Force,* ed. William A. Geller and Hans Toch (New Haven, CT: Yale University, 1996), 129–150.

2. Jerome H. Skolnick and James F. Fyfe, *Above the Law: Police and the Excessive Use of Force* (New York: The Free Press, 1993).

3. Ibid.

4. Sandra Browning, Sandra Lee Cullen, Francis T. Legun Cao, Renee Ropache, and Thomas J. Stevenson, "Race and Getting Hassled by the Police: A Research Note," *Police Studies* 17 (1994): 1–11; M. R. Gottfredson and D. M. Gottfredson, *Decision Making in Criminal Justice* (New York: Plenum Press, 1988); William Wilbanks, *The Myth of a Racist Criminal Justice System* (Monterey, CA: Brooks/Cole, 1987).

5. U.S. Congress House Committee on the Judiciary, *Police Brutality: Hearings Before the Subcommittee on Civil and Constitutional Rights of the Committee on the Judiciary,* One Hundred Second Congress, first session, March 20 and April 17, 1991 (Washington, D.C.: U.S. Government Printing Office).

6. Michael Parenti, *Democracy for the Few* (New York: St. Martin's Press, 1995).

7. *Report of the Independent Commission on the Los Angeles Police Department,* Los Angeles, CA, 1991.

8. Taylor Branch, *Parting the Waters* (New York: Simon & Schuster, 1988).

9. Ibid.

10. Charles W. Mills, *The Racial Contract* (Ithaca: Cornell University Press, 1997).

11. Alphonso Pinkney, *The Myth of Black Progress* (New York: Cambridge University Press, 1984)
.

12. Paul Takagi, "A Garrison State in 'Democratic' Society," *Crime and Social Justice* 1 (1974): 29.

13. Pinkney, *The Myth of Black Progress.*

14. Jill Nelson, "A Special Report on Police Brutality: The Blacks and the Blues," *Essence* 16 (1985): 91–156.

15. Lee May, "LA's Chief Gates Praises Philadelphia Police, Mayor: Goode Releases MOVE's Written Threat," *Los Angeles Times* 20 May 1985, part 1, p. 4.

16. Skolnick and Fyfe, *Above the Law: Police and the Excessive Use of Force.*

17. "MOVE House Is Bombed: Blaze Involves 60 Homes," *Philadelphia Inquirer,* 14 May 1985, p. Al.

18. May, "LA's Chief Gates Praises Philadelphia Police."

19. Hubert, Williams and Patrick V. Murphy, "The Evolving Strategy of Police: A Minority View," *Perspectives on Policing Series,* No. 13 (Washington, D.C.: National Institute of Justice and Kennedy School of Government, Harvard University, 1990).

20. William and Murphy; B. Wood, *Slavery in Colonial Georgia* (Athens: University of Georgia Press, 1984).

21. William and Murphy.

22. Marcus D. Pohlmann, *Black Politics in Conservative America* (New York: Longman, 1999).

23. U.S. Congress, op. cit.

24. Richard E. Sykes and John P. Clark, "A Theory of Deference Exchange in Police-Civilian Encounters," *American Journal of Sociology* 81 (1975): 584–600.

25. Ibid.

Essay/Discussion Questions

1. Why does Judson Jeffries argue that the police murder of African Americans is an epidemic?

2. Jeffries examines the subject of urban police brutality and finds a patterned response by police following the murder of their black victims. Discuss.

3. According to Jeffries, what is the purpose of growing occurrences of police murders of black people?

The Crisis of Black Middle-Class Leadership: A Critical Analysis

Maulana Karenga

The need for socially responsible and effective leadership is clearly one of the major urgencies of our time. As Burns (1978) asserts, "One of the most universal cravings of our time is a hunger for compelling and creative leadership" (p. 1). But the demand for quality leadership is met by the unsettling fact that leadership is in crisis, a crisis defined by a poverty of theory (vision and values) and practice. Moreover, if a general crisis of leadership plagues the world and U.S. society, it appears more acute in the black community, given its oppressed condition and the stringent requirements for its liberation.

Burns (1978) argues that the general "crisis in leadership is the mediocrity or irresponsibility of so many of the men and women in power" (p. 1). This general assessment can be applied, *mutatis mutandis,* to the crisis of black leadership, but it is obviously insufficient in both its factoral and contextual considerations. Beyond general contentions, a critical discussion of leadership demands a focus on other fundamental factors and especially on the specific socio-historical context in which the leadership and its crisis occurs. For it is a funda-

mental fact that social context is key to understanding social phenomena and processes. So it is, then, with the black middle-class leadership crisis which occurs in and is shaped by the overall conditions in U.S. society.

The crisis of black middle-class leadership, then, is unavoidably tied to the general crisis in U.S. society, which has economic, political, and cultural dimensions. This societal crisis sharpens the historical crisis in black leadership and makes it a more urgent and demanding task. A brief discussion of the basic dimensions of the crisis will show how it of necessity affects and aggravates the black leadership crisis both in terms of the added pressures for solutions which it brings as well as the increased difficulties it poses to reaching socially effective solutions.

The crisis in U.S. society is defined by several fundamental factors. The economic dimension of the crisis expresses itself in a high level of inflation, increasing unemployment, especially among blacks, a continuing real and contrived energy problem, a slowdown in pro-

From *The Black Scholar,* Fall 1982, pp. 16–32.

duction and consumption, and a perennially unbalanced budget. It appears that even the current [Reagan] Administration has conceded the unsolvable character of the crisis, if that solution seeks to save the socio-economic system in its current form. Budget Director Stockman's unsettling confessions of the ineptness, deception, and mystification which characterize the Administration's approach to the problem tend to confirm this (Greider, 1981).

The political dimension of the problem is marked first by substantial alienation from the political process. The low voter turnouts and the recorded distrust and disappreciation of governmental officials' moral integrity and intellectual capacity show a significant alienation from the political process and its leadership (Hadley, 1978; Kimble, 1972). Secondly, the political dimension of the crisis is expressed by the rise of the religious and political right. The Moral Majority's strident jeremiads and lamentations on moral deterioration and their desire to impose Judeo-Christian fundamentalism in the minds and media of America create unavoidable tension and conflict.

The political right has its vulgar and more respectable variants, i.e. the KKK and neo-nazi groups as well as its Orange County, Bible Belt and governmental Republicans. However, both variants of the political right come with simple solutions to complex problems, tend to reflect racist views, tend to see conspiracies in various aspects of life, over-rely on force in domestic and foreign policy, and tend to blame Third World peoples at home for the moral and material problems of society. This misfocus on Third World peoples has in fact mystified both the origin of the problem and exaggerated the anticipated effectiveness of the proposed solutions to them, which include declaring social entitlement morally wrong and financially too costly, reversing gains of the 60's and early 70's, and reducing, if not eliminating, the necessary and traditional role of government in achieving social justice and

equality for Third World peoples. It is this political indictment of Third World peoples and the resultant steps to deprive them of gains and governmental support for their struggle for rightful position and power in the social system which poses perhaps the most serious challenge to black leadership and thus contributes to its crisis.

Joined to this damning indictment is the resultant struggle over the division of social wealth and critical social space in racial, ethnic, and class terms. An assumption has been introduced and cultivated that the middle class—essentially white though including Third World members—has unjustly borne the burdens of financing the unworthy poor and lazy ethnic. This in turn has prompted fierce demands for tax cuts, reduced social services, and especially reduced and more stringently restricted social welfare.

Moreover, this struggle over social wealth and critical social space has contributed to the breakup of old allies and intense competition between them. This can be seen in the much assumed and less critically understood alliance between black and Jewish leadership groups. This split was graphically illustrated in the struggles around affirmative action (i.e., the Bakke and Weber cases), which saw former Jewish allies challenge blacks' right to these corrective measures to redress historical injustices imposed on them. It was also vividly expressed in the confrontation concerning Jews' questioning the political wisdom and right of blacks to participate in the foreign policy process and debate on the Middle East, especially when it led to the decision that the Palestinian people have as much right to a state as Jews do. This loss of or cooled relationship in a much-depended-on alliance also poses a serious problem for old line black leadership.

Finally, the crisis in U.S. society has a definite cultural dimension. It reflects Daniel Bell's (1978) concern with cultural disjunction and the "lack of a center" and sense of solidarity this implies. Using the famous Muslim historian and sociologist, Ibn Khaldun's contention that societies pass through specific phases of decline, Bell singles out Khaldun's concept of *asabiyah* to discuss the core of the cultural crisis in U.S. society. Khaldun (1958) argues that hedonism, loss of will and fortitude, competition for luxuries, and the loss of the ability to share and sacrifice leads inevitably to the loss of asabiyah. Asabiyah is a profound sense of solidarity and brotherhood and the "willingness to fight and die for each other." Bell (1978) asserts, however, that hidden in this concept is also a sense of "some moral purpose, a *telos* which provides the moral justifications for society" (p. 83). In other words, it reflects "the legitimations of society as expressed in the motivations of individuals and the moral purposes of the nation."

Bell concludes that the original implicit covenant which held U.S. society together, i.e., its belief in divine manifest destiny, and its social cement based in its uniqueness as an "open, adaptive, egalitarian and democratic system which was responsive to the many claimants that sought inclusion" and which respected principles of law, no longer obtains. Such a conclusion, though harsh, seems difficult to avoid. For if one observes U.S. society, even cursorily, one can see the age, ethnic, sexual, racial, and class divisions which plague American society, and puncture an illusion of solidarity. One can also see the hedonistic competition for luxuries, the unwillingness to share or fight for a system whose promises now seem to be so much propaganda. Moreover, one can see the entrenchment of a negative and individualistic materialism which finds identity and meaning in possessions rather than in social production (Marcuse, 1966).

Finally, it seems clear that the system can no longer meet its traditional claims or successfully mask its failures. As Bell (1978) concludes, "American capitalism . . . has lost its traditional legitimacy . . ." (p. 84) based on its claims of material abundance, mobility, and

social justice and equality. It, thus, has begun to resort to reliance on force enshrined in law as a substitute. The Cointelpro of the 60's is an example of this and the recent relaxation of rules for domestic activities of intelligence agencies as well as increased police power through law and court decisions also identify and reinforce this trend. This too poses a serious problem for black leadership in terms of its advocacy and direct action activities.

It is in this context of a societal crisis of major political, economic, and cultural dimensions that the crisis in black leadership occurs and is conditioned. Out of this general crisis, several factors tend to contribute most heavily to the pressures and problems which define the black leadership crisis. First, the loss of Democratic patronage and support for social programs from a national base has seriously weakened the middle-class leadership's capacity to deliver and thus, its legitimacy, which was based essentially on its ability to "produce" while nationalist militants and others "talked." Secondly, and directly related to this, is the Republican decision to curtail severely governmental intervention on the side of the oppressed; this deprives middle-class leadership of a powerful though often unwilling partner in pursuit of the American dream. Thirdly, the breakup of old alliances (black-Jewish) and strains in others (black-Democratic) deprives middle-class leadership of added strength and resources it sorely needs. Fourthly, the fierce competition for resources and the racist manipulation of ethnic differences, militates against much-needed alliances with other Third World peoples.

Fifthly, the reversion to raw racism, and the resultant social tendency to view blacks and other Third World peoples as freeloaders, criminals, and general threats to American social peace and prosperity, poses a particularly severe problem for black leadership. The goodwill of most whites advocated by black moderate leaders and the assumed support by Jewish allies are now called into question, and these leaders are left without an alternative approach. Finally, since the general social crisis appears unsolvable within the current social structure, and since the leadership class is not likely to countenance profound social restructuring, it will rely more and a more on "crisis management" rather than attempt real solutions. This management can only mean increasing reliance on force under cover of law to discourage, contain, and suppress social protest and challenges. This means, in turn, that black leadership—moderate and radical—will be increasingly confronted with the inability and unwillingness to practice direct action and confrontation prevalent in the 60's.

In the context of the general social crisis, then, and the fundamental problems and pressures it poses, the black middle-class leadership crisis is characterized by the two classic problems of leadership: (1) the problem of theory, and (2) the problem of practice. The problem of theory is one of definition of leadership, a poverty of vision and the possession of values which diminish leadership and social possibilities. The problem of practice is engendered by an attachment to historically exhausted and socially ineffective modes of leadership, and structural (organizational and institutional) deficiencies which result in an incapacity to achieve goals and respond effectively to challenges.

THE PROBLEMS OF THEORY

The Definitional Problem

A beginning theoretical problem which characterizes the crisis of black middle-class leadership is the problem of definition. This is expressed by an inadequate understanding and delineation of the role and responsibility of a leader. This problem of definition plagues not only those who assume the status and manner of leaders, but also is found in the confusion in the black community as to what constitutes or

ought to constitute the criteria for leadership. The criteria for leadership, which should be based on the quality of vision, values, and practice, is often reduced to style by some and status and visibility by others. Even social scientists who study black leadership have fallen into this definitional trap and contributed to this overall confusion. A critical review of the major studies on black leadership shows a tendency to reduce leadership to style. Noting this reductive translation, Charles Henry (1981b) states that "the most striking stated characteristic of these studies is their emphasis on style" (p. 464). Thompson (1963) and Gosnell (1967) stress racial-focus styles and Wilson (1960) and Ladd (1969) emphasize the moderate and militant styles. Oliver Cox (1965) discussed black leadership in terms of what he calls "five typical patterns (of) attitudes," i.e., protest, conservatism, compromise, nationalism and revolt. He then attempts to classify black leadership into categories of "spurious" or "genuine" based on its move in or in opposition to perceived social movement. However, his criteria are more subjective than objective and depend on one's perception of social tendencies rather than on how a leader objectively deals with theoretical and practical challenges.

Bardolph (1961) takes the second approach to the treatment and definition of black leadership, i.e., reductively translating it as status and visibility. In his work, *The Negro Vanguard,* Bardolph lists a mind-boggling myriad of persons as his vanguard without critical delineation of their differences and similarities. Thus, his vanguard included musicians and entertainers, athletes, artists, scientists, armed forces personnel, journalists, writers, governmental and political personalities, educators, and religious and race leaders. Although the category vanguard, unless otherwise qualified, is usually used in a political leadership sense, Bardolph translates it as anyone who has made a significant achievement.

Such a position is also seen in books on great black leaders or "Great Black Americans."

In Harold Allen's (1971) book of the same title, Jackie Robinson, an athlete, is listed and treated along with such accomplished and clearly defined leaders as Booker T. Washington, W. E. B. Du Bois, and Martin Luther King, Jr. It is in this context of equating status and visibility or achievement in any field that Muhammad Ali, a boxer, becomes a spokesman for the race; Pearl Bailey goes to the U.N.; and Stephanie Mills emerges from the land of Oz to question black concern about racism. Obviously, this approach to leadership is neither critical nor useful and ends up being used by those in power to prop up and trot out persons who support rather than challenge the established order and who are willing to criticize black leaders engaged in such a challenge. It is also in this context of the lack of a clear definition of leadership and a criteria for selecting and evaluating performance that black neo-conservatives have come to the forefront to challenge traditional black middle-class leadership which ironically was used in the same context to criticize and condemn racial leadership when and where it appeared.

Finally, the problem of leadership definition or delineation is further expressed in *Ebony*'s yearly presentation of a list of the "one hundred most influential Blacks." In discussing this "Ebony elite," Charles Henry (1981a) refers to them as leaders, but raises questions about the substantive nature of their "inherently unstable" positions due to "a relatively high degree of turnover in professional and social clubs, elections and their dependence on whites" (p. 121–122). Moreover, he, like *Ebony*, focuses on their influence rather than power and concludes that "Few of *Ebony*'s influential Blacks actually wield national power." As Henry (1981b) notes, although *Ebony* used both the reputational and decision-making method of determining their elite, they did not list the decisions or issues involved.

What one has here is not so much leadership, but prestige persons or status persons. Even though Wilson (1960) considers a prestige person a leader, the fact that his designation is based on "high personal achievement . . . in business or professional life" (pp. 256ff) rather than in activities designed to acquire power to achieve collective goals, tends to undermine the validity of his definition. For leadership is, at its core, "relational, collective and purposeful." In a word, it is "inseparable from followers' needs and goals," and the collective purpose and practices this implies and necessitates (Burns, 1978). Thus, to reduce leadership to "high personal achievement" is to vitiate its meaning and contribute to the theoretical confusion which surrounds the prestige personality approach to leadership.

The Ideological Deficiency

Joined to the problem of definition of leadership is the problem of ideological deficiency of the black middle-class leadership which, if solved, could no doubt contribute to the solution of the definitional problem. For ideology which defines the socio-historical mission of a movement suggests at the same time who and what is required to fulfill it. Studying Third World national liberation movements, Amilcar Cabral (1969) concluded that "The ideological deficiency . . . constitutes one of the greatest, if not the greatest, weaknesses of all" of these struggles (pp. 92–93). It is an assessment easily applicable to the social struggle headed by the black middle-class leadership.

The importance of ideology to social struggle is expressed in its definition. Ideology is essentially a coherent system of views and values which give its adherents a moral, material, and meaningful interpretation to life and at the same time demands allegiance and a corresponding practice. Thus, ideology provides the rationalization, inspiration, and political direction of social struggle. Given the definition above, ideology can be seen to have two main aspects—i.e., a view dimension and a value dimension. As a coherent system of views, ideology provides a social theory, a theory of change, a grand strategy which not only expresses the political, economic and cultural interests and aspirations of its adherents but a conception of social reality and the possibilities of changing it. This may also be called social vision, an effective grasp of self, society, and the world, i.e., an understanding which not only provides an interpretation of these three elements but reveals possibilities of their profound transformation.

The coherent system of values expresses a quest for a higher moral order and urges thought and practice to achieve a social situation in harmony with ideal norms. Values can be defined as categories of commitment, priorities, and possibilities. Put another way, values are goal and standard commitments and priorities which enhance human possibilities. Thus, focus on or advocacy of certain goals and standards can either increase or diminish the possibilities of liberation and a higher level of human life.

The ideological deficiency of black middle-class leadership is clearest in its lack of a grand strategy, a theory of social reality and social change which gives at the minimum a clear socio-political identity, purpose, and direction. Cruse (1968) is perhaps referring to this ideological deficiency in black middle-class leadership when he states that "The Black American, as a part of an ethnic group has no definite social theory relative to his status, presence or impact on American society" (p. 202). This is not to say black middle-class leadership lacks views, opinions, ideas, and strategies, but rather that these ideological assertions are neither coherent nor grand, though often grandiose. This example of ideological deficiency can be seen in the black middle-class leadership's inability to make a bold and incisive criticism of the established order during the Carter Administration. As I stated in another paper (Karenga, 1972), concerning their criticism of Carter, it was more moral than social, ambivalent and directed toward a person and administration rather than the system in which both operate.

This same non-systemic criticism is occurring against the Reagan Administration. The black middle-class leadership is focusing criticism almost exclusively on the Reagan Administration and avoiding the systemic criticisms. Deny what one wants, he did not come into being by himself; nor does he speak and act simply for himself. Reagan represents a class/race politics which must be confronted, not avoided and reduced to one man's personality defects. Such a partial and timid criticism expresses clear ambivalence toward the system. In his classic work on the crisis of the black intellectual, Harold Cruse (1967) points to the ambivalence, arguing that it is due to the fact that black middle-class leadership is ". . . fighting and protesting against the very social system it wants to join" (pp. 371–372). To him, "This means in effect that [Black] leadership is not really fighting against the system, but against being left out of it." Thus, there is this ambivalence of how far to push or what to dare.

What was not understood, it seems, was the socio-historical reality that produced and sustains Reagan and the political interests he represents and to whom he is obligated. Certainly, a social theory which identifies and focuses on social forces and tendencies rather than personalities would have offered such an understanding.

In addition to its inability to make a systemic criticism, the black middle class suffers ideologically also from its minimum goal approach. Thus, it seeks jobs rather than ownership, busing instead of administrative and financial control of community schools to obtain quality education; Democratic and Republican party participation rather than or in conjunction with support for an independent black party; and federal poverty programs rather than or in conjunction with shared social wealth and economic self-help. The black middle-class leadership, then, clearly faces a conflict in goal commitments and goal priorities. Wilson (1960) posed this conflict between what he calls "welfare goals" and "status goals," (p. 185), i.e., material and political goals.

Reflecting the vulgar pragmatism of the dominant society, black middle-class leadership will tend to choose the material over the political goals, material things over conditions of freedom and power, and immediate gratification over long-term struggle for a higher level of human life. Thus, they tend to reduce human aspiration to pursuit of the basic three, i.e., food, clothing, and shelter. They do not seem to grasp that a slave, even if well-fed, well-housed, and well-clothed, is still a slave or that the political goal of power is the only way to achieve and insure acquisition of life-sustaining goals as well as the ultimate human aspiration of a realm of freedom and higher levels of humanity.

THE PROBLEMS OF PRACTICE

The crisis in black leadership is also rooted in and reflective of the problems of practice. This practical dimension of the crisis is, as suggested above, both affected by and contributive to the theoretical dimension of the crisis. Thus, practical problems will appear also as theoretical problems, and theoretical problems will be certainly linked to practical problems, for the interrelatedness of the two cannot be avoided. Although there are perhaps many more problems than the ones below, those which follow seem the most substantive and requiring priority in resolution.

The Problem of Overdependence on Government

Clearly, one of the most serious problems of practice in the crisis in black middle-class leadership is its historical overdependence on governmental support for social correctives and social welfare designed to ameliorate the socio-economic and political conditions of blacks. Such overdependence has developed into what

syndicated columnist Joseph Kraft called, in a *Los Angeles Times* article, August 1, 1980, with the same title, "The pathos of Black leadership." Kraft pointed out that although "By force of habit and the pressure of professionals, black leaders are driven to call for more and more government help," these appeals find neither a positive response in the white community nor in local, state, or federal government. In fact, Kraft asserts, "white leaders, on the contrary, can expand their political influence by standing up against such help." Koch in New York, Gann and Jarvis in California, and Reagan in the White House are clear examples.

As Kraft concludes, given this, "Black leaders . . . have been thrust into losing confrontations." This, in turn, finds them "steadily reduced in stature by the experience of asking, and not getting." The solution to this, Kraft maintains, is that the middle class "shoulder responsibilities commensurate with their gains." Such a position clearly points to the middle class's historical obligation to accept the challenge of leadership, to use their skill, wealth and other resources to better the life of the masses, which in turn would yield them a real power and respected position among their people and others.

This vulnerable dependence, which was clearly evidenced during the Carter Administration, reached a new and precarious level with the actions of the Reagan Administration. John Jacobs, newly elected National Urban League President, admitted in a January 19, 1982, interview in the *Los Angeles Times* that Reagan's anti-civil rights thrust "can only be interpreted as attempts to dismantle the process of desegregating America." But when questioned about Reagan's racial approach to government, Jacobs stated that he "wouldn't say President Reagan is running a racist Administration." This was obviously said as a goodwill gesture toward the Administration in hope of its relenting.

However, regardless of Reagan's or his successor's insensitivity and savage attacks on civil rights gains, the governmental apparatus must be dealt with effectively. For how a people or group deals with government dictates how they will share in the distribution of key social space and resources. The black middle-class leadership knows that without government intervention in the slave trade, the slave system, and legal segregation, all would have lasted much longer. They also know government has monies which are vital to their programs. The National Urban League, the Opportunities Industrial Center, and the National Council of Negro Women all lost huge sums in the wake of Reagan's cutbacks and cutoffs. In fact, federal funding for the Urban League was cut last year from $29 million to $11 million, which caused an estimated layoff of 1,000 employees, one-fourth of the League work force.

The problem, then, becomes one of identifying and overcoming the source of vulnerable overdependence on government plaguing black middle-class leadership. It would appear that this vulnerability rests on three basic factors. First, the traditional support all power minorities (racial, ethnic, sexual, and age) seek from the government is always conditional and problematic. It depends first of all on their relative ability to reward or punish, be useful or disruptive to those in power. Afterwards, it depends, among other things, on political tendencies of those in power, the political climate of the country, and the strength of the opposition who might use support of minority issues against those in power.

Secondly, the black middle-class leadership, it seems, is more vulnerable by its ideological lack of a clearly positive social interpretation of the black masses' right to social wealth. It often seems ambivalent about the appropriateness and impact of social welfare. It focuses on maintenance social welfare rather than developmental welfare and on appeal to the moral conscience of the government rather than practical struggle for distributive equality or social

justice based on black historical and current contribution to the social wealth of the U.S. It is right to argue that the government is constitutionally obligated to provide for the general welfare, but its argument seems more moral than political and less a call to battle to the masses than a call for social kindness from the government. Lacking a clear positive rationale for social welfare, they have not evolved from it a rationale for struggle, only a rationale for request.

Thirdly, vulnerable overdependence on the government is rooted in the black middle-class leadership's obvious structural incapacity to reward or punish those in power. This increases the tendency of the Administration in power to disregard their demands or requests; Reagan, like Carter, understands the position of weakness from which his black critics speak. If Carter knew blacks did not elect him, but rather a Democrat, Reagan knows they did not vote for him, but for a Democrat. And the 4 percent which did vote for Reagan will no doubt do so again regardless of his performance, thus tending to project a certain amount of black support for his political and social meanness, like Carter's minions did for him.

The Rise of Black Conservatives

A second practical dimension to the crisis of black middle-class leadership is the rise of the black conservatives in and outside of government. The Reagan Administration obviously would like black representatives of its political persuasion and seems also obviously willing to sacrifice competence for conviction. It has nominated two black men to two vital commissions, the Equal Employment Opportunity Commission and the U.S. Commission on Civil Rights, whose credentials seem to be limited to their allegiance to the policies of the Administration. Thus William Bell is named as EEOC head, even though his experience seems limited to running a small job placement service in Detroit, a fact which tends to raise questions about his ability to run a major agency of such vital importance. Likewise, Reagan fired a white liberal who criticized his stance against affirmative action and replaced him with Clarence Pendleton, another black conservative. Pendleton, President of the San Diego Urban League, is a former physical education teacher who has a very limited view of government's role and responsibility in securing social justice and equality for blacks and other Third World peoples.

The appointment of these blacks is especially problematic for the black middle-class leadership for three basic reasons. First, it lessens the strength of any charge of racism or racial insensitivity against the Administration, given the fact that they are black and involved in the decision-making process, regardless of how marginally. The role "Silent Sam" Pierce, Reagan's cabinet Secretary of Housing and Urban Development, plays is perhaps illustrative. Pierce not only acquiesced in Reagan's reneging on his commitment to housing for the poor, but according to an article in *Newsweek,* January 25, 1982, "supported an effort to weaken legislation renewing the Voting Rights Act."

Secondly, such appointments, and the support for policy they imply and encourage, challenges the established middle-class leadership's claim to speak for all blacks. And thirdly, it thus justifies pursuit of and support of other policies for blacks and other Third World peoples. Reagan, no doubt, understands the purely utilitarian value of these visible blacks and uses them in crisis as in the case of the flap over his support of tax exemption for two schools practicing racial discrimination. In fact, it has been reported that until a June meeting of mayors, he had not even bothered to know his one black cabinet secretary, Pierce. At this meeting he called Pierce "Mr. Mayor," obviously mistaking him; for Hatcher of Gary until someone informed him otherwise.

The intellectuals outside the government are nevertheless philosophically allied to it. Whereas the governmental blacks pose the problem of positional replacement to the black middle-class leadership, the conservative intellectual poses the problem of being overshadowed and no longer listened to or consulted. Although Thomas Sowell, an economist at the Hoover Institution, is the most well-published and perhaps the most well-known black conservative intellectual, there are others, such as Martin Kilson, a political scientist at Harvard, Walter Williams, an economist at George Mason University in Virginia, and J. A. Y. Parker, the President of Lincoln Institute and Educational Foundation in Washington. As Willingham (1981) correctly and cogently points out, this phenomenon has its most definitive historical roots in the Washingtonian and DuBoisian approaches to black social advancement. The Washingtonian approach was characterized by rejection of black protest, vocational education, and emphasis on self-help. On the other hand, the DuBoisian approach was defined by emphasis on protest, multidimensional education, and the obligation of U.S. society to live up to its claims and of government to facilitate and insure this. Today, conservatives and liberals continue the struggle.

The rise of the white right in and out of government, then, is accompanied by the appearance of a black right which is developing intellectual arguments against the minimum wage, government intervention, affirmative action, and equal opportunity programs, and most of the other programs and proposals so key to the civil rights thrust of the black middle class. The problem of black middle-class leadership is to respond effectively to this new challenge, which is not only supported by the government, but has widespread white public support.

The rise of black conservatives, then, poses a challenge to traditional black middle-class leadership on several levels. First, they are tied politically and/or philosophically to the party in power and, thus, will benefit in stature and influence from that position. The tendency, as has been shown, will be to consult them, appoint them, and give them control of or opportunity for input in decision-making and resource allocation with regard to the black community. Secondly, the black conservatives will obviously benefit from the fact that their rise occurs at the same time the country has shifted to the right. In addition to the Administration patronage mentioned above, this could also mean more exposure, more demand for appearances, and, thus, a resultant increase in status and influence in general. It could also mean the verbal and financial backing of those whom Lee Daniels (1981) calls "resource-rich white conservatives who have never been comfortable with the Black civil-rights leadership" (p. 21).

Thirdly, given this philosophical and structural link with the Administration, the black conservatives will possibly become more "media worthy" and be given more time to introduce and establish their ideological position as the best and dominant view for black advancement. Finally, this challenge from the conservatives will certainly compel the black middle-class leadership to develop ideologically and organizationally if it is to survive and transcend the challenge to its leadership among blacks and in the eyes of the whites who have historically supported and/or deferred to them.

The Problems of Coalitions and Alliances

Certainly another key practical problem contributing to the crisis of black middle-class leadership is the problem of alliances and coalitions. As Carmichael and Hamilton (1967) noted, "All too frequently, coalitions involving Black people have been only at the leadership level, dictated by terms set by others, and for objectives not calculated to bring major improvements in the lives of the Black masses"

(pp. 59–60). Historically, the black middle-class leadership has depended on white allies—Jewish and gentile—for financial, legal, and political support. In fact, there is or seems to be a basic assumption among this leadership that blacks would not have come as far as they have if it were not for whites of goodwill. Such a conception is problematic on at least three levels and speaks to the crisis which currently plagues black middle-class leadership. First, it has been an underlying theme for misconceptions created about black/white coalitions and alliances. Secondly, it has led to a confusion of patronage with coalition and alliance. And thirdly, it has tended to encourage denial and reductive translation of blacks' contribution to their own struggle.

Two of the coalitions on which blacks have relied heavily are the Jewish and Democratic coalitions. These coalitions have produced their share of misconceptions and at the same time revealed the nature of the problem of coalitions faced by black middle-class leadership. The misconceptions which surround coalitions are many. Carmichael and Hamilton (1967) have cited three myths of coalitions that are important to understanding their weakness and unworkability. Agreeing with and incorporating some of their contentions, I have developed five misconceptions of coalitions that clearly create a problem for the coalitions in which black middle-class leadership involves itself. First, there is the misconception that the basis of coalition is long-term common interests and principles rather than short-term specific goals. This is a confusion between alliance and coalition. Alliance is a long-term ongoing unity based on common interests and common basic principles, whereas a coalition is a short-term working association based on specific short-term goals. Failure to make and observe this basic distinction has created situations in which blacks have assumed too much about their relationship with their more powerful coalition partners and left themselves vulnerable to joint actions not mutually beneficial and withdrawal of expected support at crucial times. . . .

A second misconception is that common goals on one level or in one area is a basis for unity in the other. For example, Jews might support blacks against one kind of racism (neo-nazi or KKK attacks) but oppose them on correctives for racism (affirmative action). Thirdly, there is a misconception that moral unity—assumed or real—is a substitute for unity around concrete goals and self-interests. This is clear in the case of the assumed black/Jewish unity based on common or similar suffering. But no unity is automatic, neither political nor personal; each must be built around concrete goals and interests which change or disappear and therefore, must be reinforced and renewed or replaced by others.

A fourth misconception is that a genuine coalition between the powerful and the powerless (or clearly less powerful) is always possible, rather than always problematic and often pure patronage politics. In fact, one of the problems of the Jewish and Democratic coalitions is that they often deteriorate into patronage, i.e., dependence by blacks on Jewish and Democratic patrons who may be unable or unwilling at various times to give the largesse or support blacks request or need. And the problem is that blacks cannot effectively penalize or reward these partners in any significant way to compel compliance. The Jewish withdrawal of support from SNCC and CORE as they transformed into Black Power structures and their opposition to affirmative action are examples. So are the Democratic Party's unwillingness to support fully black social justice and social welfare goals under Carter, and their unwillingness and inability to produce under Reagan. In such a coalition, the less powerful partner can lessen or eliminate such politically unhealthy arrangements in three basic ways. It can: (1) unite with other less powerful partners in the coalition to increase its power; (2) build other coalitions to offset negative effects of the problematic one;

and (3) shelter no misconception about the problems of coalitions between the powerful and clearly less powerful. Black middle-class leadership does not seem to have achieved any of these alternative options.

A final misconception about coalitions is that coalition action is a substitute for a people's or group's own initiative. Such a misconception leaves a group hopelessly and slavishly dependent on forces outside its control and often beyond its influence. There is, in fact, no substitute for the structural capacity to define, defend and develop one's interests. For regardless how numerous or sincere one's allies are, a people that cannot save itself is lost forever.

The black/Jewish coalition is a classic study in the problems of coalitions. Not only does it reflect commitment to the misconceptions which characterize coalitions in general, it also carries its own particular myths or misconceptions held mainly by its black members. Among these are, first, the myth that Jews are not white in spite of visual reality, self-definition, and social acceptance of this fact. A second myth is that the Jews are blacks' best friend, a myth which Cruse (1967) argues is misphrased. It would be far more accurate to say, he states, that "Certain Jews have been best friends of certain [Blacks], which in any case is nothing usual" (p. 467). Thirdly, there is a myth of moral affinity between blacks and Jews based on similar suffering—historical and current.

These myths suggest or seek to foster a unity and commonality of interests that do not exist and thus produce a political practice and thought based on false premises problematic to black interests. The first myth seeks to redefine Jews into the Third World to achieve unity through a contrived similarity. The second makes a claim more true for the black middle-class leadership than the black masses, and the third assumes an automatic unity and commonality of interest and implies that moral affinity, if it exists, can substitute for concrete interests and goals as a basis for a viable coalition. As Isaacs (1976) and Weisbord and Stein (1970) point out, concrete differences of interests and goals not only separate blacks and Jews, but also often place them in active opposition to each other. The Andrew Young Affair; affirmative action; the 1966 New York City referendum on a civilian review board; the fight over the Forest Hills housing project in Queens, New York; and the struggle for black community control in Brooklyn's Ocean Hill–Brownsville School District, all clearly reflect this. This is due to the fact that Jewish power, wealth, social achievement and status, and white skin privilege objectively give them a different set of priorities and interests than blacks whose race and general class character assigns them a marginal and subordinate role and status in the social process.

Since Roosevelt's New Deal in the 30's, blacks have aligned themselves with the Democratic Party. But the alliance was never of equals or semi-equals. On the contrary, like the other alliances, it was essentially a question of patronage, an alignment based on influence not power, and, thus, subject to the interests and aspirations of the patrons who control it. The Party, as a political structure, after all, is out to win votes and to do so will no doubt cater to the cutback, cut-off, and trim-down attitudes dominant now among white voters. Black middle-class leadership finds itself, then, locked into the Democratic Party, with no structural or financial ability to significantly reward or punish it to induce it into compliance with the demands of black interests. Moreover, it has developed no party alternative either with the Republican Party or through the building of a national black independent party.

There was talk in 1978 of blacks moving in significant numbers to the Republican Party as a way of increasing their bargaining power and political options, but nothing serious has come of it. Moreover, there is no current strategy to enter or construct, conduct or benefit from the proposed relations with the Republi-

cans, to pressure the Democrats or demand and get from each party a minimum set of legislative and financial concessions. It could well be that both will decide blacks are dispensable, that given their overall structural incapacity to reward or punish with organized, self-conscious voting or financial and campaign labor contributions, they are neither needed nor worthy of serious consideration. This obviously presents a practical problem for black middle-class leadership which counts so much on the Democratic alliance and talked so much about the Republican option.

Ineffective Use of the Church

Another problem of practice which confronts black middle-class leadership is its apparent inability to use effectively its relation with the black church to achieve collective social goals. It seems that black middle-class leadership understands and appreciates the socio-political possibilities of the church, but besides a warm relation with it and praise of it, it has not been able to use the church effectively since the Civil Rights Movement. Writing in the Urban League's annual *State of Black America*, Kelly M. Smith (1982), President of the National Conference of Black Churchmen, argued correctly that the black church can and must play a vital role in leading the black community in the struggle to solve the economic and political problems it currently faces. However, political desirability and possibility and political actuality diverge here rather than automatically lead to each other. This occurs because of several factors, among which are three basic ones which militate against an effective political use of the church as a self-conscious vanguard agency of social change.

One factor which militates against effective use of the church is its tendency toward support of struggles rather than leadership of struggles. It is important to realize that in spite of the church's acknowledged role in social struggle, for the most part its role has been more in support than in leadership. Except for clearly visible leadership in the Civil Rights Movement and in the Abolition Movement, the church has played more of a support role than a vanguard one. In other words, the image of the church as an openly activist and vanguard agency is perhaps an overstatement. In reality the church tends to provide leadership in morality and spiritual direction to the black community rather than social leadership.

Thus, the model of King's (1964) leading Dexter Avenue Baptist Church in its vanguard role in the struggle in Montgomery in 1955 and of other pastors leading flocks in active struggle in the South are exceptions to the kind of moderate assertion in political affairs, i.e., voter registration, candidate endorsement, etc., to which churches tend to restrict themselves.

A second factor which militates against effective use of the church is its varying contextual responses to social problems and struggles. The King model, it must be remembered, took place in the South, not the North. This tends to be reflective of the social conditions which demanded a more socially activist role of the Southern church, reducing the distinction between its social and spiritual missions and at points merging the two.

Thirdly, effective use of the church is hampered by lack of and application of a liberational theology, a theology which merges or actively links the social and spiritual missions of the church. The King model definitely shows the need for theoretical development which clearly and forcefully joins the social and spiritual mission. Although the tendency is to point to Martin Luther King's and James Cone's contribution to black liberation theology, liberation theology is not the daily fare or dominant trend in the black church. On the contrary, the dominant focus is on "salvation" as opposed to "liberation." The distinction here is suggested by Albert Cleage (1972) in his immanent criticism of black theology and his

posing black Christian nationalism as an alternative. Salvation, an essentially individualistic spiritual pursuit and escape, he argues, should give way to liberation, a collective practice and product which leads to the end of powerlessness and oppression. Without such a social liberational focus to its theology, the church will never be able to break from the tendency to suggest Hebrew myth as an answer to concrete Afro-American problems, and to stress the spiritual over the social, and divine assistance over self-conscious human intervention in the self-determination of their destiny and daily lives.

The Problem of Structural Capacity

Perhaps the most severe practical problem facing the black middle-class leadership is the problem of structural capacity, i.e., the organizational and institutional ability to define, defend, and develop black interests. The question of what is to be done is unavoidably linked to the question of how and with what it will be done. Put in other words, the question of strategy cannot be divorced from the question of structure. Invariably every practical problem I have raised necessitates a structural capacity to solve it.

Power, as a collective social capacity to realize one's will even in opposition to others, is essentially a function of structure or organization. Structural capacity gives one the ability to penalize and reward, to define, defend, and develop one's interests, to create agendas and compel a place on others' agendas. With structure, one has recognizable, measurable and respected power. One can mobilize, educate, and harness and direct mass energy. Without it, one invariably is reduced to patronage politics or an alienated marginality to the political process.

Black middle-class leadership shows its structural deficiency by its failure to develop at least three critical structures of national significance to its credibility and to the establishment, maintenance and effective use of black power. The first of these is a national deliberative, planning, and collective action body or, in popular language, a black united front. There is a Black Leadership Forum, made up of approximately sixteen national organizations, but it is not well-known or visibly active in planning, organizing, or confronting the system. Although nothing in recent times has approximated the National Convention Movement of the 1840s and 1850s, the unity and common planning of the major Civil Rights Movement leaders (King, Young, McKissick, Austin, Randolph, and Lewis) suggests the importance and value of such a relation and structure. Moreover, a truly united front would include a diversity of groups and strategies which would tend to break the middle-class monopoly on leadership and include a radical perspective and practice, which, in the final analysis, is necessary for substantive social change.

The lack of a national party, a party formation, or an adequate structural substitute to organize and mobilize black people around collective goals is also an aspect of the structural deficiency of black middle-class leadership. Power, as the social capacity to realize one's will even in opposition to others, is in the final analysis based on structural capacity, i.e., organization and institutional power. Given the power of the state, power in society can be expressed and determined by a people's ability to check, challenge, seize, control, or effectively participate in state power. To do this, one must have a party. For as I have contended, "A party—communist or capitalist—is a political structure specifically designed to seize, control, or effectively participate in state power" (Karenga, 1980, p. 66). The party, however, is only the key structure; organization of the masses on every available level around their immediate and long-range interests remains necessary.

One must admit that black parties have not had a history of unbridled success in elec-

toral politics (Walton, 1972). However, the party would not just be a vote-getting machine, but would also serve other functions equally important. Among these would be: (1) serving as political accountant, monitoring and rewarding and punishing friends and enemies respectively; (2) organizing the masses around collective interests; (3) engaging in political education concerning power issues and struggle; (4) coordinating collective community activity; and (5) serving as national and international representatives of black people. This project of party building was explored at the 1972 Gary Convention and, finally, launched in November 1980 in Philadelphia. Members of the black middle-class leadership were at Gary and absent at Philadelphia. In both cases, they denied the need and possibility.

A final problem of structure is the lack of an intellectual center which would produce the grand and minor theories vital to serious and substantive social change. The Institute of the Black World, which began in 1968–69 to bring together in Atlanta a group of black scholars to engage in critical dialogue on the history, current character, and future of black life and struggle, never received substantive assistance from the black middle class or its leadership. It would appear that black middle-class leadership places less value than necessary on building one or many intellectual centers for serious study, dialogue, and strategy. Thus, it is reduced to ad hoc and vulgarly pragmatic responses to problems which are often contradictory and never quite satisfactory.

Such an intellectual center could, in addition to being a think tank, also be a leadership training institute. This would not only professionalize leadership, but set standards for leadership which the masses could use to judge those who define themselves as such. Given the problem of definition of leadership which confronts black middle-class leadership, this should be welcomed. But the problem is that that which clarifies can also expose, and this fact may already militate against support for such intellectual centers.

BY WAY OF CONCLUSION

The crisis of black middle-class leadership, then, is rooted in the problems of theory and practice. These problems, as I have argued above, interlock and aggravate each other and demand a simultaneous solution. I have also suggested that leadership is both a political and moral task and responsibility which demands a respect for the interests and will of the masses of blacks, the drafted and volunteer followers. In both developing an effective liberational theory and practice of leadership and struggle, a certain positive, humanistic conception of human worth and possibility is necessary. Without it, leadership deteriorates—at best into transaction, at worst into manipulation.

In his seminal essay, titled "The Talented Tenth," W. E. B. Du Bois (1903) argued cogently for the academic and social cultivation of a body of men and women who, through consciousness, capacity, and commitment, would offer theoretical and practical leadership to the black community. In his own words, Du Bois sought the development of the conscious, capable, and committed intellectual who would be "as he ought to be, the group leader, the man who sets the ideals of the community where he lives, directs its thoughts and heads its social movements" (p. 54). This was and remains both a challenge and call to the black middle class to use their knowledge and skills in the service of the masses, or as Du Bois put it, to become "the leaders of a struggling people."

Based on this call and on Burns' (1978) distinction between transactional (exchange) and transformative (elevation) leadership, an operational definition of leadership can be developed. Leadership can be defined as *the self-conscious capacity to provide vision and values, and produce structures, programs, and practice which satisfies human needs and aspirations and transforms persons and society in the process.* The self-conscious capacity aspect of leadership implies and necessitates knowledge and commitment; the satisfaction of human needs and aspirations demands a structural capacity; and the transformation requires and reflects an elevation of human thought and practice. It is, therefore, this definition and kind of leadership of which the black community is in dire need and which will undoubtedly contribute definitively to the solution of the crisis of black leadership.

Bibliography

Allen, Harold. (1971) *Great Black Americans,* Westhaven, Conn.: Pendulum Press.

Bardolph, Richard. (1961) *The Negro Vanguard,* New York: Vintage Books.

Bell, Daniel. (1978) *The Cultural Contradictions of Capitalism,* New York: Basic Books.

Burns, James MacGregor. (1978) *Leadership,* New York: Harper & Row.

Cabral, Amilcar. (1969) *Revolution in Guinea,* New York: Monthly Review Press.

Carmichael, Stokely and Charles Hamilton. (1967) *Black Power,* New York: Vintage Books.

Cleage, Albert. (1972) *Black Christian Nationalism,* New York: William Morrow & Company.

Cox, Oliver. (1965) "Leadership Among Negroes in the United States," in Alvin Gouldner, *Studies in Leadership,* New York: Russell & Russell.

Daniels, Lee A. (1981) "The New Black Conservatives," *New York Times Magazine* (October 4).

Du Bois W. E. B, (1969) "The Talented Tenth," in *The Negro Problem* (ed.) Ulysses Lee, New York: Arno Press and the New York Times, pp. 31–76.

Frazier, E. Franklin. (1962) *Black Bourgeoisie,* New York: Collier Books.

Gosnell, Harold. (1967) *Negro Politicians,* Chicago: University of Chicago Press.

Greider, William (1981) "The Education of David Stockman," *The Atlantic Monthly* (December), pp. 27–54.

Hadley, Arthur. (1978) *The Empty Polling Booth,* Englewood Cliffs, N.J.: Prentice-Hall.

Hare, Nathan. (1965) *The Black Anglo Saxons,* New York: Marzni and Munsell.

Henry, Charles P. (1981) "Ebony Elite: America's Most Influential Blacks," *Phylon,* 42, 2 (June), pp. 120–132.

———. (1981) "The Political Role of the 'Bad Nigger,'" *Journal of Black Studies,* 11, 4 (June), pp. 461–482.

Hofstater, Richard. (1963) *Anti-Intellectualism in American Life,* New York: Alfred Knopf, Inc.

Isaacs, Stephen. (1974) *Jews and American Politics,* Garden City, N.Y.: Doubleday.

Karenga, Maulana. (1977) "Carter and His Black Critics: The Dialogue and Its Lessons," *The Black Scholar,* 9, 3 (November), pp. 52–54.

———. (1980) *Kawaida Theory: An Introductory Outline,* Los Angeles: Kawaida Publications.

Khaldun, Ibn. (1958) *The Muqqddimah: An Introduction to History,* New York: Pantheon Books.

King, Martin Luther, Jr. (1964) *Stride Toward Freedom,* New York: Harper & Row.

Ladd, Everett Carl, Jr. (1969) *Negro Political Leadership in the South,* New York: Atheneum.

Lukacs, Georg. (1971) *History and Class Consciousness,* Cambridge, Mass.: The MIT Press.

Marcuse, Herbert. (1966) *One Dimensional Man,* Boston: Beacon Press.

Pen, Kimble. (1972) *The Disconnected,* New York: Columbia University Press.

Thompson, Daniel. (1963) *The Negro Leadership Class,* Englewood Cliffs, N.J.: Prentice-Hall.

Tryman, Donald. (1977) "A Typology of Black Leadership," *Western Journal of Black Studies,* 1, 1 (March), pp. 8–22.

Walton, Hanes, Jr. (1972) *Black Political Parties,* New York: The Free Press.

Weisbord, Robert, and Arthur Stein. (1970) *Bittersweet Encounter: The Afro-American and the American Jew,* Westport, Conn.: Negro Universities Press.

Willingham, Alex. (1981) "The Place of the New Black Conservatives in Black Social Thought: Groundwork for the Full Critique," unpublished paper; Philadelphia (October).

Wilson, James. (1960) *Negro Politics: The Search for Leadership,* New York: The Free Press.

Essay/Discussion Questions

1. What are the elements of Maulana Karenga's criticism of African American leadership in the post–Civil Rights era?

2. According to Karenga, what societal conditions contributed to the crisis of middle-class black American leadership?

3. Karenga argues that the problems of theory and practice characterize the crisis of black middle-class leadership. Discuss.

4. In Karenga's view, what is the significance of the rise of black conservatives in the post–Civil Rights era?

5. What is Karenga's theory of leadership? What leadership practice for the African American community might flow from this theory?

Part VIII Key Terms

Alliances

Antiblack racism

Black middle-class leadership

Black Nationalism

Black Panther Party for Self-Defense

Black Power Movement

Civil disobedience campaign

Civil Rights movement

Coalitions

Conservative war on poverty

Cultural nationalism

Demographic change

Grass-roots leadership

Guerrilla warfare

Fannie Lou Hamer

Human rights

Jobless poor

Maulana Karenga

Martin Luther King, Jr.

Leadership by default

Malcolm X

Multiethnic rebellion

Huey P. Newton

Police brutality

Revolutionary black nationalism

Bobby Seale

Student Nonviolent Coordinating Committee

Symbolic leadership

US organization

Working poor

Part VIII Supplementary Readings

Allen, Robert L., *Reluctant Reformers: The Impact of Racism on American Social Reform Movements,* Washington, D.C.: Howard University Press, 1974.

_____, *Black Awakening in Capitalist America: An Analytic History,* Garden City: Doubleday and Company, Inc., 1969.

Anthony, Earl, *Picking Up the Gun: A Report on the Black Panthers,* New York: The Dial Press, 1970.

Asante, Molefi K., *Malcolm X as Cultural Hero & Other Afrocentric Essays,* Trenton: Africa World Press, 1993.

Assefa, Hizkias, and Paul Wahrhaftig, *The MOVE Crisis in Philadelphia: Extremist Groups and Conflict Resolution,* Pittsburgh: University of Pittsburgh Press, 1990.

Baldassare, Mark, ed., *The Los Angeles Riots: Lessons for the Urban Future,* Boulder: Westview Press, 1994.

Bin Wahad, Dhoruba, Mumia Abu-Jamal, and Assata Shakur, *Still Black, Still Strong: Survivors of the U.S. War Against Black Revolutionaries,* New York: Semiotext(e), 1993.

Bing, Leon, *Do or Die,* New York: HarperCollins, 1991.

Boskin, Joseph, *Urban Racial Violence in the Twentieth Century,* Beverly Hills: Glencoe Press, 1969.

Boyte, Harry C., *Common Wealth: A Return to Citizen Politics,* New York: The Free Press, 1989.

Boyte, Harry C., and Frank Riessman, eds., *The New Populism: The Politics of Empowerment,* Philadelphia: Temple University Press, 1986.

Branch, Taylor, *Parting the Waters: America in the King Years, 1954–63,* New York: Simon and Schuster, 1988.

Brisbane, Robert H., *The Black Vanguard: Origins of the Negro Social Revolution, 1900–1960,* Valley Forge: Judson Press, 1970.

Brown, Elaine, *A Taste of Power: A Black Woman's Story,* New York: Pantheon Books, 1992.

Browning, Rufus P., Dale R. Marshall, and David H. Tabb, eds., *Racial Politics in American Cities,* New York: Longman, 1990.

_____, *Protest Is Not Enough: The Struggle of Blacks and Hispanics for Equality in Urban Politics,* Berkeley: University of California Press, 1984.

Bunche, Ralph J., *The Political Status of the Negro in the Age of FDR,* Chicago: The University of Chicago Press, 1973.

Bush, Rod, ed., *The New Black Vote: Politics and Power in Four American Cities,* San Francisco: Synthesis Publications, 1984.

Button, James W., *Blacks and Social Change: Impact of the Civil Rights Movement in Southern Communities,* Princeton: Princeton University Press, 1989.

Carmichael, Stokely, and Charles V. Hamilton, *Black Power: The Politics of Liberation in America,* New York: Random House, 1967.

Carson, Clayborne, *In Struggle: SNCC and the Black Awakening of the 1960s,* Cambridge: Harvard University Press, 1981.

Chisholm, Shirley, *Unbought and Unbossed,* Boston: Houghton Mifflin Company, 1970.

Clarke, John Henrik, ed., *Marcus Garvey and the Vision of Africa,* New York: Vintage Books, 1974.

_____, ed., *Malcolm X: The Man and His Times,* New York: Collier Books, 1969.

Conant, Ralph W., *The Prospects for Revolution: A Study of Riots, Civil Disobedience, and Insurrection in Contemporary America,* New York: Harper's Magazine Press, 1971.

Cone, James H., *Martin and Malcolm and America: A Dream or a Nightmare,* Maryknoll: Orbis Books, 1991.

Cronon, Edmund D., *Black Moses: The Story of Marcus Garvey and the Universal Negro Improvement Association,* Madison: The University of Wisconsin Press, 1966.

Cruse, Harold, *Plural But Equal: Blacks and Minorities in America's Plural Society,* New York: William Morrow and Company, 1987.

Dionne, E. J., Jr., *Why Americans Hate Politics,* New York: Simon and Schuster, 1991.

Duberman, Martin B., *Paul Robeson,* New York: Alfred A. Knopf, 1988.

Durden-Smith, Jo, *Who Killed George Jackson?* New York: Alfred A. Knopf, 1976.

Duster, Alfreda M., ed., *The Autobiography of Ida B. Wells,* Chicago: The University of Chicago Press, 1976.

Dymally, Mervyn M., ed., *The Black Politician: His Struggle for Power,* Belmont: Duxbury Press, 1971.

Edsall, Thomas B., and Mary D. Edsall, *Chain Reaction: The Impact of Race, Rights, and Taxes on American Politics,* New York: W. W. Norton and Company, 1991.

Farmer, James, *Lay Bare the Heart: An Autobiography of the Civil Rights Movement,* New York: Arbor House, 1985.

Forman, James, *The Making of Black Revolutionaries,* New York: The Macmillan Company, 1972.

Franklin, John H., and August Meier, eds., *Black Leaders of the Twentieth Century,* Urbana: University of Illinois Press, 1982.

Gaines, Kevin K., *Uplifting the Race: Black Leadership, Politics, and Culture in the Twentieth Century,* Chapel Hill: The University of North Carolina Press, 1996.

Garrow, David J., *Bearing the Cross: Martin Luther King, Jr., and the Southern Christian Leadership Conference,* New York: William Morrow and Company, Inc., 1986.

_____, *Protest at Selma: Martin Luther King, Jr., and the Voting Rights Act of 1965,* New Haven: Yale University Press, 1978.

Goldman, Peter, *The Death and Life of Malcolm X,* New York: Harper and Row, Publishers, 1973.

Gooding-Williams, Robert, ed., *Reading Rodney King, Reading Urban Uprising,* New York: Routledge, 1993.

Gordon, Lewis R., *Bad Faith and Antiblack Racism,* Atlantic Highlands: Humanities Press, 1995.

_____, *Fanon and the Crisis of European Man: An Essay on Philosophy and the Human Sciences,* New York: Routledge,1995.

_____, *Existence in Black: An Anthology of Black Existential Philosophy,* New York: Routledge, 1997.

Gordon, Lewis R., T. D. Sharpley-Whiting, and R. T. White, eds., *Fanon: A Critical Reader,* Oxford: Blackwell, 1996.

Greider, William, *Who Will Tell the People: The Betrayal of American Democracy,* New York: Simon and Schuster, 1992.

Hammer, Dan, and Isaac Cronin, *Bad: The Autobiography of James Carr,* New York: Carroll & Graf Publishers, Inc., 1994.

Hamilton, Charles V., *Adam Clayton Powell, Jr.: The Political Biography of an American Dilemma,* New York: Atheneum, 1991.

_____, *The Black Experience in American Politics,* New York: G. P. Putnam's Sons, 1973.

Hayes, Floyd W., III, "Governmental Retreat and the Politics of African-American Self-Reliant Development: Public Discourse and Social Policy," *Journal of Black Studies,* Vol. 22, No. 3 (March 1992), pp. 331–348.

_____, "Fanon, Oppression, and Resentment: The Black Experience in the United States," in Gordon, Sharpley-Whiting, and White, eds., *Fanon: A Critical Reader,* Oxford: Blackwell Publishers, 1996, pp. 11–23.

_____, "The Concept of Double Vision in Richard Wright's The Outsider: Fragmented Blackness in the Age of Nihilism," in Gordon, ed., *Existence in*

Black: An Anthology of Black Existential Philosophy, New York: Routledge, 1997, pp. 173-183.

Haywood, Harry, *Black Bolshevik: Autobiography of an Afro-American Communist,* Chicago: Liberator Press, 1978.

Henry, Charles P., *Culture and African American Politics,* Bloomington: Indiana University Press, 1990.

Hilliard, David, and Lewis Cole, *This Side of Glory: The Autobiography of David Hilliard and the Story of the Black Panther Party,* Boston: Little, Brown and Company, 1993.

Holt, Rackham, *Mary McLeod Bethune,* New York: Doubleday and Company, 1964.

Jackson, Byran O., and Michael B. Preston, eds., *Racial and Ethnic Politics in California,* Berkeley: Institute of Governmental Studies/University of California, 1991.

Jackson, George, *Soledad Brother: The Prison Letters of George Jackson,* New York: Coward-McCann, Inc., 1970.

_____, *Blood in My Eye,* New York: Random House, 1972.

James, Joy A., *Radicalizing the Talented Tenth,* New York: Routledge, 1996.

_____, *Resisting State Violence in US Culture,* Minneapolis: University of Minnesota Press, 1996.

Jones, Charles E., "The Political Repression of the Black Panther Party: The Case of the Oakland Bay Area," *Journal of Black Studies,* Vol. 18, No. 4 (June 1988), pp. 415–434.

_____, ed., *The Black Panther Party Reconsidered: Reflections and Scholarship,* Baltimore: Black Classic Press, 1997.

Karagueuzian, Dikran, *Blow It Up!: The Black Student Revolt at San Francisco State and the Emergence of Dr. Hayakawa,* Boston: Gambit, Inc., 1971.

Karenga, Maulana, *The Roots of the US-Panther Conflict: The Perverse and Deadly Games Police Play,* San Diego: Kawaida Publications, 1976.

Katznelson, Ira, *City Trenches: Urban Politics and the Patterning of Class in the United States,* New York: Pantheon Books, 1981.

King, Martin Luther, Jr., *Where Do We Go from Here: Chaos or Community?* Boston: Beacon Press, 1967.

King, Mel, *Chain of Change: Struggles for Black Community Development,* Boston: South End Press, 1981.

Kornweibel, Theodore, Jr., *No Crystal Stair: Black Life and the Messenger, 1917–1928,* Westport: Greenwood Press, 1975.

Litwack, Leon, and August Meier, eds., *Black Leaders of the Nineteenth Century,* Urbana: University of Illinois Press, 1988.

Logan, Rayford, *The Betrayal of the Negro: From Rutherford B. Hayes to Woodrow Wilson,* New York: Collier Books, 1965.

Lomax, Louis E., *The Negro Revolt,* New York: Signet Book, 1963.

McAdam, Doug, *Freedom Summer,* New York: Oxford University Press, 1988.

_____, *Political Process and the Development of Black Insurgency, 1930–1970,* Chicago: The University of Chicago Press, 1982.

McLellan, Vin, and Paul Avery, *The Voices of Guns,* New York: G. P. Putnam's Sons, 1977.

Madhubuti, Haki R., *Why L.A. Happened: Implications of the '92 Los Angeles Rebellion,* Chicago: Third World Press, 1993.

Malcolm X, *The Autobiography of Malcolm X,* New York: Grove Press, Inc., 1964.

Mann, Eric, *Comrade George: An Investigation into the Life, Political Thought, and Assassination of George Jackson,* New York: Perennial Library, 1974.

Marable, Manning, *Race, Reform, and Rebellion: The Second Reconstruction in Black America, 1945–1990,* 2d. Ed., Jackson: University Press of Mississippi, 1991.

_____, *W. E. B. Du Bois: Black Radical Democrat,* Boston: Twayne Publishers, 1986.

_____, *Black American Politics: From the Washington Marches to Jesse Jackson,* London: Verso, 1985.

Marine, Gene, *The Black Panthers,* New York: Signet Books, 1969.

Martin, Tony, *Race First: The Ideological and Organizational Struggles of Marcus Garvey and the Universal Negro Improvement Association,* Westport: Greenwood Press, 1976.

Martin, Waldo E., Jr., *The Mind of Frederick Douglass,* Chapel Hill: The University of North Carolina Press, 1984.

Morris, Aldon D., *The Origins of the Civil Rights Movement: Black Communities Organizing for Change,* New York: The Free Press, 1984.

Naison, Mark, *Communism in Harlem During the Depression,* Urbana: University of Illinois Press, 1983.

Newton, Huey P., *To Die for the People: The Writings of Huey P. Newton,* New York: Random House, Inc., 1970.

_____, *Revolutionary Suicide,* New York: Harcourt Brace Jovanovich, Inc., 1973.

_____, *War Against the Panthers: A Study of Repression in America,* New York: Harlem River Press, 1996.

Omi, Michael, and Howard Winant, *Racial Formation in the United States: From the 1960s to the 1990s,* New York: Routledge and Kegan Paul, 1986.

O'Reilly, Kenneth, *"Racial Matters": The FBI's Secret File on Black America, 1960–1972,* New York: The Free Press, 1989.

Patterson, William L., *The Man Who Cried Genocide: An Autobiography,* New York: International Publishers, 1971.

Pearson, Hugh, *The Shadow of the Panther: Huey Newton and the Price of Black Power in America,* Reading: Addison-Wesley Publishing Company, 1994.

Pfeffer, Paula F., *A. Philip Randolph, Pioneer of the Civil Rights Movement,* Baton Rouge: Louisiana State University Press, 1990.

Pohlmann, Marcus D., *Black Politics in Conservative America,* New York: Longman, 1990.

Preston, Michael B., Lenneal J. Henderson, Jr., and Paul L. Puryear, eds., *The New Black Politics: The Search for Political Power,* New York: Longman Inc., 1987.

Reed, Adolph L., Jr., ed., *Race, Politics, and Culture: Critical Essays on the Radicalism of the 1960s,* Westport: Greenwood Press, 1986.

608

_____, *The Jesse Jackson Phenomenon: The Crisis of Purpose in Afro-American Politics,* New Haven: Yale University Press, 1986.

_____, Adolph, Jr., *Stirrings in the Jug: Black Politics in the Post-Segregation Era,* Minneapolis: University of Minnesota Press, 1999.

_____, ed., *Without Justice for All: The New Liberalism and Our Retreat from Racial Justice,* Boulder: Westview Press, 1999.

Rivlin, Benjamin, ed., *Ralph Bunche: The Man and His Times,* New York: Holmes and Meier, 1990.

Scott, Kody, *Monster: The Autobiography of an L. A. Gang Member,* New York: Penguin Books, 1993.

Seale, Bobby, *Seize the Time: The Story of the Black Panther Party and Huey P. Newton,* New York: Random House, Inc., 1970.

_____, *A Lonely Rage: The Autobiography of Bobby Seale,* New York: Times Books, 1978.

Shapiro, Herbert, *White Violence and Black Response: From Reconstruction to Montgomery,* Amherst: University of Massachusetts Press, 1988.

Shepperd, Gladys B., *Mary Church Terrell, Respectable Person,* Baltimore: Human Relations Press, 1959.

Sitkoff, Harvard, *A New Deal for Blacks: The Emergence of Civil Rights as a National Issue,* New York: Oxford University Press, 1978.

Smith, J. Owens, *The Politics of Racial Inequality: A Systematic Comparative Macro-Analysis from the Colonial Period to 1970,* Westport: Greenwood Press, 1987.

Smith, Robert C., *We Have No Leaders: African Americans in the Post–Civil Rights Era,* Albany: State University of New York Press, 1996.

Stone, Chuck, *Black Political Power in America,* Chicago: The Bobbs-Merrill Company, 1968.

Stone, Clarence N., *Regime Politics: Governing Atlanta, 1946–1988,* Lawrence: University Press of Kansas, 1989.

Van Deburg, William L., *New Day in Babylon: The Black Power Movement and American Culture,* Chicago: The University of Chicago Press, 1992.

Vincent, Theodore G., *Black Power and the Garvey Movement,* Berkeley: Rampart Press, nd.

Wachtel, Paul L., *Race in the Mind of America: Breaking the Vicious Circle Between Blacks and Whites,* New York: Routledge, 1999.

Walters, Ronald W., and Robert C. Smith, *African American Leadership,* Albany: State University of New York Press, 1999.

Washington, James M., ed., *A Testament of Hope: The Essential Writings of Martin Luther King, Jr.,* San Francisco: Harper & Row, Publishers, 1986.

Weisbord, Robert G., *Genocide?: Birth Control and the Black American,* Westport: Greenwood Press, 1975.

Weiss, Nancy J., *Whitney M. Young, Jr., and the Struggle for Civil Rights,* Princeton: Princeton University Press, 1989.

Wells-Barnett, Ida, *On Lynchings,* New York: Arno Press, 1960.

Wilson, William J., *Power, Racism, and Privilege: Race Relations in Theoretical and Sociohistorical Perspectives,* New York: The Macmillan Company, 1973.

Wood, Joe, ed., *Malcolm X: In Our Image,* New York: An Anchor Book/
    Doubleday, 1992.
Zinn, Howard, *SNCC: The New Abolitionists,* Boston: Beacon Press, 1965.

About the Authors

Part I: African American Studies: Trends, Developments, and Future Challenges

Carter G. Woodson, deceased, founded the Association for the Study of Negro Life and History in 1916, and later established Negro History Week. Historian, author, educator, he is considered the father of black history. He established and edited the *Journal of Negro History*. He was the author of numerous books, including *The Negro in Our History* and *Mis-Education of the Negro*.

Harold Cruse is professor emeritus of history and Afro-American Studies at the University of Michigan, where he was one of the founders of that program in 1969. He is the author of *Crisis of the Negro Intellectual, Rebellion or Revolution*, and *Plural but Equal*.

Gloria T. Hull and **Barbara Smith** are two of the most important black feminist theorists and activists to emerge during the 1970s. They, along with Patricia Bell Scott, co-edited the first black women's studies anthology—*All the Women Are White, All the Blacks Are Men, But Some of Us Are Brave*. Hull edited *Give Us Each Day: The Diary of Alice Dunbar-Nelson* and authored *Color, Sex, and Poetry: Three Women Writers of the Harlem Renaissance*. Smith edited *Home Girls: A Black Feminist Anthology* and authored *The Truth That Never Hurts: Writings on Race, Gender, and Freedom*.

Manning Marable is professor of history and director of the Institute for African-American Studies at Columbia University. He is the author of many books, including *From the Grassroots, Black American Politics, Race, Reform, and Rebellion, Beyond Black and White, Speaking Truth to Power*, and *Black Leadership*.

Part II. Africa and the Diaspora: Ties That Bind

Boniface Obichere, deceased, was professor of African history at the University of California and at the University of Ibadan.

C. L. R. James, deceased, was a Trinidadian revolutionary-intellectual and Pan-Africanist who lived for many years in England. Coming to the United States, he later taught at then Northwestern University and Federal City College in Washington, D.C. He authored many books, including *Mariners, Renegades and Castaways: A Critical Review of Herman Melville, The Black Jacobins, Facing Reality, Modern Politics, Spheres of Existence, The Future in the Present, Nkrumah and the Ghana Revolution,* and *Notes on Dialectics: Hegel, Marx, Lenin, and Modern Politics.*

Angela Davis, radical activist-intellectual, teaches in the History of Consciousness Program at the University of California, Santa Cruz. She is the author of *If They Come in the Morning: Voices of Resistance; Angela Davis: An Autobiography; Women, Race, and Class; Women, Culture, and Politics;* and *Blues Legacies and Black Feminism.*

Vincent Harding is professor of religion and social transformation at Iliff School of Theology. Among his numerous publications are *Hope and History: Why We Must Share the Story of the Movement, There Is a River,* and *The Other American Revolution.*

Michael Mitchell specializes in the study of Brazilian political and social life. He teaches Latin American politics in the Department of Political Science at Arizona State University.

Lydia Lindsey and **Carlton E. Wilson** are members of the Department of History at North Carolina Central University. Their teaching and research focus on the African and West Indian immigrant experiences in England.

Part III: Black Expressive Culture: Music and Literature

Portia Maultsby teaches in the Department of Afro-American Studies at Indiana University. She is the author *Popular Music of Black America: Socio-Cultural and Musical History* and is the co-editor of *Who's Who in Black Music.*

Daphne Duval Harrison is professor of Afro-American Studies at the University of Maryland, Baltimore County. She is the author of *Black Pearls: Blues Queens of the 1920s.*

Nelson George is an award-winning critic and author of a number of books on African American popular culture, including *The Death of Rhythm & Blues; Buppies, B-Boys, Baps & Bohos: Notes on Post-Soul Culture; Elevating the Game: Black Men and Basketball;* and *Blackface: Reflections on African-Americans and the Movies.* He also is the author of a novel, *Urban Romance.*

Richard Wright, deceased, was the author of such fictional works as *Native Son, Uncle Tom's Children, Lawd Today, Eight Men, The Outsider,* and *Savage Holiday.* His nonfiction included *Black Boy, White Man, Listen!, Black Power, The Color Curtain,* and *American Hunger.*

Larry Neal, deceased, was co-founder of the Black Arts Repertory and co-editor of *Black Fire: An Anthology of Afro-American Writing.* He taught at CCNY and at Yale and Howard Universities.

Toni Morrison is the Nobel Prize– and Pulitzer Prize–winning author of several novels, including *The Bluest Eye, Sula, Song of Solomon, Tar Baby, Beloved, Jazz,* and *Paradise.* She is the author of the nonfiction book *Playing in the Dark: Whiteness and the Literary Imagination.* She also is Robert F. Goheen Professor in the Council of the Humanities at Princeton University.

Part IV: Discovering the Meaning of Black Identity: Psychic Dimensions of Oppression

Wade Nobles is professor of Black Studies at San Francisco State University. He is a leading scholar in the development of black psychology as a field of study and practice. He also is executive director of the Institute for the Advanced Study of Black Family Life and Culture.

Kenneth M. Stampp, deceased, was a historian and author of *The Peculiar Institution: Slavery in the Ante-Bellum South.*

W. E. B. Du Bois, deceased, was an educator, activist, editor, historian, and sociologist. He authored numerous books, including *The Suppression of the African Slave Trade to the United States of America, The Philadelphia Negro, Black Reconstruction in America, The World and Africa, The Souls of Black Folk,* and *Dusk of Dawn.*

Part V: The Black Family: Historical and Policy Issues

Andrew Billingsley is professor in the Department of Family and Community Development at the University of Maryland, College Park. He is the author of a number of books, including *Black Families in White America, Climbing Jacobs Ladder: The Enduring Legacy of African American Families, Mighty Like a River: The Black Church and Social Reform,* and *Children in the Storm: Black Children and American Child Welfare.*

E. Franklin Frazier, deceased, was a professor of sociology and longtime chair of Howard University's Department of Sociology. Among his many published works were *The Negro Family in the United States, The Negro in the United States,* and *Black Bourgeoisie.*

Glenn C. Loury is University Professor and professor of economics at Boston University. He is the author of *One by One from the Inside Out.*

William A. Darity, Jr., Samuel L. Myers, Jr., Emmett D. Carson, and **William Sabol** are the authors of *The Black Underclass: Critical Essays on Race and Unwantedness.*

Part VI: The African American Struggle for Quality Education

Frederick Douglass, born a slave in the nineteenth century, became an abolitionist, orator, and statesman. He founded a weekly newspaper, *The North Star,* and wrote an autobiography, *The Life and Times of Frederick Douglass.*

Jewell R. C. Mazique, a longtime lobbyist and community activist in Washington, D.C., was educated at Spellman College and received Howard University's first M.A. degree in African Studies.

Floyd W. Hayes III teaches multidisciplinary studies and political science at North Carolina State University. He is editor of *A Turbulent Voyage: Readings in African American Studies.*

Joy James teaches political theory in the Department of Ethnic Studies at the University of Colorado, where she also is Director of the Center for Studies of Ethnicity and Race in America. She is the author of several books, including *Transcending the Talented Tenth: Black Leaders and American Intellectuals* and *Resisting State Violence: Radicalism, Gender, and Race in the US.* She is editor of *The Angela Y. Davis Reader.*

Part VII: Political Economy of the African American Situation

Harold M. Baron is the author of *The Demand for Black Labor: Historical Notes on the Political Economy of Racism.*

Daniel R. Fusfeld and **Timothy Bates** are economists and the authors of *The Political Economy of the Urban Ghetto.*

Part VIII: Racism, Resistance, and Radicalism

Lewis R. Gordon teaches Afro-American studies and philosophy of religion at Brown University. He is author of *Bad Faith and Antiblack Racism, Fanon and the Crisis of European Man: An Essay on Philosophy and the Human Sciences,* and *Her Majesty's Other Children: Philosophical Sketches from a Neocolonial Age.* He also is editor of *Existence in Black: An Anthology of Black Existential Philosophy* and co-editor of *Fanon: A Critical Reader* and *Black Texts and Textuality: Constructing and De-Constructing Blackness.*

Martin Luther King, Jr., deceased, was a major leader of the Civil Rights Movement of the late 1950s and 1960s. He was a Christian minister, head of the Southern Christian Leadership Conference, and a profound orator. He also received the Nobel Peace Prize. Among his books were *Why We Can't Wait* and *Where Do We Go From Here: Chaos or Community?*

Malcolm X (El-Hajj Malik El-Shabazz), deceased, was by any account the father of the Black Power Movement of the 1960s. While in prison, he joined the Nation of Islam and later became a Muslim minister. He made a pilgrimage to Mecca and later founded the Organization of Afro-American Unity. With Alex Haley, he wrote *The Autobiography of Malcolm X.*

Frances A. Kiene III is a graduate student in sociology at the University of Oregon.

Melvin L. Oliver, James H. Johnson, Jr., and **Walter C. Farrell, Jr.,** are the authors of *Anatomy of a Rebellion: A Political-Economic Analysis.*

Judson L. Jeffries teaches in the Department of Political Science at Purdue University. He is author of *Virginia's Native Son: The Election and Administration of L. Douglas Wilder.*

Maulana Karenga is chair of the Department of Black Studies at California State University, Long Beach, and the executive director of the Institute of Pan-African Studies in Los Angeles. In 1965 he founded the cultural nationalist US Organization and became a major intellectual, theoretician, and activist in the Black Power Movement. He has continued to be a pioneering scholar in Africana Studies. He is the creator of the African American holiday of Kwanzaa and the author of Nguzo Saba, a communitarian African value system. His numerous works include *Introduction to Black Studies, The Husia, The African American Holiday of Kwanzaa, The Book of Coming Forth By Day, Reconstructing Kemetic Culture, The Foundations of Kawaida Theory, Kawaida Theory,* and *Essays on Struggle.* He also is the co-editor of *Kemet and the African Worldview.*

Index

A

Ableman v. Booth, 374
abolition movement, 42, 71–74, 102–103, 441–442
abortion, legal, 370
Abrahams, Roger, 188
academese, 413–414
acculturation, 127, 318
action, belief and, 282
activism, in pedagogy, 417–420
addiction, as theme in women's blues lyrics, 192
aesthetic, black, 236, 237
affirmative action, 20, 30, 461, 482, 505–506, 589, 598
Africa
    colonialism in, 37
    slavery in, 59
    tribal differences in, 280–281
Africa and the Victorians (Gallagher), 46
African American Studies
    African history and, 38
    Afrocentric perspective of, 27–28
    curriculum for, 2, 10, 11–12
    defined, 24
    faculty positions for, 383
    future of, 30–33
    long-range effect of, 13
    multiculturalism and, 24–33
    trends in, 1–4, 28

African Americans
    economic situation of, 431–491
    Malcolm X on, 528
    self-hatred of, 6–7
    traveling in Europe, 138–139
African Background Outlined, The: A Handbook, 8
African Diaspora, 42–44
African Europeans, 131
African history, 59
African philosophy, 280–291
African thinkers, 413, 414
Africanisms, in New World, 288
Afro-American literature, 248–266
Afro-American Woman, The: Struggles and Images (Harley & Terborg-Penn), 22
Afrocentric European Studies, 44, 140–141
Afrocentrism, 27–28
Ahmadu Bello University, 49
Aid to Families with Dependent Children (AFDC), 475
Alabama, segregation in, 511, 514
Albert, Stewart, 538
alcohol use, 180, 191
Aldridge, Delores P., 28
Alexandre, Tio, 121
Allen, Anita, 407
Allen, Harold, 592
alliances, political, 597–599
Almeida, Aluicio, 126
American Federation of Labor, 446
American Management Association, 453

American Negro Slave Revolts (Aptheker), 40
American Telephone and Telegraph, 482
Amidon School, 403
Amin, Samir, 413, 421
Anderson, Jourdon, 329–330
Anene, J. C., 48
Annenberg, Moses L., 372
Anthony, Earl, 542, 554
Antor, Sandra, 584
Apollo Theater, 160
Appeal (Walker), 42, 104–107, 108, 110
Aptheker, Herbert, 28, 40, 89
Art of the Novel, The (Kundera), 239
art
    Afro-American, 251
    social functions of, 236
artisans, black, 340, 439 445
arts. See Black Arts Movement
asabiyah, 590
Asante, Molefi, 27, 28
Ashanti, 282, 286, 287, 290, 313, 315, 316, 317
Ashby Commission, 47
assimilation, 25
Association for the Study of Negro Life and History, 2, 5, 7–8
Association of Black Women Historians, 22
Atlanta Statement on Human Rights, 539
Atlantic Records, 207, 211–212